Index of American Periodical Verse: 1983

Rafael Catalá

and

James D. Anderson

in association with

Eric L. Ramsey

and

James Romano

The Scarecrow Press, Inc.
Metuchen, N.J., & London
1985

Library of Congress Catalog Card No. 73-3060
ISBN 0-8108-1832-9

Manufactured in the United Sates of America

CONTENTS

PREFACE

This, the thirteenth annual volume of the *Index of American Periodical Verse*, covers more English and Spanish language periodicals from Canada, the United States, and Puerto Rico than ever before. More than two hundred publications have been indexed this year, contributing more than 14,500 entries to the *Index*.

The importance of the *Index* grows as its necessity becomes more apparent in the circles of contemporary poetry research. The increasing demand for inclusion corroborates this fact. The *Index* also reveals the influences and relations between poets from other lands and ours. The growing number of translations published today tells us which poets are exerting more international influence today, since we tend to translate the poets whose poetry we like best. Thus, we find that some years Pablo Neruda gets lots of translation. Other years, it is García Lorca, Baudelaire or Aime Cesaire, Aspenström or Drummond de Andrade. Another important factor is the translator. Some translators are very prolific, which could be an indication of their poetic "worldliness." Which poets do U.S., Hispanic American and Canadian poets translate? The *Index* is a source for this type of information. Which poets of old are still being published? Which have been unearthed after years of oblivion? The *Index* can answer these questions.

James D. Anderson has made a major contribution to the *Index* by designing and refining computer programs which have greatly facilitated the indexing process. Also, I want to express my sincere appreciation to Sarah Park Anderson, Martha Park Sollberger, Eric Calaforra, and Egon Brown for their valuable assistance. Finally, I am pleased to welcome Eric L. Ramsey to the *Index* staff, joining James Romano as an Assistant Editor.

Rafael Catalá
Co-Editor

INTRODUCTION

MICRO-COMPUTER COMPILATION

The 1983 Index was compiled using an Osborne 1 microcomputer and the Wordstar word-processing program. Once all indexing was complete, the entries were sorted and formatted using a suite of programs written especially for the Index in CBasic. The Osborne 1 has a total memory capacity of 64K, not enough for sorting even 100 full index entries at one time, so sorting was done in a series of sort and merge steps, much as humans sort. After author and translator entries were sorted, entry numbers were added and title entries were extracted and sorted. Finally, cross-references were added and the final index was printed in camera-ready form on a NEC Spinwriter printer.

The principal advantage in computer-based compilation is eliminating the repetitive entry of the same data. Within a single issue of a journal, for example, the journal citation will be the same for every poem, yet in the old card-based method, the citation had to be rewritten on every card. With the computer, it is simply copied, without rekeying, to each entry. Similarly, translations no longer call for a completely new entry for the translator. Instead, the original entry is simply modified, moving the name of the translator to the lead position, and the author to the note.

Persons interested in the precise details of compilation, including the computer programs used, should write to the editors at P.O. Box 38, New Brunswick, NJ 08903-0038. The entire 1982 and 1983 Index is available from the editors on 5-1/4" Osborne format floppy disks.

NAMES AND CROSS REFERENCES

With the addition of many more poets with compound surnames and surnames containing various prefixes, we have recognized the need for systematic cross references from alternative forms of surname to the form chosen for entry in the Index. After sorting, poets with similar names are checked in the biographical sections of the journals to determine if they are the same person. If evidence indicates that they are, entries are merged using a single form of name. Alternative forms of name are indicated using the format authorized by the Anglo-American Cataloguing Rules, Second Edition. For example:

GOODENOUGH, J. B. (Judith B.)

This heading indicates that this poet has poems published under two forms of her name: J. B. Goodenough and Judith B. Goodenough. We have included cross references from alternative forms of surname whenever the form used for entry did not fall under the last element.

FORMAT AND ARRANGEMENT OF ENTRIES

The basic format and style of the Index remain unchanged. Poets are arranged alphabetically by surname and forenames. In creating this alphabetical sequence, we have adopted principles of the filing rules issued in 1980 by the American Library Association and the Library of Congress. Names are filed as spelled, rather than as pronounced, so that, for example, names beginning with 'Mac' and 'Mc' are no longer interfiled. Similarly, the space consistently counts as a filing element, so that similar compound and prefixed surnames are often separated by some distance, as illustrated in the following examples. Note that "De BOLT" precedes "DeBEVOISE" by a considerable number of entries.

De ANGELIS
De BOLT
De GRAVELLES
De LOACH
De PALCHI
De RONSARD
De VAUL
DEAL
DeBEVOISE
DeFOE
DEGUY
Del VECCHIO
DeLISLE
DeMOTT
DENNISON
Der HOVANESSIAN
DESY
DeYOUNG

Van BRUNT
Van DUYN
Van HALTEREN
Van TOORN
Van TROYER
Van WERT
Van WINCKEL
VANCE
Vander DOES
VANDERBEEK
VanDEVENTER

Abbreviations are also filed as spelled, rather than pronounced, so that "ST. JOHN" is not filed as "SAINT JOHN", but as "S+T+space+JOHN". Punctuation is not considered; a hyphen is filed as if it were a space. Finally, numerals are filed in numerical order preceding alphabetical letters rather than as if they were spelled out.

Under each poet's name, poems are filed alphabetically by title or, if there is no title, by first line. Poem titles and first lines are placed within quotation marks. All significant words of titles are capitalized, but in first lines, only the first word and proper nouns are capitalized. Incomplete excerpts from larger works are followed by the note "Excerpt" or, if they consist of complete sections, by "Selection". The title, first line or number of the excerpt, if given, follows this note. For example:

WALCOTT, Derek
"Midsummer" (Selections: XXXIV-XXXVI). Agni (18) 83, p. 5-7.

WEBB, Phyllis
"The Vision Tree" (Selection: "I Daniel"). PoetryCR (5:2) Wint 83-84, p. 11.

WAINWRIGHT, Jeffrey
"Heart's Desire" (Excerpt: "Some Propositions and Part of a Narrative"). Agni (18) 83, p. 37.

WATTEN, Barret
"One Half" (Excerpts). ParisR (24:86) Wint 82, p. 112-113.

If an excerpt is a complete "sub-work", it receives an independent entry, with reference to the larger work in a note. For example:

ANDERSON, Jack
"Magnets" (from The Clouds of That Country). PoNow (7:2, #38) 83, p. 23.

Notes about dedications, joint authors, translators, and sources follow the title, enclosed in parentheses. A poem with more than one author is entered under each author. Likewise, a translated poem is entered under each translator, as well as its author(s). Each entry includes the names of all authors and all translators. Multiple authors or translators are indicated by the abbreviation "w.", standing for "with". Translators are indicated by the abbreviation "tr. by", standing for "translated by", and original authors are indicated by the abbreviation "tr. of", standing for "translation of". For example:

AGGESTAM, Rolf
"Old Basho" (tr. by Erland Anderson and Lars Nordström). NewRena (16) Spr 83, p. 25.

ANDERSON, Erland
"Old Basho" (tr. of Rolf Aggestam, w. Lars Nordström). NewRena (16) Spr 83, p. 25.

NORDSTROM, Lars
"Old Basho" (tr. of Rolf Aggestam, w. Erland Anderson). NewRena (16) Spr 83, p. 25.

The journal citation includes an abbreviation standing for the journal title, followed by volume and issue numbers, date, and pages. The journal abbreviation is underlined. An alphabetical list of these journal abbreviations is included at the front of the volume, along with the full journal title, name of editor(s), address, the numbers of the issues indexed in this volume of the Index, and subscription information. A separate list of indexed periodicals is arranged by full journal title, with a reference to the abbreviated title. Volume and issue numbers are included within parentheses, e.g., (16:5) stands for volume 16, number 5; (21) refers to issue 21 for a journal which does not use volume numbers. Dates are given using abbreviations for months and seasons. Please see the separate list of abbreviations.

Compiling this year's Index has been an adventure into the wealth and variety of poetry published in U. S., Puerto Rican and Canadian periodicals as well as the intricacies of bringing this wealth together and organizing it into a consistent index. The world of poetry publication is a dynamic one, with new journals appearing, older journals declining, dying, reviving and thriving. This year saw the loss of thirteen journals and the addition of twenty-four new ones. These are listed at the front of the volume. Keeping up with these changes is a big order, and we solicit our reader's suggestions as to journals which should be included in future volumes of the Index, and also, journals which could be dropped. Editors who would like their journals considered for inclusion in future volumes should send sample issues to:

Rafael Catalá & James D. Anderson, Editors
Index of American Periodical Verse
P.O. Box 38
New Brunswick, NJ 08903-0038

Although indexing is indispensable for the organization of any literature so that particular works can be found when needed and scholarship and research facilitated, it is a tedious business. I know that we have made mistakes. We solicit your corrections and suggestions, which you may send to me at the above address.

James D. Anderson
Co-Editor

ABBREVIATIONS

dir., dirs.	director, directors
ed., eds.	editor, editors
(for.)	price for foreign countries
(ind.)	price for individuals
(inst.)	price for institutions
(lib.)	price for libraries
p.	page, pages
po. ed.	poetry editor
pub.	publisher
mss.	manuscripts
(stud.)	price for students
tr. by	translated by
tr. of	translation of
U.	University
w.	with

Months

Ja	January	Jl	July
F	February	Ag	August
Mr	March	S	September
Ap	April	O	October
My	May	N	November
Je	June	D	December

Seasons

Aut	Autumn, Fall	Spr	Spring
Wint	Winter	Sum	Summer

PERIODICALS ADDED

Periodical titles are followed by the acronym used in indexing.

Abatis: Abatis
Argo, Incorporating Delta: Argo
Blue Buffalo: BlueBuf
Blueline: Blueline
Calyx: Calyx
Clockwatch Review: ClockR
Crab Creek Review: CrabCR
Descant: Descant
The Harvard Advocate: HarvardA
Indiana Review: IndR
Junte del Taller Rácata: Rácata
Memphis State Review: MemphisSR
Moody Street Irregulars: MoodySI
MSS: MSS
Negative Capability: NegC
Oro Madre: OroM
Poet Lore: PoetL
Raritan: Raritan
San Fernando Poetry Journal: SanFPJ
Spirit: SpiritSH
The Spoon River Quarterly: SpoonRQ
Swallow's Tale: Swallow
The Third Wind: ThirdW
Yet Another Small Magazine: YetASM

PERIODICALS DELETED

The following periodicals have been deleted from the *Index* because 1) we have been notified that publication has ceased, or 2) no 1982 or 1983 issues have been received after repeated requests.

The Ark River Review
Aspect
Aspen Journal of the Arts
Barat Review
Caliban
Claridad
Lugar Sin Limite
Maize
Montemora
The Pikestaff Review
Puerto Norte y Sur
Unmuzzled Ox
UT Review
Zahir

PERIODICALS INDEXED

Arranged by acronym, with names of editors, addresses, issues indexed, and subscription information. New titles added to the _Index_ in 1983 are marked with an asterisk (*).

13thM: 13TH MOON, Marilyn Hacker, ed., P.O. Box 309, Cathedral Station, New York, NY 10025. Issues indexed: (6:1/2, 7:1/2). Subscriptions: $17.85/3 volumes, $11.90/2 volumes; Single issues: $5.95.

*_Abatis_: ABATIS, Duane Locke, ed., U. of Tampa, Tampa, FL 33606. Issues indexed: (1). Subscriptions: $9.50/2 issues; Single issues: $5.

Abraxas: ABRAXAS, Ingrid Swanberg, ed., 2518 Gregory St., Madison, WI 53711. Issues indexed: (27/28). Subscriptions: $8/4 issues.

Academe: ACADEME, Bulletin of the American Association of University Professors, Donald Rackin, David S. Green, Sarah G. Womack, eds., Suite 500, One Dupont Circle, Washington, DC 20036. Issues indexed: (69:1-6). Subscriptions: $30/yr., $32/yr. (for.).

Agni: THE AGNI REVIEW, Sharon Dunn, ed., P.O. Box 229, Cambridge, MA 02238. Issues indexed: (18-19). Subscriptions: $13/2 yrs., $7/yr.; Single issues: $3.50.

AmerPoR: THE AMERICAN POETRY REVIEW, David Bonanno, Stephen Berg, Arthur Vogelsang, _et al_., eds., World Poetry, Inc., Temple U Center City, 1616 Walnut St., Room 405, Philadelphia, PA 19103. Issues indexed: (12:1-6). Subscriptions: $22/3 yrs., $27/3 yrs. (for.), $15/2 yrs., $19/2 yrs. (for.), $8.50/yr., $10.50/yr. (for.); Single issues: $1.75.

AmerS: THE AMERICAN SCHOLAR, Joseph Epstein, ed., United Chapters of Phi Beta Kappa, 1811 Q St. NW, Washington, DC 20009. Issues indexed: (52:1-4). Subscriptions: $30/3 yrs., $12/yr. plus $3/yr. (for.); Single issues: $4.

Annex: ANNEX 21, Patrick Worth Gray, ed., UNO-Community Writer's Workshop, University of Nebraska at Omaha, Omaha, NE 68182. Issues indexed: "Temporarily discontinued"; Single issues: $4.95.

Antaeus: ANTAEUS, Megan Ratner, Managing ed., The Ecco Press, 18 W. 30th St., New York, NY 10001. Issues indexed: (48-51). Subscriptions: $16/yr.; Single issues: $5.

AntigR: THE ANTIGONISH REVIEW, George Sanderson, ed., St. Francis Xavier U., Antigonish, Nova Scotia B2G 1C0 Canada. Issues indexed: (52-55). Subscriptions: $8/4 issues; Single issues: $2.50.

AntR: THE ANTIOCH REVIEW, Robert S. Fogarty, ed., David St. John, Po. ed., Antioch College, P.O. Box 148, Yellow Springs, OH 45387. Issues indexed: (41:1-4). Subscriptions: $20/yr. (inst.), $15/yr. (ind.), $25/yr. (for.); Single issues: $4.50; P.O. Box 1308-R, Ft. Lee, NJ 07024.

Areito: AREITO, Max Azicri, Emilio Bejel, et al., eds., GPO Box 2174, New York, NY 10116. Issues indexed: (9:33-35). Subscriptions: $18/yr. (inst.), $8/yr. (ind)., $16/yr. (for.); Single issues: $2; Back issues: $3.

*Argo: ARGO, Incorporating DELTA, Hilary Davies, ed, Ray Fleming, U.S. ed., Dept. of Comparative Literature, Miami U., Oxford OH. Issues indexed: (4:1-3, 5:1). Subscriptions: $10/yr.; Single issues $2.50.

ArizQ: ARIZONA QUARTERLY, Albert Frank Gegenheimer, ed., U. of Arizona, Tucson, AZ 85721. Issues indexed: (39:1-4). Subscriptions: $10/3 yrs., $5/yr.; Single issues: $1.50.

Ascent: ASCENT, Daniel Curley, et al., eds., English Dept., U. of Illinois, 608 South Wright St., Urbana, IL 61801. Issues indexed: (8:2-3, 9:1). Subscriptions: $3/yr., $4.50/yr. (for.); Single issues: $1 (bookstore), $1.50 (mail).

Atlantic: THE ATLANTIC, William Whitworth, ed., Peter Davison, Po. ed., 8 Arlington St., Boston, MA 02116. Issues indexed: (251:1-6, 252:1-6). Subscriptions: $45/3 yrs., $33/2 yrs., $18/yr., plus $2/yr. (for.); Single issues: $2.

BallSUF: BALL STATE UNIVERSITY FORUM, Frances M. Rippy, Dick Renner, eds., Ball State U., Muncie, IN 47306. Issues indexed: (24:1-2). Subscriptions: (vol. 24) $8/yr., Single issues: $2.50; (vol. 25) $10/yr., Single issues: $3.

BelPoJ: THE BELOIT POETRY JOURNAL, David M. Stocking, Marion M. Stocking, eds., RFD 2, Box 154, Ellsworth, ME 04605. Issues indexed: (33:3-4, 34:1-2). Subscriptions: $17/3 yrs., $6/yr.; Single issues: $1.50.

BerksR: BERKSHIRE REVIEW, Stephen Fix, et al., eds., Williams College, Box 633, Williamstown, MA 01267. Issues indexed: (18).

BlackALF: BLACK AMERICAN LITERATURE FORUM, Joe Weixlmann, ed., PH 237, Indiana State U., Terre Haute, IN 47809. Issues indexed: (17:1-4). Subscriptions: $8/yr. (ind.), $10/yr. (inst.), $12/yr. (for.); Statesman Towers West 1005, Indiana State U., Terre Haute, IN 47809.

BlackWR: BLACK WARRIOR REVIEW, Will Blythe, ed., John C. Morrison, Po. ed., U. of Alabama, P.O. Box 2936, University, AL 35486-2936. Issues indexed: (8:1-10:1). Subscriptions: $5.50/yr. (ind.), $7.50/yr. (inst.); Single issues: $3.

*BlueBuf: BLUE BUFFALO, Claire Harris, John McDowell, et al., eds., c/o Dandelion, 922 - 9 Avenue, S.E., Calgary, Alberta, Canada, T2G 0S4. Issues indexed: (2:1).

*Blueline: BLUELINE, Alice Gilborn, ed. & publisher; Jane Z. Carroll, po. ed. Blue Mountain Lake, NY 12812. Issues indexed: (3:2, 4:1-2, 5:1). Subscriptions: $7.75/2 yrs.; $4/yr., $5/yr. (for.); Back issues: $2.25.

Bogg: BOGG, John Elsberg, ed., 422 N. Cleveland St., Arlington, VA 22201; George Cairncross, ed., 31 Belle Vue St., Filey, N. Yorks YO14 9HU, UK. Issues indexed: (50-51). Subscriptions: $6/3 issues; Single issues: $2.50.

Bound: BOUNDARY 2, William V. Spanos, ed., Dept. of English, State U. of New York, Binghamton, NY 13901. Issues indexed: (11:1-3). Subscriptions: $25/yr. (inst.), $15/yr. (ind.), $13/yr (stud.); Single issues: $8 (double), $5 (single).

CalQ: CALIFORNIA QUARTERLY, Elliot L. Gilbert, ed., Robert Swanson, Po. ed., 100 Sproul Hall, U. of California, Davis, CA 95616. Issues indexed: (22). Subscriptions: $7/yr.; Single issues: $2.

*Calyx: CALYX, Margarita Donnelly, Managing ed., P.O. Box B, Corvallis, OR 97339. Issues indexed: (7:3, 8:1). Subscriptions: $10/yr., $18/2 yrs., $24/3 yrs., plus $4/yr. (for.), $9/yr. (for. airmail); Single issue: $4.

CanLit: CANADIAN LITERATURE, W. H. New, ed., U. of British Columbia, 2021 West Mall, Vancouver, B.C. V6T 1W5 Canada. Issues indexed: (96-99). Subscriptions: $20/yr. (ind.), $25/yr. (inst.) plus $5/yr. outside Canada; Single issues: $7.50.

CapeR: THE CAPE ROCK, Harvey Hecht, et al., eds., Southeast Missouri State U., Cape Girardeau, MO 63701. Issues indexed: (18:2, 19:1). Subscriptions: $3/yr.; Single issues: $2.

CapilR: THE CAPILANO REVIEW, Ann Rosenberg, ed., Capilano College, 2055 Purcell Way, North Vancouver, B.C. V7J 3H5 Canada. Issues indexed: (26-27). Subscriptions: $17.50/8 issues (ind.), $9/4 issues (ind.), $10/4 issues (lib.), plus $1/4 issues (for.); Single issues: $3.

Caribe: CARIBE, Miguel Santiago Santana, ed., Apartado 995, San Juan, PR 00902. Issues indexed: No 1983 issues received. Subscriptions: $5/yr. (ind.), $6/yr (inst.), plus $1/yr. (USA), $2/yr. (for.); Single issues: $4.

CarolQ: CAROLINA QUARTERLY, Marc Manganaro, ed., Steve Kuusisto, Po. ed., Greenlaw Hall 066-A, U. of North Carolina, Chapel Hill, NC 27514. Issues indexed: (35:2-3). Subscriptions: $12/yr. (inst.), $9/yr. (ind.), $11/yr. (for.); Single issues: $4; Back issues: $4.

Catalyst: CATALYST, Kathleen McGann Kettern, Michael E. Kettner, eds., McKettner Publishing, P.O. Box 12067, Seattle, WA 98102. Issues indexed: No 1983 issues received. Subscriptions: $3/yr. (ind.), $5/yr. (inst., for.); Single issues: $2.

CEACritic: THE CEA CRITIC, College English Association, Michael Payne, ed., Dept. of English, Bucknell Univ., Lewisburg, PA 17837. Issues indexed: (45:2). Subscriptions: $18/yr. (lib., inst.), $15/yr. (ind.).

CEAFor: THE CEA FORUM, College English Association, Michael Payne, ed., Dept. of English, Bucknell Univ., Lewisburg, PA 17837. Issues indexed: (13:2-3/4). Subscriptions: $24/yr. (lib., inst.), $20/yr. (ind.).

CentR: THE CENTENNIAL REVIEW, Linda Wagner, ed., 110 Morrill Hall, Michigan State U., East Lansing, MI 48824-1036. Issues indexed: (27:1-4). Subscriptions: $5/2 yrs., $3/yr., plus $2/yr. (for.); Single issues: $1.50.

CharR: THE CHARITON REVIEW, Jim Barnes, ed., Division of Language and Literature, Northeast Missouri State U., Kirksville, MO 63501. Issues indexed: (9:1-2). Subscriptions: $7/4 issues; Single issues: $2.

Chelsea: CHELSEA, Sonia Raiziss, ed., P.O. Box 5880, Grand Central Station, New York, NY 10163. Issues indexed: No issues published in 1983. Subscriptions: $8/2 issues or double issue, $9 (for.); Single issues: $4.50, $5 (for.).

ChiR: CHICAGO REVIEW, Keith W. Tuma, ed., Patricia Connelly, Michael Donaghy, Po. eds., U. of Chicago, Faculty Exchange, Box C, Chicago, IL 60637. Issues indexed: (33:3-4, 34:1). Subscriptions: $35/3 yrs., $24/2 yrs., $13/yr., $10/yr. (ind.), plus $2/yr. (for.); Single issues: $3.75.

ChrC: THE CHRISTIAN CENTURY, James M. Wall, ed., 407 S. Dearborn St., Chicago, IL 60605. Issues indexed: (100:1-39). Subscriptions: $54/3 yrs., $36/2 yrs., $21/yr., plus $2.50/yr. (for.); Single issues: $.75.

CimR: CIMARRON RIVIEW, Neil J. Hackett, ed., Terry Hummer, Po. ed., 208 Life Sciences East, Oklahoma State U., Stillwater, OK 74078. Issues indexed: (62-65). Subscriptions: $10/yr.; Single issues: $2.50.

*ClockR: CLOCKWATCH REVIEW, James Plath, ed., 737 Penbrook Way, Hartland, WI 53029. Issues indexed (1:1-2, 2:1). Subscriptions: $6/yr.; Single issues: $3.

ColEng: COLLEGE ENGLISH, National Council of Teachers of English, Donald Gray, ed., Brian O'Neill, Po. cons.,

Dept. of English, Indiana U., Bloomington, IN 47405. Issues indexed: (45:1-8). Subscriptions: $35/yr. (inst.), $30/yr. (ind.), plus $4/yr. (for.); Single issues: $4; NCTE, 1111 Kenyon Rd., Urbana, IL 61801.

Comm: COMMONWEAL, James O'Gara, ed., Rosemary Deen, Marie Ponsot, Po. eds., 232 Madison Ave., New York, NY 10016. Issues indexed: (110:1-22). Subscriptions: $43/2 yrs., $47/2 yrs. (Canada), $53/2 yrs. (for.), $24/yr., $26/yr. (Canada), $29/yr. (for.); Single issues: $1.25.

ConcPo: CONCERNING POETRY, Ellwood Johnson, ed., Robert Huff, Po. ed., Dept. of English, Western Washington U., Bellingham, WA 98225. Issues Indexed: (16:1-2). Subscriptions: $6/yr. (USA, Canada), $7/yr. (for.); Single issues: $3.50.

Cond: CONDITIONS, Elly Bulkin, Jan Clausen, Rima Shore, eds., P.O. Box 56, Van Brunt Station, Brooklyn, NY 11215. Issues indexed: (3:3, issue 9). Subscriptions: $25/3 issues (inst.), $15/3 issues (ind), $9/3 issues "hardship" rate, free to women in prisons and mental institutions; Single issues: $6 (ind.), $9 (inst.).

Confr: CONFRONTATION, Martin Tucker, ed., English Dept., C. W. Post College, Long Island U., Greenvale, NY 11548. Issues indexed: (25-26). Subscriptions: $15/3 yrs., $10/2 yrs., $5/yr.; Back issues: $2; Eleanor Feleppa, Director of Public Relations, Southhampton College, Long Island U., Southhampton, NY 11968.

*CrabCR: CRAB CREEK REVIEW, Linda Clifton, Hank Buchmann, eds., 30 F Street, N.E., Ephrata, WA 98823. Issues indexed: (1:1-2). Subscriptions: $15/2 yrs., $8/yr.; Single issues: $3.

CreamCR: CREAM CITY REVIEW, Jesse Glass, Jr., ed., Robert Thompson, Po. ed., English Dept., P.O. Box 413, U. of Wisconsin-Milwaukee, Milwaukee, WI 53201. Issues indexed: (18:1-2). Subscriptions: $6/yr.

CropD: CROP DUST, Edward C. Lynskey & Heather Tervo Lynskey, eds/pubs., Route 2, Box 389-1, Bealeton, VA 22712. Issues Indexed: (4). Subscriptions: $5/2 issues (ind.), $8/2 issues (lib.); Single issues: $2.50.

CrossC: CROSS-CANADA WRITERS' QUARTERLY, Ted Plantos, ed., Bruce Hunter, Po. ed., Box 277, Station F, Toronto, Ontario M4Y 2L7 Canada. Issues indexed: (5:1-4). Subscriptions: $10/yr. (ind.), $12/yr. (inst.); Single issues: $2.95.

CutB: CUTBANK, Suzanne Hackett, Jon Davis, eds., Dept. of English, U. of Montana, Missoula, MT 59812. Issues indexed: (20-21). Subscriptions: $14/2 yrs., $7.50/yr.; Single issues: $4.

Dandel: DANDELION, Robert Hilles, Beverly Harris, eds., John McDermid, Claire Harris, Po. eds., Alexandra Centre, 922

- 9th Ave., S.E., Calgary, Alberta T2G 0S4 Canada. Issues indexed: (10:1-2). Subscriptions: $15/2 yrs., $8/yr., $12/yr. (inst.); Single issues: $4.

DekalbLAJ: THE DEKALB LITERARY ARTS JOURNAL, William S. Newman, ed., DeKalb Community College, 555 N. Indian Creek Dr., Clarkston, GA 30021. Issues indexed: (15:1/4, 16:1/4). Single issues: $3.

DenQ: DENVER QUARTERLY, Leland H. Chambers, ed., U. of Denver, Denver, CO 80208. Issues indexed: (17:4, 18:1-3). Subscriptions: $18/2 yrs., $10/yr., plus $1/yr. (for.); Single issues: $2.50

*Descant: DESCANT, Karen Mulhallen, ed., P.O. Box 314, Station P, Toronto M5S 2S8, Ontario, Canada. Issues indexed: (14:2-5, issues 40-43). Subscriptions: $18/yr (ind.), $26/yr. (inst.); Single issues: $6.50.

EngJ: ENGLISH JOURNAL, National Council of Teachers of English, Ken Donelson, Alleen Pace Nilsen, eds., College of Education, Arizona State U., Tempe, AZ 85287. Issues indexed: (72:1-8). Subscriptions: $35/yr. (inst.), $30/yr. (ind.), plus $4/yr. (for.); Single issues: $4; NCTE, 1111 Kenyon Rd., Urbana, IL 61801.

EnPas: EN PASSANT, James A. Costello, ed., 4612 Sylvanus Dr., Wilmington, DE 19803. Issues indexed: No issues published in 1983. Subscriptions: $11/6 issues, $6/3 issues; Single issues: $2.25; Back issues: $1.75.

Epoch: EPOCH, C. S. Giscombe, ed., 251 Goldwin Smith Hall, Cornell U., Ithaca, NY 14853. Issues indexed: (32:2-3, 33:1). Subscriptions: $6.50/yr.; Single issues: $2.50.

Field: FIELD, Stuart Friebert, David Young, eds., Rice Hall, Oberlin College, Oberlin, OH 44074. Issues indexed: (28-29). Subscriptions: $10/2 yrs., $6/yr.; Single issues: $3; Back issues: $10.

Focus: FOCUS/MIDWEST, Charles L. Klotzer, ed./pub., Dan Jaffe, Po. ed., 8606 Olive Blvd., St. Louis, MO 63132. Issues indexed: (15:95). No more published.

FourQt: FOUR QUARTERS, John Christopher Kleis, ed., Richard Lautz, Po. ed., La Salle College, 20th & Olney Aves., Philadelphia, PA 19141. Issues indexed: (32:2-4, 33:1). Subscriptions: $13/2 yrs., $8/yr.; Single issues: $2.

Gargoyle: GARGOYLE MAGAZINE, Richard Peabody, Jr., ed./pub., Paycock Press, P.O. Box 3567, Washington, DC 20007. Issues indexed: (22/23); 20/21 was "all fiction issue." Subscriptions: $7/yr. (ind.), $8/yr. (inst.); Single issues: $3-4.

GeoR: GEORGIA REIVEW, Stanley W. Lindberg, ed., U. of Georgia, Athens, GA 30602. Issues indexed: (37:1-4). Subscriptions: $15/2 yrs., $9/yr., plus $3/yr. (for.); Single issues: $4.

Germ: GERMINATION, Allan Cooper, ed. & pub., Leigh Faulkner, Assoc. ed., 428 Yale Ave., Riverview, New Brunswick E1B 2B5, Canada. Issues indexed: (7:1-2). Subscriptions: $6/2 issues (ind.), $8/2 issues (inst.); Single issues: $3.50.

Grain: GRAIN, Saskatchewan Writers Guild, E. F. Dyck, ed., Box 1885, Saskatoon, Saskatchewan S7K 3S2 Canada. Issues indexed: (11:1-4). Subscriptions: $10/2 yrs., $6/yr.; Single issues: $2.

HangL: HANGING LOOSE, Robert Hershon, et al., eds., 231 Wyckoff St., Brooklyn, NY 11217. Issues indexed: (44). Subscriptions: $15/9 issues, $10/6 issues, $5.50/3 issues; Single issues: $2.

Harp: HARPER'S MAGAZINE, Michael Kinsley, ed., Two Park Ave., New York, NY 10016. Issues indexed: (266:1592-1597, 267:1598-1603). Subscriptions: $18/yr., plus $2/yr. (USA possessions, Canada), plus $3/yr. (for.); Single issues: $2; P.O. Box 2622, Boulder, CO 80322.

*HarvardA: THE HARVARD ADVOCATE, Polly Saltonstall, Managing ed., Advocate House, 21 South St., Cambridge, MA 02138. Issues indexed: (117:1-3). Subscriptions: $8.50/yr. (ind.), $15/yr. (inst., for.).

HiramPoR: HIRAM POETRY REVIEW, English Department, Hiram College, David Hopes, David Anderson, eds., Box 162, Hiram, OH 44234. Issues indexed: (34-35 & Suppl. #7). Subscriptions: $2/yr.; Single issues: $1.

Hol Crit: THE HOLLINS CRITIC, John Rees Moore, ed., Hollins College, VA 24020. Issues indexed: (20:1-5). Subscriptions: $5/yr., $6.50/yr. (for.).

Hudson: THE HUDSON REVIEW, Paula Deitz, Frederick Morgan, eds., 684 Park Ave.,, New York, NY 10021. Issues indexed: (36:1-4). Subscriptions: $14/yr., $15/yr. (for.); Single issues: $4; Anniversary issue: $6.

Humanist: THE HUMANIST, Lloyd L. Morain, ed., 7 Harwood Dr., Amherst, NY 14226. Issues indexed: (43:1-6). Subscriptions: $35/3 yrs., $25/2 yrs., $15/yr., plus $3/yr. (for.); Single issues: $2.50; Back issues: $3.

Images: IMAGES, Gary Pacernick, ed., Dept. of English, Wright State U., Dayton, OH 45435. Issues indexed: (8:3). Subscriptions: $3/yr.; Single issues: $1.

*IndR: INDIANA REVIEW, Clint McCown, ed., Don Boes, Jim Brock, et al., po. eds., 316 N. Jordan Ave., Bloomington, IN 47405. Issues indexed: (5:1-3, 6:1-3). Subscriptions: $8/3 issues; Supporting subscriptions $25; Single issues: $3.

Inti: INTI, Revista de Literature Hispanica, Roger B. Carmosino, ed., Dept. of Modern Languages, Providence College, Providence, RI 02918. Issues indexed: (15). Subscriptions: $20/yr. (inst.), $16/yr. (ind.).

Iowa: IOWA REVIEW, David Hamilton, ed., 308 EPB, U. of Iowa, Iowa City, IA 52242. Issues indexed: (13:2-3/4). Subscriptions: $20/yr. (lib., inst.), $12/yr. (ind.), plus $3/yr. (for.); Single issues: $5.

KanQ: KANSAS QUARTERLY, Harold Schneider, et al., eds., Dept. of English, Kansas State U., Manhattan, KS 66506. Issues indexed: (15:1-4). Subscriptions: $20/2 yrs., $12/yr. (USA, Canada, Latin America), $22/2 yrs., $13/yr. (other countries); Single issues: $4.

Kayak: KAYAK, George Hitchcock, Marjorie Simon, Gary Fisher, eds., 325 Ocean View Ave., Santa Cruz, CA 95062. Issues indexed: (61-63). Subscriptions: $5/yr.; Single issues: $2.

LetFem: LETRAS FEMENINAS, Asociacion de Literatura Femenina Hispanica, Dr. Adelaida Martinez, ed., Texas A & M U., Asociacion de Literatura Femenina Hispanica, Modern Languages Dept., College Station, TX 77843-4238. Issues indexed: (9:1-2). Subscriptions: $15/yr.

LitR: THE LITERARY REVIEW, Walter Cummins, ed., Fairleigh Dickinson U., 285 Madison Ave., Madison, NJ 07940. Issues indexed: (26:2-4, 27:1). Subscriptions: $12/yr., $15/yr. (for.); Single issues: $4.50, $5.50/yr (for.).

LittleBR: THE LITTLE BALKANS REVIEW, Gene DeGruson, Po. ed., The Little Balkans Press, Inc., 601 Grandview Heights Terr., Pittsburg, KS 66762. Issues indexed: (3:3-4, 4:1-2). Subscriptions: $10/yr.; Single issues: $3.50.

LittleM: THE LITTLE MAGAZINE, Ginjer Buchanan, Dennis Cooney, et al., eds, Dragon Press, P.O. Box 78, Pleasantville, NY 10570. Issues Indexed: (14:1/2). Subscriptions: $13/4 issues (inst.), $12/4 issues (ind.), $14/4 issues (for.); Single issues: $3.

LittleR: THE LITTLE REVIEW, John McKernan, ed., Little Review Press, Box 205, Marshall U., Huntington, WV 25701. Issues indexed: No 1983 issues received; next issue anticipated in 1986. Subscriptions: $2.50/yr.; Single issues: $1.25.

Mairena: MAIRENA, Manuel de la Puebla, ed., Himalaya 257, Urbanizacion Monterrey, Rio Piedras, PR 00926. Issues indexed: No 1983 issues received. Subscriptions: $10/yr. (inst.), $12/yr. (for. inst.), $6/yr. (ind.), $10/yr. (for. ind.).

MalR: THE MALAHAT REVIEW, Constance Rooke, ed., P.O. Box 1700, Victoria, British Columbia, Canada V8W 2Y2. Issues indexed: (64-66). Subscriptions: $40/3 yrs., $15/yr. (USA, Canada), $50/3 yrs., $20/yr. (other countries), $10/yr. (stud.); Single issues: $7 (USA, Canada), $8 (other countries).

ManhatR: THE MANHATTAN REVIEW, Philip Fried, ed., 304 Third Ave., Apt. 4A, New York, NY 10010. Issues indexed: (3:1). Subscriptions: $8/2 issues (ind.), $12/2 issues (inst.), plus $2.50/2 issues (outside USA & Canada); Back issues: $4.

MassR: THE MASSACHUSETTS REVIEW, John Hicks, ed., Memorial Hall, U. of Massachusetts, Amherst, MA 01003. Issues indexed: (24:1-4). Subscriptions: $12/yr., $14/yr. (for.); Single issues: $4.

Meadows: THE MEADOWS, Bev Tucker, ed., Art Dept., Truckee Meadows Community College, 7000 Dandini Blvd., Reno, NV 89512. Issues indexed: (3:1, 4:1).

*MemphisSR: MEMPHIS STATE REVIEW, Willaim Page, ed., Dept. of English, Memphis State U., Memphis, TN 38152. Issues indexed: (1:2, 2:1-2, 3:1-2, 4:1). Subscriptions: $3/yr.; Single issues: $2.

MendoR: MENDOCINO REVIEW, Camille Ranker, ed., P.O. Box 888, Mendocino, CA 95460. Issues indexed: No 1983 issues received. Single issues: $5.95.

Mester: MESTER, Librada Hernandez-Lagoa, ed., Dept. of Spanish and Portuguese, U. of California, Los Angeles, CA 90024. Issues indexed: (12:1/2). Subscriptions: $14/yr. (inst.), $8/yr. (ind.), $5/yr. (stud.); Single issues: $7 (inst.), $4 (ind.)

Metam: METAMORFOSIS, Lauro Flores, Director, Centro de Estudios Chicanos, GN-09, U. of Washington, Seattle, WA 98195. Issues indexed: (4:2/5:1). Single issues: $7.

MichQR: MICHIGAN QUARTERLY REVIEW, Laurence Goldstein, ed., 3032 Rackham Bldg., U. of Michigan, Ann Arbor, MI 48109. Issues indexed: (22:1-4). Subscriptions: $24/2 yr., $13/yr. (ind.), $15/yr. (inst.); Single issues: $3.50; Back issues: $2.

MidwQ: THE MIDWEST QUARTERLY, James B. Schick, ed., Michael Heffernan, Po. ed., Pittsburg State U., Pittsburg, KS 66762. Issues indexed: (24:2-4, 25:1). Subscriptions: $6/yr. plus $2 (for.); Single issues: $2.

MinnR: THE MINNESOTA REVIEW, Fred Pfeil, Laura Rice-Sayre, Michael Sprinker, eds, Anne E. Krosby, Henry Sayre, Richard Daniels, Po. eds., Dept. of English, Oregon State U., Corvallis, OR 97331. Issues Indexed: (NS20-21). Subscriptions: $20/2 yrs. (inst. & for.), $12/2 yrs. (ind.), $12/yr. (inst. & for.), $7/yr. (ind.); Single issues: $4.

MissouriR: THE MISSOURI REVIEW, Speer Morgan, ed., Dept. of English, 231 Arts and Science, U. of Missouri, Columbia, MO 65211. Issues indexed: (6:2-3, 7:1). Subscriptions: $18/2 yrs., $10/yr.

MissR: MISSISSIPPI REVIEW, Frederick Barthelme, ed., The Center for Writers, Southern Station, Box 5144, Hattiesburg, MS 39406-5144. Issues indexed: (12:1/2 = nos. 34/35). Subscriptions: $26/3 yrs., $18/2 yrs., $10/yr., plus $2/yr. (for.); Single issues: $4.50.

ModernPS: MODERN POETRY STUDIES, Jerry McGuire, ed., 207 Delaware Ave., Buffalo, NY 14202. Issues indexed: (11:3). Subscriptions: $9/3 issues (inst.), $7.50/3 issues (ind.).

*MoodySI: MOODY STREET IRREGULARS, Joy Walsh, ed., P.O. Box 157, Clarence Center, NY 14042. Issues indexed: (1-13). Subscriptions: $5/3 issues (ind.), $6/3 issues (lib.); Single issues: $3.

*MSS: MSS, M. L. Rosenberg, J. Higgins, eds., State U. of NY at Binghamton, Binghamton, NY 13901. Issues indexed: (2:3, 3:1). Subscriptions: $18/2 yrs. (ind.), $25/2 yrs. (lib.); $10/yr. (ind.), $15/yr. (lib.); Single issues: $4., Double issues: $6.

Mund: MUNDUS ARTIUM, Rainer Schulte, ed., U. of Texas at Dallas, Box 688, Richardson, TX 75080. Issues indexed: (14:1). Subscriptions: $10/2 issues (inst.), $8/2 issues (ind.). Single issues: $4.50.

Nat: THE NATION, Victor Navasky, ed., Grace Schulman, Po. ed., 72 Fifth Ave., New York, NY 10011. Issues indexed: (236:1-25, 237:1-22). Subscriptions: $72/2 yrs., $40/yr., $20/half yr. plus $7/yr. (Mexico, Canada), plus $13/yr. (other for.); Single issues: $1.25; Nation Subscription Service, P.O. Box 1953, Marion, OH 43305.

*NegC: NEGATIVE CAPABILITY, Sue Brannam Walker, ed., 6116 Timberly Road North, Mobile, AL 36609. Issues indexed: (3:4). Subscriptions: $12/yr. (ind.), $14/yr. (inst.), $13/yr. (for.); Single issues: $3.50.

NewEngR: NEW ENGLAND REVIEW AND BREAD LOAF QUARTERLY, Sydney Lea, Jim Schley, eds., Box 170, Hanover, NH 03755. Issues indexed: (5:3-4, 6:1-2). Subscriptions: $12/yr.; Single issues: $4-7.

NewL: NEW LETTERS, David Ray, ed., U. of Missouri-Kansas City, 5346 Charlotte, Kansas City, MO 64110. Issues indexed: (49:3-4, 50:1). Subscriptions: $50/5 yrs., $25/2 yrs., $15/yr. (ind.); $60/5 yrs., $30/2 yrs., $18/yr. (lib.); Single issues: $4.

NewOR: NEW ORLEANS REVIEW, John Mosier, ed., Box 195, Loyola U., New Orleans, LA 70118. Issues indexed: (10:1-4). Subscriptions: $20/yr. (inst.), $15/yr. (ind.), $30/yr. (for.); Single issues: $6-11.

NewRena: THE NEW RENAISSANCE, Louise T. Reynolds, ed., Stanwood Bolton, Po. ed., 9 Heath Road, Arlington, MA 02174. Issues indexed: (16-17). Subscriptions: $19/6 issues, $10/3 issues; $23/6 issues, $12/3 issues (Canada, Mexico, Europe); $25/6 issues, $13/3 issues (elsewhere); Single issues: $4.25-5.

NewRep: THE NEW REPUBLIC, Martin Peretz, ed., Robert Pinsky, Po. ed., 1220 19th St., N.W., Washington, DC 20036. Issues indexed: (186:1-26, 187:1-26, 188:1-25, 189:1-4); The New Republic is the only journal which refuses to supply a complementary subscription for indexing; indexing was done by Martha Sollberger, Indiana, PA.

NewWR: NEW WORLD REVIEW, Marilyn Bechtel, ed., 162 Madison Ave., 3rd Floor, New York, NY 10016. Issues indexed: (51:1-6). Subscriptions: $5/yr. $6/yr. (for.); Single issues: $1.

NewYorker: THE NEW YORKER, Howard Moss, Po. ed., 25 W. 43rd St., New York, NY 10036. Issues indexed: (58:46-52, 59:1-45). Subscriptions: $52/2 yrs., $32/yr.; $44/yr. (Canada); $52/yr. (for.); Single issues: $1.50.

NewYRB: THE NEW YORK REVIEW OF BOOKS, Robert B. Silvers, Barbara Epstein, eds., 250 W. 57th St., New York, NY 10107. Issues indexed: (29:21-22, 30:1-20). Subscriptions: $25/yr. plus $5/yr. (Canada, Latin America), plus $7/yr. (elsewhere); Single issues: $1.50; Subscription Service Dept., P.O. Box 940, Farmingdale, NY 11737.

Nimrod: NIMROD, Francine Ringold, ed., Joan Flint, et al., Po. eds., Arts and Humanities Council of Tulsa, 2210 S. Main, Tulsa, OK 74114. Issues indexed: (27:1). Subscriptions: $10/yr., $13/yr. (for.); Single issues: $5.50, $7 (for.).

NoAmR: THE NORTH AMERICAN REVIEW, Robley Wilson, Jr., ed., Peter Cooley, Po. ed., U. of Northern Iowa, 1222 West 27th St., Cedar Falls, IA 50614. Issues indexed: (268:1-4). Subscriptions: $9/yr., $10/yr. (Canada, Latin America), $11/yr. (elsewhere); Single issues: 2.50.

Northeast: NORTHEAST, John Judson, ed., Juniper Press, 1310 Shorewood Dr., La Crosse, WI 54601. Issues indexed: (Ser. 3:15-16). Subscriptions: $25/yr.; Single issues: $2.50.

Notarte: NOTICIAS DE ARTE, Frank C. Garcia, ed./pub., Florencio Garcia Cisneros, Director, 172 E. 89th St. #5-A, New York, NY 10028. Issues indexed: No 1983 issues received. Subscriptions: No information given.

NowestR: NORTHWEST REVIEW, John Witte, ed., Maxine Scates, Po. ed., 369 PLC, U. of Oregon, Eugene, OR 97403. Issues indexed: (21:1-2/3). Subscriptions: $21/3 yrs., $14/2 yrs., $8/yr.; $13/2 yrs., $7/yr. (stud.); plus $2/yr. (for.); Single issues: $3.

Obs: OBSIDIAN, Alvin Aubert, ed./pub., Wayne State U., Detroit, MI 48202. Issues indexed: No 1983 issues received. Subscriptions: $8.50/yr., $9.50/yr. (Canada), $11.50/yr. (for.); Single issues: $3; Double issues: $6.

OhioR: THE OHIO REIVEW, Wayne Dodd, ed., Ellis Hall, Ohio U., Athens, OH 45701. Issues indexed: (30-31). Subscriptions: $30/3 yrs., $12/yr.; Single issues: $3.95-8.95.

OntR: ONTARIO REVIEW, Raymond J. Smith, ed., 9 Honey Brook Dr., Princeton, NJ 08540. Issues indexed: (18-19). Subscriptions: $21/3 yrs., $15/2 yrs., $8/yr., plus $1/yr. (for.); Single issues: $3.95.

OP: OPEN PLACES, Eleanor M. Bender, ed., Box 2085, Stephens College, Columbia, MO 65215. Issues indexed: (35-36). Subscriptions: $15/2 yrs., $8/yr. (USA, Canada), plus $6/yr. (elsewhere); Single issue: $4.

*OroM: ORO MADRE, Loss and Jan Glazier, eds., 4429 Gibraltar Dr., Fremont, CA 94536. Issues indexed: (2:1, issue 5). Subscriptions: $12/4 issues; Single issues: $3.50.

Os: OSIRIS, Andrea Moorhead, ed., Box 297, Deerfield, MA 01342. Issues indexed: (16-17). Subscriptions: $6/2 issues (USA, Canada, Mexico), $7/2 issues (elsewhere); Single issues: $3.

Outbr: OUTERBRIDGE, Charlotte Alexander, ed., English Dept. (A323), College of Staten Island, 715 Ocean Terrace, Staten Island, NY 10301. Issues indexed: (12/13). Subscriptions: $4/yr.; Single issues: $4.

Paint: PAINTBRUSH, Ben Bennani, ed., English & Foreign Languages, Georgia Southwestern College, Americus, GA 31709. Issues indexed: (10:19/20). Subscriptions: $20/3 yrs., $15/2 yrs., $8/yr.; Single issues: $5; Back issues: $5.

ParisR: THE PARIS REVIEW, George A. Plimpton, et al., eds., Jonathan Galassi, Po. ed., 541 East 72nd St., New York, NY 10021. Issues indexed: (24:84-86, 25:87-90). Subscriptions: $1000/life, $32/8 issues, $16/4 issues, plus $4/4 issues (for.); Single issues: $5; 45-39 171 Place, Flushing, NY 11358.

PartR: PARTISAN REVIEW, William Phillips, ed., Boston U., 121 Bay State Rd., Boston, MA 02215. Issues indexed: (50:1-4). Subscriptions: $36/3 yrs., $25.50/2 yrs., $14/yr.; $27.50/2 yrs., $16/yr. (for.); $20/yr. (inst.); Single issues: $4.

Peb: PEBBLE, Greg Kuzma, ed., The Best Cellar Press, Dept. of English, U. of Nebraska, Lincoln, NE 68588. Issues indexed: No issues published in 1983. Subscriptions: $15/4 issues (lib.), $12/4 issues (ind.).

Pequod: PEQUOD, David Paradis, ed., 536 Hill St., San Francisco, CA 94114; Poetry Mss. to Mark Rudman, Po. ed., 817 West End Ave., New York, NY 10025. Issues indexed: Issue No. 15 (1983) indexed in 1982 volume, but mis-dated 1982 instead of 1983. Subscriptions: $21/3 yrs., $15/2 yrs., $8/yr., plus $1/yr. (for.); Single issues: $4.50.

Pig: PIG IRON, Rose Sayre, Jim Villani, eds., Pig Iron Press, P.O. Box 237, Youngstown, OH 44501. Issues indexed: (11). Subscriptions: $12/2 yrs., $7/yr.; Single issues: 5.95.

PikeF: THE PIKESTAFF FORUM, James R. Scrimgeour, Robert D. Sutherland, eds./pubs., P.O. Box 127, Normal, IL 61761. Issues indexed: (5). Subscriptions: $10/6 issues; Single issues: $2; Back issues: $2.

Playb: PLAYBOY, Hugh M. Hefner, ed./pub., 919 N. Michigan Ave., Chicago, IL 60611. Issues indexed: (30:2-12). Subscriptions: $22/yr.; Single issues: varies.

Ploughs: PLOUGHSHARES, DeWitt Henry, Peter O'Malley, Directors, Box 529, Cambridge, MA 02139; Editorial offices: Div. of Creative Writing and Literature, Emerson College, 100 Beacon St., Boston, MA 02116; 214A Waverly Ave., Watertown, MA 02172. Issues indexed: (9:1-4). Subscriptions: $12/yr., $14/yr. (for.); Single issues: $5.

Poem: POEM, Huntsville Literary Association, Robert L. Welker, ed., U. of Alabama at Huntsville, English Dept., Huntsville, AL 35899. Issues indexed: (47-49). Subscriptions: $5.50/yr.; P.O. Box 919, Huntsville, AL 35804.

PoetC: POET AND CRITIC, Michael Martone, ed., 203 Ross Hall, Iowa State U., Ames, IA 50011. Issues indexed: (14:3, 15:1). Subscriptions: 9/yr., plus $1/yr. (for.); Single issues: $3; Iowa State U. Press, South State St., Ames, IA 50010.

*PoetL: POET LORE, Philip K. Jason, Kevin Madden, Barbara Lefcowitz, Executive eds., Heldref Publications, 4000 Albemarle St., N.W., Washington, DC 20016. Issues indexed: (77:1-4, 78:1-4). Subscriptions: $12/yr., $18/yr. (inst.), plus $5/yr. (for.); Single issues: $3.

Poetry: POETRY, John Frederick Nims, ed., 601 S. Morgan St., P.O. Box 4348, Chicago, IL 60680. Issues indexed: (141:4-6, 142:1-6, 143:1-3). Subscriptions: $20/yr., $24/yr. (for.); Single issues: $2 plus $.60 postage; Back issues: $2.25 plus $.60 postage.

PoetryCR: POETRY CANADA REVIEW, Clifton Whiten, Ed./Pub., P.O. Box 1280, Stn. 'A', Toronto, Ontario M5W 1G7 Canada. Issues indexes: (4:3-4, 5:1-2). Subscriptions: $7/yr. (Canada), $8/yr. (USA), $9.50/yr. (elsewhere); $9.50/yr. (inst., Canada); $10.50/yr. (inst., USA), $12/yr. (inst., elsewhere).

PoetryE: POETRY EAST, Richard Jones, Kate Daniels, eds., Star Route 1, Box 50, Earlysville, VA 22936. Issues indexed: (9-12). Subscriptions: $10/yr.; Single issues: $3.50.

PoetryNW: POETRY NORTHWEST, David Wagoner, ed., U. of Washington, 4045 Brooklyn Ave., NE, Seattle, WA 98105. Issues indexed: (24:1-4). Subscriptions: $8/yr., $9/yr. (for.); Single issues: $2, $2.25 (for.).

PoNow: POETRY NOW, E. V. Griffith, ed./pub., 3118 K Street, Eureka, CA 95501. Issues indexed: (7:2, issue 38). Subscriptions: $19/12 issues, $13/8 issues; $7.50/4 issues; Single issues: $2.

PortR: PORTLAND REVIEW, Nancy L. Moeller, ed., Portland State U., Box 751, Portland, OR 97207. Issues indexed: (29:1). Single issues: $3.50.

PottPort: THE POTTERSFIELD PORTFOLIO, Lesley Choyce, ed., Pottersfield Press, RR #2, Porters Lake, Nova Scotia B0J 2S0 Canada. Issues indexed: (5). Subscriptions: $10/3 yrs.; Single issues: $3.50.

PraS: PRAIRIE SCHOONER, Hugh Luke, ed., 201 Andrews Hall, U. of Nebraska, Lincoln, NE 68588. Issues indexed: (57:1-4); 57:1 numbered 51:1 by mistake on title-page. Subscriptions: $29/3 yrs., $20/2 yrs., $11/yr. (ind.); $15/yr. (lib.); Single issues: $3.25.

Prima: PRIMAVERA, Mary Biggs, Andrea Cooke, et al., eds., U. of Chicago, Ida Noyes Hall, Chicago, IL 60637. Issues indexed: (8). Single issues: $5.

Prismal: PRISMAL/CABRAL, Emma Buenaventura, et al., eds., Dept. of Spanish and Portuguese, U. of Maryland, College Park, MD 20742. Issues indexed: (11). Subscriptions: $7/yr. (ind.), $15/yr. (inst.).

Quarry: QUARRY, David Schleich, ed., Box 1061, Kingston, Ontario K7L 4Y5 Canada. Issues indexed: (32:1-4). Subscriptions: $12/yr., plus $2/yr. (for.); Single issues: $3.

QRL: QUARTERLY REVIEW OF LITERATURE, T. & R. Weiss, 26 Haslet Ave., Princeton, NJ 08540. Issues indexed: (24). Subscriptions: $15/2 volumes (paper), $20/volume (cloth, inst.) ; Single issues: $10 (paper).

QW: QUARTERLY WEST, Wyn Cooper, Robert Shapard, eds., Edward Byrne, Po. ed. 317 Olpin Union, U. of Utah, Salt Lake City, UT 84112. Issues indexed: (16-17). Subscriptions: $12/2 yrs., $6.50/yr.; Single issues: $3.50.

*Rácata: JUNTE DEL TALLER RACATA, Programa de Arte y Cultura, Colegio Comunal Eugenio María de Hostos de la Universidad de la Ciudad de Nueva York, c/o Prisma Books, Box 375, Audubon Station, New York, NY 10032. Issues indexed: (1: Esta Urticante Pasión de la Pimienta, Clemente Soto Velez, Director, Orlando José Hernández, Coordinador, Arnaldo Sepúlveda, Editor; 2: Soles Emellis, Rafael Catalá, Director, Orlando José Hernández, Coordinador, Rafael Catalá and Robertoluis Lugo, Editores).

RagMag: RAG MAG, Beverly Voldseth, ed., Box 12, Goodhue, MN 55027. Issues indexed: (2:2). Subscriptions: $10/2 yrs., $6/yr.; Single issues: $3.50; Renewals: $5/yr., $9/2 yrs.

*Raritan: RARITAN, Richard Poirier, ed., Rutgers U., 165 College Ave., New Brunswick, NJ 08903. Issues indexed: (2:3-4, 3:1-2). Subscriptions: $12/yr., $21/2 yrs.; Single issues: $4; Back issues: $4.50.

RevChic: REVISTA CHICANO-RIQUENA, Nicholas Kanellos, ed., U. of Houston, University Park, Houston, TX 77004. Issues indexed: (11:2-4). Subscriptions: $10/yr., $15/yr. (inst.); Single issues: $5.

RevIn: REVISTA/REVIEW INTERAMERICANA, John Zebrowski, ed., GPO Box 3255, San Juan, PR 00936. Issues indexed: No 1983 issues received. Subscriptions: $27/3 yrs., $20/2 yrs., $14/yr. (ind).; $45/3 yrs., $35/2 yrs., $20/yr. (inst.); $9/yr. (stud.); Single issues: $5 plus $1.50 postage & handling.

Salm: SALMAGUNDI, Robert Boyers, ed., Peggy Boyers, Exec. ed., Skidmore College, Saratoga Springs, NY 12866. Issues indexed: (60-61). Subscriptions: $25/2 yrs., $16/yr. (inst.); $15/2 yrs., $9/yr. (ind.); plus $1.50/yr. (for.); Single issues: $4.50.

Sam: SAMISDAT, Merritt Clifton, Robin Michelle Clifton, eds., Box 129, Richford, VT 05476. Issues indexed: (34:3-4, 35:1-4, 36:1-4, releases 135-144). Subscriptions: $150/all future issues, $25/1000 pages, $15/500 pages; Single issues: varies.

*SanFPJ: SAN FERNANDO POETRY JOURNAL, Richard Cloke, ed., 18301 Halsted St., Northridge, CA 91325. Issues indexed: (4:2-4, 5:1-4). Subscriptions: $10/yr., $18/2 yrs., $25/3 yrs.; Single issues: $3.

SecC: SECOND COMING, A. D. Winans, ed./pub., Box 31249, San Francisco, CA 94131. Issues indexed: (11:1/2). Subscriptions: $7.50/yr. (lib.), $5.50/yr. (ind.), $9.50 (for.)..

SenR: SENECA REVIEW, James Crenner, ed., Hobart & William Smith Colleges, Geneva, NY 14456. Issues indexed: (13:2); vol. 13, no. 1 was incorrectly labeled vol. 31, no. 1 in the 1982 Index. Single issues: $3.50; Double issues: $7.

SewanR: THE SEWANEE REVIEW, George Core, ed., U. of the South, Sewanee, TN 37375. Issues indexed: (91:1-4). Subscriptions: $37/3 yrs., $26/2 yrs., $15/yr. (inst.); $28/3 yrs., $20/2 yrs., $12/yr. (ind.); plus $3/yr. (for.); Single issues: $4; Back issues: $5-10, plus $.75/copy postage & handling.

Shen: SHENANDOAH, James Boatwright, ed., Richard Howard, Po. ed., Washington and Lee U., Box 722, Lexington, VA 24450. Issues indexed: (34:1-4). Subscriptions: $18/3 yrs., $13/2 yrs., $8/yr. plus $2/volume (for.); Single issues: $2.50; Back issues: $4.

Shout: A SHOUT IN THE STREET, Joe Cuomo, ed., Frederick Buell, Marie Ponsot, Po. eds., c/o Editorial Services,

A1310, Queens College, Flushing, NY 11367. Issues indexed: No 1983 issues received. Subscriptions: $10/yr.; Single issues: $4.

SinN: SIN NOMBRE, Nilita Vientos Gaston, Dir., Box 4391, San Juan, PR 00905-4391. Issues indexed: (13:3-4, 14:1). Subscriptions: $20/yr. (inst.), $15/yr. (ind.), $10/yr. (stud., Puerto Rico); Single issues: $4.25.

Sky: SKYWRITING, Martin Grossman, ed., 511 Campbell Ave., Kalamazoo, MI 49007. Issues indexed: No 1983 issues received. Single issues: $5.50.

SmPd: THE SMALL POND MAGAZINE OF LITERATURE, Napoleon St. Cyr, ed./pub., Box 664, Stratford, CT 06497. Issues indexed: (20:1-3, issues 57-59). Subscriptions: $5.50/yr.; Single issues: $2.25.

SoCaR: SOUTH CAROLINA REVIEW, Richard J. Calhoun, Robert W. Hill, eds., Dept. of English, Clemson U., Clemson, SC 29631. Issues indexed: (15:2, 16:1). Subscriptions: $9/2 yrs., $5/yr. (USA, Canada, Mexico); $10/2 yrs., $5.50/yr. (elsewhere); Back issues: $3.

SoDakR: SOUTH DAKOTA REVIEW, John R. Milton, ed., Dept. of English, U. of South Dakota, Box 111, U. Exchange, Vermillion, SD 57069. Issues indexed: (21:1-4). Subscriptions: $17/2 yrs., $10/yr. (USA, Canada); $20/2 yrs., $12/yr. (elsewhere); Single issues: $3.

SouthernHR: SOUTHERN HUMANITIES REVIEW, Patrick D. Morrow, James P. Hammersmith, eds., 9088 Haley Center, Auburn U., Auburn, AL 36849. Issues indexed: (17:1-4). Subscriptions: $8/yr.; Single issues: $2.50.

SouthernPR: SOUTHERN POETRY REVIEW, Robert Grey, ed., English Dept., U. of North Carolina, Charlotte, NC 28223. Issues indexed: (23:1-2?); both issues (Spr 83, Fall 83) numbered 23:2; Spr 83 issue has "Fall 82" on title-page. Subscriptions: $5/yr.; Single issues: $3.

SouthernR: SOUTHERN REVIEW, James Olney, Lewis P. Simpson, eds., Louisiana State U., 43 Allen Hall, Baton Rouge, LA 70893. Issues indexed: (19:1-4). Subscriptions: $21/3 yrs., $16/2 yrs., $9/yr.; Single issues: $2.50.

SouthwR: SOUTHWEST REVIEW, Charlotte T. Whaley, ed., Southern Methodist U., Dallas, TX 75275. Issues indexed: (68:1-4). Subscriptions: $20/3 yrs., $14/2 yrs., $8/yr.; Single issues: $2.

Sparrow: SPARROW PRESS POVERTY PAMPHLETS, Felix Stefanile, ed./Pub., Sparrow Press, 103 Waldron St., West Lafayette, IN 47906. Issues indexed: (44). Subscriptions: $6/3 issues; Single issues: $2.

Spirit: THE SPIRIT THAT MOVES US, Morty Sklar, ed., P.O. Box 1585, Iowa City, IA 52244. Issues indexed: No issues published in 1983.

*SpiritSH: SPIRIT, David Rogers, ed., Seton Hall U., South Orange, NJ 07079. Issues indexed: (48-49, 49 suppl.). Subscriptions: $4/yr.; Single issues: $2; Back issues: $3.

*SpoonRQ: THE SPOON RIVER QUARTERLY, David R. Pichaske, ed., P.O. Box 1443, Peoria, IL 61655. Issues indexed: (8:1-4). Subscriptions: $10/yr.; Single issues: $3.

Stand: STAND, Jon Silkin, et al., eds., Howard Fink, Canadian ed., 4054 Melrose Ave., Montreal, Quebec H4A 2S4 Canada. Issues indexed: (24:1-4). Subscriptions: $21.75/2 yrs., $11/yr.; Single issues: $3.

StoneC: STONE COUNTRY, Judith Neeld, ed., The Nathan Mayhew Seminars of Martha's Vineyard, P.O. Box 132, Menemsha, MA 02552. Issues indexed: (10:3/4, 11:1/2). Subscriptions: $14/2 yrs., $7.50/yr.; Single issues: $4.50.

Sulfur: SULFUR, California Institute of Technology, Clayton Eshleman, ed., 852 South Bedford St., Los Angeles, CA 90035. Issues indexed: (3:1-2, issues 7-8). Subscriptions: $22/yr. (inst.), $15/yr. (ind.), plus $3/yr. (for.); Single issues: $6; Box 228-77, California Institute of Technology, Pasadena, CA 91125.

SunM: SUN & MOON, Douglass Messerli, Literary ed., 4330 Hartwick Rd. #418, College Park, MD 20740. Issues indexed: (12-13). Single issues: $5.95.

*Swallow: SWALLOW'S TALE, Joe Taylor, ed., P.O. Box 4328, Tallahassee, FL 32315. Issues indexed: (1-2). Subscriptions: $13.50/yr. - 3 issues plus poetry books, $9.50/yr. - magazine only (ind.), $12/yr. - magazine only (inst.).

Tele: TELEPHONE, Maureen Owen, ed., 109 Dunk Rock Rd., Guildord, CT 06437. Issues indexed: (18). Subscriptions: $7/2 issues; Single issues: $4.

Telescope: TELESCOPE, Julia Wendell, Jack Stephens, eds., The Galileo Press, 15201 Wheeler Lane, Sparks, MD 21152. Issues indexed: (4-6). Subscriptions: $14/3 issues (inst.), $11/3 issues (ind.), $17.50/3 issues (for.); Single issues: $4.50; The Johns Hopkins U. Press, Journals Division, Baltimore, MD 21218.

Tendril: TENDRIL, George E. Murphy, Jr., ed., Box 512, Green Harbor, MA 02041. Issues indexed: (14-16). Subscriptions: $25/9 issues, $17/6 issues, $10/3 issues (ind.); $12/yr. (inst.); Single issues: $5.95.

*ThirdW: THE THIRD WIND, Thomas Paladino, ed., P.O. Box 8277, Boston, MA 02114. Issues indexed: (Spr 83). Single issues: $3.50.

13thM: 13TH MOON. See entry at beginning of list, prior to the 'A' entries.

ThRiPo: THREE RIVERS POETRY JOURNAL, Gerald Costanzo, ed., Three Rivers Press, P.O. Box 21, Carnegie-Mellon U., Pittsburgh, PA 15213. Issues indexed: (19/20-21/22). Subscriptions: $10/4 issues; Single issues: $2.50.

Thrpny: THE THREEPENNY REVIEW, Wendy Lesser, ed./pub., P.O. Box 9131, Berkeley, CA 94709. Issues indexed: (3:4, 4:1-3, issues 12-15). Subscriptions: $13/2 yrs., $8/yr., $16/yr. (surface for.), $24/yr. (airmail for.); Single issues: $2.

TriQ: TRIQUARTERLY, Reginald Gibbons, ed., Northwestern U., 1735 Benson Ave., Evanston, IL 60201. Issues indexed: (56-58). Subscriptions: $100/life (ind.), $200/life (inst.), $28/2 yrs. (ind.), $40/2 yrs. (inst.), $16/yr. (ind.), $22/yr. (inst.), plus $4/yr. (for.); Single issues: $6.95; Sample copies: $3.

UnderRM: UNDERGROUND RAG MAG. See: RagMag: RAG MAG.

US1: US 1 WORKSHEETS, Cindy Burd, David Keller, Rod Tulloss, Lisa Mihan, po. eds., US 1 Poets Cooperative, 21 Lake Dr., Roosevelt, NJ 08555. Issues indexed: (16/17). Subscriptions: $5/4 issues; Single issues: $2.50; Back issues: Prices on request.

UTR: UT REVIEW. No longer published; replaced by ABATIS.

VirQR: THE VIRGINIA QUARTERLY REVIEW, Staige D. Blackford, ed., Gregory Orr, Po. consultant., One West Range, Charlottsville, VA 22903. Issues indexed: (59:1-4). Subscriptions: $24/3 yrs., $18/2 yrs., $10/yr., plus $.50/yr. (Canada), $1/yr. (elsewhere); Single issues: $3.

Vis: VISIONS, Bradley R. Strahan, ed./pub., Black Buzzard Press, 4705 South 8th Rd.,Arlington, VA 22204. Issues indexed: (11-13). Subscriptions: $14/6 issues, $7/3 issues; Single issues: $2.50.

Waves: WAVES, Bernice Lever, et al., eds., 79 Denham Drive, Thornhill, Ontario L4J 1P2 Canada. Issues indexed: (11:2-4). Subscriptions: $8/yr. (ind.), $12/yr. (lib.); Single issues: $3; Back issues: $1.

WebR: WEBSTER REVIEW, Nancy Schapiro, ed., Webster U., Webster Groves, MO 63119. Issues indexed: (8:1-2). Subscriptions: $5/yr.; Single issues: $2.50.

WestB: WEST BRANCH, Karl Patten, Robert Taylor, eds., Dept. of English, Bucknell U., Lewisburg, PA 17837. Issues indexed: (12-13). Subscriptions: $8/2 yrs., $5/yr.; Single issues: $3.

WestCR: WEST COAST REVIEW, Fred Candelaria, ed., English Dept., Simon Fraser U., Burnaby, B.C. V5A 1S6 Canada. Issues indexed: (17:3-4, 18:1-2). Subscriptions: $12/yr. (Canada), $15/yr. (USA, for.), $16/yr. (inst.); Single issues: $3.50 (Canada), $4 (USA, for.).

WestHR: WESTERN HUMANITIES REVIEW, Jack Garlington, ed., U. of Utah, Salt Lake City, UT 84112. Issues indexed: (37:1-4). Subscriptions: $20/yr. (inst.), $15/yr. (ind.); Single issues: $4.

Wind: WIND, Quentin R. Howard, ed., RFD Route 1, Box 809K, Pikeville, KY 41501. Issues indexed: (13:47-49). Subscriptions: $6/3 issues (inst.), $5/3 issues (ind.), $7/3 issues (for.); Single issues: $1.50 (ind.), $1.75 (inst.), $2 (for.).

WindO: THE WINDLESS ORCHARD, Robert Novak, ed., English Dept., Indiana U.-Purdue U., Fort Wayne, IN 46805. Issues indexed: (42-43). Subscriptions: $20/3 yrs., $7/yr., $4/yr. (stud.); Single issues: $2.

WorldO: WORLD ORDER, Firuz Kazemzadeh, et al., eds., William Stafford, Po. consultant, National Spiritual Assembly of the Baha'is of the United States, 415 Linden Ave., Wilmette, IL 60091. Issues indexed: (17:2-4, 18:1). Subscriptions: $18/2 yrs., $10/yr.; $22/2 yrs., $12/yr. (for.); Single issues: $3.

WormR: THE WORMWOOD REVIEW, Marvin Malone, ed., P.O. Box 8840, Stockton, CA 95208-0840. Issues indexed: (23:1-4, issues 89-92). Subscriptions: $15/4 issues (patrons), $7/4 issues (inst.), $6/4 issues (ind.), plus $1.75 (for.); Back issues: $3; Single issues: $2.50.

WritersL: WRITER'S LIFELINE, Stephen Gill, ed., Box 1641, Cornwall, Ontario K6H 5V6 Canada. Issues indexed: (Ja-O). Subscriptions: $18/yr; Single issues: $1.50.

YaleR: THE YALE REVIEW, Kai Erikson, ed., William Meredith, Po. ed., 1902A Yale Station, New Haven, CT 06520. Issues indexed: (72:2-4, 73:1). Subscriptions: $18/yr. (inst.), $12/yr. (ind.), plus $3/yr. (for.); Single issues: $4; Back issues: Prices on request.

*YetASM: YET ANOTHER SMALL MAGAZINE, Candace Catlin Hall, ed., Box 14353, Hartford, CT 06114. Issues indexed: (1:1-2, 2:1). Single issues: $1.98.

ALPHABETICAL LIST OF JOURNALS INDEXED, WITH ACRONYMS

13TH MOON: 13thM

ABATIS: Abatis
ABRAXAS: Abraxas
ACADEME: Academe
THE AGNI REVIEW: Agni
THE AMERICAN POETRY REVIEW: AmerPoR
THE AMERICAN SCHOLAR: AmerS
ANNEX 21: Annex
ANTAEUS: Antaeus
THE ANTIGONISH REVIEW: AntigR
THE ANTIOCH REVIEW: ANTR
AREITO: Areito
ARGO, Incorporating DELTA: Argo
ARIZONA QUARTERLY: ArizQ
ASCENT: Ascent
THE ATLANTIC: Atlantic

BALL STATE UNIVERSITY FORMUM: BallSUF
THE BELOIT POETRY JOURNAL: BelPoJ
BERKSHIRE REVIEW: BerksR
BLACK AMERICAN LITERATURE FORUM: BlackALF
BLACK WARRIOR REVIEW: BlackWR
BLUE BUFFALO: BlueBuf
BLUELINE: Blueline
BOGG: Bogg
BOUNDARY 2: Bound

CALIFORNIA QUARTERLY: CalQ
CALYX: Calyx
CANADIAN LITERATURE: CanLit
THE CAPE ROCK: CapeR
THE CAPILANO REVIEW: CapilR
CARIBE: Caribe
CAROLINA QUARTERLY: CarolQ
CATALYST: Catalyst
THE CEA CRITIC: CEACritic
THE CEA FORUM: CEAFor
THE CENTENNIAL REVIEW: CentR
THE CHARITON REVIEW: CharR
CHELSEA: Chelsea
CHICAGO REVIEW: ChiR
THE CHRISTIAN CENTURY: ChrC
CIMARRON RIVIEW: CimR
CLOCKWATCH REVIEW: ClockR
COLLEGE ENGLISH: ColEng
COMMONWEAL: Comm
CONCERNING POETRY: ConcPo
CONDITIONS: Cond

CONFRONTATION: Confr
CRAB CREEK REVIEW: CrabCR
CREAM CITY REVIEW: CreamCR
CROP DUST: CropD
CROSS-CANADA WRITERS' QUARTERLY: CrossC
CUTBANK: CutB

DANDELION: Dandel
THE DEKALB LITERARY ARTS JOURNAL: DekalbLAJ
DENVER QUARTERLY: DenQ
DESCANT: Descant

EN PASSANT: EnPas
ENGLISH JOURNAL: EngJ
EPOCH: Epoch

FIELD: Field
FOCUS/MIDWEST: Focus
FOUR QUARTERS: FourQt

GARGOYLE MAGAZINE: Gargoyle
GEORGIA REIVEW: GeoR
GERMINATION: Germ
GRAIN: Grain

HANGING LOOSE: HangL
HARPER'S MAGAZINE: Harp
THE HARVARD ADVOCATE: HarvardA
HIRAM POETRY REVIEW: HiramPoR
THE HOLLINS CRITIC: Hol Crit
THE HUDSON REVIEW: Hudson
THE HUMANIST: Humanist

IMAGES: Images
INDIANA REVIEW: IndR
INTI, REVISTA DE LITERATURA HISPANICA: Inti
IOWA REVIEW: Iowa

JUNTE DEL TALLER RACATA: Rácata

KANSAS QUARTERLY: KanQ
KAYAK: Kayak

LETRAS FEMENINAS: LetFem
THE LITERARY REVIEW: LitR
THE LITTLE BALKANS REVIEW: LittleBR
THE LITTLE MAGAZINE: LittleM
THE LITTLE REVIEW: LittleR

MAIRENA: Mairena
THE MALAHAT REVIEW: MalR
THE MANHATTAN REVIEW: ManhatR
THE MASSACHUSETTS REVIEW: MassR
THE MEADOWS: Meadows
MEMPHIS STATE REVIEW: MemphisSR
MENDOCINO REVIEW: MendoR
MESTER: Mester
METAMORFOSIS: Metam
MICHIGAN QUARTERLY REVIEW: MichQR

THE MIDWEST QUARTERLY: MidwQ
THE MINNESOTA REVIEW: MinnR
MISSISSIPPI REVIEW: MissR
THE MISSOURI REVIEW: MissouriR
MODERN POETRY STUDIES: ModernPS
MOODY STREET IRREGULARS: MoodySI
MSS: MSS
MUNDUS ARTIUM: Mund

THE NATION: Nat
NEGATIVE CAPABILITY: NegC
NEW ENGLAND REVIEW AND BREAD LOAF QUARTERLY: NewEngR
NEW LETTERS: NewL
NEW ORLEANS REVIEW: NewOR
THE NEW RENAISSANCE: NewRena
THE NEW REPUBLIC: NewRep
NEW WORLD REVIEW: NewWR
THE NEW YORK REVIEW OF BOOKS: NewYRB
THE NEW YORKER: NewYorker
NIMROD: Nimrod
THE NORTH AMERICAN REVIEW: NoAmR
NORTHEAST: Northeast
NORTHWEST REVIEW: NowestR
NOTICIAS DE ARTE: Notarte

OBSIDIAN: Obs
THE OHIO REIVEW: OhioR
ONTARIO REVIEW: OntR
OPEN PLACES: OP
ORO MADRE: OroM
OSIRIS: Os
OUTERBRIDGE: Outbr

PAINTBRUSH: Paint
THE PARIS REVIEW: ParisR
PARTISAN REVIEW: PartR
PEBBLE: Peb
PEQUOD: Pequod
PIG IRON: Pig
THE PIKESTAFF FORUM: PikeF
PLAYBOY: Playb
PLOUGHSHARES: Ploughs
POEM: Poem
POET AND CRITIC: PoetC
POET LORE: PoetL
POETRY: Poetry
POETRY CANADA REVIEW: PoetryCR
POETRY EAST: PoetryE
POETRY NORTHWEST: PoetryNW
POETRY NOW: PoNow
PORTLAND REVIEW: PortR
THE POTTERSFIELD PORTFOLIO: PottPort
PRAIRIE SCHOONER: PraS
PRIMAVERA: Prima
PRISMAL/CABRAL: Prismal

QUARRY: Quarry
QUARTERLY REVIEW OF LITERATURE: QRL
QUARTERLY WEST: QW

RACATA: <u>Rácata</u>
RAG MAG: <u>RagMag</u>
RARITAN: <u>Raritan</u>
REVISTA CHICANO-RIQUENA: <u>RevChic</u>
REVISTA/REVIEW INTERAMERICANA: <u>RevIn</u>

SALMAGUNDI: <u>Salm</u>
SAMISDAT: <u>Sam</u>
SAN FERNANDO POETRY JOURNAL: <u>SanFPJ</u>
SECOND COMING: <u>SecC</u>
SENECA REVIEW: <u>SenR</u>
THE SEWANEE REVIEW: <u>SewanR</u>
SHENANDOAH: <u>Shen</u>
A SHOUT IN THE STREET: <u>Shout</u>
SIN NOMBRE: <u>SinN</u>
SKYWRITING: <u>Sky</u>
THE SMALL POND MAGAZINE OF LITERATURE: <u>SmPd</u>
SOUTH CAROLINA REVIEW: <u>SoCaR</u>
SOUTH DAKOTA REVIEW: <u>SoDakR</u>
SOUTHERN HUMANITIES REVIEW: <u>SouthernHR</u>
SOUTHERN POETRY REVIEW: <u>SouthernPR</u>
SOUTHERN REVIEW: <u>SouthernR</u>
SOUTHWEST REVIEW: <u>SouthwR</u>
SPARROW: <u>Sparrow</u>
SPIRIT: <u>SpiritSH</u>
THE SPIRIT THAT MOVES US: <u>Spirit</u>
THE SPOON RIVER QUARTERLY: <u>SpoonRQ</u>
STAND: <u>Stand</u>
STONE COUNTRY: <u>StoneC</u>
SULFUR: <u>Sulfur</u>
SUN & MOON: <u>SunM</u>
SWALLOW'S TALE: <u>Swallow</u>

TELEPHONE: <u>Tele</u>
TELESCOPE: <u>Telescope</u>
TENDRIL: <u>Tendril</u>
THE THIRD WIND: <u>ThirdW</u>
13TH MOON: <u>13thM</u>
THREE RIVERS POETRY JOURNAL: <u>ThRiPo</u>
THE THREEPENNY REVIEW: <u>Thrpny</u>
TRIQUARTERLY: <u>TriQ</u>

US 1 WORKSHEETS: <u>US1</u>
VIRGINIA QUARTERLY REVIEW: <u>VirQR</u>
VISIONS: <u>Vis</u>

WAVES: <u>Waves</u>
WEBSTER REVIEW: <u>WebR</u>
WEST BRANCH: <u>WestB</u>
WEST COAST REVIEW: <u>WestCR</u>
WESTERN HUMANITIES REVIEW: <u>WestHR</u>
WIND: <u>Wind</u>
THE WINDLESS ORCHARD: <u>WindO</u>
WORLD ORDER: <u>WorldO</u>
THE WORMWOOD REVIEW: <u>WormR</u>
WRITER'S LIFELINE: <u>WritersL</u>

THE YALE REVIEW: <u>YaleR</u>
YET ANOTHER SMALL MAGAZINE: <u>YetASM</u>

THE AUTHOR INDEX

1. AAL, Katharyn Machan
"In the Arms of Clytemnestra." Vis (13) 83, p. 26.
"Letters from My Mother." MinnR (NS 20) Spr 83, p. 52-53.
"A Second Interview with Mrs. F." Tele (18) 83, p. 80-81.

2. AARNES, William
"Accused." SoCaR (16:1) Aut 83, p. 79.
"The First" (for Arlie and Devon Hedges). SoCaR (16:1) Aut 83, p. 78.

3. ABBOTT, Mason
"Fawn Finger." Bogg (50) 83, p. 61.

4. ABERCROMBIE, V. T.
"Colorado/Fall." Poem (49) N 83, p. 50.
"The Park." Poem (49) N 83, p. 51.

5. ABHAU, Elliot
"Listen." WorldO (17:4) Sum 83, p. 26.

6. ABLEY, Mark
"Asian Mass" (Selections: "Gloria," "Credo"). Grain (11:2) My 83, p. 5-11.

7. ABRAMS, Sam
"The Definition of Dirt" (for Ma & Jimmy Yancy). Tele (18) 83, p. 7.
"Fever Cabin." Tele (18) 83, p. 6.
"Words Not Words." Tele (18) 83, p. 7.

8. ABSE, Dannie
"Quests." Poetry (142:6) S 83, p. 328.

9. ACHUGAR, Hugo
"Entre afloje y pelea" (a Angel Rama). Areito (9:35) 83, p. 41.

10. ACKER, Paul
"Swan Point, Sixth of January." Blueline (4:2) Wint-Spr 83, p. 15.

11. ACKERMAN, Diane
"Four Soccer Poems about the Rhythm of the Mind." Nimrod (27:1) Aut-Wint 83, p. 12-15.
"Golden Section, Giants Stadium." Nimrod (27:1) Aut-Wint 83, p. 13-14.
"In a Philosopher's Cottage" (for Alfonso Lingis).

AmerPoR (12:2) Mr/Ap 83, p. 15.
"Losing the Game." Nimrod (27:1) Aut-Wint 83, p. 12-13.
"Soccer at the Meadowlands." Nimrod (27:1) Aut-Wint 83, p. 12.
"Space Shuttle." MichOR (22:4) Aut 83, p. 553.
"Spiders." MichOR (22:4) Aut 83, p. 552.
"A View from the Terraces." Nimrod (27:1) Aut-Wint 83, p. 14-15.

12. ACKERMAN, Stephen
"Speculative Poem." SenR (13:2) 82-83, p. 35-36.

13. ACKERSON, Duane
"The Minotaur's Schizophrenia." PoNow (7:2, #38) 83, p. 13.
"The Reluctant Dinner." PoNow (7:2, #38) 83, p. 13.

14. ACORN, Milton
"Captain Neal MacDougal's Oath" (from Captain Neal MacDougal and the Naked Goddess). PottPort (5) 83-84, p. 42.
"The Joker Deals." Argo (4:3) 83, p. 3.
"MacDougal on the Fear of Hell" (from Captain Neal MacDougal and the Naked Goddess). PottPort (5) 83-84, p. 42.
"MacDougal's Theory of Dreams" (from Captain Neal MacDougal and the Naked Goddess). PottPort (5) 83-84, p. 42.
"More Philosophy from MacDougal" (from Captain Neal MacDougal and the Naked Goddess). PottPort (5) 83-84, p. 42.
"Politics According to MacDougal" (from Captain Neal MacDougal and the Naked Goddess). PottPort (5) 83-84, p. 42.
"Warning of Beloved Lacklove." Argo (4:3) 83, p. 3.

ACUNA, David Lopez
See: LOPEZ ACUNA, David

15. ADAM, Helen
"Margaretta's Rime." CreamCR (8:1/2) 83, p. 74.

16. ADAM, Ian
"The Big Rocks." Bluebuf (2:1) Aut 83, p. 34.

17. ADAMS, Barbara
"Camping with Marx." MinnR (NS 20) Spr 83, p. 55-56.

18. ADAMS, David
"Friday." CentR (27:2) Spr 83, p. 112.
"Lake County." CentR (27:2) Spr 83, p. 112-113.
"Leave." Wind (13:49) 83, p. 1.
"Two Windows." HiramPoR (35) Aut-Wint 83, p. 5.

19. ADAMS, Willie
"Night of Terror." PoetryE (9/10) Wint 82-Spr 83, p. 272-273.

20. ADAMSON, Arthur
"Hawk's Domain." PoetryCR (4:4) Sum 83, p. 5.
"Music." PoetryCR (5:2) Wint 83-84, p. 13.

21. ADANG, Richard
"December" (for JA). Northeast (Ser. 3:16) Wint 83-84, p. 20.
"Holding Our Own." Northeast (Ser. 3:16) Wint 83-84, p. 20.

22. ADCOCK, Betty
"To My Father, Killed in a Hunting Accident" (R.L.S. 1904-1974). SouthernPR (23:2) Aut 82 [i.e. (23:1?) Spr 83], p. 12-14.

23. ADEN, Carlin
"This Valley." SoDakR (21:4) Wint 83, p. 17.

24. ADLER, Lucile
"With Horror, Sir, Sincerely." MassR (24:3) Aut 83, p. 541-543.

25. AFROUZ, Novin
"Oriental Eyes." WritersL Mr 83, p. 17.
"Progress." WritersL Mr 83, p. 22.

26. AGGESTAM, Rolf
"Ditt Hjärta Ar Ett Rött Tag." NewRena (16) Spr 83, p. 22.
"Gamle Basko." NewRena (16) Spr 83, p. 24.
"Old Basho" (tr. by Erland Anderson and Lars Nordström). NewRena (16) Spr 83, p. 25.
"Portent" (tr. by Erland Anderson and Lars Nordström). NewRena (16) Spr 83, p. 27.
"Varsel." NewRena (16) Spr 83, p. 26.
"Your Heart Is a Red Train" (tr. by Erland Anderson and Lars Nordström). NewRena (16) Spr 83, p. 23.

AGHA SHAHID ALI
See: ALI, Agha Shahid

27. AGOOS, Julie
"Suicidio." AntR (41:4) Aut 83, p. 446-449.

28. AGOSIN, Marjorie
"Cecile and Jacqueline" (tr. by Frances Aparicio). MinnR (NS 21) Aut 83, p. 7.
"Dónde Están?" RevChic (11:3/4) 83, p. 76.
"Estados Unidos." RevChic (11:3/4) 83, p. 73.
"La Mesa de Billar en New Bedford, Mass." RevChic (11:3/4) 83, p. 72-73.
"Mis Pies." RevChic (11:3/4) 83, p. 74-75.
"United States" (tr. by Frances Aparicio). MinnR (NS 21) Aut 83, p. 8.

29. AGOSTINI, Efrain
"Al Unísono." Rácata (1) 83, p. 14.
"Encuentro." Rácata (1) 83, p. 17.
"Fábrica." Rácata (1) 83, p. 13.
"Y Seré Yo." Rácata (1) 83, p. 15-16.

30. AGTE, Bruce
"Chestnut Days." PoetC (13, i.e. 14:3) 83, p. 62-63.

31. AGUILA, Pancho
"Folsom, August 11th: A Question of Races." SecC (11:1/2) 83, p. 1-2.
"Good Morning, How Are You?" SanFPJ (4:2) 83, p. 25.

32. AGUSTINI, Delmira
"The Wings" (tr. by Beth Tornes). AmerPoR (12:1) Ja/F 83, p. 16.

33. AHEARN, Catherine
"Which Spine Are You?" PoetryCR (5:1) Aut 83, p. 6.

34. AHRENS, Robert
"The Dream Merchant." Wind (13:49) 83, p. 37.

35. AIELLO, Ralph B.
"Man's Supremacy." WritersL Ja 83, p. 2.
"Sorry Little 'Bug'." WritersL Ag 83, p. 26.

36. AIKEN, William
"Learning of the Brown World during Deer Week." SouthernHR (17:3) Sum 83, p. 264.
"The Third Rail of Beatitude." KanQ (15:1) Wint 83, p. 136.

37. AJAY, Stephen
"Avalanche." ParisR (25:87) Spr 83, p. 132.

38. AKHMADULINA, Bella
"Laughing, exulting and rebellious" (tr. by Mary Maddock). PoNow (7:2, #38) 83, p. 44.
"Sleep" (tr. by Mary Maddock). PoNow (7:2, #38) 83, p. 44.

39. AKHMATOVA, Anna
"The Last Rose" (tr. by F. D. Reeve). Nat (237:12) 22 O 83, p. 379.
"Northern Elegy" (Excerpt) (tr. by Mary Maddock). MassR (24:1) Spr 83, p. 107.
"To Alexander Blok" (tr. by Marianne Andrea). MalR (66) O 83, p. 121.
"Willow" (tr. by Marianne Andrea). MalR (66) O 83, p. 121.

AKIRA, Izumiya
See: IZUMIYA, Akira

40. AKSAL, Sabahattin Kudret
"The First Snow" (tr. by Ozcan Yalim, William A. Fielder and Dionis C. Riggs). Mund (14:1) 83, p. 51.
"Poem toward Noon" (tr. by Ozcan Yalim, William A. Fielder and Dionis C. Riggs). Mund (14:1) 83, p. 51.

AL-MU'TAZZ, Ibn
See: IBN AL-MU'TAZZ

41. ALBERHASKY, Peggy S.
"Indestructable Breeds." PortR (29:1) 83, p. 66.
"Naked Trees." PortR (29:1) 83, p. 67.

42. ALBERT, Phyllis
"Eli." YetASM (1:2) 82, p. 16.
"The Nurse Tells Me I Can See You Now." YetASM (1:2) 82, p. 5.
"The Wheelchair Waits." YetASM (1:2) 82, p. 12.

43. ALBERTI, Rafael
"Bituminous Angel" (tr. by W. A. Fahey). WebR (8:1) Spr 83, p. 56.
"Collegial Angels" (tr. by Leland H. Chambers). DevQ (18:1) Spr 83, p. 100.
"The Good Angel" (tr. by W. A. Fahey). WebR (8:1) Spr 83, p. 55.
"Invitation to the Lyre" (tr. by Leland H. Chambers). DevQ (18:1) Spr 83, p. 99.

44. ALCOSSER, Sandra
"Cry" (The Mary Elinore Smith Poetry Prize). AmerS (52:2) Spr 83, p. 170-171.
"A Fish to Feed All Hunger" (Selections: "Nightjar," "Fox Fire"). Nimrod (27:1) Aut-Wint 83, p. 88-90.
"Fox Fire." Nimrod (27:1) Aut-Wint 83, p. 89-90.
"Nightjar." Nimrod (27:1) Aut-Wint 83, p. 88-89.

45. ALDER, David
"On Top of Greenfield." Argo (5:1) 83, p. 9.

46. ALDERDICE, Eve
"After the Hunt." Wind (13:49) 83, p. 2.

47. ALDRIDGE, Richard
"The Whole Story" (Percy Larrabee, Blueberry Farmer). PoNow (7:2, #38) 83, p. 14.

48. ALEGRIA, Claribel
"I Was Born Here As Well" (tr. by Carolyn Forché). PoetryE (9/10) Wint 82-Spr 83, p. 175.
"Personal Data" (tr. by Carolyn Forché). PoetryE (9/10) Wint 82-Spr 83, p. 176.

49. ALEGRIA, Fernando
"La Ceiba Gardens" (tr. by Stephen Kessler). AmerPoR (12:5) S/O 83, p. 7.

50. ALESHIRE, Joan
"Evening." Tendril (14/15) Wint 83, p. 15.
"The Man from the Restaurant." BlackWR (10:1) Aut 83, p. 65.
"Mourning Doves: Maryland." Poetry (142:2) My 83, p. 63.
"Slipping." Poetry (142:2) My 83, p. 64.
"Still Pond, More Moving." Tendril (14/15) Wint 83, p. 16.

51. ALEXANDER, Bonnie L.
"Götterdämmerung." SouthernHR (17:1) Wint 83,

p. 29.

52. ALEXANDER, Charles
"With Eggs." CreamCR (8:1/2) 83, p. 147.

53. ALEXANDER, Francis W.
"Unemployment Poetry." SanFPJ (5:4) 83, p. 14-15.

54. ALEXANDER, Pamela
"In the Room Next to You." AntR (41:4) Aut 83, p. 445.

55. ALEXIS, Gail
"All the Way Home." BlackALF (17:4) Wint 83, p. 153.
"Athlete." BlackALF (17:4) Wint 83, p. 153.
"For Robin H--, upon Seven Years of Motherhood, at Age 21." BlackALF (17:4) Wint 83, p. 152.
"Talking Horse." BlackALF (17:4) Wint 83, p. 152.

56. ALI, Agha Shahid
"Eurydice." NewEngR (6:2) Wint 83, p. 321-322.
"Poem: O you who wear shirts ripped at the collars" (tr. of Faiz Ahmed Faiz). StoneC (10:3/4) Spr-Sum 83, p. 45.

57. ALIESAN, Jody
"Yes." NegC (3:4) Aut 83, p. 48-49.

58. ALINA, Marta
"The Art Garden" (for J.R.). MalR (64) F 83, p. 157.
"Ballad of Brecht's Soldier." MalR (64) F 83, p. 158-159.
"Bitter Sloe." MalR (64) F 83, p. 153.
"The Bower of Earthy Frights." MalR (64) F 83, p. 152-153.
"Composition after Li Po." MalR (64) F 83, p. 154.
"Crackerjack Garden: Found Loves." MalR (64) F 83, p. 154-155.
"Landscape with Starfish and Mirror." MalR (64) F 83, p. 160.
"What Kind of Myth Is This?" MalR (64) F 83, p. 156.

59. ALISHAN, Leonardo P.
"Apple tree growing in my throat." Mund (14:1) 83, p. 55.
"I've come to bury someone in the snow." Mund (14:1) 83, p. 55.
"Long winter." Mund (14:1) 83, p. 55.
"A tiger leapt at me." Mund (14:1) 83, p. 55.

60. ALKALAY, Karen
"Last Portraits: Anne Sexton." Argo (4:1) 82, p. 17.

61. ALLAN, Pat
"Collage." Bluebuf (2:1) Aut 83, p. 6.
"The Dance in the Leg-Hold." Bluebuf (2:1) Aut 83, p. 30.

62. ALLBERY, Deb
"The Reservoir" (for Lowell Jaeger). MissouriR (6:3) Sum 83, p. 30-35.

63. ALLDREDGE, C. Starr
"Dimentions of Dementia." DekalbLAJ (16:1/4) Aut 82-Sum 83, p. 84.

64. ALLEN, Blair H.
"Deep Wells." SanFPJ (5:1) 83, p. 10-11.
"Direction of Will." SanFPJ (4:4) 83, p. 79.
"Direction of Will." SanFPJ (5:1) 83, p. 53.
"Dump Kings." SanFPJ (4:3) 83, p. 76.
"A Eulogy for Choice." SanFPJ (4:4) 83, p. 78.
"Four Questions Riding Hard." SanFPJ (4:2) 83, p. 15-16.
"Neighbors." SanFPJ (4:2) 83, p. 8.
"Tripping from the Big Dipper Song." SanFPJ (5:2) 83, p. 34-35.
"Visions Don't Awaken in Stereo." SanFPJ (5:2) 83, p. 33.
"We Hold in Our Hands." SanFPJ (5:2) 83, p. 42.

65. ALLEN, Dick
"Crossing the Stars on New Year's Eve." NewYorker (58:46) 3 Ja 83, p. 38.
"Finale." NewYorker (59:29) 5 S 83, p. 46.
"The Great Wonder." MichQR (22:4) Aut 83, p. 616-617.
"Korean Veteran." SouthernR (19:3) Jl 83, p. 673.

66. ALLEN, Elizabeth
"Ranch Visit." YetASM (2:1) 83, p. 7.

67. ALLEN, Gilbert
"Morning Glories." SouthernHR (17:1) Wint 83, p. 48.

68. ALLEY, Douglas
"Initiation." EngJ (72:1) Ja 83, p. 48.

69. ALLISON, Luther
"Back Down South." ClockR (1:1) Sum 83, p. 21.

70. ALLMAN, John
"The Dog." PoetryNW (24:4) Wint 83-84, p. 42.
"Michael Collins Ambushed by Republicans on the Road to Bealnamblath, 1922." MemphisSR (3:1) Aut 82, p. 16-17.

71. ALMANZA, Antonio
"Suspended in Time." Wind (13:48) 83, p. 19.

ALMEIDA, George d'
See: D'ALMEIDA, George

72. ALMON, Bert
"Cousin Ed Gets the Family Pictures from Aunt Margaret." NewL (50:1) Aut 83, p. 41.
"Java Jive." Outbr (12/13) Aut 83-Spr 84, p. 64.
"Jurisprudence." KanQ (15:1) Wint 83, p. 24.
"Look This Way Please." CrossC (5:4) 83, p. 7.
"Le Pragmatiste." LitR (27:1) Aut 83, p. 97.
"Transformations." Waves (11:4) Spr 83, p. 63.

73. ALPERT, Pat
"The Ants in the Kitchen." AntigR (52) Wint 83, p. 120.

74. ALSCHULER, Mari
"San Miguel de Allende." AmerPoR (12:4) Jl-Ag 83, p. 31.

75. ALTA
"San Lorenzo: Library." SecC (11:1/2) 83, p. 3-4.

76. ALTHAUS, Keith
"Black Leaves." VirQR (59:4) Aut 83, p. 682-683.
"Poem: When no animals lean out of the night sky." VirQR (59:4) Aut 83, p. 681.

77. ALVARADO TENORIO, Harold
"A Principios de Junio." Inti (15) Spr 82, p. 73.
"El Tiempo Pasa en Vano." Inti (15) Spr 82, p. 74.

78. ALVAREZ, Julia
"Bedmaking." 13thM (7:1/2) 83, p. 132.
"Ironing Their Clothes." 13thM (7:1/2) 83, p. 129.
"Naming the Fabrics." 13thM (7:1/2) 83, p. 130-131.

79. AMABILE, George
"Freeze." NewYorker (58:48) 17 Ja 83, p. 42.
"The Presence of Fire." PoetryCR (5:1) Aut 83, p. 13.

80. AMATO, Joe
"A Sicilian Father." SpoonRQ (8:4) Aut 83, p. 52-53.
"Spring Daughter." SpoonRQ (8:4) Aut 83, p. 53.

81. AMICHAI, Yehuda
"All These Make a Strange Dance Rhythm." AmerPoR (12:6) N/D 83, p. 38.
"End of Summer in the Mountains of Judea." AmerPoR (12:6) N/D 83, p. 37.
"The Eternal Mystery." AmerPoR (12:6) N/D 83, p. 37.
"Eyes" (tr. by Ruth Nevo).LitR (26:2) Wint 83, p. 221.
"I Sleep Tonight to Your Memory" (To the memory of Batya B.). AmerPoR (12:6) N/D 83, p. 37.
"Instead of Words" (tr. by Gabriel Levin). LitR (26:2) Wint 83, p. 224.
"Like a Ship's Captain." AmerPoR (12:6) N/D 83, p. 38.
"Love's Over Again" (tr. by Ruth Nevo). LitR (26:2) Wint 83, p. 223.
"Second Meeting with a Father" (tr. by Ruth Nevo).LitR (26:2) Wint 83, p. 222.
"Summer Evening in the King David Hotel" (tr. by Gabriel Levin). LitR (26:2) Wint 83, p. 223-224.
"The True Hero of the Aqedah" (tr. by Edna Amir Coffin). MichQR (22:3) Sum 83, p. 445.
"When I Have Stomach Ache." AmerPoR (12:6) N/D 83, p. 37.

82. AMIEL, Henri Frédéric
"Springtime" (tr. by Virginia Scott Miner). KanQ (15:2) Spr 83, p. 172.

AMIR KHUSROW DEHLAVI
See: DEHLAVI, Amir Khusrow

83. AMMONS, A. R.
"The Ridge Farm." Hudson (36:1) Spr 83, p. 75-110.
"Serpent Country." Epoch (33:1) Aut-Wint 83, p. 38.
"Swells." OhioR (30) 83, p. 146.

84. AMPRIMOZ, Alexandre L.
"Drifting." PoetryCR (5:2) Wint 83-84, p. 16.
"For the Brilliant Lost." Waves (11:2/3) Wint 83, p. 74.
"General Delivery." Waves (11:2/3) Wint 83, p. 74.

85. ANANIA, Michael
"April Snow: An Improvisation." OP (36) Aut-Wint 83, p. 16-17.
"Such Summers." OP (36) Aut-Wint 83, p. 14-15.

86. ANDERMANN, Guri
"Becoming a Saint." Ascent (9:1) 83, p. 14.
"Disappearing Act." Ascent (9:1) 83, p. 15.
"Numbers." Calyx (7:3) Sum 83, p. 16-17.
"Pity." Calyx (7:3) Sum 83, p. 18.
"Syllogisms." Calyx (7:3) Sum 83, p. 15.

87. ANDERSDATTER, Karla
"The Gifting." SanFPJ (4:2) 83, p. 54-55.

88. ANDERSDATTER, Karla Margaret
"Shoshone Father." SecC (11:1/2) 83, p. 5.

89. ANDERSEN, Eric
"Everything Is Normal." Waves (11:4) Spr 83, p. 62.

90. ANDERSON, Barbara
"Because All Boundaries Are Subject to Slow Change." BlackWR (8:1) Aut 81, p. 45.

91. ANDERSON, C. M.
"Africa Speaks to America." LittleBR (4:1) Aut 83, p. 29.
"In His Image." LittleBR (4:1) Aut 83, p. 8.

92. ANDERSON, Catherine
"Never Leaving the City." Tendril (16) Sum 83, p. 16.
"This Woman." Tendril (16) Sum 83, p. 15.

93. ANDERSON, Douglas (Doug)
"America's Health" (for Jess Graf). SanFPJ (5:1) 83, p. 70.
"America's Health" (for Jess Graf). SanFPJ (5:2) 83, p. 96.

94. ANDERSON, Erland
"Grief in Black Tie" (tr. of Luis Cernuda). NewRena (17) Aut 83, p. 53.
"I'm Tired" (tr. of Luis Cernuda). NewRena (17) Aut 83, p. 55.
"Old Basho" (tr. of Rolf Aggestam, w. Lars

Nordström). _NewRena_ (16) Spr 83, p. 25.
"Only These Walls" (tr. of Luis Cernuda). _NewRena_ (17) Aut 83, p. 57.
"The Outsider" (tr. of Luis Cernuda). _NewRena_ (17) Aut 83, p. 27.
"Portent" (tr. of Rolf Aggestam, w. Lars Nordström). _NewRena_ (16) Spr 83, p. 27.
"A Water-Glass in Boredom's hand" (tr. of Luis Cernuda). _NewRena_ (17) Aut 83, p. 29.
"When I Was an Adolescent" (tr. of Luis Cernuda). _NewRena_ (17) Aut 83, p. 25.
"Your Heart Is a Red Train" (tr. of Rolf Aggestam, w. Lars Nordström). _NewRena_ (16) Spr 83, p. 23.

95. ANDERSON, Jack
"Blues on the Ranch." _Kayak_ (63) N 83, p. 63.
"A Good Man." _PoetryE_ (9/10) Wint 82-Spr 83, p. 138.
"Magnets" (from The Clouds of That Country). _PoNow_ (7:2, #38) 83, p. 23.
"Myself As Rain." _PoNow_ (7:2, #38) 83, p. 14.
"The Poet Who Almost Ran Over Carl Sandburg." _PoetryE_ (11) Sum 83, p. 44-46.
"Sock Lust" (from The Clouds of That Country). _PoNow_ (7:2, #38) 83, p. 23.
"A Way of Happening." _PoetryE_ (9/10) Wint 82-Spr 83, p. 135-137.

96. ANDERSON, Jack L.
"Reflective." _Confr_ (25/26) 83, p. 303.

97. ANDERSON, James
"Your Song." _NewL_ (49:3/4) Spr-Sum 83, p. 139.

98. ANDERSON, Jon
"Years." _OhioR_ (30) 83, p. 96.

99. ANDERSON, Maggie
"Related to the Sky." _PoetryE_ (12) Aut 83, p. 57.
"Spitting in the Leaves." _PoetryE_ (12) Aut 83, p. 58.

100. ANDERSON, Martin
"End of Winter on Tai Mo Shan." _WestCR_ (17:4) Ap 83, p. 39.
"Giorgionesque." _Sulfur_ (3:1, #7) 83, p. 61.
"The Pumpkin by the River." _WestCR_ (17:4) Ap 83, p. 38.
"Russian Spring." _AntigR_ (54) Sum 83, p. 38.
"Seurat's 'Port-en-Bessin, the Outer Harbour at Low Tide'." _Sulfur_ (3:1, #7) 83, p. 62.
"The Source." _AntigR_ (54) Sum 83, p. 40.
"Three Fathom Cove." _AntigR_ (54) Sum 83, p. 39.

101. ANDERSON, Michael
"Along the 401, Late Evening." _AntigR_ (53) Spr 83, p. 46.

102. ANDERSON, P. F.
"I Am the Beast." _Mund_ (14:1) 83, p. 56-57.

103. ANDERSON, Paul
"Ceremony of the Stones." SoDakR (21:2) Sum 83, p. 62.

104. ANDERSON, Peggy
"Signing Your Poetry" (for W.D. Snodgrass). KanQ (15:2) Spr 83, p. 39.

105. ANDRADE, Carlos Drummond de
"Ballad of Love through the Ages" (tr. by Mark Strand). NewYorker (58:47) 10 Ja 83, p. 32.
"Our Time" (tr. by Thomas LaBorie Burns). WebR (8:1) Spr 83, p. 26-31.

106. ANDRADE, Eugenio de
"With the Poplars" (tr. by Alexis Levitin). Confr (25/26) 83, p. 314.

107. ANDREA, Marianne
"Biography." DevQ (18:3) Aut 83, p. 69.
"For Anna Akhmatova (1888-1966)." Confr (25/26) 83, p. 306.
"Fringe of Darkness" (For B.D.). DevQ (18:3) Aut 83, p. 70.
"Pasternak to Tsvetayeva" (Paris, 1935). DevQ (18:3) Aut 83, p. 71-72.
"Stone Beach--Yalta." DevQ (18:3) Aut 83, p. 68.
"To Alexander Blok" (tr. of Anna Akhmatova). MalR (66) O 83, p. 121.
"Views." DevQ (18:3) Aut 83, p. 67.
"Willow" (tr. of Anna Akhmatova). MalR (66) O 83, p. 121.

108. ANDRESEN, Sophia de Mello Breyner
"Women beside the Sea" (tr. by Alexis Levitin). Confr (25/26) 83, p. 314.

109. ANDREWS, Bruce
"Confidence Trick" (Excerpt). ParisR (24:86) Wint 82, p. 89-90.

110. ANDREWS, Jennè R.
"The Solace in Naming." StoneC (11:1/2, Pt. 1) Aut-Wint 83, p. 20-21.

111. ANDREWS, Tom
"A Good Dream." WorldO (17:4) Sum 83, p. 26.

112. ANDROLA, Ron
"Genius Child." Bogg (50) 83, p. 9.

113. ANDRYSSON, Susan
"Aubade for Joe." PoetL (77:2) Sum 82, p. 94.
"The Red Pond." PoetL (77:2) Sum 82, p. 93.
"You Can't Go Home Again." PoetL (77:2) Sum 82, p. 95.

114. ANGELERI, Lucy
"Gold-Filled Teeth." YetASM (1:1) 82, p. 13.

ANGELIS, Milo de
See: De ANGELIS, Milo

115. ANGELL, Roger
"Greetings, Friends!" NewYorker (59:45) 26 D 83, p. 35.

116. ANGIOLIERI, Cecco
"Cecco's Rage" (tr. by David Weissmann). SouthernR (19:3) Jl 83, p. 658.

117. ANGLESEY, Zoe
"Almost Ode to the Ear" (tr. of Roberto Obregon). PoetryE (9/10) Wint 82-Spr 83, p. 178-179.
"For 'Nina', a Disappeared in Guatemala." Stand (24:1) 82-83, p. 53.
"Happy Hunters, Mill City." CrabCR (1:2) Aut 83, p. 9.
"The Importance of Place." Stand (24:1) 82-83, p. 52.
"Now As I Write" (tr. of Roberto Obregon). PoetryE (9/10) Wint 82-Spr 83, p. 181.
"Postwar Boom." PoetryE (9/10) Wint 82-Spr 83, p. 110-111.
"Ragged Saturday." NewEng (5:4) Sum 83, p. 480.
"Suddenly the Wind Ceased" (tr. of Roberto Obregon). PoetryE (9/10) Wint 82-Spr 83, p. 180.

118. ANGST, Bim
"Feet in Water." PoetL (77:4) Wint 83, p. 202.
"Sickness." SouthernHR (17:1) Wint 83, p. 76.
"Tornado Watch" (for Jim). SpoonRQ (8:4) Aut 83, p. 5-8.

119. ANONYMOUS
"Cold Mountain" (Selections: 4, 5, 16) (in Chinese, calligraphy by Hui San Sun). NowestR (21:2/3) 83, p. 76.
"Cold Mountain" (Selections: 4, 5, 16) (tr. by Red Pine). NowestR (21:2/3) 83, p. 77.
"Rights of Woman" (By a Lady, 1795). MassR (24:2) Sum 83, facsimile broadside fold-out.

120. ANSON, John
"Weather." Thrpny (3:4, issue 12) Wint 83, p. 27.

121. ANTLER
"Rexroth As He Appeared to Exist March 24, 1968, 5:15-9:00 P.M." Wind (13:48) 83, p. 1-2.
"Rexroth As He Appeared to Exist March 24, 1968, 5:15-9:00 P.M." AmerPoR (12:1) Ja/F 83, p. 18.
"Trying to Remember What I Learned." Wind (13:48) 83, p. 1.

122. APARICIO, Frances
"Cecile and Jacqueline" (tr. of Marjorie Agosin). MinnR (NS 21) Aut 83, p. 7.
"United States" (tr. of Marjorie Agosin). MinnR (NS 21) Aut 83, p. 8.

123. APOLLINAIRE, Guillaume
"4 A.M." (tr. by Karl Patten). WebR (8:1) Spr 83, p. 41.

124. APPEL, Cathy
"Climbing South." HangL (44) Sum 83, p. 8-9.
"Culprits." HangL (44) Sum 83, p. 7.

125. APPEL, Dori
"A Dream Making Many Things Better." BelPoJ (34:2) Wint 83-84, p. 11.

126. APPLEMAN, Philip
"Anniversary." Poetry (142:5) Ag 83, p. 261-262.
"Mortiphobia, the Fear of Self-Reproach." PartR (50:2) 83, p. 243.
"Phobias." Confr (25/26) 83, p. 240-241.
"Phobias." PartR (50:2) 83, p. 242-243.
"Shamanophobia, the Fear of Specialists." PartR (50:2) 83, p. 242-243.
"Staying Awake with Darwin." IndR (5:2) Sum 82, p. 17.
"The Trickle-Down Theory of Happiness." Poetry (142:5) Ag 83, p. 262.

127. APPLEWHITE, James
"Barbecue Service." Poetry (142:6) S 83, p. 313.
"A Catalogue of Trees." Poetry (142:6) S 83, p. 311-312.
"Foreseeing the Journey." AmerPoR (12:3) My-Je 83, p. 31.
"Iron River." SouthernPR (23:2) Aut 83, p. 51.
"Jonquils." SouthernHR (17:2) Spr 83, p. 147.
"Marriage Portrait." Poetry (142:6) S 83, p. 314-315.
"My Uncle's Parsonage." Ploughs (9:2/3) 83, p. 108-109.
"Road Down Home." Ploughs (9:2/3) 83, p. 107.

128. ARAKAWA
"Instantaneously and repeatedly" (w. Madeline Gins). ParisR (24:86) Wint 82, p. 123.

ARAUZ, Nicomedes Suarez
See: SUAREZ-ARAUZ, Nicomedes

ARBERET, Lorenzo d'
See: ARBERET, Lorenzo d'

129. ARBOUR, Paul
"This Window." Waves (11:4) Spr 83, p. 69.

130. ARD, Lee L.
"A Spring Vision." DekalbLAJ (16:1/4) Aut 82-Sum 83, p. 84-85.

131. ARENAS, Rosa Maria
"Quiet in a Quiet Room" (From a novel in progress entitled The Love Was Mixed Up). LittleM (14:1/2) 83, p. 113.
"The Way I Remember." 13thM (7:1/2) 83, p. 28-29.

AREND, Sylvie d'Augerot
See: AUGEROT-AREND, Sylvie d'

132. ARGUELLES, Iván
"Orion." RagMag (2:2) Aut 83, p. 23.
"El Quijote de la Máquina de Coser." RevChic (11:2) Sum 83, p. 49.
"Tamalpais Twentieth Century." SanFPJ (4:3) 83, p. 16.
"La Vida No Es Sueño." RevChic (11:2) Sum 83, p. 50.

ARIIYE, Fujiwara no
See: FUJIWARA no ARIIYE

133. ARKELL, Chris
"While Up the Hradcani" (tr. of Eugene Dubnov, w. the author). NewEng (5:4) Sum 83, p. 499.

134. ARMAND, Octavio
"Touch" (tr. by Carol Maier). NewOR (10:4) Wint 83, p. 50.

135. ARMAS, José R. de
"At the Sea" (tr. of Carmen Conde, w. Alexis Levitin). LitR (27:1) Aut 83, p. 101-102.
"A Curse on Old Age" (tr. of Carmen Conde, w. Alexis Levitin). LitR (27:1) Aut 83, p. 100.
"Drought" (tr. of Carmen Conde, w. Alexis Levitin). LitR (27:1) Aut 83, p. 101.

136. ARMSTRONG, Cherryl
"No and Yes." Ascent (8:3) 83, p. 15.

137. ARMSTRONG, Tim
"Induction." Bogg (50) 83, p. 63.
"Parable." Bogg (51) 83, p. 58.
"Teeth Ballad." Bogg (50) 83, p. 40.

138. ARNOLD, Forest D.
"Daddy's Girl" (for Toni). YetASM (1:1) 82, p. 13.

139. ARROJO, R.
"Landscape of Capibaribe" (tr. of João Cabral de Melo Neto). Mund (14:1) 83, p. 73-95.

140. ARTMANN, H. D.
"Now and Again He Was Picked Up" (tr. by Derk Wynand). Quarry (32:1) Wint 83, p. 36-38.

141. ASCHKENES, Deborah
"Cactus Eyes -- A Sijo Poem." YetASM (1:1) 82, p. 13.

142. ASCRIZZI, Lynn Ann
"The Distance Most Disturbing." WorldO (17:4) Sum 83, p. 27.

143. ASHBERY, John
"Hop o' My Thumb." OhioR (30) 83, p. 202-203.
"More Pleasant Adventures." NewYRB (30:5) 31 Mr

83, p. 10.
"The Ongoing Story." NewYorker (59:19) 27 Je 83, p. 40.
"Rain Moving In." ParisR (25:90) Wint 83, p. 60.
"The Strayed Reveller." NewYRB (30:9) 2 Je 83, p. 16.
"Variation on a Noel." Epoch (33:1) Aut-Wint 83, p. 40-41.
"A Wave." AmerPoR (12:4) Jl-Ag 83, p. 23-30.

144. ASTLEY, Neil
"Dreaming." Argo (5:1) 83, p. 3.

145. ASTOR, Susan
"Bicycle Song." PoetL (77:2) Sum 82, p. 104.
"Counterpoint for Small Talk and Percussion." Confr (25/26) 83, p. 153.
"Divorce." Outbr (12/13) Aut 83-Spr 84, p. 6.
"Dream before Sleep." Outbr (12/13) Aut 83-Spr 84, p. 9.
"Forget." Outbr (12/13) Aut 83-Spr 84, p. 5.
"Learning the Holocaust" (for Doris Kemp) (First prize, SCCA International Poetry Contest). WestB (12) 83, p. 36-37.
"Neighbors." PoetL (77:2) Sum 82, p. 103.
"One Daughter Short in Vermont." PoetL (78:1) Spr 83, p. 24-25.
"Primordial Love Poem." PoetL (78:1) Spr 83, p. 25.
"Quickening." PoetL (77:2) Sum 82, p. 102.
"Rain." PoetL (77:2) Sum 82, p. 101.
"Space Travel." Outbr (12/13) Aut 83-Spr 84, p. 7-8.
"The Wife of God II." PoetL (77:2) Sum 82, p. 105.

146. ASTRACHAN, John Mann
"Love." NegC (3:4) Aut 83, p. 123.

147. ASTRADA, Etelvina
"Death has gotten dressed up with pins and threads" (tr. by Timothy J. Rogers). LetFem (9:1) 83, p. 94.
"Just like an old dress" (tr. by Timothy J. Rogers). LetFem (9:1) 83, p. 93.
"One Tuesday my mother gave birth to me" (tr. by Timothy J. Rogers). LetFem (9:1) 83, p. 94.
"Outdoor Exercises" (tr. by Timothy J. Rogers). LetFem (9:1) 83, p. 93.
"The world is a straight-jacket" (tr. by Timothy J. Rogers). LetFem (9:1) 83, p. 95.

148. ATCHITY, Kenneth John
"Apologia, to the Other Gods" (for Jo Ann Carlton). KanQ (15:1) Wint 83, p. 22.

149. ATKINS, Kathleen
"The Collectors." Atlantic (251:6) Je 83, p. 90.

150. ATKINSON, Alan
"Stay Put." SouthernPR (23:2) Aut 82 [i.e. (23:1?) Spr 83], p. 40.

151. ATKINSON, Barbara A.
"The Best Houses Face South." Vis (13) 83, p. 12.

152. ATWOOD, Margaret
"A Boat." NoAmR (268:1) Mr 83, p. 67.
"Interlunar." Field (28) Spr 83, p. 14-15.
"Orpheus." Field (28) Spr 83, p. 9-10.
"A Painting of One Location on the Plain." Field (28) Spr 83, p. 12-13.
"The Robber Bridegroom." Field (28) Spr 83, p. 11.
"A Stone." NoAmR (268:2) Je 83, p. 39.
"Sumacs." NoAmR (268:3) S 83, p. 23.

153. AUBERT, Alvin
"All Singing in a Pie." OP (36) Aut-Wint 83, p. 41.
"Already It Concerns Us." OP (36) Aut-Wint 83, p. 44.
"Chips." PoNow (7:2, #38) 83, p. 8.
"Kong Bound." PoNow (7:2, #38) 83, p. 8.
"A Light Outside." OP (36) Aut-Wint 83, p. 44.
"My Sweet Baby Back to Me/An Interlude." OP (36) Aut-Wint 83, p. 43.
"Picasso's Etching 'Nude and Sculpture' (1933)." Epoch (32:3) Spr-Sum 83, p. 240.
"Root Beer Girl." PoNow (7:2, #38) 83, p. 8.
"Van Der Zee Extrapolation #1." OP (36) Aut-Wint 83, p. 42.
"You Read Them, Nevertheless." Epoch (32:3) Spr-Sum 83, p. 241.

154. AUBERT, Jimmy
"Baker's Dozen." Sam (35:2 138th release) 83, p. 1-14.
"Bakery Barrels." Sam (35:2 138th release) 83, p. 3.
"Fifth to Last." Sam (35:2 138th release) 83, p. 8.
"Flour Room." Sam (35:2 138th release) 83, p. 14.
"Fourteen Truckers." Sam (35:2 138th release) 83, p. 11.
"Getting the Hose." Sam (35:2 138th release) 83, p. 5.
"High Stone Falcon." Wind (13:48) 83, p. 3.
"Hooves and Shreds." Sam (34:3 135th release) 83, p. 38.
"If the Company Had a Mind." Sam (35:2 138th release) 83, p. 6.
"Little Bitch, Scorned by Nature." PoetL (77:2) Sum 82, p. 92.
"Lunchroom." Sam (35:2 138th release) 83, p. 4.
"Lye Soda." Sam (35:2 138th release) 83, p. 7.
"On the Roof (As High As We Can Go)." Sam (35:2 138th release) 83, p. 12.
"The Pie Tower." Sam (35:2 138th release) 83, p. 2.
"The Pirouette of the Fatted Pig." KanQ (15:2) Spr 83, p. 56.
"Promotion." Sam (35:2 138th release) 83, p. 3.
"Running a Trotline Like a Thief in the Midwestern Night." LittleBR (3:4) Sum 83, p. 37.
"Transfer." Sam (35:2 138th release) 83, p. 10.
"Trust." Sam (35:2 138th release) 83, p. 9.

155. AUBERT, Rosemary
"The Violins at Lunch." CrossC (5:2/3) 83, p. 30.

156. AUDEN, W. H.
"If On Account of the Political Situation." NewEngR (5:4) Sum 83, p. 439-440.

157. AUDIN, Jessica
"Reach Out and Touch." CapeR (19:1) Wint 83, p. 39.

158. AUGEROT-AREND, Sylvie d'
"A un Choix Difficile." PoetryCR (5:1) Aut 83, p. 14.

159. AUGUSTUS, Gemiann
"As Flores." SoDakR (21:1) Spr 83, p. 73.
"Flight" (tr. by Hannah Connor Tyson). SoDakR (21:1) Spr 83, p. 76.
"The Flowers" (tr. by Hannah Connor Tyson). SoDakR (21:1) Spr 83, p. 72.
"Fuga." SoDakR (21:1) Spr 83, p. 77.
"Revoada Colorida." SoDakR (21:1) Spr 83, p. 75.
"Swift Flight of Colored Birds" (tr. by Hannah Connor Tyson). SoDakR (21:1) Spr 83, p. 74.

160. AUMILLER, Emily P.
"What I Learned from the Computer." EngJ (72:2) F 83, p. 108.

161. AUSTIN, Annemarie
"Pholcus." Argo (4:3) 83, p. 35.

162. AUSTIN, Bob
"Monk's Story." Abraxas (27/28) 83, p. 20-21.

163. AUTIO, Lar
"Sunset." Argo (4:3) 83, p. 25.

AVE JEANNE
See: JEANNE, Ave

164. AVELLANEDA, Andrés
"Diario de Guerra." Prismal (11) Aut 83, p. 94-96.

165. AVIDAN, David
"Life of a Dead Dog" (tr. by Robert Friend). LitR (26:2) Wint 83, p. 246-247.
"Practical Poems" (tr. by the author). LitR (26:2) Wint 83, p. 248.
"Six Local Poems" (tr. by Robert Friend). LitR (26:2) Wint 83, p. 244-246.

166. AVILA, Haydée
"Espejo." Rácata (2) 83, p. 26.
"Lugar Común." Rácata (2) 83, p. 25.
"Química retroactiva." Rácata (2) 83, p. 130.

167. AVIS, Nick
"En Eg." Waves (11:4) Spr 83, p. 81.

168. AVISON, Margaret
"The Bible to be Believed." MichQR (22:3) Sum 83, p. 393-394.

169. AWAD, Joseph
"Checkpoint." KanQ (15:1) Wint 83, p. 77.
"Questions of Aesthetics." Poem (49) N 83, p. 4-5.
"Strolling with the Ghost of Frank O'Hara." Wind (13:48) 83, p. 4.
"There." Poem (49) N 83, p. 6.

170. AYCOCK, Shirley
"Black Felt." SanFPJ (5:3) 83, p. 12.

171. AYNE, Blythe
"This trip." SecC (11:1/2) 83, p. 6.

172. AZRAEL, Judith Anne
"Apple Tree Songs." Telescope (5/6) Spr 83, p. 129-131.

173. AZRAEL, Mary
"How to Play." PoetL (78:1) Spr 83, p. 11.

174. AZZOPARDI, Mario
"Tonight a Cross-Eyed Moon" (tr. by Grazio Falzon). Vis (13) 83, p. 28.
"Vision 22 X" (tr. by Grazio Falzon). Vis (13) 83, p. 27.

175. BAATZ, Ronald
"After a Thousand Meals I Meet Z." SmPd (20:1) Wint 83, p. 7.
"Midnight Meal during a Storm." SmPd (20:1) Wint 83, p. 8.

176. BACA, Jimmy Santiago
"Dark Innocence." RevChic (11:2) Sum 83, p. 42.
"Mr. Valdez." RevChic (11:2) Sum 83, p. 41.
"Spring Burning." RevChic (11:2) Sum 83, p. 43.

177. BACHAM, Paul
"Continuity." SanFPJ (5:1) 83, p. 49.
"Kiwanis Square." SanFPJ (5:3) 83, p. 87.
"Out of the Closet." SanFPJ (5:3) 83, p. 88.
"Up Again to Appia." SanFPJ (5:1) 83, p. 32.

178. BACHSTEIN, Michael
"The Story of the Earth." HiramPoR (34) Spr-Sum 83, p. 5.

179. BACKES, A. J.
"Starting Early." EngJ (72:8) D 83, p. 44.

180. BACKS, Kevin C.
"Summer night." WritersL Ja 83, p. 9.

181. BACON, Theresa
"The Gramma Poems" (Selection: "Four: To Weave").

SoCaR (15:2) Spr 83, p. 94-95.

182. BADOR, Bernard
"Bread and Wine" (tr. of Robert Marteau, w. Clayton Eshleman). Sulfur (3:1, #7) 83, p. 40-43.

183. BAECHLER, Lea
"Burning Season." SouthernPR (23:2) Aut 83, p. 27.

184. BAGGETT, Rebecca
"Medusa at Home." Prima (8) 83, p. 29.

185. BAIDEL, Lola
"Altankassen." SoDakR (21:1) Spr 83, p. 35.
"En Engels Talmodighed." SoDakR (21:1) Spr 83, p. 37.
"Enshrined" (tr. by Jack Brondum). SoDakR (21:1) Spr 83, p. 38.
"The Flowerbox" (tr. by Jack Brondum). SoDakR (21:1) Spr 83, p. 34.
"La Glace -- Kuren." SoDakR (21:1) Spr 83, p. 35.
"La Glace -- The Cure" (tr. by Jack Brondum). SoDakR (21:1) Spr 83, p. 34.
"The Patience of an Angel" (tr. by Jack Brondum). SoDakR (21:1) Spr 83, p. 36.
"Skrinlagt." SoDakR (21:1) Spr 83, p. 39.

186. BAILEY, Don
"Melted Ice." CrossC (5:2/3) 83, p. 12.

187. BAILEY-TYNER, Rebecca
"The Violinist Sings July." SouthernR (19:3) Jl 83, p. 685.

188. BAINES, Bill
"800325: Truckee, Highway Scene." Meadows (4:1) 83, p. 49.

189. BAIRD, Ansie
"Arrangement." SouthernR (19:3) Jl 83, p. 656.
"The Blessing." SouthernR (19:3) Jl 83, p. 652.
"The Price of Things." SouthernR (19:3) Jl 83, p. 654.
"Three Turns in the Wind." SouthernR (19:3) Jl 83, p. 653.
"Winter Accomplished." SouthernR (19:3) Jl 83, p. 655.

190. BAIRD, Scott
"The Failed Pianist." PoNow (7:2, #38) 83, p. 47.

191. BAKALIS, John
"Hotel de Ville." Kayak (61) Ap 83, p. 29.

192. BAKCHYLIDES
"Peace" (tr. by Gary Metras). PoetryE (9/10) Wint 82-Spr 83, p. 279.

193. BAKER, David
"Burrs." EngJ (72:3) Mr 83, p. 72.
"Dark Earth, 1963." PraS (57:2) Sum 83, p. 62.

"Early Love, Late Season." PraS (57:2) Sum 83, p. 60.
"The Field." NewEngR (6:1) Aut 83, p. 135-137.
"Poison." PraS (57:2) Sum 83, p. 61-62.
"Summer Sleep." OW (17) Aut-Wint 83-84, p. 64-65.
"Villanelle for Jane Fonda and Richard Simmons." EngJ (72:6) O 83, p. 58.

194. BAKER, Donald
"Naked Daughter." NewL (50:1) Aut 83, p. 66.

195. BAKER, Houston A., Jr.
"Loss/Angel-Less/Blue." BlackALF (17:4) Wint 83, p. 174.

196. BAKER, Peter
"In Sight of the Mountain" (to Karin). PoetC (15:1) Aut 83, p. 4-5.

197. BAKER, Sheridan
"Bonsai." MichQR (22:1) Wint 83, p. 32.

198. BALABAN, John
"An Afternoon's Wandering" (tr. of Kolyo Sevov, w. Elena Hristova). NewEng (5:4) Sum 83, p. 512.
"The Water Buffalo (Hanoi, 1972)" (tr. of Blaga Dimitrova, w. Vladimir Phillipov). NewEng (5:4) Sum 83, p. 497-499.

199. BALAKIAN, Peter
"Onion." ThRiPo (21/22) 83, p. 11.
"Open Pond." SouthernHR (17:1) Wint 83, p. 30-31.
"Talking over Chekov, Montauk Point" (for aunt Nona). VirQR (59:3) Sum 83, p. 440-441.

200. BALAKIER, James
"Public Furniture" (Selections: #1-13). SpiritSH (49 Suppl.) 83, p. 36-43.

201. BALAZS, Mary
"The Girl in the Torn Skirt." CapeR (18:2) Sum 83, p. 14.
"Her One Bouquet." Wind (13:49) 83, p. 4.
"Lexington Police Probe Continues: Evidence Begins to Emerge." WebR (8:2) Aut 83, p. 82-84.
"The Moment in Sunlight." Wind (13:49) 83, p. 3.
"Poet-in-the-Schools." Wind (13:49) 83, p. 4-5.

202. BALDERSTON, Jean
"The Dry-Fly Man" (found in an advertisement for fishing tackle Scotland Magazine's Annual for 1958). Tele (18) 83, p. 103.
"Our Latest Product" (found poem). Kayak (61) Ap 83, p. 27.

203. BALDRIDGE, Charlene
"The Era and the Outrage." YetASM (1:1) 82, p. 16.
"Poem Written on the Head of a Pin." YetASM (1:1) 82, p. 13.

204. BALDWIN, Tama
"Fatigue in California." Poetry (142:6) S 83, p. 338-339.

205. BALESTRIERI, Elizabeth
"Biografia Mortal" (Excerpt) (tr. of Guillermo Llanos). ClockR (2:1) 83, p. 41.

206. BALK, Christianne
"The Top Floor Window." MissouriR (7:1) Aut 83, p. 48-49.

207. BALL, Angela
"The Courtyard." BlackWR (9:1) Aut 82, p. 36-37.
"A Day at the Circus." MemphisSR (3:2) Spr 83, p. 43.
"Now Taking Place." NewOR (10:2/3) Sum-Aut 83, p. 47.

208. BALLARD, Sandra
"Seasons" (for my father). HiramPoR (35) Aut-Wint 83, p. 6-7.

209. BALLINGER, Franchot
"Waking at 5:30 AM." Poem (49) N 83, p. 57.
"Witnessing." Poem (49) N 83, p. 56.

210. BALTENSPERGER, Peter
"Dream Maker." CrossC (5:2/3) 83, p. 4.
"Lake Portrait." CrossC (5:2/3) 83, p. 4.
"Meditation." Waves (11:2/3) Wint 83, p. 53.
"Sleepwalking." WestCR (17:4) Ap 83, p. 43.

211. BANAI, Peretz
"Last Dew" (tr. by Gabriel Levin). LitR (26:2) Wint 83, p. 288.
"My Friend, Michael, From the Dust" (tr. by Gabriel Levin). LitR (26:2) Wint 83, p. 288-289.

212. BANERJI, Debashish
"The Gatherer." Os (16) 83, p. 14.

213. BANGERT, Sharon
"Looking through the Axis of DNA" (cover of Science, Feb., 1981). SanFPJ (4:4) 83, p. 36.

214. BARABAS, Gabor
"Brigatte Rosse." DekalbLAJ (16:1/4) Aut 82-Sum 83, p. 51-54.
"Racoon." DekalbLAJ (16:1/4) Aut 82-Sum 83, p. 54-55.

215. BARAKA, Amina
"Peoples Poet." PoetryE (9/10) Wint 82-Spr 83, p. 105-106.

216. BARANCZAK, Stanislaw
"Along with the Dust" (tr. by Reginald Gibbons and the author). TriQ (57, Vol. 1) Spr-Sum 83, p. 88.
"And No One Has Warned Me" (Excerpt). NewRep (187:1) 5 Jl 82, p. 30.
"December 31, 1979: Soon Now" (tr. by Magnus J. Krynski and Robert A. Maguire). TriQ (57, Vol.

1) Spr-Sum 83, p. 89.
"If China" (tr. by Reginald Gibbons and the author). TriQ (57, Vol. 1) Spr-Sum 83, p. 92.
"January 2, 1980: Eroica" (tr. by Reginald Gibbons and the author). TriQ (57, Vol. 1) Spr-Sum 83, p. 90.
"March 4, 1980: And Yet Perhaps" (tr. by Reginald Gibbons and the author). TriQ (57, Vol. 1) Spr-Sum 83, p. 91.
"This Is Not a Conversation for the Telephone" (tr. by Valeria Wasilewski). ParisR (25:87) Spr 83, p. 197.
"What Is a Verse Not to Be Thought" (tr. by Valeria Wasilewski). ParisR (25:87) Spr 83, p. 196-197.

217. BARAT, Irv
"But Not Lovable." WindO (43) Wint 83, p. 51.
"Capitalist Holiday." WindO (43) Wint 83, p. 51-52.
"My Psychiatrist Gave Me." Bogg (50) 83, p. 37.

218. BARBARESE, J. T.
"A Woman." Telescope (4) Wint 83, p. 12-15.

219. BARBER, Dave
"In Timber Country." Tendril (14/15) Wint 83, p. 17.
"South." PoetryNW (24:1) Spr 83, p. 17.
"South." Tendril (14/15) Wint 83, p. 18.
"Studebaker Luck." PoetryNW (24:1) Spr 83, p. 18-19.

220. BARBER, Jennifer
"Two Poets and a Painter." Shen (34:2) 83, p. 98-99.

221. BARBOUR, Douglas
"21.06.79." Quarry (32:3) Sum 83, p. 7.
"Art Objects for an Inner Landscape." CanLit (96) Spr 83, p. 58-59.
"Breath Ghazal #1." MalR (65) Jl 83, p. 122.
"Breath Ghazal #2." MalR (65) Jl 83, p. 122.
"Breath Ghazal #4." MalR (65) Jl 83, p. 123.
"Breath Ghazal #5." MalR (65) Jl 83, p. 123.
"Breath Ghazal #6." MalR (65) Jl 83, p. 124.
"Breath Ghazal #10." MalR (65) Jl 83, p. 124.
"Earth Song/Body Song" (Excerpts: ii, iii, vi-viii). CapilR (27) 83, p. 5-9.
"The trees, the trees suround me." Grain (11:1) F 83, p. 15.
"The Wind and the Snow." CanLit (97) Sum 83, p. 93-95.

222. BARCLAY, R. K.
"Conversation with a Victim." PoetryE (11) Sum 83, p. 54.

223. BARGEN, Walter
"Adam Canoes the Meramec River." MissouriR (7:1) Aut 83, p. 15.
"Adam Reincarnates" (on the occasion of Thomas McAfee's death). Vis (12) 83, p. 30.
"Adam Steps Out." CharR (9:2) Aut 83, p. 77.
"Advanced Linguistics/Adam Calls God." CharR (9:2)

Aut 83, p. 76.
"Dust to Dust." KanQ (15:1) Wint 83, p. 59.
"Immigrant." SpoonRQ (8:4) Aut 83, p. 57.
"Inside Tomorrow." Wind (13:47) 83, p. 1-2.
"Vision Thirst, Tucson, Arizona." Wind (13:47) 83, p. 1.

224. BARKER, Christine
"The Scene." Dandel (10:2) Aut-Wint 83, p. 31.

225. BARKER, Lucile Angela Morreale
"The Hour of the Werewolf." Descant (43) Wint 83-84, p. 34-36.

226. BARKER, Wendy
"Cores." FourQt (32:2) Wint 83, p. 14.
"Goodbye Poem" (For Elliot Gilbert). CalQ (22) Sum 83, p. 31.
"Listen, Wind" (For Sandra M. Gilbert). CalQ (22) Sum 83, p. 30.

227. BARKS, Coleman
"The Great Blue Heron." SouthernPR (23:2) Aut 83, p. 5-7.
"Hymenoptera." MemphisSR (3:2) Spr 83, p. 12-13.
"Orange Circles on Lavender Wings" (for Ashley Brewer). Ploughs (9:2/3) 83, p. 97-98.
"Sumac and Lacrimae Rerum" (for James Augustus Pennington). SenR (13:2) 82-83, p. 59-60.
"Tree Limbs Overhead" (for Ashrita Laird). SenR (13:2) 82-83, p. 61-63.

228. BARLASCINI, Neal
"Thomas More." CapeR (18:2) Sum 83, p. 19.

BARLETTA, Naomi Lockwood
See: LOCKWOOD BARLETTA, Naomi

229. BARLIN, Paul
"Experiment." SanFPJ (5:1) 83, p. 56.
"Sunday Morning Mutation." SanFPJ (5:1) 83, p. 43.

230. BARNES, Dick
"Up and Down." WorldO (17:4) Sum 83, p. 28.

231. BARNES, Jim
"Accident at Three Mile Island." NewL (49:3/4) Spr-Sum 83, p. 53.
"At the Clearance Sale." SoDakR (21:3) Aut 83, p. 88.
"Consolation." NewL (49:3/4) Spr-Sum 83, p. 231.
"Dog Days" (tr. of Rainer Brambach). MemphisSR (3:2) Spr 83, p. 30.

232. BARNES, Mike
"Cartoon." Grain (11:3) Ag 83, p. 21.
"The Conjurer." Bogg (50) 83, p. 50.
"Goldfish." Waves (11:2/3) Wint 83, p. 67.
"Post-Hiroshima Exercise (1)." Grain (11:3) Ag 83, p. 21.

233. BARNES, Richard
"Every Failure Comes to Rest." Poetry (142:2) My 83, p. 65.
"Falling." Pig (11) 83, p. 47.
"Hammond, Indiana, 1959." Pig (11) 83, p. 93.
"Learning to Be Silent." AmerPoR (12:4) Jl-Ag 83, p. 42.
"On the Strip in Liberal, Kansas." Wind (13:48) 83, p. 42.
"Red Light." Poetry (142:2) My 83, p. 67.
"The Salesman." Poetry (142:2) My 83, p. 66.
"Soliloquy of the Dead Fox." AmerPoR (12:4) Jl-Ag 83, p. 42.

234. BARNES, W. J.
"Aaron." Quarry (32:1) Wint 83, p. 30-33.

235. BARNIE, John
"Ars Moriendi." PoetryCR (5:2) Wint 83-84, p. 10.
"Botanical Gardens." AmerPoR (12:4) Jl-Ag 83, p. 16.
"December." Kayak (63) N 83, p. 44.
"Encounter." Kayak (63) N 83, p. 46.
"My Father's Brothers." PoetryCR (5:2) Wint 83-84, p. 10.
"Natural History." Kayak (63) N 83, p. 45.
"Searching." AmerPoR (12:4) Jl-Ag 83, p. 16.
"The Storm." Kayak (63) N 83, p. 45.

236. BARNSTONE, Anthony
"Another Thirst" (tr. of Francisco Brines). DevQ (18:1) Spr 83, p. 95.
"This Kingdom, the Earth" (tr. of Francisco Brines). DevQ (18:1) Spr 83, p. 94.

237. BARNSTONE, Willis
"Adventure of the Heart." NowestR (21:1) 83, p. 55.
"Antonio Machado in Segovia, Daydreaming As Usual of Soria, Baeza and Sevilla." NowestR (21:1) 83, p. 44.
"Clouds." NowestR (21:1) 83, p. 57.
"Downhill." NowestR (21:1) 83, p. 51.
"Floating after You." NowestR (21:1) 83, p. 50.
"Gandhi." NowestR (21:1) 83, p. 56.
"God the Child." NowestR (21:1) 83, p. 61.
"God the Hero." ModernPS (11:3) 83, p. 220.
"Gospel of Clouds." NoAmR (268:2) Je 83, p. 41.
"Gospel of Death." NoAmR (268:2) Je 83, p. 41.
"Gospel of Earthly Feeling." NoAmR (268:2) Je 83, p. 45.
"Gospel of Imaginary Beings." NoAmR (268:2) Je 83, p. 44.
"Gospel of Light." NoAmR (268:2) Je 83, p. 46.
"Gospel of Love." NoAmR (268:2) Je 83, p. 44.
"Gospel of Meadow." NoAmR (268:2) Je 83, p. 42.
"Gospel of Rapture." NoAmR (268:2) Je 83, p. 43.
"Gospel of Salvation." NoAmR (268:2) Je 83, p. 42.
"Gospel of the Dream." NoAmR (268:2) Je 83, p. 45.
"Gospel of the Gardener." NoAmR (268:2) Je 83, p. 45.
"Gospel of the Lonely." NoAmR (268:2) Je 83, p. 42.
"Gospel of the Losers." NoAmR (268:2) Je 83, p. 43.

"Gospel of the Meadow." NowestR (21:1) 83, p. 63.
"Gospel of the Night." NoAmR (268:2) Je 83, p. 46.
"Gospel of the Room." NoAmR (268:2) Je 83, p. 44.
"Gospel of the Sad." NoAmR (268:2) Je 83, p. 42.
"Gospel of the Singer." NoAmR (268:2) Je 83, p. 44.
"Gospel of the Way of Chaos." NoAmR (268:2) Je 83, p. 45.
"Gospel of Truth." NoAmR (268:2) Je 83, p. 43.
"Heron of the Night." NowestR (21:1) 83, p. 62.
"Icy Monday." NowestR (21:1) 83, p. 49.
"Jesus." ModernPS (11:3) 83, p. 219.
"John of the Cross in the Spring." NowestR (21:1) 83, p. 43.
"Larry Rothman." NowestR (21:1) 83, p. 54.
"Lord of the Inferno." ModernPS (11:3) 83, p. 220.
"The Luminating Experience of a Brain Scan." NowestR (21:1) 83, p. 52.
"Moonstone." PartR (50:2) 83, p. 239.
"My Heart Is in the East." NowestR (21:1) 83, p. 59.
"The Nightingale." NoAmR (268:2) Je 83, p. 46.
"The Other Gospel." NoAmR (268:2) Je 83, p. 43.
"Oxygen." NowestR (21:1) 83, p. 53.
"The Panther." PraS (51:1, i.e. 57:1) Spr 83, p. 22.
"Rain." Kayak (61) Ap 83, p. 45.
"Saul the Tentmaker." ModernPS (11:3) 83, p. 219.
"Sirens." Kayak (61) Ap 83, p. 46.
"Snow." NowestR (21:1) 83, p. 58.
"Sun." Kayak (61) Ap 83, p. 45.
"Surviving Winter." NowestR (21:1) 83, p. 48.
"Terror in the North Room." NowestR (21:1) 83, p. 47.
"Twenty Gospels & a Nightingale." NoAmR (268:2) Je 83, p. 41-46.
"Uncle Vania and the Train to Moscow." NowestR (21:1) 83, p. 46.
"The Way." NowestR (21:1) 83, p. 60.
"What Can I Do at Night?" NowestR (21:1) 83, p. 45.

238. BAROLINI, Helen
"Palazzo Backside." AntigR (53) Spr 83, p. 55-56.
"Sit Tibi Terra Levis" (from a Roman funerary inscription uncovered near Rabat in Morocco). AntigR (53) Spr 83, p. 56.
"Thinking of Milton in Rome." AntigR (53) Spr 83, p. 54.

239. BARON, John
"Grey." CanLit (96) Spr 83, p. 70-71.

240. BARON, Mary
"Reluctant Love Poem." PoNow (7:2, #38) 83, p. 11.

241. BARONE, Frank
"Contemporary Conference." EngJ (72:7) N 83, p. 36.

242. BARONE, Patricia
"The Dream and the Conception." Germ (7:1) Spr-Sum 83, p. 9-10.
"I Write a Poem with Claire Who Is Almost Four." Germ (7:2) Aut-Wint 83, p. 15.
"An Old Man Goes Shopping." Germ (7:1) Spr-Sum 83,

p. 11.

243. BARR, Tina
"Green Moths." Tendril (14/15) Wint 83, p. 19.

244. BARRACK, Jack
"Woodworker." MissouriR (6:3) Sum 83, p. 21.

245. BARRERA, Alberto
"Teología a la Liberación." Prismal (11) Aut 83, p. 100.

246. BARRESI, Dorothy
"Dorothy, Back in Kansas." Tendril (16) Sum 83, p. 17.
"Farm Wife." PoetryNW (24:4) Wint 83-84, p. 27-28.
"Mystery." PoetryNW (24:4) Wint 83-84, p. 28.
"Re-Crossing the Equator " (for Megan). Tendril (16) Sum 83, p. 18.
"When Grandfather, a World Traveller, Dies." PoetC (13, i.e. 14:3) 83, p. 28.

247. BARRETT, Carol
"Contending" (in memory of Tony Napier). KanQ (15:2) Spr 83, p. 78.

BARRETT, Donalee Moulton
See: MOULTON-BARRETT, Donalee

248. BARRETT, Joseph
"All That's Expected." Pig (11) 83, p. 23.
"Fainting Angels." Pig (11) 83, p. 72.
"Harpsicord Music." Wind (13:49) 83, p. 6.
"Solo on the Backroad." Wind (13:49) 83, p. 6.

249. BARRIENTOS, Raúl
"La Rabia, Caramba, y la Sordera." Areíto (9:35) 83, p. 37.

250. BARRON, Deborah
"On Office Stationery." BelPoJ (33:4) Sum 83, p. 1.

251. BARRON, Monica
"The Accidental End." PoetC (13, i.e. 14:3) 83, p. 19.
"The Lust Studies" (Selection: #6, "Lust Study of an Iris"). IndR (5:2) Sum 82, p. 81.

252. BARTH, R. L.
"15 April 1979." SouthernR (19:1) Ja 83, p. 150.
"Idleness: Late Summer Landscape." SouthernR (19:1) Ja 83, p. 149.

253. BARTLETT, Brian
"Bear Blood in the Tree House." Descant (41) Sum 83, p. 128.
"In a Deserted Public Park." Descant (41) Sum 83, p. 129.

254. BARTLETT, Elizabeth
"A la Brume." WebR (8:2) Aut 83, p. 58.
"A la Niebla." WebR (8:2) Aut 83, p. 59.
"Excelsior." Wind (13:49) 83, p. 7.
"Montage." SanFPJ (4:2) 83, p. 73.
"On His Parents' Anniversary." Wind (13:49) 83, p. 7.
"To the Fog." WebR (8:2) Aut 83, p. 58.
"Tripos." Argo (4:2) 82, p. 10.
"Waves." SanFPJ (4:2) 83, p. 73.

255. BARTLETT, Helen
"In the Limestone House." KanQ (15:1) Wint 83, p. 187.

256. BARTLETT, Lee
"Study for an Astronaut's Palm." IndR (6:3) Sum 83, p. 37.

257. BARTON, Fred
"Beachcombing." KanQ (15:2) Spr 83, p. 56.

258. BARTON, John
"As I Wake." Dandel (10:2) Aut-Wint 83, p. 76-78.
"Incarnation." Quarry (32:4) Aut 83, p. 38-39.
"Laughing Bear." Quarry (32:1) Wint 83, p. 42-43.
"Soon to be a Major Motion Picture." Dandel (10:2) Aut-Wint 83, p. 74-75.
"Vanquished." Quarry (32:1) Wint 83, p. 41-42.

259. BARTRAM, Phil
"The Messenger." (Excerpt, recipient of a Phillips Poetry Award, Fall/Winter 1983/84). StoneC (10:3/4) Spr-Sum 83, p. 81.

260. BASS, Ellen
"To Praise." Calyx (8:1) Aut 83, p. 13-14.

261. BASSEIN, Beth Ann
"Insular." DevQ (18:1) Spr 83, p. 28.
"To Anna." DevQ (17:4) Wint 83, p. 28.

262. BATHANTI, Joseph
"Pymatuning." HiramPoR (35) Aut-Wint 83, p. 8.

263. BATTIN, Wendy
"Christine Falls." GeoR (37:1) Spr 83, p. 166-167.

264. BATTLO, Jean
"The Don's Ode on True Love." YetASM (1:1) 82, p. 16.
"An Ode for My Analyst." YetASM (1:1) 82, p. 16.
"This Ontological Question about Susan." YetASM (1:1) 82, p. 16.

265. BAUCHMAN, Rosemary
"Advice to Writers." PottPort (5) 83-84, p. 33.

266. BAUDELAIRE, Charles
"Abyss (Le Gouffre)" (tr. by X. J. Kennedy). NegC (3:4) Aut 83, p. 105.
"The Albatross" (tr. by David Schubert). QRL (24)

83, p. 72.
"Au Lecteur." PikeF (5) Spr 83, p. 4.
"Autumn Sonnet" (tr. by David Schubert). QRL (24) 83, p. 73.
"La Cloche Felee." PikeF (5) Spr 83, p. 5.
"The Cracked Bell" (tr. by James McGowan). PikeF (5) Spr 83, p. 5.
"The Death of Lovers" (tr. by James McGowan). PikeF (5) Spr 83, p. 5.
"The Enemy" (tr. by James McGowan). PikeF (5) Spr 83, p. 5.
"L'Ennemi." PikeF (5) Spr 83, p. 5.
"Epigraph for a Banned Book (Epigraphe pour un Livre Condamne)" (tr. by X. J. Kennedy). NegC (3:4) Aut 83, p. 104.
"Les Fleurs du Mal" (Selections). PikeF (5) Spr 83, p. 4-7.
"Les Fleurs du Mal" (Selections) (tr. by James McGowan). PikeF (5) Spr 83, p. 4-7.
"Les Metamorphoses du Vampire." PikeF (5) Spr 83, p. 4.
"The Metamorphoses of the Vampire" (tr. by James McGowan). PikeF (5) Spr 83, p. 4.
"La Mort des Amants." PikeF (5) Spr 83, p. 5.
"Le Reniement de Saint Pierre." PikeF (5) Spr 83, p. 7.
"St. Peter's Denial" (tr. by James McGowan). PikeF (5) Spr 83, p. 7.
"To the Reader" (tr. by James McGowan). PikeF (5) Spr 83, p. 4.
"The Voyage" (to Maxime du Camp, tr. by David Schubert). QRL (24) 83, p. 74-79.
"Un Voyage a Cythere." PikeF (5) Spr 83, p. 6.
"A Voyage to Cythere" (tr. by James McGowan). PikeF (5) Spr 83, p. 6.

267. BAUER, Grace
"For a Boy Struck by Lightning While Playing Baseball." YetASM (2:1) 83, p. 2.
"Miss Adine." Wind (13:49) 83, p. 27.

268. BAUERLE, Claire
"Speaking of Vegetation in L.A." ThRiPo (19/20) 82, p. 29.

269. BAUMANN, Susan
"You Are Still." StoneC (10:3/4) Spr-Sum 83, p. 79.

270. BAUMEL, Judith
"Led by the Hebrew School Rabbi." Ploughs (9:1) 83, p. 164.
"Message from the Interior" (Walker Evans, No. 6: Mary Frank's Bedroom, New York City). AntR (41:1) Wint 83, p. 74-75.
"Proper Distance and Proper Time." ParisR (25:90) Wint 83, p. 178.
"Speaking in Blizzards." Nat (237:8) 24 S 83, p. 246.
"That First Angelico." Agni (19) 83, p. 73-74.

271. BAUR, Jean
"O Mom, he tells me." Confr (25/26) 83, p. 276.

272. BAYES, Ronald H.
"Theatre on the Shore" (for Fred Chappell). Abatis (1) 83, p. 10.

273. BAYRON BRUNET, Vilma
"Un Chupón de China y 6 Pepitas." Rácata (2) 83, p. 134.
"Como en el vivir." Rácata (2) 83, p. 29.
"Hoy la vida sabe a olor de casa vieja." Rácata (1) 83, p. 21.
"Me encantaría, simplemente, estar loca" (a D. C.). Rácata (2) 83, p. 27.
"No podré ya cantar." Rácata (2) 83, p. 30.
"Ocurrió en el tiempo." Rácata (2) 83, p. 28.
"Poco a poco." Rácata (1) 83, p. 22.
"Poética." Rácata (1) 83, p. 18.
"Primero, se pierde la fe en Dios." Rácata (1) 83, p. 20.
"Ten mi canción de silueta repetida." Rácata (1) 83, p. 19.

274. BEALL, Sandra
"In the Next Room." Confr (25/26) 83, p. 260.
"The Women." Confr (25/26) 83, p. 260.

275. BEAN, John
"Anniversary." IndR (6:1) Wint 83, p. 23.

276. BEARD, Susan M.
"One Patriotic Pride." SanFPJ (5:3) 83, p. 9.

277. BEARDEN, David
"Snow's Chowder." Tele (18) 83, p. 77.

278. BEARDEN, David Omer
"Marks of the Beast." SanFPJ (5:2) 83, p. 46-47.

279. BEASLEY, Bruce
"All Autumn." CutB (21) Aut-Wint 83, p. 90.

280. BEATTIE, Ann
"Heaven on a Summer Night." NewYorker (59:41) 28 N 83, p. 52.

281. BEAVERS, Herm
"A Picture of Bird." BlackALF (17:4) Wint 83, p. 154.
"Untitled: My sister and I had walked to Lawson's." BlackALF (17:4) Wint 83, p. 154.

282. BECK, Gary
"For Maggie Melvin, Weaver, Learning Italian." CrabCR (1:1) My 83, p. 16.

283. BECK-REX, Marguerite
"Devil Dance." PoetryNW (24:4) Wint 83-84, p. 21.
"Lineage." PoetryNW (24:4) Wint 83-84, p. 20-21.

284. BECKER, Therese
"Evening with a Psychic." ThirdW Spr 83, p. 88.
"Psalm." WorldO (17:4) Sum 83, p. 28.

285. BECQUER, Gustavo Adolfo
"Rimas (Excerpts: X, XVII, XXXVIII)" (tr. by Ifan Payne). KanO (15:1) Wint 83, p. 115.

BEE BEE TAN
See: TAN, Bee Bee

286. BEEDE, Gayle Jansen
"Calla Lilies." PoetC (15:1) Aut 83, p. 7.

287. BEEHR, Karen Faris
"Hill." DekalbLAJ (16:1/4) Aut 82-Sum 83, p. 56.
"January 3." DekalbLAJ (16:1/4) Aut 82-Sum 83, p. 55.

288. BEESON, Diane
"The Great American Falsie." SanFPJ (4:2) 83, p. 7.
"The Hamburger Stand." SanFPJ (4:2) 83, p. 6.

289. BEHM, Richard
"Learning to Dance, to Dance." SpoonRO (8:4) Aut 83, p. 27.
"The Mask Of Waking." SewanR (91:2) Spr 83, p. 187.
"Religion." SpoonRO (8:4) Aut 83, p. 26.

290. BEHN, Bettina
"On Such a Night" (tr. by Stuart Friebert). MemphisSR (2:2) Spr 82, p. 11.
"Precise Moment" (tr. by Stuart Friebert). MemphisSR (2:2) Spr 82, p. 10.

291. BEHN, Robin
"Distinguished Flying Cross." Field (29) Aut 83, p. 76.
"The Drowned among Us." MissouriR (7:1) Aut 83, p. 54-55.
"The First Angel" (for P.). Field (29) Aut 83, p. 75.

292. BEHRENDT, Stephen C.
"The Mammoth Tooth from the Garden: Nebraska." KanO (15:2) Spr 83, p. 80.
"Minneapolis Idyll." KanO (15:2) Spr 83, p. 79.

293. BEHRENS, Bernard
"Missing in Action." SanFPJ (5:3) 83, p. 57.

294. BEINING, Guy R.
"Ogden As Texas Traveller." SecC (11:1/2) 83, p. 7.
"Stoma 1526." Tele (18) 83, p. 68.
"Stoma 1528." Tele (18) 83, p. 69.

295. BEISSEL, Henry
"H2O." CanLit (96) Spr 83, p. 11-12.
"White Spruce." CanLit (97) Sum 83, p. 9.

296. BEJEL, Emilio
"Cruza ese recuerdo en las ventanas." Areito

(9:33) 83, p. 21.

297. BEJERANO, Maya
"Data-Processing #15" (tr. by Linda Zisquit). LitR (26:2) Wint 83, p. 295.
"First it Rained" (tr. by Gabriel Levin). LitR (26:2) Wint 83, p. 297.
"Salammbô" (tr. by Linda Zisquit). LitR (26:2) Wint 83, p. 296.
"The Tibetan Princess" (tr. by Linda Zisquit). LitR (26:2) Wint 83, p. 294.

298. BEKER, Ruth
"The New Widow." LitR (26:2) Wint 83, p. 329.
"War." LitR (26:2) Wint 83, p. 330.

299. BELFIELD, Judy
"The Day after the Bomb." SanFPJ (5:2) 83, p. 14-15.
"A December Death." SanFPJ (5:2) 83, p. 76.
"Eulogy." Poem (48) Jl 83, p. 41.
"Prophets and Lost." SanFPJ (5:1) 83, p. 83.
"Some Days, Gloom." CapeR (19:1) Wint 83, p. 38.
"Sunshine Fever." Poem (48) Jl 83, p. 42.
"Thus Far and No Further: Updating Conrad." SanFPJ (5:1) 83, p. 82.

300. BELL, Carolyn Light
"Afterwards" (for James L. White). KanQ (15:2) Spr 83, p. 98.

301. BELL, Lindolf
"On Hope" (tr. by William Jay Smith). PoNow (7:2, #38) 83, p. 46.

302. BELL, Marvin
"Balsa." MissouriR (6:2) Wint 83, p. 28.
"Draft Age." Poetry (143:1) O 83, p. 13.
"Felt But Not Touched -- Seattle." ParisR (25:90) Wint 83, p. 173.
"A Fish: On Beauty." OhioR (30) 83, p. 24.
"Fish-Feeding at Haunama Bay." Nat (236:11) 19 Mr 83, p. 346.
"A Gift of Fish" (Interlochen, Michigan) (for Jack Driscoll). Tendril (14/15) Wint 83, p. 20-21.
"Great Leaning Ferns." MissouriR (6:2) Wint 83, p. 29.
"Hawaii Too." TriQ (56) Wint 83, p. 154.
"In Two Parts." AntR (41:2) Spr 83, p. 210-211.
"Instructions to Be Left Behind." TriQ (56) Wint 83, p. 152-153.
"Landscape with Open Spaces." Poetry (143:1) O 83, p. 12.
"The Nest." NewYorker (59:22) 18 Jl 83, p. 40.
"Shoulders of Tropical Rain." MissouriR (6:2) Wint 83, p. 31.
"The Telescope on Mauna Kea." Nat (236:10) 12 Mr 83, p. 316.
"Two, When There Might Have Been Three." AntR (41:2) Spr 83, p. 209.
"A View in the Rain -- Honolulu." MissouriR (6:2)

Wint 83, p. 30.
"When I Run." Poetry (143:1) O 83, p. 14.
"White Clover." Atlantic (251:2) F 83, p. 58.

303. BELL, Melissa
"Crawling into Dali." Vis (13) 83, p. 30.

304. BELL, Sandy
"His Unfinished Sentence Would Have Told Me of Compassion, I'm Sure." PoetryCR (5:2) Wint 83-84, p. 7.
"Let Me Say All I Have to Say." PoetryCR (4:4) Sum 83, p. 15.
"Let Me Say All I Have to Say." PoetryCR (5:1) Aut 83, p. 19.

305. BELL, Wilma
"Linda." EngJ (72:4) Ap 83, p. 25.

BELLAY, Joachim du
See: Du BELLAY, Joachim

306. BELLE, Siota
"God Had a Cosmic Yoyo." Poem (48) Jl 83, p. 59.
"Odalisque." Poem (48) Jl 83, p. 57-58.

307. BELLI, Gioconda
"Estado de Animo." Areito (9:34) 83, p. 31.

308. BEMBENEK, Lawrencia
"Complications." ClockR (1:2) Wint 83-84, p. 39.

309. BEN, Menachem
"The Mother Spaceship" (tr. by Gabriel Levin). LitR (26:2) Wint 83, p. 293.
"The Sea Transparent Slices" (tr. by Gabriel Levin). LitR (26:2) Wint 83, p. 290-293.

310. BEN-SHIMON, Ezra
"Anniversary Song." PortR (29:1) 83, p. 129.

311. BEN-TOV, S.
"Didactic Sestina for White Belts." MassR (24:1) Spr 83, p. 108-109.
"During Ceasefire, in Jerusalem." BlackWR (8:2) Spr 82, p. 72-73.
"Earhart Flies through the Monsoon." PraS (57:3) Aut 83, p. 50-51.
"Earhart over Africa." PraS (57:3) Aut 83, p. 48.
"Earhart Solos." PraS (57:3) Aut 83, p. 49.
"The Summer of The Wild Artichokes." NewEng (5:4) Sum 83, p. 514-518.
"A Young Doctor in the Gardner Museum" (For Elizabeth). YaleR (72:3) Spr 83, p. 415.

312. BENCH, Carson E.
"Business Lunch." SanFPJ (4:3) 83, p. 9.
"Why is it the poet who has to analyze society?" SanFPJ (5:2) 83, p. 16.

313. BENDAH, Joshua
"Autumn Snowflakes." PoetryCR (4:3) Spr 83, p. 15.

314. BENEDETTI, David
"Baby Crying." Tele (18) 83, p. 100-102.
"Delayed Gratification." Tele (18) 83, p. 98.
"Sexual Information." Tele (18) 83, p. 99.

315. BENEDICT, Burnette B.
"Enigma of Our Time." SanFPJ (5:3) 83, p. 62.
"Presence." SanFPJ (5:3) 83, p. 63.

316. BENEDIKT, Michael
"At Vassar I taught (or, The Boston Univ. Pub on a Day I almost Ate There in '77)." MassR (24:4) Wint 83, p. 701-703.

317. BENLITT, Ben
"Battery Park: High Noon" (Selection: 2). ORL (24) 83, p. 164-165.
"The Casualty" (For David Schubert). ORL (24) 83, p. 299.

318. BENNET, Eileen
"Waiting." Wind (13:48) 83, p. 13.

319. BENNETT, Beate Hein
"I Too Look into the Fire" (tr. of Israel Eliraz). LitR (26:3) Spr 83, p. 447.
"In Halhul" (tr. of Israel Eliraz). LitR (26:3) Spr 83, p. 446.

320. BENNETT, Bruce
"At the Center." Wind (13:49) 83, p. 8-9.
"Parents As Clouds." Wind (13:49) 83, p. 8.
"Work." Wind (13:49) 83, p. 8.

321. BENNETT, J., Jr.
"To the Essential Poet." SecC (11:1/2) 83, p. 8.

322. BENNETT, Maria
"Tales of Hermes Trismegistus." Swallow (2) Aut-Wint 83, p. 10.
"Thunderstorm in New York." Swallow (2) Aut-Wint 83, p. 11.
"To Julia de Burgos" (tr. of Julia de Burgos). Swallow (2) Aut-Wint 83, p. 7, 9.

323. BENNETT, Patrick
"Rats." KanQ (15:1) Wint 83, p. 90.

324. BENNETT, Paul
"The Saga of Sam Whitfield." BelPoJ (33:4) Sum 83, p. 12-21.

325. BENSKO, John
"Mowing the Lawn." GeoR (37:3) Aut 83, p. 600.
"On Halloween the Elk Turns Detective." BlackWR (10:1) Aut 83, p. 50.
"Watching TV, the Elk Bones Up on Metaphysics."

BlackWR (10:1) Aut 83, p. 48-49.
"The Wild Horses of Asseateague Island." Poetry (142:2) My 83, p. 68-69.

326. BENTLEY, Beth
"Confessions." IndR (6:3) Sum 83, p. 59.

327. BENTLEY, Roy
"33 South." CharR (9:2) Aut 83, p. 64.
"White Handkerchief." CharR (9:2) Aut 83, p. 64-65.

328. BENTTINEN, Ted
"The Children of New England." MassR (24:3) Aut 83, p. 669.
"Provincetown, Early March." MassR (24:3) Aut 83, p. 670-671.

329. BENTZMAN, Bruce Harris
"The First Time I Saw Beauty in a Horse." WindO (43) Wint 83, p. 17.
"Foresight." HiramPoR (34) Spr-Sum 83, p. 6.
"To Linger in the Bronx Unable to Die." PoetL (78:1) Spr 83, p. 21.

330. BENVENISTE, Rachelle
"The Weekend with His Children." 13thM (6:1/2) 82, p. 20-21.

331. BENZ, Maudy
"The Lock." SouthernPR (23:2) Aut 82 [i.e. (23:1?) Spr 83], p. 39.

332. BERESFORD, Anne
"King Solomon and the Cuckoo." PoetryCR (5:1) Aut 83, p. 12.

333. BERESFORD, Larry
"Rhythms." US1 (16/17) Wint 83-84, p. 3.

334. BERESFORD, Thomas
"Charon." SouthernR (19:1) Ja 83, p. 152.
"A Child's Poem for Lucretius." SouthernR (19:1) Ja 83, p. 152.
"Epigrams." SouthernR (19:1) Ja 83, p. 153.
"The Gayhead Cliffs." SouthernR (19:1) Ja 83, p. 152.
"Mountain Waters." SouthernR (19:1) Ja 83, p. 151.
"Sun Up." SouthernR (19:1) Ja 83, p. 151.

335. BERG, Charles Ramirez
"Multiple Myeloma." SanFPJ (4:2) 83, p. 57.

336. BERG, Sharon
"The Romance." CrossC (5:1) 83, p. 12.

337. BERG, Stephen
"Bezhetsk" (from With Akhmatova at the Black Gates). Thrpny (4:2, issue 14) Sum 83, p. 7.
"January" (from With Akhmatova at the Black Gates). Thrpny (4:2, issue 14) Sum 83, p. 7.

338. BERGAMINI, L. J.
"Sisters." Blueline (4:2) Wint-Spr 83, p. 7.
"Skier's Dusk." WindO (43) Wint 83, p. 44.
"Summer Wedding." Blueline (4:1) Sum-Aut 82, p. 13.

339. BERGE, Carol
"The Power." PoNow (7:2, #38) 83, p. 27.

340. BERGER, Bruce
"Ambition." Poetry (142:5) Ag 83, p. 270.
"Stout Brahms." Poetry (142:5) Ag 83, p. 269.

341. BERGER, Irwin
"Dreams at Fifty." YetASM (1:2) 82, p. 15.
"Kaddish." YetASM (1:2) 82, p. 4.

342. BERGER, Suzanne E.
"The Meal." Tendril (14/15) Wint 83, p. 23.
"Parts." Tendril (14/15) Wint 83, p. 22.

343. BERGLAND, Martha
"Sleepwalker" (Walt Cieszynski, poet, 1946-1976). ClockR (2:1) 83, p. 5.

344. BERGMAN, David
"Aunt Ida's Last Evasion." AmerS (52:1) Wint 82/83, p. 88.
"In and Out of the Garden." Shen (34:4) 83, p. 44-45.

345. BERGMAN, Denise
"The Way He Touches Me." YetASM (1:2) 82, p. 13.

346. BERGSTROM, Vera
"Two Little Children." Bogg (51) 83, p. 3.
"Witch-Child." Bogg (51) 83, p. 26.

347. BERKE, Judith (See also BERKE, Judy)
"Les Demoiselles d'Avignon." DevQ (18:3) Aut 83, p. 35.
"Hansel and Gretel." OP (36) Aut-Wint 83, p. 49.
"If Grandpa the Buttonhole Maker Could Have Come Back." LittleM (14:1/2) 83, p. 87.
"Just Go." LitR (26:3) Spr 83, p. 450.
"Letting Go." NewL (50:1) Aut 83, p. 97.
"The Mirror." OP (36) Aut-Wint 83, p. 51.
"Mrs. Treadle and Mrs. Pocket." WormR (23:2, issue 90) 83, p. 51-52.
"Oedipus." SouthernHR (17:1) Wint 83, p. 18.
"The Other Woman." PoetryNW (24:2) Sum 83, p. 15.
"The Possibilities of Stillness." OP (36) Aut-Wint 83, p. 48-49.
"Poster." DevQ (18:3) Aut 83, p. 34.
"Recovery." NewL (50:1) Aut 83, p. 96.
"She Who Was Once the Helmet Maker's Beautiful Wife" (after Rodin). DevQ (18:3) Aut 83, p. 33.
"Smiling with the Brothers Grimm." OP (36) Aut-Wint 83, p. 52.
"The Snake." DevQ (18:3) Aut 83, p. 102.
"Soon" (for RPL). LittleM (14:1/2) 83, p. 86.
"Two Poets." WormR (23:2, issue 90) 83, p. 52.

"The Wand." OP (36) Aut-Wint 83, p. 50.

348. BERKE, Judy (See also BERKE, Judith)
"The Three-Headed Woman." Pig (11) 83, p. 62.

349. BERLIND, Bruce
"Period Piece." NewL (49:3/4) Spr-Sum 83, p. 112.

350. BERNAUER, Carol
"Bar Beastie." Sam (36:2 142nd release) 83, p. 11.
"Kid Beasties #1." Sam (36:2 142nd release) 83, p. 3.
"Modern Day Beasties." Sam (36:2 142nd release) 83, p. 1-12.
"Modern Day Beasties #2." Sam (36:2 142nd release) 83, p. 5.
"Modern Day Beasties #5." Sam (36:2 142nd release) 83, p. 9.
"Modern Day Beasties #9." Sam (36:2 142nd release) 83, p. 9.
"Modern Day Flukes #1." Sam (36:2 142nd release) 83, p. 7.
"Modern Day Flukes #7." Sam (36:2 142nd release) 83, p. 11.
"Modern Day Martyrs #4." Sam (36:2 142nd release) 83, p. 12.
"Modern Day Masochists #2." Sam (36:2 142nd release) 83, p. 12.
"The Most Enigmatic of Beasties." Sam (36:2 142nd release) 83, p. 7.

351. BERNHARD, Jeanne
"This Is the Way It Will Be." MissouriR (6:2) Wint 83, p. 88-94.

352. BERNHEIMER, Alan
"Florex Gardens." ParisR (24:86) Wint 82, p. 103.
"Topic A." ParisR (24:86) Wint 82, p. 103.

353. BERNIER, Jack
"Line-up." SanFPJ (5:4) 83, p. 15.
"One Down, Two to Go." SanFPJ (5:3) 83, p. 8.

354. BERNSTEIN, Charles
"Air Shaft." ParisR (24:86) Wint 82, p. 120.
"But Boxes Both Boats, Growing Tireder As the Day Amasses." ParisR (24:86) Wint 82, p. 119.
"Dysraphism." Sulfur (3:2, #8) 83, p. 39-45.
"Idiopathic Pathogenesis." ParisR (24:86) Wint 82, p. 120.
"Playing with a Full Deck." ParisR (24:86) Wint 82, p. 118-119.

355. BERNSTEIN, Lisa
"Anorexia" (Excerpts: "A Sequence"). MSS (3:1) Aut 83, p. 78-83.
"Eating Alone." CalQ (22) Sum 83, p. 81.
"Eating the Heart." Kayak (61) Ap 83, p. 58.
"Jumping Rope in the Yard." Kayak (61) Ap 83, p. 59.
"My Birthday." CalQ (22) Sum 83, p. 80.

356. BERRETT, Jean
"February 11." YetASM (1:2) 82, p. 11.
"The Way Back." YetASM (1:2) 82, p. 13.

357. BERRY, D. C.
"Courtney." MemphisSR (3:2) Spr 83, p. 35.
"Watercolor." OroM (2:1, #5) Sum 83, p. 12.

358. BERRY, David
"Overtures." MalR (64) F 83, p. 161.
"Urban Fishfly." MalR (64) F 83, p. 161.

359. BERRY, Donald L.
"Secondhand Theology." ChrC (100:10) 6 Ap 83, p. 308.

360. BERRY, Jan
"Duty." Sam (36:1 141st release) 83, p. 6.
"In the Footsteps of Genghis Khan." Sam (36:1 141st release) 83, p. 5.
"Late News." Sam (36:1 141st release) 83, p. 7.
"The Peace Monument." Sam (36:1 141st release) 83, p. 12.
"Reading the Names of the War Dead" (Riverside Church, December 1969). Sam (36:1 141st release) 83, p. 9.
"Sunday Morning Nap" (West Point Chapel). Sam (36:1 141st release) 83, p. 8.
"Veterans Day" (issue title). Sam (36:1 141st release) 83, p. 1-12.
"Veterans Day 1." Sam (36:1 141st release) 83, p. 2-4.
"Veterans Day 2." Sam (36:1 141st release) 83, p. 10-11.

361. BERRY, John
"On Leaving Nothing." YetASM (1:1) 82, p. 16.

362. BERTOLINO, James
"A Beginning." IndR (6:1) Wint 83, p. 45.
"The Cocoon" (for John Ashbery). IndR (6:1) Wint 83, p. 44.
"Cosmic Porcupine." ManhatR (3:1) Sum 83, p. 55.
"Dog Leader." MemphisSR (1:2) Spr 81, p. 26.
"Frog Voices" (For Philip McCracken). BelPoJ (33:3) Spr 83, p. 1.
"Tissue." ManhatR (3:1) Sum 83, p. 55.

363. BEVAN, Patricia
"In the City." Wind (13:49) 83, p. 10.

364. BEYER, Barbara Langham
"Crossing." YetASM (1:2) 82, p. 11.
"Somerset, Remembering." YetASM (1:2) 82, p. 13.

365. BIAGIONI, Amelia
"Gestalt." Mund (14:1) 83, p. 66.
"Gestalt" (tr. by Melanie Bowman). Mund (14:1) 83, p. 67.
"Tiger" (tr. by Melanie Bowman). Mund (14:1) 83, p. 67.

"Tigre." Mund (14:1) 83, p. 66.

366. BIALAS, Dan
"My Boston Aspiring Poet Friend Scoffs Whenever We Discuss My Dave Etteresque Poems." SpoonRQ (8:2) Spr 83, p. 5.

367. BIDART, Frank
"Confessional." ParisR (25:89) Aut 83, p. 52-74.
"Genesis 1-2:4." Ploughs (9:1) 83, p. 33-38.

368. BIEN, Peter
"Do Not Weep So Soon" (tr. of Stylianos Harkianakis). Paint (10:19/20) Spr-Aut 83, p. 36.
"Easy Payment Plan" (tr. of Stylianos Harkianakis). Paint (10:19/20) Spr-Aut 83, p. 33.
"For Those Who Hate the Light" (tr. of Stylianos Harkianakis). Paint (10:19/20) Spr-Aut 83, p. 32.
"My Fellow Villagers" (tr. of Stylianos Harkianakis). Paint (10:19/20) Spr-Aut 83, p. 39.
"Requiem for Poetry" (tr. of Stylianos Harkianakis). Paint (10:19/20) Spr-Aut 83, p. 40.
"Restitution" (tr. of Stylianos Harkianakis). Paint (10:19/20) Spr-Aut 83, p. 35.
"Still Life" (tr. of Stylianos Harkianakis). Paint (10:19/20) Spr-Aut 83, p. 41.
"To My Teacher L.K." (tr. of Stylianos Harkianakis). Paint (10:19/20) Spr-Aut 83, p. 37.
"The Twentieth Century" (tr. of Stylianos Harkianakis). Paint (10:19/20) Spr-Aut 83, p. 38.
"Water Color" (tr. of Stylianos Harkianakis). Paint (10:19/20) Spr-Aut 83, p. 34.

369. BIENEK, Horst
"Accused" (tr. by Paul Morris). PoetryE (9/10) Wint 82-Spr 83, p. 189.
"Afterwards" (tr. by Paul Morris). PoetryE (9/10) Wint 82-Spr 83, p. 190.
"The Defeated Conqueror" (tr. by Paul Morris). PoetryE (9/10) Wint 82-Spr 83, p. 191.
"Katorga" (tr. by Paul Morris). PoetryE (9/10) Wint 82-Spr 83, p. 186.
"Our Ashes" (tr. by Paul Morris). PoetryE (9/10) Wint 82-Spr 83, p. 187-188.
"Symbols and Propositions" (tr. by Paul Morris). PoetryE (9/10) Wint 82-Spr 83, p. 185.
"Very Far Away" (tr. by Paul Morris). PoetryE (9/10) Wint 82-Spr 83, p. 192.

370. BIENVENU, Roberta
"The Cabin in Autumn." IndR (6:2) Spr 83, p. 38.
"Something Decided." IndR (6:2) Spr 83, p. 39.

371. BIERDS, Linda
"Elegy for 41 Whales, Beached in Florence, Oregon, June 1979." NewL (49:3/4) Spr-Sum 83, p. 113.
"Fur Traders Descending the Missouri, 1845" (from the Painting by George Caleb Bingham). BlackWR (9:1) Aut 82, p. 65.
"Magicians in the Park." Outbr (12/13) Aut 83-Spr

84, p. 83.
"Nails." Outbr (12/13) Aut 83-Spr 84, p. 82.
"Open." MassR (24:3) Aut 83, p. 636.
"Tongue." Outbr (12/13) Aut 83-Spr 84, p. 81.
"Zuni Potter: Drawing the Heartline." BlackWR (9:1) Aut 82, p. 64.

372. BIGUENET, John
"Moonlight." Ploughs (9:2/3) 83, p. 227.

373. BILGERE, George
"Barnstormer." SewanR (91:4) Aut 83, p. 592-593.
"Terrapin." SewanR (91:4) Aut 83, p. 591.
"Visit from Home." Ascent (8:2) 83, p. 44-45.
"Yozu." SewanR (91:4) Aut 83, p. 590.

374. BILICKE, Tom
"Haiku." Bogg (51) 83, p. 6.
"Mary Ramirez." Bogg (50) 83, p. 19-20.
"Now." Wind (13:48) 83, p. 5.

375. BILL, Jim
"Icarus at Sunset." CrabCR (1:1) My 83, p. 5.

376. BILLINGS, Robert
"Anniversary in Late Autumn." Waves (11:2/3) Wint 83, p. 57.
"August in Sydenham Ward" (for Gail Fox). CanLit (98) Aut 83, p. 59.
"Chestwounds" (Excerpts from a sequence: 2, 5, 7, 8). Descant (42) Aut 83, p. 18-22.
"Dawn on Wellington Street West." Quarry (32:3) Sum 83, p. 41-42.
"Epiphanies on the First Cold Day" Waves (11:2/3) Wint 83, p. 56-57.
"Greenwood Hill in Winter, 1848." Quarry (32:3) Sum 83, p. 41.
"Incidental Music for Late May." PoetryCR (5:1) Aut 83, p. 8.
"Last Photographs of Pound." PikeF (5) Spr 83, p. 9.
"Morning, First of the Month." Dandel (10:1) Spr-Sum 83, p. 73.
"Moving" (for Anne). MalR (66) O 83, p. 88.
"One Walk with Kate." MalR (66) O 83, p. 87.
"Returning to Lost Bay" (for Uncle Roger). Dandel (10:1) Spr-Sum 83, p. 74.

377. BILLY, Allen T. (Also known as BILLY, Eveline Jill)
"City of Flashing Shadows." SanFPJ (4:4) 83, p. 56.
"The Dragon's Jaws." SanFPJ (5:3) 83, p. 84.
"Harvest of Evil." SanFPJ (5:3) 83, p. 84.

378. BILLY, Eveline Jill (Also known as BILLY, Allen T.)
"The New Dawn." SanFPJ (4:3) 83, p. 21.

379. BINGHAM, Ginger
"Airstream Trailer." MissouriR (6:3) Sum 83, p. 9.
"The Calendar at Avery's." MissouriR (6:3) Sum 83, p. 12.
"Songs of the Typing School." MissouriR (6:3) Sum

83, p. 10-11.

380. BINGHAM, Jo
"Winter Beach." YetASM (1:1) 82, p. 13.

381. BINGHAM, Sallie
"Slave Ship." NewL (50:1) Aut 83, p. 69.

382. BJORKLUND, Beth
"Art Trip to Oaxaca" (tr. of Wieland Schmied). DevQ (18:3) Aut 83, p. 27.
"Chess with Marcel Duchamp" (tr. of Wieland Schmied). DevQ (18:3) Aut 83, p. 28-29.
"The Things of René Magritte--I" (tr. of Wieland Schmied). DevQ (18:3) Aut 83, p. 30.

383. BIRCHAM, Doris
"Home Care." Grain (11:3) Ag 83, p. 20.

384. BIRDSALL, Jane
"Abortion." Tendril (14/15) Wint 83, p. 27.
"Blood Gravy." Tendril (14/15) Wint 83, p. 24.
"In the Palm of Her Hand." Tendril (14/15) Wint 83, p. 25.
"When I Dream of Taking My Own Life." Tendril (14/15) Wint 83, p. 26.

385. BIRKS, Lynda
"The New Depression." SanFPJ (4:4) 83, p. 77.

386. BIRNIE, Christine
"Heart Attack." Waves (11:2/3) Wint 83, p. 69.

387. BISHOP, Bonnie
"My Mother's Letters." Bluebuf (2:1) Aut 83, p. 9.

388. BISHOP, Elizabeth
"At the Fishhouses" (from The Complete Poems 1927-1979). NewRep (188:13) 4 Ap 83, p. 24-25.
"Over 2, 000 Illustrations and a Complete Concordance" (from The Complete Poems 1927-1979). NewRep (188:13) 4 Ap 83, p. 25.

389. BISHOP, Jonathan
"Entropy" (for Mary von Schlegell). Shen (34:2) 83, p. 61.
"New England Addresses." MassR (24:3) Aut 83, p. 544.

390. BISHOP, W. (Wendy)
"Addressing the Body." PoetryNW (24:1) Spr 83, p. 43.
"An Ever Open Door." MissR (12:1/2, nos. 34/35) Aut 83, p. 75.
"Gypsy Dance in Progress in a Sunlit Corner of a Courtyard of Southern Serbia." MissR (12:1/2, nos. 34/35) Aut 83, p. 74.
"The Housekeeper." Thrpny (4:2, issue 14) Sum 83, p. 6.
"Indian Women Keeping Shop at the Door of Their Adobe Hut." LitR (26:3) Spr 83, p. 350.
"Travelers Sleeping" (for R. Moore). YaleR (72:2)

Wint 83, p. 258.
"Working at Home." Thrpny (4:1, issue 13) Spr 83, p. 7.

391. BISS, Ellen
"White Skates." Blueline (3:2) Wint-Spr 82, p. 12-13.

392. BISSERT, Ellen Marie
"Insurance Agents." 13thM (6:1/2) 82, p. 121.
"Stand-Up Legacies." 13thM (6:1/2) 82, p. 122.
"Working in America" (for Amelia Etlinger & Helen (Helinka) Zihal). 13thM (7:1/2) 83, p. 113-117.

393. BISSONETTE, David
"Praise General Motors, from Whom All Blessings Flow." EngJ (72:5) S 83, p. 89.

394. BLACK, Candace
"Listening to My Uncle." Swallow (1) Spr 83, p. 86.
"What We Give Each Other." CrabCR (1:2) Aut 83, p. 14.

395. BLACK, Charles
"Conversation with a Shepherd." NewOR (10:2/3) Sum-Aut 83, p. 99.
"One of the Scholars." LittleM (14:1/2) 83, p. 17.
"Wildwood China." LittleM (14:1/2) 83, p. 16.

396. BLACK, Harold
"Yaveh." Vis (11) 83, p. 16.

397. BLACK ELK, Ben
"Red Is the Knowledge" (Excerpt). SoDakR (21:4) Wint 83, p. 37.

398. BLACKBURN, Michael
"Elegy I." Stand (24:1) 82-83, p. 6.
"Schliemann to the King of Greece." Stand (24:4) Aut 83, p. 6.
"Seaford, July '77 (for Sarah)." Stand (24:1) 82-83, p. 6.
"Tutankhamen's Antechamber." Stand (24:4) Aut 83, p. 6.

399. BLACKWELL, Will H.
"End Things." KanQ (15:2) Spr 83, p. 200.

400. BLADES, Joe
"Constable Anderson's Hat." PottPort (5) 83-84, p. 32.
"Danced with Human, Whooper Is Killed" (Baraboo, Wis., AP). PottPort (5) 83-84, p. 32.

401. BLAEUER, Mark
"The Road Taken." Wind (13:48) 83, p. 21.

402. BLAIN, Alexander
"Concord." Vis (12) 83, p. 31.

403. BLAKELY, Paul
"Your Word, a Light." BallSUF (24:2) Spr 83, p. 70.

404. BLAKEMAN, Beth
"Grandmother, they said the rice in Carolina was the best to be had." YetASM (2:1) 83, p. 12.

405. BLANCART KUBBER, Teresa
"Buscando." Rácata (2) 83, p. 33.
"Entre Tu Ser Y Mi Ser." Rácata (1) 83, p. 26.
"Mujer Camino." Rácata (1) 83, p. 24.
"Porque mis cosas." Rácata (2) 83, p. 34.
"Quechua." Rácata (2) 83, p. 32.
"Roberto lugo me habló" (a lugo, a wiso). Rácata (2) 83, p. 31.
"Tarinia" (a mi niña que partió, Baraka Basah). Rácata (1) 83, p. 23.
"Voy Cuestionando." Rácata (1) 83, p. 27.
"Yo Humanidad." Rácata (1) 83, p. 25.

406. BLANCHARD, Lucile
"I Have Sat with Madmen." NegC (3:4) Aut 83, p. 53.

407. BLANDON GUEVARA, Erick
"Un Tren Que Nunca Llega a Pablo." Areíto (9:34) 83, p. 31.

408. BLASING, Randy
"Chill." PoNow (7:2, #38) 83, p. 17.
"Gilgamesh Visits Ephesus." Poetry (142:5) Ag 83, p. 267.
"The Keys." PoNow (7:2, #38) 83, p. 17.
"Over Drinks." Poetry (142:5) Ag 83, p. 267.
"Ramazan at New Phocaea." Poetry (142:5) Ag 83, p. 268.

409. BLAUNER, Laurie
"The Woman You Wished Drowned" (for Rob Ringelstein and Richard Hugo). YetASM (1:2) 82, p. 10.

410. BLAZEK, Douglas
"Halloween Poem." Abraxas (27/28) 83, p. 8.
"Handgrenades in My Grapefruit." SecC (11:1/2) 83, p. 9.
"How the Boxcars Became Locomotives." NewL (49:3/4) Spr-Sum 83, p. 193.
"Identity." Abraxas (27/28) 83, p. 9.
"Tu Fu: Master Traveler." BelPoJ (34:2) Wint 83-84, p. 33.

411. BLEAKLEY, Alan
"Holomovement" (for Su). ManhatR (3:1) Sum 83, p. 64-65.
"I Dreamed That My Mother Died, Suddenly, While Caught in a Thunderstorm." Stand (24:3) 83, p. 60.

412. BLESSING, Tom
"Eating Names." Bogg (50) 83, p. 22.

413. BLESSINGTON, Francis
"Georgia O'Keeffe's White Rose with Larkspur." ArizQ (39:3) Aut 83, p. 245.
"The Man with the Umbrella" (from Lantskit, semi-finalist, 10th anniversary manuscript competition). StoneC (11:1/2, Pt. 1) Aut-Wint 83, p. 58.
"Nairobi in Winter." DevQ (18:3) Aut 83, p. 15.
"Photographing the Love Birds of Masai Mara: A Pastoral." DevQ (18:3) Aut 83, p. 16.
"Quabbin." Argo (4:3) 83, p. 32.

414. BLEY, Deborah L.
"Sensibility." WorldO (18:1) Aut 83, p. 37.

415. BLEYTHING, Dennis
"Mrs. Foltz Uses Molasses." YetASM (1:1) 82, p. 13.
"Violins for the Children/Bartok." YetASM (1:1) 82, p. 15.

416. BLISS, S. W.
"In the Company of Strangers." YetASM (1:1) 82, p. 8.

417. BLOCH, Chana
"Deep Calleth unto Deep" (tr. of Dahlia Ravikovitch). LitR (26:2) Wint 83, p. 261.
"The Everlasting Forests" (tr. of Dahlia Ravikovitch). LitR (26:2) Wint 83, p. 258.
"The Horns of Hittin" (tr. of Dahlia Ravikovitch). LitR (26:2) Wint 83, p. 260-261.
"King over Israel" (tr. of Dahlia Ravikovitch). LitR (26:2) Wint 83, p. 259.
"Requiem After Seventeen Years" (tr. of Dahlia Ravikovitch). LitR (26:2) Wint 83, p. 256.
"Two Songs of the Garden" (tr. of Dahlia Ravikovitch). LitR (26:2) Wint 83, p. 257-258.

418. BLOCK, Ron
"Ballade of the Back Road." Iowa (13:2) Spr 82, p. 111.
"Ballade of the Brief Life." PraS (57:3) Aut 83, p. 76.
"Ballade of the Tree." PraS (57:3) Aut 83, p. 75.

419. BLODGETT, E. D.
"Discovery" (in memoriam Shanawdithit, obit 6 June 1829). MalR (65) Jl 83, p. 132-133.
"Fall of Patriots." MalR (65) Jl 83, p. 130-131.
"Origins." MalR (65) Jl 83, p. 128-129.

420. BLOOMFIELD, Maureen
"Staircase." Ascent (8:2) 83, p. 38-39.
"Trapunto." Ascent (8:2) 83, p. 39.

421. BLOSSOM, Laurel
"Back from the Dead." Poetry (142:1) Ap 83, p. 19.
"Normal." Poetry (142:1) Ap 83, p. 18.

422. BLOSSOM, Lavina
"Choices." CalQ (22) Sum 83, p. 51.

"Him." ParisR (25:89) Aut 83, p. 129.
"Jerome." ParisR (25:89) Aut 83, p. 128.
"Staying." ParisR (25:89) Aut 83, p. 127.
"Step Two." ParisR (25:89) Aut 83, p. 128-129.

423. BLUE-ZWARTS, Janice
"The Death of You, Mother." MalR (64) F 83, p. 113-115.

424. BLUGER, Marianne
"Owned." AntigR (53) Spr 83, p. 40.
"A Song." AntigR (53) Spr 83, p. 39.

425. BLUMENTHAL, Marcia
"Quiet, Please." Wind (13:48) 83, p. 6.
"The Salt Cure." Wind (13:48) 83, p. 6-7.

426. BLUMENTHAL, Michael
"The Artichokes of Midnight." SouthernPR (23:2) Aut 83, p. 65-66.
"Blue." ThRiPo (19/20) 82, p. 32.
"Blue." ThRiPo (21/22) 83, p. 12.
"Cheers." Poetry (142:3) Je 83, p. 149-150.
"Fish Fucking." MissouriR (6:2) Wint 83, p. 72-74.
"Going Deep." KanQ (15:1) Wint 83, p. 50-51.
"Juliek's Violin." ThRiPo (19/20) 82, p. 30-31.
"October Sestina: The Shadows." KanQ (15:1) Wint 83, p. 49.
"The Old Orchard." KanQ (15:1) Wint 83, p. 50.
"Poem by Someone Else." PoetL (77:4) Wint 83, p. 222-223.
"Stones in Love." Kayak (62) Ag 83, p. 63.
"This Is It" (for John McNally). PoetL (77:4) Wint 83, p. 223-224.
"Watching La Boheme with My Father, 1981." PoetL (77:4) Wint 83, p. 221.
"Waving Good-bye to My Father" (Fleischmanns, N.Y., 31 August 1981). AmerS (52:1) Wint 82/83, p. 80.

427. BLY, Robert
"Across the Swamp" (tr. of Olav H. Hauge). PoetryE (11) Sum 83, p. 70.
"Berthold Brecht" (tr. of Olav H. Hauge). PoetryE (11) Sum 83, p. 67.
"Conversation with a Woman Not Seen for Many Years." PoetryE (11) Sum 83, p. 79.
"Dance of Death" (tr. of Federico Garcia Lorca). NewL (49:3/4) Spr-Sum 83, p. 88-91.
"December Moon in 1969" (tr. of Olav H. Hauge). PoetryE (11) Sum 83, p. 72.
"The deep parts of my life pour onward" (tr. of Rainer Maria Rilke). NewRep (186:9) 3 Mr 82, p. 27.
"Deep Winter, Snow" (tr. of Olav H. Hauge). PoetryE (11) Sum 83, p. 74.
"Don't Come to Me with the Entire Truth" (tr. of Olav H. Hauge). PoetryE (11) Sum 83, p. 66.
"Eating Poetry" (tr. of Rumi). PoetryE (11) Sum 83, p. 5.
"The Farallones Islands." OhioR (30) 83, p. 123.

"Ghazal of the Terrifying Presence" (tr. of Federico Garcia Lorca). NewL (49:3/4) Spr-Sum 83, p. 88-91.
"The Hawk" (tr. of Rumi). PoetryE (11) Sum 83, p. 7.
"I Stand Here, Yunnerstand" (tr. of Olav H. Hauge). PoetryE (11) Sum 83, p. 69.
"In the Month of May." Atlantic (251:5) My 83, p. 43.
"The Indigo Bunting." NewYorker (59:28) 29 Ag 83, p. 34.
"Listening to a Fog Horn at Port Townsend." OhioR (30) 83, p. 122-123.
"Looking at an Old Mirror" (tr. of Olav H. Hauge). PoetryE (11) Sum 83, p. 71.
"Love Poem in Twos and Threes." NewRep (187:25) 27 D 82, p. 24.
"The Mill, the Stone, and the Water" (tr. of Rumi). PoetryE (11) Sum 83, p. 8.
"A Moth with Black Eyes." OhioR (30) 83, p. 122.
"Playhouses of Leaves and Snow" (tr. of Olav H. Hauge). PoetryE (11) Sum 83, p. 68.
"That Journeys Are Good" (tr. of Rumi). PoetryE (11) Sum 83, p. 6.
"To praise is the whole thing" (tr. of Rainer Maria Rilke). NewRep (186:9) 3 Mr 82, p. 29.
"Today I Understood" (tr. of Olav H. Hauge). PoetryE (11) Sum 83, p. 75.
"Wind and Weather" (tr. of Olav H. Hauge). PoetryE (11) Sum 83, p. 73.
"You Are the Wind" (tr. of Olav H. Hauge). PoetryE (11) Sum 83, p. 76.

428. BOA, Snow
"The Little Maid." EngJ (72:3) Mr 83, p. 76.

429. BOBROWSKI, Johannes
"Always to Be Named" (tr. by Paul Morris). CutB (21) Aut-Wint 83, p. 75.
"Immer Zu Benennen." CutB (21) Aut-Wint 83, p. 74.

430. BOBYSHEV, Dmitri
"Cityscapes" (tr. by Olga Bobyshev and Elizabeth Williams). ClockR (1:2) Wint 83-84, p. 16-17.

431. BOBYSHEV, Olga
"Cityscapes" (tr. of Dmitri Bobyshev, w. Elizabeth Williams). ClockR (1:2) Wint 83-84, p. 16-17.

432. BOCCIA, Edward E.
"Foreword for an Old Artist with a Young Beard." WebR (8:2) Aut 83, p. 62.

433. BOE, Deborah
"A Dream of Running." USl (16/17) Wint 83-84, p. 8.
"Giving Warning." USl (16/17) Wint 83-84, p. 8.
"The Reason I Stay." USl (16/17) Wint 83-84, p. 8.
"Snow." LittleM (14:1/2) 83, p. 62.
"Some Permanent Ground." USl (16/17) Wint 83-84, p. 8.
"When I Think of Leaving." USl (16/17) Wint 83-84, p. 8.

434. BOES, Don
"The Room We Sit In." IndR (5:1) Wint 82, p. 9.

435. BOGAN, Don
"After the Splendid Display." MissouriR (6:2) Wint 83, p. 65-67.

436. BOGEN, Laurel Ann
"27 Years of Madness." SecC (11:1/2) 83, p. 10-12.

437. BOGIN, George
"Abraham." PoetryE (11) Sum 83, p. 17.
"Still Life." PoetryE (11) Sum 83, p. 15-16.

438. BOHM, Robert
"Too Often." MinnR (NS 21) Aut 83, p. 33.
"Writing about It As Clearly As Possible." MinnR (NS 21) Aut 83, p. 33.

439. BOLAND, Eavan
"The Hanging Judge." PoetryE (9/10) Wint 82-Spr 83, p. 214-215.

440. BOLEY, D. J.
"She Said." SanFPJ (5:2) 83, p. 61.

441. BOLLS, Imogene L.
"At Tres Piedras." SoDakR (21:2) Sum 83, p. 56.
"Glass Walker." IndR (6:1) Wint 83, p. 22.
"On a Two Gray Hills Rug." SoDakR (21:2) Sum 83, p. 57.

442. BOLTON, Joe
"In Spring." SouthernPR (23:2) Aut 82 [i.e. (23:1?) Spr 83], p. 42-44.
"Once in Autumn." Wind (13:49) 83, p. 20.

443. BOMBA, Bernard O.
"Waiting for Our Child." YetASM (2:1) 83, p. 5.

BOMBARD, Joan la
See: LaBOMBARD, Joan

444. BOND, Alec
"Rending Cars." PoetL (77:2) Sum 82, p. 98-99.

445. BOND, Anita
"He Wants Hard Poetry." KanQ (15:4) Aut 83, p. 105.

446. BONENFANT, Joseph
"En Polonais" (pour Mad Lucienne Rey, tr. of Jerzy Ficowski). Os (17) 83, p. 12-13.
"O Vision de Neige" (pour Bieta, tr. of Jerzy Ficowski). Os (17) 83, p. 18-19.
"Poème Inédit: L'attention comme un forêt qui brûle" (pour Danielle, Réjean, Céline, Alain, Ginette, Mario, et bien d'autres). Os (17) 83, p. 28.
"Recette" (tr. of Jerzy Ficowski). Os (17) 83, p. 6.

BONN, David Jay
See: JAY-BONN, David

447. BONOMO, Jacqueline
"Catching Trains." USl (16/17) Wint 83-84, p. 13.

448. BOOKER, Betty
"Nine Deer Poem." StoneC (10:3/4) Spr-Sum 83, p. 33.
"Saint John on Good Friday." ChrC (100:9) 23-30 Mr 83, p. 282.
"The Story of a Night Watcher Told in Virginia." ChrC (100:34) 16 N 83, p. 1036.

449. BOOKER, Stephen Todd
"Book of Gad." NewRena (16) Spr 83, p. 111.
"The Centrifugal Force of Orez." BlackALF (17:4) Wint 83, p. 171.
"Clarksville." Tendril (14/15) Wint 83, p. 28-29.

450. BOONE, Gene
"A Writer's Reason." WritersL Ag 83, p. 13.

451. BOOR, Jocelyn
"The House." WorldO (17:2) Wint 82-83, p. 30.

452. BOOSE, Maryetta Kelsick
"The Draining." SanFPJ (4:4) 83, p. 43.
"False Alarm." SanFPJ (4:4) 83, p. 17.
"Outraged." SanFPJ (5:2) 83, p. 80.
"Sacrificed." SanFPJ (5:4) 83, p. 49.
"With Paychecks in Their Pockets." SanFPJ (5:4) 83, p. 52.

453. BOOTH, Barbara
"Echo of Emptiness." ArizQ (39:3) Aut 83, p. 265.

454. BOOTH, Martin
"Instructions to Lord Carrington on the Construction of a Cenotaph." Bogg (51) 83, p. 45-46.

455. BOOTH, Philip
"After the Rebuilding." NewYorker (59:3) 7 Mr 83, p. 46.
"Burning the Tents." AmerPoR (12:2) Mr/Ap 83, p. 14.
"Evening." GeoR (37:3) Aut 83, p. 532.
"To Think." AmerS (52:1) Wint 82/83, p. 65-66.
"Where We Find Room." AmerPoR (12:2) Mr/Ap 83, p. 14.

456. BORGES, Jorge Luis
"1982" (tr. by Nicomedes Suarez-Arauz). AmerPoR (12:2) Mr/Ap 83, p. 48.
"The Cipher" (tr. by Anthony Kerrigan and Jeanne Cook). MalR (66) O 83, p. 147.
"El Otre [i.e. Otro] Tigre" (Excerpt: "Un tercer tigre buscaremos"). AntigR (52) Wint 83, p. 71.
"El Otre [i.e. Otro] Tigre" (Excerpt: "We'll hunt for a third tiger now, tr. by Norman Thomas di Giovanni). AntigR (52) Wint 83, p. 71.
"Seventeen Haiku" (tr. by Norman Thomas di Giovanni). NewRep (187:17) 1 N 82, p. 30.

457. BORSON, Roo
"After the Dark Flowers." Waves (11:2/3) Wint 83, p. 62.
"Fields" (for John Martin). Dandel (10:1) Spr-Sum 83, p. 23.
"Pearls." PoetryCR (4:4) Sum 83, p. 5.
"Rabbit." PoetryCR (5:2) Wint 83-84, p. 17.
"St. Francis." Waves (11:2/3) Wint 83, p. 63.
"Starfish." Dandel (10:1) Spr-Sum 83, p. 24-25.

458. BORTMAN, Bill
"Ricky Made Me Smile." WritersL O 83, p. 5.

459. BORUCH, Marianne
"Her Brown Checked Dress." Field (29) Aut 83, p. 58.
"Pushing the Stroller Under Fatalistic Elms" (for James Tate). LittleBR (4:2) Wint 83-84, p. 43.
"Static." AntR (41:4) Aut 83, p. 443.
"We Drove." Field (29) Aut 83, p. 59.

BOSCO, Rocco lo
See: Lo BOSCO, Rocco

BOSHA, Kawabata
See: KAWABATA, Bosha

460. BOSLEY, Keith
"From a Finnish Notebook." Argo (5:1) 83, p. 4-8.

461. BOSS, Laura
"Faithfuly Yours." Abraxas (27/28) 83, p. 37.

462. BOSTON, B. H.
"Postcard." BlackWR (8:2) Spr 82, p. 67.

463. BOSWORTH, Martha
"Wilderness Generation." ChrC (100:12) 20 Ap 83, p. 358.

464. BOTTOMS, David
"The Fox." AntR (41:2) Spr 83, p. 202.
"In a Jon Boat during a Florida Dawn." Swallow (1) Spr 83, p. 4.
"In a Pasture under a Cradled Moon." BlackWR (8:1) Aut 81, p. 22-23.
"Sign for My Father, Who Stressed the Bunt." Ploughs (9:2/3) 83, p. 99.
"Smoking in an Open Grave." NewL (49:3/4) Spr-Sum 83, p. 114.
"Sounding Harvey Creek." Swallow (1) Spr 83, p. 2-3.

465. BOUCHER, Alan
"Black Poem" (tr. of Thuridur Gudmundsdottir). Vis (13) 83, p. 4.
"White Light" (tr. of Steinn Steinarr, from the Icelandic poem cycle "Time and Water"). Vis (12) 83, p. 14.

466. BOUDREAU, Nicole
"Prologue au rêve Marin I." PoetryCR (4:3) Spr

83, p. 5.

467. BOUDREAUX, Laura L.
"J. V. B. - P. F. C." SanFPJ (4:3) 83, p. 52.

468. BOURAOUI, Hédi
"Rirécrire." Quarry (32:4) Aut 83, p. 8-9.
"Scribbling Laughter." Quarry (32:4) Aut 83, p. 10-11.

469. BOURBON, Nita
"Piano Player." Wind (13:49) 83, p. 11.

470. BOURNE, Daniel
"Cancer Buys a Two-Headed Calf." IndR (6:1) Wint 83, p. 59.
"Cancer Taken Hostage." IndR (6:1) Wint 83, p. 60.
"Introducing Cancer and His Concern for Higher Yields." IndR (6:1) Wint 83, p. 58.

471. BOURNE, Louis
"Alféizar en el pozo" (Un cuadro de Mercedes Gómez-Pablos). Prismal (11) Aut 83, p. 102.

472. BOURNE, Stephen R.
"Ground Zero." AntigR (55) Aut 83, p. 134.

473. BOUVARD, Marguerite Guzman
"Family Feast." WestB (12) 83, p. 5.
"The Farms on the Col des Annes." WestB (12) 83, p. 8.
"With the Sisters of the Sacred Heart, 1943." WestB (12) 83, p. 6-7.

474. BOWER, Roger
"God to the Admiral Wherein the Admiral Discovers over Lunch at the Club Where God Has Been Keeping Himself." YetASM (1:2) 82, p. 4.
"Growing." YetASM (2:1) 83, p. 2.

475. BOWERS, Neal
"Cryptography " GeoR (37:4) Wint 83, p. 833.
"Going Home." CharR (9:2) Aut 83, p. 61.
"The Golf Ball Diver." PoetryNW (24:2) Sum 83, p. 14-15.
"Rehearsal Dinner." AmerPoR (12:6) N/D 83, p. 38.
"The Washday Ascension." SouthernPR (23:2) Aut 82 [i.e. (23:1?) Spr 83], p. 5.
"Writer's Block." KanQ (15:1) Wint 83, p. 126.

476. BOWIE, Robert
"African Water Buffalo." PoetL (77:3) Aut 82, p. 156.
"Bat." PoetL (78:1) Spr 83, p. 17.
"Birds of Air." KanQ (15:2) Spr 83, p. 41.
"Canyon de Chelly." DevQ (18:3) Aut 83, p. 101.
"Great Horned Owl." PoetL (78:1) Spr 83, p. 19.
"Ifs." PoetL (78:1) Spr 83, p. 18.
"Reminders." PoetL (77:3) Aut 82, p. 156.
"Seeing Things." KanQ (15:2) Spr 83, p. 41.

477. BOWMAN, Melanie
"Gestalt" (tr. of Amelia Biagioni). Mund (14:1) 83, p. 67.
"Those Who Sing" (tr. of Maria Elena Walsh). DevQ (17:4) Wint 83, p. 22-23.
"Tiger" (tr. of Amelia Biagioni). Mund (14:1) 83, p. 67.

478. BOWMAN, P. C.
"The Projectionist." KanQ (15:3) Sum 83, p. 33.

BOWMAN, Susan Stanton
See: STANTON-BOWMAN, Susan

479. BOX, Thad
"Affirmative Action." SanFPJ (5:2) 83, p. 43.
"Conroe Creosoting Company." SanFPJ (5:3) 83, p. 64.

480. BOXER, Ray
"Worlds." ClockR (1:2) Wint 83-84, p. 15.

481. BOYCE, Robert C.
"A Helping Hand." Bogg (50) 83, p. 44.
"You Mean to Say." Bogg (50) 83, p. 37.

482. BOYD, Robert
"Might As Well." WebR (8:2) Aut 83, p. 68.

483. BOYD, Sue Abbott
"For Walt Whitman." LittleBR (4:2) Wint 83-84, p. 10.

484. BOYER, Jeff
"The Storm." KanQ (15:4) Aut 83, p. 33.

485. BOYLE, Kay
"A Poem for the Teesto Dinè of Arizona." MalR (65) Jl 83, p. 96-97.

486. BRACKENBURY, Alison
"Hill Mist." Stand (24:4) Aut 83, p. 47.

487. BRACKER, Jon
"After Being Shown Someone's." YetASM (1:2) 82, p. 5.

488. BRADBURY, Elspeth
"Pothole is not preferable.." CanLit (99) Wint 83, p. 34.
"Words to clasp the sometimes silver?" CanLit (99) Wint 83, p. 34.

489. BRADBURY, Ray
"Boys, Like Horses, Are Easily Spooked." ClockR (1:2) Wint 83-84, p. 7-8.
"Nuclear War." SanFPJ (4:4) 83, p. 3.

490. BRADLEY, Ardyth
"Repairman on the Eiffel Tower." Shen (34:2) 83, p. 66.

491. BRADLEY, George
"Black Hole." Shen (34:2) 83, p. 64.
"The Blue Giant." Shen (34:2) 83, p. 63.
"Caskets in the Fayoum." ParisR (25:90) Wint 83, p. 94-95.
"In Suspense" (at the Verrazano Narrows Bridge). ParisR (24:84) Sum 82, p. 179.
"The Life of the Stars." Shen (34:2) 83, p. 62.
"Red Giant." Shen (34:2) 83, p. 62.
"The Sound of the Sun." ParisR (24:84) Sum 82, p. 178.
"White Dwarf." Shen (34:2) 83, p. 63.

BRAKEMAN, Diane Seuss
See: SEUSS-BRAKEMAN, Diane

492. BRAMBACH, Rainer
"Dog Days" (tr. by Jim Barnes). MemphisSR (3:2) Spr 83, p. 30.

493. BRAND, Alice Glarden
"Daughters and Weekends." KanQ (15:1) Wint 83, p. 174-175.

494. BRAND, Helena S.
"Midnight Round-up." EngJ (72:1) Ja 83, p. 50.

495. BRANDI, John
"Fisherman's Song." ThirdW Spr 83, p. 35.
"A Hymn, in the Dionysian Bend." ThirdW Spr 83, p. 34.

496. BRANT, Beth
"Daddy's Story." 13thM (7:1/2) 83, p. 92-93.
"Mama's Story." 13thM (7:1/2) 83, p. 90-91.

497. BRAUER, Ann
"Virginia Woolf Walked to the River" (Excerpt). SoDakR (21:4) Wint 83, p. 60.

498. BREBNER, Diana
"The Brown Man." PoetryCR (5:2) Wint 83-84, p. 19.
"I Imagine Your Death." Grain (11:3) Ag 83, p. 18.
"The Sacred Heart." Quarry (32:3) Sum 83, p. 14.
"The Soft Heart." Quarry (32:3) Sum 83, p. 14.

499. BRECHT, Bertolt
"Changing the Wheel" (tr. by Karl Patten). WebR (8:1) Spr 83, p. 41.
"For Those Still Unborn" (tr. by James Doss). PoetryE (9/10) Wint 82-Spr 83, p. 196-198.
"General, Your Tank Is Some Strong Car" (tr. by James Doss). PoetryE (9/10) Wint 82-Spr 83, p. 195.

500. BRECHT, Stefan
"Things Falling." Confr (25/26) 83, p. 310-313.

501. BRECKENRIDGE, Jill
"Love Letter from Acapulco." KanQ (15:2) Spr 83,

p. 135.

502. BREEN, Nancy
"April 16." PikeF (5) Spr 83, p. 18.

503. BREHM, John
"Calling My Grandmother from New York." Poetry (142:2) My 83, p. 71.
"Sleep." PraS (57:3) Aut 83, p. 51.
"Supplication at the River" (for Mojgan). Poetry (142:2) My 83, p. 70.

504. BRENEMAN, Bret
"In Memory of Paul Haney, Hand of the Cause of God." WorldO (17:4) Sum 83, p. 29.
"On Time." WorldO (17:3) Spr 83, p. 23.

505. BRENNAN, Matthew
"Climax." CapeR (18:2) Sum 83, p. 24.
"The Skaters." CapeR (19:1) Wint 83, p. 1.
"Souvenir of Saint Louis." PoetL (77:2) Sum 82, p. 97.
"Waiting at a Truck Stop in Iowa at Midnight." CapeR (18:2) Sum 83, p. 25.

506. BRESLIN, Paul
"Homage to Webern." AmerS (52:2) Spr 83, p. 242.

507. BRETON, André
"The Masks & the Colored Heat" (with Philippe Soupsault, tr. by David Gascoyne). Kayak (61) Ap 83, p. 49.

508. BRETT, Brian
"Poem Beginning and Ending with a Line by Jaccottet." PoetryCR (4:3) Spr 83, p. 14.

509. BREWTON, Catherine
"Coming upon the Rainbow's End." Poem (48) Jl 83, p. 43.
"Hunting Season." PortR (29:1) 83, p. 70-71.
"Totem." Poem (48) Jl 83, p. 44.

BREYNER ANDRESEN, Sophia de Mello
See: ANDRESEN, Sophia de Mello Breyner

510. BRICUTH, John
"People Who Vanish." SouthwR (68:3) Sum 83, p. 260-265.

511. BRIDGES, Pat
"Factory Girls." YetASM (1:2) 82, p. 10.
"For David." YetASM (1:2) 82, p. 19.

512. BRIGGS, H. E., Jr.
"Tablestakes." SanFPJ (5:3) 83, p. 21.

513. BRIGGS, John
"Complaint of the Invader" (for my father). YetASM (1:1) 82, p. 3.

514. BRILLIANT, Alan
"Oil" (For Rev. Xavier Harris, o.f.m.). SouthernPR (23:2) Aut 83, p. 48-50.

515. BRINDEL, June R.
"Ballast." YetASM (1:1) 82, p. 15.
"Earth Day." Vis (11) 83, p. 36.
"Five Devils." SpoonRQ (8:4) Aut 83, p. 45.

516. BRINES, Francisco
"Another Thirst" (tr. by Anthony Barnstone). DevQ (18:1) Spr 83, p. 95.
"This Kingdom, the Earth" (tr. by Anthony Barnstone). DevQ (18:1) Spr 83, p. 94.

517. BRINKMANN, Rolf Dieter
"Red Tomatoes" (tr. by Hartmut Schnell). NewL (49:3/4) Spr-Sum 83, p. 140.

518. BRISBY, Stewart
"For Clarence Francis Brisby." SoDakR (21:3) Aut 83, p. 98-99.
"Yuletide on 9th St." SoDakR (21:3) Aut 83, p. 100-101.

519. BRISSEY, Paul
"Geri-Antics." RagMag (2:2) Aut 83, p. 6.

520. BRISTOL, David
"Sleep." PoetL (78:1) Spr 83, p. 13.

521. BRITTON, Donald
"Winter Garden" (for Robertr Dash). Epoch (33:1) Aut-Wint 83, p. 42-43.

522. BROCK, James (Jim)
"Animals That Leave Idaho." Swallow (1) Spr 83, p. 47.
"Swimming Idaho." IndR (5:3) Aut 82, p. 8-9.

523. BROCK, Randall
"Hard measure." SmPd (20:3) Aut 83, p. 27.
"Hard promise." SmPd (20:3) Aut 83, p. 27.

524. BROCK, Van K.
"Epistle for the Cicadas." Ploughs (9:2/3) 83, p. 141-142.
"For The Nazi Drawings of Mauricio Lasansky." Swallow (2) Aut-Wint 83, p. 113.

525. BROCK-BROIDO, Lucie
"Hitchcock Blue." Epoch (33:1) Aut-Wint 83, p. 44-45.

526. BROCKLEY, Michael
"The Sermon." IndR (5:1) Wint 82, p. 32.

527. BROCKWELL, Stephen
"After Visiting Hours." Quarry (32:3) Sum 83, p. 57.

528. BRODERICK, Richard
"Voices from a Folsom Kill-Site, Buffalo Creek, Colorado." ClockR (2:1) 83, p. 4.

529. BRODKEY, Harold
"Jewlove." ParisR (24:85) Aut 82, p. 27-32.

530. BRODSKY, Joseph
"Dutch Mistress." NewYRB (29:21/22) 20 Ja 83, p. 39.
"A Martial Law Carol" (For Wictor Woroszylski and Andrzei Drawicz). NewYRB (30:4) 17 Mr 83, p. 24.
"Near Alexandria" (For Carl Proffer, tr. by the author). NewYRB (30:20) 22 D 83, p. 37.
"Two Poems from 1916: I, II" (To Osip Mandelstam, tr of Marina Tsvetayeva). NewYorker (59:35) 17 O 83, p. 48.

531. BRODSKY, Louis Daniel
"A Day in the Life of Willy Sypher." SouthernR (19:2) Ap 83, p. 366-367.
"In Quest of Destinations." FourQt (32:4) Sum 83, p. 14-15.
"Inundation." CapeR (19:1) Wint 83, p. 29.
"Résumé of a Scrapegoat." SouthernR (19:2) Ap 83, p. 367-369.

532. BRODY, Harry
"Dimestore." WindO (43) Wint 83, p. 6.

533. BRODY, Polly
"The Amiable Separation." YetASM (2:1) 83, p. 8.

534. BROMLEY, Anne
"1 A.M. Memorial Day." Kayak (62) Ag 83, p. 41.

535. BRONDUM, Jack
"And the Wind Seen As Waves" (tr. of Knud Holten). SoDakR (21:1) Spr 83, p. 40.
"Crystal Day" (tr. of Klaus Lynggaard). SoDakR (21:1) Spr 83, p. 42.
"Enshrined" (tr. of Lola Baidel). SoDakR (21:1) Spr 83, p. 38.
"The Flowerbox" (tr. of Lola Baidel). SoDakR (21:1) Spr 83, p. 34.
"La Glace -- The Cure" (tr. of Lola Baidel). SoDakR (21:1) Spr 83, p. 34.
"Here come the hours" (tr. of Klaus Lynggaard). SoDakR (21:1) Spr 83, p. 42.
"Hunters--Identity" (tr. of Klaus Lynggaard). SoDakR (21:1) Spr 83, p. 44.
"Ocean View" (tr. of Knud Holten). SoDakR (21:1) Spr 83, p. 40.
"The Patience of an Angel" (tr. of Lola Baidel). SoDakR (21:1) Spr 83, p. 36.
"Sunshine in a dented windowsill" (tr. of Klaus Lynggaard). SoDakR (21:1) Spr 83, p. 46.

536. BROOK, Donna
"Final Days" (for Linda Kaufman). HangL (44) Sum 83, p. 3-4.

"March 4, 1983." HangL (44) Sum 83, p. 6.
"Ordinary New York." Tele (18) 83, p. 28.
"The Poem That I Read at Your Funeral." HangL (44) Sum 83, p. 5.
"Vanquishing Our Enemies" (for Larry Zirlin). Tele (18) 83, p. 29.

537. BROOKS, Barbara Coles
"Guarding Fears." AntigR (52) Wint 83, p. 66.

538. BROOKS, David
"Civics 101." WestB (12) 83, p. 90.

539. BROOKS, Douglas L.
"Data." PoetL (77:3) Aut 82, p. 163-164.

540. BROOKS, Gwendolyn
"Telephone Conversations" (After Discussing William Faulkner with George Kent). BlackALF (17:4) Wint 83, p. 148.

541. BROOKS, Jack
"A Leaf a Flower a Blade of Grass." WritersL Ag 83, p. 10.

542. BROOKS, James
"Sidari Village." DekalbLAJ (16:1/4) Aut 82-Sum 83, p. 56.
"Where Is Frank Polite?" (to Edward Field). DekalbLAJ (16:1/4) Aut 82-Sum 83, p. 57-58.

543. BROSMAN, Catharine Savage
"Augusta County: Perspectives in Snow." SouthernR (19:4) O 83, p. 847-848.
"Birds in the Morning." SouthernR (19:4) O 83, p. 849-850.
"Grass." SouthernR (19:4) O 83, p. 850-851.
"Lines from a Night Train." SouthernR (19:4) O 83, p. 848-849.
"Notes Toward a Journal." SouthernR (19:4) O 83, p. 842-846.

544. BROUGHTON, James
"Afternoon in Ceylon." NewL (50:1) Aut 83, p. 63.
"When You Tickle My Cravings." NewL (50:1) Aut 83, p. 64.

545. BROUGHTON, T. Alan
"Guardian of the Dump." ThRiPo (21/22) 83, p. 13-14.
"A Slant of Light." PoNow (7:2, #38) 83, p. 16.

546. BROUMAS, Olga
"No Harm Shall Come." PoetryE (9/10) Wint 82-Spr 83, p. 144-145.

547. BROWN, Allan
"The Burden of Jonah ben Amittai." Quarry (32:4) Aut 83, p. 36-37.

548. BROWN, Barry S.
"In the TTC." PoetryCR (5:1) Aut 83, p. 18.

549. BROWN, Bill
"When Chris Forgot His Pencil and Paper." EngJ (72:8) D 83, p. 21.

550. BROWN, Gregg
"Walk with the One." WorldO (17:2) Wint 82-83, p. 16.

551. BROWN, Harriet
"In Our First World." Telescope (5/6) Spr 83, p. 96.
"In Our Island World." Telescope (5/6) Spr 83, p. 98.
"In Our Perfect World, I." Telescope (5/6) Spr 83, p. 99.
"In Our Perfect World, II." Telescope (5/6) Spr 83, p. 100.
"In Our White World." Telescope (5/6) Spr 83, p. 97.
"Poem for Sigmund Freud." Telescope (5/6) Spr 83, p. 93.

552. BROWN, Melanie Beth
"If We Had Foreseen All This." CapeR (19:1) Wint 83, p. 50.

BROWN, Nicole Marchewka
See: MARCHEWKA-BROWN, Nicole

553. BROWN, Simon
"Awake." Bogg (50) 83, p. 36.
"Interrogation." Bogg (50) 83, p. 52.

554. BROWN, Steven Ford
"Conversation 1" (for Sam). Wind (13:47) 83, p. 3-4.
"Morning." Wind (13:47) 83, p. 3.

555. BROWNE, Michael Dennis
"Five Hundred and Eight Buddhas" (for Jim White). PraS (57:3) Aut 83, p. 41-43.

556. BROZOVSKY, Orise
"Across the Threshold." SanFPJ (5:3) 83, p. 32.
"Progression of Pronouns: The 60's to the 80's." SanFPJ (5:3) 83, p. 29-30.

557. BRUCE, Debra
"For the Boy Reading Playboy." MassR (24:4) Wint 83, p. 766.
"Granny Dunn Says Go Back" (For my 85-year-old-neighbor who told me, Don't get old. When you get to a certain point just turn around and go back). PoetryNW (24:4) Wint 83-84, p. 37-38.
"The Other Woman." MinnR (NS 20) Spr 83, p. 57.
"Witches' Winter." Calyx (7:3) Sum 83, p. 19-21.

558. BRUCHAC, Joseph
"Baptisms." CharR (9:1) Spr 83, p. 10.
"The Buffalo Skull." SecC (11:1/2) 83, p. 13.
"Card Players and the Stars above Paradox Lake." Blueline (4:1) Sum-Aut 82, p. 17.

"Circles." WestCR (18:2) O 83, p. 48.
"The Dream of the Guachero Bird" (Alexander Von Humboldt in Venezuela, 1799). Descant (43) Wint 83-84, p. 67-68.
"Fishing" (from Drum Songs, finalist, 10th anniversary manuscript competition). StoneC (11:1/2, Pt. 1) Aut-Wint 83, p. 47.
"In the Last Days." Hudson (36:4) Wint 83-84, p. 636.
"An Inuit Story." WestCR (18:2) O 83, p. 49.
"Lacrosse" (Mohawk Indian theme). Kayak (62) Ag 83, p. 37.
"The Lake of the Wounded." ThirdW Spr 83, p. 76-77.
"Late April Sweat." ThirdW Spr 83, p. 75.
"Long Memory." PoetryE (9/10) Wint 82-Spr 83, p. 147.
"On the Nkwatia Scarp" (from Drum Songs, finalist, 10th anniversary manuscript competition). StoneC (11:1/2, Pt. 1) Aut-Wint 83, p. 46.
"One Hot Summer Night, 1947." OhioR (30) 83, p. 83.
"Peeling Maple Poles." Descant (43) Wint 83-84, p. 65-66.
"Redwoods above Jacoby Creek." WestCR (18:2) O 83, p. 47.
"The Runner" (Mohawk Indian theme). Kayak (62) Ag 83, p. 36.
"To Visit an Island." WestCR (18:2) O 83, p. 50.
"Two Nights before the First Day of Spring." MemphisSR (2:2) Spr 82, p. 4.
"Wabikokokhasu." Descant (43) Wint 83-84, p. 69.

559. BRUEY, Alfred J.
"Dreams / At the Concert." YetASM (2:1) 83, p. 4.

560. BRUMMELS, J. V.
"At the Airport." MidwQ (24:4) Sum 83, p. 441.
"A Couple, in Town for a Saturday Night, Talk around Chickenfried Steak." KanQ (15:4) Aut 83, p. 81.
"The Francis Furter Memorial VFW Post, Cafe and Bowling Lanes" (For Bill Kloefkorn). KanQ (15:4) Aut 83, p. 84.
"The Hired Hand." MidwQ (24:4) Sum 83, p. 442-443.
"Karl." KanQ (15:4) Aut 83, p. 82-83.
"Lightfoot's Nightmare." KanQ (15:2) Spr 83, p. 40.
"Like Trees on Skis." SouthwR (68:2) Spr 83, p. 124-125.
"New Day, Central Daylight Time." MidwQ (24:4) Sum 83, p. 444-445.
"Thirty Below, Canton, Nebraska." PraS (57:4) Wint 83, p. 55.
"What's on the Young Farmer's Mind." KanQ (15:4) Aut 83, p. 85.
"Winter Solstice." PraS (57:4) Wint 83, p. 54-55.

BRUNET, Vilma Bayron
See: BAYRON BRUNET, Vilma

BRUNT, H. L. van
See: Van BRUNT, H. L.

561. BRUSH, Thomas
"Exhibition Park." PoetryNW (24:2) Sum 83, p. 41-42.

"Garage Sale." PoetryNW (24:2) Sum 83, p. 40-41.
"Love Song." PoNow (7:2, #38) 83, p. 17.
"On Finding a Dead Swallow." PoetryNW (24:2) Sum 83, p. 41.
"Reply to a Critic." PoNow (7:2, #38) 83, p. 17.
"The Shrew." OW (17) Aut-Wint 83-84, p. 22.

562. BRUTUS, Dennis
"Somehow We Survive." PoetryE (9/10) Wint 82-Spr 83, p. 278.

563. BRYAN, Sharon
"Adopted Daughter." Tendril (14/15) Wint 83, p. 30.
"Das Boot." PoetryE (12) Aut 83, p. 12-14.
"Viewing the Body." Atlantic (251:3) Mr 83, p. 54.

564. BRYNE, Vincent
"Flight." KanQ (15:2) Spr 83, p. 154.

565. BRYSMAN, Anita
"A Minute with the Man in the Moon." KanQ (15:2) Spr 83, p. 147.

566. BUCHANAN, Carl
"Last Landscape" (from The Van Gogh Poems). KanQ (15:2) Spr 83, p. 53.
"Some Arthur Poems: Gwen, Merlyn's End, Lance and Gwen (Arthur Speaks)." KanQ (15:1) Wint 83, p. 186-187.

567. BUCKAWAY, Catharine
"A very light rain." Quarry (32:3) Sum 83, p. 70.

568. BUCKHOLTS, Claudia
"Winter Morning." IndR (5:1) Wint 82, p. 4.

569. BUCKLEY, Christopher
"Insomnia." BlackWR (9:1) Aut 82, p. 38-39.
"Lost and Found" (for Kathy). OW (16) Spr-Sum 83, p. 122-123.
"Prayer." BlackWR (9:1) Aut 82, p. 40.
"Quotidiana" (for Charles Wright). AntR (41:3) Sum 83, p. 437.
"To Orsua, Years Late" (Fall '78). Telescope (5/6) Spr 83, p. 123-125.

570. BUCKNELL, Steve
"The New Wasteland." Bogg (51) 83, p. 50.
"The Tongues of the Skin." Bogg (51) 83, p. 37.

571. BUELL, Frederick
"Eros." Poetry (141:6) Mr 83, p. 325-326.
"Pattern." NewEngR (6:1) Aut 83, p. 150-152.

572. BUELL, Thomas
"The Woods Are Filling." PortR (29:1) 83, p. 72-73.

573. BUETTNER, Shirley
"Chautauqua Park" (Seaton Fourth Award Poem (2) 1983). KanQ (15:3) Sum 83, p. 12.

"Mushrooming." KanQ (15:2) Spr 83, p. 54-55.
"The Pulse." KanQ (15:2) Spr 83, p. 54.
"Village Softball League." KanQ (15:3) Sum 83, p. 11.

574. BUFIS, Paul
"A Second Story Window." Wind (13:48) 83, p. 8-9.

575. BUGEJA, Michael J.
"The Cow Is Coming: Peace Regalia." ConcPo (16:1) Spr 83, p. 57.
"The Face in Her Eyes." Wind (13:49) 83, p. 12-13.
"For Generations a Question Asked of Males." ConcPo (16:1) Spr 83, p. 58.
"Ode: Drunk on an Old Showboat Passing Charolais." SoDakR (21:3) Aut 83, p. 89.
"Snowhead, after the Accident." QW (16) Spr-Sum 83, p. 120.
"Strung with Others" (Sweden 1970). SmPd (20:1) Wint 83, p. 9-10.

576. BUKOWSKI, Charles
"About the Love Poems of the Cat." OroM (2:1, #5) Sum 83, p. 2-3.
"The Big Benefit Reading." WormR (23:4, issue 92) 83, p. 156-158.
"Crime and Punishment." OhioR (30) 83, p. 183.
"The Crunch." SecC (11:1/2) 83, p. 17-19.
"Don't Come Around But If You do." SecC (11:1/2) 83, p. 15-16.
"Gothic and Etc." PoNow (7:2, #38) 83, p. 6.
"The Green Cadillac." Abraxas (27/28) 83, p. 26.
"How to Be A Great Writer." SecC (11:1/2) 83, p. 20-22.
"Quits." WormR (23:4, issue 92) 83, p. 155-156.
"Retreat." WormR (23:1, issue 89) 83, p. 36-37.
"Sick." WormR (23:4, issue 92) 83, p. 158.
"Sloppy Day." Abraxas (27/28) 83, p. 27-31.
"A Smile to Remember." OroM (2:1, #5) Sum 83, p. 1.
"Space Creatures." WormR (23:2, issue 90) 83, p. 75-78.
"Too Late." PoNow (7:2, #38) 83, p. 6.

577. BULLIS, Jerald
"Barren Ground." Poetry (141:4) Ja 83, p. 197.
"Call to Worship." Poetry (141:4) Ja 83, p. 198-199.
"Of Ellipses and Deviations." Poetry (141:4) Ja 83, p. 200.
"Old House Journal." IndR (6:2) Spr 83, p. 43.
"Pure Poetry." Poetry (141:4) Ja 83, p. 196-197.

578. BULLOCK, Chris
"Edmonton, November 17, 1982." Bluebuf (2:1) Aut 83, p. 35.

579. BULMAN, Aaron
"Last Diaspora" (Selection: "Against the Cold"). PartR (50:1) 83, p. 82-84.

580. BURBANK, Carol
"Dead Trees: Penelope Goes to Odysseus." StoneC

(10:3/4) Spr-Sum 83, p. 65.

581. BURCHARD, Rachael C.
"Universal Message." YetASM (2:1) 83, p. 12.

582. BURD, Cindy
"We Go On." USl (16/17) Wint 83-84, p. 2.

583. BURGESS, Ed
"Twilight of the Dinosaurs." SanFPJ (5:1) 83, p. 19.

584. BURGOS, Julia de
"A Julia de Burgos." Swallow (2) Aut-Wint 83, p. 6, 8.
"To Julia de Burgos" (tr. by Maria Bennett). Swallow (2) Aut-Wint 83, p. 7, 9.

585. BURKARD, Michael
"Amnesia." LittleM (14:1/2) 83, p. 63.
"Beyond the Shadow across the Bridge." Telescope (5/6) Spr 83, p. 54.
"Directly in Shadow." Telescope (5/6) Spr 83, p. 52-53.
"Eating on a Starlit Porch." AmerPoR (12:2) Mr/Ap 83, p. 24.
"Far Sight." Telescope (5/6) Spr 83, p. 55-56.
"A Feeling from the Sea." AmerPoR (12:2) Mr/Ap 83, p. 24.
"The Ferry Boat." AmerPoR (12:2) Mr/Ap 83, p. 26.
"First Love." AmerPoR (12:2) Mr/Ap 83, p. 25.
"A Florer's Timepiece." AmerPoR (12:2) Mr/Ap 83, p. 27.
"Foolish Thing." AmerPoR (12:2) Mr/Ap 83, p. 26.
"For Him." AmerPoR (12:2) Mr/Ap 83, p. 24.
"The Hour Hand." Telescope (5/6) Spr 83, p. 59-60.
"I Entered a House." BlackWR (10:1) Aut 83, p. 68.
"In the Rain, in the Odd City." LittleM (14:1/2) 83, p. 66-67.
"Like a Receipt." AmerPoR (12:2) Mr/Ap 83, p. 27.
"A Mountain of Glass." AmerPoR (12:2) Mr/Ap 83, p. 27.
"My Sister is Not a Dollar." LittleM (14:1/2) 83, p. 68.
"North and South." Telescope (5/6) Spr 83, p. 57-58.
"Out There." AmerPoR (12:2) Mr/Ap 83, p. 26.
"The Personal Histories ('More Darkness')." AmerPoR (12:2) Mr/Ap 83, p. 24.
"Picture with No Past to It." AmerPoR (12:2) Mr/Ap 83, p. 26.
"A Small Closed Room." AmerPoR (12:2) Mr/Ap 83, p. 27.
"Stoney Lonesome." LittleM (14:1/2) 83, p. 64-65.
"The Story of Marie." AmerPoR (12:2) Mr/Ap 83, p. 25.
"Strangely Insane." BlackWR (10:1) Aut 83, p. 66-67.
"A Study in Scarlet." Telescope (5/6) Spr 83, p. 50-51.
"Time When the Day Ended." AmerPoR (12:2) Mr/Ap 83, p. 23.
"When the Sun Rises." AmerPoR (12:2) Mr/Ap 83, p. 24.

586. BURKE, Herbert
"Yesterday As I Entered." Germ (7:2) Aut-Wint 83, p. 19.

587. BURKE, Lenny
"Mistaken Identity" (Based on a newspaper article). Bogg (50) 83, p. 12.

588. BURLINGAME, Robert
"Invitation." SouthwR (68:1) Wint 83, p. 64.

589. BURNHAM, Deborah
"The Fishery: Cleaning." KanQ (15:2) Spr 83, p. 199.
"Great Bear, Little Bear." ConcPo (16:1) Spr 83, p. 83.
"Praising Their Names: the Market, Lewisburg, Pennsylvania." WestB (12) 83, p. 9.

590. BURNS, Michael
"At a Window." MidwQ (24:2) Wint 83, p. 170.
"Moving from Clear Creek." MidwQ (24:2) Wint 83, p. 169.
"Pelicans over the Missouri." LittleBR (4:1) Aut 83, p. 76.
"Renovation." NewOR (10:2/3) Sum-Aut 83, p. 136.
"State Fishkill on Shirey Bay, 1963." MidwQ (24:2) Wint 83, p. 171.
"Weather Watch." LittleBR (4:1) Aut 83, p. 76.

591. BURNS, Ralph
"Chair." IndR (6:2) Spr 83, p. 71.
"Like a Voice behind a Voice." Field (29) Aut 83, p. 60.
"Owl." CalQ (22) Sum 83, p. 78.
"Responses to a Class Questionnaire: What Is Your Career Goal." IndR (6:2) Spr 83, p. 70.
"Rid of Hogs." Poetry (141:4) Ja 83, p. 209.
"The Subnormal Girl with a Cat." IndR (5:3) Aut 82, p. 21.
"Tall Tale." ColEng (45:5) S 83, p. 492-493.
"Twins." Kayak (61) Ap 83, p. 43.
"Yes No Days." Poetry (141:4) Ja 83, p. 208.

592. BURNS, Thomas LaBorie
"Our Time" (tr. of Carlos Drummond de Andrade). WebR (8:1) Spr 83, p. 26-31.

593. BURRIS, Sidney
"Shoreline." MissouriR (6:2) Wint 83, p. 75-76.

594. BURROWS, Roland
"Craneflies." Argo (4:3) 83, p. 7.

595. BURRS, Mick
"Sanctuary." CanLit (96) Spr 83, p. 48.
"Shelf Life." CanLit (96) Spr 83, p. 101-102.

596. BURSK, Christopher
"658.386 B972." Sparrow (44) 83, p. 30.
"After Being by Myself All Day." Poetry (143:1) O

83, p. 32.
"After Waking from My Nap." Sparrow (44) 83, p. 5.
"Alien." Images (8:3) 83, p. 3.
"Antique Tree-Ornaments." Sparrow (44) 83, p. 8.
"Bedridden." Sparrow (44) 83, p. 24.
"Chores." Sparrow (44) 83, p. 14.
"The Death of a Small Beast." Sparrow (44) 83, p. 26.
"First Aid at 4 a.m." Sparrow (44) 83, p. 17.
"First Job." Sparrow (44) 83, p. 9.
"Hairs of My Body." ManhatR (3:1) Sum 83, p. 53.
"Ill at Fifteen." Sparrow (44) 83, p. 13.
"Late Afternoon Shadows." Poetry (143:1) O 83, p. 31.
"Letter to a Missing Brother." Images (8:3) 83, p. 3.
"Lies." Sparrow (44) 83, p. 18-19.
"Lord I believe. Help Me in My Unbelief." Sparrow (44) 83, p. 20.
"The Morning's Mail." Sparrow (44) 83, p. 6.
"Neither Fish Nor Fowle." Sparrow (44) 83, p. 25.
"An Ordinary Man." Sparrow (44) 83, p. 16.
"Parts of the Body." Sparrow (44) 83, p. 15.
"The Patience of the Bears." Images (8:3) 83, p. 3.
"Payment." Sparrow (44) 83, p. 12.
"Phone Call." Sparrow (44) 83, p. 31.
"Place of Residence" (Dedicated with love and gratitude to John Howard Bursk, George Richards Churchill III, Robert Fraser, Herb Frederick, Edward Lodi). Sparrow (44) 83, p. 1-31.
"Public Servant." Sparrow (44) 83, p. 23.
"Restoring the Wood." Sparrow (44) 83, p. 29.
"The Resurrection." Sparrow (44) 83, p. 27.
"Roadside Flowers." Sparrow (44) 83, p. 22.
"Rock Collection." Sparrow (44) 83, p. 7.
"The Steam Tunnels under Harvard." ManhatR (3:1) Sum 83, p. 54-55.
"Tape Recorder" (for my wife). Sparrow (44) 83, p. 28.
"Waitingroom." Sparrow (44) 83, p. 10-11.
"War Games in the Bath." Sparrow (44) 83, p. 21.

597. BURSTOW, Candace Adamson
"Strange Fields of Summer." PoetryCR (4:4) Sum 83, p. 11.

598. BURT, Johnnie F.
"Silence Grows." DekalbLAJ (16:1/4) Aut 82-Sum 83, p. 85.

599. BURTON, Ian
"Andrei Roublev" (for Ricki Seal). Stand (24:3) 83, p. 16.

600. BUSCH, Linda Ruth
"Say Goodbye to the Wind." SanFPJ (5:1) 83, p. 41.

601. BUSCH, Trent
"The Break." SouthernHR (17:4) Aut 83, p. 342.
"Ceres without Proserpine." SouthernHR (17:4) Aut 83, p. 341.
"Woman Leaving Beech Valley." MemphisSR (4:1) Aut 83, p. 10.

602. BUSH, Barney
"Blood Count." StoneC (11:1/2, Pt. 1) Aut-Wint 83, p. 18.
"Cedar Smoke." NewL (50:1) Aut 83, p. 95.

603. BUSH, Duncan
"A Generation" (tr. of Cesare Pavese). Stand (24:1) 82-83, p. 38.
"The Paper Smokers" (tr. of Cesare Pavese). Stand (24:1) 82-83, p. 39.
"Poem: Living touches us strangely." Stand (24:4) Aut 83, p. 20.

604. BUSH, Kendal
"Distance" (Vietnam War, 1968-70). Wind (13:47) 83, p. 22.

605. BUSHELL, John R.
"Suffering Servant." ChrC (100:27) 28 S 83, p. 845.

606. BUSHKOWSKY, Aaron
"Cloud Poem." Bluebuf (2:1) Aut 83, p. 5.
"Green Poem." Dandel (10:2) Aut-Wint 83, p. 72.

607. BUSSY, Jacques
"Dixains de Solitude" (Excerpts) (à F-X J). Os (17) 83, p. 26-27.

608. BUTCHER, Grace
"The Poet, Slowly Understanding How It Is, Speaks." Pig (11) 83, p. 20.
"Tell Me No Answers, I'll Ask You No Truths." Pig (11) 83, p. 21.
"Two." HiramPoR (35) Aut-Wint 83, p. 9.

609. BUTLER, Jack
"The Gunmen." PoetryNW (24:4) Wint 83-84, p. 12.
"I Wish You Could Hear the Tune I made Up for This." PoetryNW (24:4) Wint 83-84, p. 11-12.
"The Monkeys" (dedicated to Fatz). PoetryNW (24:4) Wint 83-84, p. 9-11.
"One Reason for Stars." Poetry (142:5) Ag 83, p. 263.

610. BUTLER, Marylin
"Camping Out." VirQR (59:2) Spr 83, p. 241-242.
"My Father's Canary." VirQR (59:2) Spr 83, p. 243-244.

611. BUTTERFIELD, Stephen T.
"Morris Cave." BelPoJ (33:3) Spr 83, p. 10-13.
"Purgatory Pit." BelPoJ (33:3) Spr 83, p. 8-9.

612. BUTTERWORTH, Everl
"Last Call." Poem (49) N 83, p. 19.
"Rendezvous." Poem (49) N 83, p. 20.

613. BUTTRESS, Derrick
"The Hollywood Alternative." Bogg (51) 83, p. 36.

614. BYER, Kathryn Stripling
"Indigo" (for Linda). GeoR (37:4) Wint 83, p. 814.
"Snowbird." GeoR (37:4) Wint 83, p. 815.

615. BYLES, Joan Montgomery
"The Saddest of Nights." Wind (13:48) 83, p. 7.

616. BYRNE, Vera
"The Noon Bazaar." CrossC (5:2/3) 83, p. 17.

C., R.
See: R. C.

CABRAL de MELO NETO, João
See: NETO, João Cabral de Melo

617. CACERES, Wilfredo
"Cómo me jode este saber que no sé nada."
Rácata (1) 83, p. 29.
"Conciencia de Poeta." Rácata (1) 83, p. 28.
"Epitafio para un arribista." Rácata (1) 83, p. 30.
"Génesis." Rácata (1) 83, p. 31-33.

618. CADDELL, Marsha
"Distortion." WindO (42) Sum 83, p. 38.

619. CADER, Teresa
"The Christening." Tendril (14/15) Wint 83, p. 32.
"The Strand Theatre." Tendril (14/15) Wint 83, p. 31.

620. CADSBY, Heather
"Fern." Grain (11:1) F 83, p. 11.
"What They Never Tell You." Grain (11:1) F 83, p. 11.

621. CAHN, Cynthia
"Commercial Break, World War III." SanFPJ (4:3)
83, p. 28.
"Get It?" Bogg (50) 83, p. 19.
"Tygress." SouthernHR (17:2) Spr 83, p. 120.

622. CAIN, Michael Scott
"Autoeroticism." PoetL (77:3) Aut 82, p. 135.
"Mustache." PoetL (77:3) Aut 82, p. 134.
"Picasso's Studio." PoetL (77:3) Aut 82, p. 133.

623. CAIRE, John, III
"Something Remains." Thrpny (3:4, issue 12) Wint
83, p. 8.

624. CAIRNS, Scott
"Accepting Blood." KanQ (15:4) Aut 83, p. 22.
"During Illness." CarolQ (35:3) Spr 83, p. 8.
"Harbor Seals." KanQ (15:4) Aut 83, p. 23.
"Living with the Deaf." KanQ (15:4) Aut 83, p. 21.
"The Priest Confesses" (for Marcia Vanderlip).
Swallow (1) Spr 83, p. 61.
"Selecting a Reader" (after Ted Kooser). KanQ
(15:4) Aut 83, p. 19.
"Taking Off Our Clothes." KanQ (15:4) Aut 83, p. 20.
"Trapeze Artist." IndR (6:3) Sum 83, p. 60.

"The Whale." KanQ (15:4) Aut 83, p. 21.

CAJAPE, Freddy Gómez
See: GOMEZ CAJAPE, Freddy

625. CALDWELL, Joyce Anthony
"Given Time Women Who Suckle Babies Will Wean the World Away from War." WorldO (17:4) Sum 83, p. 29.

626. CALDWELL, S. F.
"Guatemala Brother Mother Story." SanFPJ (5:2) 83, p. 77.
"USSR 0, USA 0." SanFPJ (5:2) 83, p. 78.

627. CALHOUN, Harry
"For Free." YetASM (2:1) 83, p. 6.
"Rubber Love." Bogg (51) 83, p. 16.

628. CALISCH, Richard
"Summer Snow." EngJ (72:6) O 83, p. 75.

629. CALLAWAY, Kathy
"Della's Bus." PoetL (78:2) Sum 83, p. 119-120.
"Love in the Western World." PoetL (78:2) Sum 83, p. 120.

630. CALLIMACHUS
"Talk Onward" (tr. by David Weissmann). SouthernR (19:3) Jl 83, p. 658.

631. CALMAN, Nancy Harris
"The Dog and I Watch the Cat." PoetL (77:3) Aut 82, p. 169-170.
"The Dog Meets the Devil." PoetL (78:4) Wint 84, p. 200-201.
"The Dogs in the Yards." PoetL (78:4) Wint 84, p. 202.
"Hurricane Season" (to Jack and Judith). PoetL (78:4) Wint 84, p. 203-204.

632. CALTO, Daniel
"Man Brushing a Woman's Hair." WorldO (17:4) Sum 83, p. 30.

633. CALVERT, L. D. E.
"Forced Feeding." Bogg (50) 83, p. 55.

634. CAMARA, Isabel
"Ayer Me Miraste" (mayo, 1983). Inti (15) Spr 82, p. 67.
"Entre Escombros y Tardes" (de "Las Horas, febrero, '83). Inti (15) Spr 82, p. 67.
"Neonatal" (de "Espejo", 1982). Inti (15) Spr 82, p. 68-69.
"Nuestras Voces Se Confunden" (de "En la Ausencia del Eco, 1983). Inti (15) Spr 82, p. 68.

635. CAMERON, Bella
"New Cowboys." Bogg (50) 83, p. 56-57.

636. CAMILLO, Victor
"Commodore." BallSUF (24:1) Wint 83, p. 26.

637. CAMPBELL, Mary B. (See also CAMPBELL, Mary Belle)
"Money." Atlantic (252:3) S 83, p. 80.
"Sympathy." LittleM (14:1/2) 83, p. 29.

638. CAMPBELL, Mary Belle (See also CAMPBELL, Mary B.)
"Eight." PikeF (5) Spr 83, p. 38.
"A King of Eden." CapeR (19:1) Wint 83, p. 18.
"Vines." CapeR (19:1) Wint 83, p. 19.

639. CAMPION, Dan (See also CAMPION, Daniel)
"The Epiphany." Pig (11) 83, p. 25.

640. CAMPION, Daniel (See also CAMPION, Dan)
"The Miniaturist." Ascent (8:2) 83, p. 21-22.

641. CANADA, Stephen
"Ways and Means." PoNow (7:2, #38) 83, p. 33.

642. CANAN, Craig T.
"Western Ray Gun." SanFPJ (4:4) 83, p. 20.

643. CANAWAY, Ruth Braverman
"Haiku: The sun shines through the water." StoneC (10:3/4) Spr-Sum 83, p. 19.

644. CANDELARIA, Cordelia
"Fresh Mint Garden." RevChic (11:3/4) 83, p. 66.
"Sin Raíces Hay Flor?" RevChic (11:3/4) 83, p. 65.

645. CANIZARO, Vincent, Jr.
"Empty Classrooms." WebR (8:2) Aut 83, p. 76.
"Pale Candle." Bogg (50) 83, p. 11.
"Salmon Pearl." WebR (8:2) Aut 83, p. 76.

646. CANNON, Melissa
"The Naming." ThirdW Spr 83, p. 40.

647. CANTRELL, Charles
"Baraboo's First Feminist" (after Michael Lesy's Wisconsin Death Trip). SpoonRQ (8:4) Aut 83, p. 46-47.

648. CARAM, Dick
"Author (1939-   )." OP (35) Spr-Sum 83, p. 42.
"Praying at the Phone Company." OP (35) Spr-Sum 83, p. 40-41.
"Sleeper." OP (35) Spr-Sum 83, p. 38-39.

649. CARATHEODORY, A. M.
"The Bakery Thrift Store." SanFPJ (5:3) 83, p. 72.
"Nuclear Ambush." SanFPJ (5:3) 83, p. 81.

CARBEAU, Mitchell les
See: LesCARBEAU, Mitchell

650. CARDENAL, Ernesto
"The Filibusters" (tr. by Jonathan Cohen). AmerPoR

(12:3) My-Je 83, p. 18.
"Greytown" (tr. by Jonathan Cohen). AmerPoR (12:3) My-Je 83, p. 18.
"Johan Roach, Mariner" (tr. by Jonathan Cohen). AmerPoR (12:3) My-Je 83, p. 18.
"Squier in Nicaragua" (tr. by Jonathan Cohen). DevQ (18:3) Aut 83, p. 17-25.

651. CARDOZO, Nancy
"Swamp Maple" (for Matthew Josephson). Hudson (36:3) Aut 83, p. 512-513.

652. CARELS, Peter
"I Train." Argo (4:1) 82, p. 22.

653. CAREY, Michael A.
"Early American Small Print Wallpaper." PortR (29:1) 83, p. 47-48.
"In the Close and Holy Darkness." WebR (8:1) Spr 83, p. 79.
"The Mechanical Engineer's Proposal." DekalbLAJ (16:1/4) Aut 82-Sum 83, p. 59.
"Once Again, the Combine." PoetC (15:1) Aut 83, p. 9.
"Open Season." PoetC (15:1) Aut 83, p. 12.

654. CARLILE, Henry
"In the More Recent Past." OhioR (30) 83, p. 261.

655. CARLISLE, S. E.
"At the Monument Beach Fish Market." Prima (8) 83, p. 21.
"It Is Difficult." Prima (8) 83, p. 21.

656. CARLISLE, Thomas John
"And Don't We all?" ChrC (100:18) 1 Je 83, p. 551.

657. CARLSON, Martha
"Translating." CarolQ (35:3) Spr 83, p. 62.

CARMEN, Marilyn
See: ESHE, Aisha

658. CARMI, T.
"Airborne" (tr. by Gabriel Levin). LitR (26:2) Wint 83, p. 225.
"The Almond Tree" (tr. by Grace Schulman). LitR (26:2) Wint 83, p. 228.
"Credo" (tr. by Grace Schulman). LitR (26:2) Wint 83, p. 226.
"From This Day On" (tr. by Grace Schulman). LitR (26:2) Wint 83, p. 227.
"Landing" (tr. by Gabriel Levin). LitR (26:2) Wint 83, p. 226.
"Military Funeral at High Noon" (In Memory of J.H., tr. by Grace Schulman). LitR (26:2) Wint 83, p. 228-230.
"She Sleeps" (tr. by Grace Schulman). LitR (26:2) Wint 83, p. 227.

659. CARNEVALE, Robert
"Walking by the Cliffside Dyeworks." NewYorker (58:47) 10 Ja 83, p. 38.

660. CARPATHIOS, Neil
"Dusk." YetASM (2:1) 83, p. 8.
"Infected by Morning." ThirdW Spr 83, p. 86.

661. CARPENTER, Anne Nicodemus
"Ancestor." AmerS (52:1) Wint 82/83, p. 106.

662. CARPENTER, Mack L.
"Anne's Calendar." Tele (18) 83, p. 63.

663. CARPENTER, William
"Blackout, 1944." AmerPoR (12:4) Jl-Ag 83, p. 46.
"The Ecuadorian Sailors." AmerPoR (12:4) Jl-Ag 83, p. 46.
"The Husbands." AmerPoR (12:4) Jl-Ag 83, p. 47.
"Landscape with Figures." NewEng (5:4) Sum 83, p. 529-530.
"Love." BlackWR (10:1) Aut 83, p. 13-14.
"New York City." BlackWR (8:2) Spr 82, p. 21-23.

664. CARPER, Thomas
"A Conversation." Poetry (142:2) My 83, p. 73.
"Deadalus Invents God." Poetry (142:2) My 83, p. 74.
"Hercules' Descent into the Underworld." Poetry (142:2) My 83, p. 75.
"A Picture of the Reverend's Family with the Child of One." Poetry (142:2) My 83, p. 72.
"Two Bronzes by Barlach." AntR (41:3) Sum 83, p. 332.

665. CARRADICE, Phil
"Burma Star." Bogg (51) 83, p. 55.
"Modern Nursery Rhymes." Bogg (50) 83, p. 52.

666. CARREL, Ann
"The Treacherous Death of Jesse James." ThRiPo (21/22) 83, p. 15.

667. CARRILLO, Jo
"Inside the Iron Triangle." Cond (9) Spr 83, p. 45.
"Muñeca." Cond (9) Spr 83, p. 43.
"Orden." Cond (9) Spr 83, p. 44.

668. CARRUTH, Hayden
"Lana." Kayak (63) N 83, p. 16-19.
"Living Alone" (For John Cheever, from whose writing this epigraph is taken). Iowa (13:2) Spr 82, p. 99-104.
"Paragraph 15." OhioR (30) 83, p. 204.
"Words to a Young Revolutionist." NewL (49:3/4) Spr-Sum 83, p. 26-27.

669. CARSON, Ciarán
"The Insular Celts." PoetryE (9/10) Wint 82-Spr 83, p. 218-219.
"Interior with Weaver." PoetryE (9/10) Wint 82-Spr 83, p. 216-217.

670. CARTER, Beth W.
"Balloons." DekalbLAJ (16:1/4) Aut 82-Sum 83, p. 60.

671. CARTER, Ellin
"Retracing." Tendril (14/15) Wint 83, p. 33.

672. CARTER, Jared
"Cicadas." Kayak (61) Ap 83, p. 38.
"Construction Accident." LittleBR (4:2) Wint 83-84, p. 40-41.
"Damaged Money." ClockR (1:2) Wint 83-84, p. 38.
"From the Watertower." LittleBR (3:3) Spr 83, p. 49-51.
"Waterworks." ClockR (1:1) Sum 83, p. 30-31.

673. CARTER, Nancy Corson
"For Grammy on Her 90th Birthday." YetASM (1:1) 82, p. 14.
"Katie." YetASM (1:1) 82, p. 14.

674. CARTER, Richard E.
"Root Cellar." SpoonRQ (8:4) Aut 83, p. 11.

675. CARVAJAL, José
"A La Poesía." Rácata (1) 83, p. 34.
"La Canción del Ogro" (para todos los poetas y en especial Franklin Gutiérrez). Rácata (1) 83, p. 35-37.
"Jardín de Flores Humanas." Rácata (1) 83, p. 38-39.

676. CASE, Sandra
"Autumn." WindO (42) Sum 83, p. 15.

677. CASETTA, Mike
"Preparations for Leaving Home" (For E.F.). YetASM (1:2) 82, p. 4.

678. CASEY, Deb
"Dead Possum." CropD (4) 83, p. 4.

679. CASEY, Michael
"Civil Action Group." MichQR (22:4) Aut 83, p. 558-559.

680. CASSITY, Turner
"Alfred Douglas." SouthernR (19:3) Jl 83, p. 639.
"A Dance Part Way around the Golden Calf, or, Rich within the Dreams of Avarice." ChiR (34:1) Sum 83, p. 20-21.
"Deep Depression in Key West." Ploughs (9:2/3) 83, p. 72.
"Imaginary Sargents." SouthernR (19:3) Jl 83, p. 637-640.
"J. Bruce Ismay." SouthernR (19:3) Jl 83, p. 639.
"Mainstreaming." ChiR (34:1) Sum 83, p. 17-19.
"A Member of the Mystic Krewe." ChiR (34:1) Sum 83, p. 15.
"Mrs. Leland Stanford." SouthernR (19:3) Jl 83, p. 640.

"Nellie Melba." SouthernR (19:3) Jl 83, p. 637.
"News for Loch Ness." ChiR (34:1) Sum 83, p. 16.
"U-24 Anchors off New Orleans, 1938." Ploughs (9:2/3) 83, p. 73.
"Viscount Greystoke." SouthernR (19:3) Jl 83, p. 638.

681. CASTANO, Wilfredo Q.
"Old Times." SecC (11:1/2) 83, p. 27.
"To People Who Pick Food." SecC (11:1/2) 83, p. 26.

682. CASTILLO, Ana
"The Antihero." RevChic (11:3/4) 83, p. 41.
"I Don't Want to Know." RevChic (11:3/4) 83, p. 39.
"Not Just Because My Husband Said." RevChic (11:3/4) 83, p. 40.

683. CASTILLO, Ricardo
"Ode to the Urge" (tr. by Robert L. Jones). MissouriR (7:1) Aut 83, p. 33.
"Some Reflections Beginning with the Disproportionate Length of My Feet" (tr. by Robert L. Jones). MissouriR (7:1) Aut 83, p. 32.

684. CASULLO, Joanne
"Another Woman's Lover." LitR (26:3) Spr 83, p. 386.

685. CATALA, Rafael
"Confesión." Rácata (1) 83, p. 41.
"Enfrentados a la relatividad señalan asombrados el final de su vida." Rácata (1) 83, p. 43.
"Envejecer." Rácata (1) 83, p. 45.
"La Herencia." Rácata (1) 83, p. 44.
"Hora Calibán" (para Roberto Fernández Retamar). Rácata (2) 83, p. 35.
"Isaac y Alberto." Rácata (2) 83, p. 38.
"Klemente Soto Beles." Areíto (9:33) 83, p. 21.
"Preparar un poema para el taller." Rácata (1) 83, p. 40.
"Sincretizando" (para todos los talleristas, compañeros de Rácata). Rácata (2) 83, p. 36-37.

686. CATHERS, Ken
"Hunting Ground." Quarry (32:1) Wint 83, p. 49-50.
"The Twin." Quarry (32:1) Wint 83, p. 48-49.

687. CATINA, Ray
"End Game" (from Getting There Was Half the Fun, semi-finalist, 10th anniversary manuscript competition). StoneC (11:1/2, Pt. 1) Aut-Wint 83, p. 59.
"Quality" (from Getting There Was Half the Fun, semi-finalist, 10th anniversary manuscript competition). StoneC (11:1/2, Pt. 1) Aut-Wint 83, p. 59.

688. CATLIN, Alan
"Poets in Their Youth." Abraxas (27/28) 83, p. 23.

689. CAVAGNARO, Jeanne
"After the Neutron Bomb." SanFPJ (5:4) 83, p. 76.

690. CAVALIERO, Glen
"The Prelate's Son." Argo (4:3) 83, p. 33.

691. CAVALLARO, Carol
"Being Taught." DevQ (18:1) Spr 83, p. 58-59.
"Cassandra." DevQ (17:4) Wint 83, p. 21.
"Julie in the Hospital." DevQ (18:1) Spr 83, p. 56-57.
"Songs." Calyx (8:1) Aut 83, p. 26-27.

692. CAVANAUGH, William C.
"Andromeda." SanFPJ (4:2) 83, p. 33.
"Free Falling Still Point." SanFPJ (4:2) 83, p. 33.
"Is There a Hell, Father?" SanFPJ (4:2) 83, p. 10-11.

693. CAVELIERE, Grace
"Les Jardins." PoetL (77:2) Sum 82, p. 88-91.

694. CAVERS, Gwenn
"Zucchini." Bluebuf (2:1) Aut 83, p. 26.

695. CAWS, Ian
"Sandflies." Argo (4:1) 82, p. 6.

696. CECIL, Richard
"All about Insurance." PoetryNW (24:2) Sum 83, p. 22.
"At the Franklin Planetarium." Telescope (5/6) Spr 83, p. 120-121.

697. CEDERING, Siv
"The Acrobat." SouthernPR (23:2) Aut 82 [i.e. (23:1?) Spr 83], p. 32.

698. CEDERQUIST, Druzelle
"At Liberty." WorldO (17:4) Sum 83, p. 30.
"Seasons." WorldO (17:4) Sum 83, p. 31.

699. CEELY, John
"Angry Night." Tele (18) 83, p. 24.
"Be Sure and Bring Your Bones." Tele (18) 83, p. 25.
"Burns." Tele (18) 83, p. 25.
"Green." Tele (18) 83, p. 24.
"Path." Tele (18) 83, p. 23.

700. CELAN, Paul
"In the Form of a Wild Boar" (tr. by Paul Morris). WebR (8:1) Spr 83, p. 43.
"The Years from You to Me" (tr. by Paul Morris). WebR (8:1) Spr 83, p. 42.

701. CELLUCCI, Carol
"Before, There Were Cities." KanQ (15:2) Spr 83, p. 25.
"The Eloquence of Horses" (for Laird). KanQ (15:2) Spr 83, p. 23.
"Feeding the Moon." YetASM (1:2) 82, p. 11.
"The Sky Is Not a Lie" (for Ellen). YetASM (1:2)

82, p. 13.
"Talking in the Car, Overlooking Alameda Street" (Santa Fe, New Mexico). KanQ (15:2) Spr 83, p. 24.

702. CELLY, Jean-Jacques
"Forsworn" (tr. by Hilary Davies). Argo (4:3) 83, p. 9.
"House" (tr. by Hilary Davies). Argo (4:3) 83, p. 9.
"Maison." Argo (4:3) 83, p. 8.
"Parjure." Argo (4:3) 83, p. 8.
"Passage." Argo (4:3) 83, p. 8.
"Passage" (tr. by Hilary Davies). Argo (4:3) 83, p. 9.

703. CERNIGLIA, Alice
"Anthony." Meadows (4:1) 83, p. 50.
"Love." Meadows (4:1) 83, p. 45.
"Mixers." Meadows (4:1) 83, p. 13.

704. CERNUDA, Luis
"Adolescente Fui en Dias Identicos a Nubes." NewRena (17) Aut 83, p. 24.
"Estoy Cansado." NewRena (17) Aut 83, p. 54.
"Grief in Black Tie" (tr. by Erland Anderson). NewRena (17) Aut 83, p. 53.
"I'm Tired" (tr. by Erland Anderson). NewRena (17) Aut 83, p. 55.
"El Intruso." NewRena (17) Aut 83, p. 26.
"Los Muros nada mas." NewRena (17) Aut 83, p. 56.
"Only These Walls" (tr. by Erland Anderson). NewRena (17) Aut 83, p. 57.
"The Outsider" (tr. by Erland Anderson). NewRena (17) Aut 83, p. 27.
"Remordimiento en Traje de Noche." NewRena (17) Aut 83, p. 52.
"Vidrio de Agua en Mano del Hastio." NewRena (17) Aut 83, p. 28.
"A Water-Glass in Boredom's hand" (tr. by Erland Anderson). NewRena (17) Aut 83, p. 29.
"When I Was an Adolescent" (tr. by Erland Anderson). NewRena (17) Aut 83, p. 25.

705. CERVANTES, James
"Letter to Franz Douskey." MemphisSR (4:1) Aut 83, p. 42.
"This Season." NowestR (21:1) 83, p. 25.

706. CESARANO, James
"Autobiography." NegC (3:4) Aut 83, p. 42.
"Language in Puerto Rico." SanFPJ (4:2) 83, p. 71.
"My Father Reading." YetASM (2:1) 83, p. 8.
"Visiting a Foreign Country." SanFPJ (4:2) 83, p. 71.

707. CHABRE, Virgil
"Loneliness." SanFPJ (5:2) 83, p. 64.
"A Symphony of Enchantment." SanFPJ (5:2) 83, p. 64.

708. CHAFFIN, Lillie D.
"Reasons For." Blueline (4:2) Wint-Spr 83, p. 32.

709. CHALFI, Rachel
"A Different Myth" (tr. by Linda Zisquit). LitR (26:2) Wint 83, p. 277.
"The Dolores Poems" (Selections: 1, 3, 5) (tr. by Linda Zisquit). LitR (26:2) Wint 83, p. 278-279.

710. CHAMBERLAIN, Karen
"Coast Range." Nat (236:17) 30 Ap 83, p. 547.

711. CHAMBERS, Carole
"Naked Ankles II." MalR (65) Jl 83, p. 64.

712. CHAMBERS, Henry Tim
"El Viejo y Su Muchacha." MissR (12:1/2, nos. 34/35) Aut 83, p. 73.

713. CHAMBERS, Leland H.
"Collegial Angels" (tr. of Rafael Alberti). DevQ (18:1) Spr 83, p. 100.
"Indian Woman Down in the Marketplace" (tr. of Joaquin Pasos). DevQ (18:1) Spr 83, p. 98.
"Invitation to the Lyre" (tr. of Rafael Alberti). DevQ (18:1) Spr 83, p. 99.

714. CHANDLER, Michael
"Halloween Night." NegC (3:4) Aut 83, p. 131.
"Reaching for Grief." NegC (3:4) Aut 83, p. 88.
"Under the Heavenly Mask of Marriage." ThirdW Spr 83, p. 84.

715. CHANDRA, G. S. Sharat
"The Rich Do Not Queue." MinnR (NS 20) Spr 83, p. 20.
"Sunday Afternoon." NewL (49:3/4) Spr-Sum 83, p. 252-253.

CH'ANG-LING, Wang
See: WANG, Ch'ang-ling

716. CHAPMAN, Susan
"Ice Princess." ThirdW Spr 83, p. 52.

717. CHAPPELL, Fred
"Abandoned Schoolhouse on Long Branch." Abatis (1) 83, p. 70.
"The Capacity for Pain." Abatis (1) 83, p. 68.
"Message" (for D.S.). Poetry (142:6) S 83, p. 321.
"Narcissus and Echo." Poetry (142:6) S 83, p. 320.
"Nocturne." Abatis (1) 83, p. 66.
"An Old Mountain Woman Reading the Book of Job." CharR (9:1) Spr 83, p. 8-9.
"A Prayer for the Mountains." SouthernPR (23:2) Aut 82 [i.e. (23:1?) Spr 83], p. 18.
"Proposition IVa." Abatis (1) 83, p. 67.
"Rain on Hemphill Valley." Abatis (1) 83, p. 66.
"Remodeling the Hermit's Cabin." Abatis (1) 83, p. 71-73.
"School Bully." Abatis (1) 83, p. 69.
"Song for Disembodied Voice." LittleBR (4:2) Wint 83-84, p. 59-60.
"Tate's Forty Brithdays." LittleBR (4:2) Wint 83-

84, p. 8.
"Urleid." Ploughs (9:2/3) 83, p. 30-31.
"Windows" (for Anne Newman). SouthernPR (23:2) Aut 82 [i.e. (23:1?) Spr 83], p. 17-18.

718. CHAR, René
"Conge au Vent." NegC (3:4) Aut 83, p. 98.
"Feuillets d'Hypnos, Journal de Guerre, 1943-1944" (Excerpts). NegC (3:4) Aut 83, p. 102.
"Jeunesse." NegC (3:4) Aut 83, p. 100.
"Leaves of Hypnos, a War Journal, 1943-1944" (Excerpts) (tr. by Eugene Walter). NegC (3:4) Aut 83, p. 103.
"Lily-of-the-Valley" (tr. by Eugene Walter). NegC (3:4) Aut 83, p. 99.
"Le Muguet." NegC (3:4) Aut 83, p. 98.
"Warning to the Wind" (tr. by Eugene Walter). NegC (3:4) Aut 83, p. 99.
"Youth" (tr. by Eugene Walter). NegC (3:4) Aut 83, p. 101.

719. CHARLTON, Lindsey D.
"Burn Off." AntigR (53) Spr 83, p. 126.

720. CHARNS, Alex
"Crucifixion Lunch." SanFPJ (5:4) 83, p. 17-18.

721. CHATFIELD, Hale
"Boeing 737." HiramPoR (35) Aut-Wint 83, p. 10.
"Chapter I & Chapter II." ThRiPo (21/22) 83, p. 16.

722. CHAVES, Jonathan
"Boiling Falls" (tr. of Liu E). Hudson (36:2) Sum 83, p. 286.
"The House of Red Leaves" (tr. of Liu E). Hudson (36:2) Sum 83, p. 284.
"I Remember" (tr. of Liu E). Hudson (36:2) Sum 83, p. 283.
"New Year's Eve" (tr. of Liu E). Hudson (36:2) Sum 83, p. 286.
"On the Fifteenth Day of the Eighth Month: Watching a Rainstorm from a Tower in Seoul" (tr. of Liu E). Hudson (36:2) Sum 83, p. 285.
"Pleasures of Sinbashi" (tr. of Liu E). Hudson (36:2) Sum 83, p. 284.
"Waiting for the Ferry at Inchon" (tr. of Liu E). Hudson (36:2) Sum 83, p. 281-283.

723. CHAYAT, Juliet
"Negative" (for Robert). WestB (13) 83, p. 14.

CHEN, Yüan
See: YUAN, Chên

CHENG, Gu
See: GU, Cheng

724. CHERI
"Dirge for Suzie-Q." Meadows (3:1) 82, p. 51.

725. CHERKOVSKI, Neeli
"Notes for a Basterd Angel" (to Harold Norse). SecC (11:1/2) 83, p. 29-31.

726. CHERRY, Kelly
"The Bone-Hand and the Heart." ConcPo (16:1) Spr 83, p. 82.
"Dark Confusion, Snow Scuttling Across the Street Like Blown Pages of a Newspaper." OP (36) Aut-Wint 83, p. 45.
"Forecast." OP (36) Aut-Wint 83, p. 46.
"God Whose Grief Is So Great That Nothing Can Encompass It Except Itself." DevQ (18:2) Sum 83, p. 70.
"Going Down on America." ThRiPo (21/22) 83, p. 17.
"Hide-and-Seek." DevQ (18:2) Sum 83, p. 67.
"How to Wait." ConcPo (16:1) Spr 83, p. 80-81.
"Love." DevQ (18:2) Sum 83, p. 66.
"Sighs So Deep They Seem to Speak of Death." DevQ (18:2) Sum 83, p. 68-69.
"Walking in the World" (For Mekeel McBride). OP (36) Aut-Wint 83, p. 47.
"Wind Chimes in the Deep Blue Upside-Down Heaven." NewOR (10:2/3) Sum-Aut 83, p. 42.

727. CHESS, Rick
"Mother Dating." BelPoJ (34:1) Aut 83, p. 34.

728. CHESTER, Laura
"Go Round." CreamCR (8:1/2) 83, p. 151.
"In a Motion." CreamCR (8:1/2) 83, p. 150.

729. CHETCUTI, Vincent
"Visions of Kerouac #14." MoodySI (12) Aut 82, p. 21.

730. CHEVAKO, Mari Reitsma
"Without Flowers." Thrpny (4:1, issue 13) Spr 83, p. 23.

731. CHICHETTO, James
"What Else" (tr. of Adolfo Mendez Vides). ManhatR (3:1) Sum 83, p. 59.

CH'IEN, T'ao
See: T'AO, Ch'ien

CHIH, Feng
See: FENG, Chih

732. CH'IN, Kuan
"Song" (tr. by Sam Hamill). AmerPoR (12:6) N/D 83, p. 6.

CH'ING-CHAO, Li
See: LI, Ch'ing-chao

733. CHINMOY, Sri
"Why Explain?" ArizQ (39:3) Aut 83, p. 214.

734. CHISHOLM, Jan
"Murder." CalQ (22) Sum 83, p. 57.
"Persephone." CalQ (22) Sum 83, p. 56-57.

735. CHIU, Nin
"Since You Have Gone Away" (tr. by Wang Hui-Ming). NewL (49:3/4) Spr-Sum 83, p. 64.

736. CHOPRA, Shiv
"Vagrancy." WritersL S 83, p. 12.

737. CHORLTON, David
"Common Ground." PoetL (77:2) Sum 82, p. 76-77.
"Finding the Words." PikeF (5) Spr 83, p. 29.
"Mister Lowry." PoetL (77:2) Sum 82, p. 75.
"Moving North". PikeF (5) Spr 83, p. 29.
"The Naco We Visit." PoetL (78:2) Sum 83, p. 98-99.
"St. John of the Cross in the Carmelite Priory, Toledo, 1578." PoetL (78:2) Sum 83, p. 96-97.
"The Village Painters." PoetL (78:4) Wint 84, p. 225-231.

738. CHOU, Sebastian Shin-Pan
"A Morning Song in Prose of Dry Lotus Leaves" (tr. by Gene DeGruson). LittleBR (3:4) Sum 83, p. 41.
"Searching years for fame" (tr. by Gene DeGruson). LittleBR (3:4) Sum 83, p. 44.
"When the General won his victories" (tr. by Gene DeGruson). LittleBR (3:4) Sum 83, p. 42.

739. CHOW, Mary
"Promises." Prima (8) 83, p. 74.

740. CHOYCE, Lesley
"Chasing Flies with a Vacuum Cleaner." PottPort (5) 83-84, p. 52.
"The Conjugal Visit." Quarry (32:3) Sum 83, p. 19-20.
"The Headlands." PottPort (5) 83-84, p. 40.
"Newfoundland Kitchen." Quarry (32:3) Sum 83, p. 19.
"Rocks." CrossC (5:2/3) 83, p. 5.
"Surfing before the Hurricane: Nova Scotia, September, 1981." AntigR (54) Sum 83, p. 100-101.

741. CHRISTENSEN, Erleen J.
"Across the Wide Missouri." Meadows (3:1) 82, p. 13.
"Going Home." Meadows (3:1) 82, p. 13.

742. CHRISTENSEN, Inger
"The Atom Bomb Is There" (tr. by Susanna Nied). PoetryE (9/10) Wint 82-Spr 83, p. 252-253.
"The Cobalt Bomb Is There" (tr. by Susanna Nied). PoetryE (9/10) Wint 82-Spr 83, p. 254-257.

743. CHRISTIAN, Eddena
"Vacation." NegC (3:4) Aut 83, p. 78.

744. CHRISTIAN, Joni
"Life." PortR (29:1) 83, p. 19.
"Lullabye." PortR (29:1) 83, p. 104.

745. CHRISTIAN, Paula
"My Business." SanFPJ (4:2) 83, p. 21.

746. CHRISTOPHER, Nicholas
"The House Where Lord Rochester Died." NewYorker (58:49) 24 Ja 83, p. 42.
"Mars and Venus." Nat (236:25) 25 Je 83, p. 804.
"Reflections on a Bowl of Kumquats, 1936." Nat (237:9) 1 O 83, p. 280.
"Sunday, Looking Westward." ParisR (25:90) Wint 83, p. 156-159.
"Verona, 1973." Nat (237:14) 5 N 83, p. 444.
"Voyage." Nat (236:24) 18 Je 83, p. 772.
"Winter Night." NewYorker (59:2) 28 F 83, p. 42.

747. CHRISTOPHERSEN, Bill
"Memories of Green Pastures." ModernPS (11:3) 83, p. 273.

CHUANG, Wei
See: WEI, Chuang

748. CHUBBS, Boyd
"North Atlantic." PottPort (5) 83-84, p. 32.
"Sundanced." PottPort (5) 83-84, p. 27.

749. CHUILLEANÁIN, Eiléan Ní
"Swineherd." PoetryE (9/10) Wint 82-Spr 83, p. 225.

750. CHURCH, John I.
"St. Brendan's Prayer." WindO (42) Sum 83, p. 41.

751. CHURCHILL, Sauci
"The Birthday Cake." YetASM (1:1) 82, p. 15.
"Letter from Her Aunt." YetASM (1:1) 82, p. 3.

752. CHUTE, Robert M.
"Retroactive Suit for Damages." SanFPJ (4:4) 83, p. 46.
"Search for Security and the Holy Grail." SanFPJ (4:4) 83, p. 47.

753. CIARDI, John
"Diary Entry for Any Day." LittleBR (4:2) Wint 83-84, p. 15.
"Fortieth Anniversary Poem." Poetry (143:3) D 83, p. 133-134.
"Friends." Poetry (143:3) D 83, p. 130.
"Quirks." Poetry (143:3) D 83, p. 131-132.
"True or False." Poetry (143:3) D 83, p. 132.

CICCO, Pier Giorgio di
See: Di CICCO, Pier Giorgio

754. CIRINO, Leonard
"Vanishing Species." StoneC (10:3/4) Spr-Sum 83, p. 55.

755. CISNEROS, Sandra
"Letter to Ilona from the South of France" (for

Ilona Den Blacken Nesti). RevChic (11:3/4) 83, p. 23.
"Love Poem #1." RevChic (11:3/4) 83, p. 22.
"No Mercy." RevChic (11:3/4) 83, p. 19.
"The So-and-So's." RevChic (11:3/4) 83, p. 20-21.

756. CITINO, David
"Asthma." MemphisSR (2:2) Spr 82, p. 13.
"A Brief History of Bells." WestB (13) 83, p. 56.
"The Death of Benito Mussolini." PoetL (78:3) Aut 83, p. 141.
"The Doe, Marion, Ohio, Cemetery, Dawn." PoetryNW (24:1) Spr 83, p. 39-40.
"Drugstore." CentR (27:4) Aut 83, p. 273-274.
"Emanuel Swedenborg Works Late One Night in Paris in Dr. Petit's Anatomy School." MemphisSR (2:2) Spr 82, p. 24.
"Four Short Meditations on the Body." Tendril (16) Sum 83, p. 20.
"He Shows the People What to Do with the Dead" (from Tales of Trickster). Thrpny (3:4, issue 12) Wint 83, p. 22.
"June 25, 1947: In His Own Back Yard, the Retired Pastor Looks to Heaven and the Flying Saucer Craze is Born." CimR (63) Ap 83, p. 60-61.
"Letter from Trickster: On the Nature of Beauty." CharR (9:2) Aut 83, p. 60-61.
"Life of the Bourgeoisie." PoNow (7:2, #38) 83, p. 16.
"Meditation on the Skeleton of a Prehistoric Indian at the Ohio Historical Center." SoDakR (21:4) Wint 83, p. 68.
"Poem for My Parents, Leaving Ohio for Florida, the Cuyahoga for the Caloosahatchee." HiramPoR (35) Aut-Wint 83, p. 11.
"Principles of Scarcity, Doctrines of Growth." SouthernPR (23:2) Aut 82 [i.e. (23:1?) Spr 83], p. 52.
"Redwing." YaleR (72:2) Wint 83, p. 259-260.
"The Retired Pastor Revises the Catechism." MemphisSR (2:2) Spr 82, p. 12.
"Riding." Wind (13:47) 83, p. 6-7.
"Saturday Night at the Harding High School Gym." PoetC (15:1) Aut 83, p. 12.
"Sister Mary Appassionata Lectures the Anatomy Class: Doctrines of the Nose." PoetryCR (4:3) Spr 83, p. 7.
"Sister Mary Appassionata Lectures the Eighth Grade Boys and Girls: The Family Jewels." Tendril (14/15) Wint 83, p. 34.
"Sister Mary Appassionata Lectures the Eighth-Grade Boys and Girls on the Life and Death of St. Teresa." YaleR (72:2) Wint 83, p. 259.
"Sister Mary Appassionata Lectures the History Class: Life of the Saint." HolCrit (20:1) F 83, p. 19.
"Sister Mary Appassionata Lectures the Home Ec. Class: The Feast." Wind (13:47) 83, p. 5-6.
"Sister Mary Appassionata Lectures the Quantitative Analysis Class: Proof of the Existence of the

Soul." PoetryCR (4:3) Spr 83, p. 7.
"Sister Mary Appassionata's Lecture to the Creative Writing Class: The Evangelist." ChiR (33:3) Wint 83, p. 108.
"Sister Mary Appassionata's Lecture to the Eighth Grade Boys and Girls: Flesh Willing, Spirit Weak." Wind (13:47) 83, p. 5.
"Sister Mary Appassionata's Lecture to the Eighth Grade Boys and Girls: To Punish the Cities." ChiR (33:3) Wint 83, p. 109.
"Time and the Weather." PoetL (78:3) Aut 83, p. 139-140.
"Trickster Becomes Eel and Stallion, the Face of God." Tendril (16) Sum 83, p. 19.
"Village of the Dead." CentR (27:1) Wint 83, p. 41-42.

757. CIVKIN, Shelley
"The Noah Conspiracy." PoetryCR (4:3) Spr 83, p. 15.

758. CLAMPITT, Amy
"The August Darks." NewYorker (59:28) 29 Ag 83, p. 30.
"Berceuse." NewYRB (29:21/22) 20 Ja 83, p. 8.
"Blueberrying in August." NewRep (188:17) 2 My 83, p. 34.
"The Catalpa Tree in a Back Garden on West Twelfth Street." PraS (57:4) Wint 83, p. 25-26.
"A Cure at Porlock." PraS (57:4) Wint 83, p. 29.
"Fallen Fruit." PraS (57:4) Wint 83, p. 24.
"The Godfather Returns to Color TV." PraS (57:4) Wint 83, p. 28.
"The Great Bonfire" (After Pablo Neruda). PraS (57:4) Wint 83, p. 31-32.
"Keats at Chichester." NewEngR (6:2) Wint 83, p. 317-319.
"Let the Air Circulate." PraS (57:4) Wint 83, p. 30.
"Marine Surface, Low Overcast." NewRep (186:25) 23 Je 82, p. 34.
"A New Life." NewEng (5:4) Sum 83, p. 531-533.
"Real Estate." PraS (57:4) Wint 83, p. 20.
"Real Estate: A Group of Poems." PraS (57:4) Wint 83, p. 17-32.
"Ringing Doorbells." PraS (57:4) Wint 83, p. 19.
"The Sacred Hearth Fire." MassR (24:3) Aut 83, p. 516-520.
"A Scaffold." PraS (57:4) Wint 83, p. 21-22.
"Time." NewYorker (59:42) 5 D 83, p. 54.
"Townhouse Interior with Cat." PraS (57:4) Wint 83, p. 27.
"Witness." NewRep (186:6) 10 F 82, p. 30.
"Work in Progress." PraS (57:4) Wint 83, p. 22-23.

759. CLARE, Josephine
"Cords Ropes Lines Ties & Knots Also Wreaths." SenR (13:2) 82-83, p. 41-46.
"In the Grass Biased." NewL (49:3/4) Spr-Sum 83, p. 141.

760. CLARK, Charles J.
"Windswept." SanFPJ (5:2) 83, p. 7.

761. CLARK, Katharine
"Autumnal at the Barrow." ThirdW Spr 83, p. 107.
"Devas" (to Tony). ThirdW Spr 83, p. 111.
"Fedelm's Song." ThirdW Spr 83, p. 109-110.
"The God at Winter." ThirdW Spr 83, p. 108.
"The Last Pagans." ThirdW Spr 83, p. 109.
"Mythology." ThirdW Spr 83, p. 112.

762. CLARK, Naomi
"Late Spring, Sur Coast." SecC (11:1/2) 83, p. 32.
"Letter to a Husband on an Oil Drilling Rig at Prudhoe Bay." KanQ (15:2) Spr 83, p. 42.
"Mist." PoNow (7:2, #38) 83, p. 13.

763. CLARK, Patricia
"American Lake." BlackWR (10:1) Aut 83, p. 122.
"Trees at Dusk." BlackWR (10:1) Aut 83, p. 121.

764. CLARK, Steven C.
"Commercial Sucks-X." SanFPJ (5:4) 83, p. 29.
"We Don't Make Love." SanFPJ (5:4) 83, p. 32.

765. CLARK, Susan J.
"Trick Photography." WindO (43) Wint 83, p. 50.

766. CLARK, Walter
"Grief." Iowa (13:3/4) Spr 82 (83), p. 28.

767. CLARKE, George Elliott
"CFB Stadacona" (for William Lloyd Clarke). PottPort (5) 83-84, p. 44.
"The Citizen Abroad Thinks of Home." AntigR (54) Sum 83, p. 14.
"Compassion." AntigR (54) Sum 83, p. 14.
"First Baptist Church." PottPort (5) 83-84, p. 41.
"Journey and Arrival." Quarry (32:4) Aut 83, p. 52-53.
"Primitivism." Quarry (32:4) Aut 83, p. 52.
"The stricken sun." Dandel (10:1) Spr-Sum 83, p. 43.

768. CLARKE, Kalo
"Elliott Bay." YetASM (2:1) 83, p. 8.
"Reunion." YetASM (1:2) 82, p. 17.
"Wind Dance." PortR (29:1) 83, p. 79.

769. CLARY, Killarney
"Breathless." ParisR (25:88) Sum 83, p. 80-81.
"I am used to working now." ParisR (25:88) Sum 83, p. 81.
"Larger than hand-passed dangers await us." ParisR (25:88) Sum 83, p. 80.
"Sleep was streams of red and white lights." ParisR (25:88) Sum 83, p. 81.
"There are more of us." ParisR (25:88) Sum 83, p. 79.

770. CLAUDEL, Alice Moser
"Late Depression 1940 Social Work." LitR (27:1)

Aut 83, p. 8.

771. CLEARY, Michael
"Glens Falls: Twenty-five Years Later." Blueline (4:2) Wint-Spr 83, p. 29.

772. CLEGHORN, James
"A Sequence." PoetL (78:2) Sum 83, p. 92-94.

CLEIREN, Ghislaine Sniekers
See: SNIEKERS-CLEIREN, Ghislaine

773. CLEMENTS, Arthur
"Composition in Yellow." Blueline (4:1) Sum-Aut 82, p. 16.
"Winter Storm." Blueline (4:2) Wint-Spr 83, p. 31.

774. CLEMENTS, William M.
"For Lincoln Perry." BlackALF (17:4) Wint 83, p. 174.

775. CLEWETT, Rick
"Elegy for Rusty Peach." YetASM (2:1) 83, p. 7.
"The Tasks." YetASM (1:2) 82, p. 6.

776. CLIFTON, Linda J.
"After the First Search" Calyx (7:3) Sum 83, p. 28.
"Friendly Fire." Vis (11) 83, p. 9.
"Red Cross Camp: South Mexico." Calyx (8:1) Aut 83, p. 37.

777. CLIFTON, Merritt
"Chores at the Commune." SanFPJ (4:3) 83, p. 40.
"Creating the Wealth." Sam (36:3 143rd release) 83, p. 50-52.
"Loving Couple." Sam (34:3 135th release) 83, p. 21.

778. CLINE, Charles
"Resurrection." Wind (13:48) 83, p. 56.

779. CLOCKADALE, Jill
"Disarmament." CentR (27:1) Wint 83, p. 45.

780. CLOHERTY, Pat
"The Maisie" (Excerpt). NewRep (186:20) 19 My 82, p. 39.

781. CLOKE, Kenneth
"Rooms for Rent." SanFPJ (5:4) 83, p. 83.

782. CLOKE, Richard (See also: R. C. [?])
"A 3 cent resister burns out." SanFPJ (4:3) 83, p. 1.
"ACORN is an org. of squatters." SanFPJ (5:1) 83, p. 35.
"Afflatus." SanFPJ (5:1) 83, p. 7.
"After World War I." SanFPJ (4:4) 83, p. 85.
"Ah, can I order now?" SanFPJ (5:1) 83, p. 78.
"All men are created equal." SanFPJ (5:1) 83, p. 89.
"Anthropic cosmologists." SanFPJ (5:1) 83, p. 31.
"Anti-neologisticism." SanFPJ (5:2) 83, p. 17.
"As a patriot I object." SanFPJ (4:3) 83, p. 38.

"As a reaction to dessication." _SanFPJ_ (5:3) 83, p. 9.
"Beat the Drums!" _SanFPJ_ (5:4) 83, p. 60.
"Brain synapses." _SanFPJ_ (4:2) 83, p. 8.
"But what grace has paint." _SanFPJ_ (4:2) 83, p. 29.
"A chicken is a device." _SanFPJ_ (4:4) 83, p. 19.
"A Clue to the solution." _SanFPJ_ (4:4) 83, p. 95.
"Concept of the Black Grail." _SanFPJ_ (5:1) 83, p. 56.
"Consider a cluster of ten magaton bombs." _SanFPJ_ (4:4) 83, p. 34.
"Corporations are public entities." _SanFPJ_ (5:1) 83, p. 67.
"Cousin." _SanFPJ_ (4:2) 83, p. 13-14.
"Cut Medicare reimbursibles." _SanFPJ_ (4:3) 83, p. 54.
"Disaster Headquarters." _SanFPJ_ (4:2) 83, p. 39.
"Do be subtle in your poems." _SanFPJ_ (5:2) 83, p. 69.
"Do we have political prisoners." _SanFPJ_ (4:2) 83, p. 12.
"Does space really have wormholes in it." _SanFPJ_ (4:2) 83, p. 55.
"Evacuate only the 'young fit and useful'." _SanFPJ_ (4:2) 83, p. 43.
"Every penny spent." _SanFPJ_ (4:2) 83, p. 68.
"Every time you read a book." _SanFPJ_ (5:1) 83, p. 39.
"Everyone is different." _SanFPJ_ (4:3) 83, p. 11.
"First strike use of nuclear weapons." _SanFPJ_ (4:4) 83, p. 79.
"Folio." _SanFPJ_ (4:3) 83, p. 15.
"The Force has placed us in mortal peril!" _SanFPJ_ (4:3) 83, p. 28.
"Forget about posterity." _SanFPJ_ (5:2) 83, p. 65.
"Formerly the future was given." _SanFPJ_ (4:3) 83, p. 29.
"Freedom - impossible word." _SanFPJ_ (4:4) 83, p. 71.
"Government baffled by slump in research and development." _SanFPJ_ (5:2) 83, p. 48.
"Government says 6 1/2% unemployment." _SanFPJ_ (4:4) 83, p. 67.
"Had a great idea for a new-tech venture." _SanFPJ_ (5:2) 83, p. 40.
"Hart Crane." _SanFPJ_ (4:3) 83, p. 7.
"Hosts." _SanFPJ_ (4:4) 83, p. 62.
"How to pay no taxes at all?" _SanFPJ_ (4:2) 83, p. 37.
"How to pay no taxes at all?" _SanFPJ_ (4:3) 83, p. 63.
"Humans are curious animals." _SanFPJ_ (4:2) 83, p. 70.
"I am a loser." _SanFPJ_ (4:3) 83, p. 55.
"I don't want to destroy." _SanFPJ_ (4:4) 83, p. 92.
"I had a slight headache." _SanFPJ_ (5:1) 83, p. 91.
"I have no fear of nuclear bombs." _SanFPJ_ (5:1) 83, p. 47.
"I may have to cut some corners." _SanFPJ_ (4:2) 83, p. 11.
"I sold out to the establishment." _SanFPJ_ (5:1) 83, p. 74.
"I work in a nuclear fuel processing plant." _SanFPJ_ (5:1) 83, p. 42.
"If acts of copulation." _SanFPJ_ (5:3) 83, p. 23.
"If nuclear fascists have their way." _SanFPJ_ (4:4) 83, p. 16.
"If nuclear warfare got hot enough." _SanFPJ_ (4:2)

83, p. 36.
"If the stock market goes up." _SanFPJ_ (4:4) 83, p. 91.
"If they're going to blow up the world." _SanFPJ_ (4:3) 83, p. 44.
"If you're unemployed." _SanFPJ_ (5:1) 83, p. 49.
"In the East, there was little relief." _SanFPJ_ (4:2) 83, p. 58.
"Inflation and high interest rates." _SanFPJ_ (4:3) 83, p. 35.
"Is money owed the same as money spent?" _SanFPJ_ (4:3) 83, p. 36.
"Last forty years." _SanFPJ_ (4:4) 83, p. 29.
"Let the bombs fall." _SanFPJ_ (5:2) 83, p. 42.
"Let's look at food." _SanFPJ_ (4:4) 83, p. 76.
"Logical Positivists." _SanFPJ_ (4:2) 83, p. 16.
"Love Song." _SanFPJ_ (4:4) 83, p. 6.
"A matter of priorities." _SanFPJ_ (4:2) 83, p. 24.
"May be necessary to put in anti-missile systems." _SanFPJ_ (5:1) 83, p. 68.
"Maybe I'm confused." _SanFPJ_ (4:4) 83, p. 59.
"Message: Phase A116." _SanFPJ_ (4:4) 83, p. 74.
"Message: Phase A117." _SanFPJ_ (4:4) 83, p. 75.
"Message: Phase A118." _SanFPJ_ (5:1) 83, p. 76.
"Message: Phase A119." _SanFPJ_ (5:1) 83, p. 79.
"Message: Phase A120." _SanFPJ_ (5:2) 83, p. 54.
"Message: Phase A121." _SanFPJ_ (5:2) 83, p. 55.
"Message: Phase A122." _SanFPJ_ (5:3) 83, p. 78.
"Message: Phase A123." _SanFPJ_ (5:3) 83, p. 79.
"Message: Phase A124." _SanFPJ_ (5:4) 83, p. 66.
"Message: Phase A125." _SanFPJ_ (5:4) 83, p. 67.
"Millions of Americans." _SanFPJ_ (4:4) 83, p. 13.
"Missles with a range of 1500 miles." _SanFPJ_ (4:2) 83, p. 47.
"Mortals are in danger of extinction." _SanFPJ_ (4:2) 83, p. 61.
"National debt over a trillion." _SanFPJ_ (4:4) 83, p. 15.
"Never Again." _SanFPJ_ (4:3) 83, p. 19.
"No two things equal to another." _SanFPJ_ (4:3) 83, p. 9.
"Not much fun." _SanFPJ_ (4:2) 83, p. 48.
"Nuclear bombs destroy." _SanFPJ_ (4:3) 83, p. 49.
"Nuclear fascist maniacs." _SanFPJ_ (4:3) 83, p. 31.
"Nuclear superiority." _SanFPJ_ (4:3) 83, p. 34.
"Nuclear terminology." _SanFPJ_ (4:3) 83, p. 52.
"Nuclear war at the least survival." _SanFPJ_ (4:4) 83, p. 24.
"Nuclear war can change us." _SanFPJ_ (5:2) 83, p. 54.
"Nuclear war on the horizon." _SanFPJ_ (4:3) 83, p. 32.
"Nuclear war will blind your cat." _SanFPJ_ (4:4) 83, p. 53.
"Nuclear war will kill birds." _SanFPJ_ (4:4) 83, p. 53.
"Nuclear war will ruin baseball." _SanFPJ_ (4:4) 83, p. 53.
"Nuclear war will wipe out bald eagles." _SanFPJ_ (4:4) 83, p. 56.
"Nuclear war will wreck the Rose Parade." _SanFPJ_ (4:4) 83, p. 53.

"Ok let's kill the cigarette." SanFPJ (5:1) 83, p. 74.
"Once you're dead." SanFPJ (5:1) 83, p. 51.
"Only the 'young, fit and useful' allowed to leave L.A." SanFPJ (4:2) 83, p. 59.
"Peace movements are just a rehash of old tired slogans and phrases." SanFPJ (5:1) 83, p. 35.
"People presently on SS." SanFPJ (4:4) 83, p. 77.
"Poets don't compose." SanFPJ (5:2) 83, p. 94.
"Poppy Ott and the Stuttering Parrot!" SanFPJ (5:3) 83, p. 84.
"Preparing for a Nuclear War with the Soviet Union." SanFPJ (5:1) 83, p. 23.
"Preserve endangered species." SanFPJ (4:2) 83, p. 63.
"President says unemployment is bothersome." SanFPJ (4:3) 83, p. 50.
"Real." SanFPJ (4:3) 83, p. 73.
"Rebels." SanFPJ (4:2) 83, p. 7.
"Science." SanFPJ (4:4) 83, p. 47.
"Seem to have cash-flow problems." SanFPJ (4:2) 83, p. 20.
"Selling satellites to private corps." SanFPJ (5:2) 83, p. 52.
"The slow hand of malnutrition." SanFPJ (4:4) 83, p. 89.
"Society for the prevention of cruelty to mortals." SanFPJ (4:2) 83, p. 64.
"Some friends of ours." SanFPJ (4:3) 83, p. 72.
"Some good news for a change." SanFPJ (4:4) 83, p. 72.
"Some poet said all straight lines intersect." SanFPJ (4:2) 83, p. 21.
"Some say today's a repeat of the thirties." SanFPJ (4:4) 83, p. 44.
"Spike the iambic." SanFPJ (5:1) 83, p. 93.
"Stick 'em all in jail." SanFPJ (4:2) 83, p. 69.
"The story of homo sapiens." SanFPJ (5:1) 83, p. 48.
"Survival of nuclear war?" SanFPJ (5:2) 83, p. 39.
"Tax breaks to businesses." SanFPJ (5:2) 83, p. 84.
"There are an equal number of false things." SanFPJ (4:3) 83, p. 64.
"There are more unknown things." SanFPJ (4:3) 83, p. 65.
"There's a lot of sadness." SanFPJ (4:4) 83, p. 21.
"Thinkspeak." SanFPJ (5:1) 83, p. 53.
"This century may be all over." SanFPJ (5:1) 83, p. 21.
"Those who most need." SanFPJ (4:4) 83, p. 64.
"Time." SanFPJ (4:4) 83, p. 50.
"To clearly understand." SanFPJ (5:2) 83, p. 64.
"Trade deficit soars." SanFPJ (5:3) 83, p. 21.
"Two leviathians locked." SanFPJ (5:1) 83, p. 47.
"Unbreakable computer code." SanFPJ (4:2) 83, p. 45.
"U.S. sends high voltage cattle prods to South Africa." SanFPJ (5:1) 83, p. 43.
"US opposes pipeline." SanFPJ (4:3) 83, p. 56.
"US ranks 49th in literacy rate." SanFPJ (4:4) 83, p. 20.
"US wants Egypt to build Northrop fighter planes."

<u>SanFPJ</u> (4:4) 83, p. 23.
"W.W. IV will be fought with rocks." <u>SanFPJ</u> (4:4) 83, p. 53.
"War." <u>SanFPJ</u> (5:2) 83, p. 88.
"Weapons capable of killing everyone on earth." <u>SanFPJ</u> (5:1) 83, p. 87.
"Welfare cuts, unemployment." <u>SanFPJ</u> (4:3) 83, p. 41.
"Wenseslas." <u>SanFPJ</u> (4:3) 83, p. 67.
"Went out to sell my birthright." <u>SanFPJ</u> (4:2) 83, p. 22.
"When change threatens rule." <u>SanFPJ</u> (5:1) 83, p. 32.
"When they say cut government waste." <u>SanFPJ</u> (4:2) 83, p. 62.
"When they say oust the bureaucrats." <u>SanFPJ</u> (4:3) 83, p. 57.
"Where there's a glut of oil." <u>SanFPJ</u> (4:2) 83, p. 12.
"Who discovered fire?" <u>SanFPJ</u> (5:2) 83, p. 37.
"Why they hate socialism." <u>SanFPJ</u> (4:4) 83, p. 17.
"World Awry." <u>SanFPJ</u> (5:2) 83, p. 67.
"World War I." <u>SanFPJ</u> (4:4) 83, p. 31.
"The worse the economy gets." <u>SanFPJ</u> (5:1) 83, p. 16.
"You could think of past wars." <u>SanFPJ</u> (5:1) 83, p. 31.

783. COAKLEY, William Leo
"Alderliefest, Poem as Dedication." <u>LittleM</u> (14:1/2) 83, p. 76.
"Obsessions." <u>LittleM</u> (14:1/2) 83, p. 78.
"Pigs Grazing in Tuscany." <u>LittleM</u> (14:1/2) 83, p. 77.
"Processional." <u>LittleM</u> (14:1/2) 83, p. 75.

784. COBLEY, Mark
"The Duel." <u>Bogg</u> (50) 83, p. 43.
"The Ouija Board." <u>Bogg</u> (50) 83, p. 47.

785. COCCIMIGLIO, Vic
"House Keys." <u>MSS</u> (3:1) Aut 83, p. 12.
"Portage." <u>MSS</u> (3:1) Aut 83, p. 13.

786. COCHRAN, Jo
"Another Year's Turning." <u>Cond</u> (9) Spr 83, p. 21.
"A Christmas List." <u>DevQ</u> (18:1) Spr 83, p. 29.
"Laying a Fire." <u>Cond</u> (9) Spr 83, p. 22.
"Letter from Orcas Island." <u>DevQ</u> (17:4) Wint 83, p. 24.
"Letter to Judith." <u>Cond</u> (9) Spr 83, p. 19.
"Morning Etude" (for Judy). <u>Cond</u> (9) Spr 83, p. 23.
"On Display." <u>Cond</u> (9) Spr 83, p. 24-25.
"Solstice Blanc." <u>Cond</u> (9) Spr 83, p. 20.

787. COCHRAN, Leonard
"Club Fighter." <u>SpiritSH</u> (48) 82, p. 18.
"Frames for the Picture." <u>SpiritSH</u> (49) 83, p. 1-8.
"Polonaise." <u>SpiritSH</u> (48) 82, p. 17.
"The Recruit." <u>SpiritSH</u> (48) 82, p. 19.
"The Weaver" (for Seamus Heaney). <u>SpiritSH</u> (48) 82, p. 17.

788. COCHRAN, Sally
"For a Long Time Lover Who Lost Thirty Pounds." YetASM (2:1) 83, p. 3.

789. COCHRANE, Shirley
"Warning in the Mother Tongue." Bogg (50) 83, p. 14.

790. COCKRELL, Doug
"Detective Magazine" (for David Allan Evans). YetASM (2:1) 83, p. 6.
"Hunting at Dusk" (For Dennis Sampson). YetASM (1:1) 82, p. 10.
"So It Goes." YetASM (1:1) 82, p. 14.

791. CODISH, Ed
"Coming Home: Beer Sheva, 1978." Argo (4:1) 82, p. 27.
"Intensive Care." Argo (4:1) 82, p. 26.
"Part of an Elegy for Henry Codish" (1960-1965). Argo (4:2) 82, p. 24-26.

792. COE, Dina
"Approaching the Gorillas." USl (16/17) Wint 83-84, p. 1.

793. COFER, Judith Ortiz
"In Yucatan." SouthernPR (23:2) Aut 83, p. 12-13.
"A Political Poem." SanFPJ (4:3) 83, p. 50.
"Progress Report to a Dead Father." RevChic (11:3/4) 83, p. 45.
"Returning from the Mayan Ruins." SouthernPR (23:2) Aut 83, p. 12.
"Room at the Empire." NewL (50:1) Aut 83, p. 64-65.
"To My Brother, Lately Missed." KanQ (15:1) Wint 83, p. 48.
"The Way My Mother Walked." KanQ (15:1) Wint 83, p. 48.
"What the Gypsy Said to Her Children." RevChic (11:3/4) 83, p. 46.

794. COFFEY, Marilyn
"Ariadne, of Theseus." 13thM (6:1/2) 82, p. 52-53.

795. COFFIN, Edna Amir
"The True Hero of the Aqedah" (tr. of Yehuda Amichai). MichOR (22:3) Sum 83, p. 445.

796. COFFIN, Lyn
"The Armored Girl." Focus (15:95) Ag 83, p. 19.
"Cold Venus at the Typewriter." PoetL (78:3) Aut 83, p. 138.
"Deathbed/Childbed." HolCrit (20:2) Ap 83, p. 18.
"The Empty House." PraS (57:3) Aut 83, p. 74.
"The Ending End." HolCrit (20:5) D 83, p. 18.
"Me and Me." Northeast (Ser. 3:16) Wint 83-84, p. 19.
"An Old Bachelor." KanQ (15:1) Wint 83, p. 23.
"Opium Fields in Time of War." PoetL (78:3) Aut 83, p. 137.
"Pigs on Pilgrimage." Focus (15:95) Ag 83, p. 19.
"The Sea of Children." PraS (57:3) Aut 83, p. 73.

797. COGSWELL, Fred
"At the Crucifixion." PottPort (5) 83-84, p. 20.
"The Dog." Quarry (32:3) Sum 83, p. 8.
"Haiku: In a daisy-field." Waves (11:2/3) Wint 83, p. 59.
"Of All the Forms." PottPort (5) 83-84, p. 14.
"Reverse Illusion." Quarry (32:3) Sum 83, p. 8.
"A Sonnet Is an Easy Poem to Write." CanLit (97) Sum 83, p. 38.
"Vilanelle." Waves (11:2/3) Wint 83, p. 59.

798. COHEN, Arleen
"To the One I Lost." YetASM (1:2) 82, p. 19.

799. COHEN, Helen Degen
"Snow." Prima (8) 83, p. 42.

800. COHEN, Jonathan
"The Filibusters" (tr. of Ernesto Cardenal). AmerPoR (12:3) My-Je 83, p. 18.
"Greytown" (tr. of Ernesto Cardenal). AmerPoR (12:3) My-Je 83, p. 18.
"Johan Roach, Mariner" (tr. of Ernesto Cardenal). AmerPoR (12:3) My-Je 83, p. 18.
"Squier in Nicaragua" (tr. Of Ernesto Cardenal). DevQ (18:3) Aut 83, p. 17-25.

801. COHEN, Marc
"For For Gertrude." DevQ (18:3) Aut 83, p. 90.
"Napoleon's Clock." DevQ (18:3) Aut 83, p. 91.
"Polyrhythms." DevQ (18:3) Aut 83, p. 92-93.
"Seventeen Lines." DevQ (18:3) Aut 83, p. 89.
"Silhouette." Epoch (33:1) Aut-Wint 83, p. 47.

COHEN, Maree Zukor
See: ZUKOR-COHEN, Maree

802. COHEN, Marion
"Archimedes wrote big math in the sand." SanFPJ (4:2) 83, p. 8.
"The army is doing research." SanFPJ (5:1) 83, p. 91.
"Flickering Neon." SanFPJ (5:1) 83, p. 74.
"The Infinite Loop (Dream)." SanFPJ (5:1) 83, p. 46-47.
"Masterpiece." SanFPJ (4:2) 83, p. 6.
"The Middle." SanFPJ (5:1) 83, p. 75.
"The Recent Popular Interest in Thanatology." Abraxas (27/28) 83, p. 19.
"The Road Not Taken." SanFPJ (4:2) 83, p. 72.
"Some Laws of Averages." SanFPJ (4:4) 83, p. 37.
"The Who's Who Poem." SanFPJ (4:3) 83, p. 74-75.
"Why Poetry Is Like Math." SanFPJ (4:4) 83, p. 37.

805. COHEN, Miriam (Miriam A.)
"Close-Up on This World" (For Hector). SanFPJ (5:2) 83, p. 40.
"Diana's Mother Tells Us Again & Again." Sam (36:3 143rd release) 83, p. 40.
"Displaced Frenzy." WormR (23:2, issue 90) 83, p. 74.
"The First of Ron's Vomit Stories" (for r.e.s.).

WormR (23:2, issue 90) 83, p. 74-75.
"Glitz." Bogg (51) 83, p. 28.
"Long Island City, in Queens." SanFPJ (5:2) 83, p. 37.
"Noxious News." SanFPJ (5:2) 83, p. 89.
"Visiting." Sam (34:3 135th release) 83, p. 24.

806. COHEN, Rhea (Rhea L.)
"Mary Cassatt, Pupil of Edgar Degas." PoetL (77:4) Wint 83, p. 204-205.
"My Little Treasure, Is What She Said." Swallow (1) Spr 83, p. 5.

807. COLBY, Joan
"The Attic." Ascent (8:3) 83, p. 47-48.
"Edges." NewRena (16) Spr 83, p. 58-59.
"Fire Eater." PortR (29:1) 83, p. 23.
"Four Seasons of Art." CapeR (19:1) Wint 83, p. 25.
"Math Anxiety." MemphisSR (3:2) Spr 83, p. 14.
"The Snow Poems." StoneC (10:3/4) Spr-Sum 83, p. 31.
"Travel." PortR (29:1) 83, p. 124-125.
"Writing a Poem." PortR (29:1) 83, p. 98-99.

808. COLE, Dave
"Drunk, Parked on His Father's Farm." SoDakR (21:4) Wint 83, p. 41.

809. COLE, Henri
"Of Island Animals." Nat (237:2) 9-16 Jl 83, p. 56.
"Off the Coast of Paradise." Shen (34:1) 83, p. 76-77.

810. COLE, James
"The Colonel." ModernPS (11:3) 83, p. 286-287.
"Coming to a Close in the Morning." MSS (2:3) Sum 83, p. 90-91.
"Educational Foundations, 1942." MSS (2:3) Sum 83, p. 92.

811. COLE, Michael
"Lament As Prelude to a Crime of Passion." HiramPoR (35) Aut-Wint 83, p. 12.

812. COLE, Stephen
"Ecology." Descant (42) Aut 83, p. 15-17.

813. COLEMAN, Wanda
"Ethiopian in the Fuel Supplies." BlackALF (17:4) Wint 83, p. 176.
"El Hajj Malik El-Shabazz." BlackALF (17:4) Wint 83, p. 175.
"Job Hunter." 13thM (7:1/2) 83, p. 67.
"The One Who Can." 13thM (6:1/2) 82, p. 18.
"The Wait." 13thM (6:1/2) 82, p. 19.
"Walkin' Papers Blues (Urban Blues/Jass Series)." 13thM (7:1/2) 83, p. 70.
"Worker (2)." 13thM (7:1/2) 83, p. 68-69.

814. COLES, Don
"He Let Go." Dandel (10:2) Aut-Wint 83, p. 28-29.

815. COLES, Katharine
"Before Parting." QW (16) Spr-Sum 83, p. 65.
"Datura" (On entering the Grand Canyon by moonlight). QW (16) Spr-Sum 83, p. 64.
"Ephemeral." PoetryNW (24:1) Spr 83, p. 45-46.

816. COLINAS, Antonio
"Giacomo Casanova Accepts the Office of Librarian Offered Him in Bohemia by Count Waldstein" (tr. by Anthony Kerrigan). MalR (66) O 83, p. 146.
"To Encounter Ezra Pound -- Posthumous Instructions" (tr. by Anthony Kerrigan). MalR (66) O 83, p. 145.

817. COLLIER, Michael
"Air Guitar." Ploughs (9:1) 83, p. 120-122.
"The Clasp." Agni (19) 83, p. 94.
"White Strawberries." NewRep (187:6) 9 Ag 82, p. 34.

818. COLLIER, Phyllis Herron
"Continuing." Nimrod (27:1) Aut-Wint 83, p. 51.
"Continuing" (recipient, Pablo Neruda Prize for Poetry). Nimrod (27:1) Aut-Wint 83, p. 46-53.
"A Harvest of Dreams." Nimrod (27:1) Aut-Wint 83, p. 46-47.
"Independence." Nimrod (27:1) Aut-Wint 83, p. 48-49.
"Letter to Hugo, with Feathers." Nimrod (27:1) Aut-Wint 83, p. 47-48.
"Reading the Letter." Nimrod (27:1) Aut-Wint 83, p. 51-53.
"Returning." Nimrod (27:1) Aut-Wint 83, p. 46.
"Three Aunts." Nimrod (27:1) Aut-Wint 83, p. 50.

819. COLLIER, Phyllis K.
"Crossing Over." WindO (43) Wint 83, p. 14.
"Trail No. 3256." WindO (43) Wint 83, p. 13.

820. COLLIGAN, Gretchen
"The Favor." IndR (6:2) Spr 83, p. 76.
"Suicide in White." IndR (5:2) Sum 82, p. 78.
"Taking Down the Tulip Poplar." IndR (5:2) Sum 82, p. 79.

821. COLLINGS, Michael R.
"Earth Mother." SanFPJ (5:1) 83, p. 61.
"It must have been silent that night." SanFPJ (4:4) 83, p. 8.
"Migration." SanFPJ (5:2) 83, p. 32.
"Rain shatters into small-pox scars." SanFPJ (4:4) 83, p. 32.
"Sitting on a Rock to Watch the Dawn." SanFPJ (4:4) 83, p. 73.
"Spring Showers." SanFPJ (4:4) 83, p. 73.

822. COLLINS, Denise A.
"Anger." USl (16/17) Wint 83-84, p. 9.
"Green." USl (16/17) Wint 83-84, p. 9.

823. COLLINS, Floyd
"Keepers of the Gate." CharR (9:1) Spr 83, p. 30-32.

824. COLLINS, Jeffrey
"Last Words of a Zen Fool." Poem (49) N 83, p. 12-13.
"On the Launching of Columbia." SanFPJ (4:3) 83, p. 22.
"Responsible Gardening." Poem (49) N 83, p. 11.

825. COLLINS, Martha
"April." WestB (13) 83, p. 5-11.
"Blue Roses." MassR (24:1) Spr 83, p. 177-178.
"Epiphany." Field (29) Aut 83, p. 68-69.
"Poem in Five Places." WestB (12) 83, p. 12-13.
"Prologue" (after Pissarro). Epoch (32:3) Spr-Sum 83, p. 243.
"Running Your Own Race." DevQ (18:1) Spr 83, p. 38.
"The Smallest Song." PraS (51:1, i.e. 57:1) Spr 83, p. 92.

826. COLLINS, Michael N.
"Into the Trees." Wind (13:47) 83, p. 10.
"Vision at Breakfast." Wind (13:47) 83, p. 10.

827. COLON, Salvador
"Aquí estoy de nuevo ante ti." Areíto (9:33) 83, p. 22.

828. COLON SANTIAGO, José Luis
"Ahora que penetro ese rincón de tu alma alfabética." Rácata (1) 83, p. 46-47.
"Con el pedernal azteca." Rácata (1) 83, p. 49.
"Conocí" (a Félix Rivera). Rácata (1) 83, p. 48.
"Estercolera" (a los dientes de leche de Arnaldo, Laura y Pupito). Rácata (2) 83, p. 41-43.
"El lugar común no es la flota británica." Rácata (2) 83, p. 46.
"Ojos y Rafael Catalá." Rácata (2) 83, p. 39-40.
"Quizás ahora no nos vemos los ojos" (a robertolouis lugo). Rácata (2) 83, p. 44-45.
"Tiro esta comarca de valores" (A Lucy Matos). Rácata (1) 83, p. 45.

829. COLSON, Theodore
"Snowshoeing by the First Loyalist Burial Ground." PottPort (5) 83-84, p. 32.

830. COMANN, Brad
"On the Tradition of Misdirecting Travelers." GeoR (37:4) Wint 83, p. 742.

831. COMBS, Bruce
"At Forty." Wind (13:49) 83, p. 14.
"Boogie." YetASM (2:1) 83, p. 12.

COMTE, Edward le
See: Le COMTE, Edward

832. CONDE, Carmen
"At the Sea" (tr. by José R. de Armas and Alexis Levitin). LitR (27:1) Aut 83, p. 101-102.
"A Curse on Old Age" (tr. by José R. de Armas and

Alexis Levitin). LitR (27:1) Aut 83, p. 100.
"Drought" (tr. by José R. de Armas and Alexis Levitin). LitR (27:1) Aut 83, p. 101.

833. CONN, Jan (Jan E.)
"Blue Bulls." Germ (7:1) Spr-Sum 83, p. 37.
"Cottonwood." Germ (7:1) Spr-Sum 83, p. 36.
"The End of October." Germ (7:1) Spr-Sum 83, p. 35.
"In the Spotlight of Sun" (after July's People by Nadine Gordimer). CrossC (5:2/3) 83, p. 30.
"Parable of Water." Germ (7:1) Spr-Sum 83, p. 32.
"Voice." Germ (7:1) Spr-Sum 83, p. 33.
"Where No Stars Appear." Germ (7:1) Spr-Sum 83, p. 34.

834. CONNELL, Kim
"On Chasing Younger Girls." KanQ (15:2) Spr 83, p. 79.

835. CONNELLAN, Leo
"Motel." NewEngR (6:2) Wint 83, p. 275-279.

836. CONNOR, Jean L.
"Haiku for a Summer Place." Blueline (3:2) Wint-Spr 82, p. 43.

837. CONNORS, Bruton
"With the Logic of Voltaire." Bogg (51) 83, p. 52.

838. CONOVER, Carl
"Chopin's Old Clothes." PoetL (78:2) Sum 83, p. 100.
"Postcard from Paramaribo." Outbr (12/13) Aut 83-Spr 84, p. 63.

839. CONRAD, Cherry
"Betrayal." Tendril (16) Sum 83, p. 21.
"Why I Bought You a Globe Instead of a Remote Control Corvette." Tendril (16) Sum 83, p. 22.

840. CONROY, James V.
"Coffee on Tuesday." YetASM (1:2) 82, p. 12.
"A Nondescription." YetASM (1:2) 82, p. 15.

841. CONTOSKI, Victor
"A Dream of Reverend Jim Jones." PoNow (7:2, #38) 83, p. 43.
"Hitting My Thumb with a Hammer." SouthernPR (23:2) Aut 82 [i.e. (23:1?) Spr 83], p. 70.
"Lecture." SouthernPR (23:2) Aut 82 [i.e. (23:1?) Spr 83], p. 69.
"The Message." NewL (49:3/4) Spr-Sum 83, p. 255.
"Suing a Politician." Abraxas (27/28) 83, p. 38.
"Unhappy Couple." NewL (49:3/4) Spr-Sum 83, p. 255.
"The Wolves of My Childhood." Kayak (61) Ap 83, p. 57.

842. CONTRAIRE, A. U.
"Critiquing the haiku." WindO (43) Wint 83, p. 32.
"Going out into the autumn's darkness." WindO (43) Wint 83, p. 32.

"Minding the cat." WindO (43) Wint 83, p. 32.
"The moon above your house too." WindO (43) Wint 83, p. 32.
"Not good enough to be loved." WindO (43) Wint 83, p. 32.
"Remembering last night's full sky of stars." WindO (43) Wint 83, p. 32.
"Sidewalk pools." WindO (43) Wint 83, p. 32.
"Three brothers leaving the movie." WindO (43) Wint 83, p. 32.
"The weather breaking above freezing." WindO (43) Wint 83, p. 32.

843. CONWAY, Mark
"New Liberty." DekalbLAJ (16:1/4) Aut 82-Sum 83, p. 60-61.

844. CONWAY, Rosalind Eve
"Crossing Nathan Philips Square." PoetryCR (5:2) Wint 83-84, p. 20.
"Doing Dishes." PoetryCR (5:2) Wint 83-84, p. 20.
"For Judith." PoetryCR (5:2) Wint 83-84, p. 20.
"A Man Scheduled to Die" (for Charlie Brooks). PoetryCR (5:2) Wint 83-84, p. 20.
"Sashay." PoetryCR (5:2) Wint 83-84, p. 20.

845. COOK, Donald J.
"Across the breadth of two bodies." YetASM (1:2) 82, p. 15.
"My hands move across your face." YetASM (1:2) 82, p. 13.

846. COOK, Gregory M.
"Below the Willow" (from a work in progress, My Diary of Earth, 1985). CrossC (5:4) 83, p. 7.
"Hot Arcs" (from a work in progress, Love en Route). PoetryCR (4:3) Spr 83, p. 12.

847. COOK, Jeanne
"The Cipher" (tr. of Jorge Louis Borges, w. Anthony Kerrigan). MalR (66) O 83, p. 147.

848. COOKSHAW, Marlene
"11:11 pm." Quarry (32:3) Sum 83, p. 12-13.
"After Resnais' Night and Fog." AntigR (52) Wint 83, p. 37.
"Coats #10 Chain." AntigR (52) Wint 83, p. 36.
"Late in the Afternoon While the Clouds Turn Lavender." Quarry (32:3) Sum 83, p. 11-12.
"Tracks." AntigR (52) Wint 83, p. 37.

849. COOLEY, Peter
"Attic Vase: Woman and Nurse at a Child's Tomb." MidwQ (25:1) Aut 83, p. 49.
"Certain Stars" (Honorable Mention Poem, 1982/83). KanQ (15:1) Wint 83, p. 20.
"Crepuscular Metaphysics." Telescope (4) Wint 83, back cover.
"Entracte." Telescope (4) Wint 83, p. 7.
"The Friend." MidwQ (25:1) Aut 83, p. 47.

"Frog Hunting." YaleR (72:2) Wint 83, p. 262.
"He." KanQ (15:1) Wint 83, p. 20-21.
"The History of Poetry." Ploughs (9:2/3) 83, p. 19.
"Nightfall." SouthernR (19:1) Ja 83, p. 156.
"Perish Twice." DekalbLAJ (16:1/4) Aut 82-Sum 83, p. 61.
"Psalm" (for Alissa). MemphisSR (1:2) Spr 81, p. 20.
"Song of the Drowned Man." ThRiPo (21/22) 83, p. 18-19.
"To My Daughter." MidwQ (25:1) Aut 83, p. 48.
"To the Stillborn." MissouriR (7:1) Aut 83, p. 16.
"The Untitled Poem." MemphisSR (1:2) Spr 81, p. 21.
"Waking in the Country." SouthernR (19:1) Ja 83, p. 157.

850. COON, Betty
"Mulleins." Calyx (7:3) Sum 83, p. 25.

851. COONS, Alice
"Be My Friend." Meadows (3:1) 82, p. 14.
"A Moment in Time." Meadows (3:1) 82, p. 39.
"Ruby Lake." Meadows (4:1) 83, p. 27.
"Sanctuary." Meadows (4:1) 83, p. 54.
"To Suzie." Meadows (3:1) 82, p. 39.

852. COOP, Mahlon"
"Slowpitch Softball." KanQ (15:3) Sum 83, p. 6.

853. COOPER, Allan
"The Arrow." PottPort (5) 83-84, p. 12.
"The Final Gesture" (for Alden Nowlan). PottPort (5) 83-84, p. 12.
"Men and Ship" (from cover of Kayak 57). Kayak (62) Ag 83, p. 31.
"The Sisters" (from cover of Kayak 58). Kayak (62) Ag 83, p. 31.
"The Windmill" (from cover of Kayak 54). Kayak (62) Ag 83, p. 31.

854. COOPER, Jane (See also: COOPER, Jane Todd)
"Threads: Rosa Luxemburg from Prison" (Selection: "Part I. Wronke, Spring 1917). NewEng (5:4) Sum 83, p. 551-552.

855. COOPER, Jane Todd (See also: COOPER, Jane)
"Circus Child." Gargoyle (22/23) 83, p. 14-15.
"Fast Roads." Wind (13:49) 83, p. 15.

856. COOPER, Pat
"There Are No Trains or Lovers in This Poem" (in answer to Cathryn Hankla). Outbr (12/13) Aut 83-Spr 84, p. 45.

857. COOPER, Wyn
"Marriage." BlackWR (10:1) Aut 83, p. 95.

858. COOPERMAN, Robert
"Here in Denver." KanQ (15:1) Wint 83, p. 60-61.
"The Jews of K'ai-feng." ConcPo (16:1) Spr 83, p. 86.
"Poem for My Father." KanQ (15:1) Wint 83, p. 60.

859. COPE, Wendy
"The Lavatory Attendant." Agni (18) 83, p. 45.
"Mr. Strugnell." Agni (18) 83, p. 44.
"On Finding an Old Photograph." Agni (18) 83, p. 41.
"A Policeman's Lot" (after W. S. Gilbert). Agni (18) 83, p. 42-43.
"Strugnell's Sonnets" (Selections: i-iii) (for D. M. Thomas). Agni (18) 83, p. 46-47.

860. CORBETT, William
"South End Boston Thirteen Years Later." LittleBR (4:2) Wint 83-84, p. 42.

861. CORBIN, Richard
"On Composing a Poem." EngJ (72:2) F 83, p. 82.

862. CORCORAN, Martha B.
"I Left the Window Curtain." CapeR (18:2) Sum 83, p. 29.
"She Keeps Three Clocks, Henny Litten." CapeR (18:2) Sum 83, p. 28.

863. CORDING, Robert
"Bus Ride Back." MSS (2:3) Sum 83, p. 139-143.
"Darwin Recalls the Rain Forest of Brazil." OntR (19) Aut-Wint 83-84, p. 46-47.
"The Limits of Decision." MSS (2:3) Sum 83, p. 144.
"Linnaeus: In the Garden at Uppsala." OntR (19) Aut-Wint 83-84, p. 48-49.
"Rambler Roses." OW (16) Spr-Sum 83, p. 126-127.

864. COREY, Stephen
"The Birth of Christ." KanQ (15:4) Aut 83, p. 65.
"Bread" (for Susan). GeoR (37:3) Aut 83, p. 660-661.
"Georgia O'Keeffe's 'Blue Morning Glories, New Mexico, II'." Swallow (2) Aut-Wint 83, p. 103.
"The Uselessness of American Counties." Poetry (141:5) F 83, p. 264.

865. CORKERY, Christopher Jane
"Orphan's Song." Ploughs (9:1) 83, p. 175.
"Some Things a Prisoner Knew." Poetry (141:6) Mr 83, p. 339.

866. CORLISS, Frank
"In Polish" (to Ms. Lucienne Rey, tr. of Jerzy Ficowski). Os (17) 83, p. 10-11.
"Oh Vision of Snow" (to Bieta, tr. of Jerzy Ficowski). Os (17) 83, p. 16-17.
"Recipe" (tr. of Jerzy Ficowski). Os (17) 83, p. 5.

867. CORMAN, Cid
"Cahoots" (Excerpts). Poetry (141:5) F 83, p. 259-260.

868. CORN, Alfred
"Dora Markus" (tr. of Eugenio Montale). ParisR (25:88) Sum 83, p. 61-62.
"Notes from a Child of Paradise" (Selections: XI, XIII, XXIII, XXIX). Hudson (36:4) Wint 83-84,

p. 629-632.
"Notes from a Child of Paradise" (Selection: XXVI). PartR (50:3) 83, p. 411-412.
"Prayer to Aphrodite" (tr. of Sappho). ParisR (25:88) Sum 83, p. 60.

869. CORNBERG, David
"Ago This Shimmering." StoneC (10:3/4) Spr-Sum 83, p. 49.

870. CORNELL, Brian R.
"In a Letter from Home #2." PottPort (5) 83-84, p. 36.
"The Shell." AntigR (55) Aut 83, p. 92.

871. CORNETT, Michael
"All Hallows Eve." Argo (4:3) 83, p. 34-35.

872. CORNING, Howard McKinley
"Footprints on Memaloose" (Excerpt). SoDakR (21:4) Wint 83, p. 17.

873. CORRIGAN, John
"Bringing You Home." Wind (13:49) 83, p. 16.
"Morning Photographs." Wind (13:49) 83, p. 16-17.

874. CORRIGAN, Paul
"During the Fall Turnover." Blueline (4:1) Sum-Aut 82, p. 39.
"The Poem As a Valuable Fur Bearing Animal." Blueline (4:1) Sum-Aut 82, p. 19.

875. CORRIGAN, Winifred
"A Dream." SpiritSH (48) 82, p. 40.
"Lost Drachma" (Lk 15:8-10). SpiritSH (48) 82, p. 41-42.

876. CORSE, Jennifer
"Panic." SenR (13:2) 82-83, p. 52.

877. CORSERI, Gary Steven
"Four Thousand Days and Nights" (tr. of Ryuuichi Tamura, w. Takuro Ikeda). WebR (8:1) Spr 83, p. 48.

878. CORTRIGHT, Debbi L.
"Wardrobe." SmPd (20:1) Wint 83, p. 14.

879. COSIER, Tony
"The Dayspring." WritersL Jl 83, p. 26.
"Storr Rock." Wind (13:48) 83, p. 10.
"The Water Hole." Dandel (10:1) Spr-Sum 83, p. 42.

880. COSKRAN, Kathleen
"Satellite Robot: Landsat 4." SanFPJ (5:2) 83, p. 44.

881. COSNER, John
"Guns 'n Butter." SanFPJ (5:2) 83, p. 25.

882. COSTA, Florence da
"The Queen of Dreams, Fearing." Argo (4:3) 83, p. 29.

883. COSTA, Teresa-Marta
"On the Road." Bogg (50) 83, p. 10.

884. COSTANZO, Gerald
"Dinosaurs of the Hollywood Delta." KanQ (15:4) Aut 83, p. 131-132.
"Houdini Disappearing in Philadelphia." PoNow (7:2, #38) 83, p. 9.
"Living the Good Life on the San Andreas Fault." MemphisSR (1:2) Spr 81, p. 15.
"The Poem about Blue Loons." OhioR (30) 83, p. 199.

885. COSTANZO, Gerald, ed.
"Three Rivers, Ten Years: an Anthology of Poems from Three Rivers Poetry Journal." (Pittsburgh: Carnegie-Mellon University Press, 1983). Special issue of ThRiPo (21/22) 83, p. 1-104.

886. COTT, Jonathan
"Childhood." ParisR (25:90) Wint 83, p. 61.
"Here, There, Everywhere." ParisR (25:90) Wint 83, p. 61.

887. COTTERILL, Sarah
"Airletter to Demeter." Nimrod (27:1) Aut-Wint 83, p. 73.
"Harvest Songs" (adapted from the Quechua). CarolQ (35:3) Spr 83, p. 50-51.
"Leaving Wisconsin for New York in the Sixth Month." Nimrod (27:1) Aut-Wint 83, p. 74.
"Tobit." Nimrod (27:1) Aut-Wint 83, p. 75.

888. COTTINGHAM, Michael James
"Glass of Time" (A poem from the diary of a time traveler). SanFPJ (5:4) 83, p. 8.

889. COUCH, Larry
"Crossword Puzzle." PoetL (77:3) Aut 82, p. 139.
"Disappearance." PoetL (77:3) Aut 82, p. 139.
"The Newspaper." PoetL (77:3) Aut 82, p. 138.
"The Suit." Vis (13) 83, p. 11.

890. COULETTE, Henri
"The Extras." Iowa (13:3/4) Spr 82 (83), p. 63-64.
"The Invisible Father." Iowa (13:3/4) Spr 82 (83), p. 67.
"Life with Mother." Iowa (13:3/4) Spr 82 (83), p. 68-69.
"Night Thoughts" (in memory of David Kubal). Iowa (13:3/4) Spr 82 (83), p. 130.
"Night Watch." Iowa (13:3/4) Spr 82 (83), p. 74-75.
"Petition." Iowa (13:3/4) Spr 82 (83), p. 131.
"The War of the Secret Agents" (Excerpt: XVII. "Epilogue: Author to Reader"). Iowa (13:3/4) Spr 82 (83), p. 72.

891. COUNTESS, Kathleen
"Jeanne d'Arc, Burned May 30, 1431." WindO (42) Sum 83, p. 5.
"Rocking-Chair Love." WindO (42) Sum 83, p. 5.

892. COURTNEY, Barbara
"Brief Encounter." CrabCR (1:2) Aut 83, p. 10.
"Found in the University Calendar: 'David Odden Presents a Colloquium on Sanskrit Diaspirate Again." CrabCR (1:1) My 83, p. 12.
"If You Had Six White Marbles and Six Black Marbles in Your Pocket, How Many Marbles Should You Take Out to Make Sure You Have at Least One of Each Color?" PoetryNW (24:3) Aut 83, p. 12-14.

893. COURTOISIE, Rafael
"Redoble Solo." Areito (9:35) 83, p. 37.

894. COUTO, Iremelind-Elisabeth
"Centering." PoetryCR (4:3) Spr 83, p. 15.

895. COUTO, Nancy Lee
"Broiled Haddock." PoetryNW (24:3) Aut 83, p. 33.
"Candomblé." MinnR (NS 20) Spr 83, p. 49-50.
"Irijay." PoetryNW (24:3) Aut 83, p. 30-33.
"Metempsychosis, for Aunt Susanna" (Second Award Poem, 1982/83). KanQ (15:1) Wint 83, p. 8.

896. COVINO, Michael
"You Are Here." IndR (5:2) Sum 82, p. 58-59.

897. COWELL, Bille
"The Night Cafe." Vis (13) 83, p. 9.

898. COWING, Sheila
"Versed in Country Things" (from The Round Shape of the Air, finalist, 10th anniversary manuscript competition). StoneC (11:1/2, Pt. 1) Aut-Wint 83, p. 48.
"What Happened to the Parents" (from The Round Shape of the Air, finalist, 10th anniversary manuscript competition). StoneC (11:1/2, Pt. 1) Aut-Wint 83, p. 49.

899. COX, C. B.
"The Bard at Madurai." Hudson (36:4) Wint 83-84, p. 627-628.
"Lord Ganesh." Hudson (36:4) Wint 83-84, p. 625-626.
"Nek Chand." Hudson (36:4) Wint 83-84, p. 623-625.
"Passages to India" (for Martin Banham and Yasmeen Lukmani). Hudson (36:4) Wint 83-84, p. 623-628.

900. COX, Carol
"Anxious for Failure." Ploughs (9:2/3) 83, p. 175-176.

901. COX, Jenny
"Before Rain." HarvardA (117:1) Mr 83, p. 20.

902. COX, M. V.
"Inheritance." SanFPJ (4:3) 83, p. 24.
"Migration." SanFPJ (4:3) 83, p. 21.

903. COX, Terrance
"The Beatles on Ed Sullivan" (for Debbie McConnell Dalgleish, May 12/80). Quarry (32:3) Sum 83, p. 46.
"The Five W's" (for Mahao Letsoela). Grain (11:3) Ag 83, p. 22-23.
"Rear WindoW Vision." Grain (11:1) F 83, p. 34.

904. COXE, Louis
"Constellation." NoAmR (268:2) Je 83, p. 29.
"Home from the Hill." YaleR (72:4) Sum 83, p. 600.
"Nightsong." YaleR (72:4) Sum 83, p. 600.

905. CRAIG, Connie
"For Melvin." SanFPJ (5:3) 83, p. 25.

906. CRAIG, David
"God Helps Those" (Roanoke, VA. March '82). SanFPJ (4:4) 83, p. 32.
"Spanish Walk." Wind (13:48) 83, p. 11.

907. CRAIGIE, Barbara
"Minuscule Memoirs." KanQ (15:3) Sum 83, p. 94.

908. CRAMER, Steven
"Backyards, 1959, 1971, 1953, 1942." Ploughs (9:1) 83, p. 129-130.
"Freud's Desk, Vienna, 1938." Ploughs (9:1) 83, p. 125-126.
"Homage to C.P. Cavafy." Ploughs (9:1) 83, p. 127-128.

909. CRASE, Douglas
"Once the Sole Province." Epoch (33:1) Aut-Wint 83, p. 49-50.
"The Revisionist" (Excerpts). NewRep (186:15) 14 Ap 82, p. 37.

910. CRAWFORD, John
"Desert." YetASM (1:1) 82, p. 12.

911. CRAWFORD, Tom
"Gray Lodge." PoetryE (12) Aut 83, p. 54.
"Mourning for Rue" (for Jim Stober). PoetryE (12) Aut 83, p. 56.
"Rain." PoetryE (12) Aut 83, p. 55.

912. CREELEY, Robert
"All the Way." AmerPoR (12:3) My-Je 83, p. 24.
"Be of Good Cheer." AmerPoR (12:3) My-Je 83, p. 24.
"Buffalo Evening." AmerPoR (12:3) My-Je 83, p. 24.
"Coming Home." AmerPoR (12:3) My-Je 83, p. 24.
"Question." AmerPoR (12:3) My-Je 83, p. 24.
"Rachel Had Said" (for R.G.). AmerPoR (12:3) My-Je 83, p. 23.
"Such Flowers." AmerPoR (12:3) My-Je 83, p. 24.

913. CREESE, Richard
"Hopi Inscape" (On a piece of "Yellow Sand" pottery by Robert Silas). PortR (29:1) 83, p. 107-108.

914. CRENNER, James
"Odds." CarolQ (35:3) Spr 83, p. 63.

915. CREW, Louie
"Ancient Inhospitality." Argo (4:2) 82, p. 11.

916. CREWE, Jennifer
"Stomboli." PoetC (15:1) Aut 83, p. 15.

917. CREWS, Jacquelyn
"Backdrop for Sketches." Tendril (14/15) Wint 83, p. 35.
"Stories Without a Plot." Tendril (14/15) Wint 83, p. 36.

918. CREWS, Judson
"The Clock of Moss or Else a Compass." PoNow (7:2, #38) 83, p. 9.
"Have You." PoNow (7:2, #38) 83, p. 9.
"He Was Drunk, Not On." PoNow (7:2, #38) 83, p. 9.
"How Many Bright, Darting." PoNow (7:2, #38) 83, p. 9.
"I Did Not." Abraxas (27/28) 83, p. 23.
"If I Had Sorted Out All the Quietness." BelPoJ (33:3) Spr 83, p. 7.
"In Fact." SecC (11:1/2) 83, p. 33.
"There Were Other Places We Had." BelPoJ (33:3) Spr 83, p. 7.

919. CRISP, Greg
"The Book." MemphisSR (4:1) Aut 83, p. 41.

920. CRIST, Vonnie
"Ptolemy Was Mistaken." SanFPJ (4:4) 83, p. 25-26.

921. CROCKER, Jean-Marie J.
"Saratoga Winter." Blueline (3:2) Wint-Spr 82, p. 10.

922. CROCKETT, Eleanor E.
"Cigarette Girl." Gargoyle (22/23) 83, p. 58.

923. CROCKETT-SMITH, D. L.
"Prelude to Summer." MinnR (NS 21) Aut 83, p. 22.

924. CROFT, Sally
"The Dream Garden." KanQ (15:2) Spr 83, p. 181.
"A Woman and Her Wolf Soapstone Carving from the Ural Mountains." PortR (29:1) 83, p. 82.

925. CROLLE, Kim
"An Individual." YetASM (1:2) 82, p. 17.

926. CROMWELL, Dwain
"Night Song." Swallow (1) Spr 83, p. 37.

927. CRONYN, Hume
"The Discarded Glove." Kayak (61) Ap 83, p. 17.
"Dream Room." Kayak (61) Ap 83, p. 18.
"In the Dominic Eliot Clock Shop." Kayak (61) Ap 83, p. 19.

928. CROOKER, Barbara
"Fever." WestB (13) 83, p. 41.

929. CROUCH, Annette S.
"Real Dreams." WritersL Ja 83, p. 18.
"Since Our Beginnings." WritersL Jl 83, p. 20.
"Writer's Game." WritersL F 83, p. 8.

930. CROW, Mary
"Fever." MassR (24:1) Spr 83, p. 31-32.
"Shopping in Santiago." MassR (24:1) Spr 83, p. 30-31.
"Stilts." Sam (36:3 143rd release) 83, p. 53.
"Valle del Encanto." Sam (36:3 143rd release) 83, p. 24-25.

931. CROWN, Lynne
"Peace: Act One." SanFPJ (5:3) 83, p. 42-43.

932. CRUMMETT, Vance
"Passing." NewL (50:1) Aut 83, p. 90.
"Traces of a Different Spring." NewL (50:1) Aut 83, p. 91.
"The Wreckage of Autumn." NewL (50:1) Aut 83, p. 90.

933. CRUSZ, Rienzi
"All I Ask Is My Life." Descant (43) Wint 83-84, p. 59.
"The Art of Self-Deception." Descant (43) Wint 83-84, p. 55.
"A Door Ajar to Eden or Cathay--Elizabeth Jennings." Descant (43) Wint 83-84, p. 52.
"Elegy for the Unfinished Poem" (for Ramesh). Descant (43) Wint 83-84, p. 54.
"In a Weathervane Idiom." Descant (43) Wint 83-84, p. 51.
"Mayaro Sea Sculpture." Descant (43) Wint 83-84, p. 53.
"On the Beach." Descant (43) Wint 83-84, p. 56.
"Poem in Peacock Blue." Descant (43) Wint 83-84, p. 57-58.

934. CRUZ, Fermín
"Cenoví de Sonrisa Triste." Rácata (1) 83, p. 54-56.
"Hacia el Campanario." Rácata (1) 83, p. 53.
"Persisto." Rácata (1) 83, p. 52.

935. CRYER, Jim
"Moonlit night: Hearing at the Wine Shop Accompaniment to my Lute" (tr. of Li Po). CarolQ (35:3) Spr 83, p. 30.
"Song of the Women of Yueh 5" (tr. of Li Po). CarolQ (35:3) Spr 83, p. 29.

"To a Friend" (tr. of Li Po). CarolQ (35:3) Spr 83, p. 28.

936. CSOORI, Sandor
"In the Bright Night" (tr. by Nicholas Kolumban). Abraxas (27/28) 83, p. 7.
"Poland" (tr. by Nicholas Kolumban). Abraxas (27/28) 83, p. 6.

937. CUDNEY, Bruce
"Closing." AntigR (55) Aut 83, p. 30.
"It Mocks Me." AntigR (55) Aut 83, p. 30.
"Sand Boxes." WritersL Je 83, p. 5.

938. CUELHO, Art
"Christmas Day." SecC (11:1/2) 83, p. 34.
"Whiskey and Maggie's Cries." ClockR (1:1) Sum 83, p. 55.

939. CULLUM, J. W.
"The Eucharist of the Holy Ghost at Key West." Poetry (141:4) Ja 83, p. 225-227.

940. CULVER, Marjorie
"Turn West at Jefferson." DekalbLAJ (16:1/4) Aut 82-Sum 83, p. 62-63.

941. CUMBA, David
"Cimarrón." Rácata (2) 83, p. 51.
"El gato latiga el rabo." Rácata (2) 83, p. 48.
"Guerrilla Spik." Rácata (2) 83, p. 47.
"Pájaro Náufrago." Rácata (2) 83, p. 49.
"Playerurgia." Rácata (2) 83, p. 50.

942. CUMMINGS, Darcy
"Swinging into the Light" (for Janis Somerville). CarolQ (35:2) Wint 83, p. 19.

943. CURIS, Antonio
"Con los Pies Fríos." Rácata (1) 83, p. 61.
"Esta Tarde María está Muriéndose." Rácata (2) 83, p. 54.
"Estos Ultimos Meses." Rácata (2) 83, p. 56.
"Hablando de las Musas" (a Rafael Catalá quien me enseñó por segunda vez que a las musas se les trae a tirones desde el clítoris). Rácata (1) 83, p. 58-59.
"Paréntesis del Alma." Rácata (2) 83, p. 53.
"Penetrarte." Rácata (2) 83, p. 55.
"Poema No Poema." Rácata (1) 83, p. 57.
"Sobre los Semáforos." Rácata (1) 83, p. 60.
"Soy un Ser Peligroso." Rácata (2) 83, p. 52.

944. CURLEY, Daniel
"Your Special Chair." NewL (49:3/4) Spr-Sum 83, p. 271.

945. CURRIE, John
"Insomnia." Iowa (13:3/4) Spr 82 (83), p. 125-126.

946. CURTIS, Michael
"Icarus in the Hills." Argo (4:3) 83, p. 30-31.
"The Mind Is Its Own Place." Argo (4:1) 82, p. 19.

947. CURTIS, Redmond
"Another Prufrock." AntigR (54) Sum 83, p. 79.
"Sophistication." AntigR (54) Sum 83, p. 78.

948. CURTIS, Tony
"Letting Go." Kayak (61) Ap 83, p. 36.
"Spring Fed." Kayak (61) Ap 83, p. 37.

949. CUSHING, Gloria Lane
"Kairos." ChrC (100:37) 7 D 83, p. 1132.

950. CUSHMAN, Kim
"Croatoan." CapeR (19:1) Wint 83, p. 35.
"On the Flandre Again." CapeR (19:1) Wint 83, p. 34.

951. CUTHBERT, T. D.
"Maybe you did not know the birds were all dead." Bogg (51) 83, p. 50.

952. CUTLER, Bruce
"Going Blind." BlackWR (10:1) Aut 83, p. 139.
"The Streets of La Paz." KanQ (15:2) Spr 83, p. 52-53.
"A Way of Seeing." BlackWR (10:1) Aut 83, p. 136-138.
"Your Eye." KanQ (15:2) Spr 83, p. 52.

953. CYR, Gilles
"Extraits d'après Parole." Os (16) 83, p. 2.

954. CZAPLA, Cathy Young
"Below Zero." Sam (35:3 139th release) 83, p. 11.
"Borderlands." Sam (35:3 139th release) 83, p. 3.
"Drilling near Champlain." Sam (35:3 139th release) 83, p. 6.
"Early Winter." Blueline (4:2) Wint-Spr 83, p. 30.
"Early Winter." Sam (35:3 139th release) 83, p. 4.
"Genetic Memories." Sam (35:3 139th release) 83, p. 2.
"Genetic Memories" (issue title). Sam (35:3 139th release) 83, p. 1-12.
"Killing Frost." Sam (35:3 139th release) 83, p. 5.
"Metromail: 2 Job Descriptions." Sam (36:3 143rd release) 83, p. 56.
"Quarry Hill." Blueline (3:2) Wint-Spr 82, p. 34.
"Quarry Hill." Sam (35:3 139th release) 83, p. 9.
"Refugees." Sam (35:3 139th release) 83, p. 10.
"Roaring Brook." Sam (35:3 139th release) 83, p. 7.
"Survivors." Sam (35:3 139th release) 83, p. 8.
"Woods-Runners." Sam (35:3 139th release) 83, p. 12.

955. CZERNIAWSKI, Adam
"Once in a While" (for Mieczyslaw Jastrun, tr. of Leopold Staff). Stand (24:1) 82-83, p. 7.
"Rowan" (tr. of Leopold Staff). Stand (24:1) 82-83, p. 7.

956. CZUMA, Michael
"Notes for Pat." Quarry (32:3) Sum 83, p. 35-38.

Da COSTA, Florence
See: COSTA, Florence da

957. DABNEY, Janice (Janice V.)
"Bacon." Blueline (3:2) Wint-Spr 82, p. 31.
"Bells." CapeR (18:2) Sum 83, p. 33.
"Nesting Time." CapeR (18:2) Sum 83, p. 32.
"On Learning That Falling in Love May Temporarily Cure a Migraine" (for C.R.). YetASM (1:1) 82, p. 8.

958. DABNEY, Stuart
"Divorce." Ploughs (9:2/3) 83, p. 164.
"We Never Close." Ploughs (9:2/3) 83, p. 163.

959. DABYDEEN, Cyril
"For Christl." WritersL O 83, p. 9.

960. DACEY, Florence
"Waltz with Me, Frankenstein." PoNow (7:2, #38) 83, p. 22.

961. DACEY, Philip
"Cottonwood Poem." SoDakR (21:4) Wint 83, p. 33.
"The Haircut." Vis (12) 83, p. 32.
"The Hitchhiker." PoetryNW (24:2) Sum 83, p. 6-7.
"The Laughter of the Gods." Tele (18) 83, p. 13.
"The Man of Capernaum (Mark ii, 1-12): Hopkins Prepares His Sermon for October 5, 1879." MemphisSR (1:2) Spr 81, p. 42.
"The Office Manager Locking Up." MemphisSR (1:2) Spr 81, p. 43.
"On Not Going to See the Movie about a Nuclear Holocaust's Aftermath." NewL (50:1) Aut 83, p. 99.
"Pac-Man." PoetryNW (24:2) Sum 83, p. 7-8.
"Poem in Three Parts." Outbr (12/13) Aut 83-Spr 84, p. 95.
"The Usher." PoNow (7:2, #38) 83, p. 16.
"Walking among the Ruins." PoetryNW (24:2) Sum 83, p. 5-6.

962. DAIGON, Ruth
"And the Blind" (from The Cold Touch of Time, semi-finalist, 10th anniversary manuscript competition). StoneC (11:1/2, Pt. 1) Aut-Wint 83, p. 60.
"The Simple Life." PoNow (7:2, #38) 83, p. 36.
"Since Our Dog Died." YetASM (1:1) 82, p. 15.
"Slow Return." StoneC (10:3/4) Spr-Sum 83, p. 73.
"A Temporary Visitor" (from The Cold Touch of Time, semi-finalist, 10th anniversary manuscript competition). StoneC (11:1/2, Pt. 1) Aut-Wint 83, p. 60.
"This Town." Blueline (3:2) Wint-Spr 82, p. 22.

963. DAILEY, Joel
"Against the Dark" (for my father). Paint

(10:19/20) Spr-Aut 83, p. 18.
"Because." WormR (23:2, issue 90) 83, p. 44.
"Down through Sky to Granfather." YetASM (1:1) 82, p. 11.
"Ends." Wind (13:48) 83, p. 12-13.
"Formica Daze." WormR (23:2, issue 90) 83, p. 46-47.
"In Foreign Films." WormR (23:2, issue 90) 83, p. 45-46.
"Memory." Abraxas (27/28) 83, p. 44.
"Mr. Davis, His Peccadilloes, & His Wife, Martha, Interrupt the Meat Course." WormR (23:2, issue 90) 83, p. 45.
"My Father's Indigestion." KanQ (15:2) Spr 83, p. 111.
"Obviously" (for W.). WormR (23:2, issue 90) 83, p. 47.
"Poem with Mimosa." Paint (10:19/20) Spr-Aut 83, p. 19.
"Stanzas." WormR (23:2, issue 90) 83, p. 47-48.
"These Days." WormR (23:2, issue 90) 83, p. 45.
"The Walking Wounded" (for Pose). WormR (23:2, issue 90) 83, p. 46.

964. DALE, Peter
"Short Day." SouthernR (19:3) Jl 83, p. 649.

965. DALEY, Michael
"Credo." NewEng (5:4) Sum 83, p. 564.
"Magnificat" (to the memory of Bill Evans and for Stephanie). AmerPoR (12:4) Jl-Ag 83, p. 32.

966. DALKEY, Victoria
"Chinoiserie." Abraxas (27/28) 83, p. 38.

967. DALLMAN, Elaine
"The Opening of Day Includes." YetASM (2:1) 83, p. 6.

968. D'ALMEIDA, George
"Memoirs of an Ismaric Spear" (for Alan Boegehold). YaleR (72:3) Spr 83, p. 340-365.

969. DALTON, Anne B.
"Midnight, Point Reyes." CalQ (22) Sum 83, p. 32-33.

970. DALTON, Roque B.
"Letter to Nazim Hikmet" (tr. by Richard Schaaf). MinnR (NS 21) Aut 83, p. 17-18.

971. DALY, Christopher
"At the Cabbie's Studio." WormR (23:1, issue 89) 83, p. 29.
"Courtesy Is Not Dead." WormR (23:1, issue 89) 83, p. 29.
"Like Out of Work Actors." WormR (23:1, issue 89) 83, p. 29.
"Pilgrim Day." WormR (23:1, issue 89) 83, p. 31-32.
"Rainy Day Woman #1." WormR (23:1, issue 89) 83, p. 32-33.
"Uncle Ray." WormR (23:1, issue 89) 83, p. 30.

972. DALY, Daniel
"Common Black Ants in Captivity." YetASM (1:1) 82, p. 15.
"Seven." YetASM (2:1) 83, p. 3.
"Song." Vis (12) 83, p. 7.

973. DALY, Dennis
"Industrial Sonnets." Tendril (16) Sum 83, p. 23-25.

974. DALY, Mary Ann
"For an Old Flame in Autumn." SmPd (20:1) Wint 83, p. 14.

975. D'AMBROSIO, Vinnie-Marie
"Love Upstate." Confr (25/26) 83, p. 105-107.

976. DAME, Enid
"Brighton Beach." Confr (25/26) 83, p. 88-89.

977. DANA, Robert
"Ark & Covenant." MidwQ (24:2) Wint 83, p. 168.
"Blue Iris." NewYorker (59:17) 13 Je 83, p. 91.
"Bread" (for E. L. Mayo, 1904-1979). NewL (49:3/4) Spr-Sum 83, p. 270-271.
"Burn." MidwQ (24:2) Wint 83, p. 165.
"On a View of Paradise Ridge from a Rented House." MidwQ (24:2) Wint 83, p. 166.
"A Short History of the Middle West." NewYorker (59:19) 27 Je 83, p. 34.
"Starting Out for the Difficult World." KanQ (15:4) Aut 83, p. 32.
"Sunflower State." KanQ (15:4) Aut 83, p. 31.
"Written in Winter." MidwQ (24:2) Wint 83, p. 167.

978. DANIEL, Hal J., III
"Greensboro." Sam (36:3 143rd release) 83, p. 13.

979. DANIELL, Rosemary
"The Color of Halcyon Days." Paint (10:19/20) Spr-Aut 83, p. 12.
"Yellow Birds" (for John, who gave me the gift of Guatemala before it was too late). Paint (10:19/20) Spr-Aut 83, p. 13.

980. DANIELS, Celia A.
"The Key" (For Jared Carter). LittleBR (3:3) Spr 83, p. 65.

981. DANIELS, Jim
"Blizzard." ThRiPo (19/20) 82, p. 34.
"November in Defiance, Ohio." ThRiPo (19/20) 82, p. 33.
"November in Defiance, Ohio." ThRiPo (21/22) 83, p. 20.

982. DANIELS, Kate
"Epilogue: After a Murder." VirQR (59:4) Aut 83, p. 678-679.

DANIELSON, Anita Endrezze
See: ENDREZZE-DANIELSON, Anita

983. DANSDILL, John P.
"Teachers' Son: 7:00 a.m." EngJ (72:8) D 83, p. 70.

984. D'ARBERET, Lorenzo
"The Night Splotches" (tr. [?] by Syd Weedon). Sam (34:3 135th release) 83, p. 28.
"The Opening Nonsense" (tr. [?] by Syd Weedon). Sam (34:3 135th release) 83, p. 29.

985. DARIO, Sharon
"Aspects of the Soul." HiramPoR (34) Spr-Sum 83, p. 7.
"Aspects of the Soul." WindO (43) Wint 83, p. 36.
"Bag Woman." SanFPJ (5:2) 83, p. 75.
"Has Nature No Shame?" WindO (43) Wint 83, p. 35.
"The Inside Layer." SanFPJ (5:2) 83, p. 75.
"My Mother Cried Once in Her Life." HiramPoR (34) Spr-Sum 83, p. 8.
"Song." WindO (43) Wint 83, p. 35.

986. DARLINGTON, Andrew
"Hunting Clean." Vis (11) 83, p. 40.
"Occasionally Paul Eluard." SecC (11:1/2) 83, p. 35.

987. DARLINGTON, Chris
"The Eyeball Exploder." Bogg (50) 83, p. 51.

988. DARR, Ann
"Traveling the Thames with the Queen's Own Swans." ThRiPo (21/22) 83, p. 21.

989. DARRAGH, Tina
"Ludicrous Stick." ParisR (24:86) Wint 82, p. 93.

990. DASPIT, Debra
"Untitled: How soon it is winter again." NewOR (10:2/3) Sum-Aut 83, p. 110.

D'AUGEROT-AREND, Sylvie
See: AUGEROT-AREND, Sylvie d'

991. DAUNT, Jon
"Gold Fever." SanFPJ (4:3) 83, p. 44.
"How Odin Appeared to Them in Dreams." DevQ (18:3) Aut 83, p. 87-88.
"Linda's Poem." CropD (4) 83, p. 5.
"Montauk Point, New York." SoCaR (15:2) Spr 83, p. 17.
"Pages from an Ensign's Notebook, Sea of Japan, 1943." Sam (34:3 135th release) 83, p. 39.
"Pious Ejaculations on Love and Imperialism." SanFPJ (4:3) 83, p. 7.
"Thoughts of a Senator Kissing Babies." SanFPJ (4:3) 83, p. 6.

992. DAURIO, B.
"Unsophisticated Reaction." PoetryCR (5:2) Wint 83-

84, p. 19.

993. DAVID, Almitra
"Bag Lady: A Part of Her Poem." BelPoJ (34:2) Wint 83-84, p. 22-32.

994. DAVIDSON, Anne
"In Search of Warm Shadows." Poem (47) Mr 83, p. 50.
"What You Do." Poem (47) Mr 83, p. 49.

995. DAVIDSON, Scott
"Inertia and What Emerges." CutB (21) Aut-Wint 83, p. 88-89.

996. DAVIE, Donald
"Through Bifocals." AmerS (52:2) Spr 83, p. 219-220.
"The University Of The South" (For Andrew Lytle, aged 80). SewanR (91:2) Spr 83, p. 185-186.

997. DAVIES, Alan
"Lies." ParisR (24:86) Wint 82, p. 86-88.

998. DAVIES, Cecil
"A Lucid Moment" (tr. of Richard Dehmel). Stand (24:3) 83, p. 44.

999. DAVIES, Hilary
"Forsworn" (tr. Of Jean-Jacques Celly). Argo (4:3) 83, p. 9.
"House" (tr. Of Jean-Jacques Celly). Argo (4:3) 83, p. 9.
"Passage" (tr. Of Jean-Jacques Celly). Argo (4:3) 83, p. 9.

1000. DAVIES, Nancy
"This Country." YetASM (1:2) 82, p. 2.

1001. DAVIES, Robert A.
"The Middle-Aged." FourQt (32:2) Wint 83, p. 14.

1002. DAVIS, Albert
"The Gander Gang." KanQ (15:3) Sum 83, p. 60.

1003. DAVIS, Barbara Nector
"An American in Purgatory." SanFPJ (5:1) 83, p. 64.

1004. DAVIS, Barbara Rosson
"Heat." YetASM (1:1) 82, p. 2.
"The Uttered Word Come Through." YetASM (1:1) 82, p. 6.

1005. DAVIS, Duane
"Arms Race." Sam (35:1 137th release) 83, p. 5.
"Bang-Up Futures." Sam (35:1 137th release) 83, p. 1-12.
"Economics." Sam (35:1 137th release) 83, p. 6.
"Five O'Clock News." Sam (35:1 137th release) 83, p. 7.
"Ground Zero: A Sequence." Sam (35:1 137th release) 83, p. 8-12.

"Killing." Sam (35:1 137th release) 83, p. 2.
"State of the Nation." Sam (35:1 137th release) 83, p. 3.
"Wheat Futures." Sam (35:1 137th release) 83, p. 4.

1006. DAVIS, Glover
"Barometer." SouthernR (19:3) Jl 83, p. 647-648.
"From Poland to the Orphanage, 1948." NewEngR (5:3) Spr 83, p. 362-363.
"White Pages." SouthernR (19:3) Jl 83, p. 646.

1007. DAVIS, Henry, Jr.
"Professionalsim, 1983, a Parody of Donne's 'Holy Sonnet XIV'." NegC (3:4) Aut 83, p. 130.

1008. DAVIS, Jackson
"Depth of Field." Ploughs (9:2/3) 83, p. 189-190.
"James." BlackWR (10:1) Aut 83, p. 141.

1009. DAVIS, Jon
"Blue Sky, the Girder Falling." MissouriR (7:1) Aut 83, p. 50-51.

1010. DAVIS, Ki
"Two Lovers." Poetry (141:6) Mr 83, p. 327.

1011. DAVIS, Lloyd
"Farmington No. 9: January 8, 1971." ThRiPo (21/22) 83, p. 22.

1012. DAVIS, Lydia
"Shared Nights" (tr. of Paul Eluard). ParisR (25:88) Sum 83, p. 235-238.

1013. DAVIS, Maralee G.
"The Final Lovesong." StoneC (10:3/4) Spr-Sum 83, p. 70-71.

1014. DAVIS, Roderick
"The Artist." AntigR (55) Aut 83, p. 58.

1015. DAVIS, Thadious
"Cloistered in High School." BlackALF (17:4) Wint 83, p. 148.
"New World Griot." BlackALF (17:4) Wint 83, p. 149.
"Reunion" (for Frances). BlackALF (17:4) Wint 83, p. 149.

1016. DAVIS, William Virgil
"Beatitudes." MichOR (22:3) Sum 83, p. 220.
"The Mind-Pond." DevQ (18:3) Aut 83, p. 63.
"Something I Cannot Name Has Come Close to Me." PoetL (78:4) Wint 84, p. 223.
"Wind and His Mother." Wind (13:47) 83, p. 8-9.
"Wind around the House." Wind (13:47) 83, p. 9.
"Wind As a Boy." Wind (13:47) 83, p. 8.
"Wind As a Young Man." Wind (13:47) 83, p. 8.
"Wind Settles Down." Wind (13:47) 83, p. 9-10.
"Wind Trys to Deceive His Father." Wind (13:47) 83, p. 9.

"Wind's Birth." Wind (13:47) 83, p. 8.
"The Words." MichOR (22:3) Sum 83, p. 284.

1017. DAVISON, Peter
"Impossible People." LittleBR (4:2) Wint 83-84, p. 24-25.
"Low Lands" (from Jacob van Ruisdael and for John Updike). Ploughs (9:1) 83, p. 185-186.

1018. DAWSON, Hester Jewell
"Looking Down on the Saltmarsh." StoneC (10:3/4) Spr-Sum 83, p. 30.

1019. DAY, Lucille
"The Qualifying Exam." Thrpny (4:2, issue 14) Sum 83, p. 23.
"Self-Portrait with Hand Microscope" (After the Expressionists). PortR (29:1) 83, p. 43-44.

1020. DAY, Robert
"Fairlee Creek." LittleBR (3:4) Sum 83, p. 33.
"For the Thief Who Stole My Hunting Dog." LittleBR (3:4) Sum 83, p. 65.
"Home: Late Summer." LittleBR (3:4) Sum 83, p. 30.
"Some Questions for a Boy So Badly Burned in a Prairie Fire That He Had to Tell His Doctors Who He Was: Otis, Kansas." LittleBR (3:4) Sum 83, p. 95.

De . . .
See also: Names beginning with "De" without the following space, filed below in their alphabetic positions, e.g. DeBEVOISE

De ANDRADE, Carlos Drummond de
See: ANDRADE, Carlos Drummond de

De ANDRADE, Eugenio
See: ANDRADE, Eugenio de

1021. De ANGELIS, Milo
"Anywhere Except" (tr. by Lawrence Venuti). ParisR (24:85) Aut 82, p. 163.
"Gee" (tr. by Lawrence Venuti). ParisR (24:85) Aut 82, p. 160.
"Now" (tr. by Lawrence Venuti). ParisR (24:85) Aut 82, p. 161.
"Only" (tr. by Lawrence Venuti). ParisR (24:85) Aut 82, p. 162.
"The Sounds That Arrived" (tr. by Lawrence Venuti). ParisR (24:85) Aut 82, p. 161.
"The Window" (tr. by Lawrence Venuti). ParisR (24:85) Aut 82, p. 162.

De ARMAS, José R.
See: ARMAS, José R. de

De BURGOS, Julia
See: BURGOS, Julia de

De HOYOS, Angela
See: HOYOS, Angela de

1022. De LEON, Kathie
"After the Storm." WindO (43) Wint 83, p. 26.
"Edge of Spring." WindO (43) Wint 83, p. 25.
"Roses." Poem (47) Mr 83, p. 53.
"White." Poem (47) Mr 83, p. 54.

De LEON HERNANDEZ, Víctor
See: LEON HERNANDEZ, Víctor de

1023. De LONGCHAMPS, Joanne
"A Correspondence" (Excerpt). Meadows (3:1) 82, p. 34.
"Day-Colored Cat for Orlando." Meadows (4:1) 83, p. 13.
"The Glass Hammer" (with homage to Yoko Ono who created one). SouthwR (68:4) Aut 83, p. 348.
"Lovers die but caution kills." Meadows (4:1) 83, p. 57.
"Par for What Course." Meadows (3:1) 82, p. 24.
"Take grief to bed." Meadows (4:1) 83, p. 11.
"This Body." Meadows (4:1) 83, p. 37.

De MELLO BREYNER ANDRESEN, Sophia
See: ANDRESEN, Sophia de Mello Breyner

De MELO NETO, João Cabral
See: NETO, João Cabral de Melo

De NERVAL, Gérard
See: NERVAL, Gérard de

De ORY, Carlos Edmundo
See: ORY, Carlos Edmundo de

De OYENARD, Sylvia Puentes de
See: OYENARD, Sylvia Puentes de

De PEREZ, Ilma Valenzuela
See: PEREZ, Ilma Valenzuela de

1024. De SILVA, Margot
"I Take You with Me Everywhere." YetASM (2:1) 83, p. 2.

1025. De VRIES, Carrow
"A sniffed out rabbit." WindO (42) Sum 83, p. 3.

1026. De WITT, Gene
"One of Your People." YetASM (1:2) 82, p. 2.

De . . .
See also: Names beginning with "De" followed by a space, filed above in their alphabetic positions, e.g. De ANGELIS

1027. DEAHL, James
"The 690 Level." Argo (4:3) 83, p. 21.

"In the Marsh of St.-Jean-Port-Joli." Descant (43) Wint 83-84, p. 43.
"Losses" (for R.M.N.). Quarry (32:3) Sum 83, p. 39.
"Past Dogs Nest" (for Gilda). Descant (43) Wint 83-84, p. 45-46.
"Reply in Kind." PoetryCR (4:3) Spr 83, p. 15.
"The Water's Voice." Descant (43) Wint 83-84, p. 44.

1028. DEAL, Kenneth L.
"My Hands: An Ode of Sorts." Poem (47) Mr 83, p. 20-21.
"The Pavilion: Five Poems after Han Yu." Poem (47) Mr 83, p. 22-23.
"T'zu: Filling Space." Poem (47) Mr 83, p. 19.

1029. DEAL, Susan (Susan Strayer)
"Geraniums." ThirdW Spr 83, p. 113.
"October." BlackWR (8:2) Spr 82, p. 68.
"Why Is Love Hungry." BlackWR (8:2) Spr 82, p. 69.

1030. DEAN, Clare (Clare Regina)
"Love As Refuse." NewL (50:1) Aut 83, p. 70.
"The Military Man." YetASM (2:1) 83, p. 2.

1031. DEANE, Seamus
"The Brethren." Agni (19) 83, p. 18-19.
"Fording the River." Agni (19) 83, p. 17.
"History Lessons" (For Roman Sheehan and Richard Kearney). Agni (19) 83, p. 20-21.
"Return." Agni (19) 83, p. 15.
"A Schooling." Agni (19) 83, p. 16.
"A World without a Name." Agni (19) 83, p. 22.

1034. DEANS, G. N.
"Night Child." Bogg (50) 83, p. 43.

1035. DEAVEL, Christine
"Going Out after Work." MinnR (NS 21) Aut 83, p. 26.
"The Palm Sunday Tornado." MissouriR (7:1) Aut 83, p. 34-35.

1036. DeBEVOISE, Arlene
"Room 247." ChrC (100:7) 9 Mr 83, p. 208.
"A Vigil of Maundy Thursday." ChrC (100:9) 23-30 Mr 83, p. 282.

1037. DeBOLT, William Walter
"Amnesia." ChrC (100:15) 11 My 83, p. 447.

1038. DEBRAVO, Jorge
"Hiroshima." PortR (29:1) 83, p. 24-25.
"Hiroshima" (tr. by Michael L. Johnson). PortR (29:1) 83, p. 26-27.

1039. DeCORMIER-SHEKERJIAN, Regina
"Midsummer Eve." YetASM (1:2) 82, p. 2.
"Midsummer Eve." YetASM (2:1) 83, p. 10.
"Nobody Listening." Blueline (4:2) Wint-Spr 83, p. 33.
"La Russa." LittleM (14:1/2) 83, p. 18-22.

1040. DEEN, Rosemary
"Antagonists." 13thM (6:1/2) 82, p. 8.
"Scores." 13thM (6:1/2) 82, p. 9.

1041. DEETER, Kay
"Bottoms." FourQt (32:4) Sum 83, p. 15.

1042. DeFOE, Mark
"The Accident." SoCaR (15:2) Spr 83, p. 88-89.
"After a Rain from My Third Floor Window in Early April I Consider These Correspondences." MalR (65) Jl 83, p. 18-19.
"Doing the Women's Laundry." MalR (65) Jl 83, p. 23.
"Emergency Repairs." MalR (65) Jl 83, p. 21-22.
"Jan. 27, 1979." ParisR (25:89) Aut 83, p. 134-135.
"March, from a Window (A Meditation)." DevQ (18:1) Spr 83, p. 86-87.
"Near My House There Is a Woods Where in the Summer No One Goes." MalR (65) Jl 83, p. 20.
"Neolithic." Wind (13:49) 83, p. 18-19.
"Opossum Spring." YaleR (72:3) Spr 83, p. 416.
"Self-Disgust and Resolution / Shaving at 40." MalR (65) Jl 83, p. 17.
"Telling a Child about Pain." MalR (65) Jl 83, p. 15.
"To the Person Locked in an Attic -- Now Free." MalR (65) Jl 83, p. 16.

1043. DeFREES, Madeline
"The Book of Sediments" (from "The Light Station on Tillamook Rock"). ParisR (25:89) Aut 83, p. 136-137.
"The Dovecote: Its Head Keepers." Poetry (143:1) O 83, p. 22-23.
"The Leper Graves at Spinalonga." NewEng (5:4) Sum 83, p. 525-526.

1044. DeGRUSON, Gene
"Change." LittleBR (4:2) Wint 83-84, p. 12.

1045. DEGUY, Michel
"A cup on a telegram" (tr. by Raymond Federman). ParisR (24:84) Sum 82, p. 26.
"Etc" (tr. by Clayton Eshleman). Sulfur (3:2, #8) 83, p. 109-113.
"The wall is massive, of solid stone, hard, finished" (tr. by Raymond Federman). ParisR (24:84) Sum 82, p. 26.
"When two poets come face to face" (tr. by Raymond Federman). ParisR (24:84) Sum 82, p. 26.

1046. DEHLAVI, Amir Khusrow
"Last Night" (tr. by Omar S. Pound). AntigR (55) Aut 83, p. 22.

1047. DEHMEL, Richard
"A Lucid Moment" (tr. by Cecil Davies). Stand (24:3) 83, p. 44.

1048. Del GIUDICE, Carolyn
"Holy Orders." Vis (13) 83, p. 7.
"Modesta Leaving Milan and Saint Augustine." Vis (12) 83, p. 16.

Del VALLE, María Dolores
See: VALLE, María Dolores del

1049. Del VECCHIO, Gloria
"The Bride of Caesar." USl (16/17) Wint 83-84, p. 14.

1050. DeLAMOTTE, Roy
"TV in the Kitchen." SanFPJ (5:4) 83, p. 77.

1051. DELANEY, John
"Speed Limits." SouthwR (68:4) Aut 83, p. 349.

1052. DELMAS, Annette
"Building a Fence." Wind (13:48) 83, p. 14.

1053. DeMARTINI, Brenda
"About Leaving." KanQ (15:4) Aut 83, p. 128.
"Elegy" (for my father). KanQ (15:4) Aut 83, p. 127.
"The Sleeping Gypsy" (after the painting by H. Rosseau). ThRiPo (19/20) 82, p. 35.

1054. DEMETRE, Sheila
"Mt. Pleasant Cemetery." Calyx (7:3) Sum 83, p. 29.

1055. DEMING, Alison (Alison H.)
"Letter to Nathaniel Hawthorne" (recipient, Pablo Neruda Prize for Poetry). Nimrod (27:1) Aut-Wint 83, p. 7-11.
"The Woman Painting Crates." BelPoJ (33:4) Sum 83, p. 39-40.

1056. DEMMA, Stephanie
"Claire Street." PoetL (78:4) Wint 84, p. 215.

1057. DEMPSEY, Ian
"Naturally." CrossC (5:2/3) 83, p. 11.

1058. DEMPSTER, Barry
"Accident." Waves (11:4) Spr 83, p. 58.
"My Nights Are Taken Up with Stars." Quarry (32:4) Aut 83, p. 32-35.

1059. DENHOLTZ, David Bruce
"To Awaken in Two Places Distant As an Animal." SouthernPR (23:2) Aut 83, p. 16-17.

1060. DENNER, Richard
"The Wart Cannot Be Coerced." CrabCR (1:1) My 83, p. 13.

1061. DENNIS, Carl
"Another Moses." PoetryNW (24:1) Spr 83, p. 22.
"The Art of Doylestown." GeoR (37:2) Sum 83, p. 367-370.

"At Home with Cèzanne." Salm (61) Aut 83, p. 51-52.
"Birthday." GeoR (37:3) Aut 83, p. 659.
"The Changeling." NewRep (186:13) 31 Mr 82, p. 44.
"The Connoisseur." Poetry (141:5) F 83, p. 268-269.
"For Molly." NewYorker (59:8) 11 Ap 83, p. 42.
"Hero of the Streets." PoetryNW (24:1) Spr 83, p. 20-21.
"Later." NewRep (187:26) Year End Issue 82, p. 34.
"Non Omnis Moriar." PoetryNW (24:1) Spr 83, p. 21.
"Steamboat Days." Poetry (141:5) F 83, p. 266-267.
"What Happened Then." Poetry (141:5) F 83, p. 270.
"What Jill Sees." NewRep (186:8) 24 F 82, p. 31.
"The Whole Truth." NewRep (188:8) 28 F 83, p. 28.

1062. DENT, Tory
"Luna." ParisR (25:87) Spr 83, p. 124-125.

1063. DEPTA, Victor M.
"The Basketball Coach." MemphisSR (2:1) Aut 81, p. 24-25.
"Bible Class." MemphisSR (1:2) Spr 81, p. 16.
"Old Crow." CapeR (19:1) Wint 83, p. 7.
"Saraghina." CapeR (19:1) Wint 83, p. 6.
"Unruly Boy." MemphisSR (1:2) Spr 81, p. 17.

1064. Der HOVANESSIAN, Diana
"Thinking of You As a Child." StoneC (10:3/4) Spr-Sum 83, p. 78.

1065. DERRICOTTE, Toi
"The Anesthesia Is Taking Effect." BlackALF (17:4) Wint 83, p. 155.
"Beau Monde." BlackALF (17:4) Wint 83, p. 155.
"Gynecology: The Dream of the Six Month Check." 13thM (6:1/2) 82, p. 44-45.
"The House Is the Enemy." BlackALF (17:4) Wint 83, p. 155.
"The Night She Dreamed She Was Mad." BlackALF (17:4) Wint 83, p. 155.
"The Sculpture at Night." BlackALF (17:4) Wint 83, p. 155.

1066. DERRY, Alice
"Canada Jays at Klahane Ridge." Tendril (14/15) Wint 83, p. 37.
"Eurydice." SouthernPR (23:2) Aut 82 [i.e. (23:1?) Spr 83], p. 31.
"Every Day of Her Girlhood in Montana." Poetry (142:2) My 83, p. 76-77.
"Rivers." PraS (51:1, i.e. 57:1) Spr 83, p. 54.

1067. DeRUGERIS, C. K.
"The Wetting of Alice: A Historic Fantasy." Bogg (51) 83, p. 7.

1068. DESSI, Gigi
"All Will Listen" (from L'Incomprensibile Uomo, tr. by Dominick Lepore). StoneC (10:3/4) Spr-Sum 83, p. 53.

"Di Domenica" (from _L'Incomprensibile Uomo_). _StoneC_ (10:3/4) Spr-Sum 83, p. 52.
"Sunday" (from _L'Incomprensibile Uomo_, tr. by Dominick Lepore). _StoneC_ (10:3/4) Spr-Sum 83, p. 52.
"Tutti Sentiranno" (from _L'Incomprensibile Uomo_). _StoneC_ (10:3/4) Spr-Sum 83, p. 53.

1069. DESY, Peter
"Dying Here." _NegC_ (3:4) Aut 83, p. 64.
"Father Falling." _PoetryE_ (11) Sum 83, p. 19.
"The Girl." _CutB_ (21) Aut-Wint 83, p. 14.
"Here, Now." _WindO_ (42) Sum 83, p. 31.
"Marriage Poem." _Vis_ (12) 83, p. 14.
"My Father's Picture on the Cover of a Buffalo Bison Hockey Program for 1934." _PoetryE_ (11) Sum 83, p. 18.
"Nightfall." _Images_ (8:3) 83, p. 4.
"Perspective." _MSS_ (2:3) Sum 83, p. 60.
"Summer Sunday." _WindO_ (42) Sum 83, p. 31.

1070. D'EVELYN, Thomas
"At the University" (for Sabina Johnson). _SouthernR_ (19:3) Jl 83, p. 641.
"Good Wood" (for Raymond Oliver). _SouthernR_ (19:3) Jl 83, p. 642.
"In Memory of Charlotte D'Evelyn." _SouthernR_ (19:3) Jl 83, p. 643.

1071. DEVET, Rebecca McClanahan
"To My Students, on Reading Hopkins." _EngJ_ (72:8) D 83, p. 46.

1072. DEWDNEY, Christopher
"Fovea Centralis." _MalR_ (66) O 83, p. 33.
"Ion Ore." _MalR_ (66) O 83, p. 32.
"This My Emissary." _MalR_ (66) O 83, p. 33.
"Winter Central" (from a continuation of "Log Entries"). _CanLit_ (96) Spr 83, p. 33-34.

1073. DeYOUNG, Robert
"The Owl." _KanQ_ (15:2) Spr 83, p. 74.

1074. DHARWADKER, Vinay
"The Turnaround" (tr. of Shrikant Varma). _Mund_ (14:1) 83, p. 33-34.
"The Wind" (tr. of Shrikant Varma). _Mund_ (14:1) 83, p. 33.

Di . . .
See also: Names beginning with "Di" without the following space, filed below in their alphabetic positions, e.g. DiPALMA

1075. Di CICCO, Pier Giorgio
"Concordance of the Same" (for Anna). _CrossC_ (5:2/3) 83, p. 12.

1076. Di GIOVANNI, Norman Thomas
"El Otre [i.e. Otro] Tigre" (Excerpt: "We'll hunt

for a third tiger now, tr. of Jorge Luis Borges). AntigR (52) Wint 83, p. 71.
"Seventeen Haiku" (tr. of Jorge Luis Borges). NewRep (187:17) 1 N 82, p. 30.

1077. Di MICHELE, Mary
"Entrance into Light." PoetryCR (4:4) Sum 83, p. 16.
"The Food of Love." PoetryCR (4:4) Sum 83, p. 16.
"Orchids and Blood." PoetryCR (4:4) Sum 83, p. 16.
"Sinister Clowns." PoetryCR (4:4) Sum 83, p. 16.

1078. Di PASQUALE, Emanuel"
Return to Sicily" (for X.J. Kennedy). Poem (48) Jl 83, p. 2-4.

1079. Di PIERO, W. S.
"Apache Chief." SouthernR (19:4) O 83, p. 841.
"Avery Island." SouthernR (19:4) O 83, p. 838.
"June Harvest." TriQ (56) Wint 83, p. 166-167.
"Just Around Dark." NewEngR (5:3) Spr 83, p. 415.
"Lines to a friend in trouble." TriQ (56) Wint 83, p. 170.
"Northern Lights." NoAmR (268:3) S 83, p. 60.
"The Pictures." SouthernR (19:4) O 83, p. 840-841.
"Prosody." ChiR (33:4) Sum [i.e. Spr] 83, p. 20.
"Solitaire." SouthernR (19:4) O 83, p. 839-840.
"Summer in Winter." TriQ (56) Wint 83, p. 168-169.
"To Suffice." NewEngR (5:3) Spr 83, p. 414.

1080. Di PRISCO, Joseph
"News from the Far West." PraS (51:1, i.e. 57:1) Spr 83, p. 31.

Di . . .
See also: Names beginning with "Di" followed by a space, filed above in their alphabetic positions, e.g. Di CICCO

1081. DIAZ, Rafael
"Hijo de Naturaleza." Rácata (1) 83, p. 63.
"La Muralla Femenina." Rácata (1) 83, p. 62.
"Observaré los Puntos Colgados en Tu Cola de Nieve Dormida." Rácata (1) 83, p. 66.
"Queriéndote Lucir en Mi Vuelo." Rácata (1) 83, p. 64.
"El Viento Se Lo Llevó." Rácata (1) 83, p. 65.

1082. DIAZ-DIOCARETZ, Myriam
"De una Postulante a Victima Inocente de Delito Sexual." LetFem (9:2) Aut 83, p. 91-92.
"La Llegada." LetFem (9:2) Aut 83, p. 94.
"Mujer de la Tierra." LetFem (9:2) Aut 83, p. 93.
"Mujer Nuestra de Cada Dia." LetFem (9:2) Aut 83, p. 92-93.

1083. DICKENS, Eric
"I set out on a journey" (tr. of Eeva-Liisa Manner). Stand (24:3) 83, p. 6.
"The lake is full of light without source" (tr. of Eeva-Liisa Manner). Stand (24:3) 83, p. 6.

1084. DICKEY, James
"Attempted Departure" (with Andre du Bouchet). AmerPoR (12:2) Mr/Ap 83, p. 3.
"Craters" (with Michel Leiris). AmerPoR (12:2) Mr/Ap 83, p. 4.
"Crystal." ClockR (2:1) 83, p. 16.
"Farmers" (with Andre Frenaud, a fragment). AmerPoR (12:2) Mr/Ap 83, p. 4.
"Form" (with André Frénaud). Ploughs (9:2/3) 83, p. 16-17.
"Heads" (with Lucien Becker). AmerPoR (12:2) Mr/Ap 83, p. 3.
"Lakes of Varmland" (with Andre Frenaud). AmerPoR (12:2) Mr/Ap 83, p. 3.
"Sand" (homage, Vicente Aleixandre, and acknowledging translations by Willis Barnstone and David Garrison). ClockR (2:1) 83, p. 15.

1085. DICKEY, William
"Alexander." KanQ (15:4) Aut 83, p. 57-58.
"Armageddon." NewEng (5:4) Sum 83, p. 478-479.
"Dog under False Pretenses." KanQ (15:4) Aut 83, p. 54-55.
"Larger Than a Breadbox." CarolQ (35:3) Spr 83, p. 48.
"The New Place." KanQ (15:4) Aut 83, p. 56-57.
"Rebus." PoNow (7:2, #38) 83, p. 11.

1086. DICKSON, John
"Blood Donation." SpoonRQ (8:4) Aut 83, p. 9.
"Central School." SpoonRQ (8:4) Aut 83, p. 10.
"Going by Coach." Images (8:3) 83, p. 5.
"Quiet Zone." Poetry (142:3) Je 83, p. 145.
"Reunion of the Third Platoon." AmerS (52:1) Wint 82/83, p. 78-79.
"Rollo." StoneC (10:3/4) Spr-Sum 83, p. 34.
"Rosehill." Poetry (142:3) Je 83, p. 143-144.
"The Starlight Lounge." Tendril (14/15) Wint 83, p. 38.

1087. DIEMER, Gretchen
"Victims." 13thM (6:1/2) 82, p. 87.

1088. DIESEL-HAMM, Mary
"Beginnings." PikeF (5) Spr 83, p. 18.
"The Missing Link." PikeF (5) Spr 83, p. 18.
"Precious Blood." KanQ (15:1) Wint 83, p. 190.

1089. DIETZ, Sheila
"Near Black Mesa." MassR (24:3) Aut 83, p. 658-659.

1090. DIGGES, Deborah
"Mimosa." MissouriR (6:2) Wint 83, p. 32-33.
"To S." GeoR (37:4) Wint 83, p. 790.

1091. DILLARD, R. H. W.
"What to Do (When You Want to Say So Much and You Do Not Know How)." Ploughs (9:2/3) 83, p. 20-26.

1092. DILSAVER, Paul
"Preliminary Lie." Wind (13:49) 83, p. 24.

1093. DIMITROVA, Blaga
"The Water Buffalo (Hanoi, 1972)" (tr. by John Balaban and Vladimir Phillipov). NewEng (5:4) Sum 83, p. 497-499.

1094. DINGLER, Crystal
"It's Saying the Words." IndR (6:2) Spr 83, p. 40.

DIOCARETZ, Myriam Diaz
See: DIAZ-DIOCARETZ, Myriam

1095. DIOMEDE, Matthew
"Canto 13 in Behalf of the Educational Process and System" (After E.Z.P., For My Students). CEAFor (13:2) D 82, p. 13.

1096. DiPALMA, Ray
"Hadrians Lane." ParisR (24:86) Wint 82, p. 94-95.

1097. DISCH, Tom
"Atocha Choo-Choo" (for John Ashbery). ParisR (24:84) Sum 82, p. 27-29.
"Close Your Eyes Now." OP (35) Spr-Sum 83, p. 16-17.
"Conclusive Evidence" (for James Merrill). ParisR (24:84) Sum 82, p. 29-30.
"A Cow of Our Time" (after Cuyp). Epoch (33:1) Aut-Wint 83, p. 52.
"Gossip." LittleM (14:1/2) 83, p. 45-46.
"Hopper" (at the Whitney). OP (35) Spr-Sum 83, p. 19.
"Sunday at Home." OP (35) Spr-Sum 83, p. 18.

1098. DISCHELL, Stuart
"Late Summer Night." Ploughs (9:1) 83, p. 181.
"Two Seasons" (for Seferis). Ploughs (9:1) 83, p. 182-183.

1099. DITSKY, John
"Agee." Quarry (32:3) Sum 83, p. 9.
"An Audubon Print of Jane." SmPd (20:3) Aut 83, p. 14.
"Blackjack Dealer, M/S Skyward." OntR (19) Aut-Wint 83-84, p. 51.
"Excelsior!" AntigR (54) Sum 83, p. 63.
"Excuses." Paint (10:19/20) Spr-Aut 83, p. 16.
"Extra-Terrestrial." AntigR (54) Sum 83, p. 64.
"Road Signs." OntR (19) Aut-Wint 83-84, p. 50.
"Swat." OntR (19) Aut-Wint 83-84, p. 52-53.
"A Thirst for Music." SoCaR (16:1) Aut 83, p. 24.

1100. DITTA, Joseph M.
"Boys on the Soccer Field in the Late Afternoon." MSS (3:1) Aut 83, p. 14.

1101. DIVERS, Greg
"Another True Account" (after Vladimir Mayakovsky and Frank O'Hara). PikeF (5) Spr 83, p. 31.

1102. DIXON, Stephen
"Ten Years--." LitR (27:1) Aut 83, p. 69-73.

1103. DJANIKIAN, Gregory
"Correspondence." Iowa (13:3/4) Spr 82 (83), p. 34-35.
"Farmhouse in Early Fall." GeoR (37:3) Aut 83, p. 638-639.
"Grandfather's Towers" (Hotel Bahamdoun, Lebanon, 1956). AmerS (52:3) Sum 83, p. 393.
"The Man in the Middle." PoetryNW (24:4) Wint 83-84, p. 4-5.
"Paul Gauguin: Vision after the Sermon." SoDakR (21:4) Wint 83, p. 52.
"Spring Thaw." PoetryNW (24:4) Wint 83-84, p. 3-4.

1104. DLABOHA, Lilia
"Mistaken Identity." LittleM (14:1/2) 83, p. 109.

1105. DOAR, Harriet
"In the Morning." SouthernPR (23:2) Aut 83, p. 30.

1106. DOBBERSTEIN, Michael
"East Texas Cemetery: Red Dirt" (for Terry Hummer). QW (17) Aut-Wint 83-84, p. 26.
"Soldiers." NewL (49:3/4) Spr-Sum 83, p. 228-229.

1107. DOBLER, Patricia
"1920 Photo." ThRiPo (19/20) 82, p. 36.
"Family Traits." HangL (44) Sum 83, p. 10-11.
"His Depression." ThRiPo (19/20) 82, p. 37.
"Separations." HangL (44) Sum 83, p. 12.

1108. DOBSON, Joanne
"The Great Miramichi Fire." MassR (24:1) Spr 83, p. 110-112.

1109. DOBYNS, Stephen
"Between Hamburg and Buenos Aires." Poetry (142:5) Ag 83, p. 252-254.
"Caverns of Darkness" (for Ben Tibbs). AmerPoR (12:6) N/D 83, p. 22.
"Chinese Vase." AmerPoR (12:6) N/D 83, p. 26.
"Cuidadores de Autos" (Santiago, Chile). NewYorker (59:26) 15 Ag 83, p. 32.
"Dancing in Vacationland" (for Kevin Boyle). BlackWR (10:1) Aut 83, p. 90-91.
"Dead Baby" (Helen Johnston, 1882-1968). AmerPoR (12:6) N/D 83, p. 24-25.
"The Earth from This Distance." NewYorker (58:52) 14 F 83, p. 50.
"Flight." AmerPoR (12:6) N/D 83, p. 25.
"General Matthei Drives Home Through Santiago." Poetry (142:5) Ag 83, p. 249-251.
"Gottéron Landscape." BlackWR (8:2) Spr 82, p. 27.
"Night Swimmer." AmerPoR (12:6) N/D 83, p. 22.
"The Room" (after Balthus). BlackWR (8:2) Spr 82, p. 26.
"This Life." AmerPoR (12:6) N/D 83, p. 26.
"Under the Green Ceiling." AmerPoR (12:6) N/D 83,

p. 23.
"Wedding." AmerPoR (12:6) N/D 83, p. 23.
"What Did She See?" AmerPoR (12:6) N/D 83, p. 24.
"Wind Chimes." AmerPoR (12:6) N/D 83, p. 21.

1110. DODD, Elizabeth
"Personal Annulment." GeoR (37:2) Sum 83, p. 320.

1111. DODD, Wayne
"Letter." ThRiPo (21/22) 83, p. 23.
"November." KanQ (15:4) Aut 83, p. 64.
"On All Your Fingers." GeoR (37:1) Spr 83, p. 83.
"Sometimes Music Rises." GeoR (37:1) Spr 83, p. 82-83.

1112. DODDS, Kenneth G.
"Nearly a Point." PortR (29:1) 83, p. 41.

1113. DOERING, Steven
"The New Economy." Bogg (51) 83, p. 18.

1114. DOHERTY, M. J.
"Doves." SewanR (91:1) Wint 83, p. 110-111.

1115. DOLGORUKOV, Florence
"Lines for a Young Poet." CentR (27:2) Spr 83, p. 114.
"Surreal Landscape." SanFPJ (4:4) 83, p. 33-34.

1116. DOMINA, Lynn
"Prometheus, Slightly Off-Center." MinnR (NS 20) Spr 83, p. 58.
"Shutter Speed: 1/500 Second, Distance: Infinity." KanQ (15:2) Spr 83, p. 38.

1117. DOMINGUEZ, Acacia
"Escapamos." LetFem (9:2) Aut 83, p. 73.
"La Palabra." LetFem (9:2) Aut 83, p. 74.
"Por Donde Crecera la Sombra." LetFem (9:2) Aut 83, p. 72.
"Torbellino Vertical." LetFem (9:2) Aut 83, p. 75.

1118. DONAHUE, Jack
"Late Night Movies." YetASM (2:1) 83, p. 5.
"The Tiger's Birthday." StoneC (10:3/4) Spr-Sum 83, p. 36.

1119. DONALDSON, Jeffery
"After 'Light and Color (Goethe's Theory)'." Shen (34:3) 83, p. 93.
"A Gift of Protoplasm." Quarry (32:3) Sum 83, p. 51-53.
"A Modern Prometheus." Quarry (32:4) Aut 83, p. 25.

1120. DONALSON, Mel
"On the Line" (with eleven million unemployed: 9/3/82). SanFPJ (5:1) 83, p. 88.

1121. DONAVEL, David F.
"Ars Poetica." CapeR (18:2) Sum 83, p. 34.

"Graduation." _Tendril_ (14/15) Wint 83, p. 39.
"An Historical Event." _CapeR_ (18:2) Sum 83, p. 35.

1122. DONNELL, David
"Hound." _Descant_ (43) Wint 83-84, p. 89-90.
"Lakes." _Descant_ (43) Wint 83-84, p. 85-87.
"Positions (1)." _Descant_ (43) Wint 83-84, p. 88.

1123. DONNELLY, Paul
"Aftermath." _Bogg_ (51) 83, p. 60.
"Extract from an Epic." _Bogg_ (50) 83, p. 42.
"A Man in His Time." _Bogg_ (51) 83, p. 45.

1124. DONOGHUE, John
"Lackawana." _PoetryE_ (11) Sum 83, p. 57-59.

1125. DONOVAN, Laurence
"La Belle Dame Sans Merci." _SpiritSH_ (48) 82, p. 1.
"The Butterflies" (Coconut Grove, Florida, 1955). _SpiritSH_ (48) 82, p. 8-9.
"The Moon." _SpiritSH_ (48) 82, p. 10.
"Past and Present." _SpiritSH_ (48) 82, p. 10.
"Penguin." _SpiritSH_ (48) 82, p. 11.
"Songs of the Bluely Farers." _SpiritSH_ (48) 82, p. 2-7.
"The Wind." _SpiritSH_ (48) 82, p. 12.

1126. DONOVAN, Mark
"Letter for Robert Frost." _SanFPJ_ (5:1) 83, p. 38.

1127. DONOVAN, Susan
"Why the Bride Kept a Bear" (Lola Montez, Grass Valley, California). _MassR_ (24:2) Sum 83, p. 414-416.

1128. DOR, Moshe
"Poem: The light hugs the bones of the holy East" (tr. from the Hebrew). _SoDakR_ (21:4) Wint 83, p. 31.

DORAISWAMY, T. K.
See: NAKULAN

1129. DORESKI, William
"Arrowhead Farm." _Ascent_ (8:2) 83, p. 12.
"Chrome." _CapeR_ (18:2) Sum 83, p. 6.
"Holyoke Range." _Ascent_ (8:2) 83, p. 11.

1130. DORF, Carol
"Oakland Port View." _13thM_ (7:1/2) 83, p. 126-127.

1131. DORMAN, Sonya
"The Same River." _LittleM_ (14:1/2) 83, p. 91.
"Taking It on Faith." _BelPoJ_ (34:1) Aut 83, p. 19.
"Yankee in the Desert." _LittleM_ (14:1/2) 83, p. 90.

1132. DORNEY, Dennis M.
"Driving to Kidnap Your Daughter." _Tendril_ (16) Sum 83, p. 29.
"Forgetting Music." _Tendril_ (16) Sum 83, p. 28.

"McGovern Leaving San Pedro." PoetC (15:1) Aut 83, p. 17.
"Nude on a Harley." Tendril (16) Sum 83, p. 26-27.
"Rowboat." CimR (63) Ap 83, p. 20.
"Visiting." WestB (12) 83, p. 10-11.

1133. DORSET, Gerald
"Hypothesis." Tele (18) 83, p. 71.
"Women in My Life." Bogg (51) 83, p. 18.

1134. DORSETT, Robert
"From the Observer's Platform." KanQ (15:2) Spr 83, p. 160.
"Poem Based on a Passage by Helen Waddell." KanQ (15:2) Spr 83, p. 160.

1135. DORSETT, Thomas
"The Arsonist." PoetL (77:3) Aut 82, p. 148.
"The Funeral." Wind (13:48) 83, p. 15.
"Thank You for Your Letter Bomb." Wind (13:48) 83, p. 15.

1136. DOSS, James
"For Those Still Unborn" (tr. of Bertolt Brecht). PoetryE (9/10) Wint 82-Spr 83, p. 196-198.
"General, Your Tank Is Some Strong Car" (tr. of Bertolt Brecht). PoetryE (9/10) Wint 82-Spr 83, p. 195.
"Think about It" (tr. of Gunter Eich). PoetryE (9/10) Wint 82-Spr 83, p. 193-194.

1137. DOTY, M. R. (See also: DOTY, Mark)
"Blue Weather." ThRiPo (19/20) 82, p. 38.

1138. DOTY, Mark (See also: DOTY, M. R.)
"Horses." Nimrod (27:1) Aut-Wint 83, p. 56.
"January, Waking." Tendril (14/15) Wint 83, p. 42.
"Single." OW (17) Aut-Wint 83-84, p. 27-29.
"Twentyfive Racehorses" (found poem from The Racing Form). Kayak (63) N 83, p. 15.
"Walking Home." Tendril (14/15) Wint 83, p. 40-41.

1139. DOUBIAGO, Sharon
"Ground Zero" (for Michael Daley, March 25, 1982). NewEng (5:4) Sum 83, p. 452-459.

1140. DOUGHERTY, Jay
"It Doesn't Thrill Me." SmPd (20:3) Aut 83, p. 13.
"The Language." SmPd (20:2) Spr 83, p. 18.
"Lovely." SmPd (20:3) Aut 83, p. 13.
"Sure, Sally." SmPd (20:3) Aut 83, p. 13.

1141. DOUGLAS, Randolph
"Justification." SanFPJ (5:3) 83, p. 23.
"Miami 1980." SanFPJ (5:3) 83, p. 22.

1142. DOUSKEY, Franz
"Another Night of Disillusionment Besieged by Gravity." Kayak (63) N 83, p. 29.
"Incipient Flu, or the Day I Went Out of My Mind to

Avoid the Draft." Kayak (63) N 83, p. 27-28.
"Join Us at the Harold Bloom School of Misreading." PoetryNW (24:4) Wint 83-84, p. 13-14.

1143. DOVE, Rita
"The Distinguished Lecturer Spouts a Few Obscenities." PoNow (7:2, #38) 83, p. 12.
"Magic." Nimrod (27:1) Aut-Wint 83, p. 68.
"O." OhioR (30) 83, p. 59.
"Sunday Greens." Nimrod (27:1) Aut-Wint 83, p. 68-69.

1144. DOW, Jan Henson
"Gift." YetASM (2:1) 83, p. 9.

1145. DOWDLE, Jason E.
"Leaf-Light." CarolQ (35:3) Spr 83, p. 9.

1146. DOWNES, G. V.
"Eaton's Arcade." PoetryCR (4:4) Sum 83, p. 10.

1147. DOWNIE, Glen
"Fame of the City, Hiroshima, 1981." Germ (7:1) Spr-Sum 83, p. 27.
"Hard Luck." CrossC (5:2/3) 83, p. 5.
"A Partisan in Despair after the Evening News" (for M.K.). CrossC (5:2/3) 83, p. 5.
"To One in the Path of Totality." AntigR (53) Spr 83, p. 9.
"The Tracks." Germ (7:1) Spr-Sum 83, p. 28.
"Who Loves This Country." AntigR (53) Spr 83, p. 9.
"Wishbone." Grain (11:1) F 83, p. 10.

1148. DOWNS, Susan Barker
"The Salada Tea Store." YetASM (1:2) 82, p. 15.

1149. DOWNS, Virginia
"Mary Lincoln." CropD (4) 83, p. 6.

1150. DOYLE, James
"Power." YetASM (2:1) 83, p. 8.
"Records." YetASM (2:1) 83, p. 4.

1151. DOYLE, Lynn
"The Good Hands People Know Their Bodies." PoetryNW (24:2) Sum 83, p. 45-46.
"Wake Up." PoetryNW (24:2) Sum 83, p. 47.

1152. DOYLE, Mike
"After" (to Mary di Michele). CanLit (97) Sum 83, p. 13.
"Gathered from the Air." CanLit (97) Sum 83, p. 74.

1153. DRAKE, Albert
"At the Only Wide Place between Boise and Burns." PoNow (7:2, #38) 83, p. 21.

1154. DREVNIOK, Betty
"Gloom of dusk." Quarry (32:3) Sum 83, p. 75.
"Someone calls, someone answers." Quarry (32:3)

Sum 83, p. 75.

1155. DREYER, Lynne
"Step Work" (Excerpt). ParisR (24:86) Wint 82, p. 91-92.

1156. DRISCOLL, Jack
"Asleep with My Hands." OhioR (30) 83, p. 220.
"Baseball's Religious Heart: The Umpire." Kayak (63) N 83, p. 3.
"How My Father Turned the Night into Stories." Kayak (63) N 83, p. 5.
"The Kite." Kayak (63) N 83, p. 4-5.
"Lifeguard." CalQ (22) Sum 83, p. 79-80.
"Searching for Bodies in a Glassbottom Boat." OhioR (30) 83, p. 221.
"Twins." Vis (13) 83, p. 8.

1157. DRISKELL, Leon V.
"Nunc Dimittis." NegC (3:4) Aut 83, p. 120-121.

1158. DROBNIES, Adrienne
"Birds of Prey." PoetryCR (4:4) Sum 83, p. 15.
"Maud Allen." PoetryCR (5:1) Aut 83, p. 18.

1159. DRUCKER, Sally Ann
"Dutch Church Cemetary: Brooklyn." Pig (11) 83, p. 69.
"Leftovers." Pig (11) 83, p. 69.

DRUMMOND de ANDRADE, Carlos
See: ANDRADE, Carlos Drummond de

1160. DRURY, John
"Lovers at the Zoo." SouthernPR (23:2) Aut 82 [i.e. (23:1?) Spr 83], p. 33-34.
"Soprano" (for Carolyn Long). AntR (41:3) Sum 83, p. 336-338.

1161. Du BELLAY, Joachim
"Du Bellay's Fourth Regret" (tr. by David Weissmann).1522-1560). SouthernR (19:3) Jl 83, p. 659.

1162. DUBIE, Norman
"Dream." AntR (41:1) Wint 83, p. 70.
"Elegy for Wright & Hugo." AmerPoR (12:4) Jl-Ag 83, p. 41.
"New England, Springtime." Field (29) Aut 83, p. 72-73.
"Randall Jarrell, 1914-1965." OhioR (30) 83, p. 239.
"Revelations." Poetry (142:4) Jl 83, p. 218-219.

1163. DUBNOV, Eugene
"While Up the Hradcani" (tr. by the author and Chris Arkell). NewEng (5:4) Sum 83, p. 499.

1164. DUBROFF, Susanne
"Sonnet to Orpheus XIV Series I" (tr. of Rainer Maria Rilke). PortR (29:1) 83, p. 81.

1165. DUCKETT, Ian
"I Lie on My Back This Midnight." Bogg (50) 83, p. 58.

1166. DUCKWORTH, Penelope
"Finished Hands." PoetryNW (24:2) Sum 83, p. 39.

1167. DUDDY, Patrick
"Harvest." Wind (13:48) 83, p. 16.

1168. DUDIS, Ellen Kirvin
"Dinner Hour." DevQ (18:3) Aut 83, p. 65.
"Imagery." DevQ (18:3) Aut 83, p. 64.

1169. DUENSING, Marian
"Loose." AntigR (53) Spr 83, p. 79.

1170. DUESING, Laurie
"My Sister Lets It Fall." YetASM (2:1) 83, p. 11.

1171. DUFAULT, Peter Kane
"Dear George Eliot." NewYorker (58:52) 14 F 83, p. 44.

1172. DUGAN, Alan
"Note: The Sea Grinds Things Up." AmerPoR (12:3) My-Je 83, p. 3.
"On a Baroque Clock." AmerPoR (12:3) My-Je 83, p. 4.
"To a Kid Who Believes in Astrology." AmerPoR (12:3) My-Je 83, p. 3.
"Untitled Poem: I'm waiting for you, but not purely." AmerPoR (12:3) My-Je 83, p. 3.
"Untitled Poem: The patients in the waiting room." AmerPoR (12:3) My-Je 83, p. 4.
"Untitled Poem: Why feel guilty because the death of a lover causes lust?" AmerPoR (12:3) My-Je 83, p. 3.

1173. DUGAN, Jina
"The Engagement of Orange." ThRiPo (19/20) 82, p. 39.
"Pesada." ThRiPo (19/20) 82, p. 40-41.

1174. DUGUID, Sandra R.
"Role of Nonsense." WestB (12) 83, p. 92-93.

1175. DUHAIME, A. (André)
"Automne" (Haiku). PoetryCR (5:2) Wint 83-84, p. 8.
"Autumn" (Haiku). PoetryCR (5:2) Wint 83-84, p. 8.
"Blizzard." Quarry (32:3) Sum 83, p. 72.
"Matin au motel." Quarry (32:3) Sum 83, p. 72.
"Morning at the hotel." Quarry (32:3) Sum 83, p. 72.

1176. DUMITRIU van SAANEN, Christine
"Light." Bluebuf (2:1) Aut 83, p. 4.
"Numbers." Dandel (10:2) Aut-Wint 83, p. 12.

1177. DUNGEY, Chris
"Fish Place." SanFPJ (5:2) 83, p. 31.

1178. DUNN, David
"Certain Breath." WindO (43) Wint 83, p. 48.
"Cycle of Events." WindO (43) Wint 83, p. 48.
"Gathering Footsteps." WindO (43) Wint 83, p. 47.
"Matter over Mind." WindO (43) Wint 83, p. 47.
"On Trying to Answer the Question 'How Do You Write'." WindO (43) Wint 83, p. 48.
"Poem: The heat splinters like a worn reed." Pig (11) 83, p. 50.

1179. DUNN, Douglas
"The Clear Day." NewYorker (59:24) 1 Ag 83, p. 40.

1180. DUNN, S. P.
"Summer Evening in the Suburbs, Waiting for a Movie." PikeF (5) Spr 83, p. 9.

1181. DUNN, Sharon
"Gift Invented for Easter" (for Mary and Amy). Prima (8) 83, p. 84.

1182. DUNN, Si
"Found Fragments from a Tragicomedy." Vis (12) 83, p. 33.
"Small Change." Vis (12) 83, p. 34.

1183. DUNN, Stephen
"Apples and Goodbyes." KanQ (15:4) Aut 83, p. 12.
"Blues for Another Time." KanQ (15:4) Aut 83, p. 13.
"Briefcases." NewEngR (6:1) Aut 83, p. 108-109.
"Candles." MissouriR (7:1) Aut 83, p. 70.
"The Cocked Finger." NewEng (5:4) Sum 83, p. 460-461.
"Day and Night Handball." ThRiPo (21/22) 83, p. 24-25.
"Elegy" (John Cheever 1912-1982). Poetry (142:3) Je 83, p. 141-142.
"Enough Time" (for Lyn Harrison). GeoR (37:4) Wint 83, p. 752.
"Erasures." SenR (13:2) 82-83, p. 64-65.
"Finding Your Tiger Face." KanQ (15:4) Aut 83, p. 15.
"From Port Authority." MissouriR (7:1) Aut 83, p. 72-73.
"History" (for Lois). PraS (51:1, i.e. 57:1) Spr 83, p. 33-34.
"Insomnia." MissouriR (7:1) Aut 83, p. 71.
"The Landscape." VirQR (59:2) Spr 83, p. 240-241.
"Landscape Where Children Once Played." NowestR (21:1) 83, p. 19.
"Legacy" (For my father, Charles Dunn, 1905-1967). MissouriR (7:1) Aut 83, p. 75-78.
"Living with Hornets." NewEngR (6:1) Aut 83, p. 107-108.
"Middle Class Poem." MissouriR (7:1) Aut 83, p. 74.
"Nova Scotia." NewYorker (59:23) 25 Jl 83, p. 42.
"A Private Man Confronts His Vulgarities at Dawn." ThRiPo (21/22) 83, p. 26.
"The Rain Falling Now." OhioR (30) 83, p. 207-208.
"Response to a Letter from France." AmerS (52:4)

Aut 83, p. 511-512.
"The Room and the World." AmerPoR (12:2) Mr/Ap 83, p. 39.
"Second Prelude to the Monastery." OhioR (30) 83, p. 206.
"Sick Days." AmerPoR (12:2) Mr/Ap 83, p. 39.
"Skin Diving." KanQ (15:4) Aut 83, p. 14.
"Tangier." YaleR (72:3) Spr 83, p. 419.
"To My Student Who Said He Wanted to Lead a Coherent Life." PraS (51:1, i.e. 57:1) Spr 83, p. 32.
"Visions." MissouriR (7:1) Aut 83, p. 69.
"The Winter We Had to Get Away." BlackWR (8:1) Aut 81, p. 50-51.

1184. DUNNE, Carol
"Dawn Tamer." ClockR (2:1) 83, p. 44.
"Lover's Contingency." Poem (49) N 83, p. 54.
"Protested Delivery." Poem (49) N 83, p. 55.

1185. DUNNING, Barbara
"Virgo." StoneC (10:3/4) Spr-Sum 83, p. 64.

1186. DUNNING, Stephen
"Always Later." WorldO (17:4) Sum 83, p. 31.
"Not Falling to Dogs." Focus (15:95) Ag 83, p. 18.

1187. DuPLESSIS, Rachel Blau
"Crowbar." Sulfur (3:2, #8) 83, p. 131-146.

1188. DuPREE, Don
"Forgotten Music." Ploughs (9:2/3) 83, p. 221.
"Mother." Ploughs (9:2/3) 83, p. 222.

1189. DUPREE, Edison
"Civic Song." PoetryE (11) Sum 83, p. 55.
"Ladies and Gentlemen." PoetryE (11) Sum 83, p. 56.
"A Rapid Transit." Iowa (13:2) Spr 82, p. 73.

1190. DURANTI, Riccardo
"Erbario '81" (Selections from a Roman herbiary) (tr. of Sangiuliano). Kayak (62) Ag 83, p. 12-17.

1191. DUVAL, Quinton
"Ola and Casey." TriQ (56) Wint 83, p. 171.
"On the River Road." TriQ (56) Wint 83, p. 172.

1192. DWYER, David
"A Love Letter." SoDakR (21:4) Wint 83, p. 56.

1193. DWYER, Deirdre
"Beachfeather." PoetryCR (5:2) Wint 83-84, p. 19.
"Voices in the Kitchen." PoetryCR (5:1) Aut 83, p. 18.

1194. DYBEK, Stuart
"At the Beach." MemphisSR (4:1) Aut 83, p. 6.
"Flies." Images (8:3) 83, p. 4.

E, Liu
See: LIU, E

1195. EADY, Cornelius
"Luck." PoNow (7:2, #38) 83, p. 36.
"Radio." PoNow (7:2, #38) 83, p. 36.

1196. EATON, Charles Edward
"Blue Grotto." SoCaR (16:1) Aut 83, p. 96.
"The Canal." ColEng (45:1) Ja 83, p. 47-48.
"The Dervish." SoCaR (16:1) Aut 83, p. 97.
"Hallucination of the Lost Necklace." Poem (47) Mr 83, p. 44.
"In the Garden of the Fire Plants." ColEng (45:1) Ja 83, p. 46-47.
"The Infante of Images." Poem (47) Mr 83, p. 43.
"Jugtown." Paint (10:19/20) Spr-Aut 83, p. 27.
"Liebestrauma." DekalbLAJ (16:1/4) Aut 82-Sum 83, p. 63.
"Quizzical Request." Poem (49) N 83, p. 1.
"The Rendezvous." NewL (49:3/4) Spr-Sum 83, p. 164-165.
"The Rickshaw." SouthernR (19:4) O 83, p. 852.
"Rose-Colored Glasses." Confr (25/26) 83, p. 305.
"Slightly Faded Flowers." Poem (49) N 83, p. 3.
"Vulcan at Sunrise." Poem (47) Mr 83, p. 45.
"White Lake." Poem (49) N 83, p. 2.
"The Wrench." HolCrit (20:2) Ap 83, p. 10.

1197. EBERHART, Richard
"Commas in Wintertime." AmerPoR (12:2) Mr/Ap 83, p. 41.
"Going Backward Going Forward" (For Andrew Wanning). DevQ (18:3) Aut 83, p. 78.
"River Water Music." DevQ (18:3) Aut 83, p. 79.
"Waiting to Lean to the Master's Command." PoNow (7:2, #38) 83, p. 5.

1198. EBSWORTH, Peter
"Bits of the Other." Bogg (50) 83, p. 63.
"Future Presentations." Bogg (50) 83, p. 35.

1199. ECKMAN, Frederick
"On Being Loved." NewL (49:3/4) Spr-Sum 83, p. 165.

1200. EDDY, Stephen
"Wild." PoetL (78:3) Aut 83, p. 158.

1201. EDELMAN, Lee
"Esplanade." Nat (236:17) 30 Ap 83, p. 547.

1202. EDELMAN, Sandra Prewitt
"Having Not Written a Poem." SouthwR (68:4) Aut 83, p. 337-338.
"Solitaire." SouthwR (68:3) Sum 83, p. 232-233.

1203. EDELSTEIN, Carol
"Sleeping in the Open." YetASM (1:2) 82, p. 18.

1204. EDKINS, Anthony
"For a Friend One Year Later." SpiritSH (48) 82, p. 39.

1205. EDSON, Russell
"Herman's Oyster." PoNow (7:2, #38) 83, p. 12.
"Men Floating in the Meadow." OhioR (30) 83, p. 172.
"To Look at Nature." PoNow (7:2, #38) 83, p. 12.
"Turtles." OhioR (30) 83, p. 172.
"The Way Things Are." PoNow (7:2, #38) 83, p. 12.

1206. EDWARDS, Martin
"Apology." Bogg (51) 83, p. 37.

1207. EHRHART, W. D.
"Appearances." Sam (36:3 143rd release) 83, p. 30.
"Awaiting the Inquisition." SanFPJ (5:1) 83, p. 73.
"Canoeing the Potomac." Sam (36:3 143rd release) 83, p. 29.
"Laws." SanFPJ (5:1) 83, p. 17.
"The Outer Banks" (Selection: 7) (semi-finalist, 10th anniversary manuscript competition). StoneC (11:1/2, Pt. 1) Aut-Wint 83, p. 61.
"Responsibility." PoetryE (11) Sum 83, p. 62-63.
"The Suicide" (from The Outer Banks, semi-finalist, 10th anniversary manuscript competition). StoneC (11:1/2, Pt. 1) Aut-Wint 83, p. 61.
"Surviving the Bomb One More Day." Vis (11) 83, p. 18.
"Waiting for Word from Alaska." Sam (34:3 135th release) 83, p. 26-27.
"Why I Am Certain." SanFPJ (4:2) 83, p. 24.

1208. EHRLICH, Shelley
"Lilliput." PraS (51:1, i.e. 57:1) Spr 83, p. 57-58.
"On Campus." PraS (51:1, i.e. 57:1) Spr 83, p. 56.
"Travel." SouthwR (68:1) Wint 83, p. 51.
"When the Tree Surgeon Visits." PraS (51:1, i.e. 57:1) Spr 83, p. 55.

1209. EHRMAN, Sally
"Mountains Can't Save Me." SanFPJ (4:3) 83, p. 42.
"That's Exactly What I'm Afraid Of." SanFPJ (4:3) 83, p. 38.
"What Kind of Poem." SanFPJ (4:3) 83, p. 39.

1210. EIBEL, Deborah
"Notes from a Small Clinic." StoneC (10:3/4) Spr-Sum 83, p. 71.

1211. EICH, Günter
"Abandoned Upland Farm" (tr. by Francis Golffing). PoNow (7:2, #38) 83, p. 44.
"Insight" (tr. by Francis Golffing). PoNow (7:2, #38) 83, p. 44.
"Think about It" (tr. by James Doss). PoetryE (9/10) Wint 82-Spr 83, p. 193-194.

1212. EIMERS, Nancy
"Dialogues" (to Gloria). Tendril (14/15) Wint 83, p. 44-45.
"Duets." Tendril (14/15) Wint 83, p. 43.
"The Gypsy Moth." NoAmR (268:2) Je 83, p. 19.

1213. EINHORN, Sharone
"Detectives." AmerPoR (12:6) N/D 83, p. 34.
"Dreamland." AmerPoR (12:6) N/D 83, p. 34.

1214. ELDER, Karl
"Ombrophobia." IndR (6:3) Sum 83, p. 36.

1215. ELEKTOROWICZ, Leszek
"First Move" (tr. by Magnus J. Krynski and Robert A. Maguire). TriQ (57, Vol. 1) Spr-Sum 83, p. 62.

1216. ELIOT, Eileen
"At the Animal Hospital." Vis (13) 83, p. 16.
"A Delicate Operation." Vis (13) 83, p. 18, 20.
"Don't Move." Vis (13) 83, p. 21.
"K-Mart, $2.98." Vis (13) 83, p. 15.

1217. ELIRAZ, Israel
"I Too Look into the Fire" (tr. by Beate Hein Bennett). LitR (26:3) Spr 83, p. 447.
"In Halhul" (tr. by Beate Hein Bennett). LitR (26:3) Spr 83, p. 446.

ELK, Ben Black
See: BLACK ELK, Ben

1218. ELKIN, Roger
"Thistles." Argo (4:1) 82, p. 12.

1219. ELLEN
"4,000 gather for the Stones in Worcester." SanFPJ (4:3) 83, p. 10-11.
"Blood for Oil." SanFPJ (5:3) 83, p. 26.
"Implosions and other Dimensions." SanFPJ (5:3) 83, p. 82.
"Sleeping Guardian." SanFPJ (4:3) 83, p. 11.
"Tour of a Winery." SanFPJ (5:3) 83, p. 83.
"Untitled: The thing about the five lifeguards." SanFPJ (5:3) 83, p. 27-28.

1220. ELLIOTT, Anthony
"Night Watch." Bogg (51) 83, p. 53.

1221. ELLIOTT, Harley
"Demon Trapped in a Parking Lot." MemphisSR (2:1) Aut 81, p. 6.
"For Farmers." NewL (49:3/4) Spr-Sum 83, p. 217-218.
"The Men Who Loved Everything." NewL (49:3/4) Spr-Sum 83, p. 218.
"Mr. Scoop's Listen Coin." MemphisSR (2:1) Aut 81, p. 7.

1222. ELLIS, Rebecca
"What You Say You Are." HangL (44) Sum 83, p. 13.

1223. ELLISON, Jessie T.
"The Blue Enamel Dishpan: Easter, 1963." WindO (42) Sum 83, p. 12.
"High Style." WindO (42) Sum 83, p. 15.
"The Program." WindO (42) Sum 83, p. 14.
"Ruins of a Florida Sugar Mill." Kayak (61) Ap 83, p. 28.
"Sunday Afternoon Sleep." StoneC (10:3/4) Spr-Sum 83, p. 50.
"The Waiter at the Hotel de Soledad." StoneC (10:3/4) Spr-Sum 83, p. 51.
"Why I Love the National Geographic." WindO (42) Sum 83, p. 13-14.

1224. ELON, Florence
"Bequest." Poetry (142:1) Ap 83, p. 24.
"Hothouse Art." Poetry (142:1) Ap 83, p. 23.
"Room 9639." Poetry (142:1) Ap 83, p. 22.

1225. ELOVIC, Barbara
"Saturday Morning Services." MSS (3:1) Aut 83, p. 115.
"Spring in the City." PoetC (15:1) Aut 83, p. 20.

1226. ELSON, Virginia
"And Echoes for Direction." Atlantic (252:4) O 83, p. 52.

1227. ELUARD, Paul
"Shared Nights" (tr. by Lydia Davis). ParisR (25:88) Sum 83, p. 235-238.

1228. ELYTIS, Odysseus
"The Primal Sun (Helios o Protos)" (Selections: V-VI, XII-XIII, XV, XVII-XVIII) (tr. by Lefteris Pavlides and Edward Morin). WebR (8:1) Spr 83, p. 20-25.

1229. EMANS, Elaine V.
"Cycles." CapeR (19:1) Wint 83, p. 2.
"Discovery." KanQ (15:2) Spr 83, p. 26.
"Downed Woodcock." KanQ (15:2) Spr 83, p. 26.

1230. EMANUEL, Lynn
"Frying Trout While Drunk." Poetry (142:2) My 83, p. 78.
"Grandmother Zoltana, Tunisia, Early 50's." AmerPoR (12:1) Ja/F 83, p. 17.
"The Last Two Photographs of My Father before the War." AmerPoR (12:1) Ja/F 83, p. 17.
"Of Your Father's Indiscretions and the Train to California." AmerPoR (12:1) Ja/F 83, p. 17.
"The Photograph of Ramona Posing while Father Sketches Her in Charcoal." Poetry (142:2) My 83, p. 79.
"The Picture of My Father Taken at an Early Exhibit of Arshile Gorky." AmerPoR (12:1) Ja/F 83, p. 17.
"When Father Decided He Did Not Love Her Anymore." Poetry (142:2) My 83, p. 80.

1231. EMERY, Jason
"The Shop." PikeF (5) Spr 83, p. 21.

1232. EMERY, Mary
"The Post Mortem Lounge." ThRiPo (19/20) 82, p. 42.

1233. EMERY, Michael J.
"Found Poem: Lost & Found in London." WindO (42) Sum 83, p. 39.

1234. EMERY, Thomas
"To the Dirt, the Grass and the People, Who Live with a Plutonium Plant." SanFPJ (4:2) 83, p. 46-47.

1235. ENCARNACION, Alfred
"On the Old Porch, Long Ago." CapeR (19:1) Wint 83, p. 30.
"The Plait." CapeR (19:1) Wint 83, p. 32.
"A Stone for Grandfather (dead at eighty-five of hardening of the arteries)." CapeR (19:1) Wint 83, p. 31.

1236. ENDREZZE-DANIELSON, Anita
"The Girl Who Loved the Sky." CharR (9:2) Aut 83, p. 62-63.
"Return of the Wolves." CharR (9:2) Aut 83, p. 63.
"Reviewing Past Lives While Leaf-Burning." SouthernPR (23:2) Aut 83, p. 59-60.

1237. ENGEL, Kathy
"In the Middle of the Night in July." PoetryE (9/10) Wint 82-Spr 83, p. 81-82.
"Letter to the Editor." PoetryE (9/10) Wint 82-Spr 83, p. 77-80.

1238. ENGEL, Mary
"Crucifixion" (of Martin Luther King, Jr.). SanFPJ (4:2) 83, p. 37.
"The Grass Is Greener in Scarsdale." SanFPJ (4:2) 83, p. 56.
"Preacher." SanFPJ (5:2) 83, p. 94.
"Promised Land." SanFPJ (5:2) 83, p. 95.

1239. ENGELHARDT, Helen
"A Lady Writing a Letter with Her Maid." YetASM (1:1) 82, p. 14.

1240. ENGELS, John
"A Discovery of Lovers in the Fall." BlackWR (10:1) Aut 83, p. 120.
"Panorama." GeoR (37:2) Sum 83, p. 412.

1241. ENGLE, Ed, Jr.
"In the Routine." CrabCR (1:2) Aut 83, p. 16.
"Visiting God's House Alone." CrabCR (1:2) Aut 83, p. 17.

1242. ENGLEBERT, Michel J.
"Nova II: Her Final Confession." CapeR (18:2) Sum

83, p. 20.
"Vernichtung" (For L.E.). BelPoJ (33:3) Spr 83, p. 5-6.

1243. ENGLER, Robert Klein
"Overnight by English Bay." Waves (11:2/3) Wint 83, p. 65.
"Planting Tulips." PoetL (77:2) Sum 82, p. 80-81.
"The Rocking Chair." Waves (11:2/3) Wint 83, p. 64.
"Siguenza." PoetL (77:1) Spr 82, p. 13.

1244. ENGMAN, John
"There Are Thousands of Black Wires." PoetryE (9/10) Wint 82-Spr 83, p. 139.

1245. ENRICO, Harold
"Grave at Sète" (Paul Valéry). WestCR (18:1) Je 83, p. 33.
"Margins." WestCR (18:1) Je 83, p. 31-33.
"On This Side of the Mountains Where You Have Never Been." WestCR (18:1) Je 83, p. 34.
"The Open Spaces in the Forest." WestCR (18:1) Je 83, p. 44-45.
"Photographs with and without Sound." WestCR (18:1) Je 83, p. 46-47.
"La Qual Null'altro Allegra Arbor Nè Fiore." WestCR (18:1) Je 83, p. 35.
"Quanto e'bella giovanezza, the honeyed crown of your hair." WestCR (18:1) Je 83, p. 36.
"Remembering César Vallejo." WestCR (18:1) Je 83, p. 33.
"Rip Current." WestCR (18:1) Je 83, p. 38-43.
"Tonight the Eaves Speak Ancient Hebrew." WestCR (18:1) Je 83, p. 37.

1246. ENROTH, Tess
"Anginal." YetASM (1:1) 82, p. 12.
"Lying Here." YetASM (1:1) 82, p. 4.

1247. ENSLER, Eve
"In Purple Light" (For Mac, Cape Cod, Summer 1982). ThirdW Spr 83, p. 55.

1248. ENSLIN, Theodore
"Axes 72." Sulfur (3:2, #8) 83, p. 66-72.

1249. ENTREKIN, Charles
"Point Pinole." IndR (6:3) Sum 83, p. 61.

1250. ENZENSBERGER, Hans Magnus
"Die Furie des Verschwindens Gedichte." NowestR (21:1) 83, p. 123-135.
"Labor" (for Theodor W., Adorno) (tr. by K. Lydia Schultz). NowestR (21:1) 83, p. 129.
"Land of Shadows" (tr. by Felix Pollak and Reinhold Grimm). NowestR (21:1) 83, p. 131, 133.
"Poetry Festival" (Hommage à Paul van Ostaijen). NowestR (21:1) 83, p. 124, 126.
"Poetry Festival" (Hommage à Paul van Ostaijen) (tr. by K. Lydia Schultz). NowestR (21:1) 83,

p. 125, 127.
"Schattenreich." NowestR (21:1) 83, p. 130, 132.
"Schwierige Arbeit" (für Theodor W., Adorno). NowestR (21:1) 83, p. 128.
"Those Who Have Disappeared" (for Nelly Sachs) (tr. by Felix Pollak and Reinhold Grimm). NowestR (21:1) 83, p. 135.
"Die Verschwundenen" (für Nelly Sachs). NowestR (21:1) 83, p. 134.

1251. EPLING, Kathy
"Heron." PraS (57:2) Sum 83, p. 86.
"White Freesias." Kayak (63) N 83, p. 36-37.

1252. EPSTEIN, Daniel Mark
"Paolo and Francesca." Thrpny (4:3, issue 15) Aut 83, p. 24.
"Schoolhouses." BlackWR (9:1) Aut 82, p. 7-9.

1253. EPSTEIN, Elaine
"A Question of Faith." AntR (41:3) Sum 83, p. 326.

1254. ERIAN, Soraya
"The State of an Immigrant." CrossC (5:2/3) 83, p. 25.

1255. ERICKSON, S. Leif
"Duluoz's Dirdge." MoodySI (13) Sum 83, p. 18.

1256. ERMINI, Flavio
"Isolato e Dintorni." Os (17) 83, p. 31.
"Selciato e Rotaie." Os (17) 83, p. 30.

1257. ERMLICH, Alice M.
"Pond and Sea." Poem (48) Jl 83, p. 46.
"Tar Pits." Poem (48) Jl 83, p. 45.

1258. ERNST, Kathy
"Last Night." Bogg (51) 83, p. 22.

1259. ERRANTE, Camille
"My Father." CapeR (19:1) Wint 83, p. 33.

1260. ERRINGTON, Lee Anne
"From the Fire Comes the Steel." WorldO (17:4) Sum 83, p. 32.

1261. ERWIN, Rei M.
"Last Flight." CalQ (22) Sum 83, p. 50.
"Small Dirge." CalQ (22) Sum 83, p. 50.

1262. ESCANDELL, Noemi
"Bienestar." LetFem (9:2) Aut 83, p. 96.
"Cuadros." LetFem (9:2) Aut 83, p. 96.
"Diciembre." LetFem (9:2) Aut 83, p. 97.
"Lluvia." LetFem (9:2) Aut 83, p. 95.
"Viendo Llover." LetFem (9:2) Aut 83, p. 97.

1263. ESHE, Aisha
"Black Poet Tryin' ta Rest fore School Start Nex'

Month." SanFPJ (4:2) 83, p. 66-68.
"Daydream." SanFPJ (5:3) 83, p. 77.
"Nationalist Life Marriage." SanFPJ (4:2) 83, p. 31.
"Was It You I Dreamed About (Charles)." SanFPJ (4:2) 83, p. 30.

1264. ESHLEMAN, Clayton
"Bread and Wine" (tr. of Robert Marteau, w. Bernard Bador). Sulfur (3:1, #7) 83, p. 40-43.
"Certification" (from "Fracture"). Sulfur (3:1, #7) 83, p. 58-60.
"The Color Rake of Time" (from "Fracture"). Sulfur (3:1, #7) 83, p. 52.
"Elegy" (from "Fracture"). Sulfur (3:1, #7) 83, p. 53-56.
"Etc" (tr. of Michel Deguy). Sulfur (3:2, #8) 83, p. 109-113.
"Fracture" (Selections: 4 Poems). Sulfur (3:1, #7) 83, p. 52-60.
"Manticore Vortex" (from "Fracture"). Sulfur (3:1, #7) 83, p. 56-58.
"Millenium." Epoch (32:2) Wint-Spr 83, p. 118.
"Nothing Follows." Tendril (16) Sum 83, p. 30.
"Tantrik X-ray." Epoch (32:2) Wint-Spr 83, p. 117.
"Through Breuil's Eyes." CreamCR (8:1/2) 83, p. 164-165.

1265. ESOLEN, Tony
"Shorty." CarolQ (35:2) Wint 83, p. 32-39.

1266. ESPAILLAT, Rhina (Rhina P.)
"Driving Through." PoetL (77:1) Spr 82, p. 20.
"November Music." PoetL (78:1) Spr 83, p. 20.

1267. ESPOSITO, Nancy
"Breakfast Piece." BlackWR (9:2) Spr 83, p. 82-83.
"Goodwill." Thrpny (3:4, issue 12) Wint 83, p. 23.
"In a Word" (for Desirée Pallais Checa). Nat (237:13) 29 O 83, p. 407.
"Shapeshifting." NoAmR (268:2) Je 83, p. 29.

1268. ESPRIU, Salvador
"And, Then, Silence" (tr. by Martin Paul). Mund (14:1) 83, p. 13.
"Endins de la Boira." Mund (14:1) 83, p. 12, 14.
"I, Despres, El Silenci." Mund (14:1) 83, p. 12.
"In the Fog" (tr. by Martin Paul). Mund (14:1) 83, p. 13, 15.

1269. ESTELLES, Vicent Andrés
"I see from back porches" (tr. by David H. Rosenthal). LitR (26:3) Spr 83, p. 401.
"If it's permitted" (tr. by David H. Rosenthal). LitR (26:3) Spr 83, p. 401.
"Illict Homage to Lluís Milà" (To Francesc Brines, tr. by David H. Rosenthal). LitR (26:3) Spr 83, p. 402-404.

1270. ESTESS, Sybil P.
"Wishes and Needs." SouthernHR (17:2) Spr 83, p.

119.

1271. ESTEVES, Sandra Maria
"Amor Negro." RevChic (11:3/4) 83, p. 30.
"A Celebration of Home Birth: November 15, 1981" (for Yaasmiyn Rahiyma). RevChic (11:3/4) 83, p. 31-32.
"Portraits for Shamsul Alam." RevChic (11:3/4) 83, p. 33-34.
"Transference." RevChic (11:3/4) 83, p. 34-35.

1272. ETHELSDATTAR, Karen
"Poem after the Manner of Kabir." ThirdW Spr 83, p. 87.

1273. ETTER, Dave (David Pearson)
"Black Sunflowers." Poetry (143:2) N 83, p. 89.
"Dixie Truck Stop." ClockR (1:1) Sum 83, p. 25.
"The Ellsworth Brothers" (from Boondocks). PoNow (7:2, #38) 83, p. 23.
"Gone with the Grain." Poetry (143:2) N 83, p. 88.
"Hambletonian." SpoonRQ (8:2) Spr 83, p. 13.
"Librarian." Poetry (141:4) Ja 83, p. 222-223.
"Max." CreamCR (8:1/2) 83, p. 99.
"Moonlight Yodel." Poetry (141:4) Ja 83, p. 223.
"Nina James: Writing Down the Dream." CreamCR (8:1/2) 83, p. 98.
"The Railroad Wave." Poetry (143:2) N 83, p. 89.
"Some Smart Remarks on the Closing of the Hiram Walker Distillery i Peoria." SpoonRQ (8:2) Spr 83, p. 12.
"South of Sioux Falls." SoDakR (21:4) Wint 83, p. 7.
"Tough Luck in Quincy." SpoonRQ (8:2) Spr 83, p. 14.
"Train Wreck" (from Boondocks). PoNow (7:2, #38) 83, p. 23.
"Words for Sunny." ClockR (1:1) Sum 83, p. 27.

1274. EUGSTER, Carla
"Dancing Giraffe." KanQ (15:2) Spr 83, p. 171.
"Reflections of a Retired Activist." KanQ (15:2) Spr 83, p. 171.

1275. EVANS, Bill
"Ninth Elegy" (from Rilke's Elegies, w. Andrew Gent). HangL (44) Sum 83, p. 14-16.

1276. EVANS, Christine
"A Common Failing." Stand (24:2) 83, p. 45.

1277. EVANS, Elizabeth
"One." YetASM (2:1) 83, p. 3.

1278. EVANS, James
"The Going / The Sigh." KanQ (15:1) Wint 83, p. 137.

1279. EVANS, Judson K.
"Flowering Judas." WestB (13) 83, p. 42-43.

1280. EVANS, Sharon Lynn
"Feline." Poem (47) Mr 83, p. 17.

"Your Mother's Ills." Poem (47) Mr 83, p. 18.

1281. EVARTS, Prescott, Jr.
"Coming Home from School and Going to a Game." KanQ (15:3) Sum 83, p. 58.
"Teaching." KanQ (15:1) Wint 83, p. 188-189.

1282. EVASON, Greg
"Day." PoetryCR (5:1) Aut 83, p. 18.

1283. EVATT, Julia
"Old Men." Wind (13:48) 83, p. 17.

EVELYN, Thomas d'
See: D'EVELYN, Thomas

1284. EVEN, Tom
"You Are Horribly Satanic" (Excerpt). NewRep (186:4) 27 Ja 82, p. 36.

1285. EVERETT, Barbara
"Welfare." SanFPJ (4:4) 83, p. 68.

1286. EVERMAN, Welch D.
"The Story." NewOR (10:2/3) Sum-Aut 83, p. 146-148.

1287. EVERSON, R. G.
"Herd of Stars." CanLit (97) Sum 83, p. 74.
"My Sympathy Is with the Fish." CanLit (98) Aut 83, p. 58.

1288. EVERSON, William
"Danse Macabre." Sulfur (3:2, #8) 83, p. 4-6.
"The Poet Is Dead" (A Memorial for Robinson Jeffers). SecC (11:1/2) 83, p. 45-51.
"Reaper." Sulfur (3:2, #8) 83, p. 6-7.

1289. EVERWINE, Peter
"The Burden of Decision." OhioR (30) 83, p. 100.

1290. EWART, Gavin
"The Town Mouse and the Country Mouse." Stand (24:4) Aut 83, p. 46.

1291. EWICK, David
"Still Life." IndR (6:3) Sum 83, p. 70.
"The Stone." IndR (6:3) Sum 83, p. 71.

1293. FABIAN, R. Gerry
"The 75% Factor." Sam (36:2, 142nd release [i.e. 36:4 144th release]) 83, p. 3.
"Bargaining in Good Faith." Sam (36:2, 142nd release [i.e. 36:4 144th release]) 83, p. 7.
"Bottom of the Ninth Haiku." Sam (36:2, 142nd release [i.e. 36:4 144th release]) 83, p. 12.
"Doubleheader." Sam (36:2, 142nd release [i.e. 36:4 144th release]) 83, p. 1-14.
"Hanging Curve." Sam (36:2, 142nd release [i.e. 36:4 144th release]) 83, p. 6.
"Home Stand." Sam (36:2, 142nd release [i.e. 36:4

144th release]) 83, p. 8.
"The Indicator." Sam (36:2, 142nd release [i.e. 36:4 144th release]) 83, p. 9.
"Lifetime Contract." Sam (36:2, 142nd release [i.e. 36:4 144th release]) 83, p. 3.
"Major League." Sam (36:2, 142nd release [i.e. 36:4 144th release]) 83, p. 9.
"Metaphysical Rabies." SanFPJ (4:4) 83, p. 91.
"Occasional Slaughter." SanFPJ (4:4) 83, p. 91.
"Pitch Selection." Sam (36:2, 142nd release [i.e. 36:4 144th release]) 83, p. 6.
"Pull Hitter." Sam (36:2, 142nd release [i.e. 36:4 144th release]) 83, p. 14.
"Short Relief." Sam (36:2, 142nd release [i.e. 36:4 144th release]) 83, p. 11.
"Starting Rotation." Sam (36:2, 142nd release [i.e. 36:4 144th release]) 83, p. 8.
"Stretch Drive." Sam (36:2, 142nd release [i.e. 36:4 144th release]) 83, p. 4.
"Suicide Squeeze." Sam (36:2, 142nd release [i.e. 36:4 144th release]) 83, p. 12.
"The Third Out." Sam (36:2, 142nd release [i.e. 36:4 144th release]) 83, p. 10.
"Twenty Game Winner." Sam (36:2, 142nd release [i.e. 36:4 144th release]) 83, p. 7.
"Twilight Waivers." Sam (36:2, 142nd release [i.e. 36:4 144th release]) 83, p. 5.
"The Vegetable League." Sam (36:2, 142nd release [i.e. 36:4 144th release]) 83, p. 2.

1294. FACKNITZ, Mark A. R.
"Topography." GeoR (37:2) Sum 83, p. 305.

1295. FAGAN, William Michael
"Encomium for Margaret Sanger." SanFPJ (5:4) 83, p. 72.

1296. FAGERMAN, Sherri L.
"The Pyromaniac." IndR (6:3) Sum 83, p. 65.

1297. FAGLES, Robert
"Snow Watch." OntR (18) Spr-Sum 83, p. 82-83.

1298. FAHEY, W. A.
"Again a Green River" (tr. of Salvatore Quasimodo). WebR (8:1) Spr 83, p. 57.
"Bituminous Angel" (tr. of Rafael Alberti). WebR (8:1) Spr 83, p. 56.
"Bklyn Bridge." Confr (25/26) 83, p. 186.
"Le Douanier's 'Sleeping Gypsy'." WebR (8:1) Spr 83, p. 58.
"The Good Angel" (tr. of Rafael Alberti). WebR (8:1) Spr 83, p. 55.
"Little River Song." WebR (8:1) Spr 83, p. 57.

1299. FAINLIGHT, Ruth
"Among a Thousand Others." Descant (40) Spr 83, p. 57.
"Grandmas." Poetry (141:6) Mr 83, p. 319.
"The Noonday Devil." Descant (40) Spr 83, p. 56.

"Passions." Poetry (141:6) Mr 83, p. 318.
"The Prism." Poetry (141:6) Mr 83, p. 320.
"Products of the Pig." Thrpny (3:4, issue 12) Wint 83, p. 19.

1300. FAIRCHILD, B. H., Jr.
"Hitchcock." YetASM (1:1) 82, p. 12.

1301. FAIRCHOK, Sherry
"Rowing on the Sacandaga River." Blueline (3:2) Wint-Spr 82, p. 40-41.

1302. FAIRFAX, John
"Her Song." MalR (64) F 83, p. 205-206.
"To My Mother." MalR (64) F 83, p. 204.
"The Wall, the Ants and a Green Woodpecker." MalR (64) F 83, p. 206-207.

1303. FAISON, Dossie, Jr.
"Slim Johns, Quiet Storm." NewRena (16) Spr 83, p. 67.

1304. FAIZ, Faiz Ahmed
"Poem: O you who wear shirts ripped at the collars" (in Urdu). StoneC (10:3/4) Spr-Sum 83, p. 44.
"Poem: O you who wear shirts ripped at the collars" (tr. by Agha Shahid Ali). StoneC (10:3/4) Spr-Sum 83, p. 45.

1305. FALCO, Edward
"DeWolf Point." Tendril (16) Sum 83, p. 31.

1306. FALCONE, James
"Final Entry." CrossC (5:1) 83, p. 3.
"Neptune Night." AntigR (52) Wint 83, p. 35.

1307. FALES, Nancy
"Ragtime" 13thM (6:1/2) 82, p. 86.

1308. FALK, Marcia
"Falling Asleep, I Think of My Married Friends." Prima (8) 83, p. 32.

1309. FALLON, Peter
"Mole." PoetryE (9/10) Wint 82-Spr 83, p. 222.
"Victim." PoetryE (9/10) Wint 82-Spr 83, p. 220-221.

1310. FALUDY, George
"The Ballad of the Hell-Hound" (tr. by Arthur Koestler). CanLit (98) Aut 83, p. 4-7.
"The Dancer" (tr. by Eric Johnson). CanLit (98) Aut 83, p. 7-9.

1311. FALZON, Grazio
"Tonight a Cross-Eyed Moon" (tr. of Mario Azzopardi). Vis (13) 83, p. 28.
"Vision 22 X" (tr. of Mario Azzopardi). Vis (13) 83, p. 27.

1312. FAMA, Maria
"Girl at the Bakery." Bogg (50) 83, p. 14.

1313. FANDEL, John
"75 Mirrors" (To the Chief Laureate upon Muthlabben, A Shiggaion of John, Michtam). Poetry (141:5) F 83, p. 271-273.

1314. FARBER, Norma
"Moon-Take." PoNow (7:2, #38) 83, p. 40.
"The Serpent, Urging." ChrC (100:24) 17-24 Ag 83, p. 735.

1315. FAREWELL, Patricia
"Prayer for a Journey." NewL (50:1) Aut 83, p. 38.

1316. FARGAS, Laura
"Long Distance." PoetL (78:3) Aut 83, p. 155.
"Untitled: The place where shadows wait on moonless nights." GeoR (37:1) Spr 83, p. 79.

1317. FARGNOLI, Patricia
"Going." PoetL (78:4) Wint 84, p. 205.
"Shoring." Tendril (14/15) Wint 83, p. 46-47.

1318. FARLEY, Michael
"Armillary." Stand (24:4) Aut 83, p. 48.

1319. FARNSWORTH, Jane
"A Single Life." Quarry (32:3) Sum 83, p. 24.
"Two Women and a Mirror." Quarry (32:3) Sum 83, p. 24-25.

1320. FARNSWORTH, Robert
"The Carp That Swallowed a Diamond." AmerPoR (12:2) Mr/Ap 83, p. 39.
"Pegasus." ThRiPo (21/22) 83, p. 27-28.

1321. FARRANT, Elizabeth
"Places We Come to Know." Poem (47) Mr 83, p. 59.
"Ship-Wrecked." Poem (47) Mr 83, p. 60.

1322. FARRELL, Katy
"Above Tempo." AntigR (52) Wint 83, p. 31.
"In the Storm." AntigR (52) Wint 83, p. 32.

1323. FAULKNER, Leigh
"Napoleon's Soldiers Burn Three-Thousand-Year-Old Mummies to Keep Warm in the Desert." Germ (7:1) Spr-Sum 83, p. 20.
"Song of the Blue China Horseman." Germ (7:1) Spr-Sum 83, p. 21.

1324. FAWCETT, Susan
"Bird Chasing." Prima (8) 83, p. 86.
"Fireplace with Hyacinths." Prima (8) 83, p. 30.
"For I Will Consider My Bird Ariel" (after Christopher Smart). ThirdW Spr 83, p. 38-39.
"The Slow Way of Forgiveness" (For my brother Millard 1942-1958). Nimrod (27:1) Aut-Wint 83,

p. 27-29.
"The Surfers." ThirdW Spr 83, p. 39.

1325. FAY, Julie
"Camp, 1943." 13thM (6:1/2) 82, p. 83.
"Cassiopeia's Chair." Shen (34:2) 83, p. 78.
"Felling Trees." OP (35) Spr-Sum 83, p. 14-15.
"I Think of You As in a Glass Paperweight." OP (35) Spr-Sum 83, p. 11.
"Vasari's Corridor." OP (35) Spr-Sum 83, p. 12-13.

1326. FEDERMAN, Raymond
"A cup on a telegram" (tr. of Michel Deguy). ParisR (24:84) Sum 82, p. 26.
"The wall is massive, of solid stone, hard, finished" (tr. of Michel Deguy). ParisR (24:84) Sum 82, p. 26.
"When two poets come face to face" (tr. of Michel Deguy). ParisR (24:84) Sum 82, p. 26.

1327. FEDERSPIEL, Jürg
"Bonaparte" (tr. by Eveline L. Kanes). PoetL (78:2) Sum 83, p. 81.
"Evil" (tr. by Eveline L. Kanes). PoetL (78:2) Sum 83, p. 77.
"The Expected" (tr. by Eveline L. Kanes). PoetL (78:2) Sum 83, p. 79.
"Instructor" (tr. by Eveline L. Kanes). PoetL (78:2) Sum 83, p. 82.
"Pairing Off with Ghosts" (tr. by Eveline L. Kanes). PoetL (78:2) Sum 83, p. 78.
"Paracelsus" (for Margarita, tr. by Eveline L. Kanes). PoetL (78:2) Sum 83, p. 80.

1328. FEENEY, Mary
"The middle-aged teacher lets his small son" (tr. of Jean Follain, w. William Matthews). Field (28) Spr 83, p. 63.

1329. FEENEY, Thomas (See also: FEENY, Thomas)
"Creepy People." YetASM (1:2) 82, p. 16.

1330. FEENY, Thomas (See also: FEENEY, Thomas)
"Daybreak on Plum Island." CapeR (18:2) Sum 83, p. 1.
"Homecoming." Wind (13:47) 83, p. 11-12.
"TM." WebR (8:1) Spr 83, p. 78.

1331. FEIN, Cheri
"Sunset." Confr (25/26) 83, p. 309.

1332. FEINSTEIN, Robert N.
"Energy Dialogue." NegC (3:4) Aut 83, p. 47.
"Gene Pool." SanFPJ (4:4) 83, p. 65.

1333. FELDMAN, Alan
"Für Elise." Tendril (14/15) Wint 83, p. 51.
"Grand Canyon Poem." SouthernPR (23:2) Aut 82 [i.e. (23:1?) Spr 83], p. 27-28.
"The Link." NoAmR (268:3) S 83, p. 40.

"Sailing." Tendril (14/15) Wint 83, p. 50.
"Small Losses, Small Gains." Tendril (14/15) Wint 83, p. 48-49.

1334. FELDMAN, Irving
"Art of the Haiku." Iowa (13:2) Spr 82, p. 116.
"The Labyrinth." Iowa (13:2) Spr 82, p. 116.
"Talking to Fernando" (to my son). NewRep (186:11) 17 Mr 82, p. 34.
"Widow." Nat (237:19) 10 D 83, p. 609.

1335. FELDMAN, Ruth
"Assisi." WebR (8:1) Spr 83, p. 52-53.
"Clocks and Watches." WebR (8:1) Spr 83, p. 52.
"Illumination." MalR (64) F 83, p. 126.
"A Kind of Apocalypse" (from In uno Specchio la Fenice, tr. of Gina Labriola). WebR (8:1) Spr 83, p. 49-50.
"Metallic Love" (from Alveare di Specchi, tr. of Gina Labriola). WebR (8:1) Spr 83, p. 50-51.
"Philanthropist." NewRena (16) Spr 83, p. 68.
"Timetables." WebR (8:1) Spr 83, p. 54.

1336. FELICE, Renee
"Lemon Drop Saturday." YetASM (1:2) 82, p. 14.

1337. FELIX, Catherine
"Black Woman." BlackALF (17:4) Wint 83, p. 170-171.

1338. FENG, Chih
"Here, in the full sunlight" (tr. by Cedric Dow). Germ (7:2) Aut-Wint 83, p. 31.
"Listen to the storm" (tr. by Cedric Dow). Germ (7:2) Aut-Wint 83, p. 27.
"Whether we stand on a mountain" (tr. by Cedric Dow). Germ (7:2) Aut-Wint 83, p. 28.
"You tell me the things you like best" (tr. by Cedric Dow). Germ (7:2) Aut-Wint 83, p. 29.
"You went hungry in deserted villages" (tr. by Cedric Dow). Germ (7:2) Aut-Wint 83, p. 30.

1339. FENSTERMAKER, Vesle
"Memento Mori." YetASM (1:2) 82, p. 15.

1340. FENTON, James
"Children in Exile" (to J.T.L.&S.). ParisR (25:89) Aut 83, p. 202-209.
"In a Notebook." Agni (18) 83, p. 48-49.
"Lines for Translation into Any Language." Agni (18) 83, p. 51.
"Lullaby for a Summer Recess." Agni (18) 83, p. 50.
"A Vacant Possession." Agni (18) 83, p. 52-53.
"The Wild Ones." Agni (18) 83, p. 54.

1341. FENZA, D. W.
"How Maria Rodriguez Dances with Such Authority." OP (36) Aut-Wint 83, p. 33-40.

1342. FERENCZ, Amalia
"Jubilee of Saint Elizabeth." CrabCR (1:2) Aut

83, p. 18-19.

1343. FERICANO, Paul
"Upstairs in C. Ward." SecC (11:1/2) 83, p. 52-53.

1344. FERLINGHETTI, Lawrence
"The General Song of Humanity." SecC (11:1/2) 83, p. 55-56.

1345. FERNANDEZ, Daniel
"Ice Mirror." Wind (13:48) 83, p. 51.

1346. FERNANDEZ, Eva
"The Hours." IndR (5:1) Wint 82, p. 31.
"March." IndR (5:3) Aut 82, p. 5.
"Sleep's Secret Plea." IndR (5:1) Wint 82, p. 30.

1347. FERRARELLI, Rina
"Black Orchids." Wind (13:47) 83, p. 35.
"Crowd at the Stadium." Wind (13:47) 83, p. 35.
"Hear Failure at 45." YetASM (2:1) 83, p. 5.

1348. FERRATER, Gabriel
"The Furtive Life" (tr. by David H. Rosenthal). LitR (26:3) Spr 83, p. 398.
"Idleness" (tr. by David H. Rosenthal). LitR (26:3) Spr 83, p. 400.
"A Small War" (tr. by David H. Rosenthal). LitR (26:3) Spr 83, p. 399-400.
"Two Girl Friends" (tr. by David H. Rosenthal). LitR (26:3) Spr 83, p. 398.
"Womb" (tr. by David H. Rosenthal). LitR (26:3) Spr 83, p. 400.

1349. FERREE, Joel
"St. Franics of the Suburbs." ChrC (100:12) 20 Ap 83, p. 369.

1350. FERREIRA, Christine
"Blackbird." BelPoJ (34:1) Aut 83, p. 18.

1351. FERRY, David
"In Balance" (after Jorge Guillén). Raritan (2:4) Spr 83, p. 46.
"Out at Lanesville" (In memoriam Mary Ann, 1932-1980). Raritan (2:4) Spr 83, p. 45-46.

1352. FERTIG, Mona
"4722 Rue Berri: a Poetic Journal" (Selections). Quarry (32:4) Aut 83, p. 4-5.
"And They Marry Their Hearts for Truth." Dandel (10:2) Aut-Wint 83, p. 80.
"Any Woman Can." Dandel (10:2) Aut-Wint 83, p. 81.
"For You This Letter." WestCR (17:4) Ap 83, p. 9.
"Song for Montreal." PoetryCR (5:2) Wint 83-84, p. 6.

1353. FETHERLING, Doug
"Prologue." CanLit (99) Wint 83, p. 5.

1354. FEYERABEND, Barbara
"Eve to Adam at Dawn." SenR (13:2) 82-83, p. 30.
"Fama Gloriaque" (after al-Mutanabbi, 10th century). SenR (13:2) 82-83, p. 31-32.
"Lament for Jonathan" (after Rilke). SenR (13:2) 82-83, p. 28-29.
"The Two Dogs" (from the Arabic of Ibn Al-Mu'tazz, 861-908 A.D.). SenR (13:2) 82-83, p. 33-34.

1355. FICKERT, Kurt J.
"Portrait of a Lady (from Behind)." Bogg (51) 83, p. 6.
"The Racquetball War." Wind (13:49) 83, p. 50.

1356. FICOWSKI, Jerzy
"En Polonais" (pour Mad Lucienne Rey, tr. by Joseph Bonenfant). Os (17) 83, p. 12-13.
"In Polish" (to Ms. Lucienne Rey, tr. by Frank Corliss). Os (17) 83, p. 10-11.
"O Vision de Neige" (pour Bieta, tr. by Joseph Bonenfant). Os (17) 83, p. 18-19.
"Oh Vision of Snow" (to Bieta, tr. by Frank Corliss). Os (17) 83, p. 16-17.
"Po Polsku" (pani Lucienne Rey). Os (17) 83, p. 8-9.
"Przepis." Os (17) 83, p. 4.
"Recette" (tr. by Joseph Bonenfant). Os (17) 83, p. 6.
"Recipe" (tr. by Frank Corliss). Os (17) 83, p. 5.
"Snie Sniegu." Os (17) 83, p. 14-15.

1357. FIELD, Crystal MacLean
"Eleanor of the Irises in My Yard." NewL (50:1) Aut 83, p. 71.

1358. FIELD, Edward
"Categories, Cows and Bulls." Kayak (62) Ag 83, p. 50.
"Depression." PoNow (7:2, #38) 83, p. 7.
"Income Tacks: From My Diary" (Special Section). WormR (23:4, issue 92) 83, p. 137-144.

1359. FIELDER, William A.
"Answers" (tr. of Ulku Tamer, w. Dionis C. Riggs and Ozcan Yalim). Mund (14:1) 83, p. 49-50.
"Autumn (Guz)" (tr. of Ali Puskulluoglu, w. Ozcan Yalim and Dionis Coffin Riggs). SpiritSH (48) 82, p. 48.
"The First Snow" (tr. of Sabahattin Kudret Aksal, w. Ozcan Yalim and Dionis C. Riggs). Mund (14:1) 83, p. 51.
"Hills (Tepeler)" (tr. of Ali Puskulluoglu, w. Ozcan Yalim and Dionis Coffin Riggs). SpiritSH (48) 82, p. 48.
"The Lamp" (tr. of Behcet Necatigil, w. Ozcan Yalim and Dionis C. Riggs). Mund (14:1) 83, p. 48.
"Poem toward Noon" (tr. of Sabahattin Kudret Aksal, w. Ozcan Yalim and Dionis C. Riggs). Mund (14:1) 83, p. 51.
"The Poet" (tr. of Ozcan Yalim, w. the author and Dionis C. Riggs). Mund (14:1) 83, p. 47.

"The Poet (Ozan)" (tr. of Ali Puskulluoglu, w. Ozcan Yalim and Dionis Coffin Riggs). SpiritSH (48) 82, p. 48.
"Seekers" (tr. of Ozcan Yalim, w. the author and Dionis C. Riggs). Mund (14:1) 83, p. 47.
"Summer (Yaz)" (tr. of Ali Puskulluoglu, w. Ozcan Yalim and Dionis Coffin Riggs). SpiritSH (48) 82, p. 48.
"Tale of Tales" (tr. of Nazim Hikmet, w. Ozcan Yalim and Dionis Coffin Riggs). SpiritSH (48) 82, p. 46-47.

FIELDER, William D.
See: FIELDER, William A.

1360. FIELDS, Kenneth
"It's Nothing" (after Francis Jammes). TriQ (58) Aut 83, p. 111-112.
"The Rules of the Game." TriQ (58) Aut 83, p. 113.

1361. FIERRO, Martin
"Cruz y Fierro de una estancia." NewRep (186:20) 19 My 82, p. 7.

1362. FIFER, Elizabeth
"Aghios Marina." Wind (13:48) 83, p. 18-19.
"In the Town of Copan Ruins, Honduras." MinnR (NS 21) Aut 83, p. 68.
"Up the Mountain." Wind (13:48) 83, p. 18.

1363. FIGGINS, Ross
"Haiku #281." PoetryCR (5:1) Aut 83, p. 12.
"Haiku #334." PoetryCR (5:1) Aut 83, p. 12.

1364. FILIP, Raymond
"Belladonna" (In Memory of Béla Egyedi 1913-1982). AntigR (55) Aut 83, p. 47.
"Imaginary Veillee with Gilles Vigneault." CrossC (5:2/3) 83, p. 21.

1365. FILIPKOWSKI, Zoe
"Frog Woman" (adapted from a Tlingit story). CentR (27:3) Sum 83, p. 187-189.
"Leading the Mare." NewOR (10:2/3) Sum-Aut 83, p. 60.

1366. FILLINGHAM, Patricia
"Cassandra." ThirdW Spr 83, p. 41.
"Halley's Comet." SanFPJ (5:1) 83, p. 28.
"Helen of Troy with a Broken Nose." ThirdW Spr 83, p. 42.
"Lectures in Memory of Louis the Simple (Misread Book Title)." Tele (18) 83, p. 74-75.
"Oh Say Can You See." Tele (18) 83, p. 76.

1367. FINALE, Frank
"Boarder." Vis (12) 83, p. 23.
"Digging." Vis (11) 83, p. 12.

1368. FINCH, Peter
"Strategic Targets." Stand (24:1) 82-83, p. 47-51.

1369. FINCH, Robert
"Doubles." MalR (64) F 83, p. 123.
"The Hand." MalR (64) F 83, p. 123.
"Mobile." MalR (64) F 83, p. 122.

1370. FINCH, Roger
"115 Rms, Ocn Vu" (Mar-a-Lago, the Palm Beach home of Marjorie Merriweather Post). PraS (57:4) Wint 83, p. 62.
"After the Bath." WebR (8:2) Aut 83, p. 60.
"Among the Lisu of Northern Thailand." CapeR (18:2) Sum 83, p. 18.
"Assault with Intent to Kill." BelPoJ (33:4) Sum 83, p. 5-6.
"The Authority and Power of Fire." WebR (8:2) Aut 83, p. 61.
"Autumn" (tr. of Yahya Kemal). SoDakR (21:1) Spr 83, p. 70.
"Daphne." DekalbLAJ (16:1/4) Aut 82-Sum 83, p. 64-65.
"End of September" (tr. of Yahya Kemal). SoDakR (21:1) Spr 83, p. 66.
"A Flight of Orchids." PoetL (77:1) Spr 82, p. 11-12.
"Forsythia." AntigR (53) Spr 83, p. 87.
"From a Hill" (tr. of Yahya Kemal). SoDakR (21:1) Spr 83, p. 62.
"From Another Hill" (tr. of Yahya Kemal). SoDakR (21:1) Spr 83, p. 62.
"Harakiri." PraS (57:4) Wint 83, p. 61.
"How Certain Revolving Motions Become Frozen in Time." PoetL (78:1) Spr 83, p. 14.
"In My Breast, Something Marked 'Fragile'." PoetL (78:1) Spr 83, p. 15.
"Japan Shop" (tr. of Shuntaro Tanigawa). SoDakR (21:1) Spr 83, p. 58.
"The Man the Moon Likes" (tr. of Shuntaro Tanigawa). SoDakR (21:1) Spr 83, p. 60.
"Manios med fhefhaked Numasioi, 'Manius Made Me for Numerius'" (inscription on the Praeneste gold fibula). AntigR (53) Spr 83, p. 86.
"May Crowds" (tr. of Shuntaro Tanigawa). SoDakR (21:1) Spr 83, p. 60.
"Mihriyar" (tr. of Yahya Kemal). SoDakR (21:1) Spr 83, p. 68.
"Monkeys on Mt. Miyanoura." WebR (8:2) Aut 83, p. 59.
"No Regrets." FourQt (32:3) Spr 83, p. 2.
"An Old Friend." WormR (23:4, issue 92) 83, p. 127-128.
"On the Nature of Angels." WormR (23:4, issue 92) 83, p. 126.
"On the Threshold of the Fifth Dimension" (to Thor Friedemann). PoetL (77:1) Spr 82, p. 9-10.
"Pavarotti Recalls Caruso, But Who Will Recall Pavarotti?" PoetL (77:1) Spr 82, p. 8-9.
"Pg. albricoqe, Arab. al-barqūq." AntigR (53)

Spr 83, p. 88.
"Poème d'Extase." PraS (57:4) Wint 83, p. 59-60.
"A Publicity Photograph." BelPoJ (34:2) Wint 83-84, p. 34.
"Snow Music" (tr. of Yahya Kemal). SoDakR (21:1) Spr 83, p. 64.
"Travels 1" (tr. of Shuntaro Tanigawa). SoDakR (21:1) Spr 83, p. 52.
"Travels 2" (tr. of Shuntaro Tanigawa). SoDakR (21:1) Spr 83, p. 54.
"Travels 3: Arizona" (tr. of Shuntaro Tanigawa). SoDakR (21:1) Spr 83, p. 56.
"An Unrelenting Basso Ostinato." CimR (64) Jl 83, p. 50-51.
"A Walk in Takashimadaira" (to Teruo). WormR (23:4, issue 92) 83, p. 128-129.
"What Is Written in the Wind." KanQ (15:2) Spr 83, p. 120.
"Whirlpool." CapeR (19:1) Wint 83, p. 41.
"Woman" (tr. of Shuntaro Tanigawa). SoDakR (21:1) Spr 83, p. 58.

1371. FINCKE, Gary
"B Movie." WebR (8:1) Spr 83, p. 91.
"Cornwall, Ontario." Images (8:3) 83, p. 4.
"The End of Ganster Street." WestB (12) 83, p. 80.
"The End of the Year Count." NegC (3:4) Aut 83, p. 61.
"Handing the Self Back." PoetryNW (24:3) Aut 83, p. 46-47.
"How Her Children Grew without a Man." WestB (12) 83, p. 81.
"The Neighborhood Spoke to Me." PoetL (78:3) Aut 83, p. 162.
"Oxygen." SouthernPR (23:2) Aut 83, p. 29-30.
"Running Home at Midnight." Images (8:3) 83, p. 4.
"Shaved." LittleBR (3:4) Sum 83, p. 66.
"The Smallest Park in Nova Scotia." PoetL (78:3) Aut 83, p. 163.
"Where I Was Born." PoetL (78:1) Spr 83, p. 19.
"Yoknapatawpha County." Swallow (2) Aut-Wint 83, p. 33-34.
"Your 36th Birthday." SouthernPR (23:2) Aut 82 [i.e. (23:1?) Spr 83], p. 37.

1372. FINE, Beverly K.
"The Runner." LittleBR (3:3) Spr 83, p. 34.

1373. FINE, Janice
"Dear El Salvadorians." SanFPJ (5:3) 83, p. 13.
"The Girl in the Blue Bomb Shelter." SanFPJ (4:4) 83, p. 96.

1374. FINGER, Larry
"A thin dissertation." CEAFor (13:2) D 82, p. 16.

1375. FINK, Eloise Bradley
"That Other Fellow -- from the River Front." Poetry (142:2) My 83, p. 81.

1376. FINK, Robert A.
"My Sons Ask Where God Lives." MichOR (22:3) Sum 83, p. 377.
"On Jesus, Taking His Word on Immortality." MichOR (22:3) Sum 83, p. 378.

1377. FINKEL, Donald
"At Three A.M. the Dogs." Shen (34:4) 83, p. 28.
"End of Improvement Thank You." Shen (34:4) 83, p. 26-27.

1378. FINKELSTEIN, Caroline
"Afterlife." Tendril (14/15) Wint 83, p. 53.
"High and Low." Tendril (14/15) Wint 83, p. 54.
"The Lie." Tendril (14/15) Wint 83, p. 52.
"The Sentimental Woman." Tendril (14/15) Wint 83, p. 55.

1379. FINLAY, John
"The Archaic Athena." Hudson (36:2) Sum 83, p. 324.
"Death in Asia Minor." Hudson (36:2) Sum 83, p. 324-325.
"The Wide Porch" (for M. C. F.). Hudson (36:2) Sum 83, p. 323-324.

1380. FINLEY, Michael (See also: FINLEY, Mike)
"Accident." KanQ (15:2) Spr 83, p. 75.
"The Beagles of Arkansas." KanQ (15:2) Spr 83, p. 75.
"Biker Bob Maniskalko's Living Room Decor." Northeast (Ser. 3:16) Wint 83-84, p. 15.
"Happiness." Abraxas (27/28) 83, p. 33.
"Home Trees." HiramPoR (35) Aut-Wint 83, p. 13.
"The Lost Colony." Northeast (Ser. 3:16) Wint 83-84, p. 14-15.

1381. FINLEY, Mike (See also: FINLEY, Michael)
"Taking a Job in Another Town." PoNow (7:2, #38) 83, p. 16.

1382. FINN, Michael
"I see you, and desire you in unexpected places." YetASM (1:2) 82, p. 18.

1383. FINNEGAN, James
"The Dancers." ClockR (1:2) Wint 83-84, p. 5.
"Drought." KanQ (15:1) Wint 83, p. 23.
"Five Pages from a Found Sketchbook." IndR (6:2) Spr 83, p. 10-12.
"A Ghost Story." SoDakR (21:3) Aut 83, p. 97.
"The Planting." SpoonRQ (8:4) Aut 83, p. 50.
"The Sermon." HiramPoR (34) Spr-Sum 83, p. 9.
"Wrong Exit." ClockR (1:1) Sum 83, p. 4.

1384. FINNELL, Dennis
"Oscar's Pet Pig." BlackWR (8:1) Aut 81, p. 74-75.
"Oscar's Song." BlackWR (8:1) Aut 81, p. 76-77.
"Oscar's Whistle." BlackWR (8:1) Aut 81, p. 78-79.

1385. FINNEY, Bernard
"Take Off Your Mantle." NegC (3:4) Aut 83, p. 49.

1386. FIORENTINO, Luigi
"The Rain Continues to Fall" (tr. by James E. Warren, Jr.). WebR (8:2) Aut 83, p. 48.

1387. FIRESTONE, Jon
"America: A Prophecy." SanFPJ (4:2) 83, p. 60.

1388. FIRKE, Lisa Groom
"I Love You, Mother, I Hate You, Mother." WebR (8:2) Aut 83, p. 85-86.
"To Aurora D." WebR (8:2) Aut 83, p. 87.

1389. FIRKINS, Terry
"Among Those Who Come After." Northeast (Ser. 3:15) Sum 83, p. 25.
"Taking the Train." Northeast (Ser. 3:15) Sum 83, p. 24.

1390. FISET, Joan
"Snow House." Calyx (8:1) Aut 83, p. 18-19.

1391. FISH, Karen
"Approximation." NewYorker (59:8) 11 Ap 83, p. 36.
"The Awakening." AmerPoR (12:3) My-Je 83, p. 45.
"Black Ice" (for Tom Kellogg). AmerPoR (12:3) My-Je 83, p. 46.
"Catherine of Aragon, January 1536." MissouriR (6:3) Sum 83, p. 20.
"The Cedar Canoe" (for Fred). AmerPoR (12:3) My-Je 83, p. 45.
"Equivalent." AmerPoR (12:3) My-Je 83, p. 46.
"The Ferry: Woods Hole." AntR (41:2) Spr 83, p. 216.
"Jeanne d'Arc" (for Peter Fish). AmerPoR (12:3) My-Je 83, p. 45.
"The Orchard." AntR (41:2) Spr 83, p. 214-215.
"Self-Portrait with Camellia Branch." AntR (41:2) Spr 83, p. 212-213.

1392. FISHER, David
"The Scotchman in the Fillmore." Kayak (62) Ag 83, p. 65.

1393. FISHER, Gary
"A Windy Day in Berkeley." Wind (13:48) 83, p. 2.

1394. FISHER, Sally
"Drop Everything" (from an Annunication by Tintoretto). Field (29) Aut 83, p. 71.
"Love Won't Stop" (from an Annunciation by Simone Martini). Field (29) Aut 83, p. 70.

1395. FISHMAN, Charles
"My Father." HolCrit (20:2) Ap 83, p. 17. Also HolCrit (20:3) Je 83, p. 19.
"The Tortures." Confr (25/26) 83, p. 132.

1396. FISKE, Ingrid
"Dolphin Eater." Descant (41) Sum 83, p. 93.
"Dwelling Place." Descant (41) Sum 83, p. 99.
"The Two Sherpas." Descant (41) Sum 83, p. 100.
"View of Girl." Descant (41) Sum 83, p. 98.
"Where There Is Water" (for C.C.). Descant (41) Sum 83, p. 96-97.
"Woman, Leaning Away." Descant (41) Sum 83, p. 94-95.

1397. FitzGERALD, Dora
"Annunciation above the Shepherds" (from The Life of the Virgin Mary, tr. of Rainer Maria Rilke). CapilR (26) 83, p. 27, 29.
"Annunciation to Mary" (from The Life of the Virgin Mary, tr. of Rainer Maria Rilke). CapilR (26) 83, p. 19, 21.
"Before the Passion" (from The Life of the Virgin Mary, tr. of Rainer Maria Rilke). CapilR (26) 83, p. 35, 37.
"Birth of Christ" (from The Life of the Virgin Mary, tr. of Rainer Maria Rilke). CapilR (26) 83, p. 25, 27.
"The Birth of Mary" (from The Life of the Virgin Mary, tr. of Rainer Maria Rilke). CapilR (26) 83, p. 15.
"Consolation of Mary with the Resurrected Christ" (from The Life of the Virgin Mary, tr. of Rainer Maria Rilke). CapilR (26) 83, p. 39.
"Joseph's Suspicion" (from The Life of the Virgin Mary, tr. of Rainer Maria Rilke). CapilR (26) 83, p. 23, 25.
"Of the Death of Mary" (from The Life of the Virgin Mary, tr. of Rainer Maria Rilke). CapilR (26) 83, p. 41, 43, 45.
"Of the Marriage at Cana" (from The Life of the Virgin Mary, tr. of Rainer Maria Rilke). CapilR (26) 83, p. 33, 35.
"Pieta" (from The Life of the Virgin Mary, tr. of Rainer Maria Rilke). CapilR (26) 83, p. 37.
"The Presentation of Mary in the Temple" (from The Life of the Virgin Mary, tr. of Rainer Maria Rilke). CapilR (26) 83, p. 17, 19.
"Rest on the Flight into Egypt" (from The Life of the Virgin Mary, tr. of Rainer Maria Rilke). CapilR (26) 83, p. 31.
"Visitation of the Virgin" (from The Life of the Virgin Mary, tr. of Rainer Maria Rilke). CapilR (26) 83, p. 21, 23.

1398. FITZGERALD, Judith
"In the O Zone." PoetryCR (5:1) Aut 83, p. 16.
"Narrativity" (for Daphne). PoetryCR (5:1) Aut 83, p. 16.
"Sudbury Blues." PoetryCR (5:1) Aut 83, p. 16.
"Touch of Zygosis." WestCR (17:4) Ap 83, p. 44.

1399. FITZGERALD, Robert
"The Pyres" (Aeneid Book XI, 182-209) (tr. of Virgil). ParisR (25:88) Sum 83, p. 63-64.

1400. FITZPATRICK, Mary K.
"The Family in Winter" (for Peter and Molly). CapeR (19:1) Wint 83, p. 4.

1401. FITZPATRICK, Vincent
"Amerika, You're Killing Me." SanFPJ (5:3) 83, p. 65.
"Little War Lord." SanFPJ (5:3) 83, p. 7.
"St. Mark's Place Poem." SanFPJ (4:3) 83, p. 57.
"Unemployed in Scranton, PA." SanFPJ (4:3) 83, p. 20.

1402. FITZSIMMONS, S. J.
"My Sweetheart's Grave." WritersL Ag 83, p. 13.

1403. FLANAGAN, Joanne
"Why Valentines Don't Look Like Real Hearts (One Theory)." Sam (36:3 143rd release) 83, p. 2.

1404. FLANDERS, Jane
"After Manet" (from The Students of Snow). PoNow (7:2, #38) 83, p. 24.
"Care: The Hess Children, 1912." Comm (110:9) 6 My 83, p. 280.
"Other Lives of the Romantics." Shen (34:4) 83, p. 29-30.
"Shopping in Tuckahoe." PoetryNW (24:4) Wint 83-84, p. 44.
"Wild Asters" (from The Students of Snow). PoNow (7:2, #38) 83, p. 24.

1405. FLANZBAUM, Hilene
"Schools and Schoolmasters." Ploughs (9:1) 83, p. 73-74.

1406. FLAVIN, Jack
"Two Paintings by Breughel." MidwQ (24:3) Spr 83, p. 283-284.

1407. FLECK, Richard C., Jr.
"Hobo's Still Life." YetASM (1:1) 82, p. 2.

1408. FLECK, Richard F.
"A drop of dew" (Haiku, tr. of Kawabata Bosha, w. Minoru Fujita). Paint (10:19/20) Spr-Aut 83, p. 42.
"Even disappearing tip" (Haiku, tr. of Yamaguchi Seishi, w. Minoru Fujita). Paint (10:19/20) Spr-Aut 83, p. 43.
"Eyes of Pheasant" (Haiku, tr. of Kato Shuson, w. Minoru Fujita). Paint (10:19/20) Spr-Aut 83, p. 44.
"For but an instant" (Haiku, tr. of Ishida Hakyo, w. Minoru Fujita). Paint (10:19/20) Spr-Aut 83, p. 45.
"A frogfish frozen to the bone" (Haiku, tr. of Kato Shuson, w. Minoru Fujita). Paint (10:19/20) Spr-Aut 83, p. 44.
"Gentle Fiddleheads" (Haiku, tr. of Kawabata Bosha, w. Minoru Fujita). Paint (10:19/20) Spr-Aut

83, p. 42.
"A grapefruit split open" (Haiku, tr. of Ishida Hakyo, w. Minoru Fujita). Paint (10:19/20) Spr-Aut 83, p. 45.
"In glimmer of moon" (Haiku, tr. of Kawabata Bosha, w. Minoru Fujita). Paint (10:19/20) Spr-Aut 83, p. 42.
"Waiting for a bus" (Haiku, tr. of Ishida Hakyo, w. Minoru Fujita). Paint (10:19/20) Spr-Aut 83, p. 45.
"What a crunching sound" (Haiku, tr. of Yamaguchi Seishi, w. Minoru Fujita). Paint (10:19/20) Spr-Aut 83, p. 43.

1409. FLEESON, Tyler
"The Verge of America" (for Jim Justus). IndR (6:3) Sum 83, p. 35.

1410. FLEMING, Gerald
"Eight Sketches of the Rich." PoetL (78:3) Aut 83, p. 147-149.
"Little Assonants." WebR (8:1) Spr 83, p. 88.
"Still Night with Pregnant Woman." WebR (8:1) Spr 83, p. 89.

1411. FLEMING, Harold
"Ann Belfry Causes the Gobbles." WestB (12) 83, p. 87.
"Ann's Hands." WestB (12) 83, p. 86.
"My Woods." YetASM (2:1) 83, p. 7.
"The Way Back." Wind (13:49) 83, p. 20.

1412. FLINT, Roland
"Habemus Papam." ChiR (33:4) Sum [i.e. Spr] 83, p. 21.
"In My Fashion." Tendril (16) Sum 83, p. 33.
"Pamela on February 8, 1982." Tendril (16) Sum 83, p. 32.
"Pigeon in the Night." PoetL (78:4) Wint 84, p. 238.
"Pigeon Is Jealous after Seeing." Tendril (16) Sum 83, p. 37.
"Pigeon Sees How This scratching of His." PoetL (78:4) Wint 84, p. 239.
"Pigeon Wakes Thinking How Death." Tendril (16) Sum 83, p. 35.
"Poor Pigeon without Powers." Tendril (16) Sum 83, p. 36.
"To the Only Absolute Beauty Someone." PoetL (78:4) Wint 84, p. 239.
"Transitions." Tendril (16) Sum 83, p. 34.

1413. FLINTOFF, Eddie
"In Memory" (Locvizza, 30 September 1916) (tr. of Giuseppi Ungaretti). Argo (4:2) 82, p. 29.
"A Letter from an Indonesian Merchant Home." Bogg (50) 83, p. 59.
"Nightwatch" (tr. of Giuseppi Ungaretti). Argo (4:2) 82, p. 30.
"West End Pub." Bogg (50) 83, p. 45.

1414. FLOCK, Miriam
"Afternoon with a Southwest Haze." _Shen_ (34:3) 83, p. 94.

1415. FLOOK, Maria
"Against Spring." _Poetry_ (142:6) S 83, p. 325-326.
"Discreet." _Poetry_ (142:6) S 83, p. 327.

1416. FLOSDORF, Jim
"Mel." _Blueline_ (4:2) Wint-Spr 83, p. 34.

1417. FLOWERS, M. Paulette
"Robins in a Fog at the Country Club." _ConcPo_ (16:2) Aut 83, p. 27.
"To Anne from Sylvia." _ConcPo_ (16:2) Aut 83, p. 26.

1418. FLYNN, Richard M.
"Peafowl." _CropD_ (4) 83, p. 7.

FOE, Mark de
See: DeFOE, Mark

1419. FOGEL, Alice B.
"Landscape." _PoetryE_ (9/10) Wint 82-Spr 83, p. 43-44.

1420. FOGEL, Andrea
"If Fire Were Wet." _PoetryCR_ (5:1) Aut 83, p. 18.
"Oooooo." _PoetryCR_ (4:4) Sum 83, p. 15.

1421. FOGELMAN, Betsy
"She Longs to Grow Wise in an Earthly Way." _ThirdW_ Spr 83, p. 54.

1422. FOLLAIN, Jean
"Black Meat" (tr. by Heather McHugh). _Field_ (28) Spr 83, p. 68.
"Black Meat" (tr. by W. S. Merwin). _Field_ (28) Spr 83, p. 67.
"Dawn" (tr. by W. S. Merwin). _Field_ (28) Spr 83, p. 64.
"Inhabited Interior" (tr. by Heather McHugh). _Field_ (28) Spr 83, p. 66.
"Listening" (tr. by Heather McHugh). _Field_ (28) Spr 83, p. 66.
"The middle-aged teacher lets his small son" (tr. by Mary Feeney and William Matthews). _Field_ (28) Spr 83, p. 63.
"The Students' Dog" (tr. by W. S. Merwin). _Field_ (28) Spr 83, p. 64.

1423. FOLLIN-JONES, Elizabeth
"Apprentice." _Vis_ (13) 83, p. 6.

1424. FOLSOM, Eric
"The Answer." _Quarry_ (32:3) Sum 83, p. 64.
"Care." _Quarry_ (32:3) Sum 83, p. 63.

1425. FONTAINE, Corinne
"I must not split commitments." _PoetryCR_ (4:4)

Sum 83, p. 15.

1426. FONTENOT, Ken
"Beginning Again." KanQ (15:1) Wint 83, p. 22.
"Oath of an English and French Survivor at Dien Bien Phu." KanQ (15:1) Wint 83, p. 21.

1427. FORCHE, Carolyn
"I Was Born Here As Well" (tr. of Claribel Alegría). PoetryE (9/10) Wint 82-Spr 83, p. 175.
"Personal Data" (tr. of Claribel Alegría). PoetryE (9/10) Wint 82-Spr 83, p. 176.

1428. FORD, Cathy
"Carapace" (for Jennifer, for the word, for Jean). Grain (11:3) Ag 83, p. 14-15.
"For the One Whose Moon Is Always Hung in the Right Sky, Winter Sky." Grain (11:3) Ag 83, p. 13.
"My mother said no." CanLit (98) Aut 83, p. 31-32.
"There are wolves in the timber." CanLit (98) Aut 83, p. 32.
"Together we walk the marshes to the house of his ailing bride." CanLit (98) Aut 83, p. 33.

1429. FORD, Charles Henri
"Public Haiku." CreamCR (8:1/2) 83, p. 122-126.

1430. FORD, R. A. D.
"The Coast of Childhood." CanLit (97) Sum 83, p. 72.
"Truce." CanLit (97) Sum 83, p. 25.

1431. FOREMAN, Paul
"Summer Tones." SouthernR (19:3) Jl 83, p. 660.

FORGE, P. V. le
See: LeFORGE, P. V.

1432. FORRIE, Allan
"The Stations of the Woods." Dandel (10:1) Spr-Sum 83, p. 40-41.

1433. FORT, Charles
"The Caravan #1." Argo (4:1) 82, p. 13.
"Coloratura." Argo (4:1) 82, p. 5.

1434. FORTIER, Mardelle
"In My Rounded White Bed I Lie." Swallow (1) Spr 83, p. 76.

1435. FOSS, Phillip
"Renunciation." CharR (9:1) Spr 83, p. 34-35.

1436. FOSTER, Barbara
"Winter's Waspish Herald." WritersL F 83, p. 13.

1437. FOSTER, Ben
"November Maples." YetASM (1:2) 82, p. 18.

1438. FOSTER, Linda Nemec
"Marriage." Tendril (16) Sum 83, p. 38.

1439. FOSTER, Robert
"Reflections." Quarry (32:3) Sum 83, p. 29-30.
"Refuse Dogma." Quarry (32:3) Sum 83, p. 30.
"Waking Sequence." Quarry (32:3) Sum 83, p. 29.

1440. FOURNIER, Merci
"The Performance." Waves (11:4) Spr 83, p. 65.

1441. FOWLER, Charles
"Fust." ParisR (24:84) Sum 82, p. 79.

1442. FOWLER, Gene
"Not Macho, Just Mucho." SecC (11:1/2) 83, p. 57.

1443. FOX, Dan
"Shock Day." SanFPJ (5:1) 83, p. 58.

1444. FOX, Gail
"Not Marbled." PoetryCR (5:1) Aut 83, p. 15.

1445. FOX, Hugh
"Attic (October 1, 1981)." WormR (23:1, issue 89) 83, p. 35.
"Landsmann." WormR (23:1, issue 89) 83, p. 35.
"Linda Dog." WormR (23:1, issue 89) 83, p. 35-36.
"Ordinary People." WormR (23:1, issue 89) 83, p. 34.
"Sicktime." SecC (11:1/2) 83, p. 65.
"Those Pico Della Mirandola Eyes." WormR (23:1, issue 89) 83, p. 33-34.

1446. FOX, William L.
"Hookers." Meadows (3:1) 82, p. 35.
"Losing Streak." Meadows (3:1) 82, p. 46.
"Outside." Meadows (3:1) 82, p. 37.

1447. FOY, John
"Captain's Log." PoetryCR (5:1) Aut 83, p. 18.
"Employment." PoetryCR (5:2) Wint 83-84, p. 13.
"Sailors." PoetryCR (4:4) Sum 83, p. 15.

1448. FRAJLICH, Anna
"A Twig of Rowan" (tr. by Charles Lambert). PoetL (77:3) Aut 82, p. 149.
"Untitled: And if I forget" (tr. by Charles Lambert). PoetL (77:3) Aut 82, p. 149.

1449. FRANK, Bernhard
"The Faun" (tr. of Paul Verlaine). WebR (8:1) Spr 83, p. 38.
"Lazarus Passed." AntigR (54) Sum 83, p. 8.
"My Magdalene." AntigR (54) Sum 83, p. 7.
"Present" (tr. of Zvi Ya'ir). WebR (8:1) Spr 83, p. 37.
"Rock and Billow" (tr. of Zvi Ya'ir). WebR (8:1) Spr 83, p. 36.
"Today When Christ Must Die." AntigR (54) Sum 83, p. 7.

"Woman with Cat" (tr. of Paul Verlaine). WebR (8:1) Spr 83, p. 38.

1450. FRANKLIN, Walt
"One Year." Blueline (5:1) Sum-Aut 83, p. 9.

1451. FRASER, Caroline
"Lasting." CalQ (22) Sum 83, p. 55.
"Telling." CalQ (22) Sum 83, p. 54.

1452. FRATE, Frank C.
"Mary's Cat." CapeR (19:1) Wint 83, p. 46.

1453. FRATICELLI, Marco
"On the teacher's desk." Waves (11:4) Spr 83, p. 38.
"Sitting outside the kindergarten." Waves (11:4) Spr 83, p. 38.

1454. FRATUS, David
"The Apparition, St. Louis, June 27, 1924." HiramPoR (Supp. #7) 83, p. 6.
"Atget's Gardens: Paris, 1900." HiramPoR (Supp. #7) 83, p. 3.
"The Flies: an Interrogative." HiramPoR (Supp. #7) 83, p. 22-23.
"Franklin Delano Roosevelt Meets the Vampire." HiramPoR (Supp. #7) 83, p. 16-17.
"Growing Up in the Cemetery." HiramPoR (Supp. #7) 83, p. 10-11.
"Incident at the World's Fair, St. Louis, 1904." HiramPoR (Supp. #7) 83, p. 4-5.
"The Leech: A Boyhood Memory." HiramPoR (Supp. #7) 83, p. 12-15.
"Ode to the Moosehead in Otto Moser's Saloon." HiramPoR (35) Aut-Wint 83, p. 15.
"The Old Men at the Lake: Carondelet Park, St. Louis" (Christmas Morning, 1982). HiramPoR (Supp. #7) 83, p. 7-9.
"Overheard in the Air and Space Museum, Washington, D.C., June 12, 1983." HiramPoR (Supp. #7) 83, p. 19.
"Owl Ghosts." HiramPoR (35) Aut-Wint 83, p. 14.
"Radio Gothic." HiramPoR (Supp. #7) 83, p. 18.
"The Riverman's Wedding" (Bellevue, Iowa, 1953). HiramPoR (Supp. #7) 83, p. 24-37.
"The Riverman's Wedding and Other Poems" (For my parents). HiramPoR (Supp. #7) 83, p. 3-37.
"San Francisco Bands: A Selected List." HiramPoR (Supp. #7) 83, p. 20.
"Silencing the Frogs" (for David Hopes). HiramPoR (Supp. #7) 83, p. 21.

1455. FRATUS, John
"The Rafters." HiramPoR (35) Aut-Wint 83, p. 16.
"Rome--Take II." HiramPoR (35) Aut-Wint 83, p. 17.

1456. FRAWLEY, Peter
"Babel, an Ode to Karl Marx" (concrete poem). NewL (50:1) Aut 83, p. 87.
"Birth" (concrete poem). NewL (50:1) Aut 83, p. 86.

1457. FRAZE, Candida
"Abecedarian." PoetL (78:3) Aut 83, p. 157.
"Hearts, Beating." PoetL (78:3) Aut 83, p. 156.
"Water Music: A Note to the Plumber." PoetL (78:3) Aut 83, p. 157.

1458. FRECHETTE, Jean-Marc
"Ce Pays Nous Fut Donné par la Foudre d'Après-midi." Os (16) 83, p. 13.
"Les Oiseaux du Soir." Os (16) 83, p. 12.

1459. FREEDMAN, William
"Winter Here." ConcPo (16:1) Spr 83, p. 79.

1460. FREEMAN, Anne Hobson
"As the Bumper Sticker Puts It: 'Only Love Beats Milk'." DevQ (17:4) Wint 83, p. 27.

FREES, Madeline de
See: DeFREES, Madeline

1461. FREISINGER, Randall R.
"In Front of a Small Town Radio Station." Tendril (16) Sum 83, p. 39.

1462. FRENAUD, André
"Form" (with James Dickey). Ploughs (9:2/3) 83, p. 16-17.

FRENCH, Davy James
See: JAMES-FRENCH, Davy

1463. FRETWELL, Kathy Vaughan
"For Wordsworth." PottPort (5) 83-84, p. 25.

1464. FREY, Cecelia
"Definition." PoetryCR (5:2) Wint 83-84, p. 18.
"Scarecrow." AntigR (53) Spr 83, p. 112.

1465. FREYTAG-LORINGHOVEN, Elsa von, Baroness
"Caught in Greenwich Village." CreamCR (8:1/2) 83, p. 148-149.
"Coronation." CreamCR (8:1/2) 83, p. 163.
"Lucifer Approchant." CreamCR (8:1/2) 83, p. 162.

1466. FRIAR, Kimon
"The Eels of Bracciano" (tr. of Títos Patríkios). PoNow (7:2, #38) 83, p. 45.
"Honesty" (tr. of Yánnis Rítsos). AmerPoR (12:3) My-Je 83, p. 48.
"Now Exactly" (tr. of Yánnis Rítsos). AmerPoR (12:3) My-Je 83, p. 48.

1467. FRIEBERT, Stuart
"Afterward" (tr. of Giovanni Raboni, w. Vinio Rossi). Field (29) Aut 83, p. 82.
"The Apartment" (tr. of Giovanni Raboni, w. Vinio Rossi). Field (29) Aut 83, p. 79.
"Apples, Hunger and the Law." WestB (13) 83, p. 25.
"At the Clinic." MSS (3:1) Aut 83, p. 138.

"Biography" (tr. of Walter Helmut Fritz). IndR (6:2) Spr 83, p. 41.
"Both Sides" (In memory of Hugo von Hofmannsthal). DevQ (18:2) Sum 83, p. 65.
"False and Tendentious News" (tr. of Giovanni Raboni, w. Vinio Rossi). Field (29) Aut 83, p. 77-78.
"From the Altar in the Shadows" (tr. of Giovanni Raboni, w. Vinio Rossi). DevQ (18:2) Sum 83, p. 63.
"Hospital Interns" (For Bartolo Cattafi) (tr. of Giovanni Raboni, w. Vinio Rossi). Field (29) Aut 83, p. 80-81.
"O Sausage Patty!" Tendril (14/15) Wint 83, p. 56.
"Of a Dark Room, between Their Houses." DevQ (18:2) Sum 83, p. 64.
"On Such a Night" (tr. of Bettina Behn). MemphisSR (2:2) Spr 82, p. 11.
"On Sufficiency, or Reaching the Desired Point" (tr. of Karl Krolow). IndR (5:1) Wint 82, p. 52.
"Otherwise" (tr. of Giovanni Raboni, w. Vinio Rossi). PoNow (7:2, #38) 83, p. 45.
"The Place" (for Whitt). IndR (5:1) Wint 82, p. 53.
"Precise Moment" (tr. of Bettina Behn). MemphisSR (2:2) Spr 82, p. 10.
"Steering Clear." Iowa (13:2) Spr 82, p. 112.
"Window" (tr. of Walter Helmut Fritz). Tendril (14/15) Wint 83, p. 57.
"The Window As Canvas" (for Robert Motherwell). DevQ (18:3) Aut 83, p. 37.

1468. FRIED, Philip
"At the Handball Court." KanQ (15:3) Sum 83, p. 86.
"The Hardware Drawer." CimR (63) Ap 83, p. 32.
"Testament." MassR (24:3) Aut 83, p. 563-564.

1469. FRIEDLAND, Linda
"For Loren." Dandel (10:2) Aut-Wint 83, p. 58.
"Stroke." Dandel (10:2) Aut-Wint 83, p. 57.

1470. FRIEDMAN, Jeff
"Gnats." MissouriR (7:1) Aut 83, p. 28.

1471. FRIEDMAN, Norman
"Summer Night, Fire Island, Escaping from a Party." YetASM (1:1) 82, p. 5.

1472. FRIEDRICH, Paul
"Spinoza, I Love You." BelPoJ (34:2) Wint 83-84, p. 21.

1473. FRIEND, Robert
"Dossier Zero" (tr. of Dan Pagis). LitR (26:2) Wint 83, p. 234-236.
"Life of a Dead Dog" (tr. of David Avidan). LitR (26:2) Wint 83, p. 246-247.
"The Mosquito" (tr. of Dan Pagis). LitR (26:2) Wint 83, p. 236.
"A New Lover" (tr. of Dan Pagis). LitR (26:2) Wint 83, p. 233.

"Six Local Poems" (tr. of David Avidan). LitR (26:2) Wint 83, p. 244-246.
"With Walter and Amati" (tr. of Gabriel Preil). LitR (26:2) Wint 83, p. 217-218.

1474. FRIES, Wanda
"Lot's Daughter." Wind (13:48) 83, p. 20-21.
"Narcolepsy." Wind (13:48) 83, p. 21-22.
"River." Wind (13:48) 83, p. 20.

1475. FRIMAN, Alice
"The Blind Boy and His Mother at the Rodin Museum" (Philadelphia Feb. 1981). IndR (5:3) Aut 82, p. 46.
"The Greek Bowl." Paint (10:19/20) Spr-Aut 83, p. 24.
"The Legacy." IndR (5:3) Aut 82, p. 48-49.
"Night Watch." IndR (5:3) Aut 82, p. 47.
"Township Line Road." Paint (10:19/20) Spr-Aut 83, p. 25.

1476. FRITH, David
"The Angels." WestCR (18:2) O 83, p. 8.
"I Was One with God." WestCR (18:2) O 83, p. 8.
"Migrations." WestCR (18:2) O 83, p. 9.
"No Trek Homeward." WestCR (18:2) O 83, p. 9.
"Perfect Distillation." WestCR (18:2) O 83, p. 10.
"Something Different Altogether." WestCR (18:2) O 83, p. 11.
"This Could Only Happen in Canada." WestCR (18:2) O 83, p. 11.
"The Woman I Will Marry." WestCR (18:2) O 83, p. 10.

1477. FRITZ, Walter Helmut
"Biography" (tr. by Stuart Friebert). IndR (6:2) Spr 83, p. 41.
"Window" (tr. by Stuart Friebert) Tendril (14/15) Wint 83, p. 57.

1479. FROSCH, Thomas
"Civil Defense." LittleM (14:1/2) 83, p. 43-44.
"Hume's Study." ManhatR (3:1) Sum 83, p. 60-63.

1480. FROST, Carol
"Cold Frame." AmerPoR (12:2) Mr/Ap 83, p. 41.
"The New Dog" (after 'La Premiere Nuit, ' by Jules LaForgue). NowestR (21:2/3) 83, p. 73-74.

1481. FROST, Celestine
"As a Drug That Brings Great Relief." LittleM (14:1/2) 83, p. 117.
"As Bees Breed." LittleM (14:1/2) 83, p. 115.
"Mid-Wife." LittleM (14:1/2) 83, p. 118.
"The World's House." LittleM (14:1/2) 83, p. 116.

1482. FROTHINGHAM, Rob
"At Leo's." KanQ (15:2) Spr 83, p. 120-121.
"On Tap" (Excerpts: 28, 29). KanQ (15:2) Spr 83, p. 121.

1483. FRUMKIN, Gene
"After Reading Some Poems by William Bronk." PoetryNW (24:1) Spr 83, p. 31-32.
"At Such Times." NewL (50:1) Aut 83, p. 43.
"Coming and Going." CharR (9:1) Spr 83, p. 36.
"Father to Son." NewL (50:1) Aut 83, p. 42.
"Festival of the Wolves." ThRiPo (21/22) 83, p. 29.
"How Dreams Plague the Sleepless." Kayak (61) Ap 83, p. 61.
"Land Grazing." CharR (9:1) Spr 83, p. 36.
"Nightwatcher." Kayak (61) Ap 83, p. 60.
"Saturn Is Mostly Weather." PoetryNW (24:1) Spr 83, p. 29-30.
"That Time Again." PoetryNW (24:1) Spr 83, p. 30-31.

1484. FRUTKIN, M.
"The Anarchy Impressionism Poem." Grain (11:1) F 83, p. 30-31.

1485. FRY, Elizabeth
"Coliseum Messiah." Dandel (10:1) Spr-Sum 83, p. 46-47.
"He's Not a Firm Believer in Hearts." Dandel (10:1) Spr-Sum 83, p. 44-45.

FU, Tu
See: TU, Fu

1486. FUHRINGER, Sandra
"Haiku: Everything in bloom." Waves (11:2/3) Wint 83, p. 71.
"Haiku: Funeral home." Waves (11:2/3) Wint 83, p. 71.
"Haiku: Photo album." Waves (11:2/3) Wint 83, p. 71.
"Haiku: The first snowfall." Waves (11:2/3) Wint 83, p. 71.

1487. FUJIMOTO, Stella
"Make Her Wait." TriQ (56) Wint 83, p. 165.

1488. FUJITA, Minoru
"A drop of dew" (Haiku, tr. of Kawabata Bosha, w. Richard F. Fleck). Paint (10:19/20) Spr-Aut 83, p. 42.
"Even disappearing tip" (Haiku, tr. of Yamaguchi Seishi, w. Richard F. Fleck). Paint (10:19/20) Spr-Aut 83, p. 43.
"Eyes of Pheasant" (Haiku, tr. of Kato Shuson, w. Richard F. Fleck). Paint (10:19/20) Spr-Aut 83, p. 44.
"For but an instant" (Haiku, tr. of Ishida Hakyo, w. Richard F. Fleck). Paint (10:19/20) Spr-Aut 83, p. 45.
"A frogfish frozen to the bone" (Haiku, tr. of Kato Shuson, w. Richard F. Fleck). Paint (10:19/20) Spr-Aut 83, p. 44.
"Gentle Fiddleheads" (Haiku, tr. of Kawabata Bosha, w. Richard F. Fleck). Paint (10:19/20) Spr-Aut 83, p. 42.
"A grapefruit split open" (Haiku, tr. of Ishida

Hakyo, w. Richard F. Fleck). Paint (10:19/20) Spr-Aut 83, p. 45.

"In glimmer of moon" (Haiku, tr. of Kawabata Bosha, w. Richard F. Fleck). Paint (10:19/20) Spr-Aut 83, p. 42.

"Waiting for a bus" (Haiku, tr. of Ishida Hakyo, w. Richard F. Fleck). Paint (10:19/20) Spr-Aut 83, p. 45.

"What a crunching sound" (Haiku, tr. of Yamaguchi Seishi, w. Richard F. Fleck). Paint (10:19/20) Spr-Aut 83, p. 43.

1489. FUJIWARA no ARIIYE

"Snowbound" (from The Shinkokinshu, tr. by Graeme Wilson). WestHR (37:3) Aut 83, p. 236.

1490. FUJIWARA no TOSHINARI

"Moonlit Orchard" (tr. by Graeme Wilson). WestHR (37:4) Wint 83, p. 333.

1491. FUKUHARA, Ruriko

"Goodbye, It's On the Road Time" (for Akira Izumiya, tr. Tetsuo Nakagami, w. Frank Stewart). MoodySI (10) Aut 81, p. 7-8.

"On the Wetting Road Always Splashing" (tr. of Akira Izumiya, w. Frank Stewart). MoodySI (10) Aut 81, p. 6-7.

1492. FULKER, Tina

"Love Poem." Bogg (50) 83, p. 36.

1493. FULLEN, George

"Vision in the Dream." Wind (13:49) 83, p. 21.

1494. FULTON, Alice

"The Apartment of Consumer Affairs." Ploughs (9:1) 83, p. 110-111.

"Between the Apple and the Stars." AmerS (52:3) Sum 83, p. 394-395.

"Dance Script with Electic Ballerina" (For Chris Flory). GeoR (37:2) Sum 83, p. 263-265.

"Doing the Evolution Shuffle" (for Archie). Poetry (142:4) Jl 83, p. 192.

"Everyone Knows the World Is Ending." Epoch (33:1) Aut-Wint 83, p. 54-55.

"From Our Mary to Me." Ploughs (9:1) 83, p. 112-114.

"In the Beginning." MichOR (22:1) Wint 83, p. 97.

"Needfire, This Low Heaven" (for Jon). PoetL (77:4) Wint 83, p. 225-226.

"Nursery Rhyme 1916" (in memorium: James Callahan). CarolQ (35:2) Wint 83, p. 54.

"The Perpetual Light" (to my mother, Mary Callahan Fulton). VirQR (59:4) Aut 83, p. 686-690.

"Plumbline" (In Memoriam: John Callahan). Poetry (142:4) Jl 83, p. 193.

"Reeling Back the Saffron." VirQR (59:4) Aut 83, p. 690-691.

"Sketching Uncle John, the Unsung, Till Now, Samaritan & More." CarolQ (35:2) Wint 83, p. 55.

"What I Like." Poetry (141:4) Ja 83, p. 224.

1495. FUNGE, Robert
"A Christmas Song, or, This Poem's for the Birds." SpoonRQ (8:4) Aut 83, p. 49.
"Food for Thought." SpoonRQ (8:4) Aut 83, p. 48.

1496. FUOCO, Joe A.
"My Brother Phoenix" (In the wake of fiery dreams). SanFPJ (5:1) 83, p. 37.

1497. FURTNEY, Diane
"Complementary Colors." ChiR (34:1) Sum 83, p. 42-44.
"Future Archives" (In memory of Nebio Melo Cuesta, Uruguayan journalist, arrested in Argentina, 1976, who "disappeared"). ChiR (33:4) Sum [i.e. Spr] 83, p. 34-35.
"Two Months After." Wind (13:49) 83, p. 22.

1498. GABBARD, G. N.
"The Death of the Retired Man." SanFPJ (5:4) 83, p. 74.
"Graffito" (For the Coming Unknown Soldier's Tomb). SanFPJ (5:1) 83, p. 54.
"Imperative Moods." SanFPJ (5:4) 83, p. 73.
"In the Gardens of the Twentieth Century." SanFPJ (5:1) 83, p. 57.
"A Speculation." SanFPJ (5:4) 83, p. 75.

1499. GADOL, Peter
"Looking Back." HarvardA (117:1) Mr 83, p. 35.

1500. GAFFORD, Charlotte
"Wild Kingdom." SouthernPR (23:2) Aut 82 [i.e. (23:1?) Spr 83], p. 10.

1501. GAJDA, Michael J.
"A Cry of the People." SanFPJ (4:4) 83, p. 30-31.

1502. GALA, Edward
"They Washed Me with Phisohex As a Baby." SanFPJ (5:3) 83, p. 75.

1503. GALILI, Mordechai
"Jericho" (tr. by Gabriel Levin). LitR (26:2) Wint 83, p. 305.
"Knowledge" (tr. by Gabriel Levin). LitR (26:2) Wint 83, p. 306.

1504. GALLAGHER, D. Lyons
"A penny, a nickel, a dime, a quarter." SanFPJ (4:2) 83, p. 20.
"Poor: Not having any props left." SanFPJ (5:1) 83, p. 24.
"Urban Renewal Walls." SanFPJ (4:2) 83, p. 20.

1505. GALLAGHER, Tess
"Devotion: That It Flow, That There Be Concentration." OntR (19) Aut-Wint 83-84, p. 19-23.
"Eating the Sparrows." ParisR (25:90) Wint 83, p.

154.
"Gray Eyes." NewYorker (59:42) 5 D 83, p. 60.
"Some Painful Butterflies Pass Through." ParisR (25:90) Wint 83, p. 155.

GALLAS, Louisa Loveridge
See: LOVERIDGE-GALLAS, Louisa

1506. GALLER, David
"To a Daughter." TriQ (56) Wint 83, p. 155-156.
"To the Jazz Musicians." TriQ (56) Wint 83, p. 157.

1507. GALLOWAY, Elizabeth
"Creatures." HangL (44) Sum 83, p. 19-20.

1508. GALT, Tom
"Chigetsu (ca. 1670-1700)." Poem (48) Jl 83, p. 6.
"Definition of an Optimist." SanFPJ (4:3) 83, p. 54.
"Kyoto." Poem (48) Jl 83, p. 5.
"Samurai's Diary." Poem (48) Jl 83, p. 7.
"So Long till Then." SanFPJ (4:3) 83, p. 55.

1509. GALVIN, Brendan
"Black Bear in October." Poetry (143:1) O 83, p. 35-36.
"The Brueghel Moment." SewanR (91:1) Wint 83 p. 102.
"Chickadee." NewYorker (59:11) 2 My 83, p. 95.
"Dog Love." ThRiPo (19/20) 82, p. 23.
"Heron." OhioR (30) 83, p. 231.
"Hitting the Wall." PoetL (77:3) Aut 82, p. 157-158.
"July." SewanR (91:1) Wint 83, p. 103.
"Listening to Maine Public Radio." ThRiPo (19/20) 82, p. 28.
"The Mockingbird." ThRiPo (19/20) 82, p. 19-20.
"The Mockingbird." ThRiPo (21/22) 83, p. 31-32.
"Mrs. McCandless." ThRiPo (19/20) 82, p. 24-25.
"Owl-Struck." SewanR (91:1) Wint 83, p. 101-102.
"Pollen." NewYorker (59:24) 1 Ag 83, p. 79.
"Reading the Obituaries." PoetL (77:1) Spr 82, p. 5.
"Seals in the Inner Harbor." NewRep (187:19) 15 N 82, p. 26.
"Today You Will Meet the Love of Your Life." ThRiPo (19/20) 82, p. 26-27.
"A Warning to Candidates." PoetL (77:1) Spr 82, p. 6-7.
"Whirl Is King." Poetry (143:1) O 83, p. 38.
"Winter Oysters." ThRiPo (21/22) 83, p. 30.
"With Anne at the Peabody." ThRiPo (19/20) 82, p. 21-22.
"Workout." Poetry (143:1) O 83, p. 37.
"Your New Dog." PoetL (77:3) Aut 82, p. 158-159.

1510. GALVIN, James
"Practice." CutB (21) Aut-Wint 83, p. 78-79.
"Sempiternal." NewYorker (59:9) 18 Ap 83, p. 123.
"Shadow-Casting." Agni (19) 83, p. 88-89.

1511. GALVIN, Martin
"Birthday Poem, July 19, 1866" (for Lizzie Borden). PoetL (78:2) Sum 83, p. 102.

"Circles." WindO (43) Wint 83, p. 33-34.
"Eating Around the Gizzards." Comm (110:6) 25 Mr 83, p. 182.
"Mary Cassatt." PoetL (77:4) Wint 83, p. 205.
"Pin." WindO (43) Wint 83, p. 33.
"Wild Card." WindO (43) Wint 83, p. 34.

GAN, Tanigawa
See: TANIGAWA, Gan

1512. GANNON, Tom
"Bird Poem." SoDakR (21:3) Aut 83, p. 87.

1513. GARCIA, Angeles
"Inmovil Ligadura." LetFem (9:1) 83, p. 96.

1514. GARCIA, Gloria
"Ahora." Rácata (2) 83, p. 61.
"El Amor Se LLegó." Rácata (2) 83, p. 60.
"Me preguntan si enarbolo en mi bolsillo." Rácata (2) 83, p. 58-59.
"Transito." Rácata (2) 83, p. 57.

1515. GARCIA LARINO, Marcelino
"Amores Que Matan." Prismal (11) Aut 83, p. 114.
"Medo Dos Teus Ollos." Prismal (11) Aut 83, p. 114.

GARCIA LORCA, Federico
See: LORCA, Federico Garcia

1516. GARDNER, Hall
"Come, Taste of the Sheraton Showcase" (For Joe Miller and the fifty arrested for civil disobedience at the Sheraton Arms Bazaar). SanFPJ (5:1) 83, p. 33.
"Craps (Forty Dollar Poem)." Vis (12) 83, p. 35.
"On That Final Night" (For Ground Zero). SanFPJ (5:1) 83, p. 30.

1517. GARDNER, Stephen
"Priest, Priest." HolCrit (20:3) Je 83, p. 18.

GARI, Enrique Sacerio
See: SACERIO GARI, Enrique

1518. GARIN, Marita
"Flowers." HolCrit (20:4) O 83, p. 20.

1519. GARRETT, David
"Blankets." PoetC (13, i.e. 14:3) 83, p. 63.

1520. GARRISON, David
"Chalkdust." DevQ (18:3) Aut 83, p. 94.
"Old Lives in the Neighborhood." Comm (110:9) 6 My 83, p. 280.

1521. GARRISON, Joseph
"Diving into Yourself." PoNow (7:2, #38) 83, p. 19.

1522. GARRISON, Peggy
"A Cold Snap in Peshtigo." Tele (18) 83, p. 53.
"To My Poetry Teacher" (In Memoriam). SecC (11:1/2) 83, p. 66.

1523. GARRISON, Philip
"Be Calm, Comrade, Awhile Longer" (tr. of Cesar Vallejo). NowestR (21:2/3) 83, p. 129-130.
"Between Two Stars, Losing My Footing" (tr. of Cesar Vallejo). NowestR (21:2/3) 83, p. 140-141.
"Conflict between the Eyes and the Glance" (tr. of Cesar Vallejo). NowestR (21:2/3) 83, p. 141-142.
"Faith" (tr. of Cesar Vallejo). NowestR (21:2/3) 83, p. 137.
"Far Steps" (tr. of Cesar Vallejo). NowestR (21:2/3) 83, p. 135-136.
"Good Sense" (tr. of Cesar Vallejo). NowestR (21:2/3) 83, p. 136-137.
"Un Hombre Pasa con un Pan al Hombro" (tr. of Cesar Vallejo). NowestR (21:2/3) 83, p. 126-127.
"A Masterful Demonstration of Public Heath" (tr. of Cesar Vallejo). NowestR (21:2/3) 83, p. 131-133.
"My Accent Dangles" (tr. of Cesar Vallejo). NowestR (21:2/3) 83, p. 139-140.
"Today, a Splinter Got in Her" (tr. of Cesar Vallejo). NowestR (21:2/3) 83, p. 137-138.
"Whatever, It Is a Place" (tr. of Cesar Vallejo). NowestR (21:2/3) 83, p. 138-139.

1524. GARSON, Karl
"Iowa, from Montana." CimR (63) Ap 83, p. 4.

1525. GARTON, Victoria
"Passion and After." SouthernPR (23:2) Aut 82 [i.e. (23:1?) Spr 83], p. 35-36.

1526. GASCOYNE, David
"The Masks & the Colored Heat" (from the French of André Breton & Philippe Soupsault). Kayak (61) Ap 83, p. 49.

1527. GASKELL, Ronald
"Lobsters." Stand (24:2) 83, p. 55.

1528. GASPAR, Frank
"Answering." PraS (57:2) Sum 83, p. 87.
"Deer, Swimming." NewEngR (6:2) Wint 83, p. 302-303.
"The Harbor in Winter." GeoR (37:4) Wint 83, p. 864-865.
"The Holyoke." MassR (24:3) Aut 83, p. 609-610.
"Silence." NewEngR (6:2) Wint 83, p. 303-304.

1529. GASPARINI, Len
"Full Moon." AntigR (55) Aut 83, p. 77.
"The Road to Punta Morena." AntigR (55) Aut 83, p. 78.
"Slugs." AntigR (55) Aut 83, p. 78.
"Tekahionwake." Grain (11:1) F 83, p. 33.

1530. GASSER, Frederick
"Sick room window." WindO (42) Sum 83, p. 3.
"Winter solstice." WindO (42) Sum 83, p. 3.

1531. GASTIGER, Joseph
"False Spring." SpoonRQ (8:4) Aut 83, p. 35.

1532. GASTON, Bill
"Woods Trail Marriage." PoetryCR (5:1) Aut 83, p. 18.

1533. GATES, Edward
"Riding." PottPort (5) 83-84, p. 5.

GATTUTA, Margo la
See: LaGATTUTA, Margo

1534. GAUER, Jim
"How Is This Done?" Iowa (13:2) Spr 82, p. 69.
"A Name for Anna." Iowa (13:2) Spr 82, p. 70.

1535. GAUTHIER, L.-J.
"Sur le Banc du Couvent." PoetryCR (5:1) Aut 83, p. 14.

1536. GAUTIER, Théophile
"Art" (tr. by James Michie). Poetry (142:3) Je 83, p. 153-154.

1537. GAVRON, Jackie
"Across the Mersey" (For the Robbins Family). Bogg (50) 83, p. 53-54.

1538. GAY, Mac
"Words." CutB (21) Aut-Wint 83, p. 5.

1539. GEAREN, Ann
"Genealogy" (for my father). Prima (8) 83, p. 87.

1540. GEIER, Joan L.
"Elizabeth." YetASM (1:2) 82, p. 17.

1541. GEIGER, Geoff
"Just Another Disaster." Sam (36:3 143rd release) 83, p. 38-40.

1542. GELDMAN, Mordechai
"Apollo 1" (tr. by Harold Schimmel). LitR (26:2) Wint 83, p. 286.
"Apollo 2" (tr. by Harold Schimmel). LitR (26:2) Wint 83, p. 286.
"Coastal Cities, Coastal Cities" (tr. by Gabriel Levin). LitR (26:2) Wint 83, p. 284-285.
"Fat Boy" (tr. by Harold Schimmel). LitR (26:2) Wint 83, p. 287.
"With Long Hooks" LitR (26:2) Wint 83, p. 285.

GEMIANN AUGUSTUS
See: AUGUSTUS, Gemiann

1543. GENEGA, Paul
"Descent and Sentiment." Nat (236:17) 30 Ap 83, p. 546.
"Perhaps a Castle." Swallow (2) Aut-Wint 83, p. 119-120.

1544. GENSLER, Kinereth
"Birds." Poetry (143:3) D 83, p. 140.
"December." Poetry (143:3) D 83, p. 139.

1545. GENT, Andrew
"Almanac." PoetryE (9/10) Wint 82-Spr 83, p. 146.
"The Blue Wind." PoetryE (11) Sum 83, p. 26.
"Ninth Elegy" (from Rilke's Elegies, w. Bill Evans). HangL (44) Sum 83, p. 14-16.
"The Wake" (for Franz Wright). PoetryE (11) Sum 83, p. 25.

1546. GEORGE, Emery
"Brad." PoNow (7:2, #38) 83, p. 37.

1547. GEORGE, Sharon
"At the Gates of Babylon." SpiritSH (49) 83, p. 10.
"Grey mist at morning's rising." SpiritSH (49) 83, p. 11.
"The House of Bones." SpiritSH (49) 83, p. 13.
"Noces (For St. John of the Cross)." SpiritSH (49) 83, p. 9.
"A Song for Priests." SpiritSH (49) 83, p. 12.

1548. GERMAN, Norman
"The Apprenticeship of Clay." Swallow (2) Aut-Wint 83, p. 118.
"Pygmalion's Vision." Swallow (2) Aut-Wint 83, p. 117.

1549. GERNES, Sonia
"Dust." PoetryNW (24:3) Aut 83, p. 24.

1550. GERRARD, Jill
"He Parked the Car under the Streetlight and Kissed Me and Touched My Breasts." QW (17) Aut-Wint 83-84, p. 94-95.

1551. GERSHATOR, David
"Heart Attack." Confr (25/26) 83, p. 185.

1552. GERSHGOREN, Sid
"You Go Away." CalQ (22) Sum 83, p. 23.

1553. GERSTEIN, Marvin
"The Red Kitchen." PoetL (77:4) Wint 83, p. 203.

1554. GERSTLE, Val
"The Filmstrip of My Flesh." Wind (13:48) 83, p. 23.
"Teaching Art to Children." YetASM (2:1) 83, p. 3.

1555. GERSTLER, Amy
"Perpetual Honeymoon." Gargoyle (22/23) 83, p. 5.

1556. GERVAIS, C. H.
"Learning the Fine Balance of Jean Cocteau." CrossC (5:2/3) 83, p. 21.

1557. GETSI, Lucia Cordell
"Sunday Chicken for Mrs. Minnis." SpoonRQ (8:4) Aut 83, p. 30--32.

1558. GHAI, Gail
"Green Stones." NegC (3:4) Aut 83, p. 79.

1559. GHIGNA, Charles
"Howard" (Selection: "When Howard Got All Keyed Up"). PoNow (7:2, #38) 83, p. 41.
"Howard" (Selection: "When Howard Watched His Jesus Souvenir"). PoNow (7:2, #38) 83, p. 41.
"Southern Bred." SouthernPR (23:2) Aut 83, p. 18-19.
"The Try Out." PikeF (5) Spr 83, p. 17.

1560. GHIRADELLA, Robert
"At Lake Mahopac." Kayak (63) N 83, p. 58.
"Bearers of the News." Kayak (63) N 83, p. 56-57.
"The Greatest American Poet." Kayak (63) N 83, p. 56.
"Virginia Slims." Kayak (63) N 83, p. 57.

1561. GHISELIN, Brewster
"Flame." Poetry (141:6) Mr 83, p. 321-322.
"Green Wave of Cuyutlan." Poetry (141:6) Mr 83, p. 323.
"The Well-Beloved." Poetry (141:6) Mr 83, p. 322.

1562. GIBB, Robert
"16th Street." StoneC (11:1/2, Pt. 2, 10th Anniversary Issue) 83, p. 45-46.
"The Apple Tree." StoneC (11:1/2, Pt. 2, 10th Anniversary Issue) 83, p. 16.
"At Sutter's Grave: Lititz, PA." MemphisSR (4:1) Aut 83, p. 11-12.
"At Sutter's Grave: Lititz, PA." StoneC (11:1/2, Pt. 2, 10th Anniversary Issue) 83, p. 19-20.
"Aubade." StoneC (11:1/2, Pt. 2, 10th Anniversary Issue) 83, p. 14-15.
"Camomile" (for Maggie). StoneC (11:1/2, Pt. 2, 10th Anniversary Issue) 83, p. 21.
"Carpenter Bees." StoneC (11:1/2, Pt. 2, 10th Anniversary Issue) 83, p. 47.
"Coming Again upon Mensch's Mill by Accident, after Five Years." StoneC (11:1/2, Pt. 2, 10th Anniversary Issue) 83, p. 30-31.
"Earthworks." StoneC (11:1/2, Pt. 2, 10th Anniversary Issue) 83, p. 9-10.
"For Now." StoneC (11:1/2, Pt. 2, 10th Anniversary Issue) 83, p. 17-18.
"A Friend Starts West on Melville's Birthday." StoneC (11:1/2, Pt. 2, 10th Anniversary Issue) 83, p. 39-40.
"Gatherings." StoneC (11:1/2, Pt. 2, 10th Anniversary Issue) 83, p. 53-54.
"Halfway into a Fifth of Irish Whiskey He Sings of

the Goodness of Life." StoneC (11:1/2, Pt. 2, 10th Anniversary Issue) 83, p. 41.
"Last Things." StoneC (11:1/2, Pt. 2, 10th Anniversary Issue) 83, p. 53-54.
"Lucky with Woods." StoneC (11:1/2, Pt. 2, 10th Anniversary Issue) 83, p. 58-60.
"Menses." StoneC (10:3/4) Spr-Sum 83, p. 37.
"Menses." StoneC (11:1/2, Pt. 2, 10th Anniversary Issue) 83, p. 28-29.
"Mezcal." PoetryNW (24:2) Sum 83, p. 17-18.
"Mezcal." StoneC (11:1/2, Pt. 2, 10th Anniversary Issue) 83, p. 36-38.
"The Minotaur." StoneC (11:1/2, Pt. 2, 10th Anniversary Issue) 83, p. 13.
"Monet." StoneC (11:1/2, Pt. 2, 10th Anniversary Issue) 83, p. 42-43.
"The Names of the Earth in Summer" (for Wm. O'Reilly) (winner of the 10th anniversary manuscript Competition). StoneC (11:1/2, Pt. 2, 10th Anniversary Issue) 83, p. 1-63.
"Old Men on Their Way to Pick Up the Morning Mail." NewL (49:3/4) Spr-Sum 83, p. 28.
"Requiem, Four to the Bar." Tendril (14/15) Wint 83, p. 58.
"Scything the Meadow." StoneC (11:1/2, Pt. 2, 10th Anniversary Issue) 83, p. 50.
"St. Paul's Union Church and Cemetery, Seiberlingsville, Pennsylvania." StoneC (11:1/2, Pt. 2, 10th Anniversary Issue) 83, p. 11-12.
"Stems." StoneC (11:1/2, Pt. 2, 10th Anniversary Issue) 83, p. 22-23.
"Surprised by a Flock of Canada Geese in the Field Across from My Home." StoneC (11:1/2, Pt. 2, 10th Anniversary Issue) 83, p. 61.
"This View of the Meadow." StoneC (11:1/2, Pt. 2, 10th Anniversary Issue) 83, p. 24-27.
"Vespers." StoneC (11:1/2, Pt. 2, 10th Anniversary Issue) 83, p. 57.
"Weeds." StoneC (11:1/2, Pt. 2, 10th Anniversary Issue) 83, p. 32-33.
"What the Heart can Bear." StoneC (11:1/2, Pt. 2, 10th Anniversary Issue) 83, p. 62-63.
"The White Birches." StoneC (11:1/2, Pt. 2, 10th Anniversary Issue) 83, p. 34-35.
"Widening the Road." StoneC (11:1/2, Pt. 2, 10th Anniversary Issue) 83, p. 44.
"Wind." CimR (65) O 83, p. 49-50.
"Wind." StoneC (11:1/2, Pt. 2, 10th Anniversary Issue) 83, p. 51-52.
"The Woodchuck." StoneC (11:1/2, Pt. 2, 10th Anniversary Issue) 83, p. 48-49.

1563. GIBBONS, Reginald
"Along with the Dust" (tr. of Stanislaw Baranczak, w. the author). TriQ (57, Vol. 1) Spr-Sum 83, p. 88.
"For Now" (for R. F.). Ploughs (9:2/3) 83, p. 217.
"If China" (tr. of Stanislaw Baranczak, w. the author). TriQ (57, Vol. 1) Spr-Sum 83, p. 92.

"The Instructor's Soliloquy." Ploughs (9:2/3) 83, p. 218.
"January 2, 1980: Eroica" (tr. of Stanislaw Baranczak, w. the author). TriQ (57, Vol. 1) Spr-Sum 83, p. 90.
"Make Me Hear You." Ploughs (9:2/3) 83, p. 219-220.
"March 4, 1980: And Yet Perhaps" (tr. of Stanislaw Baranczak, w. the author). TriQ (57, Vol. 1) Spr-Sum 83, p. 91.
"Prologue to a Book of American Martyrs: Some Voices." Tendril (14/15) Wint 83, p. 59-74.
"A Silence Lesson" (tr. of Tymoteusz Karpowicz, w. the author). TriQ (57, Vol. 1) Spr-Sum 83, p. 2.
"Supermarket." WebR (8:2) Aut 83, p. 77-78.

1564. GIBBS, Robert
"The Song I Have for You Is One Befitting Your Gravity." PoetryCR (4:3) Spr 83, p. 12.
"Spring Walks." CanLit (99) Wint 83, p. 18-19.
"Why Be a Poet in a Needy Time?" PoetryCR (5:2) Wint 83-84, p. 5.

1565. GIBLING, Martin
"Graveyard." PottPort (5) 83-84, p. 47.

1566. GIBSON, Margaret
"Memories of the Future" (Excerpt from The Autobiography of Tina Modotti, Written in Mexico, 1941-2). ClockR (1:2) Wint 83-84, p. 31-36.

1567. GIBSON, Margery Herwig
"The Least Skippers." PoetryCR (5:1) Aut 83, p. 18.

1568. GIBSON, Stephen M.
"The Peat Bog Finds." ThirdW Spr 83, p. 114-119.

1569. GILBERT, Celia
"Of Desire." StoneC (10:3/4) Spr-Sum 83, p. 58.
"The Walk." Ploughs (9:1) 83, p. 70.

1570. GILBERT, Chris
"Touching." Tendril (14/15) Wint 83, p. 75-76.

1571. GILBERT, Sandra (Sandra M.)
"After Long Rain." OP (36) Aut-Wint 83, p. 3.
"Hare Sitting Up." PoetryNW (24:4) Wint 83-84, p. 30-31.
"History" (for Christina). Poetry (142:4) Jl 83, p. 214.
"In the Forest of Symbols." Poetry (142:4) Jl 83, p. 213.
"The Kitchen Dream." OP (36) Aut-Wint 83, p. 5.
"A Love Journal" (Selection: "Latest Entry"). AmerPoR (12:2) Mr/Ap 83, p. 45.
"Poem Against Silence." OP (36) Aut-Wint 83, p. 4.
"Simplicity" (for E.). Poetry (142:4) Jl 83, p. 211-212.
"Sitting on Black Point Beach" (With thanks to Marlene Griffith). OP (36) Aut-Wint 83, p. 6-8.

"What He Hates / What He Loves." 13thM (6:1/2) 82, p. 84-85.

1572. GILBOA, Amir
"Gazelle, I'll Send You" (tr. by Shirley Kaufman). LitR (26:2) Wint 83, p. 220.
"To Pluck Stars" (tr. by Shirley Kaufman). LitR (26:2) Wint 83, p. 219.
"To Write the Lips of Those Asleep" (Excerpt, tr. by Shirley Kaufman). LitR (26:2) Wint 83, p. 220.

1573. GILDNER, Gary
"Johann Gaertner, 1793-1887." NewL (49:3/4) Spr-Sum 83, p. 185-187.

1574. GILL, Stephen
"My Love." WritersL Jl 83, p. 10.

1575. GILLAN, Maria
"Self-Portrait." OroM (2:1, #5) Sum 83, p. 16.

1576. GILLESPIE, Marie F.
"Journey at Dawn" (For my mother). NegC (3:4) Aut 83, p. 59.

1577. GILLET, Michelle
"Solace" (for Peter). Tendril (14/15) Wint 83, p. 77.

1578. GILLILAND, Gail
"Yaddo." AmerPoR (12:2) Mr/Ap 83, p. 5-6.

1579. GILLILAND, Mary
"Because in the Leafpile I Pitchforked a Yellowjacket Nest." Epoch (32:2) Wint-Spr 83, p. 135.
"Whoops." Epoch (32:2) Wint-Spr 83, p. 134.

1580. GILLUM, Richard F.
"Cottonwood Country" (The Second Seaton Award Poem 1983). KanQ (15:3) Sum 83, p. 34.

1581. GILSON, Estelle
"The Moment." NewRena (16) Spr 83, p. 60.
"To Dobbs Ferry with Sylvia Plath" (tr. of Gabriel Preil). NewRena (17) Aut 83, p. 65.
"Why I Became a Writer So Late in Life." NewRena (16) Spr 83, p. 62.

1582. GINS, Madeline
"Instantaneously and repeatedly" (w. Arakawa). ParisR (24:86) Wint 82, p. 123.

1583. GIOIA, Dana
"The Country Wife." Poetry (143:1) O 83, p. 8.
"Cuckoos." Poetry (143:1) O 83, p. 8.
"The Garden of the Campagna." NewYorker (59:25) 8 Ag 83, p. 40.
"Lives of the Great Composers." Epoch (33:1) Aut-Wint 83, p. 57.

"The Man in the Open Doorway." Thrpny (4:3, issue 15) Aut 83, p. 28.
"My Confessional Sestina." Poetry (143:1) O 83, p. 10-11.
"The Sunday News." Poetry (143:1) O 83, p. 9.
"Thanks for Remembering Us." Poetry (143:1) O 83, p. 7.

1584. GIOVANNI, Nikki
"I Don't Know James Tate." LittleBR (4:2) Wint 83-84, p. 7.

GIOVANNI, Norman Thomas di
See: Di GIOVANNI, Norman Thomas

1585. GIRARD, Linda Walvoord
"The Minister's Daughter Begs for Stockings." Nimrod (27:1) Aut-Wint 83, p. 67.
"The Road through the Preserve." SpoonRQ (8:4) Aut 83, p. 23.

1586. GITTLESON, Paul
"Ping Pong Poetry." WormR (23:2, issue 90) 83, p. 73.
"Surveillance." WormR (23:2, issue 90) 83, p. 72.

GIUDICE, Carolyn del
See: Del GIUDICE, Carolyn

1587. GJUKA, Norma
"Bordered by other's ecological niches." SanFPJ (4:4) 83, p. 75.
"Fighting Entropy." SanFPJ (4:4) 83, p. 75.

1588. GLADDING, Jody
"Deer Crossings." WestB (12) 83, p. 33.

1589. GLADE, Patty
"America Mystique." Pig (11) 83, p. 69.

1590. GLANCY, Diane
"It Grows Dark." LittleBR (3:3) Spr 83, p. 58.

1591. GLASER, Elton
"Acronym." ChiR (33:4) Sum [i.e. Spr] 83, p. 37.
"American Girl" (for Tom Petty and the Heartbreakers). YetASM (2:1) 83, p. 8.
"Cashier." PoNow (7:2, #38) 83, p. 22.
"Fantasia on Tchoupitoulas Wharf." GeoR (37:4) Wint 83, p. 877.
"High Ground in Louisiana." PoNow (7:2, #38) 83, p. 22.
"The History of the Foot." PoetryNW (24:3) Aut 83, p. 29-30.
"Planting the Flag." PoetryNW (24:3) Aut 83, p. 28.
"Red Beans & Rice." LittleM (14:1/2) 83, p. 100-101.

1592. GLASER, Michael S.
"Remembrance of Childhood: Itch." CimR (64) Jl 83, p. 62.

1593. GLASS, Jesse, Jr.
"Easter Poem." Bogg (50) 83, p. 13.
"Rain." SpoonRQ (8:4) Aut 83, p. 29.

1594. GLASS, Malcolm
"Building." PikeF (5) Spr 83, p. 23.
"Plague." NewL (49:3/4) Spr-Sum 83, p. 272-273.
"Tapestry." Vis (13) 83, p. 5.

1595. GLASSER, Jane Ellen
"How They Use Me." BelPoJ (33:3) Spr 83, p. 4-5.
"June Birds." BelPoJ (33:3) Spr 83, p. 3.
"Lament." BelPoJ (33:3) Spr 83, p. 2.

1596. GLAYSHER, Frederick
"Through a Tree at Night." WorldO (17:4) Sum 83, p. 32.

1597. GLAZE, Andrew
"The Rule." PoNow (7:2, #38) 83, p. 3.

1598. GLAZIER, Jan
"Late Spring." OroM (2:1, #5) Sum 83, p. 16.
"Nicaraguan Dirge." OroM (2:1, #5) Sum 83, p. 9.
"Waking." OroM (2:1, #5) Sum 83, p. 10.

1599. GLAZIER, Loss
"Puget Sound." OroM (2:1, #5) Sum 83, p. 23.
"Strip of Sun." OroM (2:1, #5) Sum 83, p. 24.

1600. GLAZNER, Greg
"Poem to Don Q., My Dog." KanQ (15:1) Wint 83, p. 173.

1601. GLEN, Emilie
"Acidosis." PikeF (5) Spr 83, p. 17.
"Botticelli Apron." SanFPJ (4:3) 83, p. 8.
"By the Cooling Towers." SanFPJ (5:3) 83, p. 33.
"Miss Lila." Wind (13:49) 83, p. 23-24.
"Popberries." SanFPJ (4:3) 83, p. 8.
"With Banana." LittleBR (3:3) Spr 83, p. 82.

1602. GLENN, Laura
"Precarious." Poetry (142:2) My 83, p. 82.

1603. GLICKMAN, Susan
"City." AntigR (52) Wint 83, p. 63.
"Grace." AntigR (52) Wint 83, p. 62.
"The Inventory of the Last Day." Grain (11:1) F 83, p. 24.
"January." PoetryCR (4:3) Spr 83, p. 5.

1604. GLOEGGLER, E. A.
"The Starved." SanFPJ (5:2) 83, p. 51.

1605. GLOWNEY, John
"At the Holiday Inn." PoetryNW (24:4) Wint 83-84, p. 36-37.

1606. GLUCK, Louise
"The Crossing." NewRep (187:1) 5 Jl 82, p. 36.
"Liberation." NewRep (186:23) 9 Je 82, p. 28.
"Night Song." NewYorker (59:36) 24 O 83, p. 50.
"A Parable." NewRep (186:15) 14 Ap 82, p. 26.

1607. GNANAKOOTHAN
"My Little World" (tr. by M. S. Ramaswami). Stand (24:1) 82-83, p. 43.

1608. GOCKER, Paula
"Patty's Poem." MassR (24:2) Sum 83, p. 479.
"Prisoner" (for all those in Argentina's prisons who cannot speak their own poems). Prima (8) 83, p. 76.

1609. GODIN, Deborah
"Dancing." Dandel (10:1) Spr-Sum 83, p. 48.

1610. GOEDICKE, Patricia
"All This Time." Tendril (14/15) Wint 83, p. 78-79.
"Beyond the Mountains." SouthernPR (23:2) Aut 83, p. 14-15.
"Coplas" (for My Students). WestB (13) 83, p. 55.
"The Entire Catch" (for Richard Hugo). PoetryE (12) Aut 83, p. 7-8.
"Full Grown." KanQ (15:4) Aut 83, p. 71.
"Greyhound." NewL (49:3/4) Spr-Sum 83, p. 30-31.
"In the Endless Dream of the Retreating." Tendril (14/15) Wint 83, p. 80.
"The Interior Music." KanQ (15:4) Aut 83, p. 67-69.
"Motel Room." KanQ (15:4) Aut 83, p. 69-70.
"Over Our Dead Bodies." ThRiPo (21/22) 83, p. 33-34.
"The People Gathering Together." NewL (49:3/4) Spr-Sum 83, p. 29-30.
"The Reading Club." NewYorker (59:6) 28 Mr 83, p. 42-43.
"The Slap." NewL (50:1) Aut 83, p. 104-105.
"Tourguide." NewL (50:1) Aut 83, p. 103-104.
"Until They Have Consumed Me Utterly." NewL (49:3/4) Spr-Sum 83, p. 31-32.

1611. GOETHE, Johann Wolfgang von
"A Wanderer's Evensong" (tr. by Geza Tatrallyay). Quarry (32:3) Sum 83, p. 31.
"Wanderers Nachlied." Quarry (32:3) Sum 83, p. 31.

1612. GOEWEY, Andrew B.
"Morning." SanFPJ (5:2) 83, p. 65.
"The Saga of Viet Nam." SanFPJ (5:2) 83, p. 91.

1613. GOGER, Joan
"Paradox." SanFPJ (5:3) 83, p. 76.

1614. GOLD, Sid
"Directions." YetASM (1:2) 82, p. 5.
"From Here to L.A." YetASM (1:2) 82, p. 4.

1615. GOLDBARTH, Albert
"35." MidwQ (25:1) Aut 83, p. 54.

"The Agnostic's Holy Sonnets" (Selection: "Raising the Dead"). Poetry (142:4) Jl 83, p. 225.
"The Agnostic's Holy Sonnets" (Selection: "The Nearerness"). MidwQ (24:4) Sum 83, p. 450.
"Apr 15." Agni (19) 83, p. 96-97.
"Assurance." LittleM (14:1/2) 83, p. 97.
"Bachelor / Acoustics." Telescope (4) Wint 83, p. 66-67.
"Ceilingfan." MidwQ (25:1) Aut 83, p. 50-51.
"The Dark." CharR (9:1) Spr 83, p. 20.
"Dead Tongues." PoetryNW (24:3) Aut 83, p. 11-12.
"Diagrams." Poetry (142:4) Jl 83, p. 226.
"Distances." AmerPoR (12:2) Mr/Ap 83, p. 40.
"Emily's Breath, 10/11/82." PoetL (78:1) Spr 83, p. 6-7.
"Epistola de Secretis Operibus, chapter 4." MidwQ (24:4) Sum 83, p. 448-449.
"Eulachon." Telescope (4) Wint 83, p. 65.
"Everyone's Ideas." MidwQ (25:1) Aut 83, p. 52-53.
"Far Pairs, Close Pairs." MemphisSR (2:2) Spr 82, p. 8.
"The First." PoetL (78:1) Spr 83, p. 10.
"The Form and Function of the Novel." OntR (18) Spr-Sum 83, p. 80-81.
"Forming Now." CharR (9:1) Spr 83, p. 22-23.
"How Could One Write on a Page So Profoundly Black?" (D.H. Lawrence). Tendril (14/15) Wint 83, p. 81.
"Images of the Soul." PoetL (78:1) Spr 83, p. 8.
"Khirbet Shemà." NewEngR (6:2) Wint 83, p. 281.
"Lines." MidwQ (24:4) Sum 83, p. 456.
"Lot's Wife." MidwQ (24:4) Sum 83, p. 446.
"Maples." PoetryNW (24:3) Aut 83, p. 10-11.
"Mars." PoetL (78:1) Spr 83, p. 5.
"Nickie Naming." MidwQ (25:1) Aut 83, p. 55.
"The Numbering at Bethlehem." Poetry (143:3) D 83, p. 141-144.
"One Thing Calls Another Thing, and the Map of Such Calls is Our Humanness." NewEngR (6:2) Wint 83, p. 280.
"Passing." Telescope (4) Wint 83, p. 68.
"Penelope." Shen (34:2) 83, p. 97.
"Phases." AmerPoR (12:2) Mr/Ap 83, p. 40-41.
"Pluto Joins the Gypsies." CharR (9:1) Spr 83, p. 21-22.
"Religious." MemphisSR (2:1) Aut 81, p. 5.
"Singsong, Whatever It Means." NowestR (21:1) 83, p. 34-35.
"Snaps." CalQ (22) Sum 83, p. 73-74.
"A Spider." BlackWR (10:1) Aut 83, p. 31-35.
"A Study of Goldb---h's Poetry in Terms of His Century's Artifacts: Prefatory Notes." MidwQ (24:4) Sum 83, p. 455.
"Thanksgiving." CalQ (22) Sum 83, p. 72.
"That Gap." Poetry (142:4) Jl 83, p. 229-230.
"A Theory." MidwQ (24:4) Sum 83, p. 447.
"The Theory of Absolute Form." BlackWR (10:1) Aut 83, p. 36.
"These Likenesses." Poetry (142:4) Jl 83, p. 227-228.

"This World." Tendril (14/15) Wint 83, p. 82-83.
"Three Anatomical Points." OhioR (30) 83, p. 25.
"Toward Notes on the Vapor Biocycle." PoetL (78:1) Spr 83, p. 9.
"Two." Telescope (4) Wint 83, p. 9-10.
"Uh-oh, I just remembered something." MidwQ (24:4) Sum 83, p. 451.
"Waking Alone in a Rented Room and Despairing Till the Phone Rings." ThRiPo (21/22) 83, p. 35.
"The Ways and Means Committee." CarolQ (35:2) Wint 83, p. 66-72.
"What Faith Means." Telescope (4) Wint 83, p. 8.
"Who We Write For." MidwQ (24:4) Sum 83, p. 452-454.
"Wings." Telescope (5/6) Spr 83, p. 148.

1616. GOLDBECK, Janne
"Shape Shifter." ConcPo (16:2) Aut 83, p. 28.

1617. GOLDBERG, Barbara
"Cautionary Tales." Poetry (142:2) My 83, p. 83.
"Ghazal: After the Fact." StoneC (10:3/4) Spr-Sum 83, p. 10.
"Her Soul to Keep." PoetL (78:4) Wint 84, p. 219.
"Song While Arranging Jasmine and Jewelweed." Tendril (16) Sum 83, p. 58-59.
"Teeth." Poetry (142:2) My 83, p. 84.

1618. GOLDBERG, Beckian Fritz
"Spring." AntR (41:2) Spr 83, p. 203.

1619. GOLDBERG, Martha
"Laundry." YetASM (2:1) 83, p. 3.

1620. GOLDBERG, Nancy Maxwell
"Intrepid Season." DekalbLAJ (16:1/4) Aut 82-Sum 83, p. 65.

1621. GOLDBERG, Natalie
"Coming Together." Calyx (7:3) Sum 83, p. 32-33.

1622. GOLDEN, Renny
"Hibakuskas" (a Japanese word for the survivors of Hiroshima and Hagasaki). Vis (11) 83, p. 22.

1623. GOLDENSOHN, Barry
"The Dream As Calculation." Salm (60) Spr-Sum 83, p. 146.
"Freeze Frame." NewRep (189:3/4) 18-25 Jl 83, p. 34.
"The Garrotted Man" (Goya). NewRep (186:17) 28 Ap 82, p. 32.
"The Kabalist." Salm (60) Spr-Sum 83, p. 142.
"Love and Work: Apple Picking." Salm (60) Spr-Sum 83, p. 143.
"The Marrano." Salm (60) Spr-Sum 83, p. 141.
"The Religion of Art (1 Feb '58)." Salm (60) Spr-Sum 83, p. 146-147.
"Simon's Dream." Salm (60) Spr-Sum 83, p. 144.
"Time-Binding." Salm (60) Spr-Sum 83, p. 145.

1624. GOLDENSOHN, Lorrie
"The Rite." MassR (24:2) Sum 83, p. 411.
"Terms." MassR (24:1) Spr 83, p. 140.

1625. GOLDERMAN, Cynthia R.
"The Contemplation and the Deed." SanFPJ (5:4) 83, p. 57.
"The Great Weapons." SanFPJ (5:4) 83, p. 58-59.
"The Neutron, Awesome Bomb." SanFPJ (5:3) 83, p. 56.
"Nuclear War." SanFPJ (5:3) 83, p. 90-91.
"The Old House." SanFPJ (5:2) 83, p. 19.

1626. GOLDIN, Grace
"The Charge." YaleR (72:2) Wint 83, p. 261.
"Lost or Found." YaleR (72:2) Wint 83, p. 260.
"Supernaturals." YaleR (72:2) Wint 83, p. 261.

1627. GOLDKORN, Isaac
"The Beginning and the End" (After Robert Frost). WritersL S 83, p. 5.
"Ernest Hemingway." WritersL F 83, p. 10.

1628. GOLDLEAF, Steven
"The Day Is Almost Gone." DevQ (18:3) Aut 83, p. 103-105.

1629. GOLDMAN, Bobbie
"Idylwood." YetASM (2:1) 83, p. 6.
"Rituals." YetASM (1:1) 82, p. 4.

1630. GOLDMAN, Judy
"My Mother's Shoes." Outbr (12/13) Aut 83-Spr 84, p. 96.

1631. GOLDMAN, Michael
"Blue Painting." OntR (18) Spr-Sum 83, p. 63.
"Christmas Scenes" (a present for Eleanor). OntR (18) Spr-Sum 83, p. 62.
"Dinner is Served." Poetry (141:6) Mr 83, p. 342.
"A Gap in the Argument." OntR (18) Spr-Sum 83, p. 61.
"Getting Away." OntR (18) Spr-Sum 83, p. 59.
"Hymeneal." OntR (18) Spr-Sum 83, p. 64.
"Recovery." Poetry (141:6) Mr 83, p. 343-344.
"Scenery." OntR (18) Spr-Sum 83, p. 60.
"So Human." OntR (18) Spr-Sum 83, p. 65.
"What It Hides." OntR (18) Spr-Sum 83, p. 66.
"What the Night Says." Poetry (141:6) Mr 83, p. 342.

1632. GOLDSTEIN, Henry
"The House with the Blue Door." Confr (25/26) 83, p. 49.

1633. GOLDSTEIN, Jonas L.
"Entrails raised to the sun." SanFPJ (5:1) 83, p. 11.
"The Force Within." SanFPJ (4:4) 83, p. 72.
"Insanity." SanFPJ (5:1) 83, p. 30.
"Nuclear proliferation." SanFPJ (4:4) 83, p. 55.
"Penance." SanFPJ (5:2) 83, p. 45.

"Rifles." SanFPJ (5:1) 83, p. 84.
"Salvation." SanFPJ (4:4) 83, p. 29.
"There's been progress." SanFPJ (5:1) 83, p. 11.
"A Woman's Chance." SanFPJ (5:1) 83, p. 31.

1634. GOLDSTEIN, Lenny
"Hunting Billie's Pad." Tele (18) 83, p. 88.
"Iodine." Tele (18) 83, p. 89.
"St. Cecilia." Tele (18) 83, p. 88.

1635. GOLDSTEIN, Marion
"It Is the Apples." StoneC (10:3/4) Spr-Sum 83, p. 42.

1636. GOLFFING, Francis
"Abandoned Upland Farm" (tr. of Günter Eich). PoNow (7:2, #38) 83, p. 44.
"Insight" (tr. of Günter Eich). PoNow (7:2, #38) 83, p. 44.

1637. GOLL, Yvan
"The Head in the Desert" (tr. by Paul Morris). WebR (8:2) Aut 83, p. 45.
"The Hours" (tr. by Paul Morris). WebR (8:2) Aut 83, p. 44.
"The Hut of Ashes" (tr. by Paul Morris). WebR (8:2) Aut 83, p. 44.
"In Every Blackbird I Loved You" (tr. by Paul Morris). WebR (8:2) Aut 83, p. 43.
"The Inner Trees" (tr. by Paul Morris). WebR (8:2) Aut 83, p. 43.

1638. GOMEZ, Jewelle L.
"Flamingoes and Bears: a Parable." Cond (9) Spr 83, p. 56.
"Pomegranate." Cond (9) Spr 83, p. 57.

1639. GOMEZ CAJAPE, Freddy
"Aquel Hombre Que Pasaba." Rácata (2) 83, p. 64.
"Detrás del árbol, acurrucada en el llanto de la tortuga." Rácata (2) 83, p. 63.
"Lluvia" (a las madres de la Plaza de Mayo). Rácata (2) 83, p. 62.
"Memorias de una Pierna Que Arrastraba Caminos." Rácata (2) 83, p. 65.
"Zapato." Rácata (2) 83, p. 133.

1640. GOMEZ-GOMOLKA, Magdalena
"Making It." MassR (24:1) Spr 83, p. 41.

GOMOLKA, Magdalena Gomez
See: GOMEZ-GOMOLKA, Magdalena

1641. GONZALEZ, Rafael Jesús
"Exhortation." SecC (11:1/2) 83, p. 67-68.

1642. GOOD, Ruth
"Wash Day." CharR (9:1) Spr 83, p. 23-24.

1643. GOODELL, Larry
"The Real Hunky-Dory." Tele (18) 83, p. 2-5.

1644. GOODENOUGH, J. B. (Judith B.)
"Afternoon Lessons." Ascent (8:3) 83, p. 31.
"Back Country." SmPd (20:1) Wint 83, p. 31.
"Bread and Shoes." NewRena (16) Spr 83, p. 49.
"Bury the Blackbird Here." DevQ (18:1) Spr 83, p. 85.
"Captive." NewRena (16) Spr 83, p. 48.
"Heartwood." SmPd (20:1) Wint 83, p. 30.
"Inland." WebR (8:1) Spr 83, p. 60.
"The Judson Place." ModernPS (11:3) 83, p. 289.
"The Local Customs." DevQ (18:3) Aut 83, p. 100.
"Mother Stones." ModernPS (11:3) 83, p. 288.
"Ox Pond." Blueline (3:2) Wint-Spr 82, p. 11.
"Primagravida." Prima (8) 83, p. 83.
"The Primitives." Blueline (5:1) Sum-Aut 83, p. 46.
"Reading It Wrong." Poem (47) Mr 83, p. 64.
"Saul's House." Blueline (4:2) Wint-Spr 83, p. 5.
"Sleight of Hand." WebR (8:1) Spr 83, p. 59.
"The Somnambulists." KanQ (15:2) Spr 83, p. 197.
"Stitchery." StoneC (10:3/4) Spr-Sum 83, p. 74.
"Times." Poem (47) Mr 83, p. 63.
"Under." ModernPS (11:3) 83, p. 287-288.

1645. GOODMAN, Michael
"Your Mother's Last Illness." PoetryE (11) Sum 83, p. 20.

1646. GOODMAN, Paul
"Ballade of the Moment After." AmerPoR (12:5) S/O 83, p. 20.
"Birthday Cake." AmerPoR (12:5) S/O 83, p. 19.
"Connary, Blodgett, Day, Hapgood." AmerPoR (12:5) S/O 83, p. 20.
"A Gravestone, August 8, 1968." AmerPoR (12:5) S/O 83, p. 20.
"In the Jury Room, in Pain." AmerPoR (12:5) S/O 83, p. 19.
"It was good when you were here." AmerPoR (12:5) S/O 83, p. 21.
"Little Prayers" (Excerpt: 14). AmerPoR (12:5) S/O 83, p. 20.
"Sentences after Defence of Poetry." AmerPoR (12:5) S/O 83, p. 20.
"Sentences for Matthew Ready, Series II" (Excerpt: 104). AmerPoR (12:5) S/O 83, p. 20.
"The Weepers Tower in Amsterdam." AmerPoR (12:5) S/O 83, p. 21.
"Woman eternal my muse, lean toward me." AmerPoR (12:5) S/O 83, p. 20.

1647. GOODMAN, Ryah Tumarkin
"The Hem Hangs." PoNow (7:2, #38) 83, p. 30.

1648. GORCZYNSKI, Renata
"Farewell" (tr. of Czeslaw Milosz, w. Robert Hass). NewYRB (30:7) 28 Ap 83, p. 6.
"It Was Winter" (tr. of Czeslaw Milosz, w. Robert

Hass and Robert Pinsky). NewRep (187:11) 13 S 82, p. 28-29.
"On the Road" (tr. of Czeslaw Milosz, w. Robert Hass). NewYRB (30:7) 28 Ap 83, p. 6.

1649. GORDETT, Marea
"The Boy Named Several." MissR (12:1/2, nos. 34/35) Aut 83, p. 82-83.
"It Seemed a Shame." MassR (24:4) Wint 83, p. 698.
"A Lighted Window." MissR (12:1/2, nos. 34/35) Aut 83, p. 86.
"A Sweet Fever." MissR (12:1/2, nos. 34/35) Aut 83, p. 87.
"Washing You." MissR (12:1/2, nos. 34/35) Aut 83, p. 84-85.

1650. GORDON, David
"Playing for Time." WestCR (17:4) Ap 83, p. 37.

1651. GORDON, Don
"In the Cell." Sam (36:3 143rd release) 83, p. 16.
"Lions." CentR (27:3) Sum 83, p. 190.

1652. GORDON, Donna
"The Estranged." YetASM (2:1) 83, p. 4.
"Geographer." PoetryNW (24:1) Spr 83, p. 44-45.

1653. GORDON, Rebecca
"Adolescence." Calyx (8:1) Aut 83, p. 9.
"Anniversary." Calyx (8:1) Aut 83, p. 10.
"The Women and the Nightmare Builders." Calyx (8:1) Aut 83, p. 6-8.

1654. GORENBERG, Gershom
"Faith." Argo (4:1) 82, p. 11.

1655. GORHAM, Sarah
"Barges" (to my father). SouthernPR (23:2) Aut 82 [i.e. (23:1?) Spr 83], p. 7.
"Dutchman's Breeches." SouthernPR (23:2) Aut 82 [i.e. (23:1?) Spr 83], p. 8.
"Harvesting." CutB (21) Aut-Wint 83, p. 21.
"Stillshot." SoDakR (21:3) Aut 83, p. 92.
"Wood Thrush." PoetL (77:3) Aut 82, p. 136.

1656. GORKA, Kris
"Scene at Sandy Hook." HangL (44) Sum 83, p. 61-63.

1657. GORLIN, Debra
"Fleshing In." MassR (24:1) Spr 83, p. 94-95.

1658. GOTRO, Paul (Paul Edmund)
"Foxes: Refuting a Post Card." Waves (11:2/3) Wint 83, p. 66.
"Nass Bay." Grain (11:1) F 83, p. 25.

1659. GOTT, George
"Father and Mother." PoetL (77:1) Spr 82, p. 21.
"The New Book." Tele (18) 83, p. 108.
"The Well." Tele (18) 83, p. 109.

1660. GOTTLIEB, Michael
"Social Realism" (Excerpts). ParisR (24:86) Wint 82, p. 106-107.

1661. GOTTSCHALK, Keith
"Cesar Mendoza, General of Chile, Collects the South African Police Star for Outstanding Services." MinnR (NS 21) Aut 83, p. 4-6.
"How the Department of Cooperation and Development Rehoused Mrs. Bhekeni Ngidi." MinnR (NS 21) Aut 83, p. 4.

1662. GOULISH, Matthew
"Blue Moon." IndR (6:2) Spr 83, p. 44-46.

1663. GOWER, David
"Hands." SanFPJ (4:4) 83, p. 89.

1664. GRABER, John
"1700 Miles to Elise." AmerPoR (12:1) Ja/F 83, p. 14.

1665. GRABILL, James
"An Earthen Night." CharR (9:1) Spr 83, p. 26-27.
"Howard Hughes Spirits Himself Still As Jeeps Are Wrecklessly Driven on Terrains Seen Only in Dream" (for Chris and Carlos). MinnR (NS 21) Aut 83, p. 23.
"A Question of Integrity." Wind (13:48) 83, p. 53.
"The Snow." StoneC (11:1/2, Pt. 1) Aut-Wint 83, p. 34-35.
"Spring Sayings." MinnR (NS 20) Spr 83, p. 47.
"The White Horse" (For Bill and Ernie). PortR (29:1) 83, p. 85-86.

1666. GRAF, Jess
"Goodnight Gang." SanFPJ (4:4) 83, p. 44.
"High Noon." SanFPJ (4:2) 83, p. 34.
"Lady Night." PikeF (5) Spr 83, p. 11.
"Semper Fi." SanFPJ (4:2) 83, p. 35.

1667. GRAF, Roger
"The Horse." Meadows (4:1) 83, p. 38.

1668. GRAHAM, Alison
"Dahlias." Stand (24:3) 83, p. 45.

1669. GRAHAM, Chael
"Gleaners." Stand (24:2) 83, p. 65.
"Tracking." PoNow (7:2, #38) 83, p. 47.

1670. GRAHAM, Greg
"One Night in Verona." AntigR (55) Aut 83, p. 64.

1671. GRAHAM, Jorie
"Evening Prayer." Tendril (16) Sum 83, p. 164.
"Expecting" (to Jim). Poetry (143:2) N 83, p. 97-100.
"Hurry." Tendril (16) Sum 83, p. 170-171.
"Mirror Prayer" (for Emily). Poetry (143:2) N 83,

p. 93-96.
"An Old Painting." Tendril (16) Sum 83, p. 169.
"Prayer" (Penelope). Tendril (16) Sum 83, p. 161-163.
"The Sacrament of Gravity." Tendril (16) Sum 83, p. 160.
"San Xavier Du Bac/For Jon" (Tuscon, Az.). Tendril (16) Sum 83, p. 165-166.
"Sundial." Tendril (16) Sum 83, p. 154-155.
"Updraft" (New York City, May 1982). Tendril (16) Sum 83, p. 158-159.
"Wind Died Down." Tendril (16) Sum 83, p. 156-157.
"With Child." Tendril (16) Sum 83, p. 167-168.

1672. GRAHAM, Matthew
"The American Falls." OP (35) Spr-Sum 83, p. 44-45.
"At the Wayne County Fair." OP (35) Spr-Sum 83, p. 43.
"Kitchen." OP (35) Spr-Sum 83, p. 46-47.
"Matthew Brady Speaks of Whitman." KanQ (15:4) Aut 83, p. 72.
"Union Town." MissouriR (7:1) Aut 83, p. 17.

1673. GRAHAM, Neile
"Anything You Say." CanLit (98) Aut 83, p. 45-46.
"High Water." CanLit (98) Aut 83, p. 44-45.
"Saltspring" (for Brenda). CanLit (98) Aut 83, p. 46.
"Swutlak Builds False Spring." CanLit (98) Aut 83, p. 44.

1674. GRANATO, Carol
"Discourse." SanFPJ (4:2) 83, p. 51.
"Once upon a Time." SanFPJ (5:2) 83, p. 74.
"Somewhere." SanFPJ (4:2) 83, p. 50.

1675. GRANT, Grell V.
"Hands." AntigR (52) Wint 83, p. 88.
"Last Voyage." AntigR (52) Wint 83, p. 88.

1676. GRAVELLE, Barbara
"Moon into Capricorn." SecC (11:1/2) 83, p. 69-70.

1677. GRAVES, Tom
"In Praise of Critics." WritersL Ap-My 83, p. 11.

1678. GRAVETT, Marilyn
"Northwest Ohio." KanQ (15:4) Aut 83, p. 30.

1679. GRAY, Cecile
"Black Dog in Oxford, Mississippi." SpiritSH (49 Suppl.) 83, p. 29.
"A Confession." SpiritSH (49 Suppl.) 83, p. 25.
"The Island Boy." SpiritSH (49 Suppl.) 83, p. 28.
"The Judge at the Witch-Burning." HiramPoR (35) Aut-Wint 83, p. 18.
"The Pontifex and the Emperor." SpiritSH (49 Suppl.) 83, p. 24.
"A Statue of Mary." SpiritSH (49 Suppl.) 83, p. 26-27.

1680. GRAY, Nelson
"Actual Sky." AntigR (52) Wint 83, p. 38.
"First Running Poem." AntigR (52) Wint 83, p. 38.

1681. GRAY, Patrick Worth
"Marion." PoetryCR (5:2) Wint 83-84, p. 10.
"Walk." PoetryCR (5:2) Wint 83-84, p. 10.

1682. GRAZIANO, Frank
"Rom" (After Jan Yoors's memoir, The Gypsies) (for Tim Correll). BelPoJ (33:3) Spr 83, p. 20-24.
"Throwing a Frog from a Bridge." CharR (9:1) Spr 83, p. 17.
"A Walk." CharR (9:1) Spr 83, p. 18.

1683. GREEN, Frank
"What Is Falling." Tele (18) 83, p. 91.

1684. GREEN, Kelly
"Layoff." SanFPJ (5:1) 83, p. 40.
"To All the Patriotic Housewives." SanFPJ (5:1) 83, p. 68.

1685. GREEN, Melissa
"The Squanicook Eclogues" (for Richard Winthrop Green, Jr. (1921-1982)) Agni (18) 83, p. 100-108.

1686. GREEN, Peter
"Christ in Our Perplexity." Comm (110:1) 14 Ja 83, p. 19.
"A Quiet Day Reading." Comm (110:1) 14 Ja 83, p. 19.

1687. GREEN, Rayna
"Mexico City Hand Game." MassR (24:1) Spr 83, p. 64.
"When I Cut My Hair." MassR (24:1) Spr 83, p. 63.

1688. GREEN, Robert
"Granny Clayton." LittleBR (3:3) Spr 83, p. 59.

1689. GREENBERG, Alvin
"1928." GeoR (37:1) Spr 83, p. 84.
"C=the Physics of Farewell." AmerPoR (12:6) N/D 83, p. 18.
"Heavy Wings" (Variations on a line by Wendy Parrish). OhioR (31) 83, p. 37-59.
"Pheasants on Ice." AmerPoR (12:6) N/D 83, p. 18.

1690. GREENBERG, Max
"Crazy, if it makes any difference to you." LittleM (14:1/2) 83, p. 40.
"In the short novel we sit bunched up." LittleM (14:1/2) 83, p. 39.

1691. GREENE, Jeffrey
"Farmhouse on the Algarve." CutB (21) Aut-Wint 83, p. 8.
"The Gathering Toward Evening." Epoch (32:2) Wint-Spr 83, p. 119.
"Makeshift." Tendril (16) Sum 83, p. 60-62.
"On Hearing Harkeness Tower." CutB (21) Aut-Wint

83, p. 6-7.
"Weldings." Epoch (32:2) Wint-Spr 83, p. 120.

1692. GREENHORN, Billy
"The Haunted House." Wind (13:48) 83, p. 24-25.

1693. GREENWALD, Roger
"But We Live" (tr. of Rolf Jacobsen). PoetryE (12) Aut 83, p. 93.
"From Above, from Below and from the Side" (tr. of Rolf Jacobsen). PoetryE (12) Aut 83, p. 90.
"Letter to the Light" (tr. of Rolf Jacobsen). PoetryE (12) Aut 83, p. 88.
"The Old Ladies" (tr. of Rolf Jacobsen). PoetryE (12) Aut 83, p. 91.
"Small Lights at Sea" (tr. of Rolf Jacobsen). PoetryE (12) Aut 83, p. 89.
"Unthinking" (tr. of Rolf Jacobsen). PoetryE (12) Aut 83, p. 92.

1694. GREENWALD, Ted
"All over the body." ParisR (24:86) Wint 82, p. 98.
"As far as I can see." ParisR (24:86) Wint 82, p. 99.
"Finally Understanding." ParisR (24:86) Wint 82, p. 100.
"How do we." ParisR (24:86) Wint 82, p. 99.
"If so." ParisR (24:86) Wint 82, p. 100.
"Industrial amazement." ParisR (24:86) Wint 82, p. 100.
"Staring Doesn't Help." ParisR (24:86) Wint 82, p. 98.
"Those is that." ParisR (24:86) Wint 82, p. 99.

1695. GREENWAY, William
"Heart." Poetry (142:2) My 83, p. 85-86.
"The Last of the Sheridans." SouthernPR (23:2) Aut 83, p. 23-24.
"The Weaning." Poetry (142:2) My 83, p. 87.

1696. GREENWOOD, G. P.
"Love under the Scouring Pad." PoetryCR (5:1) Aut 83, p. 17.
"Three A.M., Then and Now." PoetryCR (4:4) Sum 83, p. 15.
"To a Rapist." PoetryCR (5:2) Wint 83-84, p. 17.

1697. GREER, David
"Gulf Islands Fish Inspector." Grain (11:1) F 83, p. 26-27.

1698. GREER, Mary A.
"Knowledge." HiramPoR (35) Aut-Wint 83, p. 19.

1699. GREGER, Debora
"Closer." NewRep (187:20) 22 N 82, p. 26.
"The Corner of Delicious and Jonathan Streets." BlackWR (8:1) Aut 81, p. 48-49.
"Everyday Things." NewYorker (59:10) 25 Ap 83, p. 131.

"Grounds." NewRep (188:3) 24 Ja 83, p. 30.
"Incense." AntR (41:3) Sum 83, p. 334.
"Kin." Nat (237:20) 17 D 83, p. 636.
"Laundry." BlackWR (8:2) Spr 82, p. 70-71.
"Life Drawing." AmerPoR (12:3) My-Je 83, p. 40.
"Natural History." BlackWR (10:1) Aut 83, p. 81.
"No." BlackWR (10:1) Aut 83, p. 80.
"Of." Epoch (33:1) Aut-Wint 83, p. 60.
"Queen of a Small Country." AmerPoR (12:3) My-Je 83, p. 40.
"The Roman Baths at Chesters." Nat (237:20) 17 D 83, p. 636.
"To Market." Nat (237:20) 17 D 83, p. 636.
"To Speak of Water Music." Nat (237:20) 17 D 83, p. 636.
"Whitby Jet." NewRep (187:16) 18 O 82, p. 32.

1700. GREGERSON, Linda
"Halfe a Yard of Rede Sea" (Item in the records of the Coventry Cappers, Corpus Christi pageant, c. 1574). VirQR (59:2) Spr 83, p. 245-246.

1701. GREGG, Linda
"All That the Heart Owns." Tendril (14/15) Wint 83, p. 84.
"Growing Silent." Tendril (14/15) Wint 83, p. 85.
"Knowing Our Bodies Wear Out." Tendril (14/15) Wint 83, p. 86.

1702. GREGOR, Arthur
"An Illustration." PoNow (7:2, #38) 83, p. 11.
"The Pine." SouthernR (19:1) Ja 83, p. 154-155.

1703. GREGORIS. Steve
"For an Instant." PottPort (5) 83-84, p. 26.

1704. GREGORY, Horace
"Siege at Stony Point." NewL (49:3/4) Spr-Sum 83, p. 34.

1705. GREGORY, Robert
"Intersection." ModernPS (11:3) 83, p. 306-307.

1706. GREIF, Shirley
"The Gatherer." StoneC (11:1/2, Pt. 1) Aut-Wint 83, p. 25.

GRENIER, Arpine Konyalian
See: KONYALIAN-GRENIER, Arpine

1707. GRENIER, Robert
"Fool." ParisR (24:86) Wint 82, p. 105.
"Interglacial Age." ParisR (24:86) Wint 82, p. 105.
"Next Hat." ParisR (24:86) Wint 82, p. 105.
"Spawned by the Foam Intelligence." ParisR (24:86) Wint 82, p. 104.
"Thoughtless Doth." ParisR (24:86) Wint 82, p. 104.
"Two." ParisR (24:86) Wint 82, p. 104.

1708. GREY, Lucinda
"First Day at Camp." SouthernPR (23:2) Aut 82 [i.e. (23:1?) Spr 83], p. 59.

1709. GRIFFIN, Jon (See also: GRIFFIN, Jonathan)
"Wasps." NewOR (10:2/3) Sum-Aut 83, p. 26.

1710. GRIFFIN, Jonathan (See also: GRIFFIN, Jon)
"Blessed Are the Clouds." ParisR (25:87) Spr 83, p. 200.
"Laundering Song." ParisR (25:87) Spr 83, p. 201.
"Over Land and Sea." ParisR (25:87) Spr 83, p. 201.

1711. GRIFFIN, Shaun
"The Damp Face of a Cloud." Meadows (4:1) 83, p. 45.
"Daydream Driving." Meadows (3:1) 82, p. 45.
"I Woke from a Poem Evening." Meadows (3:1) 82, p. 52.
"In a Sparse Tone for Richard Shelton." Meadows (4:1) 83, p. 26.
"Just Your Average Unfinished Man." Meadows (3:1) 82, p. 54.

1712. GRIFFIN, Susan
"Prayer for Continuation." NewEng (5:4) Sum 83, p. 553-562.

1713. GRIFFIN, Walter
"Aunt Ida and Lord Byron." LitR (27:1) Aut 83, p. 99.
"Bicycle in the Rain." Wind (13:47) 83, p. 13.
"Fish Leaves." Wind (13:47) 83, p. 14-15.
"In Italy, Sons Kiss Their Fathers." Wind (13:47) 83, p. 15.
"Night Diving." WestHR (37:1) Spr 83, p. 40.
"Speed." Wind (13:47) 83, p. 13-14.

1714. GRIFFITH, Jonathan
"Still Life." Focus (15:95) Ag 83, p. 21.
"The Towns of My Poems." Focus (15:95) Ag 83, p. 21.

1715. GRIGORUK, Daniel
"The Twain Meeting Despite Kipling." WritersL F 83, p. 10.

1716. GRIGSBY, Gordon
"Rain on the Ocean." Vis (12) 83, p. 8.

1717. GRILL, Neil
"Anxiety." PoetL (77:4) Wint 83, p. 200.
"The Man behind the French Sunglasses." PoetL (77:4) Wint 83, p. 200.

1718. GRILLO, Paul
"The Roland Kirk Story." Gargoyle (22/23) 83, p. 39.

1719. GRIMM, Reinhold
"Land of Shadows" (tr. of Hans Magnus Enzensberger, w. Felix Pollak). NowestR (21:1) 83, p. 131, 133.
"Those Who Have Disappeared" (for Nelly Sachs) (tr.

of Hans Magnus Enzensberger, w. Felix Pollak). NowestR (21:1) 83, p. 135.

1720. GRINDE, Olav
"Changing Light" (tr. of Rolf Jacobsen). StoneC (11:1/2, Pt. 1) Aut-Wint 83, p. 31.
"Cobblestone" (tr. of Rolf Jacobsen). SoDakR (21:1) Spr 83, p. 16.
"Marsh" (tr. of Rolf Jacobsen). Paint (10:19/20) Spr-Aut 83, p. 46.
"Night Music" (tr. of Rolf Jacobsen). Paint (10:19/20) Spr-Aut 83, p. 47.
"Old People's Graves" (tr. of Rolf Jacobsen). SoDakR (21:1) Spr 83, p. 14.
"Old People's Graves" (tr. of Rolf Jacobsen). WebR (8:1) Spr 83, p. 19.
"Reality" (tr. of Rolf Jacobsen). SoDakR (21:1) Spr 83, p. 18.
"Rose" (tr. of Marie Takvam). PoetryE (9/10) Wint 82-Spr 83, p. 258.
"Roses--Roses" (tr. of Rolf Jacobsen). SoDakR (21:1) Spr 83, p. 22, 25.
"Saltwater" (tr. of Rolf Jacobsen). WebR (8:1) Spr 83, p. 17-19.
"Say More, Speak Like Rain" (tr. of Arne Ruste). PoetryE (9/10) Wint 82-Spr 83, p. 11-13.
"Turn Away. -- Think about Something Else!" (tr. of Rolf Jacobsen). SoDakR (21:1) Spr 83, p. 20.
"Turnip Harvest" (tr. of Rolf Jacobsen). StoneC (11:1/2, Pt. 1) Aut-Wint 83, p. 31.

1721. GROENEWOUD, Robert D.
"City Lights." CapeR (18:2) Sum 83, p. 21.

1722. GROFF, David
"Birthing." AmerPoR (12:3) My-Je 83, p. 19.
"The Crab Pickers." GeoR (37:2) Sum 83, p. 384.
"Facing East near Big Sur." MissouriR (6:3) Sum 83, p. 14-15.
"Naming Constellations." NowestR (21:2/3) 83, p. 49.
"Swing." MissR (12:1/2, nos. 34/35) Aut 83, p. 88.
"The Tomb of Lysias" (after Cavafy). AmerPoR (12:3) My-Je 83, p. 19.

1723. GROSHOLZ, Emily
"97 Rue Compans." Hudson (36:3) Aut 83, p. 492.
"Aux Balcons." Hudson (36:3) Aut 83, p. 490-491.
"Crescent Moon." PraS (57:4) Wint 83, p. 16.
"Dinner in the Courtyard." Hudson (36:3) Aut 83, p. 491.
"Five Poems for F. D." Hudson (36:3) Aut 83, p. 490-495.
"Following the Dordogne." MassR (24:2) Sum 83, p. 270-271.
"In the Garden." Hudson (36:3) Aut 83, p. 493.
"The Last of the Courtyard." Hudson (36:3) Aut 83, p. 494.

1724. GROSS, Harvey
"The Execution." Nat (237:3) 23-30 Jl 83, p. 86.

"I Believe, I Believe." VirQR (59:2) Spr 83, p. 239-240.

1725. GROSS, Philip
"A New Life" (from "News from the Other Country"). Stand (24:2) 83, p. 7.

1726. GROSSBARDT, Andrew
"Montana, Again." NewL (49:3/4) Spr-Sum 83, p. 168.

1727. GROSSMAN, Andrew J.
"After Making Love." YetASM (2:1) 83, p. 4.

1728. GROSSMAN, Florence
"Still Life." Poetry (142:1) Ap 83, p. 17.

1729. GROVE, Rex
"On Watching Jenny Go Too Fast." EngJ (72:1) Ja 83, p. 89.

1730. GROVER-ROGOFF, Jay
"Ploughing." YetASM (1:1) 82, p. 6.

1731. GRUE, Lee Meitzen
"An Open Gift." Argo (4:3) 83, p. 4.

1732. GRYNBERG, Henryk
"After the Resurrection" (tr. by Richard Lourie). PoetryE (9/10) Wint 82-Spr 83, p. 239-240.

1733. GU, Cheng
"A Generation" (tr. by Helen Siu and Zelda Stern). AmerPoR (12:2) Mr/Ap 83, p. 20.
"I Am a Willful Child" (tr. by Helen Siu and Zelda Stern). AmerPoR (12:2) Mr/Ap 83, p. 20-21.
"Shooting a Photograph" (tr. by Helen Siu and Zelda Stern). AmerPoR (12:2) Mr/Ap 83, p. 20.

1734. GUDE, Michael
"Our Viscera Kill Us." NoAmR (268:4) D 83, p. 61.

GUDMUNDSDOTTIR, Thuridur
See: THURIDUR GUDMUNDSDOTTIR

1735. GUERENA, Jacinto-Luis
"L'aube-héritage." Os (16) 83, p. 22.
"Come enneigées." Os (16) 83, p. 22.
"Comme si le chemin se brisait." Os (16) 83, p. 23.
"Je traverse à gré." Os (16) 83, p. 23.
"Les mots." Os (16) 83, p. 24.
"Paroles de rosée." Os (16) 83, p. 24.
"Poème Inédit: Le solei joue." Os (17) 83, p. 29.
"Vous disiez le sang sec." Os (16) 83, p. 24.

1736. GUERNSEY, Bruce
"The Death of the Ventriloquist." Ascent (8:3) 83, p. 17.
"The Invention of the Telephone." QW (16) Spr-Sum 83, p. 60.

"Sign Language." Ascent (8:3) 83, p. 16-17.
"This Bank Protected by Silent Alarm." Ascent (8:3) 83, p. 16.

GUEVARA, Erick Blandon
See: BLANDON GUEVARA, Erick

1737. GUILFORD, Charles
"Archaic Torso of Apollo" (tr. of Rainer Maria Rilke). KanQ (15:4) Aut 83, p. 51.
"Coyote." KanQ (15:4) Aut 83, p. 48.
"Early Apollo" (tr. of Rainer Maria Rilke). KanQ (15:4) Aut 83, p. 51.
"Entry" (tr. of Rainer Maria Rilke). KanQ (15:4) Aut 83, p. 50.
"Evening" (tr. of Rainer Maria Rilke). KanQ (15:4) Aut 83, p. 49.
"Her Amazement." ColEng (45:7) N 83, p. 676.
"Nevada." KanQ (15:4) Aut 83, p. 49.
"The Panther" (Jardin Des Palntes, Paris) (tr. of Rainer Maria Rilke). KanQ (15:4) Aut 83, p. 50.

1738. GUISTA, Mike
"Young Evangelist." PoNow (7:2, #38) 83, p. 47.

1739. GULERMA, Isabela
"Bread Pudding Days." Cond (9) Spr 83, p. 10.
"Couturier Clothes." Cond (9) Spr 83, p. 9.
"Jackson Genes." Cond (9) Spr 83, p. 13.
"The Pearl Choker." Cond (9) Spr 83, p. 11-12.

1740. GULLANS, Charles
"Anti-Faust." ChiR (33:4) Sum [i.e. Spr] 83, p. 22-23.
"Gunsmoke." SouthernR (19:3) Jl 83, p. 635.
"In Retirement." ChiR (33:4) Sum [i.e. Spr] 83, p. 24-25.
"In the Marina." SouthernR (19:3) Jl 83, p. 636.

1741. GULLAR, Ferreira
"Things of the Earth" (tr. by William Jay Smith). PoNow (7:2, #38) 83, p. 46.

1742. GUNDY, Jeff
"The Children in the Dream." IndR (5:3) Aut 82, p. 44.
"I Fall Through, or Junk Food" (for Dean Young). IndR (6:2) Spr 83, p. 6.
"Introduction to Intuitive Geometry." IndR (6:2) Spr 83, p. 7.
"The People You Meet." KanQ (15:1) Wint 83, p. 148.
"Untitled: I have sat here." KanQ (15:1) Wint 83, p. 149.

1743. GUNN, Genni
"After an Absence." Quarry (32:3) Sum 83, p. 60.
"Mirage." Quarry (32:3) Sum 83, p. 62.
"Sunday Walk in the Crescent." Quarry (32:3) Sum 83, p. 61.

1744. GUNN, George
"Ugly Couple in a Bar" (In Memoriam James Douglas Morrison 1943-1971). Bogg (50) 83, p. 61.

1745. GUNN, Thom
"Bow Down." Thrpny (4:2, issue 14) Sum 83, p. 3.

1746. GUNNELL, Bryn
"Bustard Country." Stand (24:2) 83, p. 53.

1747. GUREVITCH, Zali
"Alien Work" (tr. by Linda Zisquit). LitR (26:2) Wint 83, p. 299.
"Broken Line, Lone Trees" (tr. by Gabriel Levin). LitR (26:2) Wint 83, p. 299-301.
"Light Fever" (tr. by Linda Zisquit). LitR (26:2) Wint 83, p. 298.
"Under the Surface" (tr. by Gabriel Levin). LitR (26:2) Wint 83, p. 301-302.

1748. GURLEY, George H., Jr.
"Foxy Lady." KanQ (15:3) Sum 83, p. 102.

1749. GURLEY, James
"Monhegan Island, Maine 1918." CutB (21) Aut-Wint 83, p. 76-77.

1750. GUSS, David
"Empty" (For Blaise Cendrars, tr. of Vincente Huidobro). Pig (11) 83, p. 30.
"Horizon" (tr. of Vincente Huidobro). Pig (11) 83, p. 31.
"Spring" (tr. of Vincente Huidobro). Pig (11) 83, p. 30.
"Swimmer" (tr. of Vincente Huidobro). Pig (11) 83, p. 30.
"Woman" (tr. of Vincente Huidobro). Pig (11) 83, p. 31.

1751. GUSTAFSON, Joseph
"The Search." NewRena (17) Aut 83, p. 75-76.

1752. GUSTAFSON, Ralph
"Advice from the Wilderness." Descant (40) Spr 83, p. 50.
"Assertion about Winter." MalR (64) F 83, p. 93.
"At the Cafe at Night." MalR (64) F 83, p. 90-91.
"At the Turning of Leaves." Descant (40) Spr 83, p. 48.
"Coda." Descant (40) Spr 83, p. 47.
"A Devotion to What There Is of Grace." MalR (64) F 83, p. 92.
"Don't Listen Wholeheartedly to the Poets." Descant (40) Spr 83, p. 49.
"For a Moment, the Act." MalR (64) F 83, p. 94.
"How to Think It Out." MalR (64) F 83, p. 85-86.
"In Santa Prassede, Rome." MalR (64) F 83, p. 89-90.
"In the Everglades." CanLit (97) Sum 83, p. 24-25.
"The Instance of Lobelia and Maple Examined." MalR (64) F 83, p. 94.

"Lilies at Mount St. Helens." MalR (64) F 83, p. 91-92.
"Man Untestamented." MalR (64) F 83, p. 86.
"Meditation Sufficient for Monday." MalR (64) F 83, p. 83.
"The Mind Needs What the Poem Does." CanLit (97) Sum 83, p. 22-23.
"The Nature of Existence." MalR (64) F 83, p. 84-85.
"The Question of Winter." MalR (64) F 83, p. 88.
"Rain." CanLit (97) Sum 83, p. 23-24.
"The Reductio." MalR (64) F 83, p. 91.
"Statement." MalR (64) F 83, p. 87-88.
"To Simon Wiesenthal." Descant (40) Spr 83, p. 46.
"Toccata." MalR (64) F 83, p. 87.
"Wheel of Fire." MalR (64) F 83, p. 84.

1753. GUTIERREZ, Ernesto
"My Country Is So Tiny." Sam (36:3 143rd release) 83, p. 9.

1754. GUTIERREZ, Franklin
"Lugar Común." Rácata (1) 83, p. 67.
"MBHP." Rácata (1) 83, p. 70-71.
"NY 10032." Rácata (1) 83, p. 68-69.

1755. GUTTERIDGE, Don
"To a Daughter, Writing Her First Poem." PoetryCR (4:4) Sum 83, p. 7.

1756. GUY, Earl
"H-Bomb." SoDakR (21:4) Wint 83, p. 33.

1757. GUYER, Palmer
"The Hardworking Discovery." YetASM (1:2) 82, p. 12.

GUZMAN BOUVARD, Marguerite
See: BOUVARD, Marguerite Guzman

1758. GWYNN, R. S.
"Among Philistines." Poetry (141:6) Mr 83, p. 340-341.
"Horatio's Philosophy." Swallow (1) Spr 83, p. 105-106.

1759. GYORI, Laszlo
"The Discovery of Europe" (tr. by Timothy Kachinske). PoetryE (9/10) Wint 82-Spr 83, p. 202.
"The Weight of Earth" (tr. by Timothy Kachinske). PoetryE (9/10) Wint 82-Spr 83, p. 203.

1760. HACKENDY, K.
"Etchings." SanFPJ (5:2) 83, p. 41.
"Glacier." SanFPJ (5:2) 83, p. 52.

1761. HACKER, Marilyn
"A Chaplet for Judith Landry." Poetry (141:5) F 83, p. 261-262.
"Corona" (for Kim Vaeth). MassR (24:2) Sum 83, p. 392-394.

"Mother." 13thM (6:1/2) 82, p. 62-63.
"Part of a True Story" (for Margaret Delany). 13thM (6:1/2) 82, p. 64-66.

1762. HACKETT, Philip
"At the Benedictine Monastery in Tyniec." OroM (2:1, #5) Sum 83, p. 18.
"At the Benedictine Monastery in Tyniec." Sam (36:3 143rd release) 83, p. 49.

1763. HADAS, Pamela White
"I Heared de Angels Singin': Harriet Tubman" (for Arthur Brown). Tendril (14/15) Wint 83, p. 87-93.

1764. HADAS, Rachel
"Belated Condolence" (to Richard Reid). PartR (50:3) 83, p. 410-411.
"The Blue Snake." MassR (24:3) Aut 83, p. 585-586.
"Chester Kallman (1921-1975)." Thrpny (4:2, issue 14) Sum 83, p. 20.
"Codex Minor." Epoch (33:1) Aut-Wint 83, p. 62-63.
"Essay on Form." NewEngR (5:3) Spr 83, p. 367-369.
"The Headache" (to Charlotte Mandel and Maxine Silverman). PraS (51:1, i.e. 57:1) Spr 83, p. 76-78.
"Iris." Harp (266:1592) Ja 83, p. 44.
"On a #4 Bus, March 30. 1981." PraS (51:1, i.e. 57:1) Spr 83, p. 75-76.
"Pastoral Assignment" (For Paul Alpers). DevQ (18:1) Spr 83, p. 18.
"Salt Citizen Re-enters City." DevQ (18:1) Spr 83, p. 19.
"Shore." DevQ (18:1) Spr 83, p. 14-15.
"Sisters in Winter" (To Beth). DevQ (18:1) Spr 83, p. 16-17.
"To a Youngish Professor Who Has Waxed Eloquent over Certain Students." PraS (51:1, i.e. 57:1) Spr 83, p. 74.
"Two Landscapes." PraS (51:1, i.e. 57:1) Spr 83, p. 78.

1765. HADDON, Nancy
"Dumb." SanFPJ (4:2) 83, p. 47.
"Merchandising on a Grand Scale." SanFPJ (4:2) 83, p. 19.
"Tomorrow." SanFPJ (4:2) 83, p. 18.

1766. HADDOX, Charles
"The Light That Falls." ChrC (100:31) 26 O 83, p. 966.
"Nativity of Mary." Comm (110:1) 14 Ja 83, p. 19.

1767. HAGIWARA, Sakutaro
"Anticipation" (tr. by Ochiishi). WebR (8:2) Aut 83, p. 46.
"Bamboo (1)" (tr. by Kiyoko Miura). SoDakR (21:1) Spr 83, p. 49.
"Bamboo (2)" (tr. by Kiyoko Miura). SoDakR (21:1) Spr 83, p. 49.
"A Blade of Grass" (tr. by Kiyoko Miura). SoDakR

(21:1) Spr 83, p. 48.
"A Man Who Loves Love" (tr. by Ochiishi). WebR (8:2) Aut 83, p. 47.
"Melancholy Vista" (tr. by Kiyoko Miura). SoDakR (21:1) Spr 83, p. 51.
"Seeds in the Palm of My Hand" (tr. by Kiyoko Miura). SoDakR (21:1) Spr 83, p. 50.
"Tender Feeling" (tr. by Ochiishi). WebR (8:2) Aut 83, p. 46.
"Tortoise" (tr. by Kiyoko Miura). SoDakR (21:1) Spr 83, p. 48.
"A Withered Crime" (tr. by Kiyoko Miura). SoDakR (21:1) Spr 83, p. 50.

1768. HAGUE, Richard
"Listening Again." Wind (13:49) 83, p. 25-26.
"Washington County Suicide." Wind (13:49) 83, p. 25.

1769. HAHN, Oscar
"666 Reencarnación de los Carniceros." Prismal (11) Aut 83, p. 91.
"A la Una Mi Fortuna, a las Dos Tu Reloj." Mund (14:1) 83, p. 24.
"At One My Fortune, at Two Your Watch" (tr. by James Hoggard). Mund (14:1) 83, p. 25.
"Buenas Noches Hermosa." Mund (14:1) 83, p. 24.
"Good Night Dear" (tr. by James Hoggard). Mund (14:1) 83, p. 25.
"Hotel de las Nostalgias: Música de Elvis Presley (Q.E.P.D.)." Inti (15) Spr 82, p. 66.

1770. HAHN, Steve
"The Death of the Man Who Thought He Was Jesse James" (Little Rock, 1947). LittleBR (4:1) Aut 83, p. 10.
"John Erdman Cuts Thistles and Takes on the Lord's Passion." KanQ (15:1) Wint 83, p. 52.
"Mid-August, Alone in the Heat." KanQ (15:1) Wint 83, p. 51.
"Trinity Sunday Dawned Clear and Still." KanQ (15:1) Wint 83, p. 52.

1771. HAHN, Susan
"Looking Out on Africa." Poetry (141:4) Ja 83, p. 219.
"Melancholia." Poetry (141:4) Ja 83, p. 218.

1772. HAINES, John
"Forest without Leaves" (Selections: I-III). ClockR (2:1) 83, p. 18-20.
"Pickers." Field (28) Spr 83, p. 71.
"Whatever Is Here Is Native." Harp (266:1592) Ja 83, p. 44.

1773. HAINING, Jim
"For John Lee." SpoonRQ (8:4) Aut 83, p. 16.
"Martin Avenue." SpoonRQ (8:4) Aut 83, p. 16.
"New Boy." SpoonRQ (8:4) Aut 83, p. 16.

1774. HAISLIP, John
"A Winter Storm." PoetryNW (24:2) Sum 83, p. 37.

1775. HAKANSSON, Björn
"Napalm" (tr. by Gunnar Harding and Frederic Will). PoetryE (9/10) Wint 82-Spr 83, p. 243.

HAKYO, Ishida
See: ISHIDA, Hakyo

1776. HALES, Corrinne
"Brother Johnson's Youngest Wife." CimR (65) O 83, p. 4.

1777. HALEY, Vanessa
"Home." Poetry (142:4) Jl 83, p. 221-222.
"The Housesitter." Poetry (142:4) Jl 83, p. 220.
"Letters from My Mother." SouthernPR (23:2) Aut 82 [i.e. (23:1?) Spr 83], p. 68.

1778. HALL, Donald
"At Eagle Pond." Poetry (143:1) O 83, p. 25-26.
"The Day I Was Older." Iowa (13:3/4) Spr 82 (83), p. 20-21.
"A Difficult Marriage." Atlantic (252:1) Jl 83, p. 69.
"Mr. Wakefield on Interstate 90." NewRep (187:9) 30 Ag 82, p. 32.
"On a Literary Agent." SewanR (91:1) Wint 83, p. 166.
"On a Scholar." SewanR (91:1) Wint 83, p. 166.
"On an Ambitious Poet." SewanR (91:1) Wint 83, p. 166.
"On an Anthologist." SewanR (91:1) Wint 83, p. 166.
"On an Eminent Novelist." SewanR (91:1) Wint 83, p. 166.
"A Sister by the Pond." Iowa (13:3/4) Spr 82 (83), p. 22-25.
"The Toy Bone." OhioR (30) 83, p. 61.
"Whip-poor-will."NewRep (186:7) 17 F 82, p. 34.

1779. HALL, Frances
"Desert Dweller." SouthwR (68:4) Aut 83, p. 315.

1780. HALL, James B. (See also: HALL, James Baker; HALL, Jim)
"Elegy: My Own" (For Larry Levis). NewL (50:1) Aut 83, p. 30-31.
"Looking at the Sea." MalR (64) F 83, p. 116-117.

1781. HALL, James Baker (See also: HALL, James B.; HALL, Jim)
"Adam's Love Song." Poetry (143:3) D 83, p. 135.
"The Calling." CharR (9:2) Aut 83, p. 55-60.
"The Child." Poetry (143:3) D 83, p. 137.
"The Fox." PoetryNW (24:3) Aut 83, p. 37-39.
"Fresh Snow at Dusk." Poetry (143:3) D 83, p. 136.
"A Stillness." Ploughs (9:2/3) 83, p. 143-144.
"Swimming at Sunset." PoetryNW (24:3) Aut 83, p. 36-37.

"Traveling by Moonlight." ParisR (25:90) Wint 83, p. 152-153.

1782. HALL, Jim (See also: HALL, James B.; HALL, James Baker)
"The Black Porsche." BelPoJ (34:1) Aut 83, p. 20-21.
"Decomposing Women." ThRiPo (21/22) 83, p. 38.
"For Years." BelPoJ (34:1) Aut 83, p. 21.
"Sperm Count." NoAmR (268:1) Mr 83, p. 63.
"Woolgathering." Poetry (142:6) S 83, p. 319.

1783. HALL, Joan Joffe
"Hawk Coming." BelPoJ (33:4) Sum 83, p. 7-11.
"It's She." MinnR (NS 20) Spr 83, p. 51.
"Romance and Capitalism and the Movies." MassR (24:1) Spr 83, p. 217.

1784. HALL, Phil
"Duck Blind." Waves (11:2/3) Wint 83, p. 60.
"Singing to Sleep." Waves (11:2/3) Wint 83, p. 60-61.

1785. HALLA, Chris
"Mushroom Cloud." Northeast (Ser. 3:16) Wint 83-84, p. 37.

1786. HALLADAY, Barbara
"Dead Housewife Poem (Maggie)." Quarry (32:3) Sum 83, p. 44.
"Nobody Wants to Hire a Poet Anymore." Quarry (32:3) Sum 83, p. 44-45.

1787. HALLEY, Anne
"Enter with Flourishes." NewRep (188:10) 14 Mr 83, p. 26.
"The Street of Small Porches." NewRep (187:14) 4 O 82, p. 38.
"The Village Hears That Gold Is Unstable."NewRep (186:9) 3 Mr 82, p. 36.

1788. HALLGREN, Stephanie
"The Orbit of Forgot." BlackWR (9:2) Spr 83, p. 80-81.
"Waking before My Husband." BlackWR (8:1) Aut 81, p. 46-47.

1789. HALLIDAY, Mark
"Ballplayer at Midnight." ParisR (24:84) Sum 82, p. 145-146.
"Goosebumps." Ploughs (9:1) 83, p. 77-81.
"Jazz from Another Life." Ploughs (9:1) 83, p. 82-83.
"Thirteen-Year Old Girl." NewRep (186:22) 2 Je 82, p. 34.

1790. HALPERIN, Joan
"Fishmarket on a Winter Day." PoetL (78:1) Spr 83, p. 26.
"Pre Determination." PoetL (77:2) Sum 82, p. 78.

1791. HALPERIN, Mark
"After the Future." CrabCR (1:2) Aut 83, p. 28.
"Aunt Dunia." Telescope (5/6) Spr 83, p. 156.
"A Hummingbird for Mandelstam." Telescope (5/6) Spr 83, p. 157-158.
"Leah." DevQ (18:2) Sum 83, p. 71-74.
"March." PraS (57:2) Sum 83, p. 18.
"Nameless Indiscretions." CrabCR (1:1) My 83, p. 17.
"Quarrel." PraS (57:2) Sum 83, p. 19.

1792. HALPERN, Daniel
"The Afternoon: Mid-December." Poetry (143:3) D 83, p. 149-151.
"Another Letter." Tendril (14/15) Wint 83, p. 95.
"The Contents" (for Laurie). PartR (50:1) 83, p. 79-80.
"Low Tide Ghazal." Tendril (14/15) Wint 83, p. 94.
"On a Little Theme." ParisR (24:84) Sum 82, p. 25.
"Passing." ParisR (24:84) Sum 82, p. 25.
"The Summer Rentals." NewYorker (59:14) 23 My 83, p. 42-43.
"Summer Storm." Poetry (143:3) D 83, p. 146-149.

1793. HALPERN, Peter
"Story." KanQ (15:2) Spr 83, p. 185.

1794. HAM, Anita
"Summer Coyote's." Bluebuf (2:1) Aut 83, p. 11.

1795. HAMBLIN, Robert W.
"Hospital." CapeR (19:1) Wint 83, p. 24.
"One Looks at Two." CapeR (18:2) Sum 83, p. 37.
"The River." CapeR (18:2) Sum 83, p. 36.

1796. HAMBY, Barbara
"Eating Bees." SouthernHR (17:3) Sum 83, p. 239.
"Le Sauteur." KanQ (15:2) Spr 83, p. 182.
"Summer Cherries." SouthernHR (17:3) Sum 83, p. 240.

1797. HAMEL, Roland C.
"What's a Poet." WritersL F 83, p. 24.

1798. HAMERMESH, Cecile
"Trilogy." ThirdW Spr 83, p. 102-103.

1799. HAMILL, Sam
"After Ou-Yang Hsiu." MalR (64) F 83, p. 47.
"After the eating, the drinking and singing" (tr. of Liu Yung). CreamCR (8:1/2) 83, p. 91.
"Alone, Late, Reading a Good Friend's Poems" (after Po Chü-i). MalR (64) F 83, p. 45.
"Apologie." MalR (64) F 83, p. 44-45.
"Ashes of one world crumble upon the colors of another one" (tr. of Jaan Kaplinski, w. the author). CharR (9:2) Aut 83, p. 84-85.
"At Bamboo Lodge" (tr. of Wang Wei). MalR (64) F 83, p. 162.
"Big black hedgehog eternity descending into the valley" (tr. of Jaan Kaplinski, w. the author). CharR (9:2) Aut 83, p. 87.

"A Country Road" (tr. of Li Ho). <u>PortR</u> (29:1) 83, p. 83.
"Drinking Alone in the Rainy Season" (tr. of T'ao Ch'ien). <u>PortR</u> (29:1) 83, p. 101.
"Elegy" (tr. of Yüan Chên). <u>NowestR</u> (21:2/3) 83, p. 78.
"Everything melts" (tr. of Jaan Kaplinski, w. the author). <u>CrabCR</u> (1:2) Aut 83, p. 4.
"Honeybees through sunshine" (tr. of Jaan Kaplinski, w. the author). <u>CharR</u> (9:2) Aut 83, p. 84.
"The Horse" (tr. of Mei Yoa-ch'en). <u>CharR</u> (9:2) Aut 83, p. 89.
"In Time." <u>MalR</u> (64) F 83, p. 47.
"The Lice" (tr. of Mei Yoa-ch'en). <u>CharR</u> (9:2) Aut 83, p. 89.
"Life at the Capital" (tr. of Li Ho). <u>PortR</u> (29:1) 83, p. 127.
"Melancholic in the Manner of Li Ho" (tr. of Han Mu-Shan). <u>PortR</u> (29:1) 83, p. 10.
"Mourning a Vintner" (tr. of Li Po). <u>MalR</u> (64) F 83, p. 164.
"Near" (tr. of Jaan Kaplinski). <u>NowestR</u> (21:2/3) 83, p. 72.
"Necessities" (tr. of Mei Yoa-ch'en). <u>CharR</u> (9:2) Aut 83, p. 90.
"Our shadows are very long" (tr. of Jaan Kaplinski, w. the author). <u>CrabCR</u> (1:2) Aut 83, p. 5.
"Oven alone in the corner" (tr. of Jaan Kaplinski, w. the author). <u>CharR</u> (9:2) Aut 83, p. 85-86.
"Questions and Answers" (tr. of Li Po). <u>MalR</u> (64) F 83, p. 163.
"The same sea in us all red dark warm" (tr. of Jaan Kaplinski, w. the author). <u>CharR</u> (9:2) Aut 83, p. 87-88.
"Second Growth" (to Wendell Berry). <u>MalR</u> (64) F 83, p. 46.
"Silent at Her Window" (tr. of Wang Ch'ang-ling). <u>CreamCR</u> (8:1/2) 83, p. 91.
"Snowy River" (tr. of Liu Tsung-yüan). <u>CreamCR</u> (8:1/2) 83, p. 91.
"A Soldier's Song" (tr. of Li Po). <u>MalR</u> (64) F 83, p. 164.
"Song" (tr. of Ch'in Kuan). <u>AmerPoR</u> (12:6) N/D 83, p. 6.
"Song (Ch'i shih)" (tr. of Liu Yung). <u>AmerPoR</u> (12:6) N/D 83, p. 6.
"Song of Green Water and the Singing Girl" (tr. of Li Ho). <u>PortR</u> (29:1) 83, p. 100.
"Song (Ting Feng-po)" (tr. of Liu Yung). <u>AmerPoR</u> (12:6) N/D 83, p. 6.
"Summer's last evening" (tr. of Jaan Kaplinski, w. the author). <u>CrabCR</u> (1:2) Aut 83, p. 4.
"Swarms of daws are flying home from the west" (tr. of Jaan Kaplinski, w. the author). <u>CharR</u> (9:2) Aut 83, p. 88.
"Taking Leave of a Friend" (tr. of Li Po). <u>MalR</u> (64) F 83, p. 163.
"These Hills in Summer" (tr. of Li Po). <u>MalR</u> (64) F 83, p. 162.

"To be Icarus and fall wings aflame into the burning buttercups" (tr. of Jaan Kaplinski, w. the author). CharR (9:2) Aut 83, p. 85.
"To the Tune 'Beautiful Barbarian'" (tr. of Wei Chuang). AmerPoR (12:6) N/D 83, p. 6.
"To the Tune 'Boat of Stars'" (tr. of Li Ch'ing-chao). CrabCR (1:1) My 83, p. 6.
"To the Tune 'Magnolia Blossoms'" (tr. of Li Ch'ing-chao). CrabCR (1:1) My 83, p. 7.
"To the Tune 'Partridge Sky'" (tr. of Li Ch'ing-chao). CrabCR (1:1) My 83, p. 7.
"To the Tune 'The Washing Stream'" (tr. of Li Ch'ing-chao). CrabCR (1:1) My 83, p. 6.
"What woke us" (tr. of Jaan Kaplinski, w. the author). CrabCR (1:2) Aut 83, p. 4-5.
"You light-footed moss already on the window frame" (tr. of Jaan Kaplinski, w. the author). CharR (9:2) Aut 83, p. 86-87.
"You, you moon" (tr. of Jaan Kaplinski, w. the author). CrabCR (1:2) Aut 83, p. 5.

1800. HAMILTON, Alfred Starr
"An Ancient Mariner." CreamCR (8:1/2) 83, p. 89.
"The Blacksmith." CreamCR (8:1/2) 83, p. 89.
"Build a Big City." CreamCR (8:1/2) 83, p. 89.
"City Limits." NewL (50:1) Aut 83, p. 99.
"A Member of a Lodge." CreamCR (8:1/2) 83, p. 88.
"November." NewL (50:1) Aut 83, p. 98.
"Orange Lillies." CreamCR (8:1/2) 83, p. 88.
"The Sun and I." Epoch (32:2) Wint-Spr 83, p. 136.
"A Tree." NewL (50:1) Aut 83, p. 98.

1801. HAMILTON, Carol
"And Why Didst Thou Ever Send Me?" ChrC (100:26) 14-21 S 83, p. 804.
"Cattle Auction." Poem (47) Mr 83, p. 10-11.
"The Dance." CapeR (18:2) Sum 83, p. 15.
"Doves above the Protest Rally." Poem (48) Jl 83, p. 40.
"He, As I." Poem (47) Mr 83, p. 12.
"Photograph." StoneC (10:3/4) Spr-Sum 83, p. 26.
"South Wind." Poem (48) Jl 83, p. 39.

1802. HAMILTON, Elissa L. A.
"Plate 2-S-68, Titan" (from Improvisations after Voyager 2: Saturn). SanFPJ (4:3) 83, p. 47-48.
"Preparing for Nuclear War: Early Contamination." SanFPJ (4:3) 83, p. 45-46.

1803. HAMILTON, Fritz
"Faye." Bogg (50) 83, p. 25.
"Hard Night Aftermath" (for Phoebe). SmPd (20:3) Aut 83, p. 15.
"It's Boom Boom Time!" SanFPJ (5:2) 83, p. 49-50.
"Lanny the Lifter." PoNow (7:2, #38) 83, p. 43.
"The Miner." SecC (11:1/2) 83, p. 71.
"The Solution of 1983." SanFPJ (5:2) 83, p. 20.
"Stoic Dying!" WindO (42) Sum 83, p. 18-19.
"The Woman He's Been Looking For!" WindO (42) Sum 83, p. 19.

1804. HAMILTON, Helena
"Leonard Cohen." Waves (11:4) Spr 83, p. 56.
"Margaret Atwood." Waves (11:4) Spr 83, p. 52.
"Marie-Claire Blais." Waves (11:4) Spr 83, p. 54.

1805. HAMILTON, Horace E.
"Land after Heavy Snow." SouthwR (68:1) Wint 83, p. 25-26.

1806. HAMILTON, Robin
"Learning the Code, Coding the Life." Poetry (142:6) S 83, p. 323-324.
"Nightpiece: London, 1888." Poetry (142:6) S 83, p. 322.

HAMM, Mary Diesel
See: DIESEL-HAMM, Mary

1807. HAMMER, Louis
"Death" (for Isidoro de Blas) (tr. of Federico Garcia Lorca). Field (28) Spr 83, p. 18.
"Five Verses of Sense and One of Destiny." Kayak (61) Ap 83, p. 14-16.
"Moon and Panorama of Insects (Love Poem)" (tr. of Federico Garcia Lorca). Field (28) Spr 83, p. 19-21.
"Sleepless City (Nocturne of Brooklyn Bridge)" (tr. of Federico Garcia Lorca). Field (28) Spr 83, p. 16-17.

1808. HAMMOND, Karla (Karla M.)
"The Assailant." Paint (10:19/20) Spr-Aut 83, p. 20.
"In a Room of Henry Moores: Late 1939." DevQ (18:3) Aut 83, p. 36.
"The Linguist." SpoonRQ (8:4) Aut 83, p. 59.
"O'Connor As in Frank." SpoonRQ (8:4) Aut 83, p. 60.
"Survivors." Paint (10:19/20) Spr-Aut 83, p. 21.
"Woman." SpoonRQ (8:4) Aut 83, p. 59.

1809. HAMMOND, Mac
"The Final Note." Poetry (142:1) Ap 83, p. 32.
"Golden Age." Epoch (33:1) Aut-Wint 83, p. 64.
"High Fidelity." Poetry (142:1) Ap 83, p. 31.

1810. HAN, Mu-Shan
"Melancholic in the Manner of Li Ho" (tr. by Sam Hamill). PortR (29:1) 83, p. 10.

1811. HAN, Shan
"Cold Mountain" (in Chinese). Pig (11) 83, p. 92.
"Cold Mountain" (tr. by Joseph Lisowski). Pig (11) 83, p. 92.

1812. HAND, Jack
"City Woman, Country Wife." KanQ (15:2) Spr 83, p. 77.
"Iron." MissouriR (6:2) Wint 83, p. 25.
"Leaving the East." ThRiPo (19/20) 82, p. 43.
"No More Painters." Blueline (5:1) Sum-Aut 83, p. 4.
"Priscilla." Blueline (4:2) Wint-Spr 83, p. 35.

"Water Witch." Blueline (5:1) Sum-Aut 83, p. 5.

1813. HANDLEY, Elaine
"Meditation." YetASM (1:2) 82, p. 16.

1814. HANDY, Nixeon Civille
"Dance of the Lump." NewEngR (5:3) Spr 83, p. 320.
"Sky Wanders." Wind (13:49) 83, p. 32.

1815. HANE, Norman
"A Banal Lovers' Dialogue." Bogg (51) 83, p. 14.

1816. HANFORD, Mary
"Fatigue." Vis (12) 83, p. 31.

1817. HANKE, Peter
"The Lives of the Poets" (Selection: VI. "A Birthday Candle for John Donne"). SoCaR (16:1) Aut 83, p. 34-35.
"Mohole." SanFPJ (5:1) 83, p. 20.
"Thirteen Ways of Looking at a Jogger." SoCaR (16:1) Aut 83, p. 35-37.

1818. HANKLA, Cathryn
"Doves Bleat above Our Sleep." Telescope (4) Wint 83, p. 84-85.
"Red Giant, Black Dwarf or Degenerate." Ploughs (9:2/3) 83, p. 194-195.
"There Are Only Trains and Lovers in This Poem" (answered by Pat Cooper). Outbr (12/13) Aut 83-Spr 84, p. 44.

1819. HANLEY, Katherine, CJS
"Request." SpiritSH (48) 82, p. 38.
"Words Fail Us." SpiritSH (48) 82, p. 38.

1820. HANLEY, Patricia
"Night." Germ (7:2) Aut-Wint 83, p. 20.
"Out of the Way." Germ (7:2) Aut-Wint 83, p. 22.
"Spring." Germ (7:2) Aut-Wint 83, p. 21.

1821. HANSEN, Tom
"Butt" (a found poem). PoetryNW (24:2) Sum 83, p. 19-20.
"Morning Sounds." Northeast (Ser. 3:16) Wint 83-84, p. 18.

1822. HANSON, Charles
"Spinning Bullets." SanFPJ (5:1) 83, p. 81.

1823. HANSON, Howard G.
"Distance Makes the Difference." ArizQ (39:1) Spr 83, p. 46.

1824. HANZLICEK, C. G.
"In the Mountains." CimR (64) Jl 83, p. 49.
"Insomnia." CimR (65) O 83, p. 62.
"On a Highway South of Minneapolis." NoAmR (268:2) Je 83, p. 35.

1825. HARASYM, S. D.
"Quartet: Invocations." Quarry (32:1) Wint 83, p. 39-40, missing line corrected in Quarry (32:3) Sum 83, p. 69.
"Winter: Sketch." Quarry (32:1) Wint 83, p. 39.

1826. HARCHICK, J. W.
"Skin Play." Bogg (50) 83, p. 27.

1827. HARDER, Amy S.
"Cornflowers." Vis (13) 83, p. 35.

1828. HARDESTY, Norton
"Moonlight" (Haiku). NegC (3:4) Aut 83, p. 125.
"Silence" (Haiku). NegC (3:4) Aut 83, p. 125.

1829. HARDING, Gunnar
"Napalm" (tr. of Björn Hakansson, w. Frederic Will). PoetryE (9/10) Wint 82-Spr 83, p. 243.

1830. HARE, Jannis Allan
"The New Bears." Bluebuf (2:1) Aut 83, p. 10.
"Water Witching." Bluebuf (2:1) Aut 83, p. 24.

1831. HARGITAI, Peter
"Agamemnon." SpiritSH (49) 83, p. 25.
"For Sylvia Plath by Anne Sexton." KanQ (15:2) Spr 83, p. 76-77.
"Hera and the Peacock." SpiritSH (49) 83, p. 27.
"Isis and Godiva." SpiritSH (49) 83, p. 24-25.
"Polyphemus." SpiritSH (49) 83, p. 27-28.
"Venus Arising from the Sea." SpiritSH (49) 83, p. 26-27.
"Words." SpiritSH (49) 83, p. 28.

1832. HARINGTON, Donald
"The Villanelle." NewL (49:3/4) Spr-Sum 83, p. 194.

1833. HARJO, Joy
"Rainy Night" (for Billie Holiday). MassR (24:1) Spr 83, p. 57.
"The Woman Hanging from the Thirteenth Floor Window." MassR (24:1) Spr 83, p. 58-59.

1834. HARKIANAKIS, Stylianos
"Do Not Weep So Soon" (tr. by Peter Bien). Paint (10:19/20) Spr-Aut 83, p. 36.
"Easy Payment Plan" (tr. by Peter Bien). Paint (10:19/20) Spr-Aut 83, p. 33.
"For Those Who Hate the Light" (tr. by Peter Bien). Paint (10:19/20) Spr-Aut 83, p. 32.
"My Fellow Villagers" (tr. by Peter Bien). Paint (10:19/20) Spr-Aut 83, p. 39.
"Requiem for Poetry" (tr. by Peter Bien). Paint (10:19/20) Spr-Aut 83, p. 40.
"Restitution" (tr. by Peter Bien). Paint (10:19/20) Spr-Aut 83, p. 35.
"Still Life" (tr. by Peter Bien). Paint (10:19/20) Spr-Aut 83, p. 41.
"To My Teacher L.K." (tr. by Peter Bien). Paint

(10:19/20) Spr-Aut 83, p. 37.
"The Twentieth Century" (tr. by Peter Bien). Paint (10:19/20) Spr-Aut 83, p. 38.
"Water Color" (tr. by Peter Bien). Paint (10:19/20) Spr-Aut 83, p. 34.

1835. HARLOW, Michael
"Naming, an Occasion." SouthernHR (17:1) Wint 83, p. 31.

1836. HARMON, William
"Environmental Issues." Agni (19) 83, p. 71-72.
"A Lament in Four Fragments." Poetry (141:6) Mr 83, p. 313-317.
"Mime Polyglot." Ploughs (9:2/3) 83, p. 80-81.
"One-Finger Exercises" (Excerpts: II. "Five Quintessences, III. , Nostoi: That Every Road Is a Royal Road"). CarolQ (35:3) Spr 83, p. 85-87.
"Rousseau and Romanticism: A Letter (Eventually)." CarolQ (35:3) Spr 83, p. 80-82.
"Sundae Mourning, Blue Cigar." Kayak (61) Ap 83, p. 22-23.
"Two Cents." SouthernPR (23:2) Aut 83, p. 31.
"What's the Big Idea?" CarolQ (35:3) Spr 83, p. 83-84.

1837. HARMSTON, Richard K.
"Learning to Write." EngJ (72:4) Ap 83, p. 92.

1838. HARN, John
"Anatomy of the (Over)Loved." CutB (21) Aut-Wint 83, p. 22.
"Describing Ireland." PoetC (15:1) Aut 83, p. 23.
"Distances." PoetC (15:1) Aut 83, p. 22.

1839. HARNACK, Curtis
"Counting Time." Nat (236:8) 26 F 83, p. 244.
"Rural Development." Nat (237:22) 31 D 83-7 Ja 84, p. 702.
"The Sadness." Nat (237:22) 31 D 83-7 Ja 84, p. 702.
"White Spring." Nat (237:22) 31 D 83-7 Ja 84, p. 702.

1840. HARNEY, Stephen M.
"Prayer for the Twins" (for Erika and Denise). HarvardA (117:3) Aut 83, p. 23.

1841. HARPER, Michael S.
"The Body Polity." Iowa (13:3/4) Spr 82 (83), p. 129.
"Grandfather." OhioR (30) 83, p. 128-129.

1842. HARRELL, Ken
"Pieta." AmerPoR (12:2) Mr/Ap 83, p. 21.

1843. HARRIGAN, Stephen
"River Proposal." NewL (49:3/4) Spr-Sum 83, p. 167.

1844. HARRIS, Devorah B.
"Doubletalk." EngJ (72:5) S 83, p. 90.

1845. HARRIS, E. J.
"The Poet Compares Her Lover of Two Weeks to a Sea Creature." Prima (8) 83, p. 10.

1846. HARRIS, Ethel
"Breakfast for Two." Quarry (32:3) Sum 83, p. 49.
"Tipplers." Quarry (32:3) Sum 83, p. 50.

1847. HARRIS, Jana
"Snake at Amwell Crossing." Calyx (7:3) Sum 83, p. 36-37.

1848. HARRIS, Joseph
"The Actor's Request." NegC (3:4) Aut 83, p. 43.
"Herbal." Bogg (51) 83, p. 3.

1849. HARRIS, Judith Gail
"The China Dolls." MalR (65) Jl 83, p. 54.
"Demise." MalR (65) Jl 83, p. 52.
"Deux Femmes." MalR (65) Jl 83, p. 53.
"I Kept You in My Suitcase." MalR (65) Jl 83, p. 51.
"The Salamanders." MalR (65) Jl 83, p. 52.
"Shining One." MalR (65) Jl 83, p. 55.
"So Dangerous." MalR (65) Jl 83, p. 56.

1850. HARRIS, Maureen
"Disappearing Act." MalR (64) F 83, p. 197.
"I Spy Mother Cupboard" (for baby Katharine). MalR (64) F 83, p. 196-197.
"Still Life: Mother and Child." MalR (64) F 83, p. 198.

1851. HARRIS, William J.
"The Greek Philosopher." PoNow (7:2, #38) 83, p. 29.

1852. HARRISON, Jeanne
"Moving Through." Quarry (32:3) Sum 83, p. 21.
"Twilight." Quarry (32:3) Sum 83, p. 21.

1853. HARRISON, Keith
"Nelson." Grain (11:2) My 83, p. 17-22.

1854. HARRISON, Richard
"Iran." CrossC (5:2/3) 83, p. 30.

1855. HARRISON, Ruth
"WR 121: Impromptu Day." DevQ (18:1) Spr 83, p. 60.

1856. HARRISON, Tony
"Aqua Mortis." Agni (18) 83, p. 21.
"The Call of Nature." Agni (18) 83, p. 22.
"Long Distance." Agni (18) 83, p. 23-24.
"National Trust." Agni (18) 83, p. 20.
"On Not Being Milton" (for Sergio Vieira & Armando Guebuza (Frelimo)). Agni (18) 83, p. 18.
"Remains." Agni (18) 83, p. 25.
"Study." Agni (18) 83, p. 19.

1857. HARROLD, William
"Madonna." ClockR (1:1) Sum 83, p. 23.
"Ode to a Volkswagon." ClockR (1:1) Sum 83, p. 23.
"A Time of Apocalypse" (for William Wantling). SecC (11:1/2) 83, p. 72.

1858. HARRY, Margaret
"Laxårvogur (Hvalfjördur)." AntigR (54) Sum 83, p. 11.
"Manorbier." AntigR (54) Sum 83, p. 10.
"Reykjavík." AntigR (54) Sum 83, p. 9.

1859. HARRYMAN, Carla
"Statement." ParisR (24:86) Wint 82, p. 96-97.

1860. HARSHMAN, Marc
"A Boy's Primer." PoNow (7:2, #38) 83, p. 35.

1861. HART, Jonathan (Jonathan Locke)
"The Black Death." AntigR (55) Aut 83, p. 101-102.
"So you want novelty." Grain (11:3) Ag 83, p. 6.
"A Word on Silence." Quarry (32:3) Sum 83, p. 26-28.

1862. HARTMAN, Charles O.
"Digging In." Poetry (142:1) Ap 83, p. 40.
"New Hampshire." Poetry (142:1) Ap 83, p. 41-42.
"Pal is a Romany World." Poetry (142:1) Ap 83, p. 38-39.
"Snapshot of That." AntR (41:4) Aut 83, p. 444.
"True North." NewYorker (58:50) 31 Ja 83, p. 46.

1863. HARVEY, Andrew
"The Belief That Anything." SenR (13:2) 82-83, p. 86-87.
"Don't Let Them in." SenR (13:2) 82-83, p. 79-80.
"Fantasy Is My Persepolis." SenR (13:2) 82-83, p. 92-93.
"If God Exists." SenR (13:2) 82-83, p. 89-90.
"Lament." SenR (13:2) 82-83, p. 84-85.
"Lydia and the Eagle." SenR (13:2) 82-83, p. 77-78.
"Lydia As Hecuba." SenR (13:2) 82-83, p. 82-83.
"Lydia Walks towards Me." SenR (13:2) 82-83, p. 96-97.
"No Diamonds, No Hat, No Honey" (Selections: 12 poems). SenR (13:2) 82-83, p. 76-97.
"No Diamonds, No Hat, No Honey." SenR (13:2) 82-83, p. 94-95.
"Soak a Long Time." SenR (13:2) 82-83, p. 81.
"Spiders Love Mozart." SenR (13:2) 82-83, p. 88.
"You're Making Pasta." SenR (13:2) 82-83, p. 91.

1864. HARVEY, Gayle Elen
"Driving Home with You through July." CapeR (18:2) Sum 83, p. 23.
"Flat Lands, Altitude." Prima (8) 83, p. 45.
"From the Dardanelles." Bogg (50) 83, p. 25.
"Howl toward the Night Sky." CapeR (18:2) Sum 83, p. 22.
"Landscapes, Seascapes." Wind (13:49) 83, p. 27.
"Mere Description" (from Stones Are Sleeping Next

to Us, semi-finalist, 10th anniversary manuscript competition). StoneC (11:1/2, Pt. 1) Aut-Wint 83, p. 62.
"Moon" (from Stones Are Sleeping Next to Us, semi-finalist, 10th anniversary manuscript competition). StoneC (11:1/2, Pt. 1) Aut-Wint 83, p. 62.
"Someone Is Coming." WindO (42) Sum 83, p. 51.

1865. HARVEY, Helen Bohlen
"Brooding." Poem (47) Mr 83, p. 25.
"The Message." Poem (47) Mr 83, p. 24.
"Musing at a Red Light in Oakland, CA." Wind (13:48) 83, p. 26-27.

1866. HARWAY, Judith
"Opening the Nest." SouthernPR (23:2) Aut 82 [i.e. (23:1?) Spr 83], p. 55-57.

1867. HARWOOD, Gail L.
"To the Ancestors." Stand (24:2) 83, p. 26.

1868. HASEGAWA, Ryusei
"Paulow's Crane" (tr. by Tetsuo Kinoshita). PoetryE (9/10) Wint 82-Spr 83, p. 229-230.

1869. HASELOFF, Charles
"America." SecC (11:1/2) 83, p. 73.

1870. HASHIMOTO, Sharon
"The Embroidered Crane." CrabCR (1:1) My 83, p. 30.
"Watchmaker." CrabCR (1:1) My 83, p. 30.

1871. HASHMI, Alamgir
"Anna and Kirsten: A Photograph." Telescope (5/6) Spr 83, p. 155.
"Game and Such." Telescope (4) Wint 83, p. 71.

1872. HASKINS, Lola
"The Feasting." SouthernPR (23:2) Aut 82 [i.e. (23:1?) Spr 83], p. 15.
"The Man Who Saw the Elephant." BelPoJ (34:2) Wint 83-84, p. 12-20.
"Protection." LittleM (14:1/2) 83, p. 88.
"The Suicide." LittleM (14:1/2) 83, p. 89.

1873. HASLEY, Louis
"Sixty-Five." ArizQ (39:3) Aut 83, p. 260.

1874. HASS, Robert
"A Book in the Ruins" (Warsaw, 1942) (tr. of Czeslaw Milosz, w. the author and Robert Pinsky). NewYorker (59:1) 21 F 83, p. 49.
"Farewell" (tr. of Czeslaw Milosz, w. Renata Gorczynski). NewYRB (30:7) 28 Ap 83, p. 6.
"It Was Winter" (tr. of Czeslaw Milosz, w. Renata Gorczynski and Robert Pinsky). NewRep (187:11) 13 S 82, p. 28-29.
"A Mistake" (Paris, 1958) (tr. of Czeslaw Milosz, w. the author and Robert Pinsky). NewYorker

(59:1) 21 F 83, p. 48-49.
"Ode to a Bird" (Montgeron, 1959) (tr. of Czeslaw Milosz, w. the author and Robert Pinsky). NewYorker (59:1) 21 F 83, p. 48.
"On the Road" (tr. of Czeslaw Milosz, w. Renata Gorczynski). NewYRB (30:7) 28 Ap 83, p. 6.
"Reading the Japanese Poet Issa" (Berkely, 1978) (tr. of Czeslaw Milosz, w. the author and Robert Pinsky). NewYorker (59:1) 21 F 83, p. 48.
"Spring Rain." AmerPoR (12:5) S/O 83, p. 48.

1875. HATHAWAY, Dev
"Chocolate." KanQ (15:4) Aut 83, p. 52.
"The Peacock Feather." KanQ (15:4) Aut 83, p. 52.
"The Red Setter." KanQ (15:4) Aut 83, p. 53.

1876. HATHAWAY, Jeanine
"Recollection: Before You Sleep Come Home to Yourself." IndR (6:1) Wint 83, p. 65.

1877. HATHAWAY, Lodene Brown
"Bereavement." ChrC (100:16) 18 My 83, p. 480.

1878. HATHAWAY, William
"Alone in the House." PoNow (7:2, #38) 83, p. 18.
"Cedar Waxwings in Ligustrum Lucidum" (for Philip Dow). Ploughs (9:2/3) 83, p. 134-135.
"Concert Time." NewL (50:1) Aut 83, p. 94-95.
"A Crush." CimR (64) Jl 83, p. 30-31.
"December 18, 1944." Telescope (5/6) Spr 83, p. 122.
"Dejection at the State U." (For Ralph Adamo). AmerPoR (12:2) Mr/Ap 83, p. 22.
"Horse Sense." KanQ (15:1) Wint 83, p. 95-97.
"Little Sister." CimR (63) Ap 83, p. 40.
"The Mississippi River at Baton Rouge" (for C. deGravelles). Ploughs (9:2/3) 83, p. 136-137.
"Night Caller" (For Gary Pacernick). PoNow (7:2, #38) 83, p. 18.
"A Normal Man." AmerPoR (12:2) Mr/Ap 83, p. 22.
"The Orphan Maker." NewL (49:3/4) Spr-Sum 83, p. 166.
"Working for Wages" (for Geof Hewitt). CutB (21) Aut-Wint 83, p. 15-16.
"You Had to Know Her." AmerPoR (12:2) Mr/Ap 83, p. 22.

1879. HATLEN, Burton
"Crossing Altamont" (for Sheldon Hatlen, 1931-1983). BelPoJ (34:2) Wint 83-84, p. 2-10.

1880. HAUCK, Chris
"Undertow." CalQ (22) Sum 83, p. 84.

1881. HAUGE, Olav H.
"Across the Swamp" (tr. by Robert Bly). PoetryE (11) Sum 83, p. 70.
"Berthold Brecht" (tr. by Robert Bly). PoetryE (11) Sum 83, p. 67.
"December Moon in 1969" (tr. by Robert Bly). PoetryE (11) Sum 83, p. 72.

"Deep Winter, Snow" (tr. by Robert Bly). PoetryE (11) Sum 83, p. 74.
"Don't Come to Me with the Entire Truth" (tr. by Robert Bly). PoetryE (11) Sum 83, p. 66.
"I Stand Here, Yunnerstand" (tr. by Robert Bly). PoetryE (11) Sum 83, p. 69.
"Looking at an Old Mirror" (tr. by Robert Bly). PoetryE (11) Sum 83, p. 71.
"Playhouses of Leaves and Snow" (tr. by Robert Bly). PoetryE (11) Sum 83, p. 68.
"Today I Understood" (tr. by Robert Bly). PoetryE (11) Sum 83, p. 75.
"Wind and Weather" (tr. by Robert Bly). PoetryE (11) Sum 83, p. 73.
"You Are the Wind" (tr. by Robert Bly). PoetryE (11) Sum 83, p. 76.

1882. HAUPTFLEISCH, Susan
"Design in Stork's Foot & Old Fire." MSS (2:3) Sum 83, p. 95-96.
"Insomnias." YetASM (2:1) 83, p. 2.
"Poem for the Buddha of Wildflowers." Prima (8) 83, p. 75.
"Rainstorm on Lake Champlain." Blueline (4:2) Wint-Spr 83, p. 39.

1883. HAVEN, Richard
"Hitch-Hiker's Guide to the Universe (or Somewhere Else)." MassR (24:3) Aut 83, p. 646-647.

1884. HAVEN, Stephen
"Where Young Boys Sit along the Cement Floodwall." MissouriR (7:1) Aut 83, p. 43.

HAVRE, Rosselare le
See: ROSSELARE-LeHAVRE

1885. HAWK, Josef Sample
"Prophet of Profit." SanFPJ (5:4) 83, p. 89.

1886. HAWKES, Robert
"Message." Germ (7:2) Aut-Wint 83, p. 23.
"Unease." Germ (7:2) Aut-Wint 83, p. 24.

1887. HAWKIN, Tom
"The Gull." PortR (29:1) 83, p. 84.

1888. HAWKINS, Hunt
"Jack in the Winter." KanQ (15:1) Wint 83, p. 123.
"The Stuart Hotel." KanQ (15:1) Wint 83, p. 124.

1889. HAXTON, Brooks
"Anthropology." Tendril (14/15) Wint 83, p. 98-99.
"The Conversion Shift." Tendril (14/15) Wint 83, p. 96.
"The Excellence of a Good Breakfast." Tendril (14/15) Wint 83, p. 101.
"I Live to See Strom Thurmond Head the Judiciary Committee." Tendril (14/15) Wint 83, p. 97.
"Justice." AmerPoR (12:6) N/D 83, p. 16.

"Recess." Tendril (14/15) Wint 83, p. 100.
"Witness." Tendril (16) Sum 83, p. 63.

1890. HAY, John
"Flies, Dancing at Sundown." MassR (24:4) Wint 83, p. 704.

1891. HAYDEN, Loretta
"For Mr. Reagan & Mr. Andropov." PottPort (5) 83-84, p. 35.

1892. HAYDEN, Mahlon F.
"You are there now." YetASM (1:2) 82, p. 18.

1893. HAYES, Diana
"The Classical Torso in 1980" (for Susan Beniston). MalR (64) F 83, p. 209-213.
"Take Your Heart to the River." Quarry (32:3) Sum 83, p. 15-16.

1894. HAYES, Noreen
"Light from Light, an Ode for Candlemas." SpiritSH (49 Suppl.) 83, p. 8-12.
"Someone Stole the Watch My Mother Gave Me." SpiritSH (48) 82, p. 33.

1895. HAYS, Janice
"Net." SoDakR (21:3) Aut 83, p. 93-94.

1896. HAZARD, James
"The Healer." ClockR (1:1) Sum 83, p. 22.
"Homage to Nelson Algren" (for my son, Cael). CreamCR (8:1/2) 83, p. 106-107.
"Two Bottles of Jack Daniels, for Hoagy Carmichael." ClockR (1:1) Sum 83, p. 33-34.
"Whiskey in Whiting, Indiana." NoAmR (268:1) Mr 83, p. 26.

1897. HAZELL, Tim
"Mailroom." AntigR (54) Sum 83, p. 32.
"Music Can Come from behind Bars." AntigR (54) Sum 83, p. 33.
"Network." AntigR (54) Sum 83, p. 34.

1898. HAZEWINKEL, Julie
"A Flowing Leaf." PikeF (5) Spr 83, p. 21.

1899. HAZLEWOOD, Roy
"Nights with the Legionnaires." LittleBR (3:3) Spr 83, p. 77-78.
"Sestina of the Terrestrial Rose." LittleBR (3:3) Spr 83, p. 78-79.
"Sideshow Sestine." BelPoJ (34:1) Aut 83, p. 4-5.

1900. HAZO, Samuel
"In Convoy." ThRiPo (21/22) 83, p. 39.

1901. HEAD, Gwen
"The Blood Wedding." Telescope (5/6) Spr 83, p. 82.
"The Prize." Iowa (13:2) Spr 82, p. 105.

1902. HEAD, Robert Grady
"After Wirgil" (in memory of John Cornish). Sam (35:4 140th release) 83, p. 9.
"The Atom Bomb Is the Messiah." Sam (35:4 140th release) 83, p. 12.
"The Creek Turns into the Mississippi." Sam (35:4 140th release) 83, p. 7.
"Enrich Your Child's Speech." Sam (35:4 140th release) 83, p. 12.
"The Enriched Uranium Poems." Sam (35:4 140th release) 83, p. 1-12.
"Fawn Asked Me." Sam (35:4 140th release) 83, p. 8.
"For Jacqueline T. Bradley." Sam (35:4 140th release) 83, p. 10.
"For Richard Ettelson." Sam (35:4 140th release) 83, p. 9.
"Ghosts of America." Sam (35:4 140th release) 83, p. 8.
"God's Will in History." Sam (35:4 140th release) 83, p. 11.
"Gone Down the River." Sam (35:4 140th release) 83, p. 11.
"He Says He's a Soldier." Sam (35:4 140th release) 83, p. 7.
"Hwer Do You Believe the Langgwij Came From?" (dedicated to Joseph Carrier). Sam (35:4 140th release) 83, p. 11.
"Is the Atom Bomb God's Will?" Sam (35:4 140th release) 83, p. 12.
"Jacqueline, Patrick, & Captain Black Gold Present Their Positions." Sam (35:4 140th release) 83, p. 10.
"No Nukes." Sam (35:4 140th release) 83, p. 12.
"The Norman Conquest." Sam (35:4 140th release) 83, p. 9.
"On My Chalolithic Crystal Set." Sam (35:4 140th release) 83, p. 6.
"Our Civilisation." Sam (35:4 140th release) 83, p. 8.
"The Power of Speech" (for Katherine G.). Sam (35:4 140th release) 83, p. 10.
"They're Taking West Virginia." Sam (35:4 140th release) 83, p. 9.
"Titmouse, Juncos & Chickadees." Sam (35:4 140th release) 83, p. 7.
"To Overcome My Own Hatred." Sam (35:4 140th release) 83, p. 6.

1903. HEANEY, Seamus
"The Birthplace." NewEng (5:4) Sum 83, p. 567-568.
"An Iron Spike." AmerPoR (12:4) Jl-Ag 83, p. 48.
"Station Island" (Selections: IV, VII-IX). YaleR (73:1) Aut 83, p. 136-144.
"Station Island" (Opening sections of a longer poem). Hudson (36:2) Sum 83, p. 257-264.

1904. HEARST, James
"Abandoned Orchard." PoNow (7:2, #38) 83, p. 20.
"A Balance Sheet." SouthwR (68:3) Sum 83, p. 252.
"Claim for Damages." Focus (15:95) Ag 83, p. 20.

"Crop Inspector." PoNow (7:2, #38) 83, p. 20.
"Hope Goes Whoosh!" Focus (15:95) Ag 83, p. 20.
"The Inevitable Words Like Sign Posts." OhioR (30) 83, p. 252.
"Moments of Being Away." CharR (9:1) Spr 83, p. 16.
"There Are Those Who Say This." CharR (9:1) Spr 83, p. 16-17.
"Today Is Now." Focus (15:95) Ag 83, p. 20.
"What Time Is It Anyway?" Focus (15:95) Ag 83, p. 20.

1905. HEATH, Catherine
"First Night, Old Vic." MassR (24:1) Spr 83, p. 179.

1906. HEATH, Terrence
"Urworld." Descant (40) Spr 83, p. 25-30.

1907. HEATH-STUBBS, John
"Couperin at the Keyboard." SenR (13:2) 82-83, p. 39-40.

1908. HEBERT, Anne
"The Little Towns" (tr. by Jacklyn Potter). StoneC (10:3/4) Spr-Sum 83, p. 21-22.
"Les Petites Villes." StoneC (10:3/4) Spr-Sum 83, p. 20-21.

1909. HEBERT, Sue Ellen
"Gulf Days." KanQ (15:2) Spr 83, p. 25.

1910. HECHT-LEWIS, Rebecca
"Labor Day." Prima (8) 83, p. 85.

1911. HECKER, Teeta
"At 38 I realized there is no God." SanFPJ (4:2) 83, p. 29.

1912. HEFFERNAN, Michael
"A Feast in February." KanQ (15:4) Aut 83, p. 66.
"A Guinness at Winkle's." QW (17) Aut-Wint 83-84, p. 63.
"In the Grotto of St. Euthymius." PoetryNW (24:3) Aut 83, p. 27.
"On Completing a Fortieth Year." LittleBR (4:2) Wint 83-84, p. 39.

1913. HEFLIN, Jack
"Two Figures in Mt. Hope Cemetery." MissouriR (6:2) Wint 83, p. 15.

1914. HEGI, Ursula
"Guilt." YetASM (1:1) 82, p. 6.

HEHIR, Diana O'
See: O'HEHIR, Diana

1915. HEIDTMANN, Peter
"Vanishings." PraS (51:1, i.e. 57:1) Spr 83, p. 52-53.

1916. HEIM, Phil
"Brecht vs. the House Un-American Activities Committee." SanFPJ (5:3) 83, p. 49.
"Even in Vegas." SanFPJ (5:3) 83, p. 50.

1917. HEIMLER, Charles
"Baseball Fields in Winter." Argo (4:1) 82, p. 27.

1918. HEINE, Heinrich
"Morphine" (tr. by Felix Pollak). PraS (57:4) Wint 83, p. 45.
"The Stage Grows Dark" (tr. by Felix Pollak). PraS (57:4) Wint 83, p. 44.

1919. HEINEMAN, Lydia
"Death could come as a black shadow." Tele (18) 83, p. 10-11.
"We Were Sitting at the Lys Mykyta." Tele (18) 83, p. 12-13.

1920. HEINRICH, Peggy
"Bag People." YetASM (2:1) 83, p. 2.
"Capricorn Rising." YetASM (2:1) 83, p. 4.
"Sharing the Woods." PoetL (77:1) Spr 82, p. 17-18.

1921. HEJINIAN, Lyn
"Province." ParisR (24:86) Wint 82, p. 108-109.

1922. HEKKANEN, Ernest
"The Dancing in the Wind." CanLit (97) Sum 83, p. 38.
"Festooned with Feathers." Dandel (10:2) Aut-Wint 83, p. 79.

1923. HELLENER, M.
"Anniversary Waltz." Poem (49) N 83, p. 45.
"Morning Letter of a Bride." Poem (49) N 83, p. 46-47.
"Perfume." Poem (49) N 83, p. 42-44.

1924. HELLEW, Joyce V.
"The Ferry Stops at Orient Point." PortR (29:1) 83, p. 37-38.
"Lunch at Nanni's." PortR (29:1) 83, p. 2-3.

1925. HELLWEG, Paul
"Forty-One." SanFPJ (5:2) 83, p. 38.
"What Lies Ahead?" SanFPJ (5:2) 83, p. 39.

1926. HELWIG, David
"3 Black Birds." MalR (65) Jl 83, p. 78-79.
"Catchpenny Poems." MalR (65) Jl 83, p. 74-81.
"Cock." MalR (65) Jl 83, p. 75.
"Crofs Keys." MalR (65) Jl 83, p. 80-81.
"Fools Head." MalR (65) Jl 83, p. 74.
"Helmet." MalR (65) Jl 83, p. 76.
"Turks Head." MalR (65) Jl 83, p. 77.

1927. HELWIG, Maggie
"Dionysus and the Helmsman." CrossC (5:1) 83, p. 12.

1928. HEMAN, Bob
"Clone." Tele (18) 83, p. 54.
"Light." Tele (18) 83, p. 55.
"Moving Up." Tele (18) 83, p. 55.
"Talking." Tele (18) 83, p. 54.
"Travel." Tele (18) 83, p. 54.

1929. HEMMINGSON, Michael A.
"Clocks on the Wall." SanFPJ (4:4) 83, p. 35.
"San Onofre Nuclear Plant." SanFPJ (4:4) 83, p. 35.

1930. HENDERSON, Brian
"Disturbing the Sonnet: Flower at the Core" (for B.C.). Waves (11:4) Spr 83, p. 44.
"Dresden, Ontario: 13 Good Reasons for Turning to Drink." Waves (11:4) Spr 83, p. 43.
"A Little Nocturne with Stars." PoetryCR (4:4) Sum 83, p. 10.
"Night-Writing." Waves (11:4) Spr 83, p. 42.
"Pollen Images." Waves (11:4) Spr 83, p. 45.

1931. HENDRYSON, Barbara
"Choosing." Calyx (8:1) Aut 83, p. 24.
"Pastlife." Calyx (8:1) Aut 83, p. 23.
"A Scarcity of Air." Prima (8) 83, p. 31.

HENDY, James von
See: Von HENDY, James

1932. HENIG, Suzanne
"Lydia." Poem (47) Mr 83, p. 16.
"Usha." Poem (47) Mr 83, p. 13-15.

1933. HENLEY, Lloyd
"Driving Home" (For Jim). CapeR (18:2) Sum 83, p. 9.
"The Grasp Reflex" (for Rachel). KanQ (15:1) Wint 83, p. 192.
"Insects in the Fixture Glass." ConcPo (16:1) Spr 83, p. 84.
"Python Squeezes Infant to Death" (headline). PoetL (77:1) Spr 82, p. 16-17.
"Robert Wadlow's Shoe -- World's Tallest Man As Traveling Advertisement." CapeR (18:2) Sum 83, p. 8.
"The Seed Catalogue." WindO (42) Sum 83, p. 17.

1934. HENN, Mary Ann, Sister
"America, Thy Name I Love." SanFPJ (5:2) 83, p. 66.
"The Drift toward Disaster." SanFPJ (4:4) 83, p. 80.
"A midwinter day." WindO (42) Sum 83, p. 2.
"Of the People." SanFPJ (4:4) 83, p. 60.
"Snow falling late at night." WindO (42) Sum 83, p. 2.
"They Wouldn't Even Look" (Pentecost, May 30, 1982). SanFPJ (4:4) 83, p. 80.
"Unwritten History in El Salvador." SanFPJ (5:2) 83, p. 79.

1935. HENNEN, Tom
"I Think of Bread and Water and the Roots of a Tree

All Wet." NewL (49:3/4) Spr-Sum 83, p. 115.

1936. HENNING, Sharon
"I Like It When You Phone Back." Bluebuf (2:1) Aut 83, p. 12.
"A Picture of Grandmother." Bluebuf (2:1) Aut 83, p. 13.

1937. HENRI, Raymond
"The Bridge from Brooklyn." Confr (25/26) 83, p. 168-169.

1938. HENRIE, Carol
"Norman." Tendril (14/15) Wint 83, p. 102.
"Not Tonight." Tendril (16) Sum 83, p. 64.
"Rape." BelPoJ (33:4) Sum 83, p. 22-23.

1939. HENRY, Gerrit
"Psycho II." Epoch (33:1) Aut-Wint 83, p. 65.

1940. HENRY, Laurie
"Oldest Camper." SouthernPR (23:2) Aut 82 [i.e. (23:1?) Spr 83], p. 60-61.
"Restoring the Chateau of the Marquis De Sade." Poetry (142:2) My 83, p. 88-89.

1941. HENRY, Marie
"From Cassiopeia" YetASM (1:1) 82, p. 2.
"The Night of the Moon Geese." YetASM (1:1) 82, p. 12.

1942. HENRY, Michael
"Bramble Jelly." Bogg (51) 83, p. 51.
"Brown Study." Bogg (50) 83, p. 55.

1943. HENRY, Sarah
"The Old Scientist." SmPd (20:2) Spr 83, p. 18.
"On Reading Bob Hass." HolCrit (20:4) O 83, p. 18-19.

1944. HENSHAW, Tyler
"Anatomy of Your Beauty." WebR (8:1) Spr 83, p. 76-77.

1945. HENSON, David
"Bulls." PoNow (7:2, #38) 83, p. 31.
"The Death of Paul Bunyan." PikeF (5) Spr 83, p. 35.
"Fight." Wind (13:48) 83, p. 28.
"Her Lover Lives on the Roof." Wind (13:48) 83, p. 28-29.
"New Wings." PikeF (5) Spr 83, p. 35.
"The Reluctant Magician." PikeF (5) Spr 83, p. 35.
"Wife of the Man Who Chases Tornadoes." PoNow (7:2, #38) 83, p. 31.

1946. HENSON, Reggie
"Rallies" (for Michael). BlackALF (17:4) Wint 83, p. 175.
"Young Being." BlackALF (17:4) Wint 83, p. 175.

1947. HENSON, Stuart
"At the Curtain." Argo (4:3) 83, p. 26.

1948. HERBERT, Zbigniew (Zbigniev)
"At the Gates of the Valley" (tr. by Joanna Warwick). AmerPoR (12:1) Ja/F 83, p. 12.
"An Attempt at Description" (tr. by Joanna Warwick). Kayak (63) N 83, p. 49.
"The Chairs" (tr. by Joanna Warwick). Kayak (63) N 83, p. 50.
"The Clock" (tr. by Joanna Warwick). Kayak (63) N 83, p. 50.
"A Country" (tr. by Richard Lourie). PoetryE (9/10) Wint 82-Spr 83, p. 236.
"Fish" (tr. by Joanna Warwick). Kayak (63) N 83, p. 50.
"The Longobards" (tr. by Joanna Warwick). Kayak (63) N 83, p. 52.
"A Parable about Russian Emigrants" (tr. by Joanna Warwick). AmerPoR (12:1) Ja/F 83, p. 13.
"The Power of Taste" (tr. by Richard Lourie). PoetryE (9/10) Wint 82-Spr 83, p. 237-238.
"Report from a Besieged City" (Warsaw 1982) (tr. by Czeslaw Milosz). NewYRB (30:13) 18 Ag 83, p. 4.
"Report from a Town under Siege" (tr. by Boguslaw Rostworowski). TriQ (57, Vol. 1) Spr-Sum 83, p. 45-48.
"The Seventh Angel" (tr. by Joanna Warwick). AmerPoR (12:1) Ja/F 83, p. 13.
"She Was Setting Her Hair" (tr. by Joanna Warwick). AmerPoR (12:1) Ja/F 83, p. 13.
"A Stool" (tr. by Joanna Warwick). Kayak (63) N 83, p. 51.

1949. HERER, Paul
"The Search." SanFPJ (4:2) 83, p. 17.
"When December casts its icy frown." SanFPJ (4:2) 83, p. 45.

1950. HERMAN, Grace
"Breaking Out" (for my daugher Gail). YetASM (1:2) 82, p. 17.
"The Morning Dolores Died." YetASM (1:2) 82, p. 7.

1951. HERMAN, Peter
"An Apology." AntigR (54) Sum 83, p. 90.
"The Empty Song." CrossC (5:2/3) 83, p. 5.
"Idiot on a Bus." Waves (11:4) Spr 83, p. 66.
"My Angel." AntigR (54) Sum 83, p. 90.
"Tessa." CrossC (5:2/3) 83, p. 5.

1952. HERNAN, Owen
"To the Man I Call 'Bear'." HiramPoR (35) Aut-Wint 83, p. 20.

1953. HERNANDEZ, Carmelo Abraham
"Cruising." Rácata (2) 83, p. 69-70.
"En adelante ruegan los astros uñas." Rácata (2) 83, p. 66-67.
"Para seguir de cerca." Rácata (1) 83, p. 72.

"Paradoja Bajo el techo que habitan palomas." Rácata (2) 83, p. 68.
"Pero esta vez hallaré tu mitad inconclusa." Rácata (1) 83, p. 75-76.
"Rush Hour." Rácata (1) 83, p. 73-74.

1954. HERNANDEZ, Orlando José
"Lugar de Encuentro" (A los poetas de Casita María, en un paraíso sin cielo y sin ángeles). Rácata (2) 83, p. 71-72.
"Pergamino sin Nombre" (a ustedes, a nosotros: fundadores). Rácata (2) 83, p. 73-74.

HERNANDEZ, Víctor de Leon
See: LEON HERNANDEZ, Víctor de

1955. HERRERA, Juan Felipe
"A Poem Review of The Elephant Man." Thrpny (3:4, issue 12) Wint 83, p. 16.

1956. HERRINGTON, Neva (Neva Johnson)
"Kingdoms." SouthwR (68:2) Spr 83, p. 162.
"Original." SouthernR (19:3) Jl 83, p. 667.

1957. HERRSTROM, David (David Sten)
"The Convention of Words." USl (16/17) Wint 83-84, p. 14.
"Five Hundred Witness." ThirdW Spr 83, p. 57-62.
"Tall Walking Figure." ThirdW Spr 83, p. 63-69.

1958. HERSHON, Robert
"Earning the Living" (for Gene Brook). PoetryNW (24:4) Wint 83-84, p. 46-47.
"The Foot Has 26 Bones, the Hand Has 27." PoNow (7:2, #38) 83, p. 28.
"For Hamburger." PoNow (7:2, #38) 83, p. 28.
"Poster." PoetryNW (24:4) Wint 83-84, p. 47.

1959. HERZING, Albert
"Encounter." Kayak (63) N 83, p. 61.
"Her Song." Kayak (63) N 83, p. 62.
"Poem: Countries that have lost their legends." Kayak (63) N 83, p. 61.
"Poem: Since acting and ceasing to act." Kayak (63) N 83, p. 60.

1960. HERZON, Mary Ruth
"Manuscript." Focus (15:95) Ag 83, p. 16.

1961. HESTER, M. L.
"A Brave Man." Wind (13:49) 83, p. 28.
"The Desolation Pudding." KanQ (15:2) Spr 83, p. 187.
"Going into Saigon." PikeF (5) Spr 83, p. 7.
"Hosing Down the Gorilla." Confr (25/26) 83, p. 254.
"The Meditations of O. C. MacClean: Love Song." LittleBR (4:1) Aut 83, p. 83.
"The Night Is Dark." Bogg (51) 83, p. 52-53.
"The Poet, at the Encounter Group." Northeast (Ser. 3:15) Sum 83, p. 11.

"The Worker of Crosswords." Wind (13:49) 83, p. 28.
"Yes." PoNow (7:2, #38) 83, p. 43.

1962. HETTICH, Michael
"Cocoon." ThirdW Spr 83, p. 94.

1963. HEUVING, Jeanne
"The Girl Who Married the Sea-Being." CarolQ (35:2) Wint 83, p. 31.

1964. HEWITT, Geof
"According to Latest Reports." NewL (49:3/4) Spr-Sum 83, p. 61.
"The Challenge." NewL (50:1) Aut 83, p. 40.
"Eastern Standard." NewL (50:1) Aut 83, p. 39.
"Precision Airlines." NewL (50:1) Aut 83, p. 40-41.
"Those Stars." NewL (50:1) Aut 83, p. 39.

1965. HEWITT, John
"An Irishman in Coventry." PoetryE (9/10) Wint 82-Spr 83, p. 223-224.

1966. HEY, Phil
"Downtime." PoNow (7:2, #38) 83, p. 27.

1967. HEYD, Michael
"The Big Moose" (for Joe). WestB (13) 83, p. 70.

1968. HEYEN, William
"Between Fligts." Poetry (142:4) Jl 83, p. 210.
"The Census." Iowa (13:2) Spr 82, p. 75-76.
"The Chestnut Rain" (Selections: "Blackberry Light, 19-32). OhioR (31) 83, p. 15-36.
"The Chestnut Rain" (Selections: "The Ewe's Song, 8-18). OntR (18) Spr-Sum 83, p. 33-48.
"Mother and Son." Poetry (142:4) Jl 83, p. 209.
"Pickerel." PoetC (13, i.e. 14:3) 83, p. 65.
"The Return." PoetC (13, i.e. 14:3) 83, p. 65.
"The Swastika Poems." OhioR (30) 83, p. 217.

1969. HIATT, Ben
"David's Poem" (for David Allen Hiatt, 7/9/65 - 7/10/65). SecC (11:1/2) 83, p. 74-75.
"Folsom." SecC (11:1/2) 83, p. 76.

1970. HICKS, John V.
"Blow." KanQ (15:2) Spr 83, p. 124.
"Humorist." Grain (11:3) Ag 83, p. 10.
"One More Morning." AntigR (53) Spr 83, p. 82.
"Slip-Finger." CanLit (96) Spr 83, p. 102.
"The White Bat." Waves (11:4) Spr 83, p. 60.

1971. HIETTER, James
"Fractions of Infinity." SouthernR (19:2) Ap 83, p. 384.
"Gulf Shores: Post Frederic." SouthernR (19:2) Ap 83, p. 383-384.
"Pride of Mobile." SouthernR (19:2) Ap 83, p. 383.
"Victorian Prophets." SouthernR (19:2) Ap 83, p. 382.

1972. HIGGINBOTHAM, Keith
"Living in Quicksand." Wind (13:49) 83, p. 9.

1973. HIGGINS, Anne, Sister
"Anne Sexton's Last Reading." FourQt (32:3) Spr 83, p. 3.

1974. HIGH, Maura
"Lovers at Burrington Coombe." NewEngR (5:3) Spr 83, p. 316.
"A Shawl for my Dead Mother." NewEngR (5:3) Spr 83, p. 317.

1975. HIKMET, Nazim
"Tale of Tales" (tr. by Ozcan Yalim, William D. Fielder and Dionis Coffin Riggs). SpiritSH (48) 82, p. 46-47.

1976. HILBERRY, Conrad
"The Frog." Poetry (141:5) F 83, p. 284.
"Mexico: Explosions at 4:00 AM." VirQR (59:4) Aut 83, p. 683-686.
"Mstislav Rostropovich" (Row J, Top Balcony, Hill Auditorium, Ann Arbor). PoetryNW (24:2) Sum 83, p. 36.

1977. HILDEBIDDLE, John
"Bone Mender." HarvardA (117:1) Mr 83, p. 36.

1978. HILDUM, Robert
"Headlights." IndR (6:2) Spr 83, p. 67.

1979. HILL, Geoffrey
"The Mystery of the Charity of Charles Péguy" (An Homage to Charles Péguy). ParisR (25:88) Sum 83, p. 41-59.

1980. HILL, James E. "Boogie Red", Jr.
"24 Hours without the Sun" (for Jefferey). PikeF (5) Spr 83, p. 17.

1981. HILL, Jane Bowers
"Looking for Our Dog." KanQ (15:2) Spr 83, p. 183.
"Trying to Lie." OW (17) Aut-Wint 83-84, p. 58-59.

1982. HILL, Lindsay
"Elegy" (for April Hubinger). MemphisSR (1:2) Spr 81, p. 32-33.

1983. HILL, Nancy K.
"Ritornello." DevQ (18:1) Spr 83, p. 105-106.
"Waking to Work." DevQ (18:1) Spr 83, p. 106.

1984. HILL, Nellie
"Astronomer in Psychotherapy." PoNow (7:2, #38) 83, p. 40.
"Bird Hunting." CentR (27:2) Spr 83, p. 111.
"Coming upon Yellow Pears on a Hard Run." CentR (27:2) Spr 83, p. 111.
"Go Back." PoetryE (11) Sum 83, p. 14.

1985. HILL, Norah
"Grief. An Artist Writes a Letter Home." Stand (24:2) 83, p. 54.

1986. HILL, Robert
"Paradise." PoetryE (11) Sum 83, p. 29-30.

1987. HILL, Ruth
"Alchemist." WritersL O 83, p. 9.

1988. HILL, Victor L.
"Lookin' Where It Ain't." SanFPJ (5:1) 83, p. 24.

1989. HILLMAN, Brenda
"Common Ground." PraS (57:3) Aut 83, p. 69-70.
"Evolution." PraS (57:3) Aut 83, p. 68-69.
"If a Tree Is Struck by Lightning." AntR (41:1) Wint 83, p. 71.
"Like a Moth." AmerPoR (12:1) Ja/F 83, p. 47.
"The Ropes." AmerPoR (12:1) Ja/F 83, p. 47.

1990. HILLMAN, Elise
"Facade." SanFPJ (5:3) 83, p. 51.

1991. HILLMAN, Grady
"Big flake snowfall." SanFPJ (5:1) 83, p. 67.
"The Run." SanFPJ (5:1) 83, p. 66.

1992. HILLRINGHOUSE, Mark
"One Day Stands Out." LittleM (14:1/2) 83, p. 60.
"Russian Winter." LittleM (14:1/2) 83, p. 58-59.

1993. HILTON, David
"Across the Space That Makes Us Movies." Tele (18) 83, p. 105.
"The Cat Is Unhappy." Tele (18) 83, p. 104.
"Clothes Pile." Abraxas (27/28) 83, p. 32-33.
"Dollar Bill." PoetryNW (24:4) Wint 83-84, p. 14-15.
"Mabel, or Maybe Avis." Tele (18) 83, p. 106.
"The Man with No Face." PoetryNW (24:4) Wint 83-84, p. 17-20.
"November Burial." PoetryNW (24:4) Wint 83-84, p. 15-17.
"Science." Tele (18) 83, p. 105.

1994. HILTON, William C.
"Geometry." AntigR (55) Aut 83, p. 127.
"The Great Depression." KanQ (15:3) Sum 83, p. 101.
"The Landlady." AntigR (55) Aut 83, p. 129.
"Lines of Parting." Comm (110:14) 12 Ag 83, p. 435.
"Memory of Dried Years." AntigR (55) Aut 83, p. 128.
"Oh, Say, Can You See?" KanQ (15:2) Spr 83, p. 186.
"Summer Vacation." CapeR (18:2) Sum 83, p. 13.

1995. HIMMIRSKY, Krassin
"The Cricket" (tr. by the author and Denise Levertov). Vis (11) 83, p. 34.

1996. HIND, Steven
"Field Report." KanQ (15:1) Wint 83, p. 189.

"Walking on Raped Woman Creek." LittleBR (3:3) Spr 83, p. 27.

1997. HINDLEY, Norman
"Billfish" (for Cynthia Gauthier). StoneC (11:1/2, Pt. 1) Aut-Wint 83, p. 13.

1998. HINGHAM, Michael
"Glass of Time" (A poem from the diary of a time traveler). SanFPJ (5:1) 83, p. 9.

1999. HINRICHSEN, Dennis
"Blueberries." Tendril (14/15) Wint 83, p. 103.
"Grass." Tendril (14/15) Wint 83, p. 104-105.
"Heaven, Circa 1938." Tendril (14/15) Wint 83, p. 106-107.
"A Little Music from the House Next Door." Agni (19) 83, p. 111-112.
"On Trees." Agni (19) 83, p. 109-110.

2000. HINRICKS, Mary Mullis
"March on Seabrook." SanFPJ (4:3) 83, p. 29.

2001. HIRSCH, Edward
"Commuters." Ploughs (9:1) 83, p. 187-188.
"Dusk." NewRep (186:15) 14 Ap 82, p. 39.
"For Cesar Pavese." MemphisSR (3:2) Spr 83, p. 7.
"For the Sleepwalkers" (Excerpt). NewRep (186:15) 14 Ap 82, p. 39.
"The Season for Elegies." MemphisSR (3:2) Spr 83, p. 8.
"The Secret." MemphisSR (3:2) Spr 83, p. 9-11.
"Three Journeys." AntR (41:3) Sum 83, p. 324-325.
"The White Blackbird." Shen (34:3) 83, p. 95.
"Wild Gratitude." NewRep (186:20) 19 My 82, p. 32.

2002. HIRSCHFIELD, Jane
"In Your Hands." PoNow (7:2, #38) 83, p. 33.
"Summer Rises." PoNow (7:2, #38) 83, p. 33.

2003. HIRSCHFIELD, Robert
"David at Ein Gedi." ChrC (100:20) 22-29 Je 83, p. 612.

2004. HIRSHFIELD, Jane
"Ars Poetica." AmerPoR (12:4) Jl-Ag 83, p. 3.
"At Night." AmerPoR (12:4) Jl-Ag 83, p. 3.
"Completing the Weave." AmerPoR (12:4) Jl-Ag 83, p. 4.
"Diologue." AmerPoR (12:4) Jl-Ag 83, p. 4.
"For What Binds Us." AmerPoR (12:4) Jl-Ag 83, p. 4.
"Invocation." AmerPoR (12:4) Jl-Ag 83, p. 3.
"November, Remembering Voltaire." NewYorker (59:40) 21 N 83, p. 52.
"Osiris." AmerPoR (12:4) Jl-Ag 83, p. 3.
"See How the Roads Are Strewn." AmerPoR (12:4) Jl-Ag 83, p. 4.
"That Falling." AmerPoR (12:4) Jl-Ag 83, p. 3.
"Toward the Infinite." BlackWR (10:1) Aut 83, p. 69.

2005. HIRSHKOWITZ, Lois
"Poetry Class." EngJ (72:2) F 83, p. 76.

2006. HITCHCOCK, George
"The Hour of the Wolf" (after Bergman). ThRiPo (21/22) 83, p. 40.
"The Magnetic Arsenal, or a Birthday Bouquet for James Tate." LittleBR (4:2) Wint 83-84, p. 18.

HLUS, Carolyn D. Redl
See: REDL-HLUS, Carolyn D.

HO, Li
See: LI, Ho

2007. HOAGLAND, Everett
"Gorée." AmerPoR (12:4) Jl-Ag 83, p. 40-41.

2008. HOAGLAND, Tony
"The Balance of the Part Against the Whole." Tendril (14/15) Wint 83, p. 108-109.
"In Gratitude for Talk" (for John and Joe). Telescope (5/6) Spr 83, p. 149-150.

2009. HOBBY, Bernard
"Behind the Rented House." Bogg (50) 83, p. 41.
"Cat Nap." Bogg (51) 83, p. 36.
"My Lover." Bogg (50) 83, p. 46-47.
"Paranoia." Grain (11:1) F 83, p. 14.

2010. HODGES, Charles
"Coal Miner's Son." KanQ (15:2) Spr 83, p. 188.

2011. HOEFT, Robert D.
"The Friction of the Sun." YetASM (1:1) 82, p. 2.

2012. HOEY, Allen
"Fall." NegC (3:4) Aut 83, p. 50.
"Running at Night." CropD (4) 83, p. 8.
"The Story." Tendril (16) Sum 83, p. 65.
"The Things of August." OW (17) Aut-Wint 83-84, p. 101-103.
"Wrong Turn at Parish Corners" (for Philip Booth). Blueline (3:2) Wint-Spr 82, p. 23.

2013. HOFER, Mariann
"Radio Park." Abraxas (27/28) 83, p. 11.
"Three Things." HiramPoR (35) Aut-Wint 83, p. 21.

2014. HOFFMAN, Chris
"Orpheus, Sitting at the Mouth of the Cave." ThirdW Spr 83, p. 36-37.

2015. HOFFMAN, H. A.
"Candling Eggs (W. Va., 1980)." KanQ (15:2) Spr 83, p. 159.

2016. HOFFMAN, Jill
"7. It was O. A. Standing in line." NowestR (21:2/3) 83, p. 43-44.

"9. I cut down on my food yesterday." NowestR (21:2/3) 83, p. 45-46.
"39. May 26, 1978." NowestR (21:2/3) 83, p. 47.

2017. HOFFMAN, Judi
"Learning to Speak Papiamento." ThRiPo (19/20) 82, p. 45.
"Open City." ThRiPo (19/20) 82, p. 44.

2018. HOFFMANN, Charlotte Luise
"A Woman Reads History" (A Thought for Bertolt Brecht). SanFPJ (4:4) 83, p. 28.

2019. HOFMANN, Michael
"Author, Author." Poetry (142:4) Jl 83, p. 194.
"Changes." NewYorker (58:52) 14 F 83, p. 94.
"Furth i. Wald" (for Jan and Anja T.). Agni (18) 83, p. 67.
"Gruppenbild ohne Dame." Agni (18) 83, p. 68.
"Incident from Antiquity." Agni (18) 83, p. 65.
"Myopia in Rupert Brooke Country." Agni (18) 83, p. 69.
"Sans-Souci (L. at 22)." Agni (18) 83, p. 64.
"To a Classics Professor (1806). Agni (18) 83, p. 66.

2020. HOGAN, Linda
"Bees in Transit: Osage County." PraS (57:3) Aut 83, p. 46-47.
"Changing Weather." PraS (57:3) Aut 83, p. 45-46.
"Cities behind Glass." DevQ (18:3) Aut 83, p. 14.
"Friday Night." PraS (57:3) Aut 83, p. 44-45.
"November" (for Meridel LeSeuer). MassR (24:1) Spr 83, p. 60-61.
"Saint Coyote." MassR (24:1) Spr 83, p. 62.

2021. HOGGARD, James
"At One My Fortune, at Two Your Watch" (tr. of Oscar Hahn). Mund (14:1) 83, p. 25.
"Good Night Dear" (tr. of Oscar Hahn). Mund (14:1) 83, p. 25.

2022. HOGUE, Cynthia
"Toward Solstice" (for Knud-Erik, 1953-1982). OW (16) Spr-Sum 83, p. 124-125.

2023. HOLDEN, Jonathan
"Blizzard." ThRiPo (21/22) 83, p. 44.
"Car Showroom." BlackWR (8:1) Aut 81, p. 73.
"Casino." OW (17) Aut-Wint 83-84, p. 92-93.
"Face Up." OW (16) Spr-Sum 83, p. 63.
"Full Moon, Rising." Poetry (143:1) O 83, p. 27.
"I Lie Awake on Top of the Sheets." OhioR (30) 83, p. 140.
"The Lotus Eaters." Iowa (13:2) Spr 82, p. 77.
"Scraping the House." Poetry (143:1) O 83, p. 28.
"Seventeen." OW (16) Spr-Sum 83, p. 62.
"Shoe Store." BlackWR (8:1) Aut 81, p. 72.
"The Trick." PoetL (77:4) Wint 83, p. 227-228.
"Visiting Agnes." PoetL (77:4) Wint 83, p. 229.

2024. HOLDER, Wayne
"The Bees' Language." WestCR (18:1) Je 83, p. 18-19.
"Whose Very Blood Has Turned against Him" (for Richard Hugo - 1923-1982). WestCR (18:1) Je 83, p. 17.

2025. HOLDT, David
"The River at High Summer: Evening." StoneC (11:1/2, Pt. 1) Aut-Wint 83, p. 25.

2026. HOLINGER, Richard
"Filling in the Second Sun." WindO (42) Sum 83, p. 32-33.

2027. HOLLAMAN, Keith
"Natural History" (tr. of Benjamin Péret). Field (28) Spr 83, p. 5-8.

2028. HOLLAND, Barbara A.
"The Midday Moon: Selene." Wind (13:49) 83, p. 29-30.
"The New Sorcery." Wind (13:49) 83, p. 29.
"Northward Riding." Tele (18) 83, p. 119.
"What's Here." Tele (18) 83, p. 119.

2029. HOLLAND, William
"Notebook." PoetL (77:4) Wint 83, p. 206.

2030. HOLLANDER, Jean
"The Unforgiving Barrier." PoetL (77:1) Spr 82, p. 18.
"Unravellings." PoetL (77:1) Spr 82, p. 19-20.

2031. HOLLANDER, John
"Being Got Wrong." CarolQ (35:2) Wint 83, p. 76.
"A Corona for Wolfgang." NewYRB (30:10) 16 Je 83, p. 27.
"Cupcake to Lyrebird." OhioR (30) 83, p. 178.
"Letter." Descant (40) Spr 83, p. 31.
"Literal Account." Descant (40) Spr 83, p. 31.
"A Moment in Maine." NewYorker (59:2) 28 F 83, p. 38.
"The Sense of Unending" (for Frank Kermode). DevQ (18:3) Aut 83, p. 61-62.
"The Way Home from the Lawyer's." NewRep (188:14) 11 Ap 83, p. 36.

2032. HOLLANDER, Martha
"The Auto-Architect." Shen (34:3) 83, p. 98-99.
"Back in the Twilight Zone" (for David Leavitt). Shen (34:3) 83, p. 97-98.
"Central Park." YaleR (72:4) Sum 83, p. 604.

2033. HOLLOWAY, Geoffrey
"Railbar." Bogg (51) 83, p. 46.

2034. HOLMES, John Clellon
"Going West Alone" (for Jack). MoodySI (12) Aut 82, p. 27.

2035. HOLMES, Philip
"Brandy Bottle Inclines." Stand (24:4) Aut 83, p. 31.
"The Lead Mines of Swaledale" (Selections: 3 poems). Stand (24:4) Aut 83, p. 31-33.
"Peat Fires." Stand (24:4) Aut 83, p. 32.
"The Smelting Hearth." Stand (24:4) Aut 83, p. 32-33.

2036. HOLTEN, Knud
"And the Wind Seen As Waves" (tr. by Jack Brondum). SoDakR (21:1) Spr 83, p. 40.
"Havblik." SoDakR (21:1) Spr 83, p. 41.
"Ocean View" (tr. by Jack Brondum). SoDakR (21:1) Spr 83, p. 40.
"Og Vinden Set Som Bolger." SoDakR (21:1) Spr 83, p. 41.

2037. HOMER, Art
"I Am a Boy under Trees." MissouriR (7:1) Aut 83, p. 26-27.
"Inland with Coastal Weather." MissouriR (7:1) Aut 83, p. 25.

2038. HONGO, Garrett Kaoru
"The Legend." BlackWR (8:1) Aut 81, p. 20-21.

2039. HOOD, James W.
"Home." SouthernHR (17:2) Spr 83, p. 132.

2040. HOOGESTRAAT, Jane
"Alias." IndR (5:2) Sum 82, p. 22.

2041. HOOKER, Jeremy
"Avington: The Avenue at Dawn." Argo (4:3) 83, p. 20.

2042. HOPES, David (David Brendan)
"Advice to the Biographer." StoneC (11:1/2, Pt. 1) Aut-Wint 83, p. 32.
"Ailanthus." HiramPoR (35) Aut-Wint 83, p. 23-24.
"As They Loved Helen at the Last." ThirdW Spr 83, p. 43.
"Christmas Morning." StoneC (11:1/2, Pt. 1) Aut-Wint 83, p. 33.
"A Flower That Comes After." HiramPoR (35) Aut-Wint 83, p. 22.
"Found." KanQ (15:2) Spr 83, p. 100.
"The Front." NewRena (16) Spr 83, p. 66.
"He Comes Down Hogsback Mountain with Tablets of Iron." Wind (13:47) 83, p. 16-17.
"Lough Leane." WestB (13) 83, p. 69.
"Orpheus." ThirdW Spr 83, p. 44-46.
"September Wind." KanQ (15:2) Spr 83, p. 100.
"Where The Wife of Cain Came From." ThirdW Spr 83, p. 47-51.
"You, Walt Whitman." NewRena (16) Spr 83, p. 64-65.
"You Will Be a Stranger Here." WestB (13) 83, p. 68.

2043. HOPKINS, Leroy
"June 15, 1981 9:15 PM." Tele (18) 83, p. 59.

2044. HOPKINS, Michael F.
"One for Bird (An Open Line)." MoodySI (8) Sum-Aut 80, p. 13.

2045. HOPSON, Brenda
"Elusive Guides." WritersL Ja 83, p. 19.

2046. HORNE, Lewis
"Letter from Nga." OntR (19) Aut-Wint 83-84, p. 83-84.
"My Face Surprising." OntR (19) Aut-Wint 83-84, p. 82.
"Private Vision." OntR (19) Aut-Wint 83-84, p. 85-86.

2047. HORNIG, Doug
"Nuclear Triptych." SanFPJ (4:4) 83, p. 82-83.
"Scoliosis." Bogg (51) 83, p. 17.

2048. HOROWITZ, Mikhail
"Listening to Pharaoh Sanders." Abraxas (27/28) 83, p. 22.
"You Are the Field That No Man Dares to Till." Pig (11) 83, p. 67.

2049. HOROWITZ, Shel
"The Shape of Oklahoma." YetASM (1:2) 82, p. 5.
"Somewhere in France, there's a city." YetASM (1:2) 82, p. 3.

2050. HORTON, Barbara
"After a Workshop with Robert Bly." SpoonRQ (8:4) Aut 83, p. 13.
"Crunching through Snow toward a House." SpoonRQ (8:4) Aut 83, p. 14.
"Falling Asleep." YetASM (2:1) 83, p. 3.

2051. HORTON, David
"Tunnels." PottPort (5) 83-84, p. 36.
"Weather Observations." PottPort (5) 83-84, p. 44.

2052. HORVATH, John
"Casting from the Chinnapatkin Bridge." SanFPJ (4:3) 83, p. 73.
"Memphis." Nimrod (27:1) Aut-Wint 83, p. 60.
"Scab." Poem (48) Jl 83, p. 47.
"Winter Morning." Poem (48) Jl 83, p. 48.

2053. HOSKIN, William
"Harry Talked to Animals." Blueline (5:1) Sum-Aut 83, p. 23.

2054. HOUCHIN, Ron
"Book of the Year." Wind (13:47) 83, p. 18.
"The Drinking." ThirdW Spr 83, p. 74.
"Sea of the Dead" (After R. W. Plymale). Wind (13:47) 83, p. 19.

HOUGH, N. (Nat)
<u>See</u>: HOUGH, Natalie

2055. HOUGH, N. C.
"The Dying Cowboy." <u>SoDakR</u> (21:3) Aut 83, p. 84.

2056. HOUGH, Natalie
"Birthday." <u>SanFPJ</u> (5:1) 83, p. 69.
"The Island." <u>SanFPJ</u> (5:1) 83, p. 71.

2057. HOUGHTON, Elgar
"Driftwood." <u>SanFPJ</u> (5:3) 83, p. 95.
"Fire Power." <u>SanFPJ</u> (5:3) 83, p. 94.
"Sermons in Stone." <u>SanFPJ</u> (4:4) 83, p. 81.

2058. HOUGHTON, Tim
"Night Carving" (after a painting by Matta). <u>DevQ</u> (18:3) Aut 83, p. 31-32.

2059. HOUSE, Tom
"Coming Out." <u>PikeF</u> (5) Spr 83, p. 25.
"The Holy Primitive." <u>PikeF</u> (5) Spr 83, p. 18.
"Looking for His Mama in a Bar." <u>Bogg</u> (51) 83, p. 8.
"Politics and Pornography." <u>Bogg</u> (50) 83, p. 16.

2060. HOUSMAN, A. E.
"These, in the day when heaven was falling." <u>SanFPJ</u> (5:1) 83, p. 17.

2061. HOUSTON, Peyton
"The Art Is the Equilibrium of the Possible Impossible." <u>OP</u> (35) Spr-Sum 83, p. 23.
"Homage to the Dinosaur." <u>OP</u> (35) Spr-Sum 83, p. 21.
"In the Blackout." <u>OP</u> (35) Spr-Sum 83, p. 24.
"The Revolt of the Flowers." <u>OP</u> (35) Spr-Sum 83, p. 25.
"The Robe." <u>OP</u> (35) Spr-Sum 83, p. 22.
"The Turning." <u>OP</u> (35) Spr-Sum 83, p. 20.

HOUTEN, Lois van
<u>See</u>: Van HOUTEN, Lois

HOVANESSIAN, Diana der
<u>See</u>: Der HOVANESSIAN, Diana

2062. HOVARTH, J.
"Smuggler's Dream." <u>DekalbLAJ</u> (16:1/4) Aut 82-Sum 83, p. 66-67.

2063. HOVDE, A. J.
"Delayed Transport." <u>HolCrit</u> (20:2) Ap 83, p. 18. Also <u>HolCrit</u> (20:3) Je 83, p. 9.
"The Lure of Mountains." <u>Blueline</u> (4:1) Sum-Aut 82, p. 27.

2064. HOWARD, Ben
"Floodgates." <u>PraS</u> (51:1, i.e. 57:1) Spr 83, p. 35.
"The Keeper." <u>PraS</u> (51:1, i.e. 57:1) Spr 83, p. 36.

2065. HOWARD, Jim
"Newspaper Hats." NewL (49:3/4) Spr-Sum 83, p. 56.

2066. HOWARD, Richard
"Anatole France" (The portrait by Nadar). Nat (237:16) 19 N 83, p. 500.
"At the Monument to Pierre Louÿs" (Jardin du Luxembourg). Nat (236:7) 19 F 83, p. 216.
"Gérard de Nerval" (Taken a week before the poet's suicide). Raritan (3:2) Aut 83, p. 83-84.
"Hector Berlioz." Raritan (3:2) Aut 83, p. 81-82.
"Jean-Baptiste Camille Corot." Raritan (3:2) Aut 83, p. 85-86.
"Three Portraits by Nadar." Raritan (3:2) Aut 83, p. 81-86.

2067. HOWE, Fanny
"Tin Shoulders" (for James Tate). LittleBR (4:2) Wint 83-84, p. 44-45.

2068. HOWE, Marie
"The Fourth Visit." Poetry (143:2) N 83, p. 82.
"What Belongs to Us." Poetry (143:2) N 83, p. 81.
"What the Angels Left." Poetry (143:2) N 83, p. 79-80.

2069. HOWE, Susan
"Defenestration of Prague" (Excerpt). ParisR (24:86) Wint 82, p. 101-102.

2070. HOWELL, Christopher
"Cloudia's Angel." ChiR (33:3) Wint 83, p. 102-103.
"On the Laredo Line." MemphisSR (4:1) Aut 83, p. 12.

2071. HOWELL, Kath
"Sharpening a Serpent's Tooth." Comm (110:9) 6 My 83, p. 280.

2072. HOWELL, William
"Handles." BlackWR (8:1) Aut 81, p. 93.

2073. HOWES, Barbara
"Super Inferno: Midway Mall." TriQ (56) Wint 83, p. 159-160.

2074. HOWES, Mary
"Extra Marital Sex in the '60's." Quarry (32:3) Sum 83, p. 47.
"Still Life with Child." Quarry (32:3) Sum 83, p. 47-48.

2075. HOWSARE, Katrine
"Send Him to Play." HiramPoR (34) Spr-Sum 83, p. 10.

2076. HOYOS, Angela de
"How to Eat Crow on a Cold Sunday Morning." RevChic (11:3/4) 83, p. 43.
"Ten Dry Summers Ago." RevChic (11:3/4) 83, p. 42.

2077. HOYT, Myron S.
"Cycle of Glass." SanFPJ (5:3) 83, p. 61.

2078. HOYTE, Ralph
"Cat." Stand (24:4) Aut 83, p. 54.

2079. HRISTOVA, Elena
"An Afternoon's Wandering" (tr. of Kolyo Sevov, w. John Balaban). NewEng (5:4) Sum 83, p. 512.

2080. HRYCIUK, Marshall
"After rain." Quarry (32:3) Sum 83, p. 75.
"The bright forsythia." Quarry (32:3) Sum 83, p. 75.

2081. HUDDLE, David
"The Air Rifle." Ploughs (9:2/3) 83, p. 174.
"The House." Abatis (1) 83, p. 9.

2082. HUDGINS, Andrew
"After the Wilderness: May 3, 1863." Ploughs (9:2/3) 83, p. 28-29.
"Air View of an Industrial Scene." Poetry (141:4) Ja 83, p. 216.
"Amen." PoetryNW (24:3) Aut 83, p. 22-23.
"Appetite for Poison." MissouriR (6:3) Sum 83, p. 36-41.
"Claims." AmerPoR (12:3) My-Je 83, p. 39.
"Fire and St. Francis." OntR (19) Aut-Wint 83-84, p. 55-56.
"Julia Tutwiler State Prison for Women." Poetry (141:4) Ja 83, p. 217.
"Mary Magdalen's Left Foot." Ploughs (9:2/3) 83, p. 27.
"My Father's House." MassR (24:3) Aut 83, p. 648.
"On Sentimentality." AntR (41:3) Sum 83, p. 323.
"Sidney Lanier's Anniversary, 1868." OntR (19) Aut-Wint 83-84, p. 54.
"Sotto Voce." AmerPoR (12:3) My-Je 83, p. 39.
"Thomas Merton: First Visit to Gethsemane." CharR (9:1) Spr 83, p. 37.

2083. HUDSON, Marc
"A History of Rain." SewanR (91:3) Sum 83, p. 384.
"The Human City." PraS (57:4) Wint 83, p. 48-50.
"Last Rites." SewanR (91:3) Sum 83, p. 383.

2084. HUETER, Diane
"Josie's Tooth." KanQ (15:4) Aut 83, p. 61.
"Sneaky Poem." KanQ (15:4) Aut 83, p. 61.

2085. HUFF, Robert
"April 3, 1978." CarolQ (35:2) Wint 83, p. 75.
"In Memoriam Tennessee Williams 1911-1983." ConcPo (16:1) Spr 83, front matter.
"Ushers." CarolQ (35:2) Wint 83, p. 74.

2086. HUFF, Roland
"The Sleeping Dwarf" (A Parable for Scholars). WindO (43) Wint 83, p. 19-20.

2087. HUFFSTICKLER, Albert
"A Few More Trips to Santa Fe." Nimrod (27:1) Aut-Wint 83, p. 21.
"For Jennifer on Parting." Nimrod (27:1) Aut-Wint 83, p. 22.
"Photograph." Nimrod (27:1) Aut-Wint 83, p. 20.

2088. HUFFSTUTLER, Mickey
"A Rare Breed." LittleBR (3:3) Spr 83, p. 35-36.

2089. HUFFSTUTTER, Robert L.
"Kite Graveyard." EngJ (72:8) D 83, p. 37.

2090. HUGHES, Barbara
"Losing the Whales." Vis (11) 83, p. 30-31.

2091. HUGO, Richard
"1614 Boren" (For Guy Tucker)." CutB (20) Spr-Sum 83, p. 20.
"Aegean Islands 1940-1941." CutB (20) Spr-Sum 83, p. 29-30.
"Bear Paw." CutB (20) Spr-Sum 83, p. 34.
"Blue Stone." CutB (20) Spr-Sum 83, p. 95.
"Brown Stone." CutB (20) Spr-Sum 83, p. 94.
"Camas Prairie School." NewL (49:3/4) Spr-Sum 83, p. 24.
"Cape Nothing." CutB (20) Spr-Sum 83, p. 33-34.
"Cataldo Mission" (for Jim and Lois Welch). CutB (20) Spr-Sum 83, p. 70.
"Death of the Kapowsin Tavern." CutB (20) Spr-Sum 83, p. 67.
"Doing the House" (For Philip Levine). CutB (20) Spr-Sum 83, p. 24-26.
"Egyptian Dancer at Shubra." CutB (20) Spr-Sum 83, p. 31.
"Fort Benton" (for Jan). OhioR (30) 83, p. 240.
"From Altitude, the Diamonds." CutB (20) Spr-Sum 83, p. 73.
"Ghost in a Field of Mint" (for Sister Madeline DeFrees). CutB (20) Spr-Sum 83, p. 72.
"Gold Stone." CutB (20) Spr-Sum 83, p. 91.
"Gray Stone." CutB (20) Spr-Sum 83, p. 92.
"Green Stone." CutB (20) Spr-Sum 83, p. 89-90.
"Here, But Unable to Answer" (In memory, Herbert Hugo). NewRep (186:18) 5 My 82, p. 28.
"Houses." CutB (20) Spr-Sum 83, p. 22.
"Keen to Leaky Flowers." CutB (20) Spr-Sum 83, p. 65.
"LA Push." CutB (20) Spr-Sum 83, p. 16-17.
"Last Day There." CutB (20) Spr-Sum 83, p. 23.
"Letter to Scanlon from Whitehall." CutB (20) Spr-Sum 83, p. 74-75.
"Making Certain It Goes On." CutB (20) Spr-Sum 83, p. 146-147.
"Maratea Porto: The Dear Postmistress There." CutB (20) Spr-Sum 83, p. 69.
"Missoula Softball Tournament." CutB (20) Spr-Sum 83, p. 71.
"Montana Ranch Abandoned." CutB (20) Spr-Sum 83, p. 32-33.

"Northwest Retrospective: Mark Tobey." CutB (20) Spr-Sum 83, p. 18-19.
"Olive Trees." CutB (20) Spr-Sum 83, p. 31-32.
"Red Stone." CutB (20) Spr-Sum 83, p. 93.
"The Right Madness of Skye." CutB (20) Spr-Sum 83, p. 77-79.
"Salt Water Story." CutB (20) Spr-Sum 83, p. 6-7.
"The Small Oil Left in the House We Rented in Boulder." CutB (20) Spr-Sum 83, p. 76.
"The Tinker Camp" (for Susan Lydiatt). NewL (49:3/4) Spr-Sum 83, p. 25.
"Trout." CutB (20) Spr-Sum 83, p. 15.
"The Way a Ghost Dissolves." CutB (20) Spr-Sum 83, p. 17-18.
"West Marginal Way." CutB (20) Spr-Sum 83, p. 66.
"What the Brand New Freeway Won't Go By." CutB (20) Spr-Sum 83, p. 68.

HUI-MING, Wang
See: WANG, Hui-Ming

2092. HUIDOBRO, Vincente
"Empty" (For Blaise Cendrars, tr. by David Guss). Pig (11) 83, p. 30.
"Horizon" (tr. by David Guss). Pig (11) 83, p. 31.
"Spring" (tr. by David Guss). Pig (11) 83, p. 30.
"Swimmer" (tr. by David Guss). Pig (11) 83, p. 30.
"Woman" (tr. by David Guss). Pig (11) 83, p. 31.

2093. HULSE, Michael
"Correspondence Course." Argo (4:1) 82, p. 5.
"On Location." AntigR (54) Sum 83, p. 13.
"Tangle." AntigR (54) Sum 83, p. 12.

2094. HUMES, Harry
"Animal Skulls" (from Throwing the Compass Away, finalist, 10th anniversary manuscript competition). StoneC (11:1/2, Pt. 1) Aut-Wint 83, p. 50-51.
"Burying the Skunk." Kayak (61) Ap 83, p. 63.
"Calling in the Hawk." PoetryNW (24:2) Sum 83, p. 3-5.
"The Drought Walkers." CutB (21) Aut-Wint 83, p. 63.
"Hilltop with Voices" (after Harry Crews). CutB (21) Aut-Wint 83, p. 62.
"The History of the Apple" (from Throwing the Compass Away, finalist, 10th anniversary manuscript competition). StoneC (11:1/2, Pt. 1) Aut-Wint 83, p. 51.
"The Iola Story." LittleM (14:1/2) 83, p. 10-11.
"Leaving the Room." LittleM (14:1/2) 83, p. 9.
"A Lime Evening and White Boats." LittleM (14:1/2) 83, p. 7.
"Listening to One Thing at a Time." CutB (21) Aut-Wint 83, p. 57.
"Mountain Lake with Stumps." CutB (21) Aut-Wint 83, p. 59.
"Nijinsky's Feet." WestB (12) 83, p. 15.
"One and the Same Thing." Kayak (61) Ap 83, p. 62.
"Releasing the Minnows." LittleM (14:1/2) 83, p. 8.

"Seascape with Italian Bicycle Cap." CutB (21) Aut-Wint 83, p. 61.
"Winter Storm Watch." CutB (21) Aut-Wint 83, p. 58.
"The Woman Who Called Whales across the Fields." CutB (21) Aut-Wint 83, p. 60.

2095. HUMMER, T. R.
"Drowning: A Ghost Story." Hudson (36:1) Spr 83, p. 134-137.
"First Love: When It Falls." Hudson (36:1) Spr 83, p. 137-140.
"A Fool Is a Man Who Understands Nothing But Remembers Everything." Hudson (36:1) Spr 83, p. 132-133.
"The Lost Woman." MemphisSR (3:1) Aut 82, p. 5.
"Love Song." Hudson (36:1) Spr 83, p. 133-134.
"Or, If You Were Closer, I Might Touch You." MemphisSR (3:1) Aut 82, p. 4.
"Passion, Circumstance, What I Gave to the Air." MemphisSR (3:2) Spr 83, p. 28-29.

2096. HUNT, Leigh
"Media Man." LittleBR (3:3) Spr 83, p. 37.

2097. HUNT, Ralph
"20." WindO (42) Sum 83, p. 28.
"The Atco Drag Strip, Atco, New Jerey." PoetL (78:4) Wint 84, p. 216-217.
"How Do I Love Thee? 1947-1956. WindO (42) Sum 83, p. 29.
"The Victim of Audits." WindO (42) Sum 83, p. 30.
"Viet Nam." PoetL (77:2) Sum 82, p. 96.

2098. HUNT, William
"A Darkening Outing at Sea." NewL (49:3/4) Spr-Sum 83, p. 142.
"No Longer May We Call." NewL (49:3/4) Spr-Sum 83, p. 143.

2099. HUNTER, Donnell
"At Sea Gull Bay." PoNow (7:2, #38) 83, p. 47.

2100. HUNTER, Levona
"The Meal." KanQ (15:2) Spr 83, p. 137.

2101. HUNTINGTON, Cynthia
"In Our Former Life." Agni (19) 83, p. 90-93.
"Sleeping in the Afternoon." OhioR (30) 83, p. 173.

2102. HURLOW, Marcia L.
"Burial of the Last Rogue Valley Chief." WestB (12) 83, p. 55.
"First Calf." WestB (12) 83, p. 54.
"To Resolve a Dream." WestB (12) 83, p. 56.

2103. HURVITT, Mark
"The Bay Meditations." PoetryE (11) Sum 83, p. 84-89.

2104. HURVITZ, Yair
"Darkness Will Sweeten" (tr. by Harold Schimmel). LitR (26:2) Wint 83, p. 276.
"Listens, In Another Place" (tr. by Gabriel Levin). LitR (26:2) Wint 83, p. 274-275.
"A Map" (tr. by Harold Schimmel). LitR (26:2) Wint 83, p. 275.

2105. HUSS, Steven W.
"Neighbor's Daughter." KanQ (15:2) Spr 83, p. 74.

2106. HUSTVEDT, Siri
"Eclipse." ParisR (25:87) Spr 83, p. 129.
"Hermaphroditic Parallels." ParisR (25:87) Spr 83, p. 130-131.

2107. HUTCHINGS, Pat
"Confirmation." ClockR (1:2) Wint 83-84, p. 3.
"Dream in a Dry Time." Wind (13:48) 83, p. 30-31.
"Excavation." Calyx (8:1) Aut 83, p. 22.
"Fifty Laps for Mental Health." Northeast (Ser. 3:15) Sum 83, p. 10.
"To: Emily in Eternity, Re: Death Whose If Is Everlasting." Calyx (8:1) Aut 83, p. 20-21.
"Van Gogh's 'Road with Poplars'." CharR (9:1) Spr 83, p. 13-14.
"A Vision: Woman's Ear." ClockR (1:2) Wint 83-84, p. 13.
"Your Work on the Wall." StoneC (10:3/4) Spr-Sum 83, p. 15.

2109. HUTCHINSON, A. Scott
"Same Old Glory." SanFPJ (5:1) 83, p. 50.

2110. HUTCHINSON, Anne
"Sampler." WorldO (17:4) Sum 83, p. 33.

2111. HUTCHINSON, Robert
"Grief in Blackhawk, Colorado" (L.A.H. 1884-1968). SouthernR (19:3) Jl 83, p. 670-671.
"Out of an Old Book" (For A, J, J). SouthernR (19:3) Jl 83, p. 671-672.
"The Outcome." SouthernR (19:3) Jl 83, p. 672.

2112. HUTCHISON, Joseph
"Lamentation." Vis (11) 83, p. 13.
"Part of a Series." AmerPoR (12:1) Ja/F 83, p. 27.
"This Year." OhioR (30) 83, p. 141.
"Winter Sunrise outside a Cafe near Butte, Montana." PoNow (7:2, #38) 83, p. 21.

2113. HUTCHMAN, Laurence
"Malin Head." PoetryCR (5:1) Aut 83, p. 7.

2114. HUTNER, Herbert Hart
"What a Life." WritersL F 83, p. 18.

2115. HYUNLEE
"My Sad Friend." WritersL S 83, p. 24.
"A Rendezvous with God." WritersL O 83, p. 11.

2116. IBARAKI, Noriko
"When I Was Most Beautiful in My Life" (tr. by Tetsuo Kinoshita). PoetryE (9/10) Wint 82-Spr 83, p. 226-227.

2117. IBN AL-MU'TAZZ
"The Two Dogs" (tr. by Barbara Feyerabend). SenR (13:2) 82-83, p. 33-34.

IGLESIAS, Davide Pèrez
See: PEREZ IGLESIAS, Davide

2118. IGNATOW, David
"Air." DevQ (18:3) Aut 83, p. 77.
"And Rest with You." Ploughs (9:1) 83, p. 101.
"Childhood." Ploughs (9:1) 83, p. 100.
"A Civil Arrest." LittleBR (4:2) Wint 83-84, p. 61.
"Does this flower worry as I do." NewL (49:3/4) Spr-Sum 83, p. 116.
"Every Day." VirQR (59:1) Wint 83, p. 58-59.
"A Fact of the Weather." VirQR (59:1) Wint 83, p. 59.
"The Fly." Ploughs (9:1) 83, p. 99.
"The Garden and the Store." ThRiPo (21/22) 83, p. 36-37.
"I Am Dreaming." NewL (49:3/4) Spr-Sum 83, p. 61.
"I Listen." ClockR (2:1) 83, p. 24.
"In Memoriam: Al Lichtman." MemphisSR (2:2) Spr 82, p. 5.
"In Peace." NewL (49:3/4) Spr-Sum 83, p. 118.
"In the Graveyard." BlackWR (10:1) Aut 83, p. 93.
"Listening." VirQR (59:1) Wint 83, p. 60.
"New Year's Eve." VirQR (59:1) Wint 83, p. 57-58.
"No One." BlackWR (10:1) Aut 83, p. 94.
"Of That Fire." NewL (49:3/4) Spr-Sum 83, p. 116.
"One Definition." NewL (49:3/4) Spr-Sum 83, p. 117.
"The Poet." DevQ (18:3) Aut 83, p. 76.
"Rooting." ClockR (2:1) 83, p. 23.
"The Separate Dead." ClockR (2:1) 83, p. 25.
"Silent." PoNow (7:2, #38) 83, p. 13.
"Sleepy." NewEng (5:4) Sum 83, p. 520.
"Wherever." DevQ (18:2) Sum 83, p. 62.
"Whether." BlackWR (10:1) Aut 83, p. 92.
"The Window." NewL (49:3/4) Spr-Sum 83, p. 117.

2119. IGNATOW, Yaedi
"The Canvas." DevQ (18:3) Aut 83, p. 75.
"In the Afternoon." Images (8:3) 83, p. 6.
"The Promise." DevQ (18:3) Aut 83, p. 73.
"Spring Psalm." DevQ (18:3) Aut 83, p. 74.

2120. IKAN, Ron
"Cloud Cover." WebR (8:1) Spr 83, p. 85.
"The Park." CreamCR (8:1/2) 83, p. 80-81.

2121. IKEDA, Takuro
"Four Thousand Days and Nights" (tr. of Ryuuichi Tamura, w. Gary Steven Corseri). WebR (8:1) Spr 83, p. 48.

2122. ILLYES, Gyula
"A Winter Memory" (tr. by Nicholas Kolumban). NewL (49:3/4) Spr-Sum 83, p. 133-139.

2123. INEZ, Colette
"Along the Garonne." PoetryNW (24:1) Spr 83, p. 38-39.
"Diamond Jim and Golden Lil." ThRiPo (21/22) 83, p. 41.
"Letter from an Outpost." NewEngR (6:1) Aut 83, p. 105-106.
"Letter from the Villa." ChiR (34:1) Sum 83, p. 45-47.
"Over the Fields, Aldebaran in Taurus." MemphisSR (1:2) Spr 81, p. 31.
"Women, Priests, and Poultry Have Never Enough." Shen (34:2) 83, p. 65.

2124. INGALLS, Jeremy
"The Springtime Tour." PoNow (7:2, #38) 83, p. 28.

2125. INGRAM, Anthony L.
"Black Ain't Chic No More." SanFPJ (5:1) 83, p. 16.

2126. INGRAM, Nida E. Jones
"Haiku: Moon-lit autumn pond." LittleBR (3:3) Spr 83, p. 38.
"Haiku: With only one hoot." LittleBR (3:3) Spr 83, p. 38.

2127. INMAN, P.
"Backbite" (Excerpts) (for Bob Marley). ParisR (24:86) Wint 82, p. 117.

2128. INMAN, Will
"I Have Other Sounds." Images (8:3) 83, p. 5.

2129. IOANNOU, Susan
"In Retrospect and Anticipation" (For Sharon). Grain (11:3) Ag 83, p. 12.
"Memoriam." AntigR (53) Spr 83, p. 36-37.
"Summer Vacation." AntigR (52) Wint 83, p. 125.

2130. IORIO, Gary
"Lunch Meat." Pig (11) 83, p. 82.

2131. IRAJ
"A Veiled Girl (ca. 1900)" (tr. by Omar S. Pound). AntigR (55) Aut 83, p. 22.

2132. IRBY, Ken
"Etudes" (Excerpts). ParisR (24:86) Wint 82, p. 124.
"Requiem Etudes" (for Louis Zukofsy). ParisR (24:86) Wint 82, p. 125.

2133. IRELAND, Thelma
"Haiku: Horizon palm trees." Meadows (4:1) 83, p. 45.
"Hunting." Meadows (4:1) 83, p. 49.

2134. IRIE, Kevin
"The Auction." PoetryCR (4:3) Spr 83, p. 5.
"Cottage Country." PoetryCR (5:2) Wint 83-84, p. 7.
"The Muskellunge Alive." Argo (5:1) 83, p. 18-19.

2135. IRION, Mary Jean
"The Ant Farm." ChrC (100:23) 3-10 Ag 83, p. 710.
"Dinner for the Old Dumb Man." ChrC (100:5) 16-23 F 83, p. 144.
"The Loaves." ChrC (100:17) 25 My 83, p. 524.

2136. IRWIN, Kip
"The Four Kinds of Prayer." IndR (5:3) Aut 82, p. 27.
"The Hairs of My Body." WindO (42) Sum 83, p. 47.
"A Praise for Old Sweaters." WindO (42) Sum 83, p. 46-47.
"Shelter." IndR (5:3) Aut 82, p. 26.

2137. IRWIN, Mark
"Grandmother Making Bread" (Florence Irwin, 1889-1971). HiramPoR (35) Aut-Wint 83, p. 25.

2138. ISHIDA, Hakyo
"For but an instant" (Haiku, tr. by Minoru Fujita and Richard F. Fleck). Paint (10:19/20) Spr-Aut 83, p. 45.
"A grapefruit split open" (Haiku, tr. by Minoru Fujita and Richard F. Fleck). Paint (10:19/20) Spr-Aut 83, p. 45.
"Waiting for a bus" (Haiku, tr. by Minoru Fujita and Richard F. Fleck). Paint (10:19/20) Spr-Aut 83, p. 45.

2139. ISHIGAKI, Rin
"A Cliff" (tr. by Tetsuo Kinoshita). PoetryE (9/10) Wint 82-Spr 83, p. 227-228.

2140. ISSAIA, Nana
"Contrast." Grain (11:1) F 83, p. 19.
"That Garden." Grain (11:1) F 83, p. 19.

2141. ITZIN, Charles
"White Wing" (after the song Asa Branca by Luis Gonzaga Sr.). ThirdW Spr 83, p. 99-100.
"Winter of Gorgona." ThirdW Spr 83, p. 100.

2142. IUPPA, M. J.
"Coming into Season." NewL (50:1) Aut 83, p. 44.

2143. IWAMOTO, William
"Encounter in May." SoDakR (21:4) Wint 83, p. 30.

2144. IZUMIYA, Akira
"On the Wetting Road Always Splashing" (tr. by Frank Stewart and Ruriko Fukuhara). MoodySI (10) Aut 81, p. 6-7.

2145. JABES, Edmond
"Aely, Gallimard, 1972" (Excerpts) (tr. by Rosmarie

Waldrop). CreamCR (8:1/2) 83, p. 66-71.
"Groundless" (tr. by Keith Waldrop). Sulfur (3:2, #8) 83, p. 80-82.
"The Pact of Spring" (tr. by Keith Waldrop). Sulfur (3:2, #8) 83, p. 82-85.
"Well Water" (tr. by Keith Waldrop). Sulfur (3:2, #8) 83, p. 79-80.

2146. JACKETTI, Maria
"To a Linguist." YetASM (2:1) 83, p. 3.

2147. JACKOWSKA, Nicki
"The House of Odd Cups." Argo (5:1) 83, p. 32.

2148. JACKSON, Fleda Brown
"Maintenance." Iowa (13:3/4) Spr 82 (83), p. 33.

2149. JACKSON, Haywood
"At Cerasus." KanQ (15:1) Wint 83, p. 149.
"Hell in the Earth." SanFPJ (4:2) 83, p. 27.
"Holidays" (Excerpt, recipient of a Phillips Poetry Award, Fall/Winter 1983/84). StoneC (10:3/4) Spr-Sum 83, p. 81.
"Kansas Cats." KanQ (15:1) Wint 83, p. 150.
"The Life and Death of Jupiter." SanFPJ (4:2) 83, p. 26-27.

2150. JACKSON, Richard
"Greenwood." GeoR (37:2) Sum 83, p. 284.
"However You Say It Is." BlackWR (9:1) Aut 82, p. 62-63.
"Why We See What We See" (for Gary Margolis). NoAmR (268:3) S 83, p. 57.

JACKSON, William Haywood
See: JACKSON, Haywood

2151. JACOB, Catherine
"Kneading." PottPort (5) 83-84, p. 5.
"The Poet." PottPort (5) 83-84, p. 14.

2152. JACOBOWITZ, Judah L.
"Call to Order." CapeR (19:1) Wint 83, p. 21.
"The Moon Again." CapeR (19:1) Wint 83, p. 20.

2153. JACOBS, D. N.
"Jason's Song." SpiritSH (49 Suppl.) 83, p. 32-33.

2154. JACOBS, David
"Over and Over." Argo (4:3) 83, p. 5.
"Remember the World." Stand (24:3) 83, p. 7.

2155. JACOBS, M. G.
"Cheevy, on and on and on." KanQ (15:2) Spr 83, p. 101.
"Next Door." KanQ (15:2) Spr 83, p. 101.

2156. JACOBS, Maria
"Between Chapter and Verse" (tr. of Ankie Peypers). Waves (11:4) Spr 83, p. 75.

"But One Day" (tr. of Ankie Peypers). Waves (11:4) Spr 83, p. 71.
"Guest" (tr. of Ankie Peypers). Waves (11:4) Spr 83, p. 73.

2157. JACOBSEN, Josephine
"Paramedical." 13thM (6:1/2) 82, p. 67.

2158. JACOBSEN, Rolf
"Brosten." SoDakR (21:1) Spr 83, p. 17.
"But We Live" (tr. by Roger Greenwald). PoetryE (12) Aut 83, p. 93.
"Changing Light" (tr. by Olav Grinde). StoneC (11:1/2, Pt. 1) Aut-Wint 83, p. 31.
"Cobblestone" (tr. by Olav Grinde). SoDakR (21:1) Spr 83, p. 16.
"From Above, from Below and from the Side" (tr. by Roger Greenwald). PoetryE (12) Aut 83, p. 90.
"Gamle Foks Graver." SoDakR (21:1) Spr 83, p. 15.
"Letter to the Light" (tr. by Roger Greenwald). PoetryE (12) Aut 83, p. 88.
"Lysskifte." StoneC (11:1/2, Pt. 1) Aut-Wint 83, p. 30.
"Marsh" (tr. by Olav Grinde). Paint (10:19/20) Spr-Aut 83, p. 46.
"Night Music" (tr. by Olav Grinde). Paint (10:19/20) Spr-Aut 83, p. 47.
"The Old Ladies" (tr. by Roger Greenwald). PoetryE (12) Aut 83, p. 91.
"Old People's Graves" (tr. by Olav Grinde). WebR (8:1) Spr 83, p. 19.
"Old People's Graves" (tr. by Olav Grinde). SoDakR (21:1) Spr 83, p. 14.
"Reality" (tr. by Olav Grinde). SoDakR (21:1) Spr 83, p. 18.
"Roser--Roser." SoDakR (21:1) Spr 83, p. 23, 25.
"Roses--Roses" (tr. by Olav Grinde). SoDakR (21:1) Spr 83, p. 22, 25.
"Saltwater" (tr. by Olav Grinde). WebR (8:1) Spr 83, p. 17-19.
"Small Lights at Sea" (tr. by Roger Greenwald). PoetryE (12) Aut 83, p. 89.
"Snu Dere Bort. -- Tenk Pa Noe Annet!" SoDakR (21:1) Spr 83, p. 21.
"Turn Away. -- Think about Something Else!" (tr. by Olav Grinde). SoDakR (21:1) Spr 83, p. 20.
"Turnip Harvest" (tr. by Olav Grinde). StoneC (11:1/2, Pt. 1) Aut-Wint 83, p. 31.
"Turnipshost." StoneC (11:1/2, Pt. 1) Aut-Wint 83, p. 30.
"Unthinking" (tr. by Roger Greenwald). PoetryE (12) Aut 83, p. 92.
"Virkelighet." SoDakR (21:1) Spr 83, p. 19.

2159. JACOBSON, Jason
"Night Hike." PikeF (5) Spr 83, p. 21.

2160. JAECH, Stephen
"Child in a Well." PoetryNW (24:1) Spr 83, p. 24.
"The Garden Maze." Poem (48) Jl 83, p. 1.

"The Room with Nothing in It." PoetryNW (24:1) Spr 83, p. 25.

2161. JAEGER, Lowell
"Let's Hope This Thing Blows Over Soon" (Third prize, SCCA International Poetry Contest). WestB (12) 83, p. 44-45.

2162. JAEGER, Sharon Ann
"Zoological." YetASM (1:1) 82, p. 14.

2163. JAFFE, Dan
"Czeslaw Milosz." Focus (15:95) Ag 83, p. 21.
"The Poet's Lament" (After Heffernan). Focus (15:95) Ag 83, p. 21.
"Standing before a Lit Menorah." Focus (15:95) Ag 83, p. 21.
"We Name Him." Focus (15:95) Ag 83, p. 21.

2164. JAFFE, Maggie
"Aleph." YetASM (2:1) 83, p. 7.

2165. JAMES, David
"Afterwards." YetASM (2:1) 83, p. 11.
"Hearts." CentR (27:1) Wint 83, p. 42-43.
"The Idea of Roofs." CentR (27:1) Wint 83, p. 43-44.
"The Love of Water Faucets." CentR (27:1) Wint 83, p. 44-45.

2166. JAMES, Gary S.
"Hate the Bus." SanFPJ (5:4) 83, p. 78-79.

2167. JAMES, Joyce
"After Crossing the Nodaway River." Tendril (14/15) Wint 83, p. 112-113.
"In the Summer." Tendril (14/15) Wint 83, p. 114-115.
"Mathematics." Tendril (14/15) Wint 83, p. 116.
"Travel" (For Judy). Tendril (14/15) Wint 83, p. 110-111.

2168. JAMES, Sibyl
"Leaving the Desert." ThirdW Spr 83, p. 85.
"A View of Lake Union." Pig (11) 83, p. 66.

2169. JAMES-FRENCH, Davy
"The Daughter Recreates Her Mother." CanLit (98) Aut 83, p. 58-59.

2170. JAMIESON, Leland S.
"Not to Cry." YetASM (2:1) 83, p. 11.

2171. JAMIESON, Tim
"Grass-Grown Tracks." AntigR (54) Sum 83, p. 20.

2172. JAMMES, Francis
"The Cherry Trees" (tr. by Antony Oldknow). SoDakR (21:1) Spr 83, p. 82.
"A Cloud Is a Black" (tr. by Antony Oldknow). SoDakR (21:1) Spr 83, p. 84, 86.

"La Gomme Coule." SoDakR (21:1) Spr 83, p. 83.
"J'Aime dans le Temps." SoDakR (21:1) Spr 83, p. 81.
"My Love Is in the Past" (tr. by Antony Oldknow). SoDakR (21:1) Spr 83, p. 80.
"Un Nuage Est une Barre." SoDakR (21:1) Spr 83, p. 85, 87.
"The Sad Wind" (For Henri Ghéon, tr. by Antony Oldknow). SoDakR (21:1) Spr 83, p. 88, 90.
"Tu Seras Nue." SoDakR (21:1) Spr 83, p. 79.
"Le Vent Triste" (A Henri Ghéon). SoDakR (21:1) Spr 83, p. 89, 91.
"You'll Be Naked" (tr. by Antony Oldknow). SoDakR (21:1) Spr 83, p. 78.

2173. JANAC, Lou
"Catoctin Mountains." YetASM (1:1) 82, p. 5.
"Uncle Willie's Rose." YetASM (1:1) 82, p. 4.

2174. JANKIEWICZ, Henry
"The Night Sea Journey" (after Paul Klee's painting "Sinbad the Sailor" or "Fight Scene from the Comic Opera 'The Seafarer'"). ThirdW Spr 83, p. 89-93.
"Shadow." KanQ (15:1) Wint 83, p. 80.

2175. JANKOLA, Beth
"Crying." Quarry (32:4) Aut 83, p. 19.

2176. JANOWITZ, Phyllis
"Culmination." Ploughs (9:1) 83, p. 104-105.
"Let's All Get Up." Ploughs (9:1) 83, p. 102-103.
"Mnemonists." MichQR (22:1) Wint 83, p. 31-32.
"Tarentella." Ploughs (9:1) 83, p. 108-109.
"Theater of Operation." Ploughs (9:1) 83, p. 106-107.

2177. JANSONS, Grace Williams
"A Phinney Ridge, West Woodland Zoo Morning" (to the woman in the pink coat). YetASM (2:1) 83, p. 12.

2178. JANZEN, Jean
"The Calling." ChrC (100:7) 9 Mr 83, p. 213.
"Every Year the Bodies." PoetL (78:2) Sum 83, p. 90.

2179. JARMAN, Mark
"Ballad of Larry and Club." Kayak (61) Ap 83, p. 32-35.
"Cavafy in Redondo." NewYorker (59:11) 2 My 83, p. 44-45.
"Elegy for Redondo Beach." ThRiPo (21/22) 83, p. 42.
"Half Sonnets." OhioR (30) 83, p. 232-233.
"Mr. Numb." Kayak (62) Ag 83, p. 64.

2180. JASON, Philip K.
"Recitation." Wind (13:48) 83, p. 32-33.

2181. JASPER, Pat
"Between Toronto and Duluth" (for my sister). CrossC (5:2/3) 83, p. 17.

"Late Afternoon in Chincoteague." MalR (64) F 83, p. 200-201.
"Recycling." CanLit (97) Sum 83, p. 37-38.
"Substitutions" (for my mother). AntigR (53) Spr 83, p. 108-109.
"Trappings." MalR (64) F 83, p. 199.

2182. JASTRUN, Thomasz
"Sleeplessness" (tr. by Boguslaw Rostworowski). TriQ (57, Vol. 1) Spr-Sum 83, p. 59.

2183. JAWOLICA, Daniel
"She Touched Me." PoetryCR (5:1) Aut 83, p. 18.

2184. JAY-BONN, David
"Atom Baby." SanFPJ (4:4) 83, p. 48.

2185. JEANNE, Ave
"Balance." SanFPJ (5:4) 83, p. 25.
"Empty Tepee." SanFPJ (5:3) 83, p. 47.
"From Agent Orange." SanFPJ (5:4) 83, p. 28.
"Galactic Virginity." SanFPJ (5:3) 83, p. 47.
"Incrustations of the Vietnam War." SanFPJ (5:3) 83, p. 46.
"Is Anyone There?" SanFPJ (5:4) 83, p. 53.
"Overcast." SanFPJ (5:3) 83, p. 46.
"Overload." SanFPJ (5:4) 83, p. 56.

2186. JELLEMA, Rod
"Application." GeoR (37:3) Aut 83, p. 566-567.
"A Double Contention against the Scriptures." WestB (12) 83, p. 30.
"First Climb Up Three Surfers' Peak" (a dune at Lost Valley, on Lake Michigan, named in memory of John Jellema, Todd Eaddy, and Bill Smalligan -- d.1973). ThRiPo (21/22) 83, p. 45-46.
"I'd Like to Have a Few Words with You." WestB (12) 83, p. 32.
"Letter from Friesland to My Sons." PoetL (78:2) Sum 83, p. 69-70.
"The Self Trying to Leave the Body That It Is." WestB (12) 83, p. 29.
"Skating It Off." PoetL (78:2) Sum 83, p. 71.
"Trout Run: A Poem for Death in Seven Movements" (for John and Helen Clendenin). PoetL (77:3) Aut 82, p. 142-148.
"Wilt Dormer Going to Work." PoetL (78:2) Sum 83, p. 70.
"Wire Triangulations." WestB (12) 83, p. 31.

2187. JENCKES, Norma
"On Seeing Die Soldaten at the Boston Opera." SanFPJ (5:1) 83, p. 29.

2188. JENDRZEJCZYK, L. M.
"The River." ChrC (100:24) 17-24 Ag 83, p. 736.

2189. JENKINS, Louis
"Black Spruce." BlackWR (10:1) Aut 83, p. 118-119.
"The Painter." PoetryE (11) Sum 83, p. 37.

2190. JENKINS, Nigel
"Nostalgia." Bogg (50) 83, p. 59.

2191. JENNINGS, Catherine
"Brave Horizons." LittleM (14:1/2) 83, p. 82.
"The Ice Maiden." LittleM (14:1/2) 83, p. 79.
"Saint Munditia." LittleM (14:1/2) 83, p. 80-81.

2192. JENNINGS, Kate
"Crying in Anger." FourQt (32:4) Sum 83, p. 13.
"High Moon." PraS (57:3) Aut 83, p. 55.
"Orient & Flume" (Chico). PraS (57:3) Aut 83, p. 56-57.
"She Declines His Invitation." PraS (57:3) Aut 83, p. 54-55.
"Used Moon." SouthernPR (23:2) Aut 83, p. 52.

2193. JENNINGS, Lane
"The Ancient Voyager Remembers." ThirdW Spr 83, p. 101.
"Bottom One." Vis (11) 83, p. 35.
"Omar Khayyam and the Voyager Probes." Vis (12) 83, p. 4.

2194. JENNINGS, Michael
"A Dream Of Falling" (in memory of Karl Wallenda). SewanR (91:3) Sum 83, p. 385.

2195. JENSEN, Laura
"Adoration of the Anchor." Field (29) Aut 83, p. 64.
"George." Field (29) Aut 83, p. 62.
"Lessons." Field (29) Aut 83, p. 63.
"Mountaintop." Telescope (5/6) Spr 83, p. 147.
"Shorn." Iowa (13:2) Spr 82, p. 74.

2196. JENTZSCH, Bernd
"Beneath Clouds" (tr. by Agnes Stein). PoetL (77:4) Wint 83, p. 202.
"The Place" (tr. by Agnes Stein). PoetL (77:4) Wint 83, p. 201.

2197. JEWINSKI, Ed
"Feature of Sylvia Plath in Chatelaine." Grain (11:3) Ag 83, p. 19.

2198. JOANS, Ted
"Gallup Jack" (to J.K.). MoodySI (10) Aut 81, p. 16.
"Holy Hijinks" (in memory of Jack Kerouac). MoodySI (6/7) Wint-Spr 80, p. 15.
"The Wild Spirit of Kicks" (in memory of Jack Kerouac). MoodySI (8) Sum-Aut 80, p. 13.

JOHN of the SUN, Saint
See: ST. JOHN of the SUN

2199. JOHNSEN, Gretchen
"Love Poem for Perry Mason." Bogg (51) 83, p. 6.

2200. JOHNSON, Ann Klein
"7:35 A.M., Fluorescent Time." EngJ (72:7) N 83,

p. 79.

2201. JOHNSON, Bonnie L.
"Ankh." 13thM (6:1/2) 82, p. 27.

2202. JOHNSON, Carolyn
"Arkansas." Images (8:3) 83, p. 6.

2203. JOHNSON, Denis
"At Which This Is an Attempt." Tendril (14/15) Wint 83, p. 232.
"The Basement." Tendril (14/15) Wint 83, p. 228.
"In Palo Alto." Iowa (13:2) Spr 82, p. 71.
"Man Walking to Work." Tendril (14/15) Wint 83, p. 233.
"Movie within a Movie." Tendril (14/15) Wint 83, p. 229-230.
"The Night before the Hallowed Evening." Tendril (14/15) Wint 83, p. 235.
"Our Sadness." Tendril (14/15) Wint 83, p. 236.
"The Past." Tendril (14/15) Wint 83, p. 238-239.
"Poem: Loving you is every bit as fine." Tendril (14/15) Wint 83, p. 224.
"Proposal to Misty." Iowa (13:2) Spr 82, p. 72.
"Regarding L-." Tendril (14/15) Wint 83, p. 237.
"Sonnets Called 'On the Sacredness'." Tendril (14/15) Wint 83, p. 222-223.
"Talking Richard Wilson Blues, by Richard Clay Wilson." Tendril (14/15) Wint 83, p. 225-227.
"Travelling." Tendril (14/15) Wint 83, p. 234.
"Window." Tendril (14/15) Wint 83, p. 231.

2204. JOHNSON, Don
"Carrying Drunks Upriver." PoetL (77:1) Spr 82, p. 22-23.
"Keiko." PoetL (77:1) Spr 82, p. 24-25.

2205. JOHNSON, Eric
"The Dancer" (tr. of George Faludy). CanLit (98) Aut 83, p. 7-9.

2206. JOHNSON, Frank
"Southern Moves." PoetL (78:3) Aut 83, p. 146.

2207. JOHNSON, Greg
"Waking Blind." SouthernHR (17:3) Sum 83, p. 222-223.

2208. JOHNSON, Jean Youell
"Cocktail Party." Bogg (50) 83, p. 5.
"Missy." Bogg (51) 83, p. 8.

2209. JOHNSON, Kate Knapp
"Wanting You." Tendril (14/15) Wint 83, p. 117-118.

2210. JOHNSON, Keith Cowell
"Poem after the Subterraneans." MoodySI (13) Sum 83, p. 17.

2211. JOHNSON, Linda Wikene
"Backroad Winter." Descant (43) Wint 83-84, p. 77-79.
"Northern B.C. Notes." Descant (43) Wint 83-84, p. 76.

2212. JOHNSON, Marilyn
"The Detachment." Field (28) Spr 83, p. 24.

2213. JOHNSON, Markham
"Teresa Feldertova." IndR (6:3) Sum 83, p. 69.

2214. JOHNSON, Michael L.
"Hiroshima" (tr. of Jorge Debravo). PortR (29:1) 83, p. 26-27.
"A Hole in the Ceiling" (For Kathleen). KanQ (15:2) Spr 83, p. 102.
"Opening." Pig (11) 83, p. 23.
"Parabola." PortR (29:1) 83, p. 5.
"Seafront" (tr. of Eugenio Montale). PortR (29:1) 83, p. 75.
"To a Coquette." PortR (29:1) 83, p. 8.

2215. JOHNSON, Nancy
"Barbara" (from Paroles, tr. of Jacques Prevert). Vis (11) 83, p. 6-7.

2216. JOHNSON, Peter (See also: JOHNSON, Peter M.)
"A Fact Hitherto Unknown." YetASM (1:1) 82, p. 8.
"The Late Show." YetASM (1:1) 82, p. 7.

2217. JOHNSON, Peter M. (See also: JOHNSON, Peter)
"Beginning at the End." Tendril (14/15) Wint 83, p. 119.
"Coat." SouthernPR (23:2) Aut 82 [i.e. (23:1?) Spr 83], p. 71.
"Hanger." SouthernPR (23:2) Aut 82 [i.e. (23:1?) Spr 83], p. 71.
"A Minor Character in an Obscure Legend." Pig (11) 83, p. 80.
"One Downsmanship." Pig (11) 83, p. 64.
"A Poem to Be Translated into Russian" (for Steve Gizitsky). IndR (6:3) Sum 83, p. 64.

2218. JOHNSON, Ronald
"Ark 48, Fountain I." CreamCR (8:1/2) 83, p. 176.

2219. JOHNSON, Sam F.
"Vasectomy." YetASM (2:1) 83, p. 9.

2220. JOHNSON, Theresa (See also: JOHNSON, Theresa E.)
"Dear Mr. District Superintendent." EngJ (72:3) Mr 83, p. 88.

2221. JOHNSON, Theresa E. (See also: JOHNSON, Theresa)
"Marina." PraS (57:3) Aut 83, p. 58.

2222. JOHNSON, Thomas
"And Called, We Shall Rise." GeoR (37:4) Wint 83, p. 767.

"Inside." HolCrit (20:3) Je 83, p. 19.
"Respiratory Ode." ThRiPo (21/22) 83, p. 43.

2223. JOHNSON, William R.
"Onset." HiramPoR (35) Aut-Wint 83, p. 26.
"Some Glad Day We'll Fly Away." StoneC (10:3/4) Spr-Sum 83, p. 35.

2224. JOHNSTON, Fred
"Dead Leaves." Descant (43) Wint 83-84, p. 50.
"In Memoriam, Rahoon." Descant (43) Wint 83-84, p. 48-49.
"Old Lovers." Descant (43) Wint 83-84, p. 47.

2225. JOHNSTON, George
"Knowing" (for Betty). MalR (66) O 83, p. 104-105.
"Let Go." MalR (66) O 83, p. 102.
"Love and Marriage." MalR (66) O 83, p. 103.
"Remembering Venice" (for Bill Blissett). MalR (66) O 83, p. 105-106.

2226. JOHNSTON, Mark
"Aftermath." StoneC (10:3/4) Spr-Sum 83, p. 63.
"Beyond the Elegiac Principle." WindO (43) Wint 83, p. 37.
"Eight Unrelated Definitions." GeoR (37:4) Wint 83, p. 834.
"Into the Silver Zone." Tele (18) 83, p. 60.
"Jennings Beach at Dusk" (for Barbara). Tele (18) 83, p. 61-62.
"Kisses" (after Catullus). Argo (4:1) 82, p. 6.
"On Not Being Able to Make a Move." StoneC (10:3/4) Spr-Sum 83, p. 62-63.
"The Songs in the Branches." CentR (27:3) Sum 83, p. 191.
"War Movies in Reverse." NewEng (5:4) Sum 83, p. 550.

2227. JOHNSTON, Wayne
"Flying Fish, He Whispered, Are Superb." AntigR (52) Wint 83, p. 64-65.

2228. JOLLY, Diane L.
"Okomotos'." WorldO (17:4) Sum 83, p. 34.

2229. JONES
"Summer afternoon." PoetryCR (5:1) Aut 83, p. 18.

2230. JONES, Arlene S.
"Night Blindness." YetASM (2:1) 83, p. 3.

2231. JONES, D. G.
"For the Old Capitalist (re. a late watercolour by Rodin)." Os (16) 83, p. 5.
"Summer House: December." Os (16) 83, p. 4.

2232. JONES, Daryl
"Triangulation." BlackWR (8:1) Aut 81, p. 101.

JONES, Elizabeth Follin
See: FOLLIN-JONES, Elizabeth

2233. JONES, Emory D.
"Autumn Sunshine." NegC (3:4) Aut 83, p. 91.

2234. JONES, James David
"The Death We Give Our Children." MemphisSR (4:1) Aut 83, p. 25-26.
"The Face in the Crystal Ball." MemphisSR (3:2) Spr 83, p. 47.
"The Graves of Christ." MemphisSR (3:2) Spr 83, p. 46.
"Where the Anger Comes From." MemphisSR (4:1) Aut 83, p. 26.

2235. JONES, Paula
"Seven Bantu" (from Durable Poisons, semi-finalist, 10th anniversary manuscript competition). StoneC (11:1/2, Pt. 1) Aut-Wint 83, p. 63.

2236. JONES, Richard
"The Bell." VirQR (59:2) Spr 83, p. 235.
"In her lenity." NewL (49:3/4) Spr-Sum 83, p. 254.
"Levels of abstraction." NewL (49:3/4) Spr-Sum 83, p. 254.
"Old Lady." NewL (49:3/4) Spr-Sum 83, p. 254.

2237. JONES, Robert (See also: JONES, Robert L.)
"What Long Journey." ChrC (100:4) 2-9 F 83, p. 93.

2238. JONES, Robert L. (See also: JONES, Robert)
"Jeffrey." MissouriR (7:1) Aut 83, p. 30-31.
"Ode to the Urge" (tr. of Ricardo Castillo). MissouriR (7:1) Aut 83, p. 33.
"Some Reflections Beginning with the Disproportionate Length of My Feet" (tr. of Ricardo Castillo). MissouriR (7:1) Aut 83, p. 32.

2239. JONES, Tom
"Necklaces." KanQ (15:4) Aut 83, p. 60.

2240. JONESS, Wayne
"Why the People of Indiana Are Resorting to Violence." PoetryE (11) Sum 83, p. 49-50.

2241. JORDAN, June
"Second Poem from Nicaragua Libre: War Zone." LittleM (14:1/2) 83, p. 83.
"To Sing a Song of Palestine" (For Shulamith Koenig, an Israeli Peace Activist, 1982). PoetryE (9/10) Wint 82-Spr 83, p. 122-123.

2242. JOSEPH, Catherine
"Flesh-Eaters." HangL (44) Sum 83, p. 22-23.
"Overheard in Divorce Court." HangL (44) Sum 83, p. 21.

2243. JOSEPH, Jenny
"Extended Simile." Argo (5:1) 83, p. 17.

2244. JOSEPH, Lawrence
"Abba." Comm (110:1) 14 Ja 83, p. 19.
"The Great Society." Epoch (33:1) Aut-Wint 83, p. 66.
"I Think about Thigpen Again." ParisR (25:87) Spr 83, p. 127-128.
"In the Tenth Year of War." ParisR (25:87) Spr 83, p. 126.
"It's Not Me Shouting at No One." ParisR (25:87) Spr 83, p. 128.
"Partnership." PoetryE (11) Sum 83, p. 53.
"There I Am Again." PoetryE (11) Sum 83, p. 51-52.

2245. JOSEPHS, Laurence
"Here and There." Salm (60) Spr-Sum 83, p. 150.
"Seeing My Breath on the Air at Summer's End" (for Lynn Doe). Salm (60) Spr-Sum 83, p. 151.
"So Soon Goodbye." Salm (60) Spr-Sum 83, p. 149.
"The Vegetable Gourmet." Salm (60) Spr-Sum 83, p. 148.

2246. JOWETT, Derek
"1944, Adolescence." PottPort (5) 83-84, p. 19.

2247. JOY, Eugena
"To Alan." KanQ (15:4) Aut 83, p. 106.
"Truck Stop." KanQ (15:4) Aut 83, p. 106.

2248. JOYCE, Dianne
"Equinox." AntigR (55) Aut 83, p. 99.
"Seven O'Clock Lecture." AntigR (55) Aut 83, p. 100.

2249. JOYCE, Jane Wilson
"Timestep." YetASM (2:1) 83, p. 9.

2250. JOYCE, Jim
"Questions. Answers?" Quarry (32:4) Aut 83, p. 22.
"Seabedabbled, Fallen, Weltering." Quarry (32:4) Aut 83, p. 22-24.
"To Her Unveiling." Grain (11:1) F 83, p. 16-17.

2251. JOYCE, Thomas
"The Caged Fox." Grain (11:3) Ag 83, p. 11.
"Coming to Stone." Quarry (32:3) Sum 83, p. 4.
"Spring Bells." Quarry (32:3) Sum 83, p. 5-6.
"Stoneheart." Quarry (32:3) Sum 83, p. 4-5.

2252. JOZSEF, Attila
"My Mother" (tr. by Nicholas Kolumban). NewL (49:3/4) Spr-Sum 83, p. 137.

2253. JUANITA, Judy
"The Bus Terminal." 13thM (7:1/2) 83, p. 141.
"Three Percently." 13thM (7:1/2) 83, p. 142-144.

2254. JUBA, Shelia
"Men Working." YetASM (1:2) 82, p. 2.

2255. JUDSON, John
"Dragged out Psalm: 2 Jan. 80." ClockR (1:2) Wint 83-84, p. 37.
"Living on a Slant." OhioR (30) 83, p. 259.

2256. JUKOVSKY, Martin
"Mr. J Meditates." Bogg (50) 83, p. 11.

2257. JULANATO, Tereste
"Pasties." Bogg (51) 83, p. 26.
"The River Styx." Vis (12) 83, p. 28.

2258. JUMONVILLE, Lanier
"As I Remember It" (for L. Hennis). Wind (13:47) 83, p. 7.

2259. JUNGE, Jean
"To a Grandfather, Veteran of World War II." SanFPJ (5:2) 83, p. 90.

2260. JUNKINS, Donald
"Colors, Turnovers, 1933." SewanR (91:3) Sum 83, p. 386.
"Definition." Os (16) 83, p. 6-7.
"Hauling Traps with Theodore: A Midnight Narrative at Low Tide." MidwQ (24:4) Sum 83, p. 460-461.
"Horseshoes in Saugus, 1942." MidwQ (24:4) Sum 83, p. 462-463.
"Pickerel Fishing." NewEngR (5:3) Spr 83, p. 403-404.
"Playing Glassies with Dickie Mallar, 1943." MidwQ (24:4) Sum 83, p. 464-465.
"Talking in Spring." Os (16) 83, p. 8-9.

2261. JUSTICE, Donald
"First Death" (June 12, 1933). OhioR (30) 83, p. 236-237.
"On the Farm." Ploughs (9:2/3) 83, p. 14.
"On the Train, Heading North through Florida (And Ending with a Line from Thomas Wolfe)." NewYorker (59:43) 12 D 83, p. 52.

2262. JUSTICE, Jack R.
"Spreads Leathery Wings to Fly." HiramPoR (35) Aut-Wint 83, p. 27.

2263. KACHINSKE, Timothy
"1955" (tr. of Jozsef Utassy). PoetryE (9/10) Wint 82-Spr 83, p. 201.
"Arboretum" (tr. of Istvan Kovacs). PoetryE (9/10) Wint 82-Spr 83, p. 206.
"At a Nudist Beach" (tr. of Jozsef Utassy). PoetryE (9/10) Wint 82-Spr 83, p. 199-200.
"The Discovery of Europe" (tr. of Laszlo Gyori). PoetryE (9/10) Wint 82-Spr 83, p. 202.
"Fresco" (in the church at Csetnek) (tr. of Istvan Kovacs). PoetryE (9/10) Wint 82-Spr 83, p. 204-205.
"The Weight of Earth" (tr. of Laszlo Gyori). PoetryE (9/10) Wint 82-Spr 83, p. 203.

2264. KACHMAN, Geneva
"White Vein." WindO (43) Wint 83, p. 18.

2265. KAGEYAMA, Yuri
"Cecil Taylor." OroM (2:1, #5) Sum 83, p. 5.

2266. KALAMARAS, George
"The Hunter." Wind (13:47) 83, p. 21-22.
"Indiana, November." Wind (13:47) 83, p. 20-21.

2267. KALER, Anne K.
"Come to Bed, Sweet William." EngJ (72:5) S 83, p. 48.

2268. KALIKOFF, Beth
"Ships Ahoy! or, Thirty Years on the Uterine Canal." IndR (6:2) Spr 83, p. 68-69.

2269. KALLAS, Anthony
"And Though He Fought Like a Tiger He Went Down--He Went Down." SpoonRQ (8:4) Aut 83, p. 28.

2270. KALLET, Marilyn
"How to Get Heat without Fire." CarolQ (35:3) Spr 83, p. 21.

2271. KALLSEN, T. J.
"Anguish." WormR (23:1, issue 89) 83, p. 11.
"The Pond of the Fairmount Waterworks." Wind (13:49) 83, p. 17.
"A Pool Player's Love Poem." KanQ (15:3) Sum 83, p. 60.
"Revelation." WormR (23:1, issue 89) 83, p. 10.

2272. KALMAN, Judith
"Generation." Descant (43) Wint 83-84, p. 75.
"The House." Descant (43) Wint 83-84, p. 74.
"Lilith." Descant (43) Wint 83-84, p. 71-72.
"The Lover." Descant (43) Wint 83-84, p. 70.
"The Swimmer." Descant (43) Wint 83-84, p. 73.

2273. KALMTHOUT, Kees van
"Oldness." Vis (12) 83, p. 24.

2274. KALMUS, Morris A.
"The Graduate." SanFPJ (4:4) 83, p. 85.
"House and Street Scenes." SanFPJ (4:4) 83, p. 86-87.
"I'm Not a Ham." SanFPJ (5:3) 83, p. 60.
"Indian Story." SanFPJ (4:4) 83, p. 76.
"Man and Whale." SanFPJ (5:3) 83, p. 60.
"Walt Whitman's Song Again." SanFPJ (5:4) 83, p. 24.
"Weary Man." SanFPJ (5:2) 83, p. 53.

2275. KAMBOURELI, Smaro
"In the Second Person" (Selections: "July 7/82," "July 8/82"). Dandel (10:1) 83, p. 56-57.

2276. KAMEEN, Paul
"Motes." YetASM (2:1) 83, p. 9.

2277. KAMENETZ, Rodger
"Changing Names" (for A. Steiu (Andrei Codrescu)). Gargoyle (22/23) 83, p. 64-65.
"A Construction of Clouds." Shen (34:3) 83, p. 91.
"Elegy with Dandelions." SouthernR (19:2) Ap 83, p. 375.
"The Experimental Crossing." SouthernR (19:2) Ap 83, p. 370-374.
"Mallarme in Tournon." AntR (41:3) Sum 83, p. 335.

2278. KANE, Julie
"Airport Bar." Epoch (32:3) Spr-Sum 83, p. 242.

2279. KANE, Katherine
"George Sand, to Majorca and Back." OntR (19) Aut-Wint 83-84, p. 87-90.
"The Past at a Window Murmuring." NewL (50:1) Aut 83, p. 32.

2280. KANE, Paul
"The Whores of Algeciras." Shen (34:3) 83, p. 86-87.

2281. KANES, Eveline L.
"Bonaparte" (tr. of Jürg Federspiel). PoetL (78:2) Sum 83, p. 81.
"Evil" (tr. of Jürg Federspiel). PoetL (78:2) Sum 83, p. 77.
"The Expected" (tr. of Jürg Federspiel). PoetL (78:2) Sum 83, p. 79.
"Instructor" (tr. of Jürg Federspiel). PoetL (78:2) Sum 83, p. 82.
"Pairing Off with Ghosts" (tr. of Jürg Federspiel). PoetL (78:2) Sum 83, p. 78.
"Paracelsus" (for Margarita, tr. of Jürg Federspiel). PoetL (78:2) Sum 83, p. 80.

2282. KANFER, Allen
"Green Is for Surgeons' Gowns." NegC (3:4) Aut 83, p. 77.
"Museums." YetASM (1:1) 82, p. 6.

2283. KANGAS, J. R.
"After an Ivan Albright." WebR (8:2) Aut 83, p. 69.
"The Dreams of Vera Fielding." WebR (8:2) Aut 83, p. 70.
"The Last and Only Poem for the One and Only." Outbr (12/13) Aut 83-Spr 84, p. 43.
"Thin." WebR (8:2) Aut 83, p. 71.

2284. KANSU, Ceyan Atuf
"Raman Elegy." SpiritSH (48) 82, p. 45.

2285. KAPLINSKI, Jaan
"Ashes of one world crumble upon the colors of another one" (tr. by the author and Sam Hamill). CharR (9:2) Aut 83, p. 84-85.
"Big black hedgehog eternity descending into the valley" (tr. by the author and Sam Hamill). CharR (9:2) Aut 83, p. 87.
"Everything melts" (tr. by the author and Sam

Hamill). CrabCR (1:2) Aut 83, p. 4.
"Honeybees through sunshine" (tr. by the author and Sam Hamill). CharR (9:2) Aut 83, p. 84.
"Near" (tr. by Sam Hamill). NowestR (21:2/3) 83, p. 72.
"Our shadows are very long" (tr. by the author and Sam Hamill). CrabCR (1:2) Aut 83, p. 5.
"Oven alone in the corner" (tr. by the author and Sam Hamill). CharR (9:2) Aut 83, p. 85-86.
"The same sea in us all red dark warm" (tr. by the author and Sam Hamill). CharR (9:2) Aut 83, p. 87-88.
"Summer's last evening" (tr. by the author and Sam Hamill). CrabCR (1:2) Aut 83, p. 4.
"Swarms of daws are flying home from the west" (tr. by the author and Sam Hamill). CharR (9:2) Aut 83, p. 88.
"To be Icarus and fall wings aflame into the burning buttercups" (tr. by the author and Sam Hamill). CharR (9:2) Aut 83, p. 85.
"What woke us" (tr. by the author and Sam Hamill). CrabCR (1:2) Aut 83, p. 4-5.
"You light-footed moss already on the window frame" (tr. by the author and Sam Hamill). CharR (9:2) Aut 83, p. 86-87.
"You, you moon" (tr. by the author and Sam Hamill). CrabCR (1:2) Aut 83, p. 5.

2286. KAPTER, Kapp
"I saw, at peace in the coffin." Northeast (Ser. 3:15) Sum 83, p. 32.

2287. KARAY, Diane
"Harvesting Treasure." ChrC (100:26) 14-21 S 83, p. 810.

2288. KARP, Vickie
"Tulips: A Selected History." NewYorker (59:34) 10 O 83, p. 54.

2289. KARPOWICZ, Tymoteusz
"A Silence Lesson" (tr. by the author and Reginald Gibbons). TriQ (57, Vol. 1) Spr-Sum 83, p. 2.

2290. KARR, Mary
"Diogenes Consoles a Friend" (For Bill Knott). AntR (41:1) Wint 83, p. 76.
"Diogenes Passes the Time" (for Robert Long). Poetry (142:3) Je 83, p. 157.
"Diogenes the Bartender Closes Up" (for David St. John). Poetry (142:3) Je 83, p. 158.
"For All I Know." AntR (41:1) Wint 83, p. 77.
"For My Children." Poetry (142:3) Je 83, p. 159-60.
"Hard Knocks." Poetry (142:3) Je 83, p. 155.
"Old Mistakes" (after Marina Tsvetayeva). AntR (41:1) Wint 83, p. 78.
"Vigil." Poetry (142:3) Je 83, p. 156.

2291. KASCHNITZ, Marie Luise
"Untitled Poem in Memoriam Elizabeth Langgässer."

PraS (57:4) Wint 83, p. 43.

KASEMI MAZANDERANI, Nosrat
See: MAZANDERANI, Nosrat Kasemi

2292. KASH, Marsha Elaine
"Everybody Has to Go Home Sometime." SecC (11:1/2) 83, p. 81-82.

2293. KASHIWAGI, Hiroshi
"Haircut." SecC (11:1/2) 83, p. 80.

2294. KASISCHKE, Laura
"Five Days." YetASM (2:1) 83, p. 9.

2295. KASPER, Michael
"Human Nature Not Yet Remade: A Play." WormR (23:1, issue 89) 83, p. 5.
"When we went overland from Ismir to India." WormR (23:1, issue 89) 83, p. 4.
"While washing the spoon we examine it thoroughly." WormR (23:1, issue 89) 83, p. 6.

2296. KASTMILER, Peter
"Evening lightshow." WindO (43) Wint 83, p. 3.
"In the almond's pith." WindO (43) Wint 83, p. 3.

2297. KASZUBA, Sophia
"Cold Spring." Descant (43) Wint 83-84, p. 32.
"Icebergs Huge As Sphinxes." Descant (43) Wint 83-84, p. 33.
"Moon: First Quarter." Descant (43) Wint 83-84, p. 31.

2298. KATES, J.
"Coitus, or Journeying Together." Swallow (2) Aut-Wint 83, p. 35.
"Imaginary Runners." Swallow (2) Aut-Wint 83, p. 36.

2299. KATO, Shuson
"Eyes of Pheasant" (Haiku, tr. by Minoru Fujita and Richard F. Fleck). Paint (10:19/20) Spr-Aut 83, p. 44.
"A frogfish frozen to the bone" (Haiku, tr. by Minoru Fujita and Richard F. Fleck). Paint (10:19/20) Spr-Aut 83, p. 44.

2300. KATROVAS, Richard
"Blues' Body." NewEngR (6:2) Wint 83, p. 236.
"Crimes." NoAmR (268:1) Mr 83, p. 20.
"Our Island." AntR (41:3) Sum 83, p. 327.
"Sailors" (for David). NewEngR (6:2) Wint 83, p. 235.

2301. KATZ, Susan A.
"Borrowing." YetASM (1:2) 82, p. 12.

2302. KAUFFMAN, Janet
"The Brethren Home." BlackWR (8:2) Spr 82, p. 24.
"The Man in the Pool." AmerPoR (12:1) Ja/F 83, p.

46.
"Materializing." BlackWR (8:2) Spr 82, p. 25.
"The Prison Guard." AmerPoR (12:1) Ja/F 83, p. 46.
"The World of Men." AmerPoR (12:1) Ja/F 83, p. 46.

2303. KAUFMAN, Bob
"Heavy Water Blues." SecC (11:1/2) 83, p. 85-86.
"I Wish." SecC (11:1/2) 83, p. 83.

2304. KAUFMAN, Chris
"Green Marble." SanFPJ (5:4) 83, p. 33.
"Sweat, Thirst and Stoop." SanFPJ (5:4) 83, p. 36.

2305. KAUFMAN, Debra
"Exercises." Prima (8) 83, p. 9.
"Plain View (1)." Pig (11) 83, p. 51.
"Plain View (2)." Pig (11) 83, p. 51.

2306. KAUFMAN, Ellen
"Cash Flow." Shen (34:4) 83, p. 77.
"Fishermen." Shen (34:4) 83, p. 78.

2307. KAUFMAN, Shirley
"Autumn Crocus." VirQR (59:2) Spr 83, p. 238-239.
"Crumbs" (Jerusalem, 1982). Kayak (62) Ag 83, p. 52-53.
"Elegies Close to the Senses" (Excerpt) (tr. of Meir Wieseltier). LitR (26:2) Wint 83, p. 271-272.
"Four Jerusalem Poems" (for Sahar) LitR (26:2) Wint 83, p. 315-317.
"Gazelle, I'll Send You" (tr. of Amir Gilboa). LitR (26:2) Wint 83, p. 220.
"Stones." VirQR (59:2) Spr 83, p. 237-238.
"To Pluck Stars" (tr. of Amir Gilboa). LitR (26:2) Wint 83, p. 219.
"To Write the Lips of Those Asleep" (Excerpt, tr. of Amir Gilboa). LitR (26:2) Wint 83, p. 220.
"Wind." VirQR (59:2) Spr 83, p. 237.
"Zipporah." LitR (26:2) Wint 83, p. 317.

2308. KAWABATA, Bosha
"A drop of dew" (Haiku, tr. by Minoru Fujita and Richard F. Fleck). Paint (10:19/20) Spr-Aut 83, p. 42.
"Gentle Fiddleheads" (Haiku, tr. by Minoru Fujita and Richard F. Fleck). Paint (10:19/20) Spr-Aut 83, p. 42.
"In glimmer of moon" (Haiku, tr. by Minoru Fujita and Richard F. Fleck). Paint (10:19/20) Spr-Aut 83, p. 42.

2309. KEARNS, Sherry
"Petunias." Blueline (5:1) Sum-Aut 83, p. 39.
"Summer." Blueline (5:1) Sum-Aut 83, p. 38.
"Watching Fireworks on the 4th of July in a Boat off Bolton Landing." Blueline (4:2) Wint-Spr 83, p. 28.

2310. KEATING, Diane
"The Wife of Bath Canticles." PoetryCR (4:3) Spr 83, p. 16.

KEATING, Helane Levine
See: LEVINE-KEATING, Helane

2311. KEEBLE, Lois
"Spring Time Warmth." Meadows (4:1) 83, p. 50.

2312. KEELER, Julia
"At Josie's." PoetL (78:3) Aut 83, p. 166.
"Harvest." AntigR (52) Wint 83, p. 54.
"Memory, Flesh and Bone." PoetL (78:3) Aut 83, p. 164-165.
"Texts." AntigR (52) Wint 83, p. 53.

2313. KEENAN, Deborah
"Declaration of February." NewEngR (5:3) Spr 83, p. 318-319.
"What Will Last" (Excerpt). SoDakR (21:4) Wint 83, p. 60.

2314. KEENAN, Jean E.
"Terror." SanFPJ (5:4) 83, p. 69.

2315. KEIDA, Yusuke
"Jack." MoodySI (10) Aut 81, p. 5.

2316. KEITH, E. M.
"The Death of Peter." EngJ (72:1) Ja 83, p. 66.

2317. KEITHLEY, George
"The Lovers." PoNow (7:2, #38) 83, p. 30.

2318. KELLER, David
"The Hut in the Woods." USl (16/17) Wint 83-84, p. 6.
"True." USl (16/17) Wint 83-84, p. 6.

2319. KELLER, Emily
"Sculpture in the Gallery, 4 Horses: Butterfield." YetASM (2:1) 83, p. 10.
"Where Have All the Heroes Gone?" NewRena (17) Aut 83, p. 66.

2320. KELLEY, Shannon Keith
"Dreaming Missouri." KanQ (15:2) Spr 83, p. 21.
"Stroke." CapeR (18:2) Sum 83, p. 16-17.

2321. KELLY, Brigit Pegeen
"Christmas Eve, Old People's Guild, Mt. Angel." PoetryNW (24:3) Aut 83, p. 18-19.
"The Convent Park beneath My Window at the Hotel Charles." Poetry (141:4) Ja 83, p. 205-206.
"The Greek Alphabet" (for Christine Psathas). PoetryNW (24:3) Aut 83, p. 19-20.
"Mount Angel." Poetry (141:4) Ja 83, p. 207.
"Shepherd's Purse." BelPoJ (34:1) Aut 83, p. 22-30.
"Two Girls in a Study Lounge." PoetryNW (24:3)

Aut 83, p. 16-17.

2322. KELLY, Dennis
"Fay Wray Has Collapsed" (after Frank O'Hara, from Chicken). PoNow (7:2, #38) 83, p. 24.
"Riding the Horse" (from Chicken). PoNow (7:2, #38) 83, p. 24.

2323. KELLY, James E.
"A Land No Eyes Should See." SanFPJ (5:3) 83, p. 69.

2324. KELLY, Joseph
"Arms Race." Vis (11) 83, p. 13.

2325. KELLY, Michael
"Bad Knees." MidwQ (24:2) Wint 83, p. 180-181.
"Fixing the House." MidwQ (24:2) Wint 83, p. 178-179.
"The Scholar Turns Forty." MidwQ (24:2) Wint 83, p. 174-175.
"The Scholar Turns Forty Again." MidwQ (24:2) Wint 83, p. 176-177.

2326. KELLY, Tracey
"Poem: Sometimes I touch him." Bogg (50) 83, p. 12.

2327. KEMAL, Yahya
"Autumn" (tr. by Roger Finch). SoDakR (21:1) Spr 83, p. 70.
"Bir Baska Tepeden." SoDakR (21:1) Spr 83, p. 63.
"Bir Tepeden." SoDakR (21:1) Spr 83, p. 63.
"End of September" (tr. by Roger Finch). SoDakR (21:1) Spr 83, p. 66.
"Eylul Sonu." SoDakR (21:1) Spr 83, p. 67.
"From a Hill" (tr. by Roger Finch). SoDakR (21:1) Spr 83, p. 62.
"From Another Hill" (tr. by Roger Finch). SoDakR (21:1) Spr 83, p. 62.
"Kar Musikileri." SoDakR (21:1) Spr 83, p. 65.
"Mihriyar." SoDakR (21:1) Spr 83, p. 69.
"Mihriyar" (tr. by Roger Finch). SoDakR (21:1) Spr 83, p. 68.
"Snow Music" (tr. by Roger Finch). SoDakR (21:1) Spr 83, p. 64.
"Sonbahar." SoDakR (21:1) Spr 83, p. 71.

2328. KEMP, Penny
"Birthday." PoetryCR (5:2) Wint 83-84, p. 14.
"What trick led me to you." PoetryCR (5:1) Aut 83, p. 9.

2329. KEMPHER, Ruth Moon
"Beast Babcock: A Redneck Enigma." WindO (43) Wint 83, p. 45-46.
"Hilda Halfheart's Notes to the Milkman: #67." Swallow (2) Aut-Wint 83, p. 47.
"Sleep Lust--a Fragment." FourQt (32:3) Spr 83, p. 11.
"The Young Prince's Tale, or: The Gypsy Lady Waxes Mytho-Etymological." Bogg (51) 83, p. 27.

2330. KENNEDY, Hugh
"Motes." AntigR (53) Spr 83, p. 95.
"Note." AntigR (53) Spr 83, p. 96.
"Uncharted Territory." AntigR (53) Spr 83, p. 96.

2331. KENNEDY, Terry
"For My Sister on Her 5th Wedding Anniversary." SecC (11:1/2) 83, p. 87-89.

2332. KENNEDY, X. J.
"Abyss (Le Gouffre)" (tr. of Charles Baudelaire). NegC (3:4) Aut 83, p. 105.
"Eavesdroppings" (a nosegay of overheard verses for James Tate's birthday." LittleBR (4:2) Wint 83-84, p. 46-47.
"Epigraph for a Banned Book (Epigraphe pour un Livre Condamne)" (tr. of Charles Baudelaire). NegC (3:4) Aut 83, p. 104.
"To a Hard Core Porn Film Leading Man." PoNow (7:2, #38) 83, p. 7.

2333. KENNEY, Richard
"The Enchantadas" (Selections: 1-7, 17, 20-23) (For Capt. Leslie Buchman, 1981). Poetry (142:1) Ap 83, p. 1-17.
"Fourth." NewYorker (59:20) 4 Jl 83, p. 42.
"In June." Atlantic (251:6) Je 83, p. 44.
"Speed of Light." NewYorker (59:3) 7 Mr 83, p. 50.

2334. KENNY, Maurice
"George Segal at the Whitney" (For Paul). Tele (18) 83, p. 57.
"Tonight We Go to Hear Muriel Rukeyser Read Her Poems at SUNY Buffalo, 1978 (Now, In Memory)." Tele (18) 83, p. 56.

2335. KENYON, Jane
"Coming Home at Twilight in Late Summer." Poetry (141:5) F 83, p. 280.
"Evening Sun." Poetry (141:5) F 83, p. 279.
"Indolence in Early Winter." NewL (49:3/4) Spr-Sum 83, p. 33.
"The Little Boat." Iowa (13:3/4) Spr 82 (83), p. 31-32.
"The Sandy Hole." Iowa (13:3/4) Spr 82 (83), p. 30.
"Teacher." Poetry (141:5) F 83, p. 278.

2336. KENYON, Susan
"Never Again." Poem (47) Mr 83, p. 8.
"Rain When It Fell Used to Wash Leaves." Poem (47) Mr 83, p. 6-7.

2337. KERCHEVAL, Jesse Lee
"Mama." Prima (8) 83, p. 78.

2338. KEROUAC, Jack
"239th Chorus." MoodySI (8) Sum-Aut 80, p. 1.
"But, Wifey, I did it all." MoodySI (9) Wint-Spr 81, p. 11.
"Chair Arm, Charm Air, or, A Spontaneous Commentary

on the Diamond Sutra, with Haiku." MoodySI (10) Aut 81, p. 4.
"Kline Jungs sind Engel" (tr. by Michael Mundhenk). MoodySI (10) Aut 81, p. 15.
"Little Boys Are Angels." MoodySI (10) Aut 81, p. 15.
"To Edward Dahlberg." MoodySI (6/7) Wint-Spr 80, p. 15.

2339. KERR, J. W. R.
"The Painting." Dandel (10:1) Spr-Sum 83, p. 55.

2340. KERR, Nora
"The Hare." RagMag (2:2) Aut 83, p. 13.
"Mnemonics." RagMag (2:2) Aut 83, p. 14.
"On the Beach at Beaver River." RagMag (2:2) Aut 83, p. 12.
"Tropism." RagMag (2:2) Aut 83, p. 12.

2341. KERRIGAN, Anthony
"The Cipher" (tr. of Jorge Louis Borges, w. Jeanne Cook). MalR (66) O 83, p. 147.
"Giacomo Casanova Accepts the Office of Librarian Offered Him in Bohemia by Count Waldstein" (tr. of Antonio Colinas). MalR (66) O 83, p. 146.
"Hard Times" (tr. by Heberto Padilla). MalR (64) F 83, p. 148-149.
"Since Then" (tr. of José Emilio Pacheco). DevQ (18:1) Spr 83, p. 93.
"To Encounter Ezra Pound -- Posthumous Instructions" (tr. of Antonio Colinas). MalR (66) O 83, p. 145.
"Turn of the Century" (tr. of José Emilio Pacheco). DevQ (18:1) Spr 83, p. 92.

2342. KERSCHE, Peter
"The Mountain" (tr. of Edvard Kocbek, w. Herbert Kuhner). Confr (25/26) 83, p. 303.

2343. KERSHNER, Brandon
"3 Dialogues." ModernPS (11:3) 83, p. 200-201.
"Annals of the Invisible Cowboy." ModernPS (11:3) 83, p. 205-207.
"Doppler at Cedar Key." ModernPS (11:3) 83, p. 204-205.
"Dropping Falls, Lancashire: Brochure." ModernPS (11:3) 83, p. 203.
"Falling with Money" (for D. B. Cooper). ModernPS (11:3) 83, p. 202.
"The Gift." ModernPS (11:3) 83, p. 199.
"My grandmother meant it when she died." ModernPS (11:3) 83, p. 203-204.
"A Translation." ModernPS (11:3) 83, p. 201-202.

2344. KESSELMAN, Sandra
"Grita de Dolores." SanFPJ (5:2) 83, p. 26-27.
"The Insurance Man." SanFPJ (5:2) 83, p. 69.

2345. KESSLER, Clyde
"Grasshopper Sparrow." StoneC (10:3/4) Spr-Sum

83, p. 55.

2346. KESSLER, Jascha
"Cognition, Language, Poetry" (tr. of Lászlò Nagy). LitR (26:3) Spr 83, p. 442-443.
"Razglednica" (tr. of Miklos Radnoti). PoNow (7:2, #38) 83, p. 45.

2347. KESSLER, Milton
"Secret Love." MSS (2:3) Sum 83, p. 58-59.

2348. KESSLER, Stephen
"La Ceiba Gardens" (tr. of Fernando Alegria). AmerPoR (12:5) S/O 83, p. 7.

2349. KEVORKIAN, Karen
"Softball Dreams." MassR (24:2) Sum 83, p. 412-413.

2350. KEYS, Kerry Shawn
"One Butterfly" (for Miguel De Unamuno). DevQ (18:3) Aut 83, p. 97.
"The Predicament." DevQ (18:3) Aut 83, p. 99.
"Riddle-Dee-Dee." DevQ (18:3) Aut 83, p. 98.

2351. KGOSITSILE, Keorapetse
"My sister." PoetryE (9/10) Wint 82-Spr 83, p. 274-275.

2352. KHLEBNIKOV, Velimir
"Bakunin Baking in Baku" (Excerpt) (tr. by Paul Schmidt). Sulfur (3:1, #7) 83, p. 117.
"Bow! Wow! Bow!" (tr. by Paul Schmidt). Sulfur (3:1, #7) 83, p. 115-116.
"Crawling crying craven" (tr. by Paul Schmidt). Sulfur (3:1, #7) 83, p. 116.
"Laffers love laffing" (tr. by Paul Schmidt). Sulfur (3:1, #7) 83, p. 117-118.
"The law of the see-saw argues" (tr. by Paul Schmidt). Sulfur (3:1, #7) 83, p. 117.
"Let the plowman leave his furrow" (tr. by Paul Schmidt). Nat (237:8) 24 S 83, p. 248.
"Night's color breeding darker blues" (tr. by Paul Schmidt). Nat (237:8) 24 S 83, p. 248.
"Once more, once more" (tr. by Paul Schmidt). Nat (237:8) 24 S 83, p. 248.
"P pay o P" (tr. by Paul Schmidt). Sulfur (3:1, #7) 83, p. 116.
"Water eats at the ash-grove" (tr. by Paul Schmidt). Nat (237:8) 24 S 83, p. 248.
"Wind whose song" (tr. by Paul Schmidt). Sulfur (3:1, #7) 83, p. 115.

KHUSROW DEHLAVI, Amir
See: DEHLAVI, Amir Khusrow

2353. KICH, Martin (Marty)
"Culm Fires." WestB (12) 83, p. 57.
"Letters." ColEng (45:4) Ap 83, p. 361.

2354. KICKNOSWAY, Faye
"The Clothesline." NewL (50:1) Aut 83, p. 34-35.
"Portrait." NewL (50:1) Aut 83, p. 33-34.

2355. KIEFER, Rita B. (Rita Brady)
"Canyons." YetASM (1:1) 82, p. 10.
"It Could Have Appeared in the Annals." Vis (12) 83, p. 21.

2356. KILGORE, James C.
"Another Ecclesiastical Morning" (April 2, 1983). BlackALF (17:4) Wint 83, p. 172.
"Like the Drunk." BlackALF (17:4) Wint 83, p. 173.
"Page 3." BlackALF (17:4) Wint 83, p. 173.
"Page 3." Pig (11) 83, p. 21.
"Time Is More Than Money." BlackALF (17:4) Wint 83, p. 173.

2357. KILMER, Charles A.
"White Clapboard House in October." Ploughs (9:2/3) 83, p. 139-140.

2358. KIMBRO, Harriet
"Haiku: Light travels into and out of my mind." LittleBR (3:3) Spr 83, p. 62.

2359. KIMM, Dan
"Soliloquy." Meadows (4:1) 83, p. 49.

2360. KIMMET, Gene
"A Slight Misunderstanding." SpoonRQ (8:4) Aut 83, p. 58.
"Who's Who in Elburn." SpoonRQ (8:2) Spr 83, p. 6-7.

2361. KINDILIEN, Glenn
"Happy Trails" (for Lumpy Barnum). SmPd (20:2) Spr 83, p. 30.

2362. KING, Fred
"Jack: October Photograph." MoodySI (9) Wint-Spr 81, p. 17.

2363. KING, Lyn
"Flying." MalR (66) O 83, p. 125.
"His Waiting." MalR (66) O 83, p. 127.
"Joyce and the Broken Window." Descant (41) Sum 83, p. 89.
"Meet Jane, Dick's Wife." MalR (66) O 83, p. 126.
"On Refusing to be Born during Wartime." Descant (41) Sum 83, p. 91.
"Pictures." MalR (66) O 83, p. 124.
"The Promise." Descant (41) Sum 83, p. 90.
"Suddenly." MalR (66) O 83, p. 128.
"The Thought." Descant (41) Sum 83, p. 88.
"When It Was Before." Descant (41) Sum 83, p. 92.

2364. KING, Mary
"Easter Sunday." NewRena (16) Spr 83, p. 47.

2365. KING, Robert
"Looking for Sound." KanQ (15:2) Spr 83, p. 136.
"Morning in the Apartment." KanQ (15:2) Spr 83, p. 136.

2366. KINNELL, Galway
"Memory of Wilmington." ThRiPo (21/22) 83, p. 47-48.

2367. KINNETT, Elizabeth
"O Not with a Word." Poem (47) Mr 83, p. 27.
"Requiem." Poem (47) Mr 83, p. 26.

2368. KINNICT, Kinni
"The American Sideshow." SanFPJ (5:3) 83, p. 62.
"The American Way." SanFPJ (5:3) 83, p. 54.
"Connotations." SanFPJ (5:3) 83, p. 54.
"Contemporary Definitions." SanFPJ (4:3) 83, p. 36.
"Dust Bowl Dreamin'." SanFPJ (4:4) 83, p. 43.
"Economic Dogmas." SanFPJ (4:4) 83, p. 56.
"Executive Privilege." SanFPJ (4:2) 83, p. 36.
"Gin and Fizz." SanFPJ (5:2) 83, p. 24.
"Human Blues." SanFPJ (5:1) 83, p. 65.
"Memories of Money." SanFPJ (5:1) 83, p. 65.
"The Midway." Vis (13) 83, p. 25.
"Monster Movie." SanFPJ (4:2) 83, p. 9.
"The New Punch and Judy Show." SanFPJ (5:2) 83, p. 22-24.
"Reaganatomics." SanFPJ (5:3) 83, p. 55.
"The Space Archeologist." SanFPJ (4:4) 83, p. 42.

2369. KINOSHITA, Tetsuo
"A Cliff" (tr. of Rin Ishigaki). PoetryE (9/10) Wint 82-Spr 83, p. 227-228.
"Expulsion" (tr. of Kio Kuroda). PoetryE (9/10) Wint 82-Spr 83, p. 232-233.
"Greetings to the Tiny Herd" (tr. Takaai Yoshimoto). PoetryE (9/10) Wint 82-Spr 83, p. 233-234.
"Mao Tse-tung" (tr. of Gan Tanigawa). PoetryE (9/10) Wint 82-Spr 83, p. 230-231.
"Paulow's Crane" (tr. of Ryusei Hasegawa). PoetryE (9/10) Wint 82-Spr 83, p. 229-230.
"When I Was Most Beautiful in My Life" (tr. of Noriko Ibaraki). PoetryE (9/10) Wint 82-Spr 83, p. 226-227.

2370. KINSEY, Ralph L.
"Nothing Numinous Else." Iowa (13:3/4) Spr 82 (83), p. 128.

2371. KINZIE, Mary
"The Commissioner of Baseball." Thrpny (4:2, issue 14) Sum 83, p. 17.
"In the Queen's Chamber." ChiR (34:1) Sum 83, p. 49-50.
"Small Seasons." ChiR (34:1) Sum 83, p. 51-52.
"To the Architect." ChiR (34:1) Sum 83, p. 48.
"Words in a Garden." SouthernR (19:2) Ap 83, p. 388-392.

KIO, Kuroda
See: KURODA, Kio

2372. KIRBY, David
"After Midnight." SouthernHR (17:2) Spr 83, p. 170.
"The Clairvoyant." ThRiPo (19/20) 82, p. 46.
"Conversations with the Dead" (First Award Poem, 1982/83). KanQ (15:1) Wint 83, p. 7.
"Going after My Glasses." PoetL (78:4) Wint 84, p. 197.
"Looking for the Poem That Explains It All." Ploughs (9:2/3) 83, p. 224.
"Sexual Purvis." SouthernPR (23:2) Aut 83, p. 56-57.
"Unnatural Acts" (First Award Poem, 1982/83). KanQ (15:1) Wint 83, p. 7.

2373. KIRBY-SMITH, H. T.
"Bent Tones." Ploughs (9:2/3) 83, p. 82.
"Clocks and Crickets." Ploughs (9:2/3) 83, p. 83-84.
"Familiarity." Ploughs (9:2/3) 83, p. 87-88.
"Highland Rim." Ploughs (9:2/3) 83, p. 85-86.

2374. KIRKLAND, Will
"Song of Frustration of the Dreamer Child" (tr. of Miguel Labordeta). NewOR (10:4) Wint 83, p. 98.
"The Stars" (tr. of Carlos Edmundo de Ory). NewOR (10:4) Wint 83, p. 81.
"Weariness of Pleasure" (tr. of Carlos Edmundo de Ory). NewOR (10:4) Wint 83, p. 70.
"Winter Duck" (For Antonio, tr. of José Angel Valente). PoNow (7:2, #38) 83, p. 46.

2375. KIRKWOOD, Judith
"Another Poem from the Balcony." IndR (6:1) Wint 83, p. 64.

2376. KIRN, Walter
"Completion of Simonides." Shen (34:2) 83, p. 99.

2377. KITAGAWA, Kurtis Gene
"Dream." Dandel (10:1) Spr-Sum 83, p. 52.
"Edible Struggles." Dandel (10:1) Spr-Sum 83, p. 54.
"Thin Tin Wood Wind (Fish Creek West)." Dandel (10:1) Spr-Sum 83, p. 53.

2378. KITCHEN, Judith
"Solstice" (for Nancy). SouthernPR (23:2) Aut 82 [i.e. (23:1?) Spr 83], p. 63.
"Tell Her" (Explaining Pictures of Starvation to a Child). ThRiPo (21/22) 83, p. 49.
"Tell Her" (Explaining Pictures of Starvation to a Child). ThRiPo (19/20) 82, p. 47.
"Upstairs Window." SouthernPR (23:2) Aut 83, p. 58.

2379. KITTELL, Ronald Edward
"Aphorism." PortR (29:1) 83, p. 130.

KIYOKO, Miura
See: MIURA, Kiyoko

2380. KIZER, Carolyn
"Afternoon Happiness." Poetry (143:3) D 83, p. 156-157.
"Bitch." Poetry (143:3) D 83, p. 159.
"A Child's Guide to Central Ohio." Poetry (143:3) D 83, p. 160-161.
"Thrall." Poetry (143:3) D 83, p. 157-158.

2381. KLAPPERT, Peter
"Adolphe, or the Sad Young Man." MemphisSR (2:1) Aut 81, p. 14-15.

2382. KLAWITTER, George
"Lincoln Park." PoetL (78:4) Wint 84, p. 218.

2383. KLEIN, Binnie
"Sadness When Our Fathers Do Not Get Along." StoneC (10:3/4) Spr-Sum 83, p. 68.

2384. KLEIN, Chris
"Juggler." PoetL (77:3) Aut 82, p. 165.

2385. KLEINSCHMIDT, Edward
"Arrangement in Black." PoetryNW (24:1) Spr 83, p. 13-14.
"Election Day Speech" PoetryNW (24:1) Spr 83, p. 14-15.
"An Epileptic Watches an Eclipse of the Moon." PoetryNW (24:1) Spr 83, p. 15-16.
"Go on Living." PoetryNW (24:4) Wint 83-84, p. 7-8.
"The Magnificent Romance." PoetryNW (24:4) Wint 83-84, p. 5-6.
"Moments before the End." PoetryNW (24:2) Sum 83, p. 42-43.
"The Next Day." MSS (3:1) Aut 83, p. 185-186.
"Note for a Suicide." PoetryNW (24:4) Wint 83-84, p. 6-7.
"Onion." LittleM (14:1/2) 83, p. 12.
"Relief Map of Africa." MSS (2:3) Sum 83, p. 113-114.
"When and Where I Am Visualized." PoetryNW (24:2) Sum 83, p. 43-44.

2386. KLEINZAHLER, August
"An Autumnal Sketch." Sulfur (3:1, #7) 83, p. 150.
"Canada Geese in New Jersey." Thrpny (3:4, issue 12) Wint 83, p. 19.
"Cautionary Lines for a Thriftless Lady." Sulfur (3:1, #7) 83, p. 146-147.
"A February Idyll." Sulfur (3:1, #7) 83, p. 148-149.
"Real Hair." Sulfur (3:1, #7) 83, p. 147.
"The Tunnel of Love." Sulfur (3:1, #7) 83, p. 147-148.
"Vancouver" (with Papa K). Sulfur (3:1, #7) 83, p. 149-150.

2387. KLOEFKORN, William (Bill)
"Chief Bronze." KanQ (15:1) Wint 83, p. 98.
"Collecting for the Wichita Beacon." IndR (6:2) Spr 83, p. 75.

"An Open Prose Poem to Dave Etter." SpoonRQ (8:2) Spr 83, p. 1.
"Requiem for Cory Batt of Rural Melbeta, Nebraska." KanQ (15:1) Wint 83, p. 97.
"The Walk at Sundown." IndR (6:2) Spr 83, p. 74.

2388. KLOSTERMANN, Kerry J. W.
"The Post." CapeR (18:2) Sum 83, p. 7.

2389. KNIGHT, Ann
"Letter Home." Quarry (32:1) Wint 83, p. 44-45.
"On the First Day of Christmas." Quarry (32:1) Wint 83, p. 44.
"The Will to Live" (in memory of Judith Sloman). Quarry (32:1) Wint 83, p. 45-46.

2390. KNIGHT, Arthur W. (Arthur Winfield)
"Anniversary." SecC (11:1/2) 83, p. 90-92.
"Artists." Bogg (50) 83, p. 21.
"The Beatnik and the Fishmonger." Bogg (50) 83, p. 4.
"The Gift." Abraxas (27/28) 83, p. 34.
"The Nap." Bogg (51) 83, p. 4.
"Throwing popcorn." Bogg (51) 83, p. 52.

2391. KNIGHT, Etheridge
"At a V.A. Hospital in the Middle of the United States of America: An Act in a Play." PoetryE (9/10) Wint 82-Spr 83, p. 107-109.
"A Black Poet Leaps to His Death" (for Mbembe Milton Smith). AmerPoR (12:3) My-Je 83, p. 22.
"Once on a Night in the Delta: A Report from Hell" (for Sterling Brown). AmerPoR (12:3) My-Je 83, p. 22.

2392. KNIGHT, Kit
"Dr. Steve and Miss Molly." Bogg (51) 83, p. 9.

2393. KNOELLER, Christian
"At West Turner Lake 8/22/82." EngJ (72:5) S 83, p. 78.
"The Light." WestB (12) 83, p. 53.
"Yellow Walk." WestB (13) 83, p. 82.

2394. KNOEPFLE, John
"Another Nile for Pharoah." NewL (50:1) Aut 83, p. 73.
"Self Made in Bloomington." SpoonRQ (8:2) Spr 83, p. 2.
"WW Two Vet." NewL (50:1) Aut 83, p. 74.

2395. KNOLL, Michael
"Anna López." Confr (25/26) 83, p. 302.
"Motion" (After Edward Hopper). WestHR (37:2) Sum 83, p. 126.
"Opium." Confr (25/26) 83, p. 301.
"Vigil." Confr (25/26) 83, p. 301.

2396. KNOTT, Bill
"Lesson." ParisR (24:85) Aut 82, p. 90.

"Mitts and Gloves" (for Tom Lux). ParisR (24:85) Aut 82, p. 95-96.
"October." ParisR (24:85) Aut 82, p. 92.
"The Panther." ParisR (24:85) Aut 82, p. 91.
"Sun, Sea, Rain, Rain Season, Port Townsend, Washington" (for Tess Gallagher). ParisR (24:85) Aut 82, p. 93-94.

2397. KNOX, Caroline
"Sacagawea." MassR (24:2) Sum 83, p. 387-391.

2398. KNUTSON, Nancy Roxbury
"Anonymity." Nimrod (27:1) Aut-Wint 83, p. 58.
"Stand Off." AmerPoR (12:3) My-Je 83, p. 46.

2399. KOCBEK, Edvard
"The Mountain" (tr. by Herbert Kuhner and Peter Kersche). Confr (25/26) 83, p. 303.

2400. KOCH, Tom
"Playboy's Christmas Cards: Missives and Missiles for the Jolly Season." Playb (30:12) D 83, p. 146-147.
"To a Home Computer Owner." Playb (30:12) D 83, p. 146.
"To a Local TV Anchor Man." Playb (30:12) D 83, p. 147.
"To Hollywood's Hunks." Playb (30:12) D 83, p. 147.
"To Queen Elizabeth II." Playb (30:12) D 83, p. 147.
"To the Author of Hitler's Diaries." Playb (30:12) D 83, p. 146.

2401. KOEHN, Lala
"Letter from Poland." CrossC (5:2/3) 83, p. 15.
"Praca Jest Najlepszym Lekarstwem" (Polish proverb: "Work is the best medicine"). PoetryCR (5:2) Wint 83-84, p. 6.
"She Still Can Taste the Cold Delicious Milk." CrossC (5:2/3) 83, p. 15.

2402. KOERTGE, Ronald
"Confidential Report on the Nasty Nasty Center for Bad Habits." WormR (23:4, issue 92) 83, p. 134.
"Dick Powell." SecC (11:1/2) 83, p. 93.
"Eterna 27." WormR (23:4, issue 92) 83, p. 135.
"I Was Just Sitting." WormR (23:4, issue 92) 83, p. 136.
"On Beauty." WormR (23:4, issue 92) 83, p. 133.
"The Pasadena Freeway." WormR (23:4, issue 92) 83, p. 132-133.
"The Thing Is to Not Let Go of the Vine" -- Johnny Weissmuller. WormR (23:4, issue 92) 83, p. 135.
"This Is for Every Man Who Licks His Shoulder During Solitary Sex . . ." WormR (23:4, issue 92) 83, p. 136.
"Way Off in the Corner." WormR (23:4, issue 92) 83, p. 134.
"The Whores Were Taking Vitamins." SecC (11:1/2) 83, p. 94.

2403. KOESTENBAUM, Phyllis
"Criminal Sonnets" (Selection: V). NewEngR (6:2) Wint 83, p. 228-229.

2404. KOESTLER, Arthur
"The Ballad of the Hell-Hound" (tr. of George Faludy). CanLit (98) Aut 83, p. 4-7.

2405. KOETHE, John
"The Narrow Way." CreamCR (8:1/2) 83, p. 137-141.
"One Light." ParisR (25:90) Wint 83, p. 176-177.
"The Substitute for Time." Epoch (33:1) Aut-Wint 83, p. 68.

2406. KOETZNER, J. Michael
"El Salvador." SanFPJ (5:4) 83, p. 88.

2407. KOGAWA, Joy
"Pink Geranium." CanLit (99) Wint 83, p. 33.
"Road Building by Pick Axe." CanLit (99) Wint 83, p. 32-33.

2408. KOLLAR, Sybil
"My Mother's Tablecloth." YetASM (1:2) 82, p. 8.

2409. KOLOKITHAS, Dawn
"Love Never Stood in This Water" (for Cindy). Tele (18) 83, p. 94.
"Moving In." Tele (18) 83, p. 95.

2410. KOLUMBAN, Nicholas
"In the Bright Night" (tr. of Sandor Csoori) Abraxas (27/28) 83, p. 7.
"Inner Landscape" (tr. of Sandor Weores). MalR (64) F 83, p. 121.
"My Mother" (tr. of Attila József). NewL (49:3/4) Spr-Sum 83, p. 137.
"Poland" (tr. of Sandor Csoori) Abraxas (27/28) 83, p. 6.
"A Winter Memory" (tr. Gyula Illyes). NewL (49:3/4) Spr-Sum 83, p. 133-139.

2411. KOMUNYAKAA, Yusef
"Audacity." BlackWR (9:1) Aut 82, p. 71.
"Black String of Days." BlackWR (9:1) Aut 82, p. 69.
"By Proxy." Tendril (16) Sum 83, p. 68.
"Charmed." BlackWR (9:1) Aut 82, p. 70.
"Elegy for Thelonious." Tendril (16) Sum 83, p. 69.
"Everybody's Reading Li Po" (silk-screened on a purple t-shirt). Kayak (61) Ap 83, p. 21.
"Faith Healer." PoNow (7:2, #38) 83, p. 15.
"Happy-Go-Lucky's Wolf Skull Dream Mask." Tendril (16) Sum 83, p. 67.
"Jumping Bad Blues." PoNow (7:2, #38) 83, p. 15.
"Landscape for the Disappeared." Ploughs (9:2/3) 83, p. 104-105.
"More Girl Than Boy." Ploughs (9:2/3) 83, p. 106.
"Touch-Up Man." Tendril (16) Sum 83, p. 66.

2412. KONCEL, Mary
"Dinner Guests." Kayak (62) Ag 83, p. 30.
"Learning to Ride the Elephant." MassR (24:1) Spr 83, inside front cover.
"The Lesson." Kayak (62) Ag 83, p. 29.
"The Neighborhood Man." Kayak (62) Ag 83, p. 29.
"Of the Sun." Kayak (62) Ag 83, p. 28.

2413. KONYALIAN-GRENIER, Arpine
"Atonement." Sulfur (3:2, #8) 83, p. 46-48.
"The Covenant." Sulfur (3:2, #8) 83, p. 51-52.
"Getting Up." Sulfur (3:2, #8) 83, p. 48-50.
"Rope Song." Sulfur (3:2, #8) 83, p. 50-51.
"When Angelika Leaves." Sulfur (3:2, #8) 83, p. 53-54.

2414. KOOSER, Ted
"The Afterlife." ThRiPo (21/22) 83, p. 50.
"As the President Spoke." PraS (57:2) Sum 83, p. 35.
"Aunt Tot." PraS (57:2) Sum 83, p. 36.
"A Birthday Card." Poetry (143:2) N 83, p. 70.
"An Empty Shotgun Shell." Field (28) Spr 83, p. 23.
"The Fan in the Window." NewYorker (59:31) 19 S 83, p. 52.
"Flying at Night." PraS (57:2) Sum 83, p. 35.
"Hitchhiking." MemphisSR (1:2) Spr 81, p. 4.
"In April." MemphisSR (1:2) Spr 81, p. 4.
"In October." PraS (57:2) Sum 83, p. 37.
"The Mouse." Poetry (143:2) N 83, p. 72.
"A Quarter Moon Just before Dawn." Field (28) Spr 83, p. 22.
"The Sigh." Poetry (143:2) N 83, p. 71.
"The Urine Specimen." Poetry (143:2) N 83, p. 73.
"The Witness." Poetry (143:2) N 83, p. 69.

2415. KOPELKE, Kendra
"Letter to a Young Girl." MissouriR (7:1) Aut 83, p. 52-53.

2416. KOPP, Catherine
"Passover." CharR (9:2) Aut 83, p. 66-67.

2417. KORNEGAY, Burt
"They Crowned the Rise." Poem (47) Mr 83, p. 34-37.
"To the Open Fields." Poem (47) Mr 83, p. 38-42.

2418. KORSSUN-MARVIN, Maria
"The Feast" (Based on Picasso's etching "The Frugal Meal"). SenR (13:2) 82-83, p. 53-54.

2419. KOSITSKY, Lynne
"The Clenched Fist." CrossC (5:2/3) 83, p. 17.

2420. KOSMICKI, Greg
"It Is Too Late, or I Am Too Tired, Again." CutB (21) Aut-Wint 83, p. 17-20.

2421. KOTEK, Jo-Anne
"For Elizabeth." PoetryCR (5:2) Wint 83-84, p. 19.

2422. KOTSIUMBAS, Halyna
"True Confessions." YetASM (1:2) 82, p. 13.

2423. KOVAC, Richard
"Scenario for a Commerical." YetASM (1:1) 82, p. 5.

2424. KOVACS, Istvan
"Arboretum" (tr. by Timothy Kachinske). PoetryE (9/10) Wint 82-Spr 83, p. 206.
"Fresco" (in the church at Csetnek) (tr. by Timothy Kachinske). PoetryE (9/10) Wint 82-Spr 83, p. 204-205.

2425. KOWIT, Steve
"Kowit." Abraxas (27/28) 83, p. 43.
"Thank You." Abraxas (27/28) 83, p. 42.

2426. KOYAMA, Tina
"Ojisan after the Stroke: Three Notes to Himself" (for my uncle). PoetC (13, i.e. 14:3) 83, p. 8.

2427. KOZER, José
"Vecindario." Prismal (11) Aut 83, p. 92-93.

2428. KRAMER, Aaron
"After the Call." Vis (12) 83, p. 26.
"After the Hospital." NewEngR (6:2) Wint 83, p. 306-307.
"And On and On." SanFPJ (4:3) 83, p. 65.
"Bensonhurst Intersection." Vis (13) 83, p. 22.
"Die, Die My Outcry" (tr. of Aaron Kushnirov). Vis (11) 83, p. 4.
"Granada: First Sleep." PikeF (5) Spr 83, p. 23.
"In the Suburbs." NewEngR (6:2) Wint 83, p. 305.
"Madrid: The Ghosts of Its Defenders." PikeF (5) Spr 83, p. 23.
"Scarf." PoetL (78:2) Sum 83, p. 83.
"Seven Minutes to Traintime." PikeF (5) Spr 83, p. 7.
"Swan Song." NewEng (5:4) Sum 83, p. 533-534.
"To Ralph Waldo Emerson." SanFPJ (4:3) 83, p. 67.
"The Tour (Thanksgiving) (1982)." SanFPJ (4:3) 83, p. 13.

2429. KRAMER, Lori
"A Boy." HangL (44) Sum 83, p. 65.
"Miriam." HangL (44) Sum 83, p. 64.

2430. KRAMER, Lotte
"A Dramatist Who Was My Father." Stand (24:3) 83, p. 30.

2431. KRAPF, Norbert
"Smoke." SpoonRQ (8:4) Aut 83, p. 21.
"The Visitor." SpoonRQ (8:4) Aut 83, p. 22.

2432. KRAUSE, Judith
"The Elephant Man's Dream." Quarry (32:3) Sum 83, p. 10.

2433. KRAUSS, Janet
"The Turning" (after a Michelangelo drawing). ThirdW Spr 83, p. 56.

2434. KRESH, David
"Ruth." WebR (8:2) Aut 83, p. 65-66.
"St. Jude Pray for Us, Almost without Hope." Poetry (143:1) O 83, p. 18-19.
"To Rio." Poetry (143:1) O 83, p. 20-21.

2435. KRETZ, Thomas
"Electrical Storm." PortR (29:1) 83, p. 78.
"Flower Shop." SpoonRQ (8:4) Aut 83, p. 41.
"The Mourning Cloak." Vis (13) 83, p. 23.
"Rue and Capers." NegC (3:4) Aut 83, p. 126.
"Wedding at Quileute." Argo (5:1) 83, p. 33.

2436. KRIDLER, David
"September/The Paradox of Harvest." AntigR (55) Aut 83, p. 90.
"Slicing a Ripe Pear." AntigR (55) Aut 83, p. 91.

2437. KRIST, Gary
"Diagnosis." Pig (11) 83, p. 66.

2438. KRITSCH, Holly
"Requiem." PottPort (5) 83-84, p. 34.
"Vacancies." PottPort (5) 83-84, p. 36.

2439. KROETSCH, Robert
"Delphi: Commentary #5." CreamCR (8:1/2) 83, p. 152.
"Delphi: Commentary #7." CreamCR (8:1/2) 83, p. 153.
"Delphi: Commentary #9." CreamCR (8:1/2) 83, p. 154.

2440. KROK, Peter
"Poeta Nascitur, Non Fit." SpiritSH (49) 83, p. 32.

2441. KROLL, Ernest
"A Chink in the Armor." WebR (8:1) Spr 83, p. 71.
"Interception." Wind (13:48) 83, p. 17.
"On the First Recognition of Herman Melville." WebR (8:1) Spr 83, p. 72-73.
"Relativity." Poem (47) Mr 83, p. 32.
"Ring Lardner." WebR (8:1) Spr 83, p. 73.
"Skyline from a Rocking Chair (Costa Rica)." KanQ (15:1) Wint 83, p. 125.
"William Dean Howells." WebR (8:1) Spr 83, p. 71.

2442. KROLL, Judith
"Freedom." Poetry (142:3) Je 83, p. 147-148.
"Thinking About History" (for John Broomfield). Poetry (142:3) Je 83, p. 146.

2443. KROLOW, Karl
"On Sufficiency, or Reaching the Desired Point" (tr. by Stuart Friebert). IndR (5:1) Wint 82, p. 52.

2444. KRONENBERG, Susan
"Romora Cove." Tele (18) 83, p. 18-19.

2445. KRONENFELD, Judy
"Cause She's a Wuh-mun." Abraxas (27/28) 83, p. 41.

2446. KRONMEYER, Olga
"Reborn Again." YetASM (1:2) 82, p. 2.

2447. KROUSE, Lane
"Digital Song." SanFPJ (5:4) 83, p. 80.
"Hybrids." SanFPJ (5:4) 83, p. 94.
"Rounds." SanFPJ (5:4) 83, p. 80.

2448. KRUEGER, Donald H.
"Her Fragrance." YetASM (1:1) 82, p. 5.

2449. KRYNSKI, Magnus J.
"December 31, 1979: Soon Now" (tr. of Stanislaw Baranczak, w. Robert A. Maguire). TriQ (57, Vol. 1) Spr-Sum 83, p. 89.
"First Move" (tr. of Leszek Elektorowicz, w. Robert A. Maguire). TriQ (57, Vol. 1) Spr-Sum 83, p. 62.
"I Will Open the Window" (tr. of Anna Swirszczynska, w. Robert A. Maguire). TriQ (57, Vol. 1) Spr-Sum 83, p. 61.
"Philately" (From my childhood, tr. of Wiktor Woroszylski, w. Robert A. Maguire). TriQ (57, Vol. 1) Spr-Sum 83, p. 27-28.
"Tortures" (tr. of Wislawa Szymborska, w. Robert A. Maguire). TriQ (57, Vol. 1) Spr-Sum 83, p. 25-26.

2450. KRYSL, Marilyn
"Arms." IndR (6:3) Sum 83, p. 31.
"Artemesia." KanQ (15:4) Aut 83, p. 113.
"The Beautiful Alive Alone Illusion." KanQ (15:4) Aut 83, p. 111-112.
"Drawing." IndR (6:1) Wint 83, p. 19.
"O.K., I'll Tell You." LittleM (14:1/2) 83, p. 41-42.
"Venus." KanQ (15:4) Aut 83, p. 114.

2451. KRYSS, T. L.
"Barbershop Quartet." Abraxas (27/28) 83, p. 5.
"Evening Star." Abraxas (27/28) 83, p. 5.

KUAN, Ch'in
See: CH'IN, Kuan

2452. KUBACH, David
"Visiting the Gifted and Talented Class." PikeF (5) Spr 83, p. 23.
"White Smiles." PikeF (5) Spr 83, p. 23.

KUBBER, Teresa Blancart
See: BLANCART KUBBER, Teresa

2453. KUBICEK, J. L.
"Evening Concert." Wind (13:49) 83, p. 31.

2454. KUBY, Lolette
"Burning the Journal." DekalbLAJ (16:1/4) Aut 82-Sum 83, p. 67.

"Death Wish." PraS (57:3) Aut 83, p. 53.
"A Hitchcock Tale." PraS (57:3) Aut 83, p. 52.
"On Writing Love Poems." Pig (11) 83, p. 64.

2455. KUCHINSKY, Walter
"Indoor Geranium." WritersL Je 83, p. 18.

2456. KUFFEL, Frances
"Art and the Zen of Wall Climbing." QW (17) Aut-Wint 83-84, p. 24-25.
"Hair." QW (17) Aut-Wint 83-84, p. 23.

2457. KUHNER, Herbert
"The Mountain" (tr. of Edvard Kocbek, w. Peter Kersche). Confr (25/26) 83, p. 303.

2458. KULYCKY, Michael
"After Reading William Stafford's Eassy on Poetry." KanQ (15:2) Spr 83, p. 196-197.

2459. KUMIN, Maxine
"Shelling Jacobs Cattle Beans." NewEng (5:4) Sum 83, p. 609-611.

2460. KUMMINGS, Donald
"Jelly Roll Blues." WormR (23:2, issue 90) 83, p. 49.
"Letter for Henry: Poème Trouvé (1981)." WormR (23:2, issue 90) 83, p. 48-49.
"Listen." PoNow (7:2, #38) 83, p. 47.

2461. KUNITZ, Stanley
"The Image-Make." Atlantic (251:4) Ap 83, p. 92.
"Lamplighter, 1914." Salm (61) Aut 83, p. 4-5.
"The Long Boat." Salm (61) Aut 83, p. 5.

2462. KUO, Alex
"Gathering Children" (for MAS). MinnR (NS 21) Aut 83, p. 24-25.

2463. KURODA, Kio
"Expulsion" (tr. by Tetsuo Kinoshita). PoetryE (9/10) Wint 82-Spr 83, p. 232-233.

2464. KUSHNER, Bill
"The Itch." Tele (18) 83, p. 15.
"Lullaby." Tele (18) 83, p. 14.

2465. KUSHNER, Dale
"Barn Song." Nimrod (27:1) Aut-Wint 83, p. 58.
"Separating the Bullcalf from Its Mother at Linden Valley Farm, May 1982." Nimrod (27:1) Aut-Wint 83, p. 57.
"Waking Up." Abraxas (27/28) 83, p. 36.

2466. KUSHNIROV, Aaron
"Die, Die My Outcry" (tr. by Aaron Kramer). Vis (11) 83, p. 4.

2467. KUTNEY, Bruce
"Two Nations" (For J.D.P.). SanFPJ (4:2) 83, p. 75.

2468. KUZMA, Greg
"Archibald MacLeish." SpoonRQ (8:1) Wint 83, p. 21.
"The Beautiful and Lovely Face." SpoonRQ (8:1) Wint 83, p. 54.
"The Bird." SpoonRQ (8:1) Wint 83, p. 12.
"The Birds." BlackWR (9:1) Aut 82, p. 16-17.
"The Birds." SpoonRQ (8:1) Wint 83, p. 36.
"The Birds My Son Showed Me." CreamCR (8:1/2) 83, p. 90.
"Complete Freedom." SpoonRQ (8:1) Wint 83, p. 50.
"Crocus" (for Philip Booth). SpoonRQ (8:1) Wint 83, p. 16.
"Dark" (for Roy Scheele). SpoonRQ (8:1) Wint 83, p. 11.
"Death." IndR (6:3) Sum 83, p. 27.
"Death in Crete." SpoonRQ (8:1) Wint 83, p. 41.
"The Dream." MidwQ (24:3) Spr 83, p. 285-289.
"Dream" (for Wendell Berry). SpoonRQ (8:1) Wint 83, p. 25.
"Everyday life" (for Hugh Luke). Peoria, IL: Spoon River Poetry Press, 1983. Special issue of SpoonRQ (8:1) Wint 83, p. 1-54.
"Fair City." SpoonRQ (8:1) Wint 83, p. 29.
"The Fish." IndR (6:3) Sum 83, p. 29.
"Flesh." SpoonRQ (8:1) Wint 83, p. 52.
"For Alan Dugan." SpoonRQ (8:1) Wint 83, p. 26.
"For Weldon Kees." SpoonRQ (8:1) Wint 83, p. 20.
"The Good Part." SpoonRQ (8:1) Wint 83, p. 45.
"Homage." SpoonRQ (8:1) Wint 83, p. 24.
"Ice Skating: Across Kansas." SpoonRQ (8:1) Wint 83, p. 40.
"Ice Skating: Ten rains, and then snow." SpoonRQ (8:1) Wint 83, p. 39.
"In Canada." SpoonRQ (8:1) Wint 83, p. 48.
"In Contrast" (for Hugh Luke). SpoonRQ (8:1) Wint 83, preceding p. 1.
"Jeff." Northeast (Ser. 3:16) Wint 83-84, p. 16.
"A June Walk." SpoonRQ (8:1) Wint 83, p. 14.
"The Lawn Mowing." SpoonRQ (8:1) Wint 83, p. 32.
"Leaving Kansas." IndR (6:3) Sum 83, p. 28.
"The Loons." Tendril (14/15) Wint 83, p. 120.
"Love Poem." SpoonRQ (8:1) Wint 83, p. 51.
"The Lovers." SpoonRQ (8:1) Wint 83, p. 53.
"May." SpoonRQ (8:1) Wint 83, p. 15.
"Missles." Kayak (63) N 83, p. 35.
"Morning." SpoonRQ (8:1) Wint 83, p. 2.
"The Moth." SpoonRQ (8:1) Wint 83, p. 38.
"Muscatel." SpoonRQ (8:1) Wint 83, p. 4.
"The Music." SpoonRQ (8:1) Wint 83, p. 46.
"My Son Skating on Doane's Lake." SpoonRQ (8:1) Wint 83, p. 37.
"November." SpoonRQ (8:1) Wint 83, p. 7.
"The Owls." SpoonRQ (8:1) Wint 83, p. 10.
"The Pheasant." BlackWR (8:1) Aut 81, p. 99.
"The Poets." SpoonRQ (8:1) Wint 83, p. 19.
"Police." SpoonRQ (8:1) Wint 83, p. 33.
"Religion in America." PoetryE (9/10) Wint 82-Spr

83, p. 124.
"Remembering the Fifties." SpoonRQ (8:1) Wint 83, p. 13.
"Rhyme." SpoonRQ (8:1) Wint 83, p. 1.
"Robert Lowell Is Dead." SpoonRQ (8:1) Wint 83, p. 22-23.
"Rummy." SpoonRQ (8:1) Wint 83, p. 35.
"The Sacred Shore." SpoonRQ (8:1) Wint 83, p. 9.
"The Sexual Would Eat Up All Attention." SpoonRQ (8:1) Wint 83, p. 49.
"The Snowfall." SpoonRQ (8:1) Wint 83, p. 6.
"Songs." MemphisSR (3:1) Aut 82, p. 7.
"Sunday." SpoonRQ (8:1) Wint 83, p. 3.
"Ten Thousand Years." SpoonRQ (8:1) Wint 83, p. 8.
"The Toaster." SpoonRQ (8:1) Wint 83, p. 30.
"Travel." SpoonRQ (8:1) Wint 83, p. 47.
"The Truck." SpoonRQ (8:1) Wint 83, p. 34.
"The Two Goldfish." SpoonRQ (8:1) Wint 83, p. 31.
"Walking." NowestR (21:1) 83, p. 20.
"Who Was Killed in the Car" (for my brother Jeff). SpoonRQ (8:1) Wint 83, p. 5.
"Why I Write." OhioR (30) 83, p. 271.
"Winter." PoetryNW (24:3) Aut 83, p. 23.
"The Writer." SecC (11:1/2) 83, p. 95.

2469. KVAM, Wayne
"Below Zero" (Kent, Ohio). PoNow (7:2, #38) 83, p. 21.

2470. KWIATKOWSKI, Diana
"For You -- Young Violinist Who Created Bliss (1982)." Wind (13:48) 83, p. 34.

2471. KYLE, Solomon
"Solomon's Song." YetASM (2:1) 83, p. 7.

2472. KYNETT, Barbara
"The Roads Taken." Poetry (141:6) Mr 83, p. 328-330.

2473. L. G. M.
"Worried Writer." WritersL Ag 83, p. 17.

2474. LaBOMBARD, Joan
"Archibald MacLeish: In Memoriam." PoetryNW (24:2) Sum 83, p. 26.

2475. LABORDETA, Miguel
"Song of Frustration of the Dreamer Child" (tr. by Will Kirkland). NewOR (10:4) Wint 83, p. 98.

2476. LABRIOLA, Gina
"A Kind of Apocalypse" (from In uno Specchio la Fenice, tr. by Ruth Feldman). WebR (8:1) Spr 83, p. 49-50.
"Metallic Love" (from Alveare di Specchi, tr. by Ruth Feldman). WebR (8:1) Spr 83, p. 50-51.

2477. LACERTE, Roger
"Le Pays de Ti-Jean." MoodySI (11) Spr-Sum 82, p. 20.

2478. LACHAPELL, Côme
"Non pas le pire." PoetryCR (5:1) Aut 83, p. 14.

2479. LACHER, Lorette
"Los Desparecidos." USl (16/17) Wint 83-84, p. 2.

2480. LACKEY, Robert Sam
"Blossom." StoneC (10:3/4) Spr-Sum 83, p. 43.

2481. LaGATTUTA, Margo
"Straightening." LittleM (14:1/2) 83, p. 30.

2482. LAKE, Paul
"An American in Paris" (for Jim and Lowell). Thrpny (4:3, issue 15) Aut 83, p. 11.
"An Apparition." CalQ (22) Sum 83, p. 29.
"In Rough Weather." NewRep (188:24) 20 Je 83, p. 30.
"Rabbits." DekalbLAJ (16:1/4) Aut 82-Sum 83, p. 68.

2483. LALLY, P. T.
"Thirty." Wind (13:47) 83, p. 23-24.
"Wolves" (for my daughter." Wind (13:47) 83, p. 23.

2484. LALOUETT, J.
"New York -- Meurtre à l'Opera." PoetryCR (5:1) Aut 83, p. 14.

2485. LaMATTINA, Elaine
"Living in the Spaces between Dreams." PoetL (78:3) Aut 83, p. 169.
"Poem for the Perfect Child, Lost." PoetL (78:3) Aut 83, p. 170.

2486. LAMB, Margaret
"Not without Air." Blueline (4:2) Wint-Spr 83, p. 4.

2487. LAMBERT, Charles
"A Twig of Rowan" (tr. of Anna Frajlich). PoetL (77:3) Aut 82, p. 149.
"Untitled: And if I forget" (tr. of Anna Frajlich). PoetL (77:3) Aut 82, p. 149.

LAMOTTE, Roy de
See: DeLAMOTTE, Roy

2488. LANCE, Jeanne
"Departure No. 2." Tele (18) 83, p. 65.
"Do You Have a Gun?" Tele (18) 83, p. 64.
"The Great Escape." Tele (18) 83, p. 66.

2489. LANDALE, Zoë
"Clues." PoetryCR (5:1) Aut 83, p. 9.
"Geography: Vancouver." CrossC (5:4) 83, p. 7.
"In This Dream." Waves (11:2/3) Wint 83, p. 75.

2490. LANDER, Tim
"Another Child." WestCR (17:4) Ap 83, p. 43.

2491. LANE, Carol Bonner
"Evening at Arles." Mund (14:1) 83, p. 35.

"Sometimes the telephone rings at night." Mund (14:1) 83, p. 35.

2492. LANE, Ion
"I pray -- I know not to whom" (written somewhere in England in 1939). Wind (13:47) 83, p. 25.

2493. LANE, John
"Four Old Graves in the Viginia Woods" (Errata from Ploughs 8:2/3, 82). Ploughs (9:1) 83, p. 192.
"Seeing Wild Horses" (Errata from Ploughs 8:2/3, 82). Ploughs (9:1) 83, p. 192.

2494. LANE, M. Travis
"A Good Thought." PottPort (5) 83-84, p. 14.
"Mottos." PottPort (5) 83-84, p. 21.
"Poor Thing." PoetryCR (4:3) Spr 83, p. 12.
"Very Poetic Evening." PottPort (5) 83-84, p. 14.

2495. LANE, Patrick
"Among the Hours Women Are the Best." PoetryCR (5:1) Aut 83, p. 8.
"And of the Measure of Winter We Are Sure" (for Miriam Mandel). CanLit (97) Sum 83, p. 34.
"Chronicles" (Excerpts: 1, 3-7, 12, 16-18)." CanLit (97) Sum 83, p. 10-13.
"Meditation on Patience." PoetryCR (5:1) Aut 83, p. 8.
"White Lions in the Afternoon." Grain (11:4) N 83, p. 35.

2496. LANG, Stephen
"Fawn." Poem (48) Jl 83, p. 27.
"Gardenia." Poem (48) Jl 83, p. 23.
"Little Nietzschean Ones." Poem (48) Jl 83, p. 22.
"Music for an Autumn Afternoon." Poem (48) Jl 83, p. 29.
"Obsession." Poem (48) Jl 83, p. 24.
"On a Sad-Eyed Sunday." Poem (48) Jl 83, p. 25.
"Passion." Poem (48) Jl 83, p. 30.
"To One Practicing Older Virtures." Poem (48) Jl 83, p. 28.
"Wednesdays Have Dreams." Poem (48) Jl 83, p. 26.

2497. LANIER, Doris
"Cows." IndR (5:1) Wint 82, p. 33.

2498. LANTEIGNE, M. P.
"Chinks -- Paulatuk." PottPort (5) 83-84, p. 34.
"Weaver at Tuktoyuktuk." PottPort (5) 83-84, p. 34.

2499. LAPINGTON, S. C.
"The Adder." Stand (24:2) 83, p. 44.
"The Bones." Stand (24:2) 83, p. 44.

2500. LAPOINTE, Gatien
"Body Infinitely Other" (tr. by Andrea Moorhead). Mund (14:1) 83, p. 27.
"Book II" (tr. by Andrea Moorhead). Mund (14:1) 83, p. 27.

"Corps Autre Infiniment." Mund (14:1) 83, p. 26.
"Livre II." Mund (14:1) 83, p. 28.

2501. LAPORE, Janyce
"Crows." YetASM (1:1) 82, p. 8.

2502. LAPPIN, Linda
"From a Window near the Station." Kayak (62) Ag 83, p. 54.

2503. LARA, Omar
"Obstinado Viajero." Areito (9:35) 83, p. 37.

2504. LARDAS, Konstantinos
"Aging." NowestR (21:2/3) 83, p. 69.
"And, in a Place of Light." NowestR (21:2/3) 83, p. 70-71.

LARINO, Marcelino García
See: GARCIA LARINO, Marcelino

2505. LARKIN, Joan
"Risks." Calyx (8:1) Aut 83, p. 11.
"Self-Love." Calyx (8:1) Aut 83, p. 12.

2506. LARSEN, Jean Woodward
"Autumn moon." Quarry (32:3) Sum 83, p. 73.
"Parting." Quarry (32:3) Sum 83, p. 73.

2507. LARSEN, Jeanne
"The Badger Woman." Ploughs (9:2/3) 83, p. 79.
"The Time When the World Was Different." Ploughs (9:2/3) 83, p. 78.

2508. LARSEN, Marianne
"Limitless" (tr. by Susanna Nied). PoetryE (9/10) Wint 82-Spr 83, p. 250-251.

2509. LARSEN, Wendy
"St. Fanourious." Tendril (16) Sum 83, p. 70.

2510. LARSON, Kris
"Poem for February." StoneC (10:3/4) Spr-Sum 83, p. 75.
"Yellow Birch Hill." BelPoJ (34:1) Aut 83, p. 1.

2511. LaSALLE, Peter
"Border Town." SouthernPR (23:2) Aut 82 [i.e. (23:1?) Spr 83], p. 26.
"Jamaica." StoneC (11:1/2, Pt. 1) Aut-Wint 83, p. 14-15.

2512. LASKIN, Pamela (Pamela L.)
"Edward Hopper." YetASM (1:2) 82, p. 17.
"An Experience I Had That Changed My Life -- An Essay by a Student at City College." YetASM (2:1) 83, p. 8.

2513. LATCHAW, Joan S.
"Le Petit Zinc (on the Rue de Reine)." Wind

(13:48) 83, p. 35.

2514. LATHAM, J.
"Triangles." Bogg (50) 83, p. 44.

2515. LATTA, Catherine Evans
"Beirut: Summer of '82" (For Susan and Raya). BelPoJ (33:4) Sum 83, p. 24-36.

2516. LAUGHLIN, James
"Among the Roses." Iowa (13:3/4) Spr 82 (83), p. 132.
"Little Dog" (Stolen from Catullus: "Lugete o Veneres Cupidinesque"). ParisR (25:89) Aut 83, p. 194.
"No My Dear." Poetry (142:3) Je 83, p. 166.
"Nothing That's Lovely Can My Love Escape" (Stolen from various books about the Hindu gods). ParisR (25:89) Aut 83, p. 195.
"Professor F's Story." Iowa (13:3/4) Spr 82 (83), p. 133.
"She Seemed to Know" (Drawn from Hardy: Tess of the D'Urbervilles). ParisR (25:89) Aut 83, p. 197.
"Two Onanists" (Stolen, in general, from Juvenal). ParisR (25:89) Aut 83, p. 194.
"With My Third Eye" (Stolen from various books on Tibetan and Tanric Buddhism). ParisR (25:89) Aut 83, p. 196.

2517. LAUNIUS, Carl Judson
"Words for Ellen Gilchrist." CalQ (22) Sum 83, p. 82-83.

2518. LAURADUNN, Gayle
"Rock Climbing." Blueline (3:2) Wint-Spr 82, p. 32-33.

2519. LAURENCE, Larry
"Scenes Beginning with the Footbridge at the Lake." PoetryNW (24:3) Aut 83, p. 14-16.

2520. LAUTERBACH, Ann
"In the Garden" (for David Lauterbach). SenR (13:2) 82-83, p. 38.
"Narrow Margins." SenR (13:2) 82-83, p. 37.
"Psyche." Epoch (33:1) Aut-Wint 83, p. 70.

2521. LAUTERMILCH, Steven (Steve)
"Buddha" (tr. of Rainer Maria Rilke). SouthernR (19:3) Jl 83, p. 679.
"My God, What Will You Do, When I Die?" (tr. of Rainer Maria Rilke). DevQ (18:1) Spr 83, p. 97.
"The Song of the Mill" (for ole Fred). Abatis (1) 83, p. 12.
"Sonnets to Orpheus" (Selection: 1.24) (tr. of Rainer Maria Rilke). SouthernR (19:3) Jl 83, p. 681.
"You Are the Future, Morning Breaking Red" (tr. of Rainer Maria Rilke). DevQ (18:1) Spr 83, p. 96.

2522. LAVER, Sue
"Listen to This Train." CapilR (27) 83, p. 74-86.

2523. LAWLER, Patrick (Patrick J.)
"My Suicide Returns to Me Each Year." Iowa (13:3/4) Spr 82 (83), p. 36.
"On the Posible Death of Monsieur Smith." Iowa (13:3/4) Spr 82 (83), p. 37.
"Prison Guard." NegC (3:4) Aut 83, p. 89.
"Watching the Sailboats." HiramPoR (34) Spr-Sum 83, p. 11-12.
"The Year John Cage Was Born." Iowa (13:3/4) Spr 82 (83), p. 38.

2524. LAWRENCE, Allen
"The Editor." EngJ (72:4) Ap 83, p. 52.

2525. LAWRENCE, Robert
"Ouimet Canyon, Late Autumn." Descant (41) Sum 83, p. 84-85.
"The Steps of the M.M.A." Descant (41) Sum 83, p. 86-87.

2526. LAWRY, Mercedes
"Hide 'n Seek." Vis (11) 83, p. 19-20.
"In the Lifeguard's Chair." IndR (5:3) Aut 82, p. 24.
"The Sake of the Child." CrabCR (1:1) My 83, p. 24.
"Survivalists." Vis (11) 83, p. 20.
"The Swimmer." CrabCR (1:1) My 83, p. 25.

2527. LAWSON, Todd S. J.
"Hamburger Mary's." SecC (11:1/2) 83, p. 97.

2528. LAX, Robert
"All order, all chaos, some order, some chaos." HangL (44) Sum 83, p. 26.
"At the top of the night." HangL (44) Sum 83, p. 27.
"Black bird, green hill." HangL (44) Sum 83, p. 25.
"Cloud over hill, bird over sea." HangL (44) Sum 83, p. 24.

2529. LAYTON, Elizabeth
"Ode to a Grave Digger." LittleBR (3:4) Sum 83, p. 54-55.

2530. LAYTON, Irving
"Aristocrats." AntigR (54) Sum 83, p. 54.
"August Strindberg" (from While Waiting for the Messiah, 1984). PoetryCR (4:4) Sum 83, p. 8.
"The Flaming Maple." PoetryCR (5:1) Aut 83, p. 16.
"Hedges." PoetryCR (5:1) Aut 83, p. 16.
"I Take My Anna Everywhere" (from While Waiting for the Messiah, 1984). PoetryCR (4:4) Sum 83, p. 8.
"Kakania" (from While Waiting for the Messiah, 1984). PoetryCR (4:4) Sum 83, p. 9.
"Lady Macbeth." AntigR (54) Sum 83, p. 55.
"Lawyers" (for Linda Dranoff, from While Waiting for the Messiah, 1984). PoetryCR (4:4) Sum

83, p. 9.
"Make Room William Blake." Argo (4:3) 83, p. 29.
"The Music of Energy" (from While Waiting for the Messiah, 1984). PoetryCR (4:4) Sum 83, p. 8.
"Nostalgia When the Leaves Begin to Fall" (from While Waiting for the Messiah, 1984). PoetryCR (4:4) Sum 83, p. 9.
"Psychologists." AntigR (54) Sum 83, p. 54.
"Rendezvous at the Coffee Mill" (for Sarah, from While Waiting for the Messiah, 1984). PoetryCR (4:4) Sum 83, p. 9.
"Sex Appeal" (from While Waiting for the Messiah, 1984). PoetryCR (4:4) Sum 83, p. 9.
"Tick Tock." PoetryCR (5:1) Aut 83, p. 16.
"Yeats at Sixty-five" (from While Waiting for the Messiah, 1984). PoetryCR (4:4) Sum 83, p. 8.

2531. LAZARD, Naomi
"The Beast's Ordinance." OhioR (30) 83, p. 142.
"In Answer to Your Query." OhioR (30) 83, p. 143.

2532. LAZER, Hank
"Certain Shirts." PoetryE (11) Sum 83, p. 38.
"The Rose Garden." VirQR (59:3) Sum 83, p. 445-451.

Le . . .
See also: Names beginning with "Le" without the following space, filed below in their alphabetic positions, e.g., LeFEVRE.

2533. Le COMTE, Edward
"Saint Insane or Fractured Wrench." SpiritSH (48) 82, p. 45.

2534. Le MIEUX, Debbie
"Flying Squirrel." AntR (41:4) Aut 83, p. 440-441.
"Mere, L'Amour, Trente Ans." AntR (41:4) Aut 83, p. 438-439.

2535. Le MIEUX, Dotty
"Poem for Robert Creeley." SecC (11:1/2) 83, p. 98.
"Like There's Tomorrow." Tele (18) 83, p. 50-51.
"Love Poem." Tele (18) 83, p. 52.

Le . . .
See also: Names beginning with "Le" followed by a space, filed above in their alphabetic positions, e.g., Le COMTE.

2536. LEA, Sydney (Sidney)
"After Labor Day." NewYorker (59:33) 3 O 83, p. 38-39.
"Blessed Routine" (July 6, 1982). SewanR (91:3) Sum 83, p. 353-354.
"Burning the Christmas Tree." Hudson (36:4) Wint 83-84, p. 697.
"The Feud." KanQ (15:4) Aut 83, p. 86-96.
"From Another Shore" (in memory of DV). VirQR (59:2) Spr 83, p. 249-253.
"Horn." GeoR (37:3) Aut 83, p. 501-504.

"Issues of the Fall." Abatis (1) 83, p. 5-6.
"Making Sense." NewRep (186:12) 24 Mr 82, p. 32.
"Moves" (for George MacArthur). OW (16) Spr-Sum 83, p. 70-72.
"On Playing an Old Blues." OW (16) Spr-Sum 83, p. 68-69.
"The Return: Intensive Care." NewYorker (59:25) 8 Ag 83, p. 34.
"Self-Sermon on the Hill." SewanR (91:3) Sum 83, p. 355-356.
"White Mountain, New Year." OW (16) Spr-Sum 83, p. 73-75.

2537. LEAX, John
"Bridging the Gully." Nimrod (27:1) Aut-Wint 83, p. 30.
"Carla." Nimrod (27:1) Aut-Wint 83, p. 31.
"Good Intentions." Nimrod (27:1) Aut-Wint 83, p. 30.

2538. LEBOW, Jeanne
"Emma." MemphisSR (4:1) Aut 83, p. 24.

2539. LECHLITNER, Ruth
"August Lily." HolCrit (20:4) O 83, p. 19.
"Pet Shop." SouthwR (68:3) Sum 83, p. 251-252.

LeCOMTE, Edward
See: Le COMTE, Edward

2540. LEE, Ann
"Coming Together" (For Thomas S. Lee 1920-1972). Wind (13:49) 83, p. 32.

2541. LEE, David
"Abandoned Cabin on the Clark Ranch." MidwQ (25:1) Aut 83, p. 57.
"Fajada Butte -- Solstice" (for Dick and Lois). MidwQ (25:1) Aut 83, p. 58.
"On Turning Up a Fossil in My Garden -- May, '81." MidwQ (25:1) Aut 83, p. 61.
"Paragonah." MidwQ (25:1) Aut 83, p. 60.
"Parowan Canyon." MidwQ (25:1) Aut 83, p. 56.
"Rip-Gut Fence." MidwQ (25:1) Aut 83, p. 59.

LEE, Hyun
See: HYUNLEE

2542. LEE, John B.
"A Lesson for the Lovers of Humanity." WritersL Jl 83, p. 4.
"Ripe." PoetryCR (5:2) Wint 83-84, p. 7.
"When He Plays Harmonica." Waves (11:2/3) Wint 83, p. 70.

2543. LEE, Li-Young
"Dreaming of Hair." AmerPoR (12:5) S/O 83, p. 34.
"The Gift." AmerPoR (12:5) S/O 83, p. 33.

2544. LEE, Maria Berl
"A Bat Story." YetASM (1:1) 82, p. 10.

"I Have Vanished" (The Berber Woman Is Photographed). YetASM (1:1) 82, p. 5.

2545. LEE, Mary Hope Whitehead
"We speak." YetASM (1:2) 82, p. 14.

2546. LEE, Myra
"How Can We Be Here in Wood When We Live Burning?" SanFPJ (4:4) 83, p. 10-12.

2547. LEED, Jake
"For Jack Kerouac." MoodySI (10) Aut 81, p. 17.

2548. LEER, Norman
"Shootings." SpoonRQ (8:4) Aut 83, p. 18-19.

2549. LEET, Judith
"Returning Alive from Diverse Routes and Far Travels." Poetry (142:3) Je 83, p. 132-133.
"A Revisionist's Mozart." Poetry (142:3) Je 83, p. 131.

2550. LEFCOWITZ, Barbara (Barbara F.)
"The Amtrak Mattresses." PoetL (77:1) Spr 82, p. 7.
"Circa Berkeley, 1982." PoetL (78:2) Sum 83, p. 84-87.
"Memoirs of an Amnesiac." MinnR (NS 20) Spr 83, p. 59-61.
"Riding the Amtrak Way." WindO (42) Sum 83, p. 43.
"Rumpelstiltskin's Revenge." WebR (8:2) Aut 83, p. 63-64.

2551. LeFEVRE, Adam
"Nocturne with Cows." ParisR (24:84) Sum 82, p. 77.

2552. LeFORGE, P. V.
"The Groom." Swallow (2) Aut-Wint 83, p. 101-102.

LeHAVRE, Rosselare
See: ROSSELARE-LeHAVRE

2553. LEHMAN, David
"Exact Change." PraS (51:1, i.e. 57:1) Spr 83, p. 37-38.
"For I Will Consider Your Dog Molly." MichQR (22:3) Sum 83, p. 387-388.
"Gift Means Poison in German." VirQR (59:1) Wint 83, p. 61-62.
"The Long Goodbye." Shen (34:1) 83, p. 58.
"Love and Destiny." ParisR (24:84) Sum 82, p. 150.
"The Problem of Evil." VirQR (59:1) Wint 83, p. 60-61.
"Recent Acquisition." PartR (50:1) 83, p. 78-79.
"Wystan Hugh Auden: A Villanelle." Shen (34:1) 83, p. 59.

2554. LEIPER, Esther M.
"Family Legacy." LittleBR (3:3) Spr 83, p. 30.

2555. LEISCHNER, Dennis
"Radiation Art." SanFPJ (5:1) 83, p. 80.
"Signs." SanFPJ (5:2) 83, p. 53.

2556. LEISER, Dorothy
"Indian Summer, Donner Pass." ChrC (100:33) 9 N 83, p. 1013.
"The Light That Was There." ChrC (100:39) 21-28 D 83, p. 1179.

2557. LEITHAUSER, Brad
"The Buried Graves." NewYorker (59:37) 31 O 83, p. 48.
"Dead Elms by a River." NewRep (186:15) 14 Ap 82, p. 38.
"Miniature." Argo (4:2) 82, p. 27.
"On a Seaside Mountain, Oki Islands, Japan Sea." Harp (266:1592) Ja 83, p. 53.
"Post Coital Depression: A Sonnet." Epoch (33:1) Aut-Wint 83, p. 72.
"Two Suspensions." Atlantic (251:4) Ap 83, p. 95.

2559. LeMAIRE, Dorinda
"Limiting the Scope." PoetryNW (24:2) Sum 83, p. 16-17.

LeMIEUX, Debbie
See: Le MIEUX, Debbie

LeMIEUX, Dotty
See: Le MIEUX, Dotty

2560. LEMM, Richard
"The Immigrant Applies for Citizenship." CrossC (5:2/3) 83, p. 25.

2561. LENDENNIE, Jessie
"Thicket Road -- A Memory." Stand (24:4) Aut 83, p. 55.

2562. LENGYEL, Cornel
"He Reviews the Wisdom of the Fathers." Confr (25/26) 83, p. 276.

LEON, Kathe de
See: De LEON, Kathie

2563. LEON HERNANDEZ, Victor de
"Asuntos Resueltos." Rácata (2) 83, p. 76.
"La Cebolla." Rácata (2) 83, p. 131.
"Cuerpos de a Quintal y Pico." Rácata (2) 83, p. 78.
"En el Paraíso." Rácata (2) 83, p. 75.
"Petrificación Imposibilitada." Rácata (2) 83, p. 79.
"Rácata II." Rácata (2) 83, p. 77.

2564. LEONARD, Bill J.
"In Madrid ... at Mass." ChrC (100:1) 5-12 Ja 83, p. 15.

2565. LePONT, Henri
"Death & Stuff." Telescope (5/6) Spr 83, p. 101-107.

2566. LEPORE, Dominick
"All Will Listen" (from L'Incomprensibile Uomo, tr. of Gigi Dessi). StoneC (10:3/4) Spr-Sum 83, p. 53.
"Sunday" (from L'Incomprensibile Uomo, tr. of Gigi Dessi). StoneC (10:3/4) Spr-Sum 83, p. 52.

2567. LERER, Seth
"Gloves." SewanR (91:1) Wint 83, p. 109.
"Hansel." SewanR (91:1) Wint 83, p. 107.
"The Hun Children." SewanR (91:1) Wint 83, p. 108.

2568. LERMOND, Lucia
"The Plover Sings." YetASM (2:1) 83, p. 7.

2569. LERNER, Linda
"Maps." ColEng (45:7) N 83, p. 677.

2570. LesCARBEAU, Mitchell
"Anorexic." Tendril (16) Sum 83, p. 71-72.

2571. LESLIE, Naton
"Fascia." FourQt (33:1) Aut 83, p. 28.

2572. LESSING, Karin
"A Love Poem." Sulfur (3:1, #7) 83, p. 108-114.

2573. LESTER-MASSMAN, Gordon
"Wedding--George, Jane." HolCrit (20:3) Je 83, p. 13.

2574. LEVENS, Lance
"Return of the Titans." Poem (48) Jl 83, p. 8-9.
"Southern Preserved." Poem (48) Jl 83, p. 10.

2575. LEVERTOV, Denise
"The Cricket" (tr. of Krassin Himmirsky, w. the author). Vis (11) 83, p. 34.
"Gathered at the River" (For Beatrice Hawley and John Jagel). Ploughs (9:1) 83, p. 131-133.
"Last Night's Dream." Ploughs (9:1) 83, p. 134.
"Psalm: People Power at the Die-in." NewL (49:3/4) Spr-Sum 83, p. 54-55.
"Watching Dark Circle." NewEng (5:4) Sum 83, p. 482.

2576. LEVI, Steven
"It took the landlord two days." CropD (4) 83, p. 9.

2577. LEVI, Toni Mergentime
"Getting On." SoDakR (21:3) Aut 83, p. 95.
"Parable." Poem (48) Jl 83, p. 54.
"Temperance." Poem (48) Jl 83, p. 53.

2578. LEVIN, Amy
"These Uselss Artifacts." MSS (2:3) Sum 83, p. 115-116.

2579. LEVIN, Arthur
"In the Hall of Great Mammals." KanQ (15:1) Wint 83, p. 152-153.

2580. LEVIN, Gabriel
"Airborne" (tr. of T. Carmi). LitR (26:2) Wint 83, p. 225.
"All That We Learned, We Know" (tr. of Israel Pincas). LitR (26:2) Wint 83, p. 250-253.
"The Angel" (tr. of Pinchas Sadeh). LitR (26:2) Wint 83, p. 231-232.
"Bat Sheba" (tr. of Asher Reich). LitR (26:2) Wint 83, p. 262.
"Bat Shlomo." (tr. of Harold Schimmel). LitR (26:2) Wint 83, p. 255.
"Between Skirmish and Shadow" (tr. of Gabriel Preil). LitR (26:2) Wint 83, p. 216.
"Binyamina" (tr. of Harold Schimmel). LitR (26:2) Wint 83, p. 254.
"Broken Line, Lone Trees" (tr. of Zali Gurevitch). LitR (26:2) Wint 83, p. 299-301.
"Coastal Cities, Coastal Cities" (tr. of Mordechai Geldman). LitR (26:2) Wint 83, p. 284-285.
"The Countries We Live In" (tr. of Natan Zach). LitR (26:2) Wint 83, p. 243.
"Dantès, No" (tr. of Natan Zach). LitR (26:2) Wint 83, p. 242.
"Descriptive Poetry" (tr. of Meir Wieseltier). LitR (26:2) Wint 83, p. 271.
"First it Rained" (tr. of Maya Bejerano). LitR (26:2) Wint 83, p. 297.
"For Marilyn Monroe" (tr. of Ronnie Someck). LitR (26:2) Wint 83, p. 303.
"Instead of Words" (tr. of Yehuda Amichai). LitR (26:2) Wint 83, p. 224.
"Jericho" (tr. of Mordechai Galili). LitR (26:2) Wint 83, p. 305.
"Jerusalem: Ladders of Love" (tr. of Gabriel Preil). LitR (26:2) Wint 83, p. 216.
"Knowledge" (tr. of Mordechai Galili). LitR (26:2) Wint 83, p. 306.
"Landing" (tr. of T. Carmi). LitR (26:2) Wint 83, p. 226.
"Last Dew" (tr. of Peretz Banai). LitR (26:2) Wint 83, p. 288.
"Listens, In Another Place" (tr. of Yair Hurvitz). LitR (26:2) Wint 83, p. 274-275.
"The Mother Spaceship" (tr. of Menachem Ben). LitR (26:2) Wint 83, p. 293.
"Moving Lights" (tr. of Meir Wieseltier). LitR (26:2) Wint 83, p. 270-271.
"My Friend, Michael, From the Dust" (tr. of Peretz Banai). LitR (26:2) Wint 83, p. 288-289.
"Nine Lines on a Bedouin Who Croaked from Desert Cancer" (In memory of Achmed Abu-Rabiah, tr. of Ronnie Someck). LitR (26:2) Wint 83, p. 303.
"Our Blood is the Petrol of the World" (tr. of Asher Reich). LitR (26:2) Wint 83, p. 262.
"Restlessness on All Sides and Angels" (tr. of Natan Zach). LitR (26:2) Wint 83, p. 241.

"The Road to India" (tr. of Israel Pincas). LitR (26:2) Wint 83, p. 249-250.
"The Sea Transparent Slices" (tr. of Menachem Ben). LitR (26:2) Wint 83, p. 290-293.
"Seven Lines on the Wonder of the Yarkon" (tr. of Ronnie Someck). LitR (26:2) Wint 83, p. 304.
"Several Days After Parting from a Girl Who Lived with Me for Close to Half a Year" (tr. of Pinchas Sadeh). LitR (26:2) Wint 83, p. 232.
"Shibboleth." LitR (26:2) Wint 83, p. 327.
"Sometimes He Longs For" (tr. of Natan Zach). LitR (26:2) Wint 83, p. 240-241.
"Somewhere" (tr. of Asher Reich). LitR (26:2) Wint 83, p. 263.
"Sonnet of Air Narcissus" (tr. of Ronnie Someck). LitR (26:2) Wint 83, p. 304.
"Summer Evening in the King David Hotel" (tr. of Yehuda Amichai). LitR (26:2) Wint 83, p. 223-224.
"A Summing Up" (tr. of Gabriel Preil). LitR (26:2) Wint 83, p. 215.
"Three Sorties Out of the City Walls" (Melville, 1857). LitR (26:2) Wint 83, p. 326-327.
"Under the Surface" (tr. of Zali Gurevitch). LitR (26:2) Wint 83, p. 301-302.
"Wessex" (tr. of Natan Zach). LitR (26:2) Wint 83, p. 239-240.

2581. LEVIN, Harriet
"Thrown Out." Iowa (13:3/4) Spr 82 (83), p. 123.

2582. LEVIN, Phillis
"After a Summer of Ancient Greek" (Siracusa, Sicily). Shen (34:4) 83, p. 74-76.

2583. LEVINE, Philip
"Another Life." SecC (11:1/2) 83, p. 99-100.
"Asking." NewL (49:3/4) Spr-Sum 83, p. 190-192.
"For the Country." Poetry (143:2) N 83, p. 63-68.
"Memories of You" (for Illinois Jacquet). MissouriR (6:3) Sum 83, p. 22-23.
"New Season." OhioR (30) 83, p. 55-57.
"No One Knows the Yellow Grass." OhioR (30) 83, p. 54.
"Waiting." SecC (11:1/2) 83, p. 101-102.

2584. LEVINE, Suzanne M.
"A La Carte." Tendril (14/15) Wint 83, p. 121.

2585. LEVINE-KEATING, Helane
"Loon." MalR (65) Jl 83, p. 73.

2586. LEVIS, Larry
"After the Blue Note Closes." AmerPoR (12:1) Ja/F 83, p. 4.
"Delwyn Creed." ThRiPo (21/22) 83, p. 51-52.
"Family Romance." AmerPoR (12:1) Ja/F 83, p. 6.
"Oklahoma" (for Marcia). AmerPoR (12:1) Ja/F 83, p. 5.
"Signs." OhioR (30) 83, p. 58.
"South." AmerPoR (12:1) Ja/F 83, p. 3.

"There Are Two Worlds." AmerPoR (12:1) Ja/F 83, p. 4.
"Winter Stars." AmerPoR (12:1) Ja/F 83, p. 5.

2587. LEVITIN, Alexis
"At the Sea" (tr. of Carmen Conde, w. José R. de Armas). LitR (27:1) Aut 83, p. 101-102.
"The Betrayal" (tr. of Alexandre O'Neill). Kayak (62) Ag 83, p. 59.
"A Curse on Old Age" (tr. of Carmen Conde, w. José R. de Armas). LitR (27:1) Aut 83, p. 100.
"Drought" (tr. of Carmen Conde, w. José R. de Armas). LitR (27:1) Aut 83, p. 101.
"First Serious Warning" (tr. of Alexandre O'Neill). Kayak (62) Ag 83, p. 59.
"Table" (tr. of Alexandre O'Neill). Kayak (62) Ag 83, p. 58.
"With the Poplars" (tr. of Eugenio de Andrade). Confr (25/26) 83, p. 314.
"Women beside the Sea" (tr. of Sophia de Mello Breyner Andresen). Confr (25/26) 83, p. 314.

2588. LEVITZ, Linda
"Last Afternoon in Paris." YetASM (2:1) 83, p. 5.

2589. LEVY, Robert J.
"Juliet" (from The Enlightenment of Revolving Doors, finalist, 10th anniversary manuscript competition). StoneC (11:1/2, Pt. 1) Aut-Wint 83, p. 52.
"Noun Gathering at Dusk." Kayak (63) N 83, p. 32.
"Thanks." Kayak (63) N 83, p. 34.
"Waiting for Snow" (from The Enlightenment of Revolving Doors, finalist, 10th anniversary manuscript competition). StoneC (11:1/2, Pt. 1) Aut-Wint 83, p. 53.
"Winter Rain." Kayak (63) N 83, p. 33.

2590. LEWANDOWSKI, Stephen
"Ranger / Spruce Mountain." Abraxas (27/28) 83, p. 34.
"Susquehanna Headwaters." Blueline (4:1) Sum-Aut 82, p. 29.

2591. LEWIN, Roger A.
"On the Mailman's Daily Rounds." AntigR (55) Aut 83, p. 24.

2592. LEWIS, J. Patrick
"Birds of Russia." StoneC (11:1/2, Pt. 1) Aut-Wint 83, p. 19.

2593. LEWIS, Janet
"Lenore's Bear." Thrpny (4:2, issue 14) Sum 83, p. 13.

2594. LEWIS, Jeffrey
"Dressing Game" (Excerpt: 2,"She dresses me Debussy"). DekalbLAJ (16:1/4) Aut 82-Sum 83, p. 69.

2595. LEWIS, Kathleen P.
"Assateague." YetASM (1:2) 82, p. 3.

2596. LEWIS, Lisa
"The Consequences of Minutes." Poetry (141:6) Mr 83, p. 337-338.
"Five Rooms." CutB (21) Aut-Wint 83, p. 9-13.
"The Horses." SouthernPR (23:2) Aut 83, p. 42-43.
"Silence." Poetry (141:6) Mr 83, p. 335-336.

2597. LEWIS, Mary Gabriel
"Revelations." SanFPJ (5:4) 83, p. 87.

2598. LEWIS, Patricia (See also: LEWIS, Patricia Ann)
"Tubes." Vis (12) 83, p. 27.

2599. LEWIS, Patricia Ann (See also: LEWIS, Patricia)
"Cachet." YetASM (2:1) 83, p. 12.

LEWIS, Rebecca Hecht
See: HECHT-LEWIS, Rebecca

2600. LEWITT, Fil
"A Japanese Lesson." WindO (42) Sum 83, p. 16-17.

2601. LEZCANO, Manuel
"Read This When I Die (Again) Please." RevChic (11:2) Sum 83, p. 48.

2602. LI, Ch'ing-chao
"To the Tune 'Boat of Stars'" (tr. by Sam Hamill). CrabCR (1:1) My 83, p. 6.
"To the Tune 'Magnolia Blossoms'" (tr. by Sam Hamill). CrabCR (1:1) My 83, p. 7.
"To the Tune 'Partridge Sky'" (tr. by Sam Hamill). CrabCR (1:1) My 83, p. 7.
"To the Tune 'The Washing Stream'" (tr. by Sam Hamill). CrabCR (1:1) My 83, p. 6.

2603. LI, Ho
"A Country Road" (tr. by Sam Hamill). PortR (29:1) 83, p. 83.
"Life at the Capital" (tr. by Sam Hamill). PortR (29:1) 83, p. 127.
"Song of Green Water and the Singing Girl" (tr. by Sam Hamill). PortR (29:1) 83, p. 100.

2604. LI, Po
"Moonlit night: Hearing at the Wine Shop Accompaniment to my Lute" (tr. by Jim Cryer). CarolQ (35:3) Spr 83, p. 30.
"Mountain Dialogue" (tr. by Wang Hui-Ming). NewL (49:3/4) Spr-Sum 83, p. 65.
"Mourning a Vintner" (tr. by Sam Hamill). MalR (64) F 83, p. 164.
"Questions and Answers" (tr. by Sam Hamill). MalR (64) F 83, p. 163.
"A Soldier's Song" (tr. by Sam Hamill). MalR (64) F 83, p. 164.
"Song of the Women of Yueh 5" (tr. by Jim Cryer).

CarolQ (35:3) Spr 83, p. 29.
"Taking Leave of a Friend" (tr. by Sam Hamill). MalR (64) F 83, p. 163.
"These Hills in Summer" (tr. by Sam Hamill). MalR (64) F 83, p. 162.
"To a Friend" (tr. by Jim Cryer). CarolQ (35:3) Spr 83, p. 28.

2605. LIBBEY, Elizabeth
"The Act of Letting Go." Poetry (142:1) Ap 83, p. 45-46.
"Afterword." Poetry (142:1) Ap 83, p. 48-49.
"Eavesdropper Out Walking." Poetry (142:1) Ap 83, p. 47.
"Forcing the End." ThRiPo (21/22) 83, p. 53.
"The Kiss." Poetry (142:1) Ap 83, p. 43-44.
"A Sudden Turn of Weather" (for William MacLeish). NoAmR (268:4) D 83, p. 65.

2606. LIBERTELLI, Robert
"Sitting with a Friend Waiting to be Seen." PikeF (5) Spr 83, p. 11.

2607. LIDDELL, Julie
"Joyfulness." PortR (29:1) 83, p. 128.

2608. LIEBER, Ron
"Sentiment for an Old Notion." NewEngR (6:2) Wint 83, p. 213.

2609. LIEBERMAN, Laurence
"Cane Fires." SoCaR (16:1) Aut 83, p. 84-87.
"Fairchild Market: Meats and Mauby" (Bridgetown, Barbados, 1981). SoCaR (16:1) Aut 83, p. 80-83.
"Moonlighters." AmerPoR (12:1) Ja/F 83, p. 26.
"Siesta." Nat (237:9) 1 O 83, p. 276.
"Space and Time." SoCaR (15:2) Spr 83, p. 3.
"Suicide Attempt." SoCaR (15:2) Spr 83, p. 4.

2610. LIETZ, Robert
"After Sledding." Tendril (14/15) Wint 83, p. 122-123.
"Flying Home" (For Robert Lietz, Sr. 6/6/20 - 2/24/82). KanQ (15:4) Aut 83, p. 27-29.
"P.O.W.: In the States." CutB (21) Aut-Wint 83, p. 86-87.

2611. LIFSHIN, Lyn
"Accessory Madonna." WormR (23:4, issue 92) 83, p. 150.
"Blue Chemise." Calyx (8:1) Aut 83, p. 33.
"The Candidate." Focus (15:95) Ag 83, p. 18.
"Candidate's Madonna." WindO (42) Sum 83, p. 8.
"Channuka Madonna." NewL (49:3/4) Spr-Sum 83, p. 269.
"Charming Madonna." WormR (23:4, issue 92) 83, p. 151.
"Cherry Blossoms in Darkness." Paint (10:19/20) Spr-Aut 83, p. 14.
"Dream of Having to Talk to the Class about Masturbation." MemphisSR (2:1) Aut 81, p. 8.
"Dream of the Monster in Bloomingdale's." MemphisSR

(2:1) Aut 81, p. 9.
"The Dream When I First Woke Up." HangL (44) Sum 83, p. 28.
"Early Cool Madonna." WormR (23:4, issue 92) 83, p. 150.
"Editing Poems for the Anthology." Focus (15:95) Ag 83, p. 18.
"Fast Lane Madonna, 1." WormR (23:4, issue 92) 83, p. 150.
"Fast Lane Madonna, 2." WormR (23:4, issue 92) 83, p. 150.
"Fear." KanQ (15:1) Wint 83, p. 24.
"Going through the Notebook I Jotted Things Down in in Italy." Wind (13:49) 83, p. 33.
"Helen Marie." Calyx (8:1) Aut 83, p. 34.
"Helen Marie." Paint (10:19/20) Spr-Aut 83, p. 15.
"Hydroponics Madonna." WormR (23:4, issue 92) 83, p. 150.
"I Don't Know What You Want." SecC (11:1/2) 83, p. 105.
"I Don't Want Diana in the Palace." Bogg (51) 83, p. 20.
"I Feel like the Space a Typewriter that's Stuck Where All the Keys Keep Hitting." MemphisSR (2:2) Spr 82, p. 7.
"I Got the Bucks Figure a Long Slow." Kayak (63) N 83, p. 20-21.
"I Remember Haifa Being Lovely But." Calyx (8:1) Aut 83, p. 36.
"Insomnia Like Ants." YetASM (1:1) 82, p. 8.
"Irritation." Prima (8) 83, p. 44.
"Jealousy." NewL (49:3/4) Spr-Sum 83, p. 269.
"Journal Manuscripts Like Hair Falling, Dust." YetASM (1:1) 82, p. 10.
"The Knife Thrower's Woman." PoNow (7:2, #38) 83, p. 35.
"Leftover Madonna." WormR (23:4, issue 92) 83, p. 150.
"Like a Leaky Ball Point Pen." Wind (13:49) 83, p. 33.
"A Lover Like Sleep." MemphisSR (2:2) Spr 82, p. 47.
"Madonna Gardenia." WindO (42) Sum 83, p. 8.
"Madonna of the Excesses." Bogg (50) 83, p. 18.
"Madonna of the Mass Appeal." Bogg (51) 83, p. 23.
"Madonna of the Messy House." WormR (23:4, issue 92) 83, p. 150.
"Madonna of the Too Hard Ballet Class." Bogg (51) 83, p. 9.
"Madonna Who Gets Around." WormR (23:4, issue 92) 83, p. 150.
"Madonna Who You Have to Hand It To." WormR (23:4, issue 92) 83, p. 150.
"Mama." PoNow (7:2, #38) 83, p. 35.
"The Man in the Shoe Store." Bogg (50) 83, p. 4-5.
"The Man Married to the Midget." PoNow (7:2, #38) 83, p. 35.
"The Man with a Drill in His Head." Kayak (63) N 83, p. 23.
"More of My Mother and the Knife." ModernPS (11:3) 83, p. 270-272.
"No Deposit No Return Madonna." Bogg (50) 83, p. 8.
"Parole Madonna." WormR (23:4, issue 92) 83, p. 150.

"Phone Water Shells." AntigR (53) Spr 83, p. 17-18.
"The Poem: Like somebody who can just build band concert stages." WebR (8:1) Spr 83, p. 58.
"The Poetry Workshop Dream." AntigR (53) Spr 83, p. 18.
"Shaker Madonna." WindO (42) Sum 83, p. 9.
"Something Let Go." WindO (42) Sum 83, p. 9.
"Thirty Miles West of Chicago." Prima (8) 83, p. 44.
"To the Man Who Asked Me Why I Took So Many Showers." Bogg (50) 83, p. 9.
"Too Cold House Madonna." Bogg (50) 83, p. 15.
"Tuesday." SecC (11:1/2) 83, p. 103.
"Turned Out to Be a Rubber Check." SecC (11:1/2) 83, p. 105.
"When I'm around Carl I Don't." Kayak (63) N 83, p. 21.
"When the Borders Closed." Calyx (8:1) Aut 83, p. 35.
"Wok Madonna." WormR (23:4, issue 92) 83, p. 150.
"Yes He Says Send Your Kid to." Kayak (63) N 83, p. 22.

2612. LIFSON, Martha (Martha Ronk)
"An Exhibition of Gorky at LACMA." AmerPoR (12:5) S/O 83, p. 5.
"The Old Woman Sends Her Love Poem to Genji." ChiR (33:3) Wint 83, p. 104.

2613. LIGHT, F. L.
"Gleg the Falcon." DekalbLAJ (16:1/4) Aut 82-Sum 83, p. 70.

2614. LIGHT, Joanne
"Love Poem #1." PottPort (5) 83-84, p. 26.
"Sam Stone." Grain (11:3) Ag 83, p. 24-25.

2615. LIGI
"One Solution." StoneC (10:3/4) Spr-Sum 83, p. 46.
"Purge." StoneC (10:3/4) Spr-Sum 83, p. 46.

2616. LIGNELL, Kathleen
"Chiaroscuro." SouthwR (68:2) Spr 83, p. 134-135.
"First Snow, Death Valley" (Richard Hill, 1943-1960) (from The Range of Light, semi-finalist, 10th anniversary manuscript competition). StoneC (11:1/2, Pt. 1) Aut-Wint 83, p. 64-65.

2617. LIMA, Robert
"Throes." Images (8:3) 83, p. 6.

2618. LINDBLAD, Lois
"In Her Bath" (lines for a young husband). MissouriR (6:2) Wint 83, p. 82-83.

2619. LINDEMAN, Jack
"Utopian." CrabCR (1:2) Aut 83, p. 3.

2620. LINDHOLDT, Paul J.
"Ouzel." SouthernHR (17:1) Wint 83, p. 32.
"The Plumed Clod." AntigR (55) Aut 83, p. 65-66.
"Ptarmigan." AntigR (55) Aut 83, p. 67.

"Shrike." AntigR (55) Aut 83, p. 68.

2621. LINDNER, Carl
"Old Ladies." SouthwR (68:2) Spr 83, p. 162-163.
"Watching the Fire." StoneC (10:3/4) Spr-Sum 83, p. 48.

2622. LINDO, Hugo
"Between Words" (To Elizabeth Miller, tr. by Elizabeth Gamble Miller). Mund (14:1) 83, p. 115, 117.
"Entre Palabras" (A Elizabeth Miller). Mund (14:1) 83, p. 114, 116.
"On Poetry" (tr. by Elizabeth Gamble Miller). NewOR (10:4) Wint 83, p. 42.

2623. LINDSAY, Frannie
"1955." Tendril (16) Sum 83, p. 73.
"The Aerial Tide Coming In." PortR (29:1) 83, p. 42.
"Figure by a Chimney." TriQ (56) Wint 83, p. 147.
"The First Night in Heaven." Tendril (14/15) Wint 83, p. 124.
"The Right Side of the Brain." CutB (21) Aut-Wint 83, p. 82.

2624. LINEHAN, Don
"Calendar." Germ (7:1) Spr-Sum 83, p. 22.
"Poem: Draw the room about me like a tent." Germ (7:1) Spr-Sum 83, p. 23.

2625. LIPMAN, Ed "Foots"
"Poem for Rupert Weber, 85 Years Too Late." SecC (11:1/2) 83, p. 107-114.

2626. LIPPMAN, Amy
"The Globe Burns." HarvardA (117:1) Mr 83, p. 21.

2627. LIPSCHUTZ, Barbara
"There was nothing resembling heavy." YetASM (1:2) 82, p. 6.

2628. LIPSITZ, Lou
"Distance." SouthernPR (23:2) Aut 82 [i.e. (23:1?) Spr 83], p. 28.
"Distance, Again." SouthernPR (23:2) Aut 82 [i.e. (23:1?) Spr 83], p. 29.
"Does Romance Exist, and If So, Is It Any Good for Us?" Kayak (63) N 83, p. 59.
"Looking at a Mattress." SouthernPR (23:2) Aut 83, p. 53-55.

2629. LISK, Thomas
"Ballet Dew." KanQ (15:1) Wint 83, p. 99.
"Imitation." KanQ (15:1) Wint 83, p. 99.
"The Vise." KanQ (15:2) Spr 83, p. 6.

2630. LISOWSKI, Joseph
"At Home in the Autumn Mountain." PortR (29:1) 83, p. 77.
"Cold Mountain" (tr. of Han Shan). Pig (11) 83,

p. 92.
"In the Green Stream" (tr. of Wang Wei). LitR (26:3) Spr 83, p. 449.
"Leave-Taking" (tr. of Wang Wei). StoneC (11:1/2, Pt. 1) Aut-Wint 83, p. 17.
"Meditations" (tr. of Tu Fu, for J. P. Seaton). Pig (11) 83, p. 92.
"On Friendship." PortR (29:1) 83, p. 103.
"Visitation Rites (9)." YetASM (1:2) 82, p. 10.
"Visitation Rites (10)." YetASM (1:2) 82, p. 15.

2631. LITSEY, Sarah
"The Dark Friend." Wind (13:47) 83, p. 26-27.
"Encounter." Wind (13:47) 83, p. 26.

2632. LITTLE, Geraldine C.
"Joseph." ChrC (100:38) 14 D 83, p. 1156.

2633. LITTLE, Pippa
"Cockfight." Wind (13:48) 83, p. 36.

2634. LIU, E
"Boiling Falls" (tr. by Jonathan Chaves). Hudson (36:2) Sum 83, p. 286.
"The House of Red Leaves" (tr. by Jonathan Chaves). Hudson (36:2) Sum 83, p. 284.
"I Remember" (tr. by Jonathan Chaves). Hudson (36:2) Sum 83, p. 283.
"New Year's Eve" (tr. by Jonathan Chaves). Hudson (36:2) Sum 83, p. 286.
"On the Fifteenth Day of the Eighth Month: Watching a Rainstorm from a Tower in Seoul" (tr. by Jonathan Chaves). Hudson (36:2) Sum 83, p. 285.
"Pleasures of Sinbashi" (tr. by Jonathan Chaves). Hudson (36:2) Sum 83, p. 284.
"Waiting for the Ferry at Inchon" (tr. by Jonathan Chaves). Hudson (36:2) Sum 83, p. 281-283.

LIU, T'ieh-yün
See: LIU, E

2635. LIU, Tsung-yüan
"Snowy River" (tr. by Sam Hamil). CreamCR (8:1/2) 83, p. 91.

2636. LIU, Yung
"After the eating, the drinking and singing" (tr. by Sam Hamil). CreamCR (8:1/2) 83, p. 91.
"Song (Ch'i shih)" (tr. by Sam Hamill). AmerPoR (12:6) N/D 83, p. 6.
"Song (Ting Feng-po)" (tr. by Sam Hamill). AmerPoR (12:6) N/D 83, p. 6.

2637. LIVESAY, Dorothy
"Definitions." PoetryCR (4:4) Sum 83, p. 7.
"Wednesdays on the Island." PoetryCR (5:2) Wint 83-84, p. 17.

2638. LIVINGSTON, Albert
"Another Fall." Poem (47) Mr 83, p. 56.

"Marygold." Poem (47) Mr 83, p. 57.
"Staircase Riposte." Poem (47) Mr 83, p. 55.
"The Starving Poet to His Love." Poem (47) Mr 83, p. 58.
"A Subscriber Requests." Poem (48) Jl 83, p. 61.

2639. LLANOS, Guillermo
"Biografia Mortal" (Excerpt) (tr. by Elizabeth Balestrieri). ClockR (2:1) 83, p. 41.

2640. LLEWELLYN, Chris
"Laverne." 13thM (7:1/2) 83, p. 43.
"Rhetoric." MinnR (NS 21) Aut 83, p. 27-28.
"Stitcher" (For Judith Hall). 13thM (7:1/2) 83, p. 44-45.

LLOSA, Ricardo Pau
See: PAU-LLOSA, Ricardo

2641. LLOYD, D. H.
"Class Project." RagMag (2:2) Aut 83, p. 5.
"First Book." Abraxas (27/28) 83, p. 17.

2642. Lo BOSCO, Rocco
"Dirigible." Pig (11) 83, p. 53.
"No Disaster." Pig (11) 83, p. 74.

2643. LOCKE, Duane
"An Edwardian Lady." LitR (27:1) Aut 83, p. 64-68.

2644. LOCKE, Karen
"Moving In." YetASM (1:2) 82, p. 11.

2645. LOCKLIN, Gerald
"The 366th Day of the Year." WormR (23:4, issue 92) 83, p. 146-147.
"Après Le Métro Dernier" WormR (23:4, issue 92) 83, p. 147-148.
"The Best Year of Her Life." WormR (23:4, issue 92) 83, p. 149.
"The Blue Nun and I." WormR (23:4, issue 92) 83, p. 148.
"Cold, Straight from the Can." WormR (23:4, issue 92) 83, p. 149.
"Emeritus." WormR (23:4, issue 92) 83, p. 146.
"Final." OroM (2:1, #5) Sum 83, opposite p. 1.
"The Ladies Thank You, Ladies." Abraxas (27/28) 83, p. 40.
"The Last Unspoiled Beauty in America." WormR (23:4, issue 92) 83, p. 150.
"Maybe the Women Are Right About Us." Abraxas (27/28) 83, p. 39.
"Revised Standard Version." WormR (23:4, issue 92) 83, p. 145.
"They Insist on Calling It Overcompensation." WormR (23:4, issue 92) 83, p. 150.
"The Time I Drank with Allen Ginsberg." WormR (23:4, issue 92) 83, p. 145.
"To Live in Another Country Is to Suffer the Consequences of Our Own." OroM (2:1, #5) Sum

83, p. 3.
"Two Evenings." OroM (2:1, #5) Sum 83, p. 3-4.
"We Should Have Expected It." WormR (23:4, issue 92) 83, p. 150.
"Why There Was No Great Migration of Parisians to America." WormR (23:4, issue 92) 83, p. 150.
"Will I Ever Learn?" Bogg (51) 83, p. 24.

2646. LOCKWOOD, Margo
"Back." Ploughs (9:1) 83, p. 41-42.
"Noël Minimal." Ploughs (9:1) 83, p. 44.
"Vintage Clothes." Ploughs (9:1) 83, p. 43.

2647. LOCKWOOD BARLETTA, Naomi
"En el Norte." RevChic (11:3/4) 83, p. 71.
"El Salvador." RevChic (11:3/4) 83, p. 71.

2648. LOEHLE, Craig
"Lost Children." WorldO (17:2) Wint 82-83, p. 16.

2649. LOGAN, Chloe Hughes
"Yours/Mine." Wind (13:48) 83, p. 44.

2650. LOGAN, Henry
"Before Storm" (after Neruda). StoneC (11:1/2, Pt. 1) Aut-Wint 83, p. 38.

2651. LOGAN, John
"The Whatnot." NewRep (189:2) 11 Jl 83, p. 30.

2652. LOGAN, Thean
"Dalliance." AntigR (52) Wint 83, p. 12.
"Moon of Wakening." AntigR (52) Wint 83, p. 12.

2653. LOGAN, William
"Auden." Shen (34:4) 83, p. 100.
"Black Harbor." SouthernR (19:3) Jl 83, p. 668.
"Darwin in the Ditch." Shen (34:4) 83, p. 99.
"The English Museum." Shen (34:4) 83, p. 98.
"Money and Durer." AntR (41:3) Sum 83, p. 333.
"New York." Epoch (33:1) Aut-Wint 83, p. 73.
"The Sea." Tendril (14/15) Wint 83, p. 125.
"This Island." SouthernR (19:3) Jl 83, p. 669.

2654. LOGUE, Mary
"Watermelon in Florence." Calyx (8:1) Aut 83, p. 17.

2655. LOMAS, Herbert
"Down the Hill." Hudson (36:3) Aut 83, p. 459-460.
"How I Love My Sister." Hudson (36:3) Aut 83, p. 462.
"Mother Skin." Hudson (36:3) Aut 83, p. 461.
"With the Pike behind Her." Hudson (36:3) Aut 83, p. 460-461.

2656. LOMBARDO, Gian S.
"This Is How." YetASM (1:2) 82, p. 7.

2657. LONDON, Jonathan
"Cannery." Sam (34:3 135th release) 83, p. 54-55.

2658. LONERGAN, Frank
"Dull Day at Heart Lake in the Adirondacks." KanQ (15:2) Spr 83, p. 99.
"Mother at the Department Store." Comm (110:9) 6 My 83, p. 280.

2659. LONG, Robert
"Chelsea." NewYorker (59:12) 9 My 83, p. 50.
"Fishing Bridge" (for Robert Dash, and after his painting of the same name). Tendril (16) Sum 83, p. 76.
"Goodbye." Poetry (143:1) O 83, p. 17.
"In the Unfinished House" (For Allen Planz). Poetry (143:1) O 83, p. 16.
"Interior Decoration." Poetry (143:1) O 83, p. 15.
"Lost Assignments" (for Jeremy Cole). Tendril (16) Sum 83, p. 74-75.

2660. LONG, Susan Grafeld
"Miscarriage." PoetL (78:1) Spr 83, p. 22.
"Note from the Chesapeake." PoetL (78:1) Spr 83, p. 23.
"Womanhood." PoetL (78:1) Spr 83, p. 23.

LONGCHAMPS, Joanne de
See: De LONGCHAMPS, Joanne

2661. LONGLEY, Judy
"In the Mountains." SouthernR (19:2) Ap 83, p. 398-399.
"Mozart." SouthernR (19:2) Ap 83, p. 399-400.

2662. LONGLEY, Michael
"Casualty." Agni (19) 83, p. 11.
"Circe." Agni (19) 83, p. 9.
"Last Requests." Agni (19) 83, p. 14.
"Master of Ceremonies." Agni (19) 83, p. 13.
"The Swim." Agni (19) 83, p. 12.
"Wounds." Agni (19) 83, p. 10.

2663. LONGOBARDI, David
"As the Day Ends and I Face a Long Summer." HarvardA (117:1) Mr 83, p. 33.

2664. LOPEZ ACUNA, David
"Scherzo Fantástico" (Tras Stravinsky). Prismal (11) Aut 83, p. 101.

2665. LORCA, Federico García
"City without Sleep: Nocturne at the Brooklyn Bridge" (tr. by Greg Simon). NowestR (21:2/3) 83, p. 99, 101.
"Ciudad sin Sueño: Nocturno del Brooklyn Bridge." NowestR (21:2/3) 83, p. 98, 100.
"Dance of Death" (tr. by Robert Bly). NewL (49:3/4) Spr-Sum 83, p. 88-91.
"Death" (for Isidoro de Blas). NewL (49:3/4) Spr-Sum 83, p. 91.
"Death" (for Isidoro de Blas) (tr. by Louis Hammer). Field (28) Spr 83, p. 18.

"Double Poem of Lake Eden" (tr. by Greg Simon). NowestR (21:2/3) 83, p. 81, 83.
"Earth and Moon" (tr. by Greg Simon). NowestR (21:2/3) 83, p. 85, 87.
"Ghazal of the Terrifying Presence" (tr. by Robert Bly). NewL (49:3/4) Spr-Sum 83, p. 88-91.
"Landscape with Two Graves and an Assyrian Dog" (tr. by Greg Simon). NowestR (21:2/3) 83, p. 89.
"Moon and Panorama of Insects (Love Poem)" (tr. by Louis Hammer). Field (28) Spr 83, p. 19-21.
"Oda a Walt Whitman." NowestR (21:2/3) 83, p. 90-96.
"Ode to Walt Whitman" (tr. by Greg Simon). NowestR (21:2/3) 83, p. 91-97.
"Paisaje con Dos Tumbas y un Perro Asirio." NowestR (21:2/3) 83, p. 88.
"Poema Doble del Lago Edem." NowestR (21:2/3) 83, p. 80, 82.
"Poeta en Nueva York" (Selections) (tr. by Greg Simon). NowestR (21:2/3) 83, p. 79-101.
"Sleepless City (Nocturne of Brooklyn Bridge)" (tr. by Louis Hammer). Field (28) Spr 83, p. 16-17.
"Tierra y Luna." NowestR (21:2/3) 83, p. 84, 86.

2666. LORENZO, Eusebio
"Morremos cara ó mar mirando os horizontes." Prismal (11) Aut 83, p. 117.

2667. LORENZO, Rafael
"Sentiments in the Evening." Tele (18) 83, p. 82.
"To and Fro Lightly." Tele (18) 83, p. 83-84.

LORINGHOVEN, Elsa von Freytag, Baroness
See: FREYTAG-LORINGHOVEN, Elsa von, Baroness

2668. LORRE
"To touch your soul." Meadows (3:1) 82, p. 15.

2669. LOTT, Clarinda
"Writing on Skin." Bogg (51) 83, p. 4.

2670. LOTT, Rick
"Alabama Symphony." WestHR (37:3) Aut 83, p. 207.
"The Bamboo Cage." WestHR (37:4) Wint 83, p. 308.
"The Hurricane Party." Swallow (1) Spr 83, p. 13.

2671. LOURIE, Richard
"After the Resurrection" (tr. of Henryk Grynberg). PoetryE (9/10) Wint 82-Spr 83, p. 239-240.
"A Country" (tr. of Zbigniew Herbert). PoetryE (9/10) Wint 82-Spr 83, p. 236.
"The Power of Taste" (tr. of Zbigniew Herbert). PoetryE (9/10) Wint 82-Spr 83, p. 237-238.

2672. LOUTHAN, Robert
"Heavy Machinery." AmerPoR (12:4) Jl-Ag 83, p. 42.
"To Face Her." VirQR (59:1) Wint 83, p. 57.

2673. LOVERIDGE-GALLAS, Louisa
"The Sacred Slow Down." ClockR (2:1) 83, p. 43.

2674. LOVITT, Bob
"The Last Words." Vis (11) 83, p. 21.
"Rain on These Trees." CrabCR (1:1) My 83, p. 18.
"Seattle Pot-Shots." CrabCR (1:1) My 83, p. 18.

2675. LOW, Denise
"Rolla To Lawrence." KanQ (15:4) Aut 83, p. 34.

2676. LOWE, Elizabeth
"Absence" (tr. of Rodrigo Parra Sandoval). Mund (14:1) 83, p. 32.
"Art History" (tr. of Rodrigo Parra Sandoval). Mund (14:1) 83, p. 31.
"Possibility" (tr. of Rodrigo Parra Sandoval). Mund (14:1) 83, p. 30.
"Understanding" (tr. of Rodrigo Parra Sandoval). Mund (14:1) 83, p. 30-31.

2677. LOWE, Jonathan F.
"Braille." Poem (47) Mr 83, p. 31.

2678. LOWELL, Robert
"The Poet." NewRep (186:23) 9 Je 82, p. 37.

2679. LOWENSTEIN, Robert
"After Us." Sam (36:3 143rd release) 83, p. 10.
"Buried Treasure." SanFPJ (5:1) 83, p. 12.
"The Insects Are Restive." Sam (36:3 143rd release) 83, p. 11.
"The Oaks of Poland." Sam (34:3 135th release) 83, p. 14.
"Protective Custody." Sam (34:3 135th release) 83, p. 15.

2680. LOWRY, Betty
"Advice to a Weekend Painter." Wind (13:48) 83, p. 37.
"People Like You, with No Problems." NewRena (17) Aut 83, p. 51.
"Through the Arches: St. Severin's." ChrC (100:18) 1 Je 83, p. 544.

2681. LOWRY, Mary Ann
"Teacher Thinks about a Precocious Studnet." EngJ (72:5) S 83, p. 40.

2682. LOWRY, Ruth Agar
"Nothingness." SanFPJ (5:3) 83, p. 44.
"Under the Mushroom Cloud." SanFPJ (4:4) 83, p. 90.

2683. LUANDREW, Albert
"Be Careful How You Vote." ClockR (1:1) Sum 83, p. 20.

2684. LUBETSKY, Elsen
"Fairy Tale." SanFPJ (5:2) 83, p. 11.
"The Friendly Dow All Dead and White." SanFPJ (5:2) 83, p. 12.
"Hades Thirst." SanFPJ (5:4) 83, p. 94.
"Love That Garbage." SanFPJ (5:2) 83, p. 56.

"The Rain That Fell in Spain." SanFPJ (4:4) 83, p. 94-95.
"Revolt in El Salvador." SanFPJ (5:4) 83, p. 93.
"Rock of Ages." YetASM (2:1) 83, p. 7.
"Time Warped." SanFPJ (5:2) 83, p. 12.

2685. LUCAS, Barbara
"The Mothers." BelPoJ (34:1) Aut 83, p. 35.

2686. LUCAS, Marie B.
"Summer's End." Wind (13:48) 83, p. 38.
"Time to Change." Wind (13:48) 83, p. 38-39.

2687. LUCAS, Tom
"The Peony Fields." GeoR (37:1) Spr 83, p. 129.

2688. LUCINA, Mary, Sister
"About Vowels." StoneC (11:1/2, Pt. 1) Aut-Wint 83, p. 15.
"Choices." AntigR (54) Sum 83, p. 58.
"In the Wind." AntigR (54) Sum 83, p. 58.
"Lesson in Flying." Vis (12) 83, p. 6.
"To Eat." AntigR (54) Sum 83, p. 59.
"Where Stables Are." SouthernPR (23:2) Aut 83, p. 50.

2689. LUDVIGSON, Susan
"After Warnings from County Prosecutor Minister Agrees to Stop Using Electric Shocks to Teach Bible Students." KanQ (15:4) Aut 83, p. 18.
"Cleopatra" (after the painting by Guido Reni). BlackWR (9:1) Aut 82, p. 44.
"Embarrassment." MemphisSR (4:1) Aut 83, p. 5.
"His Confession." KanQ (15:4) Aut 83, p. 17.
"I Arrive in a Small Boat, Alone." GeoR (37:3) Aut 83, p. 516.
"Little Women." OhioR (30) 83, p. 97.
"Man Arrested in Hacking Death Tells Police He Mistook Mother-in-Law for Raccoon." KanQ (15:4) Aut 83, p. 16.
"Molasses Fumes Fatal." KanQ (15:4) Aut 83, p. 18.
"Prayer." SouthernPR (23:2) Aut 82 [i.e. (23:1?) Spr 83], p. 14.
"The Swimmer." SouthernPR (23:2) Aut 83, p. 8.
"Virginia with Artists." SouthernPR (23:2) Aut 83, p. 8-9.

2690. LUG, Sieglinde
"I Always" (tr. of Brigitte Schwaiger). DevQ (17:4) Wint 83, p. 25.

2691. LUGO, Robertoluis
"Adopto el disentimiento tranformador." Ráçata (1) 83, p. 77-78.
"Ai Juebes." Ráçata (2) 83, p. 81-83.
"Carmen: los saltos se brincan o nos qedamos gindando." Ráçata (2) 83, p. 80.
"Espejos." Ráçata (1) 83, p. 79-83.
"La espera espera a qe mutilen la primera palabra." Ráçata (2) 83, p. 84-85.

"Para Creser Cresiendo." Rácata (2) 83, p. 86.
"El sapato no inspira." Rácata (2) 83, p. 132-133.

LUM, Wing Tek
See: WING, Tek Lum

2692. LUND, Robert E.
"Bemused by the Craze." YetASM (1:2) 82, p. 19.
"Dissolving Fashion's Frenzy." YetASM (1:2) 82, p. 14.

2693. LUNDAY, Robert
"My Friends (I'm Going West)." NegC (3:4) Aut 83, p. 45.

2694. LUNDE, David
"Prize." PoNow (7:2, #38) 83, p. 13.

2695. LUNDY, Gary
"Warning Signs." PoetL (78:2) Sum 83, p. 94.

2696. LUPARDUS, Louise
"The Mockingbird." LittleBR (3:3) Spr 83, p. 33.

2697. LUSCHEI, Glenna
"Editor." SecC (11:1/2) 83, p. 125.

2698. LUTHER, Susan
"Handsome Woman Aging." NegC (3:4) Aut 83, p. 90.

2699. LUX, Thomas
"Boating with Worms" (for James Tate). LittleBR (4:2) Wint 83-84, p. 50.
"Empty Pitchforks." MemphisSR (2:1) Aut 81, p. 34.
"The Great Books of the Dead." AmerPoR (12:6) N/D 83, p. 33.
"Sleepmask Dithyrambic." ParisR (25:87) Spr 83, p. 203-204.
"Somebody's Aunt Out Swabbing Her Birdbath." ParisR (25:87) Spr 83, p. 204.
"The Thirst of Turtles." ParisR (25:87) Spr 83, p. 202.
"Triptych, Middle Panel Burning." Field (29) Aut 83, p. 83-94.

2700. LYLES, Peggy Willis
"Darkness holding stars in place." WindO (42) Sum 83, p. 2.
"His fingers on the calculator." WindO (42) Sum 83, p. 3.
"Through a maze of lilies." WindO (42) Sum 83, p. 4.
"The way the Latin teacher keeps the soccer score." WindO (42) Sum 83, p. 4.

LYN, Veronica ver
See: VerLYN, Veronica

2701. LYNCH, Thomas P.
"The Age of Reason." MidwQ (24:3) Spr 83, p. 293.
"The Exhibitionist." MidwQ (24:3) Spr 83, p. 296.

"Off Season." MidwQ (24:3) Spr 83, p. 294.
"The Orient." MidwQ (24:3) Spr 83, p. 295.
"Rotary Album." MidwQ (24:3) Spr 83, p. 290-291.
"The West Window in Moveen." MidwQ (24:3) Spr 83, p. 292.

2702. LYNGGAARD, Klaus
"Crystal Day" (tr. by Jack Brondum). SoDakR (21:1) Spr 83, p. 42.
"Here come the hours" (tr. by Jack Brondum). SoDakR (21:1) Spr 83, p. 42.
"Hunters--Identity" (tr. by Jack Brondum). SoDakR (21:1) Spr 83, p. 44.
"Jaegere--Identitet." SoDakR (21:1) Spr 83, p. 45.
"Der kommer timerne." SoDakR (21:1) Spr 83, p. 43.
"Krystaldag." SoDakR (21:1) Spr 83, p. 43.
"Solskin i en bulet vindueskarm." SoDakR (21:1) Spr 83, p. 47.
"Sunshine in a dented windowsill" (tr. by Jack Brondum). SoDakR (21:1) Spr 83, p. 46.

2703. LYNN, Robin
"Western Boys." Meadows (4:1) 83, p. 42.
"When Bobby Went to War." Meadows (4:1) 83, p. 26.

2704. LYNN, Sandra
"The Birth of Venus in the Gulf of Mexico." NewL (49:3/4) Spr-Sum 83, p. 189.

2705. LYNSKEY, Edward C.
"Burying Turnips." ColEng (45:5) S 83, p. 493.
"No Southern Comfort." CropD (4) 83, p. 10.
"The Tree Surgeon's Gift." FourQt (32:3) Spr 83, p. 18.

2706. LYON, David
"Long Distance & Here." NewL (49:3/4) Spr-Sum 83, p. 114.

2707. LYON, George Ella
"22 Hyde Park Gate." Nimrod (27:1) Aut-Wint 83, p. 16-17.
"1941." Nimrod (27:1) Aut-Wint 83, p. 19.
"At the Lodge." Nimrod (27:1) Aut-Wint 83, p. 19.
"Evidence." Nimrod (27:1) Aut-Wint 83, p. 17.
"For a Heart Leafed with Words Like a Tree." Nimrod (27:1) Aut-Wint 83, p. 16.
"In the Garden." Nimrod (27:1) Aut-Wint 83, p. 18.
"Virginia Woolf [poems]." Nimrod (27:1) Aut-Wint 83, p. 16-19.
"Visitng Monks House." Nimrod (27:1) Aut-Wint 83, p. 17-18.

2708. LYONS, Richard J.
"From the Porch." Telescope (5/6) Spr 83, p. 79-81.

2709. LYSTER, Eswyn
"Cora-Lee." Grain (11:1) F 83, p. 8.

2710. LYTLE, Leslie
"The Soybeans and The Doe: Two Stories." NewEngR (5:3) Spr 83, p. 411-413.

M., L. G.
See: L. G. M.

2711. MAASS, Arlene
"Danish Tea House (Old City)." Argo (4:1) 82, p. 4.

Mac . . .
See also: Names beginning with "Mc", filed below in their alphabetic position.

2712. MacAULAY, Dorothy Harrington
"Prodigal Son." CrossC (5:2/3) 83, p. 5.

2713. MacBAIN, Walter (Walter D.)
"House Painting." Bogg (50) 83, p. 15.
"Safehouse Mercenary." Wind (13:49) 83, p. 34.

2714. MacBETH, George
"The Leveret, in the Twilight" (for Iseult). Stand (24:4) Aut 83, p. 4.

2715. MacDONALD, Bruce
"The Cannon." AntigR (52) Wint 83, p. 29-30.
"When in a Chinese State." AntigR (52) Wint 83, p. 28-29.

2716. MacDONALD, Cynthia
"Death on the High Seas." Shen (34:4) 83, p. 109-110.
"A Perfect Binding." PoetryNW (24:2) Sum 83, p. 23.
"Two Brothers in a Field of Absence." NewYorker (59:24) 1 Ag 83, p. 34.

2717. MacDONALD, Kathryn
"Emmeline Stacks the Deck." GeoR (37:1) Spr 83, p. 156.
"Emmeline Trips the Light Fantastic." GeoR (37:1) Spr 83, p. 157.

2718. MacDOUGALL, Alan
"Time Enough." PoetL (78:3) Aut 83, p. 167.

2719. MacEWEN, Gwendolyn
"The Garden of the Thieves." PoetryCR (4:3) Spr 83, p. 9.
"Grey Owl's Poem." PoetryCR (4:3) Spr 83, p. 9.
"Languages." Descant (42) Aut 83, p. 23.
"Late Song." PoetryCR (4:3) Spr 83, p. 8.
"The Letter." PoetryCR (4:3) Spr 83, p. 9.
"Manitou Poem." PoetryCR (4:3) Spr 83, p. 9.
"The Music." PoetryCR (4:3) Spr 83, p. 9.
"The Names." CrossC (5:1) 83, p. 18.
"Open Secrets." CrossC (5:1) 83, p. 18.
"Past and Future Ghosts." Descant (42) Aut 83, p. 24.
"Sunday Morning Sermon." Descant (42) Aut 83, p. 25.

"Sunlight at Sherbourne and Bloor." PoetryCR (4:3) Spr 83, p. 8.
"The White Horse." PoetryCR (4:3) Spr 83, p. 9.

MacGAY
See: GAY, Mac

2720. MacINNES, Mairi
"At Five the Train Left Hendaye." TriQ (56) Wint 83, p. 143.
"A Complaint Answered." OntR (18) Spr-Sum 83, p. 85.
"A Linen Skirt." TriQ (56) Wint 83, p. 146.
"An Old Cat." OntR (18) Spr-Sum 83, p. 84.
"Your Eyes." TriQ (56) Wint 83, p. 144-145.

2721. MacKENZIE, Ginny
"At Home." LittleM (14:1/2) 83, p. 69.
"He Paints a Picture of His House." LittleM (14:1/2) 83, p. 70-72.
"Retreat to the Country of Pure Drought." Ploughs (9:1) 83, p. 159-160.

MacKENZIE-PORTER, Patricia
See: McKENZIE-PORTER, Patricia

2722. MACKEY, Gerald
"On Resurrecting Chaucer." EngJ (72:3) Mr 83, p. 29.

2723. MacKINNON, Bernie
"Deborah." AntigR (54) Sum 83, p. 83.
"Lionel." AntigR (54) Sum 83, p. 80.
"Margaret." AntigR (54) Sum 83, p. 81.
"Richard." AntigR (54) Sum 83, p. 82.

2724. MacQUARRIE, Lachlan
"Your Body." PottPort (5) 83-84, p. 11.

2725. MacSWEEN, R. J.
"Conspiracy." AntigR (54) Sum 83, p. 21.
"The Fall in the City." AntigR (53) Spr 83, p. 71.
"Just Born." AntigR (52) Wint 83, p. 76.
"Lulls." AntigR (54) Sum 83, p. 22.
"Reverie in Daylight." AntigR (55) Aut 83, p. 57.
"Within." AntigR (55) Aut 83, p. 56.

2726. MADDEN, Patrick
"Joseph's-of-the-Morning." MissouriR (6:2) Wint 83, p. 71.

2727. MADDOCK, Mary
"Laughing, exulting and rebellious" (tr. of Bella Akhmadulina). PoNow (7:2, #38) 83, p. 44.
"Northern Elegy" (Excerpt) (tr. of Anna Akhmatova). MassR (24:1) Spr 83, p. 107.
"Sleep" (tr. of Bella Akhmadulina). PoNow (7:2, #38) 83, p. 44.
"Workman Ascending a Staircase." Nimrod (27:1) Aut-Wint 83, p. 72.

2728. MADDOX, Everette
"Cleaning the Cruiser." Ploughs (9:2/3) 83, p. 74-75.
"Conversation with Myself at a Street Corner." Swallow (1) Spr 83, p. 74-75.
"Of Rust." Ploughs (9:2/3) 83, p. 76-77.

2729. MADONICK, Michael David
"This Winter or Any Other" (for Siena Sanderson).Nimrod (27:1) Aut-Wint 83, p. 44.

2730. MADSON, Arthur
"Artificial." WindO (43) Wint 83, p. 5.

2731. MADZELAN, P.
"Black Gold for Them / Black Lung for Me." SanFPJ (5:3) 83, p. 48.

2732. MAGARRELL, Elaine
"On Hogback Mountain." PoetL (78:2) Sum 83, p. 91.

2733. MAGGIE
"Consciousness-Raising." Argo (4:3) 83, p. 31.

2734. MAGISTRALE, Tony
"Far from Change" (for Ken Wagner, from Salvation on the Installment Plan, winner of the 1981 chapbook contest). YetASM (1:2) 82, p. 20.
"It May Have Pleased You, Henry" (from Salvation on the Installment Plan, winner of the 1981 chapbook contest). YetASM (1:2) 82, p. 20.
"November Saturday" (for Sam). Blueline (4:1) Sum-Aut 82, p. 37.

2735. MAGLIOCCO, Peter
"History." SanFPJ (5:4) 83, p. 16.
"No-Title -- 1." SanFPJ (5:4) 83, p. 13.

2736. MAGNER, James E., Jr.
"Wondrous Mariner" (For Hart Crane). HiramPoR (35) Aut-Wint 83, p. 28.

2737. MAGUIRE, Robert A.
"December 31, 1979: Soon Now" (tr. of Stanislaw Baranczak, w. Magnus J. Krynski). TriQ (57, Vol. 1) Spr-Sum 83, p. 89.
"First Move" (tr. of Leszek Elektorowicz, w. Magnus J. Krynski). TriQ (57, Vol. 1) Spr-Sum 83, p. 62.
"I Will Open the Window" (tr. of Anna Swirszczynska, w. Magnus J. Krynski). TriQ (57, Vol. 1) Spr-Sum 83, p. 61.
"Philately" (From my childhood, tr. of Wiktor Woroszylski, w. Magnus J. Krynski). TriQ (57, Vol. 1) Spr-Sum 83, p. 27-28.
"Tortures" (tr. of Wislawa Szymborska, w. Magnus J. Krynski). TriQ (57, Vol. 1) Spr-Sum 83, p. 25-26.

2738. MAHAFFEY, Phillip
"The Teaching Assistant to His Second-Semester Composition Class." CutB (21) Aut-Wint 83, p.

80-81.

2739. MAHAN, Henry
"Ben Jonson on the Poet Who Deserves Hanging." Swallow (1) Spr 83, p. 25.
"The Sub-Sub Librarian's Sestina." Swallow (1) Spr 83, p. 23-24.

2740. MAHAPATRA, Jayanta
"Dust." BlackWR (9:2) Spr 83, p. 84.
"Sunday." BlackWR (9:2) Spr 83, p. 85.

2741. MAHLER, Carol
"Hey Old Man." StoneC (11:1/2, Pt. 1) Aut-Wint 83, p. 29.
"When Shells." BelPoJ (33:3) Spr 83, p. 33-34.

2742. MAHON, Derek
"April on Toronto Island." Agni (19) 83, p. 26.
"Courtyards in Delft: Pieter De Hooch, 1659" (for Gordon Woods). Agni (19) 83, p. 28-29.
"Glengormley." Agni (19) 83, p. 23.
"My Wicked Uncle." Agni (19) 83, p. 24-25.
"Poem Beginning with a Line by Cavafy." Agni (19) 83, p. 27.
"The Terminal Bar" (for Philip Haas). Agni (19) 83, p. 30.

2743. MAHONY, Phillip
"Almost Every Cat." YetASM (1:1) 82, p. 5.
"Medical Examiner's Morgue, New York, 11/20/80." HangL (44) Sum 83, p. 29-30.

2744. MAIER, Carol
"Touch" (tr. of Octavio Armand). NewOR (10:4) Wint 83, p. 50.

2745. MAIRE, Mark
"Remembrance." SpiritSH (48) 82, p. 39.

2746. MAKER, Donald A.
"Recipe for a Well-Done Robot." SanFPJ (5:1) 83, p. 18.

2747. MAKUCK, Peter
"Last Run at La Plagne." KanQ (15:1) Wint 83, p. 62.
"Stephen Judy's Execution, That Night." NewEng (5:4) Sum 83, p. 526-528.

2748. MALDONADO, A.
"Icarus." CEACritic (45:2) Ja 83, p. 20.

2749. MALINOWITZ, Michael
"Daisy Chain." DevQ (18:3) Aut 83, p. 95.
"Glose." Epoch (33:1) Aut-Wint 83, p. 75-76.
"Poem: There I was thinking of giving it all up." DevQ (18:3) Aut 83, p. 96.

2750. MALLIN, Rupert
"A Soiled Relationship." Bogg (51) 83, p. 52.

2751. MALLINSON, J. D.
"The Cod." Stand (24:2) 83, p. 64.

2752. MALONE, Ruth
"Crazy Quilt." Calyx (7:3) Sum 83, p. 31.
"A Slow Process." Calyx (7:3) Sum 83, p. 30.

2753. MALONE, Teri L.
"The Bootleg." BlackALF (17:4) Wint 83, p. 154.

2754. MALTMAN, Kim
"Harvest." PoetryCR (4:4) Sum 83, p. 6.
"Hot Spell." Dandel (10:2) Aut-Wint 83, p. 20-21.
"The Technology of Objects." CanLit (96) Spr 83, p. 69.
"The Technology of Terror." CanLit (96) Spr 83, p. 69-70.
"The Trellis." Dandel (10:2) Aut-Wint 83, p. 22.

2755. MALYON, Carol
"Still Life." Waves (11:4) Spr 83, p. 64.

2756. MANCINELLI, Carole
"Father: Upon Leaving." NegC (3:4) Aut 83, p. 88.

2757. MANCINI, Ronald
"The Sole Companion." Wind (13:49) 83, p. 35.

2758. MANDEL, Charlotte
"A Cousin Comes to Me." WestB (13) 83, p. 12-13.
"The Screen." StoneC (10:3/4) Spr-Sum 83, p. 29.

2759. MANDEL, Peter
"Four Non-Violent Versions of a Bombing." PoetryNW (24:1) Spr 83, p. 23.

2760. MANDLOVE, Nancy
"Cocinando/What's Cooking" (to Mary Lee, tr. of Luz María Umpierre). 13thM (7:1/2) 83, p. 89.

2761. MANFRED, Frederick
"Winter Count" (Excerpt). SoDakR (21:4) Wint 83, p. 3.

2762. MANFRED, Freya
"Message from the Right Hemisphere." MichQR (22:4) Aut 83, p. 614-615.

2763. MANGAN, Kathy
"In Closing." SenR (13:2) 82-83, p. 74-75.

2764. MANLEY, Frank
"The Deified Julius." SewanR (91:1) Wint 83 p. 100.
"Hadrian." SewanR (91:1) Wint 83, p. 99.
"Zenobia." SewanR (91:1) Wint 83, p. 98.

2765. MANNER, Eeva-Liisa
"I set out on a journey" (tr. by Eric Dickens). Stand (24:3) 83, p. 6.
"The lake is full of light without source" (tr. by

Eric Dickens). Stand (24:3) 83, p. 6.

2766. MANNING, Nichola
"3 Prayers." WormR (23:1, issue 89) 83, p. 14-15.
"An Alternative Feminist Poem." WormR (23:1, issue 89) 83, p. 21.
"Armchair Types." WormR (23:1, issue 89) 83, p. 24.
"Auntie Emma." WormR (23:1, issue 89) 83, p. 19.
"Bukowski Visits a Mental Home." WormR (23:1, issue 89) 83, p. 25.
"Conperson." WormR (23:1, issue 89) 83, p. 16.
"Conversation." WormR (23:1, issue 89) 83, p. 26.
"Disability Questionnaire." WormR (23:1, issue 89) 83, p. 19.
"Feminist Poem." WormR (23:1, issue 89) 83, p. 20.
"Great Poetess." WormR (23:1, issue 89) 83, p. 17.
"Irish Church." WormR (23:1, issue 89) 83, p. 27-28.
"Lady-Like." WormR (23:1, issue 89) 83, p. 28.
"Law." WormR (23:1, issue 89) 83, p. 18.
"Long Beach Cymbalist Poem." WormR (23:1, issue 89) 83, p. 25.
"Lover." WormR (23:4, issue 92) 83, p. 152.
"Mad Doggerel." WormR (23:1, issue 89) 83, p. 26.
"Manning the Battering Ram" (Special section). WormR (23:1, issue 89) 83, p. 13-28.
"Manning the Battering Ram." WormR (23:1, issue 89) 83, p. 22-23.
"Monica." WormR (23:4, issue 92) 83, p. 153.
"Mrs. Bugg." WormR (23:1, issue 89) 83, p. 18.
"Mum." WormR (23:1, issue 89) 83, p. 18.
"My Sister." WormR (23:1, issue 89) 83, p. 17.
"Names." WormR (23:1, issue 89) 83, p. 25.
"New Book." WormR (23:1, issue 89) 83, p. 19.
"Picket Line." WormR (23:1, issue 89) 83, p. 23-24.
"Poet A and Poet B." WormR (23:1, issue 89) 83, p. 28.
"Pyramid." WormR (23:4, issue 92) 83, p. 153.
"Red Label." WormR (23:1, issue 89) 83, p. 24.
"Screamin' Art." WormR (23:1, issue 89) 83, p. 26.
"Sour German." WormR (23:1, issue 89) 83, p. 27.
"Tennis Club." WormR (23:1, issue 89) 83, p. 16.
"TV." WormR (23:4, issue 92) 83, p. 153.
"Wallpapering." WormR (23:4, issue 92) 83, p. 152.
"Wimbledon Duff." WormR (23:1, issue 89) 83, p. 15-16.
"Wool." WormR (23:1, issue 89) 83, p. 17.

2767. MANSKE, Had
"Deer Season." Northeast (Ser. 3:16) Wint 83-84, p. 21.
"Visit to the Redhouse." Northeast (Ser. 3:16) Wint 83-84, p. 22.

2768. MAPANJE, Jack
"Vigil for a Fellow Credulous Captive" (for Anenenji). Stand (24:2) 83, p. 13.
"When the Shire Valley Dries Up Patiently (or Lines Re-arranged from Megan's Letters)." Stand (24:2) 83, p. 12.

2769. MARCHAELLA, Ilona
"Cripples." Waves (11:2/3) Wint 83, p. 68.

2770. MARCHEWKA-BROWN, Nicole
"Painting by Light" (verses for Michael). Wind (13:48) 83, p. 40.

2771. MARCUS, Mordecai
"The Girls Change." SouthernPR (23:2) Aut 82 [i.e. (23:1?) Spr 83], p. 45-46.
"Going to Russia." NegC (3:4) Aut 83, p. 124-125.
"Integrity in Self-Defeat." PoetL (78:4) Wint 84, p. 222.
"A Lover for the Queen." PoetL (78:4) Wint 84, p. 221.
"Preservations." PoetL (78:4) Wint 84, p. 220.
"Return from the Desert." SoDakR (21:4) Wint 83, p. 47.
"A Simple Exchange." ClockR (2:1) 83, p. 45.

2772. MARCUS, Morton
"Defender of the Faith." TriQ (58) Aut 83, p. 78-79.
"Father and Son." TriQ (58) Aut 83, p. 80-81.
"In 1943, the Boy Images That." TriQ (58) Aut 83, p. 75-77.
"The Poet at 3: His Talents Recognized." PoetryNW (24:2) Sum 83, p. 34-35.
"The Wolf Without His Teeth." Poetry (141:5) F 83, p. 285.

2773. MARGOLIS, Gary
"Beethoven's Polish Birthday." Tendril (14/15) Wint 83, p. 126.
"Falling Awake." PoetryNW (24:2) Sum 83, p. 24.

2774. MARGOSHES, Dave
"Climbing toward Four." PoetryCR (4:3) Spr 83, p. 15.
"IOU" (for Ilya on our day). PoetryCR (5:1) Aut 83, p. 18.
"Thin Ice." Grain (11:1) F 83, p. 20-21.

2775. MARIAH, Paul
Muse Elektrique." SecC (11:1/2) 83, p. 126-127.

2776. MARIANI, Paul
"The Assassins" (for Terrence Des Pres). Tendril (14/15) Wint 83, p. 127.
"Goodnight Irene." MassR (24:4) Wint 83, p. 763-765.
"Lines I Told Myself I Wouldn't Write." Tendril (14/15) Wint 83, p. 134-135.
"News That Stays News." Hudson (36:4) Wint 83-84, p. 694-695.
"North/South" (for Bob Pack). Tendril (14/15) Wint 83, p. 132-133.
"Prime Mover." Agni (19) 83, p. 69-70.
"Promises." Tendril (14/15) Wint 83, p. 128-129.
"The Ring." Tendril (14/15) Wint 83, p. 130-131.
"Winter Meditation II: 16/I/82." Tendril (14/15) Wint 83, p. 136.

2777. MARINO, Gordon
"June Poem." StoneC (10:3/4) Spr-Sum 83, p. 26.

2778. MARION, Jeff Daniel
"Going Back Again" (for Fred Chappell). Abatis (1) 83, p. 7-8.

2779. MARION, Paul
"Dylan Sings to Kerouac." MoodySI (9) Wint-Spr 81, p. 17.

2780. MARIS, Maria R.
"Sun Woman, Anno 1632, Kolwerdam, Holland." PoetL (78:3) Aut 83, p. 142-143.

2781. MARKS, Joyce
"Reflections at Age 50." YetASM (1:1) 82, p. 7.

2782. MARLIS, Stefanie
"In the Dream." AmerPoR (12:5) S/O 83, p. 34.
"The Same Light." BlackWR (9:1) Aut 82, p. 41.
"We Women." PoetryE (9/10) Wint 82-Spr 83, p. 140.
"The World Is Not Moved by the Delicate." PoetryE (9/10) Wint 82-Spr 83, p. 141.

2783. MARNOCHA, Thomas J.
"Of Little Importance." Bogg (51) 83, p. 20.

2784. MARQUARDT, Barbara
"Doing the Time Step." KanQ (15:3) Sum 83, p. 59.

2785. MARRA, Susan
"A Ritual of Need." Bogg (51) 83, p. 16-17.

2786. MARRON, Mary Jo.
"October 21st." Wind (13:48) 83, p. 58.

2787. MARSH, Kirk
"Rain, 1967." Sam (34:3 135th release) 83, p. 42.
"Sanctuary." Sam (34:3 135th release) 83, p. 56.

2788. MARSH, William
"The First Betrayal." WormR (23:2, issue 90) 83, p. 41.
"I Told My Son." WormR (23:2, issue 90) 83, p. 42.
"Oasis in the Wilderness." WormR (23:2, issue 90) 83, p. 41.

2789. MARSHALL, J. M.
"Change." ConcPo (16:2) Aut 83, p. 66.
"The Garden of the West." KanQ (15:3) Sum 83, p. 32-33.

2790. MARSHALL, Leslie
"Bristow Hardin." Ascent (8:3) 83, p. 46.
"Your Sleeping Position." Ascent (9:1) 83, p. 49.

2791. MARSHALL, Quitman
"After the Wedding." SoCaR (15:2) Spr 83, p. 116.

2792. MARSHALL, Tom
"Dance of the Particles" (Selections: i, ii, v, ix, x, xiii-xvi, xxi). PoetryCR (4:4) Sum 83, p. 13.

2793. MARTEAU, Robert
"Bread and Wine" (tr. by Clayton Eshleman and Bernard Bador). Sulfur (3:1, #7) 83, p. 40-43.

2794. MARTIN, Carolyn, Sister, R.S.M.
"Beside the Well: Words of a Waiting Woman." Wind (13:47) 83, p. 28.
"Disillusionment of Monday Morning." Wind (13:47) 83, p. 28-29.

2795. MARTIN, Charles (See also: MARTIN, Charles Casey)
"A Happy Ending for the Lost Children." OntR (18) Spr-Sum 83, p. 86-87.
"Landscape without History." OntR (18) Spr-Sum 83, p. 88-89.
"Steal the Bacon." Thrpny (4:1, issue 13) Spr 83, p. 8.

2796. MARTIN, Charles Casey (See also: MARTIN, Charles)
"The First Famous Lady He Ever Kissed" (for John Berryman). Iowa (13:3/4) Spr 82 (83), p. 118-120.
"Foundryblack." PoetryNW (24:3) Aut 83, p. 4-5.
"Kate and John." Iowa (13:3/4) Spr 82 (83), p. 121-122.
"Our Mother Bled." PoetryNW (24:3) Aut 83, p. 3-4.
"Who Was the Valentine, Who Was the Rose?" PoetryNW (24:3) Aut 83, p. 5-6.

2797. MARTIN, Connie Lakey
"The Discussion." Poem (49) N 83, p. 53.
"Leftovers." Poem (49) N 83, p. 52.

2798. MARTIN, D. Roger (Don Roger)
"Campers." SanFPJ (4:2) 83, p. 48.
"Incident at Sand Creek." Sam (34:3 135th release) 83, p. 10-11.
"Last Exit Home." Sam (36:3 143rd release) 83, p. 18-19.
"Minor League Veteran." PikeF (5) Spr 83, p. 10.

2799. MARTIN, Herbert Woodward
"A Dreamless Winter" (For Margaret). BelPoJ (34:2) Wint 83-84, p. 1.

2800. MARTIN, James
"Residua." Shen (34:3) 83, p. 84-85.

2801. MARTIN, Jennifer
"Would You Notice, If by the Porch." IndR (6:2) Spr 83, p. 5.

2802. MARTIN, Joe
"Disappearances." SanFPJ (5:4) 83, p. 52.

2803. MARTIN, Lynne
"Binding." Pig (11) 83, p. 93.

"Notes on the Limerick of Light" (refer to Relativity/Einstein). Pig (11) 83, p. 25.

2804. MARTIN, Richard
"One of the Thieves Was Saved." IndR (5:1) Wint 82, p. 43-46.
"Time Watching." IndR (5:1) Wint 82, p. 47-49.

2805. MARTIN, Sheri
"The 6:00 O'Clock News." SanFPJ (4:4) 83, p. 92.

2806. MARTINEZ, Aida Luz
"Carmen María." Ràcata (2) 83, p. 88.
"Regreso." Ràcata (2) 83, p. 87.

2807. MARTINEZ, Dionisio (Dionisio D.)
"The Distance between Two Points." Kayak (62) Ag 83, p. 67.
"One Drawer Full of Night." Kayak (62) Ag 83, p. 66.
"Playing Dead." SouthernPR (23:2) Aut 82 [i.e. (23:1?) Spr 83], p. 41.
"Three or Four Shades of Blues" (after Charles Mingus). AmerPoR (12:6) N/D 83, p. 5.
"Three or Four Shades of Blues (2)" (for Charles Mingus). AmerPoR (12:6) N/D 83, p. 5.

MARTINEZ, Tomas Rivera
See: RIVERA MARTINEZ, Tomas

MARTINI, Brenda de
See: DeMARTINI, Brenda

2808. MARTINSON, Sue Ann
"Upper Hennepin Avenue." YetASM (1:1) 82, p. 11.

2809. MARTONE, Michael
"Perfection." WindO (42) Sum 83, p. 10.

MARVIN, Maria Korssun
See: KORSSUN-MARVIN, Maria

MARY LUCINA, Sister
See: LUCINA, Mary, Sister

2810. MASARIK, Al
"Spring Training." SecC (11:1/2) 83, p. 129.
"You See Them in the Alleys." SecC (11:1/2) 83, p. 130.

2811. MASINI, Donna
"The Consuming Passion." 13thM (7:1/2) 83, p. 63-66.

2812. MASON, Joyce
"The Mutants." SecC (11:1/2) 83, p. 131-132.

2813. MASSARO, S.A.
"Blue Peril." Tendril (16) Sum 83, p. 77.

MASSMAN, Gordon Lester
See: LESTER-MASSMAN, Gordon

2814. MASTERSON, Dan
"At the End of Sleep." PoetryNW (24:3) Aut 83, p. 42-43.
"Aunt Sadie's Carrot Juice." PoetryNW (24:3) Aut 83, p. 45-46.
"Description." MassR (24:4) Wint 83, p. 819.
"Fitz and the Gandy Dancers." MemphisSR (2:2) Spr 82, p. 14-15.
"Locked in the Icehouse." PoetryNW (24:3) Aut 83, p. 44-45.
"Night Sky." PoetryNW (24:3) Aut 83, p. 43.
"On a Hospital Porch in the Mountains, 1940." MemphisSR (2:1) Aut 81, p. 22-23.
"Opening Doors." Hudson (36:3) Aut 83, p. 514-517.
"Pool Party." MemphisSR (2:1) Aut 81, p. 36.
"Sunday Dinner." MassR (24:4) Wint 83, p. 818.
"Treehouse." YaleR (72:4) Sum 83, p. 603-604.
"Under Cover of Darkness." PoetryNW (24:3) Aut 83, p. 39-41.

2815. MATHEWS, Harry
"Condition of Desire." Epoch (33:1) Aut-Wint 83, p. 77.

2816. MATHIAS, Roland
"Cynog." SpiritSH (48) 82, p. 14-16.
"Saturday Morning: Appin." SpiritSH (48) 82, p. 13.

2817. MATHIS, Cleopatra
"After the Rose." GeoR (37:3) Aut 83, p. 599.
"August Birthday." BlackWR (9:1) Aut 82, p. 42.
"Elegy for the Other" (for my brother Jimmy, killed November, 1979). NewEngR (5:3) Spr 83, p. 297-302.
"February Thaw." DevQ (18:1) Spr 83, p. 67.
"For Blue." VirQR (59:4) Aut 83, p. 680-681.
"Louisiana Snow." BlackWR (9:1) Aut 82, p. 43.
"White Field." VirQR (59:4) Aut 83, p. 679-680.

MATRE, C. (Connie, Connetta) van
See: Van MATRE, Connetta

2818. MATSON, Clive
"Slanted Hour." CentR (27:4) Aut 83, p. 277.
"Wind Flamed." HangL (44) Sum 83, p. 31.

2819. MATSON, Suzanne
"After 'Charming'." Poetry (142:2) My 83, p. 90-91.
"The Sunbather." Poetry (142:2) My 83, p. 93.
"The Sunday Drunk." Poetry (142:2) My 83, p. 92.

2820. MATTHEWS, Jack
"The Civil War Photograph." Poetry (141:4) Ja 83, p. 203.
"Dream Signs." SewanR (91:3) Sum 83, p. 387.
"Interview with the Poet's Mother." Poetry (141:4) Ja 83, p. 202.
"Inverse Proportions." Poetry (141:4) Ja 83, p. 201.
"Speculum." SewanR (91:3) Sum 83, p. 388.

2821. MATTHEWS, William
"Another Real Estate Deal on Oahu." TriQ (58) Aut 83, p. 84-85.
"Black Box." NewEng (5:4) Sum 83, p. 519.
"A Blessing from Texas." NewRep (188:15) 18 Ap 83, p. 28.
"Country and Western." PoetryE (12) Aut 83, p. 18.
"Dance Lessons." Tendril (14/15) Wint 83, p. 137.
"Good and Bad" (Selections: "Good," "Bad"). GeoR (37:4) Wint 83, p. 738-741.
"Growing Up." PoNow (7:2, #38) 83, p. 14.
"A Happy Childhood" (Excerpts). BlackWR (9:2) Spr 83, p. 26.
"A Happy Childhood" (Excerpts). LittleBR (4:2) Wint 83-84, p. 9.
"The Hummer." NewRep (188:9) 7 Mr 83, p. 32.
"It Turns Out." Atlantic (252:6) D 83, p. 92.
"Last Words." TriQ (58) Aut 83, p. 82-83.
"Living among the Dead." OhioR (30) 83, p. 12-13.
"The middle-aged teacher lets his small son" (tr. of Jean Follain, w. Mary Feeney). Field (28) Spr 83, p. 63.
"Orthopedic Surgery Ward." BlackWR (9:2) Spr 83, p. 27.
"Prolific." TriQ (58) Aut 83, p. 86.
"The Red Studio" (After Matisse). MemphisSR (2:1) Aut 81, p. 35.
"Right" (Selections). Poetry (142:4) Jl 83, p. 187-189.
"Seattle, February." QW (16) Spr-Sum 83, p. 130-131.
"Sympathetic." QW (16) Spr-Sum 83, p. 129.
"La Tache 1962" (for Michael Cuddihy). OhioR (30) 83, p. 9.
"Taking the Train Home." OhioR (30) 83, p. 10-12.
"Wrong" (Selections). Poetry (142:4) Jl 83, p. 189-191.

2822. MATTHIAS, John
"Dry Point" (tr. of Jan Östergren). ChiR (33:4) Sum [i.e. Spr] 83, p. 36.
"E.P. in Crawfordsville" (for D.D. in South Bend lecturing on "Englightenment and Christian Dissent"). ChiR (33:3) Wint 83, p. 98-99.
"Unpleasant Letter." ChiR (33:3) Wint 83, p. 95-97.

MATTINA, Elaine la
See: LaMATTINA, Elaine

2823. MATTISON, Alice
"Looking at People." Ploughs (9:1) 83, p. 84-87.
"The Night." PoNow (7:2, #38) 83, p. 32.
"With Kate at the River." MassR (24:4) Wint 83, p. 790-792.

2824. MATYAS, Cathy
"Happiness." PoetryCR (5:1) Aut 83, p. 18.

2825. MAURA, Sister
"At the Beginning." SouthernHR (17:4) Aut 83, p. 326.
"Faith" (Matthew 8:23-27, Mark 5:35-41). ChrC

(100:14) 4 My 83, p. 430.
"Imagist At Coney Island." SewanR (91:2) Spr 83, p. 188.
"Mideast: Summer Tour." AntigR (55) Aut 83, p. 20.
"Out of Cana" (John 2:1-11). AntigR (55) Aut 83, p. 21.
"Portents." AntigR (52) Wint 83, p. 111.

2826. MAURER, Bonnie
"Eating the Still Life." IndR (5:2) Sum 82, p. 76-77.

2827. MAUSOLF, Shelly Jo
"Here we stand among the elephants' bones." DekalbLAJ (16:1/4) Aut 82-Sum 83, p. 80.
"Your noise parades through my rain." DekalbLAJ (16:1/4) Aut 82-Sum 83, p. 80.

2828. MAVIGLIA, Joseph
"Good Grape." CrossC (5:2/3) 83, p. 16.
"Vedovo (Widower)." CrossC (5:2/3) 83, p. 16.
"Wrestler." PoetryCR (4:4) Sum 83, p. 15.

2829. MAXHAM, Catherine
"Albert." PottPort (5) 83-84, p. 21.
"Judas." AntigR (55) Aut 83, p. 83.
"Untitled: I was plump and quiet and ten." PottPort (5) 83-84, p. 21.

2830. MAXSON, Gloria A.
"Lessee." ChrC (100:16) 18 My 83, p. 487.
"Northward Wending." ChrC (100:4) 2-9 F 83, p. 96.
"Perfectionist." ChrC (100:9) 23-30 Mr 83, p. 262.
"The Singers." ChrC (100:34) 16 N 83, p. 1036.
"Spared." ChrC (100:6) 2 Mr 83, p. 173.
"Zion and Bryce Canyons." ChrC (100:28) 5 O 83, p. 876.

2831. MAXWELL, Anna
"Fortune." Wind (13:48) 83, p. 41.
"In a Season." PoetL (77:4) Wint 83, p. 199.
"Lunch Hour." Wind (13:48) 83, p. 41-42.

2832. MAY, Kathy
"Rain." SouthernPR (23:2) Aut 82 [i.e. (23:1?) Spr 83], p. 22.

2833. MAYER, Gerda
"Laud to all things lavatorial." Bogg (51) 83, p. 44.
"Noli Me Tangere." Argo (4:2) 82, p. 11.

2834. MAYES, Frances
"Childhood Scene in Barfield's Drugstore." LittleM (14:1/2) 83, p. 96.
"Letter from the World." LittleM (14:1/2) 83, p. 92-93.
"October: Slash and Burn." LittleM (14:1/2) 83, p. 94-95.
"The Other Edge of June." Ploughs (9:2/3) 83, p.

169-170.

2835. MAYHALL, Jane
"Cracks." Confr (25/26) 83, p. 39.
"Seven Men on a Brooklyn Asphalt Truck." Confr (25/26) 83, p. 39.

2836. MAYHILL, Jane
"Top Song." Images (8:3) 83, p. 6.

2837. MAYNE, Seymour
"Anna." Descant (41) Sum 83, p. 144.
"At Michaelis's Café." Descant (41) Sum 83, p. 143.
"Hiroshima, Drawing by Survivor." Descant (41) Sum 83, p. 142.
"The Ottawa." Descant (41) Sum 83, p. 141.

2838. MAYOFF, Steven
"Glasgow." MalR (65) Jl 83, p. 125-127.

2839. MAZANDERANI, Nosrat Kasemi
"Said Wasp to Bee" (tr. by Omar S. Pound). AntigR (55) Aut 83, p. 23.

2840. MAZUR, Gail
"After the Fire." Hudson (36:1) Spr 83, p. 143-144.
"Jewelweed." Hudson (36:2) Sum 83, p. 291-292.
"Listening to Baseball in the Car" (for J.T.). LittleBR (4:2) Wint 83-84, p. 27.
"Mashpee, 1952." Hudson (36:1) Spr 83, p. 142.
"Mashpee, 1979." Hudson (36:1) Spr 83, p. 141.
"Mashpee Wine." Hudson (36:1) Spr 83, p. 145-146.
"Ruins." Hudson (36:1) Spr 83, p. 144-145.

MAZZIERI, Geraldo Augusto
See: AUGUSTUS, Gemiann

2841. MAZZOCCO, Robert
"Tracks." NewYorker (58:49) 24 Ja 83, p. 44.

Mc . . .
See also: Names beginning with "Mac", filed above in their alphabetic position.

2842. McAFEE, Thomas
"Brothers Meeting." NewL (49:3/4) Spr-Sum 83, p. 115.
"Claiming Lost Dances." MissouriR (6:2) Wint 83, p. 8.
"Gypsy Woman to Policeman." MemphisSR (2:1) Aut 81, p. 12.
"If There Is a Perchance." OhioR (30) 83, p. 60.
"Near Point Mallard, Decatur, Alabama." MemphisSR (2:1) Aut 81, p. 10-11.
"The Possibility of Growing Old Before It Rains." ThRiPo (19/20) 82, p. 48.
"To a Southern Lady." MissouriR (7:1) Aut 83, p. 14.
"To Miss X." MissouriR (6:2) Wint 83, p. 9.
"Trees." MissouriR (6:2) Wint 83, p. 7.

2843. McALEAVEY, David
"After." WindO (43) Wint 83, p. 12.
"Courtleigh Drive, Wichita Kansas." Epoch (32:2) Wint-Spr 83, p. 95-103.

2844. McALLISTER, Mick
"A Song of Xipe Totec." DevQ (18:1) Spr 83, p. 80.

2845. McBRIDE, Mekeel
"Evidence" (for Mark Doty). Tendril (14/15) Wint 83, p. 140.
"Growing Stones in New Hampshire." NewYorker (59:12) 9 My 83, p. 44.
"Lessons." Tendril (14/15) Wint 83, p. 138-139.

2846. McCABE, Victoria
"Grief Moves In." AntigR (55) Aut 83, p. 107.
"History, or, The Old House." AntigR (55) Aut 83, p. 108.

2847. McCAFFREY, Phillip
"Cottage Storm." NewL (50:1) Aut 83, p. 88.
"Discretion." KanQ (15:1) Wint 83, p. 75.
"The Fat Lady." PoetL (78:2) Sum 83, p. 74.
"The Old-Fashioned Farmer." PoetL (78:2) Sum 83, p. 76.
"On Burning the Ship for Light." KanQ (15:2) Spr 83, p. 22.
"Polanski's 'Repulsion'." KanQ (15:1) Wint 83, p. 75.
"The Talented Eunuch." WestHR (37:4) Wint 83, p. 319-320.
"The Technician." PoetL (78:2) Sum 83, p. 75.
"The Tight Rope Artist." KanQ (15:3) Sum 83, p. 78.
"Traditions." SouthernPR (23:2) Aut 82 [i.e. (23:1?) Spr 83], p. 62.
"Training West." KanQ (15:2) Spr 83, p. 21.

2848. McCALLUM, Paddy
"The Arsonist." Descant (43) Wint 83-84, p. 40.
"Floats." Descant (43) Wint 83-84, p. 41-42.
"In Your Version of Your Brother's Death." AntigR (54) Sum 83, p. 41.

2849. McCANN, Janet
"March Notes." Bogg (50) 83, p. 5.

2850. McCARRISTON, Linda
"Aubade: November." Poetry (143:2) N 83, p. 74.
"Barn Fire" (for Mike). OhioR (30) 83, p. 144.
"Late Afternoon." Poetry (143:2) N 83, p. 75-76.

2851. McCARTHY, William F.
"Anti-Nuclear Outcry Erupts around World." SanFPJ (5:3) 83, p. 92.
"Betrayal." SanFPJ (5:3) 83, p. 89.

2852. McCAUL, Barton
"Honky-Tonk Renaissance Man." MoodySI (4) Spr 79, p. 8.

2853. McCLAIN, John H.
"Haiku: Chasing old spiders." AntigR (53) Spr 83, p. 12.

2854. McCLATCHY, J. D.
"After a Visit." Nat (236:20) 21 My 83, p. 648.
"A Bestiary." Nat (236:9) 5 Mr 83, p. 278-279.

2855. McCLEERY, David
"Whirlwind." KanQ (15:1) Wint 83, p. 98.

2856. McCLELLAN, Jane
"To Juliet and Mae Rogers for Whom No Apology Is Needed." CapeR (19:1) Wint 83, p. 8.

2857. McCLOSKEY, Mark
"The Christmas Shows." PoetryNW (24:4) Wint 83-84, p. 43.
"The Town." PoNow (7:2, #38) 83, p. 37.

2858. McCLURE, Keith
"Our Inheritance." SouthernPR (23:2) Aut 82 [i.e. (23:1?) Spr 83], p. 23.

2859. McCONEGHEY, Nelljean
"April Snow: A Lesson." NegC (3:4) Aut 83, p. 13.

2860. McCONNEL, Frances
"Keeping the Heat Down." Iowa (13:2) Spr 82, p. 106-107.

2861. McCONNELL, Kathleen
"Children." AntigR (52) Wint 83, p. 52.

2862. McCOOL, Arvilly
"Twenty-Six Bugs for Linda Flower" (2 excerpts). YetASM (1:1) 82, p. 2, 3.

2863. McCORD, Howard
"Getting a Pig Ready for Breakfast." MemphisSR (1:2) Spr 81, p. 5.

2864. McCORKLE, James
"Homage to a Missed Season." MissouriR (6:2) Wint 83, p. 26-27.

2865. McCORMACK, Olivia
A Grammatical Rule?" SanFPJ (5:1) 83, p. 6.

2866. McCORMACK, Rohana
"The Woman Sawed in Half." Kayak (63) N 83, p. 11.

2867. McCOWN, Clint
"Fundamentalist." ColEng (45:8) D 83, p. 780-781.
"A Ten Year Old Boy Discovering the Certainly of Descent." ColEng (45:8) D 83, p. 781.

2868. McCRACKEN, Kathleen
"Paris." PoetryCR (5:1) Aut 83, p. 17.

2869. McCROBIE, C.
"Perspectives." WritersL Ag 83, p. 17.

2870. McCRORIE, Edward
"Bus 57." SpiritSH (49 Suppl.) 83, p. 13.
"The Falls at Lauterbrunnen" (for Rodney). SpiritSH (49 Suppl.) 83, p. 13.
"Poem Chain." BelPoJ (33:3) Spr 83, p. 34.

2871. McCULLOUGH, Lisa J.
"New Kid on the Block." PoetL (78:1) Spr 83, p. 12-13.
"Revision." StoneC (11:1/2, Pt. 1) Aut-Wint 83, p. 40.

2872. McCURDY, Harold
"Passing." Wind (13:49) 83, p. 36.

2873. McCUTCHEN, Annis T.
"Zoo." EngJ (72:5) S 83, p. 74.

2874. McDANIEL, Judith
"Acadia." Prima (8) 83, p. 46-47.
"November Woman." Blueline (4:2) Wint-Spr 83, p. 40-41.
"Splitting Elm." Blueline (4:2) Wint-Spr 83, p. 6.

2875. McDANIEL, Wilma Elizabeth
"Abdication Day." HangL (44) Sum 83, p. 33.
"Angelic Perspective." HangL (44) Sum 83, p. 32.
"Poets and Bottles." HangL (44) Sum 83, p. 34.

2876. McDERMOTT, Elaine M.
"Kumquats in Winter." NegC (3:4) Aut 83, p. 22.

2877. McDONALD, Walter
"Blue Skies." SouthernPR (23:2) Aut 82 [i.e. (23:1?) Spr 83], p. 19-20.
"A Brief, Familiar Story of Winter." Ascent (9:1) 83, p. 42-43.
"Burning the Limbs." Poem (49) N 83, p. 38-39.
"Digging in Escondido" (for Richard Hugo). MissouriR (7:1) Aut 83, p. 18-19.
"Fishing in Hardscrabble." CharR (9:2) Aut 83, p. 54.
"Flood Fishing." SouthernPR (23:2) Aut 82 [i.e. (23:1?) Spr 83], p. 21.
"High Plains Orchards." SoDakR (21:2) Sum 83, p. 63.
"Hunting Doves at Matador." MissouriR (7:1) Aut 83, p. 20-21.
"In a Dry Season." SpoonRQ (8:4) Aut 83, p. 2.
"In Season." WestB (13) 83, p. 45.
"Living on Hardscrabble." NoAmR (268:2) Je 83, p. 27.
"Night of the Scorpion." PoetL (78:4) Wint 84, p. 208.
"Noon." PoetL (78:4) Wint 84, p. 209-210.
"On a Saturday Afternoon in the Country." NewOR (10:4) Wint 83, p. 16.
"On the Farm." PoetL (78:1) Spr 83, p. 16.

"Rig-Sitting." BelPoJ (34:1) Aut 83, p. 31.
"Sandstorms." NegC (3:4) Aut 83, p. 93.
"The Second of Perfect Sleep." Paint (10:19/20) Spr-Aut 83, p. 26.
"Seining for Carp." CharR (9:2) Aut 83, p. 52-53.
"Slow Time Near the River." SpoonRQ (8:4) Aut 83, p. 4.
"Snow Fences." MemphisSR (4:1) Aut 83, p. 27.
"Tied Up under Trees." PoetL (78:4) Wint 84, p. 207-208.
"Two Family Men in Late Summer." PoetL (78:4) Wint 84, p. 211.
"Waiting for News." SpoonRQ (8:4) Aut 83, p. 3.
"What the Trees Hear." Poem (49) N 83, p. 40.
"What the Wind Delivers." PoetryNW (24:2) Sum 83, p. 13.
"Winning" (for Paul "Bear" Bryant). Poem (49) N 83, p. 41.
"Witching on Dry Land." SpoonRQ (8:4) Aut 83, p. 1.

2878. McDONOUGH, Kaye
"Poem for Janice Blue." SecC (11:1/2) 83, p. 135.

2879. McDONOUGH, Thomas
"The Misfit." SmPd (20:3) Aut 83, p. 28.

2880. McDOWELL, Robert
"Ballad of Maritime Mike." Kayak (63) N 83, p. 24-26.
"Coed Day at the Spa." Hudson (36:3) Aut 83, p. 441-442.
"A Formal Feeling." Kayak (61) Ap 83, p. 41.
"The Malady Lingers On." Hudson (36:3) Aut 83, p. 439-441.
"On and On." Kayak (61) Ap 83, p. 42.
"Working a #30 Sash Tool, Thinking about the Pope." Hudson (36:3) Aut 83, p. 443-444.

2881. McELROY, Colleen (Colleen J.)
"The Female as Taken from Freshman Essays." MassR (24:2) Sum 83, p. 314-316.
"How Long Does It Take to Get Away from It All" (for Kathy Newbreast). 13thM (7:1/2) 83, p. 9-10.
"Living Here Ain't Easy." Epoch (32:2) Wint-Spr 83, p. 132-133.
"The Privilege of Choice." 13thM (7:1/2) 83, p. 7-8.
"Velasquez' Juan de Pareja." MissouriR (6:2) Wint 83, p. 16-17.

2882. McFADDEN, David
"Margaret Hollingsworth's Glasses." CanLit (96) Spr 83, p. 83-84.
"Margaret Hollingsworth's Milk." CanLit (96) Spr 83, p. 84.
"Margaret Hollingsworth's Typewriter." CanLit (96) Spr 83, p. 81-82.

2883. McFARLAND, Joanne
"Bathing Beauty (Circa 1958)." CapeR (18:2) Sum 83, p. 3.

"Lipstick." CapeR (18:2) Sum 83, p. 4-5.

2884. McFARLAND, Ron
"Estelle's Antiques." SpoonRQ (8:4) Aut 83, p. 54.
"Palouse History." PoetryNW (24:1) Spr 83, p. 19-20.
"Pedestrians." IndR (6:3) Sum 83, p. 32-33.
"Rainstorm." SouthernPR (23:2) Aut 83, p. 38-39.
"Starting a Compost Heap at Forty." IndR (6:3) Sum 83, p. 34.

2885. McFEE, Michael
"Awake with Asthma." MassR (24:4) Wint 83, p. 824-825.
"Possumma" (for William Harmon). Kayak (62) Ag 83, p. 38-40.
"A Tumbleweed from Texas." SouthernPR (23:2) Aut 83, p. 39.

2886. McFERREN, Martha
"The Cowboy on the Pea: A Girl's Guide." KanQ (15:2) Spr 83, p. 184.
"Dead in Kentucky." Wind (13:47) 83, p. 30.
"Death and Bette Davis." KanQ (15:2) Spr 83, p. 185.
"Leaving Home." MissouriR (6:2) Wint 83, p. 85-87.
"Six Clips of Film Noir." Tendril (16) Sum 83, p. 91-93.

2887. McGANN, Jerome
"In Memory of Herzen." Sulfur (3:1, #7) 83, p. 48-49.
"Prose" (for Maldoror). Sulfur (3:1, #7) 83, p. 44-47.

2888. McGLINN, Sen
"Why in the Sun-Tongued Hills." WorldO (17:4) Sum 83, p. 35.

2889. McGOVERN, Martin
"Baptism of Sand." NoAmR (268:4) D 83, p. 68.

2890. McGOVERN, Robert
"Dog Days." HolCrit (20:5) D 83, p. 17.
"Driver's License." ChrC (100:10) 6 Ap 83, p. 300.

2891. McGOWAN, James (See also: McGOWAN, Jim)
"The Cracked Bell" (tr. of Charles Baudelaire). PikeF (5) Spr 83, p. 5.
"The Death of Lovers" (tr. of Charles Baudelaire). PikeF (5) Spr 83, p. 5.
"The Enemy" (tr. of Charles Baudelaire). PikeF (5) Spr 83, p. 5.
"Les Fleurs du Mal" (Selections) (tr. of Charles Baudelaire). PikeF (5) Spr 83, p. 4-7.
"The Metamorphoses of the Vampire" (tr. of Charles Baudelaire). PikeF (5) Spr 83, p. 4.
"St. Peter's Denial" (tr. of Charles Baudelaire). PikeF (5) Spr 83, p. 7.
"To the Reader" (tr. of Charles Baudelaire). PikeF (5) Spr 83, p. 4.
"A Voyage to Cythere" (tr. of Charles Baudelaire).

PikeF (5) Spr 83, p. 6.

2892. McGOWAN, Jim (See also: McGOWAN, James)
"Frail God Emperor." Bogg (51) 83, p. 38.

2893. McGRATH, Kristina
"The Kindness." LittleM (14:1/2) 83, p. 74.
"The Visits." LittleM (14:1/2) 83, p. 73.

2894. McGUCKIAN, Medbh
"Admiring the Furs." Agni (19) 83, p. 45.
"The Aphrodisiac." Agni (19) 83, p. 49.
"The Moon Pond." Agni (19) 83, p. 48.
"Not Pleasing Mama." Agni (19) 83, p. 50.
"The Perfect Mother." Agni (19) 83, p. 47.
"The Witchmark." Agni (19) 83, p. 46.

2895. McGUILL, Michael
"Two Boys." HolCrit (20:5) D 83, p. 19.

2896. McGUIRE, Irene
"Indian Summer." Quarry (32:3) Sum 83, p. 71.
"Nearing the lighthouse." Quarry (32:3) Sum 83, p. 71.

2897. McGURRIN, Ann
"The Animal in Disgrace." Meadows (4:1) 83, p. 41.
"Four Hawks Circling." Meadows (3:1) 82, p. 40.
"Looking for Halley's Comet." Meadows (3:1) 82, p. 47.
"We Who Carry Fire." Meadows (3:1) 82, p. 41.
"When on a Candle." Meadows (4:1) 83, p. 41.

2898. McHUGH, Heather
"The Amenities." SenR (13:2) 82-83, p. 70-71.
"Black Meat" (tr. of Jean Follain). Field (28) Spr 83, p. 68.
"In a World of Taking, the Mistake." NewYorker (59:43) 12 D 83, p. 56.
"In Light of Time." ThRiPo (21/22) 83, p. 54.
"Inhabited Interior" (tr. of Jean Follain). Field (28) Spr 83, p. 66.
"Listening" (tr. of Jean Follain). Field (28) Spr 83, p. 66.
"Relative." SenR (13:2) 82-83, p. 69.
"The Waco Diner." MemphisSR (3:1) Aut 82, p. 24.
"Where I'm Coming From." MemphisSR (3:1) Aut 82, p. 23.

2899. McINTYRE, Mello
"The Secrecy of Ceilings." AntigR (54) Sum 83, p. 25.
"The Sound of People." AntigR (54) Sum 83, p. 23.
"There Is an Art." AntigR (54) Sum 83, p. 24.

2900. McKAIN, David
"Doctrine of the Hands." Iowa (13:3/4) Spr 82 (83), p. 29.
"Freedom Dream." MinnR (NS 21) Aut 83, p. 16.

2901. McKAY, Don
"High Water on the Goulais." Dandel (10:2) Aut-Wint 83, p. 51.
"Sanding Down This Rocking Chair on a Windy Night." Dandel (10:2) Aut-Wint 83, p. 32-44.
"Snow Thickening on the Trans-Canada Highway." Dandel (10:2) Aut-Wint 83, p. 52-53.
"Territoriality." Dandel (10:2) Aut-Wint 83, p. 48-50.

2902. McKEAN, James
"After Listening to Jack Teagarden." MissouriR (7:1) Aut 83, p. 56.
"The Desert." QW (16) Spr-Sum 83, p. 61.
"Mountain Pass." Atlantic (252:4) O 83, p. 94.

2903. McKEE, Carrie
"Autumn in Childhood." KanQ (15:2) Spr 83, p. 114.
"Even Now." KanQ (15:2) Spr 83, p. 114.

2904. McKEE, Louis
"Song." Bogg (50) 83, p. 15.
"Too Familiar Winds." Abraxas (27/28) 83, p. 25.

2905. McKEE, Lucie
"Post Office." NewRena (17) Aut 83, p. 78-79.

2906. McKEEVER, Carmelita, C.S.J.
"Prayer." ChrC (100:25) 31 Ag-7 S 83, p. 764.
"Retreat in Spring." SpiritSH (48) 82, p. 37.

2907. McKENZIE-PORTER, Patricia
"The Fisherman." PottPort (5) 83-84, p. 43.
"Sometimes." PottPort (5) 83-84, p. 25.
"Thin As Fog." PottPort (5) 83-84, p. 11.

2908. McKEOWN, Tom
"Automatic Dream." Kayak (62) Ag 83, p. 62.
"Old Man Raking Leaves" PoNow (7:2, #38) 83, p. 30.

2909. McKERNAN, John
"Mother Writes Me in Paris to Tell Me That Grandmoter, Aged 78, Died." Pig (11) 83, p. 83.
"Something Impersonal Like Handel or Golf." SouthernPR (23:2) Aut 82 [i.e. (23:1?) Spr 83], p. 49.

2910. McKINLAY, Patricia
"Gypsy." NewL (50:1) Aut 83, p. 28-29.
"The Strangler." PoetryNW (24:1) Spr 83, p. 42-43.

2911. McKINNEY, Irene
"Deep Mining." BlackWR (9:1) Aut 82, p. 66-67.
"Little Boats." BlackWR (9:1) Aut 82, p. 68.

2912. McKINSEY, Martin
"After the Rain" (tr. of Yannis Ritsos). MassR (24:4) Wint 83, p. 722.
"With a Distant Lighting" (tr. of Yannis Ritsos). MassR (24:4) Wint 83, p. 721.

2913. McLAUGHLIN, William
"Astaire." PoetryNW (24:4) Wint 83-84, p. 34-35.
"Enigma Variation Unnumbered." Poem (48) Jl 83, p. 11.
"Home Thoughts at Home." PoetryNW (24:4) Wint 83-84, p. 32-33.
"How It's Done." Poem (48) Jl 83, p. 14.
"Victorian Images." Poem (48) Jl 83, p. 12-13.

2914. McLINTOCK, Kenneth
"Hiroshima." SanFPJ (4:3) 83, p. 30-31.
"Technology." SanFPJ (4:2) 83, p. 74.

2915. McLOUTH, Gary
"Blue Mountain." Blueline (5:1) Sum-Aut 83, p. 10.

2916. McMAHON, Jennifer
"War Night." Stand (24:4) Aut 83, p. 5.

2917. McMAHON, M. (Michael) (See also: McMAHON, Michael Beirne)
"After Winter Trees." SmPd (20:1) Wint 83, p. 20.
"Men at Otter Pond." SmPd (20:1) Wint 83, p. 19.
"On the Surprising Conversions." Blueline (4:1) Sum-Aut 82, p. 14-15.
"Taking My Sneakers Off." SmPd (20:1) Wint 83, p. 32.

2918. McMAHON, Michael Beirne (See also: McMAHON, M. (Michael))
"At the Gibbon Cage." KanQ (15:1) Wint 83, p. 100.
"Chalmers Lane." PoetL (77:2) Sum 82, p. 79.

2919. McMAKIN, James
"To William Aarnes." SoCaR (16:1) Aut 83, p. 77.

2920. McMASTER, Susan
"Performance Box: Poems for Two or More Voices, Contents: (Grief) Stillness Is at the Heart." Grain (11:4) N 83, p. 39-49.

2921. McMILLEN, Myrtis (Myrtis McMILLAN)
"Cap Gaspe." PottPort (5) 83-84, p. 13.
"Network." PottPort (5) 83-84, p. 20.

2922. McMULLEN, Richard E.
"Old Ties." FourQt (33:1) Aut 83, p. 2.
"The Peace Sign." HolCrit (20:2) Ap 83, p. 17.
"Snow on the Expressways." Focus (15:95) Ag 83, p. 16.

2923. McNAIR, Wesley
"The Longing of the Feet." Iowa (13:3/4) Spr 82 (83), p. 26-27.
"Mina Bell's Cow." Atlantic (251:2) F 83, p. 81.
"Small Towns Are Passing." Poetry (141:5) F 83, p. 286.

2924. McNAMARA, Eugene
"Crossing the River Twice in the Same Place."

CrossC (5:2/3) 83, p. 4.
"Near the Crossing." PoetryCR (5:2) Wint 83-84, p. 16.
"So It Goes." CentR (27:4) Aut 83, p. 270-271.

2925. McNEES, Eleanor
"Birds." Poem (48) Jl 83, p. 37.
"Hoard." Poem (48) Jl 83, p. 38.
"Incantation." Poem (48) Jl 83, p. 36.

2926. McNEIL, David
"Howard Sails." AntigR (52) Wint 83, p. 75.
"Parliament of Fools." AntigR (52) Wint 83, p. 74.

2927. McNEIL, Florence
"Allan Stewart." CanLit (97) Sum 83, p. 47.
"Fashions." AntigR (55) Aut 83, p. 120.
"Joseph O'Reilly." CrossC (5:2/3) 83, p. 29.
"Kirsty Kate." CanLit (97) Sum 83, p. 46.
"Remembering Captain Cook at Nootka." AntigR (55) Aut 83, p. 121-122.

2928. McPHEE, Carol
"Waiting Room." WestB (12) 83, p. 84.

2929. McPHERRON, Till
"Croquet Game" (Seaton Honorable Mention Poem (5) 1983). KanQ (15:3) Sum 83, p. 90.

2930. McPHERSON, Sandra
"The Braille Volcanos" (Oregon Museum of Science and Industry). Nat (237:7) 17 S 83, p. 219.
"Conception." AmerPoR (12:4) Jl-Ag 83, p. 15.
"Frightening Things." QW (16) Spr-Sum 83, p. 58.
"From My Notebook, Cape Cod." Field (29) Aut 83, p. 74.
"Lament, with Flesh and Blood." GeoR (37:3) Aut 83, p. 637.
"The Machinists" (for C.C.M.). QW (16) Spr-Sum 83, p. 59.
"Numbers 31" (in which Moses orders the rape of 32, 000 Midianite virgins). AmerPoR (12:4) Jl-Ag 83, p. 14.
"Ode to a Friend from the Early Sixties" (for M.S.). AmerPoR (12:4) Jl-Ag 83, p. 16.
"Poem Begun in the Haro Strait When I Was 28 and Finished When I Was 38." NewRep (188:16) 25 Ap 83, p. 36.
"Red Seeds Opening in the Shade." AmerPoR (12:4) Jl-Ag 83, p. 14.
"The Red Wig." AmerPoR (12:4) Jl-Ag 83, p. 15.
"The Way Holograms Work." NewRep (187:23) 13 D 82, p. 36.
"Young Women Talking about the Void." AmerPoR (12:4) Jl-Ag 83, p. 15.

2931. McQUILKIN, Rennie
"At the Fine Arts." Wind (13:47) 83, p. 32.
"At the New Britain Dept. of Motor Vehicles." PoNow (7:2, #38) 83, p. 27.

"Beach Fire." SmPd (20:3) Aut 83, p. 11.
"Bishop Cadigan Orders His Funeral." SmPd (20:1) Wint 83, p. 22.
"Breathing." SmPd (20:1) Wint 83, p. 21.
"Brother John Entreats His Lady." HarvardA (117:3) Aut 83, p. 12.
"Doe." PoetL (77:3) Aut 82, p. 141.
"Feedings" (for Sarah, at four). SmPd (20:3) Aut 83, p. 12.
"Girl in the Greenhouse." WindO (42) Sum 83, p. 35.
"In Conclusion" (for Lib). Wind (13:47) 83, p. 31.
"Mark's Used Parts." Atlantic (251:3) Mr 83, p. 67.
"New Cop at Blue Hills and Prospect." Wind (13:47) 83, p. 33.
"Old Man on the Night of the Eels." SmPd (20:1) Wint 83, p. 33.
"The Omen." SmPd (20:3) Aut 83, p. 14.
"The Pass." ColEng (45:6) O 83, p. 572.
"Pendergast's Garage" (after Edward Hopper). NewEngR (5:3) Spr 83, p. 416.
"Peter Farr." Poetry (141:5) F 83, p. 276-277.
"Puzzle." PoetL (78:3) Aut 83, p. 168.
"So Much Will Not Say No." Wind (13:47) 83, p. 31.
"That Time." BallSUF (24:1) Wint 83, p. 49.
"Thirteen." Wind (13:47) 83, p. 32.
"The Undoing: A Dream." YaleR (72:4) Sum 83, p. 602-603.
"When My Dog & I Dance." SmPd (20:3) Aut 83, p. 12.
"The Zenith." ColEng (45:6) O 83, p. 571.

2932. McROBBIE, Kenneth
"News Summary" (tr. of György Petri). PartR (50:4) 83, p. 586.
"To Bulcsu Bertha, with Profound Respect" (tr. of György Petri). PartR (50:4) 83, p. 586-587.
"Visigoth Sundays" (tr. of György Petri). PartR (50:4) 83, p. 587-588.

2933. McROBERTS, Robert
"Birth." PoetryCR (5:2) Wint 83-84, p. 15.

2934. McWHIRTER, George
"Finding." CanLit (97) Sum 83, p. 73.
"Successfully." CanLit (97) Sum 83, p. 73.

2935. MEADS, Kathy
"Encounter with the Devils, Race Point." KanQ (15:2) Spr 83, p. 198.

2936. MEATS, Stephen
"Bright River." KanQ (15:2) Spr 83, p. 98.
"Vacant Places" (for Tom Hemmens, killed 15 August 1981). LittleBR (3:4) Sum 83, p. 19.

2937. MEDINA, Pablo
"The Lathe of Navels." US1 (16/17) Wint 83-84, p. 12.
"Living with Shadows." StoneC (10:3/4) Spr-Sum 83, p. 27.
"Mala Suerte." StoneC (10:3/4) Spr-Sum 83, p. 27.

2938. MEEHAN, Patrick
"Treasure of the Barrio." SanFPJ (5:4) 83, p. 10-11.

2939. MEEK, Jay
"Dance Marathon." ThRiPo (21/22) 83, p. 55.
"Flowers." GeoR (37:2) Sum 83, p. 390-391.
"Four-Hand Waltzes." PoetryNW (24:1) Spr 83, p. 6-7.
"Grand Central." PoetryNW (24:1) Spr 83, p. 5-6.
"Harlequinade." PoetryNW (24:1) Spr 83, p. 4-5.
"Ramón Raquello and His Orchestra." PoetryNW (24:1) Spr 83, p. 3-4.
"Rasputin's Daughter." MemphisSR (2:2) Spr 82, p. 6.
"The Week the Dirigible Came." ThRiPo (21/22) 83, p. 56.

2940. MEGA, Paul
"Still waters, reflected blue." YetASM (1:2) 82, p. 14.

2941. MEI, Yoa-ch'en
"The Horse" (tr. by Sam Hamill). CharR (9:2) Aut 83, p. 89.
"The Lice" (tr. by Sam Hamill). CharR (9:2) Aut 83, p. 89.
"Necessities" (tr. by Sam Hamill). CharR (9:2) Aut 83, p. 90.

2942. MEILICKE, Kim J.
"For the Bahá'í Martyrs." WorldO (17:4) Sum 83, p. 36.

2943. MEINKE, Peter
"50 on 50." GeoR (37:2) Sum 83, p. 318-319.
"Atomic Pantoum." Poetry (142:1) Ap 83, p. 20-21.
"Sonnets for a Diabetic." SouthernPR (23:2) Aut 83, p. 35-36.

2944. MEISSNER, Bill (William)
"1969: The B-52 Pilot, before the Mid-Air Collision." IndR (6:1) Wint 83, p. 61.
"After Going Off the Road during the Snowstorm." ThRiPo (19/20) 82, p. 50.
"The Ann Landers Poem I've Been Meaning to Write All These Years--Finally Written After Hearing Ann and I were Both Born in Sioux City, Iowa." CharR (9:2) Aut 83, p. 73.
"Driving through an Iowa Farm Town." ThRiPo (19/20) 82, p. 49.
"The Spring Father Stopped Snowing." IndR (6:1) Wint 83, p. 62-63.

2945. MEISTER, Peter
"Afterthought." KanQ (15:2) Spr 83, p. 115.
"Headlights" (for Billy Sullivan). KanQ (15:2) Spr 83, p. 115.

2946. MELANCON, Charlotte
"Je Te Salue." Os (16) 83, p. 11.
"Pétales de roses et autres." Os (16) 83, p. 10.
"Peuplé d'oiseaux rouges." Os (16) 83, p. 11.

"Pivoines Vêtues d'orages." Os (16) 83, p. 10.

2947. MELARTIN, Riikka
"The Business Trip." AmerS (52:4) Aut 83, p. 537.
"Territories." Poetry (142:2) My 83, p. 95.
"Untitled: When we're small." Poetry (142:2) My 83, p. 94.

2948. MELFI, Mary
"The autobiography." Quarry (32:3) Sum 83, p. 73.
"The Hairdresser." Waves (11:2/3) Wint 83, p. 72.
"Like some one about to be shot." Quarry (32:3) Sum 83, p. 73.
"Mercy Killing S.I.N. 234 105 980." CrossC (5:2/3) 83, p. 11.

2949. MELHEM, D. H.
"Coney Island." Confr (25/26) 83, p. 75-76.

2950. MELLICK, Lee
"Clematis." SouthwR (68:3) Sum 83, p. 273.
"Design." YetASM (2:1) 83, p. 11.
"Onze Heures: The Sun Is Shining." Nimrod (27:1) Aut-Wint 83, p. 72.

MELLO BREYNER ANDRESEN, Sophia de
See: ANDRESEN, Sophia de Mello Breyner

2951. MELNYCZUK, Askold
"The Way of the World" (December 1980). Poetry (141:6) Mr 83, p. 324.

MELO NETO, João Cabral de
See: NETO João Cabral de Melo

2952. MELTZER, David
"7:I:82." CreamCR (8:1/2) 83, p. 78.
"24:XII:81." CreamCR (8:1/2) 83, p. 77-78.
"Back from London." SecC (11:1/2) 83, p. 138.
"Midrash." SecC (11:1/2) 83, p. 137.

2953. MEMMOTT, David
"Watching Election Returns." PortR (29:1) 83, p. 39.

2954. MENAGHAN, John Michael
"Like a Woman Saying Yes" (In Memory of Leon Bix Beiderbecke). CalQ (22) Sum 83, p. 49.
"Secrets." CalQ (22) Sum 83, p. 48.

2955. MENARD, Jean
"Boulevard Saint-Michel" (tr. by Dennis Tool). PoetL (78:2) Sum 83, p. 101.

2956. MENDELSON, Chaim
"Lessons, 47." ArizQ (39:2) Sum 83, p. 147.

2957. MENDEZ VIDES, Aldolfo
"What Else" (tr. by James Chichetto). ManhatR (3:1) Sum 83, p. 59.

2958. MENEBROKER, Ann
"The Fatties." SecC (11:1/2) 83, p. 133.
"Women Who Live Alone." Bogg (50) 83, p. 7.

2959. MENKITI, Ifeanyi
"So Help Me God." NewL (49:3/4) Spr-Sum 83, p. 74.

2960. MERCHANT, Norris
"O, Say Can You See?" Sam (34:3 135th release) 83, p. 30-31.

2961. MEREDITH, Joseph
"The Last Few Raindrops." KanQ (15:2) Spr 83, p. 102.

2962. MERRILL, James
"Dead Center." MichQR (22:1) Wint 83, p. 30.
"Domino." ParisR (24:84) Sum 82, p. 224.
"Grass." ParisR (24:84) Sum 82, p. 220.
"If U Cn Rd Ths." NewYRB (30:3) 3 Mr 83, p. 25.
"In the Dark." ParisR (24:84) Sum 82, p. 221.
"Island in the Works." ParisR (24:84) Sum 82, p. 224-225.
"Month." NewYRB (30:13) 18 Ag 83, p. 35.
"Novelettes." ParisR (24:84) Sum 82, p. 222-223.
"The Parnassians." NewYRB (30:16) 27 O 83, p. 4.
"Snapshot of Adam." Epoch (33:1) Aut-Wint 83, p. 79.
"To a Pocket Calculator." NewYorker (59:11) 2 My 83, p. 38.

2963. MERRILL, Susan
"Let's Be Maine." KanQ (15:2) Spr 83, p. 156.

2964. MERRIN, Jeredith
"Grieving" (for my father). Ploughs (9:1) 83, p. 71-72.
"Mutual Attraction." Thrpny (4:3, issue 15) Aut 83, p. 10.

2965. MERSAKHMIS, Scribe
"Praise of Amun-Re-Atum-Horakhty Who Crosses the Sky, Great of Love" (tr. by Reno Odlin). AntigR (54) Sum 83, p. 65-67.

2966. MERWIN, W. S.
"At Night." OhioR (30) 83, p. 22.
"Berryman." Nat (236:16) 23 Ap 83, p. 514.
"Black Meat" (tr. of Jean Follain). Field (28) Spr 83, p. 67.
"Dawn" (tr. of Jean Follain). Field (28) Spr 83, p. 64.
"The Fly and the Milk." OhioR (30) 83, p. 23.
"The New Seasons." NewYorker (59:34) 10 O 83, p. 50.
"Palm." Nat (236:16) 23 Ap 83, p. 514.
"Photograph." Nat (236:16) 23 Ap 83, p. 514.
"The Students' Dog" (tr. of Jean Follain). Field (28) Spr 83, p. 64.
"Talking." Nat (236:16) 23 Ap 83, p. 514.

2967. MERZ, Sandara
"Reveries." WritersL Jl 83, p. 25.

2968. MERZLAK, Regina
"As If I Saw Some Shade." SpiritSH (49 Suppl.) 83, p. 32.

2969. MESSERLI, Douglas
"Causes of the Crack Up: An Explication." ParisR (24:86) Wint 82, p. 116.

2970. METRAS, Gary
"Burning Instead of Beauty" (Selections: 3-4). PoetryE (9/10) Wint 82-Spr 83, p. 45-46.
"The Embrace." Sam (34:3 135th release) 83, p. 48-49.
"Past Impeding Present." Sam (34:3 135th release) 83, p. 32-33.
"Peace" (tr. of Bakchylides). PoetryE (9/10) Wint 82-Spr 83, p. 279.
"Progress Report on a Primitive Activity." StoneC (11:1/2, Pt. 1) Aut-Wint 83, p. 39.

2971. METTELMAN, Joyce S.
"Parenthetical Birthday Poem." YetASM (1:2) 82, p. 19.

2972. METZ, Roberta (See also: SWANN, Roberta Metz)
"Housewife." Pig (11) 83, p. 63.

2973. MEYER, Bruce
"Pictures at the Tate." Argo (4:2) 82, p. 23.

2974. MEYER, David C.
"Inner Peace." SpiritSH (48) 82, p. 24-25.
"One Condemns, the Other." SpiritSH (48) 82, p. 23.
"Prologue." SpiritSH (48) 82, p. 25.

2975. MEYER, Tim
"Art Work." IndR (5:1) Wint 82, p. 54.
"Moby Dick." IndR (5:1) Wint 82, p. 54.

2976. MEYER, William
"At the Greyhound Station." ModernPS (11:3) 83, p. 246-247.
"A Bucket-Full of Dew-Berries." WindO (43) Wint 83, p. 11.
"A Christian Cherokee Rehearses His Death" (for James E. Miller, Jr.). ModernPS (11:3) 83, p. 244.
"Night Ride Hued" (For Frances Mayhew Rippy). ModernPS (11:3) 83, p. 246.
"No Title." ModernPS (11:3) 83, p. 244.-245.
"Silent Sounds." ModernPS (11:3) 83, p. 245-246.
"Watching." ChiR (33:3) Wint 83, p. 94.

2977. MEZEY, Robert
"The Laundry" (tr. of Jacques Prévert). MemphisSR (3:1) Aut 82, p. 28-30.

2978. MICHAELS, Mary
"Funeral Procession in Carysfort Road." Argo (5:1) 83, p. 19.

2979. MICHALAK, David M.
"Sour Grapes." BelPoJ (33:3) Spr 83, p. 14-16.

MICHELE, Mary di
See: Di MICHELE, Mary

2980. MICHELINE, Jack
"Long after Midnight" (for Charles Bukowski). SecC (11:1/2) 83, p. 140-141.
"Skinny Dynamite." SecC (11:1/2) 83, p. 142-144.

2981. MICHELSON, Paul
"Vision of Durer: The Grand Schism." SanFPJ (4:2) 83, p. 32.

2982. MICHELSON, Richard
"Death and the Madonna." PoetryNW (24:1) Spr 83, p. 27.
"Nude Women Bathing, Drying Themselves and Combing Their Hair" (Fourth prize, SCCA International Poetry Contest). WestB (12) 83, p. 46-47.
"Portrait of Hortense Fiquet." PoetryNW (24:2) Sum 83, p. 31.
"Reclining Woman with Upturned Skirt." PoetryNW (24:1) Spr 83, p. 26-27.
"Wifebeating." SouthernPR (23:2) Aut 82 [i.e. (23:1?) Spr 83], p. 38.

2983. MICHIE, James
"Art" (tr. of Théophile Gautier). Poetry (142:3) Je 83, p. 153-154.

2984. MIDDLETON, Christopher
"A Young Horse." NewOR (10:2/3) Sum-Aut 83, p. 75.

MIEUX, Debbie le
See: Le MIEUX, Debbie

MIEUX, Dotty le
See: Le MIEUX, Dotty

2985. MIHAN, Lisa
"Ancient Torso of Apollo" (tr. of Rainer Maria Rilke). US1 (16/17) Wint 83-84, p. 11.
"I Love the Dark Hours" (tr. of Rainer Maria Rilke). US1 (16/17) Wint 83-84, p. 11.

2986. MIKLITSCH, Robert
"The School of Night." Shen (34:1) 83, p. 15-16.
"Sky Reading." KanQ (15:1) Wint 83, p. 177.

2987. MIKULEC, Patrick B.
"Hearing the Fugue." SanFPJ (5:4) 83, p. 42-43.

2988. MILBURN, Michael
"Bodies." MissouriR (6:3) Sum 83, p. 18-19.

"For Robert Lowell." MissouriR (6:3) Sum 83, p. 16-17.
"The Initial-Tree." Poetry (143:1) O 83, p. 24.
"Late Afternoon." PraS (57:4) Wint 83, p. 58-59.

2989. MILES, Josephine
"The Day the Winds." SecC (11:1/2) 83, p. 145.
"World." PoetryE (9/10) Wint 82-Spr 83, p. 38.

2990. MILES, Ron
"Paint." AntigR (54) Sum 83, p. 42-43.
"Poet." AntigR (54) Sum 83, p. 43.

2991. MILES, Sara
"Careers in Poetry, Part One: The Police Poet." HangL (44) Sum 83, p. 35.

2992. MILEY, Jim
"Closed Movie, Leland, Mississippi." KanQ (15:4) Aut 83, p. 62.

2993. MILLAN, Gonzalo
"La Ciudad" (Excerpt: 38). Areíto (9:35) 83, p. 39.

2994. MILLEN, Alan
"Nancy spat out a tooth." PoetryCR (5:1) Aut 83, p. 16.

2995. MILLER, A. McA.
"La Jouissance: Blackberries?" StoneC (11:1/2, Pt. 1) Aut-Wint 83, p. 28.
"Shell Mounds." BelPoJ (33:3) Spr 83, p. 29-32.

2996. MILLER, Brown
"Hiroshima's Nails." NewL (49:3/4) Spr-Sum 83, p. 62.

2997. MILLER, Carl
"Generation." KanQ (15:1) Wint 83, p. 124.

2998. MILLER, Carol
"Wisdom from the Other Side." Confr (25/26) 83, p. 309.

2999. MILLER, Elizabeth Gamble
"Between Words" (To Elizabeth Miller, tr. of Hugo Lindo). Mund (14:1) 83, p. 115, 117.
"On Poetry" (tr. of Hugo Lindo). NewOR (10:4) Wint 83, p. 42.

3000. MILLER, Heather Ross
"Adam's First Wife." Abatis (1) 83, p. 11.
"The Liberating." SouthernPR (23:2) Aut 83, p. 46.

3001. MILLER, Hollace
"Prairie Road" (Excerpt). SoDakR (21:4) Wint 83, p. 60.

3002. MILLER, J. A. (James A.)
"No Stranger Could Have Said" (for John Gardner, 1933-1982). FourQt (32:3) Spr 83, p. 4.
"Odyssey." HiramPoR (34) Spr-Sum 83, p. 13-14.

3003. MILLER, Jane
"Metaphysics at Lake Oswego." BlackWR (9:1) Aut 82, p. 92-93.
"Solstice." BlackWR (9:1) Aut 82, p. 90-91.

3004. MILLER, Leslie Adrienne
"Bookkeeping: Zanesville, Ohio, 1974." KanQ (15:4) Aut 83, p. 78-80.
"Calling on the Gypsy." PraS (51:1, i.e. 57:1) Spr 83, p. 60-62.
"Everyone Has a Single Quiet Story." PoetL (78:4) Wint 84, p. 212.
"Red on the Outside." KanQ (15:4) Aut 83, p. 74-78.
"Rhodope." PraS (51:1, i.e. 57:1) Spr 83, p. 59-60.
"The Telephone Dream." Prima (8) 83, p. 20.
"That Boy." 13thM (6:1/2) 82, p. 99.
"The Wild Ponies of Assateague Island." PoetL (78:4) Wint 84, p. 213.

3005. MILLER, Lewis H., Jr.
"Thoreau on the Lam." PoetL (77:4) Wint 83, p. 218.

3006. MILLER, Mary Ellen
"Insomnia." Wind (13:49) 83, p. 37.

3007. MILLER, Michael
"The Plant." PoetryE (9/10) Wint 82-Spr 83, p. 42.

3008. MILLER, Philip
"Attic Rummaging." Poem (49) N 83, p. 21.
"Blood Brothers." Poem (47) Mr 83, p. 9.
"Father." CapeR (19:1) Wint 83, p. 23.
"In a Mirror." Wind (13:48) 83, p. 43-44.
"The Unsmoker." WindO (43) Wint 83, p. 49.
"Winter Starlings." Poem (49) N 83, p. 22.

3009. MILLER, Thomas C.
"Transcendental Descartes." WebR (8:2) Aut 83, p. 89.

3010. MILLER, Vassar
"Cats, Dogs, and Kids I Have Known." NewL (50:1) Aut 83, p. 60.
"Demon Child." NewL (50:1) Aut 83, p. 60.
"False Alarm." NewL (50:1) Aut 83, p. 61.
"Haunt." NewL (50:1) Aut 83, p. 61.

3011. MILLER, Warren C.
"Homage à O.B." IndR (5:1) Wint 82, p. 55.

3012. MILLER, Wayne
"For Josephina." SecC (11:1/2) 83, p. 147.
"For Monique Graham." SecC (11:1/2) 83, p. 148.
"Poem for Elizabeth." SecC (11:1/2) 83, p. 146.

3013. MILLET, T. Lane
"Naked Charm." SanFPJ (5:1) 83, p. 52.

3014. MILLIS, Christopher
"Aladdin." YetASM (1:2) 82, p. 14.
"Considering a Child" (from Appearing Occupied, semi-finalist, 10th anniversary manuscript competition). StoneC (11:1/2, Pt. 1) Aut-Wint 83, p. 67.
"The Talking Bird." YetASM (1:2) 82, p. 14.
"Twelve Pirates." YetASM (1:2) 82, p. 12.
"Yale Brontosaurus Gets Head on Right at Last" (The New York Times, October 26, 1981) (from Appearing Occupied, semi-finalist, 10th anniversary manuscript competition). StoneC (11:1/2, Pt. 1) Aut-Wint 83, p. 66.

3015. MILLMAN, Lawrence
"St. Kilda Amen." NowestR (21:1) 83, p. 21-22.

3016. MILLS, Christopher
"'Deep Throat' Starring Barbara Cartland" (For Rommel Drives on Deep into Egypt, a book of poetry by Richard Brautigan). Bogg (51) 83, p. 54.

MILLS, Elizabeth Randall
See: RANDALL-MILLS, Elizabeth

3017. MILLS, George
"Rembrandt: Self Portrait" (from Each Flake Unique, semi-finalist, 10th anniversary manuscript competition). StoneC (11:1/2, Pt. 1) Aut-Wint 83, p. 68.
"She Never Cared Much" (from Each Flake Unique, semi-finalist, 10th anniversary manuscript competition). StoneC (11:1/2, Pt. 1) Aut-Wint 83, p. 68.

3018. MILLS, Ralph J., Jr.
"For the New Year." CentR (27:4) Aut 83, p. 272-273.
"In a Bar, Santa Fe" (for Dave Etter). SpoonRQ (8:2) Spr 83, p. 3.

3019. MILLS, Robert
"Comparisons." SpoonRQ (8:4) Aut 83, p. 20.
"November 1st." SpoonRQ (8:4) Aut 83, p. 20.

3020. MILLS, Sparling
"Ageing." PottPort (5) 83-84, p. 33.
"Fathers Don't Last Forever." PoetryCR (5:1) Aut 83, p. 8.
"Megan." AntigR (55) Aut 83, p. 33.
"Research." Bogg (51) 83, p. 44.
"Visitng My Parents." AntigR (55) Aut 83, p. 34.

3021. MILOSZ, Czeslaw
"Account" (tr. by Robert Pinsky and the author). NewYRB (30:7) 28 Ap 83, p. 6.
"A Book in the Ruins" (Warsaw, 1942) (tr. by the author, Robert Pinsky, and Robert Hass).

<u>NewYorker</u> (59:1) 21 F 83, p. 49.
"Farewell" (tr. by Robert Hass and Renata Gorczynski). <u>NewYRB</u> (30:7) 28 Ap 83, p. 6.
"It Was Winter" (tr. by Renata Gorczynski, Robert Hass, and Robert Pinsky). <u>NewRep</u> (187:11) 13 S 82, p. 28-29.
"A Mistake" (Paris, 1958) (tr. by the author, Robert Pinsky, and Robert Hass). <u>NewYorker</u> (59:1) 21 F 83, p. 48-49.
"My Faithful Mother Tongue." <u>ParisR</u> (25:87) Spr 83, p. 46-47.
"Ode to a Bird" (Montgeron, 1959) (tr. by the author, Robert Pinsky, and Robert Hass). <u>NewYorker</u> (59:1) 21 F 83, p. 48.
"On the Road" (tr. by Robert Hass and Renata Gorczynski). <u>NewYRB</u> (30:7) 28 Ap 83, p. 6.
"Reading the Japanese Poet Issa" (Berkely, 1978) (tr. by the author, Robert Pinsky, and Robert Hass). <u>NewYorker</u> (59:1) 21 F 83, p. 48.
"Report from a Besieged City" (Warsaw 1982) (tr. of Zbigniew Herbert). <u>NewYRB</u> (30:13) 18 Ag 83, p. 4.
"The Separate Notebooks: Pages concerning the Years of Independence" (tr. by the author and Robert Pinsky). <u>ParisR</u> (25:87) Spr 83, p. 49-54.
"A Story." <u>ParisR</u> (25:87) Spr 83, p. 48.
"Those Corridors" (tr. by Robert Pinsky). <u>Ploughs</u> (9:1) 83, p. 48.
"Veni Creator." <u>ParisR</u> (25:87) Spr 83, p. 47.

3022. MINASSIAN, Michael
"Past Present Future." <u>SanFPJ</u> (5:1) 83, p. 25-27.

3023. MINCZESKI, John
"Letters to My Death" (after Johann Froberger). <u>NegC</u> (3:4) Aut 83, p. 38-40.

3024. MINDESS, Harvey
"Hail to the Chiefs." <u>Humanist</u> (43:4) Jl-Ag 83, p. 28-29.
"I'd Rather Be a Psychologist." <u>Humanist</u> (43:4) Jl-Ag 83, p. 40.

3025. MINER, Newton
"Intuition." <u>Poem</u> (47) Mr 83, p. 65.
"To an Old Friend, at Crossroads." <u>Poem</u> (47) Mr 83, p. 66.

3026. MINER, Virginia Scott
"Springtime" (tr. of Henri Frédéric Amiel). <u>KanQ</u> (15:2) Spr 83, p. 172.

3027. MINICH, Jan
"The Reflection." <u>QW</u> (16) Spr-Sum 83, p. 121.

3028. MINOR, James
"Early Morning." <u>SoDakR</u> (21:3) Aut 83, p. 86.
"The Noose." <u>SoDakR</u> (21:3) Aut 83, p. 85.

MINORU, Fujita
<u>See</u>: FUJITA, Minoru

3029. MINTON, Helena
"August, 1981." WestB (13) 83, p. 78-79.
"Housekeeping." WestB (13) 83, p. 79.
"Taboo." BelPoJ (34:1) Aut 83, p. 2-3.

3030. MINTY, Judith
"From the Underworld." Kayak (63) N 83, p. 13-14.

3031. MINTZ, Ruth Finer
"The Peach Tree." Argo (4:1) 82, p. 29-30.
"Two Elements" (tr. of Zelda). Argo (4:3) 83, p. 32.

3032. MINUS, Ed
"Calenture." NewEngR (5:3) Spr 83, p. 366.
"Love in the '60s." NewEngR (5:3) Spr 83, p. 365.
"Now Enter." NewEngR (5:3) Spr 83, p. 364.

3033. MIRANDA, Gary
"Real Life." Argo (4:1) 82, p. 3.

3034. MIRIAM, Rivka
"Die in Me" (tr. by Linda Zisquit). LitR (26:2) Wint 83, p. 308.
"A Drunken Clown" (tr. by Linda Zisquit). LitR (26:2) Wint 83, p. 308.
"Fastening the Light of the Sabbath Candles" (tr. by Linda Zisquit). LitR (26:2) Wint 83, p. 308.
"The Girl Who Drowned in the Well" (tr. by Linda Zisquit). LitR (26:2) Wint 83, p. 309.
"Miriam's Well" (tr. by Linda Zisquit). LitR (26:2) Wint 83, p. 307.
"The Stripes in Joseph's Coat" (tr. by Linda Zisquit). LitR (26:2) Wint 83, p. 307.

3035. MIRSKIN, Jerry
"At Bay." MSS (2:3) Sum 83, p. 29.
"At the Museum." MSS (2:3) Sum 83, p. 39.
"Coming Home Drunk." MSS (2:3) Sum 83, p. 37.
"Death of a Deer." MSS (2:3) Sum 83, p. 35.
"The Fall." MSS (2:3) Sum 83, p. 33.
"Healing." MSS (2:3) Sum 83, p. 34.
"Insomnia." MSS (2:3) Sum 83, p. 40.
"Portrait." MSS (2:3) Sum 83, p. 30.
"White." MSS (2:3) Sum 83, p. 31.

3036. MISHKIN, Julia
"Adam's Lament." PortR (29:1) 83, p. 96.
"The Bad Nostalgia." Poetry (143:3) D 83, p. 152.
"Human Nature." CharR (9:1) Spr 83, p. 25-26.
"The Modern Mind." PortR (29:1) 83, p. 45.

3037. MISHLER, William
"The Bath of David Lindsay, Author of A Voyage to Arcturus." ChiR (33:4) Sum [i.e. Spr] 83, p. 40-42.

3038. MITCHAM, Judson
"Night Ride, 1965" (for John Baker). BlackWR (10:1) Aut 83, p. 85.
"Noise and a Few Words." PraS (57:2) Sum 83, p. 88.

"What You Have Need Of." PraS (57:2) Sum 83, p. 89.
"Where We Are." GeoR (37:3) Aut 83, p. 530-531.

3039. MITCHELL, Karen L.
"About 1929." 13thM (7:1/2) 83, p. 122-123.
"Belly Edge." 13thM (6:1/2) 82, p. 42-43.
"The Eating Hill." 13thM (6:1/2) 82, p. 37-39.
"The Paper Woman." 13thM (7:1/2) 83, p. 124-125.
"Sometimes." 13thM (6:1/2) 82, p. 40-41.

3040. MITCHELL, Nora
"Bells off San Salvador." Calyx (7:3) Sum 83, p. 38.
"In the Cellar." HangL (44) Sum 83, p. 36.

3041. MITCHELL, Roger
"J. P. Lundy Comes to Saranac Lake." Blueline (5:1) Sum-Aut 83, p. 36-37.
"Reuben Sanford and John Richards, Surveyors, Make Their Report, October 1827." Blueline (3:2) Wint-Spr 82, p. 24-25.

3042. MITSUI, James Masao
"Letter to Tina Koyama from Elliot Bay Park." MemphisSR (3:1) Aut 82, p. 25.

3043. MITTON, M. Anne
"Deserted." PottPort (5) 83-84, p. 25.

3044. MIURA, Kiyoko
"Bamboo (1)" (tr. of Sakutaro Hagiwara). SoDakR (21:1) Spr 83, p. 49.
"Bamboo (2)" (tr. of Sakutaro Hagiwara). SoDakR (21:1) Spr 83, p. 49.
"A Blade of Grass" (tr. of Sakutaro Hagiwara). SoDakR (21:1) Spr 83, p. 48.
"Melancholy Vista" (tr. of Sakutaro Hagiwara). SoDakR (21:1) Spr 83, p. 51.
"Seeds in the Palm of My Hand" (tr. of Sakutaro Hagiwara). SoDakR (21:1) Spr 83, p. 50.
"Tortoise" (tr. of Sakutaro Hagiwara). SoDakR (21:1) Spr 83, p. 48.
"A Withered Crime" (tr. of Sakutaro Hagiwara). SoDakR (21:1) Spr 83, p. 50.

3045. MIZE, R. W.
"The Whales of Wellfleet." CrabCR (1:1) My 83, p. 29.

3046. MIZER, Ray
"Demurrer." Poem (47) Mr 83, p. 5.
"Earth Symphony: A Cappella." Poem (47) Mr 83, p. 1.
"Harvesthome." Poem (47) Mr 83, p. 3.
"Scheduling." Poem (47) Mr 83, p. 2.
"The View from Apollo XVII." Poem (47) Mr 83, p. 4.

3047. MOE, Keith
"Visitng with Pete." BelPoJ (34:2) Wint 83-84, p. 35-36.

3048. MOELLER, Jean
"Crazy Quilt." AntigR (53) Spr 83, p. 38.
"Elegance on a Florida Lawn." AntigR (55) Aut 83, p. 133.
"Evolving." AntigR (53) Spr 83, p. 38.
"Not Here, Not Ever." AntigR (55) Aut 83, p. 133.

3049. MOFFEIT, Tony
"Adobe Wall Motel." Bogg (51) 83, p. 7.
"Five Card Stud." CrabCR (1:1) My 83, p. 14.
"Ghost Highway Past Costilla." OroM (2:1, #5) Sum 83, p. 8.
"Hopi Snake Dance." Vis (13) 83, p. 31.
"Marguerita." CrabCR (1:1) My 83, p. 14.
"Rollin Stone." Vis (13) 83, p. 31.

3050. MOFFETT, Judith
"The Greenfly Question." PraS (51:1, i.e. 57:1) Spr 83, p. 20-21.
"The Hero Worshiper." 13thM (6:1/2) 82, p. 111-119.
"Will." PraS (51:1, i.e. 57:1) Spr 83, p. 21.

3051. MOFFI, Larry
"Barbeque" (from A Simple Progression). PoNow (7:2, #38) 83, p. 25.
"Bringing Home the Dog." BlackWR (10:1) Aut 83, p. 117.
"The Demon of Elloree" (from A Simple Progression). PoNow (7:2, #38) 83, p. 25.
"The Geography of Time." PoetL (77:4) Wint 83, p. 197-198.
"To an Actress Afraid of a Dog." PoetL (77:2) Sum 82, p. 85.
"Yahrzeit." Tendril (14/15) Wint 83, p. 141.

3052. MOFFITT, John
"Jungle and Flame." Argo (4:1) 82, p. 18.
"Jungle and Flame." Argo (4:3) 83, p. 10-11.
"Testament." NegC (3:4) Aut 83, p. 41.

3053. MOIR, James M.
"Angus." Bluebuf (2:1) Aut 83, p. 21.
"Driving to Town." Bluebuf (2:1) Aut 83, p. 19.

3054. MOLESWORTH, Charles
"Breakfast in Brixton." MemphisSR (3:1) Aut 82, p. 8.

3055. MOLTON, Warren Lane
"Ascent." ChrC (100:36) 30 N 83, p. 1100.

3056. MOLYNEUX, Mary
"Dress." Tele (18) 83, p. 41.
"Gloves." Tele (18) 83, p. 41.
"Little Things, or Winter Comes." Tele (18) 83, p. 42-46.

3057. MONAGHAN, Pat
"Oakley, Kansas." YetASM (1:1) 82, p. 7.
"Spinstress." YetASM (1:1) 82, p. 10.

3058. MONAGHAN, Rita H.
"Life, Light and Love." WritersL S 83, p. 12.
"Space Brotherhood." WritersL S 83, p. 16.

3059. MONGIELLO, Raquel de
"Un Año Más." LetFem (9:2) Aut 83, p. 84.
"Apuro." LetFem (9:2) Aut 83, p. 86.
"Confidencia." LetFem (9:2) Aut 83, p. 87.
"Nostalgias." LetFem (9:2) Aut 83, p. 87.
"Te He Visto." LetFem (9:2) Aut 83, p. 85.

3060. MONROE, Jonathan
"Blue Horses." AmerPoR (12:1) Ja/F 83, p. 46.
"Mont Sainte-Victoire." PraS (57:2) Sum 83, p. 37-38.

3061. MONROE, Kent, Jr.
"Coals." SanFPJ (4:2) 83, p. 49.

3062. MONTAGUE, John
"Abbeylara." OntR (19) Aut-Wint 83-84, p. 36-37.
"Gone." OntR (19) Aut-Wint 83-84, p. 39.
"A Last Gesture." OntR (19) Aut-Wint 83-84, p. 35.
"A Murmuring Stream." OntR (19) Aut-Wint 83-84, p. 33-34.
"Process." OntR (19) Aut-Wint 83-84, p. 38.
"Turnhole." CreamCR (8:1/2) 83, p. 79.
"Upstream" (poems). OntR (19) Aut-Wint 83-84, p. 29-39.
"Upstream." OntR (19) Aut-Wint 83-84, p. 31-32.

3063. MONTALE, Eugenio
"Dora Markus" (tr. by Alfred Corn). ParisR (25:88) Sum 83, p. 61-62.
"Lungomare." PortR (29:1) 83, p. 74.
"Seafront" (tr. by Michael L. Johnson). PortR (29:1) 83, p. 75.

3064. MONTEIRO, George
"Division of Labor." CentR (27:4) Aut 83, p. 271.
"Home to the Hills." CentR (27:4) Aut 83, p. 271-272.

3065. MONTGOMERY, George
"Jumping over the Moon -- Far Far Awaaaay" (for Jack Kerouac). MoodySI (13) Sum 83, p. 9.
"A Parade You Cannot Let Pass Without Watching." SecC (11:1/2) 83, p. 149-151.

3066. MOODY, Rodger
"Black and White." YetASM (2:1) 83, p. 10.
"The Builders of Light." Wind (13:47) 83, p. 2.
"Night." ClockR (1:1) Sum 83, p. 13.
"Simple Rivers." ClockR (1:1) Sum 83, p. 5.
"Train Ride: Eugene to Portland." PoetC (15:1) Aut 83, p. 26.

3067. MOOERS, Vernon
"He Swings His Axe" (for Alden Nowlan). PottPort (5) 83-84, p. 52.

3068. MOORE, Barbara
"Van Gogh." AntR (41:1) Wint 83, p. 73.

3069. MOORE, George (George B.)
"Ghosts" (tr. of José Emilio Pacheco). MissR (12:1/2, nos. 34/35) Aut 83, p. 70.
"How Handsome a Woman Is." SouthernPR (23:2) Aut 82 [i.e. (23:1?) Spr 83], p. 46-47.
"Ratus Norvegicus" (tr. of José Emilio Pacheco). MissR (12:1/2, nos. 34/35) Aut 83, p. 71-72.
"To an Old Hotel in Quito." CharR (9:1) Spr 83, p. 18-19.

3070. MOORE, Honor
"Shenandoah." 13thM (6:1/2) 82, p. 16-17.
"Spuyten Duyvil." NewEng (5:4) Sum 83, p. 626-633.

3071. MOORE, Lenard D.
"Winter field." Wind (13:49) 83, p. 11.

3072. MOORE, Prentiss
"The 101 Views of Fuji." Poetry (143:2) N 83, p. 87.
"From the Library of Alexandria." Poetry (143:2) N 83, p. 83-84.
"Porfyry in Exile." Poetry (143:2) N 83, p. 85-86.
"Wisdom of the Mediterranean." Poetry (143:2) N 83, p. 86.

3073. MOORE, Richard
"In the Rough." Salm (60) Spr-Sum 83, p. 161-164.

3074. MOORE, Roger
"Ruins." Waves (11:4) Spr 83, p. 68.
"Walls." Waves (11:4) Spr 83, p. 68.

3075. MOORE, Todd
"Knifed Him." Bogg (51) 83, p. 22.
"Sitting in My." Bogg (50) 83, p. 11.

3076. MOORE, Tom
"Black Lake." ChrC (100:25) 31 Ag-7 S 83, p. 774.

3077. MOORE, W. T.
"Paper, Scissors, Rock." YetASM (1:2) 82, p. 18.
"Pattern: March." YetASM (1:2) 82, p. 16.

3078. MOORHEAD, Andrea
"Body Infinitely Other" (tr. of Gatien Lapointe). Mund (14:1) 83, p. 27.
"Book II" (tr. of Gatien Lapointe). Mund (14:1) 83, p. 27.
"Nomen." Os (16) 83, p. 18-21.

3079. MORA, Pat
"Bailando." RevChic (11:3/4) 83, p. 60.
"Elena." RevChic (11:3/4) 83, p. 61.

3080. MORAFF, Barbara
"And She." WormR (23:2, issue 90) 83, p. 73.
"Snowfalls." WormR (23:2, issue 90) 83, p. 73.

"Things." WormR (23:2, issue 90) 83, p. 74.

3081. MORAGA, Cherríe
"Fear, a Love Poem." 13thM (6:1/2) 82, p. 100-102.
"Like Family" (for women who travel in packs of one). 13thM (7:1/2) 83, p. 48-50.
"The Slow Dance." 13thM (7:1/2) 83, p. 46-47.

3082. MORAN, Leonard
"Brides of El Salvador" Comm (109:22) 17 D 82, p. 694 (Incorrectly listed under MORAN, Leo in the 82 index. Corrected in (110:1) 14 Ja 83, p. 18).

3083. MORAN, Ronald
"The Branch Bank." SouthernR (19:4) O 83, p. 853.
"The Termite Man." SouthernR (19:4) O 83, p. 854.

3084. MORDENSKI, Jan
"Bread and salt." SpiritSH (48) 82, p. 50.
"Christmas." SpiritSH (48) 82, p. 49.
"Szopka." SpiritSH (48) 82, p. 51.

3085. MORELAND, Jane P.
"To Mother: On Your Concern." PoetryNW (24:3) Aut 83, p. 26-27.

3086. MORGAN, Allan E., Jr.
"Run for the Pumpkins." YetASM (2:1) 83, p. 5.

3087. MORGAN, David R.
"Futuri-Manife in Northworldsville." Bogg (50) 83, p. 60.

3088. MORGAN, Frederick
"Anaktoria." SouthernR (19:1) Ja 83, p. 144.
"The Christmas Tree." Poetry (143:3) D 83, p. 162.
"Irvington." Ploughs (9:1) 83, p. 157-158.
"July 1st, 1982 - Triolet." Kayak (63) N 83, p. 19.
"The Parting." SouthernR (19:1) Ja 83, p. 143-144.

3089. MORGAN, Jan
"Outside World." WritersL Ap-My 83, p. 19.

3090. MORGAN, Jane
"Storm." WritersL Je 83, p. 5.

3091. MORGAN, Jean
"Grafting." SouthernHR (17:2) Spr 83, p. 169.

3092. MORGAN, John
"Ambush." TriQ (56) Wint 83, p. 141-142.
"The House Martins." Argo (4:3) 83, p. 22.
"The Inlet." ParisR (24:84) Sum 82, p. 149.
"The Inside Passage." AmerPoR (12:4) Jl-Ag 83, p. 47.
"Osteology of the Ants." PoetryNW (24:1) Spr 83, p. 28-29.
"Robert Lowell in Juneau." BlackWR (8:1) Aut 81, p. 17.
"The Snake-Hunt: Gallup, New Mexico" (for John

Milius). <u>BlackWR</u> (8:1) Aut 81, p. 18-19.

3093. MORGAN, Robert
"Appleglow." <u>Atlantic</u> (251:5) My 83, p. 82.
"Grandma's Bureau." <u>Epoch</u> (33:1) Aut-Wint 83, p. 80.
"Looking Homeward." <u>AmerPoR</u> (12:2) Mr/Ap 83, p. 18.
"One Fiber of a Hair Shirt." <u>Abatis</u> (1) 83, p. 13.
"Shrine." <u>MemphisSR</u> (3:1) Aut 82, p. 17.
"Thermometer Wine." <u>AmerS</u> (52:2) Spr 83, p. 172.
"Threshold." <u>PoNow</u> (7:2, #38) 83, p. 35.

3094. MORGAN, S. K.
"One Last Pepperoni Pizza." <u>SanFPJ</u> (5:4) 83, p. 27.
"Thermonuclear Wheaties." <u>SanFPJ</u> (5:1) 83, p. 48.
"Watch Repairmen Are a Dying Breed." <u>SanFPJ</u> (5:1) 83, p. 77-78.
"Wham Bam, Thank You, Ma'am." <u>SanFPJ</u> (5:4) 83, p. 26.

3095. MORGENTHALER, Sharon
"To Boom Boom." <u>Bogg</u> (51) 83, p. 15.

3096. MORICE, Dave
"Alaskan Drinking Song." <u>Epoch</u> (33:1) Aut-Wint 83, p. 82.

3097. MORIN, Edward
"The Primal Sun (Helios o Protos)" (Selections: V-VI, XII-XIII, XV, XVII-XVIII) (tr. of Odysseus Elytis, w. Lefteris Pavlides). <u>WebR</u> (8:1) Spr 83, p. 20-25.

3098. MORITZ, A. F.
"Africa." <u>AntigR</u> (54) Sum 83, p. 88-89.
"Poverty." <u>AntigR</u> (54) Sum 83, p. 87.
"They Still Kept Scribbling." <u>Quarry</u> (32:4) Aut 83, p. 12-13.

3099. MORITZ, Albert
"The Doctor." <u>MalR</u> (64) F 83, p. 49.
"Ghost Story." <u>MalR</u> (64) F 83, p. 51.
"Memory." <u>MalR</u> (64) F 83, p. 50.
"A Stranger." <u>MalR</u> (64) F 83, p. 48.

3100. MORLEY, Hilda
"After the Moon-Walk." <u>NewL</u> (49:3/4) Spr-Sum 83, p. 188.
"And I in My Bed Again." <u>SenR</u> (13:2) 82-83, p. 50-51.
"Cézanne." <u>SenR</u> (13:2) 82-83, p. 47-49.
"The Tree." <u>NewL</u> (49:3/4) Spr-Sum 83, p. 188-189.

3101. MORRILL, Donald
"For the Holidays." <u>NewEngR</u> (6:2) Wint 83, p. 320.
"For the Old Rider at the Mall in Sioux Falls." <u>CimR</u> (62) Ja 83, p. 52-53.

3102. MORRIS, Carol
"Lilacs." <u>Tendril</u> (14/15) Wint 83, p. 142-143.
"Lilacs Part II." <u>Tendril</u> (14/15) Wint 83, p. 144-

145.

3103. MORRIS, Herbert
"Atget at Ville-D'Avray Waiting for Light." MissR (12:1/2, nos. 34/35) Aut 83, p. 97-107.
"In the Storeroom." Kayak (62) Ag 83, p. 42-43.
"Kurosawa's Horses." LittleM (14:1/2) 83, p. 27-28.
"The Music." Kayak (61) Ap 83, p. 67-71.
"Some Details of Conditions on Arrival." Kayak (63) N 83, p. 53-55.
"Years Later." Salm (61) Aut 83, p. 53-54.

3104. MORRIS, John N.
"The Blacksnake in My Tree." OhioR (30) 83, p. 14.
"Bringing Up Father." NewYorker (59:39) 14 N 83, p. 180.
"Steichen at Art." NewRep (187:3/4) 19-26 Jl 82, p. 38.

3105. MORRIS, Paul
"Accused" (tr. of Horst Bienek). PoetryE (9/10) Wint 82-Spr 83, p. 189.
"Afterwards" (tr. of Horst Bienek). PoetryE (9/10) Wint 82-Spr 83, p. 190.
"Always to Be Named" (tr. of Johannes Bobrowski). CutB (21) Aut-Wint 83, p. 75.
"The Defeated Conqueror" (tr. of Horst Bienek). PoetryE (9/10) Wint 82-Spr 83, p. 191.
"The Head in the Desert" (tr. of Yvan Goll). WebR (8:2) Aut 83, p. 45.
"The Hours" (tr. of Yvan Goll). WebR (8:2) Aut 83, p. 44.
"The Hut of Ashes" (tr. of Yvan Goll). WebR (8:2) Aut 83, p. 44.
"In Every Blackbird I Loved You" (tr. of Yvan Goll). WebR (8:2) Aut 83, p. 43.
"In the Form of a Wild Boar" (tr. of Paul Celan). WebR (8:1) Spr 83, p. 43.
"The Inner Trees" (tr. of Yvan Goll). WebR (8:2) Aut 83, p. 43.
"Katorga" (tr. of Horst Bienek). PoetryE (9/10) Wint 82-Spr 83, p. 186.
"Our Ashes" (tr. of Horst Bienek). PoetryE (9/10) Wint 82-Spr 83, p. 187-188.
"Symbols and Propositions" (tr. of Horst Bienek). PoetryE (9/10) Wint 82-Spr 83, p. 185.
"Very Far Away" (tr. of Horst Bienek). PoetryE (9/10) Wint 82-Spr 83, p. 192.
"The Years from You to Me" (tr. of Paul Celan). WebR (8:1) Spr 83, p. 42.

3106. MORRIS, Peter
"Demonstrations." WormR (23:4, issue 92) 83, p. 130.
"Gravity." PoetryE (11) Sum 83, p. 40.
"It Works That Way." PoetryE (11) Sum 83, p. 41.
"Oliver." WormR (23:4, issue 92) 83, p. 129.
"Same Day Developing." WormR (23:4, issue 92) 83, p. 129.

3107. MORRIS, Richard
"Reno Nevada." SecC (11:1/2) 83, p. 153.

3108. MORRIS, Tony
"Where Rubber Plants Grow Tall." Bogg (50) 83, p. 51.

3109. MORRISON, Audrey J.
"These Days." SouthernPR (23:2) Aut 82 [i.e. (23:1?) Spr 83], p. 53.

3110. MORRISON, Madison
"Light" (Excerpts: 1-21). Epoch (32:3) Spr-Sum 83, p. 212-218.

3111. MORSE, Carl
"Atlantis Bypass." HangL (44) Sum 83, p. 38.
"Joint Letter on Poverty." HangL (44) Sum 83, p. 37.

3112. MORTON, Colin
"Anatomy of Criticism." Quarry (32:4) Aut 83, p. 15-16.
"The Autumn of the Patriarch." Quarry (32:4) Aut 83, p. 14-15.
"Two Authors in Search of a Character." Quarry (32:4) Aut 83, p. 14.

3113. MORTON, Nadine
"Redemption Dream I." MalR (64) F 83, p. 119.
"Redemption Dream II." MalR (64) F 83, p. 120.
"Sea Bed." MalR (64) F 83, p. 118.

3114. MORTON, W. C.
"A Florida Prelude." SouthernPR (23:2) Aut 82 [i.e. (23:1?) Spr 83], p. 30.

3115. MOSBY, George, Jr.
"A Kiss in Return." Images (8:3) 83, p. 7.
"Southern Snaps." Images (8:3) 83, p. 7.

3116. MOSELEY, Amelia
"Bertha Rochester during a Lucid Interval." NegC (3:4) Aut 83, p. 118-119.
"Electra in Her Old Age." NegC (3:4) Aut 83, p. 116-117.

3117. MOSER, Norman
"Cab-Driver's Lament." SecC (11:1/2) 83, p. 156.
"The Exorcism" (to Katie Austir). SecC (11:1/2) 83, p. 155.

3118. MOSES, Robert
"I Want My Bread." ParisR (25:89) Aut 83, p. 131.

3119. MOSES, W. R.
"Chipmunk Steps." Northeast (Ser. 3:15) Sum 83, p. 4.
"Coyote Creek." Northeast (Ser. 3:15) Sum 83, p. 6.
"A Dark Arrow." Northeast (Ser. 3:15) Sum 83, p. 1.
"Edges." Northeast (Ser. 3:15) Sum 83, p. 7.

"On the Road to Ferncliff Cemetery." Northeast (Ser. 3:15) Sum 83, p. 3.
"Sunday Afternoon." Northeast (Ser. 3:15) Sum 83, p. 2.
"Winter Journal Item." Northeast (Ser. 3:15) Sum 83, p. 5.

3120. MOSHMAN, Sherri
"The Poetry Reading." LittleM (14:1/2) 83, p. 13.

3121. MOSKIN, Ilene
"In Reply." OhioR (30) 83, p. 147.

3122. MOSKOVITZ, Candida Fraze
"The Balloon Is Rising." PoetL (77:3) Aut 82, p. 155.

3123. MOSKOWITZ, Faye
"The Dreams of Cora Yates Who Works at the Pants Factory in Culpeper, Virginia." 13thM (7:1/2) 83, p. 139.

3124. MOSS, Howard
"Fingerprints." NewYRB (30:6) 14 Ap 83, p. 38.
"The Light Put Out." NewYorker (59:10) 25 Ap 83, p. 48.
"Making a Bed." NewYorker (58:50) 31 Ja 83, p. 52.
"The Miles Between." Nat (237:6) 3-10 S 83, p. 187.
"Morning Glory." Raritan (3:2) Aut 83, p. 87.
"Nerves." NewYorker (59:13) 16 My 83, p. 44.
"New Hampshire." NewYorker (59:33) 3 O 83, p. 43.
"The Restaurant Window." NewYorker (59:44) 19 D 83, p. 46.
"Rome: The Night Before." NewYorker (59:17) 13 Je 83, p. 46.
"Song from the Intensive Care Unit." NewRep (188:20) 23 My 83, p. 28.
"The Swimming Pool." NewYorker (59:21) 11 Jl 83, p. 40.
"To the Islands." DevQ (18:3) Aut 83, p. 13.
"Venice: Still Life." NewYRB (30:18) 24 N 83, p. 21.

3125. MOSS, Stanley
"Letter to the Butterflies." AmerPoR (12:1) Ja/F 83, p. 34.
"The Seagull." AmerPoR (12:1) Ja/F 83, p. 34.

3126. MOTEN, Frederick
"Fragments of the Robin Island Mail." HarvardA (117:1) Mr 83, p. 34.
"The Loss of It." HarvardA (117:1) Mr 83, p. 34.
"Three Poverties." HarvardA (117:3) Aut 83, p. 13.

3127. MOTION, Andrew
"Bathing at Glymenopoulo." Agni (18) 83, p. 60-63.
"Leaving Belfast" (for Craig Raine). Agni (18) 83, p. 58.
"Letter to an Exile." Agni (18) 83, p. 55-57.
"West 23rd." Agni (18) 83, p. 59.

3128. MOTT, Michael
"Catalan." MissouriR (7:1) Aut 83, p. 38-39.
"Ffion, Foxgloves, Field Trumpets" (Stepper Point, North Cornwall). SewanR (91:2) Spr 83, p. 190.
"Geese on the Genesee." SewanR (91:2) Spr 83, p. 191.
"Tarn." SewanR (91:2) Spr 83, p. 189.

3129. MOTT, Randy
"Grandmother." PoetryNW (24:3) Aut 83, p. 25.

3130. MOULTON-BARRETT, Donalee
"Dying." PottPort (5) 83-84, p. 21.

3131. MOURE, Erin
"After All That" (for Jennifer MacKenzie, 17 years old). Bluebuf (2:1) Aut 83, p. 8.
"Clearing Trees." Bluebuf (2:1) Aut 83, p. 20.
"Curly Blond." CrossC (5:4) 83, p. 6.
"Idiom Birds." CanLit (97) Sum 83, p. 45.
"Moose by Greyhound." CrossC (5:4) 83, p. 6.
"Professional Amnesia." Bluebuf (2:1) Aut 83, p. 22.
"Safety." Dandel (10:1) Spr-Sum 83, p. 38.
"Total Artifice." Dandel (10:1) Spr-Sum 83, p. 39.
"The Words Mean What We Say, We Say." Quarry (32:4) Aut 83, p. 54.

3132. MOVIUS, Geoffrey H.
"Forgiven at Forty." LittleBR (4:2) Wint 83-84, p. 38.

3133. MOYER, Kermit
"The Far East." Tendril (16) Sum 83, p. 94.

MU-SHAN, Han
See: HAN, Mu-shan

3134. MUELLER, Lisel
"About Suffering They Were Never Wrong." NewL (50:1) Aut 83, p. 37.
"Accommodations." Atlantic (252:6) D 83, p. 52.
"Blue." AmerPoR (12:3) My-Je 83, p. 17.
"Commuter." ClockR (1:1) Sum 83, p. 28.
"Crossing Over." AmerPoR (12:3) My-Je 83, p. 17.
"The End of Science Fiction." OhioR (30) 83, p. 8.
"Into Space." BlackWR (10:1) Aut 83, p. 51-53.
"January 1st." AmerPoR (12:3) My-Je 83, p. 17.
"Letter to California." NewL (50:1) Aut 83, p. 36-37.
"Monet Refuses the Operation." ParisR (24:84) Sum 82, p. 182-183.
"Scenic Route" (For Lucy). IndR (5:3) Aut 82, p. 4.

3135. MUIR, John
"Untitled: If I could put my woods in song." Paint (10:19/20) Spr-Aut 83, p. 11.
"Untitled: Where are the joys I have met in the morning." Paint (10:19/20) Spr-Aut 83, p. 10.

3136. MULDOON, Paul
"At Martha's Deli." Agni (19) 83, p. 55.
"How to Play Championship Tennis." Agni (19) 83, p. 52.
"Lives of the Saints." Agni (19) 83, p. 51.
"Mules." Agni (19) 83, p. 54.
"Paris." Agni (19) 83, p. 53.
"Why Brownlee Left." Agni (19) 83, p. 56.

3137. MULHOLLAND, Mary Jane
"Lives of Their Own." Tendril (14/15) Wint 83, p. 146.

3138. MULLEN, Laura
"Logic." PoetryNW (24:1) Spr 83, p. 11.
"Ode for an Envelope." Thrpny (4:1, issue 13) Spr 83, p. 12.

3139. MULLIGAN, J. B.
"Requiescat." SanFPJ (4:4) 83, p. 88.
"The Unknown Soldier." Sam (34:3 135th release) 83, p. 40-41.
"The Unspeakable." Sam (34:3 135th release) 83, p. 20.

3140. MULLINS, Cecil J.
"Hymn to Tranquilizers." BallSUF (24:2) Spr 83, p. 64.

3141. MUNDHENK, Michael
"Kline Jungs sind Engel" (tr. of Jack Kerouac). MoodySI (10) Aut 81, p. 15.

3142. MUNISTERI, Joanne
"For A. J. E." YetASM (2:1) 83, p. 8.

3143. MUNOZ, Cindy McGary
"Scenes from a Haitian Refugee Camp." SanFPJ (4:3) 83, p. 68.

3144. MUNOZ, Rosalinda
"The fireman under the moonlight." YetASM (1:1) 82, p. 9.
"Morning." YetASM (1:1) 82, p. 11.

3145. MUNRO, Jane
"As Windows Shape Light." Quarry (32:1) Wint 83, p. 24-25.
"Victoria Day / East Side." Quarry (32:1) Wint 83, p. 25-27.

3146. MURABITO, S. J.
"A Box of Chestnuts." PoetL (78:2) Sum 83, p. 88.
"A Longer Arm Than God." PoetL (78:2) Sum 83, p. 89.

3147. MURATORI, Fred
"Twenty Miles from Ground Zero." QW (17) Aut-Wint 83-84, p. 96.

3148. MURAWSKI, Elisabeth
"An Address." Comm (110:9) 6 My 83, p. 277.
"The Lost Christian." ChrC (100:22) 20-27 Jl 83, p. 670.
"A New Language." MSS (3:1) Aut 83, p. 189.
"Potter's Field." WestB (13) 83, p. 26.
"Quicker Than the Eye." SouthernHR (17:3) Sum 83, p. 223.
"Saigon Woman in a Green Dress." WestB (13) 83, p. 27.
"The Second Day." HolCrit (20:2) Ap 83, p. 19.
"Study in Stained Glass." PortR (29:1) 83, p. 46.
"To Adjust to the Sky." LitR (27:1) Aut 83, p. 84.
"When the Green Is Gone." StoneC (11:1/2, Pt. 1) Aut-Wint 83, p. 37.
"The Woman Who Was Stolen." MSS (3:1) Aut 83, p. 187-188.

3149. MURGUIA, Alejandro
"Sweet Soledad." SecC (11:1/2) 83, p. 157.

3150. MURPHY, Carol Darnell
"Composition." DevQ (18:1) Spr 83, p. 88.
"For Someone Else." DevQ (17:4) Wint 83, p. 26.
"We Decide to Welcome Mortality." DevQ (18:1) Spr 83, p. 89.

3151. MURPHY, Kevin
"Sufis." CarolQ (35:3) Spr 83, p. 7.

3152. MURPHY, P. D.
"Friday, January 15, 1982." SanFPJ (4:3) 83, p. 26.
"Hand." SanFPJ (5:1) 83, p. 21.
"Will You Wait." SanFPJ (4:3) 83, p. 27.

3153. MURPHY, Paul
"Visiting the Detroit River at Night in a Sports Fury Driven by a Drunken Father" Tendril (16) Sum 83, p. 95-98.

3154. MURPHY, Rich (See also: MURPHY, Richard)
"And Every Day Is a Hard Head Day." KanQ (15:2) Spr 83, p. 198-199.
"Ezra Jones and I traveling through the Business Zone." SanFPJ (5:2) 83, p. 62.
"Fable 13." Tele (18) 83, p. 87.
"The I G W T Warheads." SanFPJ (5:2) 83, p. 63.
"The Nursemaid Is Petrified." Tele (18) 83, p. 86.
"The Same Old Story." CharR (9:1) Spr 83, p. 19.

3155. MURPHY, Richard (See also: MURPHY, Rich)
"Letterfrack Industrial School." NewYRB (30:9) 2 Je 83, p. 24.
"Stormpetrel" (Excerpt). NewRep (186:20) 19 My 82, p. 39.

3156. MURPHY, Sheila (Sheila E.)
"Consciousness." Tendril (16) Sum 83, p. 99.
"A Footnote to the Flowers." Argo (4:2) 82, p. 4.
"Hallowe'en, 1982." WindO (42) Sum 83, p. 25.

"Know to Trust the Voices." CapeR (19:1) Wint 83, p. 12.
"Mister." CapeR (19:1) Wint 83, p. 13.
"Pancakes." NegC (3:4) Aut 83, p. 129.
"The Relationship of Paranoia to Deafness." Argo (4:2) 82, p. 4.
"Taking Unemployment into My Own Hands." WindO (42) Sum 83, p. 24.

3157. MURRAY, Les A.
"Self-Portrait from a Photograph." Thrpny (4:3, issue 15) Aut 83, p. 15.

3158. MURRAY, Philip
"The Dead Dolphin." AmerS (52:4) Aut 83, p. 525-526.

3159. MUSGRAVE, Susan
"Cocktails at the Mausoleum." NegC (3:4) Aut 83, p. 14-15.
"Coming into Town, Cold." CrossC (5:2/3) 83, p. 16.
"Second Sight." ThRiPo (21/22) 83, p. 57-58.

3160. MUSINSKY, Gerry
"Bessemer Converter." Pig (11) 83, p. 65.
"Foundry." Pig (11) 83, p. 65.

3161. MUSKE, Carol
"Anna." Ploughs (9:1) 83, p. 154-156.
"Biglietto d'Ingresso." Field (28) Spr 83, p. 45-48.
"Illness As Metaphor." AmerPoR (12:5) S/O 83, p. 4.
"Surprise." NewYorker (59:9) 18 Ap 83, p. 54.
"Unheard of" (E.H.B.). AmerPoR (12:5) S/O 83, p. 3.
"Wyndmere, Windemere." AmerPoR (12:5) S/O 83, p. 4.

MU'TAZZ, Ibn al-
See: IBN AL-MU'TAZZ

3162. MUTH, Terri
"Cycles." IndR (6:3) Sum 83, p. 62.
"Passing (Segovia to Madrid)." IndR (6:3) Sum 83, p. 63.

3163. MUTSCHLECNER, David
"Currants." IndR (5:1) Wint 82, p. 8.

3164. MYCUE, Edward
"Elisions." AntigR (53) Spr 83, p. 72-73.
"Majority." SanFPJ (4:3) 83, p. 66.
"A Man Came Out of a Tree." Stand (24:3) 83, p. 31.
"Meadow, Lake, Golden Goose Chase." Wind (13:48) 83, p. 45.
"Spring That Splinters Like Stone." AntigR (53) Spr 83, p. 73-74.
"Where the Wind Begins." Wind (13:48) 83, p. 45.
"Your Wallet." SanFPJ (4:3) 83, p. 66.

3165. MYER, Neil
"For a Dead Photographer." KanQ (15:2) Spr 83, p. 152.

3166. MYERS, Jack
"As Long As You're Happy." VirQR (59:2) Spr 83, p. 246-247.
"The Diaspora." OhioR (30) 83, p. 218-219.
"How to Love Your Body." MemphisSR (3:2) Spr 83, p. 49-50.

3167. MYERS, Neil
"O Jacob." CharR (9:1) Spr 83, p. 11-13.
"Photo of My Daughter." Tendril (14/15) Wint 83, p. 147.

3168. NAGY, László
Cognition, Language, Poetry" (tr. by Jascha Kessler). LitR (26:3) Spr 83, p. 442-443.

3169. NAIL, Leslie
"At the Whirler Planetarium, Houston." BlackWR (8:2) Spr 82, p. 63.

3170. NAKAGAMI, Tetsuo
"Goodbye, It's On the Road Time" (for Akira Izumiya, tr. by Frank Stewart and Ruriko Fukuhara). MoodySI (10) Aut 81, p. 7-8.
"Poem of the Night Jack Kerouac Called Me" (tr. by Frank Stewart). MoodySI (5) Sum-Aut 79, p. 6.

3171. NAKULAN
"Step Aside" (tr. by M. S. Ramaswami). Stand (24:1) 82-83, p. 45.
"Swaha" (tr. by M. S. Ramaswami). Stand (24:1) 82-83, p. 45.
"These Are the People" (tr. by M. S. Ramaswami). Stand (24:1) 82-83, p. 44.

3172. NAMJOSHI, Suniti
"The Saint and the Robin." PoetryCR (5:2) Wint 83-84, p. 18.

3173. NANCE, K. N.
"Hunting for a Church in the City." PoetL (77:3) Aut 82, p. 151-153.

3174. NAONE, Dana
"Going to Kahoolawe." Telescope (4) Wint 83, p. 37.

3175. NAPORA, Joe
"3 Mile Rag." SanFPJ (4:3) 83, p. 49.

3176. NASH, Mildred J.
"Unfaithful Fantasy." StoneC (10:3/4) Spr-Sum 83, p. 77.

3177. NASH, Roger
"Axe." AntigR (55) Aut 83, p. 12.
"A Dream's Top Headlines." WestCR (18:2) O 83, p. 44.
"Dry Cantors." AntigR (55) Aut 83, p. 12.
"The Mound of the Viking Chocolate Bars." WestCR (18:2) O 83, p. 43-44.

"A Poem's First Remembered Experience of a Reader." Quarry (32:4) Aut 83, p. 55-56.
"Thirteenth Floor, Please." AntigR (52) Wint 83, p. 52.
"Three ways of Following Snowshoe Tracks." AntigR (55) Aut 83, p. 11.

3178. NATHAN, Leonard
"Carrying On." GeoR (37:2) Sum 83, p. 266.
"Entrance." ThRiPo (21/22) 83, p. 59.
"Harvests." Salm (60) Spr-Sum 83, p. 158.
"Homage." CalQ (22) Sum 83, p. 24.
"The Land without Ghosts." NowestR (21:1) 83, p. 18.
"The Law." NowestR (21:1) 83, p. 17.
"Renunciation." PraS (57:2) Sum 83, p. 25.
"Vows." Salm (60) Spr-Sum 83, p. 157.
"Winter Music." PraS (57:2) Sum 83, p. 26.

3179. NATHAN, Norman
"Aged In." Poem (47) Mr 83, p. 48.
"Desire." SpiritSH (49) 83, p. 22.
"The Earth My Lover." Poem (49) N 83, p. 14-15.
"Inclusive." Poem (47) Mr 83, p. 47.
"Islands." Poem (49) N 83, p. 16.
"Mood." SpiritSH (48) 82, p. 34.
"Ms. Lot of Sodom." SpiritSH (48) 82, p. 34.
"Seekers." SpiritSH (48) 82, p. 35.
"Them and/or Us." Poem (47) Mr 83, p. 46.
"Thoughts of Loneliness." SpiritSH (48) 82, p. 36.
"To a Daydream." Poem (49) N 83, p. 17.
"Visit Museums, Travel, Read." Poem (49) N 83, p. 18.
"Who's Who." SpiritSH (49) 83, p. 23.

3180. NEAL, B.
"January Hyacinths." ChrC (100:3) 26 Ja 83, p. 61.

3181. NEARY, Laura
"Chauvinist." WormR (23:4, issue 92) 83, p. 121.
"When Pigs Fly." WormR (23:4, issue 92) 83, p. 122.

3182. NECATIGIL, Behcet
"The Lamp" (tr. by Ozcan Yalim, William A. Fielder and Dionis C. Riggs). Mund (14:1) 83, p. 48.

3183. NEELD, Judith
"Dust Bowl." Wind (13:47) 83, p. 34-35.
"Lady Beetle." Wind (13:47) 83, p. 34.

3184. NEIDERBACH, Shelley
"At Odds." StoneC (10:3/4) Spr-Sum 83, p. 12.

3185. NELLES, Andrea S.
"Flossie and." MalR (66) O 83, p. 57.
"June 13, 1951." MalR (66) O 83, p. 59.
"Paisley Workshop." MalR (66) O 83, p. 56.
"Peony." MalR (66) O 83, p. 58.
"Remainder One." MalR (66) O 83, p. 55.

3186. NELMS, Sheryl L.
"Box People." SanFPJ (4:4) 83, p. 45.
"Fly." WebR (8:2) Aut 83, p. 91.
"Into Fish." WebR (8:2) Aut 83, p. 90.

3187. NELSON, Agnes M.
"Haiku: Do you hear the pines?" Meadows (4:1) 83, p. 37.
"Haiku: They say they are weeds." Meadows (4:1) 83, p. 45.
"Haiku: Tired pale morning moon." Meadows (4:1) 83, p. 45.
"The Lonely Path." Meadows (3:1) 82, p. 16.
"The pine trees whisper." Meadows (3:1) 82, p. 16.
"The Way It Is." Meadows (3:1) 82, p. 16.

3188. NELSON, D. Lloyd
"Crystal with Clouds." SanFPJ (5:2) 83, p. 36.
"The Dream, Like Music." SanFPJ (5:3) 83, p. 41.

3189. NELSON, Eric
"For the Birds." Tendril (14/15) Wint 83, p. 148.

3190. NELSON, Greg
"This Autumn Hillside." Vis (13) 83, p. 24.

3191. NELSON, Howard
"September Threadbare." Blueline (4:1) Sum-Aut 82, p. 38.

3192. NELSON, Jeremy
"Tristitia" (for Margaret Munro Clark). Agni (19) 83, p. 63-68.

3193. NELSON, Jo
"Dichotomy." SanFPJ (4:4) 83, p. 12.
"Marathon." SanFPJ (5:2) 83, p. 83.
"Mirror Echoes." SanFPJ (5:1) 83, p. 89.
"ReSteration." SanFPJ (5:2) 83, p. 82.
"The Wind Song." SanFPJ (5:1) 83, p. 13.

3194. NELSON, Paul
"Bluefish Run, Machias, Main." KanQ (15:4) Aut 83, p. 26.
"Cellars." OhioR (30) 83, p. 238.
"Confluences." BlackWR (9:1) Aut 82, p. 13.
"Frozen In." BlackWR (9:1) Aut 82, p. 12.
"Sunbath." KanQ (15:4) Aut 83, p. 25.

3195. NELSON, Shannon
"Ground Zero." SanFPJ (5:1) 83, p. 8.

3196. NELSON, Sharon H.
"Perspectives" (perspective one: us, the background). PoetryCR (4:3) Spr 83, p. 14.
"Perspectives" (perspective two: standing figure, the painter). PoetryCR (4:3) Spr 83, p. 14.

3197. NELSON, Stanley
"Atlantic Avenue." Confr (25/26) 83, p. 126.

3198. NEMEROV, Howard
"Acts of God." ParisR (25:88) Sum 83, p. 77.
"Assembly Line, Fighter Factory." ClockR (1:2) Wint 83-84, p. 26.
"Belli" (for Miller Williams). ClockR (1:2) Wint 83-84, p. 28.
"Inside the Onion." ParisR (25:88) Sum 83, p. 78.
"Runes" (Selection: XIII). Tendril (14/15) Wint 83, p. 7.
"She." Thrpny (4:3, issue 15) Aut 83, p. 24.

3199. NEPO, Mark
"I Cannot Silence Alone." MalR (65) Jl 83, p. 113-114.
"Orogeny." MalR (65) Jl 83, p. 115-116.
"Without Illusion." MalR (65) Jl 83, p. 112.

3200. NERUDA, Pablo
"The Invisible Man" (tr. by William Pitt Root). Telescope (4) Wint 83, p. 51-57.
"El mundo es una esfera de cristal." RevChic (11:2) Sum 83, p. 14.

3201. NERVAL, Gérard de
"El Desdichado: A Translation" (tr. by William Roemmich). SouthernR (19:3) Jl 83, p. 664-665.

3202. NETO, João Cabral de Melo
"Landscape of Capibaribe" (tr. by R. Arrojo). Mund (14:1) 83, p. 73-95.
"Paisagem do Capibaribe." Mund (14:1) 83, p. 72-94.

3203. NEVILLE, Mary
"Expectations of Light" (Case Institue, 1887). HiramPoR (35) Aut-Wint 83, p. 29.
"Hart Crane in Autumn: Chagrin Falls 1929." HiramPoR (35) Aut-Wint 83, p. 30.

3204. NEVILLE, Tam Lin
"The Body of a Woman." AmerPoR (12:6) N/D 83, p. 3-5.
"One Morning." IndR (6:1) Wint 83, p. 57.

3205. NEVO, Ruth
"Eyes" (tr. of Yehuda Amichai).LitR (26:2) Wint 83, p. 221.
"A Hot Wind" (tr. of Natan Zach). LitR (26:2) Wint 83, p. 237.
"Love's Over Again" (tr. of Yehuda Amichai). LitR (26:2) Wint 83, p. 223.
"Second Meeting with a Father" (tr. of Yehuda Amichai).LitR (26:2) Wint 83, p. 222.
"The Taste of Hemlock" (tr. of Natan Zach). LitR (26:2) Wint 83, p. 238.

3206. NEW, Elisa
"Hope Chest." Paint (10:19/20) Spr-Aut 83, p. 17.

3207. NEWCOMB, P. F.
"No Poems." CapeR (19:1) Wint 83, p. 37.

"She Is a Poem." CapeR (19:1) Wint 83, p. 36.

3208. NEWCOMB, Richard
"Other People's Photographs." Atlantic (252:4) O 83, p. 84.

3209. NEWLOVE, John
"The Permanent Tourist Comes Home." Grain (11:3) Ag 83, p. 4-5.

3210. NEWMAN, Lesléa
"Flies." Tele (18) 83, p. 115.
"Purple." Tele (18) 83, p. 115.
"Valentine's Day." Tele (18) 83, p. 114.

3211. NEWMAN, Michael
"Accounts Office." Bogg (50) 83, p. 38.
"Chance Meeting." Bogg (50) 83, p. 42.

3212. NEWTON-PRITCHETT, Sharon
"Sleigh Ride." WestHR (37:2) Sum 83, p. 125.

Ní CHUILLEANAIN, Eiléan
See: CHUILLEANAIN, Eiléan Ní

3213. NIATUM, Duane
"Maggie." PoNow (7:2, #38) 83, p. 31.

3214. NIBBELINK, Cynthia
"Back Then." PoNow (7:2, #38) 83, p. 32.
"Debt." PoNow (7:2, #38) 83, p. 32.

3215. NIBBELINK, Herman
"This Going Forth." SpoonRQ (8:4) Aut 83, p. 33.

3216. NICASTRO, Kathleen
"Quick Sketch." SmPd (20:3) Aut 83, p. 16.

3217. NICHOL, B. P.
"Hour 25, 2:35 a.m. to 3:35 a.m." Dandel (10:2) Aut-Wint 83, p. 7-9.
"Inchoate Road (A Partial Draft)." CapilR (27) 83, p. 51-73.

3218. NICHOLS, Martha
"Spring on Sunset Blvd." Sam (34:3 135th release) 83, p. 60.

3219. NICHOLSON, Joseph
"A Beaver Face." NewL (50:1) Aut 83, p. 102.
"Old Slant Fang." NewL (50:1) Aut 83, p. 102.
"Watching Meat-Eaters Explode." NewL (50:1) Aut 83, p. 102.

3220. NICKERSON, Sheila
"Saying Good-bye, in the Style of the Ancient Taoist Hermits." CrabCR (1:2) Aut 83, p. 11.

3221. NICKOLAUS, Audrey
"Peace Circle." SanFPJ (4:4) 83, p. 40.

3222. NICOSIA, Gerald
"At Kerouac's Grave." MoodySI (13) Sum 83, p. 16.

3223. NIDITCH, B. Z.
"At the Advent (In Warsaw)." SpiritSH (49 Suppl.) 83, p. 23.
"At the Advent (Warsaw)." SpiritSH (49 Suppl.) 83, p. 22.
"Boston (A Portrait). SpiritSH (49 Suppl.) 83, p. 14.
"Boston and Warsaw: A Sequence." SpiritSH (49 Suppl.) 83, p. 14-23.
"Boston Common." SpiritSH (49 Suppl.) 83, p. 14.
"Boston Spring." Wind (13:49) 83, p. 21.
"Boston Winter." SpiritSH (49 Suppl.) 83, p. 15.
"Cape Ann." SpiritSH (49 Suppl.) 83, p. 17.
"Dachau 1983." SpiritSH (49 Suppl.) 83, p. 21.
"December in Warsaw." SpiritSH (49 Suppl.) 83, p. 21.
"Electric Chair." SanFPJ (4:3) 83, p. 72.
"George Santayana." SpiritSH (49 Suppl.) 83, p. 16.
"Henry James." SpiritSH (49 Suppl.) 83, p. 16.
"Letter from My Mother." SpiritSH (49) 83, p. 21.
"Modern Sonata." SpiritSH (49 Suppl.) 83, p. 18.
"Moscow Vespers." SpiritSH (49) 83, p. 18.
"My Russian Friend." SpiritSH (49) 83, p. 20.
"Nerves." AntigR (52) Wint 83, p. 84.
"On the Ship S.S. Pushkin." SpiritSH (49) 83, p. 16.
"Post Dachau Visitation." SpiritSH (49 Suppl.) 83, p. 22.
"A Prayer in a Gray Church" (Warsaw, 1981). SpiritSH (48) 82, p. 22.
"A Russian Mass in America." SpiritSH (49) 83, p. 19.
"Russian Scene." SpiritSH (49) 83, p. 20.
"The Russian Steppes." SpiritSH (49) 83, p. 19.
"Russian Wolf." SpiritSH (49) 83, p. 17.
"Seventies America." SpiritSH (49) 83, p. 18.
"Sister Elizabeth of Warsaw." SpiritSH (48) 82, p. 22.
"Stalin's Breath Perfume, 1941." SpiritSH (49) 83, p. 17.
"The Tailor." SpiritSH (49) 83, p. 20.
"Tchaikovsky Bathing." AntigR (53) Spr 83, p. 97.
"Turgenev." AntigR (53) Spr 83, p. 98.
"The Unprintable" (Warsaw, 1981). SpiritSH (48) 82, p. 22.
"Visiting Robert Frost's Library (Amherst, Mass.)." SpiritSH (49 Suppl.) 83, p. 17.
"Warsaw, 1982." Abraxas (27/28) 83, p. 14.
"Warsaw, 1983." SpiritSH (49 Suppl.) 83, p. 19.
"Warsaw: A Sequence" (1941, 1945, 1951, 1971, 1981). SpiritSH (48) 82, p. 20-22.
"Warsaw, Sept. 1981." Confr (25/26) 83, p. 304.
"Warsaw Snowstorm." SpiritSH (49 Suppl.) 83, p. 18.
"Warsaw Winter (1983)." SpiritSH (49 Suppl.) 83, p. 20.

3224. NIED, Susanna
"The Atom Bomb Is There" (tr. of Inger

Christensen). PoetryE (9/10) Wint 82-Spr 83, p. 252-253.
"The Cobalt Bomb Is There" (tr. of Inger Christensen). PoetryE (9/10) Wint 82-Spr 83, p. 254-257.
"Limitless" (tr. of Marianne Larsen). PoetryE (9/10) Wint 82-Spr 83, p. 250-251.

3225. NIGHTINGALE, Barbara
"Half Time (T1/2)." SanFPJ (4:2) 83, p. 61.

3226. NIMNICHT, Nona
"The Wives." SecC (11:1/2) 83, p. 158.

3227. NIMS, John Frederick
"Elegy" (For Marion, for Jane). AmerS (52:4) Aut 83, p. 538-539.

NIN, Chiu
See: CHIU, Nin

NIPPAWANOCK
See: SANDERS, Thomas E.

3228. NIST, John
"Villanelle." NewL (49:3/4) Spr-Sum 83, p. 227.

3229. NIXON, Colin
"Conversation." Bogg (50) 83, p. 59.
"Haiku." ChrC (100:28) 5 O 83, p. 870.
"Return to Ystrad Mynach." Bogg (50) 83, p. 42.

3230. NIXON, John, Jr.
"Overkill at the Met." NewRena (17) Aut 83, p. 101.

3231. NOBLE, Charles
"Perfect Pitch." Bluebuf (2:1) Aut 83, p. 23.

3232. NOBLE, Jeanne
"A Portrait of the Last Armchair." Wind (13:48) 83, p. 5.

3233. NOCERINO, Kathryn
"Bride in the Bath." Tele (18) 83, p. 72.
"Old Blood." Tele (18) 83, p. 73.

3234. NOIPROX, Max
"Inanimates." Bogg (51) 83, p. 55.
"Red Light." Bogg (50) 83, p. 57.

3235. NOLAN, James
"Los Adulteros." GeoR (37:2) Sum 83, p. 334-335.
"The Ancient Pépère." MissR (12:1/2, nos. 34/35) Aut 83, p. 95-96.

3236. NOLAND, John
"Fishing." KanQ (15:1) Wint 83, p. 159.
"Vest." KanQ (15:2) Spr 83, p. 122.

3237. NOLL, Bink
"The Auditorium." CreamCR (8:1/2) 83, p. 73.

3238. NOMEZ, Nain
"Aquel Verano del 73." Areíto (9:35) 83, p. 40.

3239. NORCROSS, John
"Ephemeridae" (the family of Mayflies, Linnaean order Neuroptera). Sulfur (3:2, #8) 83, p. 96.
"Looking for George Washington's Teeth While My Father Hunts Dove in His Fields" Tendril (16) Sum 83, p. 100.
"Poem for My Father." Sulfur (3:2, #8) 83, p. 94.
"Things My Mother Never Had to Tell Me." Sulfur (3:2, #8) 83, p. 95.

3240. NORD, Gennie
"Ghosts in the Cold Grass" (for Greta and John Greene). YetASM (1:1) 82, p. 11.
"The Jack Pines." YetASM (1:1) 82, p. 4.

3241. NORDHAUS, Jean
"The Canonization of the Windows." PoetL (78:4) Wint 84, p. 224.

3242. NORDSTROM, Lars
"Old Basho" (tr. of Rolf Aggestam, w. Erland Anderson). NewRena (16) Spr 83, p. 25.
"Portent" (tr. of Rolf Aggestam, w. Erland Anderson). NewRena (16) Spr 83, p. 27.
"Your Heart Is a Red Train" (tr. of Rolf Aggestam, w. Erland Anderson). NewRena (16) Spr 83, p. 23.

3243. NORGREN, Constance
"Barbara Allen." WestB (13) 83, p. 77.
"Photograph - 1932" (for my mother). Tendril (16) Sum 83, p. 101.

NORIKO, Ibaraki
See: IBARAKI, Noriko

3244. NORRIS, Gunilla
"April." StoneC (10:3/4) Spr-Sum 83, p. 73.

3245. NORRIS, Ken
"Billie sings and starts you crying." Germ (7:2) Aut-Wint 83, p. 9.
"Hands." Grain (11:1) F 83, p. 17-18.
"I never thought you'd still be here." PoetryCR (5:2) Wint 83-84, p. 12.
"Look at how the snow falls." Germ (7:2) Aut-Wint 83, p. 10.
"The mistake has always been in thinking." Germ (7:2) Aut-Wint 83, p. 8.
"This poem is small but it has its power." Germ (7:2) Aut-Wint 83, p. 7.
"We're all the way out there." Germ (7:2) Aut-Wint 83, p. 6.

3246. NORSE, Harold
"The Worst Thing You Can Say to Him Is I Love You" (For Charles Bukowski). SecC (11:1/2) 83, p. 232-233.

3247. NORTH, Charles
"April." LittleM (14:1/2) 83, p. 85.

3248. NORTH SUN, Nila
"Her Boy." Meadows (4:1) 83, p. 14.
"Neckties." Meadows (3:1) 82, p. 57.
"Not Alone." Meadows (3:1) 82, p. 36.
"One Day at a Time." Meadows (3:1) 82, p. 11.
"Poets." Meadows (3:1) 82, p. 36.
"Tidbits." Meadows (4:1) 83, p. 24.

3249. NORTHEN, Philip
"Animal Behavior." HiramPoR (34) Spr-Sum 83, p. 15.

NORTHSUN, Nila
See: NORTH SUN, Nila

3250. NORTJE, Arthur
"All Hungers Pass Away." PoetryE (9/10) Wint 82-Spr 83, p. 267-268.
"Brief Thunder at Sharpeville." PoetryE (9/10) Wint 82-Spr 83, p. 266.
"Foreign Body." PoetryE (9/10) Wint 82-Spr 83, p. 269.
"Waiting." PoetryE (9/10) Wint 82-Spr 83, p. 270-271.

3251. NORTON, Rachel
"Seaside." NowestR (21:1) 83, p. 24.
"Year's End" (from Durable Poisons, semi-finalist, 10th anniversary manuscript competition). StoneC (11:1/2, Pt. 1) Aut-Wint 83, p. 69.

3252. NORTON, Scott
"Recluse." USl (16/17) Wint 83-84, p. 7.
"The Separation." USl (16/17) Wint 83-84, p. 7.

NOSRAT KASEMI MAZANDERANI
See: MAZANDERANI, Nosrat Kasemi

3253. NOSTRAND, Jennifer
"The blue jar." Tele (18) 83, p. 9.
"Cleopatra." Tele (18) 83, p. 8.
"Pandora." Tele (18) 83, p. 9.

3254. NOWLAN, Alden
"Between the Lines." Waves (11:2/3) Wint 83, p. 52.
"Field Day." PottPort (5) 83-84, p. 4.
"He" (from "Inklings"). PoetryCR (5:1) Aut 83, p. 3.
"Home from the Wars" (for Walter Learning). PottPort (5) 83-84, p. 4.
"The Morning's Mail." PottPort (5) 83-84, p. 4.
"A Song to be Whispered." Waves (11:2/3) Wint 83, p. 51.

"Two Visitors from Utah." PoetryCR (4:3) Spr 83, p. 3.
"You Can't Get There from Here." Waves (11:2/3) Wint 83, p. 50.

3255. NOWLIN, Gene
"Broken Clutch Hitch Hike 90 Miles." WindO (42) Sum 83, p. 22.

3256. NOWLIN, W. W.
"Delta Anthology: Tom Webb." ArizQ (39:2) Sum 83, p. 134.

3257. NUCK, John, II
"Photobooth Picture." ClockR (1:1) Sum 83, p. 44.

3258. NURKSE, D.
"After Music." YetASM (1:1) 82, p. 9.
"Emptiness." MSS (3:1) Aut 83, p. 55.
"Lovers." MSS (3:1) Aut 83, p. 53.
"Rockaway Point." Confr (25/26) 83, p. 87.
"Small Countries." Telescope (4) Wint 83, p. 58.
"Summer House." MSS (3:1) Aut 83, p. 54.
"Uranium." SanFPJ (4:3) 83, p. 56.
"Walking on the Highway." AmerPoR (12:1) Ja/F 83, p. 16.

NURSKE, D.
See: NURKSE, D.

3259. NYE, Naomi Shihab
"With the Greeks" (for Chrissie & Dan Anthony). GeoR (37:2) Sum 83, p. 410-411.

3260. NYSTEDT, Bob
"Spain, 1974." StoneC (10:3/4) Spr-Sum 83, p. 18.

3261. NYSTROM, Debra
"A Bridge in Florence." AmerPoR (12:6) N/D 83, p. 18.
"Passenger." AmerPoR (12:6) N/D 83, p. 18.
"A Worn Stairway." AmerPoR (12:6) N/D 83, p. 18.
"You See." PoetryE (11) Sum 83, p. 80.

3262. OAKLAND, Sam
"An Air Conditioned Theatre." YetASM (2:1) 83, p. 10.

3263. OAKS, Gladys
"Noctiluca into Woman." Nimrod (27:1) Aut-Wint 83, p. 61.
"Spark." Nimrod (27:1) Aut-Wint 83, p. 61.

3264. OATES, Joyce Carol
"Ancient Snapshots." Poetry (142:5) Ag 83, p. 257.
"In Parenthesis." TriQ (56) Wint 83, p. 161-162.
"Love Anecdote." Poetry (142:5) Ag 83, p. 258.
"The Madwoman's Repentance." SouthernR (19:2) Ap 83, p. 356-357.
"Miniatures: East Europe." DevQ (18:3) Aut 83, p.

5-12.
"Mute Mad Child." SouthernR (19:2) Ap 83, p. 357-358.
"Night." Poetry (142:5) Ag 83, p. 255-256.
"Playlet." TriQ (56) Wint 83, p. 163-164.
"The River." NewL (49:3/4) Spr-Sum 83, p. 256.
"Self-Portrait As a Still Life." SouthernR (19:2) Ap 83, p. 358-359.
"The Wren's Hunger." SouthernR (19:2) Ap 83, p. 354-355.

3265. OBEJAS, Achy
"Born in the Heat of Night." AntigR (55) Aut 83, p. 123-124.
"Kimberle." RevChic (11:3/4) 83, p. 47.
"Sugarcane." RevChic (11:3/4) 83, p. 48-49.

3266. OBERG, Robert J.
"Canticle." YetASM (2:1) 83, p. 2.

3267. OBREGON, Roberto
"Almost Ode to the Ear" (tr. by Zoe Anglesey). PoetryE (9/10) Wint 82-Spr 83, p. 178-179.
"Now As I Write" (tr. by Zoe Anglesey). PoetryE (9/10) Wint 82-Spr 83, p. 181.
"Suddenly the Wind Ceased" (tr. by Zoe Anglesey). PoetryE (9/10) Wint 82-Spr 83, p. 180.

3268. O'BRIAN, John (See also: O'BRIEN, John)
"I Am Trying to Remember." Descant (41) Sum 83, p. 131.
"Sea Road and Paper." Descant (41) Sum 83, p. 130.
"Spider." Descant (41) Sum 83, p. 133.
"Turning Back." Descant (41) Sum 83, p. 132.

3269. O'BRIEN, John (See also: O'BRIAN, John)
"The Insomniac Prays." Pig (11) 83, p. 81.
"Kenny & Leo." PoNow (7:2, #38) 83, p. 47.

3270. O'BRIEN, Tom
"Bonney Castle" (the Hiram College English Department). HiramPoR (35) Aut-Wint 83, p. 31.

3271. OCHESTER, Ed
"110-Year-Old House." OP (36) Aut-Wint 83, p. 24.
"Conversation with Artur Schnabel." OP (36) Aut-Wint 83, p. 22-23.
"Cooking." OP (36) Aut-Wint 83, p. 18-19.
"A Famous Literary Couple." PoNow (7:2, #38) 83, p. 18.
"Sunday Dinner." PoNow (7:2, #38) 83, p. 18.
"Walking Around the Farm." OP (36) Aut-Wint 83, p. 20-21.

3272. OCHIISHI
"Anticipation" (tr. of Sakutaro Hagiwara). WebR (8:2) Aut 83, p. 46.
"A Man Who Loves Love" (tr. of Sakutaro Hagiwara). WebR (8:2) Aut 83, p. 47.
"Tender Feeling" (tr. of Sakutaro Hagiwara). WebR

(8:2) Aut 83, p. 46.

3273. O'CONNELL, Kate
"Autumn Elms." Blueline (5:1) Sum-Aut 83, p. 15.

3274. O'CONNOR, Deirdre
"For the Special Collector." WestB (13) 83, p. 81.
"In the Cellar." WestB (13) 83, p. 80.

3275. O'CONNOR, John
"Give Me Your Hand" (after a song by the Chieftains). HarvardA (117:1) Mr 83, p. 22.
"Letter." HarvardA (117:2) My 83, p. 11.
"Rain Sonnet." HarvardA (117:1) Mr 83, p. 19.
"Two Sonnets." HarvardA (117:3) Aut 83, p. 23.

3276. O'CONNOR, Mark
"Pompeii." Poetry (142:1) Ap 83, p. 29.
"Source of Lake Ochrid" (Yugoslavia). Poetry (142:1) Ap 83, p. 30.

3277. ODERMAN, Kevin
"Aridities." WestB (13) 83, p. 28.
"A Charting." Wind (13:48) 83, p. 46.

3278. ODLIN, Reno
"Homily: May 1981." AntigR (53) Spr 83, p. 7.
"MacAulay's Traveler." AntigR (53) Spr 83, p. 8.
"Or He His Goddis Brocht." AntigR (53) Spr 83, p. 8.
"Praise of Amun-Re-Atum-Horakhty Who Crosses the Sky, Great of Love" (tr. of Scribe Mersakhmis). AntigR (54) Sum 83, p. 65-67.

3279. OERKE, Andrew
"Champagne." BelPoJ (34:2) Wint 83-84, p. 33.

3280. OFFER, Judith
"Strawberry Patch." Vis (11) 83, p. 32.

3281. OGDEN, Hugh
"Someday." MalR (66) O 83, p. 86.

3282. O'HARA, Frank
"For David Schubert." QRL (24) 83, p. 299-300.

3283. O'HARA, Mark
"Sea Diamonds." CutB (21) Aut-Wint 83, p. 73.

3284. O'HEHIR, Diana
"The Fisherman's Widow." Poetry (142:4) Jl 83, p. 195.
"How to Murder Your Best Friend." Poetry (142:4) Jl 83, p. 196.
"Incubus." PoetryNW (24:3) Aut 83, p. 35.
"Staying under Water Too Long." PoetryNW (24:3) Aut 83, p. 34.

3285. O'KEEFE, Kathy
"Voc Ed." EngJ (72:5) S 83, p. 54.

3286. OKTENBERG, Adrian
"Georgia O'Keeffe." Blueline (5:1) Sum-Aut 83, p. 24-25.
"Letter from Dunphy's Pasture." Blueline (4:1) Sum-Aut 82, p. 20-21.
"Looking for Home." Blueline (4:2) Wint-Spr 83, p. 26-27.
"Midnight Song., YetASM (1:1) 82, p. 2.

3287. OLDKNOW, Antony
"The Cherry Trees" (tr. of Francis Jammes). SoDakR (21:1) Spr 83, p. 82.
"A Cloud Is a Black" (tr. of Francis Jammes). SoDakR (21:1) Spr 83, p. 84, 86.
"My Love Is in the Past" (tr. of Francis Jammes). SoDakR (21:1) Spr 83, p. 80.
"The Sad Wind" (For Henri Ghéon, tr. of Francis Jammes). SoDakR (21:1) Spr 83, p. 88, 90.
"You'll Be Naked" (tr. of Francis Jammes). SoDakR (21:1) Spr 83, p. 78.

3288. OLDS, Peter
"Revisitng V8 Nostalgia." SecC (11:1/2) 83, p. 159.

3289. OLDS, Sharon
"1090 A.D." AmerPoR (12:3) My-Je 83, p. 16.
"1382 A.D." AmerPoR (12:3) My-Je 83, p. 16.
"First Love" (for Averell). AmerPoR (12:3) My-Je 83, p. 17.
"The Food-Thief" (Uganda, drought). AmerPoR (12:3) My-Je 83, p. 16.
"Free Shoes." AntR (41:1) Wint 83, p. 84.
"He Comes for the Jewish Family, 1942." Poetry (141:5) F 83, p. 263.
"The Legless Fighter Pilot" (England, 1940). Poetry (142:6) S 83, p. 318.
"The Month of June: 13 1/2." Poetry (142:6) S 83, p. 317.
"The Paths" (for Martin Garbus). NewEng (5:4) Sum 83, p. 549.
"Prayer During a Time My Son is Having Seizures." Poetry (142:6) S 83, p. 316-317.
"Summer Solstice, New York City." NewYorker (59:18) 20 Je 83, p. 34.
"When." NewEng (5:4) Sum 83, p. 500.

3290. O'LEARY, Dawn
"South Street." NowestR (21:2/3) 83, p. 50-51.

3291. OLES, Carole
"Accidents." Ploughs (9:1) 83, p. 63-64.
"Preparing for Weather." Poetry (143:1) O 83, p. 29.
"Stella's Dump" (Francestown, New Hampshire). Tendril (14/15) Wint 83, p. 150-151.
"They Set Out in Fog." Ploughs (9:1) 83, p. 61-62.
"Veterans Day, 1981." Ploughs (9:1) 83, p. 65-66.
"The Village Cyclist." Tendril (14/15) Wint 83, p. 152.
"What Shall We Name the Snow?" Tendril (14/15) Wint 83, p. 149.

3292. OLIPHANT, Dave
"Maria's Mandolin." NewL (50:1) Aut 83, p. 100.

3293. OLIVER, Mary
"American Primitive." ThRiPo (21/22) 83, p. 60-61.
"At Loxahatchie." GeoR (37:1) Spr 83, p. 113-114.
"Clam Man." OhioR (30) 83, p. 257.
"Dreams." GeoR (37:1) Spr 83, p. 114-115.
"Morning Poem." WestHR (37:3) Aut 83, p. 249-250.
"Music Lessons." OhioR (30) 83, p. 257.
"An Old Whorehouse." ThRiPo (21/22) 83, p. 62.
"Sleeping in the Forest." OhioR (30) 83, p. 256.
"Surprise." WestHR (37:4) Wint 83, p. 331-332.
"Wild Geese." WestHR (37:3) Aut 83, p. 208.

3294. OLIVER, Merrill
"It's a Mistake! I'm a Kid!" PoetL (78:3) Aut 83, p. 161.
"Or None, or Few." PoetL (78:3) Aut 83, p. 160.

3295. OLIVER, Michael Brian
"Anita." PottPort (5) 83-84, p. 19.
"Birth Is As Great" (for Stephen Blake Oliver born February 19, 1974, in Sherbrooke, Quebec). PottPort (5) 83-84, p. 11.

3296. OLIVER, Raymond
"Breakthrough." ChiR (33:3) Wint 83, p. 111.
"Recipe." NegC (3:4) Aut 83, p. 128.
"Union Street, San Francisco." ChiR (33:3) Wint 83, p. 110.

3297. OLIVIER, Lucinda C.
"I Was Riding." YetASM (2:1) 83, p. 7.

3298. OLSON, Andrew Christen
"Driving at Night." ConcPo (16:2) Aut 83, p. 64.
"Working the Late Shift at the Nebraska Computer Network." ConcPo (16:2) Aut 83, p. 65.

3299. OLSON, Elder
"Conversation Pieces." AmerS (52:4) Aut 83, p. 461-462.

3300. OLSON, Kirby
"The Romantic World." PartR (50:3) 83, p. 409-410.

3301. OLSON, Mark
"The Old." Northeast (Ser. 3:16) Wint 83-84, p. 13.

3302. OLSON, Ruby Barrett
"At the Source." Blueline (4:2) Wint-Spr 83, p. 42.

3303. ONDAATJE, Michael
"The Concessions." Descant (42) Aut 83, p. 7-11. Errata Descant (43) Wint 83-84, p. 133.
"Red Accordion: An Immigrant Song." MalR (66) O 83, p. 99-101.

3304. O'NEILL, Alexandre
"The Betrayal" (tr. by Alexis Levitin). Kayak (62) Ag 83, p. 59.
"First Serious Warning" (tr. by Alexis Levitin). Kayak (62) Ag 83, p. 59.
"Table" (tr. by Alexis Levitin). Kayak (62) Ag 83, p. 58.

3305. O'NEILL, Brian
"In Your Next Dream." ColEng (45:4) Ap 83, p. 360-361.
"Indiana Dream in Stone." ColEng (45:4) Ap 83, p. 359-360.
"Timberline." SouthernPR (23:2) Aut 82 [i.e. (23:1?) Spr 83], p. 11.

3306. O'NEILL, Maureen
"On Deliberate Unemployment" (for Carol). Prima (8) 83, p. 72-73.

3307. O'NEILL, Patrick
"The East Side." SanFPJ (5:2) 83, p. 60.
"The East Side." SanFPJ (5:3) 83, p. 20.
"The Orchard" (Observations from a Twentieth Class Reunion). SanFPJ (5:2) 83, p. 29.
"A Post Outhouse Simile." SanFPJ (5:1) 83, p. 72.
"Pour Out the Vials, or, The Blood Barrel Polka." SanFPJ (5:2) 83, p. 57-59.
"Pour Out the Vials, or, The Blood Barrel Polka." SanFPJ (5:3) 83, p. 17-19.
"Songs Sung Late." SanFPJ (4:3) 83, p. 58-59.

3308. O'NEILL, Paul
"A Sound of Seagulls." AntigR (54) Sum 83, p. 5-6.

3309. OPYR, Linda
"Soundings." EngJ (72:4) Ap 83, p. 68.

3310. ORESICK, Peter
"The Jeweler." ChrC (100:27) 28 S 83, p. 837.
"Poem for Hamid." PoetryE (11) Sum 83, p. 60-61.
"Receiving Christ" (after St. John Chrysostom). MichQR (22:3) Sum 83, p. 392.

3311. ORLEN, Steve
"The Czar's Proclamation." Ploughs (9:1) 83, p. 161-163.

3312. ORLOCK, C.
"Ninth Month." SoDakR (21:4) Wint 83, p. 64.

3313. ORMSBY, Frank
"After Mass." Agni (19) 83, p. 31.
"A Day in August." Agni (19) 83, p. 32.
"The Massage Parlour." Agni (19) 83, p. 34.
"Passing the Crematorium." Agni (19) 83, p. 35.
"The War Photographers." Agni (19) 83, p. 36.
"Winter Offerings." Agni (19) 83, p. 33.

3314. ORONO, Tatiana
"Imágenes." Areíto (9:35) 83, p. 41.

3315. O'ROURKE, David
"My Father." Quarry (32:1) Wint 83, p. 35.

3316. ORR, Bill
"Emending the First Report." CutB (21) Aut-Wint 83, p. 83-85.

3317. ORR, Gregory
"Bright Light: Blank Page." MissouriR (6:2) Wint 83, p. 22.
"The Gray Fox." MissouriR (6:2) Wint 83, p. 23.
"Padua." MissouriR (6:2) Wint 83, p. 21-21.
"The Voyages." PoetryE (12) Aut 83, p. 62.
"Walking a Small, Frozen River in Sunlight." MissouriR (6:2) Wint 83, p. 24.

3318. ORR, Verlena
"After Leaving." PortR (29:1) 83, p. 114.
"Confiding in a Map Reader" (for Scot). PortR (29:1) 83, p. 68-69.
"Night Flight." ConcPo (16:2) Aut 83, p. 10.

3319. ORTEGA, Frank
"Siege." SanFPJ (5:3) 83, p. 74.
"They Left So Little for Me." SanFPJ (5:3) 83, p. 73.
"Vacation Observation: La Paz." SanFPJ (5:3) 83, p. 76.

3320. ORTENBERG, Neil
"Dodging Bullets." MoodySI (9) Wint-Spr 81, p. 17.

3321. ORTH, Kevin
"After the Blackout." WestB (12) 83, p. 14.
"Back at the Farm after Drinking in the City." Wind (13:48) 83, p. 33.
"Deep Lock Quarry." HiramPoR (35) Aut-Wint 83, p. 33.
"Eventualities." Outbr (12/13) Aut 83-Spr 84, p. 42.
"Jehovah's Witnesses Arrive before a Thunderstorm." HiramPoR (35) Aut-Wint 83, p. 32.

3322. ORTIZ, Simon J.
"The Decapitated." PoetryE (9/10) Wint 82-Spr 83, p. 120-121.
"Just several miles to the west." PoetryE (9/10) Wint 82-Spr 83, p. 118-119.

ORTIZ COFER, Judith
See: COFER, Judith Ortiz

3323. ORTOLANI, Al
"At the State 5A Football Playoff." KanQ (15:2) Spr 83, p. 140.
"The Home Place." KanQ (15:2) Spr 83, p. 140.

3324. ORY, Carlos Edmundo de
"The Stars" (tr. by Will Kirkland). NewOR (10:4) Wint 83, p. 81.
"Weariness of Pleasure" (tr. by Will Kirkland). NewOR (10:4) Wint 83, p. 70.

3325. OSAKI, Mark
"Chinese Camp." SanFPJ (5:3) 83, p. 35.
"Shortages." SanFPJ (5:3) 83, p. 34.

3326. OSING, Gordon
"Alameda Madonna." NewL (50:1) Aut 83, p. 91.
"Betty and Benny, 1949." CimR (63) Ap 83, p. 10.

3327. OSTASZEVSKI, Krzysztof
"Allegories: Opus 24, a Tragedy" (tr. by Wojtek Stelmaszynski). AntigR (55) Aut 83, p. 86.
"Allegories: Opus 34, a Comedy" (tr. by Wojtek Stelmaszynski). AntigR (55) Aut 83, p. 87.
"Allegories: Opus 35, a Comedy" (tr. by Wojtek Stelmaszynski). AntigR (55) Aut 83, p. 88.
"Allegories: Opus 87, a Comedy" (tr. by Wojtek Stelmaszynski). AntigR (55) Aut 83, p. 88-89.
"Allegories: Opus 108, a Comedy" (tr. by Wojtek Stelmaszynski). AntigR (55) Aut 83, p. 89.

3328. OSTERGREN, Jan
"Dry Point" (tr. by John Matthias). ChiR (33:4) Sum [i.e. Spr] 83, p. 36.

3329. OSTERLUND, Steven
"Nightbirds." PoNow (7:2, #38) 83, p. 43.

3330. OSTRIKER, Alicia
"Contest." Poetry (141:4) Ja 83, p. 194-195.
"Digging to China." USl (16/17) Wint 83-84, p. 3.
"Dissolve in Slow Motion." LittleM (14:1/2) 83, p. 31.
"The Hawk's Shadow." USl (16/17) Wint 83-84, p. 3.
"Moth in April." Poetry (141:4) Ja 83, p. 193.
"Poem Beginning with a Line by Dickinson." Poetry (141:4) Ja 83, p. 189-191.
"Taking the Shuttle with Franz." Poetry (141:4) Ja 83, p. 192-193.

3331. OSTROM, Alan
"Waiting." SewanR (91:4) Aut 83, p. 594-595.

3332. OSTROM, Hans
"Winter Nocturne." SoDakR (21:3) Aut 83, p. 81.

3333. O'SULLIVAN, Sibbie
"Lawrence Shaving." YetASM (1:2) 82, p. 15.
"Live Acts." YetASM (1:2) 82, p. 14.
"Spring Spiders." Gargoyle (22/23) 83, p. 67.

OTERO, Manuel Ramos
See: RAMOS OTERO, Manuel

3334. OTT, Tom
"Subway Advertisement." YetASM (1:2) 82, p. 13.
"Wilderbeasts." YetASM (1:2) 82, p. 9.

3335. OUELLETTE, Fernand
"And the Light Just Keeps Crying" (tr. by Steve Troyanovich). Mund (14:1) 83, p. 37.
"L'Ange." Mund (14:1) 83, p. 36.
"The Angel" (tr. by Steve Troyanovich). Mund (14:1) 83, p. 37.
"Et Pleure la Lumiere." Mund (14:1) 83, p. 36.

3336. OUTRAM, Richard
"Spring at the Cottage." CanLit (98) Aut 83, p. 48.

3337. OVERTON, Ron
"The Fathers." HangL (44) Sum 83, p. 39.
"Getting to Know Your House." HangL (44) Sum 83, p. 40-41.
"The Polo Grounds." HangL (44) Sum 83, p. 42.
"Talkshow." HangL (44) Sum 83, p. 43.
"The Telephone." HangL (44) Sum 83, p. 44.

3338. OWEN, Eileen E.
"Famous Last Words." YetASM (1:2) 82, p. 8.
"Going for Wood." YetASM (1:2) 82, p. 5.
"Visiting My Friend Who Is Blind." YetASM (1:2) 82, p. 7.

3339. OWEN, Garnet
"Retention of Angels." Prima (8) 83, p. 39.

3340. OWEN, John E.
"Morale, 1980s." SanFPJ (5:3) 83, p. 36.
"Rome, Matrix of Faith." AntigR (55) Aut 83, p. 91.

3341. OWEN, Sue
"The North Star." PoNow (7:2, #38) 83, p. 37.
"The Pull of Gravity." MassR (24:3) Aut 83, p. 562.

3342. OWER, John
"Trans-Canada Train." SoDakR (21:4) Wint 83, p. 56.
"An Unpetrarchan Sonnet." Poem (48) Jl 83, p. 20.

3343. OXENHORN, Harvey
"Ibis." Atlantic (252:1) Jl 83, p. 77.

3344. OYENARD, Sylvia Puentes de
"Palabra." LetFem (9:1) 83, p. 97.

3345. PACERNIK, Gary
"Remembering." Confr (25/26) 83, p. 293.

3346. PACHECO, José Emilio
"Ghosts" (tr. by George B. Moore). MissR (12:1/2, nos. 34/35) Aut 83, p. 70.
"Ratus Norvegicus" (tr. by George B. Moore). MissR (12:1/2, nos. 34/35) Aut 83, p. 71-72.
"Since Then" (tr. by Anthony Kerrigan). DevQ (18:1) Spr 83, p. 93.

"Turn of the Century" (tr. by Anthony Kerrigan). DevQ (18:1) Spr 83, p. 92.

3347. PACK, Robert

"At the Terminal." VirQR (59:2) Spr 83, p. 247-249.
"Dear Seymour Penn." NewRep (187:2) 12 Jl 82, p. 36.
"Early and Late." NewRep (188:21) 30 My 83, p. 28.
"Ferns by the Waterfall." Hudson (36:4) Wint 83-84, p. 688-689.
"Inheritance." Tendril (14/15) Wint 83, p. 153-154.
"Landscape without Figures." PoetryNW (24:2) Sum 83, p. 32-33.
"Replacing the Elegy." AmerS (52:3) Sum 83, p. 336-338.
"Sculpting in Stone." BlackWR (10:1) Aut 83, p. 82-84.
"Sister to Brother." SouthernR (19:3) Jl 83, p. 632-634.
"Trying to Reconcile." QW (17) Aut-Wint 83-84, p. 66-67.
"Visiting the Cemetery." GeoR (37:3) Aut 83, p. 612-614.

3348. PACKIE, Susan

"Back to Love." Sam (34:3 135th release) 83, p. 9.
"Decay." Sam (34:3 135th release) 83, p. 13.
"Secretary of Armageddon." RagMag (2:2) Aut 83, p. 6.
"Unmentionables." SanFPJ (4:3) 83, p. 61.

3349. PADILLA, Heberto

"Hard Times" (tr. by Anthony Kerrigan). MalR (64) F 83, p. 148-149.

3350. PAGE, William

"Devotion." CimR (65) O 83, p. 10-11.
"The Distance." Ploughs (9:2/3) 83, p. 191-192.
"The Face." SouthwR (68:1) Wint 83, p. 26.
"For One Who Has No Heart." ThRiPo (19/20) 82, p. 51.
"The Girl in the Iron Lung." CimR (65) O 83, p. 12.
"In the Morning Like a Bitter Leaf." WebR (8:2) Aut 83, p. 88.
"Milkweed." Nimrod (27:1) Aut-Wint 83, p. 70.
"Night of the Deer." Nimrod (27:1) Aut-Wint 83, p. 70-71.
"To Begin" (In Memoriam: Columbia Miliary Academy 1905-1978). Ploughs (9:2/3) 83, p. 193.
"Trappings." CharR (9:1) Spr 83, p. 15.

3351. PAGIS, Dan

"Dossier Zero" (tr. by Robert Friend). LitR (26:2) Wint 83, p. 234-236.
"The Mosquito" (tr. by Robert Friend). LitR (26:2) Wint 83, p. 236.
"A New Lover" (tr. by Robert Friend). LitR (26:2) Wint 83, p. 233.

PAHLSON, Göran Printz
See: PRINTZ-PAHLSON, Göran

3352. PAHMEIER, Gailmarie
"Letter to an Absent Lover." YetASM (1:1) 82, p. 4.
"Sunday Baking" (for Larry). YetASM (1:1) 82, p. 7.

3353. PALADINO, Thomas
"Heraclitus in New Hampshire." ThirdW Spr 83, p. 105-106.
"The Night Sea Journey." KanQ (15:2) Spr 83, p. 138-139.
"Pericentre." KanQ (15:2) Spr 83, p. 138.
"Presences: A Poem of Decantos" (Selections: I-III). ThirdW Spr 83, p. 1-17.

3354. PALMA, Michael
"Talk." Northeast (Ser. 3:15) Sum 83, p. 17.
"Two by Two." Northeast (Ser. 3:15) Sum 83, p. 16.

PALMA, Ray di
See: DiPALMA, Ray

3355. PALMER, Graham
"Party Time." Bogg (50) 83, p. 62.

3356. PALMER, Michael
"Book of the Yellow Castle." Sulfur (3:2, #8) 83, p. 153-154.
"Miranda." PortR (29:1) 83, p. 1.
"Sign." Sulfur (3:2, #8) 83, p. 155-156.
"Tribute." PortR (29:1) 83, p. 9.

3357. PALMER, William
"At the Water Steps." Stand (24:1) 82-83, p. 28-29.
"Golfview Street." WindO (43) Wint 83, p. 43.
"Winter Dust." WindO (43) Wint 83, p. 43-44.

3358. PANKEY, Eric
"Cain." LitR (27:1) Aut 83, p. 98-99.
"The Dinner: Winter, 1569." PoetL (77:1) Spr 82, p. 14.
"The Gift." PoetL (77:1) Spr 82, p. 15.
"Tainter's Farm, Swiss, Missouri, Winter, 1979." KanQ (15:2) Spr 83, p. 5.
"Tending the Garden" (after Pierre Gascar). MissouriR (6:3) Sum 83, p. 42-48.

3359. PANTIN, Yolanda
"Lecciones de Amor y de Odio." Prismal (11) Aut 83, p. 110.
"El Ojo de la Caja." Prismal (11) Aut 83, p. 108.
"Pequeña Muerte." Prismal (11) Aut 83, p. 111.
"Pliegue de la Puerta." Prismal (11) Aut 83, p. 109.

3360. PAPANE, Matime
"Staffrider." PoetryE (9/10) Wint 82-Spr 83, p. 276.

3361. PAPE, Greg
"Endless Nights of Rain." Poetry (142:3) Je 83, p. 134-135.
"Put Your Mother on the Ceiling." BlackWR (9:2) Spr 83, p. 30-31.

"Who Was Antonio Azul?" BlackWR (9:2) Spr 83, p. 28-29.

3362. PAPENHAUSEN, Carol
"Trusting to Love." SpoonRQ (8:4) Aut 83, p. 55.

3363. PAPPAS, Theresa
"Corfu." AntR (41:4) Aut 83, p. 442.

3364. PARADIS, Philip
"Against the Drought." CimR (62) Ja 83, p. 11-12.
"Reclaiming Wetland, near the Mouth of the Connecticut." Tendril (14/15) Wint 83, p. 155.

3365. PARAFATI, Joe
"The End." YetASM (2:1) 83, p. 2.

3366. PARATTE, Henri
"Al Salam." PottPort (5) 83-84, p. 27.

3367. PARHAM, Robert
"A Jewish Uncle Dies in Miami." SoCaR (16:1) Aut 83, p. 33.
"Reflections on a Dead Bird." NegC (3:4) Aut 83, p. 52.

3368. PARIS, Cindy
"After Reading The Professor's House." PoetryE (11) Sum 83, p. 77-78.

3369. PARIS, Matthew
"Lesbic Isle" (adaption). Confr (25/26) 83, p. 205.
"Night-Song of a Wandering Asiatic Shepherd" (adaption). Confr (25/26) 83, p. 205-206.

3370. PARISH, Barbara Shirk
"Closing Hymn." Wind (13:49) 83, p. 38.
"Mustard Seed." Wind (13:49) 83, p. 38.
"Theft." LittleBR (3:3) Spr 83, p. 66.

3371. PARISI, Philip
"An Old Story." SewanR (91:4) Aut 83, p. 596-597.

3372. PARKER, Elizabeth (See also: PARKER, Lizbeth)
"The Street in Snow." Prima (8) 83, p. 43.

3373. PARKER, Lizbeth (See also: PARKER, Elizabeth)
"Lover, My Poem." Bogg (51) 83, p. 5-6.

3374. PARKER, Susan
"Cleaning House." PoetryCR (4:3) Spr 83, p. 15.

3375. PARKKARI, Emily
"Last Elegy to a Daughter." Quarry (32:3) Sum 83, p. 65-66.
"Life." Quarry (32:3) Sum 83, p. 65.

3376. PARKS, Richard
"Someone stepping off a mountain." YetASM (1:2) 82, p. 5.

"While deborah sleeps." YetASM (1:2) 82, p. 16.

3377. PARLATORE, Anselm
"Vernal Equinox at Mecox." ManhatR (3:1) Sum 83, p. 56-58.

3378. PARLETT, James
"The Balloon Pilot." CapeR (18:2) Sum 83, p. 38-39.
"The Poet in Exile." CapeR (18:2) Sum 83, p. 41.
"The Varsity Barbershop." CapeR (18:2) Sum 83, p. 40.

3379. PAROTTI, Phillip
"Steaming." SpoonRQ (8:4) Aut 83, p. 15.

3380. PARRA SANDOVAL, Rodrigo
"Absence" (tr. by Elizabeth Lowe). Mund (14:1) 83, p. 32.
"Art History" (tr. by Elizabeth Lowe). Mund (14:1) 83, p. 31.
"Possibility" (tr. by Elizabeth Lowe). Mund (14:1) 83, p. 30.
"Understanding" (tr. by Elizabeth Lowe). Mund (14:1) 83, p. 30-31.

3381. PARRIS, Peggy
"Two Cut-Up Poems: The Somnambulist's Wife, Ionisation 1929." Kayak (61) Ap 83, p. 24-25.

3382. PARSONS, Bruce
"Winter." PottPort (5) 83-84, p. 20.

3383. PARSONS, Steven C.
"Warm Morning." CapeR (19:1) Wint 83, p. 3.

3384. PARTRIDGE, Dixie L.
"Recurring Dream: Leaving the Valley Where I Grew Up." QW (17) Aut-Wint 83-84, p. 97.

3385. PASAROW, Reinee
"Once Dead, Now Dying." WorldO (17:4) Sum 83, p. 36.

3386. PASOS, Joaquin
"Indian Woman Down in the Marketplace" (tr. by Leland H. Chambers). DevQ (18:1) Spr 83, p. 98.

PASQUALE, Emanuel di
See: Di PASQUALE, Emanuel

3387. PASTAN, Linda
"At Half Century." Ploughs (9:1) 83, p. 67-68.
"At Home." ThRiPo (21/22) 83, p. 63.
"Goldwasser." NewEngR (6:1) Aut 83, p. 153.
"In the Kingdom of Midas." Tendril (16) Sum 83, p. 102.
"Last Words." NewRep (188:22) 6 Je 83, p. 34.
"Lullaby for 17." Poetry (142:5) Ag 83, p. 271-272.
"March." OhioR (30) 83, p. 130.
"Monet's Irises." PoetL (77:1) Spr 82, p. 29.
"The Moss Palace." PoetL (77:1) Spr 82, p. 30.

"Prosody 101." Atlantic (252:4) O 83, p. 63.
"Reconciliations." MichQR (22:1) Wint 83, p. 57-58.
"Remission." Ploughs (9:1) 83, p. 69.
"Screen-Memory." MemphisSR (4:1) Aut 83, p. 29.
"The Sonoran Desert, January." Poetry (142:5) Ag 83, p. 272.
"Toward Darkness." IndR (5:2) Sum 82, p. 16.
"Warm Front." Tendril (16) Sum 83, p. 103.

3388. PASTAN, Rachel
"Poem on 'Canon per Tonas': after Godel, Escher, Bach." IndR (5:2) Sum 82, p. 20-21.

3389. PATERSON, Andrea
"A Letter Following Departure." Wind (13:48) 83, p. 25.

3390. PATRIARCA, Gianna
"Perhaps." PoetryCR (5:1) Aut 83, p. 6.

3391. PATRIKIOS, Titos
"The Eels of Bracciano" (tr. by Kimon Friar). PoNow (7:2, #38) 83, p. 45.

3392. PATTEN, Karl
"4 A.M." (tr. of Guillaume Apollinaire). WebR (8:1) Spr 83, p. 41.
"Changing the Wheel" (tr. of Bertolt Brecht). WebR (8:1) Spr 83, p. 41.
"The Cloud" (tr. of Jules Supervielle). WebR (8:1) Spr 83, p. 39.
"The Wake" (tr. of Jules Supervielle). WebR (8:1) Spr 83, p. 40.

3393. PATTERSON, Cy
"The Sex Mechanic." Bogg (50) 83, p. 40.

3394. PATTON, Melinda
"All Is Calm." SanFPJ (5:3) 83, p. 93.

3395. PAU-LLOSA, Ricardo
"Onomatopoeia." ArizQ (39:2) Sum 83, p. 121.
"Terraces." MichQR (22:4) Aut 83, p. 556-557.

3396. PAUDEEN, A.
"Terminal or Gate?" SanFPJ (5:3) 83, p. 70-71.

3397. PAUL, James
"From the Country." AmerPoR (12:2) Mr/Ap 83, p. 45.
"Nothing for Rachel." AmerPoR (12:2) Mr/Ap 83, p. 45.

3398. PAUL, Jay S.
"Finding Old Photos." CimR (62) Ja 83, p. 54.
"I Think of Him on Ladders." StoneC (10:3/4) Spr-Sum 83, p. 11.
"Nap." PoetL (78:3) Aut 83, p. 154.
"Summerfield's Daughter." PoetL (78:3) Aut 83, p. 150-151.
"The Sun in March." PoetL (78:3) Aut 83, p. 152-153.

3399. PAUL, Martin
"And, Then, Silence" (tr. of Salvador Espriu). Mund (14:1) 83, p. 13.
"In the Fog" (tr. of Salvador Espriu). Mund (14:1) 83, p. 13, 15.

3400. PAULENICH, Craig
"Bringing Rain to Oconee County." Vis (13) 83, p. 33.
"Goat-Man at Home." GeoR (37:3) Aut 83, p. 628.
"Reaping." Vis (13) 83, p. 34.
"A Song of Transmutation." Blueline (3:2) Wint-Spr 82, p. 44.

3401. PAULIN, Tom
"Desertmartin." PoetryE (12) Aut 83, p. 73.
"A Lyric Afterwards." PoetryE (12) Aut 83, p. 72.
"Manichean Geography I." Agni (19) 83, p. 42.
"Manichean Geography II." Agni (19) 83, p. 43-44.
"A Nation, Yet Again" (after Pushkin). PoetryE (12) Aut 83, p. 74.
"Second-rate Republics." Agni (19) 83, p. 38.
"Settlers." Agni (19) 83, p. 37.
"Trotsky in Finland" (an incident from his memoirs). Agni (19) 83, p. 39-40.
"What Is Fixed to Happen." Agni (19) 83, p. 41.
"What Is Fixed to Happen." PoetryE (12) Aut 83, p. 70.
"Where Art Is a Midwife." PoetryE (12) Aut 83, p. 71.

3402. PAULSON, Bill
"Fool's Gold." PoetL (77:3) Aut 82, p. 164.

3403. PAVESE, Cesare
"A Generation" (tr. by Duncan Bush). Stand (24:1) 82-83, p. 38.
"The Paper Smokers" (tr. by Duncan Bush). Stand (24:1) 82-83, p. 39.

3404. PAVLICH, Walter
"Because." ConcPo (16:1) Spr 83, p. 14.
"We Carry These Stars." ConcPo (16:1) Spr 83, p. 13.

3405. PAVLIDES, Lefteris
"The Primal Sun (Helios o Protos)" (Selections: V-VI, XII-XIII, XV, XVII-XVIII) (tr. of Odysseus Elytis, w. Edward Morin). WebR (8:1) Spr 83, p. 20-25.

3406. PAYNE, Ifan
"Rimas (Excerpts: X, XVII, XXXVIII)" (tr. of Gustavo Adolfo Becquer). KanQ (15:1) Wint 83, p. 115.

3407. PAZ, Octavio
"The Branch" (tr. by David Putney). IndR (6:3) Sum 83, p. 30.
"Full Wind" (tr. by Sharon Sieber). NowestR (21:2/3) 83, p. 5-15.

"Maithuna" (tr. by Eliot Weinberger). Sulfur (3:1, #7) 83, p. 4-8.
"Poem: Between what I see and what I say" (for Roman Jakobson, tr. by Eliott Weinberger). Nat (237:1) 2 Jl 83, p. 16.
"The Same Time" (tr. by Eliot Weinberger). YaleR (72:2) Wint 83, p. 201-205.
"Viento Entero." NowestR (21:2/3) 83, p. 6-14.

3408. PEABODY, George
"Atlantis: An Elegy." PottPort (5) 83-84, p. 49-51.

3409. PEACOCK, Molly
"And You Were a Baby Girl." MissR (12:1/2, nos. 34/35) Aut 83, p. 81.
"The Distance Up Close." ParisR (25:88) Sum 83, p. 190.
"A Garden." GeoR (37:2) Sum 83, p. 383.
"How I Come to You." Shen (34:1) 83, p. 74.
"Let's Go Over Exactly What Happened." Shen (34:1) 83, p. 75.
"Mental France." ParisR (25:88) Sum 83, p. 191.
"My Vast Presumption." NewL (49:3/4) Spr-Sum 83, p. 216.
"Our Room." MissR (12:1/2, nos. 34/35) Aut 83, p. 80.
"She Lays." Epoch (33:1) Aut-Wint 83, p. 86.

3410. PEAK, Mary
"After Eden." LittleBR (4:2) Wint 83-84, p. 73.

3411. PEARLSON, F. S.
"Small Wars (Room Sounds)." LittleM (14:1/2) 83, p. 102-103.

3412. PEARSON, Fernando
"Visita al Museo Británico." Prismal (11) Aut 83, p. 103-104.

3413. PEARSON, Jean
"Inner Resources." Blueline (4:1) Sum-Aut 82, p. 36.

3414. PEASE, Deborah
"A New Home" (Excerpt). SoDakR (21:4) Wint 83, p. 56.
"Paths." NoAmR (268:2) Je 83, p. 9.
"Waking." NoAmR (268:3) S 83, p. 35.

3415. PEATTIE, Noel
"Second Coming." SecC (11:1/2) 83, p. 162.

3416. PECK, Beverly Z.
"Storm." YetASM (1:2) 82, p. 19.

3417. PECK, Gail J.
"Before the Wall." HangL (44) Sum 83, p. 45.
"Intention." Tendril (16) Sum 83, p. 104.
"Leaving Father at Landrum." Tendril (16) Sum 83, p. 105.

3418. PECK, John
"Anacreontic." Salm (60) Spr-Sum 83, p. 155.
"Assisi" (Paul Celan, Gedichte I, 108). Salm (60) Spr-Sum 83, p. 156.
"A Field of Snow on the Palatine." Salm (60) Spr-Sum 83, p. 152-153.
"Hours near the Crossing" (Excerpts). ParisR (24:85) Aut 82, p. 42-44.
"Inni Popolari." Salm (60) Spr-Sum 83, p. 154-155.
"Untitled: It seemed an eagle." TriQ (56) Wint 83, p. 150-151.
"The Well of St. Regisse." TriQ (56) Wint 83, p. 148-149.

3419. PEDEN, Margaret Sayers
"Climbing the Rag Mountain" (tr. of Luisa Valenzuela). OP (36) Aut-Wint 83, p. 56.
"A Dream about Mercedes" (tr. of Luisa Valenzuela). OP (36) Aut-Wint 83, p. 57-58.
"The Girl Who Turned into Cider" (tr. of Luisa Valenzuela). OP (36) Aut-Wint 83, p. 53.
"Manuscript Found in a Bottle" (tr. of Luisa Valenzuela). OP (36) Aut-Wint 83, p. 59.
"A Question of Chestnuts" (tr. of Luisa Valenzuela). OP (36) Aut-Wint 83, p. 54-55.

3420. PEDERSON, Cynthia S.
"Before Bittersweet." LittleBR (4:1) Aut 83, p. 18.

3421. PELIAS, Ronald J.
"On Hearing Stanley Plumly Read." NegC (3:4) Aut 83, p. 127.

3422. PELLETIER, Cathie
"Nightwatch" (for Jim Glaser). KanQ (15:1) Wint 83, p. 175.
"Quarry." KanQ (15:1) Wint 83, p. 176.

3423. PELLS, David L.
"Spring in Idaho." Wind (13:48) 83, p. 47.

3424. PENHA, James W.
"The Big Curb Maple." SanFPJ (4:2) 83, p. 44.
"A Carcassone." SanFPJ (5:3) 83, p. 68.
"Daily." YetASM (1:1) 82, p. 9.
"Royal Indian Burial Grounds at Charlestown, Rhode Island." SanFPJ (5:2) 83, p. 10.
"Salt Water Pond." YetASM (1:1) 82, p. 4.
"La Secuela." SanFPJ (4:4) 83, p. 66-67.
"Thirties/Eighties." SanFPJ (5:1) 83, p. 14.

3425. PENN, Barbara
"Ageism." YetASM (1:2) 82, p. 16.

3426. PENNANT, Edmund
"Moving Day." Confr (25/26) 83, p. 308.

3427. PENSAK, Susan
"The Desire of the Word" (from The Musical Hell, 1971, tr. of Alejandra Pizarnik). Sulfur (3:2,

#8) 83, p. 104-105.
"Fundamental Stone" (tr. of Alejandra Pizarnik). Sulfur (3:2, #8) 83, p. 106-108.
"The Hidden Ones" (tr. of Alejandra Pizarnik). Sulfur (3:2, #8) 83, p. 103.
"Sorceries" (tr. of Alejandra Pizarnik). Sulfur (3:2, #8) 83, p. 102.
"Tragedy" (tr. of Alejandra Pizarnik). Sulfur (3:2, #8) 83, p. 104.
"The Truth of the Forest" (tr. of Alejandra Pizarnik). Sulfur (3:2, #8) 83, p. 103.
"The Word of the Desire" (from The Musical Hell, 1971, tr. of Alejandra Pizarnik). Sulfur (3:2, #8) 83, p. 105-106.

3428. PENZAVECCHIA, James
"A Crash Course in Time Control." LittleM (14:1/2) 83, p. 34-35.
"The Effects of Rain." LittleM (14:1/2) 83, p. 33.
"Naming the Silence." LittleM (14:1/2) 83, p. 36-37.

3429. PERCHIK, Simon
"Again and again." PoetL (78:1) Spr 83, p. 32.
"Again the Little Dipper circling down." PoetL (78:1) Spr 83, p. 36-37.
"As a shadow brings down the dark." PoetL (78:1) Spr 83, p. 40.
"Beach Blanket Spread." SoDakR (21:4) Wint 83, p. 71.
"By tears: barbed wire." PortR (29:1) 83, p. 105.
"He allows slant." RagMag (2:2) Aut 83, p. 22.
"I let my hand shake." PoetL (78:1) Spr 83, p. 33.
"I see more with a mask." RagMag (2:2) Aut 83, p. 22.
"I want no survivors." PoetL (78:1) Spr 83, p. 31.
"My arm asleep, numb." PoetL (78:1) Spr 83, p. 34-35.
"Poem: As a stray will sniff its shadow." PoetryNW (24:2) Sum 83, p. 27.
"Rose's Wedding." NewL (49:3/4) Spr-Sum 83, p. 216.
"The stones must be small, gravel." Focus (15:95) Ag 83, p. 19.
"There is descent where your hair parted." PoetL (78:1) Spr 83, p. 38-39.
"This Battered Lamp." MSS (3:1) Aut 83, p. 56.
"This green, unsinkable wreath." Wind (13:47) 83, p. 36.
"What shy twins." SmPd (20:2) Spr 83, p. 29.
"Who can afford such risks." CapeR (19:1) Wint 83, p. 47.

3430. PEREIRA, Sam
"Cassavettes." Telescope (4) Wint 83, p. 30.
"A Science of Tuesdays." AntR (41:1) Wint 83, p. 72.

3431. PEREIRA, Terensika
"Cortázar." SinN (14:1) O-D 83, p. 37.

3432. PERELMAN, Bob
"Third & Townsend." ParisR (24:86) Wint 82, p.

114-115.
"War & Peace." Sulfur (3:1, #7) 83, p. 20-26.

3433. PERET, Benjamin
"Natural History" (tr. by Keith Hollaman). Field (28) Spr 83, p. 5-8.

3434. PEREZ, Gail Adrianne
"The Roadside Chapel." SoDakR (21:4) Wint 83, p. 59.

3435. PEREZ, Ilma Valenzuela de
"Gestación de Nuestra América." LetFem (9:2) Aut 83, p. 77-78.

3436. PEREZ IGLESIAS, Davide
"E a locura en forma de princesa perseguida." Prismal (11) Aut 83, p. 115.

3437. PERI ROSSI, Cristina
"Relación de Tripulantes Que Participaron en el Naufragio." Areíto (9:35) 83, p. 38-39.

3438. PERISH, Melanie
"Steel." 13thM (7:1/2) 83, p. 51.

3439. PERLBERG, Mark
"What Happened in the Woods." Hudson (36:3) Aut 83, p. 517-518.

3440. PERLMAN, Anne S.
"At Fifty in the Crystal-Dead Eye of the Center." ThRiPo (19/20) 82, p. 54.
"Search." ThRiPo (19/20) 82, p. 53.

3441. PERMUT, Joanna Baumer
"Atlantic Crossing, Age 17: Riccardo." YetASM (1:2) 82, p. 16.
"Paternal Grandmother." YetASM (1:2) 82, p. 11.
"Survivors." YetASM (1:2) 82, p. 12.

3442. PERREAULT, Robert B.
"Le Temps S'Enfuit." MoodySI (11) Spr-Sum 82, p. 12-13.

3443. PERRIN, Judith N.
"Present from Egypt." KanQ (15:2) Spr 83, p. 148.

3444. PERRON, Lee
"The White Bones of the Year are Scattered among Jonquils." CharR (9:1) Spr 83, p. 28-29.

3445. PERRY, Maggie
"Frivolous Things." SpoonRQ (8:4) Aut 83, p. 39.
"Going to the Drive-In" (for Dave). SpoonRQ (8:2) Spr 83, p. 8-9.
"Lily Pond." Northeast (Ser. 3:16) Wint 83-84, p. 23.
"WoodMan." SpoonRQ (8:4) Aut 83, p. 40.

3446. PERRYMAN, Marcus
"City of Night" (tr. of Vittorio Sereni, w. Peter Robinson). Argo (5:1) 83, p. 20.
"Italian in Greece" (tr. of Vittorio Sereni, w. Peter Robinson). Argo (5:1) 83, p. 20.

3447. PERSUN, Terry L.
"Princess of the Block." YetASM (1:1) 82, p. 2.

3448. PERTTU, Charmian
"Ice on the River." HiramPoR (35) Aut-Wint 83, p. 34.

3449. PESEROFF, Joyce
"Spring Dress." Ploughs (9:1) 83, p. 171-172.

3450. PETACCIA, Mario A.
"First Poems." YetASM (1:1) 82, p. 7.

3451. PETERFREUND, Stuart
"Fan." PoNow (7:2, #38) 83, p. 41.
"A Grade Crossing in Ayer." PoNow (7:2, #38) 83, p. 41.
"Harvesting Cantaloupe." PoNow (7:2, #38) 83, p. 41.
"Lilacs." StoneC (10:3/4) Spr-Sum 83, p. 12.
"Mardi Gras Poem" (for Debbie). NewL (49:3/4) Spr-Sum 83, p. 232.
"The Old Dirt." NewOR (10:4) Wint 83, p. 36.
"Places We Can Never Live." StoneC (10:3/4) Spr-Sum 83, p. 13.

3452. PETERS, Anne
"Cult Goddesses." SpiritSH (49) 83, p. 15.
"The Well of St. Claire." SpiritSH (49) 83, p. 14.

3453. PETERS, Robert
"All Is the Idea, the Idea Is All." PoetL (77:2) Sum 82, p. 70-71.
"Bewitched Animals." PoetL (77:2) Sum 82, p. 69.
"First Storm in Paradise." PoetL (77:2) Sum 82, p. 72-73.
"Gyp, My Loving Big Black Pig: An Acrostic Poem." BelPoJ (33:3) Spr 83, p. 18-19.
"His Mother's Burial." WormR (23:4, issue 92) 83, p. 154.
"His Sister." WormR (23:4, issue 92) 83, p. 155.
"How to Gain the Evil Eye." PoetL (77:2) Sum 82, p. 71.
"Mother-Death." WormR (23:4, issue 92) 83, p. 154.
"Opium Pipe." Abraxas (27/28) 83, p. 9.
"Sweet Macho Nothings." Gargoyle (22/23) 83, p. 15.
"Tamar River Cornish Pie." BelPoJ (33:3) Spr 83, p. 19.
"Why Don't They Go Back to Transylvania?" SecC (11:1/2) 83, p. 160.

3454. PETERSEN, Carol Miles
"Untitled: We are out looking for signs of early spring." KanQ (15:2) Spr 83, p. 123.

3455. PETERSON, Eugene H.
"Even the Fringe" (Mark 6:53-56). ChrC (100:6) 2 Mr 83, p. 181.

3456. PETERSON, Geoff
"Listening to Rain." YetASM (1:1) 82, p. 3.
"The Rapture." Vis (11) 83, p. 28-29.

3457. PETERSON, Jan
"In the Hour of Exile." KanQ (15:1) Wint 83, p. 118.

3458. PETERSON, Jim
"Silence." CharR (9:2) Aut 83, p. 72.

3459. PETERSON, Karen
"Her Hair, Her Arms Become Flame." Prima (8) 83, p. 97.

3460. PETERSON, Robert
"Kicking It Around with Spats Longo, a Serious Contender" (for M. A. Ashley). PoetryNW (24:2) Sum 83, p. 20-21.
"La Paz." Kayak (62) Ag 83, p. 61.
"The Silver Bell" (found poem, from a Las Vegas wedding chapel advertisement). Kayak (63) N 83, p. 31.

3461. PETERSON, Sue (Susan)
"The Name Collector" (for Dave Etter). SpoonRQ (8:2) Spr 83, p. 10.
"Today, Rain." SpoonRQ (8:4) Aut 83, p. 38.

3462. PETESCH, Donald A.
"Dreaming about the Bomb." YetASM (2:1) 83, p. 6.
"On the Line in Oakland, California" (for Jim Daniels). PoetryNW (24:3) Aut 83, p. 7-9.

3463. PETIC, Zorika
"After a Limited Nuclear Excursion" (Adapted from Dennis Tedlock's translation of the Mayan Popol Vuh). SanFPJ (4:3) 83, p. 41.

3464. PETRAKOS, Chris
"All the World Is Sleep." PoetryE (11) Sum 83, p. 12-13.
"Call Them Back." PoetryE (11) Sum 83, p. 10.
"Like Any Other." PoetryE (11) Sum 83, p. 11.
"Now Will Be Tomorrow." PoetryE (12) Aut 83, p. 61.
"Such Beauty." PoetryE (11) Sum 83, p. 9.
"Testing, Testing." PoetryE (12) Aut 83, p. 59.
"Tightrope." PoetryE (12) Aut 83, p. 60.

3465. PETRE, Michele
"We have it all." SanFPJ (4:4) 83, p. 22-23.

3466. PETREMAN, David A.
"Mariposa." Poem (49) N 83, p. 25.
"Shark Eyes." Poem (49) N 83, p. 24.
"Whale Toy" (for Jonathan). Poem (49) N 83, p. 26.

3467. PETRI, György
"News Summary" (tr. by Kenneth McRobbie). PartR (50:4) 83, p. 586.
"To Bulcsu Bertha, with Profound Respect" (tr. by Kenneth McRobbie). PartR (50:4) 83, p. 586-587.
"Visigoth Sundays" (tr. by Kenneth McRobbie). PartR (50:4) 83, p. 587-588.

3468. PETRIE, Paul
"Biography." WestHR (37:4) Wint 83, p. 306-307.
"Grandmother." ChrC (100:25) 31 Ag-7 S 83, p. 768.
"Report Card Time." KanQ (15:1) Wint 83, p. 135.
"Youth and Age." KanQ (15:1) Wint 83, p. 134.

3469. PETT, Stephen
"An Eagle, by Jesus." CimR (65) O 83, p. 32.
"Where the Woods Meet the World" (for John Gardner, September 15, 1982). CimR (65) O 83, p. 58.

3470. PETTIT, Michael
"Cape Work." BlackWR (9:1) Aut 82, p. 34.
"Fire and Ice." BlackWR (9:1) Aut 82, p. 35.
"Looney Tunes." MissouriR (6:2) Wint 83, p. 78-81.
"Self Portrait Approaching Promontory, Utah." BlackWR (9:1) Aut 82, p. 32-33.

3471. PEYPERS, Ankie
"Between Chapter and Verse" (tr. by Maria Jacobs). Waves (11:4) Spr 83, p. 75.
"But One Day" (tr. by Maria Jacobs). Waves (11:4) Spr 83, p. 71.
"Gast." Waves (11:4) Spr 83, p. 72.
"Guest" (tr. by Maria Jacobs). Waves (11:4) Spr 83, p. 73.
"Maar Op Een Dag." Waves (11:4) Spr 83, p. 70.
"Tussen Tekst En Uitleg." Waves (11:4) Spr 83, p. 74.

3472. PFEFFERLE, Susan G.
"My father the pacifist." SanFPJ (5:2) 83, p. 93.
"Question: What would life be without Trees?" SanFPJ (5:1) 83, p. 62.

3473. PFEIFER, Michael
"The Clam Plays the Accordion." KanQ (15:4) Aut 83, p. 59.
"The Outfielder." KanQ (15:4) Aut 83, p. 59.
"Spinner, Carolina Cotton Mill, 1908." MissouriR (7:1) Aut 83, p. 24.

3474. PFINGSTON, Roger
"Bird Seed." Images (8:3) 83, p. 7.
"A Dancing Fool." Confr (25/26) 83, p. 259.
"Radio Hill." Tendril (16) Sum 83, p. 106.
"Stealing Ice, 1948." PoetL (78:4) Wint 84, p. 198-199.

3475. PFLUM, Richard
"At the Concert." Kayak (61) Ap 83, p. 40.
"Poem Beginning with a Line by Walt Whitman."

Kayak (61) Ap 83, p. 39.
"The Uncertainty of It All." Kayak (61) Ap 83, p. 39.

3476. PHIFER, Rob
"From Harmon's Creek." SouthernPR (23:2) Aut 83, p. 20-22.

3477. PHILLIPOV, Vladimir
"The Water Buffalo (Hanoi, 1972)" (tr. of Blaga Dimitrova, w. John Balaban). NewEng (5:4) Sum 83, p. 497-499.

3478. PHILLIPS, A. P. (Alma Payne)
"Flowers and Bones." ArizQ (39:2) Sum 83, p. 100.

3479. PHILLIPS, Ben
"The Goldberg Variations." WestCR (17:4) Ap 83, p. 38.
"In the Mourning." WritersL Je 83, p. 27.
"The Moon Sits." WestCR (17:4) Ap 83, p. 37.
"What Is There about the Snow." WritersL Ja 83, p. 18.

3480. PHILLIPS, Dennis
"Three-Part Requiem." Sulfur (3:2, #8) 83, p. 92-93.

3481. PHILLIPS, Hilda
"A Mother's Legacy." WritersL S 83, p. 24.

3482. PHILLIPS, James
"Her Sadness." Vis (12) 83, p. 10.
"The Open Book." PortR (29:1) 83, p. 95.

3483. PHILLIPS, Louis
"Census." WindO (43) Wint 83, p. 40.
"For My Sisters." CapeR (19:1) Wint 83, p. 5.
"The Krazy Kat of the Poetry Set Begs an Indulgence from His Reader." KanQ (15:2) Spr 83, p. 155.
"This Is Where We Are." SpiritSH (48) 82, p. 37.

3484. PHILLIPS, Robert
"Inside and Out." NewYorker (59:29) 5 S 83, p. 93.
"The Land: A Love Letter." ParisR (24:84) Sum 82, p. 147.
"Queen Anne's Lace" (In memory of Isabella Gardner, 1915-1981). Hudson (36:4) Wint 83-84, p. 690-692.
"The Well-Tempered Performer." Shen (34:4) 83, p. 96-97.

3485. PICHE, Alphonze
"Quai." Mund (14:1) 83, p. 68.
"Quai" (tr. by Gary Wilson). Mund (14:1) 83, p. 69.
"Remous." Mund (14:1) 83, p. 70.
"Retraite." Mund (14:1) 83, p. 70.
"Retreat" (tr. by Gary Wilson). Mund (14:1) 83, p. 71.
"Whirlpool" (tr. by Gary Wilson). Mund (14:1) 83, p. 71.

3486. PICKARD, Deanna Louise
"For Louise Nevelson." PoetL (77:4) Wint 83, p. 219.

3487. PICKETT, Thomas
"Waiting the Ride Beyond." Wind (13:48) 83, p. 48-49.

3488. PIEKUNKA, Thomas L.
"Black: The Leopard." SanFPJ (5:4) 83, p. 38-39.

3489. PIEMONTE, Philip
"Grandma Cranks Up." Wind (13:48) 83, p. 11.

3490. PIERCE, Constance
"The Villa Capri" (Second prize, SCCA International Poetry Contest). WestB (12) 83, p. 38-43.

3491. PIERCE, Neal
"Afternoon." Wind (13:48) 83, p. 31.

3492. PIERCEY, Wallace, Jr.
"Snapshots." Bluebuf (2:1) Aut 83, p. 7.

3493. PIERCY, Marge
"Building Is Taming." Tendril (14/15) Wint 83, p. 158-159.
"For the Furies." 13thM (6:1/2) 82, p. 5-7.
"Listening to a Speech." 13thM (7:1/2) 83, p. 119.
"Out of Sight." 13thM (7:1/2) 83, p. 120-121.
"Reconciled." Tendril (14/15) Wint 83, p. 157.
"Six Underrated Pleasures." OP (36) Aut-Wint 83, p. 25-32.

3494. PIERMAN, Carol J.
"The Word." CentR (27:4) Aut 83, p. 276-277.

PIERO, W. S. di
See: Di PIERO, W. S.

3495. PIERSON, Philip
"To a Child Bride at the Rose Lane Tourist." OhioR (30) 83, p. 174-175.

3496. PIES, Stacy
"Lagrasse." Cond (9) Spr 83, p. 76-77.
"Raw Autumn." Cond (9) Spr 83, p. 74-75.

PIGNO, Antonia Quintana
See: QUINTANA PIGNO, Antonia

3498. PIGOTT, Yvonne
"Gone." AntigR (55) Aut 83, p. 85.
"Leaf by Leaf." AntigR (55) Aut 83, p. 84.
"A Single Leaf." AntigR (55) Aut 83, p. 85.
"Winter's Hide." AntigR (55) Aut 83, p. 84.

3499. PILCHER, Barry Edgar
"Chartreuse Microbus." Bogg (50) 83, p. 53.

3500. PILKINGTON, Kevin
"Directions Through a Changing Scene." Poetry (142:6) S 83, p. 332-333.
"Jogging on the Beach." Poetry (142:6) S 83, p. 334-335.
"A Spruce in Vermont." Poetry (142:6) S 83, p. 336-337.

3501. PIMPL, Bill E.
"Soon." Meadows (3:1) 82, p. 41.

3502. PINCAS, Israel
"All That We Learned, We Know" (tr. by Gabriel Levin). LitR (26:2) Wint 83, p. 250-253.
"The Road to India" (tr. by Gabriel Levin). LitR (26:2) Wint 83, p. 249-250.

3503. PINE, Red
"Cold Mountain" (Selections: 4, 5, 16) (tr. of Anonymous). NowestR (21:2/3) 83, p. 77.

3504. PINEGAR, Ruth
"Limits at the Mansfield Training School." YetASM (1:2) 82, p. 3.
"The Properties of Water." YetASM (1:2) 82, p. 6.

3505. PINKWATER, Susan
"Submitting." BelPoJ (33:3) Spr 83, p. 16-17.

3506. PINSKY, Robert
"Account" (tr. of Czeslaw Milosz, w. the author). NewYRB (30:7) 28 Ap 83, p. 6.
"A Book in the Ruins" (Warsaw, 1942) (tr. of Czeslaw Milosz, w. the author and Robert Hass). NewYorker (59:1) 21 F 83, p. 49.
"The Figured Wheel." Ploughs (9:1) 83, p. 45-47.
"History of My Heart." Poetry (141:5) F 83, p. 251-258.
"Icicles." NewYorker (59:44) 19 D 83, p. 50.
"It Was Winter" (tr. of Czeslaw Milosz, w. Renata Gorczynski and Robert Hass). NewRep (187:11) 13 S 82, p. 28-29.
"A Long Branch Song." SoCaR (16:1) Aut 83, p. 95.
"A Mistake" (Paris, 1958) (tr. of Czeslaw Milosz, w. the author and Robert Hass). NewYorker (59:1) 21 F 83, p. 48-49.
"The New Saddhus." NewYorker (59:31) 19 S 83, p. 46.
"Ode to a Bird" (Montgeron, 1959) (tr. of Czeslaw Milosz, w. the author and Robert Hass). NewYorker (59:1) 21 F 83, p. 48.
"Reading the Japanese Poet Issa" (Berkely, 1978) (tr. of Czeslaw Milosz, w. the author and Robert Hass). NewYorker (59:1) 21 F 83, p. 48.
"The Separate Notebooks: Pages concerning the Years of Independence" (tr. of Czeslaw Milosz, w. the author). ParisR (25:87) Spr 83, p. 49-54.
"Those Corridors" (tr. of Czeslaw Milosz). Ploughs (9:1) 83, p. 48.

3507. PIRKLE, Thomas
"Days of January." StoneC (10:3/4) Spr-Sum 83, p. 41.
"Stump." StoneC (10:3/4) Spr-Sum 83, p. 41.

3508. PITZEN, Jim
"Memory's Slave." WritersL Ag 83, p. 27.

3509. PIZARNIK, Alejandra
"The Desire of the Word" (from The Musical Hell, 1971, tr. by Susan Pensak). Sulfur (3:2, #8) 83, p. 104-105.
"Fundamental Stone" (tr. by Susan Pensak). Sulfur (3:2, #8) 83, p. 106-108.
"The Hidden Ones" (tr. by Susan Pensak). Sulfur (3:2, #8) 83, p. 103.
"Sorceries" (tr. by Susan Pensak). Sulfur (3:2, #8) 83, p. 102.
"Tragedy" (tr. by Susan Pensak). Sulfur (3:2, #8) 83, p. 104.
"The Truth of the Forest" (tr. by Susan Pensak). Sulfur (3:2, #8) 83, p. 103.
"The Word of the Desire" (from The Musical Hell, 1971, tr. by Susan Pensak). Sulfur (3:2, #8) 83, p. 105-106.

3510. PLATH, James
"The Aerial Photo Looked Impressive" (a.l. championship game Milwaukee County stadium October 10, 1982). SpoonRQ (8:4) Aut 83, p. 43.

PLESSIS, Rachel Blau du
See: DuPLESSIS, Rachel Blau

3511. PLINER, Susan
"Something I Couldn't Tell You." AmerPoR (12:6) N/D 83, p. 34.

3512. PLUMLY, Stanley
"Coalbrookdale at Night, by Phillipe Jacques de Loutherbourg." GeoR (37:1) Spr 83, p. 190-191.
"Commelina Virginica." NewYorker (59:15) 30 My 83, p. 40.
"Denn, Herr, Die Grossen Stadte Sind" (after Rilke). MemphisSR (2:2) Spr 82, p. 25.
"Early Meadow-Rue." OhioR (30) 83, p. 99.
"In Passing." NewYorker (59:18) 20 Je 83, p. 40.
"The Mother." ThRiPo (21/22) 83, p. 64.
"My Mother's Feet." Poetry (142:3) Je 83, p. 169.
"One of Us." NewL (49:3/4) Spr-Sum 83, p. 163.
"Out-of-the-Body Travel." OhioR (30) 83, p. 98.
"Posthumous Keats." Poetry (142:3) Je 83, p. 167-168.
"This Poem." OhioR (30) 83, p. 99.

3513. PLYBON, Amy
"Grandfather House." Argo (4:3) 83, p. 21.

3514. PLYMELL, Charles
"Neal Cassady." SecC (11:1/2) 83, p. 166.

"Ten Years before the Blast (An After Dinner Monologue Interior)." SecC (11:1/2) 83, p. 167-169.

PO, Li
See: LI, Po

3515. POBO, Kenneth
"Aaron Sees a Ghost." PikeF (5) Spr 83, p. 16.
"Here." IndR (6:2) Spr 83, p. 72.
"Letter." PikeF (5) Spr 83, p. 16.
"The Pennsylvania Line." ThirdW Spr 83, p. 103.
"Sanctuary." PikeF (5) Spr 83, p. 16.
"Sometimes at Night." StoneC (11:1/2, Pt. 1) Aut-Wint 83, p. 35.
"Van Gogh: A Study in Amethyst." IndR (5:2) Sum 82, p. 82-85.

3516. POGGE, Mary
"The Natural." KanQ (15:1) Wint 83, p. 151.

3517. POGSON, Patricia
"Abandonment of the Union Building." Bogg (51) 83, p. 51.
"Cornflowers." Bogg (50) 83, p. 39.

3518. POHL, Evelyn
"Leaves." YetASM (1:1) 82, p. 7.

3519. POIRIER, Thelma
"Clotheslines." AntigR (53) Spr 83, p. 45.
"Gull Path." AntigR (53) Spr 83, p. 44.
"My Sundress Inside Out." Grain (11:1) F 83, p. 12.

3520. POLENTAS, Manolis S.
"Last Words to Hermes." YetASM (1:1) 82, p. 6.
"Lost." YetASM (1:1) 82, p. 3.

3521. POLITE, Frank
"God's Ill, A." PoNow (7:2, #38) 83, p. 34.
"Masloff Is Not In Zagreb." PoNow (7:2, #38) 83, p. 34.

3522. POLITO, Robert
"Cigarette Lighter." Ploughs (9:1) 83, p. 60.
"First Love." Ploughs (9:1) 83, p. 57-59.
"Weekend at the Biltmore." Ploughs (9:1) 83, p. 55-56.

3523. POLK, Noel
"I Sonned a Father." SouthernR (19:2) Ap 83, p. 387.

3524. POLLAK, Felix
"Dedication" (For Reinhold Grimm). NewL (50:1) Aut 83, p. 92.
"Land of Shadows" (tr. of Hans Magnus Enzensberger, w. Reinhold Grimm). NowestR (21:1) 83, p. 131, 133.
"Morphine" (tr. of Heinrich Heine). PraS (57:4) Wint 83, p. 45.

"The Stage Grows Dark" (tr. of Heinrich Heine). PraS (57:4) Wint 83, p. 44.
"They." PraS (57:4) Wint 83, p. 45-46.
"Those Who Have Disappeared" (for Nelly Sachs) (tr. of Hans Magnus Enzensberger, w. Reinhold Grimm). NowestR (21:1) 83, p. 135.

3525. POLLITT, Katha
"Blue Window." NewRep (186:15) 14 Ap 82, p. 38.
"Composition in Black and White." NewRep (186:15) 14 Ap 82, p. 38.
"Night Blooming Flowers." NewRep (186:15) 14 Ap 82, p. 38.

3526. POLLOK, Estill
"State of the Art." Wind (13:47) 83, p. 19.

3527. POLSON, Don
"And Then My Lungs." AntigR (53) Spr 83, p. 122.
"Autumn Rhyme." AntigR (53) Spr 83, p. 122.
"The Chafe of Re-arrangements." PottPort (5) 83-84, p. 33.
"Completing the Circle." AntigR (53) Spr 83, p. 123.
"Heron." BallSUF (24:1) Wint 83, p. 18.
"Our Eldest Son Calls Home." AntigR (53) Spr 83, p. 121.
"A Short But Sweetly Conceived Epitaph" (with apologies to W.H. Auden). CrossC (5:1) 83, p. 12.
"Solstice Prayer." PottPort (5) 83-84, p. 26.
"What's in a Name" (for Len Gasparini). PoetryCR (5:1) Aut 83, p. 19.
"Winter Poverty." AntigR (53) Spr 83, p. 123.

3528. POMERANTZ, Marsha
"Lucy." LitR (26:2) Wint 83, p. 323.
"Lucy: Her Fear." LitR (26:2) Wint 83, p. 325.
"Lucy Speaks." LitR (26:2) Wint 83, p. 324.

3529. POMERANZE, Julius
"Salicidal." SanFPJ (5:1) 83, p. 44.

3530. POMEROY, Ralph
"The Dream." PoNow (7:2, #38) 83, p. 5.
"Weather." MemphisSR (2:1) Aut 81, p. 51.

3531. PONSOT, Marie
"1900, near Lyon." 13thM (6:1/2) 82, p. 105.
"Fear Is Known by the Taste, After." OP (35) Spr-Sum 83, p. 34-35.
"For Frances Von Stechow." OP (35) Spr-Sum 83, p. 33.
"June, 1940." OP (35) Spr-Sum 83, p. 36.
"Museum Out of Mind." 13thM (6:1/2) 82, p. 103-104.
"Myopia Makes All Light-Sources Radiant." OP (35) Spr-Sum 83, p. 37.
"Skambha, Guess-Worker, Both Within and Beyond." 13thM (6:1/2) 82, p. 107-108.

PONT, Henri le
See: LePONT, Henri

3532. POOLE, Thomas
"Mules Sometimes." CimR (64) Jl 83, p. 36.

3533. POPE, Dan
"Anglia." Quarry (32:3) Sum 83, p. 67.

3534. POPE, Deborah
"What We Meant to Say." SouthernPR (23:2) Aut 82 [i.e. (23:1?) Spr 83], p. 66-67.

3535. PORTER, Anne
"Cause of Our Joy." Comm (110:20) 18 N 83, p. 633.
"Fire." Comm (110:20) 18 N 83, p. 632.
"From Denver to Albuquerque." Comm (110:14) 12 Ag 83, p. 435.
"Red Sky at Night." Comm (110:20) 18 N 83, p. 633.
"The Vendanger." Comm (110:20) 18 N 83, p. 632.
"Wartime Sunday" (In honor of Eugene Atget, photographer of Paris). Comm (110:20) 18 N 83, p. 632.

3536. PORTER, Helen
"The Remedy." PottPort (5) 83-84, p. 48.

PORTER, Patricia McKenzie
See: McKENZIE-PORTER, Patricia

3537. PORTWOOD, Pamela
"Ashes." MemphisSR (2:2) Spr 82, p. 46-47.
"Origami." MemphisSR (1:2) Spr 81, p. 8.
"The Purple Air." MemphisSR (2:1) Aut 81, p. 52.
"The Voice: Carlos Fuentes on Tape." MemphisSR (3:1) Aut 82, p. 39.
"Waiting." MemphisSR (2:1) Aut 81, p. 52.

3538. POST, Peter
"Katie Burned." Tendril (16) Sum 83, p. 107.

3539. POSTER, Carol
"Bag Ladies Never Beg." Ploughs (9:2/3) 83, p. 182-183.

3540. POTASH, L.
"Final Judgement." SanFPJ (5:3) 83, p. 58-59.
"Statue of Liberty." SanFPJ (5:3) 83, p. 50.
"They Say that They're Good Christians." SanFPJ (4:3) 83, p. 51.

3541. POTTER, Carol
"In the Chair, Root Canal, Day #2." MassR (24:2) Sum 83, p. 305.
"Incident at Port." MinnR (NS 20) Spr 83, p. 26-27.
"Leaping for the Imaginary Fly." MinnR (NS 20) Spr 83, p. 27-28.

3542. POTTER, Jacklyn
"The Little Towns" (tr. of Anne Hébert). StoneC (10:3/4) Spr-Sum 83, p. 21-22.

3543. POTTER, Robin
"Pacing." Quarry (32:1) Wint 83, p. 34.

3544. POTTS, Charles
"A Grudg against Boston." SecC (11:1/2) 83, p. 161.

3545. POULIN, A. (Al), Jr.
"Calco di Cadevere di Donna: Pompeii." DevQ (18:2) Sum 83, p. 80-82.
"The French Notebooks" (Excerpts: "Fragments") (tr. of Rainer Maria Rilke). DevQ (18:2) Sum 83, p. 59-61.
"Saltimbanques." DevQ (18:2) Sum 83, p. 75-77.
"September 1, 1979" (To Basilike). DevQ (18:2) Sum 83, p. 78-79.
"Siamese in Sunlight." MemphisSR (3:2) Spr 83, p. 44-45.
"The Singers" (for W. D. Snodgrass). ChiR (33:3) Wint 83, p. 105-107.

3546. POUND, Omar S.
"The Almshouse." AntigR (54) Sum 83, p. 30-31.
"The Dalai Lama's Appointment." AntigR (54) Sum 83, p. 28.
"Last Night" (tr. of Amir Khusrow Dehlavi). AntigR (55) Aut 83, p. 22.
"Said Wasp to Bee" (tr. of Nosrat Kasemi Mazanderani). AntigR (55) Aut 83, p. 23.
"A Veiled Girl (ca. 1900)" (tr. of Iraj). AntigR (55) Aut 83, p. 22.
"A Witch." AntigR (54) Sum 83, p. 29.

3547. POWELL, Craig
"A Woman at 4 A.M." CanLit (97) Sum 83, p. 74.

3548. POWELL, David B.
"Barn Swallows" (to my brother Darrell). SpiritSH (48) 82, p. 54-55.
"Pie Berries" (from Wyeth Watercolors). SpiritSH (48) 82, p. 55-56.

3549. POWELL, J. A. (James A.)
"Captives." ChiR (33:3) Wint 83, p. 91-93.
"Home Free." Thrpny (4:3, issue 15) Aut 83, p. 8.

3550. POWELL, Richard R.
"I Doubt Meadows." WestCR (18:2) O 83, p. 42.
"Owl Progression." WestCR (18:2) O 83, p. 42.
"Visions of a World." WestCR (18:2) O 83, p. 41.

3551. POWELL, Tony
"Excuses." WormR (23:2, issue 90) 83, p. 43.
"The Lost Senses." WormR (23:2, issue 90) 83, p. 43.
"Waiting in Line at Lenin's Tomb." WormR (23:2, issue 90) 83, p. 43.

3552. POWER, Marjorie
"Through Kitchen Windows." CrabCR (1:1) My 83, p. 26.

3553. POWERS, Richard S.
"Common Grave." WindO (43) Wint 83, p. 8.
"A Tour of the Curse." WindO (43) Wint 83, p. 7.

3554. POWERS, Shirley
"Visiting Hour." YetASM (1:2) 82, p. 10.
"Wisconsin Winter." YetASM (1:2) 82, p. 9.

3555. POYNER, Ken
"Backwaters." PoetL (78:4) Wint 84, p. 214.
"Cooling Passions." WestB (12) 83, p. 59.
"The Farmer's Daughter, the Traveling Salesman." WestHR (37:1) Spr 83, p. 22.
"The Great Fourth of July Parade." WestB (12) 83, p. 58.
"Salvation." WindO (43) Wint 83, p. 24.

3556. POZIER, Bernard
"Emotion Monographe." Os (16) 83, p. 3.

3557. PRATT, Annis
"Lammas Elegy." Prima (8) 83, p. 88.

3558. PRATT, C. W. (Charles W.)
"Band Concert in Regent's Park." LitR (26:3) Spr 83, p. 384.
"Fibonacci Sequence." Comm (110:14) 12 Ag 83, p. 435.
"For My Daughter Coming of Age in the Nuclear Age." HiramPoR (34) Spr-Sum 83, p. 16.
"Relativity" (for Lotte Jacobi). Atlantic (251:1) Ja 83, p. 76.
"Verses to One Rhyme." HiramPoR (34) Spr-Sum 83, p. 17.

3559. PRATT, Claire
"Darkened branch." Quarry (32:3) Sum 83, p. 71.
"Rose petal tellin." Quarry (32:3) Sum 83, p. 71.

3560. PRATT, Gerry (Gerry Dillon)
"Dear Dave Etter." SpoonRQ (8:2) Spr 83, p. 11.
"Dream Suite." Northeast (Ser. 3:15) Sum 83, p. 9.
"I Haven't Forgotten." Northeast (Ser. 3:15) Sum 83, p. 8.

3561. PRATT, Minnie Bruce
"Strange Flesh." NewEng (5:4) Sum 83, p. 611-615.

3562. PRECIOUS, Jocelyn
"If I." Bogg (51) 83, p. 52.

PREE, Don du
See: DuPREE, Don

3563. PREIL, Gabriel
"Between Skirmish and Shadow" (tr. by Gabriel Levin). LitR (26:2) Wint 83, p. 216.
"Jerusalem: Ladders of Love" (tr. by Gabriel Levin). LitR (26:2) Wint 83, p. 216.
"A Summing Up" (tr. by Gabriel Levin). LitR

(26:2) Wint 83, p. 215.
"To Dobbs Ferry with Sylvia Plath" (tr. by Estelle Gilson). NewRena (17) Aut 83, p. 65.
"To Dobbs Ferry with Sylvia Plath (in Hebrew)." NewRena (17) Aut 83, p. 64.
"With Walter and Amati" (tr. by Robert Friend). LitR (26:2) Wint 83, p. 217-218.

3564. PRESS, Marcia
"Need Keeps the Songs Alive." IndR (5:2) Sum 82, p. 46.

3565. PRESTON, Edward
"Naya" (Excerpts: 3, 5, 6, 9-12) (for Stevie Smith). LittleM (14:1/2) 83, p. 104-108.

3566. PRESTON, Kathleen
"Spring." WritersL O 83, p. 9.

3567. PREVERT, Jacques
"Barbara" (from Paroles, tr. by Nancy Johnson). Vis (11) 83, p. 6-7.
"The Laundry" (tr. by Robert Mezey). MemphisSR (3:1) Aut 82, p. 28-30.

3568. PRICE, Alice L.
"Massacre at Marais Des Cygnes." LittleBR (3:4) Sum 83, p. 20.

3569. PRICE, Charles
"A Night on the Town." SecC (11:1/2) 83, p. 164.
"A Poem for Captian Cool." SecC (11:1/2) 83, p. 163.

3570. PRICE, Gale
"Lammas, 1984." SanFPJ (5:4) 83, p. 85-86.

3571. PRICE, Reynolds
"Ambrosia." Poetry (143:2) N 83, p. 90-92.

3572. PRICE-ROUSH, Joy L.
"Let's Pretend." SanFPJ (5:1) 83, p. 34-35.

3573. PRIEST, Robert
"Poem for a Tall Woman." PoetryCR (5:1) Aut 83, p. 15.

3574. PRINCIPE, Luis
"El Cometa" (al científico). Rácata (2) 83, p. 89.
"Latente." Rácata (2) 83, p. 90.

3575. PRINTZ-PAHLSON, Göran
"Comedians" (for Kenneth Koch) ChiR (33:3) Wint 83, p. 100-101.

3576. PRIORE, Allan
"Virginia Woolf." Tendril (14/15) Wint 83, p. 156.

PRISCO, Joseph di
See: Di PRISCO, Joseph

PRITCHETT, Sharon Newton
See: NEWTON-PRITCHETT, Sharon

3577. PRIVETT, Katharine
"Sign Language." Sam (36:3 143rd release) 83, p. 45.

3578. PROBECK, William R.
"All But the Wedding" (for John). YetASM (2:1) 83, p. 5.

3579. PROCHASKA, Robert
"Anniversary of Words." SanFPJ (4:3) 83, p. 53.
"To Here and Back." MoodySI (12) Aut 82, p. 21.

3580. PROPPER, Dan
"A Chagall (#1)." SecC (11:1/2) 83, p. 165.
"For Kerouac in Heaven." MoodySI (3) Wint 79, p. 7.

3581. PROSPERE, Susan
"Affinities." Poetry (142:2) My 83, p. 96.
"Ministering Angels." Poetry (142:2) My 83, p. 99-100.
"Oxford, on an Ancient Crossroads Beside the Thames." Poetry (142:2) My 83, p. 97-98.

3582. PROST, R.
"Garden." WormR (23:2, issue 90) 83, p. 71.
"Touch." WormR (23:2, issue 90) 83, p. 70.

3583. PROVOST, Sarah
"The Namer." MichQR (22:4) Aut 83, p. 618.
"The Orphans Construct." HolCrit (20:1) F 83, p. 20.
"Why Standing Still Was a Lot Like Walking, Walking Like Letting Go." PraS (57:4) Wint 83, p. 57.

3584. PRUNTY, Wyatt
"Mother and Spring." Ploughs (9:2/3) 83, p. 172-173.
"Our Neighbor." Ploughs (9:2/3) 83, p. 171.

PUENTES de OYENARD, Sylvia
See: OYENARD, Sylvia Puentes de

3585. PUGHE, Bronwyn G.
"Green Snakes and Wolves." ThRiPo (19/20) 82, p. 52.

3586. PUIG, Salvador
"Historias." Areíto (9:35) 83, p. 38.

3587. PUIGDOLLERS, Carmen
"Con Nombre" (A Nilita: mi meditación por su ausencia). SinN (13:3) Abril-Junio 83, p. 49-51.

3588. PULTZ, Constance
"Alumnus at the Window" (University Club, 1982). StoneC (10:3/4) Spr-Sum 83, p. 39.
"Hospital Room." NegC (3:4) Aut 83, p. 72-75.
"Porcus Porcellus." StoneC (10:3/4) Spr-Sum 83, p. 38.
"Psychology." CrabCR (1:2) Aut 83, p. 8.

3589. PURDY, Al
"For Eurithe." PoetryCR (4:3) Spr 83, p. 6.
"In Cabbagetown." PoetryCR (4:4) Sum 83, p. 6.
"In Cabbagetown." PoetryCR (5:1) Aut 83, p. 19.

3590. PURDY, Brian
"Letter to a Quasi-Fictional Former Self." PoetryCR (4:3) Spr 83, p. 13.
"Poem to be Placed in a Property-owner's Mailbox." CrossC (5:1) 83, p. 12.

3591. PURDY, Nigel
"After This." Stand (24:3) 83, p. 4.
"The Field." Stand (24:3) 83, p. 4.

3592. PURENS, Ilmars
"First Snow." Kayak (61) Ap 83, p. 26-27.

3593. PURSER, Ralph, Jr.
"Niger." KanQ (15:1) Wint 83, p. 119.

3594. PURSIFULL, Carmen M.
"Going for the Land of the Living." RevChic (11:2) Sum 83, p. 47.
"Papá" (In memory of my father, Pedro C. Padilla). RevChic (11:2) Sum 83, p. 45-46.
"The Poltergeist." RevChic (11:2) Sum 83, p. 44.

3595. PUSKULLUOGLU, Ali
"Autumn (Guz)" (tr. by Ozcan Yalim, William D. Fielder and Dionis Coffin Riggs). SpiritSH (48) 82, p. 48.
"Hills (Tepeler)" (tr. by Ozcan Yalim, William D. Fielder and Dionis Coffin Riggs). SpiritSH (48) 82, p. 48.
"The Poet (Ozan)" (tr. by Ozcan Yalim, William D. Fielder and Dionis Coffin Riggs). SpiritSH (48) 82, p. 48.
"Summer (Yaz)" (tr. by Ozcan Yalim, William D. Fielder and Dionis Coffin Riggs). SpiritSH (48) 82, p. 48.

3596. PUTNAM, Robert
"A Sparrow." CrabCR (1:1) My 83, p. 19.

3597. PUTNEY, David
"The Branch" (tr. of Octavio Paz). IndR (6:3) Sum 83, p. 30.

3598. PYE, Virginia
"Adam Climbing Mount Pisgah." NewRena (17) Aut 83, p. 103.
"Stepping Back." NewRena (17) Aut 83, p. 102-103.

3599. PYLE, John V.
"Thank You." EngJ (72:2) F 83, p. 104.

3600. PYTKO, J. F.
Mise un Scene." SanFPJ (4:4) 83, p. 54-55.

3601. QUALLS, Betty
"A Contagious Person." Wind (13:48) 83, p. 61.

3602. QUASIMODO, Salvatore
"Again a Green River" (tr. by W. A. Fahey). WebR (8:1) Spr 83, p. 57.

3603. QUETCHENBACH, Bernard
"Acid Rain." Blueline (4:1) Sum-Aut 82, p. 30.

3604. QUINN, Carol A.
"All Hallow's Eve." NegC (3:4) Aut 83, p. 131.

3605. QUINN, Doris Kerns
"Time's End." Wind (13:48) 83, p. 50-51.

3606. QUINN, John (See also: QUINN, John Robert)
"Things I Didn't Tell Madjid." ThRiPo (21/22) 83, p. 65.

3607. QUINN, John Robert (See also: QUINN, John)
"A Day in Pennsylvania." Wind (13:49) 83, p. 5.
"Farm Gate." SpiritSH (49) 83, p. 29.
"Measurements." Wind (13:49) 83, p. 39.
"Notes for a Sonnet." SpiritSH (49) 83, p. 29.
"Ohio Woodland." SpiritSH (49) 83, p. 30.
"Pears Falling on a Tin Roof." ChrC (100:33) 9 N 83, p. 1004.
"Picnic." PoNow (7:2, #38) 83, p. 20.
"Such Small Things." ChrC (100:12 [i.e. 13]) 27 Ap 83, p. 402.
"This Evening As Usual." SpoonRQ (8:4) Aut 83, p. 56.
"Time Loves a Hedgerow." SpiritSH (48) 82, p. 41.

3608. QUINTANA PIGNO, Antonia
"December's Picture" (for Felix). KanQ (15:1) Wint 83, p. 117-118.
"Isleta." RevChic (11:3/4) 83, p. 67-70.
"Verano." KanQ (15:1) Wint 83, p. 117.

3609. QUINTERO, Salomón
"Esquinas." Metam (4:2/5:1) 82-83, p. 58.
"Oficio." Metam (4:2/5:1) 82-83, p. 57.
"El Terrorista." Metam (4:2/5:1) 82-83, p. 55.

3610. R. C. (See also: CLOKE, Richard [?])
"1300 billion gov. debt." SanFPJ (5:4) 83, p. 69.
"About 5 billion people on earth." SanFPJ (5:4) 83, p. 43.
"As to who's most likely to launch a first strike." SanFPJ (5:3) 83, p. 49.
"Been eating an apple a day." SanFPJ (5:2) 83, p. 16.
"Blacks, women now wictims of double-reverse discrimination." SanFPJ (5:2) 83, p. 41.
"Border between Honduras and Nicaragua." SanFPJ (5:3) 83, p. 74.
"Cost of Living up 3.5%." SanFPJ (5:3) 83, p. 41.

"Depends on who pilfers." SanFPJ (5:3) 83, p. 34.
"Enter the chambers of darkness." SanFPJ (5:3) 83, p. 38.
"Feynman domains are two dimensional." SanFPJ (5:4) 83, p. 35.
"First they stole money." SanFPJ (5:4) 83, p. 76.
"Former CIA director Colby." SanFPJ (5:4) 83, p. 31.
"Goethe once said." SanFPJ (5:3) 83, p. 66.
"Got a job last week." SanFPJ (5:4) 83, p. 37.
"Great publicity about the holocaust." SanFPJ (5:2) 83, p. 59.
"Hard times not only means no money." SanFPJ (5:3) 83, p. 35.
"Having weapons you can never use." SanFPJ (5:2) 83, p. 29.
"Hot shit!" SanFPJ (5:4) 83, p. 39.
"How to fix the Dow." SanFPJ (5:4) 83, p. 79.
"I don't want to hear about nuclear bombs." SanFPJ (5:1) 83, p. 72.
"I hitched a ride with an errant neutrino." SanFPJ (5:1) 83, p. 95.
"If merit pay's to be the rule." SanFPJ (5:4) 83, p. 83.
"Jake's wife left him." SanFPJ (5:4) 83, p. 24.
"James Watt says that we are God's chosen people." SanFPJ (5:2) 83, p. 11.
"Just think we now have the power." SanFPJ (5:3) 83, p. 53.
"A move by Senate body to increase health insurance." SanFPJ (5:4) 83, p. 50.
"New dictator in Guatemala." SanFPJ (5:4) 83, p. 11.
"New law in Germany." SanFPJ (5:3) 83, p. 13.
"Not wild about the gringos." SanFPJ (5:2) 83, p. 50.
"Obliterate earth and what have you got?" SanFPJ (5:1) 83, p. 88.
"On the other hand." SanFPJ (5:1) 83, p. 80.
"Pershing and cruise missles." SanFPJ (5:3) 83, p. 78.
"Sincere Liars." SanFPJ (5:3) 83, p. 19.
"Social security funds are held in Trust by the government." SanFPJ (5:4) 83, p. 63.
"Something worse than being old or poor." SanFPJ (5:4) 83, p. 90.
"SS may be cut off at 67 years." SanFPJ (5:3) 83, p. 30.
"There is always an undercurrent of hysteria." SanFPJ (5:1) 83, p. 66.
"Thirteen pious women." SanFPJ (5:2) 83, p. 24.
"Those who devise our nuclear weapons." SanFPJ (5:3) 83, p. 73.
"U.S. troops maneuver in Central America." SanFPJ (5:3) 83, p. 75.
"US aid to Somozista rebels." SanFPJ (5:3) 83, p. 91.
"US will not police the world." SanFPJ (5:4) 83, p. 27.
"Very simple: 1 - 1 = 2." SanFPJ (5:3) 83, p. 54.
"Watch out when they attack the bureaucrats." SanFPJ (5:4) 83, p. 89.

"We're a nuclear family." SanFPJ (5:2) 83, p. 6.
"When a politician says 'I hate war'." SanFPJ (5:3) 83, p. 52.
"When fleets converge." SanFPJ (5:4) 83, p. 59.
"When from the mystery of comparative secureness." SanFPJ (5:3) 83, p. 22.

3611. RAAB, Lawrence
"Letter Home." AmerS (52:2) Spr 83, p. 192.
"Listening to a Certain Song." ParisR (25:89) Aut 83, p. 132-133.
"Other Children." Poetry (142:3) Je 83, p. 125-130.
"The Witch's Story." NewYorker (59:37) 31 O 83, p. 42.

3612. RABBITT, Thomas
"Christmas Gifts." BlackWR (10:1) Aut 83, p. 166-167.
"Losses." BlackWR (10:1) Aut 83, p. 170.
"September 1, 1983." BlackWR (10:1) Aut 83, p. 168.
"Timber Sales." BlackWR (10:1) Aut 83, p. 165.
"Tortoise." BlackWR (10:1) Aut 83, p. 169.
"Your Father's Watch." Ploughs (9:2/3) 83, p. 177.

3613. RABOFF, Paul
"Altar." MichQR (22:3) Sum 83, p. 446.

3614. RABONI, Giovanni
"Afterward" (tr. by Stuart Friebert and Vinio Rossi). Field (29) Aut 83, p. 82.
"The Apartment" (tr. by Stuart Friebert and Vinio Rossi). Field (29) Aut 83, p. 79.
"False and Tendentious News" (tr. by Stuart Friebert and Vinio Rossi). Field (29) Aut 83, p. 77-78.
"From the Altar in the Shadows" (tr. by Vinio Rossi and Stuart Friebert). DevQ (18:2) Sum 83, p. 63.
"Hospital Interns" (For Bartolo Cattafi) (tr. by Stuart Friebert and Vinio Rossi). Field (29) Aut 83, p. 80-81.
"Otherwise" (tr. by Vinio Rossi and Stuart Friebert). PoNow (7:2, #38) 83, p. 45.

3615. RABORG, Frederick A., Jr.
"Curiosity." PortR (29:1) 83, p. 50.
"Eating Out." Tendril (16) Sum 83, p. 108.
"Looking toward Manhattan." SanFPJ (5:1) 83, p. 42.
"Mummy Wrap." PortR (29:1) 83, p. 20-22.
"Taking Care of Dad." Wind (13:48) 83, p. 52-53.
"VJ Day, Portsmouth: Joy." CapeR (18:2) Sum 83, p. 30-31.

3616. RACHEL, Naomi
"Joyce & the Poem." Outbr (12/13) Aut 83-Spr 84, p. 78.
"The Saint." Outbr (12/13) Aut 83-Spr 84, p. 80.
"Scapegoat." Outbr (12/13) Aut 83-Spr 84, p. 77.
"Simon the Super-Realist." Outbr (12/13) Aut 83-Spr 84, p. 79.

3617. RADIN, Doris
"The Generations." MinnR (NS 21) Aut 83, p. 34-35.
"Hymn to Rivka's Forehead." MinnR (NS 21) Aut 83, p. 35-36.
"Rivka Reveals the Facts of Life." MinnR (NS 21) Aut 83, p. 36-37.

3618. RADNER, Rebecca
"The Second Waitress." NewL (50:1) Aut 83, p. 68-69.

3619. RADNOTI, Miklos
"Razglednica" (tr. by Jascha Kessler). PoNow (7:2, #38) 83, p. 45.

3620. RADU, Kenneth
"Adele Hugo: after Truffaut's Film." Quarry (32:4) Aut 83, p. 17-18.
"Demonstration in Quebec City: Jan. 30/83." AntigR (55) Aut 83, p. 97.
"Objectivity." AntigR (55) Aut 83, p. 98.

3621. RAE, Simon
"Chestnuts." Argo (5:1) 83, p. 9.

3622. RAFFA, Joseph
"Before the Night." SanFPJ (4:4) 83, p. 9.

3623. RAFFEL, Burton
"Summer Morality." StoneC (10:3/4) Spr-Sum 83, p. 23.
"There Are Ways." StoneC (11:1/2, Pt. 1) Aut-Wint 83, p. 39.

3624. RAGLAND, Cindy
"Small Town Girls." Calyx (8:1) Aut 83, p. 16.

3625. RAINE, Craig
"Beware the Vibes of Marx." Agni (18) 83, p. 30.
"The Grey Boy." PartR (50:2) 83, p. 240-242.
"The Grocer." Agni (18) 83, p. 29.
"In the Kalahari Desert." Agni (18) 83, p. 31-33.
"A Martian Sends a Postcard Home." Agni (18) 83, p. 26-27.
"Sexual Couplets." Agni (18) 83, p. 28.

3626. RAKOSI, Carl
"I Was Listening to Jean Redpath." DevQ (18:3) Aut 83, p. 59.
"Making an Apocalypse." DevQ (18:3) Aut 83, p. 60.

3627. RAMASWAMI, M. S.
"My Little World" (tr. of Gnanakoothan). Stand (24:1) 82-83, p. 43.
"Step Aside" (tr. of Nakulan). Stand (24:1) 82-83, p. 45.
"Swaha" (tr. of Nakulan). Stand (24:1) 82-83, p. 45.
"These Are the People" (tr. of Nakulan). Stand (24:1) 82-83, p. 44.

RAMIREZ BERG, Charles
See: BERG, Charles Ramirez

3628. RAMKE, Bin
"Another Small Town in Georgia." Ploughs (9:2/3) 83, p. 100.
"Bathing Boys." Ploughs (9:2/3) 83, p. 101.
"The Facts of Life." Paint (10:19/20) Spr-Aut 83, p. 22.
"A Nod toward True Love and Fidelity." OhioR (30) 83, p. 35.
"Syllogism." GeoR (37:1) Spr 83, p. 128.
"Tourists and Bad Weather." Paint (10:19/20) Spr-Aut 83, p. 23.
"Westminster Chimes." OhioR (30) 83, p. 34.

3629. RAMOS OTERO, Manuel
"Epitafios." SinN (13:3) Abril-Junio 83, p. 60-63.

3630. RAMSEY, Anthony
"The Limits of Cartology." PoetryCR (4:3) Spr 83, p. 15.

3631. RAMSEY, Mark
"In - com - mu - ni - ca - do (Sp.) of a Prisoner, Deprived of Communication with Other People." Meadows (4:1) 83, p. 27.

3632. RAMSEY, Paul
"As in Paradise" (suggested by parts of Petrarch's Sonnet 98). Ploughs (9:2/3) 83, p. 18.
"Smoke." FourQt (32:3) Spr 83, p. 12.

3633. RANDALL, David
"Reprise." SanFPJ (4:4) 83, p. 87.

3634. RANDALL, Dudley
"Be Kind to Me." BlackALF (17:4) Wint 83, p. 168.
"For Kim." BlackALF (17:4) Wint 83, p. 169.
"For Vivian." BlackALF (17:4) Wint 83, p. 170.
"The Girls in Booths." BlackALF (17:4) Wint 83, p. 170.
"Motown Polka." BlackALF (17:4) Wint 83, p. 168.
"Old Detroit" (For Sister Barbara Johns). BlackALF (17:4) Wint 83, p. 168.
"Silly Jim" (After Mother Goose). BlackALF (17:4) Wint 83, p. 169.
"To Poets Who Preach in Prose." BlackALF (17:4) Wint 83, p. 169.
"Woman of Ghana." BlackALF (17:4) Wint 83, p. 169.

3635. RANDALL, Margaret
"Yesterday's Rain Is Not Today's." Calyx (8:1) Aut 83, p. 38.

3636. RANDALL-MILLS, Elizabeth
"Alone." SpiritSH (49) 83, p. 22.
"Now." SpiritSH (49 Suppl.) 83, p. 33.

RANGANATHAN, R.
See: GNANAKOOTHAN

3637. RANGEL, Rubén
"Corrido de Rudy Lozano." Metam (4:2/5:1) 82-83, p. 54.

3638. RANKIN, Paula
"The Dolls." MemphisSR (1:2) Spr 81, p. 24.
"Glossolalia." MissouriR (7:1) Aut 83, p. 44-46.
"On Possibilities." ThRiPo (21/22) 83, p. 66.
"Somewhere Else." QW (16) Spr-Sum 83, p. 114.
"Stigmata." MemphisSR (1:2) Spr 81, p. 25.

3639. RANKIN, Rush
"Husband." Stand (24:2) 83, p. 40-41.

3640. RANNIT, Aleksis
"I hear your tiny cyprinoid fish" (written on reading James Still's poem 'Leap, Minnows Leap'). Wind (13:48) 83, p. 54.

3641. RANSOM, Cherra S.
"After Armageddon." AntigR (52) Wint 83, p. 100.

3642. RANSOM, John Crowe
"The Eye Can Tell." SouthernR (19:4) O 83, p. 836-837.

3643. RAPOPORT, Larry
"Walt Whitman Faints in the Vegetable Garden." YetASM (1:2) 82, p. 6.

3644. RATCLIFFE, Stephen
"Highway 56." PoNow (7:2, #38) 83, p. 21.

3645. RATNER, Rochelle
"Wednesday at the Wall." Confr (25/26) 83, p. 89.

3646. RATZLAFF, Keith
"Armstice Day." PoetryNW (24:2) Sum 83, p. 11.
"Displacement." Kayak (61) Ap 83, p. 44.
"Driving at the Edge of Winter." IndR (5:1) Wint 82, p. 5.
"The Hawks We Have Never Seen." Wind (13:47) 83, p. 49.
"Pig Drive." KanQ (15:2) Spr 83, p. 155.
"Solstice." SouthernPR (23:2) Aut 83, p. 26.

3647. RAULERSON, Robert
"35 Dead Haitians." SanFPJ (4:2) 83, p. 70.
"Looking for the Mushroom." SanFPJ (4:2) 83, p. 12.

3648. RAVICZ, Tanyo
"The Falling Out." HarvardA (117:2) My 83, p. 23.
"Homage to the Avant-Garde." HarvardA (117:3) Aut 83, p. 14.

3649. RAVIKOVITCH, Dahlia
"Deep Calleth unto Deep" (tr. by Chana Bloch).

LitR (26:2) Wint 83, p. 261.
"The Everlasting Forests" (tr. by Chana Bloch). LitR (26:2) Wint 83, p. 258.
"The Horns of Hittin" (tr. by Chana Bloch). LitR (26:2) Wint 83, p. 260-261.
"King over Israel" (tr. by Chana Bloch). LitR (26:2) Wint 83, p. 259.
"Requiem After Seventeen Years" (tr. by Chana Bloch). LitR (26:2) Wint 83, p. 256.
"Two Songs of the Garden" (tr. by Chana Bloch). LitR (26:2) Wint 83, p. 257-258.

3650. RAY, Daniel G.
"Jazz." Bluebuf (2:1) Aut 83, p. 29.
"Mask." Bluebuf (2:1) Aut 83, p. 7.

3651. RAY, David
"Agra near the Taj." MissouriR (7:1) Aut 83, p. 40-42.
"The Cathedral." CharR (9:1) Spr 83, p. 6-7.
"The Child's Concept of Aging" (found poem, from a University of Missouri Education Dept. disseration). Kayak (63) N 83, p. 30.
"Extreme Unction in Pa." NewL (49:3/4) Spr-Sum 83, p. 55.
"La Familia de Pescadores." CharR (9:1) Spr 83, p. 5-6.
"The Ganges at Dawn." SouthernPR (23:2) Aut 83, p. 32-33.
"Heading South along the Nebraska Border." Iowa (13:2) Spr 82, p. 108.
"In Bombay." MissouriR (6:2) Wint 83, p. 84.
"Mother in Phoenix, 1950." Confr (25/26) 83, p. 274-275.
"The Optometrist." CharR (9:2) Aut 83, p. 78-80.
"A Round-The-World Balloon." CharR (9:2) Aut 83, p. 80-81.
"A Statue of Gandhiji." PoetryE (11) Sum 83, p. 81.
"The Telephone." PoNow (7:2, #38) 83, p. 20.
"Throwing the Racetrack Cats at Saratoga." Iowa (13:2) Spr 82, p. 109-110.
"Toffee Cantata." CharR (9:2) Aut 83, p. 81-82.

3652. RAY, Judy
"Rose Bay Willow Herb." NewL (49:3/4) Spr-Sum 83, p. 58-59.

3653. REA, Susan Irene
"Patterns." FourQt (32:3) Spr 83, p. 28.

3654. REAGLER, Robin Lee
"A Launched Bomb Is Immutable." SanFPJ (5:2) 83, p. 9.

3655. REANEY, James
"Animated Film, a Sequence of Emblem Poems." Descant (42) Aut 83, p. 29-33.
"Triads I." Descant (42) Aut 83, p. 26-27.
"Triads II." Descant (42) Aut 83, p. 28.

3656. REARDON, Patrick
"The Bullet Enters Lincoln's Skull." Tele (18) 83, p. 49.
"Let Me Tell You of My Illness." Tele (18) 83, p. 48.
"Providence." StoneC (10:3/4) Spr-Sum 83, p. 56.
"Two Deaths." Wind (13:49) 83, p. 39.

3657. REBELSKY, Freda
"Summer Collecting, On-Island." StoneC (10:3/4) Spr-Sum 83, p. 79.

3658. RECTOR, K. K.
"Demoiselle." ConcPo (16:1) Spr 83, p. 85.

3659. RECTOR, Liam
"An Origin of A-R-T." ParisR (25:87) Spr 83, p. 198-199.

3660. REDEL, Victoria
"Third Unit, State Hospital." NewEngR (6:1) Aut 83, p. 110-111.

3661. REDGROVE, Peter
"Hieroglyph." Argo (4:1) 82, p. 16.
"The Idea of Entropy at Maenporth Beach" (To John Layard). ManhatR (3:1) Sum 83, p. 51-52.
"Lesson on the Banjo." Descant (40) Spr 83, p. 60-61.
"Or Was That When I Was Grass." ManhatR (3:1) Sum 83, p. 52-53.
"Paper Door." Descant (40) Spr 83, p. 58-59.
"The Volets." Argo (4:1) 82, p. 14.

3662. REDL-HLUS, Carolyn D.
"Wheeling." Bluebuf (2:1) Aut 83, p. 14.

3663. REDMAN, Blanche
"The Visit." DekalbLAJ (16:1/4) Aut 82-Sum 83, p. 70.

3664. REDMOND, Chris
"Postscript." Bogg (50) 83, p. 38.

3665. REED, Alison
"Poetry Out of Almost Stone." StoneC (10:3/4) Spr-Sum 83, p. 32-33.

3666. REED, Crystal
"Pictures on the Roof." MSS (2:3) Sum 83, p. 138.
"Schoolyard." MSS (2:3) Sum 83, p. 137.

3667. REED, Jeremy
"Riddles." MalR (64) F 83, p. 189.

3668. REED, John R.
"Chopin." LittleM (14:1/2) 83, p. 125-126.
"Dusk at Verrazano Narrows." FourQt (32:3) Spr 83, p. 12.
"Morning Paper Route--January, 1953." KanQ (15:1)

Wint 83, p. 61.
"Old Loves." LittleM (14:1/2) 83, p. 123-124.
"Paestum." ParisR (25:89) Aut 83, p. 130.
"The Sniper." SanFPJ (4:4) 83, p. 61-62.
"Trash." TriQ (56) Wint 83, p. 158.
"An Unguided Tour" (a suite on Dante's Inferno). NewOR (10:2/3) Sum-Aut 83, p. 15-19.

3669. REED, Judith
"The Looking Glass." Germ (7:1) Spr-Sum 83, p. 29.
"Poem: My pain is my mentor." Germ (7:1) Spr-Sum 83, p. 30.

3670. REED, Louis
"Sweet Jane." HarvardA (117:3) Aut 83, p. 11.

3671. REES, Elizabeth
"The 75 Year Old Sabbath Queen." PartR (50:4) 83, p. 588-589.
"A Topography of Anguish." Wind (13:49) 83, p. 40.

3672. REES, Ennis
"The Low Country." SouthernR (19:2) Ap 83, p. 401-402.

3673. REEVE, F. D.
"The Last Rose" (tr. of Anna Akhmatova). Nat (237:12) 22 O 83, p. 379.
"Nightway." KanQ (15:4) Aut 83, p. 42-47.
"What Color Is the Sun?" WestHR (37:1) Spr 83, p. 52.

3674. REIBSTEIN, R. (Regina)
"February Bud." Poem (49) N 83, p. 28.
"Grown Children." SouthwR (68:1) Wint 83, p. 66.
"The Heart Has Reasons." SoDakR (21:3) Aut 83, p. 96.
"I Have Been Careful." Poem (49) N 83, p. 29.
"My Father Loved Me Once." Poem (49) N 83, p. 27.

3675. REICH, Asher
"Bat Sheba" (tr. by Gabriel Levin). LitR (26:2) Wint 83, p. 262.
"Our Blood is the Petrol of the World" (tr. by Gabriel Levin). LitR (26:2) Wint 83, p. 262.
"Somewhere" (tr. by Gabriel Levin). LitR (26:2) Wint 83, p. 263.

3676. REICHOW, V. L.
"Les Etrangers." IndR (5:2) Sum 82, p. 19.
"The Step-Father." IndR (5:2) Sum 82, p. 18.

3677. REID, Jeffrey
"Sacrilege, Sacre Coeur." CrossC (5:2/3) 83, p. 21.

3678. REID, Monty
"Chimes." Dandel (10:2) Aut-Wint 83, p. 59.
"The Dream of the Snowy Owls." CapilR (26) 83, p. 4-9.
"Feb. 12." Bluebuf (2:1) Aut 83, p. 27.

"For a Daughter." PoetryCR (4:4) Sum 83, p. 7.
"For the Wed." PoetryCR (5:2) Wint 83-84, p. 16.
"Snowfall." Bluebuf (2:1) Aut 83, p. 27.
"Sweet Tooth." Grain (11:1) F 83, p. 9.
"Walking Tour." Bluebuf (2:1) Aut 83, p. 18-19.

3679. REID, Robin Anne
"Bus Trip." YetASM (1:2) 82, p. 3.
"Turning of the Season." YetASM (1:2) 82, p. 8.

3680. REIMAN, Susan
"Eating at the Elephant Burial Ground." US1 (16/17) Wint 83-84, p. 6.

3681. REINER, Gary York
"The Death of Bartok." ThirdW Spr 83, p. 125.
"The Death of Dylan Thomas." ThirdW Spr 83, p. 120.
"The Death of Faith: Ellington and Coltrane." ThirdW Spr 83, p. 132.
"The Death of Forster." ThirdW Spr 83, p. 129.
"The Death of Hammerskojld." ThirdW Spr 83, p. 131.
"The Death of Housman." ThirdW Spr 83, p. 130.
"The Death of Kafka." ThirdW Spr 83, p. 126.
"The Death of Lenin." ThirdW Spr 83, p. 122-123.
"The Death of Mandelstam." ThirdW Spr 83, p. 121.
"The Death of Mozart." ThirdW Spr 83, p. 121.
"The Death of Saul Alinsky." ThirdW Spr 83, p. 124.
"The Death of Thurber." ThirdW Spr 83, p. 127.
"The Death of Virginia Woolf." ThirdW Spr 83, p. 128.

3682. REINSBERG, Carol
"A Thank-You Note to My Student." EngJ (72:7) N 83, p. 82.

3683. REISS, James
"Rimsky, Nijinsky, and a Pile of Wet Blankets." NewL (49:3/4) Spr-Sum 83, p. 162.

3684. REITER, Thomas
"Burning through the Winter." NowestR (21:2/3) 83, p. 75.
"Diamond Ohio Matches." QW (16) Spr-Sum 83, p. 128.

3685. REITZ, Del
"After the Bomb." SanFPJ (5:4) 83, p. 92.
"Anniversary Sermon" (My Lai, 3/16/68). SanFPJ (5:1) 83, p. 90.
"Balanced." SanFPJ (4:2) 83, p. 69.
"Cold and Hungry." SanFPJ (4:4) 83, p. 16.
"Coming of Age" (When the visit was expected). SanFPJ (4:3) 83, p. 34.
"Fish Story." SanFPJ (4:3) 83, p. 33.
"Flowers for the Baby." SanFPJ (4:4) 83, p. 14-15.
"Lubricant." SanFPJ (5:2) 83, p. 73.
"Mars Brew." SanFPJ (5:4) 83, p. 65.
"Safe." SanFPJ (4:2) 83, p. 22.
"Smoke Chains." SanFPJ (4:4) 83, p. 58.
"There Can Be No Garbage." SanFPJ (4:4) 83, p. 59.
"Unemployed." SanFPJ (4:4) 83, p. 13.

"Unrequited." SanFPJ (4:2) 83, p. 23.

3686. RENNER-TANA, Patti
"Countdown at Ground Zero." SanFPJ (4:2) 83, p. 40.
"The Machine." SanFPJ (4:2) 83, p. 40.
"Resolution." SanFPJ (5:2) 83, p. 85.

3687. REPP, John
"Peas." KanQ (15:1) Wint 83, p. 178.
"Reading the Confucian Odes on a Cement Patio." Vis (12) 83, p. 6.
"Working for the Summit" (For Ted Kremer). Blueline (4:1) Sum-Aut 82, p. 18.

3688. RESINA, Juan Ramón
"Ciclos." Inti (15) Spr 82, p. 70-72.
"Verano en la Ciudad." Inti (15) Spr 82, p. 72.

3689. RETALLACK, Joan
"Murder Mystery." LittleM (14:1/2) 83, p. 14-15.

3690. REVARD, Carter
"Outside in Oxford." WestCR (17:4) Ap 83, p. 32-33.
"Outside in St. Louis." WestCR (17:4) Ap 83, p. 33-35.
"To the Muse in Oklahoma." WestCR (17:4) Ap 83, p. 35-36.

3691. REVELL, Donald
"Graves in East Tennessee." BlackWR (9:1) Aut 82, p. 100-101.
"Gymnopedie: the Exhibition." NewEngR (5:3) Spr 83, p. 339-340.
"Near Life." BlackWR (9:1) Aut 82, p. 102.

3692. REWA, Michael
"Cleaning a Spring." Blueline (4:1) Sum-Aut 82, p. 26-27.
"Naming Creatures from a Porch in the Country." Blueline (3:2) Wint-Spr 82, p. 42.

3693. REWAK, William J.
"The Orphan Bear." KanQ (15:3) Sum 83, p. 67.

REX, Marguerite Beck
See: BECK-REX, Marguerite

3694. REXROTH, Kenneth
"Bride and groom." OhioR (30) 83, p. 124.
"Four Poems Written in Kyoto." OhioR (30) 83, p. 124.
"Hototogisu -- horobirete." OhioR (30) 83, p. 124.
"Late Spring." OhioR (30) 83, p. 124.
"Only the sea mist." OhioR (30) 83, p. 124.

3695. REYES, Carlos
"Poem for Seven Years" (for Karen). CrabCR (1:2) Aut 83, p. 12.
"The Spanish Poet." MinnR (NS 20) Spr 83, p. 48.

3696. REYES, Ellen
"The Palladium View." Wind (13:49) 83, p. 41-42.
"The Rabbit Laughs." Wind (13:49) 83, p. 41.

3697. REYES, Sandra
"The Rat" (tr. of Manuel Silva). NewOR (10:2/3) Sum-Aut 83, p. 78.

3698. REYNOLDS, Diane
"The Case of the Loaded Beam's a Familiar One." Nimrod (27:1) Aut-Wint 83, p. 62-63.
"Coming in from the Rain." Nimrod (27:1) Aut-Wint 83, p. 59.

3699. REYNOLDS, Richard
"Point Pleasant." HiramPoR (34) Spr-Sum 83, p. 18.

3700. REZMERSKI, John Calvin
"Male Chauvinist Roadside Pig." ThRiPo (21/22) 83, p. 67.

3701. RHENISCH, Harold
"Spring Wood." CanLit (98) Aut 83, p. 34.
"Stone." CanLit (98) Aut 83, p. 34.

3702. RHODES, Mary
"Blending Auras." EngJ (72:2) F 83, p. 78.

3703. RIBOVICH, John
"The Children's Crusade." Poem (47) Mr 83, p. 61.
"Mother and Son." Poem (47) Mr 83, p. 62.

3704. RICE, Chris
"You Do Not Know." Stand (24:3) 83, p. 5.

3705. RICE, Paul
"For My Unborn." DekalbLAJ (16:1/4) Aut 82-Sum 83, p. 71.

3706. RICH, Adrienne
"Trying to Talk with a Man." OhioR (30) 83, p. 32-33.

3707. RICHARDS, G. D.
"The Snag." NegC (3:4) Aut 83, p. 65.

3708. RICHARDSON, James
"Compositae." Shen (34:1) 83, p. 90.
"Ending an End." Shen (34:1) 83, p. 89.
"Have It Your Way." Shen (34:1) 83, p. 87-88.
"Lines Separated by Years." Shen (34:1) 83, p. 88.

3709. RICHMOND, Kevin
"Full Circle." Bogg (51) 83, p. 60.
"Natural Rhythm." Bogg (50) 83, p. 58.
"Tiger Tiger." Bogg (50) 83, p. 35.

3710. RICHMOND, Steve
"1 a: I would rather write badly and have fun." WormR (23:3, issue 91) 83, p. 107.

"The cat had the orange and black striped butterfly." WormR (23:3, issue 91) 83, p. 104.
"Fan." WormR (23:3, issue 91) 83, p. 113.
"Gagaku." SecC (11:1/2) 83, p. 183.
"Gagaku: A touch of hysteria." WormR (23:3, issue 91) 83, p. 93.
"Gagaku: I fed the sparrows this morning." WormR (23:3, issue 91) 83, p. 97.
"Gagaku: I have not written." WormR (23:3, issue 91) 83, p. 105.
"Gagaku: I like it more when my lines move about the page." WormR (23:3, issue 91) 83, p. 100.
"Gagaku: I like things that are bashed in on their right." WormR (23:3, issue 91) 83, p. 90.
"Gagaku: I like to beat on a drum." WormR (23:3, issue 91) 83, p. 91-92.
"Gagaku: I still put wild bird see out." WormR (23:3, issue 91) 83, p. 95.
"Gagaku: I think I've lost it." WormR (23:3, issue 91) 83, p. 101.
"Gagaku: I was sent to clean out a dead woman's apartment." WormR (23:3, issue 91) 83, p. 97.
"Gagaku: I watch them dance." WormR (23:3, issue 91) 83, p. 92.
"Gagaku: I'd call more women." WormR (23:3, issue 91) 83, p. 96.
"Gagaku: I'd swear aphrodite herself." WormR (23:3, issue 91) 83, p. 89.
"Gagaku: I'd travel but I can't afford it." WormR (23:3, issue 91) 83, p. 112.
"Gagaku: I'm in Juice." WormR (23:3, issue 91) 83, p. 88.
"Gagaku: I'm typing my poems." WormR (23:3, issue 91) 83, p. 110.
"Gagaku: It's a rhythm." WormR (23:3, issue 91) 83, p. 109.
"Gagaku: It's become rather automatic." WormR (23:3, issue 91) 83, p. 83.
"Gagaku: I've decided to flood the world." WormR (23:3, issue 91) 83, p. 94.
"Gagaku: I've got nothing to say." WormR (23:3, issue 91) 83, p. 87.
"Gagaku: I've tried much." WormR (23:3, issue 91) 83, p. 86.
"Gagaku: Let me raise demons here." WormR (23:3, issue 91) 83, p. 84.
"Gagaku: Maybe I'll write a poem that works." WormR (23:3, issue 91) 83, p. 103.
"Gagaku: Poetry will survive the joggers." WormR (23:3, issue 91) 83, p. 99.
"Gagaku: The demons toss balls." WormR (23:3, issue 91) 83, p. 111.
"Gagaku: The forecast possible 12 foot waves." WormR (23:3, issue 91) 83, p. 87.
"Gagaku: There's a man singing." WormR (23:3, issue 91) 83, p. 114.
"Gagaku: They carry a banner." WormR (23:3, issue 91) 83, p. 85.
"Gagaku: They wave their index fingers in all directions." WormR (23:3, issue 91) 83, p. 100.

"Gagaku: This is the first poem." WormR (23:3, issue 91) 83, p. 102.
"Grow a little fat and write in relative peace." WormR (23:3, issue 91) 83, p. 107.
"I didn't have to scrape for the royalties." WormR (23:3, issue 91) 83, p. 108.
"I read my own work." WormR (23:3, issue 91) 83, p. 106.
"It is like." WormR (23:3, issue 91) 83, p. 113.
"It's best." WormR (23:3, issue 91) 83, p. 114.
"The last reading." WormR (23:3, issue 91) 83, p. 96.
"Love sign." WormR (23:3, issue 91) 83, p. 98.
"My." WormR (23:3, issue 91) 83, p. 90.
"The phone has not rung today." WormR (23:3, issue 91) 83, p. 99.
"Prospects" (A Wormwood Chapbook). WormR (23:3, issue 91) 83, p. 81-114.
"Prospects." WormR (23:3, issue 91) 83, p. 81-82.
"The speckled trout." WormR (23:3, issue 91) 83, p. 120.
"They asked what I believed in." WormR (23:3, issue 91) 83, p. 120.
"Travel." WormR (23:3, issue 91) 83, p. 112.
"When I want time to fly." WormR (23:3, issue 91) 83, p. 106.

3711. RICHTER, Harvena
"Scenes from Meditation II (Living Walls and Loving Leaves)." SoDakR (21:2) Sum 83, p. 58-61.

3712. RICKABAUGH, René
"Baby Me." NowestR (21:2/3) 83, p. 42.
"Digging." NowestR (21:2/3) 83, p. 40.
"Tidy Work." NowestR (21:2/3) 83, p. 41.

3713. RICKEL, Boyer
"Alexandrian." AntR (41:3) Sum 83, p. 331.

3714. RICKERT, Robert
"A Riddle." Swallow (2) Aut-Wint 83, p. 70.
"Sleeper." Swallow (1) Spr 83, p. 46.
"The Stockpond." Swallow (2) Aut-Wint 83, p. 69.

3715. RICKS, Jim
"The Secret." Quarry (32:3) Sum 83, p. 40.

3716. RIDLAND, John
"Another Easter" (Errata from Ploughs 8:2/3, 82). Ploughs (9:1) 83, p. 193-194.

3717. RIECKEN, Lara
"A Day in the Life of the White Blanket." Grain (11:1) F 83, p. 7.
"Feather in Paw." MalR (66) O 83, p. 84.

3718. RIELLY, Edward J.
"A Matter of Light." WebR (8:1) Spr 83, p. 74.
"My Son." WebR (8:1) Spr 83, p. 75.

3719. RIEMER, Frances J. (Frances Julia)
"Descent." YetASM (1:2) 82, p. 9.
"Enid and Merlin." CrabCR (1:1) My 83, p. 28.

3720. RIFBJERG, Klaus
"Sex Roles" (tr. by Alexander Taylor). MinnR (NS 20) Spr 83, p. 25.

3721. RIGGIO, Michael
"Ocean Ranger -- February 13, 1982." PottPort (5) 83-84, p. 51.

3722. RIGGS, Dionis C. (Dionis Coffin)
"Answers" (tr. of Ulku Tamer, w. Ozcan Yalim and William A. Fielder). Mund (14:1) 83, p. 49-50.
"Autumn (Guz)" (tr. of Ali Puskulluoglu, w. Ozcan Yalim and William D. Fielder). SpiritSH (48) 82, p. 48.
"Defenses." StoneC (10:3/4) Spr-Sum 83, p. 78.
"The First Snow" (tr. of Sabahattin Kudret Aksal, w. Ozcan Yalim and William A. Fielder). Mund (14:1) 83, p. 51.
"Hills (Tepeler)" (tr. of Ali Puskulluoglu, w. Ozcan Yalim and William D. Fielder). SpiritSH (48) 82, p. 48.
"The Lamp" (tr. of Behcet Necatigil, w. Ozcan Yalim and William A. Fielder). Mund (14:1) 83, p. 48.
"Poem toward Noon" (tr. of Sabahattin Kudret Aksal, w. Ozcan Yalim and William A. Fielder). Mund (14:1) 83, p. 51.
"The Poet" (tr. of Ozcan Yalim, w. the author and William A. Fielder). Mund (14:1) 83, p. 47.
"The Poet (Ozan)" (tr. of Ali Puskulluoglu, w. Ozcan Yalim and William D. Fielder). SpiritSH (48) 82, p. 48.
"Seekers" (tr. of Ozcan Yalim, w. the author and William A. Fielder). Mund (14:1) 83, p. 47.
"Summer (Yaz)" (tr. of Ali Puskulluoglu, w. Ozcan Yalim and William D. Fielder). SpiritSH (48) 82, p. 48.
"Tale of Tales" (tr. of Nazim Hikmet, w. Ozcan Yalim and William D. Fielder). SpiritSH (48) 82, p. 46-47.

3723. RIGSBEE, David
"The Next I Know." BlackWR (10:1) Aut 83, p. 134-135.

3724. RILEY, Bill
"Salmon." WestCR (17:4) Ap 83, p. 8.
"Teacher, June 27." WestCR (17:4) Ap 83, p. 8.

3725. RILEY, Joanne M.
"The Midnight Cloud." WindO (43) Wint 83, p. 39.

3726. RILKE, Rainer Maria
"Ancient Torso of Apollo" (tr. by Lisa Mihan). USl (16/17) Wint 83-84, p. 11.
"Annunciation above the Shepherds" (from The Life of the Virgin Mary, tr. by Dora FitzGerald).

CapilR (26) 83, p. 27, 29.

"Annunciation to Mary" (from The Life of the Virgin Mary, tr. by Dora FitzGerald). CapilR (26) 83, p. 19, 21.

"Archaic Torso of Apollo" (tr. by Charles Guilford). KanQ (15:4) Aut 83, p. 51.

"Argwohn Josephs" (from Das Marienleben). CapilR (26) 83, p. 22, 24.

"Autumn" (tr. by Paul Wadden). Nimrod (27:1) Aut-Wint 83, p. 54.

"Before the Passion" (from The Life of the Virgin Mary, tr. by Dora FitzGerald). CapilR (26) 83, p. 35, 37.

"Birth of Christ" (from The Life of the Virgin Mary, tr. by Dora FitzGerald). CapilR (26) 83, p. 25, 27.

"The Birth of Mary" (from The Life of the Virgin Mary, tr. by Dora FitzGerald). CapilR (26) 83, p. 15.

"Buddha." SouthernR (19:3) Jl 83, p. 678.

"Buddha" (tr. by Steven Lautermilch). SouthernR (19:3) Jl 83, p. 679.

"Come, you last of those I will see" (tr. by Franz Wright). Field (28) Spr 83, p. 59.

"Consolation of Mary with the Resurrected Christ" (from The Life of the Virgin Mary, tr. by Dora FitzGerald). CapilR (26) 83, p. 39.

"Die Darstellung Maria im Tempel" (from Das Marienleben). CapilR (26) 83, p. 16, 18.

"The deep parts of my life pour onward" (tr. by Robert Bly). NewRep (186:9) 3 Mr 82, p. 27.

"Early Apollo" (tr. by Charles Guilford). KanQ (15:4) Aut 83, p. 51.

"Entry" (tr. by Charles Guilford). KanQ (15:4) Aut 83, p. 50.

"Evening" (tr. by Charles Guilford). KanQ (15:4) Aut 83, p. 49.

"The French Notebooks" (Excerpts: "Fragments") (tr. by A. Poulin, Jr.). DevQ (18:2) Sum 83, p. 59-61.

"Geburt Christi" (from Das Marienleben). CapilR (26) 83, p. 24, 26.

"Geburt Maria" (from Das Marienleben). CapilR (26) 83, p. 14.

"I Love the Dark Hours" (tr. by Lisa Mihan). USl (16/17) Wint 83-84, p. 11.

"Joseph's Suspicion" (from The Life of the Virgin Mary, tr. by Dora FitzGerald). CapilR (26) 83, p. 23, 25.

"Maria Heimsuchung" (from Das Marienleben). CapilR (26) 83, p. 20, 22.

"Maria Verkundigung" (from Das Marienleben). CapilR (26) 83, p. 18, 20.

"My God, What Will You Do, When I Die?" (tr. by Steve Lautermilch). DevQ (18:1) Spr 83, p. 97.

"Now it is time the gods stepped out of everyday things" (tr. by Franz Wright). Field (28) Spr 83, p. 58.

"Now nothing can prevent me completing my appointed orbit" (tr. by Franz Wright). Field (28) Spr 83, p. 57.

"Of the Death of Mary" (from The Life of the Virgin Mary, tr. by Dora FitzGerald). CapilR (26) 83, p. 41, 43, 45.
"Of the Marriage at Cana" (from The Life of the Virgin Mary, tr. by Dora FitzGerald). CapilR (26) 83, p. 33, 35.
"Oh haven't you known nights of love?" (tr. by Franz Wright). PoNow (7:2, #38) 83, p. 45.
"Oh, not to be excluded" (tr. by Franz Wright). Field (28) Spr 83, p. 56.
"The Panther" (Jardin Des Palntes, Paris) (tr. by Charles Guilford). KanQ (15:4) Aut 83, p. 50.
"Pieta" (from Das Marienleben). CapilR (26) 83, p. 36.
"Pieta" (from The Life of the Virgin Mary, tr. by Dora FitzGerald). CapilR (26) 83, p. 37.
"The Presentation of Mary in the Temple" (from The Life of the Virgin Mary, tr. by Dora FitzGerald). CapilR (26) 83, p. 17, 19.
"Rast auf der Flucht in Agypten" (from Das Marienleben). CapilR (26) 83, p. 30.
"Rest on the Flight into Egypt" (from The Life of the Virgin Mary, tr. by Dora FitzGerald). CapilR (26) 83, p. 31.
"Song of Love" (tr. by Paul Wadden). Nimrod (27:1) Aut-Wint 83, p. 55.
"Sonnet to Orpheus XIV Series I" (tr. by Susanne Dubroff). PortR (29:1) 83, p. 81.
"Die Sonnetee an Orpheus I" (Selection: XIV). PortR (29:1) 83, p. 80.
"Sonnets from Orpheus" (Selections: I.3, I.10, II.4, II.10, I.19) (tr. by John Rosenwald). Northeast (Ser. 3:15) Sum 83, p. 18-22.
"The Sonnets to Orpheus" (Selection: I, 8: "Nur im Raum der Rühmung darf die Klage"). SouthernHR (17:3) Sum 83, p. 224.
"The Sonnets to Orpheus" (Selection: I, 8: "Only in that place where praise is") (tr. by Paul Wadden). SouthernHR (17:3) Sum 83, p. 224.
"Sonnets to Orpheus" (Selection: 1.24). SouthernR (19:3) Jl 83, p. 680.
"Sonnets to Orpheus" (Selection: 1.24) (tr. by Steven Lautermilch). SouthernR (19:3) Jl 83, p. 681.
"Stillung Maria mit dem Auferstandenen" (from Das Marienleben). CapilR (26) 83, p. 38.
"Title Page" (tr. by Paul Wadden). Nimrod (27:1) Aut-Wint 83, p. 54.
"To praise is the whole thing" (tr. by Robert Bly). NewRep (186:9) 3 Mr 82, p. 29.
"Vase Painting: Supper of the Dead" (tr. by Franz Wright). Field (28) Spr 83, p. 55.
"Verkundigung uber den Hirten" (from Das Marienleben). CapilR (26) 83, p. 26, 28.
"Visitation of the Virgin" (from The Life of the Virgin Mary, tr. by Dora FitzGerald). CapilR (26) 83, p. 21, 23.
"Vom Tode Maria" (from Das Marienleben). CapilR (26) 83, p. 40, 42, 44.
"Von der Hochzeit zu Kana" (from Das Marienleben).

CapilR (26) 83, p. 32, 34.
"Vor der Passion" (from Das Marienleben). CapilR (26) 83, p. 34, 36.
"You Are the Future, Morning Breaking Red" (tr. by Steve Lautermilch). DevQ (18:1) Spr 83, p. 96.

RIN, Ishigaki
See: ISHIGAKI, Rin

3727. RINALDI, Nicholas
"The Artillerymen." IndR (5:1) Wint 82, p. 51.
"Auschwitz." PoetL (77:4) Wint 83, p. 216-217.
"Balloons." Pig (11) 83, p. 80.
"Boat on the Highway." KanQ (15:1) Wint 83, p. 125.
"The Dead." LitR (27:1) Aut 83, p. 127.
"Hermann Goring." PoetL (77:4) Wint 83, p. 214-215.
"Hitler in the Trenches: White Crow." Abraxas (27/28) 83, p. 16.
"Lemons." KanQ (15:1) Wint 83, p. 126.
"The Luftwaffe in Chaos." PoetL (77:4) Wint 83, p. 215-216.
"Miracle of the Tongues." NegC (3:4) Aut 83, p. 11-12.
"Pharmacopoeia." SouthwR (68:2) Spr 83, p. 187.
"The Saint Dies, Recovers, Remembers How It Was." NegC (3:4) Aut 83, p. 9-10.
"Shagging Flies in Flushing Meadow Park." IndR (5:1) Wint 82, p. 50.

3728. RIND, Sherry
"The Pig Invades." PoetryNW (24:2) Sum 83, p. 38.

3729. RINGROSE, Katrina V.
"The Dancing Class" (after a painting by Edgar Degas). YetASM (1:1) 82, p. 8.
"Entering an Old House." CalQ (22) Sum 83, p. 52.
"Returning." YetASM (1:1) 82, p. 12.
"Signals." CalQ (22) Sum 83, p. 52.
"Stars Are the Dead." YetASM (1:1) 82, p. 4.

3730. RIOS, Alberto
"Combing My Hair in the Hall." AmerPoR (12:5) S/O 83, p. 9.
"I Held His Name." AmerPoR (12:5) S/O 83, p. 8.
"I Would Visit Him in the Corner." BlackWR (8:2) Spr 82, p. 28.
"The Job of a Shirt." AmerPoR (12:5) S/O 83, p. 8.
"Perhaps Harder Contours." AmerPoR (12:5) S/O 83, p. 8.
"The Scent of Unbought Flowers." AmerPoR (12:5) S/O 83, p. 9.
"The Seeds That Come through the Air." BlackWR (8:2) Spr 82, p. 29.

3731. RITCH, Luana J.
"Morning Light." Meadows (3:1) 82, p. 47.

3732. RITCHIE, Elisavietta
"Anise, Uses of." StoneC (10:3/4) Spr-Sum 83, p. 14.
"Harvestimes." PoetL (77:2) Sum 82, p. 74.

"Homecoming from Indonesia." Vis (12) 83, p. 15.
"In Kraljevo." PoNow (7:2, #38) 83, p. 16.

3733. RITSOS, Yánnis
"After the Rain" (tr. by Martin McKinsey). MassR (24:4) Wint 83, p. 722.
"Honesty" (tr. by Kimon Friar). AmerPoR (12:3) My-Je 83, p. 48.
"Now Exactly" (tr. by Kimon Friar). AmerPoR (12:3) My-Je 83, p. 48.
"With a Distant Lighting" (tr. by Martin McKinsey). MassR (24:4) Wint 83, p. 721.

3734. RITTY, Joan
"Electricity." LittleBR (3:3) Spr 83, p. 60.
"Transference." LittleBR (3:3) Spr 83, p. 60.

3735. RIVARD, David
"Autumn." BlackWR (8:1) Aut 81, p. 56-57.
"Walking By." BlackWR (8:1) Aut 81, p. 55.

3736. RIVARD, Ken
"First Chapter of Its Blood." CrossC (5:2/3) 83, p. 11.
"Ice-Cream Bars and the Lone Ranger." Quarry (32:3) Sum 83, p. 17.
"Looking into My Daughter's Nightmare." MalR (66) O 83, p. 85.
"Pulling the Sunset Tighter." Quarry (32:3) Sum 83, p. 17-18.

3737. RIVERA, Carmen
"Conmemorando a Cristo resucitado." Rácata (2) 83, p. 92.
"Dios en ti en mi, en la nada." Rácata (2) 83, p. 95-96.
"Llego hasta aquí." Rácata (2) 83, p. 93.
"Manos ruedan llorando al pie del flamboyán." Rácata (2) 83, p. 91.
"Semillas en latas plantitas." Rácata (2) 83, p. 94.

3738. RIVERA, Félix
"1er Poema Grueso." Rácata (2) 83, p. 97.
"2do Poema Grueso." Rácata (2) 83, p. 98.
"3er Poema Grueso." Rácata (2) 83, p. 99.
"Bola de Fuego (o Bolero 'Besos de Fuego')." Rácata (2) 83, p. 100.

3739. RIVERA, Juan Manuel
"Amores y Cicutas." Rácata (2) 83, p. 104.
"La Cebolla." Rácata (2) 83, p. 129.
"La Dialesía" (a José Colón Santiago (Wiso) ese torvo querubín de misas infernales). Rácata (1) 83, p. 87.
"Es Bobby Sands Que Enamorado Pasa." Rácata (2) 83, p. 105-106.
"Hondo Tú Viejo Niño Que Cruzas Culebreando por Mi Pecho Como una Antigua Cicatriz Recién Nacida" (Para lano rivera amigo-amigo).

Rácata (2) 83, p. 102.
"Invitación a los Poetas Sin Cobija." Rácata (1) 83, p. 88-90.
"Oficio de Escribiente." Rácata (2) 83, p. 101.
"Safari." Rácata (1) 83, p. 86.
"Yo También Le Escribo Poemas a la Luna." Rácata (2) 83, p. 103.

3740. RIVERA, Virginia
"Entrega." Rácata (2) 83, p. 109.
"Evolucionando Aquí." Rácata (2) 83, p. 107.
"Taponada." Rácata (2) 83, p. 108.

3741. RIVERA MARTINEZ, Tomas
"América" (a Rafael Catalá). Rácata (1) 83, p. 91-92.
"La Marcha de los Condenados." Rácata (1) 83, p. 95-96.
"No es mucho Lo Sé." Rácata (1) 83, p. 93.
"Que me dejes amarte voy pidiendo." Rácata (1) 83, p. 94.

3742. RIVERO, Eliana
"En el Lugar Que Corresponde" (Para Margarita). RevChic (11:3/4) 83, p. 36.
"Gloria." RevChic (11:3/4) 83, p. 38.
"Salutación: Ave" (de mal agüero para tantos). RevChic (11:3/4) 83, p. 37.
"Tan Lejos del Azúcar." Areíto (9:33) 83, p. 21.

3743. RIVERS, Ann
"Commencement." StoneC (11:1/2, Pt. 1) Aut-Wint 83, p. 23.

3744. RIVERS, J. W.
"An American Reporter in Tabasco, Mexico, 1926." SanFPJ (4:2) 83, p. 63.
"En Route from Charleston to Cape Fear, the Marquis de Lafayette Stops at Diggs Plantation." SoCaR (15:2) Spr 83, p. 19.
"For Rulfo." SouthwR (68:2) Spr 83, p. 125.
"In His Revolutionary Uniform, the Marquis de Lafayette Attends a Fish Fry." SoCaR (15:2) Spr 83, p. 20.
"The Marquis de Lafayette Steps Ashore in the New World and Goes to Charleston." SoCaR (15:2) Spr 83, p. 18.
"On a Glendale Arizona Citrus Ranch Work Crew." SouthernPR (23:2) Aut 82 [i.e. (23:1?) Spr 83], p. 24-25.
"Picking Little Green Onions - Glendale, Arizona." SanFPJ (4:2) 83, p. 62.

3745. ROBBINS, Martin
"Dateline: Spring Training." FourQt (32:2) Wint 83, p. 2.
"Exercise for a New Season." CapeR (18:2) Sum 83, p. 42.
"Graph on the Spring Equinox." WebR (8:1) Spr 83, p. 90.

"Little Dance Suite." SewanR (91:1) Wint 83 p. 105-106.
"Morning Song." SewanR (91:1) Wint 83, p. 104.
"On a March Bass Lake." StoneC (10:3/4) Spr-Sum 83, p. 72.
"Slow Movement/Quartet." SewanR (91:1) Wint 83, p. 106.
"Towards the Light." StoneC (10:3/4) Spr-Sum 83, p. 72.

3746. ROBBINS, Richard (Rick)
"October: Resetting the Clocks." ThirdW Spr 83, p. 104.
"Swainson's Hawk." KanQ (15:2) Spr 83, p. 55.
"The Way It Works." CrabCR (1:2) Aut 83, p. 19.

3747. ROBBINS, Shellie Keir
"Inside a Purse." SpoonRQ (8:4) Aut 83, p. 12.

3748. ROBBINS, Tim
"January 29 and I Wait." HangL (44) Sum 83, p. 69.
"Rhythm and Affection." HangL (44) Sum 83, p. 68.
"You Know As the Street Knows." HangL (44) Sum 83, p. 70.

3749. ROBERTS, Betty
"Drought Breaker." Bogg (50) 83, p. 45.

3750. ROBERTS, Dorothy
"The Poets of Home." Hudson (36:2) Sum 83, p. 326.

3751. ROBERTS, Gordi
"Faces and Phases." SanFPJ (5:4) 83, p. 41.
"The Main Thing." SanFPJ (5:2) 83, p. 81.
"Religion Part I." SanFPJ (5:4) 83, p. 41.
"Steeple People." SanFPJ (5:4) 83, p. 44.

3752. ROBERTS, Kevin
"Genesis." MalR (64) F 83, p. 150-151.
"Of the Stars" (for Jon Roberts). CanLit (96) Spr 83, p. 36.
"Surprise." CanLit (96) Spr 83, p. 85-86.

3753. ROBERTS, Len
"Catching Eels." PraS (51:1, i.e. 57:1) Spr 83, p. 67-68.
"The Dead Leaves." Pig (11) 83, p. 22.
"Eggshells." Pig (11) 83, p. 23.
"Homer." CalQ (22) Sum 83, p. 76-77.
"My Father's Whistle" (for Gerald Stern). MinnR (NS 20) Spr 83, p. 54.
"Pyracantha." PraS (51:1, i.e. 57:1) Spr 83, p. 66.
"Stealing." CalQ (22) Sum 83, p. 75.
"Vide's Pension." WestB (12) 83, p. 63.
"Walking through a Family Graveyard and Thinking of the Italian Stone Builders." WestB (12) 83, p. 62.

3754. ROBERTS, Rebecca
"The Squirrel on the Limb." BelPoJ (33:3) Spr 83,

p. 35.
"Versal's New Hip." WorldO (17:4) Sum 83, p. 37.

3755. ROBERTS, Susan
"Willow." Tele (18) 83, p. 120-121.

3756. ROBERTSON, Howard
"The Barber Did Just What I Told Him." YetASM (2:1) 83, p. 5.

3757. ROBERTSON, Kell
"For Hank Williams." SecC (11:1/2) 83, p. 185-187.
"Merlene." SecC (11:1/2) 83, p. 184.

3758. ROBERTSON, Kirk
"Dry Spell." Meadows (3:1) 82, p. 53.
"Lovelock to Twin Falls." Meadows (3:1) 82, p. 48.
"The Misfits" (Excerpt). SoDakR (21:4) Wint 83, p. 73.
"One Night." Meadows (3:1) 82, p. 47.
"Teddy Blue Abbot's Recipe." Meadows (3:1) 82, p. 48.
"Things to Do at Jane's Cabin." OroM (2:1, #5) Sum 83, p. 4.
"Twin Falls to St. Ignatius." Meadows (3:1) 82, p. 49.
"Water." Meadows (3:1) 82, p. 49.

3759. ROBERTSON, William B.
"Horse Knees." CanLit (99) Wint 83, p. 67.

3760. ROBINETTE, Janice
"Birthmark." Tendril (14/15) Wint 83, p. 160-161.

3761. ROBINSON, Gillian
"The Submission of Allan." PottPort (5) 83-84, p. 5.

3762. ROBINSON, James Miller
"The Book of Mormon." SouthernHR (17:4) Aut 83, p. 340-341.
"In the Waiting Room of a Psychiatrist's Office." SouthernHR (17:4) Aut 83, p. 339.
"Learning to Live with Mice." Poem (48) Jl 83, p. 31.

3763. ROBINSON, Peter
"At St. David's." MalR (65) Jl 83, p. 100-101.
"City of Night" (tr. of Vittorio Sereni, w. Marcus Perryman). Argo (5:1) 83, p. 20.
"The East Window: St. Mary's, Muker." MalR (65) Jl 83, p. 98.
"The Empty Shed" (for Dylan Thomas). MalR (65) Jl 83, p. 102-103.
"The House." AntigR (52) Wint 83, p. 77.
"Italian in Greece" (tr. of Vittorio Sereni, w. Marcus Perryman). Argo (5:1) 83, p. 20.
"Scavenger of Images." MalR (65) Jl 83, p. 99.

3764. ROBISON, Margaret
"Come." Vis (12) 83, p. 9.

3765. ROBLES, Al
"Rapping with One Million Carabaos in the Dark." SecC (11:1/2) 83, p. 188-190.

3766. ROBSON, Ruthann
"For the Arapesh." MinnR (NS 20) Spr 83, p. 76.
"Kore." ThirdW Spr 83, p. 53-54.

3767. ROBY, Gayle
"Still Life." PraS (57:3) Aut 83, p. 57.

3768. ROCHELEAU, Linda
"Joe Paul." Vis (12) 83, p. 25.

3769. RODD, Valerie
"Apropos Reality." WestCR (18:1) Je 83, p. 22.
"Eve Revisited." WestCR (18:1) Je 83, p. 21.
"In the Beginning." WestCR (18:1) Je 83, p. 21.
"Look Out upon the Wind with Glorious Fear." WestCR (18:1) Je 83, p. 20.
"To Argue the Laurel." WestCR (18:1) Je 83, p. 20.

3770. RODGERS, Gordon
"Acids." Waves (11:4) Spr 83, p. 76.
"Scaling." PottPort (5) 83-84, p. 43.

3771. RODRIGUEZ, Aleida
"Little Cuba Stories / Cuentos de Cuba." 13thM (6:1/2) 82, p. 25-26.

3772. RODRIGUEZ, Carlos
"Jarcha #1-#5." Rácata (2) 83, p. 110-112.
"Jarchas Místicas." Rácata (1) 83, p. 99-101.
"La Sangre." Rácata (1) 83, p. 97-98.

3773. RODRIGUEZ, Sandra
"A Edwin Reyes: Poeta de la Obsesión Errante." Rácata (1) 83, p. 102.
"Cebolla." Rácata (2) 83, p. 130.
"Censura." Rácata (2) 83, p. 116.
"De Paso." Rácata (2) 83, p. 114.
"Me gusta mi cara." Rácata (2) 83, p. 115.
"Mujer con Sombrero." Rácata (1) 83, p. 104.
"La mujer que quiero." Rácata (2) 83, p. 113.
"Poema a la Negritud." Rácata (1) 83, p. 103.
"Ser Mujer." Rácata (1) 83, p. 105-106.

3774. RODRIGUEZ, W. R.
"Little Spic & Big Man." Abraxas (27/28) 83, p. 12-14.

3775. ROE SONYE S.
"We All Eat Pigs in a Blanket at Weddings." LittleM (14:1/2) 83, p. 61.

3776. ROEMER, Kenneth M.
"In Thanksgiving." SouthwR (68:3) Sum 83, p. 250.

3777. ROEMER, Marjorie
"General Delivery: West Chatham." EngJ (72:7) N

83, p. 31.
"Monday Morning." EngJ (72:1) Ja 83, p. 45.

3778. ROEMMICH, William
"The Allegory of the Cave." SouthernR (19:3) Jl 83, p. 664.
"El Desdichado: A Translation" (tr. of Gérard de Nerval (1808-1855). SouthernR (19:3) Jl 83, p. 664-665.

3779. ROESKE, Paulette
"7:00 A.M. Lakefront." Poetry (141:5) F 83, p. 289.
"Anger." WebR (8:1) Spr 83, p. 67.
"Looking for You One Year Later" (to My Sister). Poetry (141:5) F 83, p. 287-288.
"Refugees at Avila Beach." Poetry (141:5) F 83, p. 290.
"Wintering at A Summer Resort." Poetry (141:5) F 83, p. 288.

3780. ROGERS, Bernard
"Mirage." ArizQ (39:1) Spr 83, p. 61.

3781. ROGERS, Larry S.
"The Good Old Days (1952)." PikeF (5) Spr 83, p. 17.

3782. ROGERS, Linda
"Equinox." MalR (64) F 83, p. 124.
"The Fat Man Dreams." MalR (64) F 83, p. 125.

3783. ROGERS, Pattiann
"Angel of the Atom." PraS (57:2) Sum 83, p. 21-22.
"The Art of Becoming." GeoR (37:1) Spr 83, p. 168.
"Aspects of Unity." ChiR (33:3) Wint 83, p. 115-116.
"Betrayal: The Reflection of the Cattail." CarolQ (35:2) Wint 83, p. 8.
"The Body as Window." Poetry (143:1) O 83, p. 4.
"The Body Is Filled with Light." PoetryNW (24:4) Wint 83-84, p. 22-23.
"The Compassion of the Iris." PoetryNW (24:1) Spr 83, p. 9-10.
"The Creation of Sin." HiramPoR (34) Spr-Sum 83, p. 19.
"I Thought I Heard a White-Haired Man with a Purple Tie Say, 'The Mind Creates What It Perceives.'" MassR (24:4) Wint 83, p. 719-720.
"Intermediary" (For John A. and Arthur). PraS (57:2) Sum 83, p. 20-21.
"Light as Condition." CarolQ (35:2) Wint 83, p. 7.
"Nude Standing Alone in the Forest: A Study of Place." Poetry (143:1) O 83, p. 5-6.
"The Pieces of Heaven." PoetryNW (24:1) Spr 83, p. 8-9.
"The Place of Juxtaposition." PoetryNW (24:4) Wint 83-84, p. 23.
"The Power of Toads." Iowa (13:2) Spr 82, p. 67-68.
"The Puzzle of Beauty." HiramPoR (34) Spr-Sum 83, p. 20.
"Reaching the Audience" (From the introduction to The First Book of Iridaceae). Iowa (13:2)

Spr 82, p. 65-66.
"The Second Witness." VirQR (59:2) Spr 83, p. 244-245.
"Seminar: Dominoes, Zebras, and the Full Moon." Kayak (62) Ag 83, p. 47-48.
"The Shape of Sorrow." Kayak (62) Ag 83, p. 49.
"Statement Preliminary to the Invention of Solace." Poetry (143:1) O 83, p. 3.
"The Tongues of Angels" (1 Cor. 13:1). CarolQ (35:2) Wint 83, p. 9.
"The Tree Has Captured By Soul" (for van Gogh). PoetryNW (24:1) Spr 83, p. 10-11.
"The Verification of Vulnerability: Bog Turtle." Poetry (143:1) O 83, p. 1-2.

3784. ROGERS, Timothy J.
"Death has gotten dressed up with pins and threads" (tr. of Etelvina Astrada). LetFem (9:1) 83, p. 94.
"Just like an old dress" (tr. of Etelvina Astrada). LetFem (9:1) 83, p. 93.
"One Tuesday my mother gave birth to me" (tr. of Etelvina Astrada). LetFem (9:1) 83, p. 94.
"Outdoor Exercises" (tr. of Etelvina Astrada). LetFem (9:1) 83, p. 93.
"The world is a straight-jacket" (tr. of Etelvina Astrada). LetFem (9:1) 83, p. 95.

ROGOFF, Jay Grover
See: GROVER-ROGOFF, Jay

3785. ROHRER, Daniela
"Buenos Aires (Air Mail 1)." Prismal (11) Aut 83, p. 97.
"Provisorias Desvalijas." Prismal (11) Aut 83, p. 98.

3786. ROJAS, Luis
"Niña Enamorada." Rácata (2) 83, p. 118.
"Nombre Olvidado." Rácata (2) 83, p. 119.
"Tiempo y Muerte." Rácata (2) 83, p. 117.

3787. ROLLER, Sarah
"In Final Seasons." MalR (64) F 83, p. 202-203.

3788. ROLLER, Tom
"Fred Astaire." YetASM (1:2) 82, p. 6.

3789. ROLLINGS, Alane
"Life Expectancies." TriQ (58) Aut 83, p. 92-93.
"Spectacles of Ourselves." TriQ (58) Aut 83, p. 90-91.

3790. ROLLINS, Cal E.
"Metempsychosis: Sunday Morning." WorldO (17:4) Sum 83, p. 38.
"Upon Flying Puffer Kites for Inge." WorldO (18:1) Aut 83, p. 37.

3791. ROLLINS, Edgar M.
"Equinox." DekalbLAJ (16:1/4) Aut 82-Sum 83, p. 72.

3792. ROMA, Hedy
"A Peace for My Mother." HangL (44) Sum 83, p. 71.
"Spring of Winter." HangL (44) Sum 83, p. 72.

3793. ROMANI, Ana
"Compostela, cidade atemporal da historia." Prismal (11) Aut 83, p. 116.

3794. ROMTVEDT, David
"Flight." MemphisSR (4:1) Aut 83, p. 28.
"Gisenyi, Rwanda, Club Edelweiss." CrabCR (1:2) Aut 83, p. 26-27.

3795. RONAN, John
"Last Laugh." Thrpny (4:2, issue 14) Sum 83, p. 6.

3796. RONAN, Richard
"July/Here." NowestR (21:2/3) 83, p. 52-53.
"Lachrymae Rerum." AmerPoR (12:5) S/O 83, p. 18.
"A Lady in a Northern Province." Telescope (4) Wint 83, p. 16-17.
"A Sighting of Whales." AmerPoR (12:5) S/O 83, p. 18.
"Sleepwalk Watercolour." Telescope (4) Wint 83, p. 11.

3797. RONER, C. J.
"Seismic Apology from Diablo Canyon." SanFPJ (5:4) 83, p. 54-55.

3798. RONIS, A.
"Two Widowers." YetASM (1:2) 82, p. 7.

3799. ROOT, Judith (Judith C.)
"Beachcombing the Planets in Mendocino." PoetryNW (24:4) Wint 83-84, p. 41.
"Naming the Shells." Nat (237:3) 23-30 Jl 83, p. 90.
"Round Dance." ThRiPo (21/22) 83, p. 68.

3800. ROOT, William Pitt
"La Charmeuse de Serpents" (after Rousseau). MemphisSR (3:2) Spr 83, p. 23.
"Fever Breaking." SouthwR (68:4) Aut 83, p. 338.
"The Invisible Man" (tr. of Pablo Neruda). Telescope (4) Wint 83, p. 51-57.
"Late Twentieth Century Pastoral." SouthernPR (23:2) Aut 83, p. 10-11.
"A Note on Nostalgia as the Corruption of Innocence" (for Fred). Abatis (1) 83, p. 10.
"The Perfect Day." MemphisSR (3:2) Spr 83, p. 16.
"Screen of Birds and Flowers (for a Fifteenth Birthday)." MemphisSR (3:2) Spr 83, p. 51.
"The Unbroken Diamond: Nightletter to the Mujahadeen." Telescope (4) Wint 83, p. 40-49.

3801. RORIPAUGH, Robert
"After the Steers Are Shipped." SoDakR (21:3) Aut

83, p. 83.
"Wintering." SpoonRQ (8:4) Aut 83, p. 51.

3802. ROSBERG, Rose
"Ambush." Wind (13:48) 83, p. 55.
"Enclosures." Poem (48) Jl 83, p. 55.
"Glass Girls." Poem (48) Jl 83, p. 56.
"Tourist at Taormina." Wind (13:48) 83, p. 55-56.

3803. ROSE, Dorothy
"Ready for Business." SanFPJ (5:3) 83, p. 96.

3804. ROSE, Harriet
"The Lost Princess." PoetryCR (5:2) Wint 83-84, p. 10.
"Sheerah." PoetryCR (5:1) Aut 83, p. 12.
"The Succubus." PoetryCR (5:1) Aut 83, p. 12.
"The Wedding Dress." PoetryCR (5:2) Wint 83-84, p. 10.

3805. ROSE, Lynne Cheney
"Sibyl Takes to the Sky." Wind (13:48) 83, p. 57.

3806. ROSE, Mike
"The Day Mack Sennett Dined with Ingmar Bergman." Vis (13) 83, p. 38-39.
"Dream of the White Room." Bogg (50) 83, p. 9.
"Green." Vis (13) 83, p. 36.
"Ice Box Coloratura." Vis (13) 83, p. 37.
"Transplant." Bogg (50) 83, p. 22.

3807. ROSE, Wilga (Wilga M.)
"Crow Country." Bogg (51) 83, p. 49.
"Early Morning Swimmers." Bogg (51) 83, p. 58.
"Elegy for a Drowned Car." Bogg (50) 83, p. 46.

3808. ROSEBURY, Pauline P.
"Golden Age of Chivalry." SanFPJ (4:3) 83, p. 14-15.
"Have a Good Day, Death Is on the Way." SanFPJ (5:3) 83, p. 53.
"Invisible Killer." SanFPJ (4:4) 83, p. 57.
"Power." SanFPJ (4:4) 83, p. 69.

3809. ROSELIEP, Raymond
"After Augustine." ChrC (100:2) 19 Ja 83, p. 44.
"Equinox." ChrC (100:16) 18 My 83, p. 478.
"The Fine Arts." SpoonRQ (8:4) Aut 83, p. 24-25.
"Gregorian." ChrC (100:2) 19 Ja 83, p. 36.
"House." NewL (49:3/4) Spr-Sum 83, p. 214.
"Noël." ChrC (100:39) 21-28 D 83, p. 1185.
"Noël." SpoonRQ (8:4) Aut 83, p. 25.
"Scenario." PoNow (7:2, #38) 83, p. 34.
"Shore." PoNow (7:2, #38) 83, p. 34.

3810. ROSEN, Kenneth
"After the Race" (for R.L.R. 1942-1980). Poetry (141:5) F 83, p. 275.
"Breakfast." QW (17) Aut-Wint 83-84, p. 19.
"The Clam Flats." AntR (41:3) Sum 83, p. 328.
"Flying." AntR (41:3) Sum 83, p. 329.

"Peeping Tom." Poetry (141:5) F 83, p. 274.

3811. ROSEN, Lisa
"Growing Wild." SanFPJ (5:1) 83, p. 92.

3812. ROSEN, Michael J.
"The Age When Parents Don't Need Reasons." Nat (236:3) 22 Ja 83, p. 90.

3813. ROSENBERG, David
"Pentacostal Voice." Nat (237:5) 20-27 Ag 83, p. 154.

3814. ROSENBERG, L. M.
"At the Common Table." Ploughs (9:1) 83, p. 123.
"Children." Ploughs (9:1) 83, p. 124.
"Further Adventures of the Vegetable Kingdom." CimR (64) Jl 83, p. 4.
"The Mourner's Christmas." NewYorker (59:45) 26 D 83, p. 38.
"Snowbound in Lanesboro, Pennsylvania." BlackWR (10:1) Aut 83, p. 140.
"Survival." CimR (64) Jl 83, p. 52.

3815. ROSENBERGER, F. C.
"Young Poet." ArizQ (39:2) Sum 83, p. 155.

3816. ROSENBLATT, Herta
"Image (a Gold Pin for a Theologian)." SpiritSH (49) 83, p. 31.
"To the Still House." SpiritSH (49) 83, p. 30-31.

3817. ROSENBLATT, Joe
"The Black Flower" (from Top Soil). PoetryCR (5:1) Aut 83, p. 10.
"Bride of My Brain" (from Virgins & Vampires). PoetryCR (5:1) Aut 83, p. 11.
"Cockroach Poem" (to commemorate the invoking of the War Measures Act in Canada, from Top Soil). PoetryCR (5:1) Aut 83, p. 11.
"The Dream Apprentice" (from Top Soil). PoetryCR (5:1) Aut 83, p. 11.
"Groundhogs & Appearnaces" (from Top Soil). PoetryCR (5:1) Aut 83, p. 10.
"I Want to Hijack a Bumblebee" (from Top Soil). PoetryCR (5:1) Aut 83, p. 11.
"The Mandrill Baboon" (for Milton Acorn, from Top Soil). PoetryCR (5:1) Aut 83, p. 11.
"Mother Nature's Helpers" (from Top Soil). PoetryCR (5:1) Aut 83, p. 11.
"The Oyster Farm" (from Top Soil). PoetryCR (5:1) Aut 83, p. 10.
"Poem for a Dying Bumblebee" (from Top Soil). PoetryCR (5:1) Aut 83, p. 11.
"Spiderman" (from Top Soil). PoetryCR (5:1) Aut 83, p. 11.
"Trout Poem" (from Top Soil). PoetryCR (5:1) Aut 83, p. 11.

3818. ROSENTHAL, David H.
"The Furtive Life" (tr. of Gabriel Ferrater). LitR (26:3) Spr 83, p. 398.
"I see from back porches" (tr. of Vicent Andrés Estellés). LitR (26:3) Spr 83, p. 401.
"Idleness" (tr. of Gabriel Ferrater). LitR (26:3) Spr 83, p. 400.
"If it's permitted" (tr. of Vicent Andrés Estellés). LitR (26:3) Spr 83, p. 401.
"Illict Homage to Lluis Milà" (To Francesc Brines, tr. of Vicent Andrés Estellés). LitR (26:3) Spr 83, p. 402-404.
"A Small War" (tr. of Gabriel Ferrater). LitR (26:3) Spr 83, p. 399-400.
"Two Girl Friends" (tr. of Gabriel Ferrater). LitR (26:3) Spr 83, p. 398.
"Womb" (tr. of Gabriel Ferrater). LitR (26:3) Spr 83, p. 400.

3819. ROSENTHAL, M. L.
"Water Lilies, White Violets." GeoR (37:2) Sum 83, p. 248.

3820. ROSENWALD, John
"Sonnets from Orpheus" (Selections: I.3, I.10, II.4, II.10, I.19) (tr. of Rainer Maria Rilke). Northeast (Ser. 3:15) Sum 83, p. 18-22.

3821. ROSKOLENKO, Harry
"Nationalism." NewL (49:3/4) Spr-Sum 83, p. 211-212.
"Only God Can Make Me." NewL (49:3/4) Spr-Sum 83, p. 212.
"View." NewL (49:3/4) Spr-Sum 83, p. 211.

3822. ROSOVSKY, Candace
"Sleeping with Ghosts" (To Stuart Purser). NegC (3:4) Aut 83, p. 55-57.

3823. ROSSELARE-LeHAVRE
"Bread vs. Poem" (for Raymond the Cabdriver). Tele (18) 83, p. 96.
"Letter to the Edge of a Field." Tele (18) 83, p. 97.
"Queen Camel's Song." Tele (18) 83, p. 97.

ROSSI, Cristina Peri
See: PERI ROSSI, Cristina

3824. ROSSI, Vinio
"Afterward" (tr. of Giovanni Raboni, w. Stuart Friebert). Field (29) Aut 83, p. 82.
"The Apartment" (tr. of Giovanni Raboni, w. Stuart Friebert). Field (29) Aut 83, p. 79.
"False and Tendentious News" (tr. of Giovanni Raboni, w. Stuart Friebert). Field (29) Aut 83, p. 77-78.
"From the Altar in the Shadows" (tr. of Giovanni Raboni, w. Stuart Friebert). DevQ (18:2) Sum 83, p. 63.
"Hospital Interns" (For Bartolo Cattafi) (tr. of

Giovanni Raboni, w. Stuart Friebert). Field (29) Aut 83, p. 80-81.
"Otherwise" (tr. of Giovanni Raboni, w. Stuart Friebert). PoNow (7:2, #38) 83, p. 45.

3825. ROSTWOROWSKI, Boguslaw
"Absence" (tr. of Wiktor Woroszylski). TriQ (57, Vol. 1) Spr-Sum 83, p. 87.
"The Belly of Barbara N." (tr. of Wiktor Woroszylski). TriQ (57, Vol. 1) Spr-Sum 83, p. 85.
"Diary of Internment (Darlowko, 1982)" (Selections: 3 poems) (tr. of Wiktor Woroszylski). TriQ (57, Vol. 1) Spr-Sum 83, p. 85-87.
"Golden Times" (tr. by the author). TriQ (57, Vol. 1) Spr-Sum 83, p. 63.
"Just till Spring" (tr. of Wiktor Woroszylski). TriQ (57, Vol. 1) Spr-Sum 83, p. 86.
"Report from a Town under Siege" (tr. of Zbigniew Herbert). TriQ (57, Vol. 1) Spr-Sum 83, p. 45-48.
"Sleeplessness" (tr. of Thomasz Jastrun). TriQ (57, Vol. 1) Spr-Sum 83, p. 59.

3826. ROTH, Ann
"Hanging the Swings." HiramPoR (35) Aut-Wint 83, p. 36.
"A Sense of Place." HiramPoR (35) Aut-Wint 83, p. 35.
"Sisters." YetASM (2:1) 83, p. 5.

3827. ROTH, Michael P.
"Canto del Refugiado" (Song of the Refugee). SanFPJ (5:2) 83, p. 72.

3828. ROTHENBERG, Jerome
"An Ikon." Sulfur (3:2, #8) 83, p. 128-130.
"Setchin the Singer" (a working--not more 'free' than most translations--from a French translation of a series of Vogul shaman songs). Sulfur (3:2, #8) 83, p. 124-128.

3829. ROTHOLZ, Susan
"Dog Poem with Snow." NewRena (17) Aut 83, p. 74.
"What We Have Become." NewRena (17) Aut 83, p. 73-74.

3830. ROUGHTON, Becke
"The Other." Poetry (142:2) My 83, p. 101.
"Poem for Richard." PoetL (77:1) Spr 82, p. 25.

3831. ROUSE, Irene
"Making the Best of It." Bogg (50) 83, p. 8.

ROUSH, Joy L. Price
See: PRICE-ROUSH, Joy L.

3832. ROWDON, Larry
"Field Trip." PottPort (5) 83-84, p. 21.

3833. ROWLAND, Jon
"The Chorale." Grain (11:1) F 83, p. 29.

3834. ROY, André
"Lent Amour" (I). PoetryCR (4:3) Spr 83, p. 12.
"Lent Amour" (II). PoetryCR (5:2) Wint 83-84, p. 8.
"Lent Amour" (III). PoetryCR (5:2) Wint 83-84, p. 8.

3835. ROYSTER, Philip M.
"Grandma's House." KanQ (15:1) Wint 83, p. 76-77.

3836. RUARK, Gibbons
"Late Word from Corcomroe Abbey." MidwQ (24:2) Wint 83, p. 172-173.
"Love Letter from Clarity in Chartres." MemphisSR (3:2) Spr 83, p. 15-16.
"Wildflowers Left to Live on Knocknarea." Ploughs (9:2/3) 83, p. 132-133.
"Words Full of Wind from the Poulnabrone Dolmen" (for Fred Chappell). Abatis (1) 83, p. 3-4.
"Written in the Guest Book at Thoor Ballylee." Swallow (1) Spr 83, p. 1.

3837. RUBIA, Geraldine
"I Am Tormented." PottPort (5) 83-84, p. 10.
"I'd Like To." PottPort (5) 83-84, p. 11.
"Sparable II." PottPort (5) 83-84, p. 27.

3838. RUBIN, Larry
"The Death of the Drugist." Images (8:3) 83, p. 7.
"The Guest." Vis (13) 83, p. 25.
"The Houses of Emily Dickinson." SewanR (91:2) Spr 83, p. 235.
"Lines at My Father's Grave." SouthernR (19:2) Ap 83, p. 386.
"Miami Boy, Northbound." SouthernR (19:2) Ap 83, p. 385.
"Venice, Once More." Argo (4:3) 83, p. 5.

3839. RUBIN, Louis D., Jr.
"In Memory Of Elliott Coleman, Variations On A Mockingbird." SewanR (91:4) Aut 83, p. 585-589.

3840. RUBNER, Irene Masiker
"L'Envoi." Vis (12) 83, p. 29.

3841. RUCKER, Trish
"Armistice." DekalbLAJ (16:1/4) Aut 82-Sum 83, p. 102.
"Elegy: After Love." DekalbLAJ (16:1/4) Aut 82-Sum 83, p. 102.
"Equinox." DekalbLAJ (16:1/4) Aut 82-Sum 83, p. 103.

3842. RUDMAN, Mark
"Conflagrations at the End of Summer." Tendril (14/15) Wint 83, p. 164.
"Negative." PoetryE (12) Aut 83, p. 63.
"Orphanos." PoetryE (12) Aut 83, p. 67.
"Peripheral Vision." PoetryE (12) Aut 83, p. 68-69.
"Solitaire." ParisR (25:90) Wint 83, p. 68-70.

"Solstice." PoetryE (12) Aut 83, p. 64-65.
"Threshold." PoetryE (12) Aut 83, p. 66.
"The Unknowable." Tendril (14/15) Wint 83, p. 162-163.

3843. RUEFLE, Mary
"Almost As If to Tell Me." BlackWR (10:1) Aut 83, p. 107.
"As Many as Nine." BlackWR (10:1) Aut 83, p. 104.
"Dead Silence on a Beautiful Day." BlackWR (10:1) Aut 83, p. 103.
"Lady Throwing Crackers to the Sea." BlackWR (10:1) Aut 83, p. 110.
"More Nights." BlackWR (10:1) Aut 83, p. 106.
"Stamina." BlackWR (10:1) Aut 83, p. 105.
"Who Shall Have This." BlackWR (10:1) Aut 83, p. 109.
"The Wife of Mission Rock." BlackWR (10:1) Aut 83, p. 108.

3844. RUENZEL, David
"Finis." KanQ (15:1) Wint 83, p. 114.

3845. RUESCHER, Scott
"Gold Mining." Agni (19) 83, p. 108.
"I Look into the Pothole." Agni (19) 83, p. 106-107.
"Objects of Love." Agni (19) 83, p. 105.
"Paper Airplanes." PoetryNW (24:4) Wint 83-84, p. 39-40.
"Personnel." PoetryNW (24:4) Wint 83-84, p. 38-39.
"To the Memory of a Bought-Out Farmer." Ploughs (9:1) 83, p. 173-174.

3846. RUETTIMANN, Donna
"Even Those." CalQ (22) Sum 83, p. 88.

3847. RUFFIN, Paul
"Teaching You to Fly: Taking Off." MemphisSR (3:2) Spr 83, p. 42.

3848. RUGGLES, Eugene
"Lines from an Alcohoic Ward." SecC (11:1/2) 83, p. 191.
"Why Most of Us Are Limping Away from Life." SecC (11:1/2) 83, p. 193.

3849. RUGO, Mariève
"Marriage." SouthernPR (23:2) Aut 83, p. 61.
"Now." PraS (51:1, i.e. 57:1) Spr 83, p. 39.
"Places Are Not Where We Are." Tendril (14/15) Wint 83, p. 165.
"Red Bird in a White Tree" (for Philip Booth). BlackWR (8:1) Aut 81, p. 98.
"Sequence toward a Beginning." PraS (51:1, i.e. 57:1) Spr 83, p. 40-41.
"Two Sides of a Three-Sided Figure." Tendril (14/15) Wint 83, p. 166.
"Vigil." PraS (51:1, i.e. 57:1) Spr 83, p. 42.

3850. RUMENS, Carol
"Letter from South London." Stand (24:2) 83, p. 4-5.

3851. RUMI
"Eating Poetry" (tr. by Robert Bly). PoetryE (11) Sum 83, p. 5.
"The Hawk" (tr. by Robert Bly). PoetryE (11) Sum 83, p. 7.
"The Mill, the Stone, and the Water" (tr. by Robert Bly). PoetryE (11) Sum 83, p. 8.
"That Journeys Are Good" (tr. by Robert Bly). PoetryE (11) Sum 83, p. 6.

3852. RUNCIMAN, Lex
"December 7." NowestR (21:2/3) 83, p. 48.
"Jerome, Arizona." ColEng (45:1) Ja 83, p. 48.

3853. RUNTE, Roseann
"Cinq Vautours." PoetryCR (4:4) Sum 83, p. 14.

RURIKO, Fukuhara
See: FUKUHARA, Ruriko

3854. RUSS, Lisa
"Insomnia." StoneC (10:3/4) Spr-Sum 83, p. 17.
"A Marriage." PoetL (78:3) Aut 83, p. 144.
"Pregnancy." Tendril (14/15) Wint 83, p. 168.
"Soup." PoetL (78:3) Aut 83, p. 145.
"Vespers." Tendril (14/15) Wint 83, p. 167.

3855. RUSSELL, Carolann
"The Black Brother Poems to Etheridge Knight." MidwQ (24:4) Sum 83, p. 457-459.
"Halloween Song for Black Brother." MidwQ (24:4) Sum 83, p. 458.
"Solitary Song for Black Brother Gone Home to Indianapolis." MidwQ (24:4) Sum 83, p. 457.
"The Train Always Goes Home." PoetC (15:1) Aut 83, p. 30.
"Unsung Song for Black Brother." MidwQ (24:4) Sum 83, p. 459.
"Visiting an Abandoned Farmhouse." PoetC (15:1) Aut 83, p. 29.

3856. RUSSELL, Frank
"An Exclusive Drag." PoetryNW (24:1) Spr 83, p. 12-13.
"Have You Ever or Are You Now?." Poetry (143:2) N 83, p. 77-78.
"Invitation to the Robber." MemphisSR (1:2) Spr 81, p. 22.
"Passionate Cousins." MemphisSR (1:2) Spr 81, p. 23.

3857. RUSSELL, Norman H.
"First Class." SmPd (20:1) Wint 83, p. 15.
"Smoke and Fog." SmPd (20:1) Wint 83, p. 16.

3858. RUSSELL, Thomas
"Lavonder." NowestR (21:1) 83, p. 23.

3859. RUSTE, Arne
"Say More, Speak Like Rain" (tr. by Olav Grinde). PoetryE (9/10) Wint 82-Spr 83, p. 11-13.

3860. RUTAN, Catherine
"The Wedding." OhioR (30) 83, p. 125.

3861. RUTH, Gloria
"Racing." FourQt (32:4) Sum 83, p. 2.

3862. RUTSALA, Vern
"Bravado and Rage: A Memoir." BlackWR (10:1) Aut 83, p. 46-47.
"The Cheap Hotel." SewanR (91:3) Sum 83, p. 391.
"Disappearing." OhioR (30) 83, p. 179.
"Explication de Texte." SewanR (91:3) Sum 83, p. 393-394.
"Leaks." SewanR (91:3) Sum 83, p. 392-393.
"A Little Night Music." BlackWR (8:1) Aut 81, p. 54.
"The Other Room." SewanR (91:3) Sum 83, p. 389-390.
"Something Like Spinks." ThRiPo (21/22) 83, p. 69-70.
"Speaking Her Lonely Greek." BlackWR (8:1) Aut 81, p. 52-53.

3863. RYAN, Michael
"My Dream by Henry James." NewYorker (59:27) 22 Ag 83, p. 30.
"The Myth." OhioR (30) 83, p. 253.
"Tourists on Paros." NewYorker (59:22) 18 Jl 83, p. 34.

3864. RYERSON, Alice
"Aikido Is a Martial Art." SpoonRQ (8:4) Aut 83, p. 34-35.
"Architect." Prima (8) 83, p. 40-41.

RYUSEI, Hasegawa
See: HASEGAWA, Ryusei

RYUUICHI, Tamura
See: TAMURA, Ryuuichi

S., Roe Sonye
See: ROE SONYE S.

SAANEN, Christine Dumitriu van
See: DUMITRIU van SAANEN, Christine

3865. SACERIO GARI, Enrique
"Se despierta un reflejo niuyorquino." Areíto (9:33) 83, p. 22.

3866. SACKETT, Lori
"Fireflies." PoetL (77:3) Aut 82, p. 165.

3867. SACKS, Peter
"Change of Address." GeoR (37:1) Spr 83, p. 189.
"For Richard Turner Assassinated January 8, 1978." AntR (41:4) Aut 83, p. 450-452.

"In Time." SenR (13:2) 82-83, p. 7-8.

3868. SADEH, Pinchas
"The Angel" (tr. by Gabriel Levin). LitR (26:2) Wint 83, p. 231-232.
"Several Days After Parting from a Girl Who Lived with Me for Close to Half a Year" (tr. by Gabriel Levin). LitR (26:2) Wint 83, p. 232.

3869. SADOFF, Ira
"After a Disappointing Visit with Old Friends I Try in Vain to Recover the Joys of Childhood." YaleR (72:3) Spr 83, p. 418.
"The Day We Learned Manners." OhioR (30) 83, p. 260.
"Ginseng Root." MissouriR (6:3) Sum 83, p. 26-27.
"Labor Day." Ploughs (9:1) 83, p. 167-168.
"Labor Day: The Women of Fifth Avenue." NewRep (188:25) 27 Je 83, p. 30.
"Scars." Ploughs (9:1) 83, p. 169-170.
"Why We Always Take Vacations by the Water." Ploughs (9:1) 83, p. 165-166.

3870. SAFARIK, Allan
"The Abstract Self." MalR (64) F 83, p. 34.
"Crab." CanLit (98) Aut 83, p. 47-48.
"The Dead Man's Eye." MalR (64) F 83, p. 38-39.
"The Evergreens Shine Like Poison in Their Winter Coats of Rain." MalR (64) F 83, p. 35-36.
"God Loves Us Like Earthworms Love Wood." MalR (64) F 83, p. 33.
"Horticulture." PoetryCR (5:1) Aut 83, p. 6.
"Jelly Fish Tofino Harbour." MalR (64) F 83, p. 36-37.
"Knock Knock the Air Is Empty of Sound." MalR (64) F 83, p. 42.
"The Lions at Coombs." MalR (64) F 83, p. 40-41.
"Meat in the Silo." MalR (64) F 83, p. 34.
"Rivals for the Sun." CanLit (98) Aut 83, p. 46-47.

3871. SAFIR, Natale
"Coecles Harbor 1981." Images (8:3) 83, p. 8.
"Shifting." NegC (3:4) Aut 83, p. 94.
"Variations on Round Form." Images (8:3) 83, p. 8.

3872. SAGAN, Miriam
"Aegean Doorway." IndR (6:2) Spr 83, p. 73.

3873. SAGARIS, Lake
"Fragments: or How Is Life in Chile?" MinnR (NS 21) Aut 83, p. 70-71.
"Resolving Differences." MinnR (NS 20) Spr 83, p. 45-46.
"Two Visions in One World." MinnR (NS 20) Spr 83, p. 44.-45.
"Waiting." MinnR (NS 21) Aut 83, p. 69.

3874. SAGER, Deborah
"Landscape in December." SpiritSH (49 Suppl.) 83, p. 34.
"Mirror." SpiritSH (49 Suppl.) 83, p. 34.

"Morning." SpiritSH (49 Suppl.) 83, p. 35.
"She." SpiritSH (49 Suppl.) 83, p. 35.

3875. SAID, Amina
"Une Femme Retarde la Venue de la Mer et Leur Mouvance se Brise." PoetryCR (5:2) Wint 83-84, p. 8.
"Nous remettrons-nous seulement." PoetryCR (4:3) Spr 83, p. 11.

3876. SAIGYO, Priest
"Body" (tr. by Graeme Wilson). WestHR (37:4) Wint 83, p. 334.

SAINT . . .
See: ST. . . ., filed below as spelled.

3877. SAKELLARIOU, Becky (Becky Dennison)
"What Some Women Do." 13thM (6:1/2) 82, p. 24.
"Women Who." YetASM (2:1) 83, p. 6.

3878. SAKON, Lady
"The Hearts of Men" (from The Shinkokinshu, tr. by Graeme Wilson). WestHR (37:2) Sum 83, p. 146.

SAKUTARO, Hagiwara
See: HAGIWARA, Sakutaro

3879. SALANGA, Alfredo
"By my bidding and mine alone." Dandel (10:2) Aut-Wint 83, p. 26-27.
"This is no way to begin the year." Dandel (10:2) Aut-Wint 83, p. 24-25.

3880. SALASIN, Robert
"Three Pieces for Karl Radek, 1885-1937." NewRena (17) Aut 83, p. 23.

3881. SALEH, Dennis
"1949." MissouriR (7:1) Aut 83, p. 22-23.
"Fear of Whites." SouthernPR (23:2) Aut 83, p. 67-74.
"Paul." SecC (11:1/2) 83, p. 194-195.

3882. SALEMI, Joseph
"Propertius, III.24." PortR (29:1) 83, p. 6-7.
"Tribulus, 11.4." PortR (29:1) 83, p. 4.

3883. SALIM, Hassan K.
"Change." SanFPJ (4:4) 83, p. 21.
"December." SanFPJ (5:4) 83, p. 71.
"From Rags to Riches." SanFPJ (4:4) 83, p. 18.
"In America, Not of America." SanFPJ (4:4) 83, p. 19.
"Things Are Worse Than Bad." SanFPJ (5:4) 83, p. 70.

3884. SALINAS, Luis Omar
"After I'm Gone." Telescope (5/6) Spr 83, p. 154.
"For Good Pablo." Telescope (5/6) Spr 83, p. 153.
"Ode to Cervantes." Telescope (5/6) Spr 83, p.

151-152.

3885. SALINGER, Wendy
"The Eternal Boy." ParisR (24:84) Sum 82, p. 148.

3886. SALKEY, Andrew
"Mountains, Rivers, and Caribbea" (For Eliot and Jason). NewL (49:3/4) Spr-Sum 83, p. 82-83.
"A Recollection of Caribbea." NewL (49:3/4) Spr-Sum 83, p. 82.
"A Year Afterwards." NewL (49:3/4) Spr-Sum 83, p. 81.

SALLE, Peter la
See: LaSALLE, Peter

3887. SALLIS, James
"Apostrophe." CharR (9:2) Aut 83, p. 83.
"Jazz." Bogg (51) 83, p. 19.
"P.S." BlackWR (10:1) Aut 83, p. 156-159.

3888. SALMI, Shelly
"I Believe." Meadows (3:1) 82, p. 44.
"No More." Meadows (3:1) 82, p. 44.

3889. SALMON, Jenny
"The Addams' Ingenuity." Tele (18) 83, p. 58.
"Magi." Tele (18) 83, p. 59.

3890. SALSICH, Albert
"Portraiture." SouthwR (68:1) Wint 83, p. 41.

3891. SALTER, Mary Jo
"Amphitheater with Trees." Nat (237:1) 2 Jl 83, p. 26.
"Anthropod." Nat (236:4) 29 Ja 83, p. 118.
"At the Public Baths" (Kyoto, 1982). Nat (236:23) 11 Je 83, p. 740.
"At the Public Baths" (Kyoto, 1982) (incomplete). Nat (236:17) 30 Ap 83, p. 546.
"Henry Purcell in Japan." NewYorker (59:9) 18 Ap 83, p. 134.
"Japanese Characters." Poetry (142:4) Jl 83, p. 202-206.
"Luminary." Nat (237:1) 2 Jl 83, p. 26.
"Officer and Laughing Girl." Nat (236:4) 29 Ja 83, p. 118.
"On Removing Summer from the Public Gardens." Nat (236:4) 29 Ja 83, p. 118.
"Rocky Harbour Newfoundland." NewRep (186:5) 3 F 82, p. 35.
"Welcome to Hiroshima." Atlantic (252:2) Ag 83, p. 44.

3892. SALTMAN, Benjamin
"Always toward Evening." Epoch (32:3) Spr-Sum 83, p. 245.
"Neutral Zone." Epoch (32:3) Spr-Sum 83, p. 244.
"The Purchase." PoetryNW (24:4) Wint 83-84, p. 45.

3893. SALVAGGIO, Ruth
"Frostbite." Poem (49) N 83, p. 23.

3894. SALZMAN, Eva
"Historic House on the River-Bank." PoetC (13, i.e. 14:3) 83, p. 23-24.

3895. SALZMANN, Jerome
"Mark's Mushroom." LittleBR (3:3) Spr 83, p. 83.
"Rose the Mourner." Wind (13:49) 83, p. 43.

3896. SAMARAS, Nicholas
"Tracking the Bears." NewYorker (59:38) 7 N 83, p. 48.

3897. SAMPSON, Dennis
"Joy of Living Aone." BlackWR (9:2) Spr 83, p. 54-55.

3898. SAMUELS, Diana Reed
"The Tribes of Light." SanFPJ (4:4) 83, p. 7.

3899. SANCHEZ, Nardelis
"Río Piedras." Areíto (9:33) 83, p. 22.

3900. SANDEEN, Ernest
"Tricycle." NewRep (187:10) 6 S 82, p. 32.

3901. SANDERS, Ed
"Sappho on East Seventh." Sulfur (3:2, #8) 83, p. 8-38.

3902. SANDERS, Lewis
"Dawn the old dog's gaping mouth." WindO (42) Sum 83, p. 2.

3903. SANDERS, Mark
"Hasp." LittleBR (3:3) Spr 83, p. 81.

3904. SANDERS, Thomas E. (Nippawanock)
"Dad's Signs--Now Mine" (Excerpt). SoDakR (21:4) Wint 83, p. 39.
"Machine out of the God." SoDakR (21:4) Wint 83, p. 62.

SANDOVAL, Rodrigo Parra
See: PARRA SANDOVAL, Rodrigo

3905. SANDY, Stephen
"Bridge of Abandonment." ParisR (24:84) Sum 82, p. 177.
"Landscape with the Body of Judas." Poetry (141:4) Ja 83, p. 204.
"Lhasa Flea Market." LittleBR (4:2) Wint 83-84, p. 49.
"Pirandello, Pirandello." NewEngR (6:1) Aut 83, p. 149.
"Potala, Colorado." LittleBR (4:2) Wint 83-84, p. 48-49.
"Tender Gothic." PoNow (7:2, #38) 83, p. 9.

"Tom and Henry, Camping Out." ParisR (24:84) Sum 82, p. 176.

3906. SANER, Reg
"Anne, Your Name's Mouth and Kiss." PraS (57:2) Sum 83, p. 53-54.
"Aspen Oktoberfest." PraS (57:2) Sum 83, p. 57-59.
"August Night." KanQ (15:4) Aut 83, p. 130.
"Beggar." PoNow (7:2, #38) 83, p. 14.
"Blue Ruin." PraS (57:2) Sum 83, p. 48-49.
"The Boulderfield." KanQ (15:4) Aut 83, p. 130.
"Earth and Sky and Light's Offer." PraS (57:2) Sum 83, p. 41-42.
"Faces, Campus Faces." Outbr (12/13) Aut 83-Spr 84, p. 98-99.
"Fairgrounds." PraS (57:2) Sum 83, p. 46.
"The Fifth Season." ParisR (24:85) Aut 82, p. 144-145.
"The Fire Thief." PraS (57:2) Sum 83, p. 45.
"Fireweed My Wand." KanQ (15:4) Aut 83, p. 129.
"For the Irish Humming at Gregory Gulch." PraS (57:2) Sum 83, p. 56-57.
"Guessing the Right Hand of Love." PraS (57:2) Sum 83, p. 44.
"Jane." PraS (57:2) Sum 83, p. 43.
"Light's Offer: A Group of Poems." PraS (57:2) Sum 83, p. 39-59.
"The Moon's Secret Face." PraS (57:2) Sum 83, p. 46-47.
"Mountain Conifer." PraS (57:2) Sum 83, p. 48.
"North." PraS (57:2) Sum 83, p. 50.
"Poem: Waxy, glistering thickets." MemphisSR (3:2) Spr 83, p. 13.
"Return to Tundra at Bighorn Flats: for Anne." ThRiPo (21/22) 83, p. 71.
"Road Life." ParisR (24:85) Aut 82, p. 140-143.
"Song for Sisyphus." PraS (57:2) Sum 83, p. 53.
"The Sun's Perfect Works." Outbr (12/13) Aut 83-Spr 84, p. 97.
"Swimming to China." MemphisSR (3:2) Spr 83, p. 52.
"To Escape the High Country." PraS (57:2) Sum 83, p. 51.
"The Tongue As Red Dog." ThRiPo (21/22) 83, p. 72.
"The Vesuvius Variations." OhioR (31) 83, p. 5-12.
"View." PraS (57:2) Sum 83, p. 52.
"West." PraS (57:2) Sum 83, p. 49.
"The Westerly Jet, The Newlywed Snails." PraS (57:2) Sum 83, p. 55.
"Words for Them." Telescope (4) Wint 83, p. 64.

3907. SANFILIPPO, Amelia
"An American Dream II." SanFPJ (4:3) 83, p. 35.
"From the Depths of Suburbia." Wind (13:49) 83, p. 52.

3908. SANFORD, Richard
"October Lights." YetASM (2:1) 83, p. 8.

3909. SANFORD, William W.
"Error." Poem (48) Jl 83, p. 32-33.

3910. SANGER, Peter M.
"On Hokusai's 'The Great Wave'." PoetryCR (5:2) Wint 83-84, p. 9.
"Properties of Wood." PoetryCR (5:2) Wint 83-84, p. 9.

3911. SANGIULIANO
"Erbario '81" (Selections from a Roman herbiary) (tr. by Riccardo Duranti). Kayak (62) Ag 83, p. 12-17.

3912. SANTELLI, Richard
"The Busses Are on Time." SoDakR (21:4) Wint 83, p. 36.

SANTIAGO, José Luis Colon
See: COLON SANTIAGO, José Luis

SANTIAGO BACA, Jimmy
See: BACA, Jimmy Santiago

3913. SANTOS, Sherod
"Drag & Shackle." OhioR (30) 83, p. 176.
"The Dream of Nothing." Poetry (141:6) Mr 83, p. 345.
"Eurydice." Poetry (141:6) Mr 83, p. 348.
"Evening Refrain." Poetry (141:6) Mr 83, p. 346.
"The Harvest Season." Poetry (141:6) Mr 83, p. 347.

3914. SAPIA, Yvonne
"Del Medio del Sueño." RevChic (11:3/4) 83, p. 58.
"The Landlord's Dream of Hell." RevChic (11:3/4) 83, p. 57.
"The Posture of the Dance." RevChic (11:3/4) 83, p. 59.
"South Beach: Proteus, S-Shaped in the Sand." KanQ (15:1) Wint 83, p. 191.
"Southern Boulevard." RevChic (11:3/4) 83, p. 56.

3915. SAPPHO
"Prayer to Aphrodite" (tr. by Alfred Corn). ParisR (25:88) Sum 83, p. 60.

3916. SARABIA, Gilbert M.
"The Harvest." SanFPJ (5:3) 83, p. 14.
"Star Dancer." SanFPJ (5:3) 83, p. 14.

3917. SARAH, Robyn
"A Meditation between Claims." AntigR (52) Wint 83, p. 10-11.
"Sounding an Old Chord in October." AntigR (52) Wint 83, p. 9-10.
"Suckers for Truth." AntigR (54) Sum 83, p. 56-57.

3918. SARGENT, Colin W.
"Down to Earth." Sam (36:3 143rd release) 83, p. 17.

3919. SARPER, Ayse
"At the Photographer." NewL (49:3/4) Spr-Sum 83, p. 74.

3920. SARRETT, Sylvia G.
"Poetic License?" EngJ (72:7) N 83, p. 72.

3921. SARTON, May
"A Farewell." ParisR (25:89) Aut 83, p. 111.
"Letters from Maine." ParisR (25:89) Aut 83, p. 112-117.
"Mourning to Do." NegC (3:4) Aut 83, p. 16-17.

3922. SASSI, Mary Elizabeth
"From the Betrothed to a Seagull." YetASM (2:1) 83, p. 3.

3923. SASSO, Laurence J. (See also: SASSO, Laurence J., Jr.)
"The Burial." Wind (13:48) 83, p. 4.

3924. SASSO, Laurence J., Jr. (See also: SASSO, Laurence J.)
"Farm Futures." Confr (25/26) 83, p. 277.

3925. SATEL, Sally
"Arctic Ferry." Prima (8) 83, p. 48.

3926. SATHERLEY, David
"B.C." PottPort (5) 83-84, p. 47.
"For Hagen, Antigonish 1977." AntigR (53) Spr 83, p. 80.
"Half Condition Blind to the Cause." AntigR (53) Spr 83, p. 81-82.
"Lorne (Pictou County, N.S.)." PottPort (5) 83-84, p. 41.

3927. SAULS, Roger
"Mallards and Partridges." Ploughs (9:2/3) 83, p. 188.

3928. SAUNDERS, Geraldine
"Coming Apart" (Excerpt). USl (16/17) Wint 83-84, p. 16.
"We Bolt In." USl (16/17) Wint 83-84, p. 16.
"When I Dance with You." USl (16/17) Wint 83-84, p. 16.

3929. SAUVAGE, Ken
"Flashback." SpoonRQ (8:4) Aut 83, p. 47.

3930. SAVAGE, Gail
"Early November." SpoonRQ (8:4) Aut 83, p. 42.

3931. SAVAGE, Tom
"Syncopation." LittleM (14:1/2) 83, p. 110.
"Welcome to Your Body." LittleM (14:1/2) 83, p. 111.

3932. SAVILLE, Ken
"Tokay!" CreamCR (8:1/2) 83, p. 72.

3933. SAVITT, Lynne
"I'm Glad You Are Casually Interested in Why I Was an Hour Late / or Take Your Fucking Hands Off My Throat." SecC (11:1/2) 83, p. 199-200.
"On the Hospitalization of My Daughter for

Diabetes." SecC (11:1/2) 83, p. 197.

3934. SAVOIE, Terry
"1951." Iowa (13:3/4) Spr 82 (83), p. 124.

3935. SAWYER, Laurie
"Harpo." DekalbLAJ (16:1/4) Aut 82-Sum 83, p. 81.

3936. SCALF, Sue
"Newspaper Photo, 1920" (For my mother). NegC (3:4) Aut 83, p. 62-63.
"Star Children." EngJ (72:4) Ap 83, p. 56.

3937. SCARBROUGH, George
"Address." SpiritSH (49 Suppl.) 83, p. 2.
"Leathers." SpiritSH (49 Suppl.) 83, p. 5.
"Matins." SpiritSH (49 Suppl.) 83, p. 1.
"Ploughing." SewanR (91:3) Sum 83, p. 395-396.
"Sunday School Picnic." SpiritSH (49 Suppl.) 83, p. 3-4.
"Tenantry." PoNow (7:2, #38) 83, p. 19.

3938. SCARPA, Vivien C.
"Life retreats from disintegration." SanFPJ (4:4) 83, p. 51.
"Memories." SanFPJ (4:4) 83, p. 39.
"A Presence." SanFPJ (5:2) 83, p. 68.
"Revelations." SanFPJ (4:4) 83, p. 38.

3939. SCATES, Maxine
"1956." AmerPoR (12:2) Mr/Ap 83, p. 6.
"Floorplans." MassR (24:3) Aut 83, p. 634-635.
"Wartime." AntR (41:2) Spr 83, p. 208.

3940. SCHAAF, Richard
"Burn the KKK: Rally around the Flag Boys." MinnR (NS 21) Aut 83, p. 19-20.
"Letter to Nazim Hikmet" (tr. of Roque B. Dalton). MinnR (NS 21) Aut 83, p. 17-18.

3941. SCHACHTER, Sandy
"Then and Now." YetASM (2:1) 83, p. 9.

3942. SCHAEFER, Ted
"Anxiety Pastorale." NewL (49:3/4) Spr-Sum 83, p. 213.
"The Waltz of Nuclear Physics." NewL (49:3/4) Spr-Sum 83, p. 213.

3943. SCHAEFFER, Susan (See also: SCHAEFFER, Susan Fromberg)
"And Who Is the Doorman." SoCaR (15:2) Spr 83, p. 58-59.
"The River." SoCaR (15:2) Spr 83, p. 60.

3944. SCHAEFFER, Susan Fromberg (See also: SCHAEFFER, Susan)
"The Black Mountain." Confr (25/26) 83, p. 130-132.
"The Garden." ThRiPo (21/22) 83, p. 77-78.
"The House of Snow." KanQ (15:1) Wint 83, p. 78-79.
"In the Garden." Salm (60) Spr-Sum 83, p. 159-160.
"The Lion." OP (35) Spr-Sum 83, p. 52-53.

"Poetry Writing." SoDakR (21:4) Wint 83, p. 29.
"Rising." SoDakR (21:4) Wint 83, p. 64.
"The Story of My Life." OP (35) Spr-Sum 83, p. 48-51.

3945. SCHECHTER, Robert
"A Worthwhile Exercise." PoetryE (11) Sum 83, p. 27-28.

3946. SCHECHTER, Ruth Lisa
"Before Thunder Struck." Images (8:3) 83, p. 10.

3947. SCHEDLER, Gilbert
"Celibacy." WindO (42) Sum 83, p. 34.
"Easter Sunday." ChrC (100:9) 23-30 Mr 83, p. 282.
"My Brother Loves Diversity." WindO (42) Sum 83, p. 34.

3948. SCHEEL, Jean
"Equinox." PoetL (77:1) Spr 82, p. 26.
"War of White and Yellow." PoetL (77:1) Spr 82, p. 26.

3949. SCHEEL, Mark
"Rain." LittleBR (4:1) Aut 83, p. 9.

3950. SCHEELE, Roy
"A Crossing." KanQ (15:2) Spr 83, p. 168.

3951. SCHEFFLEIN, Susan
"Sunrise in a Beanfield." Wind (13:48) 83, p. 58.

3952. SCHEIER, Libby
"Clarity." Descant (40) Spr 83, p. 37-38.
"Dwarfs and War." Descant (40) Spr 83, p. 34-35.
"The Hard Work of Flying." Descant (40) Spr 83, p. 32-33.
"Ideas." Descant (40) Spr 83, p. 40-41.
"Linguistic Analysis." Descant (40) Spr 83, p. 42-43.
"Tight Space." Descant (40) Spr 83, p. 39.
"Violence." Descant (40) Spr 83, p. 44-45.
"Why Poems Should Not Be Fictions" (a polemic). Descant (40) Spr 83, p. 36.

3953. SCHERMERHORN, D. R.
"Night Sequence." Waves (11:4) Spr 83, p. 39-41.
"Poem: This emotion must gain the authority." Dandel (10:1) Spr-Sum 83, p. 51.
"Reconciliation." AntigR (55) Aut 83, p. 69.

3954. SCHEVILL, James
"Clown at Crafts Fair." PoNow (7:2, #38) 83, p. 3.
"Confidential Data on the Loyalty Investigation of Herbert Ashenfoot" (from The American Fantasies: Collected Poems 1945-1981). PoNow (7:2, #38) 83, p. 38.
"The Difficult Task of Mentioning." StoneC (11:1/2, Pt. 1) Aut-Wint 83, p. 27.
"The Dream of Fathers." PoNow (7:2, #38) 83, p. 2.

"Flood." PoNow (7:2, #38) 83, p. 3.
"The Jovial Mortician" (from The American Fantasies: Collected Poems 1945-1981). PoNow (7:2, #38) 83, p. 38.
"Marriage of Horse and Wood." PoNow (7:2, #38) 83, p. 2.
"Mr. Castle's Vacation Drive" (from The American Fantasies: Collected Poems 1945-1981). PoNow (7:2, #38) 83, p. 38.
"The Murderer." PoNow (7:2, #38) 83, p. 2.

3955. SCHEXNAYDER, Kenneth
"The Rocker and the Dog." SouthernPR (23:2) Aut 82 [i.e. (23:1?) Spr 83], p. 54.
"Toward Distant Water." AmerPoR (12:2) Mr/Ap 83, p. 44.

3956. SCHICKELE, Susan
"Too Small for Cards." WestB (12) 83, p. 16-17.

3957. SCHIFF, Jeff
"Balance." Tendril (16) Sum 83, p. 109.
"In Praise: Say Hey." WindO (43) Wint 83, p. 22.
"Misogyny." WindO (43) Wint 83, p. 21.
"Preservation." IndR (6:1) Wint 83, p. 21.
"Saturday on the Drag." WindO (43) Wint 83, p. 23.
"Unemployment." Tendril (16) Sum 83, p. 110.

3958. SCHIMMEL, Harold
"All" (tr. of Avoth Yeshurun). LitR (26:2) Wint 83, p. 211.
"Apollo 1" (tr. of Mordechai Geldman). LitR (26:2) Wint 83, p. 286.
"Apollo 2" (tr. of Mordechai Geldman). LitR (26:2) Wint 83, p. 286.
"The Ballad of Berl Schlosser" (tr. of Avoth Yeshurun) LitR (26:2) Wint 83, p. 213-214.
"Bat Shlomo." (tr. by Gabriel Levin). LitR (26:2) Wint 83, p. 255.
"Before the Surgeon" (tr. of Avoth Yeshurun). LitR (26:2) Wint 83, p. 212.
"Binyamina" (tr. by Gabriel Levin). LitR (26:2) Wint 83, p. 254.
"Cruel Heart" (tr. of Yona Wollach). LitR (26:2) Wint 83, p. 280-281.
"Darkness Will Sweeten" (tr. of Yair Hurvitz). LitR (26:2) Wint 83, p. 276.
"Domestic Poem" (tr. of Aharon Shabtai). LitR (26:2) Wint 83, p. 264-269.
"Family Pictures" (Excerpt) (tr. of Meir Wieseltier). LitR (26:2) Wint 83, p. 273.
"Fat Boy" (tr. of Mordechai Geldman). LitR (26:2) Wint 83, p. 287.
"Fruit" (tr. of Meir Wieseltier). LitR (26:2) Wint 83, p. 273.
"A Map" (tr. of Yair Hurvitz). LitR (26:2) Wint 83, p. 275.
"My Father and My Mother Went Out to Hunt" (tr. of Yona Wollach). LitR (26:2) Wint 83, p. 281.
"My sins" (tr. of Yona Wollach). LitR (26:2) Wint

83, p. 280.
"Prelude on the Demise of the Mulberry Tree" (tr. of Avoth Yeshurun). LitR (26:2) Wint 83, p. 213.
"With Long Hooks" (tr. of Mordechai Geldman). LitR (26:2) Wint 83, p. 285.

3959. SCHLOSSER, Robert
"The Bamboo Ocean / A Sailor Speaks." Sam (36:3 143rd release) 83, p. 22.

3960. SCHMID, Vernon
"Baptism." ChrC (100:12 [i.e. 13]) 27 Ap 83, p. 398.
"Passing through Oklahoma." Wind (13:48) 83, p. 59.

3961. SCHMIDT, Claudia
"River of Tears." ClockR (2:1) 83, p. 29.

3962. SCHMIDT, Paul
"After Cambridge." Shen (34:3) 83, p. 88-89.
"Bakunin Baking in Baku" (Excerpt) (tr. of Velimir Khlebnikov). Sulfur (3:1, #7) 83, p. 117.
"Bow! Wow! Bow!" (tr. of Velimir Khlebnikov). Sulfur (3:1, #7) 83, p. 115-116.
"Crawling crying craven" (tr. of Velimir Khlebnikov). Sulfur (3:1, #7) 83, p. 116.
"Laffers love laffing" (tr. of Velimir Khlebnikov). Sulfur (3:1, #7) 83, p. 117-118.
"The law of the see-saw argues" (tr. of Velimir Khlebnikov). Sulfur (3:1, #7) 83, p. 117.
"Let the plowman leave his furrow" (tr. of Velimir Khlebnikov). Nat (237:8) 24 S 83, p. 248.
"New York: Museum of Modern Art" (for Annette Michelson). Shen (34:3) 83, p. 90.
"Night's color breeding darker blues" (tr. of Velimir Khlebnikov). Nat (237:8) 24 S 83, p. 248.
"Once more, once more" (tr. of Velimir Khlebnikov). Nat (237:8) 24 S 83, p. 248.
"P pay o P" (tr. of Velimir Khlebnikov). Sulfur (3:1, #7) 83, p. 116.
"Water eats at the ash-grove" (tr. of Velimir Khlebnikov). Nat (237:8) 24 S 83, p. 248.
"Wind whose song" (tr. of Velimir Khlebnikov). Sulfur (3:1, #7) 83, p. 115.

3963. SCHMIDT, Steven
"Station House." Blueline (3:2) Wint-Spr 82, p. 26.

3964. SCHMIDT, William J.
"To Robert Frost (Died January 29, 1963)." ChrC (100:3) 26 Ja 83, p. 66.

3965. SCHMIED, Wieland
"Art Trip to Oaxaca" (tr. by Beth Bjorklund). DevQ (18:3) Aut 83, p. 27.
"Chess with Marcel Duchamp" (tr. by Beth Bjorklund). DevQ (18:3) Aut 83, p. 28-29.
"The Things of René Magritte--I" (tr. by Beth Bjorklund). DevQ (18:3) Aut 83, p. 30.

3966. SCHMITT, E. B.
"The Goddess Laments." DekalbLAJ (16:1/4) Aut 82-Sum 83, p. 104.
"Reckoning." DekalbLAJ (16:1/4) Aut 82-Sum 83, p. 103.

3967. SCHMITZ, Barbara
"Danny." Tele (18) 83, p. 117.
"Going." Tele (18) 83, p. 118.
"He clears his throat." Tele (18) 83, p. 117.
"Shorter." Tele (18) 83, p. 116.

3968. SCHMITZ, Dennis
"Auto-." NewL (49:3/4) Spr-Sum 83, p. 253.
"Gill Boy" (for John, my son). TriQ (56) Wint 83, p. 140.
"The Knot." TriQ (56) Wint 83, p. 137.
"A Man & a Woman." Field (28) Spr 83, p. 49.
"News." TriQ (56) Wint 83, p. 138-139.
"Sabotage." Tendril (14/15) Wint 83, p. 169-170.
"Stung." Field (28) Spr 83, p. 50.
"La Traviata." Tendril (14/15) Wint 83, p. 171-172.

3969. SCHNEIDER, Aaron
"The Gadgets." AntigR (53) Spr 83, p. 10.
"The Great Escape Artist" (for Harry Houdini). AntigR (53) Spr 83, p. 11-12.

3970. SCHNELL, Hartmut
"Red Tomatoes" (tr. of Rolf Dieter Brinkmann). NewL (49:3/4) Spr-Sum 83, p. 140.

3971. SCHNORBUS, Frank
"The Meadowlands." SanFPJ (5:4) 83, p. 12.
"The Meadowlands." SanFPJ (5:4) 83, p. 45.

3972. SCHOECK, R. J.
"Winter Scene." AntigR (55) Aut 83, p. 70.

3973. SCHOENBERGER, Nancy
"God's Sun." AmerPoR (12:6) N/D 83, p. 33.
"Her Story: Bathsheba." SouthernR (19:3) Jl 83, p. 645.
"Horse." AmerPoR (12:6) N/D 83, p. 33.
"In Street Light" (for my sister). AmerPoR (12:6) N/D 83, p. 33.
"In This City." SouthernR (19:3) Jl 83, p. 644.

3974. SCHOENFELDT, Stephanie Mara
"Just Once More, for Old Times Sake." YetASM (1:2) 82, p. 7.
"Silly Goose." YetASM (1:2) 82, p. 11.

3975. SCHOONOVER, Amy Jo
"Judging Poetry at the Homemakers' Show." WindO (43) Wint 83, p. 52.
"Turn the calendar page." WindO (42) Sum 83, p. 4.

3976. SCHOR, Sandra
"Have you heard the still lifes of Morandi" (For

Georgio Morandi). LittleM (14:1/2) 83, p. 23.

SCHORBUS, Frank
See: SCHNORBUS, Frank

3977. SCHRAMM, Darrell G. H.
"Pat and Banjo." KanQ (15:2) Spr 83, p. 158-159.

3978. SCHREIBER, Ron
"Gregoria, on the Street." HangL (44) Sum 83, p. 47.
"John, at Home." HangL (44) Sum 83, p. 49.
"The Middle of May." Wind (13:47) 83, p. 37.
"Nico, Presiding." HangL (44) Sum 83, p. 48.
"Pictures in Black & White." HangL (44) Sum 83, p. 52.
"Sex." HangL (44) Sum 83, p. 50-51.
"What You're Teaching Me." HangL (44) Sum 83, p. 46.

3979. SCHROCK, Glenda
"Grandmother Bryan." Thrpny (3:4, issue 12) Wint 83, p. 3.
"In Memory of Will, Drowned." Thrpny (4:2, issue 14) Sum 83, p. 19.
"Part of That Particular Circus." Thrpny (3:4, issue 12) Wint 83, p. 3.
"When You Were Gone from Home." Thrpny (4:1, issue 13) Spr 83, p. 4.

3980. SCHUBERT, David
"The Adoration." QRL (24) 83, p. 109-110.
"Advice." QRL (24) 83, p. 117-118.
"The Albatross" (tr. of Charles Baudelaire). QRL (24) 83, p. 72.
"Another Poet Called David." QRL (24) 83, p. 69.
"Autumn Sonnet" (tr. of Charles Baudelaire). QRL (24) 83, p. 73.
"BA (On the Same Theme)." QRL (24) 83, p. 21.
"Boy of the Arrowy Thoughts." QRL (24) 83, p. 98-99.
"The Christmas Tree and the Terror." QRL (24) 83, p. 30-32.
"A Corsage." QRL (24) 83, p. 66-67.
"Cortez." QRL (24) 83, p. 88-90.
"The Creation of Others." QRL (24) 83, p. 68.
"Crooked Road Crooked Year." QRL (24) 83, p. 8-10.
"Crow on the Husk." QRL (24) 83, p. 13.
"The Darkness of the Night." QRL (24) 83, p. 14.
"Dissertation on the Detroit Free Press." QRL (24) 83, p. 37-38.
"Dream." QRL (24) 83, p. 95.
"Faustus, The End (a revision)." QRL (24) 83, p. 105-107.
"For a Boy Infant's Wreath." QRL (24) 83, p. 29.
"Gawayn and the Green Knight." QRL (24) 83, p. 39-40.
"Getting a Mosquito." QRL (24) 83, p. 19.
"Gold Chariot." QRL (24) 83, p. 12.
"The Happy Traveller." QRL (24) 83, p. 35-36.
"Hunter." QRL (24) 83, p. 111-113.
"Incidental." QRL (24) 83, p. 103-104.
"Intersection." QRL (24) 83, p. 7.

"Invitation." _QRL_ (24) 83, p. 94.
"It Is Sticky in the Subway." _QRL_ (24) 83, p. 48.
"Kind Valentine." _QRL_ (24) 83, p. 3-4.
"The Lake." _QRL_ (24) 83, p. 28.
"The Letter." _QRL_ (24) 83, p. 26.
"Lighthouse Mission." _QRL_ (24) 83, p. 11.
"Looking for a House." _QRL_ (24) 83, p. 18.
"Lullaby from the Japanese." _QRL_ (24) 83, p. 220.
"Lunar." _QRL_ (24) 83, p. 115-116.
"The Mark." _QRL_ (24) 83, p. 20.
"The Meaning of Winter." _QRL_ (24) 83, p. 58.
"Memory." _QRL_ (24) 83, p. 101.
"Midston House." _QRL_ (24) 83, p. 56-57.
"Monterey." _QRL_ (24) 83, p. 16.
"Morning." _QRL_ (24) 83, p. 93.
"Narcissus." _QRL_ (24) 83, p. 83-86.
"Night Piece." _QRL_ (24) 83, p. 97-98.
"No Finis." _QRL_ (24) 83, p. 70.
"No Title." _QRL_ (24) 83, p. 64-65.
"Old Story." _QRL_ (24) 83, p. 91.
"Peter and Mother." _QRL_ (24) 83, p. 24-25.
"The Picnic." _QRL_ (24) 83, p. 44-45.
"Pier I." _QRL_ (24) 83, p. 27.
"Poem: Greenhorn a popcorn five cents a piece." _QRL_ (24) 83, p. 136-139.
"Poem: Lift up your voice to a new song, you said." _QRL_ (24) 83, p. 121-122.
"Poem: While the valley was blistering baby suns." _QRL_ (24) 83, p. 87-88.
"Predicament." _QRL_ (24) 83, p. 62-63.
"Prospect Park." _QRL_ (24) 83, p. 55.
"Question." _QRL_ (24) 83, p. 87.
"Reflections on Violence." _QRL_ (24) 83, p. 54.
"The Simple Scale." _QRL_ (24) 83, p. 46-47.
"The Skeleton in the Closet." _QRL_ (24) 83, p. 49.
"A Small Girl And." _QRL_ (24) 83, p. 99-100.
"The Snow in the Mouse Wind." _QRL_ (24) 83, p. 41-43.
"A Successful Summer." _QRL_ (24) 83, p. 61.
"To Ra." _QRL_ (24) 83, p. 120-121.
"The Transformation." _QRL_ (24) 83, p. 50-52.
"Victor Record Catalog." _QRL_ (24) 83, p. 59-60.
"The Visitor." _QRL_ (24) 83, p. 33.
"Voyage." _QRL_ (24) 83, p. 122-123.
"The Voyage" (to Maxime du Camp, tr. of Charles Baudelaire). _QRL_ (24) 83, p. 74-79.
"Voyage (Revision)." _QRL_ (24) 83, p. 124-125.
"Wanda." _QRL_ (24) 83, p. 92-93.
"West by the Rain." _QRL_ (24) 83, p. 23.
"The Wheel." _QRL_ (24) 83, p. 173-176.
"When Apples on the Lilac." _QRL_ (24) 83, p. 5-6.
"With Japanese Lanterns." _QRL_ (24) 83, p. 17.

3981. SCHUCHAT, Simon
"Across the creek are the masses." _Tele_ (18) 83, p. 38.
"Auto-Critique." _Tele_ (18) 83, p. 37.
"Bloomingdales." _Tele_ (18) 83, p. 34.
"Brass boots pounding out of the cave." _Tele_ (18) 83, p. 33.
"The Camera Eye." _Tele_ (18) 83, p. 30.

"Dejection." Tele (18) 83, p. 31.
"Erdnusskerne." Tele (18) 83, p. 34.
"A Field of Experts." Tele (18) 83, p. 40.
"Heavenly Ford Road Anecdote." Tele (18) 83, p. 36.
"I hear the Voice of America calling." Tele (18) 83, p. 35.
"In the Multi-Storied Hotel." Tele (18) 83, p. 30.
"Lake Li." Tele (18) 83, p. 39.
"New Year." Tele (18) 83, p. 39.
"Poem: Houses fill in the interior of a block." Tele (18) 83, p. 38.
"Spring & Autumn." Tele (18) 83, p. 32.
"Tiny Romance." Tele (18) 83, p. 31.
"Wind and water and cold penetrating." Tele (18) 83, p. 35.
"Written in Red: Spring & Autumn" (Selections). Tele (18) 83, p. 30-40.

3982. SCHULER, Ruth Wildes
"The Boat People, San Francisco, 1979." Sam (36:3 143rd release) 83, p. 54-55.
"Kathy." Sam (34:3 135th release) 83, p. 22.
"Rhino." Sam (36:3 143rd release) 83, p. 20.

3983. SCHULMAN, Grace
"The Almond Tree" (tr. of T. Carmi). LitR (26:2) Wint 83, p. 228.
"Birds on a Blighted Tree." OntR (19) Aut-Wint 83-84, p. 43.
"Credo" (tr. of T. Carmi). LitR (26:2) Wint 83, p. 226.
"From This Day On" (tr. of T. Carmi). LitR (26:2) Wint 83, p. 227.
"The Marsh." Shen (34:3) 83, p. 96.
"Military Funeral at High Noon" (In Memory of J.H., tr. of T. Carmi). LitR (26:2) Wint 83, p. 228-230.
"New Year." Poetry (142:3) Je 83, p. 152.
"Port of Many Names." Poetry (142:3) Je 83, p. 151.
"She Sleeps" (tr. of T. Carmi). LitR (26:2) Wint 83, p. 227.

3984. SCHULMAN, Norma
"Lot's Wife." PoetL (77:2) Sum 82, p. 73.

3985. SCHULTZ, K. Lydia
"Labor" (for Theodor W., Adorno) (tr. of Hans Magnus Enzensberger). NowestR (21:1) 83, p. 129.
"Poetry Festival" (Hommage à Paul van Ostaijen) (tr. of Hans Magnus Enzensberger). NowestR (21:1) 83, p. 125, 127.

3986. SCHULTZ, Philip
"Anemone." Nat (236:6) 12 F 83, p. 186.
"The Garden of Honor." Poetry (141:5) F 83, p. 283.
"His Face." Nat (236:24) 18 Je 83, p. 776.
"Lines to a Jewish Cossack: For Isaac Babel." Poetry (141:5) F 83, p. 281-282.
"The Ogre." MichQR (22:1) Wint 83, p. 96.
"Personal History." MichQR (22:1) Wint 83, p. 95.

"The View." NewYorker (58:46) 3 Ja 83, p. 32.
"The Wish." Nat (236:12) 26 Mr 83, p. 375.

3987. SCHULTZ, Robert
"Antarctica." VirQR (59:1) Wint 83, p. 62-65.

3988. SCHUSTER, Anne
"Ambidextrous." YetASM (2:1) 83, p. 7.

3989. SCHUSTER, David
"124th Street Song." Abraxas (27/28) 83, p. 11.

3990. SCHWAIGER, Brigitte
"I Always" (tr. by Sieglinde Lug). DevQ (17:4) Wint 83, p. 25.

3991. SCHWARTZ, Hillel
"The Baroness Renata, Her Magic Shop." AntigR (52) Wint 83, p. 89.
"Camel Watcher." NewRena (16) Spr 83, p. 30.
"Countless Collectibles." Pig (11) 83, p. 68.
"Douc Langur: 'An Unusual Leaf-Eating Monkey of Indochina'." BelPoJ (34:1) Aut 83, p. 16-17.
"Flotsam." AntigR (52) Wint 83, p. 90.
"Long Division." Tendril (14/15) Wint 83, p. 173.
"Out of the Wreckage." NewRena (16) Spr 83, p. 28-29.
"Pulling Up the Tents." PoetL (78:3) Aut 83, p. 171-172.
"Rita, Sue, Gwendolyn, Agnes, Linda, Marge, Queens for a Day." BallSUF (24:1) Wint 83, p. 53.
"Rocks, Gate, Winter." PoetL (77:3) Aut 82, p. 154.
"Thousands of Small Hands." NewOR (10:2/3) Sum-Aut 83, p. 153.
"Vizier Sweets." StoneC (10:3/4) Spr-Sum 83, p. 16.
"Why after All Octave Chanute Encouraged the Two Brothers." Comm (110:11) 3 Je 83, p. 340.

3992. SCHWARTZ, Jeffrey
"Night Driving." LittleM (14:1/2) 83, p. 112.

3993. SCHWARTZ, Lloyd
"Artie Matteosian." Shen (34:1) 83, p. 47.
"Danny and Mary Kelleher." Shen (34:1) 83, p. 48.
"Estelle's Testimony." NewRep (186:15) 14 Ap 82, p. 38-39.
"Fourteen People" (after a portrait series by Ralph Hamilton). Shen (34:1) 83, p. 41-48.
"Frank Bidart." Shen (34:1) 83, p. 42.
"Friendships and Time." Ploughs (9:1) 83, p. 75-76.
"Gail Mazur." Shen (34:1) 83, p. 42.
"Jane Struss." Shen (34:1) 83, p. 43.
"Joyce Peseroff." Shen (34:1) 83, p. 44.
"Lloyd Schwartz." Shen (34:1) 83, p. 41.
"Margo Lockwood." Shen (34:1) 83, p. 46.
"Mr. and Mrs. Hamilton." Shen (34:1) 83, p. 43-44.
"Ralph Hamilton." Shen (34:1) 83, p. 41.
"Robert Pinsky." Shen (34:1) 83, p. 45.
"Tom Joanides." Shen (34:1) 83, p. 46.

3994. SCHWEIZER, Lauren
"Why I Left Houston." YetASM (2:1) 83, p. 11.

3995. SCOTT, Greg
"War Is a Whore." SanFPJ (4:3) 83, p. 32.

3996. SCOTT, Jo
"Continuum." SanFPJ (4:4) 83, p. 27.
"Jane Doe." SanFPJ (5:4) 83, p. 68.
"Man's Hunger for War." SanFPJ (5:2) 83, p. 8.
"Science." SanFPJ (5:2) 83, p. 13.

3997. SCOTT, Nancy
"As I Lay Drowning." Tele (18) 83, p. 112.
"The Oak." Tele (18) 83, p. 112.
"Thruway." Tele (18) 83, p. 113.
"To a Young Lover." Tele (18) 83, p. 113.

3998. SCOTT, Shelley
"Apologies to 'Berlin' (To Ray Madachy). Vis (12) 83, p. 13.
"Folding Clothes." Vis (12) 83, p. 12.

3999. SCRIBNER, Douglas
"My Days Are Numbered." SanFPJ (4:3) 83, p. 60.

4000. SEABURG, Alan
"Not Everyone Has Been So Lucky." CapeR (18:2) Sum 83, p. 11.
"The Old Goat." CapeR (19:1) Wint 83, p. 22.
"Rebecca and Ann." CapeR (18:2) Sum 83, p. 12.
"Silent Movies." CapeR (18:2) Sum 83, p. 10.

4001. SEALE, Jan
"In Praise of Woman Chief." Calyx (7:3) Sum 83, p. 22-24.
"Trailride." Wind (13:48) 83, p. 60-61.

4002. SEARS, Peter
"To a Young Woman Considering Suicide." Field (28) Spr 83, p. 54.

4003. SEATON, Maureen Therese
"New Versa." YetASM (1:2) 82, p. 10.
"New Versa." YetASM (2:1) 83, p. 4.

4004. SEATON, Peter
"Need from a Wound Would Do It." ParisR (24:86) Wint 82, p. 79-81.

4005. SEATOR, Lynette
"Seer." YetASM (2:1) 83, p. 7.

4006. SEETCH, Beth
"Little Apocalypses." PoetryNW (24:3) Aut 83, p. 21.

4007. SEGALL, Pearl B.
"No-Win Situation." SanFPJ (5:4) 83, p. 50.
"Who Stole Hallowe'en?" SanFPJ (5:4) 83, p. 51-52.

4008. SEIBLES, Timothy
"The Ring around the Moon." SouthwR (68:3) Sum 83, p. 281.

4009. SEID, Christopher
"Fable." IndR (5:2) Sum 82, p. 47.

4010. SEIDEL, Frederick
"A Dimpled Cloud." Raritan (2:3) Wint 83, p. 88-90.

4011. SEIDMAN, Hugh
"Ars Poetica" (for the poet RD). ParisR (24:84) Sum 82, p. 73-75.
"Coast of Maine." OhioR (30) 83, p. 234-235.
"Kaddish." ParisR (24:84) Sum 82, p. 76.

4012. SEILER, Barry
"Dark World." IndR (5:3) Aut 82, p. 7.
"In Passing." Swallow (2) Aut-Wint 83, p. 48.
"In Vermeer's Delft." NewRep (188:11) 21 Mr 83, p. 32.

SEISHI, Yamaguchi
See: YAMAGUCHI, Seishi

4013. SELINGER, Eric
"Don't Get Cute." HarvardA (117:2) My 83, p. 12-13.

4014. SELLERS, Bettie
"Another Innisfree." Blueline (3:2) Wint-Spr 82, p. 39.
"State Highway over Brasstown Gap." PikeF (5) Spr 83, p. 10.
"Thirteen Lines for Stephen." PikeF (5) Spr 83, p. 10.

4015. SELTZER, Joanne
"Lines to a Future Soldier." Vis (11) 83, p. 8.
"Scandal at the Hyde House: Glen Falls, New York." Blueline (3:2) Wint-Spr 82, p. 35.
"Waxwings at Ampersand." Blueline (5:1) Sum-Aut 83, p. 37.

4016. SELVAGGIO, Marc
"The Curious Looking In." WestB (12) 83, p. 85.

4017. SEMENOVICH, Joseph
"Lonely and Insecure." PikeF (5) Spr 83, p. 34.
"A Machiavellian Thought." Abraxas (27/28) 83, p. 17.
"My arch enemy peter." Wind (13:47) 83, p. 38-39.

4018. SEMONES, Charles
"Elegy in the Red-Light District." Wind (13:47) 83, p. 40.

4019. SEPULVEDA, Arnaldo
"Angélica de Madrugada." Rácata (1) 83, p. 111.
"Autobiografía Común." Rácata (1) 83, p. 108.
"Definición de la Cebolla." Rácata (2) 83, p.

129.
"Di á Logo de Taller" (a y por Rácata). Rácata (2) 83, p. 123.
"Las lagunas entre los dedos" (A Josefina, Al Grupo Contadores de Historias). Rácata (1) 83, p. 110.
"Mi amor es un extraño." Rácata (1) 83, p. 109.
"Ojo por Tuerto." Rácata (2) 83, p. 122.
"Poética del Ocio." Rácata (2) 83, p. 121.
"Teleología (Sonsa) de un Chupón." Rácata (2) 83, p. 120.
"Tener el ocio de la venganza a distancia." Rácata (1) 83, p. 107.

4020. SERCHUK, Peter
"For Poppa, Asleep in the Smithtown Madhouse." AmerPoR (12:3) My-Je 83, p. 31.

4021. SERENI, Vittorio
"City of Night" (tr. by Marcus Perryman and Peter Robinson). Argo (5:1) 83, p. 20.
"Italian in Greece" (tr. by Marcus Perryman and Peter Robinson). Argo (5:1) 83, p. 20.

4022. SERGEANT, Howard
"Crazy Love Poem for an Unseen Lady." Waves (11:4) Spr 83, p. 59.

4023. SEROTE, Mongane
"A Poem: Everyone of us." PoetryE (9/10) Wint 82-Spr 83, p. 277.

4024. SERVID, Carolyn
"Recollecting Jasmine." WorldO (17:4) Sum 83, p. 39.

4025. SESSIONS, W. A.
"Plato's Poet." CalQ (22) Sum 83, p. 85.

4026. SEUSS-BRAKEMAN, Diane
"Whities." IndR (5:3) Aut 82, p. 42-43.

4027. SEVOV, Kolyo
"An Afternoon's Wandering":(tr. by John Balaban and Elena Hristova). NewEng (5:4) Sum 83, p. 512.

4028. SEYFRIED, Robin
"The National Anthem." Poetry (142:2) My 83, p. 102-103.

4029. SHABTAI, Aharon
"Domestic Poem" (tr. by Harold Schimmel). LitR (26:2) Wint 83, p. 264-269.

SHAEFFER, Susan Fromberg
See: SCHAEFFER, Susan Fromberg

4030. SHAFFER, Craig C.
"Groundhog Day in Maggie Valley." PoetC (13, i.e. 14:3) 83, p. 32-33.

4031. SHAFFER, Greg
"Father." Wind (13:47) 83, p. 45.

SHAHID ALI, Agha
See: ALI, Agha Shahid

SHAN, Han
See: HAN, Shan

4032. SHANAHAN, Deidre
"Sunday Service." Argo (4:2) 82, p. 17.

4033. SHANNON, Laura
"Food for Thought." HangL (44) Sum 83, p. 73.

4034. SHAPIRO, Alan
"Bedtime Story." TriQ (58) Aut 83, p. 87.
"Fossils." SouthernR (19:1) Ja 83, p. 147-148.
"Genie." TriQ (58) Aut 83, p. 89.
"His Happy Hour." TriQ (58) Aut 83, p. 88.
"Long Days." SouthernR (19:1) Ja 83, p. 147.
"Perfect Son." ChiR (33:4) Sum [i.e. Spr] 83, p. 38-39.
"Someone Else." AmerS (52:3) Sum 83, p. 363-364.
"Song for a Time of Year." SouthernR (19:1) Ja 83, p. 145-146.
"What Makes You Think It's Fear." SouthernR (19:1) Ja 83, p. 148.
"Without Warning." SouthernR (19:1) Ja 83, p. 146.

4035. SHAPIRO, David
"St. Barnabas." ParisR (24:85) Aut 82, p. 76-79.

4036. SHAPIRO, Harvey
"Blue Eyes." Confr (25/26) 83, p. 21.
"Causing Anguish." Confr (25/26) 83, p. 20.
"Discovery." Nat (236:10) 12 Mr 83, p. 310.
"Experiences." Confr (25/26) 83, p. 18-19.
"On a Sunday." ParisR (24:84) Sum 82, p. 78.

SHARAT CHANDRA, G. S.
See: CHANDRA, G. S. Sharat

4037. SHARPE, Peter
"Farmer in Welsh Fog." MassR (24:3) Aut 83, p. 500.

4038. SHATTUCK, Roger
"Cher Ami" (for Henri Peyre at eighty). AmerS (52:1) Wint 82/83, p. 38-39.
"A Little Night Music (Borborygmes)." PoetryE (11) Sum 83, p. 83.
"The Shirt." NewYorker (59:35) 17 O 83, p. 52.

4039. SHAW, Robert B.
"Chronometrics." Poetry (142:4) Jl 83, p. 215-217.

4040. SHEDD, Kenn
"The Divine Miss M" (after Jonathan Holden). KanQ (15:3) Sum 83, p. 89.

4041. SHEEHAN, Marc J.
"On the Decline of the Furniture Industry in Grand Rapids." MinnR (NS 20) Spr 83, p. 24.

4042. SHEEHAN, Tom
"Bare Ribbed Talisman." Vis (12) 83, p. 20.
"There Are Rivets." WindO (43) Wint 83, p. 42.
"Things That Happen Only If You Watch." WindO (43) Wint 83, p. 41.

4043. SHEFTEL, Harry B.
"Heirlooms." YetASM (1:2) 82, p. 9.

4044. SHEILDS, Carol
"Daddy." AntigR (54) Sum 83, p. 72.
"Getting." AntigR (54) Sum 83, p. 71.
"Learning to Read." AntigR (54) Sum 83, p. 70.
"Waking." AntigR (54) Sum 83, p. 71.

SHEKERJIAN, Regina deCormier
See: DeCORMIER-SHEKERJIAN, Regina

4045. SHELDON, Anne Lane
"July 8." YetASM (1:1) 82, p. 3.
"May 4." YetASM (1:1) 82, p. 2.

4046. SHELLEY, Pat
"Eggs in Basket." Calyx (8:1) Aut 83, p. 15.

4047. SHELTON, Richard
"Another Darkness." OhioR (30) 83, p. 95.
"The Unbetrayed." ThRiPo (21/22) 83, p. 79.

4048. SHEPARD, Neil
"After the Wishing Star Goes Down." Nimrod (27:1) Aut-Wint 83, p. 45.
"Atchafalaya November." SouthernR (19:2) Ap 83, p. 393-394.
"Autumn at the Farm." SouthernR (19:2) Ap 83, p. 395-396.
"For Vivian." Nimrod (27:1) Aut-Wint 83, p. 44.
"In the Dark." Vis (11) 83, p. 37.
"Learning to Ride the Train." SouthernR (19:2) Ap 83, p. 396-397.
"Notes on Human Evolution from the Museum of Natural History." Vis (12) 83, p. 18.

4049. SHEPHERD, J. Barrie
"Advent Haiku." ChrC (100:36) 30 N 83, p. 1109.
"And of All Things Visible and Invisible." ChrC (100:32) 2 N 83, p. 988.
"Regalia." ChrC (100:39) 21-28 D 83, p. 1176.
"Winter Garden." ChrC (100:5) 16-23 F 83, p. 143.

4050. SHEPPARD, Patricia
"The Commuter's Poem." Hudson (36:2) Sum 83, p. 327.

4051. SHER, Steven
"Distant Cousin." KanQ (15:1) Wint 83, p. 158.
"Dog Aura." KanQ (15:1) Wint 83, p. 158-159.

4052. SHERER, Joan M.
"Away from the Emptiness." PortR (29:1) 83, p. 49.
"The Bag Ladies." SanFPJ (5:4) 83, p. 81-82.
"Happy Birthday, Husband!" SanFPJ (5:4) 83, p. 30-31.
"Within Us All." SanFPJ (5:3) 83, p. 31.

4053. SHERIDAN, David
"Easter Garden." Abraxas (27/28) 83, p. 18.

4054. SHERIDAN, Michael
"Days." OhioR (30) 83, p. 254-255.

4055. SHERMAN, Alana
"Why Rebecca Is Not Allowed to Kill Fireflies." YetASM (1:1) 82, p. 10.

4056. SHERMAN, Ken (See also: SHERMAN, Kenneth)
"Aquarium" (from The Elephant Man). Descant (40) Spr 83, p. 64-65.
"Into the Workhouse" (from The Elephant Man). Descant (40) Spr 83, p. 67.
"A Pretty Lady" (from The Elephant Man). Descant (40) Spr 83, p. 71.
"The Wrong One Died" (from The Elephant Man). Descant (40) Spr 83, p. 69.

4057. SHERMAN, Kenneth (See also: SHERMAN, Ken)
"Diane Arbus: Ground Glass." CanLit (96) Spr 83, p. 80-81.

4058. SHERRY, James
"Epistle Apology." ParisR (24:86) Wint 82, p. 121-122.

4059. SHERWIN, Judith Johnson
"Steenweg." SouthwR (68:1) Wint 83, p. 65-66.

4060. SHETTERLY, Susan Hand
"Pastoral." BelPoJ (33:4) Sum 83, p. 37-38.

4061. SHIELDS, Carol
"The Methodist Jesus." Quarry (32:1) Wint 83, p. 47.

4062. SHIMER, Michael
"Midnight Ritual." SmPd (20:1) Wint 83, p. 17-19.

SHIMON, Ezra ben
See: Ben-SHIMON, Ezra

4063. SHIPLEY, Vivian
"Scientific Knives Are Sharp But Now Mythical." SanFPJ (4:4) 83, p. 70-71.

4064. SHIRLEY, Aleda
"The Feel of Not to Feel It." Poetry (142:5) Ag 83, p. 264-265.
"One of a Number of Good Intentions." Poetry (142:5) Ag 83, p. 266.
"The Waiting, the Sailing." CimR (62) Ja 83, p. 4.

SHNORBUS, Frank
See: SCHNORBUS, Frank

4065. SHOEMAKER, Lynn
"Lullabye." SoDakR (21:4) Wint 83, p. 71.

4066. SHOEMAKER, Tom
"Attack of the Killer Amenities." SanFPJ (5:1) 83, p. 86-87.

4067. SHOLL, Betsy
"Wisps." BelPoJ (33:3) Spr 83, p. 25.

4068. SHOMER, Enid
"Song of the Disaster." Outbr (12/13) Aut 83-Spr 84, p. 40.
"They May Throw Silver Nets." Outbr (12/13) Aut 83-Spr 84, p. 41.

4069. SHORB, Michael
"The Gills of Prometheus." ThirdW Spr 83, p. 73.
"Harp Seal Harvest." Vis (11) 83, p. 27.
"In Memory of Beauty Douglas." Os (16) 83, p. 15.
"Lincoln." ThirdW Spr 83, p. 72.
"The Man Who Killed for Love." Vis (11) 83, p. 23.
"More Fish Than Ever." Vis (11) 83, p. 26.
"The Rain Forest Massacre." Vis (11) 83, p. 25.

4070. SHORE, Jane
"German Weather-House." NewRep (187:18) 8 N 82, p. 30.
"The Glass Slipper." NewRep (187:12/13) 20-27 S 82, p. 30.
"The Other Woman." Ploughs (9:1) 83, p. 49-51.
"Philemon and Baucis." Ploughs (9:1) 83, p. 53-54.
"Triangle." NewRep (187:5) 2 Ag 82, p. 28.
"Two Figures." Ploughs (9:1) 83, p. 51-52.

4071. SHORT, Gary
"Benjamin (Bugsy) Siegel 1906-1947 Businessman." Meadows (4:1) 83, p. 51.

4072. SHOWALTER, Link
"Frosted Faces and Freight Trains." SanFPJ (5:3) 83, p. 15.

4073. SHUKWIT, Christen, Sister
"Sterility." EngJ (72:3) Mr 83, p. 112.

4074. SHULLENBERGER, William
"Newborn." YetASM (1:1) 82, p. 5.

4075. SHULMAN, Susie
"An Everyday Integrity." Poetry (142:6) S 83, p. 331.
"The Going-Part." Poetry (142:6) S 83, p. 330.

4076. SHUMAKER, Peggy
"Esperanza's Hair." MissouriR (6:2) Wint 83, p. 77.

SHUNTARO, Tanigawa
See: TANIGAWA, Shuntaro

4077. SHURIN, Aaron
"Multiple Heart" (Selections). Sulfur (3:1, #7) 83, p. 140-142.

SHUSON, Kato
See: KATO, Shuson

4078. SIBUM, Norm
"And Heaven Has a Lonely Sound." Dandel (10:1) Spr-Sum 83, p. 61.
"Breaking and Entering the Hungarian's Place." Dandel (10:1) Spr-Sum 83, p. 58.
"Lutenists in the Morning." Dandel (10:1) Spr-Sum 83, p. 64.
"Marriage by Arrangement." Dandel (10:1) Spr-Sum 83, p. 62-63.
"On the Eve of a Certain Madness." Dandel (10:1) Spr-Sum 83, p. 60.
"The Shadows of Beauty Lengthen." Dandel (10:1) Spr-Sum 83, p. 59.

4079. SICOLI, Dan
"Ghosts." Bogg (50) 83, p. 23.

4080. SIEBER, Sharon
"Full Wind" (tr. of Octavio Paz). NowestR (21:2/3) 83, p. 5-15.

4081. SIEGEL, Melanie
"The Business." HiramPoR (34) Spr-Sum 83, p. 21.
"Food Shopping." HiramPoR (34) Spr-Sum 83, p. 22.

4082. SIEGEL, Robert
"Alphabeasts." KanQ (15:4) Aut 83, p. 35-40.
"A Dream of Feeding Pigs." KanQ (15:4) Aut 83, p. 40-41.
"The Great Northern Diver." PraS (57:2) Sum 83, p. 23-24.

4083. SIEGFRIED, Rodney
"Gas Line." WormR (23:2, issue 90) 83, p. 69.
"Mike." WormR (23:2, issue 90) 83, p. 69.
"Poison Tree." WormR (23:2, issue 90) 83, p. 69.

4084. SIEVERS, Wendy
"Changes." CapeR (19:1) Wint 83, p. 44.

4085. SIGUROSSON, Olafur Johann
"Steeple-Sign." Vis (11) 83, p. 38-39.

4086. SILESKY, Barry
"Jackpine." KanQ (15:2) Spr 83, p. 167.
"Working on the Roof." BlackWR (10:1) Aut 83, p. 70-71.

4087. SILK, Dennis
"At Large." Stand (24:2) 83, p. 42.

"Difficulties of an Actress." AmerPoR (12:5) S/O 83, p. 40.
"Grand Central." AmerPoR (12:5) S/O 83, p. 40.
"Guide to Jerusalem" (Selections from the 3rd ed.)." LitR (26:2) Wint 83, p. 318-320.
"Memories of '57." AmerPoR (12:5) S/O 83, p. 40.
"Pastoral of the Fast Talkers" (For Hilda O'Connell and Adeli di Cruz). AmerPoR (12:5) S/O 83, p. 41.
"Politics." LitR (26:2) Wint 83, p. 320.

4088. SILKIN, Jon
"Absence and Light." Telescope (4) Wint 83, p. 6.
"Crossing to Europe." Telescope (4) Wint 83, p. 38-39.
"Footsteps on the Downcast Path." MichQR (22:3) Sum 83, p. 352-359.
"We Were Evacuated in the War." Stand (24:1) 82-83, p. 4-5.
"What We Have Held." PraS (57:4) Wint 83, p. 56.

4089. SILLIMAN, Ron
"Blue" (for Gil Ott). ParisR (24:86) Wint 82, p. 84-85.

4090. SILVA, Chanel
"The Dr. Turmoil Diet." Poem (48) Jl 83, p. 19.
"God in His Winter." Poem (48) Jl 83, p. 16-18.
"Reptilian Crack-up." Poem (48) Jl 83, p. 15.

4091. SILVA, Manuel
"The Rat" (tr. by Sandra Reyes). NewOR (10:2/3) Sum-Aut 83, p. 78.

SILVA, Margot de
See: De SILVA, Margot

4092. SILVA, Sam
"Fusion on the Outer Banks." SanFPJ (4:4) 83, p. 24.

4093. SILVER, William
"Small Excursions of the Hour." KanQ (15:1) Wint 83, p. 190-191.

4094. SILVERBERG, Dan
"Future Draft." Sam (34:3 135th release) 83, p. 56.

4095. SILVERMAN, Stuart Jay
"Standing Before and Standing About." HolCrit (20:5) D 83, p. 17.

4096. SILVERSTEIN, Ronn
"And Loving Her, Flows My Blood." WestCR (18:2) O 83, p. 19.
"Ave Maria." WestCR (18:2) O 83, p. 18.
"Go to her/tell her." WestCR (18:2) O 83, p. 20.
"A Spasm of Miracles." WestCR (18:2) O 83, p. 19.
"Today, I am at a loss for words." WestCR (18:2) O 83, p. 17.

4097. SIMBECK, Rob
"Beer in a Glass." KanQ (15:2) Spr 83, p. 149.
"Catacomb." KanQ (15:2) Spr 83, p. 149.

4098. SIMIC, Charles
"The Childhood of Parmenides." ParisR (24:84) Sum 82, p. 180.
"Cold Blue Tinge." ParisR (24:84) Sum 82, p. 181.
"Fool's Paradise" (for Keith). AmerPoR (12:4) Jl-Ag 83, p. 5.
"For the Lovers of the Absolute." AmerPoR (12:4) Jl-Ag 83, p. 6.
"In Midsummer Quiet." AmerPoR (12:4) Jl-Ag 83, p. 5.
"Northern Exposure." Field (28) Spr 83, p. 25.
"A Quiet Talk with Oneself." Field (28) Spr 83, p. 26.
"The Riddle." OhioR (30) 83, p. 7.
"Sheep Delivered by Truckloads." GeoR (37:3) Aut 83, p. 629.
"Trees in the Open Country" (For Jim). LittleBR (4:2) Wint 83-84, p. 16.
"William and Cynthia." AmerPoR (12:4) Jl-Ag 83, p. 5.
"Without a Sough of Wind." AmerPoR (12:4) Jl-Ag 83, p. 6.

4099. SIMISON, Greg
"Longbeach." CanLit (99) Wint 83, p. 32.

4100. SIMMERMAN, Jim
"Black Angel." QW (16) Spr-Sum 83, p. 116-117.
"Child's Grave, Hale County, Alabama" (after the photograph by Walker Evans). KanQ (15:4) Aut 83, p. 63.
"If: On Learning of a Friend's Miscarriage." MissouriR (6:2) Wint 83, p. 36.
"What Is Wrong with This Picture?" (Halloween, 1980). MissouriR (6:2) Wint 83, p. 34-35.

4101. SIMMONS, Thomas
"Candles" (to L.W., April 1978). SouthernR (19:3) Jl 83, p. 662.
"The Companion." SouthernR (19:3) Jl 83, p. 661.
"Hunting Phantoms" (Los Trancos Preserve, California). SouthernR (19:3) Jl 83, p. 663.
"Waking." Thrpny (4:1, issue 13) Spr 83, p. 17.

4102. SIMMS, Michael
"The Inner Ear." Telescope (5/6) Spr 83, p. 83.

4103. SIMMS, Norman
"A Two-Part Poem of Penang." Bogg (50) 83, p. 41.

4104. SIMNER, Barry
"Levellers." Stand (24:3) 83, p. 17.

4105. SIMON, Greg
"City without Sleep: Nocturne at the Brooklyn Bridge" (tr. of Federico García Lorca). NowestR (21:2/3) 83, p. 99, 101.

"Double Poem of Lake Eden" (tr. of Federico García Lorca). NowestR (21:2/3) 83, p. 81, 83.
"Earth and Moon" (tr. of Federico García Lorca). NowestR (21:2/3) 83, p. 85, 87.
"Elegy for a Sleeping Negress Seized by Captain Lancarote in the Spring of 1442." AmerPoR (12:2) Mr/Ap 83, p. 44.
"Landscape with Two Graves and an Assyrian Dog" (tr. of Federico García Lorca). NowestR (21:2/3) 83, p. 89.
"Ode to Walt Whitman" (tr. of Federico García Lorca). NowestR (21:2/3) 83, p. 91-97.
"Poeta en Nueva York" (Selections) (tr. of Federico García Lorca). NowestR (21:2/3) 83, p. 79-101.

4106. SIMON, John Oliver
"In Swarthmore College Ethics Class." SecC (11:1/2) 83, p. 196.

4107. SIMONS, Michelle Blake
"Almost Asleep." Ploughs (9:1) 83, p. 180.

4108. SIMPSON, Grace Pow
"Buzzard Invading Our Field." PoetL (77:4) Wint 83, p. 209-210.
"The Clay Eaters." PoetL (77:4) Wint 83, p. 207-208.
"Waking on the Beach." PoetL (77:4) Wint 83, p. 210-211.

4109. SIMPSON, Louis
"Elegy for Jake." VirQR (59:3) Sum 83, p. 441-445.
"The Eleventh Commandment." NewL (50:1) Aut 83, p. 27-28.
"How to Live on Long Island." Hudson (36:2) Sum 83, p. 289-291.
"Periodontics." VirQR (59:1) Wint 83, p. 52-57.
"Physical Universe." Hudson (36:2) Sum 83, p. 287-289.
"The Previous Tenant." Hudson (36:1) Spr 83, p. 30-44.
"A Remembrance of Things Past." PoetryE (11) Sum 83, p. 42-43.
"Why Do You Write about Russia." OhioR (30) 83, p. 84-86.

4110. SIMPSON, Nancy
"Paris." SouthernPR (23:2) Aut 82 [i.e. (23:1?) Spr 83], p. 64.

4111. SINASON, Valerie
"Rumpelstiltskin." Argo (4:3) 83, p. 12-13.

4112. SINGER, Rosanne
"Hadrian's Villa." CapeR (19:1) Wint 83, p. 40.
"My Suit with Padded Shoulders." Poem (49) N 83, p. 10.
"Quaint Exhibition." Poem (49) N 83, p. 9.

4113. SINIKKA
"Decades." Waves (11:4) Spr 83, p. 67.

4114. SIO, Hilary
"In a New Voice." Tele (18) 83, p. 78-79.
"You Paint Me." YetASM (1:1) 82, p. 11.

4115. SIPE, D. D.
"The Thistle Feeder." Wind (13:49) 83, p. 44.

4116. SIROWITZ, Hal
"Designing Women's Clothes." Abraxas (27/28) 83, p. 43.
"Invisible Stars." YetASM (1:1) 82, p. 3.
"Rings under My Eyes." NewRena (16) Spr 83, p. 70.
"The Talking Flame." NewRena (16) Spr 83, p. 69.

4117. SISSON, Jonathan
"The Prisoner of Dry Rock." LittleM (14:1/2) 83, p. 48-49.
"The Tree Sitter of 1930." LittleM (14:1/2) 83, p. 50.
"Tryst, 21 March 1952." LittleM (14:1/2) 83, p. 47.

SISTER MARY LUCINA
See: LUCINA, Mary, Sister

SISTER MAURA
See: MAURA, Sister

4118. SIU, Helen
"A Generation" (tr. of Gu Cheng, w. Zelda Stern). AmerPoR (12:2) Mr/Ap 83, p. 20.
"I Am a Willful Child" (tr. of Gu Cheng, w. Zelda Stern). AmerPoR (12:2) Mr/Ap 83, p. 20.
"Shooting a Photograph" (tr. of Gu Cheng, w. Zelda Stern). AmerPoR (12:2) Mr/Ap 83, p. 20.

4119. SKARSTEDT, S. A.
"The Bus Driver." AntigR (53) Spr 83, p. 111.
"The Roomer." AntigR (53) Spr 83, p. 110.

4120. SKEATE, Jeffery
"Each moment tacking." Northeast (Ser. 3:15) Sum 83, p. 12.
"Sunset: darkness invading." Northeast (Ser. 3:15) Sum 83, p. 12.
"Your falling hair." Northeast (Ser. 3:15) Sum 83, p. 12.

4121. SKELLEY, Jack
"Smogman Laments His Task." Tele (18) 83, p. 47-48.

4122. SKELTON, Robin
"Come in, Anyway." Kayak (61) Ap 83, p. 53.
"Door to Door to Door." Kayak (61) Ap 83, p. 53.
"Emergence." Kayak (61) Ap 83, p. 52.
"Her Wisdom." Waves (11:2/3) Wint 83, p. 49.
"How." Descant (40) Spr 83, p. 52-53.
"Is Not and Is." PoetryCR (5:2) Wint 83-84, p. 13.
"Not Grief But Thanks." PoetryCR (5:2) Wint 83-84, p. 6.
"The Performance." Kayak (61) Ap 83, p. 51.

"Poetry." Waves (11:2/3) Wint 83, p. 48.
"Prestidigitation." Kayak (61) Ap 83, p. 50.
"The Secret." Descant (40) Spr 83, p. 51.
"Wild Mushrooms" (For Brigid). Descant (40) Spr 83, p. 54-55.
"With Help from Stein and Stevens." PoetryCR (4:4) Sum 83, p. 5.

4123. SKIADOPOULOU, Irini
"On Heroics." Stand (24:4) Aut 83, p. 56.

4124. SKILLMAN, Judith
"Black Ice." CrabCR (1:1) My 83, p. 15.
"Canoe." CrabCR (1:1) My 83, p. 15.
"My Parents' Yard Revisited." YetASM (1:1) 82, p. 8.

4125. SKINNER, Knute
"The American College Dictionary (Copyright 1962 by Random House)" (from Friends and Relations, finalist, 10th anniversary manuscript competition). StoneC (11:1/2, Pt. 1) Aut-Wint 83, p. 5
"A Double Monopoly Game" (from Friends and Relations, finalist, 10th anniversary manuscript competition). StoneC (11:1/2, Pt. 1) Aut-Wint 83, p. 54-55.
"The Mastodon in the Wall." Bogg (50) 83, p. 45.

4126. SKLAR, Morty
"I Put the Telephone Back on Its Receiver." Tele (18) 83, p. 46.
"A Man Lies in White Linen." NewL (49:3/4) Spr-Sum 83, p. 231.
"Poem to the Sun." NewL (49:3/4) Spr-Sum 83, p. 57.

4127. SKLOOT, Floyd
"Diggings." Confr (25/26) 83, p. 307.
"The Resort" (Long Beach, NY, 1982). Tendril (14/15) Wint 83, p. 174-175.
"Seeing Wind." SouthwR (68:4) Aut 83, p. 324.

4128. SKOYLES, John
"No Thank You." OhioR (30) 83, p. 171.
"White Nights" (after a line by Montale). VirQR (59:2) Spr 83, p. 235-236.

4129. SKY-PECK, Kathryn
"Fugue." AntR (41:2) Spr 83, p. 204.
"Lesson." AntR (41:2) Spr 83, p. 205.

4130. SLATER, Dave (See also: SLATER, David)
"Joggers." Bogg (50) 83, p. 38.

4131. SLATER, David (See also: SLATER, Dave)
"Jean-Louis." SecC (11:1/2) 83, p. 201-202.

4132. SLAVOV, Atanas
"Pavarotti Is Her Man." Vis (12) 83, p. 22.

4133. SLEIGH, Tom
"In the Hospital for Tests." Ploughs (9:1) 83, p.

39-40.
"Three Horses." NewYorker (59:30) 12 S 83, p. 46.
"The Very End" (For my Grandmother). Poetry (143:1) O 83, p. 30.

4134. SLOSS, Henry
"Your Picture at the House of Love" (Granada, '81). Shen (34:1) 83, p. 60.

4135. SMALLWOOD, Randy
"The Resident." Wind (13:47) 83, p. 41-43.

4136. SMART, Carolyn
"Afterwards." MalR (64) F 83, p. 193.
"Blood Is Sap Is Desire." MalR (64) F 83, p. 192.
"Now" (for Gillian Robinson). MalR (64) F 83, p. 194.
"Rain: Liverpool, 1980." MalR (64) F 83, p. 191.
"Snow Warning." MalR (64) F 83, p. 195.

4137. SMETZER, Michael
"Apple Trees." KanQ (15:2) Spr 83, p. 150.
"Shadows." KanQ (15:2) Spr 83, p. 150.

4138. SMIDDY, Nena
"Bones." ThirdW Spr 83, p. 97-98.
"Legend of the Box" (after Vasko Popa). ThirdW Spr 83, p. 96-97.
"My Brother Finding the I Ching" (for Robin Hemley). ThirdW Spr 83, p. 95.

4139. SMILLIE, Bill
"Celebration." KanQ (15:1) Wint 83, p. 154.
"The Four Minute Mile." KanQ (15:1) Wint 83, p. 153-154.
"There." PraS (51:1, i.e. 57:1) Spr 83, p. 72-73.

4140. SMITH, Arthur
"Lines on a Tenth Anniversary." NewYorker (59:40) 21 N 83, p. 56.
"Quarry, 1962." ChiR (33:4) Sum [i.e. Spr] 83, p. 43-44.

4141. SMITH, Barbara
"Spoilage." Abatis (1) 83, p. 8.

4142. SMITH, Barbara Leavell
"Meaning." YetASM (1:1) 82, p. 9.
"The Puppy." YetASM (1:1) 82, p. 6.

4143. SMITH, Bill
"Cut -- A Marriage Poem." Stand (24:2) 83, p. 27.

4144. SMITH, Bobbie Jean
"To Chris." Quarry (32:3) Sum 83, p. 56.

4145. SMITH, Bruce
"How Garnett Mims and the Enchanters Came into Your Life." NewRep (187:17) 25 O 82, p. 26.
"In My Father's House." NewEngR (6:2) Wint 83, p.

177-182.

4146. SMITH, Cathryn
"After the Tea Dance, Michigan 1947." Tendril (14/15) Wint 83, p. 176.

4147. SMITH, Charlie
"What It's Like When You're Doing Fine." SouthernPR (23:2) Aut 82 [i.e. (23:1?) Spr 83], p. 48.

SMITH, D. L. Crockett
See: CROCKETT-SMITH, D. L.

4148. SMITH, Dave (See also: SMITH, David)
"Along the Underground Railroad." MemphisSR (2:2) Spr 82, p. 9.
"Bats." Ploughs (9:2/3) 83, p. 110-111.
"Caravati's Salvage: Richmond, Virginia." GeoR (37:2) Sum 83, p. 345.
"A Day with No Clouds." ThRiPo (21/22) 83, p. 80-81.
"A Friend of the Family." NoAmR (268:3) S 83, p. 28.
"Ironclad." SewanR (91:3) Sum 83, p. 378-379.
"Kitchen Windows." NewYorker (59:41) 28 N 83, p. 58.
"Leafless Trees, Chickahominy Swamp." NewYorker (59:32) 26 S 83, p. 50.
"Lion Weather." TriQ (58) Aut 83, p. 104-105.
"Lovesong after Flood." ThRiPo (21/22) 83, p. 82-83.
"Men Drafted." SewanR (91:3) Sum 83, p. 380-382.
"Mosquito Biting." PartR (50:1) 83, p. 80-82.
"Night Traffic near Winchester." TriQ (58) Aut 83, p. 102-103.
"No Return Address." BlackWR (9:1) Aut 82, p. 58-61.
"The Peach Orchard." TriQ (58) Aut 83, p. 106-107.
"The Purpose of the Chesapeake & Ohio Canal." Poetry (142:6) S 83, p. 347.
"Reaction at the Site of a Field Hospital." NoAmR (268:1) Mr 83, p. 46.
"Runaway." Poetry (142:6) S 83, p. 345-346.
"Seven Pines: Taking Shelter from the Rain." NewEngR (6:2) Wint 83, p. 230-234.
"Skating." GeoR (37:4) Wint 83, p. 878-879.
"Squirrel Season." Poetry (142:6) S 83, p. 348-349.
"Winesaps." SewanR (91:3) Sum 83, p. 376-378.

4149. SMITH, David (See also: SMITH, Dave)
"Reliable Heat." Atlantic (251:5) My 83, p. 60.

4150. SMITH, Delphia Frazier
"Fingers of Winter." WritersL Ag 83, p. 10.

4151. SMITH, Douglas
"The Knife-Thrower's Partner." Kayak (63) N 83, p. 10.

4152. SMITH, H. Anne
"Specialties." EngJ (72:5) S 83, p. 46.

SMITH, H. T. Kirby
See: KIRBY-SMITH, H. T.

4153. SMITH, Iain Crichton
"The Loved Place." MalR (64) F 83, p. 208.

4154. SMITH, J. D.
"Earth." SanFPJ (4:2) 83, p. 41.
"Emigrating." SanFPJ (4:2) 83, p. 41.
"Ocean." SanFPJ (4:2) 83, p. 41.

4155. SMITH, Jack
"Mill Closing, 1980." ThRiPo (19/20) 82, p. 55.

4156. SMITH, James Sutherland (See also: SMITH, Jim)
"A Performance of Shakespeare." Outbr (12/13) Aut 83-Spr 84, p. 61-62.

4157. SMITH, Jim (See also: SMITH, James Sutherland)
"Baby Film Review" (for Megan). PoetryCR (4:4) Sum 83, p. 15.
"Imperatives." WestCR (17:4) Ap 83, p. 41.
"It All Comes From." WestCR (17:4) Ap 83, p. 42.

4158. SMITH, Larry (Larry R.) (See also: SMITH, Lawrence R.)
"Let Them Eat Cheese." SanFPJ (4:4) 83, p. 64.
"A Plant Is a Moon." Pig (11) 83, p. 50.

4159. SMITH, Larry E.
"Rainy Time People." Wind (13:48) 83, p. 29.

4160. SMITH, Lawrence R. (See also: SMITH, Larry)
"Vibrio" (Selections: "Social Relations"). Kayak (62) Ag 83, p. 21-27.

4161. SMITH, LeRoy, Jr.
"Adam Rational." Comm (110:1) 14 Ja 83, p. 19.

4162. SMITH, Marcus
"Eight-Fingered America, Land of Fear." MoodySI (10) Aut 81, p. 16.

4163. SMITH, Mbembe Milton
"The Black Messiah." BlackALF (17:4) Wint 83, p. 151.
"The Broken Church Window." BlackALF (17:4) Wint 83, p. 151.
"Bucks." NewL (50:1) Aut 83, p. 5.
"The Eyes of the Ancestors." BlackALF (17:4) Wint 83, p. 150.
"GIGO (Garbage In, Garbage Out)." BlackALF (17:4) Wint 83, p. 150.
"Hawker." NewL (50:1) Aut 83, p. 11.
"Hour of Need: Outer & Inner Sanctuary." NewL (50:1) Aut 83, p. 6-7.
"Lyric for the Girl with Holes in Her Jeans." NewL (50:1) Aut 83, p. 8-9.
"Meditation." NewL (50:1) Aut 83, p. 13-14.
"Meditation in Action." NewL (50:1) Aut 83, p. 14.
"Mysterioso" (after Thelonious Monk). NewL (50:1) Aut 83, p. 8.
"Poor But Happy -- American Television." NewL (50:1) Aut 83, p. 10.

"Prophecy." NewL (50:1) Aut 83, p. 5.
"Reality." NewL (50:1) Aut 83, p. 10.
"The Silent Clouds." NewL (50:1) Aut 83, p. 3.
"Third Page News, or the Rent Problem." NewL (50:1) Aut 83, p. 9.
"What I'm Talking About." BlackALF (17:4) Wint 83, p. 151.
"What I'm Talking About." NewL (50:1) Aut 83, p. 6.
"What Would Give Meaning." NewL (50:1) Aut 83, p. 3.
"Yourself Fulfilling History." BlackALF (17:4) Wint 83, p. 151.

4164. SMITH, Patricia Keeney
"Heritage." CrossC (5:2/3) 83, p. 29.

4165. SMITH, R. A.
"Inflation." Grain (11:1) F 83, p. 22-23.

4166. SMITH, R. T.
"Before Chickamauga." Poem (49) N 83, p. 35.
"Birthmark." SoCaR (16:1) Aut 83, p. 98.
"The Casualty." Poem (49) N 83, p. 34.
"Correspondence" (For Jim Mathis). SouthernHR (17:3) Sum 83, p. 238-239.
"A Cosmological Discovery in the Hollow Log Lounge." Poem (49) N 83, p. 32.
"Farm, Waiting." SpoonRQ (8:4) Aut 83, p. 36-37.
"Goat." PoetL (78:3) Aut 83, p. 136.
"He Rejects a Tract in the Holiday Inn Parking Lot on the Way to Happy Hour." Wind (13:49) 83, p. 45.
"Indian Summer." KanQ (15:2) Spr 83, p. 116.
"Long Distance." PoetL (77:2) Sum 82, p. 84.
"Medicine Shirt, 1892." PoetL (78:3) Aut 83, p. 134-135.
"Miller's Best." Poem (49) N 83, p. 30-31.
"No Masks" (on Ossabaw Island). PoetL (77:2) Sum 82, p. 82-83.
"Rehearsing the Migration." Poem (49) N 83, p. 33.
"Remembering Brady at Gettysburg." MemphisSR (4:1) Aut 83, p. 47.
"Young Bandit Queen Formally Surrenders As Thousands Watch (AP)." PoetL (78:3) Aut 83, p. 133-134.

4167. SMITH, Susan M.
"God Came Crashing Down." PottPort (5) 83-84, p. 20.

4168. SMITH, Sybil
"The Origin of the Dog." Prima (8) 83, p. 98.

4169. SMITH, Thomas R. (See also: SMITH, Tom)
"The Birdsfoot Trefoil." Germ (7:1) Spr-Sum 83, p. 12.
"The White Turtle." Germ (7:1) Spr-Sum 83, p. 13.

4170. SMITH, Tom (See also: SMITH, Thomas R.)
"Lichens (Winter 81-82)." BelPoJ (34:1) Aut 83, p. 6-15.

4171. SMITH, William Jay
"On Hope" (tr. of Lindolf Bell). PoNow (7:2, #38) 83, p. 46.
"Things of the Earth" (tr. of Ferreira Gullar). PoNow (7:2, #38) 83, p. 46.

SMITH WALLACE, Terry H.
See: WALLACE, Terry H. Smith

4172. SMYTH, Deborah
"A Roof Broad Enough." YetASM (1:2) 82, p. 9.
"Running Unconscious." YetASM (1:2) 82, p. 13.

4173. SMYTH, Ethel
"The March of the Women" (Dedicated to the Women's Social and Political Union, c1911). MassR (24:1) Spr 83, p. 131.

4174. SMYTHE, Colin
"Death and the Mole." SpiritSH (49 Suppl.) 83, p. 30.
"Evening." SpiritSH (49 Suppl.) 83, p. 31.
"Why is it that lengths of rail." SpiritSH (49 Suppl.) 83, p. 30.

4175. SNELLING, Lynn
"This and Us." PoetryCR (4:4) Sum 83, p. 15.

4176. SNEYD, Steve
"Face of the Waters." Bogg (51) 83, p. 64.
"Frontier Country." Bogg (51) 83, p. 64.
"A Magnificent Gesture." Bogg (51) 83, p. 52.
"Where Did You Hide the Canoe?" Bogg (51) 83, p. 46.

4177. SNIDER, Francis J. (Frank J.)
"Plain Talk to the People of Nicaragua." SanFPJ (5:4) 83, p. 9.
"Speaking of Hot Lines." SanFPJ (5:4) 83, p. 19.
"To the Mayan Indians." SanFPJ (5:4) 83, p. 49.

4178. SNIEKERS-CLEIREN, Ghislaine
"Overseas." Bluebuf (2:1) Aut 83, p. 11.

4179. SNIVELY, Susan
"To an Artist Going Blind." GeoR (37:3) Aut 83, p. 577.

4180. SNODGRASS, Ann
"Will." CarolQ (35:3) Spr 83, p. 49.

4181. SNODGRASS, W. D.
"Manet: The Execution of the Emperor Maximilian." MemphisSR (3:2) Spr 83, p. 31-34.

SNOW, Bao
See: BAO, Snow

4182. SNOW, Margaret
"Wave Goodbye." MalR (64) F 83, p. 43.

4183. SNYDAL, James
"The Dark Wood." HiramPoR (34) Spr-Sum 83, p. 23-31.

4184. SNYDER, Gary
"Fear Not." Sulfur (3:1, #7) 83, p. 63-64.
"Hers." Sulfur (3:1, #7) 83, p. 64.
"Talking Late with the Governor about the Budget." OhioR (30) 83, p. 126.
"Uluru Wild Fig Song." Sulfur (3:1, #7) 83, p. 64-67.
"Walked Two Days in Light Snow, Then It Cleared for Five" (for Masa). OhioR (30) 83, p. 127.

4185. SOBIN, Anthony
"The Calculation." Gargoyle (22/23) 83, p. 49.

4186. SOCOLOW, Elizabeth Anne
"Marriage Poem" (for Scott and Cindy). USl (16/17) Wint 83-84, p. 12.
"On Dreaming I Was in Normandy, with You This Time." YetASM (1:1) 82, p. 15.
"Winning the Lottery" (for Hai Tai). USl (16/17) Wint 83-84, p. 12.

SOKAN, Yamazaki
See: YAMAZAKI, Sokan

4187. SOKOLSKY, Helen H.
"Two Sides of a Ticket." YetASM (1:1) 82, p. 12.

4188. SOLARCZYK, Bart
"The Death of the Industrial Revolution" SanFPJ (5:3) 83, p. 39.

4189. SOLDO, John J.
"Epistle to an Exile." Wind (13:49) 83, p. 46-50.

4190. SOLHEIM, James
"Barry Gray's Painful Decision." MissR (12:1/2, nos. 34/35) Aut 83, p. 93.
"Callie Lida's Pain." MissR (12:1/2, nos. 34/35) Aut 83, p. 92.
"Faith of Our Fathers." Poetry (143:3) D 83, p. 153-154.
"Harley Greenfield's Frustration." MissR (12:1/2, nos. 34/35) Aut 83, p. 94.
"My Father after a Day's Work at Otto Steel." Poetry (143:3) D 83, p. 155.
"The Paree Visit." MissR (12:1/2, nos. 34/35) Aut 83, p. 89-90.
"The Question of Jones's Intentions." NowestR (21:2/3) 83, p. 39.
"Rodeo Time." NowestR (21:2/3) 83, p. 38.
"Tom Thompson's Transcendence." MissR (12:1/2, nos. 34/35) Aut 83, p. 91.

4191. SOLT, Cindy
"Some Things Better Off Said." Bogg (50) 83, p. 3.

4192. SOLYN, Paul
"Schoolcraft." Northeast (Ser. 3:15) Sum 83, p. 14-15.

4193. SOMAN, Jeanne (Jeanne B.)
"Affirmation." SanFPJ (5:1) 83, p. 59.
"Day of Reckoning" (Yom Kippur, '82). SanFPJ (5:1) 83, p. 60.
"Dear Editor." SanFPJ (4:4) 83, p. 84.
"Demographic Dilemma." SanFPJ (5:4) 83, p. 20.
"Respite in Minor Key." SanFPJ (4:3) 83, p. 37.
"Transport." SanFPJ (4:3) 83, p. 12.

4194. SOMECK, Ronnie
"For Marilyn Monroe" (tr. by Gabriel Levin). LitR (26:2) Wint 83, p. 303.
"Nine Lines on a Bedouin Who Croaked from Desert Cancer" (In memory of Achmed Abu-Rabiah, tr. by Gabriel Levin). LitR (26:2) Wint 83, p. 303.
"Seven Lines on the Wonder of the Yarkon" (tr. by Gabriel Levin). LitR (26:2) Wint 83, p. 304.
"Sonnet of Air Narcissus" (tr. by Gabriel Levin). LitR (26:2) Wint 83, p. 304.

4195. SOMMER, Jason
"The Numbered Set of Human Faces." ChiR (33:3) Wint 83, p. 114.

4196. SOMMER, Sheyla
"Adieu." AntigR (52) Wint 83, p. 78.

4197. SONG, Cathy
"Blue Lantern." Tendril (14/15) Wint 83, p. 180-181.
"Father and Daughter." Tendril (14/15) Wint 83, p. 178-179.
"For My Brother." Tendril (14/15) Wint 83, p. 187-188.
"Girl Powdering Her Neck" (from a Ukiyo-e print by Utamaro). Tendril (14/15) Wint 83, p. 182-183.
"January." Tendril (14/15) Wint 83, p. 177.
"A Pale Arrangement of Hands." Tendril (14/15) Wint 83, p. 184-186.

4198. SONIAT, Katherine
"Drawing in Boundaries." MichQR (22:1) Wint 83, p. 58.
"Fiding a Resting Place" (For my mother, 1918-1972). NegC (3:4) Aut 83, p. 58-59.
"Missing." Poetry (142:1) Ap 83, p. 28.
"Proximity." ColEng (45:6) O 83, p. 570.

SONYE S., Roe
See: ROE SONYE S.

4199. SOOS, Richard
"Keep On Rockin' Baby" (for Erin Marie, age 2). Sam (36:3 143rd release) 83, p. 44.

4200. SORESTAD, Glen
"Aging Poet." Waves (11:2/3) Wint 83, p. 54.

"Cedar Waxwings in January." CrossC (5:1) 83, p. 11.
"Fourteen." MalR (64) F 83, p. 190.
"Morning of Hoar Frost." Quarry (32:1) Wint 83, p. 23.
"The Outdoorsman" (The Chalkboard Poems). PoetryCR (5:1) Aut 83, p. 9.
"The Road from Medicine Hat to Lethbridge." CrossC (5:1) 83, p. 11.
"The Stone." MalR (64) F 83, p. 190.
"Tough Vernal Sentiments." Dandel (10:2) Aut-Wint 83, p. 73.
"Woman at the Poetry Reading." Waves (11:2/3) Wint 83, p. 55.

4201. SORETSKY, Barbara
"Bronx Landscape." SanFPJ (5:3) 83, p. 37-38.
"Nightmare U.S.A." SanFPJ (5:3) 83, p. 40.

4202. SORNBERGER, Judith
"Musings in the Garden at Poissy." Calyx (8:1) Aut 83, p. 29-32.
"My Grandmother's Dolls." Calyx (8:1) Aut 83, p. 28.
"One Time in Mississippi." KanQ (15:1) Wint 83, p. 138.

4203. SORRELLS, Helen
"The Quarrel." KanQ (15:2) Spr 83, p. 157.

SOSA, María Vasquez
See: VASQUEZ SOSA, María

4204. SOSAYA, Elizabeth G.
"The Shed." AntigR (55) Aut 83, p. 7-8.

4205. SOSKIS, David A.
"The Satyr Replies." Confr (25/26) 83, p. 54.

4206. SOTO, Gary
"Black Hair." RevChic (11:2) Sum 83, p. 8.
"Brown Girl, Blonde Okie." PoNow (7:2, #38) 83, p. 10.
"Come Back." PoNow (7:2, #38) 83, p. 10.
"Eating." RevChic (11:2) Sum 83, p. 10.
"Envying the Children of San Francisco." Poetry (142:2) Je 83, p. 164-165.
"The Estonian Comes to Dinner." Poetry (141:4) Ja 83, p. 221.
"Getting Serious." Poetry (141:4) Ja 83, p. 220.
"Girls among Waves, 1967." RevChic (11:2) Sum 83, p. 9.
"Hard Times." RevChic (11:2) Sum 83, p. 7.
"Hitchhiking with a Friend and a Book That Explains the Pacific Ocean" (from Where Sparrows Work Hard). PoNow (7:2, #38) 83, p. 25.
"In the Madness of Love." RevChic (11:2) Sum 83, p. 13.
"Kearney Park." AmerPoR (12:3) My-Je 83, p. 19.
"Learning to Bargain." MissouriR (6:3) Sum 83, p. 13.
"Mission Tire Factory, 1969" (from Where Sparrows

Work Hard). PoNow (7:2, #38) 83, p. 25.
"Ode to the Yard Sale." Telescope (4) Wint 83, p. 18-20.
"Oranges." Poetry (142:3) Je 83, p. 161-162.
"Ritual." RevChic (11:2) Sum 83, p. 11.
"Saturday Under the Sky." Poetry (142:3) Je 83, p. 163.
"Telephoning God For." SecC (11:1/2) 83, p. 203.
"Where We Could Go." Nat (237:1) 2 Jl 83, p. 24.
"Who Are You?" RevChic (11:2) Sum 83, p. 12.

4207. SOUPAULT, Philippe
"The Masks & the Colored Heat" (with André Breton, tr. by David Gascoyne). Kayak (61) Ap 83, p. 49.

4208. SOUSTER, Raymond
"Earliest History." CanLit (99) Wint 83, p. 47.

4209. SOUTHWARD, Keith
"Bullrushes explode." Quarry (32:3) Sum 83, p. 70.

4210. SOUTHWICK, Marcia
"Kaspar Hauser" (A boy abandoned by his parents and raised in a cell by a prison guard). OhioR (30) 83, p. 53.

4211. SPACKS, Barry
"Bronze Jar." IndR (6:2) Spr 83, p. 8.
"Defining It." ParisR (25:90) Wint 83, p. 96.
"Ease." CarolQ (35:3) Spr 83, p. 60.
"The Gift." ParisR (25:90) Wint 83, p. 96.
"Little Things." Ascent (8:3) 83, p. 21-22.
"Loners." SouthernPR (23:2) Aut 82 [i.e. (23:1?) Spr 83], p. 6-7.
"Spoons." Ascent (8:3) 83, p. 22.
"We Tartars." IndR (6:2) Spr 83, p. 9.

4212. SPANGLE, Douglas
"At Cheshire Cheese -- a Dialogue, Yeats and Beardsley." Swallow (2) Aut-Wint 83, p. 12.
"Jennings." Blueline (5:1) Sum-Aut 83, p. 7.

4213. SPARSHOTT, Francis
"Blank." CrossC (5:4) 83, p. 6.
"Exhalations of a Dying Metaphor." PoetryCR (5:2) Wint 83-84, p. 13.
"The Filling." PoetryCR (4:4) Sum 83, p. 11.
"Loaded for Bard." CrossC (5:4) 83, p. 6.
"Recessional." PoetryCR (5:1) Aut 83, p. 16.

4214. SPEAKES, Richard
"Beer." Tendril (16) Sum 83, p. 111.
"Driving on Ice." QW (16) Spr-Sum 83, p. 119.
"For Heather, on Her 12th Birthday." PoetryNW (24:2) Sum 83, p. 25.
"The Nurturing of Darkness." QW (16) Spr-Sum 83, p. 118.
"One Ghost's Pranks." Tendril (16) Sum 83, p. 114-115.

"Ordinary Blessings." Tendril (16) Sum 83, p. 113.
"Relationships." Tendril (16) Sum 83, p. 116.
"Water." Tendril (16) Sum 83, p. 112.

4215. SPEAR, Roberta
"A Map for the Unborn." MemphisSR (3:1) Aut 82, p. 12-13.
"The Moravian Cemetery: 'God's Acre'." MemphisSR (3:1) Aut 82, p. 14.
"Oi-Dle-Doi-Dle-Doi." Poetry (142:3) Je 83, p. 136-137.
"The Old City." MemphisSR (3:2) Spr 83, p. 6.
"Two Trees." MemphisSR (3:2) Spr 83, p. 4-5.

4216. SPEARS, Heather
"The Foot Therapist." PoetryCR (4:3) Spr 83, p. 7.

4217. SPEECE, Merry
"Arms." Abatis (1) 83, p. 9.

4218. SPEER, J.
"Hitchhiking in Southeast Kansas." LittleBR (3:4) Sum 83, p. 56-57.
"Pittsburg Kansas Summer." LittleBR (3:4) Sum 83, p. 57-58.

4219. SPEER, Laurel
"Bodies drape the wire like Puttees." NewL (50:1) Aut 83, p. 72.
"The Cat Sits Inside." CapeR (19:1) Wint 83, p. 26.
"Commitment." CapeR (19:1) Wint 83, p. 27.
"D.C." CropD (4) 83, p. 11-13.
"Dear Steve/Love Mother." WindO (42) Sum 83, p. 21.
"The Freckle in My Mother's Eye." LittleM (14:1/2) 83, p. 24-26.
"Rented Rooms." ClockR (1:1) Sum 83, p. 14.
"The Room with Green Walls." ClockR (1:1) Sum 83, p. 14.
"That's Callas Singing the Casta Diva." WindO (42) Sum 83, p. 20.

4220. SPENCE, Michael
"Prayer to the Lord of Speed." PortR (29:1) 83, p. 97.

4221. SPICER, David
"The Boy and the Lights." MemphisSR (1:2) Spr 81, p. 18.
"Ethyl." MemphisSR (1:2) Spr 81, p. 19.
"I Fuck Only Ugly Women." Bogg (51) 83, p. 5.
"Strawberry." MemphisSR (1:2) Spr 81, p. 18.
"This Poem Again." Gargoyle (22/23) 83, p. 22-25.
"Waiting for the Woman." Ploughs (9:2/3) 83, p. 223.

4222. SPIERS, Margaret Ann
"Orogeny." Calyx (8:1) Aut 83, p. 25.

4223. SPINA, Vincent
"Living in China." PoetryE (11) Sum 83, p. 47-48.

4224. SPINGARN, Lawrence P.
"Jacob and Rachel." Confr (25/26) 83, p. 154.
"Minimum Duck." SecC (11:1/2) 83, p. 204.

4225. SPIRES, Elizabeth
"Bertram at Fat Camp." ThRiPo (21/22) 83, p. 84.
"Dreams of Plants." MemphisSR (2:1) Aut 81, p. 50.
"Letter from Swan's Island." AntR (41:1) Wint 83, p. 79-81.
"My Daughter" (After a theme by Carlos Drummond de Andrade). Poetry (143:1) O 83, p. 34.
"The Playground." Poetry (143:1) O 83, p. 33.
"Second Story." ParisR (25:89) Aut 83, p. 138.
"Sleeping in a Church." NewRep (188:6) 14 F 83, p. 32.

4226. SPIVACK, Kathleen
"First Warm Day." PoNow (7:2, #38) 83, p. 8.
"In This Urban Corner." 13thM (7:1/2) 83, p. 19.
"Poem in Three Parts." KanQ (15:4) Aut 83, p. 107-108.
"The Separation Agreement." MassR (24:4) Wint 83, p. 699-700.
"Windows." Poetry (141:4) Ja 83, p. 230-231.
"The Young Wife Who Went Deaf." Poetry (141:4) Ja 83, p. 228-229.

4227. SPIVACK, Susan F. (Susan Fantl)
"Desire." 13thM (6:1/2) 82, p. 15.
"Last Day of School." Images (8:3) 83, p. 9.
"One-Legged Man." Images (8:3) 83, p. 9.
"Two Women Moving Stones." Images (8:3) 83, p. 9.

4228. SPIVEY, Ted R.
"Memphis, Muddy River." SouthernR (19:2) Ap 83, p. 403.

4229. SPLAKE, T. Kilgore
"Technology." SanFPJ (4:2) 83, p. 28.
"Trout Fishing." SanFPJ (4:2) 83, p. 65.
"Untitled Alaskan Letter I." MoodySI (13) Sum 83, p. 24.
"Veteran." SanFPJ (4:2) 83, p. 65.

4230. SPOTTSWOOD, H. M.
"Billie Jane." CapeR (19:1) Wint 83, p. 48.
"Last Get-Together." CapeR (19:1) Wint 83, p. 49.
"Never to Be Caught Maudlin." Poem (48) Jl 83, p. 34-35.

4231. SPRINKLE, M. K.
"In Protest: One-Ninety-Three." SanFPJ (5:2) 83, p. 70-71.
"Protection." SanFPJ (5:4) 83, p. 25.

SRI CHINMOY
See: CHINMOY, Sri

4232. ST. JOHN, David
"33." GeoR (37:2) Sum 83, p. 317.

"The Ash Tree." MissouriR (6:2) Wint 83, p. 12-14.
"Dancing." MissouriR (6:2) Wint 83, p. 10-11.
"The Party's Over." NewRep (188:12) 28 Mr 83, p. 34.
"Shadow." NewYorker (59:13) 16 My 83, p. 38.
"Stand by Me." SenR (13:2) 82-83, p. 66-68.
"Thinking of Cuba." PartR (50:2) 83, p. 239-240.
"Woman and Leopard" (Jardin des Plantes, the zoo). Poetry (142:3) Je 83, p. 138-140.

4233. ST. JOHN of the SUN
"Millennium." ThirdW Spr 83, p. 134.
"Of Old and New Jerusalems" (for my brother). ThirdW Spr 83, p. 133.
"Of Time, Men and Flowers: meditations on the Spirit of Man" (Selections). ThirdW Spr 83, p. 19-33.

4234. ST. PAT'S MIDDLE SCHOOL, 7th Grade, Clinton, Iowa
"Alley" (Collaboration Poem, correction of entry in 1982 index). PikeF (4) Spr 82, p. 20.

4235. ST. PIERRE, Pat
"Life Once Had Meaning." Wind (13:48) 83, p. 39.

4236. STACH, Carl L.
"The Final Prospect." GeoR (37:1) Spr 83, p. 32.

4237. STAFF, Leopold
"Once in a While" (for Mieczyslaw Jastrun, tr. by Adam Czerniawski). Stand (24:1) 82-83, p. 7.
"Rowan" (tr. by Adam Czerniawski). Stand (24:1) 82-83, p. 7.

4238. STAFFORD, Kim R.
"The Surface." ThRiPo (21/22) 83, p. 73.
"Waiting to Be Born." ThRiPo (21/22) 83, p. 74.

4239. STAFFORD, William
"After a Cold Goodby." ClockR (1:2) Wint 83-84, p. 23.
"Both Ways." ThRiPo (21/22) 83, p. 75.
"A Briefing for Visitors to Our Planet." LittleBR (4:2) Wint 83-84, p. 21-22.
"Cannon Beach." Tendril (14/15) Wint 83, p. 191.
"Childish Things." WorldO (17:4) Sum 83, p. 40.
"The Color of an Old Friend's Eyes." CutB (20) Spr-Sum 83, p. 5.
"The Company." PoNow (7:2, #38) 83, p. 7.
"Coronado Heights." LittleBR (4:2) Wint 83-84, p. 22-23.
"First Grade." OntR (19) Aut-Wint 83-84, p. 69.
"For the Governor's Inaugural." WorldO (17:4) Sum 83, p. 41.
"Forget." OntR (19) Aut-Wint 83-84, p. 75.
"From Up High." PoNow (7:2, #38) 83, p. 7.
"A Game and a Brother." MichQR (22:4) Aut 83, p. 555.
"Ground Zero." Field (28) Spr 83, p. 38.
"Ground Zero." OntR (19) Aut-Wint 83-84, p. 72.
"Honeysuckle." IndR (5:2) Sum 82, p. 49.

"Knowing." Field (28) Spr 83, p. 76.
"Lights and Las Vegas." LittleBR (4:2) Wint 83-84, p. 23.
"Lost in the Centuries." MemphisSR (2:1) Aut 81, p. 4.
"Mr. or Mrs. Nobody." OntR (19) Aut-Wint 83-84, p. 70.
"My Name Is William Tell: Poems from the Tradition of Total Experience." OntR (19) Aut-Wint 83-84, p. 67-75.
"Network." Tendril (14/15) Wint 83, p. 189.
"New Times, New People." MichQR (22:4) Aut 83, p. 554.
"Next Time." NewEng (5:4) Sum 83, p. 616.
"Not Saying Anything." IndR (5:2) Sum 82, p. 48.
"Old Ways, New Ways." LittleBR (4:2) Wint 83-84, p. 22.
"On the Road Last Night" (from A Glass Face in the Rain). PoNow (7:2, #38) 83, p. 26.
"Querencia." AmerS (52:4) Aut 83, p. 460.
"Rover" (from A Glass Face in the Rain). PoNow (7:2, #38) 83, p. 26.
"Run before Dawn." OntR (19) Aut-Wint 83-84, p. 74.
"Scripture." MichQR (22:3) Sum 83, p. 165.
"So What?" OntR (19) Aut-Wint 83-84, p. 73.
"Some Day." Field (28) Spr 83, p. 39.
"Someone You Don't Know." ClockR (1:2) Wint 83-84, p. 25.
"Something I Was Thinking About." Tendril (14/15) Wint 83, p. 190.
"The Sparkle Depends on Flaws in the Diamond." OntR (19) Aut-Wint 83-84, p. 71.
"There Is Blindness." Field (28) Spr 83, p. 73.
"Troubleshooting" (from A Glass Face in the Rain). PoNow (7:2, #38) 83, p. 26.
"Unknown Beings." ThRiPo (21/22) 83, p. 76.
"Uplifting Thoughts." OhioR (30) 83, p. 200.
"A Voice from the Past." OntR (19) Aut-Wint 83-84, p. 68.
"What Lasts." OhioR (30) 83, p. 200.
"Yellow Cars." Field (28) Spr 83, p. 73.

4240. STAHL, Laura
"This Grief So New." LittleBR (4:1) Aut 83, p. 85.

4241. STAINTON, Albert
"Dog Day." PoNow (7:2, #38) 83, p. 29.

4242. STAIRRETT, Claire R.
"Entropy." LittleBR (4:1) Aut 83, p. 15.
"Seven O'Clock" (after Williams' "Nantucket"). LittleBR (4:1) Aut 83, p. 23.

4243. STALEY, George
"Night Images." FourQt (32:2) Wint 83, p. 13.

4244. STALL, Lindon
"Good Friday." SouthernR (19:4) O 83, p. 858-862.

4245. STALLMAN, R. W.
"Agrippina." SouthernR (19:2) Ap 83, p. 378.
"The Cloak." SouthernR (19:2) Ap 83, p. 380.
"Death and the Maiden." SouthernR (19:2) Ap 83, p. 381.
"Domitian." SouthernR (19:2) Ap 83, p. 377.
"In the Roman Forum." SouthernR (19:2) Ap 83, p. 376-377.
"Mad Messalina." SouthernR (19:2) Ap 83, p. 379.
"Nero's Letter To An Unknown Friend" (Dictated to Epaphroditus, Nero's Secretary, 64 A.D.). SewanR (91:1) Wint 83, p. 97.

4246. STALLWORTHY, Jon
"At Half Past Three in the Afternoon." Epoch (33:1) Aut-Wint 83, p. 89-90.

4247. STAMBLER, Peter
"Camp Meeting. Abraxas (27/28) 83, p. 35.

4248. STANDEN, Michael
"Someone mentioned it." Stand (24:2) 83, p. 6.

4249. STANDIFORD, Les
"The Magic of Hands." WestB (12) 83, p. 18.

4250. STANDING, Sue
"Getting Off the Train." PoetL (77:4) Wint 83, p. 230.
"Heartprint." PoetL (77:4) Wint 83, p. 231.
"Hopper's Women." AmerPoR (12:1) Ja/F 83, p. 40.
"Radio Waves: July." Tendril (14/15) Wint 83, p. 192.
"Vocabulary." PoetL (77:4) Wint 83, p. 232.

4251. STANDISH, Lorranie
"Grandmother." NegC (3:4) Aut 83, p. 63-64.

4252. STANFORD, Ann
"Despite All That." SecC (11:1/2) 83, p. 205.

4253. STANGE, Ken
"Advice to Travellers" (Selections)." Quarry (32:1) Wint 83, p. 4-11.

4254. STANHOPE, Patrick
"Elk County." WebR (8:1) Spr 83, p. 87.
"The Great Bass Expedition." WebR (8:1) Spr 83, p. 86.

4255. STANHOPE, Rosamund
"Chelone." WebR (8:1) Spr 83, p. 70.
"The Lapsing, Unsoilable, Whispering." WebR (8:1) Spr 83, p. 69.

4256. STANTON, Joseph
"Bruegel's 'Harvesters'." WindO (42) Sum 83, p. 37.
"Porte d'Orleans." WindO (42) Sum 83, p. 36.

4257. STANTON, Maura
"Carol" (for Greenville, N.C.). PoNow (7:2, #38) 83, p. 11.
"Sunday Graveyard." MemphisSR (4:1) Aut 83, p. 4.

4258. STANTON-BOWMAN, Susan
"In Spring." CrossC (5:2/3) 83, p. 11.
"Spring Stretch." CrossC (5:2/3) 83, p. 11.

4259. STAP, Don
"Trying to Write." Poetry (142:6) S 83, p. 344.

4260. STAPLES, William F., III
"Who Am I?" SanFPJ (5:2) 83, p. 84.

4261. STARBUCK, George
"Canon Fanin's Apology." Iowa (13:2) Spr 82, p. 115.
"Commencement Address." Nat (237:12) 22 O 83, p. 370.
"Errand at the Lone Tree Mall" (for Winifred and Winfield Scott). TriQ (58) Aut 83, p. 94-101.
"High Renaissance." Nat (237:12) 22 O 83, p. 371.
"New Strain." Nat (237:12) 22 O 83, p. 371.
"Said." Nat (237:12) 22 O 83, p. 371.
"The Well-Trained English Critic Surveys the American Scene." Nat (237:12) 22 O 83, p. 370.
"Working Habits" (Excerpts). OhioR (30) 83, p. 201.

4262. STARCK, Clemens
"In the Meantime." Kayak (62) Ag 83, p. 34.
"Job No. 75 - 14." Kayak (62) Ag 83, p. 32.
"Journeyman's Wages." Kayak (62) Ag 83, p. 35.
"On the Job - 5 poems." Kayak (62) Ag 83, p. 32-35.
"Putting in Footings." Kayak (62) Ag 83, p. 33.
"Willamette River (Marion St.) Bridge, Pier 5, General Details." Kayak (62) Ag 83, p. 34.

4263. STARK, David
"For Michael." Nimrod (27:1) Aut-Wint 83, p. 69.

4264. STARK, Sharon (Sharon Sheehe)
"Drought Crops." Epoch (32:2) Wint-Spr 83, p. 143-145.
"For Linda Hoyer Updike." Epoch (32:2) Wint-Spr 83, p. 146.
"Watching the Road." Tendril (16) Sum 83, p. 117-118.

4265. STARZEC, Larry
"The Balloon Man at Union Station." PikeF (5) Spr 83, p. 9.
"Wedding Party." KanQ (15:3) Sum 83, p. 74.

4266. STASIOWSKI, Carole A.
"Christmas Cactus." YetASM (2:1) 83, p. 7.
"Fossil Bed." YetASM (1:2) 82, p. 17.

4267. STAVEN, Kurt
"Revolver." Vis (11) 83, p. 10-11.

4268. STAVEN, Leland
"Beacon Fire." SanFPJ (4:2) 83, p. 76.
"Jurassic Attendant." SanFPJ (4:2) 83, p. 76.

4269. STAW, Jane
"Fishing in the Truckee." Iowa (13:2) Spr 82, p. 113-114.

4270. STEARNS, Catherine
"Border People." ModernPS (11:3) 83, p. 266-269.
"Lilac Scarf." ModernPS (11:3) 83, p. 269-270.
"The Summerhouse." ModernPS (11:3) 83, p. 269.

4271. STEBBINS, Mary
"Repentances." Blueline (5:1) Sum-Aut 83, p. 11.

4272. STEELE, Paul Curry
"Crux et Corpus." AmerPoR (12:2) Mr/Ap 83, p. 46.
"Filles de Joie." AmerPoR (12:2) Mr/Ap 83, p. 46.
"The Hat." AmerPoR (12:6) N/D 83, p. 29.
"Sans Essence." AmerPoR (12:2) Mr/Ap 83, p. 46.

4273. STEELE, Timothy
"Angel." Poetry (143:3) D 83, p. 127.
"Chanson Philosophique." Poetry (142:5) Ag 83, p. 260.
"The Chorus." Poetry (142:5) Ag 83, p. 259.
"From a Rooftop." ParisR (25:88) Sum 83, p. 188-189.
"The Library." Poetry (143:3) D 83, p. 128-129.
"Timothy." ParisR (25:88) Sum 83, p. 187.

4274. STEFANILE, Felix
"August." CentR (27:4) Aut 83, p. 275-276.
"The Veteran." CentR (27:4) Aut 83, p. 274-275.

4275. STEFENHAGENS, Lyn
"Domesticities." WindO (42) Sum 83, p. 6-7.
"The Last Day of the World." WindO (42) Sum 83, p. 6.
"Photograph." SmPd (20:2) Spr 83, p. 32.

4276. STEIN, Agnes
"Beneath Clouds" (tr. of Bernd Jentzsch). PoetL (77:4) Wint 83, p. 202.
"Hampstead Heath Walk." SanFPJ (4:3) 83, p. 51.
"The Place" (tr. of Bernd Jentzsch). PoetL (77:4) Wint 83, p. 201.
"The Unimaginable." SanFPJ (4:3) 83, p. 17-19.

4277. STEIN, Dona
"The Bison of Lascaux." DevQ (18:3) Aut 83, p. 66.
"The Imilchil Betrothal Fair." StoneC (11:1/2, Pt. 1) Aut-Wint 83, p. 12.
"Pain." StoneC (10:3/4) Spr-Sum 83, p. 67.
"Translation" (Figures and Inscriptions on a Tomb). StoneC (11:1/2, Pt. 1) Aut-Wint 83, p. 11.

4278. STEIN, Hadassah
"Raking Leaves." SoDakR (21:3) Aut 83, p. 90.
"These Few Days Alone." SoDakR (21:3) Aut 83, p. 91.

4279. STEIN, Kevin
"A Field of Wings" (for Dean Young). IndR (6:1) Wint 83, p. 20.
"A Theory of Poetry in Wood." IndR (5:1) Wint 82, p. 56-57.

4280. STEIN, Paul
"Goat." OhioR (30) 83, p. 145.

4281. STEINARR, Steinn
"White Light" (tr. from the Icelandic poem cycle "Time and Water" by Alan Boucher). Vis (12) 83, p. 14.

4282. STEINBERGH, Judith (Judith W.)
"Arguing with Joyce." Calyx (7:3) Sum 83, p. 14.
"Jugglers." Tendril (14/15) Wint 83, p. 193.
"One Evening When I Was Busy Typing, My Daughter" (from Chat Book, finalist, 10th anniversary manuscript competition). StoneC (11:1/2, Pt. 1) Aut-Wint 83, p. 57.
"Planting Holland Bulbs in November." StoneC (10:3/4) Spr-Sum 83, p. 66-67.
"Planting Holland Bulbs in November" (Excerpt, recipient of a Phillips Poetry Award, Spring/Summer 1983). StoneC (11:1/2, Pt. 1) Aut-Wint 83, p. 44.
"Silver" (for Robin, from Chat Book, finalist, 10th anniversary manuscript competition). StoneC (11:1/2, Pt. 1) Aut-Wint 83, p. 56.

4283. STEINER, Karen
"Definition." StoneC (11:1/2, Pt. 1) Aut-Wint 83, p. 24.
"Paint." YetASM (1:2) 82, p. 8.
"That Summer You Left." BallSUF (24:1) Wint 83, p. 37.

4284. STEINGASS, Dave
"The American Porch." ThRiPo (21/22) 83, p. 85.

4285. STEINICHEN, Paul
"In the Silence." DekalbLAJ (16:1/4) Aut 82-Sum 83, p. 104.

4286. STEINKE, Paul David
"South Point Fish Co.: Ocracoke, N. C." SmPd (20:2) Spr 83, p. 19.

4287. STEINMAN, Lisa M.
"The Dove Returns, Bedraggled and with Something to Say." WebR (8:2) Aut 83, p. 79.
"Landgods Are Not Easily Transportable." WebR (8:2) Aut 83, p. 81.
"The Passion for Imitation Tries." WebR (8:2) Aut 83, p. 80.

4288. STELMASZYNSKI, Wojtek
"Allegories: Opus 24, a Tragedy" (tr. of Krzysztof Ostaszewski). AntigR (55) Aut 83, p. 86.

"Allegories: Opus 34, a Comedy" (tr. of Krzysztof Ostaszewski). AntigR (55) Aut 83, p. 87.
"Allegories: Opus 35, a Comedy" (tr. of Krzysztof Ostaszewski). AntigR (55) Aut 83, p. 88.
"Allegories: Opus 87, a Comedy" (tr. of Krzysztof Ostaszewski). AntigR (55) Aut 83, p. 88-89.
"Allegories: Opus 108, a Comedy" (tr. of Krzysztof Ostaszewski). AntigR (55) Aut 83, p. 89.

4289. STELZIG, Eugene
"Home." CrabCR (1:1) My 83, p. 27.

4290. STEPHEN, Ian
"Byname." PoetryCR (4:3) Spr 83, p. 7.
"Provisions." PoetryCR (4:3) Spr 83, p. 8.

4291. STEPHENS, Jack
"Ab Ovo." PoetryNW (24:2) Sum 83, p. 12-13.

4292. STEPHENS, Jan M.
"Window Treatment." PoetryCR (5:1) Aut 83, p. 12.

4293. STEPHENSON, Harry
"Fingertips of the left hand hold the paper." YetASM (1:1) 82, p. 9.

4294. STERLING, Gary
"Convergence." SanFPJ (5:4) 83, p. 64.
"Howling of a pack of words." SanFPJ (5:4) 83, p. 61.
"Terror comes from the ground." SanFPJ (5:4) 83, p. 64.

4295. STERN, Gerald
"Bee Balm." NewYorker (59:21) 11 Jl 83, p. 44.
"For Song." ParisR (25:90) Wint 83, p. 65.
"Honey Locust." ThRiPo (21/22) 83, p. 87.
"Leaving Another Kingdom." ParisR (25:90) Wint 83, p. 62-63.
"Near Perigord." ParisR (25:90) Wint 83, p. 66-67.
"Peddler's Village." ThRiPo (21/22) 83, p. 86.
"Romania, Romania." Field (29) Aut 83, p. 95-96.
"Saying the First Words." ParisR (25:90) Wint 83, p. 64.
"Two Trees." Field (29) Aut 83, p. 97.
"Vivaldi Years." ParisR (25:90) Wint 83, p. 64.

4296. STERN, Robert
"Ruth and Boaz." AntigR (52) Wint 83, p. 121.
"Satan at His Desk." AntigR (52) Wint 83, p. 122.
"Solstice." AntigR (52) Wint 83, p. 121-122.

4297. STERN, Zelda
"A Generation" (tr. of Gu Cheng, w. Helen Siu). AmerPoR (12:2) Mr/Ap 83, p. 20.
"I Am a Willful Child" (tr. of Gu Cheng, w. Helen Siu). AmerPoR (12:2) Mr/Ap 83, p. 20.
"Shooting a Photograph" (tr. of Gu Cheng, w. Helen Siu). AmerPoR (12:2) Mr/Ap 83, p. 20.

4298. STERNLIEB, Barry
"The Confines." PoetryNW (24:1) Spr 83, p. 35-36.
"For the Farm Ghost." PoetryNW (24:1) Spr 83, p. 34.
"Kinship." PoetryNW (24:1) Spr 83, p. 34-35.
"Provision." PoetryNW (24:1) Spr 83, p. 37-38.
"Wood Lesson." PoetryNW (24:1) Spr 83, p. 36-37.

4299. STETLER, Charles
"'A' Student." WormR (23:2, issue 90) 83, p. 67.
"Advice." WormR (23:2, issue 90) 83, p. 66.
"At the Paddock." WormR (23:2, issue 90) 83, p. 66.
"The Best of Carson." WormR (23:2, issue 90) 83, p. 58.
"A Chance Meeting." WormR (23:2, issue 90) 83, p. 63.
"Check under the Hood." WormR (23:2, issue 90) 83, p. 64.
"Come Again Another Day." WormR (23:2, issue 90) 83, p. 67.
"The Day I Lost My Catholicism." WormR (23:2, issue 90) 83, p. 56.
"Enrolled." WormR (23:2, issue 90) 83, p. 65.
"Expert Appraisal." WormR (23:2, issue 90) 83, p. 64.
"Gangway!" (Special section). WormR (23:2, issue 90) 83, p. 53-68.
"Gangway!" WormR (23:2, issue 90) 83, p. 54.
"Happy Holiday." WormR (23:2, issue 90) 83, p. 65.
"A Hopeful Pun." WormR (23:2, issue 90) 83, p. 64.
"In Between Courses." WormR (23:2, issue 90) 83, p. 61.
"In the Can." WormR (23:2, issue 90) 83, p. 62.
"Lesson." WormR (23:2, issue 90) 83, p. 57.
"Life Imitates Art, Again." WormR (23:2, issue 90) 83, p. 62.
"Literature and Biography." WormR (23:2, issue 90) 83, p. 60.
"A Man of Many Moves." WormR (23:2, issue 90) 83, p. 63.
"Rationalism." WormR (23:2, issue 90) 83, p. 57.
"A Refund." Abraxas (27/28) 83, p. 18.
"Rerun." WormR (23:2, issue 90) 83, p. 54.
"Salvage." WormR (23:2, issue 90) 83, p. 55.
"To Wilt Chamberlain." WormR (23:2, issue 90) 83, p. 56.
"Transmission." WormR (23:2, issue 90) 83, p. 61.
"Vocabulary." WormR (23:2, issue 90) 83, p. 55.
"Where Have You Gone?" WormR (23:2, issue 90) 83, p. 60.
"A Wish Fulfilled." WormR (23:2, issue 90) 83, p. 59.
"A Withdrawal Slip." WormR (23:2, issue 90) 83, p. 68.

4300. STEURY, Tim
"The Stranger Loses His Way." SouthernPR (23:2) Aut 83, p. 25-26.

4301. STEVENS, Alex
"An American General Dies in Exile." Shen (34:3)

83, p. 92-93.
"Cardinal Points." GeoR (37:1) Spr 83, p. 130.
"Connections in a Field." NewYorker (59:27) 22 Ag 83, p. 36.
"A Midwest Mezzotint." Poetry (141:6) Mr 83, p. 333-334.
"The Plain-Speech Symposium." Poetry (141:6) Mr 83, p. 331-332.
"Western Nocturne." Poetry (143:3) D 83, p. 138.

4302. STEVENS, Ralph S., III
"Night Watch." CrabCR (1:2) Aut 83, p. 15.

4303. STEVENSON, Diane
"The Diurnal." Wind (13:49) 83, p. 51.
"Last Rites." AmerPoR (12:4) Jl-Ag 83, p. 30.
"Night-Time." Wind (13:49) 83, p. 51-52.
"Original Sin." AmerPoR (12:4) Jl-Ag 83, p. 30.
"Resurrection." AmerPoR (12:4) Jl-Ag 83, p. 30.
"Waiting for Sleep." SouthernPR (23:2) Aut 82 [i.e. (23:1?) Spr 83], p. 36.

4304. STEVENSON, Eugene
"The Compass, at Night." Hudson (36:4) Wint 83-84, p. 693-694.

4305. STEVENSON, Richard
"The American Film Institute Salute to Alfred Hitchcock." PoetryCR (5:2) Wint 83-84, p. 14.
"Ba Light." Descant (41) Sum 83, p. 105-106.
"Beep Beep and Beep Beep, Ya!" Grain (11:1) F 83, p. 13.
"Clifford Olson." Grain (11:3) Ag 83, p. 25-27.
"Dusk, During Harmattan." CanLit (99) Wint 83, p. 31.
"He Sees Himself in the Dishes." Quarry (32:3) Sum 83, p. 43.
"Juju Magani." Descant (41) Sum 83, p. 101-102.
"Look, a Deer!" Germ (7:2) Aut-Wint 83, p. 13-14.
"New Oxford Catechism: Say 'Plato's Cave'." Sam (34:3 135th release) 83, p. 50.
"Sunday Sermon, Wulari Ward." Descant (41) Sum 83, p. 104.
"Why Does It Cry So." Descant (41) Sum 83, p. 103.

4306. STEVER, Margo
"Ascension." WebR (8:2) Aut 83, p. 73.
"Bringing a Father Back." WebR (8:2) Aut 83, p. 72.
"Dance of the Jackrabbit." PoetL (77:3) Aut 82, p. 168.
"Entering the Box." WestB (12) 83, p. 60.
"Sloane's Window." YetASM (2:1) 83, p. 10.
"The Treehouse." WestB (12) 83, p. 61.

4307. STEWART, Frank
"Christmas Birds" (for Shawhan). SouthernPR (23:2) Aut 83, p. 44-45.
"Flying the Red Eye." IndR (6:3) Sum 83, p. 66.
"Goodbye, It's On the Road Time" (for Akira Izumiya, tr. Tetsuo Nakagami, w. Ruriko

Fukuhara). MoodySI (10) Aut 81, p. 7-8.
"On the Wetting Road Always Splashing" (tr. of Akira Izumiya, w. Ruriko Fukuhara). MoodySI (10) Aut 81, p. 6-7.
"Poem of the Night Jack Kerouac Called Me" (tr. of Tetsuo Nakagami). MoodySI (5) Sum-Aut 79, p. 6.
"Summer 1964/'O, Freedom over Me'." IndR (6:3) Sum 83, p. 67.

4308. STEWART, Jack
"Familiarities." PoetryE (11) Sum 83, p. 23-24.
"El Greco." PoetryE (11) Sum 83, p. 21-22.

4309. STEWART, Pamela
"Witnessing the Pankot Hills, 1942." AntR (41:2) Spr 83, p. 201.

4310. STEWART, Robert
"The Plumber Arrives at Three Mile Island." NewL (49:3/4) Spr-Sum 83, p. 59.

4311. STEWART, Susan
"Blue Willow." GeoR (37:4) Wint 83, p. 847-849.
"Consecration." Poetry (142:1) Ap 83, p. 33-35.
"Fire Ceremony." Poetry (142:1) Ap 83, p. 36-37.
"The Sleeping Gypsy." Kayak (62) Ag 83, p. 3-4.

4312. STIEDA, Vivian
"From Continent." AntigR (55) Aut 83, p. 75.
"Puzzle." AntigR (55) Aut 83, p. 76.

4313. STILLWELL, Marie
"At Logan Pass." WebR (8:1) Spr 83, p. 83-84.
"Once upon a Time." WebR (8:1) Spr 83, p. 82.

4314. STILLWELL, Mary Kathryn
"Greetings from the New Year to Nancy." LittleM (14:1/2) 83, p. 98.
"The Night the Monsky-Lewis Showroom Burned Down." LittleM (14:1/2) 83, p. 99.

4315. STIVERSON, James A.
"Truth." WritersL Mr 83, p. 5.

4316. STOCK, Bud
"The Briar Month." Poem (49) N 83, p. 48.
"On Blackened Branch." Poem (49) N 83, p. 49.

4317. STOCKDALE, John C.
"Between Us." PottPort (5) 83-84, p. 41.

4318. STOKES, Denis
"After the Film." Descant (43) Wint 83-84, p. 27.
"Closet News." Descant (43) Wint 83-84, p. 25.
"Damsels." Descant (43) Wint 83-84, p. 28-30.
"Lament to Orpheus." Descant (43) Wint 83-84, p. 26.

4319. STOKES, Terry
"Child's Song." MemphisSR (1:2) Spr 81, p. 44.
"Cloud Cover." Shen (34:1) 83, p. 78.

"Damp Panties" (for Gussie). _ChiR_ (33:3) Wint 83, p. 112-113.
"The Innkeeper's Daughter." _ThRiPo_ (21/22) 83, p. 88.

4320. STOKESBURY, Leon
"Airport Bars." _Swallow_ (1) Spr 83, p. 92-95.
"A Skeptical View of the Tarot." _QW_ (17) Aut-Wint 83-84, p. 62.

4321. STOLOFF, Carolyn
"The Sneeze." _Kayak_ (61) Ap 83, p. 47.

4322. STONE, Carole
"Dream in Sweet Briar." _WestB_ (12) 83, p. 83.
"Early November." _WestB_ (12) 83, p. 82.
"Earthquake." _KanQ_ (15:2) Spr 83, p. 186-187.

4323. STONE, Joan
"The Shadow Hunter." _IndR_ (6:1) Wint 83, p. 42-43.

4324. STONE, John
"The Bass." _MidwQ_ (24:4) Sum 83, p. 466-467.
"Forecast." _SouthernPR_ (23:2) Aut 83, p. 37.

4325. STONE, Ken
"A Brazen Theme." _WritersL_ S 83, p. 24.

4326. STONE, Sandra
"A Primer." _Calyx_ (7:3) Sum 83, p. 34-35.

4327. STORACE, Patricia
"The Archaeology of Divorce." _MichQR_ (22:1) Wint 83, p. 56.
"Still Life." _ParisR_ (25:90) Wint 83, p. 160.

4328. STOTT, Sandy
"Offshore Poem." _Vis_ (12) 83, p. 7.

4329. STOUT, Robert Joe
"The Coot." _PikeF_ (5) Spr 83, p. 13.
"Could I Give You a Better World, Children?" _Northeast_ (Ser. 3:16) Wint 83-84, p. 17.
"Ft. Laramie, Wyoming." _CapeR_ (18:2) Sum 83, p. 26.
"Gail." _Vis_ (12) 83, p. 11.
"The Radio Goes on Playing after We Make Love." _Images_ (8:3) 83, p. 10.

4330. STRAHAN, B. R. (Bradley Russel)
"Against the Dying." _Vis_ (11) 83, p. 5.
"Chilly Scenes of Winter." _NegC_ (3:4) Aut 83, p. 95.
"An Inquiry into the Presumed Death of Richard M. Nixon." _SanFPJ_ (5:1) 83, p. 55.
"Net." _SanFPJ_ (5:1) 83, p. 54.

4331. STRAHAN, Barak D.
"A Door into Tomorrow." _Vis_ (11) 83, p. 41.

4332. STRALEY, John
"This Is a Letter to Rachel Jean Greenough on the

Occasion of Her 18th Birthday, February 17, 2001." WorldO (17:4) Sum 83, p. 42-43.

4333. STRAND, Mark
"Ballad of Love through the Ages" (tr. of Carlos Drummond de Andrade). NewYorker (58:47) 10 Ja 83, p. 32.

4334. STRAUS, Austin
"Old Ladies." Vis (13) 83, p. 14.

4335. STRECKER, James
"Gulls" (for Ira Progoff). Waves (11:4) Spr 83, p. 61.
"In His Way." Quarry (32:1) Wint 83, p. 50-51.

4336. STRINGER, A. E.
"The Community" (after the poem by Bill Tremblay). CarolQ (35:2) Wint 83, p. 18.
"Wire Figures." PoetryNW (24:2) Sum 83, p. 44-45.

4337. STROBERG, Paul
"Conversation Piece." WormR (23:1, issue 89) 83, p. 9.
"Discovering Great Writers." WormR (23:1, issue 89) 83, p. 9.
"Family Portraits." WormR (23:1, issue 89) 83, p. 9.
"Learning Something." WormR (23:1, issue 89) 83, p. 9.
"Meterological." WormR (23:1, issue 89) 83, p. 7.
"One of the Silly Things." WormR (23:1, issue 89) 83, p. 9.
"Sparrow Feathers." WormR (23:1, issue 89) 83, p. 10.
"Spring Training." WormR (23:1, issue 89) 83, p. 8.

4338. STROBLAS, Laurie
"The Clara Hold." PoetL (78:2) Sum 83, p. 95.
"Sleep." NegC (3:4) Aut 83, p. 122-123.

4339. STROHM, Paul Martin
"A Child's Letter to a Brother in the Army." NegC (3:4) Aut 83, p. 40.

4340. STROMBERG, Scott
"The Afternoon Ladies." Wind (13:47) 83, p. 29.

4341. STRUTHERS, Ann
"Old Women at Church." NewL (49:3/4) Spr-Sum 83, p. 230.

4342. STRUTHERS, Betsy
"Cottage Country" (Windy Pine, Lake Kushog). Quarry (32:3) Sum 83, p. 58-59.
"Sleeping Alone." Grain (11:1) F 83, p. 23.
"The Slow Loris" (for Timothy). Quarry (32:3) Sum 83, p. 58.

4343. STRUTHERS, Carolyn
"Beyond Strawberry Bank" (near Kendal, England).

Quarry (32:3) Sum 83, p. 33.
"Blood Shed (for Many)." Quarry (32:3) Sum 83, p. 33-34.

4344. STRYK, Dan
"The Chimney" (after Thoreau). MissouriR (7:1) Aut 83, p. 36-37.
"Driving near Rockford in Late Fall." PikeF (5) Spr 83, p. 27.
"Fish-Bowl." Poem (48) Jl 83, p. 60.

4345. STRYK, Lucien
"The Great Exception." TriQ (56) Wint 83, p. 173-174.
"Savants." GeoR (37:3) Aut 83, p. 500.
"Watching War Movies." Confr (25/26) 83, p. 255.

4346. STUART, Dabney
"The Birds." VirQR (59:3) Sum 83, p. 436-440.
"The Girl at the Pool." QW (16) Spr-Sum 83, p. 115.
"Once More for My Lady." SouthernR (19:2) Ap 83, p. 360-365.
"Snapshots of the Writer Entering Middle Age." PoetryE (11) Sum 83, p. 82.

4347. STUART, Floyd C.
"Lake Williamstown." KanQ (15:1) Wint 83, p. 160.
"Last Things." StoneC (10:3/4) Spr-Sum 83, p. 80.

STUBBS, John Heath
See: HEATH-STUBBS, John

4348. STUCKEY, Elma
"Reprobate." BlackALF (17:4) Wint 83, p. 171.

4349. STULL, Dalene Workman
"At the Window." KanQ (15:1) Wint 83, p. 137.

4350. STULL, Richard
"Notes toward a Discourse." Epoch (33:1) Aut-Wint 83, p. 91.

4351. STURGES, Mark
"The Second Coming." Sam (34:3 135th release) 83, p. 36.

4352. STURM, John Edward
"On Art and Life." SpoonRQ (8:4) Aut 83, p. 56.

4353. SU, Tung-p'o
"Tin-Fong-Po" (tr. by Gene DeGruson). LittleBR (3:4) Sum 83, p. 47.

4354. SUAREZ-ARAUZ, Nicomedes
"1982" (tr. of Jorge Luis Borges). AmerPoR (12:2) Mr/Ap 83, p. 48.

4355. SUBLETT, Dyan
"Simple Rituals." GeoR (37:2) Sum 83, p. 282-283.

4356. SUCH, Peter
"The Expedition." PoetryCR (5:1) Aut 83, p. 20.
"In Praise of Ishtar." PoetryCR (5:1) Aut 83, p. 20.

4357. SUK, Julie
"A Cut in the Mountain." SouthernHR (17:3) Sum 83, p. 237.
"Falling to Sleep." KanQ (15:2) Spr 83, p. 169.
"Pantheon." SouthernPR (23:2) Aut 82 [i.e. (23:1?) Spr 83], p. 65.
"Stepping on Cracks." KanQ (15:2) Spr 83, p. 168.
"Stones." NegC (3:4) Aut 83, p. 21.
"Waiting for the Storyteller." GeoR (37:3) Aut 83, p. 515.

4358. SULLIVAN, Chuck
"Pilgrim Arrows: For Teilhard de Chardin." SouthernPR (23:2) Aut 83, p. 47.

4359. SUMMERHAYES, Don (Donald C.)
"Après la Guerre Finie." PoetryCR (5:2) Wint 83-84, p. 12.
"Chimaera." PoetryCR (4:4) Sum 83, p. 11.
"I Didn't Tell You." PoetryCR (5:2) Wint 83-84, p. 12.
"Looking in the Mirror." Descant (43) Wint 83-84, p. 82-84.
"This Old Man Reclines on the Field of Heaven." Descant (43) Wint 83-84, p. 80-81.

4360. SUMMERS, Hollis
"Snapshots Taken with a Timer." PoNow (7:2, #38) 83, p. 35.

4361. SUMMERS, Rod
"Rain." CreamCR (8:1/2) 83, p. 142.

SUN, Nila North
See: NORTH SUN, Nila

SUN, Saint John of the
See: ST. JOHN of the SUN

4362. SUPERVIELLE, Jules
"The Cloud" (tr. by Karl Patten). WebR (8:1) Spr 83, p. 39.
"The Wake" (tr. by Karl Patten). WebR (8:1) Spr 83, p. 40.

4363. SUPRANER, Robyn
"Labyrinth." SouthernPR (23:2) Aut 82 [i.e. (23:1?) Spr 83], p. 50.
"While Chopping Green Cabbage." MassR (24:1) Spr 83, p. 12.

4364. SUSSKIND, Harriet
"Crownings of Uncut Grass." Prima (8) 83, p. 96.
"Lean Benefits." NegC (3:4) Aut 83, p. 18-20.
"Three Moods of Winter." GeoR (37:4) Wint 83, p. 768-769.

4365. SUTHER, Judith D.
"Midwife My Love." WebR (8:1) Spr 83, p. 61.

4366. SVEHLA, John
"Snow Patterns." PortR (29:1) 83, p. 64.
"Treasure Island." Wind (13:48) 83, p. 66.
"Woodpecker Hills." Wind (13:48) 83, p. 65.

4367. SVENSON, Robert
"Heat Lightning." PoetL (77:3) Aut 82, p. 160-161.

4368. SVOBODA, Robert J.
"A Rogue's Thesaurus: A." SmPd (20:1) Wint 83, p. 34-35.
"A Rogue's Thesaurus: B." SmPd (20:2) Spr 83, p. 7-9.
"A Rogue's Thesaurus: C." SmPd (20:3) Aut 83, p. 29-30.

4369. SVOBODA, Terese
"After You Tried to Strangle Me." NewL (50:1) Aut 83, p. 68.
"Each Season Contains the Last." Nat (236:23) 11 Je 83, p. 742.

4370. SWAN, Diane
"Anniversary." Tendril (16) Sum 83, p. 119.
"Family Portrait." Tendril (16) Sum 83, p. 120.

4371. SWANBERG, Christine
"The Principle of It." EngJ (72:2) F 83, p. 61.

4372. SWANBERG, Ingrid
"Dear California." Abraxas (27/28) 83, p. 24.

4373. SWANDER, Mary
"Cessna 180." AntR (41:1) Wint 83, p. 82-83.
"Novena." GeoR (37:1) Spr 83, p. 31.
"Sweater." OhioR (30) 83, p. 223.

4374. SWANGER, David
"Matinee." CharR (9:2) Aut 83, p. 82-83.

4375. SWANN, Brian
"Afterimage." BlackWR (8:1) Aut 81, p. 96-97.
"Binocular." MemphisSR (3:1) Aut 82, p. 38-39.
"Biography." Germ (7:1) Spr-Sum 83, p. 6.
"The Mice and the Walam Olum." WormR (23:4, issue 92) 83, p. 123.
"The Morning of the First Day." LitR (26:3) Spr 83, p. 385.
"Mouse of the Year." Germ (7:1) Spr-Sum 83, p. 7-8.
"The National Debt." MinnR (NS 20) Spr 83, p. 22-23.
"The Other Side." LitR (26:3) Spr 83, p. 385.
"The Reinvention of Action Photography." WormR (23:4, issue 92) 83, p. 122-123.
"Scarlatti and the Black Stove." BlackWR (8:1) Aut 81, p. 94-95.
"Singing." ConcPo (16:1) Spr 83, p. 28.
"Singing Up the Snow." PraS (51:1, i.e. 57:1) Spr

83, p. 63-64.
"Stick Boy." WormR (23:4, issue 92) 83, p. 124-125.
"Stories." PraS (51:1, i.e. 57:1) Spr 83, p. 64-65.
"Untitled: The real things, them." ConcPo (16:1) Spr 83, p. 26-27.

4376. SWANN, Don
"Locusts." SanFPJ (5:3) 83, p. 10-11.

4377. SWANN, Roberta Metz (See also: METZ, Roberta)
"Brightwork." PikeF (5) Spr 83, p. 33.
"Doll House." PikeF (5) Spr 83, p. 10.
"Gloves." Swallow (1) Spr 83, p. 114.
"Grey Fox." PoetL (78:3) Aut 83, p. 159.
"Noon." IndR (5:3) Aut 82, p. 45.

4378. SWANSON, Robert
"Amelia Earhart, Aviator (1898-1937)." CalQ (22) Sum 83, p. 19.
"Arkansas River." Wind (13:47) 83, p. 33.
"Grandfather Takes His Grandson to the Basketball Game." CentR (27:2) Spr 83, p. 115.
"Leon Rappolo, Jazz Musician (1902-1943)." CalQ (22) Sum 83, p. 23.
"Roald Amundsen, Explorer (1872-1928)." CalQ (22) Sum 83, p. 20-21.
"Robert Johnson, Blues Musician (1912-1938)." CalQ (22) Sum 83, p. 22.
"Some Things Remember Us." CentR (27:2) Spr 83, p. 116.

4379. SWARD, Robert
"Blind Poet." PoetryCR (5:1) Aut 83, p. 17.
"Meditations of a Journalist" (Based on yogic instructions for meditation). PoetryCR (5:1) Aut 83, p. 17.
"Ned Hanlan (1855-1908)--Champion of Canada." Descant (43) Wint 83-84, p. 38-39.
"There's No Way Out." Descant (43) Wint 83-84, p. 37.
"A Walk in the Scenery." PoetryCR (5:1) Aut 83, p. 17.

4380. SWARTS, Helene
"Amnesty." ChrC (100:1) 5-12 Ja 83, p. 13.

4381. SWARTS, William
"Organic Gardening." YetASM (1:2) 82, p. 9.
"Reading to Students." YetASM (1:2) 82, p. 8.

4382. SWARTZ, David
"Madonna." StoneC (10:3/4) Spr-Sum 83, p. 47.

4383. SWASKEY, Christine A.
"A Trifle, Glaring." Quarry (32:4) Aut 83, p. 57-58.

4384. SWEDE, George
"Descending." PoetryCR (5:2) Wint 83-84, p. 12.

4385. SWEENEY, Gael
"Late Dating the Holy Spirit." HiramPoR (35) Aut-Wint 83, p. 37.

4386. SWEENEY, Kevin
"An Educated Man." Bogg (50) 83, p. 7-8.

4387. SWEET, Eileen
"The Santa Ana." YetASM (1:1) 82, p. 9.

4388. SWEET, Nanora
"If in the Movies of Jean Luc Godard." Ascent (8:2) 83, p. 52-53.

4389. SWENSON, Karen
"Androgyny." DevQ (18:1) Spr 83, p. 37.
"The Bear Went Over the Mountain." DevQ (18:1) Spr 83, p. 36.
"The Burden." Nimrod (27:1) Aut-Wint 83, p. 65.
"I Have Lost the Address of My Country." PraS (51:1, i.e. 57:1) Spr 83, p. 69.
"The Love Poem." PraS (51:1, i.e. 57:1) Spr 83, p. 70-71.
"The Rand McNally Atlas." PraS (51:1, i.e. 57:1) Spr 83, p. 71.
"The Runaway." Nimrod (27:1) Aut-Wint 83, p. 64-65.
"Surface and Structure: Bonaventure Hotel, Los Angeles." KanQ (15:4) Aut 83, p. 24.

4390. SWENSON, May
"Birthday Bush." Atlantic (252:3) S 83, p. 92.
"Double Exposure." NewYorker (59:5) 21 Mr 83, p. 46.
"A Thank-You Letter." Atlantic (251:5) My 83, p. 66.
"Three White Vases." NewYorker (59:16) 6 Je 83, p. 36.

4391. SWETMAN, Glenn R.
"A.M. the Woman's Liberationist." KanQ (15:2) Spr 83, p. 172.

4392. SWICKARD, David
"After-Dinner Coffee." Nimrod (27:1) Aut-Wint 83, p. 66-67.
"Coming Home: David Smith." Blueline (5:1) Sum-Aut 83, p. 35.

4393. SWIFT, Joan
"Poem: Someday we will take this chance again." PoetryNW (24:2) Sum 83, p. 10.
"Silent." PoetryNW (24:2) Sum 83, p. 9.
"Strip Mining, Atrim Cemetery." PoetryNW (24:2) Sum 83, p. 10.

4394. SWILKY, Jody
"Tenants." YaleR (72:4) Sum 83, p. 601.

4395. SWIRSZCZYNSKA, Anna
"I Will Open the Window" (tr. by Magnus J. Krynski and Robert A. Maguire). TriQ (57, Vol. 1) Spr-Sum 83, p. 61.

4396. SWISS, Thomas
"August Outing." BlackWR (9:2) Spr 83, p. 52-53.
"The Wake in the Mansion." CimR (63) Ap 83, p. 30-31.

4397. SYKES, Graham
"Into My Hand." Waves (11:2/3) Wint 83, p. 73.
"With Round Eyes." Waves (11:2/3) Wint 83, p. 73.

4398. SYLVESTER, Bill
"Feedback." LitR (27:1) Aut 83, p. 26-27.

4399. SYLVESTER, Janet
"Cambridge, 1981." OntR (18) Spr-Sum 83, p. 94.
"Hard Strain in a Delicate Place." OntR (18) Spr-Sum 83, p. 95.
"My Grandmother Marries My Grandfather." SenR (13:2) 82-83, p. 25-26.
"The Woman in the Wall." SenR (13:2) 82-83, p. 27.

4400. SYTSMA, Curt
"A Humanist Manifesto." Humanist (43:3) My-Je 83, p. 32.

4401. SZEMAN, Sheri
"Halcedama" (Novum Testamentum, Matt. 27:3-8). PortR (29:1) 83, p. 126.

4402. SZIRTES, George
"John Aubrey in a Junk Shop in Hell." Argo (4:2) 82, p. 3.

4403. SZUMIGALSKI, Anne
"The Farm." Dandel (10:1) Spr-Sum 83, p. 18-19.
"H Died 16:1:62." Dandel (10:1) Spr-Sum 83, p. 20.
"Jazzing at the Vatican." Grain (11:2) My 83, p. 14-16.
"A Man on a Bus Decides to Eat Lunch." Grain (11:3) Ag 83, p. 8-9.
"She's Writing Her Memoirs" (for Tessa). Dandel (10:1) Spr-Sum 83, p. 21.

4404. SZYMBORSKA, Wislawa
"Tortures" (tr. by Magnus J. Krynski and Robert A. Maguire). TriQ (57, Vol. 1) Spr-Sum 83, p. 25-26.

TABLIABUE, John
See: TAGLIABUE, John

4405. TAFOLLA, Carmen
"Casa." RevChic (11:3/4) 83, p. 27.
"MotherMother" (they see Hiroshima and speak of nuclear "defense"). RevChic (11:3/4) 83, p. 26.
"Soulpain." RevChic (11:3/4) 83, p. 25.
"Woman-Hole." RevChic (11:3/4) 83, p. 24.

4406. TAGGART, John
"Nativity." CreamCR (8:1/2) 83, p. 166-172.

4407. TAGLIABUE, John
"Art Lesson." MassR (24:3) Aut 83, p. 611-612.
"Dojoji (or the Lust of Jealousy)." PraS (51:1, i.e. 57:1) Spr 83, p. 13.
"Green river." Kayak (62) Ag 83, p. 57.
"Maine Vastly Covered with Much Snow." PoNow (7:2, #38) 83, p. 8.
"No One Can Count How Often We Can Be Born." StoneC (10:3/4) Spr-Sum 83, p. 59.
"We Are Notes and Laughter on the Great Musical Scale." StoneC (10:3/4) Spr-Sum 83, p. 59.
"When after Learning There Is Yearning There's Grand Opera." Kayak (62) Ag 83, p. 55.
"Who Juggles Tonight?" Kayak (62) Ag 83, p. 56.

TAKAAI, Yoshimoto
See: YOSHIMOTO, Takaai

4408. TAKSA, Mark
"After the Theft." Wind (13:48) 83, p. 62.
"Hill House." IndR (6:3) Sum 83, p. 68.

TAKURO, Ikeda
See: IKEDA, Takuro

4409. TAKVAM, Marie
"Rose" (tr. by Olav Grinde). PoetryE (9/10) Wint 82-Spr 83, p. 258.

4410. TALARICO, Ross
"Creationism or Evolution: After Canoeing the Jack's Forks in Southern Missouri" (for Jerry Farwell). QW (17) Aut-Wint 83-84, p. 98-99.
"When You Do." PoetL (77:4) Wint 83, p. 212-213.

4411. TALBOT, Kathrine
"The Sword." Argo (4:3) 83, p. 24-25.

4412. TALL, Deborah
"December Field." IndR (5:2) Sum 82, p. 80.
"This Winter." PartR (50:4) 83, p. 589.

4413. TALLY, Susan Dahl
"Ricardo's Poem." EngJ (72:3) Mr 83, p. 70.

4414. TAMER, Ulku
"Answers" (tr. by Dionis C. Riggs, Ozcan Yalim and William A. Fielder). Mund (14:1) 83, p. 49-50.

4415. TAMURA, Ryuuichi
"Four Thousand Days and Nights" (tr. by Gary Steven Corseri and Takuro Ikeda). WebR (8:1) Spr 83, p. 48.

4416. TAN, Bee Bee
"Hsi Shih: Daughter of Silence." CrabCR (1:1) My 83, p. 8.
"Insomnia." CrabCR (1:2) Aut 83, p. 13.

TANA, Patti Renner
See: RENNER-TANA, Patti

4417. TANE, Miriam
"Rescue." SmPd (20:2) Spr 83, p. 19.

4418. TANER, Renato O.
"Sometimes I like to enter the house." PoetryCR (5:2) Wint 83-84, p. 19.

4419. TANIGAWA, Gan
"Mao Tse-tung" (tr. by Tetsuo Kinoshita). PoetryE (9/10) Wint 82-Spr 83, p. 230-231.

4420. TANIGAWA, Shuntaro
"Gogatsu-No Hitogomi." SoDakR (21:1) Spr 83, p. 61.
"Japan Shop" (tr. by Roger Finch). SoDakR (21:1) Spr 83, p. 58.
"The Man the Moon Likes" (tr. by Roger Finch). SoDakR (21:1) Spr 83, p. 60.
"May Crowds" (tr. by Roger Finch). SoDakR (21:1) Spr 83, p. 60.
"Nippon-Ya." SoDakR (21:1) Spr 83, p. 59.
"Onna." SoDakR (21:1) Spr 83, p. 59.
"Tabi 1." SoDakR (21:1) Spr 83, p. 53.
"Tabi 2." SoDakR (21:1) Spr 83, p. 55.
"Tabi 3: Arizona." SoDakR (21:1) Spr 83, p. 57.
"Travels 1" (tr. by Roger Finch). SoDakR (21:1) Spr 83, p. 52.
"Travels 2" (tr. by Roger Finch). SoDakR (21:1) Spr 83, p. 54.
"Travels 3: Arizona" (tr. by Roger Finch). SoDakR (21:1) Spr 83, p. 56.
"Tsuki-No Suki-Na Otoko." SoDakR (21:1) Spr 83, p. 61.
"Woman" (tr. by Roger Finch). SoDakR (21:1) Spr 83, p. 58.

4421. TANKSLEY, Sheila
"The Prolonged Wakefulness." Comm (110:4) 25 F 83, p. 108.

4422. TANZI, Diane
"The Rising Sun" (For my father, John Spring Tanzi, who died on this date, February 18, 1982). WebR (8:1) Spr 83, p. 80-81.
"Sticks." WebR (8:1) Spr 83, p. 81.

4423. T'AO, Ch'ien (Chi'ien)
"Drinking Alone in the Rainy Season" (tr. by Sam Hamill). PortR (29:1) 83, p. 101.

4424. TAPLEY, Katherine (Kathy)
"Hate." WritersL Ap-My 83, p. 19.
"The Writers Twenty-Third Psalm." WritersL Ag 83, p. 12.

4425. TAPSCOTT, Stephen
"Forger of Vermeer." Tendril (14/15) Wint 83, p. 194.

"Herbs." SenR (13:2) 82-83, p. 55-58.
"I write." NewEngR (5:3) Spr 83, p. 338.
"Letter from Maine." AmerPoR (12:4) Jl-Ag 83, p. 6.
"Parable: Evening." ThRiPo (21/22) 83, p. 89-90.
"When the Water Broke." MissouriR (6:3) Sum 83, p. 24-25.

4426. TARASOVIC, Marcia M.
"Landscape." PortR (29:1) 83, p. 87.
"Metamorphosis." PortR (29:1) 83, p. 11-12.

4427. TARLEN, Carol
"Alicia (on Her 16th Brithday)." SanFPJ (4:2) 83, p. 42.
"April 30th." SanFPJ (4:2) 83, p. 38-39.
"Believe in My Hands (Which Are Ending)" (for Silvio Rodriguez who lives in Cuba). ModernPS (11:3) 83, p. 307-308.
"For the Children of El Salvador" (dedicated to Cesar Vallejo). SanFPJ (4:2) 83, p. 43.

4428. TARN, Nathaniel
"Dog Viewing Deer: Songs of Death, Resurrection and the Movie Market." Sulfur (3:2, #8) 83, p. 86-91.

4429. TARVER, John
"Death of His Mother" (for R.D.). Telescope (4) Wint 83, p. 69-70.
"Speaking, with Razor." Telescope (4) Wint 83, p. 36.

4430. TARWOOD, James
"Burning Like Green Wood." AmerPoR (12:1) Ja/F 83, p. 40.

TASSEL, Katrina van
See: Van TASSEL, Katrina

4431. TATE, James
"A Beer Ain't Got No Bone." Ploughs (9:1) 83, p. 119.
"The End of an Era." Iowa (13:3/4) Spr 82 (83), p. 116.
"Hanging-Out with Howard, Looking around for Charmagne." DevQ (18:3) Aut 83, p. 80-81.
"Hurry Up and Wait." Kayak (61) Ap 83, p. 8.
"If It Is Peace You Seek." Kayak (61) Ap 83, p. 7.
"Jelka Revisited." Ploughs (9:1) 83, p. 115-117.
"Love Gets Ornery." Ploughs (9:1) 83, p. 118.
"Minus Something." Kayak (61) Ap 83, p. 9.
"The Motorcyclists." Iowa (13:3/4) Spr 82 (83), p. 117.
"Pigs of the Deep." Kayak (61) Ap 83, p. 11.
"Poem for the Sandman." Tendril (16) Sum 83, p. 121.
"Poem to Some of My Recent Poems." Tendril (16) Sum 83, p. 122.
"The Refugees." DevQ (18:3) Aut 83, p. 82-83.
"Save the Mosquitoes." BlackWR (9:2) Spr 83, p. 50.
"Sensitive Ears." SecC (11:1/2) 83, p. 206.
"Smart and Final Iris." PoNow (7:2, #38) 83, p. 15.

"Some Beneficial Rays." Tendril (16) Sum 83, p. 123.
"The Spring Tour." DevQ (18:3) Aut 83, p. 84.
"Storm." MissouriR (7:1) Aut 83, p. 9.
"Thoughts While Reading The Sand Reckoner." MissouriR (7:1) Aut 83, p. 10-11.
"To a Bunch of Rotten Bananas." BlackWR (9:2) Spr 83, p. 49.
"Who Is Jenny?" Kayak (61) Ap 83, p. 10.

4432. TATRALLYAY, Geza
"Autumnal Question" (tr. by the author). Quarry (32:3) Sum 83, p. 32.
"Oszi Kérdés." Quarry (32:3) Sum 83, p. 32.
"A Wanderer's Evensong" (tr. of Johann Wolfgang von Goethe). Quarry (32:3) Sum 83, p. 31.

4433. TAWESE
"Tía Ester" (a song of remembrance). RevChic (11:3/4) 83, p. 62-64.

4434. TAYLOR, Alexander
"Sex Roles" (tr. of Klaus Rifbjerg). MinnR (NS 20) Spr 83, p. 25.

4435. TAYLOR, Charles (See also: TAYLOR, Chuck)
"White Night." PikeF (5) Spr 83, p. 11.

4436. TAYLOR, Christopher
"Mercy Mother Don't Leave Me Out Here." Grain (11:2) My 83, p. 12-13.

4437. TAYLOR, Chuck (See also: TAYLOR, Charles)
"The Library in Beaumont, Texas" (for Phil Dunn). OroM (2:1, #5) Sum 83, p. 18-19.

4438. TAYLOR, Eleanor Ross
"Lucinda Comes to Visit." Ploughs (9:2/3) 83, p. 228-229.

4439. TAYLOR, Henry
"Landscape with Tractor." Ploughs (9:2/3) 83, p. 102-103.

4440. TAYLOR, Joan (See also: TAYLOR, Joan Imig)
"Untitled: Dishes slide in and out of soapy water." Bluebuf (2:1) Aut 83, p. 24.
"Untitled: I chop vegetables in the kitchen." Bluebuf (2:1) Aut 83, p. 26.

4441. TAYLOR, Joan Imig (See also: TAYLOR, Joan)
"Hawaiian Fireside." WorldO (17:4) Sum 83, p. 44.

4442. TAYLOR, John
"Good Bye?" (To Karen, wherever she is). Bogg (50) 83, p. 56.

4443. TAYLOR, Laurie
"Flights." WindO (43) Wint 83, p. 38.

4444. TAYLOR, Leslie E., Jr.
"A Model Railway Enthusiast: The Forfeiture of Trains." VirQR (59:4) Aut 83, p. 691-692.

4445. TAYLOR, Ross
"Crimson." Shen (34:4) 83, p. 46.

4446. TEM, Steve Rasnic
"After the Collapse." Piq (11) 83, p. 24.

TENORIO, Harold Alvarado
See: ALVARADO TENORIO, Harold

4447. TERRILL, Richard
"A Cafe Terrace at Night." BlackWR (9:1) Aut 82, p. 14.
"Casals." BlackWR (9:1) Aut 82, p. 15.

4448. TERRIS, Susan
"Baited." Prima (8) 83, p. 77.
"Redstone, Colorado." SanFPJ (4:2) 83, p. 52.
"Two." Prima (8) 83, p. 77.

4449. TERRIS, Virginia (Virginia R.)
"Genesis Revisited." PoetryE (9/10) Wint 82-Spr 83, p. 40-41.
"The Hoof." PraS (57:4) Wint 83, p. 51.
"Invocation." PraS (57:4) Wint 83, p. 53.
"The Little Woman." PraS (57:4) Wint 83, p. 54.
"The Preparer." PraS (57:4) Wint 83, p. 52.

4450. TETI, Zona
"Christmas Poem of the Lukan Mary." Comm (110:22) 16 D 83, p. 691.
"Florentine Painters after Giotto" (for Ruby Zagoren). Comm (110:22) 16 D 83, p. 691.

TETSUO, Kinoshita
See: KINOSHITA, Tetsuo

TETSUO, Nakagami
See: NAKAGAMI, Tetsuo

4451. THACKER, Julia
"Cape Sound." Tendril (16) Sum 83, p. 125.
"How the Sun Sees Us." Tendril (16) Sum 83, p. 124.

4452. THESEN, Sharon
"Interference for Sharon" (a homolinguistic translation by Richard Truhlar of Sharon Thesen's poems Radio New France Radio). CapilR (26) 83, p. 50-53.

4453. THIBAULT, Mary Ann
"The Wallflower." YetASM (2:1) 83, p. 6.

4454. THIEL, Robert
"I, Palinurus." AntigR (52) Wint 83, p. 123-124.
"Preference." PottPort (5) 83-84, p. 11.

4455. THOMAS, Donna
"The Final Conflict" (a fable). LittleBR (3:3) Spr 83, p. 32.

4456. THOMAS, Gail
"Photo: Four Sisters at the Piano." YetASM (1:2) 82, p. 8.
"The Woman Who Sings in the Cellar." YetASM (1:2) 82, p. 7.

4457. THOMAS, Harry
"Three Tiny Poems." SouthernR (19:3) Jl 83, p. 666.

4458. THOMAS, Jim
"Bedtime Story." KanQ (15:2) Spr 83, p. 151.
"Escape." EngJ (72:4) Ap 83, p. 38.
"The Fire Bubbles." KanQ (15:2) Spr 83, p. 151.
"On Vocations." CapeR (19:1) Wint 83, p. 28.
"Rescue Mission." KanQ (15:1) Wint 83, p. 135.
"Salt in the Beer." KanQ (15:1) Wint 83, p. 136.

4459. THOMAS, Julia
"Revelation." AntigR (52) Wint 83, p. 72-73.

4460. THOMAS, Michael
"A Madras Gent Receives His 'Dear John' Letter." Grain (11:3) Ag 83, p. 7.

4461. THOMAS, Peter
"Of Meetings and Departures." SpiritSH (48) 82, p. 26-29.

THOMAS di GIOVANNI, Norman
See: Di GIOVANNI, Norman Thomas

4462. THOMPSON, Hilary
"Hair" (for Evelyn Garbary). PottPort (5) 83-84, p. 52.

4463. THOMPSON, J. (See also: THOMPSON, Jeanie)
"After All." Poem (48) Jl 83, p. 51.
"A Bridge Too Narrow." Poem (48) Jl 83, p. 52.

4464. THOMPSON, Jeanie (See also: THOMPSON, J.)
"At the Wheeler Wildlife Refuge." MissouriR (6:3) Sum 83, p. 29.
"Birch Street, 1960." MissouriR (6:3) Sum 83, p. 28.
"Returning." NoAmR (268:4) D 83, p. 77.
"Snowy Egrets Flying before a Storm." Ploughs (9:2/3) 83, p. 138.

4465. THOMPSON, Perry
"Miracles." DekalbLAJ (16:1/4) Aut 82-Sum 83, p. 81-82.
"To Flynn." DekalbLAJ (16:1/4) Aut 82-Sum 83, p. 82-83.
"When I Was a Farmer I Carried." DekalbLAJ (16:1/4) Aut 82-Sum 83, p. 83.

4466. THOMPSON, Phil
"Old Charlie Leaves the Tavern." PottPort (5) 83-84, p. 27.
"The Parting." PottPort (5) 83-84, p. 47.

4467. THOMPSON, Phyllis
"The Ghosts of Who We Were." Hudson (36:4) Wint 83-84, p. 696.

4468. THOMPSON, Sue Ellen
"Birthday." Tendril (14/15) Wint 83, p. 195.
"The Death of Uncles." NewL (50:1) Aut 83, p. 93.
"Family Portrait." Tendril (14/15) Wint 83, p. 196.

4469. THOMSEN, Barbara
"Boston Fern." SouthernR (19:3) Jl 83, p. 682-683.
"Coming Home." ChiR (34:1) Sum 83, p. 41.
"Dolphins." SouthernR (19:3) Jl 83, p. 684.
"Summer Litter." ChiR (33:4) Sum [i.e. Spr] 83, p. 26.
"Widow." ChiR (33:4) Sum [i.e. Spr] 83, p. 27.

4470. THOMSON, Sharon
"Pigeons." Confr (25/26) 83, p. 16.

4471. THORNE, Evelyn
"Not Flood nor Fire Next Time" (after seeing a PBS program on hydro-chemical poisons). SanFPJ (5:2) 83, p. 86.
"Now." SanFPJ (5:2) 83, p. 87.

4472. THORNTON, Laura
"The Peace of Worldly Detachment." Tendril (16) Sum 83, p. 126.
"A Trident Submarine Soaks in Water Thirty Miles From My Home." Tendril (16) Sum 83, p. 127.

4473. THORNTON, Russell
"Seagulls Twist Air." CanLit (96) Spr 83, p. 85.
"Story." CanLit (98) Aut 83, p. 30-31.

4474. THORNTON, Susan
"Songs for the Death of the Hero." Paint (10:19/20) Spr-Aut 83, p. 7-9.

4475. THORPE, Michael
"The Burning of Louisbourg Town Hall." AntigR (54) Sum 83, p. 104.
"Greater Expectations." AntigR (54) Sum 83, p. 105.

4476. THURIDUR GUDMUNDSDOTTIR
"Black Poem" (tr. by Alan Boucher). Vis (13) 83, p. 4.

4477. THURSTON, Harry
"Cabbages Reading Newspapers." PottPort (5) 83-84, p. 13.
"Revelations." PottPort (5) 83-84, p. 44.
"Time Zone." PottPort (5) 83-84, p. 12.

4478. TICHY, Susan
"October." BlackWR (9:1) Aut 82, p. 96-97.
"Travel." BlackWR (9:1) Aut 82, p. 94-95.

4479. TIDWELL, Charles
"Pastoral." Bluebuf (2:1) Aut 83, p. 36.
"September Sabbath." Bluebuf (2:1) Aut 83, p. 25.
"Still Life." Bluebuf (2:1) Aut 83, p. 28.

4480. TIERNEY, Terry
"How to Build a House." ConcPo (16:1) Spr 83, p. 43.
"Turning Back at the Rubicon." ConcPo (16:1) Spr 83, p. 44.

4481. TIFFT, Ellen
"Nuclear Land." NewL (49:3/4) Spr-Sum 83, p. 60.

4482. TIHANYI, Eva
"Blind Man." CanLit (99) Wint 83, p. 46-47.
"Branding." Germ (7:2) Aut-Wint 83, p. 16.
"Dust to Dust: The Last Survivor." Germ (7:2) Aut-Wint 83, p. 18.
"Focus." AntigR (52) Wint 83, p. 112.
"Wanting." Germ (7:2) Aut-Wint 83, p. 17.

4483. TILLINGHAST, Richard
"Fossils, Metal, and the Blue Limit." Tendril (14/15) Wint 83, p. 197-204.
"Our Flag Was Still There." NewEngR (6:2) Wint 83, p. 211-212.

4484. TIMI, Jeri Dawn
"This Night Is Ours" (with music). LittleBR (3:4) Sum 83, p. 31-33.

4485. TINER, E.
"Birds at Dawn." SpiritSH (48) 82, p. 43.
"Echoes of Seasons." SpiritSH (48) 82, p. 42.
"Prayer for Peace." SpiritSH (48) 82, p. 43.

4486. TISDALE, Charles (Charles P. R.)
"Easter Words." MichQR (22:3) Sum 83, p. 515.
"Not Meaning to End." CentR (27:1) Wint 83, p. 46.
"Swimming Hole." SouthernPR (23:2) Aut 82 [i.e. (23:1?) Spr 83], p. 58.

4487. TISERA, Mary
"Alchemical Change." PortR (29:1) 83, p. 106.
"The Blessing." Calyx (7:3) Sum 83, p. 26-27.
"Fall Out." WestB (12) 83, p. 64-66.
"Man on the Iron Fire Escape." PortR (29:1) 83, p. 40.
"Prescription" (for Robert Bly). Tendril (16) Sum 83, p. 128.

4488. TKACH, Michael S.
"Across the Table." ColEng (45:3) Mr 83, p. 264.
"Love and Resistance." ColEng (45:3) Mr 83, p. 263-264.

4489. TODD, Theodora
"The Future of Crab." YetASM (2:1) 83, p. 9.

4490. TOLSON, Melvin B.
"Chittling Sue." NewL (49:3/4) Spr-Sum 83, p. 144-145.
"The Underdog." NewL (49:3/4) Spr-Sum 83, p. 145-146.

4491. TOMLINSON, Charles
"Above Manhattan." Hudson (36:1) Spr 83, p. 130.
"All Afternoon." Hudson (36:4) Wint 83-84, p. 635.
"At the Trade Center." Hudson (36:4) Wint 83-84, p. 633.
"Byzantium." Hudson (36:4) Wint 83-84, p. 635-636.
"Dunnett Landing." Hudson (36:1) Spr 83, p. 131.
"History of a Malady." Hudson (36:1) Spr 83, p. 127-129.
"Ice Cream at Blauenberg." OntR (19) Aut-Wint 83-84, p. 44-45.
"In Verdi Square." Hudson (36:4) Wint 83-84, p. 634.

4492. TOMPKINS, Leslie C.
"By Owner." Northeast (Ser. 3:15) Sum 83, p. 23.

4493. TONG, Raymond
"Donkeys." WormR (23:1, issue 89) 83, p. 7.
"Enlightenment." WormR (23:4, issue 92) 83, p. 132.
"Holy Bathing Place: Allahabad." WormR (23:4, issue 92) 83, p. 131.
"A Professor Dreaming." WormR (23:4, issue 92) 83, p. 130.
"Tea ceremony." WormR (23:1, issue 89) 83, p. 7.
"Transgressions." WormR (23:4, issue 92) 83, p. 131.

4494. TOOL, Dennis
"Boulevard Saint-Michel" (tr. of Jean Ménard). PoetL (78:2) Sum 83, p. 101.

TOORN, Peter van
See: Van TOORN, Peter

4495. TORGERSEN, Eric
"No Dancer Still Walking." PoNow (7:2, #38) 83, p. 29.
"The Spring the Old, the Lyric." MemphisSR (2:1) Aut 81, p. 37.

4496. TORNES, Beth
"The Wings" (tr. of Delmira Agustini). AmerPoR (12:1) Ja/F 83, p. 16.

4497. TORNLUND, Niklas
"Breaking Points" (Rolf Nilsson's paintings) (tr. by John Tritica). Argo (4:2) 82, p. 13.
"Bristningsgranser" (Rolf Nilssons tavlor). Argo (4:2) 82, p. 12.
"Djungeln." Argo (4:2) 82, p. 15.
"The Jungle" (tr. by John Tritica). Argo (4:2) 82, p. 15.

4498. TORRES, Juan
"A la Pañueleta." Rácata (2) 83, p. 134.
"Canción de Madrugada frente al Mapa de América" (A Mario Hernández Sánchez-Barba, Historiador). Rácata (2) 83, p. 125.
"Flash Back." Rácata (2) 83, p. 124.
"Marea Alta." Rácata (2) 83, p. 127.
"Operador de Signos." Rácata (1) 83, p. 112.
"Querían vestirme de Cid." Rácata (2) 83, p. 126.
"La Realidad, y el Deseo (framentos)." Rácata (1) 83, p. 113-115.

4499. TORRES, Pedro
"City." NewRena (17) Aut 83, p. 67.

TOSHINARI, Fujiwara no
See: FUJIWARA no TOSHINARI

4500. TOSTESON, Heather
"Martinique." SmPd (20:1) Wint 83, p. 36-37.

TOV, S. Ben
See: BEN-TOV, S.

4501. TOWELL, Larry
"Night Cannot Be Turned Off" (from Burning Cadillacs). Descant (41) Sum 83, p. 119-120.
"The Orphan Boys at Pipe Road" (from Burning Cadillacs). Descant (41) Sum 83, p. 121-122.
"Shishu Bhavan" (for Sister Rosilda) (from Burning Cadillacs). Descant (41) Sum 83, p. 117-118.

4502. TOWLE, Parker
"Dawn from the Hill." CapeR (18:2) Sum 83, p. 2.
"Renewal Reminds Me of the End." SanFPJ (4:3) 83, p. 64.
"This Weather Is No Womb." StoneC (10:3/4) Spr-Sum 83, p. 60.

4503. TRAINA, Joe
"Lost Love Ghazal." Wind (13:49) 83, p. 42.

4504. TRANBARGER, Ossie E.
"The Same Name." LittleBR (3:3) Spr 83, p. 16.

4505. TRASK, Mavis Loretta
"A Poem: I think I will never see." WritersL Ag 83, p. 10.
"Smiles." WritersL Ag 83, p. 13.
"Somewhere." WritersL Ag 83, p. 26.
"Success." WritersL Ag 83, p. 10.

4506. TRAVIS, Byll
"Mole Digging." MissouriR (7:1) Aut 83, p. 47.

4507. TRAXLER, Patricia
"The Cowboy in Dreams." KanQ (15:1) Wint 83, p. 176.
"Why She Waits." KanQ (15:1) Wint 83, p. 176.

4508. TREBY, Ivor
"Miz' Pretty." Argo (4:1) 82, p. 20.

4509. TREFETHEN, Florence N.
"An Iceberg Is Towed to Jidda." StoneC (10:3/4) Spr-Sum 83, p. 61.

4510. TREGEBOV, Rhea
"People Change." PoetryCR (4:4) Sum 83, p. 10.

4511. TREITEL, Margot
"A Charmed Life." WestB (13) 83, p. 67.
"First Principles." SmPd (20:1) Wint 83, p. 29.
"The Handwriting on the Wall." Tele (18) 83, p. 85.
"Journey by Mammy Wagon." WebR (8:1) Spr 83, p. 68.
"The Legends of Timbuctoo." HolCrit (20:2) Ap 83, p. 16.
"Living Apart." NewRena (16) Spr 83, p. 46.
"The Quick Change Artist." RagMag (2:2) Aut 83, p. 23.
"The Road to Ife." HiramPoR (34) Spr-Sum 83, p. 32.
"A Stage You Are Passing Through." Ascent (8:2) 83, p. 54.

4512. TREJO, Ernesto
"The Cloud Unfolding." SecC (11:1/2) 83, p. 207-208.

4513. TREMBLAY, Bill
"The Second Sun." MinnR (NS 21) Aut 83, p. 21.
"The Wolf." MassR (24:4) Wint 83, p. 746.

4514. TREMMEL, Robert
"Devotions for Today's Couple." Ascent (9:1) 83, p. 44-45.
"Your First Early Easter in the North." Ascent (9:1) 83, p. 45-46.

4515. TRETHEWEY, Eric
"After Holding Out." MalR (66) O 83, p. 123.
"Cross-Purposes." AmerS (52:3) Sum 83, p. 326.
"Dreaming of Rivers." CanLit (97) Sum 83, p. 35-36.
"Leaving." NegC (3:4) Aut 83, p. 92.
"Looking Back across the Water." Northeast (Ser. 3:15) Sum 83, p. 13.
"Rabbits for Sale." BlackWR (8:1) Aut 81, p. 69.
"Snowbound." BlackWR (9:2) Spr 83, p. 51.
"Thinking of Them." BlackWR (8:1) Aut 81, p. 70.

4516. TRITEL, Barbara
"Aunt Bertha's Poem." MassR (24:1) Spr 83, p. 82-83.
"The Blind-Woman at Fourth of July." BelPoJ (34:1) Aut 83, p. 32-33.

4517. TRITICA, John
"Breaking Points" (Rolf Nilsson's paintings) (tr. of Niklas Tornlund). Argo (4:2) 82, p. 13.
"The Jungle" (tr. of Niklas Tornlund). Argo (4:2) 82, p. 15.
"The Ways of Lizards." Argo (5:1) 83, p. 30-31.

4518. TRIVELPIECE, Laurel
"Blinked Out." IndR (5:2) Sum 82, p. 44-45.
"Feeding the Wild Cats." IndR (5:2) Sum 82, p. 43.
"The Potato Planters." SouthernPR (23:2) Aut 83, p. 41.
"Rehearsing." IndR (5:2) Sum 82, p. 42.

4519. TROPP, M.
"Personal Critique." WritersL Jl 83, p. 11.

4520. TROUPE, Quincy
"New Times." Mund (14:1) 83, p. 44.
"Riff." Mund (14:1) 83, p. 45.
"The Sky Empties Down Ice." Mund (14:1) 83, p. 46.
"Whose Death Is This Walking." Mund (14:1) 83, p. 45.

4521. TROWBRIDGE, William
"Beginners Class" (to Randy). PraS (57:3) Aut 83, p. 78.
"The Knack of Jumping." PraS (57:3) Aut 83, p. 79-80.
"Looking for Uncle Al." NewL (50:1) Aut 83, p. 89.
"Orbis Terrarum Descriptio Duobis Planis Hemisphaerus Comprehesa" (1632). PraS (57:3) Aut 83, p. 80-81.
"Plain Geometry." Tendril (14/15) Wint 83, p. 205.
"Sophia." KanQ (15:2) Spr 83, p. 170.
"Visiting Grandma at St. Luke's." PraS (57:3) Aut 83, p. 77.
"Walking Out: The Death of Karl Wallenda." MissouriR (6:2) Wint 83, p. 19.

4522. TROWELL, Ian
"Haiku: His subtleties" (Of and For Lesley Choyce). PottPort (5) 83-84, p. 13.
"Wordless Tolstoys." PottPort (5) 83-84, p. 13.

4523. TROYANOVICH, Steve
"And the Light Just Keeps Crying" (tr. of Fernand Ouellette). Mund (14:1) 83, p. 37.
"The Angel" (tr. of Fernand Ouellette). Mund (14:1) 83, p. 37.
"Harlequin Autumn." Abraxas (27/28) 83, p. 35.

4524. TRUDELL, Dennis
"Music." GeoR (37:2) Sum 83, p. 346.

4525. TRUESDALE, C. W.
"Totem." Abraxas (27/28) 83, p. 10.

4526. TRUHLAR, Richard
"Chanteuse" (from Interference for Sharon). CapilR (26) 83, p. 52.
"Ghosting" (from Interference for Sharon). CapilR (26) 83, p. 53.
"In the Waiting Room" (from Interference for Sharon). CapilR (26) 83, p. 50.
"Interference for Sharon" (a homolinguistic translation of Sharon Thesen's poems Radio New

France Radio). CapilR (26) 83, p. 50-53.
"Mirage" (from Interference for Sharon). CapilR (26) 83, p. 53.
"Obscure Disaster" (from Interference for Sharon). CapilR (26) 83, p. 51.
"Obscure Disaster II" (from Interference for Sharon). CapilR (26) 83, p. 52.
"Snapping Open Suitcases" (from Interference for Sharon). CapilR (26) 83, p. 51.
"Temporary Positions" (from Interference for Sharon). CapilR (26) 83, p. 50.
"Temporary Positions II" (from Interference for Sharon). CapilR (26) 83, p. 51.
"Temporary Positions III" (from Interference for Sharon). CapilR (26) 83, p. 53.
"Traffic" (from Interference for Sharon). CapilR (26) 83, p. 51.
"The Writer on Holiday" (from Interference for Sharon). CapilR (26) 83, p. 52.

4527. TRUSS, Jan
"Dancing Frigid." Bluebuf (2:1) Aut 83, p. 31.
"Untitled: My daughter tells me how I failed her." Bluebuf (2:1) Aut 83, p. 9.

4528. TSCHANNEN, Mary M.
"Nicaragua Rojo." SanFPJ (5:4) 83, p. 22-23.

4529. TSIGANE
"Washed Up on the Grau du Roi, Provence." CrossC (5:1) 83, p. 7.

4530. TSONGAS, George
"20 Years of Irreversible Brain Damage." SecC (11:1/2) 83, p. 209-210.
"Keep Your Face." SecC (11:1/2) 83, p. 211.

TSUNG-YUAN, Liu
See: LIU, Tsung-yüan

4531. TSVETAYEVA, Marina
"Two Poems from 1916: I, II" (To Osip Mandelstam, tr by Joseph Brodsky). NewYorker (59:35) 17 O 83, p. 48.

4532. TU, Fu
"Meditations" (in Chinese). Pig (11) 83, p. 92.
"Meditations" (tr. by Joseph Lisowski, for J. P. Seaton). Pig (11) 83, p. 92.

4533. TUCKER, Jean
"Articles of Faith." NewL (50:1) Aut 83, p. 26.

4534. TUCKER, Jim
"Bear Dreams." Poem (49) N 83, p. 37.
"Vicksburg." Poem (49) N 83, p. 36.

4535. TUCKER, Martin
"Brooklyn and the World." Confr (25/26) 83, p. 186.

4536. TUCKER, Memye Curtis
"Finding the Dog." Poem (47) Mr 83, p. 30.
"In the Clinic Waiting Room." Poem (47) Mr 83, p. 28.
"Normal Fabric." Poem (47) Mr 83, p. 29.

4537. TUCKER, Scott
"Prissyllogisms." PoetL (77:2) Sum 82, p. 100.

4538. TUELL, Cynthia
"Power Out." Kayak (61) Ap 83, p. 30.
"Strategies for Dealing with a Full Moon." Kayak (61) Ap 83, p. 31.

4539. TULLOSS, Rod
"1954" (for E.S.D. Hutchins). Gargoyle (22/23) 83, p. 39.
"Imitations of Saigyo." USl (16/17) Wint 83-84, p. 9.
"Joshu on Hatteras Island." USl (16/17) Wint 83-84, p. 9.
"On a Gold-Flecked Green Pear." USl (16/17) Wint 83-84, p. 9.

TUNG-P'O, Su
See: SU, Tung-p'o

4540. TUPPER, Jean L.
"Photo of Carrie." YetASM (2:1) 83, p. 9.

4541. TURCO, Lewis
"Albums." CreamCR (8:1/2) 83, p. 118.
"The Amherst Fire, July 4, 1879." CentR (27:3) Sum 83, p. 186.
"The Cage." SewanR (91:2) Spr 83, p. 238.
"Home." CentR (27:3) Sum 83, p. 186.
"Mansions of Mirage." SewanR (91:2) Spr 83, p. 237.
"Marble Rooms." SewanR (91:2) Spr 83, p. 239.
"The Naked Eye." SewanR (91:2) Spr 83, p. 236.
"Nocturne." CentR (27:3) Sum 83, p. 186-187.
"A Sampler of Hours" (Selections: 4 poems) (On lines from Emily Dickinson's letter). SewanR (91:2) Spr 83, p. 236-239.
"The Skater" (for Richard Emil Braun). CreamCR (8:1/2) 83, p. 119.
"Three Poems on Lines from Emily Dickinson's letters." CentR (27:3) Sum 83, p. 186-187.

4542. TURGEON, Gregoire
"Edward Hopper, 1960." WestB (12) 83, p. 89.
"Empty November." WestB (12) 83, p. 88.

4543. TURMAN, Laura K.
"Waiting for the Rapture." SanFPJ (5:2) 83, p. 48.

4544. TURNBULL, Gael
"Sixty One Entries" (from a Book of Interesting Things, being part of a log of 367 consecutive entries from 19 October 1979 to 19 October 1980). Sulfur (3:2, #8) 83, p. 147-152.

4545. TURNER, Alberta
"From a Dictionary of Common Terms." <u>MemphisSR</u> (3:1) Aut 82, p. 11.

4546. TURNER, Doug
"The Painting." <u>Grain</u> (11:1) F 83, p. 28.

4547. TURNER, Frederick
"The Agape." <u>Poetry</u> (142:5) Ag 83, p. 276.
"Dumbarton Oaks." <u>Poetry</u> (142:5) Ag 83, p. 273-275.

4548. TURNER, Gordon
"A Poem As Big As a Mountain." <u>CanLit</u> (96) Spr 83, p. 68-69.

4549. TURNER, Keith
"Death Wishes." <u>Argo</u> (4:2) 82, p. 16-17.

4550. TUSIANI, Joseph
"A Definition of Poetry." <u>SpiritSH</u> (49 Suppl.) 83, p. 6.
"End of May." <u>SpiritSH</u> (49 Suppl.) 83, p. 7.
"For Pablo Casals" (Obit Oct. 22, 1973). <u>SpiritSH</u> (49 Suppl.) 83, p. 7.

4551. TWICHELL, Chase
"Abandoned House in Late Light." <u>Poetry</u> (142:2) My 83, p. 105.
"Blurry Cow." <u>Poetry</u> (142:2) My 83, p. 104.
"The Hotel du Nord." <u>BlackWR</u> (9:1) Aut 82, p. 10-11.
"The Iris, That Sexual Flower." <u>OhioR</u> (30) 83, p. 79.
"Not Like Water." <u>Field</u> (29) Aut 83, p. 61.
"Partita for Solo Violin." <u>Telescope</u> (5/6) Spr 83, p. 76-77.

TYNER, Rebecca Bailey
<u>See</u>: BAILEY-TYNER, Rebecca

4552. TYSH, Chris
"The Day We Threw Out the Xmas Tree." <u>Tele</u> (18) 83, p. 16.
"Winter." <u>Tele</u> (18) 83, p. 17.

4553. TYSON, Hannah Connor
"Flight" (tr. of Gemiann Augustus). <u>SoDakR</u> (21:1) Spr 83, p. 76.
"The Flowers" (tr. of Gemiann Augustus). <u>SoDakR</u> (21:1) Spr 83, p. 72.
"Swift Flight of Colored Birds" (tr. of Gemiann Augustus). <u>SoDakR</u> (21:1) Spr 83, p. 74.

UCHUK, Pamela
<u>See</u>: UZCHUK, Pamela

4554. UGOLNIK, Anthony
"Sermon in a Greek Orthodox Church." <u>ChrC</u> (100:20) 22-29 Je 83, p. 604.

4555. UGUAY, Marie
"Pluie du soir." Os (16) 83, p. 31.

4556. UHER, Lorna
"Albino Bull." MalR (64) F 83, p. 30-31.
"Pariah." MalR (64) F 83, p. 29-30.
"Stepping Stones." MalR (64) F 83, p. 32.
"What the Mind Turns Over." MalR (64) F 83, p. 28.

4557. ULLMAN, Leslie
"Care." Descant (41) Sum 83, p. 81.
"The Move." Descant (41) Sum 83, p. 79-80.
"Rain in the Desert." Descant (41) Sum 83, p. 82-83.
"The Split." ThRiPo (21/22) 83, p. 91.

4558. ULMER, James
"Before the Harvest." Poetry (142:4) Jl 83, p. 208.
"The Birthmark" (for my sister). QW (16) Spr-Sum 83, p. 113.
"Catalpa." QW (16) Spr-Sum 83, p. 112.
"From a Box of Old Photographs." Poetry (142:4) Jl 83, p. 207.
"Play Dead." BlackWR (8:1) Aut 81, p. 71.
"The Vigil." MissouriR (6:2) Wint 83, p. 18.

4559. UMPHREY, Michael
"Alone in the Grove." CarolQ (35:3) Spr 83, p. 61.
"Teaching The Grapes of Wrath to Middle Class High School Students As Refugees Wander the World Unwelcome and American Guns Murder Salvadoran Peasants . . ." EngJ (72:3) Mr 83, p. 78.

4560. UMPIERRE, Luz María
"Cocinando/What's Cooking" (to Mary Lee, tr. by Nancy Mandlove). 13thM (7:1/2) 83, p. 89.
"Neoteny." 13thM (7:1/2) 83, p. 88.

4561. UNGARETTI, Giuseppe
"In Memoria" (Locvizza il 30 settembre 1916). Argo (4:2) 82, p. 28.
"In Memory" (Locvizza, 30 September 1916) (tr. by Eddie Flintoff). Argo (4:2) 82, p. 29.
"Nightwatch" (tr. by Eddie Flintoff). Argo (4:2) 82, p. 30.
"Veglia." Argo (4:2) 82, p. 30.

4562. UNGER, Barbara
"Cassandra on Eighth Avenue." StoneC (11:1/2, Pt. 1) Aut-Wint 83, p. 22.
"The Snakeskin." MassR (24:2) Sum 83, p. 337.

4563. UNTERECKER, John
"The Betrayal." NewL (49:3/4) Spr-Sum 83, p. 269.

4564. UPDIKE, John
"The Fleckings." NewRep (186:3) 20 Ja 82, p. 36.
"L. A." NewYorker (59:9) 18 Ap 83, p. 48.
"The Rockettes." NewYorker (59:29) 5 S 83, p. 42.
"Two Hoppers" (On Display at the National Gallery). NewRep (188:4) 31 Ja 83, p. 35.

4565. UPTON, Lee
"Barbara's Story." Gargoyle (22/23) 83, p. 5.
"Book of Seasons." BlackWR (10:1) Aut 83, p. 26-27.
"Lou Anne in the House of Glass." WebR (8:2) Aut 83, p. 67.
"Plank Hill Farm." MassR (24:2) Sum 83, p. 328.
"The Servant of Snow." LittleBR (4:2) Wint 83-84, p. 62.
"The Tail of Robert E. Lee's Horse." CimR (65) O 83, p. 57.
"Window Seat at the Paradise." BlackWR (10:1) Aut 83, p. 28-29.
"You Are Not a Child." BlackWR (10:1) Aut 83, p. 30.

4566. URDANG, Constance
"Rain." PoNow (7:2, #38) 83, p. 15.
"Ways of Returning." Ploughs (9:1) 83, p. 184.

4567. URIARTE, Ivan
"Un Rostro en la Multitud." Areíto (9:34) 83, p. 32.

4568. URQUHART, Jane
"The One Before" (from a manuscript, The Little Flowers of Mme de Montespan). Waves (11:4) Spr 83, p. 49.
"Somewhere Else." Waves (11:4) Spr 83, p. 51.
"Words." Waves (11:4) Spr 83, p. 50.

4569. URSELL, Geoffrey
"Apnoea." Grain (11:3) Ag 83, p. 16.
"Drinking David Han Is Possible." Grain (11:3) Ag 83, p. 17.
"Elegance." Grain (11:3) Ag 83, p. 16.

4570. USACK, Kendra
"Dark Easter Nights." SanFPJ (4:3) 83, p. 25.
"Emily Dickenson's Basket." SanFPJ (4:3) 83, p. 25.
"Politics." SanFPJ (4:3) 83, p. 25.

USCHUK, Pamela
See: UZCHUK, Pamela

4571. UTASSY, Jozsef
"1955" (tr. by Timothy Kachinske). PoetryE (9/10) Wint 82-Spr 83, p. 201.
"At a Nudist Beach" (tr. by Timothy Kachinske). PoetryE (9/10) Wint 82-Spr 83, p. 199-200.

4572. UTZ, Stephen
"Avignon Days." SouthernR (19:3) Jl 83, p. 650.
"Et Progreditur ut Luna." SouthernR (19:3) Jl 83, p. 651.
"I Imagine Saying." SouthernR (19:3) Jl 83, p. 651.
"Un Rêve." SouthernR (19:3) Jl 83, p. 650.

4573. UZCHUK, Pamela
"A Gift Blue As Light." CimR (62) Ja 83, p. 24-26.

4574. VAISIUS, Andrew
"Main Street and Kingston Road." Waves (11:4) Spr 83, p. 48.
"You were born in a confusion of flesh" (to Emma). Waves (11:4) Spr 83, p. 47.
"You were delivered swathed in the slime of centuries" (for Daniel). Waves (11:4) Spr 83, p. 46.

4575. VAKAR, Anna
"A bruised apricot." WindO (42) Sum 83, p. 2.

4576. VALAORITIS, Nanos
"The Hunchback of Notre Dame." Kayak (63) N 83, p. 41.
"Language or Silence?" Kayak (63) N 83, p. 42.
"Moving Targets." Kayak (63) N 83, p. 41-42.

4577. VALENTA, Helen
"Surveillance." KanQ (15:2) Spr 83, p. 170.

4578. VALENTE, José Angel
"Winter Duck" (For Antonio, tr. by Will Kirkland). PoNow (7:2, #38) 83, p. 46.

4579. VALENZUELA, Luisa
"Climbing the Rag Mountain" (tr. by Margaret Sayers Peden). OP (36) Aut-Wint 83, p. 56.
"A Dream about Mercedes" (tr. by Margaret Sayers Peden). OP (36) Aut-Wint 83, p. 57-58.
"The Girl Who Turned into Cider" (tr. by Margaret Sayers Peden). OP (36) Aut-Wint 83, p. 53.
"Manuscript Found in a Bottle" (tr. by Margaret Sayers Peden). OP (36) Aut-Wint 83, p. 59.
"A Question of Chestnuts" (tr. by Margaret Sayers Peden). OP (36) Aut-Wint 83, p. 54-55.

VALENZUELA de PEREZ, Ilma
See: PEREZ, Ilma Valenzuela de

4580. VALGARDSON, W. D.
"In a Dry Season." Grain (11:2) My 83, p. 23-30.

4581. VALIS, Noel M.
"Last Message." Wind (13:48) 83, p. 59.
"Rag Player." Wind (13:48) 83, p. 63.

4582. VALLE, María Dolores del
"Un Niño." Prismal (11) Aut 83, p. 99.

4583. VALLEJO, Cesar
"Be Calm, Comrade, Awhile Longer" (tr. by Philip Garrison). NowestR (21:2/3) 83, p. 129-130.
"Between Two Stars, Losing My Footing" (tr. by Philip Garrison). NowestR (21:2/3) 83, p. 140-141.
"Conflict between the Eyes and the Glance" (tr. by Philip Garrison). NowestR (21:2/3) 83, p. 141-142.
"Faith" (tr. by Philip Garrison). NowestR

(21:2/3) 83, p. 137.
"Far Steps" (tr. by Philip Garrison). NowestR (21:2/3) 83, p. 135-136.
"Good Sense" (tr. by Philip Garrison). NowestR (21:2/3) 83, p. 136-137.
"Un Hombre Pasa con un Pan al Hombro" (tr. by Philip Garrison). NowestR (21:2/3) 83, p. 126-127.
"A Masterful Demonstration of Public Heath" (tr. by Philip Garrison). NowestR (21:2/3) 83, p. 131-133.
"My Accent Dangles" (tr. by Philip Garrison). NowestR (21:2/3) 83, p. 139-140.
"Today, a Splinter Got in Her" (tr. by Philip Garrison). NowestR (21:2/3) 83, p. 137-138.
"Whatever, It Is a Place" (tr. by Philip Garrison). NowestR (21:2/3) 83, p. 138-139.

Van . . .
See also: Names beginning with "Van" without the following space, filed below in their alphabetic positions, e.g., VanderMOLEN.

4584. Van BRUNT, H. L.
"Alba." NewL (49:3/4) Spr-Sum 83, p. 83.
"Ardent Spirits" (in memory of Archibald MacLeish). SouthernPR (23:2) Aut 82 [i.e. (23:1?) Spr 83], p. 16.
"Homage to Li Po." Wind (13:47) 83, p. 44-45.
"Lake/Man/Bird." SoDakR (21:4) Wint 83, p. 39.
"Wingin' On" (the name of a crossroads in the prairie country of eastern Oklahoma). PoNow (7:2, #38) 83, p. 30.

4585. Van HOUTEN, Lois
"Masks." StoneC (10:3/4) Spr-Sum 83, p. 25.
"Olive Tree." StoneC (10:3/4) Spr-Sum 83, p. 24.

Van KALMTHOUT, Kees
See: KALMTHOUT, Kees van

4586. Van MATRE, C. (Connie, Connetta)
"Each New Day." SanFPJ (5:4) 83, p. 61.
"Memories at Thirty." SanFPJ (5:4) 83, p. 34-35.
"Poem Untitled: I watch as children play." SanFPJ (5:4) 83, p. 37.
"'Twas Nineteen Eighty Four." SanFPJ (5:4) 83, p. 40.

Van SAANEN, Christine Dumitriu
See: DUMITRIU van SAANEN, Christine

4587. Van TASSEL, Katrina
"The Trespasser." StoneC (10:3/4) Spr-Sum 83, p. 76.

4588. Van TOORN, Peter
"Mountain Memo" (from Tu Fu). AntigR (52) Wint 83, p. 8.
"Mountain Snail" (from Giusti). AntigR (52) Wint 83, p. 7-8.

4589. Van WALLEGHEN, Michael
"The Foot." Iowa (13:3/4) Spr 82 (83), p. 39-40.
"Hanging on Like Death." Iowa (13:3/4) Spr 82 (83), p. 41-42.

4590. Van WINCKEL, Nance
"The 24 Doors: Advent Calendar Poems" (Selections: December 19-21, 23-24) (for my nephew, turning 7). Telescope (4) Wint 83, p. 80-83.
"Crossing the Solomon South Fork." MalR (65) Jl 83, p. 104.
"Eclipse, 609 B.C." (for Thales). PoetryNW (24:2) Sum 83, p. 29-30.
"Kepler Lectures on Satellitc Deportment." PoetryNW (24:2) Sum 83, p. 28-29.

Van . . .
See also: Names beginning with "Van" followed by a space, filed above in their alphabetic positions, e.g., Van BRUNT.

4591. VANDERLIP, Brian
"The Dancer." Quarry (32:4) Aut 83, p. 50.
"Word-digger's Lament." Quarry (32:4) Aut 83, p. 51.

4592. VanderMOLEN, Robert
"About Indians." Epoch (32:3) Spr-Sum 83, p. 267-269.
"Light." Epoch (32:3) Spr-Sum 83, p. 271.
"Marilyn." Epoch (32:3) Spr-Sum 83, p. 274-275.
"My Room." Epoch (32:3) Spr-Sum 83, p. 272-273.
"The Return." Images (8:3) 83, p. 11.
"The Road." Epoch (32:3) Spr-Sum 83, p. 270.
"She and Me." Epoch (32:3) Spr-Sum 83, p. 270-271.
"The Snowplows." Images (8:3) 83, p. 11.
"Swimming." Images (8:3) 83, p. 11.

4593. VANDERSEE, Charles
"Family Reunion." PoetryE (11) Sum 83, p. 39.
"Remembering the Present." Poetry (142:6) S 83, p. 340-343.
"Spring at Arm's Length." GeoR (37:1) Spr 83, p. 80-81.

VanMATRE, C. (Connie, Connetta)
See: Van MATRE, C.

4594. VARGA, Jon
"The Man in the Dark." Wind (13:48) 83, p. 27.

4595. VARGAS, Roberto
"To a Rebel." SecC (11:1/2) 83, p. 212-213.

4596. VARMA, Shrikant
"The Turnaround" (tr. by Vinay Dharwadker). Mund (14:1) 83, p. 33-34.
"The Wind" (tr. by Vinay Dharwadker). Mund (14:1) 83, p. 33.

4597. VASQUEZ SOSA, María
"Ronca el Ruiseñor." _Rácata_ (2) 83, p. 128.

4598. VAVRA, Linda
"After the Operation" (for my mother). _IndR_ (5:3) Aut 82, p. 22.
"The Girl and the Geese." _IndR_ (5:3) Aut 82, p. 23.

VECCHIO, Gloria del
See: Del VECCHIO, Gloria

4599. VEGA, Vilma
"De Mi Hermano." _LetFem_ (9:2) Aut 83, p. 80-81.
"Retrospectiva" ((A Nilda). _LetFem_ (9:2) Aut 83, p. 81-82.

4600. VEIGA, Marisella
"Sky Falling Orange Woman Fields: Carrots." _WindO_ (42) Sum 83, p. 23.

4601. VENTADOUR, Fanny
"Ad Rest: The Right." _SanFPJ_ (5:2) 83, p. 17.
"Delayed Green." _SanFPJ_ (5:2) 83, p. 18.

4602. VENUTI, Lawrence
"Anywhere Except" (tr. of Milo De Angelis). _ParisR_ (24:85) Aut 82, p. 163.
"Gee" (tr. of Milo De Angelis). _ParisR_ (24:85) Aut 82, p. 160.
"Now" (tr. of Milo De Angelis). _ParisR_ (24:85) Aut 82, p. 161.
"Only" (tr. of Milo De Angelis). _ParisR_ (24:85) Aut 82, p. 162.
"The Sounds That Arrived" (tr. of Milo De Angelis). _ParisR_ (24:85) Aut 82, p. 161.
"The Window" (tr. of Milo De Angelis). _ParisR_ (24:85) Aut 82, p. 162.

Ver LYN, Veronica
See: VerLYN, Veronica

Ver SYN, Veronica
See: VerLYN, Veronica

4603. VERDICCHIO, Pasquale
"Tides." _Bluebuf_ (2:1) Aut 83, p. 35.

4604. VERDUCCI, Florence
"Briseis." _Thrpny_ (4:3, issue 15) Aut 83, p. 13.

4605. VERLAINE, Paul
"The Faun" (tr. by Bernhard Frank). _WebR_ (8:1) Spr 83, p. 38.
"Woman with Cat" (tr. by Bernhard Frank). _WebR_ (8:1) Spr 83, p. 38.

4606. VerLYN, Veronica
"Testify or Die." _SanFPJ_ (5:4) 83, p. 91.
"A Time to Protest." _SanFPJ_ (5:4) 83, p. 90.

4607. VERNON, William (William J.)
"Animal Adjustment." Sam (34:4 136th release) 83, p. 8.
"The Bypass of Rendville, Ohio." Sam (34:4 136th release) 83, p. 10.
"Cao Gio." Sam (34:4 136th release) 83, p. 2.
"The Cold Springs Public Preserve." Sam (34:4 136th release) 83, p. 5.
"The Fourth Son." SanFPJ (5:3) 83, p. 67.
"Land of Sinkholes." Sam (34:4 136th release) 83, p. 9.
"On the Surface at Castalia." RagMag (2:2) Aut 83, p. 4.
"Outside During the Six O'Clock News." Sam (34:4 136th release) 83, p. 7.
"Pink Pearls in Clamshells." Sam (34:4 136th release) 83, p. 6.
"Praising the Sand." Sam (34:4 136th release) 83, p. 1-12.
"The Prisoner." Sam (34:4 136th release) 83, p. 11.
"Raising a Child: Praising the Sand." Sam (34:4 136th release) 83, p. 12.
"Rhythms." Sam (34:4 136th release) 83, p. 4.
"Rodin's Polish Soldier." PikeF (5) Spr 83, p. 10.
"To the First Black Appointed." SanFPJ (5:3) 83, p. 66.
"Whittler's Mother." Sam (34:4 136th release) 83, p. 3.

4608. VERSHEL, Laurence
"Here Is Your Evening." Argo (4:3) 83, p. 27.
"To Build a Quiet City in His Mind." Argo (4:3) 83, p. 27.

4609. VESAAS, Halldis Moren
"Bladrik Grein." SoDakR (21:1) Spr 83, p. 27.
"Den Andre Skogen." SoDakR (21:1) Spr 83, p. 33.
"The Other Forest" (tr. by Ron Wakefield). SoDakR (21:1) Spr 83, p. 32.
"Rich Leafy Branch" (tr. by Ron Wakefield). SoDakR (21:1) Spr 83, p. 26.
"The Tree" (tr. by Ron Wakefield). SoDakR (21:1) Spr 83, p. 28, 30.
"Treet." SoDakR (21:1) Spr 83, p. 29, 31.

4610. VEST, Debra Kay
"Airport." PikeF (5) Spr 83, p. 18.
"The Extra." PikeF (5) Spr 83, p. 11.
"Pine Cone and Variations" (for Robert Bly). PikeF (5) Spr 83, p. 31.

4611. VEVERKA, Marian
"Dead of Winter." SanFPJ (4:4) 83, p. 49.

4612. VIANT, William
"Pruning." StoneC (10:3/4) Spr-Sum 83, p. 54.

4613. VICUNA, Cecilia
"Golpes, Nada Más." Areíto (9:35) 83, p. 39.

VIDES, Aldolfo Mendez
See: MENDEZ VIDES, Aldolfo

4614. VIERECK, Peter
"Gladness Ode." PoNow (7:2, #38) 83, p. 4.
"New-Icarus Is Alive & Well, Only a Little Wet." PoNow (7:2, #38) 83, p. 4.
"To My Underwater Moon." PoNow (7:2, #38) 83, p. 4-5.

4615. VIGIL, Evangelina
"The Bridge People." RevChic (11:3/4) 83, p. 50-51.
"Dumb Broad!." RevChic (11:3/4) 83, p. 51-53.
"Telephone Line." RevChic (11:3/4) 83, p. 54-55.

4616. VIGNOLA, R. A.
"Farewell Everything." SanFPJ (5:1) 83, p. 23.
"Lost Lives." SanFPJ (5:2) 83, p. 92.
"Love Consumed." SanFPJ (5:1) 83, p. 63.
"Sackcloth and Ashes." SanFPJ (5:1) 83, p. 93.
"Sins of Our Fathers." SanFPJ (5:1) 83, p. 62.
"Those Who Cry Out." SanFPJ (4:3) 83, p. 70.
"Tranquilizer." SanFPJ (5:1) 83, p. 22.

4617. VINZ, Mark
"Along the Way." SpoonRQ (8:2 i.e. 8:3) Sum 83, p. 62.
"Anthropologist." SpoonRQ (8:2 i.e. 8:3) Sum 83, p. 43.
"Bedtime Story." SpoonRQ (8:2 i.e. 8:3) Sum 83, p. 1.
"Business As Usual." SpoonRQ (8:2 i.e. 8:3) Sum 83, p. 22.
"Can You Believe It? (for Dave Etter). SpoonRQ (8:2) Spr 83, p. 4.
"Ceremonial." SpoonRQ (8:2 i.e. 8:3) Sum 83, p. 58.
"Changing the Guard." SpoonRQ (8:2 i.e. 8:3) Sum 83, p. 13.
"Charter Line." SpoonRQ (8:2 i.e. 8:3) Sum 83, p. 45.
"Climbing the Stairs." Peoria, IL: Spoon River Poetry Press, 1983. Special issue of SpoonRQ (8:2 i.e. 8:3) Sum 83, p. 1-54.
"Climbing the Stairs." SpoonRQ (8:2 i.e. 8:3) Sum 83, p. 17.
"Collection." SpoonRQ (8:2 i.e. 8:3) Sum 83, p. 27.
"Contingency Plan." OhioR (30) 83, p. 258.
"Contingency Plan." SpoonRQ (8:2 i.e. 8:3) Sum 83, p. 25.
"Currents." SpoonRQ (8:2 i.e. 8:3) Sum 83, p. 35.
"Death Wish." SpoonRQ (8:2 i.e. 8:3) Sum 83, p. 57.
"Déjà Vu." SpoonRQ (8:2 i.e. 8:3) Sum 83, p. 4.
"Discount Shopping" (for Jim Stevens). SpoonRQ (8:2 i.e. 8:3) Sum 83, p. 39.
"Dream House." SpoonRQ (8:2 i.e. 8:3) Sum 83, p. 8.
"A Dream of Fish." SpoonRQ (8:2 i.e. 8:3) Sum 83, p. 15.
"A Dream of Snow." SpoonRQ (8:2 i.e. 8:3) Sum 83, p. 16.
"Endangered Species." SpoonRQ (8:2 i.e. 8:3) Sum

83, p. 48.
"Exploring the Natural History Museum." SpoonRQ (8:2 i.e. 8:3) Sum 83, p. 23.
"Feast of All Fools." SpoonRQ (8:2 i.e. 8:3) Sum 83, p. 32.
"Festival of Light." SpoonRQ (8:2 i.e. 8:3) Sum 83, p. 64.
"First Light" (for James L. White). SpoonRQ (8:2 i.e. 8:3) Sum 83, p. 31.
"The Funeral." SpoonRQ (8:2 i.e. 8:3) Sum 83, p. 63.
"Genesis." SpoonRQ (8:2 i.e. 8:3) Sum 83, p. 59.
"A Harvest." SpoonRQ (8:2 i.e. 8:3) Sum 83, p. 72.
"Holiday Inn." SpoonRQ (8:2 i.e. 8:3) Sum 83, p. 47.
"Hometown Blues." SpoonRQ (8:2 i.e. 8:3) Sum 83, p. 65.
"Householder." SpoonRQ (8:2 i.e. 8:3) Sum 83, p. 33.
"Hunter." SpoonRQ (8:2 i.e. 8:3) Sum 83, p. 69.
"In a Drought Year" (for Joe Richardson). SpoonRQ (8:2 i.e. 8:3) Sum 83, p. 71.
"Indian Corn." SpoonRQ (8:2 i.e. 8:3) Sum 83, p. 19.
"Insomniac" (for Wayne and Sylvia Branum). SpoonRQ (8:2 i.e. 8:3) Sum 83, p. 11.
"Into the Dark." SpoonRQ (8:2 i.e. 8:3) Sum 83, p. 70.
"Journey." SpoonRQ (8:2 i.e. 8:3) Sum 83, p. 26.
"Junta." SpoonRQ (8:2 i.e. 8:3) Sum 83, p. 40.
"Keeping in Touch." SpoonRQ (8:2 i.e. 8:3) Sum 83, p. 42.
"A Kind of Victory." SpoonRQ (8:2 i.e. 8:3) Sum 83, p. 41.
"Letter to the Outside." SpoonRQ (8:2 i.e. 8:3) Sum 83, p. 21.
"Life of the Party." SpoonRQ (8:2 i.e. 8:3) Sum 83, p. 7.
"Line Storm" (for Gene Frumkin). SpoonRQ (8:2 i.e. 8:3) Sum 83, p. 68.
"A Matter of Angels." SpoonRQ (8:2 i.e. 8:3) Sum 83, p. 14.
"Midcontinent." SpoonRQ (8:2 i.e. 8:3) Sum 83, p. 61.
"Missing Persons." SpoonRQ (8:2 i.e. 8:3) Sum 83, p. 37.
"Music Lesson." SpoonRQ (8:2 i.e. 8:3) Sum 83, p. 24.
"North Dakota Gothic." SpoonRQ (8:2 i.e. 8:3) Sum 83, p. 67.
"North of North." SoDakR (21:3) Aut 83, p. 82.
"North of North." SoDakR (21:4) Wint 83, p. 76.
"Our Lady of the Table." GeoR (37:4) Wint 83, p. 850.
"Patriarch." SpoonRQ (8:2 i.e. 8:3) Sum 83, p. 56.
"Photo from an Album Never Kept." LittleM (14:1/2) 83, p. 38.
"Poet, Seeking Credentials, Pulls Daring Daylight Robbery of Small Town Iowa Bank." SpoonRQ (8:2 i.e. 8:3) Sum 83, p. 44.
"Postcards." SpoonRQ (8:2 i.e. 8:3) Sum 83, p. 49-51.
"Proposition." SpoonRQ (8:2 i.e. 8:3) Sum 83, p. 53.
"The Prowler." SpoonRQ (8:2 i.e. 8:3) Sum 83, p. 10.

"Quilt Song" (for Alec Bond). SpoonRQ (8:2 i.e. 8:3) Sum 83, p. 28.
"Recluse." SpoonRQ (8:2 i.e. 8:3) Sum 83, p. 5.
"Resolution." SpoonRQ (8:2 i.e. 8:3) Sum 83, p. 54.
"Revolutionary." SpoonRQ (8:2 i.e. 8:3) Sum 83, p. 6.
"Ripoff Artist." SpoonRQ (8:2 i.e. 8:3) Sum 83, p. 52.
"Sleepless, Reading Machado." SpoonRQ (8:2 i.e. 8:3) Sum 83, p. 29-30.
"Sleepwalking." SpoonRQ (8:2 i.e. 8:3) Sum 83, p. 3.
"Soda Fountain." SpoonRQ (8:2 i.e. 8:3) Sum 83, p. 66.
"Southside." SpoonRQ (8:2 i.e. 8:3) Sum 83, p. 12.
"State of the Economy." SpoonRQ (8:2 i.e. 8:3) Sum 83, p. 55.
"Still Life: A Good All-Night Cafe." Focus (15:95) Ag 83, p. 15.
"Still Life: Barber Shop in a Small Town." Focus (15:95) Ag 83, p. 14.
"Still Life: Below Zero." Focus (15:95) Ag 83, p. 14.
"Still Life: The Pleasures of Home." Focus (15:95) Ag 83, p. 15.
"Survival Manual" (for George Roberts). SpoonRQ (8:2 i.e. 8:3) Sum 83, p. 9.
"Talk Show." SpoonRQ (8:2 i.e. 8:3) Sum 83, p. 38.
"Vigil." Focus (15:95) Ag 83, p. 19.
"The World's Greatest Two-Piece Band." SpoonRQ (8:2 i.e. 8:3) Sum 83, p. 46.

4618. VIOLI, Paul
"Fable." HangL (44) Sum 83, p. 54-56.
"Index." Epoch (33:1) Aut-Wint 83, p. 93-94.
"Midnight Shift." LittleM (14:1/2) 83, p. 6.
"Parkway." LittleM (14:1/2) 83, p. 5.
"Vanity." HangL (44) Sum 83, p. 53.

4619. VIRGIL
"The Pyres" (Aeneid Book XI, 182-209) (tr. by Robert Fitzgerald). ParisR (25:88) Sum 83, p. 63-64.

4620. VITALI, Karyn Van Kirk
"Soup." CrabCR (1:1) My 83, p. 13.

4621. VLASAK, Keith
"Photograph." NewRena (17) Aut 83, p. 77.
"To See a Tall Maple." StoneC (10:3/4) Spr-Sum 83, p. 40.

4622. VODREY, Catherine
"The Game." PoetC (13, i.e. 14:3) 83, p. 63-64.

4623. VOGT, Mary
"Grant Woods: 'American Gothic'." Wind (13:48) 83, p. 63.
"In Central Illinois." WestB (12) 83, p. 79.

4624. VOIGT, Ellen Bryant
"For My Mother." NewRep (188:5) 7 F 83, p. 36.
"The Last Class." TriQ (58) Aut 83, p. 68-69.
"The Lotus Flowers." NewYorker (59:30) 12 S 83, p. 91.
"Nocturne." Ploughs (9:2/3) 83, p. 167-168.
"The Wish." Atlantic (252:5) N 83, p. 102.

Von FREYTAG-LORINGHOVEN, Elsa, Baroness
See: FREYTAG-LORINGHOVEN, Elsa von, Baroness

Von GOETHE, Johann Wolfgang
See: GOETHE, Johann Wolfgang von

4625. Von HENDY, James
"After Making Love." KanQ (15:1) Wint 83, p. 151.
"The Match." KanQ (15:1) Wint 83, p. 150.

4626. VOORE, M.
"Child of Refugees." AntigR (55) Aut 83, p. 31.
"Cursed with Bark." AntigR (55) Aut 83, p. 32.
"Have You Seen It." AntigR (55) Aut 83, p. 32.

4627. VOSSEKUIL, Cheryl
"Why I No Longer Eat Lunch." Tendril (14/15) Wint 83, p. 206-208.

4628. VRETTAKOS, Nikiforos
"The Seven Elegies" (tr. by Robert Zaller). SpiritSH (48) 82, p. 30-32.

VRIES, Carrow de
See: De VRIES, Carrow

4629. WAAGE, Fred
"Up on the Hudson." Stand (24:3) 83, p. 61.

4630. WADDEN, Paul
"Autumn" (tr. of Rainer Maria Rilke). Nimrod (27:1) Aut-Wint 83, p. 54.
"Song of Love" (tr. of Rainer Maria Rilke). Nimrod (27:1) Aut-Wint 83, p. 55.
"The Sonnets to Orpheus" (Selection: I, 8: "Only in that place where praise is") (tr. of Rainer Maria Rilke). SouthernHR (17:3) Sum 83, p. 224.
"Title Page" (tr. of Rainer Maria Rilke). Nimrod (27:1) Aut-Wint 83, p. 54.

4631. WADE, Jennifer
"Boundaries." AntigR (55) Aut 83, p. 29.

4632. WADE, Seth
"Alba." Tendril (16) Sum 83, p. 129.
"Boll Weevil." Tendril (16) Sum 83, p. 132-133.
"Elegy for Maureen." Tendril (16) Sum 83, p. 130-131.
"Wordsworth on the Banks of the Rio Grande." SoDakR (21:4) Wint 83, p. 7.

4633. WADE, Sidney
"The Crab." PraS (57:4) Wint 83, p. 48.
"A Little Romance." PraS (57:4) Wint 83, p. 47.

4634. WAGNER, John Dean
"House Sitting." QW (17) Aut-Wint 83-84, p. 100.

4635. WAGNER, Linda
"The Story of Anorexia." KanQ (15:4) Aut 83, p. 115-117.

4636. WAGONER, David
"Aerial Act." PraS (51:1, i.e. 57:1) Spr 83, p. 15.
"The Best Slow Dancer." Kayak (62) Ag 83, p. 51.
"Bitter Cherry." Nat (236:25) 25 Je 83, p. 808.
"By Starlight." Poetry (142:4) Jl 83, p. 200.
"Danse Macabre." MemphisSR (2:2) Spr 82, p. 27.
"Elephant Ride." MemphisSR (2:2) Spr 82, p. 26.
"Eruption." NewRep (186:24) 16 Je 82, p. 36.
"The Gardener's Dream." WestHR (37:2) Sum 83, p. 138.
"Getting Away." NewYorker (59:7) 4 Ap 83, p. 48.
"A Guide to the Field." Poetry (142:4) Jl 83, p. 197-198.
"The Illusionist." Nat (236:19) 14 My 83, p. 616.
"In Love." WestHR (37:2) Sum 83, p. 135.
"Jack and the Beanstalk." PraS (51:1, i.e. 57:1) Spr 83, p. 17-18.
"Kinglet." NewYorker (58:51) 7 F 83, p. 112.
"Loons Mating." WestHR (37:2) Sum 83, p. 136.
"Medusa's Lover." Telescope (4) Wint 83, p. 31.
"My Father in the Basement." NewRep (188:19) 16 My 83, p. 38.
"Our Blindness." Poetry (142:4) Jl 83, p. 199.
"The Padded Cell." PraS (51:1, i.e. 57:1) Spr 83, p. 19.
"Pandora's Dream." Nat (236:2) 15 Ja 83, p. 56.
"Peacock Display." PraS (51:1, i.e. 57:1) Spr 83, p. 14.
"Replanting a Garden." WestHR (37:2) Sum 83, p. 137.
"The Shape." Iowa (13:3/4) Spr 82 (83), p. 127.
"That Moment." IndR (6:2) Spr 83, p. 4.
"Waking Up in a Garden." AmerPoR (12:1) Ja/F 83, p. 45.
"Walking on the Ceiling." PraS (51:1, i.e. 57:1) Spr 83, p. 16.
"The Waterlily." Poetry (142:4) Jl 83, p. 201.
"A Woman Feeding Gulls." Nat (236:2) 15 Ja 83, p. 56.
"A Young Woman Found in the Woods." Atlantic (252:3) S 83, p. 62.

4637. WAHLE, F. Keith
"Horses." WestB (13) 83, p. 54.
"The Man in the Black Hat." WestB (13) 83, p. 52-53.

4638. WAINIO, Ken
"Getting Rid of the Ego." SecC (11:1/2) 83, p. 216.

4639. WAINWRIGHT, Jeffrey
"Before Battle." Agni (18) 83, p. 36.
"Heart's Desire" (Excerpt: "Some Propositions and Part of a Narrative"). Agni (18) 83, p. 37.
"Sea Dreams." Agni (18) 83, p. 38-40.
"Sentimental Education." Agni (18) 83, p. 34-35.

4640. WAKEFIELD, Ron
"The Other Forest" (tr. of Halldis Moren Vesaas). SoDakR (21:1) Spr 83, p. 32.
"Rich Leafy Branch" (tr. of Halldis Moren Vesaas). SoDakR (21:1) Spr 83, p. 26.
"The Tree" (tr. of Halldis Moren Vesaas). SoDakR (21:1) Spr 83, p. 28, 30.

4641. WAKOSKI, Diane
"For the Girl with Her Face in a Rose." Sulfur (3:1, #7) 83, p. 30-31.
"Joyce Carol Oates Plays the Saturn Piano" (for Joyce Carol Oates, who, several years ago, began to study the piano again). Sulfur (3:1, #7) 83, p. 31-35.
"Molokai" (for Travis Summersgill). MemphisSR (2:2) Spr 82, p. 48-51.
"Personal & Impersonal Landscapes." LittleBR (4:2) Wint 83-84, p. 19-20.
"The Ring of Irony." Sulfur (3:1, #7) 83, p. 27-29.
"Sleeping in the Ring of Fire." Tendril (14/15) Wint 83, p. 209-210.

4642. WALCOTT, Derek
"August." Nat (237:5) 20-27 Ag 83, p. 150.
"Certain Things." Nat (237:5) 20-27 Ag 83, p. 150.
"Midsummer." NewYorker (59:20) 4 Jl 83, p. 38.
"Midsummer" (Selections: XXXIV-XXXVI). Agni (18) 83, p. 5-7.
"Tropic Zone." NewYorker (59:4) 14 Mr 83, p. 48-49.
"Two Poems: XXVI, XLVIII." NewYRB (30:17) 10 N 83, p. 42.

4643. WALD, Diane
"What She Said, When She Sat Up." AmerPoR (12:6) N/D 83, p. 17.

4644. WALDRIDGE, Robert
"Poem for Late Fall." SoDakR (21:4) Wint 83, p. 41.

4645. WALDROP, Keith
"Groundless" (tr. of Edmond Jabès). Sulfur (3:2, #8) 83, p. 80-82.
"The Pact of Spring" (tr. of Edmond Jabès). Sulfur (3:2, #8) 83, p. 82-85.
"Well Water" (tr. of Edmond Jabès). Sulfur (3:2, #8) 83, p. 79-80.

4646. WALDROP, Rosmarie
"Actaeon: 11 Glosses on an Alibi." OP (35) Spr-Sum 83, p. 3-10.
"Aely, Gallimard, 1972" (Excerpts) (tr. of Edmond Jabès). CreamCR (8:1/2) 83, p. 66-71.

"Difficulties of a Heavy Body." CreamCR (8:1/2) 83, p. 173-175.

4647. WALKER, Alice
"Early Losses: a Requiem." NewL (49:3/4) Spr-Sum 83, p. 75-80.

4648. WALKER, Jim
"Iceman." AntigR (53) Spr 83, p. 111.

4649. WALKER, Lois V.
"The War Came to Illinois." PikeF (5) Spr 83, p. 27.
"Words to a Pioneer Husband: After the Fact." LittleBR (3:4) Sum 83, p. 48.

4650. WALLACE, Robert
"Ann 2." Images (8:3) 83, p. 12.
"Ellie." Images (8:3) 83, p. 12.
"A Fresco of Swans and Bears." ThRiPo (21/22) 83, p. 93.
"God's Wonderful Drowning Machine." ThRiPo (21/22) 83, p. 92.
"Leslie." Images (8:3) 83, p. 12.

4651. WALLACE, Ronald
"At Half-Moon Bay." NoAmR (268:1) Mr 83, p. 53.
"The Facts of Life." PoetL (77:4) Wint 83, p. 235.
"Fat: in Love." PoetL (77:4) Wint 83, p. 234.
"Fish Magic." PoetL (77:4) Wint 83, p. 233-234.
"The Poetry Lesson" (for Molly, age 6). PoetryNW (24:4) Wint 83-84, p. 35.
"Requiem." ClockR (1:1) Sum 83, p. 15.
"Softball." PoetryNW (24:1) Spr 83, p. 46-47.
"Tupperware" (for Linda). ClockR (1:2) Wint 83-84, p. 44-45.
"Words, Words." PoetryNW (24:1) Spr 83, p. 47.

4652. WALLACE, Terry H. Smith
"Indian Summer in the Delaware." FourQt (33:1) Aut 83, p. 2.

WALLEGHEN, Michael van
See: Van WALLEGHEN, Michael

4653. WALLER, Adele Haverty
"Another Season." MemphisSR (2:1) Aut 81, p. 13.

4654. WALLER, Gary (Gary F.)
"European Vacation." Poetry (142:4) Jl 83, p. 223.
"Grave Meeting." Poetry (142:4) Jl 83, p. 224.
"Jackson Pollock: Albright-Knox Gallery." SpiritSH (48) 82, p. 52-53.
"Just Kidding: More Trials of a Suburban Father." PoetryCR (4:4) Sum 83, p. 15.
"Troilus in Hell." Quarry (32:1) Wint 83, p. 28-29.

4655. WALLS, Doyle Wesley
"The Grasshopper Interviews." PikeF (5) Spr 83, p. 17.

4656. WALSH, Joy
"Kerouac." MoodySI (8) Sum-Aut 80, p. 13.

4657. WALSH, María Elena
"Those Who Sing" (tr. by Melanie Bowman). DevQ (17:4) Wint 83, p. 22-23.

4658. WALSH, Marty
"Angel of Misfits and Loose Change." StoneC (11:1/2, Pt. 1) Aut-Wint 83, p. 36-37.
"Grendel." BelPoJ (33:4) Sum 83, p. 2-5.

4659. WALSH, Phyllis
"Awakened before birdsong." WindO (42) Sum 83, p. 3.
"Bond." SmPd (20:3) Aut 83, p. 11.

4660. WALSH, Rosemary
"On the Road to Making You a Memory." Bogg (50) 83, p. 6.

4661. WALTER, Eugene
"Leaves of Hypnos, a War Journal, 1943-1944" (Excerpts) (tr. of René Char). NegC (3:4) Aut 83, p. 103.
"Lily-of-the-Valley" (tr. of René Char). NegC (3:4) Aut 83, p. 99.
"Warning to the Wind" (tr. of René Char). NegC (3:4) Aut 83, p. 99.
"Youth" (tr. of René Char). NegC (3:4) Aut 83, p. 101.

4662. WALTERS, LaWanda
"On Being Alive at the Same Time." SouthernPR (23:2) Aut 83, p. 34.

4663. WALTERS, Robert
"The Fifth Horseman of the Apocalypse." Poem (49) N 83, p. 60.
"On Greyhound Buses." Poem (49) N 83, p. 58-59.
"The Return." Poem (49) N 83, p. 61.
"The Snow Goose." NegC (3:4) Aut 83, p. 51.

4664. WALTHALL, Hugh
"Hunki-Dori." Gargoyle (22/23) 83, p. 6.
"Otiose Bones." Gargoyle (22/23) 83, p. 6.

4665. WAMPLER, Martin
"Nights in San Francisco after the Chemical-Biological-Neutron Bomb Disaster." SanFPJ (5:1) 83, p. 96.

4666. WAMPLER, Pamela
"Walking into Water: Virginia Woolf 1941." IndR (5:2) Sum 82, p. 23.

4667. WANG, Ch'ang-ling
"Silent at Her Window" (tr. by Sam Hamil). CreamCR (8:1/2) 83, p. 91.

4668. WANG, Hui-Ming
"The Flowers outside My Window." LittleBR (4:2) Wint 83-84, p. 71.
"A Marble-white full moon." LittleBR (4:2) Wint 83-84, p. 85.
"Mountain Dialogue" (tr. of Li Po). NewL (49:3/4) Spr-Sum 83, p. 65.
"Reply to Chang Shao-Fu, the Keeper of Archives" (tr. of Wang Wei). NewL (49:3/4) Spr-Sum 83, p. 66.
"Since You Have Gone Away" (tr. of Chiu Nin). NewL (49:3/4) Spr-Sum 83, p. 64.
"Sloops in the Bay." LittleBR (4:2) Wint 83-84, p. 14.
"Where the Deer Live" (tr. of Wang Wei). NewL (49:3/4) Spr-Sum 83, p. 63.

4669. WANG, Karl
"From the Cinema, Friday Night." PikeF (5) Spr 83, p. 9.

4670. WANG, Wei
"At Bamboo Lodge" (tr. by Sam Hamill). MalR (64) F 83, p. 162.
"In the Green Stream" (tr. by Joseph Lisowski). LitR (26:3) Spr 83, p. 449.
"Leave-Taking" (in Chinese). StoneC (11:1/2, Pt. 1) Aut-Wint 83, p. 16.
"Leave-Taking" (tr. by Joseph Lisowski). StoneC (11:1/2, Pt. 1) Aut-Wint 83, p. 17.
"Reply to Chang Shao-Fu, the Keeper of Archives" (tr. by Wang Hui-Ming). NewL (49:3/4) Spr-Sum 83, p. 66.
"Where the Deer Live" (tr. by Wang Hui-Ming). NewL (49:3/4) Spr-Sum 83, p. 63.

4671. WANIEK, Marilyn Nelson
"It's All in Your Head" (For Deborah M.). GeoR (37:4) Wint 83, p. 787-789.

4672. WANTLING, William
"For Ernie Marshall" (if he's still around). SecC (11:1/2) 83, p. 214.
"Style 7, Alive, Alive." SecC (11:1/2) 83, p. 215.

4673. WARD, Diane
"Approximately." ParisR (24:86) Wint 82, p. 82-83.

4674. WARD, Joanne
"Climbing." 13thM (6:1/2) 82, p. 47-49.
"Substation." 13thM (6:1/2) 82, p. 50-51.

4675. WARD, Robert R.
"Aubade for George." OroM (2:1, #5) Sum 83, p. 25.
"Safe Anchor." OroM (2:1, #5) Sum 83, p. 25.

4676. WARDEN, Marine Robert
"My Father-in-Law Remembers the Argonne, September, 1918." Abraxas (27/28) 83, p. 15.

4677. WARMBROD, Nancy Compton
"The Exhibit." Poem (49) N 83, p. 8.
"Keystone." Poem (49) N 83, p. 7.

4678. WARNER, S. A.
"Bald Hills Road." SanFPJ (4:2) 83, p. 59.
"Battlefield Parade." SanFPJ (5:2) 83, p. 28.
"Dry Creek Braceros." SanFPJ (4:2) 83, p. 58.
"Hardhats on Avenue of the Americas" SanFPJ (5:2) 83, p. 28.
"One Day." SanFPJ (4:4) 83, p. 52.

4679. WARREN, Charlotte Gould
"Quiet Down" (after reading Scott Momaday's Gourd Dancer). SouthernPR (23:2) Aut 82 [i.e. (23:1?) Spr 83], p. 9.

4680. WARREN, James E., Jr.
"The Rain Continues to Fall" (tr. of Luigi Fiorentino). WebR (8:2) Aut 83, p. 48.

4681. WARREN, Larkin
"Labor Day." Tendril (16) Sum 83, p. 135.
"Solstice." Tendril (16) Sum 83, p. 134.

4682. WARREN, Robert Penn
"Amazing Grace in the Back Country." OhioR (30) 83, p. 80-82.
"Breaking the Code." Nat (236:18) 7 My 83, p. 583.
"Breaking the Code." SouthernR (19:2) Ap 83, p. 352-353.
"Delusion?--No!." SewanR (91:4) Aut 83, p. 566-567.
"It Is Not Dead." NewYorker (58:48) 17 Ja 83, p. 36.
"Marble." NewYorker (59:36) 24 O 83, p. 46.
"Minnesota Recollection." SouthernR (19:2) Ap 83, p. 345-347.
"Mortal Limit." SewanR (91:4) Aut 83, p. 566.
"Muted Music." GeoR (37:2) Sum 83, p. 247.
"New Dawn." NewYorker (59:39) 14 N 83, p. 46-48.
"Old Covered Bridge." SouthernR (19:2) Ap 83, p. 342-343.
"Old Dog." Nat (237:18) 3 D 83, p. 572-573.
"Paradigm of Seasons." Ploughs (9:2/3) 83, p. 11-12.
"Personal History." SewanR (91:4) Aut 83, p. 565.
"The Place." NewYorker (59:23) 25 Jl 83, p. 26.
"Problem of Autobiography: Vague Recollection or Dream." SewanR (91:4) Aut 83, p. 568.
"Question at Cliff-Thrust." SouthernR (19:2) Ap 83, p. 351-352.
"Seasons." GeoR (37:4) Wint 83, p. 750-751.
"Self." Nat (236:18) 7 My 83, p. 583.
"Snowfall." Atlantic (251:3) Mr 83, p. 86-87.
"Sunset." Ploughs (9:2/3) 83, p. 13.
"Three Darknesses." NewYorker (58:51) 7 F 83, p. 40-41.
"True Love." SouthernR (19:2) Ap 83, p. 343-345.
"Why You Climbed Up." GeoR (37:3) Aut 83, p. 565.
"Why You Climbed Up." SewanR (91:4) Aut 83, p. 567-568.
"Wind and Gibbon." SouthernR (19:2) Ap 83, p. 349-

351.
"Winter Dreams." SouthernR (19:2) Ap 83, p. 348-349.

4683. WARREN, Rosanna
"A Cypress." ChiR (33:4) Sum [i.e. Spr] 83, p. 17-19.
"Renoir" (for Donald Davie). Shen (34:2) 83, p. 79.
"Rocamadour." SenR (13:2) 82-83, p. 13-15.
"Theora" (for Theora Hamblett, painter, Oxford, Mississippi, 1895-1977). SenR (13:2) 82-83, p. 9-12.

4684. WARSH, Lewis
"Eye Opener." SunM (13) 83, p. 7-31.
"The Genetic Ode." SunM (13) 83, p. 32-52.
"High Fidelity." SunM (13) 83, p. 53-72.
"Methods of Birth Control." SunM (13) 83, p. 73-98.
"Methods of Birth Control" (for Peggy DeCoursey). Washington: Sun & Moon Press, 1983. Also SunM (13) 83, p. 1-98.

4685. WARWICK, Joanna
"At the Gates of the Valley" (tr. of Zbigniew Herbert). AmerPoR (12:1) Ja/F 83, p. 12.
"An Attempt at Description" (tr. of Zbigniev Herbert). Kayak (63) N 83, p. 49.
"The Chairs" (tr. of Zbigniev Herbert). Kayak (63) N 83, p. 50.
"The Clock" (tr. of Zbigniev Herbert). Kayak (63) N 83, p. 50.
"Fish" (tr. of Zbigniev Herbert). Kayak (63) N 83, p. 50.
"The Longobards" (tr. of Zbigniev Herbert). Kayak (63) N 83, p. 52.
"A Parable about Russian Emigrants" (tr. of Zbigniew Herbert). AmerPoR (12:1) Ja/F 83, p. 13.
"The Seventh Angel" (tr. of Zbigniew Herbert). AmerPoR (12:1) Ja/F 83, p. 13.
"She Was Setting Her Hair" (tr. of Zbigniew Herbert). AmerPoR (12:1) Ja/F 83, p. 13.
"A Stool" (tr. of Zbigniev Herbert). Kayak (63) N 83, p. 51.

4686. WASHINGTON, Thomas
"I Never Learned the Names of Flowers." WorldO (17:3) Spr 83, p. 43.

4687. WASILEWSKI, Valeria
"This Is Not a Conversation for the Telephone" (tr. of Stanislaw Barańczak). ParisR (25:87) Spr 83, p. 197.
"What Is a Verse Not to Be Thought" (tr. of Stanislaw Barańczak). ParisR (25:87) Spr 83, p. 196-197.

4688. WATERMAN, Charles
"The Powerline Poles." Sam (36:3 143rd release) 83, p. 23.

4689. WATERS, Mary Ann
"Blueprint." SenR (13:2) 82-83, p. 72-73.
"Glasses" (for my mother). KanQ (15:4) Aut 83, p. 109.
"Illumination." PoetryNW (24:1) Spr 83, p. 33.
"The Narrows." PoetryNW (24:1) Spr 83, p. 32-33.
"Three Reasons Why It Is Called Isla Mujeres" (Quintanna Roo, Mexico). OroM (2:1, #5) Sum 83, p. 11-12.
"Woman Running." KanQ (15:4) Aut 83, p. 110.

4690. WATERS, Michael
"American Bandstand." MissouriR (6:2) Wint 83, p. 37.
"Body Language" (for Deborah Tall & David Weiss). MemphisSR (3:1) Aut 82, p. 9.
"Carousel." MemphisSR (3:1) Aut 82, p. 10-11.
"The Faithful." GeoR (37:1) Spr 83, p. 39.
"The Furniture-Maker." ThRiPo (21/22) 83, p. 94.
"Green Shoes." MissouriR (6:2) Wint 83, p. 40.
"Independence Day." OhioR (30) 83, p. 222.
"Matinee." KanQ (15:3) Sum 83, p. 73.
"Monopoly." MissouriR (6:2) Wint 83, p. 38-39.
"The Story of the Caul." YaleR (72:3) Spr 83, p. 417.

4691. WATERS, Susan C.
"Seagulls on Lake Ontario." CapeR (19:1) Wint 83, p. 45.

4692. WATKINS, Edward
"Chandler Country, 1954." PikeF (5) Spr 83, p. 35.
"The Undertaker." PikeF (5) Spr 83, p. 23.
"A Villanelle for Myself." PikeF (5) Spr 83, p. 35.

4693. WATSON, Karl
"Dover (AFB), Delaware." SoCaR (15:2) Spr 83, p. 26.
"The Iceman." PoetL (77:3) Aut 82, p. 140.

4694. WATSON, Thomas Ramey
"On Botticelli's 'Modonna of the Magnificat'." Comm (110:22) 16 D 83, p. 691.

4695. WATSON, Wilfred
"Deconstruction chez Flahiff." Descant (41) Sum 83, p. 108-109.
"Picasso and Gertrude Stein." Descant (41) Sum 83, p. 110-112.
"Putting an Old Environment inside a New One." Descant (41) Sum 83, p. 115.
"Re March 3, 1980." Descant (41) Sum 83, p. 113-114.
"Re Narcissus." Descant (41) Sum 83, p. 116.

4696. WATTEN, Barret
"One Half" (Excerpts). ParisR (24:86) Wint 82, p. 112-113.

4697. WATTS, Enos
"A la Recherche du Temps Perdu." AntigR (53) Spr 83, p. 68.

"For One Who Dies Alone in the Night." PottPort (5) 83-84, p. 5.
"Intruder." PottPort (5) 83-84, p. 19.
"Patience." PottPort (5) 83-84, p. 27.
"The Pieta: Madonna della Febbre." AntigR (53) Spr 83, p. 67.

4698. WAUGAMAN, Charles A.
"Mother's Memorabilia." CapeR (18:2) Sum 83, p. 27.

4699. WAYMAN, Tom
"Bosses" (after Nicanor Parra). MinnR (NS 20) Spr 83, p. 21.
"Breath: For Fred Wah." CanLit (99) Wint 83, p. 66.
"Broken Toes." LittleM (14:1/2) 83, p. 121-122.
"East Kootenay Illumination." CanLit (96) Spr 83, p. 34-36.
"Feeding Time at the Tiger House of the Detroit Zoo" (for Philip Levine). MassR (24:3) Aut 83, p. 587-589.
"The Ladies" (found poem). Kayak (62) Ag 83, p. 11.
"A Man's World" (found poem). Kayak (62) Ag 83, p. 10.
"Nuance." OntR (18) Spr-Sum 83, p. 92-93.
"Planetary Consciousness Sonnet" (found poem). Kayak (62) Ag 83, p. 11.
"Raising a Relationship." LittleM (14:1/2) 83, p. 119-120.
"Salmonwater." WestCR (17:4) Ap 83, p. 40.
"Saving the World." OntR (18) Spr-Sum 83, p. 90-91.
"Urban Housing" (found poem). Kayak (62) Ag 83, p. 10.

4700. WAYNE, Jane O.
"Playing from Memory." MassR (24:1) Spr 83, p. 81.
"Slipping." AmerS (52:2) Spr 83, p. 228.
"Tooth and Nail." Ascent (8:3) 83, p. 48.

4701. WEAVER, Margaret
"The Hawk." PoetL (77:3) Aut 82, p. 166.
"Lullaby." PoetL (77:3) Aut 82, p. 166-167.

4702. WEAVER, Roger
"The Way It Goes." ConcPo (16:2) Aut 83, p. 22.

4703. WEBB, Anthony Lee
"Heightened Sensitivity." PottPort (5) 83-84, p. 25.

4704. WEBB, Bernice Larson
"Private Parts." StoneC (10:3/4) Spr-Sum 83, p. 28.

4705. WEBB, Phyllis
"The Authors are in Eternity, or so Blake said." MalR (65) Jl 83, p. 13.
"Dentelle, she-teeth, milk-tooth, a mouthful of lace." MalR (65) Jl 83, p. 11.
"Frivolities: Seven Anti-ghazals." MalR (65) Jl 83, p. 7-13.
"History and Secrecy." MalR (65) Jl 83, p. 14.
"Is there such a thing as a vulgar plant?" MalR

(65) Jl 83, p. 10.
"A lozenge of dream sticks on my tongue." MalR (65) Jl 83, p. 7.
"Mulberry tree with innocent eyes." MalR (65) Jl 83, p. 9.
"My soul, my soul, who said that?" MalR (65) Jl 83, p. 8.
"Reserved books, Reserved land, Reserved flight, And still property is theft." MalR (65) Jl 83, p. 12.
"The Vision Tree" (Selection: "I Daniel"). PoetryCR (5:2) Wint 83-84, p. 11.

4706. WEBER, Elizabeth
"All Gone." Calyx (7:3) Sum 83, p. 39.
"The North Cape." Ascent (9:1) 83, p. 21-22.
"The Wind Taking My Name." Calyx (7:3) Sum 83, p. 40.

4707. WEBER, Joanne
"Heloise." Grain (11:3) Ag 83, p. 15.
"Heloise: White Martyrdom." Grain (11:3) Ag 83, p. 15.

4708. WEBER, R. B.
"A Day of Walking." Blueline (4:1) Sum-Aut 82, p. 28.

4709. WEBSTER, Diane
"Baking Cookies." Bogg (50) 83, p. 21.
"Generations." Wind (13:49) 83, p. 14.
"On Water." SmPd (20:3) Aut 83, p. 16.

4710. WEDGE, Philip
"Catechism" (Seaton Fourth Award Poem (2) 1983). KanQ (15:3) Sum 83, p. 88.

4711. WEED, Lynn
"An Emily Dickinson Poem." YetASM (2:1) 83, p. 2.

4712. WEEDON, Syd
"Hands convey warmth with a touch." SanFPJ (5:4) 83, p. 3.
"The Night Splotches" (tr. [?] of Lorenzo D'Arberet). Sam (34:3 135th release) 83, p. 28.
"The Opening Nonsense" (tr. [?] of Lorenzo D'Arberet). Sam (34:3 135th release) 83, p. 29.
"Ronko's Dream." SanFPJ (4:2) 83, p. 64.
"Rose Garden." RagMag (2:2) Aut 83, p. 4.

4713. WEEKS, Ramona
"After the Storm." WindO (43) Wint 83, p. 16-17.
"Einstein's Son." CapeR (19:1) Wint 83, p. 9.
"Farewell." PoNow (7:2, #38) 83, p. 28.
"Savage of the Aveyron." WindO (43) Wint 83, p. 15.
"Tree Ornament." CapeR (19:1) Wint 83, p. 11.
"The Wagon Man." CapeR (19:1) Wint 83, p. 10.

4714. WEERASINGHE, Asoka
"Apartheid." WritersL S 83, p. 26.

"The Killdeer." WritersL O 83, p. 11.
"Summer Image." WritersL Jl 83, p. 10.

4715. WEI, Chuang
"To the Tune 'Beautiful Barbarian'" (tr. by Sam Hamill). AmerPoR (12:6) N/D 83, p. 6.

WEI, Wang
See: WANG, Wei

4716. WEIDMAN, Phil
"Absence." WormR (23:1, issue 89) 83, p. 2.
"Can Man." WormR (23:1, issue 89) 83, p. 3.
"Common Deceit." WormR (23:1, issue 89) 83, p. 2.
"Continuation Students." WormR (23:1, issue 89) 83, p. 3.
"Deck Hawk." WormR (23:1, issue 89) 83, p. 2.
"Headway." WormR (23:1, issue 89) 83, p. 3.
"Horse Shoes." WormR (23:1, issue 89) 83, p. 3.
"Jurisdiction." WormR (23:1, issue 89) 83, p. 2.
"Mike's Magic." WormR (23:1, issue 89) 83, p. 2.
"Mind of Its Own." WormR (23:1, issue 89) 83, p. 2.
"Quick Stop." WormR (23:1, issue 89) 83, p. 3.
"Sitting." WormR (23:1, issue 89) 83, p. 1.
"Taste of Notoriety." WormR (23:1, issue 89) 83, p. 3.

4717. WEIGEL, Tom
"Elegy to Natalie Wood." Tele (18) 83, p. 26-27.
"Foretop to Rigging (After Melville)." Tele (18) 83, p. 27.

4718. WEIGL, Bruce
"1955." Field (28) Spr 83, p. 53.
"Burning Shit at An Khe." QW (16) Spr-Sum 83, p. 66-67.
"Killing Chickens." Field (28) Spr 83, p. 51-52.
"The Life before Fear." OhioR (30) 83, p. 170.
"Song for Private Charlie Fitzgerald." PoNow (7:2, #38) 83, p. 10.

4719. WEIL, James L.
"This House, My Garden." Confr (25/26) 83, p. 304.

4720. WEINBERG, Sylvia Turk
"Epitaph." Wind (13:48) 83, p. 64-65.
"Unhealed." Wind (13:48) 83, p. 64.

4721. WEINBERGER, Eliot
"Maithuna" (tr. of Octavio Paz). Sulfur (3:1, #7) 83, p. 4-8.
"Poem: Between what I see and what I say" (for Roman Jakobson, tr. of Octavio Paz). Nat (237:1) 2 Jl 83, p. 16.
"The Same Time" (tr. of Octavio Paz). YaleR (72:2) Wint 83, p. 201-205.

4722. WEINER, Hannah
"Spoke" (Excerpts). ParisR (24:86) Wint 82, p. 110-111.

4723. WEINER, Rebecca
"Getting It Right." SenR (13:2) 82-83, p. 22-23.
"Survival." SenR (13:2) 82-83, p. 24.

4724. WEINGARTEN, Roger
"For the Reader." Poetry (141:5) F 83, p. 265.
"Gulf Stream." NewL (50:1) Aut 83, p. 62.
"In Retreat." MemphisSR (4:1) Aut 83, p. 14.
"Intermissions." Tendril (14/15) Wint 83, p. 211.
"Memorial Day in the Present Tense: The Eagle Has Black Bones." MemphisSR (4:1) Aut 83, p. 13.
"Rage." MemphisSR (4:1) Aut 83, p. 15.
"Sonata of My Approach to Public Readings." Shen (34:2) 83, p. 80-82.

4725. WEINMAN, Paul
"The Connection." PikeF (5) Spr 83, p. 9.
"Episode in Civil War." Wind (13:47) 83, p. 46.
"In Joking They Began." SouthernHR (17:3) Sum 83, p. 254.
"People in Ermine Robes." Tele (18) 83, p. 107.
"Preacher man." DekalbLAJ (16:1/4) Aut 82-Sum 83, p. 73.
"There's a Turn-Off." Tele (18) 83, p. 107.
"Watching a Lady with Her X." Wind (13:47) 83, p. 46.

4726. WEISER, Dennis
"Self-Help." NewL (50:1) Aut 83, p. 101.

4727. WEISMAN, Ann
"Driving the Hi-Line" (for Yeats and Dwight Billideaux, Jr.). KanQ (15:1) Wint 83, p. 119.

4728. WEISS, David
"After All." Poetry (141:4) Ja 83, p. 210-211.
"Air Inversions." GeoR (37:1) Spr 83, p. 154-155.
"Alders." PartR (50:3) 83, p. 408-409.
"A Little Treasury of Love Poems." SenR (13:2) 82-83, p. 16-19.
"The Pail of Steam." Kayak (62) Ag 83, p. 18-19.
"Parabola." Kayak (62) Ag 83, p. 19-20.
"Starling." SenR (13:2) 82-83, p. 20-21.
"This World." Poetry (141:4) Ja 83, p. 212-215.
"Traveler's Advisory." PartR (50:3) 83, p. 407-408.
"Untitled: Like any girl with red, brown or blond hair." BlackWR (8:1) Aut 81, p. 100.

4729. WEISS, Dora
"Dear Author." SanFPJ (4:4) 83, p. 50.
"Ode to LILCO." SanFPJ (5:3) 83, p. 24.

4730. WEISS, Mike
"Waiting for the Buddha Express on Telegraph Hill." OroM (2:1, #5) Sum 83, p. 17-18.

4731. WEISS, Ruth
"Coyote" (for John Rampley). SecC (11:1/2) 83, p. 218.
"Sena." SecC (11:1/2) 83, p. 217.

4732. WEISS, Sanford
"The Broom." PoNow (7:2, #38) 83, p. 29.

4733. WEISS, Sigmund
"Apologism." SanFPJ (5:1) 83, p. 45.
"The Awakening." SanFPJ (5:3) 83, p. 16.
"Gibberish of Violence." SanFPJ (4:4) 83, p. 41.

4734. WEISS, Theodore
"After Five Years." QRL (24) 83, p. 302-304.
"The Dance Called David." QRL (24) 83, p. 295-297.
"The Inn." MichQR (22:3) Sum 83, p. 379-380.
"The Inn II." MichQR (22:3) Sum 83, p. 380.

4735. WEISSBORT, Daniel
"My London." Poetry (142:6) S 83, p. 329.
"Thwarted." Poetry (142:6) S 83, p. 329.

4736. WEISSMANN, David
"Cecco's Rage" (tr. of Cecco Angiolieri, 1250-1319). SouthernR (19:3) Jl 83, p. 658.
"Du Bellay's Fourth Regret" (tr. of Joachim Du Bellay, 1522-1560). SouthernR (19:3) Jl 83, p. 659.
"Meditation." SouthernR (19:3) Jl 83, p. 657.
"Talk Onward" (tr. of Callimachus). SouthernR (19:3) Jl 83, p. 658.

4737. WEITZMAN, Sarah Brown
"When the Sea." KanQ (15:2) Spr 83, p. 196.

4738. WELCH, Don
"American Venus." SpoonRQ (8:4) Aut 83, p. 44.
"The Eye of the Cyclops." ThirdW Spr 83, p. 71.
"The White Jaguar" (Peru, 1549). ThirdW Spr 83, p. 70.

4739. WELCH, James
"The Man from Washington." SoDakR (21:4) Wint 83, p. 21.

4740. WELCH, Jennifer
"Side Streets." HiramPoR (35) Aut-Wint 83, p. 38.

4741. WELCH, Liliane
"Composing the Glass." Grain (11:1) F 83, p. 21.
"Cutting the Trees." PoetryCR (4:4) Sum 83, p. 11.
"The Eagles" (for Silvio Simoni). AntigR (52) Wint 83, p. 92.
"Landscape." PottPort (5) 83-84, p. 14.
"September." AntigR (52) Wint 83, p. 91.
"The Wedding Band." Grain (11:1) F 83, p. 22.

4742. WELCH, Michael Irene
"Light Jewelry." Tele (18) 83, p. 90.
"She Has No Dance Card." Tele (18) 83, p. 90.

4743. WELISH, Marjorie
"Portable Lights." Epoch (33:1) Aut-Wint 83, p. 96-97.

4744. WELLS, Chris
"Fear." PoetL (77:3) Aut 82, p. 161-162.

4745. WELLS, Valerie
"Artificial Devices." Nimrod (27:1) Aut-Wint 83, p. 23-25.

4746. WELLS, Will
"For Gavin Who Cries during Bach's 'Come Sweetest Death'." NegC (3:4) Aut 83, p. 54.
"Puberty/Sandusky Shoals." KanQ (15:1) Wint 83, p. 120.

4747. WENDELL, Julia
"For You, Elizabeth." QW (17) Aut-Wint 83-84, p. 20-21.

4748. WENDT, Ingrid
"Endangered Species." PoetryNW (24:2) Sum 83, p. 30.
"Inflorescence." CharR (9:2) Aut 83, p. 68-71.

4749. WENTWORTH, Don
"Tiptoeing through the Laurencing Neutrons." SanFPJ (5:1) 83, p. 95.
"Turnpike/Inferno." SanFPJ (5:1) 83, p. 94-95.

4750. WEORES, Sandor
"Inner Landscape" (tr. by Nicholas Kolumban). MalR (64) F 83, p. 121.

4751. WERBE, Bonnie
"Cicada sits large on thin branch." Northeast (Ser. 3:15) Sum 83, p. 35.
"Fall echoes." Northeast (Ser. 3:15) Sum 83, p. 35.

4752. WERN, Randal
"Opening." KanQ (15:2) Spr 83, p. 188.

4753. WESLOWSKI, Dieter
"Brother." SouthernPR (23:2) Aut 83, p. 40.
"Exhortation to an April Day Feigning, El Dia de Los Muertos." MSS (3:1) Aut 83, p. 139.

4754. WEST, Bob
"The Wait." SanFPJ (4:3) 83, p. 43.

4755. WEST, Michael
"Slow Watch." Vis (12) 83, p. 10.

4756. WEST, Thomas A., Jr.
"Auntie Flood." PoetL (78:4) Wint 84, p. 206.

4757. WESTERFIELD, Hargis
"Brahms' Second Symphony and Martinez" (Killed in Action, 26 June 1944). Wind (13:49) 83, p. 53.
"Tryst with Sparrows and Rails." ChrC (100:35) 23 N 83, p. 1071.
"Veterans' Cadence." NegC (3:4) Aut 83, p. 44.

4758. WESTERFIELD, Nancy G.
"End of an Orchard." PoetL (78:2) Sum 83, p. 72.
"Sister Annamary as Mermaid." Confr (25/26) 83, p. 300.
"Tabula Rasa." Comm (110:14) 12 Ag 83, p. 435.
"Weathergrams." PoetL (78:2) Sum 83, p. 73.

4759. WETTEROTH, Bruce
"Media in Vita." OhioR (30) 83, p. 205.
"Remembering Rosalind." OhioR (30) 83, p. 205.
"Still Lives." WindO (42) Sum 83, p. 50.

4760. WHALEN, Damian
"Morning Aperture." MissouriR (7:1) Aut 83, p. 29.

4761. WHARTON, Calvin
"Ten (The Sky, Heaven)." WestCR (17:4) Ap 83, p. 39.

4762. WHEATLEY, Patience
"Black Hole." AntigR (52) Wint 83, p. 101-102.
"Just Visiting." AntigR (52) Wint 83, p. 102-103.
"Outage at Key Biscayne." AntigR (52) Wint 83, p. 103-104.

4763. WHEELER, Emily
"Strategies of Confession." Tendril (14/15) Wint 83, p. 212.

4764. WHEELER, Sylvia
"Another Barn Painting." NewL (49:3/4) Spr-Sum 83, p. 215.

4765. WHISLER, Robert F.
"Sheroo." SanFPJ (4:4) 83, p. 63.

4766. WHITE, Gail
"The Brown Recluse." Outbr (12/13) Aut 83-Spr 84, p. 11.
"Donkey Skin." Outbr (12/13) Aut 83-Spr 84, p. 10.
"My Neighbor's Ghost." Outbr (12/13) Aut 83-Spr 84, p. 12.
"Out of the Ordinary." Ascent (9:1) 83, p. 33-34.

4767. WHITE, J. Shelly (Janet Shelly)
"After apocolypse." SanFPJ (5:4) 83, p. 21.
"In the Face of the News: I Helicopter Raid in Guatemala." SanFPJ (5:4) 83, p. 46.
"In the Face of the News: II USA Reporters Killed by Land Mine in Honduras." SanFPJ (5:4) 83, p. 47.
"In the Face of the News: III Issues in the News." SanFPJ (5:4) 83, p. 48.
"Lebanon's Children." SanFPJ (4:4) 83, p. 93.
"Left, right." SanFPJ (4:4) 83, p. 93.

4769. WHITE, Jean
"Columbine." Bogg (51) 83, p. 24.

4770. WHITE, Julie Herrick
"Division of the Bear." PoetryNW (24:4) Wint 83-84, p. 25.
"The Mailman's Wife." PoetryNW (24:4) Wint 83-84, p. 24-25.
"Short Story." PoetryNW (24:4) Wint 83-84, p. 26.

4771. WHITE, Michael K.
"Dracula Was a Sinner But God Forgame Him." HiramPoR (34) Spr-Sum 83, p. 33.

4772. WHITE, Mimi
"Lullaby." Tendril (14/15) Wint 83, p. 213.
"Melancholia." Tendril (16) Sum 83, p. 138.
"Penises" (for C.S.). Tendril (16) Sum 83, p. 136-137.

4773. WHITE, Randy
"Between not speech but light & echo." Sulfur (3:1, #7) 83, p. 36.
"In a ring of stone." Sulfur (3:1, #7) 83, p. 37-38.
"In sight the falls." Sulfur (3:1, #7) 83, p. 37.
"O moon head." Sulfur (3:1, #7) 83, p. 38-39.

4774. WHITE, Roger
"Possession." WorldO (17:4) Sum 83, p. 44.

4775. WHITE, William M.
"Grace Abounding." Poem (47) Mr 83, p. 52.
"Leave-Taking." Poem (47) Mr 83, p. 51.
"Nightly News." NegC (3:4) Aut 83, p. 17.

4776. WHITEHEAD, James (James E.)
"For Ellen after the Publication of Her Stories." SouthernR (19:4) O 83, p. 856-857.
"A Natural Theology." SouthernR (19:4) O 83, p. 857.
"Sestina in Celebration of the Voice of Johnny Cash" (with special thanks to Tom Royals and Tom T. Hall, Fox Hollow, February 25, 1983). SouthernR (19:4) O 83, p. 855-856.
"This is an Elegy for Charlie Harry -- Pilot, Agent, Bounty Hunter, Friend." CimR (63) Ap 83, p. 62.

4777. WHITEN, Clifton
"Flailing Out There in the Ocean." Descant (43) Wint 83-84, p. 64.
"Waiting and Watching." Descant (43) Wint 83-84, p. 63.
"A Week of settling in" (In Memoriam: Alden Nowlan -- 1933-1983). PoetryCR (5:1) Aut 83, p. 3.
"We're Only Given One Liver." Descant (43) Wint 83-84, p. 60.
"While She's Eating Spaghetti He Blows Smoke in Her Face." Descant (43) Wint 83-84, p. 61.
"The World, or People in It." Descant (43) Wint 83-84, p. 62.

4778. WHITING, Nathan
"Clean Orally Only." HangL (44) Sum 83, p. 57.

"Left Signal Interference." PoNow (7:2, #38) 83, p. 33.
"The Racewalker Finds a Racewalker Pacer." HangL (44) Sum 83, p. 58.
"Ventrillo's Delighted Imp Negentropy." PoNow (7:2, #38) 83, p. 33.
"Waking on a Track during the Race." LittleBR (4:2) Wint 83-84, p. 17.

4779. WHITLOCK, Fred
"How a Flannel Shirt Cracks at the Seams/San Francisco-New York City Night Bop" (for Jack). MoodySI (13) Sum 83, p. 14-15.

4780. WHITLOW, Carolyn Beard
"Rockin' a Man, Stone Blind." MassR (24:2) Sum 83, p. 329.

4781. WHITMAN, Cedric
"Snowman." Poetry (143:3) D 83, p. 145.

4782. WHITMAN, Ruth
"Messengers." IndR (6:2) Spr 83, p. 42.

4783. WHITT, L. A. (Laurie Anne)
"Fermata." PoetryCR (5:2) Wint 83-84, p. 15.
"Les Matins." CrossC (5:2/3) 83, p. 16.

4784. WHITTAKER, A. R.
"Cryonyx." Bogg (51) 83, p. 50.

4785. WHYATT, Frances
"Offering." PoNow (7:2, #38) 83, p. 27.

4786. WICKER, Nina A.
"The Prey." Wind (13:47) 83, p. 47.

4787. WICKLESS, Robert
"Industrial Revolution Comes to the Old Country." PoetC (15:1) Aut 83, p. 32.
"Three views: August from This Town." PoetC (15:1) Aut 83, p. 33-34.

4788. WIDERKEHR, Richard
"At Sandy Neck." YetASM (2:1) 83, p. 2.

4789. WIDERSHIEN, Marc
"Venice 1976." WormR (23:4, issue 92) 83, p. 125-126.

4790. WIEBER, Wendy
"Belling the Flock." MissouriR (6:2) Wint 83, p. 68-70.

4791. WIECZOROWSKI, A.
"A Marriage in Marmaros." PoetC (13, i.e. 14:3) 83, p. 16.

4792. WIEGMAN, Robyn
"Come Winter." Swallow (2) Aut-Wint 83, p. 85-86.

"Echo." FourQt (32:3) Spr 83, p. 11.
"La Mujer." ArizQ (39:3) Aut 83, p. 196.

4793. WIER, Dara
"Another and Another." ThRiPo (21/22) 83, p. 95.

4794. WIESELTIER, Meir
"Descriptive Poetry" (tr. by Gabriel Levin). LitR (26:2) Wint 83, p. 271.
"Elegies Close to the Senses" (Excerpt) (tr. by Shirley Kaufman). LitR (26:2) Wint 83, p. 271-272.
"Family Pictures" (Excerpt) (tr. by Harold Schimmel). LitR (26:2) Wint 83, p. 273.
"Fruit" (tr. by Harold Schimmel). LitR (26:2) Wint 83, p. 273.
"Moving Lights" (tr. by Gabriel Levin). LitR (26:2) Wint 83, p. 270-271.

4795. WIGGIN, Neurine
"Visit of a Young Sister." BallSUF (24:2) Spr 83, p. 71.

4796. WILBUR, Richard
"Advice to a Prophet." NewRep (186:12) 24 Mr 82, p. 30.
"The Catch." SewanR (91:4) Aut 83, p. 551-552.
"Lying." NewYorker (58:49) 24 Ja 83, p. 36.

4797. WILD, John
"The High School Dance." IndR (6:1) Wint 83, p. 24-25.

4798. WILD, Peter
"Babylon." Images (8:3) 83, p. 11.
"Florist." QW (17) Aut-Wint 83-84, p. 60-61.
"Free Will." MemphisSR (2:1) Aut 81, p. 27.
"Good Catholics." SouthernPR (23:2) Aut 82 [i.e. (23:1?) Spr 83], p. 51.
"House Painter." LitR (26:3) Spr 83, p. 444.
"Living in Sin." Nimrod (27:1) Aut-Wint 83, p. 29.
"Miner." ThRiPo (21/22) 83, p. 96.
"Mysterious Farmhouse." MemphisSR (2:1) Aut 81, p. 26.
"Opera Singers." LittleM (14:1/2) 83, p. 32.
"Ornaments." CropD (4) 83, p. 14.
"The Owner." SecC (11:1/2) 83, p. 219.
"Painting the Mormon Church." BlackWR (8:2) Spr 82, p. 64-65.
"Perfect Romances." CharR (9:2) Aut 83, p. 74.
"Picking Up Nails." MemphisSR (1:2) Spr 81, p. 6.
"Pioneers #2." MemphisSR (1:2) Spr 81, p. 7.
"Planting Cactus." LitR (26:3) Spr 83, p. 445.
"Salt River Project." SecC (11:1/2) 83, p. 220.
"Tetons." BlackWR (8:2) Spr 82, p. 66.
"Wedding." CharR (9:2) Aut 83, p. 75.
"Yard Sale." GeoR (37:3) Aut 83, p. 578.

4799. WILDRICK, Annmarie
"The Runaway Lollie Pops." PikeF (5) Spr 83, p. 21.

4800. WILER, Jack
"We Cut Lawns." _US1_ (16/17) Wint 83-84, p. 4.

4801. WILJER, Robert
"After Death the Doctor." _AntigR_ (53) Spr 83, p. 124.
"Responsibilities." _PoetryCR_ (5:2) Wint 83-84, p. 15.
"Your Figure." _AntigR_ (53) Spr 83, p. 125.

4802. WILKERSON
"Dreaming of America." _WindO_ (43) Wint 83, p. 9-10.

4803. WILKES, Lyall
"Bud Flanagan." _Stand_ (24:1) 82-83, p. 16.
"The Incomers." _Stand_ (24:1) 82-83, p. 17.

4804. WILKINS, Charles
"Poem: She reads." _WestCR_ (17:4) Ap 83, p. 29-31.

4805. WILKINSON, Robert
"Travelers' Advisory." _Kayak_ (62) Ag 83, p. 1.

4806. WILL, Frederic
"Napalm" (tr. of Björn Hakansson, w. Gunnar Harding). _PoetryE_ (9/10) Wint 82-Spr 83, p. 243.
"A Robitussin Novena for Jim." _LittleBR_ (4:2) Wint 83-84, p. 56-58.
"Self-Portrait in Painted Glass." _MassR_ (24:4) Wint 83, p. 743-745.

4807. WILLARD, Nancy
"Saint Pumpkin." _Field_ (28) Spr 83, p. 80-81.
"The Sleep of the Painted Ladies." _Field_ (28) Spr 83, p. 78-79.

4808. WILLERTON, Chris
"Our Speaker This Morning." _KanQ_ (15:1) Wint 83, p. 172-173.

4809. WILLEY, Edward P.
"Mortality Clings." _Meadows_ (4:1) 83, p. 23.

4810. WILLHOUSE, Susan Going
"Days after Trinity (or 'Hell, I Was Only Going Fission')." _SanFPJ_ (4:3) 83, p. 62-63.

4811. WILLIAMS, Ann
"Trapped in the Spartan Motel." _LittleM_ (14:1/2) 83, p. 84.

4812. WILLIAMS, C. K.
"The Dog." _AmerPoR_ (12:5) S/O 83, p. 5.
"My Mother's Lips." _NewYorker_ (59:7) 4 Ap 83, p. 44.
"Neglect." _TriQ_ (58) Aut 83, p. 70-72.
"One of the Muses." _ParisR_ (25:87) Spr 83, p. 88-103.
"Tar." _NewRep_ (187:24) 20 D 82, p. 35.
"Waking Jed." _TriQ_ (58) Aut 83, p. 73-74.

4813. WILLIAMS, David
"Rio Escondido." PoetryE (11) Sum 83, p. 64.

4814. WILLIAMS, Elizabeth
"Cityscapes" (tr. of Dmitri Bobyshev, w. Olga Bobyshev). ClockR (1:2) Wint 83-84, p. 16-17.

4815. WILLIAMS, Miller
"Late Show." ThRiPo (21/22) 83, p. 97-98.
"Learning to Read." AmerPoR (12:1) Ja/F 83, p. 14.
"Living on the Surface." Thrpny (4:3, issue 15) Aut 83, p. 10.
"The Man Who Believes in Five." Ploughs (9:2/3) 83, p. 225.
"The Muse." Ploughs (9:2/3) 83, p. 226.
"The Story." AmerPoR (12:1) Ja/F 83, p. 14.

4816. WILLIAMS, Phil
"Regarding Shoes." KanQ (15:2) Spr 83, p. 182.

4817. WILLIAMS, Russ
"Long Rod: The Mettawee at Dawn." Blueline (5:1) Sum-Aut 83, p. 33.

4818. WILLIAMS, Shirely
"I Want Aretha to Set This to Music." SecC (11:1/2) 83, p. 221.

4819. WILLIAMS, William Carlos
"Between Walls." Field (29) Aut 83, p. 9.
"The Birth of Venus." Field (29) Aut 83, p. 50-51.
"Canthara." Field (29) Aut 83, p. 41.
"Death." Field (29) Aut 83, p. 32-33.
"Dedication for a Plot of Ground." Field (29) Aut 83, p. 14-15.
"The Horse Show." Field (29) Aut 83, p. 45-46.
"Nantucket." Field (29) Aut 83, p. 22.
"The Polar Bear." Field (29) Aut 83, p. 29.
"Sketch for a Primer of Present Day Poetic Practice" (1 hr. of continuous writing -- aside from 6 telephone calls, May 4, 1933). Sulfur (3:1, #7) 83, p. 151-156.
"The Term." Field (29) Aut 83, p. 38.

4820. WILLIAMSON, Alan
"Mr. Brown." NewRep (188:7) 21 F 83, p. 33.

4821. WILLIAMSON, Ann
"Noon tips on her pedestal." YetASM (2:1) 83, p. 10.

4822. WILLIS, Lionel
"In the Implement Shed." Descant (41) Sum 83, p. 134-140.

4823. WILLIS, Meredith Sue
"Cloud Poem." Vis (11) 83, p. 14.

4824. WILLSON, John
"Hunger Strike." CalQ (22) Sum 83, p. 46-47.

4825. WILNER, Eleanor
"The Continuous Is Broken, and Resumes." ThirdW Spr 83, p. 80-81.
"The End of the Line." ThirdW Spr 83, p. 78-79.
"Recovery." ThirdW Spr 83, p. 82-83.

4826. WILSON, Barbara
"We each hunt our own quarry." PoetryCR (5:1) Aut 83, p. 18.
"Woman." PoetryCR (4:3) Spr 83, p. 15.

4827. WILSON, Bill
"The Green Room." Sulfur (3:1, #7) 83, p. 123-124.
"Kokoschka's Water." Sulfur (3:1, #7) 83, p. 121.
"Tomato Soup." Sulfur (3:1, #7) 83, p. 122.

4828. WILSON, Carroll
"Looking beyond the Guards at the Gates to Pantex." SanFPJ (5:1) 83, p. 39.

4829. WILSON, Gary
"Quai" (tr. of Alphonze Piché). Mund (14:1) 83, p. 69.
"Retreat" (tr. of Alphonze Piché). Mund (14:1) 83, p. 71.
"Whirlpool" (tr. of Alphonze Piché). Mund (14:1) 83, p. 71.

4830. WILSON, Graeme
"Body" (tr. of Priest Saigyo). WestHR (37:4) Wint 83, p. 334.
"Death Bed" (tr. of Yamazaki Sokan). WestHR (37:3) Aut 83, p. 235.
"The Hearts of Men" (from The Shinkokinshu, tr. of Lady Sakon). WestHR (37:2) Sum 83, p. 146.
"Moonlit Orchard" (tr. of Fujiwara no Toshinari). WestHR (37:4) Wint 83, p. 333.
"Snowbound" (from The Shinkokinshu, tr. of Fujiwara no Ariiye). WestHR (37:3) Aut 83, p. 236.

4831. WILSON, Jeffrey (See also: WILSON, Jeffrey B.)
"Columbus Days." YetASM (2:1) 83, p. 4.

4832. WILSON, Jeffrey B. (See also: WILSON, Jeffrey)
"River." PikeF (5) Spr 83, p. 38.

4833. WILSON, Jonathan
"The Nursery." LitR (26:2) Wint 83, p. 322.
"Prayer." LitR (26:2) Wint 83, p. 321.

4834. WILSON, Joseph
"We: Two Death Songs." StoneC (10:3/4) Spr-Sum 83, p. 69.

4835. WILSON, Keith
"The Day of the Sculptor." Hudson (36:3) Aut 83, p. 510.
"Pecos Valley Poems." Hudson (36:3) Aut 83, p. 511.

4836. WILSON, Matthew
"Allah Akbar." Outbr (12/13) Aut 83-Spr 84, p. 14-15.
"The Kafir on the Bus." Outbr (12/13) Aut 83-Spr 84, p. 13.
"The Street of Flies." Outbr (12/13) Aut 83-Spr 84, p. 15.

4837. WILSON, Miles
"The Promise Keepers." GeoR (37:1) Spr 83, p. 158.

4838. WILSON, R. T.
"The Black Bridge." KanQ (15:4) Aut 83, p. 9.
"Downriver." KanQ (15:4) Aut 83, p. 8.
"Driving." KanQ (15:4) Aut 83, p. 10.
"Life and Art." KanQ (15:4) Aut 83, p. 7.
"Pearl Road Monologue" (Joey Conlan: 1955-1981). NewEngR (6:2) Wint 83, p. 214-215.
"The Snow-Man." NewEngR (6:2) Wint 83, p. 216.
"Something Broke." KanQ (15:4) Aut 83, p. 11.

4839. WILSON, Robert D.
"Ashes." SanFPJ (5:2) 83, p. 21.
"In Sleep I See." SanFPJ (5:3) 83, p. 52.
"Tunes of Contradiction." SanFPJ (5:3) 83, p. 45.

4840. WILSON, Robert N.
"Conversations with Death." NegC (3:4) Aut 83, p. 33-37.

4841. WILSON, Robley, Jr.
"Ice." BlackWR (9:2) Spr 83, p. 25.
"In Early Morning Traffic." Poetry (142:1) Ap 83, p. 25.
"Keys." Poetry (142:1) Ap 83, p. 27.
"A Lady in Charcoal." Poetry (142:1) Ap 83, p. 26-27.
"Persons." PoetryNW (24:1) Spr 83, p. 40-41.
"When We Are Old." PoetryNW (24:1) Spr 83, p. 41-42.

4842. WINANS, A. D.
"Excuse the Harshness Excuse the Grime But Seriousness Ain't No Crime." SecC (11:1/2) 83, p. 228-230.
"I Paid $3.00 to See Bukowski Read." SecC (11:1/2) 83, p. 223-227.

WINCKEL, Nance van
See: Van WINCKEL, Nance

4843. WINDER, Barbara
"If You Know the Answer, Don't Tell Me." ColEng (45:2) F 83, p. 150.
"You Look Past Me into the Dark." ColEng (45:2) F 83, p. 149-150.

4844. WINDER, Louise Somers
"Haiku: Drought shrinks the old pond." LittleBR (3:3) Spr 83, p. 38.
"Haiku: Just a few red coals." LittleBR (3:3) Spr

83, p. 39.
"Haiku: Soil turning to dust." LittleBR (3:3) Spr 83, p. 38.

4845. WINE, James
"'A' Oboe." SunM (12) Spr 83, p. 38.
"Aspiration." SunM (12) Spr 83, p. 49.
"Esplanade." SunM (12) Spr 83, p. 42.
"Estuary." SunM (12) Spr 83, p. 52-56.
"Formentera." SunM (12) Spr 83, p. 41.
"From Castile or Castalie." SunM (12) Spr 83, p. 39.
"L'Heure, Seulement le Saule Pleure." SunM (12) Spr 83, p. 50.
"Intransit." SunM (12) Spr 83, p. 28.
"The Law of the Sea" (for my father). SunM (12) Spr 83, p. 31-35.
"Longwalks" (for Charlie, in memory of our mother). Washington: Sun & Moon Press, 1983. Also SunM (12) Spr 83, p. 1-61.
"The Loom and the Weave." SunM (12) Spr 83, p. 23-27.
"Overlooking, Lac Léman." SunM (12) Spr 83, p. 47.
"Plein-Air." SunM (12) Spr 83, p. 48.
"Ruska." SunM (12) Spr 83, p. 46.
"Segno." SunM (12) Spr 83, p. 37.
"Seiche." SunM (12) Spr 83, p. 30.
"Shoals." SunM (12) Spr 83, p. 40.
"A Shout at Morning." SunM (12) Spr 83, p. 43-45.
"Sotto Voce" (for Doublas). SunM (12) Spr 83, p. 57-61.
"Thence, 1914." SunM (12) Spr 83, p. 29.
"To Lose La Trek." SunM (12) Spr 83, p. 36.
"Västansjö" (for Eva). SunM (12) Spr 83, p. 9-22.
"Where Snow Is Blue." SunM (12) Spr 83, p. 51.

4846. WINEMAN, Andrew
"A Ballad." EngJ (72:4) Ap 83, p. 98.

4847. WINFIELD, William
"Birthday." Nimrod (27:1) Aut-Wint 83, p. 43.
"Loss." Tendril (16) Sum 83, p. 139.
"The Visitor." CapeR (19:1) Wint 83, p. 42.
"Waking at Night." CapeR (19:1) Wint 83, p. 43.
"Wolf Poem." PortR (29:1) 83, p. 65.

4848. WING, Betsey
"Nursery Rhymes." Argo (4:1) 82, p. 7-10.

4849. WING, Tek Lum
"Pine Trees." Tele (18) 83, p. 121.

4850. WINKLER, J. S.
"February." SouthernPR (23:2) Aut 83, p. 28.

4851. WINN, Howard
"Emancipation." Wind (13:47) 83, p. 48.
"Futile Gesture." KanQ (15:1) Wint 83, p. 157.
"Group Picture." KanQ (15:1) Wint 83, p. 157.
"Husband." Wind (13:47) 83, p. 48-49.

4852. WINNER, Robert
"Death." AmerPoR (12:3) My-Je 83, p. 40.
"The Instrument." PoNow (7:2, #38) 83, p. 34.

4853. WINNING, Rebecca
"Sometimes." KanQ (15:1) Wint 83, p. 188.

4854. WINSLOW, Pete
"In the air picketed by hours with missing minutes." SecC (11:1/2) 83, p. 231.
"The invisible telephones of the wind are ringing." SecC (11:1/2) 83, p. 231.

4855. WISCHNER, Claudia (Claudia March)
"The Child." CarolQ (35:3) Spr 83, p. 22.
"When the Dead Step." WebR (8:1) Spr 83, p. 66.

4856. WISEMAN, Christopher
"Canadian Content." CrossC (5:2/3) 83, p. 25.
"Needs." CanLit (99) Wint 83, p. 20.

4857. WISMER, Leslie E.
"Open Future." WritersL Ap-My 83, p. 33.

4858. WITEK, John
"The Phantom of Flamingo Night." Tele (18) 83, p. 110-111.

4859. WITHAM, Fran
"In the Park." SpiritSH (48) 82, p. 44.
"Song." SpiritSH (48) 82, p. 44.

WITT, Gene de
See: De WITT, Gene

4860. WITT, Harold
"Aunt Tisnelda Keeps Up with the Times." MidwQ (25:1) Aut 83, p. 62.
"Bebe Dixon." Focus (15:95) Ag 83, p. 16.
"Beethoven's Ninth." SouthwR (68:1) Wint 83, p. 40.
"Clarence Holmes Jr.'s Vision." Images (8:3) 83, p. 10.
"The Dental Hygienist." NewL (50:1) Aut 83, p. 67.
"Gaylord Markwartz, Sunshine Home for Seniors." WormR (23:2, issue 90) 83, p. 50.
"Johnny Walsh, Checkered Cab Co." ThRiPo (21/22) 83, p. 99.
"Marjorie Tetlow, M.L.S., Tries for Whitman." MidwQ (25:1) Aut 83, p. 63.
"Mrs. Asquith's Scarlet Letter." CropD (4) 83, p. 15.
"My Brother Still Goes to the Barber." CharR (9:1) Spr 83, p. 32-33.
"The Peacock's Sheen." WormR (23:2, issue 90) 83, p. 50.
"Peter Lorenzo, Chairperson, City College English Department." WormR (23:2, issue 90) 83, p. 51.
"Rancher Hermann Schrader Rejoices over the $1, 000, 000 Sale of His Property to Walt Disney, Inc." Bogg (50) 83, p. 20.

"Sara Teasdale." WestB (12) 83, p. 91.
"Sara Teasdale." WestB (13) 83, p. 44.
"Sit-Out." PoNow (7:2, #38) 83, p. 31.

4861. WITTE, John
"Just When." AmerPoR (12:1) Ja/F 83, p. 45.
"Switchyard." AmerPoR (12:1) Ja/F 83, p. 45.

4862. WITTLINGER, Ellen
"Birthday." AntR (41:3) Sum 83, p. 330.
"Breakfast at the Track" (for Annette). Ploughs (9:1) 83, p. 178-179.
"Inside the Mushroom." Ploughs (9:1) 83, p. 176-177.

4863. WOESSNER, Warren
"Atoms for Peace." SanFPJ (4:3) 83, p. 69.
"Bad Timing." Abraxas (27/28) 83, p. 45.
"Report from Iowa." SoDakR (21:4) Wint 83, p. 36.

4864. WOJAHN, David
"Alan." Ploughs (9:1) 83, p. 149-150.
"Beyond This." Tendril (14/15) Wint 83, p. 216.
"The Bicycle." Ploughs (9:1) 83, p. 147-148.
"Cool Nights of October." Tendril (14/15) Wint 83, p. 214-215.
"Dark-House Spearing." Ploughs (9:1) 83, p. 151-153.
"Leaving New Orleans" (for Richard). MSS (3:1) Aut 83, p. 116-117.
"New Orleans: Poem on His Birthday." MemphisSR (3:1) Aut 82, p. 27.
"Outside the Story." Telescope (5/6) Spr 83, p. 126-127.
"The Railroad Bridge and Cemetery at Marine." MemphisSR (3:1) Aut 82, p. 26.
"This Journey on Bach's Birthday." Telescope (5/6) Spr 83, p. 128.
"The Truth" (for Steve Orlen, after Jarrell). AmerS (52:4) Aut 83, p. 447-448.

4865. WOJCIECHOWSKI, Judith
"Becoming of Age." SanFPJ (5:2) 83, p. 30.

4866. WOLF, Mindy
"Approaching Sound -- Cross Village." CapeR (19:1) Wint 83, p. 17.
"Losing Friends at the Tent Revival." CapeR (19:1) Wint 83, p. 15.
"A Stepmother's Dream." Pig (11) 83, p. 73.
"There Is a Greeting As Well As a Parting." CapeR (19:1) Wint 83, p. 16.

4867. WOLF, Virginia
"Miller Park." PikeF (5) Spr 83, p. 11.

4868. WOLFE, Cary
"Fishing for Blues." CarolQ (35:2) Wint 83, p. 53.

4869. WOLFF, Daniel
"The Marriage Vow." NewL (50:1) Aut 83, p. 59.

4870. WOLFF, Milton
"Dear Editor." SanFPJ (5:4) 83, p. 84.
"Deterrence." SanFPJ (5:3) 83, p. 86.
"A Seasonal Carol for a Writer's Group." SanFPJ (5:3) 83, p. 85-86.

4871. WOLFIRE, Douglas
"What Is Left." LittleBR (3:3) Spr 83, p. 26.

4872. WOLLACH, Yona
"Cassius" (tr. by Linda Zisquit). LitR (26:2) Wint 83, p. 283.
"Cruel Heart" (tr. by Harold Schimmel). LitR (26:2) Wint 83, p. 280-281.
"Jonathan" (tr. by Linda Zisquit). LitR (26:2) Wint 83, p. 282.
"My Father and My Mother Went Out to Hunt" (tr. by Harold Schimmel). LitR (26:2) Wint 83, p. 281.
"My sins" (tr. by Harold Schimmel). LitR (26:2) Wint 83, p. 280.

4873. WONNACOTT, Richard
"Chopped Up Prose." Bogg (50) 83, p. 58.

4874. WOOD, Denis
"Getting" (Selections). KanQ (15:2) Spr 83, p. 112-113.

4875. WOOD, James
"The Perfect Day." MassR (24:3) Aut 83, p. 672.

4876. WOOD, John A.
"The Wastes of Resurrection." Swallow (2) Aut-Wint 83, p. 46.

4877. WOOD, Patricia W.
"Guide and contribute." YetASM (1:1) 82, p. 4.

4878. WOOD, Peter
"Losing Ground." USl (16/17) Wint 83-84, p. 2.

4879. WOOD, Susan
"January 1946." AntR (41:2) Spr 83, p. 206-207.

4880. WOODBURY, James E. A.
"Carrousel." NewRena (17) Aut 83, p. 30.

4881. WOODMAN, Allen
"Listening to Late Night A.M. Radio." PoetC (13, i.e. 14:3) 83, p. 5.
"Something about My Childhood." PoetC (13, i.e. 14:3) 83, p. 4.

4882. WOODS, Christopher
"Easter Sunday." CapeR (19:1) Wint 83, p. 14.
"Epidermis." YetASM (2:1) 83, p. 12.

4883. WOODS, Cindy
"Found Sign: Clubhouse 3 -- Lobby." Kayak (61) Ap 83, back cover.

4884. WOODS, John
"To the Chairperson of the Sonnets." OhioR (30) 83, p. 87.

4885. WOOLFOLK, Ann
"The Uncles." USl (16/17) Wint 83-84, p. 7.
"A Winter Sestina: After a Portuguese Sestina." USl (16/17) Wint 83-84, p. 7.

4886. WOOLSON, Peter
"Hole Theory." Bogg (50) 83, p. 24.

4887. WORLEY, Demetrice Anntia
"I Am Waiting for a Sign to Begin Speaking in Tongues." SpoonRQ (8:4) Aut 83, p. 17.

4888. WORLEY, James
"The Newest Adam." ChrC (100:32) 2 N 83, p. 980.
"Photograph: Victorian Waif Asleep in a London Park." ChrC (100:17) 25 My 83, p. 518.

4889. WORLEY, Jeff
"Dad Writes from the Sunbelt." LitR (26:3) Spr 83, p. 370.
"Honky-Tonk." Focus (15:95) Ag 83, p. 19.
"Man in Overcoat and Kneesocks." Tendril (14/15) Wint 83, p. 217.
"Marriage Proposal." KanQ (15:3) Sum 83, p. 68.
"Storm Watch (3/15/76). Wind (13:47) 83, p. 50.
"Whitley at Three O'Clock." Thrpny (4:2, issue 14) Sum 83, p. 17.

4890. WORLEY, Stella
"Multiple Choice." SanFPJ (4:2) 83, p. 53.

4891. WORMSER, Baron
"Essay: The Hudson River School." ParisR (25:90) Wint 83, p. 181.
"Europe." NewEngR (5:3) Spr 83, p. 402.
"Good Trembling." ParisR (25:90) Wint 83, p. 179.
"An Inclusive Letter." Poetry (141:4) Ja 83, p. 234-235.
"More of the Singular Implausible, Please." Tendril (14/15) Wint 83, p. 219.
"On the Suicide of a Poet-Friend." Tendril (14/15) Wint 83, p. 218.
"The Oxymoron As Taoist Vision." ParisR (25:90) Wint 83, p. 180.
"Shards." Poetry (141:4) Ja 83, p. 232-233.
"Some Happiness" (for Maisie). Poetry (141:4) Ja 83, p. 236.
"Walk" (for Janet) AmerS (52:1) Wint 82/83, p. 40.
"Werewolfness." GeoR (37:1) Spr 83, p. 40.

4892. WOROSZYLSKI, Wiktor
"Absence" (tr. by Boguslaw Rostworowski). TriQ (57, Vol. 1) Spr-Sum 83, p. 87.
"The Belly of Barbara N." (tr. by Boguslaw Rostworowski). TriQ (57, Vol. 1) Spr-Sum 83, p. 85.

"Diary of Internment (Darlowko, 1982)" (Selections: 3 poems) (tr. by Boguslaw Rostworowski). TriQ (57, Vol. 1) Spr-Sum 83, p. 85-87.
"Just till Spring" (tr. by Boguslaw Rostworowski). TriQ (57, Vol. 1) Spr-Sum 83, p. 86.
"Philately" (From my childhood, tr. by Magnus J. Krynski and Robert A. Maguire). TriQ (57, Vol. 1) Spr-Sum 83, p. 27-28.

4893. WORSHAM, Fabian
"Ossabaw: The Inspirational Island." PoetL (77:3) Aut 82, p. 137.

4894. WORTH, Douglas
"This Land Is Your Land." SanFPJ (4:3) 83, p. 71.

4895. WORTMAN, Tamela
"The Blacksmith." Meadows (4:1) 83, p. 56.

4896. WRIGHT, A. J.
"Cotton Field in Winter." WebR (8:2) Aut 83, p. 74.
"The Last Resort." WebR (8:2) Aut 83, p. 75.

4897. WRIGHT, C. D.
"Alla Breve Loving." BlackWR (8:2) Spr 82, p. 74.
"Bent Tones." Ploughs (9:2/3) 83, p. 82.
"Falling Beasts." Field (28) Spr 83, p. 82-83.
"Fascination." Field (28) Spr 83, p. 85.
"Jazz Impressions in the Garden." Field (28) Spr 83, p. 84.

4898. WRIGHT, Carolyne
"After All Is Said and Done." SouthernPR (23:2) Aut 83, p. 62-64.
"American Still Life." OP (35) Spr-Sum 83, p. 32.
"Attraction-repulsion" (for Harriet Pappas). Kayak (61) Ap 83, p. 5.
"The Conjure Woman." Kayak (61) Ap 83, p. 3-4.
"Couple Having an Argument" (Park Street Station, Boston). MinnR (NS 21) Aut 83, p. 67.
"Dictating the Answers." OP (35) Spr-Sum 83, p. 26-27.
"Farm Outside Oswego." AmerPoR (12:1) Ja/F 83, p. 27.
"Josie Bliss, October 1971." BlackWR (10:1) Aut 83, p. 7-10.
"Masquerade." Ploughs (9:2/3) 83, p. 165-166.
"A Memory of Islands" (for Nicholas Samaras). PraS (57:3) Aut 83, p. 72-73.
"Message to César Vallejo." BlackWR (10:1) Aut 83, p. 11-12.
"The Miracle Room" (Nossa Senhora de Bomfim Church: São Salvador, Bahia). OP (35) Spr-Sum 83, p. 28-29.
"The Mythology of Guns." GeoR (37:2) Sum 83, p. 306.
"The Peace Corps Volunteer Comes Home." Kayak (61) Ap 83, p. 6.
"The Peace Corps Volunteer Comes Home." OP (35) Spr-Sum 83, p. 30-31.
"Under the Sign of Cancer." MissouriR (7:1) Aut

83, p. 12-13.
"Walk to the Russian Monastery Garden." PraS (57:3) Aut 83, p. 71.
"Woman and Luna Moth in a Telephone Booth: Late Evening." Stand (24:4) Aut 83, p. 7.

4899. WRIGHT, Celeste Turner
"Reprieve." CalQ (22) Sum 83, p. 25.

4900. WRIGHT, Charles
"California Dreaming." ParisR (25:90) Wint 83, p. 88-91.
"Cloud River." ThRiPo (21/22) 83, p. 100.
"Driving to Passalacqua, 1960." Ploughs (9:2/3) 83, p. 15.
"Roma I." ParisR (25:90) Wint 83, p. 92.
"Roma II." ParisR (25:90) Wint 83, p. 93.
"T'ang Notebook." NewYorker (59:5) 21 Mr 83, p. 40.
"To Giacomo Leopardi in the Sky." Field (28) Spr 83, p. 40-44.
"Virgo Descending." OhioR (30) 83, p. 262-263.
"Wishes." OhioR (30) 83, p. 263.

4901. WRIGHT, Franz
"Birthday." Field (29) Aut 83, p. 65.
"Come, you last of those I will see" (tr. of Rainer Maria Rilke). Field (28) Spr 83, p. 59.
"Joeph Come Back As the Dusk." Field (29) Aut 83, p. 67.
"Now it is time the gods stepped out of everyday things" (tr. of Rainer Maria Rilke). Field (28) Spr 83, p. 58.
"Now nothing can prevent me completing my appointed orbit" (tr. of Rainer Maria Rilke). Field (28) Spr 83, p. 57.
"Oh haven't you known nights of love?" (tr. of Rainer Maria Rilke). PoNow (7:2, #38) 83, p. 45.
"Oh, not to be excluded" (tr. of Rainer Maria Rilke). Field (28) Spr 83, p. 56.
"Untitled: Will I always be eleven." Field (29) Aut 83, p. 66.
"Vase Painting: Supper of the Dead" (tr. of Rainer Maria Rilke). Field (28) Spr 83, p. 55.

4902. WRIGHT, Fred W., Jr.
"Beach Walk." RagMag (2:2) Aut 83, p. 5.
"Leaving." YetASM (2:1) 83, p. 8.

4903. WRIGHT, James
"Beautiful Ohio." OhioR (30) 83, p. 26.
"The Fruits of the Season." OhioR (30) 83, p. 27.
"Honey." Field (28) Spr 83, p. 93.
"Ohioan Pastoral." Field (28) Spr 83, p. 89.
"Petition to the Terns." ThRiPo (21/22) 83, p. 101.
"The Sumac in Ohio." Field (28) Spr 83, p. 88.
"Time." Field (28) Spr 83, p. 90.
"A Winter Daybreak above Vence." Field (28) Spr 83, p. 94-95.
"Yes, But." Field (28) Spr 83, p. 92.

4904. WRIGHT, Jonathan
"Atomic vibration." Germ (7:1) Spr-Sum 83, p. 17.
"Cracking eggs for breakfast." Germ (7:1) Spr-Sum 83, p. 19.
"Falcon hunting." Germ (7:1) Spr-Sum 83, p. 17.
"In a curve of empty space." Germ (7:1) Spr-Sum 83, p. 17.
"Inside the stems of the smallest plants." Germ (7:1) Spr-Sum 83, p. 19.
"O human voice." Germ (7:1) Spr-Sum 83, p. 19.
"One full moon." Germ (7:1) Spr-Sum 83, p. 18.
"Only the chill." Germ (7:1) Spr-Sum 83, p. 18.
"The secret scents." Germ (7:1) Spr-Sum 83, p. 18.
"Spring rain." Germ (7:1) Spr-Sum 83, p. 17.
"Waking from a dream." Germ (7:1) Spr-Sum 83, p. 19.

4905. WRIGHT, M. Fay
"Christening." PoetL (77:1) Spr 82, p. 28.
"He Becomes Father" (for Gary). PoetL (77:1) Spr 82, p. 27.

4906. WRIGHT, Terry
"The Divine Porno Movie." Pig (11) 83, p. 19.

4907. WRIGHT, Thomas B.
"El Salvador." SanFPJ (5:3) 83, p. 80.

4908. WRIGLEY, Robert
"Aubade for Mothers and Their Lives." QW (17) Aut-Wint 83-84, p. 57.

4909. WUEST, Barbara McInturff
"Between Hills." BelPoJ (33:3) Spr 83, p. 26-28.

4910. WUNDERLICH, Joachim
"Circe." WormR (23:1, issue 89) 83, p. 11.
"Error." WormR (23:1, issue 89) 83, p. 12.
"Unique." WormR (23:1, issue 89) 83, p. 12.

4911. WURSTER, Michael
"On the Beach." Descant (42) Aut 83, p. 14.
"The Snake Charmer's Daughter." Descant (42) Aut 83, p. 12-13.

4912. WYATT, David
"Inviting a Woman to Dinner." NowestR (21:1) 83, p. 31.
"Tonight As Usual." NowestR (21:1) 83, p. 32-33.
"Travelogue" (for Phil Woods). PoetC (15:1) Aut 83, p. 35-36.

4913. WYATT, Jiri
"Survivor." SouthernR (19:3) Jl 83, p. 677.
"Table and Plates." SouthernR (19:3) Jl 83, p. 675-676.
"Thaw." SouthernR (19:3) Jl 83, p. 674-675.

4914. WYNAND, Derk
"Afloat a Long Time Ago" (from Dead Man's Float). Quarry (32:4) Aut 83, p. 6.

"Dead Man's Float" (Selections). Quarry (32:4) Aut 83, p. 6-7.
"Now and Again He Was Picked Up" (tr. of H. C. Artmann). Quarry (32:1) Wint 83, p. 36-38.
"Plume." CalQ (22) Sum 83, p. 87.
"Talking and Not Talking" (from Dead Man's Float). Quarry (32:4) Aut 83, p. 7.
"Twine." CalQ (22) Sum 83, p. 86.

4915. WYTTENBERG, Victoria
"The Curse." PoetryNW (24:4) Wint 83-84, p. 29.

YAHYA, Kemal
See: KEMAL, Yahya

4916. YA'IR, Zvi
"Present" (tr. by Bernhard Frank). WebR (8:1) Spr 83, p. 37.
"Rock and Billow" (tr. by Bernhard Frank). WebR (8:1) Spr 83, p. 36.

4917. YALIM, Ozcan
"Answers" (tr. of Ulku Tamer, w. Dionis C. Riggs and William A. Fielder). Mund (14:1) 83, p. 49-50.
"Autumn (Guz)" (tr. of Ali Puskulluoglu, w. William D. Fielder and Dionis Coffin Riggs). SpiritSH (48) 82, p. 48.
"The First Snow" (tr. of Sabahattin Kudret Aksal, w. William A. Fielder and Dionis C. Riggs). Mund (14:1) 83, p. 51.
"Hills (Tepeler)" (tr. of Ali Puskulluoglu, w. William D. Fielder and Dionis Coffin Riggs). SpiritSH (48) 82, p. 48.
"The Lamp" (tr. of Behcet Necatigil, w. William A. Fielder and Dionis C. Riggs). Mund (14:1) 83, p. 48.
"Poem toward Noon" (tr. of Sabahattin Kudret Aksal, w. William A. Fielder and Dionis C. Riggs). Mund (14:1) 83, p. 51.
"The Poet" (tr. by the author, William A. Fielder and Dionis C. Riggs). Mund (14:1) 83, p. 47.
"The Poet (Ozan)" (tr. of Ali Puskulluoglu, w. William D. Fielder and Dionis Coffin Riggs). SpiritSH (48) 82, p. 48.
"Seekers" (tr. by the author, William A. Fielder and Dionis C. Riggs). Mund (14:1) 83, p. 47.
"Summer (Yaz)" (tr. of Ali Puskulluoglu, w. William D. Fielder and Dionis Coffin Riggs). SpiritSH (48) 82, p. 48.
"Tale of Tales" (tr. of Nazim Hikmet, w. William D. Fielder and Dionis Coffin Riggs). SpiritSH (48) 82, p. 46-47.

4918. YALKUT, Carolyn
"The Solace of Summer Is the Solstice" (to Janet, leaving for England). PoetC (13, i.e. 14:3) 83, p. 14.

4919. YAMAGUCHI, Seishi
"Even disappearing tip" (Haiku, tr. by Minoru Fujita and Richard F. Fleck). <u>Paint</u> (10:19/20) Spr-Aut 83, p. 43.
"What a crunching sound" (Haiku, tr. by Minoru Fujita and Richard F. Fleck). <u>Paint</u> (10:19/20) Spr-Aut 83, p. 43.

4920. YAMAZAKI, Sokan
"Death Bed" (tr. by Graeme Wilson). <u>WestHR</u> (37:3) Aut 83, p. 235.

4921. YAMRUS, John
"In a Car." <u>Abraxas</u> (27/28) 83, p. 20.
"Sex Appeal." <u>Bogg</u> (51) 83, p. 14.
"These Old Bullshit Poets." <u>Bogg</u> (51) 83, p. 15.

4922. YANCEY, Mama Estella
"Four O'Clock Blues." <u>ClockR</u> (1:2) Wint 83-84, p. 21.
"Maybe I'll Cry." <u>ClockR</u> (1:2) Wint 83-84, p. 20.

4923. YATES, Ernest
"Facades." <u>Poem</u> (48) Jl 83, p. 49.
"The Things That Last." <u>Poem</u> (48) Jl 83, p. 50.

4924. YATES, J. Michael
"The Queen Charlotte Islands Meditations." <u>OP</u> (36) Aut-Wint 83, p. 9-13.
"The Queen Charlotte Islands Meditations" (Selections: 2, 9, 11). <u>PoetryCR</u> (4:4) Sum 83, p. 11.

4925. YAU, John
"The Pleasures of Exile." <u>BlackWR</u> (9:1) Aut 82, p. 98-99.

4926. YEAGLEY, Joan
"Baptist Primitive--A Christmas Poem." <u>Focus</u> (15:95) Ag 83, p. 17.
"Blackberry Summer." <u>LittleBR</u> (4:2) Wint 83-84, p. 13.
"Hank Williams Done It This Way." <u>Focus</u> (15:95) Ag 83, p. 17.
"When Cold Gathers the Woods Close." <u>Focus</u> (15:95) Ag 83, p. 17.

4927. YEATS, William Butler
"Portent of Nuclear War?" <u>SanFPJ</u> (4:4) 83, p. 3.

4928. YELLEN, Samuel
"As I Sit on the Dinosaur Egg." <u>DevQ</u> (18:3) Aut 83, p. 85-86.
"A Letter to Sei Shonagon." <u>CalQ</u> (22) Sum 83, p. 26-28.

4929. YESHURUN, Avoth
"All" (tr. by Harold Schimmel). <u>LitR</u> (26:2) Wint 83, p. 211.
"The Ballad of Berl Schlosser" (tr. by Harold

Schimmel) LitR (26:2) Wint 83, p. 213-214.
"Before the Surgeon" (tr. by Harold Schimmel). LitR (26:2) Wint 83, p. 212.
"Prelude on the Demise of the Mulberry Tree" (tr. by Harold Schimmel). LitR (26:2) Wint 83, p. 213.

4930. YORK, James F.
"Salt and Pepper." SanFPJ (5:1) 83, p. 85.

4931. YORK, Judy
"Church of Fourviere" (Lyon, France). WestCR (18:2) O 83, p. 46.
"The Dweller." WestCR (18:2) O 83, p. 46.
"The Ghosts of Kejimkujik." WestCR (18:2) O 83, p. 45.

4932. YOSHIMOTO, Takaai
"Greetings to the Tiny Herd" (tr. by Tetsuo Kinoshita). PoetryE (9/10) Wint 82-Spr 83, p. 233-234.

4933. YOTS, Michael
"A Crash Course in American Social History." PikeF (5) Spr 83, p. 17.

4934. YOUMANS, Marlene
"The Cherry Trees." Ploughs (9:2/3) 83, p. 186-187.

4935. YOUNG, Al
"Saudades: The Portuguese Blues." TriQ (58) Aut 83, p. 108-109.
"Sweet Sixteen Lines." TriQ (58) Aut 83, p. 110.

4936. YOUNG, Bernard
"A Family Show." Bogg (51) 83, p. 38.
"The Mini's Back in Fashion." Bogg (50) 83, p. 39.

4937. YOUNG, David
"Two Trips to Ireland." IndR (6:1) Wint 83, p. 46-47.

4938. YOUNG, Dean
"Casting Off." MSS (3:1) Aut 83, p. 119.
"Counter Provisions to the NRC Acceptable Death Ratio Re: Nuclear Accident: 1% over 10 Years within Vicinity." IndR (5:3) Aut 82, p. 25.
"Every Light in the House" (for Ralph Burns). NowestR (21:1) 83, p. 29-30.
"Failing." IndR (5:1) Wint 82, p. 7.
"Hush." IndR (5:1) Wint 82, p. 6.
"Lifeguard." Tendril (16) Sum 83, p. 152.
"Renovations for a Sister." PoetC (13, i.e. 14:3) 83, p. 11.

4939. YOUNG, Ellen Roberts
"Lessons." YetASM (2:1) 83, p. 4.
"Palm Sunday." ChrC (100:8) 16 Mr 83, p. 248.
"Twilight." ChrC (100:34) 16 N 83, p. 1046.

4940. YOUNG, Gary
"Seven Days of Rain." OntR (19) Aut-Wint 83-84, p. 80.
"To Raise a Chimney." OntR (19) Aut-Wint 83-84, p. 81.

4941. YOUNG, Geoffrey
"Life Size." Sulfur (3:2, #8) 83, p. 55-57.

4942. YOUNG, J. T.
"Reclaimed Shore, Schleswig-Holstein." Argo (4:3) 83, p. 20.

4943. YOUNG, Karl
"Middle American Dialogues" (Excerpts from the "Book of Openings" section) (Based on the Myan Popol Vuh). CreamCR (8:1/2) 83, p. 104-105.

4944. YOUNG, Kathryn
"Death Has a Face" (for Doris Young). PoetL (77:2) Sum 82, p. 86-87.

4945. YOUNG, Kathy Jo
"Childhood Memories." Meadows (4:1) 83, p. 54.

4946. YOUNG, Linda
"Air Head." AntigR (55) Aut 83, p. 9.
"The Birthday Boy" (for J. T. McMoran Anderson). AntigR (55) Aut 83, p. 10.

4947. YOUNG, Patricia
"The Casual Fall." MalR (66) O 83, p. 13.
"Clean-up." MalR (66) O 83, p. 16-17.
"Inland." MalR (66) O 83, p. 14-15.
"Lucky." MalR (66) O 83, p. 18-19.
"Melancholy." MalR (66) O 83, p. 20-21.
"What about Wood." MalR (66) O 83, p. 22-25.

4948. YOUNG, Ree
"Jozepha--1900." SouthernHR (17:4) Aut 83, p. 325.

YOUNG, Robert de
See: DeYOUNG, Robert

4949. YOUNG, Roz
"For Barbara (on the Death of Her Student)." EngJ (72:4) Ap 83, p. 70.

4950. YOUNG, William
"Becoming Another Person and Hearing Different Melodies." Agni (19) 83, p. 95.

4951. YOUNGER, Virginia
"Remnants." Wind (13:49) 83, p. 54.

4952. YOUNT, Lisa
"She Carries Him in a Dream." Prima (8) 83, p. 22.

4953. YUAN, Chên
"Elegy" (tr. by Sam Hamill). NowestR (21:2/3) 83,

p. 78.

YUNG, Liu
See: LIU, Yung

4954. YURKIEVICH, Saúl
"Don Domingo." Inti (15) Spr 82, p. 62-65.

YUSUKE, Keida
See: KEIDA, Yusuke

4955. ZABLE, Jeffrey A. Z.
"Imagine." SoDakR (21:4) Wint 83, p. 52.

4956. ZACH, Natan
"The Countries We Live In" (tr. by Gabriel Levin). LitR (26:2) Wint 83, p. 243.
"Dantès, No" (tr. by Gabriel Levin). LitR (26:2) Wint 83, p. 242.
"A Hot Wind" (tr. by Ruth Nevo). LitR (26:2) Wint 83, p. 237.
"Restlessness on All Sides and Angels" (tr. by Gabriel Levin). LitR (26:2) Wint 83, p. 241.
"Sometimes He Longs For" (tr. by Gabriel Levin). LitR (26:2) Wint 83, p. 240-241.
"The Taste of Hemlock" (tr. by Ruth Nevo). LitR (26:2) Wint 83, p. 238.
"Wessex" (tr. by Gabriel Levin). LitR (26:2) Wint 83, p. 239-240.

4957. ZACHARIN, Noah
"Forests Swallow My Walking." Quarry (32:3) Sum 83, p. 68-69.

4958. ZALLER, Robert
"The Seven Elegies" (tr. of Nikiforos Vrettakos). SpiritSH (48) 82, p. 30-32.

4959. ZANCA, Kenneth J.
"Good Friday." ChrC (100:9) 23-30 Mr 83, p. 261.

4960. ZANETTI, C.
"Four of a kind beats a flush." Meadows (4:1) 83, p. 16.

4961. ZAPOCAS, Andrés
"Eclipse (IV)." Metam (4:2/5:1) 82-83, p. 59.
"Eclipse (V)." Metam (4:2/5:1) 82-83, p. 60.
"Hi, Jack." Metam (4:2/5:1) 82-83, p. 61.
"El Jardín de los Héroes." Metam (4:2/5:1) 82-83, p. 62.
"Perfil." Metam (4:2/5:1) 82-83, p. 61.

4962. ZARANKA, William
"Blessing's Adultery." MissR (12:1/2, nos. 34/35) Aut 83, p. 79.
"Blessing's Envoi." NewEng (5:4) Sum 83, p. 481.
"Blessing's Gulf Assignment." WebR (8:1) Spr 83, p. 62.
"Blessing's Limitations." WebR (8:1) Spr 83, p. 63.

"Blessing's Medium." WebR (8:1) Spr 83, p. 64-65.
"He Swallows a Ball Bearing." MissR (12:1/2, nos. 34/35) Aut 83, p. 77-78.
"The Third Culture." MissR (12:1/2, nos. 34/35) Aut 83, p. 76.

4963. ZARIN, Cynthia
"Field Guide." NewYorker (59:26) 15 Ag 83, p. 36.

4964. ZAVRIAN, Suzanne (Suzanne Ostro)
"Autobiography." Tele (18) 83, p. 67.
"California Coast 1977." Images (8:3) 83, p. 11.

4965. ZAWADIWSKY, Christine
"Dust in the Outer World." LittleM (14:1/2) 83, p. 114.
"Exterminating Angel." MemphisSR (3:1) Aut 82, p. 15.

4966. ZBORNIK, Richard
"Hiram (Pop. 652)." HiramPoR (35) Aut-Wint 83, p. 39-40.

4967. ZEIDNER, Lisa
"Bach." ThRiPo (19/20) 82, p. 56.
"Kafka Poem." ThRiPo (21/22) 83, p. 102.
"Needlepoint Guernica." MissR (12:1/2, nos. 34/35) Aut 83, p. 56-69.

4968. ZEIGER, Gene
"Orbiting." StoneC (11:1/2, Pt. 1) Aut-Wint 83, p. 26.
"Something about Fruit" (For my mother). NegC (3:4) Aut 83, p. 60.

4969. ZEIGER, L. I.
"Bargemusic" (For Olga Bloom). Confr (25/26) 83, p. 53-54.

4970. ZEKE
"If There Is No Tomorrow." Meadows (4:1) 83, p. 37.
"Nevada Desert." Meadows (4:1) 83, p. 42.

4971. ZELDA
"Two Elements" (tr. by Ruth Finer Mintz). Argo (4:3) 83, p. 32.

4972. ZEMBOWER, T.
"Note Left under the Left-over Flowers" (to James Tate). Kayak (61) Ap 83, p. 12.

4973. ZERFAS, Jan
"The Caving Grounds." WorldO (17:4) Sum 83, p. 45.

4974. ZIEROTH, Dale
"Harvest." PoetryCR (4:4) Sum 83, p. 7.

4975. ZIKA, B. Lynne
"By Storm." Tele (18) 83, p. 122.
"Esther's Going to Prayer-Meetin' Sundy Evenin'."

Tele (18) 83, p. 123.
"Hollywood Oasis." *Tele* (18) 83, p. 122.
"Two Days after the Toadfrog." *Tele* (18) 83, p. 123.

4976. ZIMMER, Paul
"Because of Duties the King Had Forgotten the Forest." *ThRiPo* (19/20) 82, p. 57.
"Father Animus and Zimmer." *ThRiPo* (21/22) 83, p. 103-104.
"The King Drunk and Alone." *Paint* (10:19/20) Spr-Aut 83, p. 29.
"The King's Insomnia." *Paint* (10:19/20) Spr-Aut 83, p. 28.
"The Queen." *ThRiPo* (19/20) 82, p. 58.
"Rollo's Miracle." *OhioR* (30) 83, p. 177.
"Two Drinking Songs." *MemphisSR* (3:1) Aut 82, p. 6.

4977. ZISQUIT, Linda
"Alien Work" (tr. of Zali Gurevitch). *LitR* (26:2) Wint 83, p. 299.
"Cassius" (tr. of Yona Wollach). *LitR* (26:2) Wint 83, p. 283.
"Data-Processing #15" (tr. of Maya Bejerano). *LitR* (26:2) Wint 83, p. 295.
"Die in Me" (tr. of Rivka Miriam). *LitR* (26:2) Wint 83, p. 308.
"A Different Myth" (tr. of Rachel Chalfi). *LitR* (26:2) Wint 83, p. 277.
"The Dolores Poems" (Selections: 1, 3, 5) (tr. of Rachel Chalfi). *LitR* (26:2) Wint 83, p. 278-279.
"A Drunken Clown" (tr. of Rivka Miriam). *LitR* (26:2) Wint 83, p. 308.
"Fastening the Light of the Sabbath Candles" (tr. of Rivka Miriam). *LitR* (26:2) Wint 83, p. 308.
"The Girl Who Drowned in the Well" (tr. of Rivka Miriam). *LitR* (26:2) Wint 83, p. 309.
"Istehar Returning." *LitR* (26:2) Wint 83, p. 328.
"Jonathan" (tr. of Yona Wollach). *LitR* (26:2) Wint 83, p. 282.
"Light Fever" (tr. of Zali Gurevitch). *LitR* (26:2) Wint 83, p. 298.
"Miriam's Well" (tr. of Rivka Miriam). *LitR* (26:2) Wint 83, p. 307.
"Salammbô" (tr. of Maya Bejerano). *LitR* (26:2) Wint 83, p. 296.
"The Stripes in Joseph's Coat" (tr. of Rivka Miriam). *LitR* (26:2) Wint 83, p. 307.
"The Tibetan Princess" (tr. of Maya Bejerano). *LitR* (26:2) Wint 83, p. 294.

4978. ZIVKEVIC, Peter D. (ZIVKOVIC, Peter D.)
"Missionary (Amateur Sufferer)." *Wind* (13:48) 83, p. 66.
"Reaping This Year's Harvest." *SanFPJ* (5:1) 83, p. 36.

4979. ZLOTKOWSKI, Edward
"Claustrophobia." *Kayak* (61) Ap 83, p. 54.
"Nursery Rhyme." *Kayak* (61) Ap 83, p. 55.

4980. ZOLLER, Ann (Ann L.)
"New Pony on a Carousel." LittleBR (3:3) Spr 83, p. 31.
"Night Babies." Vis (13) 83, p. 10.
"The Perfect Couple" (Selection: "Making the Baby"). Nimrod (27:1) Aut-Wint 83, p. 25.
"Target." YetASM (2:1) 83, p. 7.

4981. ZUCKERMAN, Phyllis
"A Dialogue between Gertrude Stein and Karl Marx." MinnR (NS 20) Spr 83, p. 5-6.

4982. ZUKOR-COHEN, Maree
"Impromptu for Mouse: A Fantasy in Adagio, Allemande and Allegro." Vis (13) 83, p. 32.

ZWARTS, Janice Blue
See: BLUE-ZWARTS, Janice

4983. ZWEIG, Ellen
"Black Dog Dreams." Tele (18) 83, p. 92-93.

4984. ZWEIG, Paul
"The Dance of Death." ParisR (25:90) Wint 83, p. 175.
"Parting the Sea." ParisR (25:90) Wint 83, p. 174.
"The River." NewYorker (59:13) 16 My 83, p. 105.

4985. ZYDEK, Fredrick
"Apple Orchard." AntigR (55) Aut 83, p. 122.

TITLE INDEX

Titles are arranged alphanumerically, with numerals filed in numerical order before letters. Each title is followed by one or more author entry numbers, which refer to the numbered entries in the first part of the volume. Poems with the title "Untitled" are filed under that title, followed by the first line.

All That We Learned, We Know: 2580, 3502.
All That's Expected: 248.
All the Way: 912.
All the Way Home: 55.
All the World Is Sleep: 3464.
All These Make a Strange Dance Rhythm: 81.
All This Time: 1610.
All Will Listen: 1068, 2566.
Alla Breve Loving: 4897.
Allah Akbar: 4836.
Allan Stewart: 2927.
Allegories: Opus 24, a Tragedy: 3327, 4288.
Allegories: Opus 34, a Comedy: 3327, 4288.
Allegories: Opus 35, a Comedy: 3327, 4288.
Allegories: Opus 87, a Comedy: 3327, 4288.
Allegories: Opus 108, a Comedy: 3327, 4288.
The Allegory of the Cave: 3778.
Alley: 4234.
Almanac: 1545.
The Almond Tree: 658, 3983.
Almost As If to Tell Me: 3843.
Almost Asleep: 4107.
Almost Every Cat: 2743.
Almost Ode to the Ear: 117, 3267.
The Almshouse: 3546.
Alone: 3636.
Alone in the Grove: 4559.
Alone in the House: 1878.
Alone, Late, Reading a Good Friend's Poems: 1799.
Along the 401, Late Evening: 101.
Along the Garonne: 2123.
Along the Underground Railroad: 4148.
Along the Way: 4617.
Along with the Dust: 216, 1563.
Alphabeasts: 4082.
Already It Concerns Us: 153.
Altankassen: 185.
Altar: 3613.
An Alternative Feminist Poem: 2766.
Alumnus at the Window (University Club, 1982): 3588.
Always Later: 1186.
Always to Be Named: 429, 3105.
Always toward Evening: 3892.
Amazing Grace in the Back Country: 4682.
Ambidextrous: 3988.
Ambition: 340.
Ambrosia: 3571.
Ambush: 3092, 3802.
Amelia Earhart, Aviator (1898-1937): 4378.
Amen: 2082.
The Amenities: 2898.
America: 1869.
América: 3741.
America: A Prophecy: 1387.
America Mystique: 1589.
America, Thy Name I Love: 1934.
American Bandstand: 4690.
The American College Dictionary (Copyright 1962 by Random House): 4125.
An American Dream II: 3907.
The American Falls: 1672.
The American Film Institute Salute to Alfred Hitchcock: 4305.
An American General Dies in Exile: 4301.
American Girl: 1591.
An American in Paris: 2482.
An American in Purgatory: 1003.
American Lake: 763.
The American Porch: 4284.
American Primitive: 3293.
An American Reporter in Tabasco, Mexico, 1926: 3744.
The American Sideshow: 2368.
American Still Life: 4898.
American Venus: 4738.
The American Way: 2368.
America's Health: 93, 93.
Amerika, You're Killing Me: 1401.
The Amherst Fire, July 4, 1879: 4541.
The Amiable Separation: 533.
Amnesia: 585, 1037.
Amnesty: 4380.
Among a Thousand Others: 1299.
Among Philistines: 1758.
Among the Hours Women Are the Best: 2495.
Among the Lisu of Northern Thailand: 1370.
Among the Roses: 2516.
Among Those Who Come After: 1389.
Amor Negro: 1271.
El Amor Se LLegó: 1514.
Amores Que Matan: 1515.
Amores y Cicutas: 3739.
Amphitheater with Trees: 3891.
The Amtrak Mattresses: 2550.
Anacreontic: 3418.
Anaktoria: 3088.
The Anarchy Impressionism Poem: 1484.
Anatole France (The portrait by Nadar): 2066.
Anatomy of Criticism: 3112.
Anatomy of the (Over)Loved: 1838.

Anatomy of Your Beauty: 1944.
Ancestor: 661.
Ancient Inhospitality: 915.
An Ancient Mariner: 1800.
The Ancient Pépère: 3235.
Ancient Snapshots: 3264.
Ancient Torso of Apollo: 2985, 3726.
The Ancient Voyager Remembers: 2193.
And Called, We Shall Rise: 2222.
And Don't We all?: 656.
And Echoes for Direction: 1226.
And Every Day Is a Hard Head Day: 3154.
And Heaven Has a Lonely Sound: 4078.
And I in My Bed Again: 3100.
And, in a Place of Light: 2504.
And Loving Her, Flows My Blood: 4096.
And No One Has Warned Me (Excerpt): 216.
And of All Things Visible and Invisible: 4049.
And of the Measure of Winter We Are Sure: 2495.
And On and On: 2428.
And Rest with You: 2118.
And She: 3080.
And the Blind: 962.
And the Light Just Keeps Crying: 3335, 4523.
And the Wind Seen As Waves: 535, 2036.
And Then My Lungs: 3527.
And, Then, Silence: 1268, 3399.
And They Marry Their Hearts for Truth: 1352.
And Though He Fought Like a Tiger He Went Down--He Went Down: 2269.
And Who Is the Doorman: 3943.
And Why Didst Thou Ever Send Me?: 1801.
And You Were a Baby Girl: 3409.
Andrei Roublev: 599.
Androgyny: 4389.
Andromeda: 692.
Anemone: 3986.
The Anesthesia Is Taking Effect: 1065.
L'Ange: 3335.
Angel: 4273.
The Angel: 2580, 3335, 3868, 4523.
Angel of Misfits and Loose Change: 4658.
Angel of the Atom: 3783.
Angelic Perspective: 2875.
Angélica de Madrugada: 4019.
The Angels: 1476.
Anger: 822, 3779.
Anginal: 1246.
Anglia: 3533.
Angry Night: 699.
Anguish: 2271.
Angus: 3053.
Animal Adjustment: 4607.
Animal Behavior: 3249.
The Animal in Disgrace: 2897.
Animal Skulls: 2094.
Animals That Leave Idaho: 522.
Animated Film, a Sequence of Emblem Poems: 3655.
Anise, Uses of: 3732.
Anita: 3295.
Ankh: 2201.
Ann 2: 4650.
Ann Belfry Causes the Gobbles: 1411.
The Ann Landers Poem I've Been Meaning to Write All These Years--Finally Written After Hearing Ann and I were Both Born in Sioux City, Iowa: 2944.
Anna: 2837, 3161.
Anna and Kirsten: A Photograph: 1871.
Anna López: 2395.
Annals of the Invisible Cowboy: 2343.
Anne Sexton's Last Reading: 1973.
Anne, Your Name's Mouth and Kiss: 3906.
Anne's Calendar: 662.
Anniversary: 126, 275, 1653, 2390, 4370.
Anniversary in Late Autumn: 376.
Anniversary of Words: 3579.
Anniversary Sermon (My Lai, 3/16/68): 3685.
Anniversary Song: 310.
Anniversary Waltz: 1923.
Ann's Hands: 1411.
Annunciation above the Shepherds: 1397, 3726.
Annunciation to Mary: 1397, 3726.
Un Año Más: 3059.
Anonymity: 2398.
Anorexia (Exceprts: A Sequence): 355.
Anorexic: 2570.
Another and Another: 4793.
Another Barn Painting: 4764.
Another Child: 2490.
Another Darkness: 4047.
Another Easter: 3716.
Another Ecclesiastical Morning: 2356.
Another Fall: 2638.
Another Innisfree: 4014.
Another Letter: 1792.

Afternoon: 4246.
At Half-Moon Bay: 4651.
At Home: 2721, 3387.
At Home in the Autumn Mountain: 2630.
At Home with Cézanne: 1061.
At Josie's: 2312.
At Kerouac's Grave: 3222.
At Lake Mahopac: 1560.
At Large: 4087.
At Leo's: 1482.
At Liberty: 698.
At Logan Pass: 4313.
At Loxahatchie: 3293.
At Martha's Deli: 3136.
At Michaelis's Café: 2837.
At Night: 2004, 2966.
At Odds: 3184.
At One My Fortune, at Two Your Watch: 1769, 2021.
At Sandy Neck: 4788.
At Sea Gull Bay: 2099.
At St. David's: 3763.
At Such Times: 1483.
At Sutter's Grave: Lititz, PA: 1562, 1562.
At the Advent (In Warsaw): 3223.
At the Advent (Warsaw): 3223.
At the Airport: 560.
At the Animal Hospital: 1216.
At the Beach: 1194.
At the Beginning: 2825.
At the Benedictine Monastery in Tyniec: 1762, 1762.
At the Cabbie's Studio: 971.
At the Cafe at Night: 1752.
At the Center: 320.
At the Clearance Sale: 231.
At the Clinic: 1467.
At the Common Table: 3814.
At the Concert: 3475.
At the Crucifixion: 797.
At the Curtain: 1947.
At the End of Sleep: 2814.
At the Fine Arts: 2931.
At the Fishhouses: 388.
At the Franklin Planetarium: 696.
At the Gates of Babylon: 1547.
At the Gates of the Valley: 1948, 4685.
At the Gibbon Cage: 2918.
At the Greyhound Station: 2976.
At the Handball Court: 1468.
At the Holiday Inn: 1605.
At the Lodge: 2707.
At the Monument Beach Fish Market: 655.
At the Monument to Pierre Louÿs (Jardin du Luxembourg): 2066.
At the Museum: 3035.
At the New Britain Dept. of Motor Vehicles: 2931.
At the Only Wide Place between Boise and Burns: 1153.
At the Paddock: 4299.
At the Photographer: 3919.
At the Public Baths (Kyoto, 1982): 3891, 3891.
At the Sea: 135, 832, 2587.
At the Source: 3302.
At the State 5A Football Playoff: 3323.
At the Terminal: 3347.
At the top of the night: 2528.
At the Trade Center: 4491.
At the Turning of Leaves: 1752.
At the University: 1070.
At the Water Steps: 3357.
At the Wayne County Fair: 1672.
At the Wheeler Wildlife Refuge: 4464.
At the Whirler Planetarium, Houston: 3169.
At the Window: 4349.
At Three A.M. the Dogs: 1377.
At Tres Piedras: 441.
At Vassar I taught (or, The Boston Univ. Pub on a Day I almost Ate There in '77): 316.
At West Turner Lake 8/22/82: 2393.
At Which This Is an Attempt: 2203.
Atchafalaya November: 4048.
The Atco Drag Strip, Atco, New Jerey: 2097.
Atget at Ville-D'Avray Waiting for Light: 3103.
Atget's Gardens: Paris, 1900: 1454.
Athlete: 55.
Atlantic Avenue: 3197.
Atlantic Crossing, Age 17: Riccardo: 3441.
Atlantis: An Elegy: 3408.
Atlantis Bypass: 3111.
Atocha Choo-Choo: 1097.
Atom Baby: 2184.
The Atom Bomb Is the Messiah: 1902.
The Atom Bomb Is There: 742, 3224.
Atomic Pantoum: 2943.
Atomic vibration: 4904.
Atoms for Peace: 4863.
Atonement: 2413.
Attack of the Killer Amenities: 4066.
An Attempt at Description: 1948, 4685.
Attempted Departure: 1084.
The Attic: 807.
Attic (October 1, 1981): 1445.
Attic Rummaging: 3008.
Attic Vase: Woman and Nurse at

Baited: 4448.
Baker's Dozen: 154.
Bakery Barrels: 154.
The Bakery Thrift Store: 649.
Baking Cookies: 4709.
Bakunin Baking in Baku (Excerpt): 2352, 3962.
Balance: 2185, 3957.
The Balance of the Part Against the Whole: 2008.
A Balance Sheet: 1904.
Balanced: 3685.
Bald Hills Road: 4678.
A Ballad: 4846.
The Ballad of Berl Schlosser: 3958, 4929.
Ballad of Brecht's Soldier: 58.
Ballad of Larry and Club: 2179.
Ballad of Love through the Ages: 105, 4333.
Ballad of Maritime Mike: 2880.
The Ballad of the Hell-Hound: 1310, 2404.
Ballade of the Back Road: 418.
Ballade of the Brief Life: 418.
Ballade of the Moment After: 1646.
Ballade of the Tree: 418.
Ballast: 515.
Ballet Dew: 2629.
The Balloon Is Rising: 3122.
The Balloon Man at Union Station: 4265.
The Balloon Pilot: 3378.
Balloons: 670, 3727.
Ballplayer at Midnight: 1789.
Balsa: 302.
Bamboo (1): 1767, 3044.
Bamboo (2): 1767, 3044.
The Bamboo Cage: 2670.
The Bamboo Ocean / A Sailor Speaks: 3959.
A Banal Lovers' Dialogue: 1815.
Band Concert in Regent's Park: 3558.
Bang-Up Futures: 1005.
Baptism: 3960.
Baptism of Sand: 2889.
Baptisms: 558.
Baptist Primitive--A Christmas Poem: 4926.
Bar Beastie: 350.
Baraboo's First Feminist: 647.
Barbara: 2215, 3567.
Barbara Allen: 3243.
Barbara's Story: 4565.
Barbecue Service: 127.
Barbeque: 3051.
The Barber Did Just What I Told Him: 3756.
Barbershop Quartet: 2451.
The Bard at Madurai: 899.
Bare Ribbed Talisman: 4042.
Bargaining in Good Faith: 1293.
Bargemusic: 4969.
Barges: 1655.
Barn Fire: 2850.
Barn Song: 2465.
Barn Swallows: 3548.
Barnstormer: 373.
Barometer: 1006.
The Baroness Renata, Her Magic Shop: 3991.
Barren Ground: 577.
Barry Gray's Painful Decision: 4190.
Baseball Fields in Winter: 1917.
Baseball's Religious Heart: The Umpire: 1156.
The Basement: 2203.
The Basketball Coach: 1063.
The Bass: 4324.
Bat: 476.
Bat Sheba: 2580, 3675.
Bat Shlomo: 2580, 3958.
A Bat Story: 2544.
The Bath of David Lindsay, Author of _A Voyage to Arcturus_: 3037.
Bathing at Glymenopoulo: 3127.
Bathing Beauty (Circa 1958): 2883.
Bathing Boys: 3628.
Bats: 4148.
Battery Park: High Noon (Selection: 2): 317.
Battlefield Parade: 4678.
The Bay Meditations: 2103.
Be Calm, Comrade, Awhile Longer: 1523, 4583.
Be Careful How You Vote: 2683.
Be Kind to Me: 3634.
Be My Friend: 851.
Be of Good Cheer: 912.
Be Sure and Bring Your Bones: 699.
Beach Blanket Spread: 3429.
Beach Fire: 2931.
Beach Walk: 4902.
Beachcombing: 257.
Beachcombing the Planets in Mendocino: 3799.
Beachfeather: 1193.
Beacon Fire: 4268.
The Beagles of Arkansas: 1380.
Bear Blood in the Tree House: 253.
Bear Dreams: 4534.
Bear Paw: 2091.
The Bear Went Over the Mountain: 4389.
Bearers of the News: 1560.
Beast Babcock: A Redneck Enigma: 2329.
The Beast's Ordinance: 2531.
Beat the Drums!: 782.

echo: 4773.
Between Skirmish and Shadow: 2580, 3563.
Between the Apple and the Stars: 1494.
Between the Lines: 3254.
Between Toronto and Duluth: 2181.
Between Two Stars, Losing My Footing: 1523, 4583.
Between Us: 4317.
Between Walls: 4819.
Between Words: 2622, 2999.
Beware the Vibes of Marx: 3625.
Bewitched Animals: 3453.
Beyond Strawberry Bank (near Kendal, England): 4343.
Beyond the Elegiac Principle: 2226.
Beyond the Mountains: 1610.
Beyond the Shadow across the Bridge: 585.
Beyond This: 4864.
Bezhetsk: 337.
Bible Class: 1063.
The Bible to be Believed: 168.
The Bicycle: 4864.
Bicycle in the Rain: 1713.
Bicycle Song: 145.
Bienestar: 1262.
The Big Benefit Reading: 576.
Big black hedgehog eternity descending into the valley: 1799, 2285.
The Big Curb Maple: 3424.
Big flake snowfall: 1991.
The Big Moose: 1967.
The Big Rocks: 16.
Biglietto d'Ingresso: 3161.
Biker Bob Maniskalko's Living Room Decor: 1380.
Billfish: 1997.
Billie Jane: 4230.
Billie sings and starts you crying: 3245.
Binding: 2803.
Binocular: 4375.
Binyamina: 2580, 3958.
Biografia Mortal (Excerpt): 205, 2639.
Biography: 107, 1467, 1477, 3468, 4375.
Bir Baska Tepeden: 2327.
Bir Tepeden: 2327.
Birch Street, 1960: 4464.
The Bird: 2468.
Bird Chasing: 1324.
Bird Hunting: 1984.
Bird Poem: 1512.
Bird Seed: 3474.
Birds: 1544, 2925.
The Birds: 2468, 2468, 4346.
Birds at Dawn: 4485.
Birds in the Morning: 543.
The Birds My Son Showed Me: 2468.
Birds of Air: 476.
Birds of Prey: 1158.
Birds of Russia: 2592.
Birds on a Blighted Tree: 3983.
The Birdsfoot Trefoil: 4169.
Birth: 2933.
Birth (concrete poem): 1456.
Birth Is As Great: 3295.
Birth of Christ: 1397, 3726.
The Birth of Christ: 864.
The Birth of Mary: 1397, 3726.
The Birth of Venus: 4819.
The Birth of Venus in the Gulf of Mexico: 2704.
Birthday: 1061, 2056, 2328, 4468, 4847, 4862, 4901.
The Birthday Boy: 4946.
Birthday Bush: 4390.
Birthday Cake: 1646.
The Birthday Cake: 751.
A Birthday Card: 2414.
Birthday Poem, July 19, 1866: 1511.
Birthing: 1722.
Birthmark: 3760, 4166.
The Birthmark: 4558.
The Birthplace: 1903.
Bishop Cadigan Orders His Funeral: 2931.
The Bison of Lascaux: 4277.
Bitch: 2380.
Bits of the Other: 1198.
Bitter Cherry: 4636.
Bitter Sloe: 58.
Bituminous Angel: 43, 1298.
Bklyn Bridge: 1298.
Black Ain't Chic No More: 2125.
Black and White: 3066.
Black Angel: 4100.
Black Bear in October: 1509.
Black bird, green hill: 2528.
Black Box: 2821.
The Black Bridge: 4838.
The Black Brother Poems to Etheridge Knight: 3855.
The Black Death: 1861.
Black Dog Dreams: 4983.
Black Dog in Oxford, Mississippi: 1679.
Black Felt: 170.
The Black Flower: 3817.
Black Gold for Them / Black Lung for Me: 2731.
Black Hair: 4206.
Black Harbor: 2653.
Black Hole: 491, 4762.
Black Ice: 1391, 4124.
Black Lake: 3076.
Black Leaves: 76.
Black Meat: 1422, 1422, 2898, 2966.
The Black Messiah: 4163.
The Black Mountain: 3944.

1942): 1874, 3021, 3506.
Book of Gad: 449.
The Book of Mormon: 3762.
Book of Seasons: 4565.
The Book of Sediments (from The Light Station on Tillamook Rock): 1043.
Book of the Year: 2054.
Book of the Yellow Castle: 3356.
Bookkeeping: Zanesville, Ohio, 1974: 3004.
Das Böot: 563.
The Bootleg: 2753.
Border between Honduras and Nicaragua: 3610.
Border People: 4270.
Border Town: 2511.
Bordered by other's ecological niches: 1587.
Borderlands: 954.
Born in the Heat of Night: 3265.
Borrowing: 2301.
Bosses: 4699.
Boston (A Portrait): 3223.
Boston and Warsaw: A Sequence: 3223.
Boston Common: 3223.
Boston Fern: 4469.
Boston Spring: 3223.
Boston Winter: 3223.
Botanical Gardens: 235.
Both Sides: 1467.
Both Ways: 4239.
Botticelli Apron: 1601.
Bottom of the Ninth Haiku: 1293.
Bottom One: 2193.
Bottoms: 1041.
The Boulderfield: 3906.
Boulevard Saint-Michel: 2955, 4494.
Boundaries: 4631.
Bow Down: 1745.
Bow! Wow! Bow!: 2352, 3962.
The Bower of Earthy Frights: 58.
A Box of Chestnuts: 3146.
Box People: 3186.
A Boy: 2429.
The Boy and the Lights: 4221.
The Boy Named Several: 1649.
Boy of the Arrowy Thoughts: 3980.
Boys, Like Horses, Are Easily Spooked: 489.
Boys on the Soccer Field in the Late Afternoon: 1100.
A Boy's Primer: 1860.
Brad: 1546.
Brahms' Second Symphony and Martinez: 4757.
Braille: 2677.
The Braille Volcanos (Oregon Museum of Science and Industry): 2930.
Brain synapses: 782.
Bramble Jelly: 1942.
The Branch: 3407, 3597.
The Branch Bank: 3083.
Branding: 4482.
Brandy Bottle Inclines: 2035.
Brass boots pounding out of the cave: 3981.
Bravado and Rage: A Memoir: 3862.
Brave Horizons: 2191.
A Brave Man: 1961.
A Brazen Theme: 4325.
Bread: 864, 977.
Bread and salt: 3084.
Bread and Shoes: 1644.
Bread and Wine: 182, 1264, 2793.
Bread Pudding Days: 1739.
Bread vs. Poem: 3823.
The Break: 601.
Breakfast: 3810.
Breakfast at the Track: 4862.
Breakfast for Two: 1846.
Breakfast in Brixton: 3054.
Breakfast Piece: 1267.
Breaking and Entering the Hungarian's Place: 4078.
Breaking Out: 1950.
Breaking Points: 4497, 4517.
Breaking the Code: 4682, 4682.
Breakthrough: 3296.
Breath: For Fred Wah: 4699.
Breath Ghazal #1: 221.
Breath Ghazal #2: 221.
Breath Ghazal #4: 221.
Breath Ghazal #5: 221.
Breath Ghazal #6: 221.
Breath Ghazal #10: 221.
Breathing: 2931.
Breathless: 769.
Brecht vs. the House Un-American Activities Committee: 1916.
The Brethren: 1031.
The Brethren Home: 2302.
The Briar Month: 4316.
Bride and groom: 3694.
Bride in the Bath: 3233.
The Bride of Caesar: 1049.
Bride of My Brain: 3817.
Brides of El Salvador: 3082.
The Bridge from Brooklyn: 1937.
A Bridge in Florence: 3261.
Bridge of Abandonment: 3905.
The Bridge People: 4615.
A Bridge Too Narrow: 4463.
Bridging the Gully: 2537.
Brief Encounter: 892.
A Brief, Familiar Story of Winter: 2877.
A Brief History of Bells: 756.
Brief Thunder at Sharpeville: 3250.

Coastal Cities, Coastal Cities: 1542, 2580.
Coat: 2217.
Coats #10 Chain: 848.
The Cobalt Bomb Is There: 742, 3224.
Cobblestone: 1720, 2158.
Cocinando/What's Cooking: 2760, 4560.
Cock: 1926.
The Cocked Finger: 1183.
Cockfight: 2633.
Cockroach Poem: 3817.
Cocktail Party: 2208.
Cocktails at the Mausoleum: 3159.
Cocoon: 1962.
The Cocoon: 362.
The Cod: 2751.
Coda: 1752.
Codex Minor: 1764.
Coecles Harbor 1981: 3871.
Coed Day at the Spa: 2880.
Coffee on Tuesday: 840.
Cognition, Language, Poetry: 2346, 3168.
Coitus, or Journeying Together: 2298.
Cold and Hungry: 3685.
Cold Blue Tinge: 4098.
Cold Frame: 1480.
Cold Mountain: 1811, 2630.
Cold Mountain (in Chinese): 1811.
Cold Mountain (Selections: 4, 5, 16): 119, 119, 3503.
A Cold Snap in Peshtigo: 1522.
Cold Spring: 2297.
The Cold Springs Public Preserve: 4607.
Cold, Straight from the Can: 2645.
Cold Venus at the Typewriter: 796.
Coliseum Messiah: 1485.
Collage: 61.
Collecting for the Wichita Beacon: 2387.
Collection: 4617.
The Collectors: 149.
Collegial Angels: 43, 713.
The Colonel: 810.
The Color of an Old Friend's Eyes: 4239.
The Color of Halcyon Days: 979.
The Color Rake of Time: 1264.
Colorado/Fall: 4.
Coloratura: 1433.
Colors, Turnovers, 1933: 2260.
Columbine: 4769.
Columbus Days: 4831.
Combing My Hair in the Hall: 3730.
Come: 3764.
Come Again Another Day: 4299.
Come Back: 4206.
Come enneigées: 1735.
Come in, Anyway: 4122.
Come, Taste of the Sheraton Showcase: 1516.
Come to Bed, Sweet William: 2267.
Come Winter: 4792.
Come, you last of those I will see: 3726, 4901.
Comedians: 3575.
El Cometa: 3574.
Coming Again upon Mensch's Mill by Accident, after Five Years: 1562.
Coming and Going: 1483.
Coming Apart (Excerpt): 3928.
Coming Home: 912, 4469.
Coming Home at Twilight in Late Summer: 2335.
Coming Home: Beer Sheva, 1978: 791.
Coming Home: David Smith: 4392.
Coming Home Drunk: 3035.
Coming Home from School and Going to a Game: 1281.
Coming in from the Rain: 3698.
Coming into Season: 2142.
Coming into Town, Cold: 3159.
Coming of Age (When the visit was expected): 3685.
Coming Out: 2059.
Coming to a Close in the Morning: 810.
Coming to Stone: 2251.
Coming Together: 1621, 2540.
Coming upon the Rainbow's End: 509.
Coming upon Yellow Pears on a Hard Run: 1984.
Commas in Wintertime: 1197.
Comme si le chemin se brisait: 1735.
Commelina Virginica: 3512.
Commencement: 3743.
Commencement Address: 4261.
Commercial Break, World War III: 621.
Commercial Sucks-X: 764.
The Commissioner of Baseball: 2371.
Commitment: 4219.
Commodore: 636.
Common Black Ants in Captivity: 972.
Common Deceit: 4716.
A Common Failing: 1276.
Common Grave: 3553.
Common Ground: 737, 1989.
The Community: 4336.
Commuter: 3134.
Commuters: 2001.
The Commuter's Poem: 4050.
Como en el vivir: 273.
Cómo me jode este saber que

x, xiii-xvi, xxi): 2792.
A Dance Part Way around the Golden Calf, or, Rich within the Dreams of Avarice: 680.
Dance Script with Electic Ballerina: 1494.
Danced with Human, Whooper Is Killed: 400.
The Dancer: 1310, 2205, 4591.
The Dancers: 1383.
Dancing: 1609, 4232.
The Dancing Class: 3729.
A Dancing Fool: 3474.
Dancing Frigid: 4527.
Dancing Giraffe: 1274.
The Dancing in the Wind: 1922.
Dancing in Vacationland: 1109.
Danish Tea House (Old City): 2711.
Danny: 3967.
Danny and Mary Kelleher: 3993.
Danse Macabre: 1288, 4636.
Dantès, No: 2580, 4956.
Daphne: 1370.
Dark: 2468.
The Dark: 1615.
A Dark Arrow: 3119.
Dark Confusion, Snow Scuttling Across the Street Like Blown Pages of a Newspaper: 726.
Dark Earth, 1963: 193.
Dark Easter Nights: 4570.
The Dark Friend: 2631.
Dark-House Spearing: 4864.
Dark Innocence: 176.
The Dark Wood: 4183.
Dark World: 4012.
Darkened branch: 3559.
A Darkening Outing at Sea: 2098.
Darkness holding stars in place: 2700.
The Darkness of the Night: 3980.
Darkness Will Sweeten: 2104, 3958.
Die Darstellung Maria im Tempel: 3726.
Darwin in the Ditch: 2653.
Darwin Recalls the Rain Forest of Brazil: 863.
Data: 539.
Data-Processing #15: 297, 4977.
Dateline: Spring Training: 3745.
Datura (On entering the Grand Canyon by moonlight): 815.
The Daughter Recreates Her Mother: 2169.
Daughters and Weekends: 493.
David at Ein Gedi: 2003.
David's Poem: 1969.
Dawn: 1422, 2966.
Dawn from the Hill: 4502.
Dawn on Wellington Street West: 376.
Dawn Tamer: 1184.
Dawn the old dog's gaping mouth: 3902.
Day: 1282.
The Day after the Bomb: 299.
Day and Night Handball: 1183.
A Day at the Circus: 207.
Day-Colored Cat for Orlando: 1023.
The Day I Lost My Catholicism: 4299.
The Day I Was Older: 1778.
A Day in August: 3313.
A Day in Pennsylvania: 3607.
A Day in the Life of the White Blanket: 3717.
A Day in the Life of Willy Sypher: 531.
The Day Is Almost Gone: 1628.
The Day Mack Sennett Dined with Ingmar Bergman: 3806.
Day of Reckoning (Yom Kippur, '82): 4193.
The Day of the Sculptor: 4835.
A Day of Walking: 4708.
The Day the Winds: 2989.
The Day We Learned Manners: 3869.
The Day We Threw Out the Xmas Tree: 4552.
A Day with No Clouds: 4148.
Daybreak on Plum Island: 1330.
Daydream: 1263.
Daydream Driving: 1711.
Days: 4054.
Days after Trinity (or 'Hell, I Was Only Going Fission'): 4810.
Days of January: 3507.
The Dayspring: 879.
De Mi Hermano: 4599.
De Paso: 3773.
De una Postulante a Victima Inocente de Delito Sexual: 1082.
The Dead: 3727.
Dead Baby: 1109.
Dead Center: 2962.
The Dead Dolphin: 3158.
Dead Elms by a River: 2557.
Dead Housewife Poem (Maggie): 1786.
Dead in Kentucky: 2886.
Dead Leaves: 2224.
The Dead Leaves: 3753.
The Dead Man's Eye: 3870.
Dead Man's Float (Selections): 4914.
Dead of Winter: 4611.
Dead Possum: 678.
Dead Silence on a Beautiful Day: 3843.
Dead Tongues: 1615.

Definitions: 2637.
The Deified Julius: 2764.
Déjà Vu: 4617.
Dejection: 3981.
Dejection at the State U: 1878.
Del Medio del Sueño: 3914.
Delayed Gratification: 314.
Delayed Green: 4601.
Delayed Transport: 2063.
A Delicate Operation: 1216.
Della's Bus: 629.
Delphi: Commentary #5: 2439.
Delphi: Commentary #7: 2439.
Delphi: Commentary #9: 2439.
Delta Anthology: Tom Webb: 3256.
Delusion?--No!: 4682.
Delwyn Creed: 2586.
Demise: 1849.
Demographic Dilemma: 4193.
Demoiselle: 3658.
Les Demoiselles d'Avignon: 347.
Demon Child: 3010.
The Demon of Elloree: 3051.
Demon Trapped in a Parking Lot: 1221.
Demonstration in Quebec City: Jan. 30/83: 3620.
Demonstrations: 3106.
Demurrer: 3046.
Den Andre Skogen: 4609.
Denn, Herr, Die Grossen Stadte Sind: 3512.
The Dental Hygienist: 4860.
Dentelle, she-teeth, milk-tooth, a mouthful of lace: 4705.
Departure No. 2: 2488.
Depends on who pilfers: 3610.
Depression: 1358.
Depth of Field: 1008.
The Dervish: 1196.
Descending: 4384.
Descent: 3719.
Descent and Sentiment: 1543.
Describing Ireland: 1838.
Description: 2814.
Descriptive Poetry: 2580, 4794.
El Desdichado: A Translation: 3201, 3778.
Desert: 910.
The Desert: 2902.
Desert Dweller: 1779.
Deserted: 3043.
Desertmartin: 3401.
Design: 2950.
Design in Stork's Foot & Old Fire: 1882.
Designing Women's Clothes: 4116.
Desire: 3179, 4227.
The Desire of the Word: 3427, 3509.
The Desolation Pudding: 1961.
Los Desparecidos: 2479.
Despite All That: 4252.
The Detachment: 2212.
Detective Magazine: 790.
Detectives: 1213.
Deterrence: 4870.
Detrás del árbol, acurrucada en el llanto de la tortuga: 1639.
Deux Femmes: 1849.
Devas: 761.
Devil Dance: 283.
Devotion: 3350.
Devotion: That It Flow, That There Be Concentration: 1505.
A Devotion to What There Is of Grace: 1752.
Devotions for Today's Couple: 4514.
DeWolf Point: 1305.
Di á Logo de Taller: 4019.
Di Domenica: 1068.
Diagnosis: 2437.
Diagrams: 1615.
La Dialesia: 3739.
A Dialogue between Gertrude Stein and Karl Marx: 4981.
Dialogues: 1212.
Diamond Jim and Golden Lil: 2123.
Diamond Ohio Matches: 3684.
Diana's Mother Tells Us Again & Again: 805.
Diane Arbus: Ground Glass: 4057.
Diario de Guerra: 164.
Diary Entry for Any Day: 753.
Diary of Internment (Darlowko, 1982) (Selections: 3 poems): 3825, 4892.
The Diaspora: 3166.
Dichotomy: 3193.
Diciembre: 1262.
Dick Powell: 2402.
Dictating the Answers: 4898.
Didactic Sestina for White Belts: 311.
Die, Die My Outcry: 2428, 2466.
Die in Me: 3034, 4977.
A Different Myth: 709, 4977.
A Difficult Marriage: 1778.
The Difficult Task of Mentioning: 3954.
Difficulties of a Heavy Body: 4646.
Difficulties of an Actress: 4087.
Digging: 1367, 3712.
Digging In: 1862.
Digging in Escondido: 2877.
Digging to China: 3330.
Diggings: 4127.
Digital Song: 2447.

Earliest History: 4208.
Early American Small Print Wallpaper: 653.
Early and Late: 3347.
Early Apollo: 1737, 3726.
Early Cool Madonna: 2611.
Early Losses: a Requiem: 4647.
Early Love, Late Season: 193.
Early Meadow-Rue: 3512.
Early Morning: 3028.
Early Morning Swimmers: 3807.
Early November: 3930, 4322.
Early Winter: 954, 954.
Earning the Living: 1958.
Earth: 4154.
Earth and Moon: 2665, 4105.
Earth and Sky and Light's Offer: 3906.
Earth Day: 515.
The Earth from This Distance: 1109.
Earth Mother: 821.
The Earth My Lover: 3179.
Earth Song/Body Song (Excerpts: ii, iii, vi-viii): 221.
Earth Symphony: A Cappella: 3046.
An Earthen Night: 1665.
Earthquake: 4322.
Earthworks: 1562.
Ease: 4211.
East Kootenay Illumination: 4699.
The East Side: 3307, 3307.
East Texas Cemetery: Red Dirt: 1106.
The East Window: St. Mary's, Muker: 3763.
Easter Garden: 4053.
Easter Poem: 1593.
Easter Sunday: 2364, 3947, 4882.
Easter Words: 4486.
Eastern Standard: 1964.
Easy Payment Plan: 368, 1834.
Eating: 4206.
Eating Alone: 355.
Eating Around the Gizzards: 1511.
Eating at the Elephant Burial Ground: 3680.
Eating Bees: 1796.
The Eating Hill: 3039.
Eating Names: 412.
Eating on a Starlit Porch: 585.
Eating Out: 3615.
Eating Poetry: 427, 3851.
Eating the Heart: 355.
Eating the Sparrows: 1505.
Eating the Still Life: 2826.
Eaton's Arcade: 1146.
Eavesdropper Out Walking: 2605.
Eavesdroppings: 2332.
Echo: 4792.
Echo of Emptiness: 453.
Echoes of Seasons: 4485.
Eclipse: 2106.
Eclipse (IV): 4961.
Eclipse (V): 4961.
Eclipse, 609 B.C: 4590.
Ecology: 812.
Economic Dogmas: 2368.
Economics: 1005.
The Ecuadorian Sailors: 663.
Edge of Spring: 1022.
Edges: 807, 3119.
Edible Struggles: 2377.
Editing Poems for the Anthology: 2611.
Editor: 2697.
The Editor: 2524.
Edmonton, November 17, 1982: 578.
An Educated Man: 4386.
Educational Foundations, 1942: 810.
Edward Hopper: 2512.
Edward Hopper, 1960: 4542.
An Edwardian Lady: 2643.
The Eels of Bracciano: 1466, 3391.
The Effects of Rain: 3428.
Eggs in Basket: 4046.
Eggshells: 3753.
Egyptian Dancer at Shubra: 2091.
Eight: 638.
Eight-Fingered America, Land of Fear: 4162.
Eight Sketches of the Rich: 1410.
Eight Unrelated Definitions: 2226.
Einstein's Son: 4713.
El Salvador: 2406, 2647, 4907.
Eleanor of the Irises in My Yard: 1357.
Election Day Speech: 2385.
Electra in Her Old Age: 3116.
Electric Chair: 3223.
Electrical Storm: 2435.
Electricity: 3734.
Elegance: 4569.
Elegance on a Florida Lawn: 3048.
Elegies Close to the Senses (Excerpt): 2307, 4794.
Elegy: 1053, 1183, 1264, 1799, 1982, 3227, 4953.
Elegy I: 398.
Elegy: After Love: 3841.
Elegy for 41 Whales, Beached in Florence, Oregon, June 1979: 371.
Elegy for a Drowned Car: 3807.
Elegy for a Sleeping Negress Seized by Captain Lancarote in the Spring of 1442: 4105.

1902.
The Enriched Uranium Poems: 1902.
Enrolled: 4299.
Enshrined: 185, 535.
Enter the chambers of darkness: 3610.
Enter with Flourishes: 1787.
Entering an Old House: 3729.
Entering the Box: 4306.
The Entire Catch: 1610.
Entracte: 849.
Entrails raised to the sun: 1633.
Entrance: 3178.
Entrance into Light: 1077.
Entre afloje y pelea: 9.
Entre Escombros y Tardes: 634.
Entre Palabras: 2622.
Entre Tu Ser Y Mi Ser: 405.
Entrega: 3740.
Entropy: 389, 4242.
Entry: 1737, 3726.
Envejecer: 685.
Environmental Issues: 1836.
L'Envoi: 3840.
Envying the Children of San Francisco: 4206.
Ephemeral: 815.
Ephemeridae (the family of Mayflies, Linnaean order Neuroptera): 3239.
Epidermis: 4882.
Epigrams: 334.
Epigraph for a Banned Book (Epigraphe pour un Livre Condamne): 266, 2332.
An Epileptic Watches an Eclipse of the Moon: 2385.
Epilogue: After a Murder: 982.
Epiphanies on the First Cold Day: 376.
Epiphany: 825.
The Epiphany: 639.
Episode in Civil War: 4725.
Epistle Apology: 4058.
Epistle for the Cicadas: 524.
Epistle to an Exile: 4189.
Epistola de Secretis Operibus, chapter 4: 1615.
Epitafio para un arribista: 617.
Epitafios: 3629.
Epitaph: 4720.
Equinox: 2248, 3782, 3791, 3809, 3841, 3948.
Equivalent: 1391.
The Era and the Outrage: 203.
Erasures: 1183.
Erbario '81 (Selections from a Roman herbiary): 1190, 3911.
Erdnusskerne: 3981.
Ernest Hemingway: 1627.
Eros: 571.
Errand at the Lone Tree Mall: 4261.
Error: 3909, 4910.
Eruption: 4636.
Es Bobby Sands Que Enamorado Pasa: 3739.
Escapamos: 1117.
Escape: 4458.
Espejo: 166.
Espejos: 2691.
La espera espera a qe mutilen la primera palabra: 2691.
Esperanza's Hair: 4076.
Esplanade: 1201, 4845.
Esquinas: 3609.
Essay on Form: 1764.
Essay: The Hudson River School: 4891.
Esta Tarde María está Muriéndose: 943.
Estado de Animo: 307.
Estados Unidos: 28.
Estelle's Antiques: 2884.
Estelle's Testimony: 3993.
Estercolera: 828.
Esther's Going to Prayer-Meetin' Sundy Evenin': 4975.
The Estonian Comes to Dinner: 4206.
Estos Ultimos Meses: 943.
Estoy Cansado: 704.
The Estranged: 1652.
Estuary: 4845.
Et Pleure la Lumiere: 3335.
Et Progreditur ut Luna: 4572.
Etc: 1045, 1264.
Etchings: 1760.
Eterna 27: 2402.
The Eternal Boy: 3885.
The Eternal Mystery: 81.
Ethiopian in the Fuel Supplies: 813.
Ethyl: 4221.
Les Etrangers: 3676.
Etudes (Excerpts): 2132.
The Eucharist of the Holy Ghost at Key West: 939.
Eulachon: 1615.
Eulogy: 299.
A Eulogy for Choice: 64.
Europe: 4891.
European Vacation: 4654.
Eurydice: 56, 1066, 3913.
Evacuate only the 'young fit and useful': 782.
Eve Revisited: 3769.
Eve to Adam at Dawn: 1354.
Even disappearing tip: 1408, 1488, 4919.
Even in Vegas: 1916.
Even Now: 2903.
Even the Fringe: 3455.
Even Those: 3846.
Evening: 50, 455, 1737, 3726, 4174.
Evening at Arles: 2491.

The Facts of Life: 3628, 4651.
The Failed Pianist: 190.
Failing: 4938.
Fainting Angels: 248.
Fair City: 2468.
Fairchild Market: Meats and Mauby (Bridgetown, Barbados, 1981): 2609.
Fairgrounds: 3906.
Fairlee Creek: 1020.
Fairy Tale: 2684.
Faith: 1523, 1654, 2825, 4583.
Faith Healer: 2411.
Faith of Our Fathers: 4190.
The Faithful: 4690.
Faithfuly Yours: 461.
Fajada Butte -- Solstice: 2541.
Falcon hunting: 4904.
Fall: 2012.
The Fall: 3035.
Fall echoes: 4751.
The Fall in the City: 2725.
Fall of Patriots: 419.
Fall Out: 4487.
Fallen Fruit: 758.
Falling: 233.
Falling Asleep: 2050.
Falling Asleep, I Think of My Married Friends: 1308.
Falling Awake: 2773.
Falling Beasts: 4897.
The Falling Out: 3648.
Falling to Sleep: 4357.
Falling with Money: 2343.
The Falls at Lauterbrunnen: 2870.
False Alarm: 452, 3010.
False and Tendentious News: 1467, 3614, 3824.
False Spring: 1531.
Fama Gloriaque: 1354.
Fame of the City, Hiroshima, 1981: 1147.
La Familia de Pescadores: 3651.
Familiarities: 4308.
Familiarity: 2373.
Family Feast: 473.
The Family in Winter: 1400.
Family Legacy: 2554.
Family Pictures (Excerpt): 3958, 4794.
Family Portrait: 4370, 4468.
Family Portraits: 4337.
Family Reunion: 4593.
Family Romance: 2586.
A Family Show: 4936.
Family Traits: 1107.
Famous Last Words: 3338.
A Famous Literary Couple: 3271.
Fan: 3451, 3710.
The Fan in the Window: 2414.
Fantasia on Tchoupitoulas Wharf: 1591.
Fantasy Is My Persepolis: 1863.
The Far East: 3133.
Far from Change: 2734.
Far Pairs, Close Pairs: 1615.
Far Sight: 585.
Far Steps: 1523, 4583.
The Farallones Islands: 427.
Farewell: 1648, 1874, 3021, 4713.
A Farewell: 3921.
Farewell Everything: 4616.
The Farm: 4403.
Farm Futures: 3924.
Farm Gate: 3607.
Farm Outside Oswego: 4898.
Farm, Waiting: 4166.
Farm Wife: 246.
Farmer in Welsh Fog: 4037.
Farmers: 1084.
The Farmer's Daughter, the Traveling Salesman: 3555.
Farmhouse in Early Fall: 1103.
Farmhouse on the Algarve: 1691.
Farmington No. 9: January 8, 1971: 1011.
The Farms on the Col des Annes: 473.
Fascia: 2571.
Fascination: 4897.
Fashions: 2927.
Fast Lane Madonna, 1: 2611.
Fast Lane Madonna, 2: 2611.
Fast Roads: 855.
Fastening the Light of the Sabbath Candles: 3034, 4977.
Fat Boy: 1542, 3958.
Fat: in Love: 4651.
The Fat Lady: 2847.
The Fat Man Dreams: 3782.
Father: 3008, 4031.
Father and Daughter: 4197.
Father and Mother: 1659.
Father and Son: 2772.
Father Animus and Zimmer: 4976.
Father Falling: 1069.
Father to Son: 1483.
Father: Upon Leaving: 2756.
The Fathers: 3337.
Fathers Don't Last Forever: 3020.
Fatigue: 1816.
Fatigue in California: 204.
The Fatties: 2958.
The Faun: 1449, 4605.
Faustus, The End (a revision): 3980.
The Favor: 820.
Fawn: 2496.
Fawn Asked Me: 1902.
Fawn Finger: 3.
Fay Wray Has Collapsed: 2322.
Faye: 1803.

Fear: 2611, 4744.
Fear, a Love Poem: 3081.
Fear Is Known by the Taste, After: 3531.
Fear Not: 4184.
Fear of Whites: 3881.
The Feast: 2418.
A Feast in February: 1912.
Feast of All Fools: 4617.
The Feasting: 1872.
Feather in Paw: 3717.
Feature of Sylvia Plath in Chatelaine: 2197.
Feb. 12: 3678.
February: 4850.
February 11: 356.
February Bud: 3674.
A February Idyll: 2386.
February Thaw: 2817.
Fedelm's Song: 761.
Feedback: 4398.
Feeding the Moon: 701.
Feeding the Wild Cats: 4518.
Feeding Time at the Tiger House of the Detroit Zoo: 4699.
Feedings: 2931.
The Feel of Not to Feel It: 4064.
A Feeling from the Sea: 585.
Feet in Water: 118.
Feline: 1280.
Felling Trees: 1325.
Felt But Not Touched -- Seattle: 302.
The Female as Taken from Freshman Essays: 2881.
Feminist Poem: 2766.
Une Femme Retarde la Venue de la Mer et Leur Mouvance se Brise: 3875.
Fermata: 4783.
Fern: 620.
Ferns by the Waterfall: 3347.
The Ferry Boat: 585.
The Ferry Stops at Orient Point: 1924.
The Ferry: Woods Hole: 1391.
Festival of Light: 4617.
Festival of the Wolves: 1483.
Festooned with Feathers: 1922.
The Feud: 2536.
Feuillets d'Hypnos, Journal de Guerre, 1943-1944 (Excerpts): 718.
Fever: 928, 930.
Fever Breaking: 3800.
Fever Cabin: 7.
A Few More Trips to Santa Fe: 2087.
Feynman domains are two dimensional: 3610.
Ffion, Foxgloves, Field Trumpets: 3128.
Fibonacci Sequence: 3558.
Fiding a Resting Place: 4198.
The Field: 193, 3591.
Field Day: 3254.
Field Guide: 4963.
A Field of Experts: 3981.
A Field of Snow on the Palatine: 3418.
A Field of Wings: 4279.
Field Report: 1996.
Field Trip: 3832.
Fields: 457.
The Fifth Horseman of the Apocalypse: 4663.
The Fifth Season: 3906.
Fifth to Last: 154.
Fifty Laps for Mental Health: 2107.
Fight: 1945.
Fighting Entropy: 1587.
Figure by a Chimney: 2623.
The Figured Wheel: 3506.
The Filibusters: 650, 800.
Filles de Joie: 4272.
The Filling: 4213.
Filling in the Second Sun: 2026.
The Filmstrip of My Flesh: 1554.
Final: 2645.
The Final Conflict (a fable): 4455.
Final Days: 536.
Final Entry: 1306.
The Final Gesture: 853.
Final Judgement: 3540.
The Final Lovesong: 1013.
The Final Note: 1809.
The Final Prospect: 4236.
Finale: 65.
Finally Understanding: 1694.
Finding: 2934.
Finding Old Photos: 3398.
Finding the Dog: 4536.
Finding the Words: 737.
Finding Your Tiger Face: 1183.
The Fine Arts: 3809.
Fingerprints: 3124.
Fingers of Winter: 4150.
Fingertips of the left hand hold the paper: 4293.
Finis: 3844.
Finished Hands: 1166.
Fire: 3535.
Fire and Ice: 3470.
Fire and St. Francis: 2082.
The Fire Bubbles: 4458.
Fire Ceremony: 4311.
Fire Eater: 807.
Fire Power: 2057.
The Fire Thief: 3906.
Fireflies: 3866.
The fireman under the moonlight: 3144.
Fireplace with Hyacinths: 1324.
Fireweed My Wand: 3906.
The First: 2, 1615.

A Flower That Comes After: 2042.
The Flowerbox: 185, 535.
Flowering Judas: 1279.
Flowers: 1518, 2939.
The Flowers: 159, 4553.
Flowers and Bones: 3478.
Flowers for the Baby: 3685.
The Flowers outside My Window: 4668.
A Flowing Leaf: 1898.
Fly: 3186.
The Fly: 2118.
The Fly and the Milk: 2966.
Flying: 2363, 3810.
Flying at Night: 2414.
Flying Fish, He Whispered, Are Superb: 2227.
Flying Home: 2610.
Flying Squirrel: 2534.
Flying the Red Eye: 4307.
Focus: 4482.
Folding Clothes: 3998.
Folio: 782.
Following the Dordogne: 1723.
Folsom: 1969.
Folsom, August 11th: A Question of Races: 31.
Food for Thought: 1495, 4033.
The Food of Love: 1077.
Food Shopping: 4081.
The Food-Thief (Uganda, drought): 3289.
Fool: 1707.
A Fool Is a Man Who Understands Nothing But Remembers Everything: 2095.
Foolish Thing: 585.
Fool's Gold: 3402.
Fools Head: 1926.
Fool's Paradise: 4098.
The Foot: 4589.
The Foot Has 26 Bones, the Hand Has 27: 1958.
The Foot Therapist: 4216.
A Footnote to the Flowers: 3156.
Footprints on Memaloose (Excerpt): 872.
Footsteps on the Downcast Path: 4088.
For a Boy Infant's Wreath: 3980.
For a Boy Struck by Lightning While Playing Baseball: 267.
For a Daughter: 3678.
For a Dead Photographer: 3165.
For a Friend One Year Later: 1204.
For a Heart Leafed with Words Like a Tree: 2707.
For A. J. E: 3142.
For a Long Time Lover Who Lost Thirty Pounds: 788.
For a Moment, the Act: 1752.
For Alan Dugan: 2468.
For All I Know: 2290.
For an Instant: 1703.
For an Old Flame in Autumn: 974.
For Anna Akhmatova (1888-1966): 107.
For Barbara (on the Death of Her Student): 4949.
For Blue: 2817.
For but an instant: 1408, 1488, 2138.
For Cesar Pavese: 2001.
For Christl: 959.
For Clarence Francis Brisby: 518.
For David: 511.
For David Schubert: 3282.
For Elizabeth: 2421.
For Ellen after the Publication of Her Stories: 4776.
For Ernie Marshall (if he's still around): 4672.
For Eurithe: 3589.
For Farmers: 1221.
For For Gertrude: 801.
For Frances Von Stechow: 3531.
For Free: 627.
For Gavin Who Cries during Bach's 'Come Sweetest Death': 4746.
For Generations a Question Asked of Males: 575.
For Good Pablo: 3884.
For Grammy on Her 90th Birthday: 673.
For Hagen, Antigonish 1977: 3926.
For Hamburger: 1958.
For Hank Williams: 3757.
For Heather, on Her 12th Birthday: 4214.
For Him: 585.
For I Will Consider My Bird Ariel: 1324.
For I Will Consider Your Dog Molly: 2553.
For Jack Kerouac: 2547.
For Jacqueline T. Bradley: 1902.
For Jennifer on Parting: 2087.
For John Lee: 1773.
For Josephina: 3012.
For Judith: 844.
For Kerouac in Heaven: 3580.
For Kim: 3634.
For Lincoln Perry: 774.
For Linda Hoyer Updike: 4264.
For Loren: 1469.
For Louise Nevelson: 3486.
For Maggie Melvin, Weaver, Learning Italian: 282.
For Marilyn Monroe: 2580, 4194.
For Melvin: 905.

Machine: 4650.
Goethe once said: 3610.
Gogatsu-No Hitogomi: 4420.
Going: 1317, 3967.
Going after My Glasses: 2372.
Going Back Again: 2778.
Going Backward Going Forward: 1197.
Going Blind: 952.
Going by Coach: 1086.
Going Deep: 426.
Going Down on America: 726.
Going for the Land of the Living: 3594.
Going for Wood: 3338.
Going Home: 475, 741.
Going into Saigon: 1961.
Going Out after Work: 1035.
Going out into the autumn's darkness: 842.
The Going-Part: 4075.
The Going / The Sigh: 1278.
Going through the Notebook I Jotted Things Down in in Italy: 2611.
Going to Kahoolawe: 3174.
Going to Russia: 2771.
Going to the Drive-In: 3445.
Going West Alone: 2034.
Gold Chariot: 3980.
Gold Fever: 991.
Gold-Filled Teeth: 114.
Gold Mining: 3845.
Gold Stone: 2091.
The Goldberg Variations: 3479.
Golden Age: 1809.
Golden Age of Chivalry: 3808.
Golden Section, Giants Stadium: 11.
Golden Times: 3825.
Goldfish: 232.
Goldwasser: 3387.
The Golf Ball Diver: 475.
Golfview Street: 3357.
Golpes, Nada Más: 4613.
La Gomme Coule: 2172.
Gone: 3062, 3498.
Gone Down the River: 1902.
Gone with the Grain: 1273.
Good and Bad (Selections: Good, Bad): 2821.
The Good Angel: 43, 1298.
Good Bye?: 4442.
Good Catholics: 4798.
A Good Dream: 111.
Good Friday: 4244, 4959.
Good Grape: 2828.
The Good Hands People Know Their Bodies: 1151.
Good Intentions: 2537.
A Good Man: 95.
Good Morning, How Are You?: 31.
Good Night Dear: 1769, 2021.
The Good Old Days (1952): 3781.
The Good Part: 2468.
Good Sense: 1523, 4583.
A Good Thought: 2494.
Good Trembling: 4891.
Good Wood: 1070.
Goodbye: 2659.
Goodbye, It's On the Road Time: 1491, 3170, 4307.
Goodbye Poem: 226.
Goodnight Gang: 1666.
Goodnight Irene: 2776.
Goodwill: 1267.
Goosebumps: 1789.
Gorée: 2007.
Gospel of Clouds: 237.
Gospel of Death: 237.
Gospel of Earthly Feeling: 237.
Gospel of Imaginary Beings: 237.
Gospel of Light: 237.
Gospel of Love: 237.
Gospel of Meadow: 237.
Gospel of Rapture: 237.
Gospel of Salvation: 237.
Gospel of the Dream: 237.
Gospel of the Gardener: 237.
Gospel of the Lonely: 237.
Gospel of the Losers: 237.
Gospel of the Meadow: 237.
Gospel of the Night: 237.
Gospel of the Room: 237.
Gospel of the Sad: 237.
Gospel of the Singer: 237.
Gospel of the Way of Chaos: 237.
Gospel of Truth: 237.
Gossip: 1097.
Got a job last week: 3610.
Gothic and Etc: 576.
Götterdämmerung: 51.
Gottéron Landscape: 1109.
Government baffled by slump in research and development: 782.
Government says 6 1/2% unemployment: 782.
Grace: 1603.
Grace Abounding: 4775.
A Grade Crossing in Ayer: 3451.
The Graduate: 2274.
Graduation: 1121.
Graffito (For the Coming Unknown Soldier's Tomb): 1498.
Grafting: 3091.
The Gramma Poems (Selection: Four: To Weave): 181.
A Grammatical Rule?: 2865.
Granada: First Sleep: 2428.
Grand Canyon Poem: 1333.
Grand Central: 2939, 4087.
Grandfather: 1841.
Grandfather House: 3513.
Grandfather Takes His Grandson

Hamburger Mary's: 2527.
The Hamburger Stand: 288.
Hammond, Indiana, 1959: 233.
Hampstead Heath Walk: 4276.
Hand: 3152.
The Hand: 1369.
Handgrenades in My Grapefruit: 410.
Handing the Self Back: 1371.
Handles: 2072.
Hands: 1663, 1675, 3245.
Hands convey warmth with a touch: 4712.
Handsome Woman Aging: 2698.
The Handwriting on the Wall: 4511.
Hanger: 2217.
Hanging Curve: 1293.
The Hanging Judge: 439.
Hanging on Like Death: 4589.
Hanging-Out with Howard, Looking around for Charmagne: 4431.
Hanging the Swings: 3826.
Hank Williams Done It This Way: 4926.
Hansel: 2567.
Hansel and Gretel: 347.
Happiness: 1380, 2824.
Happy Birthday, Husband!: 4052.
A Happy Childhood (Excerpts): 2821, 2821.
A Happy Ending for the Lost Children: 2795.
Happy-Go-Lucky's Wolf Skull Dream Mask: 2411.
Happy Holiday: 4299.
Happy Hunters, Mill City: 117.
Happy Trails: 2361.
The Happy Traveller: 3980.
Harakiri: 1370.
The Harbor in Winter: 1528.
Harbor Seals: 624.
Hard Knocks: 2290.
Hard Luck: 1147.
Hard measure: 523.
Hard Night Aftermath: 1803.
Hard promise: 523.
Hard Strain in a Delicate Place: 4399.
Hard Times: 2341, 3349, 4206.
Hard times not only means no money: 3610.
The Hard Work of Flying: 3952.
Hardhats on Avenue of the Americas: 4678.
The Hardware Drawer: 1468.
The Hardworking Discovery: 1757.
The Hare: 2340.
Hare Sitting Up: 1571.
Harlequin Autumn: 4523.
Harlequinade: 2939.
Harley Greenfield's Frustration: 4190.
Harp Seal Harvest: 4069.
Harpo: 3935.
Harpsicord Music: 248.
Harry Talked to Animals: 2053.
Hart Crane: 782.
Hart Crane in Autumn: Chagrin Falls 1929: 3203.
Harvest: 1167, 2312, 2754, 4974.
A Harvest: 4617.
The Harvest: 3916.
A Harvest of Dreams: 818.
Harvest of Evil: 377.
The Harvest Season: 3913.
Harvest Songs: 887.
Harvesthome: 3046.
Harvestimes: 3732.
Harvesting: 1655.
Harvesting Cantaloupe: 3451.
Harvesting Treasure: 2287.
Harvests: 3178.
Has Nature No Shame?: 985.
Hasp: 3903.
The Hat: 4272.
Hate: 4424.
Hate the Bus: 2166.
Hauling Traps with Theodore: A Midnight Narrative at Low Tide: 2260.
Haunt: 3010.
The Haunted House: 1692.
Havblik: 2036.
Have a Good Day, Death Is on the Way: 3808.
Have It Your Way: 3708.
Have You: 918.
Have You Ever or Are You Now?: 3856.
Have you heard the still lifes of Morandi: 3976.
Have You Seen It: 4626.
Having Not Written a Poem: 1202.
Having weapons you can never use: 3610.
Hawaii Too: 302.
Hawaiian Fireside: 4441.
The Hawk: 427, 3851, 4701.
Hawk Coming: 1783.
Hawker: 4163.
Hawk's Domain: 20.
The Hawk's Shadow: 3330.
The Hawks We Have Never Seen: 3646.
He: 849, 3254.
He allows slant: 3429.
He, As I: 1801.
He Becomes Father: 4905.
He clears his throat: 3967.
He Comes Down Hogsback Mountain with Tablets of Iron: 2042.
He Comes for the Jewish Family, 1942: 3289.
He Let Go: 814.
He Paints a Picture of His

High Ground in Louisiana: 1591.
High Moon: 2192.
High Noon: 1666.
High Plains Orchards: 2877.
High Renaissance: 4261.
The High School Dance: 4797.
High Stone Falcon: 154.
High Style: 1223.
High Water: 1673.
High Water on the Goulais: 2901.
Highland Rim: 2373.
Highway 56: 3644.
Hijo de Naturaleza: 1081.
Hilda Halfheart's Notes to the Milkman: #67: 2329.
Hill: 287.
Hill House: 4408.
Hill Mist: 486.
Hills (Tepeler): 1359, 3595, 3722, 4917.
Hilltop with Voices: 2094.
Him: 422.
Hiram (Pop. 652): 4966.
The Hired Hand: 560.
Hiroshima: 1038, 1038, 2214, 2914.
Hiroshima, Drawing by Survivor: 2837.
Hiroshima's Nails: 2996.
His Confession: 2689.
His Depression: 1107.
His Face: 3986.
His fingers on the calculator: 2700.
His Happy Hour: 4034.
His Mother's Burial: 3453.
His Sister: 3453.
His Unfinished Sentence Would Have Told Me of Compassion, I'm Sure: 304.
His Waiting: 2363.
Historias: 3586.
Historic House on the River-Bank: 3894.
An Historical Event: 1121.
History: 1183, 1571, 2735.
History and Secrecy: 4705.
History of a Malady: 4491.
History of My Heart: 3506.
The History of Poetry: 849.
A History of Rain: 2083.
The History of the Apple: 2094.
The History of the Foot: 1591.
History, or, The Old House: 2846.
History Lessons: 1031.
Hitchcock: 1300.
Hitchcock Blue: 525.
A Hitchcock Tale: 2454.
The Hitchhiker: 961.
Hitch-Hiker's Guide to the Universe (or Somewhere Else): 1883.
Hitchhiking: 2414.
Hitchhiking in Southeast Kansas: 4218.
Hitchhiking with a Friend and a Book That Explains the Pacific Ocean: 4206.
Hitler in the Trenches: White Crow: 3727.
Hitting My Thumb with a Hammer: 841.
Hitting the Wall: 1509.
Hoard: 2925.
Hobo's Still Life: 1407.
Holding Our Own: 21.
A Hole in the Ceiling: 2214.
Hole Theory: 4886.
Holiday Inn: 4617.
Holidays: 2149.
The Hollywood Alternative: 613.
Hollywood Oasis: 4975.
Holomovement: 411.
Holy Bathing Place: Allahabad: 4493.
Holy Hijinks: 2198.
Holy Orders: 1048.
The Holy Primitive: 2059.
The Holyoke: 1528.
Holyoke Range: 1129.
Homage: 2468, 3178.
Homage à O.B: 3011.
Homage to a Missed Season: 2864.
Homage to C.P. Cavafy: 908.
Homage to Li Po: 4584.
Homage to Nelson Algren: 1896.
Homage to the Avant-Garde: 3648.
Homage to the Dinosaur: 2061.
Homage to Webern: 506.
Un Hombre Pasa con un Pan al Hombro: 1523, 4583.
Home: 1777, 2039, 4289, 4541.
Home Care: 383.
Home Free: 3549.
Home from the Hill: 904.
Home from the Wars: 3254.
Home: Late Summer: 1020.
The Home Place: 3323.
Home Stand: 1293.
Home Thoughts at Home: 2913.
Home to the Hills: 3064.
Home Trees: 1380.
Homecoming: 1330.
Homecoming from Indonesia: 3732.
Homer: 3753.
Hometown Blues: 4617.
Homily: May 1981: 3278.
Hondo Tú Viejo Niño Que Cruzas Culebreando por Mi Pecho Como una Antigua Cicatriz Recién Nacida: 3739.
Honesty: 1466, 3733.
Honey: 4903.

In the Silence: 4285.
In the Spotlight of Sun: 833.
In the Storeroom: 3103.
In the Storm: 1322.
In the Suburbs: 2428.
In the Summer: 2167.
In the Tenth Year of War: 2244.
In the Town of Copan Ruins, Honduras: 1362.
In the TTC: 548.
In the Unfinished House: 2659.
In the Waiting Room: 4526.
In the Waiting Room of a Psychiatrist's Office: 3762.
In the Wind: 2688.
In This City: 3973.
In This Dream: 2489.
In This Urban Corner: 4226.
In Timber Country: 219.
In Time: 1799, 3867.
In Two Parts: 302.
In Verdi Square: 4491.
In Vermeer's Delft: 4012.
In Your Hands: 2002.
In Your Next Dream: 3305.
In Your Version of Your Brother's Death: 2848.
In Yucatan: 793.
Inanimates: 3234.
Incantation: 2925.
Incarnation: 258.
Incense: 1699.
Inchoate Road (A Partial Draft): 3217.
Incident at Port: 3541.
Incident at Sand Creek: 2798.
Incident at the World's Fair, St. Louis, 1904: 1454.
Incident from Antiquity: 2019.
Incidental: 3980.
Incidental Music for Late May: 376.
Incipient Flu, or the Day I Went Out of My Mind to Avoid the Draft: 1142.
Inclusive: 3179.
An Inclusive Letter: 4891.
Income Tacks: From My Diary: 1358.
The Incomers: 4803.
Incrustations of the Vietnam War: 2185.
Incubus: 3284.
Independence: 818.
Independence Day: 4690.
Indestructable Breeds: 41.
Index: 4618.
Indian Corn: 4617.
Indian Story: 2274.
Indian Summer: 2896, 4166.
Indian Summer, Donner Pass: 2556.
Indian Summer in the Delaware: 4652.
Indian Woman Down in the Marketplace: 713, 3386.
Indian Women Keeping Shop at the Door of Their Adobe Hut: 390.
Indiana Dream in Stone: 3305.
Indiana, November: 2266.
The Indicator: 1293.
Indigo: 614.
The Indigo Bunting: 427.
An Individual: 925.
Indolence in Early Winter: 2335.
Indoor Geranium: 2455.
Induction: 137.
Industrial amazement: 1694.
Industrial Revolution Comes to the Old Country: 4787.
Industrial Sonnets: 973.
Inertia and What Emerges: 995.
The Inevitable Words Like Sign Posts: 1904.
The Infante of Images: 1196.
Infected by Morning: 660.
The Infinite Loop (Dream): 802.
Inflation: 4165.
Inflation and high interest rates: 782.
Inflorescence: 4748.
Inhabited Interior: 1422, 2898.
Inheritance: 902, 3347.
The Initial-Tree: 2988.
Initiation: 68.
Inland: 1644, 4947.
Inland with Coastal Weather: 2037.
The Inlet: 3092.
Inmovil Ligadura: 1513.
The Inn: 4734.
The Inn II: 4734.
The Inner Ear: 4102.
Inner Landscape: 2410, 4750.
Inner Peace: 2974.
Inner Resources: 3413.
The Inner Trees: 1637, 3105.
Inni Popolari: 3418.
The Innkeeper's Daughter: 4319.
An Inquiry into the Presumed Death of Richard M. Nixon: 4330.
Insanity: 1633.
The Insects Are Restive: 2679.
Insects in the Fixture Glass: 1933.
Inside: 2222.
Inside a Purse: 3747.
Inside and Out: 3484.
The Inside Layer: 985.
The Inside Passage: 3092.
Inside the Iron Triangle: 667.
Inside the Mushroom: 4862.
Inside the Onion: 3198.
Inside the stems of the

800.
Johann Gaertner, 1793-1887: 1573.
John, at Home: 3978.
John Aubrey in a Junk Shop in Hell: 4402.
John Erdman Cuts Thistles and Takes on the Lord's Passion: 1770.
John of the Cross in the Spring: 237.
Johnny Walsh, Checkered Cab Co: 4860.
Join Us at the Harold Bloom School of Misreading: 1142.
Joint Letter on Poverty: 3111.
The Joker Deals: 14.
Jonathan: 4872, 4977.
Jonquils: 127.
Joseph: 2632.
Joseph O'Reilly: 2927.
Joseph's-of-the-Morning: 2726.
Joseph's Suspicion: 1397, 3726.
Joshu on Hatteras Island: 4539.
Josie Bliss, October 1971: 4898.
Josie's Tooth: 2084.
La Jouissance: Blackberries?: 2995.
Journal Manuscripts Like Hair Falling, Dust: 2611.
Journey: 4617.
Journey and Arrival: 767.
Journey at Dawn: 1576.
Journey by Mammy Wagon: 4511.
Journeyman's Wages: 4262.
The Jovial Mortician: 3954.
Joy of Living Aone: 3897.
Joyce and the Broken Window: 2363.
Joyce & the Poem: 3616.
Joyce Carol Oates Plays the Saturn Piano: 4641.
Joyce Peseroff: 3993.
Joyfulness: 2607.
Jozepha--1900: 4948.
Jubilee of Saint Elizabeth: 1342.
Judas: 2829.
The Judge at the Witch-Burning: 1679.
Judging Poetry at the Homemakers' Show: 3975.
The Judson Place: 1644.
Juggler: 2384.
Jugglers: 4282.
Jugtown: 1196.
Juju Magani: 4305.
Julia Tutwiler State Prison for Women: 2082.
Julie in the Hospital: 691.
Juliek's Violin: 426.
Juliet: 2589.
July: 1509.
July 1st, 1982 - Triolet: 3088.
July 8: 4045.
July/Here: 3796.
Jumping Bad Blues: 2411.
Jumping over the Moon -- Far Far Awaaaay: 3065.
Jumping Rope in the Yard: 355.
June 13, 1951: 3185.
June 15, 1981 9:15 PM: 2043.
June 25, 1947: In His Own Back Yard, the Retired Pastor Looks to Heaven and the Flying Saucer Craze is Born: 756.
June, 1940: 3531.
June Birds: 1595.
June Harvest: 1079.
June Poem: 2777.
A June Walk: 2468.
The Jungle: 4497, 4517.
Jungle and Flame: 3052, 3052.
Junta: 4617.
Jurassic Attendant: 4268.
Jurisdiction: 4716.
Jurisprudence: 72.
Just Another Disaster: 1541.
Just Around Dark: 1079.
Just Born: 2725.
Just Go: 347.
Just Kidding: More Trials of a Suburban Father: 4654.
Just like an old dress: 147, 3784.
Just Once More, for Old Times Sake: 3974.
Just several miles to the west: 3322.
Just think we now have the power: 3610.
Just till Spring: 3825, 4892.
Just Visiting: 4762.
Just When: 4861.
Just Your Average Unfinished Man: 1711.
Justice: 1889.
Justification: 1141.
K-Mart, $2.98: 1216.
The Kabalist: 1623.
Kaddish: 341, 4011.
The Kafir on the Bus: 4836.
Kafka Poem: 4967.
Kairos: 949.
Kakania: 2530.
Kansas Cats: 2149.
Kar Musikileri: 2327.
Karl: 560.
Kaspar Hauser (A boy abandoned by his parents and raised in a cell by a prison guard): 4210.
Kate and John: 2796.
Kathy: 3982.
Katie: 673.
Katie Burned: 3538.
Katorga: 369, 3105.

A Lament in Four Fragments: 1836.
Lament to Orpheus: 4318.
Lament, with Flesh and Blood: 2930.
Lamentation: 2112.
Lammas, 1984: 3570.
Lammas Elegy: 3557.
The Lamp: 1359, 3182, 3722, 4917.
Lamplighter, 1914: 2461.
Lana: 668.
The Land: A Love Letter: 3484.
Land after Heavy Snow: 1805.
Land Grazing: 1483.
A Land No Eyes Should See: 2323.
Land of Shadows: 1250, 1719, 3524.
Land of Sinkholes: 4607.
The Land without Ghosts: 3178.
Landgods Are Not Easily Transportable: 4287.
Landing: 658, 2580.
The Landlady: 1994.
The Landlord's Dream of Hell: 3914.
Landscape: 1419, 4426, 4741.
The Landscape: 1183.
Landscape for the Disappeared: 2411.
Landscape in December: 3874.
Landscape of Capibaribe: 139, 3202.
Landscape Where Children Once Played: 1183.
Landscape with Figures: 663.
Landscape with Open Spaces: 302.
Landscape with Starfish and Mirror: 58.
Landscape with the Body of Judas: 3905.
Landscape with Tractor: 4439.
Landscape with Two Graves and an Assyrian Dog: 2665, 4105.
Landscape without Figures: 3347.
Landscape without History: 2795.
Landscapes, Seascapes: 1864.
Landsmann: 1445.
The Language: 1140.
Language in Puerto Rico: 706.
Language or Silence?: 4576.
Languages: 2719.
Lanny the Lifter: 1803.
The Lapsing, Unsoilable, Whispering: 4255.
Larger Than a Breadbox: 1085.
Larger than hand-passed dangers await us: 769.
Larry Rothman: 237.
Last Afternoon in Paris: 2588.
The Last and Only Poem for the One and Only: 2283.
Last Call: 612.
The Last Class: 4624.
Last Day of School: 4227.
The Last Day of the World: 4275.
Last Day There: 2091.
Last Dew: 211, 2580.
Last Diaspora (Selection: Against the Cold): 579.
Last Elegy to a Daughter: 3375.
Last Exit Home: 2798.
The Last Few Raindrops: 2961.
Last Flight: 1261.
Last forty years: 782.
A Last Gesture: 3062.
Last Get-Together: 4230.
Last Landscape (from The Van Gogh Poems): 566.
Last Laugh: 3795.
Last Message: 4581.
Last Night: 1046, 1258, 3546.
Last Night's Dream: 2575.
The Last of the Courtyard: 1723.
The Last of the Sheridans: 1695.
The Last Pagans: 761.
Last Photographs of Pound: 376.
Last Portraits: Anne Sexton: 60.
The last reading: 3710.
Last Requests: 2662.
The Last Resort: 4896.
Last Rites: 2083, 4303.
The Last Rose: 39, 3673.
Last Run at La Plagne: 2747.
Last Things: 1562, 4347.
The Last Two Photographs of My Father before the War: 1230.
The Last Unspoiled Beauty in America: 2645.
Last Voyage: 1675.
Last Words: 2821, 3387.
The Last Words: 2674.
Last Words of a Zen Fool: 824.
Last Words to Hermes: 3520.
Lasting: 1451.
Late Afternoon: 2850, 2988.
Late Afternoon in Chincoteague: 2181.
Late Afternoon Shadows: 596.
Late April Sweat: 558.
Late Dating the Holy Spirit: 4385.
Late Depression 1940 Social Work: 770.
Late in the Afternoon While the Clouds Turn Lavender: 848.
Late News: 360.
Late Night Movies: 1118.
Late Show: 4815.

The Late Show: 2216.
Late Song: 2719.
Late Spring: 1598, 3694.
Late Spring, Sur Coast: 762.
Late Summer Night: 1098.
Late Twentieth Century Pastoral: 3800.
Late Word from Corcomroe Abbey: 3836.
Latente: 3574.
Later: 1061.
The Lathe of Navels: 2937.
Laud to all things lavatorial: 2833.
Laughing Bear: 258.
Laughing, exulting and rebellious: 38, 2727.
The Laughter of the Gods: 961.
A Launched Bomb Is Immutable: 3654.
Laundering Song: 1710.
Laundry: 1619, 1699.
The Laundry: 2977, 3567.
The Lavatory Attendant: 859.
Laverne: 2640.
Lavonder: 3858.
Law: 2766.
The Law: 3178.
The Law of the Sea: 4845.
The law of the see-saw argues: 2352, 3962.
The Lawn Mowing: 2468.
Lawrence Shaving: 3333.
Laws: 1207.
Lawyers: 2530.
Laxårvogur (Hvalfjördur): 1858.
Laying a Fire: 786.
Layoff: 1684.
Lazarus Passed: 1449.
The Lead Mines of Swaledale (Selections: 3 poems): 2035.
Leading the Mare: 1365.
A Leaf a Flower a Blade of Grass: 541.
Leaf by Leaf: 3498.
Leaf-Light: 1145.
Leafless Trees, Chickahominy Swamp: 4148.
Leah: 1791.
Leaks: 3862.
Lean Benefits: 4364.
Leaping for the Imaginary Fly: 3541.
Learning of the Brown World during Deer Week: 36.
Learning Something: 4337.
Learning the Code, Coding the Life: 1806.
Learning the Fine Balance of Jean Cocteau: 1556.
Learning the Holocaust: 145.
Learning to Bargain: 4206.
Learning to Be Silent: 233.
Learning to Dance, to Dance: 289.
Learning to Live with Mice: 3762.
Learning to Read: 4044, 4815.
Learning to Ride the Elephant: 2412.
Learning to Ride the Train: 4048.
Learning to Speak Papiamento: 2017.
Learning to Write: 1837.
The Least Skippers: 1567.
Leathers: 3937.
Leave: 18.
Leave-Taking: 2630, 4670, 4775.
Leave-Taking (in Chinese): 4670.
Leaves: 3518.
Leaves of Hypnos, a War Journal, 1943-1944 (Excerpts): 718, 4661.
Leaving: 4515, 4902.
Leaving Another Kingdom: 4295.
Leaving Belfast: 3127.
Leaving Father at Landrum: 3417.
Leaving Home: 2886.
Leaving Kansas: 2468.
Leaving New Orleans: 4864.
Leaving the Desert: 2168.
Leaving the East: 1812.
Leaving the Room: 2094.
Leaving Wisconsin for New York in the Sixth Month: 887.
Lebanon's Children: 4767.
Lecciones de Amor y de Odio: 3359.
Lecture: 841.
Lectures in Memory of Louis the Simple (Misread Book Title): 1366.
Led by the Hebrew School Rabbi: 270.
The Leech: A Boyhood Memory: 1454.
Left, right: 4767.
Left Signal Interference: 4778.
Leftover Madonna: 2611.
Leftovers: 1159, 2797.
Legacy: 1183.
The Legacy: 1475.
The Legend: 2038.
Legend of the Box: 4138.
The Legends of Timbuctoo: 4511.
The Legless Fighter Pilot (England, 1940): 3289.
Lemon Drop Saturday: 1336.
Lemons: 3727.
Lenore's Bear: 2593.
Lent Amour (I): 3834.
Lent Amour (II): 3834.
Lent Amour (III): 3834.
Leon Rappolo, Jazz Musician

(1902-1943): 4378.
Leonard Cohen: 1804.
The Leper Graves at Spinalonga: 1043.
Lesbic Isle: 3369.
Leslie: 4650.
Lessee: 2830.
Lesson: 2396, 4129, 4299.
The Lesson: 2412.
A Lesson for the Lovers of Humanity: 2542.
Lesson in Flying: 2688.
Lesson on the Banjo: 3661.
Lessons: 2195, 2845, 4939.
Lessons, 47: 2956.
Let Go: 2225.
Let Me Say All I Have to Say: 304, 304.
Let Me Tell You of My Illness: 3656.
Let the Air Circulate: 758.
Let the bombs fall: 782.
Let the plowman leave his furrow: 2352, 3962.
Let Them Eat Cheese: 4158.
Let's All Get Up: 2176.
Let's Be Maine: 2963.
Let's Go Over Exactly What Happened: 3409.
Let's Hope This Thing Blows Over Soon: 2161.
Let's look at food: 782.
Let's Pretend: 3572.
Letter: 1111, 2031, 3275, 3515.
The Letter: 2719, 3980.
A Letter Following Departure: 3389.
Letter for Henry: Poème Trouvé (1981): 2460.
Letter for Robert Frost: 1126.
A Letter from an Indonesian Merchant Home: 1413.
Letter from an Outpost: 2123.
Letter from Dunphy's Pasture: 3286.
Letter from Friesland to My Sons: 2186.
Letter from Her Aunt: 751.
Letter from Maine: 4425.
Letter from My Mother: 3223.
Letter from Nga: 2046.
Letter from Orcas Island: 786.
Letter from Poland: 2401.
Letter from South London: 3850.
Letter from Swan's Island: 4225.
Letter from the Villa: 2123.
Letter from the World: 2834.
Letter from Trickster: On the Nature of Beauty: 756.
Letter Home: 2389, 3611.
Letter to a Husband on an Oil Drilling Rig at Prudhoe Bay: 762.
Letter to a Missing Brother: 596.
Letter to a Quasi-Fictional Former Self: 3590.
Letter to a Young Girl: 2415.
Letter to an Absent Lover: 3352.
Letter to an Exile: 3127.
Letter to California: 3134.
Letter to Franz Douskey: 705.
Letter to Hugo, with Feathers: 818.
Letter to Ilona from the South of France: 755.
Letter to Judith: 786.
Letter to Nathaniel Hawthorne: 1055.
Letter to Nazim Hikmet: 970, 3940.
Letter to Scanlon from Whitehall: 2091.
A Letter to Sei Shonagon: 4928.
Letter to the Butterflies: 3125.
Letter to the Edge of a Field: 3823.
Letter to the Editor: 1237.
Letter to the Light: 1693, 2158.
Letter to the Outside: 4617.
Letter to Tina Koyama from Elliot Bay Park: 3042.
Letterfrack Industrial School: 3155.
Letters: 2353.
Letters from Maine: 3921.
Letters from My Mother: 1, 1777.
Letters to My Death: 3023.
Letting Go: 347, 948.
Levellers: 4104.
Levels of abstraction: 2236.
The Leveret, in the Twilight: 2714.
Lexington Police Probe Continues: Evidence Begins to Emerge: 201.
Lhasa Flea Market: 3905.
The Liberating: 3000.
Liberation: 1606.
Librarian: 1273.
The Library: 4273.
The Library in Beaumont, Texas: 4437.
The Lice: 1799, 2941.
Lichens (Winter 81-82): 4170.
The Lie: 1378.
Liebestrauma: 1196.
Lies: 596, 997.
Life: 744, 3375.
Life and Art: 4838.
The Life and Death of Jupiter: 2149.
Life at the Capital: 1799, 2603.

Looking for Halley's Comet: 2897.
Looking for His Mama in a Bar: 2059.
Looking for Home: 3286.
Looking for Our Dog: 1981.
Looking for Sound: 2365.
Looking for the Mushroom: 3647.
Looking for the Poem That Explains It All: 2372.
Looking for Uncle Al: 4521.
Looking for You One Year Later: 3779.
The Looking Glass: 3669.
Looking Homeward: 3093.
Looking in the Mirror: 4359.
Looking into My Daughter's Nightmare: 3736.
Looking Out on Africa: 1771.
Looking through the Axis of DNA (cover of Science, Feb., 1981): 213.
Looking toward Manhattan: 3615.
The Loom and the Weave: 4845.
Loon: 2585.
Looney Tunes: 3470.
The Loons: 2468.
Loons Mating: 4636.
Loose: 1169.
Lord Ganesh: 899.
Lord I believe. Help Me in My Unbelief: 596.
Lord of the Inferno: 237.
Lorne (Pictou County, N.S.): 3926.
Losing Friends at the Tent Revival: 4866.
Losing Ground: 4878.
Losing Streak: 1446.
Losing the Game: 11.
Losing the Whales: 2090.
Loss: 4847.
Loss/Angel-Less/Blue: 195.
The Loss of It: 3126.
Losses: 1027, 3612.
Lost: 3520.
Lost and Found: 569.
Lost Assignments: 2659.
Lost Children: 2648.
The Lost Christian: 3148.
The Lost Colony: 1380.
Lost Drachma (Lk 15:8-10): 875.
Lost in the Centuries: 4239.
Lost Lives: 4616.
Lost Love Ghazal: 4503.
Lost or Found: 1626.
The Lost Princess: 3804.
The Lost Senses: 3551.
The Lost Woman: 2095.
Lot's Daughter: 1474.
Lot's Wife: 1615, 3984.
The Lotus Eaters: 2023.
The Lotus Flowers: 4624.
Lou Anne in the House of Glass: 4565.
Lough Leane: 2042.
Louisiana Snow: 2817.
Love: 146, 663, 703, 726.
Love and Destiny: 2553.
Love and Marriage: 2225.
Love and Resistance: 4488.
Love and Work: Apple Picking: 1623.
Love Anecdote: 3264.
Love As Refuse: 1030.
Love Consumed: 4616.
Love Gets Ornery: 4431.
Love in the '60s: 3032.
Love in the Western World: 629.
A Love Journal (Selection: Latest Entry): 1571.
A Love Letter: 1192.
Love Letter from Acapulco: 501.
Love Letter from Clarity in Chartres: 3836.
Love Never Stood in This Water: 2409.
The Love of Water Faucets: 2165.
Love Poem: 1492, 2468, 2535.
A Love Poem: 2572.
The Love Poem: 4389.
Love Poem #1: 755, 2614.
Love Poem for Perry Mason: 2199.
Love Poem in Twos and Threes: 427.
Love sign: 3710.
Love Song: 561, 782, 2095.
Love That Garbage: 2684.
Love under the Scouring Pad: 1696.
Love Upstate: 975.
Love Won't Stop: 1394.
The Loved Place: 4153.
Lovelock to Twin Falls: 3758.
Lovely: 1140.
Lover: 2766.
The Lover: 2272.
A Lover for the Queen: 2771.
A Lover Like Sleep: 2611.
Lover, My Poem: 3373.
Lovers: 3258.
The Lovers: 2317, 2468.
Lovers at Burrington Coombe: 1974.
Lovers at the Zoo: 1160.
Lover's Contingency: 1184.
Lovers die but caution kills: 1023.
Love's Over Again: 81, 3205.
Lovesong after Flood: 4148.
Loving Couple: 777.
The Low Country: 3672.
Low Lands: 1017.
Low Tide Ghazal: 1792.
A lozenge of dream sticks on

my tongue: 4705.
Lubricant: 3685.
A Lucid Moment: 998, 1047.
Lucifer Approchant: 1465.
Lucinda Comes to Visit: 4438.
Luck: 1195.
Lucky: 4947.
Lucky with Woods: 1562.
Lucy: 3528.
Lucy: Her Fear: 3528.
Lucy Speaks: 3528.
Ludicrous Stick: 989.
The Luftwaffe in Chaos: 3727.
Lugar Común: 166, 1754.
El lugar común no es la flota británica: 828.
Lugar de Encuentro: 1954.
Lullaby: 2464, 4701, 4772.
Lullaby for 17: 3387.
Lullaby for a Summer Recess: 1340.
Lullaby from the Japanese: 3980.
Lullabye: 744, 4065.
Lulls: 2725.
Luminary: 3891.
The Luminating Experience of a Brain Scan: 237.
Luna: 1062.
Lunar: 3980.
Lunch at Nanni's: 1924.
Lunch Hour: 2831.
Lunch Meat: 2130.
Lunchroom: 154.
Lungomare: 3063.
The Lure of Mountains: 2063.
The Lust Studies (Selection: #6, Lust Study of an Iris,: 251.
Lutenists in the Morning: 4078.
Lydia: 1932.
Lydia and the Eagle: 1863.
Lydia As Hecuba: 1863.
Lydia Walks towards Me: 1863.
Lye Soda: 154.
Lying: 4796.
Lying Here: 1246.
A Lyric Afterwards: 3401.
Lyric for the Girl with Holes in Her Jeans: 4163.
Lysskifte: 2158.
Maar Op Een Dag: 3471.
Mabel, or Maybe Avis: 1993.
MacAulay's Traveler: 3278.
MacDougal on the Fear of Hell: 14.
MacDougal's Theory of Dreams: 14.
A Machiavellian Thought: 4017.
The Machine: 3686.
Machine out of the God: 3904.
The Machinists: 2930.
Mad Doggerel: 2766.
Mad Messalina: 4245.
Madonna: 1857, 4382.
Madonna Gardenia: 2611.
Madonna of the Excesses: 2611.
Madonna of the Mass Appeal: 2611.
Madonna of the Messy House: 2611.
Madonna of the Too Hard Ballet Class: 2611.
Madonna Who Gets Around: 2611.
Madonna Who You Have to Hand It To: 2611.
A Madras Gent Receives His 'Dear John' Letter: 4460.
Madrid: The Ghosts of Its Defenders: 2428.
The Madwoman's Repentance: 3264.
Maggie: 3213.
Magi: 3889.
Magic: 1143.
The Magic of Hands: 4249.
Magicians in the Park: 371.
The Magnetic Arsenal, or a Birthday Bouquet for James Tate: 2006.
Magnets: 95.
Magnificat: 965.
A Magnificent Gesture: 4176.
The Magnificent Romance: 2385.
The Mailman's Wife: 4770.
Mailroom: 1897.
Main Street and Kingston Road: 4574.
The Main Thing: 3751.
Maine Vastly Covered with Much Snow: 4407.
Mainstreaming: 680.
Maintenance: 2148.
The Maisie (Excerpt): 780.
Maison: 702.
Maithuna: 3407, 4721.
Major League: 1293.
Majority: 3164.
Make Her Wait: 1487.
Make Me Hear You: 1563.
Make Room William Blake: 2530.
Makeshift: 1691.
Making a Bed: 3124.
Making an Apocalypse: 3626.
Making Certain It Goes On: 2091.
Making It: 1640.
Making Sense: 2536.
Making the Best of It: 3831.
Mala Suerte: 2937.
The Malady Lingers On: 2880.
Male Chauvinist Roadside Pig: 3700.
Malin Head: 2113.
Mallards and Partridges: 3927.
Mallarme in Tournon: 2277.
Mama: 2337, 2611.
Mama's Story: 496.
The Mammoth Tooth from the Garden: Nebraska: 292.
A Man & a Woman: 3968.

Man and Whale: 2274.
Man Arrested in Hacking Death Tells Police He Mistook Mother-in-Law for Raccoon: 2689.
The Man behind the French Sunglasses: 1717.
Man Brushing a Woman's Hair: 632.
A Man Came Out of a Tree: 3164.
The Man from the Restaurant: 50.
The Man from Washington: 4739.
A Man in His Time: 1123.
Man in Overcoat and Kneesocks: 4889.
The Man in the Black Hat: 4637.
The Man in the Dark: 4594.
The Man in the Middle: 1103.
The Man in the Open Doorway: 1583.
The Man in the Pool: 2302.
The Man in the Shoe Store: 2611.
A Man Lies in White Linen: 4126.
The Man Married to the Midget: 2611.
The Man of Capernaum (Mark ii, 1-12): Hopkins Prepares His Sermon for October 5, 1879: 961.
A Man of Many Moves: 4299.
A Man on a Bus Decides to Eat Lunch: 4403.
Man on the Iron Fire Escape: 4487.
A Man Scheduled to Die: 844.
The Man the Moon Likes: 1370, 4420.
Man Untestamented: 1752.
Man Walking to Work: 2203.
The Man Who Believes in Five: 4815.
The Man Who Killed for Love: 4069.
A Man Who Loves Love: 1767, 3272.
The Man Who Saw the Elephant: 1872.
The Man with a Drill in His Head: 2611.
The Man with No Face: 1993.
The Man with the Umbrella: 413.
The Mandrill Baboon: 3817.
Manet: The Execution of the Emperor Maximilian: 4181.
Manichean Geography I: 3401.
Manichean Geography II: 3401.
Manios med fhefhaked Numasioi, 'Manius Made Me for Numerius': 1370.
Manitou Poem: 2719.
Manning the Battering Ram: 2766.
Manning the Battering Ram (Special section): 2766.
Manorbier: 1858.
Manos ruedan llorando al pie del flamboyàn: 3737.
Man's Hunger for War: 3996.
Man's Supremacy: 35.
A Man's World (found poem): 4699.
Mansions of Mirage: 4541.
Manticore Vortex: 1264.
Manuscript: 1960.
Manuscript Found in a Bottle: 3419, 4579.
Mao Tse-tung: 2369, 4419.
A Map: 2104, 3958.
A Map for the Unborn: 4215.
Maples: 1615.
Maps: 2569.
Maratea Porto: The Dear Postmistress There: 2091.
Marathon: 3193.
Marble: 4682.
Marble Rooms: 4541.
A Marble-white full moon: 4668.
March: 1346, 1791, 3387.
March 4, 1980: And Yet Perhaps: 216, 1563.
March 4, 1983: 536.
March, from a Window (A Meditation): 1042.
March Notes: 2849.
The March of the Women: 4173.
March on Seabrook: 2000.
La Marcha de los Condenados: 3741.
Mardi Gras Poem: 3451.
Marea Alta: 4498.
Margaret: 2723.
Margaret Atwood: 1804.
Margaret Hollingsworth's Glasses: 2882.
Margaret Hollingsworth's Milk: 2882.
Margaret Hollingsworth's Typewriter: 2882.
Margaretta's Rime: 15.
Margins: 1245.
Margo Lockwood: 3993.
Marguerita: 3049.
Maria Heimsuchung: 3726.
Maria Verkundigung: 3726.
Maria's Mandolin: 3292.
Marie-Claire Blais: 1804.
Marilyn: 4592.
Marina: 2221.
Marine Surface, Low Overcast: 758.
Marion: 1681.
Mariposa: 3466.
Marjorie Tetlow, M.L.S., Tries for Whitman: 4860.
The Mark: 3980.

Mark's Mushroom: 3895.
Marks of the Beast: 278.
Mark's Used Parts: 2931.
The Marquis de Lafayette Steps Ashore in the New World and Goes to Charleston: 3744.
The Marrano: 1623.
Marriage: 857, 1438, 3849.
A Marriage: 3854.
Marriage by Arrangement: 4078.
A Marriage in Marmaros: 4791.
Marriage of Horse and Wood: 3954.
Marriage Poem: 1069, 4186.
Marriage Portrait: 127.
Marriage Proposal: 4889.
The Marriage Vow: 4869.
Mars: 1615.
Mars and Venus: 746.
Mars Brew: 3685.
Marsh: 1720, 2158.
The Marsh: 3983.
A Martial Law Carol: 530.
A Martian Sends a Postcard Home: 3625.
Martin Avenue: 1773.
Martinique: 4500.
Mary Cassatt: 1511.
Mary Cassatt, Pupil of Edgar Degas: 806.
Mary Lincoln: 1149.
Mary Magdalen's Left Foot: 2082.
Mary Ramirez: 374.
Marygold: 2638.
Mary's Cat: 1452.
Mashpee, 1952: 2840.
Mashpee, 1979: 2840.
Mashpee Wine: 2840.
Mask: 3650.
The Mask Of Waking: 289.
Masks: 4585.
The Masks & the Colored Heat: 507, 1526, 4207.
Masloff Is Not In Zagreb: 3521.
Masquerade: 4898.
Massacre at Marais Des Cygnes: 3568.
The Massage Parlour: 3313.
Master of Ceremonies: 2662.
A Masterful Demonstration of Public Heath: 1523, 4583.
Masterpiece: 802.
The Mastodon in the Wall: 4125.
The Match: 4625.
Materializing: 2302.
Math Anxiety: 807.
Mathematics: 2167.
Matin au motel: 1175.
Matinee: 4374, 4690.
Matins: 3937.
Les Matins: 4783.
A Matter of Angels: 4617.
A Matter of Light: 3718.
A matter of priorities: 782.
Matter over Mind: 1178.
Matthew Brady Speaks of Whitman: 1672.
Maud Allen: 1158.
Max: 1273.
May: 2468.
May 4: 4045.
May be necessary to put in anti-missile systems: 782.
May Crowds: 1370, 4420.
Mayaro Sea Sculpture: 933.
Maybe I'll Cry: 4922.
Maybe I'm confused: 782.
Maybe the Women Are Right About Us: 2645.
Maybe you did not know the birds were all dead: 951.
MBHP: 1754.
McGovern Leaving San Pedro: 1132.
Me and Me: 796.
Me encantaria, simplemente, estar loca: 273.
Me gusta mi cara: 3773.
Me preguntan si enarbolo en mi bolsillo: 1514.
Meadow, Lake, Golden Goose Chase: 3164.
The Meadowlands: 3971, 3971.
The Meal: 342, 2100.
Meaning: 4142.
The Meaning of Winter: 3980.
Measurements: 3607.
Meat in the Silo: 3870.
The Mechanical Engineer's Proposal: 653.
Media in Vita: 4759.
Media Man: 2096.
Medical Examiner's Morgue, New York, 11/20/80: 2743.
Medicine Shirt, 1892: 4166.
Meditation: 210, 1813, 4163, 4736.
A Meditation between Claims: 3917.
Meditation in Action: 4163.
Meditation on Patience: 2495.
Meditation on the Skeleton of a Prehistoric Indian at the Ohio Historical Center: 756.
Meditation Sufficient for Monday: 1752.
Meditations: 2630, 4532.
Meditations (in Chinese): 4532.
Meditations of a Journalist: 4379.
The Meditations of O. C. MacClean: Love Song: 1961.
Medo Dos Teus Ollos: 1515.
Medusa at Home: 184.
Medusa's Lover: 4636.
Meet Jane, Dick's Wife: 2363.
Megan: 3020.

Modern Day Flukes #7: 350.
Modern Day Martyrs #4: 350.
Modern Day Masochists #2: 350.
The Modern Mind: 3036.
Modern Nursery Rhymes: 665.
A Modern Prometheus: 1119.
Modern Sonata: 3223.
Modesta Leaving Milan and Saint Augustine: 1048.
Mohole: 1817.
Molasses Fumes Fatal: 2689.
Mole: 1309.
Mole Digging: 4506.
Molokai: 4641.
The Moment: 1581.
A Moment in Maine: 2031.
The Moment in Sunlight: 201.
A Moment in Time: 851.
Moments before the End: 2385.
Moments of Being Away: 1904.
Monday Morning: 3777.
Monet: 1562.
Monet Refuses the Operation: 3134.
Monet's Irises: 3387.
Money: 637.
Money and Durer: 2653.
Monhegan Island, Maine 1918: 1749.
Monica: 2766.
The Monkeys: 609.
Monkeys on Mt. Miyanoura: 1370.
Monk's Story: 162.
Monopoly: 4690.
Monster Movie: 2368.
Mont Sainte-Victoire: 3060.
Montage: 254.
Montana, Again: 1726.
Montana Ranch Abandoned: 2091.
Montauk Point, New York: 991.
Monterey: 3980.
Month: 2962.
The Month of June: 13 1/2: 3289.
Mood: 3179.
Moon: 1864.
The Moon: 1125.
The moon above your house too: 842.
The Moon Again: 2152.
Moon and Panorama of Insects (Love Poem): 1807, 2665.
Moon: First Quarter: 2297.
Moon into Capricorn: 1676.
Moon of Wakening: 2652.
The Moon Pond: 2894.
The Moon Sits: 3479.
Moon-Take: 1314.
Moonlight: 372.
Moonlight (Haiku): 1828.
Moonlight Yodel: 1273.
Moonlighters: 2609.
Moonlit night: Hearing at the Wine Shop Accompaniment to my Lute: 935, 2604.
Moonlit Orchard: 1490, 4830.
The Moon's Secret Face: 3906.
Moonstone: 237.
Moose by Greyhound: 3131.
Morale, 1980s: 3340.
The Moravian Cemetery: 'God's Acre': 4215.
More Fish Than Ever: 4069.
More Girl Than Boy: 2411.
More Nights: 3843.
More of My Mother and the Knife: 2611.
More of the Singular Implausible, Please: 4891.
More Philosophy from MacDougal: 14.
More Pleasant Adventures: 143.
Morning: 554, 1612, 2468, 3144, 3874, 3980.
Morning Aperture: 4760.
Morning at the hotel: 1175.
The Morning Dolores Died: 1950.
Morning Etude: 786.
Morning, First of the Month: 376.
Morning Glories: 67.
Morning Glory: 3124.
Morning in the Apartment: 2365.
Morning Letter of a Bride: 1923.
Morning Light: 3731.
Morning of Hoar Frost: 4200.
The Morning of the First Day: 4375.
Morning Paper Route--January, 1953: 3668.
Morning Photographs: 873.
Morning Poem: 3293.
Morning Song: 3745.
A Morning Song in Prose of Dry Lotus Leaves: 738.
Morning Sounds: 1821.
The Morning's Mail: 596, 3254.
Morphine: 1918, 3524.
Morremos cara ó mar mirando os horizontes: 2666.
Morris Cave: 611.
La Mort des Amants: 266.
Mortal Limit: 4682.
Mortality Clings: 4809.
Mortals are in danger of extinction: 782.
Mortiphobia, the Fear of Self-Reproach: 126.
Moscow Vespers: 3223.
The Mosquito: 1473, 3351.
Mosquito Biting: 4148.
The Moss Palace: 3387.
The Most Enigmatic of Beasties: 350.
Motel: 835.
Motel Room: 1610.
Motes: 2276, 2330.
The Moth: 2468.

Moth in April: 3330.
A Moth with Black Eyes: 427.
Mother: 1188, 1761.
The Mother: 3512.
Mother and Son: 1968, 3703.
Mother and Spring: 3584.
Mother at the Department Store: 2658.
Mother Dating: 727.
Mother-Death: 3453.
Mother in Phoenix, 1950: 3651.
Mother Nature's Helpers: 3817.
Mother Skin: 2655.
The Mother Spaceship: 309, 2580.
Mother Stones: 1644.
Mother Writes Me in Paris to Tell Me That Grandmoter, Aged 78, Died: 2909.
MotherMother (they see Hiroshima and speak of nuclear defense): 4405.
The Mothers: 2685.
A Mother's Legacy: 3481.
Mother's Memorabilia: 4698.
Motion: 2395.
The Motorcyclists: 4431.
Motown Polka: 3634.
Les mots: 1735.
Mottos: 2494.
The Mound of the Viking Chocolate Bars: 3177.
Mount Angel: 2321.
The Mountain: 2342, 2399, 2457.
Mountain Conifer: 3906.
Mountain Dialogue: 2604, 4668.
Mountain Lake with Stumps: 2094.
Mountain Memo: 4588.
A Mountain of Glass: 585.
Mountain Pass: 2902.
Mountain Snail: 4588.
Mountain Waters: 334.
Mountains Can't Save Me: 1209.
Mountains, Rivers, and Caribbea: 3886.
Mountaintop: 2195.
The Mourner's Christmas: 3814.
Mourning a Vintner: 1799, 2604.
The Mourning Cloak: 2435.
Mourning Doves: Maryland: 50.
Mourning for Rue: 911.
Mourning to Do: 3921.
The Mouse: 2414.
Mouse of the Year: 4375.
The Move: 4557.
A move by Senate body to increase health insurance: 3610.
Moves: 2536.
Movie within a Movie: 2203.
Moving: 376.
Moving Day: 3426.
Moving from Clear Creek: 590.
Moving In: 2409, 2644.
Moving Lights: 2580, 4794.
Moving North: 737.
Moving Targets: 4576.
Moving Through: 1852.
Moving Up: 1928.
Mowing the Lawn: 325.
Mozart: 2661.
Mr. and Mrs. Hamilton: 3993.
Mr. Brown: 4820.
Mr. Castle's Vacation Drive: 3954.
Mr. Davis, His Peccadilloes, & His Wife, Martha, Interrupt the Meat Course: 963.
Mr. J Meditates: 2256.
Mr. Numb: 2179.
Mr. or Mrs. Nobody: 4239.
Mr. Scoop's Listen Coin: 1221.
Mr. Strugnell: 859.
Mr. Valdez: 176.
Mr. Wakefield on Interstate 90: 1778.
Mrs. Asquith's Scarlet Letter: 4860.
Mrs. Bugg: 2766.
Mrs. Foltz Uses Molasses: 415.
Mrs. Leland Stanford: 680.
Mrs. McCandless: 1509.
Mrs. Treadle and Mrs. Pocket: 347.
Ms. Lot of Sodom: 3179.
Mstislav Rostropovich (Row J, Top Balcony, Hill Auditorium, Ann Arbor): 1976.
Mt. Pleasant Cemetery: 1054.
Le Muguet: 718.
La Mujer: 4792.
Mujer Camino: 405.
Mujer con Sombrero: 3773.
Mujer de la Tierra: 1082.
Mujer Nuestra de Cada Dia: 1082.
La mujer que quiero: 3773.
Mulberry tree with innocent eyes: 4705.
Mules: 3136.
Mules Sometimes: 3532.
Mulleins: 850.
Multiple Choice: 4890.
Multiple Heart (Selections): 4077.
Multiple Myeloma: 335.
Mum: 2766.
Mummy Wrap: 3615.
El mundo es una esfera de cristal: 3200.
Muñeca: 667.
La Muralla Femenina: 1081.
Murder: 734.
Murder Mystery: 3689.
The Murderer: 3954.
A Murmuring Stream: 3062.
Los Muros nada más: 704.
Muscatel: 2468.

The Muse: 4815.
Muse Elektrique: 2775.
Museum Out of Mind: 3531.
Museums: 2282.
Mushroom Cloud: 1785.
Mushrooming: 573.
Music: 20, 4524.
The Music: 2468, 2719, 3103.
Music Can Come from behind Bars: 1897.
Music for an Autumn Afternoon: 2496.
Music Lesson: 4617.
Music Lessons: 3293.
The Music of Energy: 2530.
Musing at a Red Light in Oakland, CA: 1865.
Musings in the Garden at Poissy: 4202.
The Muskellunge Alive: 2134.
Mustache: 622.
Mustard Seed: 3370.
The Mutants: 2812.
Mute Mad Child: 3264.
Muted Music: 4682.
Mutual Attraction: 2964.
My: 3710.
My Accent Dangles: 1523, 4583.
My Angel: 1951.
My arch enemy peter: 4017.
My arm asleep, numb: 3429.
My Birthday: 355.
My Boston Aspiring Poet Friend Scoffs Whenever We Discuss My Dave Etteresque Poems: 366.
My Brother Finding the I Ching: 4138.
My Brother Loves Diversity: 3947.
My Brother Phoenix (In the wake of fiery dreams): 1496.
My Brother Still Goes to the Barber: 4860.
My Business: 745.
My Confessional Sestina: 1583.
My Country Is So Tiny: 1753.
My Daughter: 4225.
My Days Are Numbered: 3999.
My Dream by Henry James: 3863.
My Face Surprising: 2046.
My Faithful Mother Tongue: 3021.
My Father: 1259, 1395, 3315.
My Father after a Day's Work at Otto Steel: 4190.
My Father and My Mother Went Out to Hunt: 3958, 4872.
My Father-in-Law Remembers the Argonne, September, 1918: 4676.
My Father in the Basement: 4636.
My Father Loved Me Once: 3674.
My Father Reading: 706.
My father the pacifist: 3472.
My Father's Brothers: 235.
My Father's Canary: 610.
My Father's House: 2082.
My Father's Indigestion: 963.
My Father's Picture on the Cover of a Buffalo Bison Hockey Program for 1934: 1069.
My Father's Whistle: 3753.
My Fellow Villagers: 368, 1834.
My Friend, Michael, From the Dust: 211, 2580.
My Friends (I'm Going West): 2693.
My God, What Will You Do, When I Die?: 2521, 3726.
My Grandmother Marries My Grandfather: 4399.
My grandmother meant it when she died: 2343.
My Grandmother's Dolls: 4202.
My Hands: An Ode of Sorts: 1028.
My hands move across your face: 845.
My Heart Is in the East: 237.
My Little Treasure, Is What She Said: 806.
My Little World: 1607, 3627.
My London: 4735.
My Love: 1574.
My Love Is in the Past: 2172, 3287.
My Lover: 2009.
My Magdalene: 1449.
My Mother: 2252, 2410.
My Mother Cried Once in Her Life: 985.
My mother said no: 1428.
My Mother's Feet: 3512.
My Mother's Letters: 387.
My Mother's Lips: 4812.
My Mother's Shoes: 1630.
My Mother's Tablecloth: 2408.
My Name Is William Tell: Poems from the Tradition of Total Experience: 4239.
My Neighbor's Ghost: 4766.
My Nights Are Taken Up with Stars: 1058.
My Parents' Yard Revisited: 4124.
My Psychiatrist Gave Me: 217.
My Room: 4592.
My Russian Friend: 3223.
My Sad Friend: 2115.
My sins: 3958, 4872.
My sister: 2351.
My Sister: 2766.
My Sister is Not a Dollar: 585.
My Sister Lets It Fall: 1170.
My Son: 3718.
My Son Skating on Doane's

Neolithic: 1042.
Neonatal: 634.
Neoteny: 4560.
Neptune Night: 1306.
Nero's Letter To An Unknown Friend: 4245.
Nerves: 3124, 3223.
The Nest: 302.
Nesting Time: 957.
Net: 1895, 4330.
Network: 1897, 2921, 4239.
Neutral Zone: 3892.
The Neutron, Awesome Bomb: 1625.
Nevada: 1737.
Nevada Desert: 4970.
Never Again: 782, 2336.
Never Leaving the City: 92.
Never to Be Caught Maudlin: 4230.
The New Bears: 1830.
New Book: 2766.
The New Book: 1659.
New Boy: 1773.
New Cop at Blue Hills and Prospect: 2931.
New Cowboys: 635.
New Dawn: 4682.
The New Dawn: 378.
New Day, Central Daylight Time: 560.
The New Depression: 385.
New dictator in Guatemala: 3610.
The New Dog: 1480.
The New Economy: 1113.
New England Addresses: 389.
New England, Springtime: 1162.
New Hampshire: 1862, 3124.
A New Home (Excerpt): 3414.
New-Icarus Is Alive & Well, Only a Little Wet: 4614.
New Kid on the Block: 2871.
A New Language: 3148.
New law in Germany: 3610.
New Liberty: 843.
A New Life: 758, 1725.
A New Lover: 1473, 3351.
New Orleans: Poem on His Birthday: 4864.
New Oxford Catechism: Say 'Plato's Cave': 4305.
The New Place: 1085.
New Pony on a Carousel: 4980.
The New Punch and Judy Show: 2368.
The New Saddhus: 3506.
New Season: 2583.
The New Seasons: 2966.
The New Sorcery: 2028.
New Strain: 4261.
New Times: 4520.
New Times, New People: 4239.
New Versa: 4003, 4003.
The New Wasteland: 570.
The New Widow: 298.
New Wings: 1945.
New World Griot: 1015.
New Year: 3981, 3983.
New Year's Eve: 722, 2118, 2634.
New York: 2653.
New York City: 663.
New York -- Meurtre à l'Opera: 2484.
New York: Museum of Modern Art: 3962.
Newborn: 4074.
The Newest Adam: 4888.
Newfoundland Kitchen: 740.
News: 3968.
News for Loch Ness: 680.
News from the Far West: 1080.
News Summary: 2932, 3467.
News That Stays News: 2776.
The Newspaper: 889.
Newspaper Hats: 2065.
Newspaper Photo, 1920: 3936.
The Next Day: 2385.
Next Door: 2155.
Next Hat: 1707.
The Next I Know: 3723.
Next Time: 4239.
Nicaragua Rojo: 4528.
Nicaraguan Dirge: 1598.
Nickie Naming: 1615.
Nico, Presiding: 3978.
Niger: 3593.
Night: 1820, 3066, 3264.
The Night: 2823.
Night Babies: 4980.
The Night before the Hallowed Evening: 2203.
Night Blindness: 2230.
Night Blooming Flowers: 3525.
The Night Cafe: 897.
Night Caller: 1878.
Night Cannot Be Turned Off: 4501.
Night Carving: 2058.
Night Child: 1034.
Night Diving: 1713.
Night Driving: 3992.
Night Flight: 3318.
Night Hike: 2159.
Night Images: 4243.
The Night Is Dark: 1961.
Night Music: 1720, 2158.
Night of Terror: 19.
Night of the Deer: 3350.
The Night of the Moon Geese: 1941.
Night of the Scorpion: 2877.
A Night on the Town: 3569.
Night Piece: 3980.
Night Ride, 1965: 3038.
Night Ride Hued: 2976.
The Night Sea Journey: 2174, 3353.
Night Sequence: 3953.
The Night She Dreamed She Was Mad: 1065.

Northern Lights: 1079.
Northward Riding: 2028.
Northward Wending: 2830.
Northwest Ohio: 1678.
Northwest Retrospective: Mark Tobey: 2091.
Nostalgia: 2190.
Nostalgia When the Leaves Begin to Fall: 2530.
Nostalgias: 3059.
Not Alone: 3248.
Not Everyone Has Been So Lucky: 4000.
Not Falling to Dogs: 1186.
Not Flood nor Fire Next Time (after seeing a PBS program on hydro-chemical poisons): 4471.
Not good enough to be loved: 842.
Not Grief But Thanks: 4122.
Not Here, Not Ever: 3048.
Not Just Because My Husband Said: 682.
Not Like Water: 4551.
Not Macho, Just Mucho: 1442.
Not Marbled: 1444.
Not Meaning to End: 4486.
Not much fun: 782.
Not Pleasing Mama: 2894.
Not Saying Anything: 4239.
Not to Cry: 2170.
Not Tonight: 1938.
Not wild about the gringos: 3610.
Not without Air: 2486.
Note: 2330.
Note for a Suicide: 2385.
Note from the Chesapeake: 2660.
Note Left under the Left-over Flowers: 4972.
A Note on Nostalgia as the Corruption of Innocence: 3800.
Note: The Sea Grinds Things Up: 1172.
Notebook: 2029.
Notes for a Basterd Angel: 725.
Notes for a Sonnet: 3607.
Notes for Pat: 956.
Notes from a Child of Paradise (Selection: XXVI): 868.
Notes from a Child of Paradise (Selections: XI, XIII, XXIII, XXIX): 868.
Notes from a Small Clinic: 1210.
Notes on Human Evolution from the Museum of Natural History: 4048.
Notes on the Limerick of Light (refer to Relativity/Einstein): 2803.
Notes toward a Discourse: 4350.
Notes Toward a Journal: 543.
Nothing Follows: 1264.
Nothing for Rachel: 3397.
Nothing Numinous Else: 2370.
Nothing That's Lovely Can My Love Escape: 2516.
Nothingness: 2682.
Noun Gathering at Dusk: 2589.
Nous remettrons-nous seulement: 3875.
Nova II: Her Final Confession: 1242.
Nova Scotia: 1183.
Novelettes: 2962.
November: 1111, 1800, 2020, 2468.
November 1st: 3019.
November Burial: 1993.
November in Defiance, Ohio: 981, 981.
November Maples: 1437.
November Music: 1266.
November, Remembering Voltaire: 2004.
November Saturday: 2734.
November Woman: 2874.
Novena: 4373.
Now: 374, 1021, 3636, 3849, 4136, 4471, 4602.
Now and Again He Was Picked Up: 140, 4914.
Now As I Write: 117, 3267.
Now Enter: 3032.
Now Exactly: 1466, 3733.
Now it is time the gods stepped out of everyday things: 3726, 4901.
Now nothing can prevent me completing my appointed orbit: 3726, 4901.
Now Taking Place: 207.
Now Will Be Tomorrow: 3464.
Noxious News: 805.
Un Nuage Est une Barre: 2172.
Nuance: 4699.
Nuclear Ambush: 649.
Nuclear bombs destroy: 782.
Nuclear fascist maniacs: 782.
Nuclear Land: 4481.
Nuclear proliferation: 1633.
Nuclear superiority: 782.
Nuclear terminology: 782.
Nuclear Triptych: 2047.
Nuclear War: 489, 1625.
Nuclear war at the least survival: 782.
Nuclear war can change us: 782.
Nuclear war on the horizon: 782.
Nuclear war will blind your cat: 782.
Nuclear war will kill birds: 782.
Nuclear war will ruin

baseball: 782.
Nuclear war will wipe out bald eagles: 782.
Nuclear war will wreck the Rose Parade: 782.
Nude on a Harley: 1132.
Nude Standing Alone in the Forest: A Study of Place: 3783.
Nude Women Bathing, Drying Themselves and Combing Their Hair: 2982.
Nuestras Voces Se Confunden: 634.
The Numbered Set of Human Faces: 4195.
The Numbering at Bethlehem: 1615.
Numbers: 86, 1176.
Numbers 31 (in which Moses orders the rape of 32, 000 Midianite virgins): 2930.
Nunc Dimittis: 1157.
The Nurse Tells Me I Can See You Now: 42.
The Nursemaid Is Petrified: 3154.
The Nursery: 4833.
Nursery Rhyme: 4979.
Nursery Rhyme 1916: 1494.
Nursery Rhymes: 4848.
The Nurturing of Darkness: 4214.
NY 10032: 1754.
O: 1143.
O human voice: 4904.
O Jacob: 3167.
O.K., I'll Tell You: 2450.
O K let's kill the cigarette: 782.
O Mom, he tells me: 271.
O moon head: 4773.
O Not with a Word: 2367.
O Sausage Patty!: 1467.
O, Say Can You See?: 2960.
O Vision de Neige: 446, 1356.
The Oak: 3997.
Oakland Port View: 1130.
Oakley, Kansas: 3057.
The Oaks of Poland: 2679.
Oasis in the Wilderness: 2788.
Oath of an English and French Survivor at Dien Bien Phu: 1426.
Objectivity: 3620.
Objects of Love: 3845.
Obliterate earth and what have you got?: 3610.
Obscure Disaster: 4526.
Obscure Disaster II: 4526.
Observaré los Puntos Colgados en Tu Cola de Nieve Dormida: 1081.
Obsession: 2496.
Obsessions: 783.
Obstinado Viajero: 2503.
Obviously: 963.
Occasional Slaughter: 1293.
Occasionally Paul Eluard: 986.
Ocean: 4154.
Ocean Ranger -- February 13, 1982: 3721.
Ocean View: 535, 2036.
O'Connor As in Frank: 1808.
October: 1029, 2396, 4478.
October 21st: 2786.
October Lights: 3908.
October: Resetting the Clocks: 3746.
October Sestina: The Shadows: 426.
October: Slash and Burn: 2834.
Ocurrió en el tiempo: 273.
Oda a Walt Whitman: 2665.
Odalisque: 306.
Odds: 914.
Ode: Drunk on an Old Showboat Passing Charolais: 575.
Ode for an Envelope: 3138.
An Ode for My Analyst: 264.
Ode to a Bird (Montgeron, 1959): 1874, 3021, 3506.
Ode to a Friend from the Early Sixties: 2930.
Ode to a Grave Digger: 2529.
Ode to a Volkswagon: 1857.
Ode to Cervantes: 3884.
Ode to LILCO: 4729.
Ode to the Moosehead in Otto Moser's Saloon: 1454.
Ode to the Urge: 683, 2238.
Ode to the Yard Sale: 4206.
Ode to Walt Whitman: 2665, 4105.
Odyssey: 3002.
Oedipus: 347.
Of: 1699.
Of a Dark Room, between Their Houses: 1467.
Of All the Forms: 797.
Of Desire: 1569.
Of Ellipses and Deviations: 577.
Of Island Animals: 809.
Of Little Importance: 2783.
Of Meetings and Departures: 4461.
Of Old and New Jerusalems: 4233.
Of Rust: 2728.
Of That Fire: 2118.
Of the Death of Mary: 1397, 3726.
Of the Marriage at Cana: 1397, 3726.
Of the People: 1934.
Of the Stars: 3752.
Of the Sun: 2412.
Of Time, Men and Flowers: meditations on the Spirit of Man (Selections): 4233.
Of Your Father's Indiscretions

2917.
On the teacher's desk: 1453.
On the Threshold of the Fifth Dimension: 1370.
On the Tradition of Misdirecting Travelers: 830.
On the Train, Heading North through Florida (And Ending with a Line from Thomas Wolfe): 2261.
On the Wetting Road Always Splashing: 1491, 2144, 4307.
On This Side of the Mountains Where You Have Never Been: 1245.
On Time: 504.
On Top of Greenfield: 45.
On Trees: 1999.
On Trying to Answer the Question 'How Do You Write': 1178.
On Turning Up a Fossil in My Garden -- May, '81: 2541.
On Vocations: 4458.
On Watching Jenny Go Too Fast: 1729.
On Water: 4709.
On Writing Love Poems: 2454.
Once Again, the Combine: 653.
Once Dead, Now Dying: 3385.
Once in a While: 955, 4237.
Once in Autumn: 442.
Once More for My Lady: 4346.
Once more, once more: 2352, 3962.
Once on a Night in the Delta: A Report from Hell: 2391.
Once the Sole Province: 909.
Once upon a Time: 1674, 4313.
Once you're dead: 782.
One: 1277.
One and the Same Thing: 2094.
The One Before: 4568.
One Butterfly: 2350.
One Condemns, the Other: 2974.
One Daughter Short in Vermont: 145.
One Day: 4678.
One Day at a Time: 3248.
One Day Stands Out: 1992.
One Definition: 2118.
One Down, Two to Go: 353.
One Downsmanship: 2217.
One Drawer Full of Night: 2807.
One Evening When I Was Busy Typing, My Daughter: 4282.
One Fiber of a Hair Shirt: 3093.
One-Finger Exercises (Excerpts: II. Five Quintessences, III. , Nostoi: That Every Road Is a Royal Road): 1836.
One for Bird (An Open Line): 2044.
One full moon: 4904.
One Ghost's Pranks: 4214.
One Half (Excerpts): 4696.
One Hot Summer Night, 1947: 558.
One Last Pepperoni Pizza: 3094.
One-Legged Man: 4227.
One Light: 2405.
One Looks at Two: 1795.
One More Morning: 1970.
One Morning: 3204.
One Night: 3758.
One Night in Verona: 1670.
One of a Number of Good Intentions: 4064.
One of the Muses: 4812.
One of the Scholars: 395.
One of the Silly Things: 4337.
One of the Thieves Was Saved: 2804.
One of Us: 3512.
One of Your People: 1026.
One Patriotic Pride: 276.
One Reason for Stars: 609.
One Solution: 2615.
One Thing Calls Another Thing, and the Map of Such Calls is Our Humanness: 1615.
One Time in Mississippi: 4202.
One Tuesday my mother gave birth to me: 147, 3784.
One Walk with Kate: 376.
The One Who Can: 813.
One Year: 1450.
The Ongoing Story: 143.
Onion: 199, 2385.
Only: 1021, 4602.
Only God Can Make Me: 3821.
Only the chill: 4904.
Only the sea mist: 3694.
Only the 'young, fit and useful' allowed to leave L.A: 782.
Only These Walls: 94, 704.
Onna: 4420.
Onomatopoeia: 3395.
Onset: 2223.
Onze Heures: The Sun Is Shining: 2950.
Oooooo: 1420.
Open: 371.
The Open Book: 3482.
Open City: 2017.
Open Future: 4857.
An Open Gift: 1731.
Open Pond: 199.
An Open Prose Poem to Dave Etter: 2387.
Open Season: 653.
Open Secrets: 2719.
The Open Spaces in the Forest: 1245.
Opening: 2214, 4752.

Opening Doors: 2814.
The Opening Nonsense: 984, 4712.
The Opening of Day Includes: 967.
Opening the Nest: 1866.
Opera Singers: 4798.
Operador de Signos: 4498.
Opium: 2395.
Opium Fields in Time of War: 796.
Opium Pipe: 3453.
Opossum Spring: 1042.
The Optometrist: 3651.
Or He His Goddis Brocht: 3278.
Or, If You Were Closer, I Might Touch You: 2095.
Or None, or Few: 3294.
Or Was That When I Was Grass: 3661.
Orange Circles on Lavender Wings: 227.
Orange Lillies: 1800.
Oranges: 4206.
Orbis Terrarum Descriptio Duobis Planis Hemisphaerus Comprehesa: 4521.
The Orbit of Forgot: 1788.
Orbiting: 4968.
The Orchard: 1391.
The Orchard (Observations from a Twentieth Class Reunion): 3307.
Orchids and Blood: 1077.
Orden: 667.
Ordinary Blessings: 4214.
An Ordinary Man: 596.
Ordinary New York: 536.
Ordinary People: 1445.
Organic Gardening: 4381.
The Orient: 2701.
Orient & Flume: 2192.
Oriental Eyes: 25.
Origami: 3537.
An Origin of A-R-T: 3659.
The Origin of the Dog: 4168.
Original: 1956.
Original Sin: 4303.
Origins: 419.
Orion: 132.
Ornaments: 4798.
Orogeny: 3199, 4222.
The Orphan Bear: 3693.
The Orphan Boys at Pipe Road: 4501.
The Orphan Maker: 1878.
Orphanos: 3842.
The Orphans Construct: 3583.
Orphan's Song: 865.
Orpheus: 152, 2042.
Orpheus, Sitting at the Mouth of the Cave: 2014.
Orthopedic Surgery Ward: 2821.
Oscar's Pet Pig: 1384.
Oscar's Song: 1384.
Oscar's Whistle: 1384.
Osiris: 2004.
Ossabaw: The Inspirational Island: 4893.
Osteology of the Ants: 3092.
Oszi Kérdés: 4432.
The Other: 3830.
Other Children: 3611.
The Other Edge of June: 2834.
The Other Forest: 4609, 4640.
The Other Gospel: 237.
Other Lives of the Romantics: 1404.
Other People's Photographs: 3208.
The Other Room: 3862.
The Other Side: 4375.
The Other Woman: 347, 557, 4070.
Otherwise: 1467, 3614, 3824.
Otiose Bones: 4664.
El Otre [i.e. Otro] Tigre (Excerpt: Un tercer tigre buscaremos): 456.
El Otre [i.e. Otro] Tigre (Excerpt: We'll hunt for a third tiger now, tr. by Norman Thomas di Giovanni): 456.
El Otre [i.e. Otro] Tigre (Excerpt: We'll hunt for a third tiger now, tr. of Jorge Luis Borges): 1076.
The Ottawa: 2837.
The Ouija Board: 784.
Ouimet Canyon, Late Autumn: 2525.
Our Ashes: 369, 3105.
Our Blindness: 4636.
Our Blood is the Petrol of the World: 2580, 3675.
Our Civilisation: 1902.
Our Eldest Son Calls Home: 3527.
Our Flag Was Still There: 4483.
Our Inheritance: 2858.
Our Island: 2300.
Our Lady of the Table: 4617.
Our Latest Product (found poem): 202.
Our Mother Bled: 2796.
Our Neighbor: 3584.
Our Room: 3409.
Our Sadness: 2203.
Our shadows are very long: 1799, 2285.
Our Speaker This Morning: 4808.
Our Time: 105, 592.
Our Viscera Kill Us: 1734.
Out at Lanesville: 1351.
Out of an Old Book: 2111.
Out of Cana: 2825.
Out of Sight: 3493.
Out-of-the-Body Travel: 3512.
Out of the Closet: 177.

Preparing for Weather: 3291.
Prescription: 4487.
Presence: 315.
A Presence: 3938.
The Presence of Fire: 79.
Presences: A Poem of Decantos (Selections: I-III): 3353.
Present: 1449, 4916.
Present from Egypt: 3443.
The Presentation of Mary in the Temple: 1397, 3726.
Preservation: 3957.
Preservations: 2771.
Preserve endangered species: 782.
President says unemployment is bothersome: 782.
Prestidigitation: 4122.
A Pretty Lady: 4056.
The Previous Tenant: 4109.
The Prey: 4786.
The Price of Things: 189.
Pride of Mobile: 1971.
The Priest Confesses: 624.
Priest, Priest: 1517.
Primagravida: 1644.
The Primal Sun (Helios o Protos) (Selections: V-VI, XII-XIII, XV, XVII-XVIII): 1228, 3097, 3405.
Prime Mover: 2776.
A Primer: 4326.
Primero, se pierde la fe en Dios: 273.
The Primitives: 1644.
Primitivism: 767.
Primordial Love Poem: 145.
Princess of the Block: 3447.
A Principios de Junio: 77.
The Principle of It: 4371.
Principles of Scarcity, Doctrines of Growth: 756.
Priscilla: 1812.
The Prism: 1299.
Prison Guard: 2523.
The Prison Guard: 2302.
Prisoner: 1608.
The Prisoner: 4607.
The Prisoner of Dry Rock: 4117.
Prissyllogisms: 4537.
A Private Man Confronts His Vulgarities at Dawn: 1183.
Private Parts: 4704.
Private Vision: 2046.
The Privilege of Choice: 2881.
Prize: 2694.
The Prize: 1901.
Problem of Autobiography: Vague Recollection or Dream: 4682.
The Problem of Evil: 2553.
Process: 3062.
Processional: 783.
Prodigal Son: 2712.
Products of the Pig: 1299.
Professional Amnesia: 3131.
Professionalsim, 1983, a Parody of Donne's 'Holy Sonnet XIV': 1007.
A Professor Dreaming: 4493.
Professor F's Story: 2516.
The Program: 1223.
Progress: 25.
Progress Report on a Primitive Activity: 2970.
Progress Report to a Dead Father: 793.
Progression of Pronouns: The 60's to the 80's: 556.
The Projectionist: 478.
Prolific: 2821.
Prologue: 825, 1353, 2974.
Prologue au rêve Marin I: 466.
Prologue to a Book of American Martyrs: Some Voices: 1563.
The Prolonged Wakefulness: 4421.
Prometheus, Slightly Off-Center: 1116.
The Promise: 2119, 2363.
The Promise Keepers: 4837.
Promised Land: 1238.
Promises: 739, 2776.
Promotion: 154.
Proper Distance and Proper Time: 270.
The Properties of Water: 3504.
Properties of Wood: 3910.
Propertius, III.24: 3882.
Prophecy: 4163.
Prophet of Profit: 1885.
Prophets and Lost: 299.
Proposal to Misty: 2203.
Proposition: 4617.
Proposition IVa: 717.
Prose: 2887.
Prosody: 1079.
Prosody 101: 3387.
Prospect Park: 3980.
Prospects: 3710.
Prospects (A Wormwood Chapbook): 3710.
Protection: 1872, 4231.
Protective Custody: 2679.
Protested Delivery: 1184.
Providence: 3656.
Province: 1921.
Provincetown, Early March: 328.
Provision: 4298.
Provisions: 4290.
Provisorias Desvalijas: 3785.
The Prowler: 4617.
Proximity: 4198.
Pruning: 4612.
Przepis: 1356.
Psalm: 284, 849.
Psalm: People Power at the Die-in: 2575.
Psyche: 2520.

Rachel Had Said: 912.
Racing: 3861.
Racoon: 214.
The Racquetball War: 1355.
Radiation Art: 2555.
Radio: 1195.
The Radio Goes on Playing after We Make Love: 4329.
Radio Gothic: 1454.
Radio Hill: 3474.
Radio Park: 2013.
Radio Waves: July: 4250.
The Rafters: 1455.
Rag Player: 4581.
Rage: 4724.
Ragged Saturday: 117.
Ragtime: 1307.
Railbar: 2033.
The Railroad Bridge and Cemetery at Marine: 4864.
The Railroad Wave: 1273.
Rain: 145, 237, 911, 1593, 1752, 2832, 3949, 4361, 4566.
Rain, 1967: 2787.
The Rain Continues to Fall: 1386, 4680.
The Rain Falling Now: 1183.
The Rain Forest Massacre: 4069.
Rain in the Desert: 4557.
Rain: Liverpool, 1980: 4136.
Rain Moving In: 143.
Rain on Hemphill Valley: 717.
Rain on the Ocean: 1716.
Rain on These Trees: 2674.
Rain shatters into small-pox scars: 821.
Rain Sonnet: 3275.
The Rain That Fell in Spain: 2684.
Rain When It Fell Used to Wash Leaves: 2336.
Rainstorm: 2884.
Rainstorm on Lake Champlain: 1882.
Rainy Day Woman #1: 971.
Rainy Night: 1833.
Rainy Time People: 4159.
Raising a Child: Praising the Sand: 4607.
Raising a Relationship: 4699.
Raking Leaves: 4278.
Rallies: 1946.
Ralph Hamilton: 3993.
Raman Elegy: 2284.
Ramazan at New Phocaea: 408.
Rambler Roses: 863.
Ramón Raquello and His Orchesta: 2939.
Ranch Visit: 66.
Rancher Hermann Schrader Rejoices over the $1, 000, 000 Sale of His Property to Walt Disney, Inc: 4860.
The Rand McNally Atlas: 4389.
Randall Jarrell, 1914-1965: 1162.
Ranger / Spruce Mountain: 2590.
Rape: 1938.
A Rapid Transit: 1189.
Rapping with One Million Carabaos in the Dark: 3765.
The Rapture: 3456.
A Rare Breed: 2088.
Rasputin's Daughter: 2939.
Rast auf der Flucht in Agypten: 3726.
The Rat: 3697, 4091.
Rationalism: 4299.
Rats: 323.
Ratus Norvegicus: 3069, 3346.
Raw Autumn: 3496.
Razglednica: 2346, 3619.
Re-Crossing the Equator : 246.
Re March 3, 1980: 4695.
Re Narcissus: 4695.
Reach Out and Touch: 157.
Reaching for Grief: 714.
Reaching the Audience: 3783.
Reaction at the Site of a Field Hospital: 4148.
Read This When I Die (Again) Please: 2601.
The Reading Club: 1610.
Reading It Wrong: 1644.
Reading the Confucian Odes on a Cement Patio: 3687.
Reading the Japanese Poet Issa (Berkely, 1978): 1874, 3021, 3506.
Reading the Letter: 818.
Reading the Names of the War Dead (Riverside Church, December 1969): 360.
Reading the Obituaries: 1509.
Reading to Students: 4381.
Ready for Business: 3803.
Reaganatomics: 2368.
Real: 782.
Real Dreams: 929.
Real Estate: 758.
Real Estate: A Group of Poems: 758.
Real Hair: 2386.
The Real Hunky-Dory: 1643.
Real Life: 3033.
La Realidad, y el Deseo (framentos): 4498.
Reality: 1720, 2158, 4163.
Reaper: 1288.
Reaping: 3400.
Reaping This Year's Harvest: 4978.
Rear WindoW Vision: 903.
The Reason I Stay: 433.
Reasons For: 708.
Rebecca and Ann: 4000.
Rebels: 782.
Reborn Again: 2446.
Rebus: 1085.

Receiving Christ: 3310.
Recent Acquisition: 2553.
The Recent Popular Interest in thanatology: 802.
Recess: 1889.
Recessional: 4213.
Recette: 446, 1356.
Recipe: 866, 1356, 3296.
Recipe for a Well-Done Robot: 2746.
Recitation: 2180.
Reckoning: 3966.
Reclaimed Shore, Schleswig-Holstein: 4942.
Reclaiming Wetland, near the Mouth of the Connecticut: 3364.
Reclining Woman with Upturned Skirt: 2982.
Recluse: 3252, 4617.
Recollecting Jasmine: 4024.
Recollection: Before You Sleep Come Home to Yourself: 1876.
A Recollection of Caribbea: 3886.
Reconciled: 3493.
Reconciliation: 3953.
Reconciliations: 3387.
Records: 1150.
Recovery: 347, 1631, 4825.
The Recruit: 787.
Recurring Dream: Leaving the Valley Where I Grew Up: 3384.
Recycling: 2181.
Red Accordion: An Immigrant Song: 3303.
Red Beans & Rice: 1591.
Red Bird in a White Tree: 3849.
Red Cross Camp: South Mexico: 776.
Red Giant: 491.
Red Giant, Black Dwarf or Degenerate: 1818.
Red Is the Knowledge (Excerpt): 397.
The Red Kitchen: 1553.
Red Label: 2766.
Red Light: 233, 3234.
Red on the Outside: 3004.
The Red Pond: 113.
Red Seeds Opening in the Shade: 2930.
The Red Setter: 1875.
Red Sky at Night: 3535.
Red Stone: 2091.
The Red Studio: 2821.
Red Tomatoes: 517, 3970.
The Red Wig: 2930.
Redemption Dream I: 3113.
Redemption Dream II: 3113.
Redoble Solo: 893.
Redstone, Colorado: 4448.
The Reductio: 1752.
Redwing: 756.
Redwoods above Jacoby Creek: 558.
Reeling Back the Saffron: 1494.
The Reflection: 3027.
Reflections: 1439.
Reflections at Age 50: 2781.
Reflections of a Retired Activist: 1274.
Reflections on a Bowl of Kumquats, 1936: 746.
Reflections on a Dead Bird: 3367.
Reflections on Violence: 3980.
Reflective: 96.
Refugees: 954.
The Refugees: 4431.
Refugees at Avila Beach: 3779.
A Refund: 4299.
Refuse Dogma: 1439.
Regalia: 4049.
Regarding L-: 2203.
Regarding Shoes: 4816.
Regreso: 2806.
Rehearsal Dinner: 475.
Rehearsing: 4518.
Rehearsing the Migration: 4166.
The Reinvention of Action Photography: 4375.
Relación de Tripulantes Que Participaron en el Naufragio: 3437.
Related to the Sky: 99.
The Relationship of Paranoia to Deafness: 3156.
Relationships: 4214.
Relative: 2898.
Relativity: 2441, 3558.
Releasing the Minnows: 2094.
Reliable Heat: 4149.
Relief Map of Africa: 2385.
Religion: 289.
Religion in America: 2468.
The Religion of Art (1 Feb '58): 1623.
Religion Part I: 3751.
Religious: 1615.
The Reluctant Dinner: 13.
Reluctant Love Poem: 240.
The Reluctant Magician: 1945.
Remainder One: 3185.
Remains: 1856.
Rembrandt: Self Portrait: 3017.
The Remedy: 3536.
Remember the World: 2154.
Remembering: 3345.
Remembering Brady at Gettysburg: 4166.
Remembering Captain Cook at Nootka: 2927.
Remembering César Vallejo: 1245.
Remembering last night's full

sky of stars: 842.
Remembering Rosalind: 4759.
Remembering the Fifties: 2468.
Remembering the Present: 4593.
Remembering Venice: 2225.
Remembrance: 2745.
Remembrance of Childhood: Itch: 1592.
A Remembrance of Things Past: 4109.
Reminders: 476.
Remission: 3387.
Remnants: 4951.
Remodeling the Hermit's Cabin: 717.
Remordimiento en Traje de Noche: 704.
Remous: 3485.
Rendezvous: 612.
The Rendezvous: 1196.
Rendezvous at the Coffee Mill: 2530.
A Rendezvous with God: 2115.
Rending Cars: 444.
Renewal Reminds Me of the End: 4502.
Le Reniement de Saint Pierre: 266.
Reno Nevada: 3107.
Renoir: 4683.
Renovation: 590.
Renovations for a Sister: 4938.
Rented Rooms: 4219.
Renunciation: 1435, 3178.
Repairman on the Eiffel Tower: 490.
Repentances: 4271.
Replacing the Elegy: 3347.
Replanting a Garden: 4636.
Reply in Kind: 1027.
Reply to a Critic: 561.
Reply to Chang Shao-Fu, the Keeper of Archives: 4668, 4670.
Report Card Time: 3468.
Report from a Besieged City (Warsaw 1982): 1948, 3021.
Report from a Town under Siege: 1948, 3825.
Report from Iowa: 4863.
Reprieve: 4899.
Reprise: 3633.
Reprobate: 4348.
Reptilian Crack-up: 4090.
Request: 1819.
Requiem: 2367, 2438, 4651.
Requiem After Seventeen Years: 417, 3649.
Requiem Etudes: 2132.
Requiem for Cory Batt of Rural Melbeta, Nebraska: 2387.
Requiem for Poetry: 368, 1834.
Requiem, Four to the Bar: 1562.
Requiescat: 3139.
Rerun: 4299.
Rescue: 4417.
Rescue Mission: 4458.
Research: 3020.
Reserved books, Reserved land, Reserved flight, And still property is theft: 4705.
The Reservoir: 62.
The Resident: 4135.
Residua: 2800.
Resolution: 3686, 4617.
Resolving Differences: 3873.
The Resort (Long Beach, NY, 1982): 4127.
Respiratory Ode: 2222.
Respite in Minor Key: 4193.
Response to a Letter from France: 1183.
Responses to a Class Questionnaire: What Is Your Career Goal: 591.
Responsibilities: 4801.
Responsibility: 1207.
Responsible Gardening: 824.
Rest on the Flight into Egypt: 1397, 3726.
The Restaurant Window: 3124.
ReSteration: 3193.
Restitution: 368, 1834.
Restlessness on All Sides and Angels: 2580, 4956.
Restoring the Chateau of the Marquis De Sade: 1940.
Restoring the Wood: 596.
Résumé of a Scrapegoat: 531.
Resurrection: 778, 4303.
The Resurrection: 596.
Retention of Angels: 3339.
The Retired Pastor Revises the Catechism: 756.
Retracing: 671.
Retraite: 3485.
Retreat: 576, 3485, 4829.
Retreat in Spring: 2906.
Retreat to the Country of Pure Drought: 2721.
Retroactive Suit for Damages: 752.
Retrospectiva: 4599.
Return: 1031.
The Return: 1968, 4592, 4663.
Return from the Desert: 2771.
The Return: Intensive Care: 2536.
Return of the Titans: 2574.
Return of the Wolves: 1236.
Return to Sicily: 1078.
Return to Tundra at Bighorn Flats: for Anne: 3906.
Return to Ystrad Mynach: 3229.
Returning: 818, 3729, 4464.
Returning Alive from Diverse Routes and Far Travels: 2549.
Returning from the Mayan

The Second Day: 3148.
Second Growth: 1799.
A Second Interview with Mrs. F: 1.
Second Meeting with a Father: 81, 3205.
The Second of Perfect Sleep: 2877.
Second Poem from Nicaragua Libre: War Zone: 2241.
Second Prelude to the Monastery: 1183.
Second-rate Republics: 3401.
Second Sight: 3159.
Second Story: 4225.
A Second Story Window: 574.
The Second Sun: 4513.
The Second Waitress: 3618.
The Second Witness: 3783.
Secondhand Theology: 359.
The Secrecy of Ceilings: 2899.
The Secret: 2001, 3715, 4122.
Secret Love: 2347.
The secret scents: 4904.
Secretary of Armageddon: 3348.
Secrets: 2954.
La Secuela: 3424.
See How the Roads Are Strewn: 2004.
The Seed Catalogue: 1933.
Seeds in the Palm of My Hand: 1767, 3044.
The Seeds That Come through the Air: 3730.
Seeing My Breath on the Air at Summer's End: 2245.
Seeing Things: 476.
Seeing Wild Horses: 2493.
Seeing Wind: 4127.
Seekers: 1359, 3179, 3722, 4917.
Seem to have cash-flow problems: 782.
Seer: 4005.
Segno: 4845.
Seiche: 4845.
Seining for Carp: 2877.
Seismic Apology from Diablo Canyon: 3797.
Selciato e Rotaie: 1256.
Selecting a Reader: 624.
Self: 4682.
Self-Disgust and Resolution / Shaving at 40: 1042.
Self-Help: 4726.
Self-Love: 2505.
Self Made in Bloomington: 2394.
Self-Portrait: 1575.
Self Portrait Approaching Promontory, Utah: 3470.
Self-Portrait As a Still Life: 3264.
Self-Portrait from a Photograph: 3157.
Self-Portrait in Painted Glass: 4806.
Self-Portrait with Camellia Branch: 1391.
Self-Portrait with Hand Microscope: 1019.
Self-Sermon on the Hill: 2536.
The Self Trying to Leave the Body That It Is: 2186.
Selling satellites to private corps: 782.
Semillas en latas plantitas: 3737.
Seminar: Dominoes, Zebras, and the Full Moon: 3783.
Semper Fi: 1666.
Sempiternal: 1510.
Sena: 4731.
Send Him to Play: 2075.
A Sense of Place: 3826.
The Sense of Unending: 2031.
Sensibility: 414.
Sensitive Ears: 4431.
Sentences after <u>Defence of Poetry</u>: 1646.
Sentences for Matthew Ready, Series II (Excerpt: 104): 1646.
Sentiment for an Old Notion: 2608.
Sentimental Education: 4639.
The Sentimental Woman: 1378.
Sentiments in the Evening: 2667.
The Separate Dead: 2118.
The Separate Notebooks: Pages concerning the Years of Independence: 3021, 3506.
Separating the Bullcalf from Its Mother at Linden Valley Farm, May 1982: 2465.
The Separation: 3252.
The Separation Agreement: 4226.
Separations: 1107.
September: 4741.
September 1, 1979: 3545.
September 1, 1983: 3612.
September Sabbath: 4479.
September/The Paradox of Harvest: 2436.
September Threadbare: 3191.
September Wind: 2042.
A Sequence: 772.
Sequence toward a Beginning: 3849.
Ser Mujer: 3773.
The Sermon: 526, 1383.
Sermon in a Greek Orthodox Church: 4554.
Sermons in Stone: 2057.
Serpent Country: 83.
The Serpent, Urging: 1314.
The Servant of Snow: 4565.
Sestina in Celebration of the Voice of Johnny Cash: 4776.
Sestina of the Terrestrial

Shorter: 3967.
Shorty: 1265.
Shoshone Father: 88.
Shoulders of Tropical Rain: 302.
A Shout at Morning: 4845.
The Shrew: 561.
Shrike: 2620.
Shrine: 3093.
Shutter Speed: 1/500 Second, Distance: Infinity: 1116.
Siamese in Sunlight: 3545.
Sibyl Takes to the Sky: 3805.
A Sicilian Father: 80.
Sick: 576.
Sick Days: 1183.
Sick room window: 1530.
Sickness: 118.
Sicktime: 1445.
Sidari Village: 542.
Side Streets: 4740.
Sideshow Sestine: 1899.
Sidewalk pools: 842.
Sidney Lanier's Anniversary, 1868: 2082.
Siege: 3319.
Siege at Stony Point: 1704.
Siesta: 2609.
The Sigh: 2414.
Sighs So Deep They Seem to Speak of Death: 726.
A Sighting of Whales: 3796.
Sign: 3356.
Sign for My Father, Who Stressed the Bunt: 464.
Sign Language: 1736, 3577.
Signals: 3729.
Signing Your Poetry: 104.
Signs: 2555, 2586.
Siguenza: 1243.
Silence: 1528, 2596, 3458.
Silence (Haiku): 1828.
Silence Grows: 598.
A Silence Lesson: 1563, 2289.
Silencing the Frogs: 1454.
Silent: 2118, 4393.
Silent at Her Window: 1799, 4667.
The Silent Clouds: 4163.
Silent Movies: 4000.
Silent Sounds: 2976.
Silhouette: 801.
Silly Goose: 3974.
Silly Jim: 3634.
Silver: 4282.
The Silver Bell: 3460.
Simon the Super-Realist: 3616.
Simon's Dream: 1623.
A Simple Exchange: 2771.
The Simple Life: 962.
Simple Rituals: 4355.
Simple Rivers: 3066.
The Simple Scale: 3980.
Simplicity: 1571.
Sin Raíces Hay Flor?: 644.
Since Our Beginnings: 929.
Since Our Dog Died: 962.
Since Then: 2341, 3346.
Since You Have Gone Away: 735, 4668.
Sincere Liars: 3610.
Sincretizando: 685.
The Singers: 2830, 3545.
Singing: 4375.
Singing to Sleep: 1784.
Singing Up the Snow: 4375.
Single: 1138.
A Single Leaf: 3498.
A Single Life: 1319.
Singsong, Whatever It Means: 1615.
Sinister Clowns: 1077.
Sins of Our Fathers: 4616.
Sirens: 237.
Sister Annamary as Mermaid: 4758.
A Sister by the Pond: 1778.
Sister Elizabeth of Warsaw: 3223.
Sister Mary Appassionata Lectures the Anatomy Class: Doctrines of the Nose: 756.
Sister Mary Appassionata Lectures the Eighth-Grade Boys and Girls on the Life and Death of St. Teresa: 756.
Sister Mary Appassionata Lectures the Eighth Grade Boys and Girls: The Family Jewels: 756.
Sister Mary Appassionata Lectures the History Class: Life of the Saint: 756.
Sister Mary Appassionata Lectures the Home Ec. Class: The Feast: 756.
Sister Mary Appassionata Lectures the Quantitative Analysis Class: Proof of the Existence of the Soul: 756.
Sister Mary Appassionata's Lecture to the Creative Writing Class: The Evangelist: 756.
Sister Mary Appassionata's Lecture to the Eighth Grade Boys and Girls: Flesh Willing, Spirit Weak: 756.
Sister Mary Appassionata's Lecture to the Eighth Grade Boys and Girls: To Punish the Cities: 756.
Sister to Brother: 3347.
Sisters: 338, 3826.
The Sisters: 853.
Sisters in Winter: 1764.
Sit-Out: 4860.
Sit Tibi Terra Levis: 238.
Sitting: 4716.
Sitting in My: 3075.

Arrival: 3103.
Some friends of ours: 782.
Some Glad Day We'll Fly Away: 2223.
Some good news for a change: 782.
Some Happiness: 4891.
Some Laws of Averages: 802.
Some Painful Butterflies Pass Through: 1505.
Some Permanent Ground: 433.
Some poet said all straight lines intersect: 782.
Some Questions for a Boy So Badly Burned in a Prairie Fire That He Had to Tell His Doctors Who He Was: Otis, Kansas: 1020.
Some Reflections Beginning with the Disproportionate Length of My Feet: 683, 2238.
Some say today's a repeat of the thirties: 782.
Some Smart Remarks on the Closing of the Hiram Walker Distillery i Peoria: 1273.
Some Things a Prisoner Knew: 865.
Some Things Better Off Said: 4191.
Some Things Remember Us: 4378.
Somebody's Aunt Out Swabbing Her Birdbath: 2699.
Someday: 3281.
Somehow We Survive: 562.
Someone calls, someone answers: 1154.
Someone Else: 4034.
Someone Is Coming: 1864.
Someone mentioned it: 4248.
Someone stepping off a mountain: 3376.
Someone Stole the Watch My Mother Gave Me: 1894.
Someone You Don't Know: 4239.
Somerset, Remembering: 364.
Something about Fruit: 4968.
Something about My Childhood: 4881.
Something Broke: 4838.
Something Decided: 370.
Something Different Altogether: 1476.
Something I Cannot Name Has Come Close to Me: 1016.
Something I Couldn't Tell You: 3511.
Something I Was Thinking About: 4239.
Something Impersonal Like Handel or Golf: 2909.
Something Let Go: 2611.
Something Like Spinks: 3862.
Something Remains: 623.
Something worse than being old or poor: 3610.
Sometimes: 2907, 3039, 4853.
Sometimes at Night: 3515.
Sometimes He Longs For: 2580, 4956.
Sometimes I like to enter the house: 4418.
Sometimes Music Rises: 1111.
Sometimes the telephone rings at night: 2491.
Somewhere: 1674, 2580, 3675, 4505.
Somewhere Else: 3638, 4568.
Somewhere in France, there's a city: 2049.
The Somnambulists: 1644.
Sonata of My Approach to Public Readings: 4724.
Sonbahar: 2327.
Song: 732, 972, 985, 1799, 2904, 4859.
A Song: 424.
Song (Ch'i shih): 1799, 2636.
Song (Ting Feng-po): 1799, 2636.
Song for a Time of Year: 4034.
Song for Disembodied Voice: 717.
Song for Montreal: 1352.
A Song for Priests: 1547.
Song for Private Charlie Fitzgerald: 4718.
Song for Sisyphus: 3906.
Song from the Intensive Care Unit: 3124.
The Song I Have for You Is One Befitting Your Gravity: 1564.
Song of Frustration of the Dreamer Child: 2374, 2475.
Song of Green Water and the Singing Girl: 1799, 2603.
Song of Love: 3726, 4630.
Song of the Blue China Horseman: 1323.
Song of the Disaster: 4068.
Song of the Drowned Man: 849.
The Song of the Mill: 2521.
Song of the Women of Yueh 5: 935, 2604.
A Song of Transmutation: 3400.
A Song of Xipe Totec: 2844.
Song (Ting Feng-po): 1799, 2636.
A Song to be Whispered: 3254.
Song While Arranging Jasmine and Jewelweed: 1617.
Songs: 691, 2468.
Songs for the Death of the Hero: 4474.
The Songs in the Branches: 2226.
Songs of the Bluely Farers: 1125.
Songs of the Typing School: 379.

Spring at the Cottage: 3336.
Spring Bells: 2251.
Spring Burning: 176.
Spring Daughter: 80.
Spring Dress: 3449.
The Spring Father Stopped Snowing: 2944.
Spring Fed: 948.
Spring in Idaho: 3423.
Spring in the City: 1225.
Spring of Winter: 3792.
Spring on Sunset Blvd: 3218.
Spring Psalm: 2119.
Spring Rain: 1874.
Spring rain: 4904.
Spring Sayings: 1665.
Spring Showers: 821.
Spring Spiders: 3333.
Spring Stretch: 4258.
Spring That Splinters Like Stone: 3164.
Spring Thaw: 1103.
The Spring the Old, the Lyric: 4495.
Spring Time Warmth: 2311.
The Spring Tour: 4431.
Spring Training: 2810, 4337.
A Spring Vision: 130.
Spring Walks: 1564.
Spring Wood: 3701.
Springtime: 82, 3026.
The Springtime Tour: 2124.
A Spruce in Vermont: 3500.
Spuyten Duyvil: 3070.
The Squanicook Eclogues: 1685.
Squier in Nicaragua: 650, 800.
The Squirrel on the Limb: 3754.
Squirrel Season: 4148.
SS may be cut off at 67 years: 3610.
St. . . .: See also: Saint . . .
St. Barnabas: 4035.
St. Brendan's Prayer: 750.
St. Cecilia: 1634.
St. Fanourious: 2509.
St. Francis: 457.
St. Franics of the Suburbs: 1349.
St. John of the Cross in the Carmelite Priory, Toledo, 1578: 737.
St. Jude Pray for Us, Almost without Hope: 2434.
St. Kilda Amen: 3015.
St. Mark's Place Poem: 1401.
St. Paul's Union Church and Cemetery, Seiberlingsville, Pennsylvania: 1562.
St. Peter's Denial: 266, 2891.
Staffrider: 3360.
The Stage Grows Dark: 1918, 3524.
A Stage You Are Passing Through: 4511.
Staircase: 420.
Staircase Riposte: 2638.
Stalin's Breath Perfume, 1941: 3223.
Stamina: 3843.
Stand by Me: 4232.
Stand Off: 2398.
Stand-Up Legacies: 392.
Standing before a Lit Menorah: 2163.
Standing Before and Standing About: 4095.
Stanzas: 963.
Star Children: 3936.
Star Dancer: 3916.
Starfish: 457.
Staring Doesn't Help: 1694.
The Starlight Lounge: 1086.
Starling: 4728.
The Stars: 2374, 3324.
Stars Are the Dead: 3729.
Starting a Compost Heap at Forty: 2884.
Starting Early: 179.
Starting Out for the Difficult World: 977.
Starting Rotation: 1293.
The Starved: 1604.
The Starving Poet to His Love: 2638.
State Fishkill on Shirey Bay, 1963: 590.
State Highway over Brasstown Gap: 4014.
The State of an Immigrant: 1254.
State of the Art: 3526.
State of the Economy: 4617.
State of the Nation: 1005.
Statement: 1752, 1859.
Statement Preliminary to the Invention of Solace: 3783.
Static: 459.
Station House: 3963.
Station Island: 1903.
Station Island (Selections: IV, VII-IX): 1903.
The Stations of the Woods: 1432.
A Statue of Gandhiji: 3651.
Statue of Liberty: 3540.
A Statue of Mary: 1679.
Stay Put: 150.
Staying: 422.
Staying Awake with Darwin: 126.
Staying under Water Too Long: 3284.
Steal the Bacon: 2795.
Stealing: 3753.
Stealing Ice, 1948: 3474.
The Steam Tunnels under Harvard: 596.
Steamboat Days: 1061.
Steaming: 3379.
Steel: 3438.

Study in Stained Glass: 3148.
A Study of Goldb---h's Poetry in Terms of His Century's Artifacts: Prefatory Notes: 1615.
Stump: 3507.
Stung: 3968.
Style 7, Alive, Alive: 4672.
The Sub-Sub Librarian's Sestina: 2739.
The Submission of Allan: 3761.
Submitting: 3505.
The Subnormal Girl with a Cat: 591.
A Subscriber Requests: 2638.
Substation: 4674.
The Substitute for Time: 2405.
Substitutions: 2181.
Subway Advertisement: 3334.
Success: 4505.
A Successful Summer: 3980.
Successfully: 2934.
The Succubus: 3804.
Such Beauty: 3464.
Such Flowers: 912.
Such Small Things: 3607.
Such Summers: 85.
Suckers for Truth: 3917.
Sudbury Blues: 1398.
A Sudden Turn of Weather: 2605.
Suddenly: 2363.
Suddenly the Wind Ceased: 117, 3267.
Suffering Servant: 605.
Sufis: 3151.
Sugarcane: 3265.
The Suicide: 1207, 1872.
Suicide Attempt: 2609.
Suicide in White: 820.
Suicide Squeeze: 1293.
Suicidio: 27.
Suing a Politician: 841.
The Suit: 889.
Sumac and Lacrimae Rerum: 227.
The Sumac in Ohio: 4903.
Sumacs: 152.
Summer: 2309.
Summer (Yaz): 1359, 3595, 3722, 4917.
Summer 1964/'O, Freedom over Me': 4307.
Summer afternoon: 2229.
Summer Cherries: 1796.
Summer Collecting, On-Island: 3657.
Summer Coyote's: 1794.
Summer Evening in the King David Hotel: 81, 2580.
Summer Evening in the Suburbs, Waiting for a Movie: 1180.
Summer House: 3258.
Summer House: December: 2231.
Summer Image: 4714.
Summer in Winter: 1079.
Summer Litter: 4469.
Summer Morality: 3623.
Summer night: 180.
Summer Night, Fire Island, Escaping from a Party: 1471.
The Summer of The Wild Artichokes: 311.
The Summer Rentals: 1792.
Summer Rises: 2002.
Summer Sleep: 193.
Summer Snow: 628.
Summer Solstice, New York City: 3289.
Summer Storm: 1792.
Summer Sunday: 1069.
Summer Tones: 1431.
Summer Vacation: 1994, 2129.
Summer Wedding: 338.
Summer (Yaz): 1359, 3595, 3722, 4917.
Summerfield's Daughter: 3398.
The Summerhouse: 4270.
Summer's End: 2686.
Summer's last evening: 1799, 2285.
A Summing Up: 2580, 3563.
Sun: 237.
The Sun and I: 1800.
The Sun in March: 3398.
Sun, Sea, Rain, Rain Season, Port Townsend, Washington: 2396.
Sun Up: 334.
Sun Woman, Anno 1632, Kolwerdam, Holland: 2780.
Sunbath: 3194.
The Sunbather: 2819.
Sundae Mourning, Blue Cigar: 1836.
Sundanced: 748.
Sunday: 1068, 2468, 2566, 2740.
Sunday Afternoon: 715, 3119.
Sunday Afternoon Sleep: 1223.
Sunday at Home: 1097.
Sunday Baking: 3352.
Sunday Chicken for Mrs. Minnis: 1557.
Sunday Dinner: 2814, 3271.
The Sunday Drunk: 2819.
Sunday Graveyard: 4257.
Sunday Greens: 1143.
Sunday, Looking Westward: 746.
Sunday Morning Mutation: 229.
Sunday Morning Nap (West Point Chapel): 360.
Sunday Morning Sermon: 2719.
The Sunday News: 1583.
Sunday School Picnic: 3937.
Sunday Sermon, Wulari Ward: 4305.
Sunday Service: 4032.
Sunday Walk in the Crescent: 1743.
Sundial: 1671.

Thin Ice: 2774.
Thin Tin Wood Wind (Fish Creek West): 2377.
The Thing Is to Not Let Go of the Vine -- Johnny Weissmuller: 2402.
Things: 3080.
Things Are Worse Than Bad: 3883.
Things Falling: 500.
Things I Didn't Tell Madjid: 3606.
Things My Mother Never Had to Tell Me: 3239.
The Things of August: 2012.
The Things of René Magritte--I: 382, 3965.
Things of the Earth: 1741, 4171.
Things That Happen Only If You Watch: 4042.
The Things That Last: 4923.
Things to Do at Jane's Cabin: 3758.
Think about It: 1136, 1211.
Thinking About History: 2442.
Thinking of Cuba: 4232.
Thinking of Milton in Rome: 238.
Thinking of Them: 4515.
Thinking of You As a Child: 1064.
Thinkspeak: 782.
Third & Townsend: 3432.
The Third Culture: 4962.
The Third Out: 1293.
Third Page News, or the Rent Problem: 4163.
The Third Rail of Beatitude: 36.
Third Unit, State Hospital: 3660.
A Thirst for Music: 1099.
The Thirst of Turtles: 2699.
Thirteen: 2931.
Thirteen Lines for Stephen: 4014.
Thirteen pious women: 3610.
Thirteen Ways of Looking at a Jogger: 1817.
Thirteen-Year Old Girl: 1789.
Thirteenth Floor, Please: 3177.
Thirties/Eighties: 3424.
Thirty: 2483.
Thirty Below, Canton, Nebraska: 560.
Thirty Miles West of Chicago: 2611.
This and Us: 4175.
This Autumn Hillside: 3190.
This Bank Protected by Silent Alarm: 1736.
This Battered Lamp: 3429.
This Body: 1023.
This century may be all over: 782.
This Could Only Happen in Canada: 1476.
This Country: 1000.
This Evening As Usual: 3607.
This Going Forth: 3215.
This green, unsinkable wreath: 3429.
This Grief So New: 4240.
This House, My Garden: 4719.
This Is a Letter to Rachel Jean Greenough on the Occasion of Her 18th Birthday, February 17, 2001: 4332.
This is an Elegy for Charlie Harry -- Pilot, Agent, Bounty Hunter, Friend: 4776.
This Is for Every Man Who Licks His Shoulder During Solitary Sex . . .: 2402.
This Is How: 2656.
This Is It: 426.
This is no way to begin the year: 3879.
This Is Not a Conversation for the Telephone: 216, 4687.
This Is the Way It Will Be: 351.
This Is Where We Are: 3483.
This Island: 2653.
This Journey on Bach's Birthday: 4864.
This Kingdom, the Earth: 236, 516.
This Land Is Your Land: 4894.
This Life: 1109.
This My Emissary: 1072.
This Night Is Ours: 4484.
This Old Man Reclines on the Field of Heaven: 4359.
This Ontological Question about Susan: 264.
This Poem: 3512.
This Poem Again: 4221.
This poem is small but it has its power: 3245.
This Season: 705.
This Town: 962.
This trip: 171.
This Valley: 23.
This View of the Meadow: 1562.
This Weather Is No Womb: 4502.
This Window: 129.
This Winter: 4412.
This Winter or Any Other: 2729.
This Woman: 92.
This World: 1615, 4728.
This Year: 2112.
The Thistle Feeder: 4115.
Thistles: 1218.
Thomas Merton: First Visit to Gethsemane: 2082.
Thomas More: 228.

Thoreau on the Lam: 3005.
Those Corridors: 3021, 3506.
Those is that: 1694.
Those Pico Della Mirandola Eyes: 1445.
Those Stars: 1964.
Those Who Cry Out: 4616.
Those who devise our nuclear weapons: 3610.
Those Who Have Disappeared: 1250, 1719, 3524.
Those who most need: 782.
Those Who Sing: 477, 4657.
The Thought: 2363.
Thoughtless Doth: 1707.
Thoughts of a Senator Kissing Babies: 991.
Thoughts of Loneliness: 3179.
Thoughts While Reading _The Sand Reckoner_: 4431.
Thousands of Small Hands: 3991.
Thrall: 2380.
Threads: Rosa Luxemburg from Prison (Selection: Part I. Wronke, Spring 1917): 854.
Three A.M., Then and Now: 1696.
Three Anatomical Points: 1615.
Three Aunts: 818.
Three brothers leaving the movie: 842.
Three Darknesses: 4682.
Three Fathom Cove: 100.
The Three-Headed Woman: 348.
Three Horses: 4133.
Three Journeys: 2001.
Three Moods of Winter: 4364.
Three or Four Shades of Blues: 2807.
Three or Four Shades of Blues (2): 2807.
Three-Part Requiem: 3480.
Three Percently: 2253.
Three Pieces for Karl Radek, 1885-1937: 3880.
Three Poems on Lines from Emily Dickinson's letters: 4541.
Three Portraits by Nadar: 2066.
Three Poverties: 3126.
Three Reasons Why It Is Called Isla Mujeres (Quintanna Roo, Mexico): 4689.
Three Rivers, Ten Years: an Anthology of Poems from _Three Rivers Poetry Journal_: 885.
Three Sorties Out of the City Walls: 2580.
Three Things: 2013.
Three Tiny Poems: 4457.
Three Turns in the Wind: 189.
Three views: August from This Town: 4787.
Three ways of Following Snowshoe Tracks: 3177.
Three White Vases: 4390.
Threshold: 3093, 3842.
Throes: 2617.
Through a maze of lilies: 2700.
Through a Tree at Night: 1596.
Through Bifocals: 996.
Through Breuil's Eyes: 1264.
Through Kitchen Windows: 3552.
Through the Arches: St. Severin's: 2680.
Throwing a Frog from a Bridge: 1682.
Throwing popcorn: 2390.
Throwing the Racetrack Cats at Saratoga: 3651.
Thrown Out: 2581.
Thruway: 3997.
Thunderstorm in New York: 322.
Thus Far and No Further: Updating Conrad: 299.
Thwarted: 4735.
Tía Ester (a song of remembrance): 4433.
The Tibetan Princess: 297, 4977.
Tick Tock: 2530.
Tidbits: 3248.
Tides: 4603.
Tidy Work: 3712.
Tied Up under Trees: 2877.
El Tiempo Pasa en Vano: 77.
Tiempo y Muerte: 3786.
Tierra y Luna: 2665.
Tiger: 365, 477.
A tiger leapt at me: 59.
Tiger Tiger: 3709.
The Tiger's Birthday: 1118.
The Tight Rope Artist: 2847.
Tight Space: 3952.
Tightrope: 3464.
Tigre: 365.
Timber Sales: 3612.
Timberline: 3305.
Time: 758, 782, 4903.
Time and the Weather: 756.
Time-Binding: 1623.
Time Enough: 2718.
The Time I Drank with Allen Ginsberg: 2645.
Time Is More Than Money: 2356.
Time Loves a Hedgerow: 3607.
A Time of Apocalypse: 1857.
Time to Change: 2686.
A Time to Protest: 4606.
Time Warped: 2684.
Time Watching: 2804.
Time When the Day Ended: 585.
The Time When the World Was Different: 2507.
Time Zone: 4477.
Times: 1644.
Time's End: 3605.
Timestep: 2249.

Timetables: 1335.
Timothy: 4273.
Tin-Fong-Po: 4353.
Tin Shoulders: 2067.
The Tinker Camp: 2091.
Tiny Romance: 3981.
Tipplers: 1846.
Tiptoeing through the Laurencing Neutrons: 4749.
Tiro esta comarca de valores: 828.
Tissue: 362.
Title Page: 3726, 4630.
Titmouse, Juncos & Chickadees: 1902.
TM: 1330.
To a Bunch of Rotten Bananas: 4431.
To a Child Bride at the Rose Lane Tourist: 3495.
To a Classics Professor (1806): 2019.
To a Coquette: 2214.
To a Daughter: 1506.
To a Daughter, Writing Her First Poem: 1755.
To a Daydream: 3179.
To a Friend: 935, 2604.
To a Grandfather, Veteran of World War II: 2259.
To a Hard Core Porn Film Leading Man: 2332.
To a Home Computer Owner: 2400.
To a Kid Who Believes in Astrology: 1172.
To a Linguist: 2146.
To a Local TV Anchor Man: 2400.
To a Pocket Calculator: 2962.
To a Rapist: 1696.
To a Rebel: 4595.
To a Southern Lady: 2842.
To a Young Lover: 3997.
To a Young Woman Considering Suicide: 4002.
To a Youngish Professor Who Has Waxed Eloquent over Certain Students: 1764.
To Adjust to the Sky: 3148.
To Alan: 2247.
To Alexander Blok: 39, 107.
To All the Patriotic Housewives: 1684.
To an Actress Afraid of a Dog: 3051.
To an Artist Going Blind: 4179.
To an Old Friend, at Crossroads: 3025.
To an Old Hotel in Quito: 3069.
To and Fro Lightly: 2667.
To Anna: 261.
To Anne from Sylvia: 1417.
To Argue the Laurel: 3769.
To Aurora D: 1388.
To Awaken in Two Places Distant As an Animal: 1059.
To be Icarus and fall wings aflame into the burning buttercups: 1799, 2285.
To Begin: 3350.
To Boom Boom: 3095.
To Build a Quiet City in His Mind: 4608.
To Bulcsu Bertha, with Profound Respect: 2932, 3467.
To Chris: 4144.
To clearly understand: 782.
To Dobbs Ferry with Sylvia Plath: 1581, 3563.
To Dobbs Ferry with Sylvia Plath (in Hebrew): 3563.
To Eat: 2688.
To Edward Dahlberg: 2338.
To: Emily in Eternity, Re: Death Whose If Is Everlasting: 2107.
To Encounter Ezra Pound -- Posthumous Instructions: 816, 2341.
To Escape the High Country: 3906.
To Face Her: 2672.
To Flynn: 4465.
To Giacomo Leopardi in the Sky: 4900.
To Her Unveiling: 2250.
To Here and Back: 3579.
To Hollywood's Hunks: 2400.
To Julia de Burgos: 322, 584.
To Juliet and Mae Rogers for Whom No Apology Is Needed: 2856.
To Linger in the Bronx Unable to Die: 329.
To Live in Another Country Is to Suffer the Consequences of Our Own: 2645.
To Look at Nature: 1205.
To Lose La Trek: 4845.
To Market: 1699.
To Miss X: 2842.
To Mother: On Your Concern: 3085.
To My Brother, Lately Missed: 793.
To My Daughter: 849.
To My Father, Killed in a Hunting Accident: 22.
To My Mother: 1302.
To My Poetry Teacher (In Memoriam): 1522.
To My Student Who Said He Wanted to Lead a Coherent Life: 1183.
To My Students, on Reading Hopkins: 1071.
To My Teacher L.K: 368, 1834.
To My Underwater Moon: 4614.

Two Days after the Toadfrog: 4975.
Two Deaths: 3656.
The Two Dogs: 1354, 2117.
Two Drinking Songs: 4976.
Two Elements: 3031, 4971.
Two Evenings: 2645.
Two Family Men in Late Summer: 2877.
Two Figures: 4070.
Two Figures in Mt. Hope Cemetery: 1913.
Two Girl Friends: 1348, 3818.
Two Girls in a Study Lounge: 2321.
The Two Goldfish: 2468.
Two Hoppers (On Display at the National Gallery): 4564.
Two Landscapes: 1764.
Two leviathians locked: 782.
Two Little Children: 346.
Two Lovers: 1010.
Two Months After: 1497.
Two Nations: 2467.
Two Nights before the First Day of Spring: 558.
Two Onanists: 2516.
Two Paintings by Breughel: 1406.
A Two-Part Poem of Penang: 4103.
Two Poems: XXVI, XLVIII: 4642.
Two Poems from 1916: I, II: 530, 4531.
Two Poets: 347.
Two Poets and a Painter: 220.
Two Seasons: 1098.
The Two Sherpas: 1396.
Two Sides of a Three-Sided Figure: 3849.
Two Sides of a Ticket: 4187.
Two Songs of the Garden: 417, 3649.
Two Sonnets: 3275.
Two Suspensions: 2557.
Two Trees: 4215, 4295.
Two Trips to Ireland: 4937.
Two Visions in One World: 3873.
Two Visitors from Utah: 3254.
Two, When There Might Have Been Three: 302.
Two Widowers: 3798.
Two Windows: 18.
Two Women and a Mirror: 1319.
Two Women Moving Stones: 4227.
Tygress: 621.
T'zu: Filling Space: 1028.
U-24 Anchors off New Orleans, 1938: 680.
U.S.: <u>See also</u> US . . .
U.S. sends high voltage cattle prods to South Africa: 782.
U.S. troops maneuver in Central America: 3610.
Ugly Couple in a Bar: 1744.
Uh-oh, I just remembered something: 1615.
Uluru Wild Fig Song: 4184.
The Unbetrayed: 4047.
Unbreakable computer code: 782.
The Unbroken Diamond: Nightletter to the Mujahadeen: 3800.
The Uncertainty of It All: 3475.
Uncharted Territory: 2330.
Uncle Ray: 971.
Uncle Vania and the Train to Moscow: 237.
Uncle Willie's Rose: 2173.
The Uncles: 4885.
Under: 1644.
Under Cover of Darkness: 2814.
Under the Green Ceiling: 1109.
Under the Heavenly Mask of Marriage: 714.
Under the Mushroom Cloud: 2682.
Under the Sign of Cancer: 4898.
Under the Surface: 1747, 2580.
The Underdog: 4490.
Understanding: 2676, 3380.
The Undertaker: 4692.
Undertow: 1880.
The Undoing: A Dream: 2931.
Unease: 1886.
Unemployed: 3685.
Unemployed in Scranton, PA: 1401.
Unemployment: 3957.
Unemployment Poetry: 53.
Unfaithful Fantasy: 3176.
The Unforgiving Barrier: 2030.
An Unguided Tour: 3668.
Unhappy Couple: 841.
Unhealed: 4720.
Unheard of: 3161.
The Unimaginable: 4276.
Union Street, San Francisco: 3296.
Union Town: 1672.
Unique: 4910.
United States: 28, 122.
Universal Message: 581.
The University Of The South: 996.
The Unknowable: 3842.
Unknown Beings: 4239.
The Unknown Soldier: 3139.
Unmentionables: 3348.
Unnatural Acts: 2372.
An Unpetrarchan Sonnet: 3342.
Unpleasant Letter: 2822.
The Unprintable (Warsaw, 1981): 3223.
Unravellings: 2030.
An Unrelenting <u>Basso Ostinato</u>: 1370.
Unrequited: 3685.

Unruly Boy: 1063.
The Unsmoker: 3008.
Unsophisticated Reaction: 992.
The Unspeakable: 3139.
Unsung Song for Black Brother: 3855.
Unthinking: 1693, 2158.
Until They Have Consumed Me Utterly: 1610.
Untitled Alaskan Letter I: 4229.
Untitled: And if I forget: 1448, 2487.
Untitled: Dishes slide in and out of soapy water: 4440.
Untitled: How soon it is winter again: 990.
Untitled: I chop vegetables in the kitchen: 4440.
Untitled: I have sat here: 1742.
Untitled: I was plump and quiet and ten: 2829.
Untitled: If I could put my woods in song: 3135.
Untitled: It seemed an eagle: 3418.
Untitled: Like any girl with red, brown or blond hair: 4728.
Untitled: My daughter tells me how I failed her: 4527.
Untitled: My sister and I had walked to Lawson's: 281.
The Untitled Poem: He is a man at the end of himself: 849.
Untitled Poem: I'm waiting for you, but not purely: 1172.
Untitled Poem in Memoriam Elizabeth Langgässer: 2291.
Untitled Poem: The patients in the waiting room: 1172.
Untitled Poem: Why feel guilty because the death of a lover causes lust?: 1172.
Untitled: The place where shadows wait on moonless nights: 1316.
Untitled: The real things, them: 4375.
Untitled: The thing about the five lifeguards: 1219.
Untitled: We are out looking for signs of early spring: 3454.
Untitled: When we're small: 2947.
Untitled: Where are the joys I have met in the morning: 3135.
Untitled: Will I always be eleven: 4901.
Unwritten History in El Salvador: 1934.
Up Again to Appia: 177.
Up and Down: 230.
Up on the Hudson: 4629.
Up the Mountain: 1362.
Updraft (New York City, May 1982): 1671.
Uplifting Thoughts: 4239.
Upon Flying Puffer Kites for Inge: 3790.
Upper Hennepin Avenue: 2808.
Upstairs in C. Ward: 1343.
Upstairs Window: 2378.
Upstream: 3062.
Upstream (poems): 3062.
Uranium: 3258.
Urban Fishfly: 358.
Urban Housing (found poem): 4699.
Urban Renewal Walls: 1504.
The Urine Specimen: 2414.
Urleid: 717.
Urworld: 1906.
US aid to Somozista rebels: 3610.
US opposes pipeline: 782.
US ranks 49th in literacy rate: 782.
US wants Egypt to build Northrop fighter planes: 782.
US will not police the world: 3610.
Used Moon: 2192.
The Uselessness of American Counties: 864.
Usha: 1932.
The Usher: 961.
Ushers: 2085.
USSR 0, USA 0: 626.
Utopian: 2619.
The Uttered Word Come Through: 1004.
Vacancies: 2438.
Vacant Places: 2936.
A Vacant Possession: 1340.
Vacation: 743.
Vacation Observation: La Paz: 3319.
Vagrancy: 736.
Valentine's Day: 3210.
Valle del Encanto: 930.
Van Der Zee Extrapolation #1: 153.
Van Gogh: 3068.
Van Gogh: A Study in Amethyst: 3515.
Van Gogh's 'Road with Poplars': 2107.
Vancouver: 2386.
Vanishing Species: 754.
Vanishings: 1915.
Vanity: 4618.
Vanquished: 258.
Vanquishing Our Enemies: 536.
Variation on a Noel: 143.
Variations on Round Form: 3871.

Varsel: 26.
The Varsity Barbershop: 3378.
Vasari's Corridor: 1325.
Vase Painting: Supper of the Dead: 3726, 4901.
Vasectomy: 2219.
Västansjö: 4845.
Vecindario: 2427.
Vedovo (Widower): 2828.
The Vegetable Gourmet: 2245.
The Vegetable League: 1293.
Veglia: 4561.
A Veiled Girl (ca. 1900): 2131, 3546.
Velasquez' Juan de Pareja: 2881.
The Vendanger: 3535.
Veni Creator: 3021.
Venice 1976: 4789.
Venice, Once More: 3838.
Venice: Still Life: 3124.
Le Vent Triste: 2172.
Ventrillo's Delighted Imp Negentropy: 4778.
Venus: 2450.
Venus Arising from the Sea: 1831.
Verano: 3608.
Verano en la Ciudad: 3688.
The Verge of America: 1409.
The Verification of Vulnerability: Bog Turtle: 3783.
Verkundigung uber den Hirten: 3726.
Vernal Equinox at Mecox: 3377.
Vernichtung: 1242.
Verona, 1973: 746.
Versal's New Hip: 3754.
Die Verschwundenen: 1250.
Versed in Country Things: 898.
Verses to One Rhyme: 3558.
The Very End: 4133.
Very Far Away: 369, 3105.
A very light rain: 567.
Very Poetic Evening: 2494.
Very simple: 1 - 1 = 2: 3610.
Vespers: 1562, 3854.
Vest: 3236.
The Vesuvius Variations: 3906.
Veteran: 4229.
The Veteran: 4274.
Veterans' Cadence: 4757.
Veterans Day: 360.
Veterans Day 1: 360.
Veterans Day 2: 360.
Veterans Day, 1981: 3291.
Vibrio (Selections: Social Relations): 4160.
Vicksburg: 4534.
Victim: 1309.
The Victim of Audits: 2097.
Victims: 1087.
Victor Record Catalog: 3980.
Victoria Day / East Side: 3145.
Victorian Images: 2913.
Victorian Prophets: 1971.
La Vida No Es Sueño: 132.
Vide's Pension: 3753.
Vidrio de Agua en Mano del Hastío: 704.
El Viejo y Su Muchacha: 712.
Viendo Llover: 1262.
Viento Entero: 3407.
El Viento Se Lo Llevó: 1081.
Viet Nam: 2097.
View: 3821, 3906.
The View: 3986.
The View from Apollo XVII: 3046.
A View from the Terraces: 11.
A View in the Rain -- Honolulu: 302.
View of Girl: 1396.
A View of Lake Union: 2168.
Viewing the Body: 563.
Views: 107.
Vigil: 2290, 2395, 3849, 4617.
The Vigil: 4558.
Vigil for a Fellow Credulous Captive: 2768.
A Vigil of Maundy Thursday: 1036.
Vilanelle: 797.
The Villa Capri: 3490.
The Village Cyclist: 3291.
The Village Hears That Gold Is Unstable. NewRep (186:9) 3 Mr 82,: 1787.
Village of the Dead: 756.
The Village Painters: 737.
Village Softball League: 573.
Villanelle: 3228.
The Villanelle: 1832.
Villanelle for Jane Fonda and Richard Simmons: 193.
A Villanelle for Myself: 4692.
Vines: 638.
Vintage Clothes: 2646.
Violence: 3952.
The Violinist Sings July: 187.
The Violins at Lunch: 155.
Violins for the Children/Bartok: 415.
Virginia Slims: 1560.
Virginia with Artists: 2689.
Virginia Woolf: 3576.
Virginia Woolf [poems]: 2707.
Virginia Woolf Walked to the River (Excerpt): 497.
Virgo: 1185.
Virgo Descending: 4900.
Virkelighet: 2158.
Viscount Greystoke: 680.
The Vise: 2629.
Visigoth Sundays: 2932, 3467.
Vision 22 X: 174, 1311.
Vision at Breakfast: 826.
Vision in the Dream: 1493.
Vision of Durer: The Grand Schism: 2981.

Vision Thirst, Tucson, Arizona: 223.
The Vision Tree (Selection: I Daniel): 4705.
A Vision: Woman's Ear: 2107.
Visions: 1183.
Visions Don't Awaken in Stereo: 64.
Visions of a World: 3550.
Visions of Kerouac #14: 729.
The Visit: 3663.
Visit from Home: 373.
Visit Museums, Travel, Read: 3179.
Visit of a Young Sister: 4795.
Visit to the Redhouse: 2767.
Visita al Museo Británico: 3412.
Visitation of the Virgin: 1397, 3726.
Visitation Rites (9): 2630.
Visitation Rites (10): 2630.
Visiting: 805, 1132.
Visiting a Foreign Country: 706.
Visiting Agnes: 2023.
Visiting an Abandoned Farmhouse: 3855.
Visiting God's House Alone: 1241.
Visiting Grandma at St. Luke's: 4521.
Visiting Hour: 3554.
Visiting My Friend Who Is Blind: 3338.
Visiting Robert Frost's Library (Amherst, Mass.): 3223.
Visiting the Cemetery: 3347.
Visiting the Detroit River at Night in a Sports Fury Driven by a Drunken Father: 3153.
Visiting the Gifted and Talented Class: 2452.
Visitng Monks House: 2707.
Visitng My Parents: 3020.
Visitng with Pete: 3047.
The Visitor: 2431, 3980, 4847.
The Visits: 2893.
Vivaldi Years: 4295.
Vizier Sweets: 3991.
VJ Day, Portsmouth: Joy: 3615.
Voc Ed: 3285.
Vocabulary: 4250, 4299.
Voice: 833.
The Voice: Carlos Fuentes on Tape: 3537.
A Voice from the Past: 4239.
Voices from a Folsom Kill-Site, Buffalo Creek, Colorado: 528.
Voices in the Kitchen: 1193.
The Volets: 3661.
Vom Tode Maria: 3726.
Von der Hochzeit zu Kana: 3726.
Vor der Passion: 3726.
Vous disiez le sang sec: 1735.
Vows: 3178.
Voy Cuestionando: 405.
Voyage: 746, 3980.
The Voyage: 266, 3980.
Un Voyage a Cythere: 266.
Voyage (Revision): 3980.
A Voyage to Cythere: 266, 2891.
The Voyages: 3317.
Vulcan at Sunrise: 1196.
W.W. IV will be fought with rocks: 782.
W.W. Two Vet: 2394.
Wabikokokhasu: 558.
The Waco Diner: 2898.
The Wagon Man: 4713.
The Wait: 813, 4754.
The Waiter at the Hotel de Soledad: 1223.
Waiting: 318, 2583, 3250, 3331, 3537, 3873.
Waiting and Watching: 4777.
Waiting at a Truck Stop in Iowa at Midnight: 505.
Waiting for a bus: 1408, 1488, 2138.
Waiting for News: 2877.
Waiting for Our Child: 443.
Waiting for Sleep: 4303.
Waiting for Snow: 2589.
Waiting for the Buddha Express on Telegraph Hill: 4730.
Waiting for the Ferry at Inchon: 722, 2634.
Waiting for the Rapture: 4543.
Waiting for the Storyteller: 4357.
Waiting for the Woman: 4221.
Waiting for Word from Alaska: 1207.
Waiting in Line at Lenin's Tomb: 3551.
Waiting Room: 2928.
Waiting the Ride Beyond: 3487.
The Waiting, the Sailing: 4064.
Waiting to Be Born: 4238.
Waiting to Lean to the Master's Command: 1197.
Waitingroom: 596.
The Wake: 1545, 3392, 4362.
The Wake in the Mansion: 4396.
Wake Up: 1151.
Waking: 1598, 3414, 4044, 4101.
Waking Alone in a Rented Room and Despairing Till the Phone Rings: 1615.
Waking at 5:30 AM: 209.
Waking at Night: 4847.
Waking before My Husband: 1788.
Waking Blind: 2207.

Waking from a dream: 4904.
Waking in the Country: 849.
Waking Jed: 4812.
Waking on a Track during the Race: 4778.
Waking on the Beach: 4108.
Waking Sequence: 1439.
Waking to Work: 1983.
Waking Up: 2465.
Waking Up in a Garden: 4636.
Walk: 1681, 4891.
A Walk: 1682.
The Walk: 1569.
The Walk at Sundown: 2387.
A Walk in Takashimadaira: 1370.
A Walk in the Scenery: 4379.
Walk to the Russian Monastery Garden: 4898.
Walk with the One: 550.
Walked Two Days in Light Snow, Then It Cleared for Five: 4184.
Walkin' Papers Blues (Urban Blues/Jass Series): 813.
Walking: 2468.
Walking a Small, Frozen River in Sunlight: 3317.
Walking among the Ruins: 961.
Walking Around the Farm: 3271.
Walking By: 3735.
Walking by the Cliffside Dyeworks: 659.
Walking Home: 1138.
Walking in the World: 726.
Walking into Water: Virginia Woolf 1941: 4666.
Walking on Raped Woman Creek: 1996.
Walking on the Ceiling: 4636.
Walking on the Highway: 3258.
Walking Out: The Death of Karl Wallenda: 4521.
Walking through a Family Graveyard and Thinking of the Italian Stone Builders: 3753.
Walking Tour: 3678.
The Walking Wounded: 963.
The wall is massive, of solid stone, hard, finished: 1045, 1326.
The Wall, the Ants and a Green Woodpecker: 1302.
The Wallflower: 4453.
Wallpapering: 2766.
Walls: 3074.
Walt Whitman Faints in the Vegetable Garden: 3643.
Walt Whitman's Song Again: 2274.
The Waltz of Nuclear Physics: 3942.
Waltz with Me, Frankenstein: 960.
The Wand: 347.
Wanda: 3980.
A Wanderer's Evensong: 1611, 4432.
Wanderers Nachlied: 1611.
Wanting: 4482.
Wanting You: 2209.
War: 298, 782.
War & Peace: 3432.
The War Came to Illinois: 4649.
War Games in the Bath: 596.
War Is a Whore: 3995.
War Movies in Reverse: 2226.
War Night: 2916.
The War of the Secret Agents (Excerpt: XVII. Epilogue: Author to Reader): 890.
War of White and Yellow: 3948.
The War Photographers: 3313.
Wardrobe: 878.
Warm Front: 3387.
Warm Morning: 3383.
Warning in the Mother Tongue: 789.
Warning of Beloved Lacklove: 14.
Warning Signs: 2695.
A Warning to Candidates: 1509.
Warning to the Wind: 718, 4661.
Warsaw, 1982: 3223.
Warsaw, 1983: 3223.
Warsaw: A Sequence (1941, 1945, 1951, 1971, 1981): 3223.
Warsaw, Sept. 1981: 3223.
Warsaw Snowstorm: 3223.
Warsaw Winter (1983): 3223.
The Wart Cannot Be Coerced: 1060.
Wartime: 3939.
Wartime Sunday: 3535.
Was It You I Dreamed About (Charles): 1263.
Wash Day: 1642.
The Washday Ascension: 475.
Washed Up on the Grau du Roi, Provence: 4529.
Washing You: 1649.
Washington County Suicide: 1768.
Wasps: 1709.
The Wastes of Resurrection: 4876.
Watch out when they attack the bureaucrats: 3610.
Watch Repairmen Are a Dying Breed: 3094.
Watching: 2976.
Watching a Lady with Her X: 4725.
Watching Dark Circle: 2575.
Watching Election Returns: 2953.
Watching Fireworks on the 4th of July in a Boat off